POKÉDEX

Pokémon BLACK VERSION Pokémon WHITE VERSION

The Official Unova Pokédex & Guide

W9-CCE-449

Staff

PUBLISHED BY
The Pokémon Company
International
333 108th Ave NE, Suite 1900
Bellevue, WA 98004

TM, ®, and © The Pokémon
Company International.
All rights reserved.

EDITOR-IN-CHIEF
Michael G. Ryan

TRANSLATORS
Hisato Yamamori
Tim Hove
Sayuri Munday

EDITORS
Kellyn Ballard
Blaise Selby
Hollie Beg
Wolfgang Baur

COVER DESIGN
Eric Medalle
Bridget O'Neill

ACKNOWLEDGEMENTS
Heather Dalgleish
Yasuhiro Usui
Mikiko Ryu
David Numrich
Rey Perez
Antoin Johnson

Naoya Sugie
Eoin Sanders

DESIGN & PRODUCTION
Prima Games
Mario De Govia
Shaida Boroumand
Stephanie Sanchez
Melissa Smith
Jamie Bryson

99 Lives Design, LLC

Adam Crowell
Emily Crowell
Oliver Crowell
Sonja Morris

ISBN: 9780307890634

11 12 13 14 GG 10 9 8 7 6 5 4 3 2

Published in the United States using materials from the
Pokémon Black and Pokémon White Official Unova Pokédex
Completion Guide. Published in Japan by Media Factory, Inc.

SPECIAL THANKS TO:
Editor: Shusuke Motomiya and ONEUP, Inc.
Design & Layout: RAGTIME CO., LTD., and SUZUKIKOUBOU, Inc.

Let's complete the Unova Pokédex!

"I want you three to travel to many distant places and meet all of the Pokémon in the Unova region!" This is a big dream that Professor Juniper asked you to make come true. This is also your own dream as a Pokémon Trainer. Exciting encounters with Pokémon that you've never seen before are waiting for you in the Unova region!

The Official Unova Pokédex & Guide

Unova Pokédex Index 6

Unova Pokédex 9

How to Use the Unova Pokédex 10

Unova Pokédex Completion Guide 91

Complete the Unova Pokédex 92

Techniques for Catching Wild Pokémon 94
Use Pokémon Moves and Abilities 96
Catch Pokémon That Appear in the Wild 98
Catch Pokémon While Surfing 101
Catch Specially Appearing Wild Pokémon 102
Obtain Pokémon through Evolution 104
Evolve Pokémon by Using Stones 106
Evolve Pokémon through Friendship 107
Obtain Pokémon by Restoring Fossils 108
Get Certain Pokémon
during Story Events 109
Link Trade for Pokémon 110
Catch Cobalion, Terrakion, and Virizion! 112
Catch Tornadus or Thundurus 113
Find Zorua and Zoroark 114

Complete the National Pokédex 115

Catch Pokémon from Other Regions 116
Obtain Pokémon by Hatching Eggs 122
Pokémon Egg Groups—
Unova Pokémon 124
Transfer Pokémon with Poké Transfer 126

Communication Features Guide 127

Try the Communication Features 128

C-Gear

How to Use the C-Gear 130
Collect Data Using Tag Mode 131

Infrared

Battle over Infrared 134
Link Trade Pokémon with Infrared 137
Check Compatibility with Feeling Check 138
Exchange Friend Codes with Lots of Friends ... 139

Wireless

Talk to Your Friends with the Xtransceiver 140
Explore Other Players' Worlds
with the Entralink 142
Expand Black City or White Forest 146
Greet Other Players in the Union Room 147
Enjoy Battles in the Union Room 148
Link Trade Pokémon in the Union Room 149
Have Fun Drawing in the Union Room 150
Spin Trade Eggs in the Union Room 151

Online

Accessing Nintendo Wi-Fi Connection 152
Use the Xtransceiver in the Wi-Fi Club 153
Enjoy Battles in the Wi-Fi Club 154
Link Trade Pokémon in the Wi-Fi Club 155
Battle Trainers Worldwide
with Random Matchups 156
Trade Pokémon Worldwide Using GTS 158
Check Out Other Players' Musical Photos 160
Watch Other Players' Battle Videos 161
Use the Vs. Recorder to Record Battles 162

Pokémon Global Link

Access the Pokémon Global Link 163
Befriend Pokémon in
the Pokémon Dream World 164
Bring Back Pokémon from Other Regions in
the Pokémon Dream World 166
Minigames in the Pokémon Dream World 167
Grow Berries in Your Garden 169
Decorate Your Home 170
Dream Catalogue 171
Swap Items on Share Shelves 172
Bring Back Berries and Items 173
Set Up Your Profile 174
Communicate with Your Game Pals
with E-Z Mail 175
Customize the Game 176
Check Your Ranking at
the Global Battle Union 177

Pokémon Battle Primer 179

New Pokémon Battles
in the Unova Region 180
Master All the Battle Formats to Win 184
Connect with Link Battle
and Battle Anyone 190
Master Type Matchups 192
Know Stats for Battling
and Raising Pokémon 196
Inflict Status Conditions to Get an Edge.......... 198
Become a Pokémon Move Master 200
Take Advantage of Pokémon Abilities 210
Use Items to Develop New Strategies.............215
Adapt Your Strategy to Win Battles.............. 220
Master the Art of the Combo 224
When a Battle Is Lost, Consider This 230
Find the Right Pokémon to Train 232
Raise Pokémon from Eggs 235
Master the Art of Strengthening Pokémon 240
Plan Ahead to Raise Pokémon
That Fit Your Strategy.......................... 246
Put Your Team to the Ultimate Test at
the Pokémon World Championships 248

Battle Subway Strategies 249

Win on the Battle Subway 250
Learn Battle Subway Basics 250
Take On the Single and Super Single Trains 253
Take On the Double and Super Double Trains... 254
Take On the Multi and Super Multi Trains 255
Take On the Wi-Fi Train 256
Techniques for Winning
on the Battle Subway 257

Pokémon Musical Stratagies 259

Be a Star in the Pokémon Musical................... 260
Learn All About the Pokémon Musical.............. 260
Dress Up Your Pokémon 263
Give Performances
for Good Reviews 267
After the Pokémon Musical Performance 268
Perform with Your Friends.......................... 269

Adventure Data 271

Pokémon Moves 272
Field Moves/Moves Learned from People 283
TMs 284
HMs 285
Pokémon Abilities 286
Items Obtained with the Pickup Ability 290
Pokémon's Natures and Characteristics........ 291
Items 292
Items Held by Wild Pokémon:
Unova Pokémon 306
Items That Certain
People Will Buy from You.......................... 307
Pokémon Musical Props.......................... 308
Pokémon Moves Reverse Lookup—
Unova Pokémon 310
Pokémon Abilities Reverse Lookup—
Unova Pokémon 334
How and Where to Meet Special Pokémon 338
Pokémon Weakness Chart—
National Pokédex 340
Type Matchup Chart 352

Special Sections

Shiny Pokémon and
the Mysterious Pokérus 90
Use Battle-Combo Moves That the Three Starter
Pokémon Can Learn 178
Teach Your Pokémon
the Ultimate Move 258
Upgrade Your Trainer Card 270

A • B

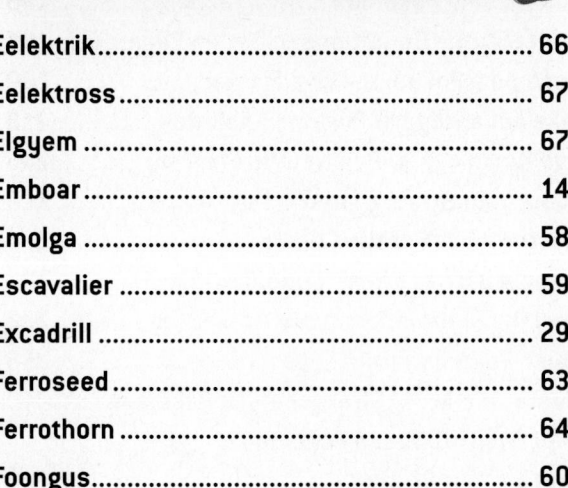

Accelgor 73

Alomomola 62

Amoonguss 60

Archen 48

Archeops 48

Audino 30

Axew 70

Basculin (Blue-Striped Form) 40

Basculin (Red-Striped Form) 39

Beartic 72

Beheeyem 68

Bisharp 77

Blitzle 25

Boldore 27

Bouffalant 78

Braviary 79

C • D

Carracosta 47

Chandelure 69

Cinccino 51

Cobalion 84

Cofagrigus 46

Conkeldurr 31

Cottonee 37

Crustle 44

Cryogonal 72

Cubchoo 71

Darmanitan (Standard & Zen Modes) ... 42

Darumaka 42

Deerling (Spring, Summer, Autumn &

Winter Forms) 57

Deino 81

Dewott 15

Drilbur 29

Druddigon 75

Ducklett 55

Duosion 54

Durant 81

Dwebble 43

E • F

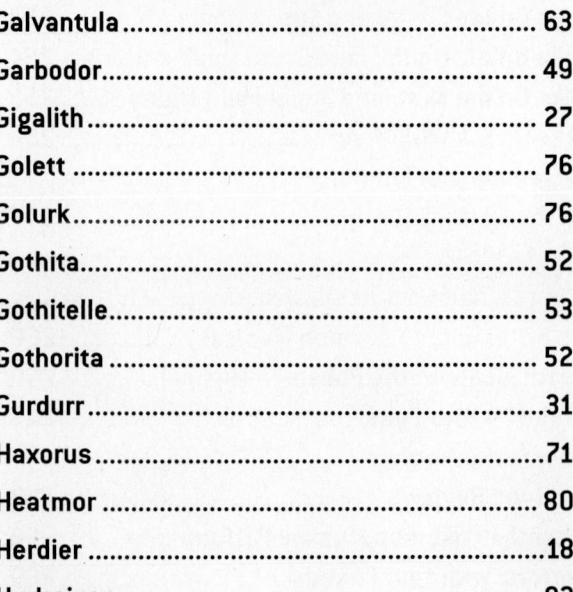

Eelektrik 66

Eelektross 67

Elgyem 67

Emboar 14

Emolga 58

Escavalier 59

Excadrill 29

Ferroseed 63

Ferrothorn 64

Foongus 60

Fraxure 70

Frillish 61

G • H

Galvantula 63

Garbodor 49

Gigalith 27

Golett 76

Golurk 76

Gothita 52

Gothitelle 53

Gothorita 52

Gurdurr 31

Haxorus 71

Heatmor 80

Herdier 18

Hydreigon 82

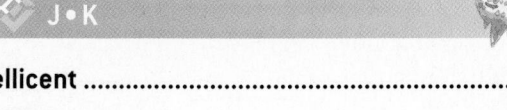

J • K

Jellicent 61
Joltik 62
Karrablast 59
Klang 65
Klink 64
Klinklang 65
Krokorok 41
Krookodile 41
Kyurem 88

L • M

Lampent 69
Landorus 87
Larvesta 83
Leavanny 35
Liepard 19
Lilligant 39
Lillipup 17
Litwick 68
Mandibuzz 80
Maractus 43
Mienfoo 74
Mienshao 75
Minccino 51
Munna 23
Musharna 23

O • P

Oshawott 15
Palpitoad 32
Panpour 22
Pansage 20
Pansear 21
Patrat 16

Pawniard 77
Petilil 38
Pidove 24
Pignite 14
Purrloin 19

R • S

Reshiram 86
Reuniclus 54
Roggenrola 26
Rufflet 78
Samurott 16
Sandile 40
Sawk 34
Sawsbuck (Spring, Summer, Autumn & Winter Forms) 58
Scolipede 37
Scrafty 45
Scraggy 44
Seismitoad 33
Serperior 13
Servine 12
Sewaddle 34
Shelmet 73
Sigilyph 45
Simipour 22
Simisage 20
Simisear 21
Snivy 12
Solosis 53
Stoutland 18
Stunfisk 74
Swadloon 35
Swanna 55
Swoobat 28

T • U

Tepig 13

Terrakion 84

Throh 33

Thundurus 86

Timburr 30

Tirtouga 47

Tornadus 85

Tranquill 24

Trubbish...................................... 49

Tympole 32

Tynamo.. 66

Unfezant..................................... 25

V • W • Y • Z

Vanillish....................................... 56

Vanillite 56

Vanilluxe 57

Venipede 36

Victini 89

Virizion 85

Volcarona 83

Vullaby 79

Watchog 17

Whimsicott 38

Whirlipede 36

Woobat 28

Yamask... 46

Zebstrika 26

Zekrom 87

Zoroark 50

Zorua 50

Zweilous 82

Unova Region Pokédex

Pokémon Black Version and *Pokémon White Version* Official Unova Pokédex Completion Guide

How to Use the Unova Pokédex

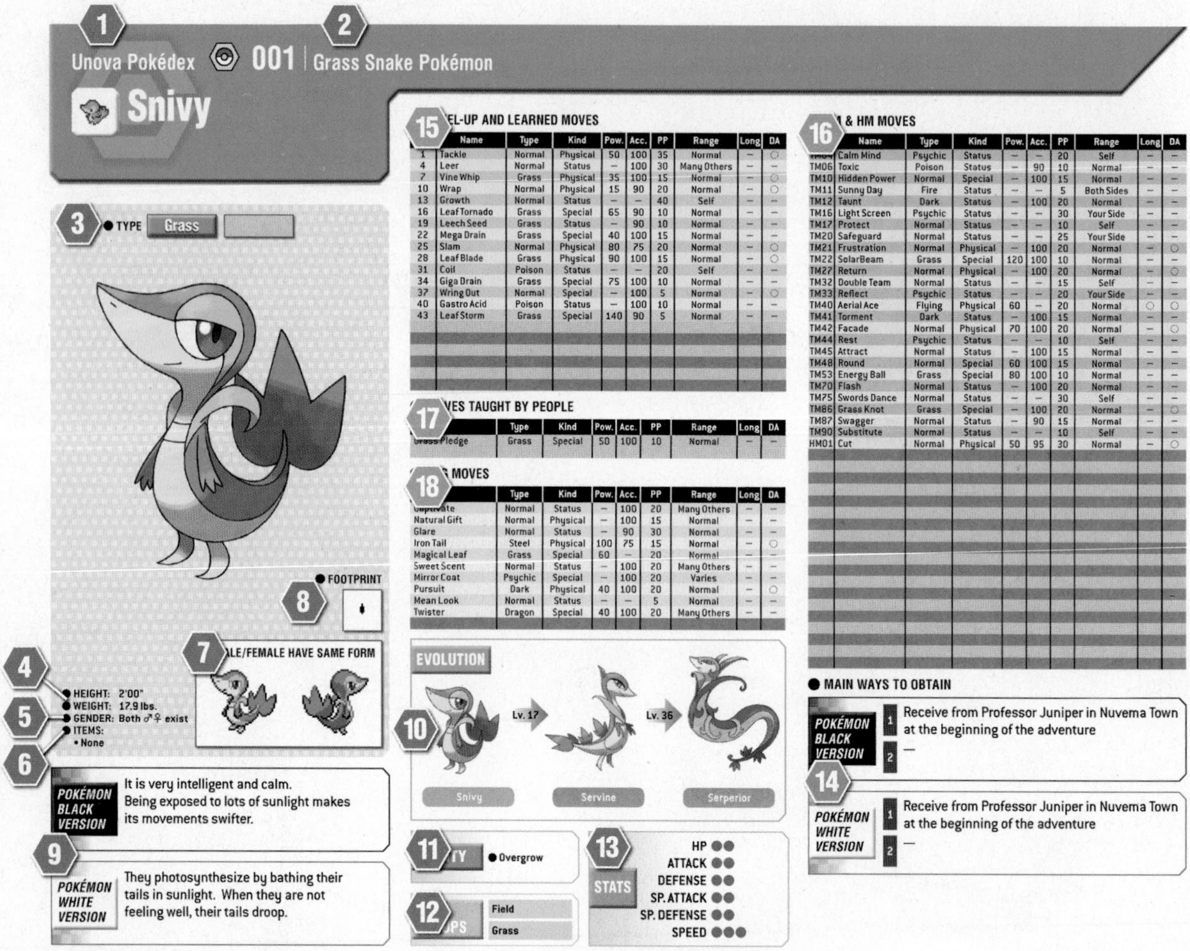

1 Unova Pokédex ⬡ **001** | **2** Grass Snake Pokémon

Snivy

3 ● TYPE Grass

4
- ● HEIGHT: 2'00"

5
- ● WEIGHT: 17.9 lbs.
- ● GENDER: Both ♂♀ exist

6
- ● ITEMS:
  - • None

● FOOTPRINT **8**

7 MALE/FEMALE HAVE SAME FORM

POKÉMON BLACK VERSION
It is very intelligent and calm. Being exposed to lots of sunlight makes its movements swifter.

9
POKÉMON WHITE VERSION
They photosynthesize by bathing their tails in sunlight. When they are not feeling well, their tails droop.

15 LEVEL-UP AND LEARNED MOVES

Lv.	Name	Type	Kind	Pow.	Acc.	PP	Range	Long	DA
1	Tackle	Normal	Physical	50	100	35	Normal	—	○
4	Leer	Normal	Status	—	100	30	Many Others	—	—
7	Vine Whip	Grass	Physical	35	100	15	Normal	—	○
10	Wrap	Normal	Physical	15	90	20	Normal	—	○
13	Growth	Normal	Status	—	—	40	Self	—	—
16	Leaf Tornado	Grass	Special	65	90	10	Normal	—	—
19	Leech Seed	Grass	Status	—	90	10	Normal	—	—
22	Mega Drain	Grass	Special	40	100	15	Normal	—	—
25	Slam	Normal	Physical	80	75	20	Normal	—	○
28	Leaf Blade	Grass	Physical	90	100	15	Normal	—	○
31	Coil	Poison	Status	—	—	20	Self	—	—
34	Giga Drain	Grass	Special	75	100	10	Normal	—	—
37	Wring Out	Normal	Special	—	100	5	Normal	—	○
40	Gastro Acid	Poison	Status	—	100	10	Normal	—	—
43	Leaf Storm	Grass	Special	140	90	5	Normal	—	—

16 TM & HM MOVES

No.	Name	Type	Kind	Pow.	Acc.	PP	Range	Long	DA
TM04	Calm Mind	Psychic	Status	—	—	20	Self	—	—
TM06	Toxic	Poison	Status	—	90	10	Normal	—	—
TM10	Hidden Power	Normal	Special	—	100	15	Normal	—	—
TM11	Sunny Day	Fire	Status	—	—	5	Both Sides	—	—
TM12	Taunt	Dark	Status	—	100	20	Normal	—	—
TM16	Light Screen	Psychic	Status	—	—	30	Your Side	—	—
TM17	Protect	Normal	Status	—	—	10	Self	—	—
TM20	Safeguard	Normal	Status	—	—	25	Your Side	—	—
TM21	Frustration	Normal	Physical	—	100	20	Normal	—	○
TM22	SolarBeam	Grass	Special	120	100	10	Normal	—	—
TM27	Return	Normal	Physical	—	100	20	Normal	—	○
TM32	Double Team	Normal	Status	—	—	15	Self	—	—
TM33	Reflect	Psychic	Status	—	—	20	Your Side	—	—
TM40	Aerial Ace	Flying	Physical	60	—	20	Normal	○	○
TM41	Torment	Dark	Status	—	100	15	Normal	—	—
TM42	Facade	Normal	Physical	70	100	20	Normal	—	○
TM44	Rest	Psychic	Status	—	—	10	Self	—	—
TM45	Attract	Normal	Status	—	100	15	Normal	—	—
TM49	Round	Normal	Special	60	100	15	Normal	—	—
TM53	Energy Ball	Grass	Special	80	100	10	Normal	—	—
TM70	Flash	Normal	Status	—	100	20	Normal	—	—
TM75	Swords Dance	Normal	Status	—	—	30	Self	—	—
TM86	Grass Knot	Grass	Special	—	100	20	Normal	—	○
TM87	Swagger	Normal	Status	—	90	15	Normal	—	—
TM90	Substitute	Normal	Status	—	—	10	Self	—	—
HM01	Cut	Normal	Physical	50	95	30	Normal	—	○

17 MOVES TAUGHT BY PEOPLE

Name	Type	Kind	Pow.	Acc.	PP	Range	Long	DA
Grass Pledge	Grass	Special	50	100	10	Normal	—	—

18 EGG MOVES

Name	Type	Kind	Pow.	Acc.	PP	Range	Long	DA
Captivate	Normal	Status	—	100	20	Many Others	—	—
Natural Gift	Normal	Physical	—	100	15	Normal	—	—
Glare	Normal	Status	—	90	30	Normal	—	—
Iron Tail	Steel	Physical	100	75	15	Normal	—	○
Magical Leaf	Grass	Special	60	—	20	Normal	—	—
Sweet Scent	Normal	Status	—	100	20	Many Others	—	—
Mirror Coat	Psychic	Special	—	100	20	Varies	—	—
Pursuit	Dark	Physical	40	100	20	Normal	—	○
Mean Look	Normal	Status	—	—	5	Normal	—	—
Twister	Dragon	Special	40	100	20	Many Others	—	—

EVOLUTION

Lv. 17   Lv. 36

Snivy   Servine   Serperior

10

11 ABILITY ● Overgrow

12 EGG GROUPS
Field
Grass

13 STATS
- HP ●●
- ATTACK ●●
- DEFENSE ●●
- SP.ATTACK ●●
- SP.DEFENSE ●●
- SPEED ●●●

● MAIN WAYS TO OBTAIN

POKÉMON BLACK VERSION
1. Receive from Professor Juniper in Nuvema Town at the beginning of the adventure
2. —

14
POKÉMON WHITE VERSION
1. Receive from Professor Juniper in Nuvema Town at the beginning of the adventure
2. —

Basic Data

1 Unova Pokédex Number

The Unova Pokédex number of the Pokémon.

2 Pokémon Category

The Pokémon's category tells you what kind of features it has.

3 Type

The Pokémon's type. Some Pokémon have two types.

4 Height and Weight

The height and weight of the Pokémon.

5 Gender

It shows whether the Pokémon has two genders. Some Pokémon's genders are unknown.

6 Held Item

The item that is sometimes held by the Pokémon when you encounter it in the wild in places such as tall grass, caves, and while surfing.

7 ⟩ In-Game Form

This is a picture of how the Pokémon is shown in the game. Here you can see how the Pokémon looks from both the front and the back. If the male and female have different forms, they will be shown here. If the Pokémon has special forms, they'll be shown here, too.

8 ⟩ Footprint

This is the Pokémon's footprint. Some Pokémon don't have footprints.

9 ⟩ Pokédex Entry

This is the summary of the Pokémon's characteristics given in the Pokédex. Both the *Pokémon Black Version* and *Pokémon White Version* entries are included.

10 ⟩ Evolution

If the Pokémon evolves, this shows the course of evolution for the Pokémon as well as any conditions governing its evolution.

11 ⟩ Abilities

The Pokémon's Ability. If two Abilities are listed, each individual Pokémon will have one of the two.

12 ⟩ Egg Groups

The Egg group the Pokémon belongs to. When two Egg groups are listed, the Pokémon belongs to both.

13 ⟩ Stat Levels

The levels of the Pokémon's stats are listed here. The number of ● is calculated by comparing the stat to the stats of the other Pokémon in the Unova Pokédex. The maximum number of ● is six.

How to Obtain

14 ⟩ Main Ways to Obtain

Two main methods to obtain the Pokémon for registration in the Unova Pokédex are shown. Ways to obtain it will be shown for both the *Pokémon Black* and *Pokémon White Versions*.

Moves

15 ⟩ Level-Up Moves

A list of the moves the Pokémon can learn by leveling up.

16 ⟩ TM & HM Moves

A list of the moves the Pokémon can learn by using a TM or an HM.

17 ⟩ Moves Taught by People

A list of moves that people can teach to the Pokémon.

18 ⟩ Egg Moves

These moves are occasionally learned by the Pokémon upon hatching from an Egg, as long as they are known by the male Pokémon you left at the Pokémon Day Care.

Explanations of Lists

Lv. .... The level at which the move can be learned

No. .... The TM or HM's number

Type .... The move's type

Kind .... Whether the move is a physical, special, or status move

Pow. .... The move's attack power

Acc. .... The move's accuracy

PP .... How many times the move can be used

Range .... The number and type of targets the move affects

Long .... Whether the move is a long-range move that can affect faraway targets during a Triple Battle

DA .... Whether the move is a direct attack that makes physical contact with the target

Range Guide

■ **Adjacent:** The move affects the surrounding Pokémon simultaneously. If the move is used by a Pokémon in the middle position during Triple Battles, the move will affect the other five Pokémon (this includes its allies) simultaneously. If the move is used by a Pokémon in the left or right position, the move will affect the three surrounding Pokémon (including its ally) simultaneously.

■ **Both Sides:** The move affects the entire playing field without regard to opposing and ally Pokémon. Since the move affects the field, the move's effects will continue even if the user is swapped out (except for moves that only work for one turn).

■ **Other Side:** The move affects the opponent's side of the field. Since the move affects the field, the move's effects will continue even if the user is swapped out (except for moves that only work for one turn).

■ **Many Others:** The move affects multiple opposing Pokémon simultaneously. If the move is used by a Pokémon in the middle position during Triple Battles, the move will affect all three opposing Pokémon. If the move is used by a Pokémon in the left or right position, the move will affect two opposing Pokémon.

■ **Normal:** The move affects the selected target. If the move is used by a Pokémon in the middle position during Triple Battles, the move can target any of the other five Pokémon (including allies). If the move is used by a Pokémon in the left or right position, the move can target any of the three surrounding Pokémon (including its ally).

■ **1 Ally:** The move affects an adjacent ally. It has no effect in a Single Battle.

■ **1 Random:** The move affects one of the opposing Pokémon at random.

■ **Self:** This move affects only the user.

■ **Self/Ally:** The move affects the user or one of its allies at random. (In a Single Battle, it affects only the user.)

■ **Varies:** The move is influenced by things like the opposing Pokémon's move or the user's type, so the effect and range are not fixed.

■ **Your Party:** The move affects your entire party, including party Pokémon who are still in their Poké Balls.

■ **Your Side:** The move affects the side of the field where your Pokémon are. Since the move affects the field, the move's effects will continue even if the user is swapped out (except for moves that only work for one turn).

Snivy

● TYPE | Grass

● LEVEL-UP AND LEARNED MOVES

Lv.	Name	Type	Kind	Pow.	Acc.	PP	Range	Long	DA
1	Tackle	Normal	Physical	50	100	35	Normal	—	○
4	Leer	Normal	Status	—	100	30	Many Others	—	—
7	Vine Whip	Grass	Physical	35	100	15	Normal	—	○
10	Wrap	Normal	Physical	15	90	20	Normal	—	○
13	Growth	Normal	Status	—	—	40	Self	—	—
16	Leaf Tornado	Grass	Special	65	90	10	Normal	—	—
19	Leech Seed	Grass	Status	—	90	10	Normal	—	—
22	Mega Drain	Grass	Special	40	100	15	Normal	—	—
25	Slam	Normal	Physical	80	75	20	Normal	—	○
28	Leaf Blade	Grass	Physical	90	100	15	Normal	—	○
31	Coil	Poison	Status	—	—	20	Self	—	—
34	Giga Drain	Grass	Special	75	100	10	Normal	—	—
37	Wring Out	Normal	Special	—	100	5	Normal	—	○
40	Gastro Acid	Poison	Status	—	100	10	Normal	—	—
43	Leaf Storm	Grass	Special	140	90	5	Normal	—	—

● MOVES TAUGHT BY PEOPLE

Name	Type	Kind	Pow.	Acc.	PP	Range	Long	DA
Grass Pledge	Grass	Special	50	100	10	Normal	—	—

● EGG MOVES

Name	Type	Kind	Pow.	Acc.	PP	Range	Long	DA
Captivate	Normal	Status	—	100	20	Many Others	—	—
Natural Gift	Normal	Physical	—	100	15	Normal	—	—
Glare	Normal	Status	—	90	30	Normal	—	—
Iron Tail	Steel	Physical	100	75	15	Normal	—	○
Magical Leaf	Grass	Special	60	—	20	Normal	—	—
Sweet Scent	Normal	Status	—	100	20	Many Others	—	—
Mirror Coat	Psychic	Special	—	100	20	Varies	—	—
Pursuit	Dark	Physical	40	100	20	Normal	—	—
Mean Look	Normal	Status	—	—	5	Normal	—	—
Twister	Dragon	Special	40	100	20	Many Others	—	—

● TM & HM MOVES

No.	Name	Type	Kind	Pow.	Acc.	PP	Range	Long	DA
TM04	Calm Mind	Psychic	Status	—	—	20	Self	—	—
TM06	Toxic	Poison	Status	—	90	10	Normal	—	—
TM10	Hidden Power	Normal	Special	—	100	15	Normal	—	—
TM11	Sunny Day	Fire	Status	—	—	5	Both Sides	—	—
TM12	Taunt	Dark	Status	—	100	20	Normal	—	—
TM16	Light Screen	Psychic	Status	—	—	30	Your Side	—	—
TM17	Protect	Normal	Status	—	—	10	Self	—	—
TM20	Safeguard	Normal	Status	—	—	25	Your Side	—	—
TM21	Frustration	Normal	Physical	—	100	20	Normal	—	○
TM22	SolarBeam	Grass	Special	120	100	10	Normal	—	—
TM27	Return	Normal	Physical	—	100	20	Normal	—	○
TM32	Double Team	Normal	Status	—	—	15	Self	—	—
TM33	Reflect	Psychic	Status	—	—	20	Your Side	—	—
TM40	Aerial Ace	Flying	Physical	60	—	20	Normal	○	○
TM41	Torment	Dark	Status	—	100	15	Normal	—	—
TM42	Facade	Normal	Physical	70	100	20	Normal	—	○
TM44	Rest	Psychic	Status	—	—	10	Self	—	—
TM45	Attract	Normal	Status	—	100	15	Normal	—	—
TM48	Round	Normal	Special	60	100	15	Normal	—	—
TM53	Energy Ball	Grass	Special	80	100	10	Normal	—	—
TM70	Flash	Normal	Status	—	100	20	Normal	—	—
TM75	Swords Dance	Normal	Status	—	—	30	Self	—	—
TM86	Grass Knot	Grass	Special	—	100	20	Normal	—	○
TM87	Swagger	Normal	Status	—	90	15	Normal	—	—
TM90	Substitute	Normal	Status	—	—	10	Self	—	—
HM01	Cut	Normal	Physical	50	95	30	Normal	—	○

● HEIGHT: 2'00"
● WEIGHT: 17.9 lbs.
● GENDER: Both ♂♀ exist
● ITEMS:
  • None

● FOOTPRINT

● MALE/FEMALE HAVE SAME FORM

● EVOLUTION

Snivy → Lv. 17 → Servine → Lv. 36 → Serperior

POKÉMON BLACK VERSION
It is very intelligent and calm. Being exposed to lots of sunlight makes its movements swifter.

POKÉMON WHITE VERSION
They photosynthesize by bathing their tails in sunlight. When they are not feeling well, their tails droop.

● ABILITY ● Overgrow

● EGG GROUPS: Field / Grass

● STATS
HP ●●
ATTACK ●●
DEFENSE ●●
SP. ATTACK ●●
SP. DEFENSE ●●
SPEED ●●●

● MAIN WAYS TO OBTAIN

POKÉMON BLACK VERSION
1 Receive from Professor Juniper in Nuvema Town at the beginning of the adventure
2 —

POKÉMON WHITE VERSION
1 Receive from Professor Juniper in Nuvema Town at the beginning of the adventure
2 —

Servine

● TYPE | Grass

● LEVEL-UP AND LEARNED MOVES

Lv.	Name	Type	Kind	Pow.	Acc.	PP	Range	Long	DA
1	Tackle	Normal	Physical	50	100	35	Normal	—	○
1	Leer	Normal	Status	—	100	30	Many Others	—	—
1	Vine Whip	Grass	Physical	35	100	15	Normal	—	○
1	Wrap	Normal	Physical	15	90	20	Normal	—	○
4	Leer	Normal	Status	—	100	30	Many Others	—	—
7	Vine Whip	Grass	Physical	35	100	15	Normal	—	○
10	Wrap	Normal	Physical	15	90	20	Normal	—	○
13	Growth	Normal	Status	—	—	40	Self	—	—
16	Leaf Tornado	Grass	Special	65	90	10	Normal	—	—
20	Leech Seed	Grass	Status	—	90	10	Normal	—	—
24	Mega Drain	Grass	Special	40	100	15	Normal	—	—
28	Slam	Normal	Physical	80	75	20	Normal	—	○
32	Leaf Blade	Grass	Physical	90	100	15	Normal	—	○
36	Coil	Poison	Status	—	—	20	Self	—	—
40	Giga Drain	Grass	Special	75	100	10	Normal	—	—
44	Wring Out	Normal	Special	—	100	5	Normal	—	○
48	Gastro Acid	Poison	Status	—	100	10	Normal	—	—
52	Leaf Storm	Grass	Special	140	90	5	Normal	—	—

● MOVES TAUGHT BY PEOPLE

Name	Type	Kind	Pow.	Acc.	PP	Range	Long	DA
Grass Pledge	Grass	Special	50	100	10	Normal	—	—

● TM & HM MOVES

No.	Name	Type	Kind	Pow.	Acc.	PP	Range	Long	DA
TM04	Calm Mind	Psychic	Status	—	—	20	Self	—	—
TM06	Toxic	Poison	Status	—	90	10	Normal	—	—
TM10	Hidden Power	Normal	Special	—	100	15	Normal	—	—
TM11	Sunny Day	Fire	Status	—	—	5	Both Sides	—	—
TM12	Taunt	Dark	Status	—	100	20	Normal	—	—
TM16	Light Screen	Psychic	Status	—	—	30	Your Side	—	—
TM17	Protect	Normal	Status	—	—	10	Self	—	—
TM20	Safeguard	Normal	Status	—	—	25	Your Side	—	—
TM21	Frustration	Normal	Physical	—	100	20	Normal	—	○
TM22	SolarBeam	Grass	Special	120	100	10	Normal	—	—
TM27	Return	Normal	Physical	—	100	20	Normal	—	○
TM32	Double Team	Normal	Status	—	—	15	Self	—	—
TM33	Reflect	Psychic	Status	—	—	20	Your Side	—	—
TM40	Aerial Ace	Flying	Physical	60	—	20	Normal	○	○
TM41	Torment	Dark	Status	—	100	15	Normal	—	—
TM42	Facade	Normal	Physical	70	100	20	Normal	—	○
TM44	Rest	Psychic	Status	—	—	10	Self	—	—
TM45	Attract	Normal	Status	—	100	15	Normal	—	—
TM48	Round	Normal	Special	60	100	15	Normal	—	—
TM53	Energy Ball	Grass	Special	80	100	10	Normal	—	—
TM70	Flash	Normal	Status	—	100	20	Normal	—	—
TM75	Swords Dance	Normal	Status	—	—	30	Self	—	—
TM86	Grass Knot	Grass	Special	—	100	20	Normal	—	○
TM87	Swagger	Normal	Status	—	90	15	Normal	—	—
TM90	Substitute	Normal	Status	—	—	10	Self	—	—
HM01	Cut	Normal	Physical	50	95	30	Normal	—	○

● HEIGHT: 2'07"
● WEIGHT: 35.3 lbs.
● GENDER: Both ♂♀ exist
● ITEMS:
  • None

● FOOTPRINT

● MALE/FEMALE HAVE SAME FORM

● EVOLUTION

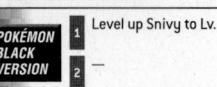

Snivy → Lv. 17 → Servine → Lv. 36 → Serperior

POKÉMON BLACK VERSION
It moves along the ground as if sliding. Its swift movements befuddle its foes, and it then attacks with a vine whip.

POKÉMON WHITE VERSION
They avoid attacks by sinking into the shadows of thick foliage. They retaliate with masterful whipping techniques.

● ABILITY ● Overgrow

● EGG GROUPS: Field / Grass

● STATS
HP ●●
ATTACK ●●●
DEFENSE ●●●
SP. ATTACK ●●●
SP. DEFENSE ●●●
SPEED ●●●●

● MAIN WAYS TO OBTAIN

POKÉMON BLACK VERSION
1 Level up Snivy to Lv. 17
2 —

POKÉMON WHITE VERSION
1 Level up Snivy to Lv. 17
2 —

Serperior

● TYPE **Grass**

● FOOTPRINT

● MALE/FEMALE HAVE SAME FORM

- ● HEIGHT: 10'10"
- ● WEIGHT: 138.9 lbs.
- ● GENDER: Both ♂♀ exist
- ● ITEMS:
  - • None

POKÉMON BLACK VERSION
It can stop its opponents' movements with just a glare. It takes in solar energy and boosts it internally.

POKÉMON WHITE VERSION
They raise their heads to intimidate opponents but only give it their all when fighting a powerful opponent.

● LEVEL-UP AND LEARNED MOVES

Lv.	Name	Type	Kind	Pow.	Acc.	PP	Range	Long	DA
1	Tackle	Normal	Physical	50	100	35	Normal	—	○
1	Leer	Normal	Status	—	100	30	Many Others	—	—
1	Vine Whip	Grass	Physical	35	100	15	Normal	—	○
1	Wrap	Normal	Physical	15	90	20	Normal	—	○
4	Leer	Normal	Status	—	100	30	Many Others	—	—
7	Vine Whip	Grass	Physical	35	100	15	Normal	—	○
10	Wrap	Normal	Physical	15	90	20	Normal	—	○
13	Growth	Normal	Status	—	—	40	Self	—	—
16	Leaf Tornado	Grass	Special	65	90	10	Normal	—	—
20	Leech Seed	Grass	Status	—	90	10	Normal	—	—
24	Mega Drain	Grass	Special	40	100	15	Normal	—	—
28	Slam	Normal	Physical	80	75	20	Normal	—	○
32	Leaf Blade	Grass	Physical	90	100	15	Normal	—	○
38	Coil	Poison	Status	—	—	20	Self	—	—
44	Giga Drain	Grass	Special	75	100	10	Normal	—	—
50	Wring Out	Normal	Special	—	100	5	Normal	—	○
56	Gastro Acid	Poison	Status	—	100	10	Normal	—	—
62	Leaf Storm	Grass	Special	140	90	5	Normal	—	—

● MOVES TAUGHT BY PEOPLE

Name	Type	Kind	Pow.	Acc.	PP	Range	Long	DA
Grass Pledge	Grass	Special	50	100	10	Normal	—	—
Frenzy Plant	Grass	Special	150	90	5	Normal	—	—

● TM & HM MOVES

No.	Name	Type	Kind	Pow.	Acc.	PP	Range	Long	DA
TM04	Calm Mind	Psychic	Status	—	—	20	Self	—	—
TM06	Toxic	Poison	Status	—	90	10	Normal	—	—
TM10	Hidden Power	Normal	Special	—	100	15	Normal	—	—
TM11	Sunny Day	Fire	Status	—	—	5	Both Sides	—	—
TM12	Taunt	Dark	Status	—	100	20	Normal	—	—
TM15	Hyper Beam	Normal	Special	150	90	5	Normal	—	—
TM16	Light Screen	Psychic	Status	—	—	30	Your Side	—	—
TM17	Protect	Normal	Status	—	—	10	Self	—	—
TM20	Safeguard	Normal	Status	—	—	25	Your Side	—	—
TM21	Frustration	Normal	Physical	—	100	20	Normal	—	○
TM22	SolarBeam	Grass	Special	120	100	10	Normal	—	—
TM27	Return	Normal	Physical	—	100	20	Normal	—	○
TM32	Double Team	Normal	Status	—	—	15	Self	—	—
TM33	Reflect	Psychic	Status	—	—	20	Your Side	—	—
TM40	Aerial Ace	Flying	Physical	60	—	20	Normal	—	○
TM41	Torment	Dark	Status	—	100	15	Normal	—	—
TM42	Facade	Normal	Physical	70	100	20	Normal	—	○
TM44	Rest	Psychic	Status	—	—	10	Self	—	—
TM45	Attract	Normal	Status	—	100	15	Normal	—	—
TM48	Round	Normal	Special	60	100	15	Normal	—	—
TM53	Energy Ball	Grass	Special	80	100	10	Normal	—	—
TM68	Giga Impact	Normal	Physical	150	90	5	Normal	—	○
TM70	Flash	Normal	Status	—	100	20	Normal	—	—
TM75	Swords Dance	Normal	Status	—	—	30	Self	—	—
TM82	Dragon Tail	Dragon	Physical	60	90	10	Normal	—	○
TM86	Grass Knot	Grass	Special	—	100	20	Normal	—	○
TM87	Swagger	Normal	Status	—	90	15	Normal	—	—
TM90	Substitute	Normal	Status	—	—	10	Self	—	—
TM94	Rock Smash	Fighting	Physical	40	100	15	Normal	—	○
HM01	Cut	Normal	Physical	50	95	30	Normal	—	○
HM04	Strength	Normal	Physical	80	100	15	Normal	—	○

EVOLUTION

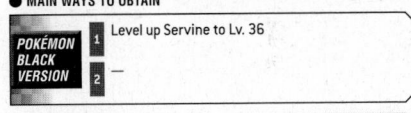

Snivy → Lv. 17 → Servine → Lv. 36 → Serperior

ABILITY ● Overgrow

EGG GROUPS Field / Grass

STATS
HP ●●●
ATTACK ●●●
DEFENSE ●●●●
SP. ATTACK ●●●
SP. DEFENSE ●●●●
SPEED ●●●●●

● MAIN WAYS TO OBTAIN

POKÉMON BLACK VERSION	1	Level up Servine to Lv. 36
	2	—

POKÉMON WHITE VERSION	1	Level up Servine to Lv. 36
	2	—

Tepig

● TYPE **Fire**

● FOOTPRINT

● MALE/FEMALE HAVE SAME FORM

- ● HEIGHT: 1'08"
- ● WEIGHT: 21.8 lbs.
- ● GENDER: Both ♂♀ exist
- ● ITEMS:
  - • None

POKÉMON BLACK VERSION
It can deftly dodge its foe's attacks while shooting fireballs from its nose. It roasts berries before it eats them.

POKÉMON WHITE VERSION
It blows fire through its nose. When it catches a cold, the fire becomes pitch-black smoke instead.

● LEVEL-UP AND LEARNED MOVES

Lv.	Name	Type	Kind	Pow.	Acc.	PP	Range	Long	DA
1	Tackle	Normal	Physical	50	100	35	Normal	—	○
3	Tail Whip	Normal	Status	—	100	30	Many Others	—	—
7	Ember	Fire	Special	40	100	25	Normal	—	—
9	Odor Sleuth	Normal	Status	—	—	40	Normal	—	—
13	Defense Curl	Normal	Status	—	—	40	Self	—	—
15	Flame Charge	Fire	Physical	50	100	20	Normal	—	○
19	Smog	Poison	Special	30	70	20	Normal	—	—
21	Rollout	Rock	Physical	30	90	20	Normal	—	○
25	Take Down	Normal	Physical	90	85	20	Normal	—	○
27	Heat Crash	Fire	Physical	—	100	10	Normal	—	○
31	Assurance	Dark	Physical	50	100	10	Normal	—	○
33	Flamethrower	Fire	Special	95	100	15	Normal	—	—
37	Head Smash	Rock	Physical	150	80	5	Normal	—	○
39	Roar	Normal	Status	—	100	20	Normal	—	—
43	Flare Blitz	Fire	Physical	120	100	15	Normal	—	○

● MOVES TAUGHT BY PEOPLE

Name	Type	Kind	Pow.	Acc.	PP	Range	Long	DA
Fire Pledge	Fire	Special	50	100	10	Normal	—	—

● EGG MOVES

Name	Type	Kind	Pow.	Acc.	PP	Range	Long	DA
Covet	Normal	Physical	60	100	40	Normal	—	○
Body Slam	Normal	Physical	85	100	15	Normal	—	○
Thrash	Normal	Physical	120	100	10	1 Random	—	○
Magnitude	Ground	Physical	—	100	30	Adjacent	—	○
Superpower	Fighting	Physical	120	100	5	Normal	—	○
Curse	Ghost	Status	—	—	10	Varies	—	—
Endeavor	Normal	Physical	—	100	5	Normal	—	○
Yawn	Normal	Status	—	—	10	Normal	—	—
Sleep Talk	Normal	Status	—	—	10	Self	—	—
Heavy Slam	Steel	Physical	—	100	10	Normal	—	○

● TM & HM MOVES

No.	Name	Type	Kind	Pow.	Acc.	PP	Range	Long	DA
TM05	Roar	Normal	Status	—	100	20	Normal	—	—
TM06	Toxic	Poison	Status	—	90	10	Normal	—	—
TM10	Hidden Power	Normal	Special	—	100	15	Normal	—	—
TM11	Sunny Day	Fire	Status	—	—	5	Both Sides	—	—
TM12	Taunt	Dark	Status	—	100	20	Normal	—	—
TM17	Protect	Normal	Status	—	—	10	Self	—	—
TM21	Frustration	Normal	Physical	—	100	20	Normal	—	○
TM22	SolarBeam	Grass	Special	120	100	10	Normal	—	—
TM27	Return	Normal	Physical	—	100	20	Normal	—	○
TM32	Double Team	Normal	Status	—	—	15	Self	—	—
TM35	Flamethrower	Fire	Special	95	100	15	Normal	—	—
TM38	Fire Blast	Fire	Special	120	85	5	Normal	—	—
TM39	Rock Tomb	Rock	Physical	50	80	10	Normal	—	○
TM42	Facade	Normal	Physical	70	100	20	Normal	—	○
TM43	Flame Charge	Fire	Physical	50	100	20	Normal	—	○
TM44	Rest	Psychic	Status	—	—	10	Self	—	—
TM45	Attract	Normal	Status	—	100	15	Normal	—	—
TM48	Round	Normal	Special	60	100	15	Normal	—	—
TM49	Echoed Voice	Normal	Special	40	100	15	Normal	—	—
TM50	Overheat	Fire	Special	140	90	5	Normal	—	—
TM59	Incinerate	Fire	Special	30	100	15	Many Others	—	—
TM61	Will-O-Wisp	Fire	Status	—	75	15	Normal	—	—
TM74	Gyro Ball	Steel	Physical	—	100	5	Normal	—	○
TM86	Grass Knot	Grass	Special	—	100	20	Normal	—	○
TM87	Swagger	Normal	Status	—	90	15	Normal	—	—
TM90	Substitute	Normal	Status	—	—	10	Self	—	—
TM93	Wild Charge	Electric	Physical	90	100	15	Normal	—	○
TM94	Rock Smash	Fighting	Physical	40	100	15	Normal	—	○
HM04	Strength	Normal	Physical	80	100	15	Normal	—	○

EVOLUTION

Tepig → Lv. 17 → Pignite → Lv. 36 → Emboar

ABILITY ● Blaze

EGG GROUP Field

STATS
HP ●●
ATTACK ●●●
DEFENSE ●●
SP. ATTACK ●●
SP. DEFENSE ●●
SPEED ●●

● MAIN WAYS TO OBTAIN

POKÉMON BLACK VERSION	1	Receive from Professor Juniper in Nuvema Town at the beginning of the adventure
	2	—

POKÉMON WHITE VERSION	1	Receive from Professor Juniper in Nuvema Town at the beginning of the adventure
	2	—

Pignite

● TYPE Fire Fighting

● LEVEL-UP AND LEARNED MOVES

Lv.	Name	Type	Kind	Pow.	Acc.	PP	Range	Long	DA
1	Tackle	Normal	Physical	50	100	35	Normal	–	○
1	Tail Whip	Normal	Status	–	100	30	Many Others	–	–
1	Ember	Fire	Special	40	100	25	Normal	–	–
1	Odor Sleuth	Normal	Status	–	–	40	Normal	–	–
3	Tail Whip	Normal	Status	–	100	30	Many Others	–	–
7	Ember	Fire	Special	40	100	25	Normal	–	–
9	Odor Sleuth	Normal	Status	–	–	40	Normal	–	–
13	Defense Curl	Normal	Status	–	–	40	Self	–	–
15	Flame Charge	Fire	Physical	50	100	20	Normal	–	–
17	Arm Thrust	Fighting	Physical	15	100	20	Normal	–	○
20	Smog	Poison	Special	20	70	20	Normal	–	–
23	Rollout	Rock	Physical	30	90	20	Normal	–	○
28	Take Down	Normal	Physical	90	85	20	Normal	–	○
31	Heat Crash	Fire	Physical	–	100	10	Normal	–	–
36	Assurance	Dark	Physical	50	100	10	Normal	–	–
39	Flamethrower	Fire	Special	95	100	15	Normal	–	–
44	Head Smash	Rock	Physical	150	80	5	Normal	–	○
47	Roar	Normal	Status	–	100	20	Normal	–	○
52	Flare Blitz	Fire	Physical	120	100	15	Normal	–	○

● MOVES TAUGHT BY PEOPLE

Name	Type	Kind	Pow.	Acc.	PP	Range	Long	DA
Fire Pledge	Fire	Special	50	100	10	Normal	–	–

● TM & HM MOVES

No.	Name	Type	Kind	Pow.	Acc.	PP	Range	Long	DA
TM05	Roar	Normal	Status	–	100	20	Normal	–	–
TM06	Toxic	Poison	Status	–	90	10	Normal	–	–
TM10	Hidden Power	Normal	Special	–	100	15	Normal	–	–
TM11	Sunny Day	Fire	Status	–	–	5	Both Sides	–	–
TM17	Protect	Normal	Status	–	–	10	Self	–	–
TM21	Frustration	Normal	Physical	–	100	20	Normal	–	○
TM22	SolarBeam	Grass	Special	120	100	10	Normal	–	–
TM27	Return	Normal	Physical	–	100	20	Normal	–	○
TM31	Brick Break	Fighting	Physical	75	100	15	Normal	–	–
TM32	Double Team	Normal	Status	–	–	15	Self	–	–
TM35	Flamethrower	Fire	Special	95	100	15	Normal	–	–
TM38	Fire Blast	Fire	Special	120	85	5	Normal	–	–
TM39	Rock Tomb	Rock	Physical	50	80	10	Normal	–	–
TM42	Facade	Normal	Physical	70	100	20	Normal	–	○
TM43	Flame Charge	Fire	Physical	50	100	20	Normal	–	–
TM44	Rest	Psychic	Status	–	–	10	Self	–	–
TM45	Attract	Normal	Status	–	100	15	Normal	–	–
TM47	Low Sweep	Fighting	Physical	60	100	20	Normal	–	–
TM48	Round	Normal	Special	60	100	15	Normal	–	–
TM49	Echoed Voice	Normal	Special	40	100	15	Normal	–	–
TM50	Overheat	Fire	Special	140	90	5	Normal	–	–
TM52	Focus Blast	Fighting	Special	120	70	5	Normal	–	–
TM56	Fling	Dark	Physical	–	100	10	Normal	–	○
TM59	Incinerate	Fire	Special	30	100	15	Many Others	–	–
TM61	Will-O-Wisp	Fire	Status	–	75	15	Normal	–	–
TM71	Stone Edge	Rock	Physical	100	80	5	Normal	–	○
TM74	Gyro Ball	Steel	Physical	–	100	5	Normal	–	○
TM78	Bulldoze	Ground	Physical	60	100	20	Adjacent	–	–
TM80	Rock Slide	Rock	Physical	75	90	10	Many Others	–	–
TM83	Work Up	Normal	Status	–	–	30	Self	–	–
TM84	Poison Jab	Poison	Physical	80	100	20	Normal	–	○
TM86	Grass Knot	Grass	Special	–	100	20	Normal	–	–
TM87	Swagger	Normal	Status	–	90	15	Normal	–	–
TM90	Substitute	Normal	Status	–	–	10	Self	–	–
TM93	Wild Charge	Electric	Physical	90	100	15	Normal	–	–
TM94	Rock Smash	Fighting	Physical	40	100	15	Normal	–	○
HM04	Strength	Normal	Physical	80	100	15	Normal	–	○

● FOOTPRINT

● MALE/FEMALE HAVE SAME FORM

● HEIGHT: 3'03"
● WEIGHT: 122.4 lbs.
● GENDER: Both ♂♀ exist
● ITEMS:
  • None

POKÉMON BLACK VERSION
When its internal fire flares up, its movements grow sharper and faster. When in trouble, it emits smoke.

POKÉMON WHITE VERSION
Whatever it eats becomes fuel for the flame in its stomach. When it is angered, the intensity of the flame increases.

EVOLUTION
Tepig — Lv. 17 → Pignite — Lv. 36 → Emboar

ABILITY ● Blaze

EGG GROUP Field

STATS
HP ●●●
ATTACK ●●●●
DEFENSE ●●
SP. ATTACK ●●●
SP. DEFENSE ●●
SPEED ●●●

● MAIN WAYS TO OBTAIN

POKÉMON BLACK VERSION
1 Level up Tepig to Lv. 17
2 —

POKÉMON WHITE VERSION
1 Level up Tepig to Lv. 17
2 —

Emboar

● TYPE Fire Fighting

● LEVEL-UP AND LEARNED MOVES

Lv.	Name	Type	Kind	Pow.	Acc.	PP	Range	Long	DA
1	Hammer Arm	Fighting	Physical	100	90	10	Normal	–	–
1	Tackle	Normal	Physical	50	100	35	Normal	–	○
1	Tail Whip	Normal	Status	–	100	30	Many Others	–	–
1	Ember	Fire	Special	40	100	25	Normal	–	–
1	Odor Sleuth	Normal	Status	–	–	40	Normal	–	–
3	Tail Whip	Normal	Status	–	100	30	Many Others	–	–
7	Ember	Fire	Special	40	100	25	Normal	–	–
9	Odor Sleuth	Normal	Status	–	–	40	Normal	–	–
13	Defense Curl	Normal	Status	–	–	40	Self	–	–
15	Flame Charge	Fire	Physical	50	100	20	Normal	–	–
17	Arm Thrust	Fighting	Physical	15	100	20	Normal	–	○
20	Smog	Poison	Special	20	70	20	Normal	–	–
23	Rollout	Rock	Physical	30	90	20	Normal	–	○
28	Take Down	Normal	Physical	90	85	20	Normal	–	○
31	Heat Crash	Fire	Physical	–	100	10	Normal	–	–
38	Assurance	Dark	Physical	50	100	10	Normal	–	–
43	Flamethrower	Fire	Special	95	100	15	Normal	–	–
50	Head Smash	Rock	Physical	150	80	5	Normal	–	○
55	Roar	Normal	Status	–	100	20	Normal	–	○
62	Flare Blitz	Fire	Physical	120	100	15	Normal	–	○

● MOVES TAUGHT BY PEOPLE

Name	Type	Kind	Pow.	Acc.	PP	Range	Long	DA
Fire Pledge	Fire	Special	50	100	10	Normal	–	–
Blast Burn	Fire	Special	150	90	5	Normal	–	–

● TM & HM MOVES

No.	Name	Type	Kind	Pow.	Acc.	PP	Range	Long	DA
TM05	Roar	Normal	Status	–	100	20	Normal	–	–
TM06	Toxic	Poison	Status	–	90	10	Normal	–	–
TM08	Bulk Up	Fighting	Status	–	–	20	Self	–	–
TM10	Hidden Power	Normal	Special	–	100	15	Normal	–	–
TM11	Sunny Day	Fire	Status	–	–	5	Both Sides	–	–
TM12	Taunt	Dark	Status	–	100	20	Normal	–	–
TM15	Hyper Beam	Normal	Special	150	90	5	Normal	–	–
TM17	Protect	Normal	Status	–	–	10	Self	–	–
TM21	Frustration	Normal	Physical	–	100	20	Normal	–	○
TM22	SolarBeam	Grass	Special	120	100	10	Normal	–	–
TM23	Smack Down	Rock	Physical	50	100	15	Normal	–	–
TM26	Earthquake	Ground	Physical	100	100	10	Adjacent	–	–
TM27	Return	Normal	Physical	–	100	20	Normal	–	○
TM31	Brick Break	Fighting	Physical	75	100	15	Normal	–	–
TM32	Double Team	Normal	Status	–	–	15	Self	–	–
TM35	Flamethrower	Fire	Special	95	100	15	Normal	–	–
TM38	Fire Blast	Fire	Special	120	85	5	Normal	–	–
TM39	Rock Tomb	Rock	Physical	50	80	10	Normal	–	–
TM42	Facade	Normal	Physical	70	100	20	Normal	–	○
TM43	Flame Charge	Fire	Physical	50	100	20	Normal	–	–
TM44	Rest	Psychic	Status	–	–	10	Self	–	–
TM45	Attract	Normal	Status	–	100	15	Normal	–	–
TM47	Low Sweep	Fighting	Physical	60	100	20	Normal	–	–
TM48	Round	Normal	Special	60	100	15	Normal	–	–
TM49	Echoed Voice	Normal	Special	40	100	15	Normal	–	–
TM50	Overheat	Fire	Special	140	90	5	Normal	–	–
TM52	Focus Blast	Fighting	Special	120	70	5	Normal	–	–
TM55	Scald	Water	Special	80	100	15	Normal	–	–
TM56	Fling	Dark	Physical	–	100	10	Normal	–	○
TM59	Incinerate	Fire	Special	30	100	15	Many Others	–	–
TM61	Will-O-Wisp	Fire	Status	–	75	15	Normal	–	–
TM68	Giga Impact	Normal	Physical	150	90	5	Normal	–	–
TM71	Stone Edge	Rock	Physical	100	80	5	Normal	–	○
TM74	Gyro Ball	Steel	Physical	–	100	5	Normal	–	○
TM78	Bulldoze	Ground	Physical	60	100	20	Adjacent	–	–
TM80	Rock Slide	Rock	Physical	75	90	10	Many Others	–	–
TM83	Work Up	Normal	Status	–	–	30	Self	–	–
TM84	Poison Jab	Poison	Physical	80	100	20	Normal	–	○
TM86	Grass Knot	Grass	Special	–	100	20	Normal	–	–
TM87	Swagger	Normal	Status	–	90	15	Normal	–	–
TM90	Substitute	Normal	Status	–	–	10	Self	–	–
TM93	Wild Charge	Electric	Physical	90	100	15	Normal	–	–
TM94	Rock Smash	Fighting	Physical	40	100	15	Normal	–	○
HM04	Strength	Normal	Physical	80	100	15	Normal	–	○

● FOOTPRINT

● MALE/FEMALE HAVE SAME FORM

● HEIGHT: 5'03"
● WEIGHT: 330.7 lbs.
● GENDER: Both ♂♀ exist
● ITEMS:
  • None

POKÉMON BLACK VERSION
It can throw a fire punch by setting its fists on fire with its fiery chin. It cares deeply about its friends.

POKÉMON WHITE VERSION
It has mastered fast and powerful fighting moves. It grows a beard of fire.

EVOLUTION
Tepig — Lv. 17 → Pignite — Lv. 36 → Emboar

ABILITY ● Blaze

EGG GROUP Field

STATS
HP ●●●●
ATTACK ●●●●
DEFENSE ●●●
SP. ATTACK ●●●
SP. DEFENSE ●●
SPEED ●●●

● MAIN WAYS TO OBTAIN

POKÉMON BLACK VERSION
1 Level up Pignite to Lv. 36
2 —

POKÉMON WHITE VERSION
1 Level up Pignite to Lv. 36
2 —

Oshawott

● TYPE Water

● HEIGHT: 1'08"
● WEIGHT: 13.0 lbs.
● GENDER: Both ♂♀ exist
● ITEMS:
  • None

● FOOTPRINT

● MALE/FEMALE HAVE SAME FORM

POKÉMON BLACK VERSION
It fights using the scalchop on its stomach. In response to an attack, it retaliates immediately by slashing.

POKÉMON WHITE VERSION
The scalchop on its stomach is made from the same elements as claws. It detaches the scalchop for use as a blade.

● LEVEL-UP AND LEARNED MOVES

Lv.	Name	Type	Kind	Pow.	Acc.	PP	Range	Long	DA
1	Tackle	Normal	Physical	50	100	35	Normal	—	○
5	Tail Whip	Normal	Status	—	100	30	Many Others	—	—
7	Water Gun	Water	Special	40	100	25	Normal	—	—
11	Water Sport	Water	Status	—	—	15	Both Sides	—	—
13	Focus Energy	Normal	Status	—	—	30	Self	—	—
17	Razor Shell	Water	Physical	75	95	10	Normal	—	○
19	Fury Cutter	Bug	Physical	20	95	20	Normal	—	○
23	Water Pulse	Water	Special	60	100	20	Normal	○	—
25	Revenge	Fighting	Physical	60	100	10	Normal	—	○
29	Aqua Jet	Water	Physical	40	100	20	Normal	—	○
31	Encore	Normal	Status	—	100	5	Normal	—	—
35	Aqua Tail	Water	Physical	90	90	10	Normal	—	○
37	Retaliate	Normal	Physical	70	100	5	Normal	—	○
41	Swords Dance	Normal	Status	—	—	30	Self	—	—
43	Hydro Pump	Water	Special	120	80	5	Normal	—	—

● MOVES TAUGHT BY PEOPLE

Name	Type	Kind	Pow.	Acc.	PP	Range	Long	DA
Water Pledge	Water	Special	50	100	10	Normal	—	—

● EGG MOVES

Name	Type	Kind	Pow.	Acc.	PP	Range	Long	DA
Copycat	Normal	Status	—	—	20	Self	—	—
Detect	Fighting	Status	—	—	5	Self	—	—
Air Slash	Flying	Special	75	95	20	Normal	○	—
Assurance	Dark	Physical	50	100	10	Normal	—	○
Brine	Water	Special	65	100	10	Normal	—	—
Night Slash	Dark	Physical	70	100	15	Normal	—	○
Trump Card	Normal	Special	—	—	5	Normal	—	—
Screech	Normal	Status	—	85	40	Normal	—	—

● TM & HM MOVES

No.	Name	Type	Kind	Pow.	Acc.	PP	Range	Long	DA
TM06	Toxic	Poison	Status	—	90	10	Normal	—	—
TM07	Hail	Ice	Status	—	—	10	Both Sides	—	—
TM10	Hidden Power	Normal	Special	—	100	15	Normal	—	—
TM12	Taunt	Dark	Status	—	100	20	Normal	—	—
TM13	Ice Beam	Ice	Special	95	100	10	Normal	—	—
TM14	Blizzard	Ice	Special	120	70	5	Many Others	—	—
TM17	Protect	Normal	Status	—	—	10	Self	—	—
TM18	Rain Dance	Water	Status	—	—	5	Both Sides	—	—
TM21	Frustration	Normal	Physical	—	100	20	Normal	—	○
TM27	Return	Normal	Physical	—	100	20	Normal	—	○
TM28	Dig	Ground	Physical	80	100	10	Normal	—	○
TM32	Double Team	Normal	Status	—	—	15	Self	—	—
TM40	Aerial Ace	Flying	Physical	60	—	20	Normal	○	○
TM42	Facade	Normal	Physical	70	100	20	Normal	—	○
TM44	Rest	Psychic	Status	—	—	10	Self	—	—
TM45	Attract	Normal	Status	—	100	15	Normal	—	—
TM48	Round	Normal	Special	60	100	15	Normal	—	—
TM54	False Swipe	Normal	Physical	40	100	40	Normal	—	○
TM55	Scald	Water	Special	80	100	15	Normal	—	—
TM56	Fling	Dark	Physical	—	100	10	Normal	—	○
TM67	Retaliate	Normal	Physical	70	100	5	Normal	—	○
TM75	Swords Dance	Normal	Status	—	—	30	Self	—	—
TM81	X-Scissor	Bug	Physical	80	100	15	Normal	—	○
TM86	Grass Knot	Grass	Special	—	100	20	Normal	—	○
TM87	Swagger	Normal	Status	—	90	15	Normal	—	—
TM90	Substitute	Normal	Status	—	—	10	Self	—	—
TM94	Rock Smash	Fighting	Physical	40	100	15	Normal	—	○
HM01	Cut	Normal	Physical	50	95	30	Normal	—	○
HM03	Surf	Water	Special	95	100	15	Adjacent	—	—
HM05	Waterfall	Water	Physical	80	100	15	Normal	—	○
HM06	Dive	Water	Physical	80	100	10	Normal	—	—

EVOLUTION

Oshawott — Lv. 17 → Dewott — Lv. 36 → Samurott

ABILITY
● Torrent

EGG GROUP
Field

STATS
HP ●●
ATTACK ●●
DEFENSE ●●●
SP. ATTACK ●●●
SP. DEFENSE ●●●
SPEED ●●

● MAIN WAYS TO OBTAIN

| POKÉMON BLACK VERSION | 1 | Receive from Professor Juniper in Nuvema Town at the beginning of the adventure |
| | 2 | — |

| POKÉMON WHITE VERSION | 1 | Receive from Professor Juniper in Nuvema Town at the beginning of the adventure |
| | 2 | — |

Dewott

● TYPE Water

● HEIGHT: 2'07"
● WEIGHT: 54.0 lbs.
● GENDER: Both ♂♀ exist
● ITEMS:
  • None

● FOOTPRINT

● MALE/FEMALE HAVE SAME FORM

POKÉMON BLACK VERSION
Strict training is how it learns its flowing double-scalchop technique.

POKÉMON WHITE VERSION
Scalchop techniques differ from one Dewott to another. It never neglects maintaining its scalchops.

● LEVEL-UP AND LEARNED MOVES

Lv.	Name	Type	Kind	Pow.	Acc.	PP	Range	Long	DA
1	Tackle	Normal	Physical	50	100	35	Normal	—	○
1	Tail Whip	Normal	Status	—	100	30	Many Others	—	—
1	Water Gun	Water	Special	40	100	25	Normal	—	—
1	Water Sport	Water	Status	—	—	15	Both Sides	—	—
5	Tail Whip	Normal	Status	—	100	30	Many Others	—	—
7	Water Gun	Water	Special	40	100	25	Normal	—	—
11	Water Sport	Water	Status	—	—	15	Both Sides	—	—
13	Focus Energy	Normal	Status	—	—	30	Self	—	—
17	Razor Shell	Water	Physical	75	95	10	Normal	—	○
20	Fury Cutter	Bug	Physical	20	95	20	Normal	—	○
25	Water Pulse	Water	Special	60	100	20	Normal	○	—
28	Revenge	Fighting	Physical	60	100	10	Normal	—	○
33	Aqua Jet	Water	Physical	40	100	20	Normal	—	○
36	Encore	Normal	Status	—	100	5	Normal	—	—
41	Aqua Tail	Water	Physical	90	90	10	Normal	—	○
44	Retaliate	Normal	Physical	70	100	5	Normal	—	○
49	Swords Dance	Normal	Status	—	—	30	Self	—	—
52	Hydro Pump	Water	Special	120	80	5	Normal	—	—

● MOVES TAUGHT BY PEOPLE

Name	Type	Kind	Pow.	Acc.	PP	Range	Long	DA
Water Pledge	Water	Special	50	100	10	Normal	—	—

● TM & HM MOVES

No.	Name	Type	Kind	Pow.	Acc.	PP	Range	Long	DA
TM06	Toxic	Poison	Status	—	90	10	Normal	—	—
TM07	Hail	Ice	Status	—	—	10	Both Sides	—	—
TM10	Hidden Power	Normal	Special	—	100	15	Normal	—	—
TM12	Taunt	Dark	Status	—	100	20	Normal	—	—
TM13	Ice Beam	Ice	Special	95	100	10	Normal	—	—
TM14	Blizzard	Ice	Special	120	70	5	Many Others	—	—
TM17	Protect	Normal	Status	—	—	10	Self	—	—
TM18	Rain Dance	Water	Status	—	—	5	Both Sides	—	—
TM21	Frustration	Normal	Physical	—	100	20	Normal	—	○
TM27	Return	Normal	Physical	—	100	20	Normal	—	○
TM28	Dig	Ground	Physical	80	100	10	Normal	—	○
TM32	Double Team	Normal	Status	—	—	15	Self	—	—
TM40	Aerial Ace	Flying	Physical	60	—	20	Normal	○	○
TM42	Facade	Normal	Physical	70	100	20	Normal	—	○
TM44	Rest	Psychic	Status	—	—	10	Self	—	—
TM45	Attract	Normal	Status	—	100	15	Normal	—	—
TM48	Round	Normal	Special	60	100	15	Normal	—	—
TM54	False Swipe	Normal	Physical	40	100	40	Normal	—	○
TM55	Scald	Water	Special	80	100	15	Normal	—	—
TM56	Fling	Dark	Physical	—	100	10	Normal	—	○
TM67	Retaliate	Normal	Physical	70	100	5	Normal	—	○
TM75	Swords Dance	Normal	Status	—	—	30	Self	—	—
TM81	X-Scissor	Bug	Physical	80	100	15	Normal	—	○
TM86	Grass Knot	Grass	Special	—	100	20	Normal	—	○
TM87	Swagger	Normal	Status	—	90	15	Normal	—	—
TM90	Substitute	Normal	Status	—	—	10	Self	—	—
TM94	Rock Smash	Fighting	Physical	40	100	15	Normal	—	○
HM01	Cut	Normal	Physical	50	95	30	Normal	—	○
HM03	Surf	Water	Special	95	100	15	Adjacent	—	—
HM05	Waterfall	Water	Physical	80	100	15	Normal	—	○
HM06	Dive	Water	Physical	80	100	10	Normal	—	—

EVOLUTION

Oshawott — Lv. 17 → Dewott — Lv. 36 → Samurott

ABILITY
● Torrent

EGG GROUP
Field

STATS
HP ●●●
ATTACK ●●
DEFENSE ●●
SP. ATTACK ●●●●
SP. DEFENSE ●●
SPEED ●●●

● MAIN WAYS TO OBTAIN

| POKÉMON BLACK VERSION | 1 | Level up Oshawott to Lv. 17 |
| | 2 | — |

| POKÉMON WHITE VERSION | 1 | Level up Oshawott to Lv. 17 |
| | 2 | — |

Samurott

● TYPE **Water**

● HEIGHT: 4'11"
● WEIGHT: 208.6 lbs.
● GENDER: Both ♂♀ exist
● ITEMS:
• None

● FOOTPRINT

● MALE/FEMALE HAVE SAME FORM

One swing of the sword incorporated in its armor can fell an opponent. A simple glare from one of them quiets everybody.

Part of the armor on its anterior legs becomes a giant sword. Its cry alone is enough to intimidate most enemies.

● LEVEL-UP AND LEARNED MOVES

Lv.	Name	Type	Kind	Pow.	Acc.	PP	Range	Long	DA
1	Megahorn	Bug	Physical	120	85	10	Normal	–	○
1	Tackle	Normal	Physical	50	100	35	Normal	–	○
1	Tail Whip	Normal	Status	–	100	30	Many Others	–	–
1	Water Gun	Water	Special	40	100	25	Normal	–	○
1	Water Sport	Water	Status	–	–	15	Both Sides	–	–
5	Tail Whip	Normal	Status	–	100	30	Many Others	–	–
7	Water Gun	Water	Special	40	100	25	Normal	–	○
11	Water Sport	Water	Status	–	–	15	Both Sides	–	–
13	Focus Energy	Normal	Status	–	–	30	Self	–	–
17	Razor Shell	Water	Physical	75	95	10	Normal	–	○
20	Fury Cutter	Bug	Physical	20	95	20	Normal	–	○
25	Water Pulse	Water	Special	60	100	20	Normal	–	○
28	Revenge	Fighting	Physical	60	100	10	Normal	○	–
33	Aqua Jet	Water	Physical	40	100	20	Normal	–	○
36	Slash	Normal	Physical	70	100	20	Normal	–	○
38	Encore	Normal	Status	–	100	5	Normal	–	–
45	Aqua Tail	Water	Physical	90	90	10	Normal	–	○
50	Retaliate	Normal	Physical	70	100	5	Normal	–	○
57	Swords Dance	Normal	Status	–	–	30	Self	–	–
62	Hydro Pump	Water	Special	120	80	5	Normal	–	○

● MOVES TAUGHT BY PEOPLE

Name	Type	Kind	Pow.	Acc.	PP	Range	Long	DA
Water Pledge	Water	Special	50	100	10	Normal	–	–
Hydro Cannon	Water	Special	150	90	5	Normal	–	–

● TM & HM MOVES

No.	Name	Type	Kind	Pow.	Acc.	PP	Range	Long	DA
TM06	Toxic	Poison	Status	–	90	10	Normal	–	–
TM07	Hail	Ice	Status	–	–	10	Both Sides	–	–
TM10	Hidden Power	Normal	Special	–	100	15	Normal	–	–
TM12	Taunt	Dark	Status	–	100	20	Normal	–	–
TM13	Ice Beam	Ice	Special	95	100	10	Normal	–	○
TM14	Blizzard	Ice	Special	120	70	5	Normal	–	○
TM15	Hyper Beam	Normal	Special	150	90	5	Normal	–	○
TM17	Protect	Normal	Status	–	–	10	Self	–	–
TM18	Rain Dance	Water	Status	–	–	5	Both Sides	–	–
TM21	Frustration	Normal	Physical	–	100	20	Normal	–	○
TM27	Return	Normal	Physical	–	100	20	Normal	–	○
TM28	Dig	Ground	Physical	80	100	10	Normal	–	○
TM32	Double Team	Normal	Status	–	–	15	Self	–	–
TM40	Aerial Ace	Flying	Physical	60	–	20	Normal	○	–
TM42	Facade	Normal	Physical	70	100	20	Normal	–	○
TM44	Rest	Psychic	Status	–	–	10	Self	–	–
TM45	Attract	Normal	Status	–	100	15	Normal	–	–
TM48	Round	Normal	Special	60	100	15	Normal	–	–
TM54	False Swipe	Normal	Physical	40	100	40	Normal	–	○
TM55	Scald	Water	Special	80	100	15	Normal	–	○
TM56	Fling	Dark	Physical	–	100	10	Normal	–	○
TM67	Retaliate	Normal	Physical	70	100	5	Normal	–	○
TM68	Giga Impact	Normal	Physical	150	90	5	Normal	–	○
TM75	Swords Dance	Normal	Status	–	–	30	Self	–	–
TM81	X-Scissor	Bug	Physical	80	100	15	Normal	–	○
TM82	Dragon Tail	Dragon	Physical	60	90	10	Normal	–	○
TM86	Grass Knot	Grass	Special	–	100	20	Normal	–	○
TM87	Swagger	Normal	Status	–	90	15	Normal	–	–
TM90	Substitute	Normal	Status	–	–	10	Self	–	–
TM94	Rock Smash	Fighting	Physical	40	100	15	Normal	–	○
HM01	Cut	Normal	Physical	50	95	30	Normal	–	○
HM03	Surf	Water	Special	95	100	15	Adjacent	–	○
HM04	Strength	Normal	Physical	80	100	15	Normal	–	○
HM05	Waterfall	Water	Physical	80	100	15	Normal	–	○
HM06	Dive	Water	Physical	80	100	10	Normal	–	○

● EVOLUTION

Oshawott → Lv. 17 → Dewott → Lv. 36 → Samurott

ABILITY ● Torrent

EGG GROUP: Field

STATS
HP ●●●●
ATTACK ●●●●
DEFENSE ●●●
SP. ATTACK ●●●●●
SP. DEFENSE ●●●
SPEED ●●●

● MAIN WAYS TO OBTAIN

	POKÉMON BLACK VERSION	
1	Level up Dewott to Lv. 36	
2	—	

	POKÉMON WHITE VERSION	
1	Level up Dewott to Lv. 36	
2	—	

Patrat

● TYPE **Normal**

● HEIGHT: 1'08"
● WEIGHT: 25.6 lbs.
● GENDER: Both ♂♀ exist
● ITEMS:
• None

● FOOTPRINT

● MALE/FEMALE HAVE SAME FORM

Using food stored in cheek pouches, they can keep watch for days. They use their tails to communicate with others.

Extremely cautious, they take shifts to maintain a constant watch of their nest. They feel insecure without a lookout.

● LEVEL-UP AND LEARNED MOVES

Lv.	Name	Type	Kind	Pow.	Acc.	PP	Range	Long	DA
1	Tackle	Normal	Physical	50	100	35	Normal	–	○
3	Leer	Normal	Status	–	100	30	Many Others	–	–
6	Bite	Dark	Physical	60	100	25	Normal	–	○
8	Bide	Normal	Physical	–	–	10	Self	–	○
11	Detect	Fighting	Status	–	–	5	Self	–	–
13	Sand-Attack	Ground	Status	–	100	15	Normal	–	–
16	Crunch	Dark	Physical	80	100	15	Normal	–	○
18	Hypnosis	Psychic	Status	–	60	20	Normal	–	–
21	Super Fang	Normal	Physical	–	90	10	Normal	–	○
23	After You	Normal	Status	–	–	15	Normal	–	–
26	Work Up	Normal	Status	–	–	30	Self	–	–
28	Hyper Fang	Normal	Physical	80	90	15	Normal	–	○
31	Mean Look	Normal	Status	–	–	5	Normal	–	–
33	Baton Pass	Normal	Status	–	–	40	Self	–	–
36	Slam	Normal	Physical	80	75	20	Normal	–	○

● MOVES TAUGHT BY PEOPLE

Name	Type	Kind	Pow.	Acc.	PP	Range	Long	DA

● EGG MOVES

Name	Type	Kind	Pow.	Acc.	PP	Range	Long	DA
Foresight	Normal	Status	–	–	40	Normal	–	–
Iron Tail	Steel	Physical	100	75	15	Normal	–	○
Screech	Normal	Status	–	85	40	Normal	–	–
Assurance	Dark	Physical	50	100	10	Normal	–	○
Pursuit	Dark	Physical	40	100	20	Normal	–	○
Revenge	Fighting	Physical	60	100	10	Normal	○	–
Flail	Normal	Physical	–	100	15	Normal	–	○

● TM & HM MOVES

No.	Name	Type	Kind	Pow.	Acc.	PP	Range	Long	DA
TM06	Toxic	Poison	Status	–	90	10	Normal	–	–
TM10	Hidden Power	Normal	Special	–	100	15	Normal	–	–
TM11	Sunny Day	Fire	Status	–	–	5	Both Sides	–	–
TM17	Protect	Normal	Status	–	–	10	Self	–	–
TM18	Rain Dance	Water	Status	–	–	5	Both Sides	–	–
TM21	Frustration	Normal	Physical	–	100	20	Normal	–	○
TM24	Thunderbolt	Electric	Special	95	100	15	Normal	–	○
TM27	Return	Normal	Physical	–	100	20	Normal	–	○
TM28	Dig	Ground	Physical	80	100	10	Normal	–	○
TM30	Shadow Ball	Ghost	Special	80	100	15	Normal	–	○
TM32	Double Team	Normal	Status	–	–	15	Self	–	–
TM42	Facade	Normal	Physical	70	100	20	Normal	–	○
TM44	Rest	Psychic	Status	–	–	10	Self	–	–
TM45	Attract	Normal	Status	–	100	15	Normal	–	–
TM48	Round	Normal	Special	60	100	15	Normal	–	–
TM56	Fling	Dark	Physical	–	100	10	Normal	–	○
TM67	Retaliate	Normal	Physical	70	100	5	Normal	–	○
TM75	Swords Dance	Normal	Status	–	–	30	Self	–	–
TM83	Work Up	Normal	Status	–	–	30	Self	–	–
TM86	Grass Knot	Grass	Special	–	100	20	Normal	–	○
TM87	Swagger	Normal	Status	–	90	15	Normal	–	–
TM90	Substitute	Normal	Status	–	–	10	Self	–	–
HM01	Cut	Normal	Physical	50	95	30	Normal	–	○

● EVOLUTION

Patrat → Lv. 20 → Watchog

ABILITIES ● Run Away ● Keen Eye

EGG GROUP: Field

STATS
HP ●●
ATTACK ●●
DEFENSE ●●
SP. ATTACK ●
SP. DEFENSE ●
SPEED ●●

● MAIN WAYS TO OBTAIN

	POKÉMON BLACK VERSION	
1	Route 1	
2	Route 2	

	POKÉMON WHITE VERSION	
1	Route 1	
2	Route 2	

UNOVA POKÉDEX

009 SAMUROTT

010 PATRAT

Watchog

● TYPE Normal

● FOOTPRINT

● MALE/FEMALE HAVE SAME FORM

● HEIGHT: 3'07"
● WEIGHT: 59.5 lbs.
● GENDER: Both ♂♀ exist
● ITEMS:
• None

POKÉMON BLACK VERSION
When they see an enemy, their tails stand high, and they spit the seeds of berries stored in their cheek pouches.

POKÉMON WHITE VERSION
They make the patterns on their bodies shine in order to threaten predators. Keen eyesight lets them see in the dark.

● LEVEL-UP AND LEARNED MOVES

Lv.	Name	Type	Kind	Pow.	Acc.	PP	Range	Long	DA
1	Tackle	Normal	Physical	50	100	35	Normal	—	—
1	Leer	Normal	Status	—	100	30	Many Others	—	—
1	Bite	Dark	Physical	60	100	25	Normal	—	○
1	Low Kick	Fighting	Physical	—	100	20	Normal	—	○
3	Leer	Normal	Status	—	100	30	Many Others	—	—
6	Bite	Dark	Physical	60	100	25	Normal	—	○
8	Bide	Normal	Physical	—	—	10	Self	—	—
11	Detect	Fighting	Status	—	—	5	Self	—	—
13	Sand-Attack	Ground	Status	—	100	15	Normal	—	—
16	Crunch	Dark	Physical	80	100	15	Normal	—	○
18	Hypnosis	Psychic	Status	—	60	20	Normal	—	—
20	Confuse Ray	Ghost	Status	—	100	10	Normal	—	—
22	Super Fang	Normal	Physical	—	90	10	Normal	—	—
25	After You	Normal	Status	—	—	15	Normal	—	—
29	Psych Up	Normal	Status	—	—	10	Normal	—	—
32	Hyper Fang	Normal	Physical	80	90	15	Normal	—	○
36	Mean Look	Normal	Status	—	—	5	Normal	—	—
39	Baton Pass	Normal	Status	—	—	40	Self	—	—
43	Slam	Normal	Physical	80	75	20	Normal	—	○

● MOVES TAUGHT BY PEOPLE

Name	Type	Kind	Pow.	Acc.	PP	Range	Long	DA

● TM & HM MOVES

No.	Name	Type	Kind	Pow.	Acc.	PP	Range	Long	DA
TM06	Toxic	Poison	Status	—	90	10	Normal	—	—
TM10	Hidden Power	Normal	Special	—	100	15	Normal	—	—
TM11	Sunny Day	Fire	Status	—	—	5	Both Sides	—	—
TM15	Hyper Beam	Normal	Special	150	90	5	Normal	—	—
TM16	Light Screen	Psychic	Status	—	—	30	Your Side	—	—
TM17	Protect	Normal	Status	—	—	10	Self	—	—
TM18	Rain Dance	Water	Status	—	—	5	Both Sides	—	—
TM21	Frustration	Normal	Physical	—	100	20	Normal	—	○
TM24	Thunderbolt	Electric	Special	95	100	15	Normal	—	—
TM25	Thunder	Electric	Special	120	70	10	Normal	—	—
TM27	Return	Normal	Physical	—	100	20	Normal	—	○
TM28	Dig	Ground	Physical	80	100	10	Normal	—	○
TM30	Shadow Ball	Ghost	Special	80	100	15	Normal	—	—
TM32	Double Team	Normal	Status	—	—	15	Self	—	—
TM35	Flamethrower	Fire	Special	95	100	15	Normal	—	—
TM42	Facade	Normal	Physical	70	100	20	Normal	—	○
TM44	Rest	Psychic	Status	—	—	10	Self	—	—
TM45	Attract	Normal	Status	—	100	15	Normal	—	—
TM48	Round	Normal	Special	60	100	15	Normal	—	—
TM52	Focus Blast	Fighting	Special	120	70	5	Normal	—	—
TM56	Fling	Dark	Physical	—	100	10	Normal	—	○
TM67	Retaliate	Normal	Physical	70	100	5	Normal	—	—
TM68	Giga Impact	Normal	Physical	150	90	5	Normal	—	○
TM70	Flash	Normal	Status	—	100	20	Normal	—	—
TM73	Thunder Wave	Electric	Status	—	100	20	Normal	—	—
TM75	Swords Dance	Normal	Status	—	—	30	Self	—	—
TM77	Psych Up	Normal	Status	—	—	10	Self	—	—
TM83	Work Up	Normal	Status	—	—	30	Self	—	—
TM85	Dream Eater	Psychic	Special	100	100	15	Normal	—	—
TM86	Grass Knot	Grass	Special	—	100	20	Normal	—	—
TM87	Swagger	Normal	Status	—	90	15	Normal	—	—
TM90	Substitute	Normal	Status	—	—	10	Self	—	—
TM94	Rock Smash	Fighting	Physical	40	100	15	Normal	—	○
HM01	Cut	Normal	Physical	50	95	30	Normal	—	○
HM04	Strength	Normal	Physical	80	100	15	Normal	—	○

EVOLUTION

Patrat — Lv. 20 → Watchog

ABILITIES
● Illuminate
● Keen Eye

EGG GROUP Field

STATS
HP ●●
ATTACK ●●●●
DEFENSE ●●●
SP. ATTACK ●●●
SP. DEFENSE ●●●
SPEED ●●●

● MAIN WAYS TO OBTAIN

POKÉMON BLACK VERSION
1 Route 7
2 Level up Patrat to Lv. 20

POKÉMON WHITE VERSION
1 Route 7
2 Level up Patrat to Lv. 20

Unova Pokédex 012 | Puppy Pokémon

Lillipup

● TYPE Normal

● FOOTPRINT

● MALE/FEMALE HAVE SAME FORM

● HEIGHT: 1'04"
● WEIGHT: 9.0 lbs.
● GENDER: Both ♂♀ exist
● ITEMS:
• None

POKÉMON BLACK VERSION
It faces strong opponents with great courage. But, when at a disadvantage in a fight, this intelligent Pokémon flees.

POKÉMON WHITE VERSION
The long hair around its face provides an amazing radar that lets it sense subtle changes in its surroundings.

● LEVEL-UP AND LEARNED MOVES

Lv.	Name	Type	Kind	Pow.	Acc.	PP	Range	Long	DA
1	Leer	Normal	Status	—	100	30	Many Others	—	—
1	Tackle	Normal	Physical	50	100	35	Normal	—	—
5	Odor Sleuth	Normal	Status	—	—	40	Normal	—	—
8	Bite	Dark	Physical	60	100	25	Normal	—	○
12	Helping Hand	Normal	Status	—	—	20	1 Ally	—	—
15	Take Down	Normal	Physical	90	85	20	Normal	—	○
19	Work Up	Normal	Status	—	—	30	Self	—	—
22	Crunch	Dark	Physical	80	100	15	Normal	—	○
26	Roar	Normal	Status	—	100	20	Normal	—	—
29	Retaliate	Normal	Physical	70	100	5	Normal	—	—
33	Reversal	Fighting	Physical	—	100	15	Normal	—	○
36	Last Resort	Normal	Physical	140	100	5	Normal	—	—
40	Giga Impact	Normal	Physical	150	90	5	Normal	—	○

● MOVES TAUGHT BY PEOPLE

Name	Type	Kind	Pow.	Acc.	PP	Range	Long	DA

● EGG MOVES

Name	Type	Kind	Pow.	Acc.	PP	Range	Long	DA
Howl	Normal	Status	—	—	40	Self	—	—
Sand-Attack	Ground	Status	—	100	15	Normal	—	—
Mud-Slap	Ground	Special	20	100	10	Normal	—	—
Lick	Ghost	Physical	20	100	30	Normal	—	○
Charm	Normal	Status	—	100	20	Normal	—	—
Endure	Normal	Status	—	—	10	Self	—	—
Yawn	Normal	Status	—	—	10	Normal	—	—
Pursuit	Dark	Physical	40	100	20	Normal	—	○
Fire Fang	Fire	Physical	65	95	15	Normal	—	○
Thunder Fang	Electric	Physical	65	95	15	Normal	—	○
Ice Fang	Ice	Physical	65	95	15	Normal	—	○

● TM & HM MOVES

No.	Name	Type	Kind	Pow.	Acc.	PP	Range	Long	DA
TM05	Roar	Normal	Status	—	100	20	Normal	—	—
TM06	Toxic	Poison	Status	—	90	10	Normal	—	—
TM10	Hidden Power	Normal	Special	—	100	15	Normal	—	—
TM11	Sunny Day	Fire	Status	—	—	5	Both Sides	—	—
TM17	Protect	Normal	Status	—	—	10	Self	—	—
TM18	Rain Dance	Water	Status	—	—	5	Both Sides	—	—
TM21	Frustration	Normal	Physical	—	100	20	Normal	—	○
TM24	Thunderbolt	Electric	Special	95	100	15	Normal	—	—
TM27	Return	Normal	Physical	—	100	20	Normal	—	○
TM28	Dig	Ground	Physical	80	100	10	Normal	—	○
TM30	Shadow Ball	Ghost	Special	80	100	15	Normal	—	—
TM32	Double Team	Normal	Status	—	—	15	Self	—	—
TM39	Rock Tomb	Rock	Physical	50	80	10	Normal	—	—
TM40	Aerial Ace	Flying	Physical	60	—	20	Normal	○	○
TM42	Facade	Normal	Physical	70	100	20	Normal	—	○
TM44	Rest	Psychic	Status	—	—	10	Self	—	—
TM45	Attract	Normal	Status	—	100	15	Normal	—	—
TM48	Round	Normal	Special	60	100	15	Normal	—	—
TM67	Retaliate	Normal	Physical	70	100	5	Normal	—	—
TM68	Giga Impact	Normal	Physical	150	90	5	Normal	—	○
TM73	Thunder Wave	Electric	Status	—	100	20	Normal	—	—
TM83	Work Up	Normal	Status	—	—	30	Self	—	—
TM87	Swagger	Normal	Status	—	90	15	Normal	—	—
TM90	Substitute	Normal	Status	—	—	10	Self	—	—
TM93	Wild Charge	Electric	Physical	90	100	15	Normal	—	○
TM94	Rock Smash	Fighting	Physical	40	100	15	Normal	—	○

EVOLUTION

Lillipup — Lv. 16 → Herdier — Lv. 32 → Stoutland

● MAIN WAYS TO OBTAIN

POKÉMON BLACK VERSION
1 Route 1
2 Route 2

POKÉMON WHITE VERSION
1 Route 1
2 Route 2

ABILITIES
● Vital Spirit
● Pickup

EGG GROUP Field

STATS
HP ●●
ATTACK ●●●
DEFENSE ●●●
SP. ATTACK ●●
SP. DEFENSE ●●
SPEED ●●●

🐾 Herdier

● TYPE Normal

● FOOTPRINT

● MALE/FEMALE HAVE SAME FORM

● HEIGHT: 2'11"
● WEIGHT: 32.4 lbs.
● GENDER: Both ♂♀ exist
● ITEMS:
　• None

POKÉMON BLACK VERSION
It has black, cape-like fur that is very hard and decreases the amount of damage it receives.

POKÉMON WHITE VERSION
It loyally follows its Trainer's orders. For ages, they have helped Trainers raise Pokémon.

● LEVEL-UP AND LEARNED MOVES

Lv.	Name	Type	Kind	Pow.	Acc.	PP	Range	Long	DA
1	Leer	Normal	Status	—	100	30	Many Others	—	—
1	Tackle	Normal	Physical	50	100	35	Normal	—	○
1	Odor Sleuth	Normal	Status	—	—	40	Normal	—	—
1	Bite	Dark	Physical	60	100	25	Normal	—	○
5	Odor Sleuth	Normal	Status	—	—	40	Normal	—	—
8	Bite	Dark	Physical	60	100	25	Normal	—	○
12	Helping Hand	Normal	Status	—	—	20	1 Ally	—	—
15	Take Down	Normal	Physical	90	85	20	Normal	—	○
20	Work Up	Normal	Status	—	—	30	Self	—	—
24	Crunch	Dark	Physical	80	100	15	Normal	—	○
29	Roar	Normal	Status	—	100	20	Normal	—	—
33	Retaliate	Normal	Physical	70	100	5	Normal	—	○
38	Reversal	Fighting	Physical	—	100	15	Normal	—	○
42	Last Resort	Normal	Physical	140	100	5	Normal	—	○
47	Giga Impact	Normal	Physical	150	90	5	Normal	—	○

● MOVES TAUGHT BY PEOPLE

Name	Type	Kind	Pow.	Acc.	PP	Range	Long	DA

● TM & HM MOVES

No.	Name	Type	Kind	Pow.	Acc.	PP	Range	Long	DA
TM05	Roar	Normal	Status	—	100	20	Normal	—	—
TM06	Toxic	Poison	Status	—	90	10	Normal	—	—
TM10	Hidden Power	Normal	Special	—	100	15	Normal	—	—
TM11	Sunny Day	Fire	Status	—	—	5	Both Sides	—	—
TM17	Protect	Normal	Status	—	—	10	Self	—	—
TM18	Rain Dance	Water	Status	—	—	5	Both Sides	—	—
TM21	Frustration	Normal	Physical	—	100	20	Normal	—	○
TM24	Thunderbolt	Electric	Special	95	100	15	Normal	—	—
TM27	Return	Normal	Physical	—	100	20	Normal	—	○
TM28	Dig	Ground	Physical	80	100	10	Normal	—	○
TM30	Shadow Ball	Ghost	Special	80	100	15	Normal	—	—
TM32	Double Team	Normal	Status	—	—	15	Self	—	—
TM39	Rock Tomb	Rock	Physical	50	80	10	Normal	—	○
TM40	Aerial Ace	Flying	Physical	60	—	20	Normal	○	○
TM42	Facade	Normal	Physical	70	100	20	Normal	—	○
TM44	Rest	Psychic	Status	—	—	10	Self	—	—
TM45	Attract	Normal	Status	—	100	15	Normal	—	—
TM48	Round	Normal	Special	60	100	15	Normal	—	—
TM66	Payback	Dark	Physical	50	100	10	Normal	—	○
TM67	Retaliate	Normal	Physical	70	100	5	Normal	—	○
TM68	Giga Impact	Normal	Physical	150	90	5	Normal	—	○
TM73	Thunder Wave	Electric	Status	—	100	20	Normal	—	—
TM83	Work Up	Normal	Status	—	—	30	Self	—	—
TM87	Swagger	Normal	Status	—	90	15	Normal	—	—
TM90	Substitute	Normal	Status	—	—	10	Self	—	—
TM93	Wild Charge	Electric	Physical	90	100	15	Normal	—	○
TM94	Rock Smash	Fighting	Physical	40	100	15	Normal	—	○
HM03	Surf	Water	Special	95	100	15	Adjacent	—	—
HM04	Strength	Normal	Physical	80	100	15	Normal	—	○

● MAIN WAYS TO OBTAIN

POKÉMON BLACK VERSION
1 Cold Storage Area
2 Level up Lillipup to Lv. 16

POKÉMON WHITE VERSION
1 Cold Storage Area
2 Level up Lillipup to Lv. 16

● EVOLUTION

Lillipup → Lv. 16 → Herdier → Lv. 32 → Stoutland

ABILITIES
● Intimidate
● Sand Rush

STATS
HP ●●
ATTACK ●●●
DEFENSE ●●●
SP. ATTACK ●
SP. DEFENSE ●●
SPEED ●●●

EGG GROUP Field

🐾 Stoutland

● TYPE Normal

● FOOTPRINT

● MALE/FEMALE HAVE SAME FORM

● HEIGHT: 3'11"
● WEIGHT: 134.5 lbs.
● GENDER: Both ♂♀ exist
● ITEMS:
　• None

POKÉMON BLACK VERSION
It rescues people stranded by blizzards in the mountains. Its shaggy fur shields it from the cold.

POKÉMON WHITE VERSION
This extremely wise Pokémon excels at rescuing people stranded at sea or in the mountains.

● LEVEL-UP AND LEARNED MOVES

Lv.	Name	Type	Kind	Pow.	Acc.	PP	Range	Long	DA
1	Ice Fang	Ice	Physical	65	95	15	Normal	—	○
1	Fire Fang	Fire	Physical	65	95	15	Normal	—	○
1	Thunder Fang	Electric	Physical	65	95	15	Normal	—	○
1	Leer	Normal	Status	—	100	30	Many Others	—	—
1	Tackle	Normal	Physical	50	100	35	Normal	—	○
1	Odor Sleuth	Normal	Status	—	—	40	Normal	—	—
1	Bite	Dark	Physical	60	100	25	Normal	—	○
5	Odor Sleuth	Normal	Status	—	—	40	Normal	—	—
8	Bite	Dark	Physical	60	100	25	Normal	—	○
12	Helping Hand	Normal	Status	—	—	20	1 Ally	—	—
15	Take Down	Normal	Physical	90	85	20	Normal	—	○
20	Work Up	Normal	Status	—	—	30	Self	—	—
24	Crunch	Dark	Physical	80	100	15	Normal	—	○
29	Roar	Normal	Status	—	100	20	Normal	—	—
36	Retaliate	Normal	Physical	70	100	5	Normal	—	○
42	Reversal	Fighting	Physical	—	100	15	Normal	—	○
51	Last Resort	Normal	Physical	140	100	5	Normal	—	○
59	Giga Impact	Normal	Physical	150	90	5	Normal	—	○

● MOVES TAUGHT BY PEOPLE

Name	Type	Kind	Pow.	Acc.	PP	Range	Long	DA

● TM & HM MOVES

No.	Name	Type	Kind	Pow.	Acc.	PP	Range	Long	DA
TM05	Roar	Normal	Status	—	100	20	Normal	—	—
TM06	Toxic	Poison	Status	—	90	10	Normal	—	—
TM10	Hidden Power	Normal	Special	—	100	15	Normal	—	—
TM11	Sunny Day	Fire	Status	—	—	5	Both Sides	—	—
TM15	Hyper Beam	Normal	Special	150	90	5	Normal	—	—
TM17	Protect	Normal	Status	—	—	10	Self	—	—
TM18	Rain Dance	Water	Status	—	—	5	Both Sides	—	—
TM21	Frustration	Normal	Physical	—	100	20	Normal	—	○
TM24	Thunderbolt	Electric	Special	95	100	15	Normal	—	—
TM25	Thunder	Electric	Special	120	70	10	Normal	—	—
TM27	Return	Normal	Physical	—	100	20	Normal	—	○
TM28	Dig	Ground	Physical	80	100	10	Normal	—	○
TM30	Shadow Ball	Ghost	Special	80	100	15	Normal	—	—
TM32	Double Team	Normal	Status	—	—	15	Self	—	—
TM39	Rock Tomb	Rock	Physical	50	80	10	Normal	—	○
TM40	Aerial Ace	Flying	Physical	60	—	20	Normal	○	○
TM42	Facade	Normal	Physical	70	100	20	Normal	—	○
TM44	Rest	Psychic	Status	—	—	10	Self	—	—
TM45	Attract	Normal	Status	—	100	15	Normal	—	—
TM48	Round	Normal	Special	60	100	15	Normal	—	—
TM66	Payback	Dark	Physical	50	100	10	Normal	—	○
TM67	Retaliate	Normal	Physical	70	100	5	Normal	—	○
TM68	Giga Impact	Normal	Physical	150	90	5	Normal	—	○
TM73	Thunder Wave	Electric	Status	—	100	20	Normal	—	—
TM83	Work Up	Normal	Status	—	—	30	Self	—	—
TM87	Swagger	Normal	Status	—	90	15	Normal	—	—
TM90	Substitute	Normal	Status	—	—	10	Self	—	—
TM93	Wild Charge	Electric	Physical	90	100	15	Normal	—	○
TM94	Rock Smash	Fighting	Physical	40	100	15	Normal	—	○
HM03	Surf	Water	Special	95	100	15	Adjacent	—	—
HM04	Strength	Normal	Physical	80	100	15	Normal	—	○

● MAIN WAYS TO OBTAIN

POKÉMON BLACK VERSION
1 Cold Storage Area (Rustling Grass)
2 Level up Herdier to Lv. 32

POKÉMON WHITE VERSION
1 Cold Storage Area (Rustling Grass)
2 Level up Herdier to Lv. 32

● EVOLUTION

Lillipup → Lv. 16 → Herdier → Lv. 32 → Stoutland

ABILITIES
● Intimidate
● Sand Rush

STATS
HP ●●●
ATTACK ●●●●
DEFENSE ●●●
SP. ATTACK ●●
SP. DEFENSE ●●●
SPEED ●●●●

EGG GROUP Field

UNOVA POKÉDEX
013 HERDIER
014 STOUTLAND

Purrloin

● TYPE Dark

● LEVEL-UP AND LEARNED MOVES

Lv.	Name	Type	Kind	Pow.	Acc.	PP	Range	Long	DA
1	Scratch	Normal	Physical	40	100	35	Normal	–	–
3	Growl	Normal	Status	–	100	40	Many Others	–	–
6	Assist	Normal	Status	–	–	20	Self	–	–
10	Sand-Attack	Ground	Status	–	100	15	Normal	–	–
12	Fury Swipes	Normal	Physical	18	80	15	Normal	–	○
15	Pursuit	Dark	Physical	40	100	20	Normal	–	–
19	Torment	Dark	Status	–	100	15	Normal	–	–
21	Fake Out	Normal	Physical	40	100	10	Normal	–	○
24	Hone Claws	Dark	Status	–	–	15	Self	–	–
28	Assurance	Dark	Physical	50	100	10	Normal	–	○
30	Slash	Normal	Physical	70	100	20	Normal	–	–
33	Captivate	Normal	Status	–	100	20	Many Others	–	–
37	Night Slash	Dark	Physical	70	100	15	Normal	–	○
39	Snatch	Dark	Status	–	–	10	Self	–	–
42	Nasty Plot	Dark	Status	–	–	20	Self	–	–
46	Sucker Punch	Dark	Physical	80	100	5	Normal	–	○

● MOVES TAUGHT BY PEOPLE

Name	Type	Kind	Pow.	Acc.	PP	Range	Long	DA

● EGG MOVES

Name	Type	Kind	Pow.	Acc.	PP	Range	Long	DA
Pay Day	Normal	Physical	40	100	20	Normal	–	–
Foul Play	Dark	Physical	95	100	15	Normal	–	○
Faint Attack	Dark	Physical	60	–	20	Normal	–	○
Fake Tears	Dark	Status	–	100	20	Normal	–	–
Charm	Normal	Status	–	100	20	Normal	–	–
Encore	Normal	Status	–	100	5	Normal	–	–
Yawn	Normal	Status	–	–	10	Normal	–	–
Covet	Normal	Physical	60	100	40	Normal	–	○

● TM & HM MOVES

No.	Name	Type	Kind	Pow.	Acc.	PP	Range	Long	DA
TM01	Hone Claws	Dark	Status	–	–	15	Self	–	–
TM06	Toxic	Poison	Status	–	90	10	Normal	–	–
TM10	Hidden Power	Normal	Special	–	100	15	Normal	–	–
TM11	Sunny Day	Fire	Status	–	–	5	Both Sides	–	–
TM12	Taunt	Dark	Status	–	100	20	Normal	–	–
TM17	Protect	Normal	Status	–	–	10	Self	–	–
TM18	Rain Dance	Water	Status	–	–	5	Both Sides	–	–
TM21	Frustration	Normal	Physical	–	100	20	Normal	–	○
TM27	Return	Normal	Physical	–	100	20	Normal	–	○
TM30	Shadow Ball	Ghost	Special	80	100	15	Normal	–	–
TM32	Double Team	Normal	Status	–	–	15	Self	–	–
TM40	Aerial Ace	Flying	Physical	60	–	20	Normal	○	○
TM41	Torment	Dark	Status	–	100	15	Normal	–	–
TM42	Facade	Normal	Physical	70	100	20	Normal	–	○
TM44	Rest	Psychic	Status	–	–	10	Self	–	–
TM45	Attract	Normal	Status	–	100	15	Normal	–	–
TM46	Thief	Dark	Physical	40	100	10	Normal	–	○
TM48	Round	Normal	Special	60	100	15	Normal	–	–
TM49	Echoed Voice	Normal	Special	40	100	15	Normal	–	–
TM63	Embargo	Dark	Status	–	100	15	Normal	–	–
TM65	Shadow Claw	Ghost	Physical	70	100	15	Normal	–	○
TM66	Payback	Dark	Physical	50	100	10	Normal	–	○
TM73	Thunder Wave	Electric	Status	–	100	20	Normal	–	–
TM77	Psych Up	Normal	Status	–	–	10	Self	–	–
TM85	Dream Eater	Psychic	Special	100	100	15	Normal	–	–
TM86	Grass Knot	Grass	Special	–	100	20	Normal	–	○
TM87	Swagger	Normal	Status	–	90	15	Normal	–	–
TM90	Substitute	Normal	Status	–	–	10	Self	–	–
HM01	Cut	Normal	Physical	50	95	30	Normal	–	–

● MAIN WAYS TO OBTAIN

POKÉMON BLACK VERSION	1	Route 2
	2	Dreamyard

POKÉMON WHITE VERSION	1	Route 2
	2	Dreamyard

● FOOTPRINT

● MALE/FEMALE HAVE SAME FORM

● HEIGHT: 1'04"
● WEIGHT: 22.3 lbs.
● GENDER: Both ♂♀ exist
● ITEMS:
  • None

POKÉMON BLACK VERSION
They steal from people for fun, but their victims can't help but forgive them. Their deceptively cute act is perfect.

POKÉMON WHITE VERSION
Its cute act is a ruse. When victims let down their guard, they find their items taken. It attacks with sharp claws.

EVOLUTION

Purrloin → Lv. 20 → Liepard

ABILITIES ● Limber ● Unburden

EGG GROUP Field

STATS
HP ●
ATTACK ●●
DEFENSE ●●
SP. ATTACK ●●
SP. DEFENSE ●●
SPEED ●●●

Liepard

● TYPE Dark

● LEVEL-UP AND LEARNED MOVES

Lv.	Name	Type	Kind	Pow.	Acc.	PP	Range	Long	DA
1	Scratch	Normal	Physical	40	100	35	Normal	–	○
1	Growl	Normal	Status	–	100	40	Many Others	–	–
1	Assist	Normal	Status	–	–	20	Self	–	–
1	Sand-Attack	Ground	Status	–	100	15	Normal	–	–
3	Growl	Normal	Status	–	100	40	Many Others	–	–
6	Assist	Normal	Status	–	–	20	Self	–	–
10	Sand-Attack	Ground	Status	–	100	15	Normal	–	–
12	Fury Swipes	Normal	Physical	18	80	15	Normal	–	○
15	Pursuit	Dark	Physical	40	100	20	Normal	–	–
17	Torment	Dark	Status	–	100	15	Normal	–	–
22	Fake Out	Normal	Physical	40	100	10	Normal	–	○
26	Hone Claws	Dark	Status	–	–	15	Self	–	–
31	Assurance	Dark	Physical	50	100	10	Normal	–	○
34	Slash	Normal	Physical	70	100	20	Normal	–	–
38	Taunt	Dark	Status	–	100	20	Normal	–	–
43	Night Slash	Dark	Physical	70	100	15	Normal	–	○
47	Snatch	Dark	Status	–	–	10	Self	–	–
50	Nasty Plot	Dark	Status	–	–	20	Self	–	–
55	Sucker Punch	Dark	Physical	80	100	5	Normal	–	○

● MOVES TAUGHT BY PEOPLE

Name	Type	Kind	Pow.	Acc.	PP	Range	Long	DA

● TM & HM MOVES

No.	Name	Type	Kind	Pow.	Acc.	PP	Range	Long	DA
TM01	Hone Claws	Dark	Status	–	–	15	Self	–	–
TM06	Toxic	Poison	Status	–	90	10	Normal	–	–
TM10	Hidden Power	Normal	Special	–	100	15	Normal	–	–
TM11	Sunny Day	Fire	Status	–	–	5	Both Sides	–	–
TM12	Taunt	Dark	Status	–	100	20	Normal	–	–
TM15	Hyper Beam	Normal	Special	150	90	5	Normal	–	–
TM17	Protect	Normal	Status	–	–	10	Self	–	–
TM18	Rain Dance	Water	Status	–	–	5	Both Sides	–	–
TM21	Frustration	Normal	Physical	–	100	20	Normal	–	○
TM27	Return	Normal	Physical	–	100	20	Normal	–	○
TM30	Shadow Ball	Ghost	Special	80	100	15	Normal	–	–
TM32	Double Team	Normal	Status	–	–	15	Self	–	–
TM40	Aerial Ace	Flying	Physical	60	–	20	Normal	○	○
TM41	Torment	Dark	Status	–	100	15	Normal	–	–
TM42	Facade	Normal	Physical	70	100	20	Normal	–	○
TM44	Rest	Psychic	Status	–	–	10	Self	–	–
TM45	Attract	Normal	Status	–	100	15	Normal	–	–
TM46	Thief	Dark	Physical	40	100	10	Normal	–	○
TM48	Round	Normal	Special	60	100	15	Normal	–	–
TM49	Echoed Voice	Normal	Special	40	100	15	Normal	–	–
TM63	Embargo	Dark	Status	–	100	15	Normal	–	–
TM65	Shadow Claw	Ghost	Physical	70	100	15	Normal	–	○
TM66	Payback	Dark	Physical	50	100	10	Normal	–	○
TM68	Giga Impact	Normal	Physical	150	90	5	Normal	–	○
TM73	Thunder Wave	Electric	Status	–	100	20	Normal	–	–
TM77	Psych Up	Normal	Status	–	–	10	Self	–	–
TM85	Dream Eater	Psychic	Special	100	100	15	Normal	–	–
TM86	Grass Knot	Grass	Special	–	100	20	Normal	–	○
TM87	Swagger	Normal	Status	–	90	15	Normal	–	–
TM90	Substitute	Normal	Status	–	–	10	Self	–	–
TM94	Rock Smash	Fighting	Physical	40	100	15	Normal	–	○
HM01	Cut	Normal	Physical	50	95	30	Normal	–	○

● MAIN WAYS TO OBTAIN

POKÉMON BLACK VERSION	1	Route 5
	2	Level up Purrloin to Lv. 20

POKÉMON WHITE VERSION	1	Route 5
	2	Level up Purrloin to Lv. 20

● FOOTPRINT

● MALE/FEMALE HAVE SAME FORM

● HEIGHT: 3'07"
● WEIGHT: 82.7 lbs.
● GENDER: Both ♂♀ exist
● ITEMS:
  • None

POKÉMON BLACK VERSION
These Pokémon vanish and appear unexpectedly. Many Trainers are drawn to their beautiful form and fur.

POKÉMON WHITE VERSION
Stealthily, it sneaks up on its target, striking from behind before its victim has a chance to react.

EVOLUTION

Purrloin → Lv. 20 → Liepard

ABILITIES ● Limber ● Unburden

EGG GROUP Field

STATS
HP ●●
ATTACK ●●●●
DEFENSE ●●●
SP. ATTACK ●●●●
SP. DEFENSE ●●
SPEED ●●●●

🐵 Pansage

● TYPE Grass

● FOOTPRINT

● HEIGHT: 2'00"
● WEIGHT: 23.1 lbs.
● GENDER: Both ♂ ♀ exist
● ITEMS:
  • Oran Berry
  • Occa Berry

● MALE/FEMALE HAVE SAME FORM

POKÉMON BLACK VERSION
This Pokémon dwells deep in the forest. Eating a leaf from its head whisks weariness away as if by magic.

POKÉMON WHITE VERSION
It shares the leaf on its head with weary-looking Pokémon. These leaves are known to relieve stress.

● LEVEL-UP AND LEARNED MOVES

Lv.	Name	Type	Kind	Pow.	Acc.	PP	Range	Long	DA
1	Scratch	Normal	Physical	40	100	35	Normal	–	○
4	Leer	Normal	Status	–	100	30	Many Others	–	–
7	Lick	Ghost	Physical	20	100	30	Normal	–	○
10	Vine Whip	Grass	Physical	35	100	15	Normal	–	○
13	Fury Swipes	Normal	Physical	18	80	15	Normal	–	○
16	Leech Seed	Grass	Status	–	90	10	Normal	–	–
19	Bite	Dark	Physical	60	100	25	Normal	–	○
22	Seed Bomb	Grass	Physical	80	100	15	Normal	–	–
25	Torment	Dark	Status	–	100	15	Normal	–	–
28	Fling	Dark	Physical	–	100	10	Normal	–	○
31	Acrobatics	Flying	Physical	55	100	15	Normal	○	○
34	Grass Knot	Grass	Special	–	100	20	Normal	–	○
37	Recycle	Normal	Status	–	–	10	Self	–	–
40	Natural Gift	Normal	Physical	–	100	15	Normal	–	–
43	Crunch	Dark	Physical	80	100	15	Normal	–	○

● MOVES TAUGHT BY PEOPLE

Name	Type	Kind	Pow.	Acc.	PP	Range	Long	DA

● EGG MOVES

Name	Type	Kind	Pow.	Acc.	PP	Range	Long	DA
Covet	Normal	Physical	60	100	40	Normal	–	○
Low Kick	Fighting	Physical	–	100	20	Normal	–	○
Tickle	Normal	Status	–	100	20	Normal	–	–
Nasty Plot	Dark	Status	–	–	20	Self	–	–
Role Play	Psychic	Status	–	–	10	Normal	–	–
Astonish	Ghost	Physical	30	100	15	Normal	–	○
GrassWhistle	Grass	Status	–	55	15	Normal	–	–
Magical Leaf	Grass	Special	60	–	20	Normal	–	–
Bullet Seed	Grass	Physical	25	100	30	Normal	–	–
Leaf Storm	Grass	Special	140	90	5	Normal	–	–

● TM & HM MOVES

No.	Name	Type	Kind	Pow.	Acc.	PP	Range	Long	DA
TM01	Hone Claws	Dark	Status	–	–	15	Self	–	–
TM06	Toxic	Poison	Status	–	90	10	Normal	–	–
TM10	Hidden Power	Normal	Special	–	100	15	Normal	–	–
TM11	Sunny Day	Fire	Status	–	–	5	Both Sides	–	–
TM12	Taunt	Dark	Status	–	100	20	Normal	–	–
TM17	Protect	Normal	Status	–	–	10	Self	–	–
TM21	Frustration	Normal	Physical	–	100	20	Normal	–	○
TM22	SolarBeam	Grass	Special	120	100	10	Normal	–	–
TM27	Return	Normal	Physical	–	100	20	Normal	–	○
TM28	Dig	Ground	Physical	80	100	10	Normal	–	–
TM32	Double Team	Normal	Status	–	–	15	Self	–	–
TM39	Rock Tomb	Rock	Physical	50	80	10	Normal	–	–
TM41	Torment	Dark	Status	–	100	15	Normal	–	–
TM42	Facade	Normal	Physical	70	100	20	Normal	–	–
TM44	Rest	Psychic	Status	–	–	10	Self	–	–
TM45	Attract	Normal	Status	–	100	15	Normal	–	–
TM46	Thief	Dark	Physical	40	100	10	Normal	–	○
TM47	Low Sweep	Fighting	Physical	60	100	20	Normal	–	○
TM48	Round	Normal	Special	60	100	15	Normal	–	–
TM53	Energy Ball	Grass	Special	80	100	10	Normal	–	–
TM56	Fling	Dark	Physical	–	100	10	Normal	–	○
TM62	Acrobatics	Flying	Physical	55	100	15	Normal	○	○
TM65	Shadow Claw	Ghost	Physical	70	100	15	Normal	–	○
TM66	Payback	Dark	Physical	50	100	10	Normal	–	○
TM70	Flash	Normal	Status	–	100	20	Normal	–	–
TM83	Work Up	Normal	Status	–	–	30	Self	–	–
TM86	Grass Knot	Grass	Special	–	100	20	Normal	–	○
TM87	Swagger	Normal	Status	–	90	15	Normal	–	–
TM90	Substitute	Normal	Status	–	–	10	Self	–	–
TM94	Rock Smash	Fighting	Physical	40	100	15	Normal	–	–
HM01	Cut	Normal	Physical	50	95	30	Normal	–	–

EVOLUTION

Pansage → (Use Leaf Stone) → Simisage

● MAIN WAYS TO OBTAIN

POKÉMON BLACK VERSION
1 Receive from a girl in the Dreamyard (if your starter Pokémon is Tepig)
2 Pinwheel Forest (Rustling Grass)

POKÉMON WHITE VERSION
1 Receive from a girl in the Dreamyard (if your starter Pokémon is Tepig)
2 Pinwheel Forest (Rustling Grass)

ABILITY ● Gluttony

EGG GROUP Field

STATS
HP ●●
ATTACK ●●
DEFENSE ●●
SP. ATTACK ●●
SP. DEFENSE ●●
SPEED ●●●

🐵 Simisage

● TYPE Grass

● FOOTPRINT

● HEIGHT: 3'07"
● WEIGHT: 67.2 lbs.
● GENDER: Both ♂ ♀ exist
● ITEMS:
  • None

● MALE/FEMALE HAVE SAME FORM

POKÉMON BLACK VERSION
Ill tempered, it fights by swinging its barbed tail around wildly. The leaf growing on its head is very bitter.

POKÉMON WHITE VERSION
It attacks enemies with strikes of its thorn-covered tail. This Pokémon is wild tempered.

● LEVEL-UP AND LEARNED MOVES

Lv.	Name	Type	Kind	Pow.	Acc.	PP	Range	Long	DA
1	Leer	Normal	Status	–	100	30	Many Others	–	–
1	Lick	Ghost	Physical	20	100	30	Normal	–	○
1	Fury Swipes	Normal	Physical	18	80	15	Normal	–	○
1	Seed Bomb	Grass	Physical	80	100	15	Normal	–	–

● MOVES TAUGHT BY PEOPLE

Name	Type	Kind	Pow.	Acc.	PP	Range	Long	DA

● TM & HM MOVES

No.	Name	Type	Kind	Pow.	Acc.	PP	Range	Long	DA
TM01	Hone Claws	Dark	Status	–	–	15	Self	–	–
TM06	Toxic	Poison	Status	–	90	10	Normal	–	–
TM10	Hidden Power	Normal	Special	–	100	15	Normal	–	–
TM11	Sunny Day	Fire	Status	–	–	5	Both Sides	–	–
TM12	Taunt	Dark	Status	–	100	20	Normal	–	–
TM15	Hyper Beam	Normal	Special	150	90	5	Normal	–	–
TM17	Protect	Normal	Status	–	–	10	Self	–	–
TM21	Frustration	Normal	Physical	–	100	20	Normal	–	○
TM22	SolarBeam	Grass	Special	120	100	10	Normal	–	–
TM27	Return	Normal	Physical	–	100	20	Normal	–	○
TM28	Dig	Ground	Physical	80	100	10	Normal	–	–
TM31	Brick Break	Fighting	Physical	75	100	15	Normal	–	–
TM32	Double Team	Normal	Status	–	–	15	Self	–	–
TM39	Rock Tomb	Rock	Physical	50	80	10	Normal	–	–
TM41	Torment	Dark	Status	–	100	15	Normal	–	–
TM42	Facade	Normal	Physical	70	100	20	Normal	–	–
TM44	Rest	Psychic	Status	–	–	10	Self	–	–
TM45	Attract	Normal	Status	–	100	15	Normal	–	–
TM46	Thief	Dark	Physical	40	100	10	Normal	–	○
TM47	Low Sweep	Fighting	Physical	60	100	20	Normal	–	○
TM48	Round	Normal	Special	60	100	15	Normal	–	–
TM52	Focus Blast	Fighting	Special	120	70	5	Normal	–	–
TM53	Energy Ball	Grass	Special	80	100	10	Normal	–	–
TM56	Fling	Dark	Physical	–	100	10	Normal	–	○
TM62	Acrobatics	Flying	Physical	55	100	15	Normal	○	○
TM65	Shadow Claw	Ghost	Physical	70	100	15	Normal	–	○
TM66	Payback	Dark	Physical	50	100	10	Normal	–	○
TM68	Giga Impact	Normal	Physical	150	90	5	Normal	–	–
TM70	Flash	Normal	Status	–	100	20	Normal	–	–
TM80	Rock Slide	Rock	Physical	75	90	10	Many Others	–	–
TM83	Work Up	Normal	Status	–	–	30	Self	–	–
TM86	Grass Knot	Grass	Special	–	100	20	Normal	–	○
TM87	Swagger	Normal	Status	–	90	15	Normal	–	–
TM90	Substitute	Normal	Status	–	–	10	Self	–	–
TM94	Rock Smash	Fighting	Physical	40	100	15	Normal	–	–
HM01	Cut	Normal	Physical	50	95	30	Normal	–	–

EVOLUTION

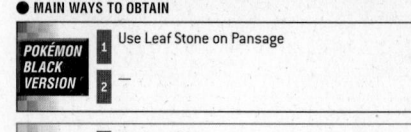

Pansage → (Use Leaf Stone) → Simisage

● MAIN WAYS TO OBTAIN

POKÉMON BLACK VERSION
1 Use Leaf Stone on Pansage
2 —

POKÉMON WHITE VERSION
1 Use Leaf Stone on Pansage
2 —

ABILITY ● Gluttony

EGG GROUP Field

STATS
HP ●●●
ATTACK ●●●●
DEFENSE ●●●
SP. ATTACK ●●●●
SP. DEFENSE ●●●
SPEED ●●●●

Pansear

● TYPE | Fire

● LEVEL-UP AND LEARNED MOVES

Lv.	Name	Type	Kind	Pow.	Acc.	PP	Range	Long	DA
1	Scratch	Normal	Physical	40	100	35	Normal	—	—
4	Leer	Normal	Status	—	100	30	Many Others	—	—
7	Lick	Ghost	Physical	20	100	30	Normal	—	○
10	Incinerate	Fire	Special	30	100	15	Many Others	—	—
13	Fury Swipes	Normal	Physical	18	80	15	Normal	—	—
16	Yawn	Normal	Status	—	—	10	Normal	—	—
19	Bite	Dark	Physical	60	100	25	Normal	—	○
22	Flame Burst	Fire	Special	70	100	15	Normal	—	—
25	Amnesia	Psychic	Status	—	—	20	Self	—	—
28	Fling	Dark	Physical	—	100	10	Normal	—	○
31	Acrobatics	Flying	Physical	55	100	15	Normal	○	○
34	Fire Blast	Fire	Special	120	85	5	Normal	—	—
37	Recycle	Normal	Status	—	—	10	Self	—	—
40	Natural Gift	Normal	Physical	—	100	15	Normal	—	○
43	Crunch	Dark	Physical	80	100	15	Normal	—	○

● MOVES TAUGHT BY PEOPLE

Name	Type	Kind	Pow.	Acc.	PP	Range	Long	DA

● EGG MOVES

Name	Type	Kind	Pow.	Acc.	PP	Range	Long	DA
Covet	Normal	Physical	60	100	40	Normal	—	○
Low Kick	Fighting	Physical	—	100	20	Normal	—	○
Tickle	Normal	Status	—	100	20	Normal	—	—
Nasty Plot	Dark	Status	—	—	20	Self	—	—
Role Play	Psychic	Status	—	—	10	Normal	—	—
Astonish	Ghost	Physical	30	100	15	Normal	—	○
Sleep Talk	Normal	Status	—	—	10	Self	—	—
Fire Spin	Fire	Special	35	85	15	Normal	—	—
Fire Punch	Fire	Physical	75	100	15	Normal	—	○
Heat Wave	Fire	Special	100	90	10	Many Others	—	—

● TM & HM MOVES

No.	Name	Type	Kind	Pow.	Acc.	PP	Range	Long	DA
TM01	Hone Claws	Dark	Status	—	—	15	Self	—	—
TM06	Toxic	Poison	Status	—	90	10	Normal	—	—
TM10	Hidden Power	Normal	Special	—	100	15	Normal	—	—
TM11	Sunny Day	Fire	Status	—	—	5	Both Sides	—	—
TM12	Taunt	Dark	Status	—	100	20	Normal	—	—
TM17	Protect	Normal	Status	—	—	10	Self	—	—
TM21	Frustration	Normal	Physical	—	100	20	Normal	—	○
TM22	SolarBeam	Grass	Special	120	100	10	Normal	—	—
TM27	Return	Normal	Physical	—	100	20	Normal	—	○
TM28	Dig	Ground	Physical	80	100	10	Normal	—	○
TM32	Double Team	Normal	Status	—	—	15	Self	—	—
TM35	Flamethrower	Fire	Special	95	100	15	Normal	—	—
TM38	Fire Blast	Fire	Special	120	85	5	Normal	—	—
TM39	Rock Tomb	Rock	Physical	50	80	10	Normal	—	○
TM41	Torment	Dark	Status	—	100	15	Normal	—	—
TM42	Facade	Normal	Physical	70	100	20	Normal	—	○
TM43	Flame Charge	Fire	Physical	50	100	20	Normal	—	○
TM44	Rest	Psychic	Status	—	—	10	Self	—	—
TM45	Attract	Normal	Status	—	100	15	Normal	—	—
TM46	Thief	Dark	Physical	40	100	10	Normal	—	○
TM47	Low Sweep	Fighting	Physical	60	100	20	Normal	—	○
TM48	Round	Normal	Special	60	100	15	Normal	—	—
TM50	Overheat	Fire	Special	140	90	5	Normal	—	—
TM56	Fling	Dark	Physical	—	100	10	Normal	—	○
TM59	Incinerate	Fire	Special	30	100	15	Many Others	—	—
TM61	Will-O-Wisp	Fire	Status	—	75	15	Normal	—	—
TM62	Acrobatics	Flying	Physical	55	100	15	Normal	○	○
TM65	Shadow Claw	Ghost	Physical	70	100	15	Normal	—	○
TM66	Payback	Dark	Physical	50	100	10	Normal	—	○
TM83	Work Up	Normal	Status	—	—	30	Self	—	—
TM86	Grass Knot	Grass	Special	—	100	20	Normal	—	○
TM87	Swagger	Normal	Status	—	90	15	Normal	—	—
TM90	Substitute	Normal	Status	—	—	10	Self	—	—
TM94	Rock Smash	Fighting	Physical	40	100	15	Normal	—	○
HM01	Cut	Normal	Physical	50	95	30	Normal	—	—

● MAIN WAYS TO OBTAIN

POKÉMON BLACK VERSION	1	Receive from a girl in the Dreamyard (if your starter Pokémon is Oshawott)
	2	Pinwheel Forest (Rustling Grass)

POKÉMON WHITE VERSION	1	Receive from a girl in the Dreamyard (if your starter Pokémon is Oshawott)
	2	Pinwheel Forest (Rustling Grass)

● FOOTPRINT

● MALE/FEMALE HAVE SAME FORM

- ● HEIGHT: 2'00"
- ● WEIGHT: 24.3 lbs.
- ● GENDER: Both ♂♀ exist
- ● ITEMS:
  - • Oran Berry
  - • Passho Berry

POKÉMON BLACK VERSION
When it is angered, the temperature of its head tuft reaches 600° F. It uses its tuft to roast berries.

POKÉMON WHITE VERSION
This Pokémon lives in caves in volcanoes. The fire within the tuft on its head can reach 600° F.

EVOLUTION

Use Fire Stone

Pansear → Simisear

ABILITY ● Gluttony

EGG GROUP Field

STATS
- HP ●●
- ATTACK ●●
- DEFENSE ●●
- SP. ATTACK ●●
- SP. DEFENSE ●●
- SPEED ●●●

Simisear

● TYPE | Fire

● LEVEL-UP AND LEARNED MOVES

Lv.	Name	Type	Kind	Pow.	Acc.	PP	Range	Long	DA
1	Leer	Normal	Status	—	100	30	Many Others	—	—
1	Lick	Ghost	Physical	20	100	30	Normal	—	○
1	Fury Swipes	Normal	Physical	18	80	15	Normal	—	—
1	Flame Burst	Fire	Special	70	100	15	Normal	—	—

● MOVES TAUGHT BY PEOPLE

Name	Type	Kind	Pow.	Acc.	PP	Range	Long	DA

● TM & HM MOVES

No.	Name	Type	Kind	Pow.	Acc.	PP	Range	Long	DA
TM01	Hone Claws	Dark	Status	—	—	15	Self	—	—
TM06	Toxic	Poison	Status	—	90	10	Normal	—	—
TM10	Hidden Power	Normal	Special	—	100	15	Normal	—	—
TM11	Sunny Day	Fire	Status	—	—	5	Both Sides	—	—
TM12	Taunt	Dark	Status	—	100	20	Normal	—	—
TM15	Hyper Beam	Normal	Special	150	90	5	Normal	—	—
TM17	Protect	Normal	Status	—	—	10	Self	—	—
TM21	Frustration	Normal	Physical	—	100	20	Normal	—	○
TM22	SolarBeam	Grass	Special	120	100	10	Normal	—	—
TM27	Return	Normal	Physical	—	100	20	Normal	—	○
TM28	Dig	Ground	Physical	80	100	10	Normal	—	○
TM31	Brick Break	Fighting	Physical	75	100	15	Normal	—	○
TM32	Double Team	Normal	Status	—	—	15	Self	—	—
TM35	Flamethrower	Fire	Special	95	100	15	Normal	—	—
TM38	Fire Blast	Fire	Special	120	85	5	Normal	—	—
TM39	Rock Tomb	Rock	Physical	50	80	10	Normal	—	○
TM41	Torment	Dark	Status	—	100	15	Normal	—	—
TM42	Facade	Normal	Physical	70	100	20	Normal	—	○
TM43	Flame Charge	Fire	Physical	50	100	20	Normal	—	○
TM44	Rest	Psychic	Status	—	—	10	Self	—	—
TM45	Attract	Normal	Status	—	100	15	Normal	—	—
TM46	Thief	Dark	Physical	40	100	10	Normal	—	○
TM47	Low Sweep	Fighting	Physical	60	100	20	Normal	—	○
TM48	Round	Normal	Special	60	100	15	Normal	—	—
TM50	Overheat	Fire	Special	140	90	5	Normal	—	—
TM52	Focus Blast	Fighting	Special	120	70	5	Normal	—	—
TM56	Fling	Dark	Physical	—	100	10	Normal	—	○
TM59	Incinerate	Fire	Special	30	100	15	Many Others	—	—
TM61	Will-O-Wisp	Fire	Status	—	75	15	Normal	—	—
TM62	Acrobatics	Flying	Physical	55	100	15	Normal	○	○
TM65	Shadow Claw	Ghost	Physical	70	100	15	Normal	—	○
TM66	Payback	Dark	Physical	50	100	10	Normal	—	○
TM68	Giga Impact	Normal	Physical	150	90	5	Normal	—	○
TM80	Rock Slide	Rock	Physical	75	90	10	Many Others	—	○
TM83	Work Up	Normal	Status	—	—	30	Self	—	—
TM86	Grass Knot	Grass	Special	—	100	20	Normal	—	○
TM87	Swagger	Normal	Status	—	90	15	Normal	—	—
TM90	Substitute	Normal	Status	—	—	10	Self	—	—
TM94	Rock Smash	Fighting	Physical	40	100	15	Normal	—	○
HM01	Cut	Normal	Physical	50	95	30	Normal	—	—

● MAIN WAYS TO OBTAIN

POKÉMON BLACK VERSION	1	Use Fire Stone on Pansear
	2	—

POKÉMON WHITE VERSION	1	Use Fire Stone on Pansear
	2	—

● FOOTPRINT

● MALE/FEMALE HAVE SAME FORM

- ● HEIGHT: 3'03"
- ● WEIGHT: 61.7 lbs.
- ● GENDER: Both ♂♀ exist
- ● ITEMS:
  - • None

POKÉMON BLACK VERSION
It loves sweets because they become energy for the fire burning inside its body.

POKÉMON WHITE VERSION
A flame burns inside its body. It scatters embers from its head and tail to sear its opponents.

EVOLUTION

Use Fire Stone

Pansear → Simisear

ABILITY ● Gluttony

EGG GROUP Field

STATS
- HP ●●●
- ATTACK ●●●●
- DEFENSE ●●●
- SP. ATTACK ●●●●
- SP. DEFENSE ●●●
- SPEED ●●●●

Panpour

● TYPE **Water**

● FOOTPRINT

● MALE/FEMALE HAVE SAME FORM

● HEIGHT: 2'00"
● WEIGHT: 29.8 lbs.
● GENDER: Both ♂♀ exist
● ITEMS:
  • Oran Berry
  • Rindo Berry

POKÉMON BLACK VERSION
The water stored inside the tuft on its head is full of nutrients. Plants that receive its water grow large.

POKÉMON WHITE VERSION
It does not thrive in dry environments. It keeps itself damp by shooting water stored in its head tuft from its tail.

● **LEVEL-UP AND LEARNED MOVES**

Lv.	Name	Type	Kind	Pow.	Acc.	PP	Range	Long	DA
1	Scratch	Normal	Physical	40	100	35	Normal	—	○
4	Leer	Normal	Status	—	100	30	Many Others	—	—
7	Lick	Ghost	Physical	20	100	30	Normal	—	○
10	Water Gun	Water	Special	40	100	25	Normal	—	○
13	Fury Swipes	Normal	Physical	18	80	15	Normal	—	○
16	Water Sport	Water	Status	—	—	15	Both Sides	—	—
19	Bite	Dark	Physical	60	100	25	Normal	—	○
22	Scald	Water	Special	80	100	15	Normal	—	○
25	Taunt	Dark	Status	—	100	20	Normal	—	—
28	Fling	Dark	Physical	—	100	10	Normal	—	○
31	Acrobatics	Flying	Physical	55	100	15	Normal	○	○
34	Brine	Water	Special	65	100	10	Normal	—	○
37	Recycle	Normal	Status	—	—	10	Self	—	—
40	Natural Gift	Normal	—	—	100	15	Normal	—	—
43	Crunch	Dark	Physical	80	100	15	Normal	—	○

● **MOVES TAUGHT BY PEOPLE**

Name	Type	Kind	Pow.	Acc.	PP	Range	Long	DA

● **EGG MOVES**

Name	Type	Kind	Pow.	Acc.	PP	Range	Long	DA
Covet	Normal	Physical	60	100	40	Normal	—	○
Low Kick	Fighting	Physical	—	100	20	Normal	—	○
Tickle	Normal	Status	—	100	20	Normal	—	—
Nasty Plot	Dark	Status	—	—	20	Self	—	—
Role Play	Psychic	Status	—	—	10	Normal	—	—
Astonish	Ghost	Physical	30	100	15	Normal	—	○
Aqua Ring	Water	Status	—	—	20	Self	—	—
Aqua Tail	Water	Physical	90	90	10	Normal	—	○
Mud Sport	Ground	Status	—	—	15	Both Sides	—	—
Hydro Pump	Water	Special	120	80	5	Normal	—	—

● **TM & HM MOVES**

No.	Name	Type	Kind	Pow.	Acc.	PP	Range	Long	DA
TM01	Hone Claws	Dark	Status	—	—	15	Self	—	—
TM06	Toxic	Poison	Status	—	90	10	Normal	—	—
TM07	Hail	Ice	Status	—	—	10	Both Sides	—	—
TM10	Hidden Power	Normal	Special	—	100	15	Normal	—	—
TM12	Taunt	Dark	Status	—	100	20	Normal	—	—
TM13	Ice Beam	Ice	Special	95	100	10	Normal	—	○
TM14	Blizzard	Ice	Special	120	70	5	Many Others	—	○
TM17	Protect	Normal	Status	—	—	10	Self	—	—
TM18	Rain Dance	Water	Status	—	—	5	Both Sides	—	—
TM21	Frustration	Normal	Physical	—	100	20	Normal	—	○
TM27	Return	Normal	Physical	—	100	20	Normal	—	○
TM28	Dig	Ground	Physical	80	100	10	Normal	—	○
TM32	Double Team	Normal	Status	—	—	15	Self	—	—
TM39	Rock Tomb	Rock	Physical	50	80	10	Normal	—	○
TM41	Torment	Dark	Status	—	100	15	Normal	—	—
TM42	Facade	Normal	Physical	70	100	20	Normal	—	○
TM44	Rest	Psychic	Status	—	—	10	Self	—	—
TM45	Attract	Normal	Status	—	100	15	Normal	—	—
TM46	Thief	Dark	Physical	40	100	10	Normal	—	○
TM47	Low Sweep	Fighting	Physical	60	100	20	Normal	—	○
TM48	Round	Normal	Special	60	100	15	Normal	—	—
TM55	Scald	Water	Special	80	100	15	Normal	—	○
TM56	Fling	Dark	Physical	—	100	10	Normal	—	○
TM62	Acrobatics	Flying	Physical	55	100	15	Normal	○	○
TM65	Shadow Claw	Ghost	Physical	70	100	15	Normal	—	○
TM66	Payback	Dark	Physical	50	100	10	Normal	—	○
TM83	Work Up	Normal	Status	—	—	30	Self	—	—
TM86	Grass Knot	Grass	Special	—	100	20	Normal	—	○
TM87	Swagger	Normal	Status	—	90	15	Normal	—	—
TM90	Substitute	Normal	Status	—	—	10	Self	—	—
TM94	Rock Smash	Fighting	Physical	40	100	15	Normal	—	○
HM01	Cut	Normal	Physical	50	95	30	Normal	—	○
HM03	Surf	Water	Special	95	100	15	Adjacent	—	○
HM05	Waterfall	Water	Physical	80	100	15	Normal	—	○
HM06	Dive	Water	Physical	80	100	10	Normal	—	○

● **EVOLUTION**

Panpour → Use Water Stone → Simipour

● **MAIN WAYS TO OBTAIN**

POKÉMON BLACK VERSION
1 Receive from a girl in the Dreamyard (if your starter Pokémon is Snivy)
2 Pinwheel Forest (Rustling Grass)

POKÉMON WHITE VERSION
1 Receive from a girl in the Dreamyard (if your starter Pokémon is Snivy)
2 Pinwheel Forest (Rustling Grass)

● ABILITY • Gluttony

● EGG GROUP Field

● STATS
HP ●●
ATTACK ●●
DEFENSE ●●
SP. ATTACK ●●
SP. DEFENSE ●●
SPEED ●●●

Simipour

● TYPE **Water**

● FOOTPRINT

● MALE/FEMALE HAVE SAME FORM

● HEIGHT: 3'03"
● WEIGHT: 63.9 lbs.
● GENDER: Both ♂♀ exist
● ITEMS:
  • None

POKÉMON BLACK VERSION
The tuft on its head holds water. When the level runs low, it replenishes the tuft by siphoning up water with its tail.

POKÉMON WHITE VERSION
The high-pressure water expelled from its tail is so powerful, it can destroy a concrete wall.

● **LEVEL-UP AND LEARNED MOVES**

Lv.	Name	Type	Kind	Pow.	Acc.	PP	Range	Long	DA
1	Leer	Normal	Status	—	100	30	Many Others	—	—
1	Lick	Ghost	Physical	20	100	30	Normal	—	○
1	Fury Swipes	Normal	Physical	18	80	15	Normal	—	○
1	Scald	Water	Special	80	100	15	Normal	—	○

● **MOVES TAUGHT BY PEOPLE**

Name	Type	Kind	Pow.	Acc.	PP	Range	Long	DA

● **TM & HM MOVES**

No.	Name	Type	Kind	Pow.	Acc.	PP	Range	Long	DA
TM01	Hone Claws	Dark	Status	—	—	15	Self	—	—
TM06	Toxic	Poison	Status	—	90	10	Normal	—	—
TM07	Hail	Ice	Status	—	—	10	Both Sides	—	—
TM10	Hidden Power	Normal	Special	—	100	15	Normal	—	—
TM12	Taunt	Dark	Status	—	100	20	Normal	—	—
TM13	Ice Beam	Ice	Special	95	100	10	Normal	—	○
TM14	Blizzard	Ice	Special	120	70	5	Many Others	—	○
TM15	Hyper Beam	Normal	Special	150	90	5	Normal	—	—
TM17	Protect	Normal	Status	—	—	10	Self	—	—
TM18	Rain Dance	Water	Status	—	—	5	Both Sides	—	—
TM21	Frustration	Normal	Physical	—	100	20	Normal	—	○
TM27	Return	Normal	Physical	—	100	20	Normal	—	○
TM28	Dig	Ground	Physical	80	100	10	Normal	—	○
TM31	Brick Break	Fighting	Physical	75	100	15	Normal	—	○
TM32	Double Team	Normal	Status	—	—	15	Self	—	—
TM39	Rock Tomb	Rock	Physical	50	80	10	Normal	—	○
TM41	Torment	Dark	Status	—	100	15	Normal	—	—
TM42	Facade	Normal	Physical	70	100	20	Normal	—	○
TM44	Rest	Psychic	Status	—	—	10	Self	—	—
TM45	Attract	Normal	Status	—	100	15	Normal	—	—
TM46	Thief	Dark	Physical	40	100	10	Normal	—	○
TM47	Low Sweep	Fighting	Physical	60	100	20	Normal	—	○
TM48	Round	Normal	Special	60	100	15	Normal	—	—
TM52	Focus Blast	Fighting	Special	120	70	5	Normal	—	—
TM55	Scald	Water	Special	80	100	15	Normal	—	○
TM56	Fling	Dark	Physical	—	100	10	Normal	—	○
TM62	Acrobatics	Flying	Physical	55	100	15	Normal	○	○
TM65	Shadow Claw	Ghost	Physical	70	100	15	Normal	—	○
TM66	Payback	Dark	Physical	50	100	10	Normal	—	○
TM68	Giga Impact	Normal	Physical	150	90	5	Normal	—	○
TM80	Rock Slide	Rock	Physical	75	90	10	Many Others	—	○
TM83	Work Up	Normal	Status	—	—	30	Self	—	—
TM86	Grass Knot	Grass	Special	—	100	20	Normal	—	○
TM87	Swagger	Normal	Status	—	90	15	Normal	—	—
TM90	Substitute	Normal	Status	—	—	10	Self	—	—
TM94	Rock Smash	Fighting	Physical	40	100	15	Normal	—	○
HM01	Cut	Normal	Physical	50	95	30	Normal	—	○
HM03	Surf	Water	Special	95	100	15	Adjacent	—	○
HM05	Waterfall	Water	Physical	80	100	15	Normal	—	○
HM06	Dive	Water	Physical	80	100	10	Normal	—	○

● **EVOLUTION**

Panpour → Use Water Stone → Simipour

● **MAIN WAYS TO OBTAIN**

POKÉMON BLACK VERSION
1 Use Water Stone on Panpour
2 —

POKÉMON WHITE VERSION
1 Use Water Stone on Panpour
2 —

● ABILITY • Gluttony

● EGG GROUP Field

● STATS
HP ●●●
ATTACK ●●●●
DEFENSE ●●●
SP. ATTACK ●●●●
SP. DEFENSE ●●●
SPEED ●●●●

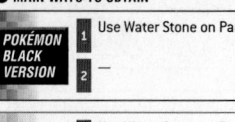

Munna

● TYPE Psychic

● **LEVEL-UP AND LEARNED MOVES**

Lv.	Name	Type	Kind	Pow.	Acc.	PP	Range	Long	DA
1	Psywave	Psychic	Special	—	80	15	Normal	—	—
1	Defense Curl	Normal	Status	—	—	40	Self	—	—
5	Lucky Chant	Normal	Status	—	—	30	Your Side	—	—
7	Yawn	Normal	Status	—	—	10	Normal	—	—
11	Psybeam	Psychic	Special	65	100	20	Normal	—	—
13	Imprison	Psychic	Status	—	—	10	Normal	—	—
17	Moonlight	Normal	Status	—	—	5	Self	—	—
19	Hypnosis	Psychic	Status	—	60	20	Normal	—	—
23	Zen Headbutt	Psychic	Physical	80	90	15	Normal	—	—
25	Synchronoise	Psychic	Special	70	100	15	Adjacent	—	○
29	Nightmare	Ghost	Status	—	100	15	Normal	—	—
31	Future Sight	Psychic	Special	100	100	10	Normal	—	—
35	Calm Mind	Psychic	Status	—	—	20	Self	—	—
37	Psychic	Psychic	Special	90	100	10	Normal	—	—
41	Dream Eater	Psychic	Special	100	100	15	Normal	—	—
43	Telekinesis	Psychic	Status	—	—	15	Normal	—	—
47	Stored Power	Psychic	Special	20	100	10	Normal	—	—

● **MOVES TAUGHT BY PEOPLE**

Name	Type	Kind	Pow.	Acc.	PP	Range	Long	DA

● **EGG MOVES**

Name ○	Type	Kind	Pow.	Acc.	PP	Range	Long	DA
Sleep Talk	Normal	Status	—	—	10	Self	—	—
Secret Power	Normal	Physical	70	100	20	Normal	—	—
Barrier	Psychic	Status	—	—	30	Self	—	—
Magic Coat	Psychic	Status	—	—	15	Self	—	—
Helping Hand	Normal	Status	—	—	20	1 Ally	—	—
Baton Pass	Normal	Status	—	—	40	Self	—	—
Swift	Normal	Special	60	—	20	Many Others	—	—
Curse	Ghost	Status	—	—	10	Varies	—	—
SonicBoom	Normal	Special	—	90	20	Normal	—	—

● **TM & HM MOVES**

No.	Name	Type	Kind	Pow.	Acc.	PP	Range	Long	DA
TM03	Psyshock	Psychic	Special	80	100	10	Normal	—	—
TM04	Calm Mind	Psychic	Status	—	—	20	Self	—	—
TM06	Toxic	Poison	Status	—	90	10	Normal	—	—
TM10	Hidden Power	Normal	Special	—	100	15	Normal	—	—
TM16	Light Screen	Psychic	Status	—	—	30	Your Side	—	—
TM17	Protect	Normal	Status	—	—	10	Self	—	—
TM18	Rain Dance	Water	Status	—	—	5	Both Sides	—	—
TM19	Telekinesis	Psychic	Status	—	—	15	Normal	—	—
TM20	Safeguard	Normal	Status	—	—	25	Your Side	—	—
TM21	Frustration	Normal	Physical	—	100	20	Normal	—	○
TM27	Return	Normal	Physical	—	100	20	Normal	—	○
TM29	Psychic	Psychic	Special	90	100	10	Normal	—	—
TM30	Shadow Ball	Ghost	Special	80	100	15	Normal	—	—
TM32	Double Team	Normal	Status	—	—	15	Self	—	—
TM33	Reflect	Psychic	Status	—	—	20	Your Side	—	—
TM39	Rock Tomb	Rock	Physical	50	80	10	Normal	—	—
TM41	Torment	Dark	Status	—	100	15	Normal	—	—
TM42	Facade	Normal	Physical	70	100	20	Normal	—	○
TM44	Rest	Psychic	Status	—	—	10	Self	—	—
TM45	Attract	Normal	Status	—	100	15	Normal	—	—
TM48	Round	Normal	Special	60	100	15	Normal	—	—
TM53	Energy Ball	Grass	Special	80	100	10	Normal	—	—
TM57	Charge Beam	Electric	Special	50	90	10	Normal	—	—
TM70	Flash	Normal	Status	—	100	20	Normal	—	—
TM73	Thunder Wave	Electric	Status	—	100	20	Normal	—	—
TM74	Gyro Ball	Steel	Physical	—	100	5	Normal	—	○
TM77	Psych Up	Normal	Status	—	—	10	Normal	—	—
TM80	Rock Slide	Rock	Physical	75	90	10	Many Others	—	—
TM85	Dream Eater	Psychic	Special	100	100	15	Normal	—	—
TM87	Swagger	Normal	Status	—	90	15	Normal	—	—
TM90	Substitute	Normal	Status	—	—	10	Self	—	—
TM92	Trick Room	Psychic	Status	—	—	5	Both Sides	—	—

● FOOTPRINT

● **MALE/FEMALE HAVE SAME FORM**

● HEIGHT: 2′00″
● WEIGHT: 51.4 lbs.
● GENDER: Both ♂♀ exist
● ITEMS:
  • None

POKÉMON BLACK VERSION
Munna always float in the air. People whose dreams are eaten by them forget what the dreams had been about.

POKÉMON WHITE VERSION
It eats the dreams of people and Pokémon. When it eats a pleasant dream, it expels pink-colored mist.

EVOLUTION

Use Moon Stone

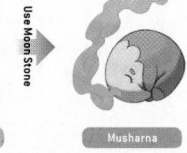

Munna → Musharna

ABILITIES
● Forewarn
● Synchronize
● Telepathy

EGG GROUP Field

STATS
HP ●●●
ATTACK ●
DEFENSE ●●
SP. ATTACK ●●●
SP. DEFENSE ●●
SPEED ●

● **MAIN WAYS TO OBTAIN**

| POKÉMON BLACK VERSION | 1 | Dreamyard |
| | 2 | — |

| POKÉMON WHITE VERSION | 1 | Dreamyard |
| | 2 | — |

● Munna with the Hidden Ability Telepathy do not appear in the wild.

Musharna

● TYPE Psychic

● **LEVEL-UP AND LEARNED MOVES**

Lv.	Name	Type	Kind	Pow.	Acc.	PP	Range	Long	DA
1	Defense Curl	Normal	Status	—	—	40	Self	—	—
1	Lucky Chant	Normal	Status	—	—	30	Your Side	—	—
1	Psybeam	Psychic	Special	65	100	20	Normal	—	—
1	Hypnosis	Psychic	Status	—	60	20	Normal	—	—

● **MOVES TAUGHT BY PEOPLE**

Name	Type	Kind	Pow.	Acc.	PP	Range	Long	DA

● **TM & HM MOVES**

No.	Name	Type	Kind	Pow.	Acc.	PP	Range	Long	DA
TM03	Psyshock	Psychic	Special	80	100	10	Normal	—	—
TM04	Calm Mind	Psychic	Status	—	—	20	Self	—	—
TM06	Toxic	Poison	Status	—	90	10	Normal	—	—
TM10	Hidden Power	Normal	Special	—	100	15	Normal	—	—
TM15	Hyper Beam	Normal	Special	150	90	5	Normal	—	—
TM16	Light Screen	Psychic	Status	—	—	30	Your Side	—	—
TM17	Protect	Normal	Status	—	—	10	Self	—	—
TM18	Rain Dance	Water	Status	—	—	5	Both Sides	—	—
TM19	Telekinesis	Psychic	Status	—	—	15	Normal	—	—
TM20	Safeguard	Normal	Status	—	—	25	Your Side	—	—
TM21	Frustration	Normal	Physical	—	100	20	Normal	—	○
TM27	Return	Normal	Physical	—	100	20	Normal	—	○
TM29	Psychic	Psychic	Special	90	100	10	Normal	—	—
TM30	Shadow Ball	Ghost	Special	80	100	15	Normal	—	—
TM32	Double Team	Normal	Status	—	—	15	Self	—	—
TM33	Reflect	Psychic	Status	—	—	20	Your Side	—	—
TM39	Rock Tomb	Rock	Physical	50	80	10	Normal	—	—
TM41	Torment	Dark	Status	—	100	15	Normal	—	—
TM42	Facade	Normal	Physical	70	100	20	Normal	—	○
TM44	Rest	Psychic	Status	—	—	10	Self	—	—
TM45	Attract	Normal	Status	—	100	15	Normal	—	—
TM48	Round	Normal	Special	60	100	15	Normal	—	—
TM53	Energy Ball	Grass	Special	80	100	10	Normal	—	—
TM57	Charge Beam	Electric	Special	50	90	10	Normal	—	—
TM68	Giga Impact	Normal	Physical	150	90	5	Normal	—	○
TM70	Flash	Normal	Status	—	100	20	Normal	—	—
TM73	Thunder Wave	Electric	Status	—	100	20	Normal	—	—
TM74	Gyro Ball	Steel	Physical	—	100	5	Normal	—	○
TM77	Psych Up	Normal	Status	—	—	10	Normal	—	—
TM80	Rock Slide	Rock	Physical	75	90	10	Many Others	—	—
TM85	Dream Eater	Psychic	Special	100	100	15	Normal	—	—
TM87	Swagger	Normal	Status	—	90	15	Normal	—	—
TM90	Substitute	Normal	Status	—	—	10	Self	—	—
TM92	Trick Room	Psychic	Status	—	—	5	Both Sides	—	—

● FOOTPRINT

● **MALE/FEMALE HAVE SAME FORM**

● HEIGHT: 3′07″
● WEIGHT: 133.4 lbs.
● GENDER: Both ♂♀ exist
● ITEMS:
  • None

POKÉMON BLACK VERSION
The mist emanating from their foreheads is packed with the dreams of people and Pokémon.

POKÉMON WHITE VERSION
With the mist from its forehead, it can create shapes of things from dreams it has eaten.

EVOLUTION

Use Moon Stone

Munna → Musharna

ABILITIES
● Forewarn
● Synchronize
● Telepathy

EGG GROUP Field

STATS
HP ●●●●●
ATTACK ●●●
DEFENSE ●●●
SP. ATTACK ●●●●●
SP. DEFENSE ●●●●
SPEED ●

● **MAIN WAYS TO OBTAIN**

| POKÉMON BLACK VERSION | 1 | Dreamyard (Rustling Grass) |
| | 2 | Use Moon Stone on Munna |

| POKÉMON WHITE VERSION | 1 | Dreamyard (Rustling Grass) |
| | 2 | Use Moon Stone on Munna |

● Musharna with the Hidden Ability Telepathy appear on Fridays in the basement of the Dreamyard after finishing the main story.

 Pidove

● TYPE **Normal** **Flying**

● FOOTPRINT

● HEIGHT: 1'00"
● WEIGHT: 4.6 lbs.
● GENDER: Both ♂♀ exist
● ITEMS:
  • None

● MALE/FEMALE HAVE SAME FORM

POKÉMON BLACK VERSION — Each follows its Trainer's orders as best it can, but they sometimes fail to understand complicated commands.

POKÉMON WHITE VERSION — These Pokémon live in cities. They are accustomed to people. Flocks often gather in parks and plazas.

● LEVEL-UP AND LEARNED MOVES

Lv.	Name	Type	Kind	Pow.	Acc.	PP	Range	Long	DA
1	Gust	Flying	Special	40	100	35	Normal	○	—
4	Growl	Normal	Status	—	100	40	Many Others	—	—
8	Leer	Normal	Status	—	100	30	Many Others	—	—
11	Quick Attack	Normal	Physical	40	100	30	Normal	—	○
15	Air Cutter	Flying	Special	55	95	25	Many Others	○	—
18	Roost	Flying	Status	—	—	10	Self	—	—
22	Detect	Fighting	Status	—	—	5	Self	—	—
25	Taunt	Dark	Status	—	100	20	Normal	—	—
29	Air Slash	Flying	Special	75	95	20	Normal	○	—
32	Razor Wind	Normal	Special	80	100	10	Normal	○	—
36	FeatherDance	Flying	Status	—	100	15	Normal	—	—
39	Swagger	Normal	Status	—	90	15	Normal	—	—
43	Facade	Normal	Physical	70	100	20	Normal	—	—
46	Tailwind	Flying	Status	—	—	30	Your Side	○	—
50	Sky Attack	Flying	Physical	140	90	5	Normal	○	—

● MOVES TAUGHT BY PEOPLE

Name	Type	Kind	Pow.	Acc.	PP	Range	Long	DA

● EGG MOVES

Name	Type	Kind	Pow.	Acc.	PP	Range	Long	DA
Steel Wing	Steel	Physical	70	90	25	Normal	—	○
Hypnosis	Psychic	Status	—	60	20	Normal	—	—
Uproar	Normal	Special	90	100	10	1 Random	—	—
Bestow	Normal	Status	—	—	15	Normal	—	—
Wish	Normal	Status	—	—	10	Self	—	—
Morning Sun	Normal	Status	—	—	5	Self	—	—
Lucky Chant	Normal	Status	—	—	30	Your Side	—	—

● TM & HM MOVES

No.	Name	Type	Kind	Pow.	Acc.	PP	Range	Long	DA
TM06	Toxic	Poison	Status	—	90	10	Normal	—	—
TM10	Hidden Power	Normal	Special	—	100	15	Normal	—	—
TM11	Sunny Day	Fire	Status	—	—	5	Both Sides	—	—
TM12	Taunt	Dark	Status	—	100	20	Normal	—	—
TM17	Protect	Normal	Status	—	—	10	Self	—	—
TM18	Rain Dance	Water	Status	—	—	5	Both Sides	—	—
TM21	Frustration	Normal	Physical	—	100	20	Normal	—	○
TM27	Return	Normal	Physical	—	100	20	Normal	—	○
TM32	Double Team	Normal	Status	—	—	15	Self	—	—
TM40	Aerial Ace	Flying	Physical	60	—	20	Normal	○	—
TM42	Facade	Normal	Physical	70	100	20	Normal	—	—
TM44	Rest	Psychic	Status	—	—	10	Self	—	—
TM45	Attract	Normal	Status	—	100	15	Normal	—	—
TM48	Round	Normal	Special	60	100	15	Normal	—	—
TM49	Echoed Voice	Normal	Special	40	100	15	Normal	—	—
TM83	Work Up	Normal	Status	—	—	30	Self	—	—
TM87	Swagger	Normal	Status	—	90	15	Normal	—	—
TM88	Pluck	Flying	Physical	60	100	20	Normal	○	—
TM89	U-turn	Bug	Physical	70	100	20	Normal	—	○
TM90	Substitute	Normal	Status	—	—	10	Self	—	—
HM02	Fly	Flying	Physical	90	95	15	Normal	○	—

EVOLUTION

Pidove — Lv. 21 → Tranquill — Lv. 32 → Unfezant

ABILITIES
● Big Pecks
● Super Luck

EGG GROUP
Flying

STATS
HP ●●
ATTACK ●●
DEFENSE ●●
SP. ATTACK ●
SP. DEFENSE ●
SPEED ●●

● MAIN WAYS TO OBTAIN

POKÉMON BLACK VERSION
1. Route 3
2. Pinwheel Forest Entrance

POKÉMON WHITE VERSION
1. Route 3
2. Pinwheel Forest Entrance

Tranquill

● TYPE **Normal** **Flying**

● FOOTPRINT

● MALE/FEMALE HAVE SAME FORM

● HEIGHT: 2'00"
● WEIGHT: 33.1 lbs.
● GENDER: Both ♂♀ exist
● ITEMS:
  • None

POKÉMON BLACK VERSION — It can return to its Trainer's location regardless of the distance separating them.

POKÉMON WHITE VERSION — Many people believe that, deep in the forest where Tranquill live, there is a peaceful place where there is no war.

● LEVEL-UP AND LEARNED MOVES

Lv.	Name	Type	Kind	Pow.	Acc.	PP	Range	Long	DA
1	Gust	Flying	Special	40	100	35	Normal	○	—
1	Growl	Normal	Status	—	100	40	Many Others	—	—
1	Leer	Normal	Status	—	100	30	Many Others	—	—
1	Quick Attack	Normal	Physical	40	100	30	Normal	—	○
4	Growl	Normal	Status	—	100	40	Many Others	—	—
8	Leer	Normal	Status	—	100	30	Many Others	—	—
11	Quick Attack	Normal	Physical	40	100	30	Normal	—	○
15	Air Cutter	Flying	Special	55	95	25	Many Others	○	—
18	Roost	Flying	Status	—	—	10	Self	—	—
23	Detect	Fighting	Status	—	—	5	Self	—	—
27	Taunt	Dark	Status	—	100	20	Normal	—	—
32	Air Slash	Flying	Special	75	95	20	Normal	○	—
36	Razor Wind	Normal	Special	80	100	10	Many Others	○	—
41	FeatherDance	Flying	Status	—	100	15	Normal	—	—
45	Swagger	Normal	Status	—	90	15	Normal	—	—
50	Facade	Normal	Physical	70	100	20	Normal	—	—
54	Tailwind	Flying	Status	—	—	30	Your Side	—	—
59	Sky Attack	Flying	Physical	140	90	5	Normal	○	—

● MOVES TAUGHT BY PEOPLE

Name	Type	Kind	Pow.	Acc.	PP	Range	Long	DA

● TM & HM MOVES

No.	Name	Type	Kind	Pow.	Acc.	PP	Range	Long	DA
TM06	Toxic	Poison	Status	—	90	10	Normal	—	—
TM10	Hidden Power	Normal	Special	—	100	15	Normal	—	—
TM11	Sunny Day	Fire	Status	—	—	5	Both Sides	—	—
TM12	Taunt	Dark	Status	—	100	20	Normal	—	—
TM17	Protect	Normal	Status	—	—	10	Self	—	—
TM18	Rain Dance	Water	Status	—	—	5	Both Sides	—	—
TM21	Frustration	Normal	Physical	—	100	20	Normal	—	○
TM27	Return	Normal	Physical	—	100	20	Normal	—	○
TM32	Double Team	Normal	Status	—	—	15	Self	—	—
TM40	Aerial Ace	Flying	Physical	60	—	20	Normal	○	—
TM42	Facade	Normal	Physical	70	100	20	Normal	—	—
TM44	Rest	Psychic	Status	—	—	10	Self	—	—
TM45	Attract	Normal	Status	—	100	15	Normal	—	—
TM48	Round	Normal	Special	60	100	15	Normal	—	—
TM49	Echoed Voice	Normal	Special	40	100	15	Normal	—	—
TM83	Work Up	Normal	Status	—	—	30	Self	—	—
TM87	Swagger	Normal	Status	—	90	15	Normal	—	—
TM88	Pluck	Flying	Physical	60	100	20	Normal	○	—
TM89	U-turn	Bug	Physical	70	100	20	Normal	—	○
TM90	Substitute	Normal	Status	—	—	10	Self	—	—
HM02	Fly	Flying	Physical	90	95	15	Normal	○	—

EVOLUTION

Pidove — Lv. 21 → Tranquill — Lv. 32 → Unfezant

ABILITIES
● Big Pecks
● Super Luck

EGG GROUP
Flying

STATS
HP ●●
ATTACK ●●●
DEFENSE ●●
SP. ATTACK ●●
SP. DEFENSE ●●
SPEED ●●●

● MAIN WAYS TO OBTAIN

POKÉMON BLACK VERSION
1. Lostlorn Forest
2. Level up Pidove to Lv. 21

POKÉMON WHITE VERSION
1. Lostlorn Forest
2. Level up Pidove to Lv. 21

Unfezant

● TYPE Normal Flying

● HEIGHT: 3'11"
● WEIGHT: 63.9 lbs.
● GENDER: Both ♂♀ exist
● ITEMS:
• None

● FOOTPRINT

● MALE FORM ● FEMALE FORM

POKÉMON BLACK VERSION
Males swing their head plumage to threaten opponents. The females' flying abilities surpass those of the males.

POKÉMON WHITE VERSION
Males have plumage on their heads. They will never let themselves feel close to anyone other than their Trainers.

● LEVEL-UP AND LEARNED MOVES

Lv.	Name	Type	Kind	Pow.	Acc.	PP	Range	Long	DA
1	Gust	Flying	Special	40	100	35	Normal	○	—
1	Growl	Normal	Status	—	100	40	Many Others	—	—
1	Leer	Normal	Status	—	100	30	Many Others	—	—
1	Quick Attack	Normal	Physical	40	100	30	Normal	—	○
4	Growl	Normal	Status	—	100	40	Many Others	—	—
8	Leer	Normal	Status	—	100	30	Many Others	—	—
11	Quick Attack	Normal	Physical	40	100	30	Normal	—	○
15	Air Cutter	Flying	Special	55	95	25	Many Others	○	—
18	Roost	Flying	Status	—	—	10	Self	—	—
23	Detect	Fighting	Status	—	—	5	Self	—	—
27	Taunt	Dark	Status	—	100	20	Normal	—	—
33	Air Slash	Flying	Special	75	95	20	Normal	○	—
38	Razor Wind	Normal	Special	80	100	10	Many Others	○	—
44	FeatherDance	Flying	Status	—	100	15	Normal	—	—
49	Swagger	Normal	Status	—	90	15	Normal	—	—
55	Facade	Normal	Physical	70	100	20	Normal	—	○
60	Tailwind	Flying	Status	—	—	30	Your Side	—	—
66	Sky Attack	Flying	Physical	140	90	5	Normal	○	—

● MOVES TAUGHT BY PEOPLE

Name	Type	Kind	Pow.	Acc.	PP	Range	Long	DA

● TM & HM MOVES

No.	Name	Type	Kind	Pow.	Acc.	PP	Range	Long	DA
TM06	Toxic	Poison	Status	—	90	10	Normal	—	—
TM10	Hidden Power	Normal	Special	—	100	15	Normal	—	—
TM11	Sunny Day	Fire	Status	—	—	5	Both Sides	—	—
TM12	Taunt	Dark	Status	—	100	20	Normal	—	—
TM15	Hyper Beam	Normal	Special	150	90	5	Normal	○	—
TM17	Protect	Normal	Status	—	—	10	Self	—	—
TM18	Rain Dance	Water	Status	—	—	5	Both Sides	—	—
TM21	Frustration	Normal	Physical	—	100	20	Normal	—	○
TM27	Return	Normal	Physical	—	100	20	Normal	—	○
TM32	Double Team	Normal	Status	—	—	15	Self	—	—
TM40	Aerial Ace	Flying	Physical	60	—	20	Normal	○	○
TM42	Facade	Normal	Physical	70	100	20	Normal	—	○
TM44	Rest	Psychic	Status	—	—	10	Self	—	—
TM45	Attract	Normal	Status	—	100	15	Normal	—	—
TM48	Round	Normal	Special	60	100	15	Normal	—	—
TM49	Echoed Voice	Normal	Special	40	100	15	Normal	—	—
TM68	Giga Impact	Normal	Physical	150	90	5	Normal	○	—
TM77	Psych Up	Normal	Status	—	—	10	Self	—	—
TM83	Work Up	Normal	Status	—	—	30	Self	—	—
TM87	Swagger	Normal	Status	—	90	15	Normal	—	—
TM88	Pluck	Flying	Physical	60	100	20	Normal	○	○
TM89	U-turn	Bug	Physical	70	100	20	Normal	—	○
TM90	Substitute	Normal	Status	—	—	10	Self	—	—
HM02	Fly	Flying	Physical	90	95	15	Normal	○	○

EVOLUTION

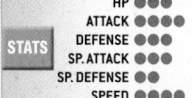

Pidove — Lv. 21 → Tranquill — Lv. 32 → Unfezant

ABILITIES
● Big Pecks
● Super Luck

EGG GROUP Flying

STATS
HP ●●●
ATTACK ●●●●
DEFENSE ●●●
SP. ATTACK ●●●
SP. DEFENSE ●●
SPEED ●●●●

● MAIN WAYS TO OBTAIN

POKÉMON BLACK VERSION
1 Lostlorn Forest (Rustling Grass)
2 Level up Tranquill to Lv. 32

POKÉMON WHITE VERSION
1 Lostlorn Forest (Rustling Grass)
2 Level up Tranquill to Lv. 32

Blitzle

● TYPE Electric

● FOOTPRINT

● MALE/FEMALE HAVE SAME FORM

● HEIGHT: 2'07"
● WEIGHT: 65.7 lbs.
● GENDER: Both ♂♀ exist
● ITEMS:
• Cheri Berry

POKÉMON BLACK VERSION
Its mane shines when it discharges electricity. They use their flashing manes to communicate with one another.

POKÉMON WHITE VERSION
When thunderclouds cover the sky, it will appear. It can catch lightning with its mane and store the electricity.

● LEVEL-UP AND LEARNED MOVES

Lv.	Name	Type	Kind	Pow.	Acc.	PP	Range	Long	DA
1	Quick Attack	Normal	Physical	40	100	30	Normal	—	○
4	Tail Whip	Normal	Status	—	100	30	Many Others	—	—
8	Charge	Electric	Status	—	—	20	Self	—	—
11	Shock Wave	Electric	Special	60	—	20	Normal	—	—
15	Thunder Wave	Electric	Status	—	100	20	Normal	—	—
18	Flame Charge	Fire	Physical	50	100	20	Normal	—	○
22	Pursuit	Dark	Physical	40	100	20	Normal	—	○
25	Spark	Electric	Physical	65	100	20	Normal	—	○
29	Stomp	Normal	Physical	65	100	20	Normal	—	○
32	Discharge	Electric	Special	80	100	15	Adjacent	—	—
36	Agility	Psychic	Status	—	—	30	Self	—	—
39	Wild Charge	Electric	Physical	90	100	15	Normal	—	○
43	Thrash	Normal	Physical	120	100	10	1 Random	—	○

● MOVES TAUGHT BY PEOPLE

Name	Type	Kind	Pow.	Acc.	PP	Range	Long	DA

● EGG MOVES

Name	Type	Kind	Pow.	Acc.	PP	Range	Long	DA
Me First	Normal	Status	—	—	20	Varies	—	○
Take Down	Normal	Physical	90	85	20	Normal	—	○
Sand-Attack	Ground	Status	—	100	15	Normal	—	—
Double Kick	Fighting	Physical	30	100	30	Normal	—	○
Screech	Normal	Status	—	85	40	Normal	—	—
Rage	Normal	Physical	20	100	20	Normal	—	○
Endure	Normal	Status	—	—	10	Self	—	—
Double-Edge	Normal	Physical	120	100	15	Normal	—	○
Shock Wave	Electric	Special	60	—	20	Normal	—	—

● TM & HM MOVES

No.	Name	Type	Kind	Pow.	Acc.	PP	Range	Long	DA
TM06	Toxic	Poison	Status	—	90	10	Normal	—	—
TM10	Hidden Power	Normal	Special	—	100	15	Normal	—	—
TM16	Light Screen	Psychic	Status	—	—	30	Your Side	—	—
TM17	Protect	Normal	Status	—	—	10	Self	—	—
TM18	Rain Dance	Water	Status	—	—	5	Both Sides	—	—
TM21	Frustration	Normal	Physical	—	100	20	Normal	—	○
TM24	Thunderbolt	Electric	Special	95	100	15	Normal	—	—
TM25	Thunder	Electric	Special	120	70	10	Normal	—	—
TM27	Return	Normal	Physical	—	100	20	Normal	—	○
TM32	Double Team	Normal	Status	—	—	15	Self	—	—
TM42	Facade	Normal	Physical	70	100	20	Normal	—	○
TM43	Flame Charge	Fire	Physical	50	100	20	Normal	—	○
TM44	Rest	Psychic	Status	—	—	10	Self	—	—
TM45	Attract	Normal	Status	—	100	15	Normal	—	—
TM48	Round	Normal	Special	60	100	15	Normal	—	—
TM57	Charge Beam	Electric	Special	50	90	10	Normal	—	—
TM70	Flash	Normal	Status	—	100	20	Normal	—	—
TM72	Volt Switch	Electric	Special	70	100	20	Normal	—	○
TM73	Thunder Wave	Electric	Status	—	100	20	Normal	—	—
TM87	Swagger	Normal	Status	—	90	15	Normal	—	—
TM90	Substitute	Normal	Status	—	—	10	Self	—	—
TM93	Wild Charge	Electric	Physical	90	100	15	Normal	—	○

EVOLUTION

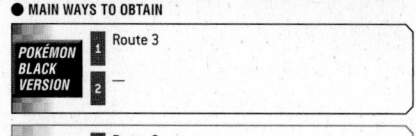

Blitzle — Lv. 27 → Zebstrika

ABILITIES
● Lightningrod
● Motor Drive

EGG GROUP Field

STATS
HP ●●
ATTACK ●●●
DEFENSE ●
SP. ATTACK ●●
SP. DEFENSE ●
SPEED ●●●

● MAIN WAYS TO OBTAIN

POKÉMON BLACK VERSION
1 Route 3
2 —

POKÉMON WHITE VERSION
1 Route 3
2 —

Zebstrika

● **TYPE** Electric

● FOOTPRINT

● MALE/FEMALE HAVE SAME FORM

● HEIGHT: 5'03"
● WEIGHT: 175.3 lbs.
● GENDER: Both ♂ ♀ exist
● ITEMS:
 • Cheri Berry

POKÉMON BLACK VERSION
They have lightning-like movements. When Zebstrika run at full speed, the sound of thunder reverberates.

POKÉMON WHITE VERSION
This ill-tempered Pokémon is dangerous because when it's angry, it shoots lightning from its mane in all directions.

● LEVEL-UP AND LEARNED MOVES

Lv.	Name	Type	Kind	Pow.	Acc.	PP	Range	Long	DA
1	Quick Attack	Normal	Physical	40	100	30	Normal	—	○
1	Tail Whip	Normal	Status	—	100	30	Many Others	—	—
1	Charge	Electric	Status	—	—	20	Self	—	—
1	Thunder Wave	Electric	Status	—	100	20	Normal	—	—
4	Tail Whip	Normal	Status	—	100	30	Many Others	—	—
8	Charge	Electric	Status	—	—	20	Self	—	—
11	Shock Wave	Electric	Special	60	—	20	Normal	—	—
15	Thunder Wave	Electric	Status	—	100	20	Normal	—	—
18	Flame Charge	Fire	Physical	50	100	20	Normal	—	○
22	Pursuit	Dark	Physical	40	100	20	Normal	—	○
25	Spark	Electric	Physical	65	100	20	Normal	—	○
31	Stomp	Normal	Physical	65	100	20	Normal	—	○
36	Discharge	Electric	Special	80	100	15	Adjacent	—	○
42	Agility	Psychic	Status	—	—	30	Self	—	—
47	Wild Charge	Electric	Physical	90	100	15	Normal	—	○
53	Thrash	Normal	Physical	120	100	10	1 Random	—	○

● MOVES TAUGHT BY PEOPLE

Name	Type	Kind	Pow.	Acc.	PP	Range	Long	DA

● TM & HM MOVES

No.	Name	Type	Kind	Pow.	Acc.	PP	Range	Long	DA
TM06	Toxic	Poison	Status	—	90	10	Normal	—	—
TM10	Hidden Power	Normal	Special	—	100	15	Normal	—	—
TM15	Hyper Beam	Normal	Special	150	90	5	Normal	—	—
TM16	Light Screen	Psychic	Status	—	—	30	Your Side	—	—
TM17	Protect	Normal	Status	—	—	10	Self	—	—
TM18	Rain Dance	Water	Status	—	—	5	Both Sides	—	—
TM21	Frustration	Normal	Physical	—	100	20	Normal	—	○
TM24	Thunderbolt	Electric	Special	95	100	15	Normal	—	—
TM25	Thunder	Electric	Special	120	70	10	Normal	—	—
TM27	Return	Normal	Physical	—	100	20	Normal	—	○
TM32	Double Team	Normal	Status	—	—	15	Self	—	—
TM42	Facade	Normal	Physical	70	100	20	Normal	—	○
TM43	Flame Charge	Fire	Physical	50	100	20	Normal	—	○
TM44	Rest	Psychic	Status	—	—	10	Self	—	—
TM45	Attract	Normal	Status	—	100	15	Normal	—	—
TM48	Round	Normal	Special	60	100	15	Normal	—	—
TM50	Overheat	Fire	Special	140	90	5	Normal	—	—
TM57	Charge Beam	Electric	Special	50	90	10	Normal	—	—
TM68	Giga Impact	Normal	Physical	150	90	5	Normal	—	—
TM70	Flash	Normal	Status	—	100	20	Normal	—	—
TM72	Volt Switch	Electric	Special	70	100	20	Normal	—	—
TM73	Thunder Wave	Electric	Status	—	100	20	Normal	—	—
TM87	Swagger	Normal	Status	—	90	15	Normal	—	—
TM90	Substitute	Normal	Status	—	—	10	Self	—	—
TM93	Wild Charge	Electric	Physical	90	100	15	Normal	—	○
TM94	Rock Smash	Fighting	Physical	40	100	15	Normal	—	○

EVOLUTION

Blitzle → Lv. 27 → Zebstrika

ABILITIES
● Lightningrod
● Motor Drive

EGG GROUP
Field

STATS
HP ●●●
ATTACK ●●●●
DEFENSE ●●●
SP. ATTACK ●●●●
SP. DEFENSE ●●
SPEED ●●●●●

● MAIN WAYS TO OBTAIN

POKÉMON BLACK VERSION
1 Route 7
2 Level up Blitzle to Lv. 27

POKÉMON WHITE VERSION
1 Route 7
2 Level up Blitzle to Lv. 27

Roggenrola

● **TYPE** Rock

● FOOTPRINT

● MALE/FEMALE HAVE SAME FORM

● HEIGHT: 1'04"
● WEIGHT: 39.7 lbs.
● GENDER: Both ♂ ♀ exist
● ITEMS:
 • Everstone
 • Hard Stone

POKÉMON BLACK VERSION
Its ear is hexagonal in shape. Compressed underground, its body is as hard as steel.

POKÉMON WHITE VERSION
They were discovered a hundred years ago in an earthquake fissure. Inside each one is an energy core.

● LEVEL-UP AND LEARNED MOVES

Lv.	Name	Type	Kind	Pow.	Acc.	PP	Range	Long	DA
1	Tackle	Normal	Physical	50	100	35	Normal	—	○
4	Harden	Normal	Status	—	—	30	Self	—	—
7	Sand-Attack	Ground	Status	—	100	15	Normal	—	—
10	Headbutt	Normal	Physical	70	100	15	Normal	—	○
14	Rock Blast	Rock	Physical	25	90	10	Normal	—	—
17	Mud-Slap	Ground	Special	20	100	10	Normal	—	—
20	Iron Defense	Steel	Status	—	—	15	Self	—	—
23	Smack Down	Rock	Physical	50	100	15	Normal	—	—
27	Rock Slide	Rock	Physical	75	90	10	Many Others	—	—
30	Stealth Rock	Rock	Status	—	—	20	Other Side	—	—
33	Sandstorm	Rock	Status	—	—	10	Both Sides	—	—
36	Stone Edge	Rock	Physical	100	80	5	Normal	—	—
40	Explosion	Normal	Physical	250	100	5	Adjacent	—	—

● MOVES TAUGHT BY PEOPLE

Name	Type	Kind	Pow.	Acc.	PP	Range	Long	DA

● EGG MOVES

Name	Type	Kind	Pow.	Acc.	PP	Range	Long	DA
Magnitude	Ground	Physical	—	100	30	Adjacent	—	—
Curse	Ghost	Status	—	—	10	Varies	—	—
Autotomize	Steel	Status	—	—	15	Self	—	—
Rock Tomb	Rock	Physical	50	80	10	Normal	—	—
Lock-On	Normal	Status	—	—	5	Normal	—	—
Heavy Slam	Steel	Physical	—	100	10	Normal	—	○
Take Down	Normal	Physical	90	85	20	Normal	—	○
Gravity	Psychic	Status	—	—	5	Both Sides	—	—

● TM & HM MOVES

No.	Name	Type	Kind	Pow.	Acc.	PP	Range	Long	DA
TM06	Toxic	Poison	Status	—	90	10	Normal	—	—
TM10	Hidden Power	Normal	Special	—	100	15	Normal	—	—
TM17	Protect	Normal	Status	—	—	10	Self	—	—
TM21	Frustration	Normal	Physical	—	100	20	Normal	—	○
TM23	Smack Down	Rock	Physical	50	100	15	Normal	—	—
TM26	Earthquake	Ground	Physical	100	100	10	Adjacent	—	—
TM27	Return	Normal	Physical	—	100	20	Normal	—	○
TM32	Double Team	Normal	Status	—	—	15	Self	—	—
TM37	Sandstorm	Rock	Status	—	—	10	Both Sides	—	—
TM39	Rock Tomb	Rock	Physical	50	80	10	Normal	—	—
TM42	Facade	Normal	Physical	70	100	20	Normal	—	○
TM44	Rest	Psychic	Status	—	—	10	Self	—	—
TM45	Attract	Normal	Status	—	100	15	Normal	—	—
TM48	Round	Normal	Special	60	100	15	Normal	—	—
TM64	Explosion	Normal	Physical	250	100	5	Adjacent	—	—
TM69	Rock Polish	Rock	Status	—	—	20	Self	—	—
TM71	Stone Edge	Rock	Physical	100	80	5	Normal	—	—
TM78	Bulldoze	Ground	Physical	60	100	20	Adjacent	—	—
TM80	Rock Slide	Rock	Physical	75	90	10	Many Others	—	—
TM87	Swagger	Normal	Status	—	90	15	Normal	—	—
TM90	Substitute	Normal	Status	—	—	10	Self	—	—
TM91	Flash Cannon	Steel	Special	80	100	10	Normal	—	—
TM94	Rock Smash	Fighting	Physical	40	100	15	Normal	—	○
HM04	Strength	Normal	Physical	80	100	15	Normal	—	—

EVOLUTION

Roggenrola → Lv. 25 → Boldore → Link Trade → Gigalith

ABILITY
● Sturdy

EGG GROUP
Mineral

STATS
HP ●●
ATTACK ●●●
DEFENSE ●●●
SP. ATTACK ●
SP. DEFENSE ●
SPEED ●

● MAIN WAYS TO OBTAIN

POKÉMON BLACK VERSION
1 Wellspring Cave 1F
2 —

POKÉMON WHITE VERSION
1 Wellspring Cave 1F
2 —

Boldore

● LEVEL-UP AND LEARNED MOVES

Lv.	Name	Type	Kind	Pow.	Acc.	PP	Range	Long	DA
1	Tackle	Normal	Physical	50	100	35	Normal	—	○
1	Harden	Normal	Status	—	—	30	Self	—	—
1	Sand-Attack	Ground	Status	—	100	15	Normal	—	—
1	Headbutt	Normal	Physical	70	100	15	Normal	—	○
4	Harden	Normal	Status	—	—	30	Self	—	—
7	Sand-Attack	Ground	Status	—	100	15	Normal	—	—
10	Headbutt	Normal	Physical	70	100	15	Normal	—	○
14	Rock Blast	Rock	Physical	25	90	10	Normal	—	—
17	Mud-Slap	Ground	Special	20	100	10	Normal	—	—
20	Iron Defense	Steel	Status	—	—	15	Self	—	—
23	Smack Down	Rock	Physical	50	100	15	Normal	—	—
25	Power Gem	Rock	Special	70	100	20	Normal	—	—
30	Rock Slide	Rock	Physical	75	90	10	Many Others	—	—
36	Stealth Rock	Rock	Status	—	—	20	Other Side	—	—
42	Sandstorm	Rock	Status	—	—	10	Both Sides	—	—
48	Stone Edge	Rock	Physical	100	80	5	Normal	—	—
55	Explosion	Normal	Physical	250	100	5	Adjacent	—	—

● MOVES TAUGHT BY PEOPLE

Name	Type	Kind	Pow.	Acc.	PP	Range	Long	DA

● TM & HM MOVES

No.	Name	Type	Kind	Pow.	Acc.	PP	Range	Long	DA
TM06	Toxic	Poison	Status	—	90	10	Normal	—	—
TM10	Hidden Power	Normal	Special	—	100	15	Normal	—	—
TM17	Protect	Normal	Status	—	—	10	Self	—	—
TM21	Frustration	Normal	Physical	—	100	20	Normal	—	○
TM23	Smack Down	Rock	Physical	50	100	15	Normal	—	—
TM26	Earthquake	Ground	Physical	100	100	10	Adjacent	—	○
TM27	Return	Normal	Physical	—	100	20	Normal	—	○
TM32	Double Team	Normal	Status	—	—	15	Self	—	—
TM37	Sandstorm	Rock	Status	—	—	10	Both Sides	—	—
TM39	Rock Tomb	Rock	Physical	50	80	10	Normal	—	—
TM42	Facade	Normal	Physical	70	100	20	Normal	—	—
TM44	Rest	Psychic	Status	—	—	10	Self	—	—
TM45	Attract	Normal	Status	—	100	15	Normal	—	—
TM48	Round	Normal	Special	60	100	15	Normal	—	—
TM64	Explosion	Normal	Physical	250	100	5	Adjacent	—	—
TM69	Rock Polish	Rock	Status	—	—	20	Self	—	—
TM71	Stone Edge	Rock	Physical	100	80	5	Normal	—	—
TM78	Bulldoze	Ground	Physical	60	100	20	Adjacent	—	—
TM80	Rock Slide	Rock	Physical	75	90	10	Many Others	—	—
TM87	Swagger	Normal	Status	—	90	15	Normal	—	—
TM90	Substitute	Normal	Status	—	—	10	Self	—	—
TM91	Flash Cannon	Steel	Special	80	100	10	Normal	—	—
TM94	Rock Smash	Fighting	Physical	40	100	15	Normal	—	○
HM04	Strength	Normal	Physical	80	100	15	Normal	—	○

● TYPE Rock

● FOOTPRINT

● HEIGHT: 2'11"
● WEIGHT: 224.9 lbs.
● GENDER: Both ♂♀ exist
● ITEMS:
  • Everstone
  • Hard Stone

● MALE/FEMALE HAVE SAME FORM

POKÉMON BLACK VERSION
When it overflows with power, the orange crystal on its body glows. It looks for underground water in caves.

POKÉMON WHITE VERSION
Because its energy was too great to be contained, the energy leaked and formed orange crystals.

EVOLUTION

Roggenrola → (Lv. 25) Boldore → (Link Trade) Gigalith

ABILITY ● Sturdy

EGG GROUP Mineral

STATS
HP ●●●
ATTACK ●●●●
DEFENSE ●●●●
SP. ATTACK ●●
SP. DEFENSE ●
SPEED ●

● MAIN WAYS TO OBTAIN

POKÉMON BLACK VERSION
1 Twist Mountain Upper level
2 Level up Roggenrola to Lv. 25

POKÉMON WHITE VERSION
1 Twist Mountain Upper level
2 Level up Roggenrola to Lv. 25

Gigalith

● LEVEL-UP AND LEARNED MOVES

Lv.	Name	Type	Kind	Pow.	Acc.	PP	Range	Long	DA
1	Tackle	Normal	Physical	50	100	35	Normal	—	○
1	Harden	Normal	Status	—	—	30	Self	—	—
1	Sand-Attack	Ground	Status	—	100	15	Normal	—	—
1	Headbutt	Normal	Physical	70	100	15	Normal	—	○
4	Harden	Normal	Status	—	—	30	Self	—	—
7	Sand-Attack	Ground	Status	—	100	15	Normal	—	—
10	Headbutt	Normal	Physical	70	100	15	Normal	—	○
14	Rock Blast	Rock	Physical	25	90	10	Normal	—	—
17	Mud-Slap	Ground	Special	20	100	10	Normal	—	—
20	Iron Defense	Steel	Status	—	—	15	Self	—	—
23	Smack Down	Rock	Physical	50	100	15	Normal	—	—
25	Power Gem	Rock	Special	70	100	20	Normal	—	—
30	Rock Slide	Rock	Physical	75	90	10	Many Others	—	—
36	Stealth Rock	Rock	Status	—	—	20	Other Side	—	—
42	Sandstorm	Rock	Status	—	—	10	Both Sides	—	—
48	Stone Edge	Rock	Physical	100	80	5	Normal	—	—
55	Explosion	Normal	Physical	250	100	5	Adjacent	—	—

● MOVES TAUGHT BY PEOPLE

Name	Type	Kind	Pow.	Acc.	PP	Range	Long	DA

● TM & HM MOVES

No.	Name	Type	Kind	Pow.	Acc.	PP	Range	Long	DA
TM06	Toxic	Poison	Status	—	90	10	Normal	—	—
TM10	Hidden Power	Normal	Special	—	100	15	Normal	—	—
TM15	Hyper Beam	Normal	Special	150	90	5	Normal	—	—
TM17	Protect	Normal	Status	—	—	10	Self	—	—
TM21	Frustration	Normal	Physical	—	100	20	Normal	—	○
TM22	SolarBeam	Grass	Special	120	100	10	Normal	—	—
TM23	Smack Down	Rock	Physical	50	100	15	Normal	—	—
TM26	Earthquake	Ground	Physical	100	100	10	Adjacent	—	○
TM27	Return	Normal	Physical	—	100	20	Normal	—	○
TM32	Double Team	Normal	Status	—	—	15	Self	—	—
TM37	Sandstorm	Rock	Status	—	—	10	Both Sides	—	—
TM39	Rock Tomb	Rock	Physical	50	80	10	Normal	—	—
TM42	Facade	Normal	Physical	70	100	20	Normal	—	—
TM44	Rest	Psychic	Status	—	—	10	Self	—	—
TM45	Attract	Normal	Status	—	100	15	Normal	—	—
TM48	Round	Normal	Special	60	100	15	Normal	—	—
TM64	Explosion	Normal	Physical	250	100	5	Adjacent	—	—
TM68	Giga Impact	Normal	Physical	150	90	5	Normal	—	○
TM69	Rock Polish	Rock	Status	—	—	20	Self	—	—
TM71	Stone Edge	Rock	Physical	100	80	5	Normal	—	—
TM78	Bulldoze	Ground	Physical	60	100	20	Adjacent	—	—
TM80	Rock Slide	Rock	Physical	75	90	10	Many Others	—	—
TM87	Swagger	Normal	Status	—	90	15	Normal	—	—
TM90	Substitute	Normal	Status	—	—	10	Self	—	—
TM91	Flash Cannon	Steel	Special	80	100	10	Normal	—	—
TM94	Rock Smash	Fighting	Physical	40	100	15	Normal	—	○
HM04	Strength	Normal	Physical	80	100	15	Normal	—	○

● TYPE Rock

● FOOTPRINT

● HEIGHT: 5'07"
● WEIGHT: 573.2 lbs.
● GENDER: Both ♂♀ exist
● ITEMS:
  • None

● MALE/FEMALE HAVE SAME FORM

POKÉMON BLACK VERSION
Compressing the energy from its internal core lets it fire off an attack capable of blowing away a mountain.

POKÉMON WHITE VERSION
The solar energy absorbed by its body's orange crystals is magnified internally and fired from its mouth.

EVOLUTION

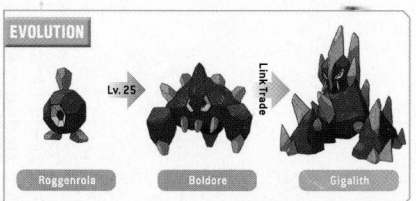

Roggenrola → (Lv. 25) Boldore → (Link Trade) Gigalith

ABILITY ● Sturdy

EGG GROUP Mineral

STATS
HP ●●●
ATTACK ●●●●
DEFENSE ●●●●●
SP. ATTACK ●●●
SP. DEFENSE ●●●
SPEED ●

● MAIN WAYS TO OBTAIN

POKÉMON BLACK VERSION
1 Link trade Boldore
2 —

POKÉMON WHITE VERSION
1 Link trade Boldore
2 —

Woobat

● TYPE: Psychic / Flying

● LEVEL-UP AND LEARNED MOVES

Lv.	Name	Type	Kind	Pow.	Acc.	PP	Range	Long	DA
1	Confusion	Psychic	Special	50	100	25	Normal	—	—
4	Odor Sleuth	Normal	Status	—	—	40	Normal	—	—
8	Gust	Flying	Special	40	100	35	Normal	○	—
12	Assurance	Dark	Physical	50	100	10	Normal	—	○
15	Heart Stamp	Psychic	Physical	60	100	25	Normal	—	—
19	Imprison	Psychic	Status	—	—	10	Self	—	—
21	Air Cutter	Flying	Special	55	95	25	Many Others	—	—
25	Attract	Normal	Status	—	100	15	Normal	—	—
29	Amnesia	Psychic	Status	—	—	20	Self	—	—
29	Calm Mind	Psychic	Status	—	—	20	Self	—	—
32	Air Slash	Flying	Special	75	95	20	Normal	○	—
36	Future Sight	Psychic	Special	100	100	10	Normal	—	—
41	Psychic	Psychic	Special	90	100	10	Normal	—	—
47	Endeavor	Normal	Physical	—	100	5	Normal	—	○

● MOVES TAUGHT BY PEOPLE

Name	Type	Kind	Pow.	Acc.	PP	Range	Long	DA

● EGG MOVES

Name	Type	Kind	Pow.	Acc.	PP	Range	Long	DA
Charm	Normal	Status	—	100	20	Normal	—	—
Knock Off	Dark	Physical	20	100	20	Normal	—	○
Fake Tears	Dark	Status	—	100	20	Normal	—	—
Supersonic	Normal	Status	—	55	20	Normal	—	—
Synchronoise	Psychic	Special	70	100	15	Adjacent	—	—
Stored Power	Psychic	Special	20	100	10	Normal	—	—
Roost	Flying	Status	—	—	10	Self	—	—
Flatter	Dark	Status	—	100	15	Normal	—	—
Helping Hand	Normal	Status	—	—	20	1 Ally	—	—

● TM & HM MOVES

No.	Name	Type	Kind	Pow.	Acc.	PP	Range	Long	DA
TM03	Psyshock	Psychic	Special	80	100	10	Normal	—	—
TM04	Calm Mind	Psychic	Status	—	—	20	Self	—	—
TM06	Toxic	Poison	Status	—	90	10	Normal	—	—
TM10	Hidden Power	Normal	Special	—	100	15	Normal	—	—
TM12	Taunt	Dark	Status	—	100	20	Normal	—	—
TM16	Light Screen	Psychic	Status	—	—	30	Your Side	—	—
TM17	Protect	Normal	Status	—	—	10	Self	—	—
TM18	Rain Dance	Water	Status	—	—	5	Both Sides	—	—
TM19	Telekinesis	Psychic	Status	—	—	15	Normal	—	—
TM20	Safeguard	Normal	Status	—	—	25	Your Side	—	—
TM21	Frustration	Normal	Physical	—	100	20	Normal	—	○
TM27	Return	Normal	Physical	—	100	20	Normal	—	○
TM29	Psychic	Psychic	Special	90	100	10	Normal	—	—
TM30	Shadow Ball	Ghost	Special	80	100	15	Normal	—	—
TM32	Double Team	Normal	Status	—	—	15	Self	—	—
TM33	Reflect	Psychic	Status	—	—	20	Your Side	—	—
TM40	Aerial Ace	Flying	Physical	60	—	20	Normal	○	○
TM41	Torment	Dark	Status	—	100	15	Normal	—	—
TM42	Facade	Normal	Physical	70	100	20	Normal	—	○
TM44	Rest	Psychic	Status	—	—	10	Self	—	—
TM45	Attract	Normal	Status	—	100	15	Normal	—	—
TM46	Thief	Dark	Physical	40	100	10	Normal	—	○
TM48	Round	Normal	Special	60	100	15	Normal	—	—
TM53	Energy Ball	Grass	Special	80	100	10	Normal	—	—
TM57	Charge Beam	Electric	Special	50	90	10	Normal	—	—
TM62	Acrobatics	Flying	Physical	55	100	15	Normal	○	○
TM63	Embargo	Dark	Status	—	100	15	Normal	—	—
TM70	Flash	Normal	Status	—	100	20	Normal	—	—
TM73	Thunder Wave	Electric	Status	—	100	20	Normal	—	—
TM74	Gyro Ball	Steel	Physical	—	100	5	Normal	—	—
TM77	Psych Up	Normal	Status	—	—	10	Normal	—	—
TM85	Dream Eater	Psychic	Special	100	100	15	Normal	—	—
TM87	Swagger	Normal	Status	—	90	15	Normal	—	—
TM88	Pluck	Flying	Physical	60	100	20	Normal	—	○
TM89	U-turn	Bug	Physical	70	100	20	Normal	—	○
TM90	Substitute	Normal	Status	—	—	10	Self	—	—
TM92	Trick Room	Psychic	Status	—	—	5	Both Sides	—	—
HM02	Fly	Flying	Physical	90	95	15	Normal	—	—

● FOOTPRINT

● HEIGHT: 1'04"
● WEIGHT: 4.6 lbs.
● GENDER: Both ♂♀ exist
● ITEMS:
  • None

● MALE/FEMALE HAVE SAME FORM

EVOLUTION

Level up with high friendship

Woobat → Swoobat

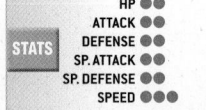

● MAIN WAYS TO OBTAIN

POKÉMON BLACK VERSION	1	Wellspring Cave 1F
	2	Twist Mountain Upper level

POKÉMON WHITE VERSION	1	Wellspring Cave 1F
	2	Twist Mountain Upper level

POKÉMON BLACK VERSION: Its habitat is dark forests and caves. It emits ultrasonic waves from its nose to learn about its surroundings.

POKÉMON WHITE VERSION: Suction from its nostrils enables it to stick to cave walls during sleep. It leaves a heart-shaped mark behind.

ABILITIES
• Unaware
• Klutz

EGG GROUPS
Field
Flying

STATS
HP ●●
ATTACK ●●
DEFENSE ●●
SP. ATTACK ●●
SP. DEFENSE ●●
SPEED ●●●

Swoobat

● TYPE: Psychic / Flying

● LEVEL-UP AND LEARNED MOVES

Lv.	Name	Type	Kind	Pow.	Acc.	PP	Range	Long	DA
1	Confusion	Psychic	Special	50	100	25	Normal	—	—
1	Odor Sleuth	Normal	Status	—	—	40	Normal	—	—
1	Gust	Flying	Special	40	100	35	Normal	○	—
1	Assurance	Dark	Physical	50	100	10	Normal	—	○
4	Odor Sleuth	Normal	Status	—	—	40	Normal	—	—
8	Gust	Flying	Special	40	100	35	Normal	○	—
12	Assurance	Dark	Physical	50	100	10	Normal	—	○
15	Heart Stamp	Psychic	Physical	60	100	25	Normal	—	—
19	Imprison	Psychic	Status	—	—	10	Self	—	—
21	Air Cutter	Flying	Special	55	95	25	Many Others	—	—
25	Attract	Normal	Status	—	100	15	Normal	—	—
29	Amnesia	Psychic	Status	—	—	20	Self	—	—
29	Calm Mind	Psychic	Status	—	—	20	Self	—	—
32	Air Slash	Flying	Special	75	95	20	Normal	○	—
36	Future Sight	Psychic	Special	100	100	10	Normal	—	—
41	Psychic	Psychic	Special	90	100	10	Normal	—	—
47	Endeavor	Normal	Physical	—	100	5	Normal	—	○

● MOVES TAUGHT BY PEOPLE

Name	Type	Kind	Pow.	Acc.	PP	Range	Long	DA

● TM & HM MOVES

No.	Name	Type	Kind	Pow.	Acc.	PP	Range	Long	DA
TM03	Psyshock	Psychic	Special	80	100	10	Normal	—	—
TM04	Calm Mind	Psychic	Status	—	—	20	Self	—	—
TM06	Toxic	Poison	Status	—	90	10	Normal	—	—
TM10	Hidden Power	Normal	Special	—	100	15	Normal	—	—
TM12	Taunt	Dark	Status	—	100	20	Normal	—	—
TM15	Hyper Beam	Normal	Special	150	90	5	Normal	—	—
TM16	Light Screen	Psychic	Status	—	—	30	Your Side	—	—
TM17	Protect	Normal	Status	—	—	10	Self	—	—
TM18	Rain Dance	Water	Status	—	—	5	Both Sides	—	—
TM19	Telekinesis	Psychic	Status	—	—	15	Normal	—	—
TM20	Safeguard	Normal	Status	—	—	25	Your Side	—	—
TM21	Frustration	Normal	Physical	—	100	20	Normal	—	○
TM27	Return	Normal	Physical	—	100	20	Normal	—	○
TM29	Psychic	Psychic	Special	90	100	10	Normal	—	—
TM30	Shadow Ball	Ghost	Special	80	100	15	Normal	—	—
TM32	Double Team	Normal	Status	—	—	15	Self	—	—
TM33	Reflect	Psychic	Status	—	—	20	Your Side	—	—
TM40	Aerial Ace	Flying	Physical	60	—	20	Normal	○	○
TM41	Torment	Dark	Status	—	100	15	Normal	—	—
TM42	Facade	Normal	Physical	70	100	20	Normal	—	○
TM44	Rest	Psychic	Status	—	—	10	Self	—	—
TM45	Attract	Normal	Status	—	100	15	Normal	—	—
TM46	Thief	Dark	Physical	40	100	10	Normal	—	○
TM48	Round	Normal	Special	60	100	15	Normal	—	—
TM53	Energy Ball	Grass	Special	80	100	10	Normal	—	—
TM57	Charge Beam	Electric	Special	50	90	10	Normal	—	—
TM62	Acrobatics	Flying	Physical	55	100	15	Normal	○	○
TM63	Embargo	Dark	Status	—	100	15	Normal	—	—
TM68	Giga Impact	Normal	Physical	150	90	5	Normal	—	—
TM70	Flash	Normal	Status	—	100	20	Normal	—	—
TM73	Thunder Wave	Electric	Status	—	100	20	Normal	—	—
TM74	Gyro Ball	Steel	Physical	—	100	5	Normal	—	—
TM77	Psych Up	Normal	Status	—	—	10	Normal	—	—
TM85	Dream Eater	Psychic	Special	100	100	15	Normal	—	—
TM87	Swagger	Normal	Status	—	90	15	Normal	—	—
TM88	Pluck	Flying	Physical	60	100	20	Normal	—	○
TM89	U-turn	Bug	Physical	70	100	20	Normal	—	○
TM90	Substitute	Normal	Status	—	—	10	Self	—	—
TM92	Trick Room	Psychic	Status	—	—	5	Both Sides	—	—
HM02	Fly	Flying	Physical	90	95	15	Normal	—	—

● FOOTPRINT

● MALE/FEMALE HAVE SAME FORM

● HEIGHT: 2'11"
● WEIGHT: 23.1 lbs.
● GENDER: Both ♂♀ exist
● ITEMS:
  • None

EVOLUTION

Level up with high friendship

Woobat → Swoobat

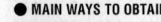

● MAIN WAYS TO OBTAIN

POKÉMON BLACK VERSION	1	Level up Woobat with high friendship
	2	—

POKÉMON WHITE VERSION	1	Level up Woobat with high friendship
	2	—

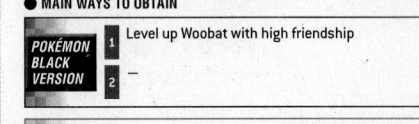

POKÉMON BLACK VERSION: It emits sound waves of various frequencies from its nose, including some powerful enough to destroy rocks.

POKÉMON WHITE VERSION: Anyone who comes into contact with the ultrasonic waves emitted by a courting male experiences a positive mood shift.

ABILITIES
• Unaware
• Klutz

EGG GROUPS
Field
Flying

STATS
HP ●●
ATTACK ●●
DEFENSE ●●
SP. ATTACK ●●●
SP. DEFENSE ●●
SPEED ●●●●●

UNOVA POKÉDEX
033 WOOBAT
034 SWOOBAT

Drilbur

● TYPE Ground

● FOOTPRINT

● MALE/FEMALE HAVE SAME FORM

● HEIGHT: 1'00"
● WEIGHT: 18.7 lbs.
● GENDER: Both ♂ ♀ exist
● ITEMS:
• None

● LEVEL-UP AND LEARNED MOVES

Lv.	Name	Type	Kind	Pow.	Acc.	PP	Range	Long	DA
1	Scratch	Normal	Physical	40	100	35	Normal	—	○
1	Mud Sport	Ground	Status	—	—	15	Both Sides	—	—
5	Rapid Spin	Normal	Physical	20	100	40	Normal	—	—
8	Mud-Slap	Ground	Special	20	100	10	Normal	—	—
12	Fury Swipes	Normal	Physical	18	80	15	Normal	—	—
15	Metal Claw	Steel	Physical	50	95	35	Normal	—	—
19	Dig	Ground	Physical	80	100	10	Normal	—	—
22	Hone Claws	Dark	Status	—	—	15	Self	—	—
26	Slash	Normal	Physical	70	100	20	Normal	—	—
29	Rock Slide	Rock	Physical	75	90	10	Many Others	—	—
33	Earthquake	Ground	Physical	100	100	10	Adjacent	—	—
36	Swords Dance	Normal	Status	—	—	30	Self	—	—
40	Sandstorm	Rock	Status	—	—	10	Both Sides	—	—
43	Drill Run	Ground	Physical	80	95	10	Normal	—	○
47	Fissure	Ground	Physical	—	30	5	Normal	—	—

● MOVES TAUGHT BY PEOPLE

Name	Type	Kind	Pow.	Acc.	PP	Range	Long	DA

● EGG MOVES

Name	Type	Kind	Pow.	Acc.	PP	Range	Long	DA
Iron Defense	Steel	Status	—	—	15	Self	—	—
Rapid Spin	Normal	Physical	20	100	40	Normal	—	○
Earth Power	Ground	Special	90	100	10	Normal	—	○
Crush Claw	Normal	Physical	75	95	10	Normal	—	○
Metal Sound	Steel	Status	—	85	40	Normal	—	○
Submission	Fighting	Physical	80	80	25	Normal	—	○
Skull Bash	Normal	Physical	100	100	15	Normal	—	○
Rock Climb	Normal	Physical	90	85	20	Normal	—	○

● TM & HM MOVES

No.	Name	Type	Kind	Pow.	Acc.	PP	Range	Long	DA
TM01	Hone Claws	Dark	Status	—	—	15	Self	—	—
TM06	Toxic	Poison	Status	—	90	10	Normal	—	—
TM10	Hidden Power	Normal	Special	—	100	15	Normal	—	—
TM17	Protect	Normal	Status	—	—	10	Self	—	—
TM21	Frustration	Normal	Physical	—	100	20	Normal	—	○
TM26	Earthquake	Ground	Physical	100	100	10	Adjacent	—	—
TM27	Return	Normal	Physical	—	100	20	Normal	—	○
TM28	Dig	Ground	Physical	80	100	10	Normal	—	○
TM31	Brick Break	Fighting	Physical	75	100	15	Normal	—	○
TM32	Double Team	Normal	Status	—	—	15	Self	—	—
TM36	Sludge Bomb	Poison	Special	90	100	10	Normal	—	—
TM37	Sandstorm	Rock	Status	—	—	10	Both Sides	—	—
TM39	Rock Tomb	Rock	Physical	50	80	10	Normal	—	○
TM40	Aerial Ace	Flying	Physical	60	—	20	Normal	○	○
TM42	Facade	Normal	Physical	70	100	20	Normal	—	○
TM44	Rest	Psychic	Status	—	—	10	Self	—	—
TM45	Attract	Normal	Status	—	100	15	Normal	—	—
TM48	Round	Normal	Special	60	100	15	Normal	—	—
TM56	Fling	Dark	Physical	—	100	10	Normal	—	○
TM65	Shadow Claw	Ghost	Physical	70	100	15	Normal	—	○
TM75	Swords Dance	Normal	Status	—	—	30	Self	—	—
TM78	Bulldoze	Ground	Physical	60	100	20	Adjacent	—	○
TM80	Rock Slide	Rock	Physical	75	90	10	Many Others	—	—
TM81	X-Scissor	Bug	Physical	80	100	15	Normal	—	○
TM84	Poison Jab	Poison	Physical	80	100	20	Normal	—	○
TM87	Swagger	Normal	Status	—	90	15	Normal	—	—
TM90	Substitute	Normal	Status	—	—	10	Self	—	—
TM94	Rock Smash	Fighting	Physical	40	100	15	Normal	—	○
HM01	Cut	Normal	Physical	50	95	30	Normal	—	○
HM04	Strength	Normal	Physical	80	100	15	Normal	—	○

EVOLUTION

Drilbur → Lv. 31 → Excadrill

ABILITIES
● Sand Rush
● Sand Force

EGG GROUP
Field

STATS
HP ●●
ATTACK ●●●●
DEFENSE ●●
SP. ATTACK ●●
SP. DEFENSE ●●
SPEED ●●●

POKÉMON BLACK VERSION
It can dig through the ground at a speed of 30 mph. It could give a car running aboveground a good race.

POKÉMON WHITE VERSION
It makes its way swiftly through the soil by putting both claws together and rotating at high speed.

● MAIN WAYS TO OBTAIN

POKÉMON BLACK VERSION
1 Wellspring Cave 1F (Dust Cloud)
2 Chargestone Cave 1F (Dust Cloud)

POKÉMON WHITE VERSION
1 Wellspring Cave 1F (Dust Cloud)
2 Chargestone Cave 1F (Dust Cloud)

Excadrill

● TYPE Ground Steel

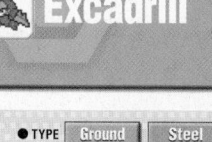

● FOOTPRINT

● MALE/FEMALE HAVE SAME FORM

● HEIGHT: 2'04"
● WEIGHT: 89.1 lbs.
● GENDER: Both ♂ ♀ exist
● ITEMS:
• None

● LEVEL-UP AND LEARNED MOVES

Lv.	Name	Type	Kind	Pow.	Acc.	PP	Range	Long	DA
1	Scratch	Normal	Physical	40	100	35	Normal	—	○
1	Mud Sport	Ground	Status	—	—	15	Both Sides	—	—
1	Rapid Spin	Normal	Physical	20	100	40	Normal	—	—
1	Mud-Slap	Ground	Special	20	100	10	Normal	—	—
5	Rapid Spin	Normal	Physical	20	100	40	Normal	—	—
8	Mud-Slap	Ground	Special	20	100	10	Normal	—	—
12	Fury Swipes	Normal	Physical	18	80	15	Normal	—	—
15	Metal Claw	Steel	Physical	50	95	35	Normal	—	—
19	Dig	Ground	Physical	80	100	10	Normal	—	—
22	Hone Claws	Dark	Status	—	—	15	Self	—	—
26	Slash	Normal	Physical	70	100	20	Normal	—	—
29	Rock Slide	Rock	Physical	75	90	10	Many Others	—	—
31	Horn Drill	Normal	Physical	—	30	5	Normal	—	—
36	Earthquake	Ground	Physical	100	100	10	Adjacent	—	—
42	Swords Dance	Normal	Status	—	—	30	Self	—	—
49	Sandstorm	Rock	Status	—	—	10	Both Sides	—	—
55	Drill Run	Ground	Physical	80	95	10	Normal	—	○
62	Fissure	Ground	Physical	—	30	5	Normal	—	—

● MOVES TAUGHT BY PEOPLE

Name	Type	Kind	Pow.	Acc.	PP	Range	Long	DA

● TM & HM MOVES

No.	Name	Type	Kind	Pow.	Acc.	PP	Range	Long	DA
TM01	Hone Claws	Dark	Status	—	—	15	Self	—	—
TM06	Toxic	Poison	Status	—	90	10	Normal	—	—
TM10	Hidden Power	Normal	Special	—	100	15	Normal	—	—
TM15	Hyper Beam	Normal	Special	150	90	5	Normal	—	—
TM17	Protect	Normal	Status	—	—	10	Self	—	—
TM21	Frustration	Normal	Physical	—	100	20	Normal	—	○
TM26	Earthquake	Ground	Physical	100	100	10	Adjacent	—	—
TM27	Return	Normal	Physical	—	100	20	Normal	—	○
TM28	Dig	Ground	Physical	80	100	10	Normal	—	○
TM31	Brick Break	Fighting	Physical	75	100	15	Normal	—	○
TM32	Double Team	Normal	Status	—	—	15	Self	—	—
TM36	Sludge Bomb	Poison	Special	90	100	10	Normal	—	—
TM37	Sandstorm	Rock	Status	—	—	10	Both Sides	—	—
TM39	Rock Tomb	Rock	Physical	50	80	10	Normal	—	○
TM40	Aerial Ace	Flying	Physical	60	—	20	Normal	○	○
TM42	Facade	Normal	Physical	70	100	20	Normal	—	○
TM44	Rest	Psychic	Status	—	—	10	Self	—	—
TM45	Attract	Normal	Status	—	100	15	Normal	—	—
TM48	Round	Normal	Special	60	100	15	Normal	—	—
TM52	Focus Blast	Fighting	Special	120	70	5	Normal	—	—
TM56	Fling	Dark	Physical	—	100	10	Normal	—	○
TM65	Shadow Claw	Ghost	Physical	70	100	15	Normal	—	○
TM68	Giga Impact	Normal	Physical	150	90	5	Normal	—	○
TM75	Swords Dance	Normal	Status	—	—	30	Self	—	—
TM78	Bulldoze	Ground	Physical	60	100	20	Adjacent	—	○
TM80	Rock Slide	Rock	Physical	75	90	10	Many Others	—	—
TM81	X-Scissor	Bug	Physical	80	100	15	Normal	—	○
TM84	Poison Jab	Poison	Physical	80	100	20	Normal	—	○
TM87	Swagger	Normal	Status	—	90	15	Normal	—	—
TM90	Substitute	Normal	Status	—	—	10	Self	—	—
TM94	Rock Smash	Fighting	Physical	40	100	15	Normal	—	○
HM01	Cut	Normal	Physical	50	95	30	Normal	—	○
HM04	Strength	Normal	Physical	80	100	15	Normal	—	○

EVOLUTION

Drilbur → Lv. 31 → Excadrill

ABILITIES
● Sand Rush
● Sand Force

EGG GROUP
Field

STATS
HP ●●●●
ATTACK ●●●●●●
DEFENSE ●●
SP. ATTACK ●●
SP. DEFENSE ●●
SPEED ●●●●

POKÉMON BLACK VERSION
It can help in tunnel construction. Its drill has evolved into steel strong enough to bore through iron plates.

POKÉMON WHITE VERSION
More than 300 feet below the surface, they build mazelike nests. Their activity can be destructive to subway tunnels.

● MAIN WAYS TO OBTAIN

POKÉMON BLACK VERSION
1 Victory Road 1F (Dust Cloud)
2 Level up Drilbur to Lv. 31

POKÉMON WHITE VERSION
1 Victory Road 1F (Dust Cloud)
2 Level up Drilbur to Lv. 31

Unova Pokédex 037 | Hearing Pokémon

Audino

● TYPE Normal

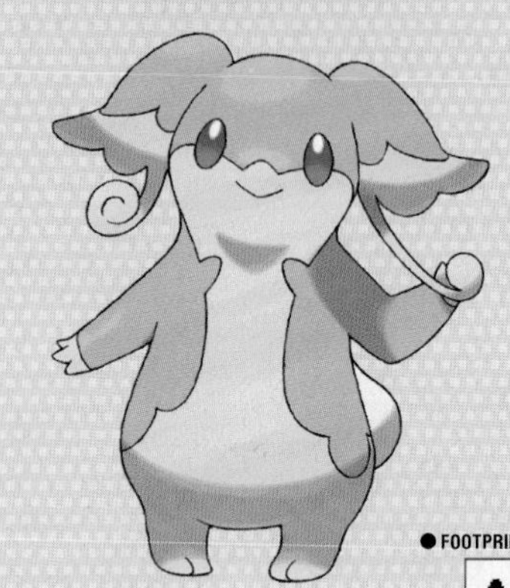

● FOOTPRINT

● MALE/FEMALE HAVE SAME FORM

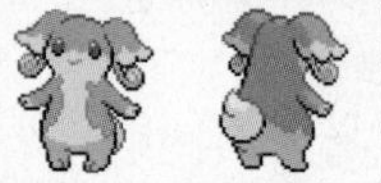

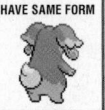

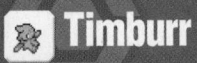

- HEIGHT: 3'07"
- WEIGHT: 68.3 lbs.
- GENDER: Both ♂♀ exist
- ITEMS:
  - Oran Berry
  - Sitrus Berry

POKÉMON BLACK VERSION It touches others with the feelers on its ears, using the sound of their heartbeats to tell how they are feeling.

POKÉMON WHITE VERSION Its auditory sense is astounding. It has a radarlike ability to understand its surroundings through slight sounds.

● LEVEL-UP AND LEARNED MOVES

Lv.	Name	Type	Kind	Pow.	Acc.	PP	Range	Long	DA
1	Pound	Normal	Physical	40	100	35	Normal	–	○
1	Growl	Normal	Status	–	100	40	Many Others	–	–
1	Helping Hand	Normal	Status	–	–	20	1 Ally	–	–
5	Refresh	Normal	Status	–	–	20	Self	–	–
10	DoubleSlap	Normal	Physical	15	85	10	Normal	–	○
15	Attract	Normal	Status	–	100	15	Normal	–	–
20	Secret Power	Normal	Physical	70	100	20	Normal	–	–
25	Entrainment	Normal	Status	–	100	15	Normal	–	–
30	Take Down	Normal	Physical	90	85	20	Normal	–	○
35	Heal Pulse	Psychic	Status	–	–	10	Normal	○	–
40	After You	Normal	Status	–	–	15	Normal	–	–
45	Simple Beam	Normal	Status	–	100	15	Normal	–	–
50	Double-Edge	Normal	Physical	120	100	15	Normal	–	○
55	Last Resort	Normal	Physical	140	100	5	Normal	–	○

● MOVES TAUGHT BY PEOPLE

Name	Type	Kind	Pow.	Acc.	PP	Range	Long	DA

● EGG MOVES

Name	Type	Kind	Pow.	Acc.	PP	Range	Long	DA
Wish	Normal	Status	–	–	10	Self	–	–
Heal Bell	Normal	Status	–	–	5	Your Party	–	–
Lucky Chant	Normal	Status	–	–	30	Your Side	–	–
Encore	Normal	Status	–	100	5	Normal	–	–
Bestow	Normal	Status	–	–	15	Normal	–	–
Sweet Kiss	Normal	Status	–	75	10	Normal	–	–
Yawn	Normal	Status	–	–	10	Normal	–	–
Sleep Talk	Normal	Status	–	–	10	Self	–	–
Healing Wish	Psychic	Status	–	–	10	Self	–	–
Amnesia	Psychic	Status	–	–	20	Self	–	–

EVOLUTION

Does not evolve

ABILITIES
- Healer
- Regenerator

EGG GROUP Fairy

STATS
- HP ●●●●
- ATTACK ●●●
- DEFENSE ●●●
- SP. ATTACK ●●●
- SP. DEFENSE ●●●
- SPEED ●●

● TM & HM MOVES

No.	Name	Type	Kind	Pow.	Acc.	PP	Range	Long	DA
TM03	Psyshock	Psychic	Special	80	100	10	Normal	–	–
TM04	Calm Mind	Psychic	Status	–	–	20	Self	–	–
TM06	Toxic	Poison	Status	–	90	10	Normal	–	–
TM10	Hidden Power	Normal	Special	–	100	15	Normal	–	–
TM11	Sunny Day	Fire	Status	–	–	5	Both Sides	–	–
TM13	Ice Beam	Ice	Special	95	100	10	Normal	–	–
TM14	Blizzard	Ice	Special	120	70	5	Many Others	–	–
TM15	Hyper Beam	Normal	Special	150	90	5	Normal	–	–
TM16	Light Screen	Psychic	Status	–	–	30	Your Side	–	–
TM17	Protect	Normal	Status	–	–	10	Self	–	–
TM18	Rain Dance	Water	Status	–	–	5	Both Sides	–	–
TM19	Telekinesis	Psychic	Status	–	–	15	Normal	–	–
TM20	Safeguard	Normal	Status	–	–	25	Your Side	–	–
TM21	Frustration	Normal	Physical	–	100	20	Normal	–	○
TM22	SolarBeam	Grass	Special	120	100	10	Normal	–	–
TM24	Thunderbolt	Electric	Special	95	100	15	Normal	–	–
TM25	Thunder	Electric	Special	120	70	10	Normal	–	–
TM27	Return	Normal	Physical	–	100	20	Normal	–	○
TM28	Dig	Ground	Physical	80	100	10	Normal	–	○
TM29	Psychic	Psychic	Special	90	100	10	Normal	–	–
TM30	Shadow Ball	Ghost	Special	80	100	15	Normal	–	–
TM32	Double Team	Normal	Status	–	–	15	Self	–	–
TM33	Reflect	Psychic	Status	–	–	20	Your Side	–	–
TM35	Flamethrower	Fire	Special	95	100	15	Normal	–	–
TM38	Fire Blast	Fire	Special	120	85	5	Normal	–	–
TM42	Facade	Normal	Physical	70	100	20	Normal	–	○
TM44	Rest	Psychic	Status	–	–	10	Self	–	–
TM45	Attract	Normal	Status	–	100	15	Normal	–	–
TM48	Round	Normal	Special	60	100	15	Normal	–	–
TM49	Echoed Voice	Normal	Special	40	100	15	Normal	–	–
TM56	Fling	Dark	Physical	–	100	10	Normal	–	–
TM57	Charge Beam	Electric	Special	50	90	10	Normal	–	–
TM59	Incinerate	Fire	Special	30	100	15	Many Others	–	–
TM67	Retaliate	Normal	Physical	70	100	5	Normal	–	○
TM70	Flash	Normal	Status	–	100	20	Normal	–	–
TM73	Thunder Wave	Electric	Status	–	100	20	Normal	–	–
TM77	Psych Up	Normal	Status	–	–	10	Normal	–	–
TM83	Work Up	Normal	Status	–	–	30	Self	–	–
TM85	Dream Eater	Psychic	Special	100	100	15	Normal	–	–
TM86	Grass Knot	Grass	Special	–	100	20	Normal	–	○
TM87	Swagger	Normal	Status	–	90	15	Normal	–	–
TM90	Substitute	Normal	Status	–	–	10	Self	–	–
TM92	Trick Room	Psychic	Status	–	–	5	Both Sides	–	–
TM93	Wild Charge	Electric	Physical	90	100	15	Normal	–	○
HM03	Surf	Water	Special	95	100	15	Adjacent	–	–

● MAIN WAYS TO OBTAIN

POKÉMON BLACK VERSION
1. Route 1 (Rustling Grass)
2. Route 2 (Rustling Grass)

POKÉMON WHITE VERSION
1. Route 1 (Rustling Grass)
2. Route 2 (Rustling Grass)

Unova Pokédex 038 | Muscular Pokémon

Timburr

● TYPE Fighting

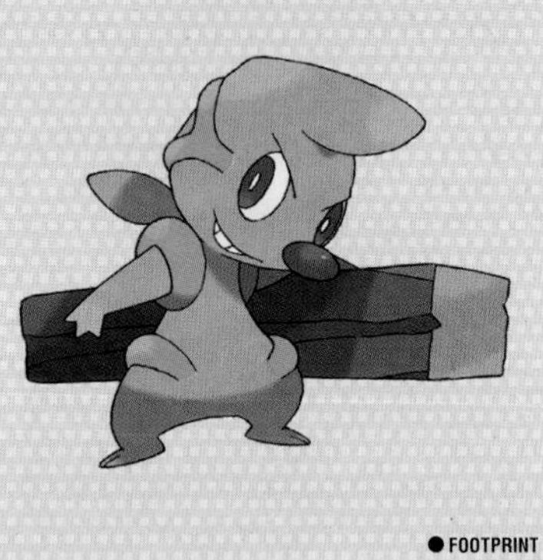

● FOOTPRINT

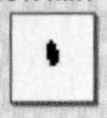

● MALE/FEMALE HAVE SAME FORM

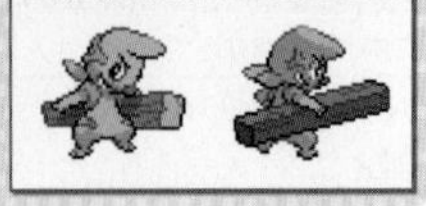

- HEIGHT: 2'00"
- WEIGHT: 27.6 lbs.
- GENDER: Both ♂♀ exist
- ITEMS:
  - None

POKÉMON BLACK VERSION It fights by swinging a piece of lumber around. It is close to evolving when it can handle the lumber without difficulty.

POKÉMON WHITE VERSION These Pokémon appear at building sites and help out with construction. They always carry squared logs.

● LEVEL-UP AND LEARNED MOVES

Lv.	Name	Type	Kind	Pow.	Acc.	PP	Range	Long	DA
1	Pound	Normal	Physical	40	100	35	Normal	–	○
1	Leer	Normal	Status	–	100	30	Many Others	–	–
4	Focus Energy	Normal	Status	–	–	30	Self	–	–
8	Bide	Normal	Physical	–	–	10	Self	–	○
12	Low Kick	Fighting	Physical	–	100	20	Normal	–	○
16	Rock Throw	Rock	Physical	50	90	15	Normal	–	–
20	Wake-Up Slap	Fighting	Physical	60	100	10	Normal	–	○
24	Chip Away	Normal	Physical	70	100	20	Normal	–	○
28	Bulk Up	Fighting	Status	–	–	20	Self	–	–
31	Rock Slide	Rock	Physical	75	90	10	Many Others	–	–
34	DynamicPunch	Fighting	Physical	100	50	5	Normal	–	○
37	Scary Face	Normal	Status	–	100	10	Normal	–	–
40	Hammer Arm	Fighting	Physical	100	90	10	Normal	–	○
43	Stone Edge	Rock	Physical	100	80	5	Normal	–	–
46	Focus Punch	Fighting	Physical	150	100	20	Normal	–	○
49	Superpower	Fighting	Physical	120	100	5	Normal	–	○

● MOVES TAUGHT BY PEOPLE

Name	Type	Kind	Pow.	Acc.	PP	Range	Long	DA

● EGG MOVES

Name	Type	Kind	Pow.	Acc.	PP	Range	Long	DA
Drain Punch	Fighting	Physical	75	100	10	Normal	–	○
Endure	Normal	Status	–	–	10	Self	–	–
Counter	Fighting	Physical	–	100	20	Varies	–	○
Comet Punch	Normal	Physical	18	85	15	Normal	–	○
Foresight	Normal	Status	–	–	40	Normal	–	–
SmellingSalt	Normal	Physical	60	100	10	Normal	–	○
Detect	Fighting	Status	–	–	5	Self	–	–
Wide Guard	Rock	Status	–	–	10	Your Side	–	–
Force Palm	Fighting	Physical	60	100	10	Normal	–	○
Reversal	Fighting	Physical	–	100	15	Normal	–	○
Mach Punch	Fighting	Physical	40	100	30	Normal	–	○

EVOLUTION

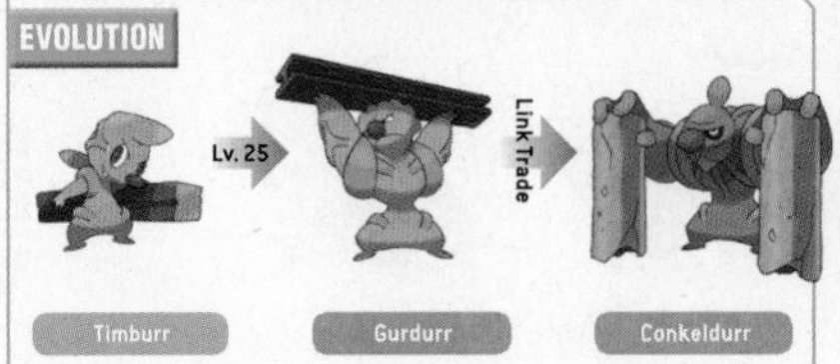
Lv. 25
Link Trade
Timburr
Gurdurr
Conkeldurr

ABILITIES
- Guts
- Sheer Force

EGG GROUP Human-Like

STATS
- HP ●●●
- ATTACK ●●●
- DEFENSE ●●
- SP. ATTACK ●
- SP. DEFENSE ●
- SPEED ●●

● TM & HM MOVES

No.	Name	Type	Kind	Pow.	Acc.	PP	Range	Long	DA
TM06	Toxic	Poison	Status	–	90	10	Normal	–	–
TM08	Bulk Up	Fighting	Status	–	–	20	Self	–	–
TM10	Hidden Power	Normal	Special	–	100	15	Normal	–	–
TM11	Sunny Day	Fire	Status	–	–	5	Both Sides	–	–
TM12	Taunt	Dark	Status	–	100	20	Normal	–	–
TM17	Protect	Normal	Status	–	–	10	Self	–	–
TM18	Rain Dance	Water	Status	–	–	5	Both Sides	–	–
TM21	Frustration	Normal	Physical	–	100	20	Normal	–	○
TM23	Smack Down	Rock	Physical	50	100	15	Normal	–	–
TM27	Return	Normal	Physical	–	100	20	Normal	–	○
TM28	Dig	Ground	Physical	80	100	10	Normal	–	○
TM31	Brick Break	Fighting	Physical	75	100	15	Normal	–	○
TM32	Double Team	Normal	Status	–	–	15	Self	–	–
TM39	Rock Tomb	Rock	Physical	50	80	10	Normal	–	–
TM42	Facade	Normal	Physical	70	100	20	Normal	–	○
TM44	Rest	Psychic	Status	–	–	10	Self	–	–
TM45	Attract	Normal	Status	–	100	15	Normal	–	–
TM47	Low Sweep	Fighting	Physical	60	100	20	Normal	–	○
TM48	Round	Normal	Special	60	100	15	Normal	–	–
TM52	Focus Blast	Fighting	Special	120	70	5	Normal	–	–
TM56	Fling	Dark	Physical	–	100	10	Normal	–	–
TM66	Payback	Dark	Physical	50	100	10	Normal	–	○
TM67	Retaliate	Normal	Physical	70	100	5	Normal	–	○
TM71	Stone Edge	Rock	Physical	100	80	5	Normal	–	–
TM80	Rock Slide	Rock	Physical	75	90	10	Many Others	–	–
TM83	Work Up	Normal	Status	–	–	30	Self	–	–
TM84	Poison Jab	Poison	Physical	80	100	20	Normal	–	○
TM86	Grass Knot	Grass	Special	–	100	20	Normal	–	○
TM87	Swagger	Normal	Status	–	90	15	Normal	–	–
TM90	Substitute	Normal	Status	–	–	10	Self	–	–
TM94	Rock Smash	Fighting	Physical	40	100	15	Normal	–	○
HM04	Strength	Normal	Physical	80	100	15	Normal	–	○

● MAIN WAYS TO OBTAIN

POKÉMON BLACK VERSION
1. Pinwheel Forest Entrance
2. Cold Storage Area

POKÉMON WHITE VERSION
1. Pinwheel Forest Entrance
2. Cold Storage Area

Gurdurr

● TYPE Fighting

● FOOTPRINT

● MALE/FEMALE HAVE SAME FORM

● HEIGHT: 3'11"
● WEIGHT: 88.2 lbs.
● GENDER: Both ♂♀ exist
● ITEMS:
 • None

POKÉMON BLACK VERSION
This Pokémon is so muscular and strongly built that even a group of wrestlers could not make it budge an inch.

POKÉMON WHITE VERSION
They strengthen their bodies by carrying steel beams. They show off their big muscles to their friends.

● LEVEL-UP AND LEARNED MOVES

Lv.	Name	Type	Kind	Pow.	Acc.	PP	Range	Long	DA
1	Pound	Normal	Physical	40	100	35	Normal	—	○
1	Leer	Normal	Status	—	100	30	Many Others	—	—
1	Focus Energy	Normal	Status	—	—	30	Self	—	—
1	Bide	Normal	Physical	—	—	10	Self	—	○
4	Focus Energy	Normal	Status	—	—	30	Self	—	—
8	Bide	Normal	Physical	—	—	10	Self	—	○
12	Low Kick	Fighting	Physical	—	100	20	Normal	—	○
16	Rock Throw	Rock	Physical	50	90	15	Normal	—	—
20	Wake-Up Slap	Fighting	Physical	60	100	10	Normal	—	○
24	Chip Away	Normal	Physical	70	100	20	Normal	—	○
29	Bulk Up	Fighting	Status	—	—	20	Self	—	—
33	Rock Slide	Rock	Physical	75	90	10	Many Others	—	—
37	DynamicPunch	Fighting	Physical	100	50	5	Normal	—	○
41	Scary Face	Normal	Status	—	100	10	Normal	—	—
45	Hammer Arm	Fighting	Physical	100	90	10	Normal	—	○
49	Stone Edge	Rock	Physical	100	80	5	Normal	—	—
53	Focus Punch	Fighting	Physical	150	100	20	Normal	—	○
57	Superpower	Fighting	Physical	120	100	5	Normal	—	○

● MOVES TAUGHT BY PEOPLE

Name	Type	Kind	Pow.	Acc.	PP	Range	Long	DA

● TM & HM MOVES

No.	Name	Type	Kind	Pow.	Acc.	PP	Range	Long	DA
TM06	Toxic	Poison	Status	—	90	10	Normal	—	—
TM08	Bulk Up	Fighting	Status	—	—	20	Self	—	—
TM10	Hidden Power	Normal	Special	—	100	15	Normal	—	—
TM11	Sunny Day	Fire	Status	—	—	5	Both Sides	—	—
TM12	Taunt	Dark	Status	—	100	20	Normal	—	—
TM17	Protect	Normal	Status	—	—	10	Self	—	—
TM18	Rain Dance	Water	Status	—	—	5	Both Sides	—	—
TM21	Frustration	Normal	Physical	—	100	20	Normal	—	○
TM23	Smack Down	Rock	Physical	50	100	15	Normal	—	—
TM27	Return	Normal	Physical	—	100	20	Normal	—	○
TM28	Dig	Ground	Physical	80	100	10	Normal	—	○
TM31	Brick Break	Fighting	Physical	75	100	15	Normal	—	○
TM32	Double Team	Normal	Status	—	—	15	Self	—	—
TM39	Rock Tomb	Rock	Physical	50	80	10	Normal	—	—
TM42	Facade	Normal	Physical	70	100	20	Normal	—	○
TM44	Rest	Psychic	Status	—	—	10	Self	—	—
TM45	Attract	Normal	Status	—	100	15	Normal	—	—
TM47	Low Sweep	Fighting	Physical	60	100	20	Normal	—	○
TM48	Round	Normal	Special	60	100	15	Normal	—	—
TM52	Focus Blast	Fighting	Special	120	70	5	Normal	—	—
TM56	Fling	Dark	Physical	—	100	10	Normal	—	○
TM66	Payback	Dark	Physical	50	100	10	Normal	—	○
TM67	Retaliate	Normal	Physical	70	100	5	Normal	—	—
TM71	Stone Edge	Rock	Physical	100	80	5	Normal	—	—
TM80	Rock Slide	Rock	Physical	75	90	10	Many Others	—	—
TM83	Work Up	Normal	Status	—	—	30	Self	—	—
TM84	Poison Jab	Poison	Physical	80	100	20	Normal	—	○
TM86	Grass Knot	Grass	Special	—	100	20	Normal	—	○
TM87	Swagger	Normal	Status	—	90	15	Normal	—	—
TM90	Substitute	Normal	Status	—	—	10	Self	—	—
TM94	Rock Smash	Fighting	Physical	40	100	15	Normal	—	○
HM04	Strength	Normal	Physical	80	100	15	Normal	—	○

● EVOLUTION

Timburr → Lv. 25 → Gurdurr → Link Trade → Conkeldurr

ABILITIES ● Guts ● Sheer Force

EGG GROUP Human-Like

STATS
HP ●●●
ATTACK ●●●●
DEFENSE ●●●●
SP. ATTACK ●●●
SP. DEFENSE ●●●
SPEED ●●

● MAIN WAYS TO OBTAIN

POKÉMON BLACK VERSION
1 Twist Mountain Upper level
2 Level up Timburr to Lv. 25

POKÉMON WHITE VERSION
1 Twist Mountain Upper level
2 Level up Timburr to Lv. 25

Conkeldurr

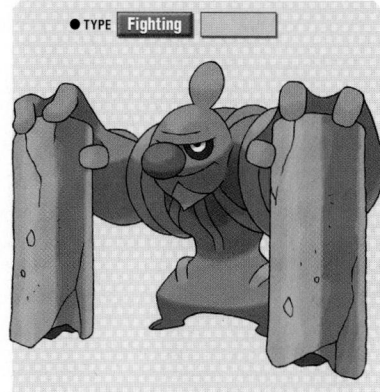

● TYPE Fighting

● FOOTPRINT

● MALE/FEMALE HAVE SAME FORM

● HEIGHT: 4'07"
● WEIGHT: 191.8 lbs.
● GENDER: Both ♂♀ exist
● ITEMS:
 • None

POKÉMON BLACK VERSION
It is thought that Conkeldurr taught humans how to make concrete more than 2,000 years ago.

POKÉMON WHITE VERSION
They use concrete pillars as walking canes. They know moves that enable them to swing the pillars freely in battle.

● LEVEL-UP AND LEARNED MOVES

Lv.	Name	Type	Kind	Pow.	Acc.	PP	Range	Long	DA
1	Pound	Normal	Physical	40	100	35	Normal	—	○
1	Leer	Normal	Status	—	100	30	Many Others	—	—
1	Focus Energy	Normal	Status	—	—	30	Self	—	—
1	Bide	Normal	Physical	—	—	10	Self	—	○
4	Focus Energy	Normal	Status	—	—	30	Self	—	—
8	Bide	Normal	Physical	—	—	10	Self	—	○
12	Low Kick	Fighting	Physical	—	100	20	Normal	—	○
16	Rock Throw	Rock	Physical	50	90	15	Normal	—	—
20	Wake-Up Slap	Fighting	Physical	60	100	10	Normal	—	○
24	Chip Away	Normal	Physical	70	100	20	Normal	—	○
29	Bulk Up	Fighting	Status	—	—	20	Self	—	—
33	Rock Slide	Rock	Physical	75	90	10	Many Others	—	—
37	DynamicPunch	Fighting	Physical	100	50	5	Normal	—	○
41	Scary Face	Normal	Status	—	100	10	Normal	—	—
45	Hammer Arm	Fighting	Physical	100	90	10	Normal	—	○
49	Stone Edge	Rock	Physical	100	80	5	Normal	—	—
53	Focus Punch	Fighting	Physical	150	100	20	Normal	—	○
57	Superpower	Fighting	Physical	120	100	5	Normal	—	○

● MOVES TAUGHT BY PEOPLE

Name	Type	Kind	Pow.	Acc.	PP	Range	Long	DA

● TM & HM MOVES

No.	Name	Type	Kind	Pow.	Acc.	PP	Range	Long	DA
TM06	Toxic	Poison	Status	—	90	10	Normal	—	—
TM08	Bulk Up	Fighting	Status	—	—	20	Self	—	—
TM10	Hidden Power	Normal	Special	—	100	15	Normal	—	—
TM11	Sunny Day	Fire	Status	—	—	5	Both Sides	—	—
TM12	Taunt	Dark	Status	—	100	20	Normal	—	—
TM15	Hyper Beam	Normal	Special	150	90	5	Normal	—	—
TM17	Protect	Normal	Status	—	—	10	Self	—	—
TM18	Rain Dance	Water	Status	—	—	5	Both Sides	—	—
TM21	Frustration	Normal	Physical	—	100	20	Normal	—	○
TM23	Smack Down	Rock	Physical	50	100	15	Normal	—	—
TM26	Earthquake	Ground	Physical	100	100	10	Adjacent	—	○
TM27	Return	Normal	Physical	—	100	20	Normal	—	○
TM28	Dig	Ground	Physical	80	100	10	Normal	—	○
TM31	Brick Break	Fighting	Physical	75	100	15	Normal	—	○
TM32	Double Team	Normal	Status	—	—	15	Self	—	—
TM39	Rock Tomb	Rock	Physical	50	80	10	Normal	—	—
TM42	Facade	Normal	Physical	70	100	20	Normal	—	○
TM44	Rest	Psychic	Status	—	—	10	Self	—	—
TM47	Low Sweep	Fighting	Physical	60	100	20	Normal	—	○
TM48	Round	Normal	Special	60	100	15	Normal	—	—
TM52	Focus Blast	Fighting	Special	120	70	5	Normal	—	—
TM56	Fling	Dark	Physical	—	100	10	Normal	—	○
TM66	Payback	Dark	Physical	50	100	10	Normal	—	○
TM67	Retaliate	Normal	Physical	70	100	5	Normal	—	—
TM68	Giga Impact	Normal	Physical	150	90	5	Normal	—	—
TM71	Stone Edge	Rock	Physical	100	80	5	Normal	—	—
TM78	Bulldoze	Ground	Physical	60	100	20	Adjacent	—	○
TM80	Rock Slide	Rock	Physical	75	90	10	Many Others	—	—
TM83	Work Up	Normal	Status	—	—	30	Self	—	—
TM84	Poison Jab	Poison	Physical	80	100	20	Normal	—	○
TM86	Grass Knot	Grass	Special	—	100	20	Normal	—	○
TM87	Swagger	Normal	Status	—	90	15	Normal	—	—
TM90	Substitute	Normal	Status	—	—	10	Self	—	—
TM94	Rock Smash	Fighting	Physical	40	100	15	Normal	—	○
HM04	Strength	Normal	Physical	80	100	15	Normal	—	○

● EVOLUTION

Timburr → Lv. 25 → Gurdurr → Link Trade → Conkeldurr

ABILITIES ● Guts ● Sheer Force

EGG GROUP Human-Like

STATS
HP ●●●●
ATTACK ●●●●
DEFENSE ●●●●
SP. ATTACK ●●
SP. DEFENSE ●●
SPEED ●●●

● MAIN WAYS TO OBTAIN

POKÉMON BLACK VERSION
1 Link trade Gurdurr
2 —

POKÉMON WHITE VERSION
1 Link trade Gurdurr
2 —

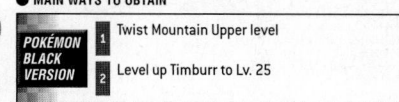

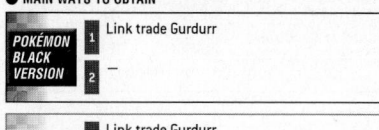

Unova Pokédex ◉ 041 | Tadpole Pokémon

 Tympole

● TYPE Water

● LEVEL-UP AND LEARNED MOVES

Lv.	Name	Type	Kind	Pow.	Acc.	PP	Range	Long	DA
1	Bubble	Water	Special	20	100	30	Many Others	—	—
5	Growl	Normal	Status	—	100	40	Many Others	—	—
5	Supersonic	Normal	Status	—	55	20	Normal	—	—
9	Round	Normal	Special	60	100	15	Normal	—	—
12	BubbleBeam	Water	Special	65	100	20	Normal	—	—
16	Mud Shot	Ground	Special	55	95	15	Normal	—	—
20	Aqua Ring	Water	Status	—	—	20	Self	—	—
23	Uproar	Normal	Special	90	100	10	1 Random	—	—
27	Muddy Water	Water	Special	95	85	10	Many Others	—	—
31	Rain Dance	Water	Status	—	—	5	Both Sides	—	—
34	Flail	Normal	Physical	—	100	15	Normal	—	○
38	Echoed Voice	Normal	Special	40	100	15	Normal	—	—
42	Hydro Pump	Water	Special	120	80	5	Normal	—	—
45	Hyper Voice	Normal	Special	90	100	10	Many Others	—	—

● MOVES TAUGHT BY PEOPLE

Name	Type	Kind	Pow.	Acc.	PP	Range	Long	DA

● EGG MOVES

Name	Type	Kind	Pow.	Acc.	PP	Range	Long	DA
Water Pulse	Water	Special	60	100	20	Normal	○	—
Refresh	Normal	Status	—	—	20	Self	—	—
Mud Sport	Ground	Status	—	—	15	Both Sides	—	—
Mud Bomb	Ground	Special	65	85	10	Normal	—	—
Sleep Talk	Normal	Status	—	—	10	Self	—	—
Snore	Normal	Special	40	100	15	Normal	—	—
Mist	Ice	Status	—	—	30	Your Side	—	—
Earth Power	Ground	Special	90	100	10	Normal	—	—

● TM & HM MOVES

No.	Name	Type	Kind	Pow.	Acc.	PP	Range	Long	DA
TM06	Toxic	Poison	Status	—	90	10	Normal	—	—
TM07	Hail	Ice	Status	—	—	10	Both Sides	—	—
TM10	Hidden Power	Normal	Special	—	100	15	Normal	—	—
TM17	Protect	Normal	Status	—	—	10	Self	—	—
TM18	Rain Dance	Water	Status	—	—	5	Both Sides	—	—
TM21	Frustration	Normal	Physical	—	100	20	Normal	—	○
TM27	Return	Normal	Physical	—	100	20	Normal	—	○
TM32	Double Team	Normal	Status	—	—	15	Self	—	—
TM34	Sludge Wave	Poison	Special	95	100	10	Adjacent	—	—
TM36	Sludge Bomb	Poison	Special	90	100	10	Normal	—	—
TM42	Facade	Normal	Physical	70	100	20	Normal	—	○
TM44	Rest	Psychic	Status	—	—	10	Self	—	—
TM45	Attract	Normal	Status	—	100	15	Normal	—	—
TM48	Round	Normal	Special	60	100	15	Normal	—	—
TM49	Echoed Voice	Normal	Special	40	100	15	Normal	—	—
TM55	Scald	Water	Special	80	100	15	Normal	—	—
TM87	Swagger	Normal	Status	—	90	15	Normal	—	—
TM90	Substitute	Normal	Status	—	—	10	Self	—	—
HM03	Surf	Water	Special	95	100	15	Adjacent	—	—

● FOOTPRINT

● MALE/FEMALE HAVE SAME FORM

● HEIGHT: 1'08"
● WEIGHT: 9.9 lbs.
● GENDER: Both ♂♀ exist
● ITEMS:
• Persim Berry

EVOLUTION

Tympole → Lv. 25 → Palpitoad → Lv. 36 → Seismitoad

● MAIN WAYS TO OBTAIN

POKÉMON BLACK VERSION	1	Pinwheel Forest Entrance
	2	—

POKÉMON WHITE VERSION	1	Pinwheel Forest Entrance
	2	—

POKÉMON BLACK VERSION: They warn others of danger by vibrating their cheeks to create a high-pitched sound.

POKÉMON WHITE VERSION: By vibrating its cheeks, it emits sound waves imperceptible to humans. It uses the rhythm of these sounds to talk.

ABILITIES
● Swift Swim
● Hydration

EGG GROUP
Water 1

STATS
HP ●●
ATTACK ●●
DEFENSE ●●
SP. ATTACK ●●
SP. DEFENSE ●
SPEED ●●●

Unova Pokédex ◉ 042 | Vibration Pokémon

Palpitoad

● TYPE Water Ground

● LEVEL-UP AND LEARNED MOVES

Lv.	Name	Type	Kind	Pow.	Acc.	PP	Range	Long	DA
1	Bubble	Water	Special	20	100	30	Many Others	—	—
1	Growl	Normal	Status	—	100	40	Many Others	—	—
1	Supersonic	Normal	Status	—	55	20	Normal	—	—
1	Round	Normal	Special	60	100	15	Normal	—	—
5	Supersonic	Normal	Status	—	55	20	Normal	—	—
9	Round	Normal	Special	60	100	15	Normal	—	—
12	BubbleBeam	Water	Special	65	100	20	Normal	—	—
16	Mud Shot	Ground	Special	55	95	15	Normal	—	—
20	Aqua Ring	Water	Status	—	—	20	Self	—	—
23	Uproar	Normal	Special	90	100	10	1 Random	—	—
28	Muddy Water	Water	Special	95	85	10	Many Others	—	—
33	Rain Dance	Water	Status	—	—	5	Both Sides	—	—
37	Flail	Normal	Physical	—	100	15	Normal	—	○
42	Echoed Voice	Normal	Special	40	100	15	Normal	—	—
47	Hydro Pump	Water	Special	120	80	5	Normal	—	—
51	Hyper Voice	Normal	Special	90	100	10	Many Others	—	—

● MOVES TAUGHT BY PEOPLE

Name	Type	Kind	Pow.	Acc.	PP	Range	Long	DA

● TM & HM MOVES

No.	Name	Type	Kind	Pow.	Acc.	PP	Range	Long	DA
TM06	Toxic	Poison	Status	—	90	10	Normal	—	—
TM07	Hail	Ice	Status	—	—	10	Both Sides	—	—
TM10	Hidden Power	Normal	Special	—	100	15	Normal	—	—
TM17	Protect	Normal	Status	—	—	10	Self	—	—
TM18	Rain Dance	Water	Status	—	—	5	Both Sides	—	—
TM21	Frustration	Normal	Physical	—	100	20	Normal	—	○
TM27	Return	Normal	Physical	—	100	20	Normal	—	○
TM32	Double Team	Normal	Status	—	—	15	Self	—	—
TM34	Sludge Wave	Poison	Special	95	100	10	Adjacent	—	—
TM36	Sludge Bomb	Poison	Special	90	100	10	Normal	—	—
TM42	Facade	Normal	Physical	70	100	20	Normal	—	○
TM44	Rest	Psychic	Status	—	—	10	Self	—	—
TM45	Attract	Normal	Status	—	100	15	Normal	—	—
TM48	Round	Normal	Special	60	100	15	Normal	—	—
TM49	Echoed Voice	Normal	Special	40	100	15	Normal	—	—
TM55	Scald	Water	Special	80	100	15	Normal	—	—
TM78	Bulldoze	Ground	Physical	60	100	20	Adjacent	—	—
TM87	Swagger	Normal	Status	—	90	15	Normal	—	—
TM90	Substitute	Normal	Status	—	—	10	Self	—	—
TM94	Rock Smash	Fighting	Physical	40	100	15	Normal	—	○
HM03	Surf	Water	Special	95	100	15	Adjacent	—	—

● FOOTPRINT

● MALE/FEMALE HAVE SAME FORM

● HEIGHT: 2'07"
● WEIGHT: 37.5 lbs.
● GENDER: Both ♂♀ exist
● ITEMS:
• Persim Berry

EVOLUTION

Tympole → Lv. 25 → Palpitoad → Lv. 36 → Seismitoad

● MAIN WAYS TO OBTAIN

POKÉMON BLACK VERSION	1	Icirrus City (spring/summer/autumn only)
	2	Level up Tympole to Lv. 25

POKÉMON WHITE VERSION	1	Icirrus City (spring/summer/autumn only)
	2	Level up Tympole to Lv. 25

POKÉMON BLACK VERSION: When they vibrate the bumps on their heads, they can make waves in water or earthquake-like vibrations on land.

POKÉMON WHITE VERSION: It lives in the water and on land. It uses its long, sticky tongue to capture prey.

ABILITIES
● Swift Swim
● Hydration

EGG GROUP
Water 1

STATS
HP ●●●
ATTACK ●●
DEFENSE ●●
SP. ATTACK ●●●
SP. DEFENSE ●●
SPEED ●●●

Seismitoad

● TYPE Water Ground

● FOOTPRINT

● MALE/FEMALE HAVE SAME FORM

● HEIGHT: 4'11"
● WEIGHT: 136.7 lbs.
● GENDER: Both ♂♀ exist
● ITEMS:
 • Persim Berry

POKÉMON BLACK VERSION They shoot paralyzing liquid from their head bumps. They use vibration to hurt their opponents.

POKÉMON WHITE VERSION It increases the power of its punches by vibrating the bumps on its fists. It can turn a boulder to rubble with one punch.

● LEVEL-UP AND LEARNED MOVES

Lv.	Name	Type	Kind	Pow.	Acc.	PP	Range	Long	DA
1	Bubble	Water	Special	20	100	30	Many Others	—	—
1	Growl	Normal	Status	—	100	40	Many Others	—	—
1	Supersonic	Normal	Status	—	55	20	Normal	—	—
1	Round	Normal	Special	60	100	15	Normal	—	—
5	Supersonic	Normal	Status	—	55	20	Normal	—	—
9	Round	Normal	Special	60	100	15	Normal	—	—
12	BubbleBeam	Water	Special	65	100	20	Normal	—	—
16	Mud Shot	Ground	Special	55	95	15	Normal	—	—
20	Aqua Ring	Water	Status	—	—	20	Self	—	—
23	Uproar	Normal	Special	90	100	10	1 Random	—	—
28	Muddy Water	Water	Special	95	85	10	Many Others	—	—
33	Rain Dance	Water	Status	—	—	5	Both Sides	—	—
36	Acid	Poison	Special	40	100	30	Many Others	—	—
39	Flail	Normal	Physical	—	100	15	Normal	—	○
44	Drain Punch	Fighting	Physical	75	100	10	Normal	—	○
49	Echoed Voice	Normal	Special	40	100	15	Normal	—	—
53	Hydro Pump	Water	Special	120	80	5	Normal	—	—
59	Hyper Voice	Normal	Special	90	100	10	Many Others	—	—

● MOVES TAUGHT BY PEOPLE

Name	Type	Kind	Pow.	Acc.	PP	Range	Long	DA

● TM & HM MOVES

No.	Name	Type	Kind	Pow.	Acc.	PP	Range	Long	DA
TM06	Toxic	Poison	Status	—	90	10	Normal	—	—
TM07	Hail	Ice	Status	—	—	10	Both Sides	—	—
TM09	Venoshock	Poison	Special	65	100	10	Normal	—	—
TM10	Hidden Power	Normal	Special	—	100	15	Normal	—	—
TM15	Hyper Beam	Normal	Special	150	90	5	Normal	—	—
TM17	Protect	Normal	Status	—	—	10	Self	—	—
TM18	Rain Dance	Water	Status	—	—	5	Both Sides	—	—
TM21	Frustration	Normal	Physical	—	100	20	Normal	—	○
TM26	Earthquake	Ground	Physical	100	100	10	Adjacent	—	—
TM27	Return	Normal	Physical	—	100	20	Normal	—	○
TM28	Dig	Ground	Physical	80	100	10	Normal	—	○
TM31	Brick Break	Fighting	Physical	75	100	15	Normal	—	○
TM32	Double Team	Normal	Status	—	—	15	Self	—	—
TM34	Sludge Wave	Poison	Special	95	100	10	Adjacent	—	—
TM36	Sludge Bomb	Poison	Special	90	100	10	Normal	—	—
TM39	Rock Tomb	Rock	Physical	50	80	10	Normal	—	—
TM42	Facade	Normal	Physical	70	100	20	Normal	—	○
TM44	Rest	Psychic	Status	—	—	10	Self	—	—
TM45	Attract	Normal	Status	—	100	15	Normal	—	—
TM48	Round	Normal	Special	60	100	15	Normal	—	—
TM49	Echoed Voice	Normal	Special	40	100	15	Normal	—	—
TM52	Focus Blast	Fighting	Special	120	70	5	Normal	—	—
TM55	Scald	Water	Special	80	100	15	Normal	—	—
TM56	Fling	Dark	Physical	—	100	10	Normal	—	○
TM66	Payback	Dark	Physical	50	100	10	Normal	—	○
TM68	Giga Impact	Normal	Physical	150	90	5	Normal	—	○
TM78	Bulldoze	Ground	Physical	60	100	20	Adjacent	—	—
TM80	Rock Slide	Rock	Physical	75	90	10	Many Others	—	—
TM84	Poison Jab	Poison	Physical	80	100	20	Normal	—	○
TM86	Grass Knot	Grass	Special	—	100	20	Normal	—	○
TM87	Swagger	Normal	Status	—	90	15	Normal	—	—
TM90	Substitute	Normal	Status	—	—	10	Self	—	—
TM94	Rock Smash	Fighting	Physical	40	100	15	Normal	—	○
HM03	Surf	Water	Special	95	100	15	Adjacent	—	—
HM04	Strength	Normal	Physical	80	100	15	Normal	—	○

EVOLUTION

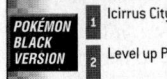

Tympole → Lv. 25 → Palpitoad → Lv. 36 → Seismitoad

ABILITIES
● Swift Swim
● Poison Touch

EGG GROUP Water 1

STATS
HP ●●●●
ATTACK ●●●●
DEFENSE ●●●
SP. ATTACK ●●●
SP. DEFENSE ●●●
SPEED ●●●

● MAIN WAYS TO OBTAIN

POKÉMON BLACK VERSION
1 Icirrus City (Ripples in Water)
2 Level up Palpitoad to Lv. 36

POKÉMON WHITE VERSION
1 Icirrus City (Ripples in Water)
2 Level up Palpitoad to Lv. 36

Throh

● TYPE Fighting

● FOOTPRINT

● MALE FORM

● HEIGHT: 4'03"
● WEIGHT: 122.4 lbs.
● GENDER: Only ♂ exist
● ITEMS:
 • Black Belt
 • Expert Belt

POKÉMON BLACK VERSION When it tightens its belt, it becomes stronger. Wild Throh use vines to weave their own belts.

POKÉMON WHITE VERSION When they encounter foes bigger than themselves, they try to throw them. They always travel in packs of five.

● LEVEL-UP AND LEARNED MOVES

Lv.	Name	Type	Kind	Pow.	Acc.	PP	Range	Long	DA
1	Bind	Normal	Physical	15	85	20	Normal	—	○
1	Leer	Normal	Status	—	100	30	Many Others	—	—
5	Bide	Normal	Physical	—	—	10	Self	—	—
9	Focus Energy	Normal	Status	—	—	30	Self	—	—
13	Seismic Toss	Fighting	Physical	—	100	20	Normal	—	—
17	Vital Throw	Fighting	Physical	70	—	10	Normal	—	—
21	Revenge	Fighting	Physical	60	100	10	Normal	—	—
25	Storm Throw	Fighting	Physical	40	100	10	Normal	—	—
29	Body Slam	Normal	Physical	85	100	15	Normal	—	—
33	Bulk Up	Fighting	Status	—	—	20	Self	—	—
37	Circle Throw	Fighting	Physical	60	90	10	Normal	—	—
41	Endure	Normal	Status	—	—	10	Self	—	—
45	Wide Guard	Rock	Status	—	—	10	Your Side	—	—
49	Superpower	Fighting	Physical	120	100	5	Normal	—	—
53	Reversal	Fighting	Physical	—	100	15	Normal	—	—

● MOVES TAUGHT BY PEOPLE

Name	Type	Kind	Pow.	Acc.	PP	Range	Long	DA

● EGG MOVES

Name	Type	Kind	Pow.	Acc.	PP	Range	Long	DA

● TM & HM MOVES

No.	Name	Type	Kind	Pow.	Acc.	PP	Range	Long	DA
TM06	Toxic	Poison	Status	—	90	10	Normal	—	—
TM08	Bulk Up	Fighting	Status	—	—	20	Self	—	—
TM10	Hidden Power	Normal	Special	—	100	15	Normal	—	—
TM11	Sunny Day	Fire	Status	—	—	5	Both Sides	—	—
TM12	Taunt	Dark	Status	—	100	20	Normal	—	—
TM17	Protect	Normal	Status	—	—	10	Self	—	—
TM18	Rain Dance	Water	Status	—	—	5	Both Sides	—	—
TM21	Frustration	Normal	Physical	—	100	20	Normal	—	○
TM26	Earthquake	Ground	Physical	100	100	10	Adjacent	—	—
TM27	Return	Normal	Physical	—	100	20	Normal	—	○
TM28	Dig	Ground	Physical	80	100	10	Normal	—	○
TM31	Brick Break	Fighting	Physical	75	100	15	Normal	—	○
TM32	Double Team	Normal	Status	—	—	15	Self	—	—
TM39	Rock Tomb	Rock	Physical	50	80	10	Normal	—	—
TM42	Facade	Normal	Physical	70	100	20	Normal	—	○
TM44	Rest	Psychic	Status	—	—	10	Self	—	—
TM45	Attract	Normal	Status	—	100	15	Normal	—	—
TM48	Low Sweep	Fighting	Physical	60	100	20	Normal	—	—
TM48	Round	Normal	Special	60	100	15	Normal	—	—
TM52	Focus Blast	Fighting	Special	120	70	5	Normal	—	—
TM56	Fling	Dark	Physical	—	100	10	Normal	—	○
TM66	Payback	Dark	Physical	50	100	10	Normal	—	○
TM67	Retaliate	Normal	Physical	70	100	5	Normal	—	—
TM68	Giga Impact	Normal	Physical	150	90	5	Normal	—	○
TM71	Stone Edge	Rock	Physical	100	80	5	Normal	—	—
TM78	Bulldoze	Ground	Physical	60	100	20	Adjacent	—	—
TM80	Rock Slide	Rock	Physical	75	90	10	Many Others	—	—
TM83	Work Up	Normal	Status	—	—	30	Self	—	—
TM84	Poison Jab	Poison	Physical	80	100	20	Normal	—	○
TM86	Grass Knot	Grass	Special	—	100	20	Normal	—	○
TM87	Swagger	Normal	Status	—	90	15	Normal	—	—
TM90	Substitute	Normal	Status	—	—	10	Self	—	—
TM94	Rock Smash	Fighting	Physical	40	100	15	Normal	—	○
HM04	Strength	Normal	Physical	80	100	15	Normal	—	○

EVOLUTION

Does not evolve

ABILITIES
● Guts
● Inner Focus

EGG GROUP Human-Like

STATS
HP ●●●●●
ATTACK ●●●●
DEFENSE ●●●
SP. ATTACK ●
SP. DEFENSE ●●●
SPEED ●●

● MAIN WAYS TO OBTAIN

POKÉMON BLACK VERSION
1 Pinwheel Forest Entrance (Rustling Grass)
2 Route 18 (Rustling Grass)

POKÉMON WHITE VERSION
1 Pinwheel Forest Entrance
2 Route 18

Sawk

● TYPE **Fighting**

LEVEL-UP AND LEARNED MOVES

Lv.	Name	Type	Kind	Pow.	Acc.	PP	Range	Long	DA
1	Rock Smash	Fighting	Physical	40	100	15	Normal	—	○
1	Leer	Normal	Status	—	100	30	Many Others	—	—
5	Bide	Normal	Physical	—	—	10	Self	—	○
9	Focus Energy	Normal	Status	—	—	30	Self	—	—
13	Double Kick	Fighting	Physical	30	100	30	Normal	—	○
17	Low Sweep	Fighting	Physical	60	100	20	Normal	—	○
21	Counter	Fighting	Physical	—	100	20	Varies	—	○
25	Karate Chop	Fighting	Physical	50	100	25	Normal	—	○
29	Brick Break	Fighting	Physical	75	100	15	Normal	—	○
33	Bulk Up	Fighting	Status	—	—	20	Self	—	—
37	Retaliate	Normal	Physical	70	100	5	Normal	—	○
41	Endure	Normal	Status	—	—	10	Self	—	—
45	Quick Guard	Fighting	Status	—	—	15	Your Side	—	—
49	Close Combat	Fighting	Physical	120	100	5	Normal	—	○
53	Reversal	Fighting	Physical	—	100	15	Normal	—	○

MOVES TAUGHT BY PEOPLE

Name	Type	Kind	Pow.	Acc.	PP	Range	Long	DA

EGG MOVES

Name	Type	Kind	Pow.	Acc.	PP	Range	Long	DA

TM & HM MOVES

No.	Name	Type	Kind	Pow.	Acc.	PP	Range	Long	DA
TM06	Toxic	Poison	Status	—	90	10	Normal	—	—
TM08	Bulk Up	Fighting	Status	—	—	20	Self	—	—
TM10	Hidden Power	Normal	Special	—	100	15	Normal	—	—
TM11	Sunny Day	Fire	Status	—	—	5	Both Sides	—	—
TM12	Taunt	Dark	Status	—	100	20	Normal	—	—
TM17	Protect	Normal	Status	—	—	10	Self	—	—
TM18	Rain Dance	Water	Status	—	—	5	Both Sides	—	—
TM21	Frustration	Normal	Physical	—	100	20	Normal	—	○
TM26	Earthquake	Ground	Physical	100	100	10	Adjacent	—	○
TM27	Return	Normal	Physical	—	100	20	Normal	—	○
TM28	Dig	Ground	Physical	80	100	10	Normal	—	○
TM31	Brick Break	Fighting	Physical	75	100	15	Normal	—	○
TM32	Double Team	Normal	Status	—	—	15	Self	—	—
TM39	Rock Tomb	Rock	Physical	50	80	10	Normal	—	○
TM42	Facade	Normal	Physical	70	100	20	Normal	—	○
TM44	Rest	Psychic	Status	—	—	10	Self	—	—
TM45	Attract	Normal	Status	—	100	15	Normal	—	—
TM47	Low Sweep	Fighting	Physical	60	100	20	Normal	—	○
TM48	Round	Normal	Special	60	100	15	Normal	—	—
TM52	Focus Blast	Fighting	Special	120	70	5	Normal	—	○
TM56	Fling	Dark	Physical	—	100	10	Normal	—	○
TM66	Payback	Dark	Physical	50	100	10	Normal	—	○
TM67	Retaliate	Normal	Physical	70	100	5	Normal	—	○
TM68	Giga Impact	Normal	Physical	150	90	5	Normal	—	○
TM71	Stone Edge	Rock	Physical	100	80	5	Normal	—	○
TM78	Bulldoze	Ground	Physical	60	100	20	Adjacent	—	○
TM80	Rock Slide	Rock	Physical	75	90	10	Many Others	—	○
TM83	Work Up	Normal	Status	—	—	30	Self	—	—
TM84	Poison Jab	Poison	Physical	80	100	20	Normal	—	○
TM86	Grass Knot	Grass	Special	—	100	20	Normal	—	○
TM87	Swagger	Normal	Status	—	90	15	Normal	—	—
TM90	Substitute	Normal	Status	—	—	10	Self	—	—
TM94	Rock Smash	Fighting	Physical	40	100	15	Normal	—	○
HM04	Strength	Normal	Physical	80	100	15	Normal	—	—

● FOOTPRINT

● MALE FORM

● HEIGHT: 4'07"
● WEIGHT: 112.4 lbs.
● GENDER: Only ♂ exist
● ITEMS:
• Black Belt
• Expert Belt

EVOLUTION

Does not evolve

MAIN WAYS TO OBTAIN

POKÉMON BLACK VERSION	1	Pinwheel Forest Entrance
	2	Route 18

POKÉMON WHITE VERSION	1	Pinwheel Forest Entrance (Rustling Grass)
	2	Route 18 (Rustling Grass)

POKÉMON BLACK VERSION — The sound of Sawk punching boulders and trees can be heard all the way from the mountains where they train.

POKÉMON WHITE VERSION — Tying their belts gets them pumped and makes their punches more destructive. Disturbing their training angers them.

ABILITIES
● Sturdy
● Inner Focus

EGG GROUP: Human-Like

STATS
HP ●●●
ATTACK ●●●●●
DEFENSE ●●●
SP. ATTACK ●●
SP. DEFENSE ●●●
SPEED ●●●●

Sewaddle

● TYPE **Bug** **Grass**

LEVEL-UP AND LEARNED MOVES

Lv.	Name	Type	Kind	Pow.	Acc.	PP	Range	Long	DA
1	Tackle	Normal	Physical	50	100	35	Normal	—	○
1	String Shot	Bug	Status	—	95	40	Many Others	—	—
8	Bug Bite	Bug	Physical	60	100	20	Normal	—	○
15	Razor Leaf	Grass	Physical	55	95	25	Many Others	—	—
22	Struggle Bug	Bug	Special	30	100	20	Many Others	—	—
29	Endure	Normal	Status	—	—	10	Self	—	—
36	Bug Buzz	Bug	Special	90	100	10	Normal	—	○
43	Flail	Normal	Physical	—	100	15	Normal	—	○

MOVES TAUGHT BY PEOPLE

Name	Type	Kind	Pow.	Acc.	PP	Range	Long	DA

EGG MOVES

Name	Type	Kind	Pow.	Acc.	PP	Range	Long	DA
Silver Wind	Bug	Special	60	100	5	Normal	—	—
Screech	Normal	Status	—	85	40	Normal	—	—
Razor Wind	Normal	Special	80	100	10	Many Others	—	—
Mind Reader	Normal	Status	—	—	5	Normal	—	—
Agility	Psychic	Status	—	—	30	Self	—	—
Me First	Normal	Status	—	—	20	Varies	—	—
Baton Pass	Normal	Status	—	—	40	Self	—	—
Camouflage	Normal	Status	—	—	20	Self	—	—
Air Slash	Flying	Special	75	95	20	Normal	○	—

TM & HM MOVES

No.	Name	Type	Kind	Pow.	Acc.	PP	Range	Long	DA
TM04	Calm Mind	Psychic	Status	—	—	20	Self	—	—
TM06	Toxic	Poison	Status	—	90	10	Normal	—	—
TM10	Hidden Power	Normal	Special	—	100	15	Normal	—	—
TM11	Sunny Day	Fire	Status	—	—	5	Both Sides	—	—
TM16	Light Screen	Psychic	Status	—	—	30	Your Side	—	—
TM17	Protect	Normal	Status	—	—	10	Self	—	—
TM20	Safeguard	Normal	Status	—	—	25	Your Side	—	—
TM21	Frustration	Normal	Physical	—	100	20	Normal	—	○
TM22	SolarBeam	Grass	Special	120	100	10	Normal	—	○
TM27	Return	Normal	Physical	—	100	20	Normal	—	○
TM32	Double Team	Normal	Status	—	—	15	Self	—	—
TM42	Facade	Normal	Physical	70	100	20	Normal	—	○
TM44	Rest	Psychic	Status	—	—	10	Self	—	—
TM45	Attract	Normal	Status	—	100	15	Normal	—	—
TM48	Round	Normal	Special	60	100	15	Normal	—	—
TM53	Energy Ball	Grass	Special	80	100	10	Normal	—	○
TM66	Payback	Dark	Physical	50	100	10	Normal	—	○
TM70	Flash	Normal	Status	—	100	20	Normal	—	—
TM76	Struggle Bug	Bug	Special	30	100	20	Many Others	—	—
TM85	Dream Eater	Psychic	Special	100	100	15	Normal	—	○
TM86	Grass Knot	Grass	Special	—	100	20	Normal	—	○
TM87	Swagger	Normal	Status	—	90	15	Normal	—	—
TM90	Substitute	Normal	Status	—	—	10	Self	—	—
HM01	Cut	Normal	Physical	50	95	30	Normal	—	—

● FOOTPRINT

● MALE/FEMALE HAVE SAME FORM

● HEIGHT: 1'00"
● WEIGHT: 5.5 lbs.
● GENDER: Both ♂♀ exist
● ITEMS:
• Mental Herb

EVOLUTION

Sewaddle → Lv. 20 → Swadloon → Level up with high friendship → Leavanny

MAIN WAYS TO OBTAIN

POKÉMON BLACK VERSION	1	Pinwheel Forest
	2	—

POKÉMON WHITE VERSION	1	Pinwheel Forest
	2	—

POKÉMON BLACK VERSION — Leavanny dress it in clothes they made for it when it hatched. It hides its head in its hood while it is sleeping.

POKÉMON WHITE VERSION — This Pokémon makes clothes for itself. It chews up leaves and sews them with sticky thread extruded from its mouth.

ABILITIES
● Swarm
● Chlorophyll

EGG GROUP: Bug

STATS
HP ●●
ATTACK ●●●
DEFENSE ●●●
SP. ATTACK ●●
SP. DEFENSE ●●
SPEED ●●

Swadloon

● TYPE Bug Grass

● FOOTPRINT

● MALE/FEMALE HAVE SAME FORM

● HEIGHT: 1'08"
● WEIGHT: 16.1 lbs.
● GENDER: Both ♂♀ exist
● ITEMS:
  • Mental Herb

POKÉMON BLACK VERSION
Forests where Swadloon live have superb foliage because the nutrients they make from fallen leaves nourish the plant life.

POKÉMON WHITE VERSION
It protects itself from the cold by wrapping up in leaves. It stays on the move, eating leaves in forests.

● LEVEL-UP AND LEARNED MOVES

Lv.	Name	Type	Kind	Pow.	Acc.	PP	Range	Long	DA
1	GrassWhistle	Grass	Status	—	55	15	Normal	—	—
1	Tackle	Normal	Physical	50	100	35	Normal	—	○
1	String Shot	Bug	Status	—	95	40	Many Others	—	—
1	Bug Bite	Bug	Physical	60	100	20	Normal	—	○
1	Razor Leaf	Grass	Physical	55	95	25	Many Others	—	—
20	Protect	Normal	Status	—	—	10	Self	—	—

● MOVES TAUGHT BY PEOPLE

Name	Type	Kind	Pow.	Acc.	PP	Range	Long	DA

● TM & HM MOVES

No.	Name	Type	Kind	Pow.	Acc.	PP	Range	Long	DA
TM04	Calm Mind	Psychic	Status	—	—	20	Self	—	—
TM06	Toxic	Poison	Status	—	90	10	Normal	—	—
TM10	Hidden Power	Normal	Special	—	100	15	Normal	—	—
TM11	Sunny Day	Fire	Status	—	—	5	Both Sides	—	—
TM16	Light Screen	Psychic	Status	—	—	30	Your Side	—	—
TM17	Protect	Normal	Status	—	—	10	Self	—	—
TM20	Safeguard	Normal	Status	—	—	25	Your Side	—	—
TM21	Frustration	Normal	Physical	—	100	20	Normal	—	○
TM22	SolarBeam	Grass	Special	120	100	10	Normal	—	—
TM27	Return	Normal	Physical	—	100	20	Normal	—	○
TM32	Double Team	Normal	Status	—	—	15	Self	—	—
TM42	Facade	Normal	Physical	70	100	20	Normal	—	○
TM44	Rest	Psychic	Status	—	—	10	Self	—	—
TM45	Attract	Normal	Status	—	100	15	Normal	—	—
TM48	Round	Normal	Special	60	100	15	Normal	—	—
TM53	Energy Ball	Grass	Special	80	100	10	Normal	—	—
TM66	Payback	Dark	Physical	50	100	10	Normal	—	○
TM70	Flash	Normal	Status	—	100	20	Normal	—	—
TM76	Struggle Bug	Bug	Special	30	100	20	Many Others	—	—
TM85	Dream Eater	Psychic	Special	100	100	15	Normal	—	—
TM86	Grass Knot	Grass	Special	—	100	20	Normal	—	○
TM87	Swagger	Normal	Status	—	90	15	Normal	—	—
TM90	Substitute	Normal	Status	—	—	10	Self	—	—
HM01	Cut	Normal	Physical	50	95	30	Normal	—	○

EVOLUTION

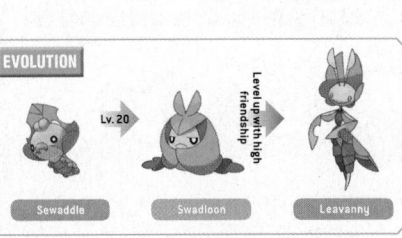

Sewaddle → Lv. 20 → Swadloon → Level up with high friendship → Leavanny

ABILITIES
● Leaf Guard
● Chlorophyll

EGG GROUP Bug

STATS
HP ●●
ATTACK ●●●
DEFENSE ●●●●
SP. ATTACK ●●●
SP. DEFENSE ●●●
SPEED ●●

● MAIN WAYS TO OBTAIN

POKÉMON BLACK VERSION
1 Lostlorn Forest
2 Level up Sewaddle to Lv. 20

POKÉMON WHITE VERSION
1 Lostlorn Forest
2 Level up Sewaddle to Lv. 20

Leavanny

● TYPE Bug Grass

● FOOTPRINT

● MALE/FEMALE HAVE SAME FORM

● HEIGHT: 3'11"
● WEIGHT: 45.2 lbs.
● GENDER: Both ♂♀ exist
● ITEMS:
  • Mental Herb

POKÉMON BLACK VERSION
Upon finding a small Pokémon, it weaves clothing for it from leaves, using the cutters on its arms and sticky silk.

POKÉMON WHITE VERSION
It keeps its eggs warm with heat from fermenting leaves. It also uses leaves to make warm wrappings for Sewaddle.

● LEVEL-UP AND LEARNED MOVES

Lv.	Name	Type	Kind	Pow.	Acc.	PP	Range	Long	DA
1	False Swipe	Normal	Physical	40	100	40	Normal	—	○
1	Tackle	Normal	Physical	50	100	35	Normal	—	○
1	String Shot	Bug	Status	—	95	40	Many Others	—	—
1	Bug Bite	Bug	Physical	60	100	20	Normal	—	○
1	Razor Leaf	Grass	Physical	55	95	25	Many Others	—	—
8	Bug Bite	Bug	Physical	60	100	20	Normal	—	○
15	Razor Leaf	Grass	Physical	55	95	25	Many Others	—	—
22	Struggle Bug	Bug	Special	30	100	20	Many Others	—	—
29	Slash	Normal	Physical	70	100	20	Normal	—	○
32	Helping Hand	Normal	Status	—	—	20	1 Ally	—	—
36	Leaf Blade	Grass	Physical	90	100	15	Normal	—	○
39	X-Scissor	Bug	Physical	80	100	15	Normal	—	○
43	Entrainment	Normal	Status	—	100	15	Normal	—	—
46	Swords Dance	Normal	Status	—	—	30	Self	—	—
50	Leaf Storm	Grass	Special	140	90	5	Normal	—	—

● MOVES TAUGHT BY PEOPLE

Name	Type	Kind	Pow.	Acc.	PP	Range	Long	DA

● TM & HM MOVES

No.	Name	Type	Kind	Pow.	Acc.	PP	Range	Long	DA
TM01	Hone Claws	Dark	Status	—	—	15	Self	—	—
TM04	Calm Mind	Psychic	Status	—	—	20	Self	—	—
TM06	Toxic	Poison	Status	—	90	10	Normal	—	—
TM10	Hidden Power	Normal	Special	—	100	15	Normal	—	—
TM11	Sunny Day	Fire	Status	—	—	5	Both Sides	—	—
TM15	Hyper Beam	Normal	Special	150	90	5	Normal	—	—
TM16	Light Screen	Psychic	Status	—	—	30	Your Side	—	—
TM17	Protect	Normal	Status	—	—	10	Self	—	—
TM20	Safeguard	Normal	Status	—	—	25	Your Side	—	—
TM21	Frustration	Normal	Physical	—	100	20	Normal	—	○
TM22	SolarBeam	Grass	Special	120	100	10	Normal	—	—
TM27	Return	Normal	Physical	—	100	20	Normal	—	○
TM32	Double Team	Normal	Status	—	—	15	Self	—	—
TM33	Reflect	Psychic	Status	—	—	20	Your Side	—	—
TM40	Aerial Ace	Flying	Physical	60	—	20	Normal	○	○
TM42	Facade	Normal	Physical	70	100	20	Normal	—	○
TM44	Rest	Psychic	Status	—	—	10	Self	—	—
TM45	Attract	Normal	Status	—	100	15	Normal	—	—
TM48	Round	Normal	Special	60	100	15	Normal	—	—
TM53	Energy Ball	Grass	Special	80	100	10	Normal	—	—
TM54	False Swipe	Normal	Physical	40	100	40	Normal	—	○
TM65	Shadow Claw	Ghost	Physical	70	100	15	Normal	—	○
TM66	Payback	Dark	Physical	50	100	10	Normal	—	○
TM67	Retaliate	Normal	Physical	70	100	5	Normal	—	○
TM68	Giga Impact	Normal	Physical	150	90	5	Normal	—	○
TM70	Flash	Normal	Status	—	100	20	Normal	—	—
TM75	Swords Dance	Normal	Status	—	—	30	Self	—	—
TM76	Struggle Bug	Bug	Special	30	100	20	Many Others	—	—
TM81	X-Scissor	Bug	Physical	80	100	15	Normal	—	○
TM84	Poison Jab	Poison	Physical	80	100	20	Normal	—	○
TM85	Dream Eater	Psychic	Special	100	100	15	Normal	—	—
TM86	Grass Knot	Grass	Special	—	100	20	Normal	—	○
TM87	Swagger	Normal	Status	—	90	15	Normal	—	—
TM90	Substitute	Normal	Status	—	—	10	Self	—	—
HM01	Cut	Normal	Physical	50	95	30	Normal	—	○

EVOLUTION

Sewaddle → Lv. 20 → Swadloon → Level up with high friendship → Leavanny

ABILITIES
● Swarm
● Chlorophyll

EGG GROUP Bug

STATS
HP ●●●
ATTACK ●●●●
DEFENSE ●●●
SP. ATTACK ●●●
SP. DEFENSE ●●●
SPEED ●●●●

● MAIN WAYS TO OBTAIN

POKÉMON BLACK VERSION
1 Lostlorn Forest (Rustling Grass)
2 Level up Swadloon with high friendship

POKÉMON WHITE VERSION
1 Lostlorn Forest (Rustling Grass)
2 Level up Swadloon with high friendship

Venipede

● TYPE **Bug** **Poison**

● LEVEL-UP AND LEARNED MOVES

Lv.	Name	Type	Kind	Pow.	Acc.	PP	Range	Long	DA
1	Defense Curl	Normal	Status	—	—	40	Self	—	—
1	Rollout	Rock	Physical	30	90	20	Normal	—	○
5	Poison Sting	Poison	Physical	15	100	35	Normal	—	—
8	Screech	Normal	Status	—	85	40	Normal	—	—
12	Pursuit	Dark	Physical	40	100	20	Normal	—	○
15	Protect	Normal	Status	—	—	10	Self	—	—
19	Poison Tail	Poison	Physical	50	100	25	Normal	—	○
22	Bug Bite	Bug	Physical	60	100	20	Normal	—	○
26	Venoshock	Poison	Special	65	100	10	Normal	—	—
29	Agility	Psychic	Status	—	—	30	Self	—	—
33	Steamroller	Bug	Physical	65	100	20	Normal	—	○
36	Toxic	Poison	Status	—	90	10	Normal	—	—
40	Rock Climb	Normal	Physical	90	85	20	Normal	—	○
43	Double-Edge	Normal	Physical	120	100	15	Normal	—	○

● TM & HM MOVES

No.	Name	Type	Kind	Pow.	Acc.	PP	Range	Long	DA
TM06	Toxic	Poison	Status	—	90	10	Normal	—	—
TM09	Venoshock	Poison	Special	65	100	10	Normal	—	—
TM10	Hidden Power	Normal	Special	—	100	15	Normal	—	—
TM11	Sunny Day	Fire	Status	—	—	5	Both Sides	—	—
TM17	Protect	Normal	Status	—	—	10	Self	—	—
TM21	Frustration	Normal	Physical	—	100	20	Normal	—	○
TM22	SolarBeam	Grass	Special	120	100	10	Normal	—	—
TM27	Return	Normal	Physical	—	100	20	Normal	—	○
TM32	Double Team	Normal	Status	—	—	15	Self	—	—
TM36	Sludge Bomb	Poison	Special	90	100	10	Normal	—	—
TM42	Facade	Normal	Physical	70	100	20	Normal	—	○
TM44	Rest	Psychic	Status	—	—	10	Self	—	—
TM45	Attract	Normal	Status	—	100	15	Normal	—	—
TM48	Round	Normal	Special	60	100	15	Normal	—	—
TM66	Payback	Dark	Physical	50	100	10	Normal	—	○
TM74	Gyro Ball	Steel	Physical	—	100	5	Normal	—	—
TM76	Struggle Bug	Bug	Special	30	100	20	Many Others	—	—
TM84	Poison Jab	Poison	Physical	80	100	20	Normal	—	○
TM87	Swagger	Normal	Status	—	90	15	Normal	—	—
TM90	Substitute	Normal	Status	—	—	10	Self	—	—
TM94	Rock Smash	Fighting	Physical	40	100	15	Normal	—	—

● MOVES TAUGHT BY PEOPLE

Name	Type	Kind	Pow.	Acc.	PP	Range	Long	DA

● EGG MOVES

Name	Type	Kind	Pow.	Acc.	PP	Range	Long	DA
Twineedle	Bug	Physical	25	100	20	Normal	—	—
Pin Missile	Bug	Physical	14	85	20	Normal	—	—
Toxic Spikes	Poison	Status	—	—	20	Other Side	—	—
Spikes	Ground	Status	—	—	20	Other Side	—	—
Take Down	Normal	Physical	90	85	20	Normal	—	—
Rock Climb	Normal	Physical	90	85	20	Normal	—	○

● FOOTPRINT

● MALE/FEMALE HAVE SAME FORM

● HEIGHT: 1'04"
● WEIGHT: 11.7 lbs.
● GENDER: Both ♂♀ exist
● ITEMS:
 • Pecha Berry
 • Poison Barb

POKÉMON BLACK VERSION
Its bite injects a potent poison, enough to paralyze large bird Pokémon that try to prey on it.

POKÉMON WHITE VERSION
It discovers what is going on around it by using the feelers on its head and tail. It is brutally aggressive.

EVOLUTION

Venipede → Lv. 22 → Whirlipede → Lv. 30 → Scolipede

ABILITIES
 • Poison Point
 • Swarm

EGG GROUP **Bug**

STATS
HP ●
ATTACK ●●
DEFENSE ●●
SP. ATTACK ●
SP. DEFENSE ●
SPEED ●●●

● MAIN WAYS TO OBTAIN

POKÉMON BLACK VERSION
1 Pinwheel Forest
2 Lostlorn Forest

POKÉMON WHITE VERSION
1 Pinwheel Forest
2 Lostlorn Forest

Whirlipede

● TYPE **Bug** **Poison**

● LEVEL-UP AND LEARNED MOVES

Lv.	Name	Type	Kind	Pow.	Acc.	PP	Range	Long	DA
1	Defense Curl	Normal	Status	—	—	40	Self	—	—
1	Rollout	Rock	Physical	30	90	20	Normal	—	○
1	Poison Sting	Poison	Physical	15	100	35	Normal	—	—
1	Screech	Normal	Status	—	85	40	Normal	—	—
5	Poison Sting	Poison	Physical	15	100	35	Normal	—	—
8	Screech	Normal	Status	—	85	40	Normal	—	—
12	Pursuit	Dark	Physical	40	100	20	Normal	—	○
15	Protect	Normal	Status	—	—	10	Self	—	—
19	Poison Tail	Poison	Physical	50	100	25	Normal	—	○
22	Iron Defense	Steel	Status	—	—	15	Self	—	—
23	Bug Bite	Bug	Physical	60	100	20	Normal	—	○
28	Venoshock	Poison	Special	65	100	10	Normal	—	—
32	Agility	Psychic	Status	—	—	30	Self	—	—
37	Steamroller	Bug	Physical	65	100	20	Normal	—	○
41	Toxic	Poison	Status	—	90	10	Normal	—	—
46	Rock Climb	Normal	Physical	90	85	20	Normal	—	○
50	Double-Edge	Normal	Physical	120	100	15	Normal	—	○

● TM & HM MOVES

No.	Name	Type	Kind	Pow.	Acc.	PP	Range	Long	DA
TM06	Toxic	Poison	Status	—	90	10	Normal	—	—
TM09	Venoshock	Poison	Special	65	100	10	Normal	—	—
TM10	Hidden Power	Normal	Special	—	100	15	Normal	—	—
TM11	Sunny Day	Fire	Status	—	—	5	Both Sides	—	—
TM17	Protect	Normal	Status	—	—	10	Self	—	—
TM21	Frustration	Normal	Physical	—	100	20	Normal	—	○
TM22	SolarBeam	Grass	Special	120	100	10	Normal	—	—
TM27	Return	Normal	Physical	—	100	20	Normal	—	○
TM32	Double Team	Normal	Status	—	—	15	Self	—	—
TM36	Sludge Bomb	Poison	Special	90	100	10	Normal	—	—
TM42	Facade	Normal	Physical	70	100	20	Normal	—	○
TM44	Rest	Psychic	Status	—	—	10	Self	—	—
TM45	Attract	Normal	Status	—	100	15	Normal	—	—
TM48	Round	Normal	Special	60	100	15	Normal	—	—
TM66	Payback	Dark	Physical	50	100	10	Normal	—	○
TM74	Gyro Ball	Steel	Physical	—	100	5	Normal	—	—
TM76	Struggle Bug	Bug	Special	30	100	20	Many Others	—	—
TM84	Poison Jab	Poison	Physical	80	100	20	Normal	—	○
TM87	Swagger	Normal	Status	—	90	15	Normal	—	—
TM90	Substitute	Normal	Status	—	—	10	Self	—	—
TM94	Rock Smash	Fighting	Physical	40	100	15	Normal	—	—

● MOVES TAUGHT BY PEOPLE

Name	Type	Kind	Pow.	Acc.	PP	Range	Long	DA

● FOOTPRINT

● MALE/FEMALE HAVE SAME FORM

● HEIGHT: 3'11"
● WEIGHT: 129.0 lbs.
● GENDER: Both ♂♀ exist
● ITEMS:
 • Pecha Berry
 • Poison Barb

POKÉMON BLACK VERSION
Protected by a hard shell, it spins its body like a wheel and crashes furiously into its enemies.

POKÉMON WHITE VERSION
It is usually motionless, but when attacked, it rotates at high speed and then crashes into its opponent.

EVOLUTION

Venipede → Lv. 22 → Whirlipede → Lv. 30 → Scolipede

ABILITIES
 • Poison Point
 • Swarm

EGG GROUP **Bug**

STATS
HP ●
ATTACK ●●
DEFENSE ●●●●
SP. ATTACK ●●
SP. DEFENSE ●●●
SPEED ●●

● MAIN WAYS TO OBTAIN

POKÉMON BLACK VERSION
1 Pinwheel Forest (Dark Grass)
2 Level up Venipede to Lv. 22

POKÉMON WHITE VERSION
1 Pinwheel Forest (Dark Grass)
2 Level up Venipede to Lv. 22

Scolipede

● TYPE Bug Poison

● FOOTPRINT

● HEIGHT: 8'02"
● WEIGHT: 442.0 lbs.
● GENDER: Both ♂♀ exist
● ITEMS:
 • None

● MALE/FEMALE HAVE SAME FORM

● LEVEL-UP AND LEARNED MOVES

Lv.	Name	Type	Kind	Pow.	Acc.	PP	Range	Long	DA
1	Megahorn	Bug	Physical	120	85	10	Normal	—	○
1	Defense Curl	Normal	Status	—	—	40	Self	—	—
1	Rollout	Rock	Physical	30	90	20	Normal	—	—
1	Poison Sting	Poison	Physical	15	100	35	Normal	—	—
1	Screech	Normal	Status	—	85	40	Normal	—	—
5	Poison Sting	Poison	Physical	15	100	35	Normal	—	—
8	Screech	Normal	Status	—	85	40	Normal	—	—
12	Pursuit	Dark	Physical	40	100	20	Normal	—	○
15	Protect	Normal	Status	—	—	10	Self	—	—
19	Poison Tail	Poison	Physical	50	100	25	Normal	—	—
23	Bug Bite	Bug	Physical	60	100	20	Normal	—	○
28	Venoshock	Poison	Special	65	100	10	Normal	—	—
30	Baton Pass	Normal	Status	—	—	40	Self	—	—
33	Agility	Psychic	Status	—	—	30	Self	—	—
39	Steamroller	Bug	Physical	65	100	20	Normal	—	○
44	Toxic	Poison	Status	—	90	10	Normal	—	—
50	Rock Climb	Normal	Physical	90	85	20	Normal	—	○
55	Double-Edge	Normal	Physical	120	100	15	Normal	—	○

● MOVES TAUGHT BY PEOPLE

Name	Type	Kind	Pow.	Acc.	PP	Range	Long	DA

● TM & HM MOVES

No.	Name	Type	Kind	Pow.	Acc.	PP	Range	Long	DA
TM06	Toxic	Poison	Status	—	90	10	Normal	—	—
TM09	Venoshock	Poison	Special	65	100	10	Normal	—	—
TM10	Hidden Power	Normal	Special	—	100	15	Normal	—	—
TM11	Sunny Day	Fire	Status	—	—	5	Both Sides	—	—
TM15	Hyper Beam	Normal	Special	150	90	5	Normal	—	○
TM17	Protect	Normal	Status	—	—	10	Self	—	—
TM21	Frustration	Normal	Physical	—	100	20	Normal	—	○
TM22	SolarBeam	Grass	Special	120	100	10	Normal	—	—
TM26	Earthquake	Ground	Physical	100	100	10	Adjacent	—	—
TM27	Return	Normal	Physical	—	100	20	Normal	—	○
TM28	Dig	Ground	Physical	80	100	10	Normal	—	○
TM32	Double Team	Normal	Status	—	—	15	Self	—	—
TM36	Sludge Bomb	Poison	Special	90	100	10	Normal	—	—
TM39	Rock Tomb	Rock	Physical	50	80	10	Normal	—	—
TM42	Facade	Normal	Physical	70	100	20	Normal	—	—
TM44	Rest	Psychic	Status	—	—	10	Self	—	—
TM45	Attract	Normal	Status	—	100	15	Normal	—	—
TM48	Round	Normal	Special	60	100	15	Normal	—	—
TM66	Payback	Dark	Physical	50	100	10	Normal	—	○
TM68	Giga Impact	Normal	Physical	150	90	5	Normal	—	○
TM74	Gyro Ball	Steel	Physical	—	100	5	Normal	—	○
TM75	Swords Dance	Normal	Status	—	—	30	Self	—	—
TM76	Struggle Bug	Bug	Special	30	100	20	Many Others	—	—
TM78	Bulldoze	Ground	Physical	60	100	20	Adjacent	—	—
TM80	Rock Slide	Rock	Physical	75	90	10	Many Others	—	—
TM81	X-Scissor	Bug	Physical	80	100	15	Normal	—	○
TM84	Poison Jab	Poison	Physical	80	100	20	Normal	—	○
TM87	Swagger	Normal	Status	—	90	15	Normal	—	—
TM90	Substitute	Normal	Status	—	—	10	Self	—	—
TM94	Rock Smash	Fighting	Physical	40	100	15	Normal	—	○
HM01	Cut	Normal	Physical	50	95	30	Normal	—	○
HM04	Strength	Normal	Physical	80	100	15	Normal	—	○

● MAIN WAYS TO OBTAIN

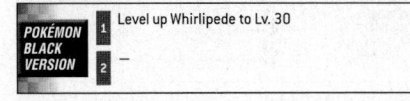

POKÉMON BLACK VERSION	1	Level up Whirlipede to Lv. 30
	2	—

POKÉMON WHITE VERSION	1	Level up Whirlipede to Lv. 30
	2	—

EVOLUTION

Venipede — Lv. 22 → Whirlipede — Lv. 30 → Scolipede

POKÉMON BLACK VERSION
With quick movements, it chases down its foes, attacking relentlessly with its horns until it prevails.

POKÉMON WHITE VERSION
Highly aggressive, it uses the claws near its neck to dig into its opponents and poison them.

● ABILITIES: Poison Point, Swarm

● EGG GROUP: Bug

● STATS:
HP ●●
ATTACK ●●●●
DEFENSE ●●●●
SP. ATTACK ●●
SP. DEFENSE ●●●
SPEED ●●●●●

Cottonee

● TYPE Grass

● FOOTPRINT

● MALE/FEMALE HAVE SAME FORM

● HEIGHT: 1'00"
● WEIGHT: 1.3 lbs.
● GENDER: Both ♂♀ exist
● ITEMS:
 • None

● LEVEL-UP AND LEARNED MOVES

Lv.	Name	Type	Kind	Pow.	Acc.	PP	Range	Long	DA
1	Absorb	Grass	Special	20	100	25	Normal	—	—
4	Growth	Normal	Status	—	—	40	Self	—	—
8	Leech Seed	Grass	Status	—	90	10	Normal	—	—
10	Stun Spore	Grass	Status	—	75	30	Normal	—	—
13	Mega Drain	Grass	Special	40	100	15	Normal	—	—
17	Cotton Spore	Grass	Status	—	100	40	Normal	—	—
19	Razor Leaf	Grass	Physical	55	95	25	Many Others	—	—
22	PoisonPowder	Poison	Status	—	75	35	Normal	—	—
26	Giga Drain	Grass	Special	75	100	10	Normal	—	—
28	Charm	Normal	Status	—	100	20	Normal	—	—
31	Helping Hand	Normal	Status	—	—	20	1 Ally	—	—
35	Energy Ball	Grass	Special	80	100	10	Normal	—	—
37	Cotton Guard	Grass	Status	—	—	10	Self	—	—
40	Sunny Day	Fire	Status	—	—	5	Both Sides	—	—
44	Endeavor	Normal	Physical	—	100	5	Normal	—	○
46	SolarBeam	Grass	Special	120	100	10	Normal	—	—

● MOVES TAUGHT BY PEOPLE

● EGG MOVES

Name	Type	Kind	Pow.	Acc.	PP	Range	Long	DA
Natural Gift	Normal	Physical	—	100	15	Normal	—	—
Encore	Normal	Status	—	100	5	Normal	—	—
Tickle	Normal	Status	—	100	20	Normal	—	—
Fake Tears	Dark	Status	—	100	20	Normal	—	—
GrassWhistle	Grass	Status	—	55	15	Normal	—	—
Memento	Dark	Status	—	100	10	Normal	—	—
Beat Up	Dark	Physical	—	100	10	Normal	—	—
Switcheroo	Dark	Status	—	100	10	Normal	—	—
Worry Seed	Grass	Status	—	100	10	Normal	—	—

● TM & HM MOVES

No.	Name	Type	Kind	Pow.	Acc.	PP	Range	Long	DA
TM06	Toxic	Poison	Status	—	90	10	Normal	—	—
TM10	Hidden Power	Normal	Special	—	100	15	Normal	—	—
TM11	Sunny Day	Fire	Status	—	—	5	Both Sides	—	—
TM12	Taunt	Dark	Status	—	100	20	Normal	—	—
TM17	Protect	Normal	Status	—	—	10	Self	—	—
TM20	Safeguard	Normal	Status	—	—	25	Your Side	—	—
TM21	Frustration	Normal	Physical	—	100	20	Normal	—	○
TM22	SolarBeam	Grass	Special	120	100	10	Normal	—	—
TM27	Return	Normal	Physical	—	100	20	Normal	—	○
TM32	Double Team	Normal	Status	—	—	15	Self	—	—
TM42	Facade	Normal	Physical	70	100	20	Normal	—	—
TM44	Rest	Psychic	Status	—	—	10	Self	—	—
TM45	Attract	Normal	Status	—	100	15	Normal	—	—
TM48	Round	Normal	Special	60	100	15	Normal	—	—
TM53	Energy Ball	Grass	Special	80	100	10	Normal	—	—
TM70	Flash	Normal	Status	—	100	20	Normal	—	—
TM85	Dream Eater	Psychic	Special	100	100	15	Normal	—	—
TM86	Grass Knot	Grass	Special	—	100	20	Normal	—	○
TM87	Swagger	Normal	Status	—	90	15	Normal	—	—
TM90	Substitute	Normal	Status	—	—	10	Self	—	—

● MAIN WAYS TO OBTAIN

POKÉMON BLACK VERSION	1	Pinwheel Forest
	2	Lostlorn Forest

POKÉMON WHITE VERSION	1	Trade Petilil in a house in Nacrene City
	2	—

EVOLUTION

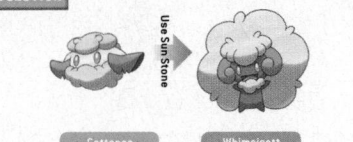

Cottonee — Use Sun Stone → Whimsicott

POKÉMON BLACK VERSION
When attacked, it escapes by shooting cotton from its body. The cotton serves as a decoy to distract the attacker.

POKÉMON WHITE VERSION
They go wherever the wind takes them. On rainy days, their bodies are heavier, so they take shelter beneath big trees.

● ABILITIES: Prankster, Infiltrator

● EGG GROUPS: Grass, Fairy

● STATS:
HP ●
ATTACK ●
DEFENSE ●●
SP. ATTACK ●●
SP. DEFENSE ●●●
SPEED ●●●

Whimsicott

● TYPE Grass

● MALE/FEMALE HAVE SAME FORM

● FOOTPRINT

● HEIGHT: 2'04"
● WEIGHT: 14.6 lbs.
● GENDER: Both ♂♀ exist
● ITEMS:
• None

POKÉMON BLACK VERSION
Like the wind, it can slip through any gap, no matter how small. It leaves balls of white fluff behind.

POKÉMON WHITE VERSION
Riding whirlwinds, they appear. These Pokémon sneak through gaps into houses and cause all sorts of mischief.

● LEVEL-UP AND LEARNED MOVES

Lv.	Name	Type	Kind	Pow.	Acc.	PP	Range	Long	DA
1	Growth	Normal	Status	—	—	40	Self	●	—
1	Leech Seed	Grass	Status	—	90	10	Normal	●	—
1	Mega Drain	Grass	Special	40	100	15	Normal	●	—
1	Cotton Spore	Grass	Status	—	100	40	Normal	●	—
10	Gust	Flying	Special	40	100	35	Normal	○	—
28	Tailwind	Flying	Status	—	—	30	Your Side	●	—
46	Hurricane	Flying	Special	120	70	10	Normal	○	—

● MOVES TAUGHT BY PEOPLE

Name	Type	Kind	Pow.	Acc.	PP	Range	Long	DA

● TM & HM MOVES

No.	Name	Type	Kind	Pow.	Acc.	PP	Range	Long	DA
TM06	Toxic	Poison	Status	—	90	10	Normal	—	—
TM10	Hidden Power	Normal	Special	—	100	15	Normal	—	—
TM11	Sunny Day	Fire	Status	—	—	5	Both Sides	—	—
TM12	Taunt	Dark	Status	—	100	20	Normal	—	—
TM15	Hyper Beam	Normal	Special	150	90	5	Normal	○	—
TM16	Light Screen	Psychic	Status	—	—	30	Your Side	—	—
TM17	Protect	Normal	Status	—	—	10	Self	—	—
TM20	Safeguard	Normal	Status	—	—	25	Your Side	—	—
TM21	Frustration	Normal	Physical	—	100	20	Normal	—	○
TM22	SolarBeam	Grass	Special	120	100	10	Normal	—	—
TM27	Return	Normal	Physical	—	100	20	Normal	—	○
TM29	Psychic	Psychic	Special	90	100	10	Normal	—	—
TM30	Shadow Ball	Ghost	Special	80	100	15	Normal	—	—
TM32	Double Team	Normal	Status	—	—	15	Self	—	—
TM42	Facade	Normal	Physical	70	100	20	Normal	—	○
TM44	Rest	Psychic	Status	—	—	10	Self	—	—
TM45	Attract	Normal	Status	—	100	15	Normal	—	—
TM46	Thief	Dark	Physical	40	100	10	Normal	—	○
TM48	Round	Normal	Special	60	100	15	Normal	—	—
TM53	Energy Ball	Grass	Special	80	100	10	Normal	—	—
TM56	Fling	Dark	Physical	—	100	10	Normal	—	○
TM68	Giga Impact	Normal	Physical	150	90	5	Normal	—	○
TM70	Flash	Normal	Status	—	100	20	Normal	—	—
TM85	Dream Eater	Psychic	Special	100	100	15	Normal	—	—
TM86	Grass Knot	Grass	Special	—	100	20	Normal	—	○
TM87	Swagger	Normal	Status	—	90	15	Normal	—	—
TM89	U-turn	Bug	Physical	70	100	20	Normal	—	○
TM90	Substitute	Normal	Status	—	—	10	Self	—	—
TM92	Trick Room	Psychic	Status	—	—	5	Both Sides	—	—

EVOLUTION

Cottonee → Whimsicott (Use Sun Stone)

ABILITIES
● Prankster
● Infiltrator

EGG GROUPS: Grass / Fairy

STATS
HP ●●
ATTACK ●●●
DEFENSE ●●●
SP. ATTACK ●●●
SP. DEFENSE ●●●
SPEED ●●●●●

● MAIN WAYS TO OBTAIN

POKÉMON BLACK VERSION
1 Pinwheel Forest (Rustling Grass)
2 Use Sun Stone on Cottonee

POKÉMON WHITE VERSION
1 Use Sun Stone on Cottonee
2 —

Petilil

● TYPE Grass

● FEMALE FORM

● FOOTPRINT

● HEIGHT: 1'08"
● WEIGHT: 14.6 lbs.
● GENDER: Only ♀ exist
● ITEMS:
• None

POKÉMON BLACK VERSION
The leaves on its head are very bitter. Eating one of these leaves is known to refresh a tired body.

POKÉMON WHITE VERSION
Since they prefer moist, nutrient-rich soil, the areas where Petilil live are known to be good for growing plants.

● LEVEL-UP AND LEARNED MOVES

Lv.	Name	Type	Kind	Pow.	Acc.	PP	Range	Long	DA
1	Absorb	Grass	Special	20	100	25	Normal	—	—
4	Growth	Normal	Status	—	—	40	Self	—	—
8	Leech Seed	Grass	Status	—	90	10	Normal	—	—
10	Sleep Powder	Grass	Status	—	75	15	Normal	—	—
13	Mega Drain	Grass	Special	40	100	15	Normal	—	—
17	Synthesis	Grass	Status	—	—	5	Self	—	—
19	Magical Leaf	Grass	Special	60	—	20	Normal	—	—
22	Stun Spore	Grass	Status	—	75	30	Normal	—	—
26	Giga Drain	Grass	Special	75	100	10	Normal	—	—
28	Aromatherapy	Grass	Status	—	—	5	Your Party	—	—
31	Helping Hand	Normal	Status	—	—	20	1 Ally	—	—
35	Energy Ball	Grass	Special	80	100	10	Normal	—	—
37	Entrainment	Normal	Status	—	100	15	Normal	—	—
40	Sunny Day	Fire	Status	—	—	5	Both Sides	—	—
44	After You	Normal	Status	—	—	15	Normal	—	—
46	Leaf Storm	Grass	Special	140	90	5	Normal	—	—

● MOVES TAUGHT BY PEOPLE

Name	Type	Kind	Pow.	Acc.	PP	Range	Long	DA

● EGG MOVES

Name	Type	Kind	Pow.	Acc.	PP	Range	Long	DA
Natural Gift	Normal	Physical	—	100	15	Normal	—	—
Charm	Normal	Status	—	100	20	Normal	—	—
Endure	Normal	Status	—	—	10	Self	—	—
Ingrain	Grass	Status	—	—	20	Self	—	—
Worry Seed	Grass	Status	—	100	10	Normal	—	—
GrassWhistle	Grass	Status	—	55	15	Normal	—	—
Sweet Scent	Normal	Status	—	100	20	Many Others	—	—
Bide	Normal	Physical	—	—	10	Self	—	○
Healing Wish	Psychic	Status	—	—	10	Self	—	—

● TM & HM MOVES

No.	Name	Type	Kind	Pow.	Acc.	PP	Range	Long	DA
TM06	Toxic	Poison	Status	—	90	10	Normal	—	—
TM10	Hidden Power	Normal	Special	—	100	15	Normal	—	—
TM11	Sunny Day	Fire	Status	—	—	5	Both Sides	—	—
TM17	Protect	Normal	Status	—	—	10	Self	—	—
TM20	Safeguard	Normal	Status	—	—	25	Your Side	—	—
TM21	Frustration	Normal	Physical	—	100	20	Normal	—	○
TM22	SolarBeam	Grass	Special	120	100	10	Normal	—	—
TM27	Return	Normal	Physical	—	100	20	Normal	—	○
TM32	Double Team	Normal	Status	—	—	15	Self	—	—
TM42	Facade	Normal	Physical	70	100	20	Normal	—	○
TM44	Rest	Psychic	Status	—	—	10	Self	—	—
TM45	Attract	Normal	Status	—	100	15	Normal	—	—
TM48	Round	Normal	Special	60	100	15	Normal	—	—
TM53	Energy Ball	Grass	Special	80	100	10	Normal	—	—
TM70	Flash	Normal	Status	—	100	20	Normal	—	—
TM85	Dream Eater	Psychic	Special	100	100	15	Normal	—	—
TM86	Grass Knot	Grass	Special	—	100	20	Normal	—	○
TM87	Swagger	Normal	Status	—	90	15	Normal	—	—
TM90	Substitute	Normal	Status	—	—	10	Self	—	—
HM01	Cut	Normal	Physical	50	95	30	Normal	—	○

EVOLUTION

Petilil → Lilligant (Use Sun Stone)

ABILITIES
● Chlorophyll
● Own Tempo

EGG GROUP: Grass

STATS
HP ●●
ATTACK ●●
DEFENSE ●●
SP. ATTACK ●●●
SP. DEFENSE ●●
SPEED ●

● MAIN WAYS TO OBTAIN

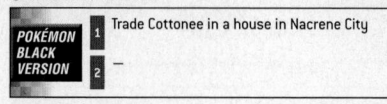

POKÉMON BLACK VERSION
1 Trade Cottonee in a house in Nacrene City
2 —

POKÉMON WHITE VERSION
1 Pinwheel Forest
2 Lostlorn Forest

UNOVA POKÉDEX
053 WHIMSICOTT
054 PETILIL

Lilligant

● TYPE Grass

● FOOTPRINT
♣

● FEMALE FORM

● HEIGHT: 3'07"
● WEIGHT: 35.9 lbs.
● GENDER: Only ♀ exist
● ITEMS:
  • None

POKÉMON BLACK VERSION
Even veteran Trainers face a challenge in getting its beautiful flower to bloom. This Pokémon is popular with celebrities.

POKÉMON WHITE VERSION
The fragrance of the garland on its head has a relaxing effect. It withers if a Trainer does not take good care of it.

● LEVEL-UP AND LEARNED MOVES

Lv.	Name	Type	Kind	Pow.	Acc.	PP	Range	Long	DA
1	Growth	Normal	Status	–	–	40	Self	–	–
1	Leech Seed	Grass	Status	–	90	10	Normal	–	–
1	Mega Drain	Grass	Special	40	100	15	Normal	–	–
1	Synthesis	Grass	Status	–	–	5	Self	–	–
10	Teeter Dance	Normal	Status	–	100	20	Adjacent	–	–
28	Quiver Dance	Bug	Status	–	–	20	Self	–	–
46	Petal Dance	Grass	Special	120	100	10	1 Random	–	○

● MOVES TAUGHT BY PEOPLE

Name	Type	Kind	Pow.	Acc.	PP	Range	Long	DA

● TM & HM MOVES

No.	Name	Type	Kind	Pow.	Acc.	PP	Range	Long	DA
TM06	Toxic	Poison	Status	–	90	10	Normal	–	–
TM10	Hidden Power	Normal	Special	–	100	15	Normal	–	–
TM11	Sunny Day	Fire	Status	–	–	5	Both Sides	–	–
TM15	Hyper Beam	Normal	Special	150	90	5	Normal	–	○
TM16	Light Screen	Psychic	Status	–	–	30	Your Side	–	–
TM17	Protect	Normal	Status	–	–	10	Self	–	–
TM20	Safeguard	Normal	Status	–	–	25	Your Side	–	–
TM21	Frustration	Normal	Physical	–	100	20	Normal	–	○
TM22	SolarBeam	Grass	Special	120	100	10	Normal	–	○
TM27	Return	Normal	Physical	–	100	20	Normal	–	○
TM32	Double Team	Normal	Status	–	–	15	Self	–	–
TM42	Facade	Normal	Physical	70	100	20	Normal	–	○
TM44	Rest	Psychic	Status	–	–	10	Self	–	–
TM45	Attract	Normal	Status	–	100	15	Normal	–	–
TM48	Round	Normal	Special	60	100	15	Normal	–	–
TM53	Energy Ball	Grass	Special	80	100	10	Normal	–	○
TM68	Giga Impact	Normal	Physical	150	90	5	Normal	–	○
TM70	Flash	Normal	Status	–	100	20	Normal	–	–
TM75	Swords Dance	Normal	Status	–	–	30	Self	–	–
TM85	Dream Eater	Psychic	Special	100	100	15	Normal	–	○
TM86	Grass Knot	Grass	Special	–	100	20	Normal	–	○
TM87	Swagger	Normal	Status	–	90	15	Normal	–	–
TM90	Substitute	Normal	Status	–	–	10	Self	–	–
HM01	Cut	Normal	Physical	50	95	30	Normal	–	○

EVOLUTION

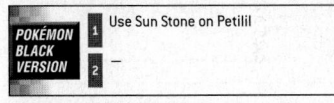

Petilil → (Use Sun Stone) → Lilligant

● ABILITIES
  ● Chlorophyll
  ● Own Tempo

● EGG GROUP Grass

● STATS
  HP ●●●
  ATTACK ●●●
  DEFENSE ●●●
  SP. ATTACK ●●●●●
  SP. DEFENSE ●●●●
  SPEED ●●●●

● MAIN WAYS TO OBTAIN

POKÉMON BLACK VERSION
1 Use Sun Stone on Petilil
2 —

POKÉMON WHITE VERSION
1 Pinwheel Forest (Rustling Grass)
2 Use Sun Stone on Petilil

Basculin
(Red-Striped Form)

● TYPE Water

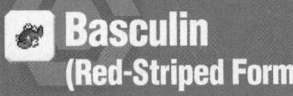

● FOOTPRINT

● MALE/FEMALE HAVE SAME FORM

● HEIGHT: 3'03"
● WEIGHT: 39.7 lbs.
● GENDER: Both ♂♀ exist
● ITEMS:
  • DeepSeaTooth

POKÉMON BLACK VERSION
Red and blue Basculin get along so poorly, they'll start fighting instantly. These Pokémon are very hostile.

POKÉMON WHITE VERSION
Red and blue Basculin usually do not get along, but sometimes members of one school mingle with the other's school.

● LEVEL-UP AND LEARNED MOVES

Lv.	Name	Type	Kind	Pow.	Acc.	PP	Range	Long	DA
1	Tackle	Normal	Physical	50	100	35	Normal	–	–
1	Water Gun	Water	Special	40	100	25	Normal	–	–
4	Uproar	Normal	Special	90	100	10	1 Random	–	–
7	Headbutt	Normal	Physical	70	100	15	Normal	–	○
10	Bite	Dark	Physical	60	100	25	Normal	–	○
13	Aqua Jet	Water	Physical	40	100	20	Normal	–	–
16	Chip Away	Normal	Physical	70	100	20	Normal	–	–
20	Take Down	Normal	Physical	90	85	20	Normal	–	○
24	Crunch	Dark	Physical	80	100	15	Normal	–	○
28	Aqua Tail	Water	Physical	90	90	10	Normal	–	○
32	Soak	Water	Status	–	100	20	Normal	–	–
36	Double-Edge	Normal	Physical	120	100	15	Normal	–	○
41	Scary Face	Normal	Status	–	100	10	Normal	–	–
46	Flail	Normal	Physical	–	100	15	Normal	–	–
51	Final Gambit	Fighting	Special	–	100	5	Normal	–	–
56	Thrash	Normal	Physical	120	100	10	1 Random	–	○

● MOVES TAUGHT BY PEOPLE

Name	Type	Kind	Pow.	Acc.	PP	Range	Long	DA

● EGG MOVES

Name	Type	Kind	Pow.	Acc.	PP	Range	Long	DA
Swift	Normal	Special	60	–	20	Many Others	–	–
BubbleBeam	Water	Special	65	100	20	Normal	–	–
Mud Shot	Ground	Special	55	95	15	Normal	–	–
Muddy Water	Water	Special	95	85	10	Many Others	–	–
Agility	Psychic	Status	–	–	30	Self	–	–
Whirlpool	Water	Special	35	85	15	Normal	–	–
Rage	Normal	Physical	20	100	20	Normal	–	○
Brine	Water	Special	65	100	10	Normal	–	–
Revenge	Fighting	Physical	60	100	10	Normal	–	–

● TM & HM MOVES

No.	Name	Type	Kind	Pow.	Acc.	PP	Range	Long	DA
TM06	Toxic	Poison	Status	–	90	10	Normal	–	–
TM07	Hail	Ice	Status	–	–	10	Both Sides	–	–
TM10	Hidden Power	Normal	Special	–	100	15	Normal	–	–
TM12	Taunt	Dark	Status	–	100	20	Normal	–	–
TM13	Ice Beam	Ice	Special	95	100	10	Normal	–	–
TM17	Protect	Normal	Status	–	–	10	Self	–	–
TM18	Rain Dance	Water	Status	–	–	5	Both Sides	–	–
TM21	Frustration	Normal	Physical	–	100	20	Normal	–	○
TM27	Return	Normal	Physical	–	100	20	Normal	–	○
TM32	Double Team	Normal	Status	–	–	15	Self	–	–
TM42	Facade	Normal	Physical	70	100	20	Normal	–	○
TM44	Rest	Psychic	Status	–	–	10	Self	–	–
TM45	Attract	Normal	Status	–	100	15	Normal	–	–
TM48	Round	Normal	Special	60	100	15	Normal	–	–
TM55	Scald	Water	Special	80	100	15	Normal	–	–
TM87	Swagger	Normal	Status	–	90	15	Normal	–	–
TM90	Substitute	Normal	Status	–	–	10	Self	–	–
HM01	Cut	Normal	Physical	50	95	30	Normal	–	○
HM03	Surf	Water	Special	95	100	15	Adjacent	–	–
HM05	Waterfall	Water	Physical	80	100	15	Normal	–	○
HM06	Dive	Water	Physical	80	100	10	Normal	–	○

EVOLUTION

Does not evolve

● ABILITIES
  ● Reckless
  ● Adaptability

● EGG GROUP Water 2

● STATS
  HP ●●●
  ATTACK ●●●●
  DEFENSE ●●●
  SP. ATTACK ●●●●
  SP. DEFENSE ●●
  SPEED ●●●●

● MAIN WAYS TO OBTAIN

POKÉMON BLACK VERSION
1 Route 1 (Water Surface)
2 Dragonspiral Tower 1F Outside (Water Surface)

POKÉMON WHITE VERSION
1 Route 1 (Ripples in Water)
2 Dragonspiral Tower 1F Outside (Ripples in Water)

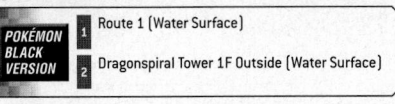

Basculin
(Blue-Striped Form)

● TYPE Water

● HEIGHT: 3'03"
● WEIGHT: 39.7 lbs.
● GENDER: Both ♂♀ exist
● ITEMS:
• DeepSeaScale

● MALE/FEMALE HAVE SAME FORM

● FOOTPRINT

POKÉMON BLACK VERSION
Red and blue Basculin get along so poorly, they'll start fighting instantly. These Pokémon are very hostile.

POKÉMON WHITE VERSION
Red and blue Basculin usually do not get along, but sometimes members of one school mingle with the other's school.

● LEVEL-UP AND LEARNED MOVES

Lv.	Name	Type	Kind	Pow.	Acc.	PP	Range	Long	DA
1	Tackle	Normal	Physical	50	100	35	Normal	–	○
1	Water Gun	Water	Special	40	100	25	Normal	–	–
4	Uproar	Normal	Special	90	100	10	1 Random	–	–
7	Headbutt	Normal	Physical	70	100	15	Normal	–	○
10	Bite	Dark	Physical	60	100	25	Normal	–	○
13	Aqua Jet	Water	Physical	40	100	20	Normal	–	○
16	Chip Away	Normal	Physical	70	100	20	Normal	–	○
20	Take Down	Normal	Physical	90	85	20	Normal	–	○
24	Crunch	Dark	Physical	80	100	15	Normal	–	○
28	Aqua Tail	Water	Physical	90	90	10	Normal	–	○
32	Soak	Water	Status	–	100	20	Normal	–	–
36	Double-Edge	Normal	Physical	120	100	15	Normal	–	○
41	Scary Face	Normal	Status	–	100	10	Normal	–	–
46	Flail	Normal	Physical	–	100	15	Normal	–	○
51	Final Gambit	Fighting	Special	–	100	5	Normal	–	–
56	Thrash	Normal	Physical	120	100	10	1 Random	–	○

● MOVES TAUGHT BY PEOPLE

Name	Type	Kind	Pow.	Acc.	PP	Range	Long	DA

● EGG MOVES

Name	Type	Kind	Pow.	Acc.	PP	Range	Long	DA
Swift	Normal	Special	60	–	20	Many Others	–	–
BubbleBeam	Water	Special	65	100	20	Normal	–	–
Mud Shot	Ground	Special	55	95	15	Normal	–	–
Muddy Water	Water	Special	95	85	10	Many Others	–	–
Agility	Psychic	Status	–	–	30	Self	–	–
Whirlpool	Water	Special	35	85	15	Normal	–	–
Rage	Normal	Physical	20	100	20	Normal	–	○
Brine	Water	Special	65	100	10	Normal	–	–
Revenge	Fighting	Physical	60	100	10	Normal	–	○

● TM & HM MOVES

No.	Name	Type	Kind	Pow.	Acc.	PP	Range	Long	DA
TM06	Toxic	Poison	Status	–	90	10	Normal	–	–
TM07	Hail	Ice	Status	–	–	10	Both Sides	–	–
TM10	Hidden Power	Normal	Special	–	100	15	Normal	–	–
TM12	Taunt	Dark	Status	–	100	20	Normal	–	–
TM13	Ice Beam	Ice	Special	95	100	10	Normal	–	–
TM17	Protect	Normal	Status	–	–	10	Self	–	–
TM18	Rain Dance	Water	Status	–	–	5	Both Sides	–	–
TM21	Frustration	Normal	Physical	–	100	20	Normal	–	○
TM27	Return	Normal	Physical	–	100	20	Normal	–	○
TM32	Double Team	Normal	Status	–	–	15	Self	–	–
TM42	Facade	Normal	Physical	70	100	20	Normal	–	○
TM44	Rest	Psychic	Status	–	–	10	Self	–	–
TM45	Attract	Normal	Status	–	100	15	Normal	–	–
TM48	Round	Normal	Special	60	100	15	Normal	–	–
TM55	Scald	Water	Special	80	100	15	Normal	–	–
TM87	Swagger	Normal	Status	–	90	15	Normal	–	–
TM90	Substitute	Normal	Status	–	–	10	Self	–	–
HM01	Cut	Normal	Physical	50	95	30	Normal	–	○
HM03	Surf	Water	Special	95	100	15	Adjacent	–	–
HM05	Waterfall	Water	Physical	80	100	15	Normal	–	○
HM06	Dive	Water	Physical	80	100	10	Normal	–	○

EVOLUTION

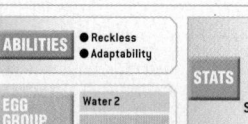

Does not evolve

ABILITIES ● Reckless ● Adaptability

EGG GROUP Water 2

STATS
HP ●●●
ATTACK ●●●●
DEFENSE ●●●
SP. ATTACK ●●●●
SP. DEFENSE ●●
SPEED ●●●●

● MAIN WAYS TO OBTAIN

POKÉMON BLACK VERSION
1 Route 1 (Ripples in Water)
2 Dragonspiral Tower 1F Outside (Ripples in Water)

POKÉMON WHITE VERSION
1 Route 1 (Water Surface)
2 Dragonspiral Tower 1F Outside (Water Surface)

Sandile

● TYPE Ground Dark

● HEIGHT: 2'04"
● WEIGHT: 33.5 lbs.
● GENDER: Both ♂♀ exist
● ITEMS:
• None

● MALE/FEMALE HAVE SAME FORM

● FOOTPRINT

POKÉMON BLACK VERSION
They live buried in the sands of the desert. The sun-warmed sands prevent their body temperature from dropping.

POKÉMON WHITE VERSION
It moves along below the sand's surface, except for its nose and eyes. A dark membrane shields its eyes from the sun.

● LEVEL-UP AND LEARNED MOVES

Lv.	Name	Type	Kind	Pow.	Acc.	PP	Range	Long	DA
1	Leer	Normal	Status	–	100	30	Many Others	–	–
1	Rage	Normal	Physical	20	100	20	Normal	–	○
4	Bite	Dark	Physical	60	100	25	Normal	–	○
7	Sand-Attack	Ground	Status	–	100	15	Normal	–	–
10	Torment	Dark	Status	–	100	15	Normal	–	–
13	Sand Tomb	Ground	Physical	35	85	15	Normal	–	–
16	Assurance	Dark	Physical	50	100	10	Normal	–	○
19	Mud-Slap	Ground	Special	20	100	10	Normal	–	–
22	Embargo	Dark	Status	–	100	15	Normal	–	–
25	Swagger	Normal	Status	–	90	15	Normal	–	–
28	Crunch	Dark	Physical	80	100	15	Normal	–	○
31	Dig	Ground	Physical	80	100	10	Normal	–	○
34	Scary Face	Normal	Status	–	100	10	Normal	–	–
37	Foul Play	Dark	Physical	95	100	15	Normal	–	○
40	Sandstorm	Rock	Status	–	–	10	Both Sides	–	–
43	Earthquake	Ground	Physical	100	100	10	Adjacent	–	–
46	Thrash	Normal	Physical	120	100	10	1 Random	–	○

● MOVES TAUGHT BY PEOPLE

Name	Type	Kind	Pow.	Acc.	PP	Range	Long	DA

● EGG MOVES

Name	Type	Kind	Pow.	Acc.	PP	Range	Long	DA
Double-Edge	Normal	Physical	120	100	15	Normal	–	○
Rock Climb	Normal	Physical	90	85	20	Normal	–	○
Pursuit	Dark	Physical	40	100	20	Normal	–	○
Uproar	Normal	Special	90	100	10	1 Random	–	–
Fire Fang	Fire	Physical	65	95	15	Normal	–	○
Thunder Fang	Electric	Physical	65	95	15	Normal	–	○
Beat Up	Dark	Physical	–	100	10	Normal	–	○
Focus Energy	Normal	Status	–	–	30	Self	–	–
Counter	Fighting	Physical	–	100	20	Varies	–	–
Mean Look	Normal	Status	–	–	5	Normal	–	–

● TM & HM MOVES

No.	Name	Type	Kind	Pow.	Acc.	PP	Range	Long	DA
TM01	Hone Claws	Dark	Status	–	–	15	Self	–	–
TM05	Roar	Normal	Status	–	100	20	Normal	–	–
TM06	Toxic	Poison	Status	–	90	10	Normal	–	–
TM10	Hidden Power	Normal	Special	–	100	15	Normal	–	–
TM12	Taunt	Dark	Status	–	100	20	Normal	–	–
TM17	Protect	Normal	Status	–	–	10	Self	–	–
TM21	Frustration	Normal	Physical	–	100	20	Normal	–	○
TM26	Earthquake	Ground	Physical	100	100	10	Adjacent	–	–
TM27	Return	Normal	Physical	–	100	20	Normal	–	○
TM28	Dig	Ground	Physical	80	100	10	Normal	–	○
TM32	Double Team	Normal	Status	–	–	15	Self	–	–
TM36	Sludge Bomb	Poison	Special	90	100	10	Normal	–	–
TM37	Sandstorm	Rock	Status	–	–	10	Both Sides	–	–
TM39	Rock Tomb	Rock	Physical	50	80	10	Normal	–	–
TM41	Torment	Dark	Status	–	100	15	Normal	–	–
TM42	Facade	Normal	Physical	70	100	20	Normal	–	○
TM44	Rest	Psychic	Status	–	–	10	Self	–	–
TM45	Attract	Normal	Status	–	100	15	Normal	–	–
TM46	Thief	Dark	Physical	40	100	10	Normal	–	○
TM48	Round	Normal	Special	60	100	15	Normal	–	–
TM59	Incinerate	Fire	Special	30	100	15	Many Others	–	–
TM63	Embargo	Dark	Status	–	100	15	Normal	–	–
TM66	Payback	Dark	Physical	50	100	10	Normal	–	○
TM67	Retaliate	Normal	Physical	70	100	5	Normal	–	○
TM71	Stone Edge	Rock	Physical	100	80	5	Normal	–	–
TM78	Bulldoze	Ground	Physical	60	100	20	Adjacent	–	–
TM80	Rock Slide	Rock	Physical	75	90	10	Many Others	–	–
TM87	Swagger	Normal	Status	–	90	15	Normal	–	–
TM90	Substitute	Normal	Status	–	–	10	Self	–	–
HM01	Cut	Normal	Physical	50	95	30	Normal	–	○

EVOLUTION

Sandile → Lv. 29 → Krokorok → Lv. 40 → Krookodile

ABILITIES ● Intimidate ● Moxie

EGG GROUP Field

STATS
HP ●●
ATTACK ●●●
DEFENSE ●●
SP. ATTACK ●
SP. DEFENSE ●
SPEED ●●●

● MAIN WAYS TO OBTAIN

POKÉMON BLACK VERSION
1 Route 4
2 Desert Resort Entrance

POKÉMON WHITE VERSION
1 Route 4
2 Desert Resort Entrance

Krokorok

● TYPE: Ground | Dark

● LEVEL-UP AND LEARNED MOVES

Lv.	Name	Type	Kind	Pow.	Acc.	PP	Range	Long	DA
1	Leer	Normal	Status	—	100	30	Many Others	—	—
1	Rage	Normal	Physical	20	100	20	Normal	—	—
1	Bite	Dark	Physical	60	100	25	Normal	—	○
1	Sand-Attack	Ground	Status	—	100	15	Normal	—	—
4	Bite	Dark	Physical	60	100	25	Normal	—	○
7	Sand-Attack	Ground	Status	—	100	15	Normal	—	—
10	Torment	Dark	Status	—	100	15	Normal	—	—
13	Sand Tomb	Ground	Physical	35	85	15	Normal	—	—
16	Assurance	Dark	Physical	50	100	10	Normal	—	○
19	Mud-Slap	Ground	Special	20	100	10	Normal	—	—
22	Embargo	Dark	Status	—	100	15	Normal	—	—
25	Swagger	Normal	Status	—	90	15	Normal	—	—
28	Crunch	Dark	Physical	80	100	15	Normal	—	○
32	Dig	Ground	Physical	80	100	10	Normal	—	—
36	Scary Face	Normal	Status	—	100	10	Normal	—	—
40	Foul Play	Dark	Physical	95	100	15	Normal	—	○
44	Sandstorm	Rock	Status	—	—	10	Both Sides	—	—
48	Earthquake	Ground	Physical	100	100	10	Adjacent	—	—
52	Thrash	Normal	Physical	120	100	10	1 Random	—	—

● MOVES TAUGHT BY PEOPLE

Name	Type	Kind	Pow.	Acc.	PP	Range	Long	DA

● TM & HM MOVES

No.	Name	Type	Kind	Pow.	Acc.	PP	Range	Long	DA
TM01	Hone Claws	Dark	Status	—	—	15	Self	—	—
TM05	Roar	Normal	Status	—	100	20	Normal	—	—
TM06	Toxic	Poison	Status	—	90	10	Normal	—	—
TM10	Hidden Power	Normal	Special	—	100	15	Normal	—	—
TM12	Taunt	Dark	Status	—	100	20	Normal	—	—
TM17	Protect	Normal	Status	—	—	10	Self	—	—
TM21	Frustration	Normal	Physical	—	100	20	Normal	—	—
TM26	Earthquake	Ground	Physical	100	100	10	Adjacent	—	—
TM27	Return	Normal	Physical	—	100	20	Normal	—	—
TM28	Dig	Ground	Physical	80	100	10	Normal	—	○
TM31	Brick Break	Fighting	Physical	75	100	15	Normal	—	—
TM32	Double Team	Normal	Status	—	—	15	Self	—	—
TM36	Sludge Bomb	Poison	Special	90	100	10	Normal	—	—
TM37	Sandstorm	Rock	Status	—	—	10	Both Sides	—	—
TM39	Rock Tomb	Rock	Physical	50	80	10	Normal	—	—
TM41	Torment	Dark	Status	—	100	15	Normal	—	—
TM42	Facade	Normal	Physical	70	100	20	Normal	—	—
TM44	Rest	Psychic	Status	—	—	10	Self	—	—
TM45	Attract	Normal	Status	—	100	15	Normal	—	—
TM46	Thief	Dark	Physical	40	100	10	Normal	—	○
TM47	Low Sweep	Fighting	Physical	60	100	20	Normal	—	—
TM48	Round	Normal	Special	60	100	15	Normal	—	—
TM56	Fling	Dark	Physical	—	100	10	Normal	—	—
TM59	Incinerate	Fire	Special	30	100	15	Many Others	—	—
TM63	Embargo	Dark	Status	—	100	15	Normal	—	—
TM65	Shadow Claw	Ghost	Physical	70	100	15	Normal	—	○
TM66	Payback	Dark	Physical	50	100	10	Normal	—	○
TM67	Retaliate	Normal	Physical	70	100	5	Normal	—	—
TM71	Stone Edge	Rock	Physical	100	80	5	Normal	—	—
TM78	Bulldoze	Ground	Physical	60	100	20	Adjacent	—	—
TM80	Rock Slide	Rock	Physical	75	90	10	Many Others	—	—
TM86	Grass Knot	Grass	Special	—	100	20	Normal	—	—
TM87	Swagger	Normal	Status	—	90	15	Normal	—	—
TM90	Substitute	Normal	Status	—	—	10	Self	—	—
TM94	Rock Smash	Fighting	Physical	40	100	15	Normal	—	—
HM01	Cut	Normal	Physical	50	95	30	Normal	—	—
HM04	Strength	Normal	Physical	80	100	15	Normal	—	—

● HEIGHT: 3'03"
● WEIGHT: 73.6 lbs.
● GENDER: Both ♂♀ exist
● ITEMS:
• None

● FOOTPRINT

● MALE/FEMALE HAVE SAME FORM

EVOLUTION

Sandile → Lv. 29 → Krokorok → Lv. 40 → Krookodile

POKÉMON BLACK VERSION
They live in groups of a few individuals. Protective membranes shield their eyes from sandstorms.

POKÉMON WHITE VERSION
The special membrane covering its eyes can sense the heat of objects, so it can see its surroundings even in darkness.

ABILITIES
● Intimidate
● Moxie

EGG GROUP
Field

STATS
HP ●●
ATTACK ●●●
DEFENSE ●●●
SP. ATTACK ●●●
SP. DEFENSE ●●●
SPEED ●●●

● MAIN WAYS TO OBTAIN

POKÉMON BLACK VERSION
1 Relic Castle B2F
2 Level up Sandile to Lv. 29

POKÉMON WHITE VERSION
1 Relic Castle B2F
2 Level up Sandile to Lv. 29

Krookodile

● TYPE: Ground | Dark

● LEVEL-UP AND LEARNED MOVES

Lv.	Name	Type	Kind	Pow.	Acc.	PP	Range	Long	DA
1	Leer	Normal	Status	—	100	30	Many Others	—	—
1	Rage	Normal	Physical	20	100	20	Normal	—	○
1	Bite	Dark	Physical	60	100	25	Normal	—	○
1	Sand-Attack	Ground	Status	—	100	15	Normal	—	—
4	Bite	Dark	Physical	60	100	25	Normal	—	○
7	Sand-Attack	Ground	Status	—	100	15	Normal	—	—
10	Torment	Dark	Status	—	100	15	Normal	—	—
13	Sand Tomb	Ground	Physical	35	85	15	Normal	—	—
16	Assurance	Dark	Physical	50	100	10	Normal	—	○
19	Mud-Slap	Ground	Special	20	100	10	Normal	—	—
22	Embargo	Dark	Status	—	100	15	Normal	—	—
25	Swagger	Normal	Status	—	90	15	Normal	—	—
28	Crunch	Dark	Physical	80	100	15	Normal	—	○
32	Dig	Ground	Physical	80	100	10	Normal	—	—
36	Scary Face	Normal	Status	—	100	10	Normal	—	—
42	Foul Play	Dark	Physical	95	100	15	Normal	—	○
48	Sandstorm	Rock	Status	—	—	10	Both Sides	—	—
54	Earthquake	Ground	Physical	100	100	10	Adjacent	—	—
60	Outrage	Dragon	Physical	120	100	10	1 Random	—	—

● MOVES TAUGHT BY PEOPLE

Name	Type	Kind	Pow.	Acc.	PP	Range	Long	DA

● TM & HM MOVES

No.	Name	Type	Kind	Pow.	Acc.	PP	Range	Long	DA
TM01	Hone Claws	Dark	Status	—	—	15	Self	—	—
TM02	Dragon Claw	Dragon	Physical	80	100	15	Normal	—	○
TM05	Roar	Normal	Status	—	100	20	Normal	—	—
TM06	Toxic	Poison	Status	—	90	10	Normal	—	—
TM08	Bulk Up	Fighting	Status	—	—	20	Self	—	—
TM10	Hidden Power	Normal	Special	—	100	15	Normal	—	—
TM12	Taunt	Dark	Status	—	100	20	Normal	—	—
TM15	Hyper Beam	Normal	Special	150	90	5	Normal	—	—
TM17	Protect	Normal	Status	—	—	10	Self	—	—
TM21	Frustration	Normal	Physical	—	100	20	Normal	—	—
TM23	Smack Down	Rock	Physical	50	100	15	Normal	—	—
TM26	Earthquake	Ground	Physical	100	100	10	Adjacent	—	—
TM27	Return	Normal	Physical	—	100	20	Normal	—	—
TM28	Dig	Ground	Physical	80	100	10	Normal	—	○
TM31	Brick Break	Fighting	Physical	75	100	15	Normal	—	—
TM32	Double Team	Normal	Status	—	—	15	Self	—	—
TM36	Sludge Bomb	Poison	Special	90	100	10	Normal	—	—
TM37	Sandstorm	Rock	Status	—	—	10	Both Sides	—	—
TM39	Rock Tomb	Rock	Physical	50	80	10	Normal	—	—
TM40	Aerial Ace	Flying	Physical	60	—	20	Normal	○	—
TM41	Torment	Dark	Status	—	100	15	Normal	—	—
TM42	Facade	Normal	Physical	70	100	20	Normal	—	—
TM44	Rest	Psychic	Status	—	—	10	Self	—	—
TM45	Attract	Normal	Status	—	100	15	Normal	—	—
TM46	Thief	Dark	Physical	40	100	10	Normal	—	○
TM47	Low Sweep	Fighting	Physical	60	100	20	Normal	—	—
TM48	Round	Normal	Special	60	100	15	Normal	—	—
TM52	Focus Blast	Fighting	Special	120	70	5	Normal	—	—
TM56	Fling	Dark	Physical	—	100	10	Normal	—	—
TM59	Incinerate	Fire	Special	30	100	15	Many Others	—	—
TM63	Embargo	Dark	Status	—	100	15	Normal	—	—
TM65	Shadow Claw	Ghost	Physical	70	100	15	Normal	—	○
TM66	Payback	Dark	Physical	50	100	10	Normal	—	○
TM67	Retaliate	Normal	Physical	70	100	5	Normal	—	—
TM68	Giga Impact	Normal	Physical	150	90	5	Normal	—	—
TM71	Stone Edge	Rock	Physical	100	80	5	Normal	—	—
TM78	Bulldoze	Ground	Physical	60	100	20	Adjacent	—	—
TM80	Rock Slide	Rock	Physical	75	90	10	Many Others	—	—
TM82	Dragon Tail	Dragon	Physical	60	90	10	Normal	—	—
TM86	Grass Knot	Grass	Special	—	100	20	Normal	—	—
TM87	Swagger	Normal	Status	—	90	15	Normal	—	—
TM90	Substitute	Normal	Status	—	—	10	Self	—	—
TM94	Rock Smash	Fighting	Physical	40	100	15	Normal	—	—
HM01	Cut	Normal	Physical	50	95	30	Normal	—	—
HM04	Strength	Normal	Physical	80	100	15	Normal	—	—

● HEIGHT: 4'11"
● WEIGHT: 212.3 lbs.
● GENDER: Both ♂♀ exist
● ITEMS:
• None

● FOOTPRINT

● MALE/FEMALE HAVE SAME FORM

EVOLUTION

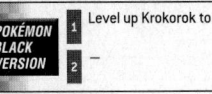

Sandile → Lv. 29 → Krokorok → Lv. 40 → Krookodile

POKÉMON BLACK VERSION
They never allow prey to escape. Their jaws are so powerful, they can crush the body of an automobile.

POKÉMON WHITE VERSION
It can expand the focus of its eyes, enabling it to see objects in the far distance as if it were using binoculars.

ABILITIES
● Intimidate
● Moxie

EGG GROUP
Field

STATS
HP ●●●●
ATTACK ●●●●●
DEFENSE ●●●
SP. ATTACK ●●●
SP. DEFENSE ●●●
SPEED ●●●●

● MAIN WAYS TO OBTAIN

POKÉMON BLACK VERSION
1 Level up Krokorok to Lv. 40
2 —

POKÉMON WHITE VERSION
1 Level up Krokorok to Lv. 40
2 —

Darumaka

● TYPE Fire

● LEVEL-UP AND LEARNED MOVES

Lv.	Name	Type	Kind	Pow.	Acc.	PP	Range	Long	DA
1	Tackle	Normal	Physical	50	100	35	Normal	—	○
3	Rollout	Rock	Physical	30	90	20	Normal	—	○
6	Rollout	Rock	Physical	30	90	20	Normal	—	○
9	Rollout	Rock	Physical	30	90	20	Normal	—	○
11	Fire Fang	Fire	Physical	65	95	15	Normal	—	○
14	Headbutt	Normal	Physical	70	100	15	Normal	—	○
17	Uproar	Normal	Special	90	100	10	1 Random	—	—
19	Facade	Normal	Physical	70	100	20	Normal	—	○
22	Fire Punch	Fire	Physical	75	100	15	Normal	—	○
25	Work Up	Normal	Status	—	—	30	Self	—	—
27	Thrash	Normal	Physical	120	100	10	1 Random	—	○
30	Belly Drum	Normal	Status	—	—	10	Self	—	—
33	Flare Blitz	Fire	Physical	120	100	15	Normal	—	○
35	Taunt	Dark	Status	—	100	20	Normal	—	—
39	Superpower	Fighting	Physical	120	100	5	Normal	—	○
42	Overheat	Fire	Special	140	90	5	Normal	—	—

● MOVES TAUGHT BY PEOPLE

Name	Type	Kind	Pow.	Acc.	PP	Range	Long	DA

● EGG MOVES

Name	Type	Kind	Pow.	Acc.	PP	Range	Long	DA
Sleep Talk	Normal	Status	—	—	10	Self	—	—
Focus Punch	Fighting	Physical	150	100	20	Normal	—	○
Focus Energy	Normal	Status	—	—	30	Self	—	—
Endure	Normal	Status	—	—	10	Self	—	—
Hammer Arm	Fighting	Physical	100	90	10	Normal	—	○
Take Down	Normal	Physical	90	85	20	Normal	—	○
Flame Wheel	Fire	Physical	60	100	25	Normal	—	○
Encore	Normal	Status	—	100	5	Normal	—	—
Yawn	Normal	Status	—	—	10	Normal	—	—

● FOOTPRINT

● MALE/FEMALE HAVE SAME FORM

● HEIGHT: 2'00"
● WEIGHT: 82.7 lbs.
● GENDER: Both ♂♀ exist
● ITEMS:
• Rawst Berry

● TM & HM MOVES

No.	Name	Type	Kind	Pow.	Acc.	PP	Range	Long	DA
TM05	Roar	Normal	Status	—	100	20	Normal	—	—
TM06	Toxic	Poison	Status	—	90	10	Normal	—	—
TM10	Hidden Power	Normal	Special	—	100	15	Normal	—	—
TM11	Sunny Day	Fire	Status	—	—	5	Both Sides	—	—
TM12	Taunt	Dark	Status	—	100	20	Normal	—	—
TM17	Protect	Normal	Status	—	—	10	Self	—	—
TM21	Frustration	Normal	Physical	—	100	20	Normal	—	○
TM22	SolarBeam	Grass	Special	120	100	10	Normal	—	—
TM27	Return	Normal	Physical	—	100	20	Normal	—	○
TM28	Dig	Ground	Physical	80	100	10	Normal	—	○
TM31	Brick Break	Fighting	Physical	75	100	15	Normal	—	○
TM32	Double Team	Normal	Status	—	—	15	Self	—	—
TM35	Flamethrower	Fire	Special	95	100	15	Normal	—	—
TM38	Fire Blast	Fire	Special	120	85	5	Normal	—	—
TM39	Rock Tomb	Rock	Physical	50	80	10	Normal	—	○
TM42	Facade	Normal	Physical	70	100	20	Normal	—	○
TM43	Flame Charge	Fire	Physical	50	100	20	Normal	—	○
TM44	Rest	Psychic	Status	—	—	10	Self	—	—
TM45	Attract	Normal	Status	—	100	15	Normal	—	—
TM46	Thief	Dark	Physical	40	100	10	Normal	—	○
TM48	Round	Normal	Special	60	100	15	Normal	—	—
TM50	Overheat	Fire	Special	140	90	5	Normal	—	—
TM56	Fling	Dark	Physical	—	100	10	Normal	—	○
TM59	Incinerate	Fire	Special	30	100	15	Many Others	—	—
TM61	Will-O-Wisp	Fire	Status	—	75	15	Normal	—	—
TM74	Gyro Ball	Steel	Physical	—	100	5	Normal	—	○
TM80	Rock Slide	Rock	Physical	75	90	10	Many Others	—	○
TM83	Work Up	Normal	Status	—	—	30	Self	—	—
TM86	Grass Knot	Grass	Special	—	100	20	Normal	—	—
TM87	Swagger	Normal	Status	—	90	15	Normal	—	—
TM89	U-turn	Bug	Physical	70	100	20	Normal	—	○
TM90	Substitute	Normal	Status	—	—	10	Self	—	—
TM94	Rock Smash	Fighting	Physical	40	100	15	Normal	—	○
HM04	Strength	Normal	Physical	80	100	15	Normal	—	—

● EVOLUTION

Lv. 35

Darumaka → Darmanitan

● MAIN WAYS TO OBTAIN

POKÉMON BLACK VERSION	1	Route 4
	2	Desert Resort Entrance

POKÉMON WHITE VERSION	1	Route 4
	2	Desert Resort Entrance

● Darumaka with the Hidden Ability Inner Focus do not appear in the wild.

POKÉMON BLACK VERSION
When its internal fire is burning, it cannot calm down and it runs around. When the fire diminishes, it falls asleep.

POKÉMON WHITE VERSION
Darumaka's droppings are hot, so people used to put them in their clothes to keep themselves warm.

ABILITIES
● Hustle
● Inner Focus

EGG GROUP
Field

STATS
HP ●●●
ATTACK ●●●●
DEFENSE ●●
SP. ATTACK ●
SP. DEFENSE ●●
SPEED ●●

Darmanitan

● TYPE (Standard Mode) Fire
● TYPE (Zen Mode) Fire Psychic

● LEVEL-UP AND LEARNED MOVES

Lv.	Name	Type	Kind	Pow.	Acc.	PP	Range	Long	DA
1	Tackle	Normal	Physical	50	100	35	Normal	—	○
1	Rollout	Rock	Physical	30	90	20	Normal	—	○
1	Incinerate	Fire	Special	30	100	15	Many Others	—	—
1	Rage	Normal	Physical	20	100	20	Normal	—	○
3	Rollout	Rock	Physical	30	90	20	Normal	—	○
6	Incinerate	Fire	Special	30	100	15	Many Others	—	—
9	Rage	Normal	Physical	20	100	20	Normal	—	○
11	Fire Fang	Fire	Physical	65	95	15	Normal	—	○
14	Headbutt	Normal	Physical	70	100	15	Normal	—	○
17	Swagger	Normal	Status	—	90	15	Normal	—	—
19	Facade	Normal	Physical	70	100	20	Normal	—	○
22	Fire Punch	Fire	Physical	75	100	15	Normal	—	○
25	Work Up	Normal	Status	—	—	30	Self	—	—
27	Thrash	Normal	Physical	120	100	10	1 Random	—	○
30	Belly Drum	Normal	Status	—	—	10	Self	—	—
33	Flare Blitz	Fire	Physical	120	100	15	Normal	—	○
35	Hammer Arm	Fighting	Physical	100	90	10	Normal	—	○
39	Taunt	Dark	Status	—	100	20	Normal	—	—
47	Superpower	Fighting	Physical	120	100	5	Normal	—	○
54	Overheat	Fire	Special	140	90	5	Normal	—	—

● MOVES TAUGHT BY PEOPLE

Name	Type	Kind	Pow.	Acc.	PP	Range	Long	DA

● EVOLUTION

Lv. 35

Darumaka → Darmanitan

● HEIGHT: 4'03"
● WEIGHT: 204.8 lbs.
● GENDER: Both ♂♀ exist
● ITEMS:
• Rawst Berry

● FOOTPRINT

● STANDARD MODE
● ZEN MODE

● TM & HM MOVES

No.	Name	Type	Kind	Pow.	Acc.	PP	Range	Long	DA
TM05	Roar	Normal	Status	—	100	20	Normal	—	—
TM06	Toxic	Poison	Status	—	90	10	Normal	—	—
TM08	Bulk Up	Fighting	Status	—	—	20	Self	—	—
TM10	Hidden Power	Normal	Special	—	100	15	Normal	—	—
TM11	Sunny Day	Fire	Status	—	—	5	Both Sides	—	—
TM12	Taunt	Dark	Status	—	100	20	Normal	—	—
TM15	Hyper Beam	Normal	Special	150	90	5	Normal	—	—
TM17	Protect	Normal	Status	—	—	10	Self	—	—
TM21	Frustration	Normal	Physical	—	100	20	Normal	—	○
TM22	SolarBeam	Grass	Special	120	100	10	Normal	—	—
TM23	Smack Down	Rock	Physical	50	100	15	Normal	—	○
TM26	Earthquake	Ground	Physical	100	100	10	Adjacent	—	—
TM27	Return	Normal	Physical	—	100	20	Normal	—	○
TM28	Dig	Ground	Physical	80	100	10	Normal	—	○
TM29	Psychic	Psychic	Special	90	100	10	Normal	—	—
TM31	Brick Break	Fighting	Physical	75	100	15	Normal	—	○
TM32	Double Team	Normal	Status	—	—	15	Self	—	—
TM35	Flamethrower	Fire	Special	95	100	15	Normal	—	—
TM38	Fire Blast	Fire	Special	120	85	5	Normal	—	—
TM39	Rock Tomb	Rock	Physical	50	80	10	Normal	—	○
TM41	Torment	Dark	Status	—	100	15	Normal	—	—
TM42	Facade	Normal	Physical	70	100	20	Normal	—	○
TM43	Flame Charge	Fire	Physical	50	100	20	Normal	—	○
TM44	Rest	Psychic	Status	—	—	10	Self	—	—
TM45	Attract	Normal	Status	—	100	15	Normal	—	—
TM46	Thief	Dark	Physical	40	100	10	Normal	—	○
TM48	Round	Normal	Special	60	100	15	Normal	—	—
TM50	Overheat	Fire	Special	140	90	5	Normal	—	—
TM52	Focus Blast	Fighting	Special	120	70	5	Normal	—	—
TM56	Fling	Dark	Physical	—	100	10	Normal	—	○
TM59	Incinerate	Fire	Special	30	100	15	Many Others	—	—
TM61	Will-O-Wisp	Fire	Status	—	75	15	Normal	—	—
TM66	Payback	Dark	Physical	50	100	10	Normal	—	○
TM68	Giga Impact	Normal	Physical	150	90	5	Normal	—	○
TM71	Stone Edge	Rock	Physical	100	80	5	Normal	—	○
TM74	Gyro Ball	Steel	Physical	—	100	5	Normal	—	○
TM78	Bulldoze	Ground	Physical	60	100	20	Adjacent	—	—
TM80	Rock Slide	Rock	Physical	75	90	10	Many Others	—	○
TM83	Work Up	Normal	Status	—	—	30	Self	—	—
TM86	Grass Knot	Grass	Special	—	100	20	Normal	—	—
TM87	Swagger	Normal	Status	—	90	15	Normal	—	—
TM89	U-turn	Bug	Physical	70	100	20	Normal	—	○
TM90	Substitute	Normal	Status	—	—	10	Self	—	—
TM94	Rock Smash	Fighting	Physical	40	100	15	Normal	—	○
HM04	Strength	Normal	Physical	80	100	15	Normal	—	—

● MAIN WAYS TO OBTAIN

POKÉMON BLACK VERSION	1	Use a RageCandyBar on a Pokémon statue near the Relic Castle
	2	Level up Darumaka to Lv. 35

POKÉMON WHITE VERSION	1	Use a RageCandyBar on a Pokémon statue near the Relic Castle
	2	Level up Darumaka to Lv. 35

● A Darmanitan with the Hidden Ability Zen Mode appears when you give a RageCandyBar to a Pokémon statue near the Relic Castle after finishing the main story.

● If Darmanitan has the Hidden Ability Zen Mode, its mode will become the Zen Mode when its HP becomes half or less. Its mode will return to Standard Mode after the battle.

ABILITIES
● Sheer Force
● Zen Mode

EGG GROUP
Field

POKÉMON BLACK VERSION
Its internal fire burns at 2,500° F, making enough power that it can destroy a dump truck with one punch.

POKÉMON WHITE VERSION
When weakened in battle, it transforms into a stone statue. Then it sharpens its mind and fights on mentally.

● STATS

	● STANDARD MODE	● ZEN MODE
HP	●●●●	●●●●
ATTACK	●●●●●●●	●
DEFENSE	●●●●	●●●●
SP. ATTACK	●●	●●●●●●
SP. DEFENSE	●●	●●●●●●
SPEED	●●●●	●●●●

Maractus

● TYPE Grass

● HEIGHT: 3'03"
● WEIGHT: 61.7 lbs.
● GENDER: Both ♂♀ exist
● ITEMS:
  • Miracle Seed

● MALE/FEMALE HAVE SAME FORM

● FOOTPRINT

● LEVEL-UP AND LEARNED MOVES

Lv.	Name	Type	Kind	Pow.	Acc.	PP	Range	Long	DA
1	Peck	Flying	Physical	35	100	35	Normal	○	–
1	Absorb	Grass	Special	20	100	25	Normal	–	–
3	Sweet Scent	Normal	Status	–	100	20	Many Others	–	–
6	Growth	Normal	Status	–	–	40	Self	–	–
10	Pin Missile	Bug	Physical	14	85	20	Normal	–	–
13	Mega Drain	Grass	Special	40	100	15	Normal	–	–
15	Synthesis	Grass	Status	–	–	5	Self	–	–
18	Cotton Spore	Grass	Status	–	100	40	Normal	–	–
22	Needle Arm	Grass	Physical	60	100	15	Normal	–	○
26	Giga Drain	Grass	Special	75	100	10	Normal	–	–
29	Acupressure	Normal	Status	–	–	30	Self/Ally	–	–
33	Ingrain	Grass	Status	–	–	20	Self	–	–
38	Petal Dance	Grass	Special	120	100	10	1 Random	–	○
42	Sucker Punch	Dark	Physical	80	100	5	Normal	–	○
45	Sunny Day	Fire	Status	–	–	5	Both Sides	–	–
50	SolarBeam	Grass	Special	120	100	10	Normal	–	–
55	Cotton Guard	Grass	Status	–	–	10	Self	–	–
57	After You	Normal	Status	–	–	15	Normal	–	–

● MOVES TAUGHT BY PEOPLE

Name	Type	Kind	Pow.	Acc.	PP	Range	Long	DA

● EGG MOVES

Name	Type	Kind	Pow.	Acc.	PP	Range	Long	DA
Bullet Seed	Grass	Physical	25	100	30	Normal	–	–
Bounce	Flying	Physical	85	85	5	Normal	○	○
Worry Seed	Grass	Status	–	100	10	Normal	–	–
Leech Seed	Grass	Status	–	90	10	Normal	–	–
Seed Bomb	Grass	Physical	80	100	15	Normal	–	–
Wood Hammer	Grass	Physical	120	100	15	Normal	–	○
Spikes	Ground	Status	–	–	20	Other Side	–	–
GrassWhistle	Grass	Status	–	55	15	Normal	–	–

EVOLUTION

Does not evolve

● TM & HM MOVES

No.	Name	Type	Kind	Pow.	Acc.	PP	Range	Long	DA
TM06	Toxic	Poison	Status	–	90	10	Normal	–	–
TM10	Hidden Power	Normal	Special	–	100	15	Normal	–	–
TM11	Sunny Day	Fire	Status	–	–	5	Both Sides	–	–
TM17	Protect	Normal	Status	–	–	10	Self	–	–
TM20	Safeguard	Normal	Status	–	–	25	Your Side	–	–
TM21	Frustration	Normal	Physical	–	100	20	Normal	–	○
TM22	SolarBeam	Grass	Special	120	100	10	Normal	–	–
TM27	Return	Normal	Physical	–	100	20	Normal	–	○
TM32	Double Team	Normal	Status	–	–	15	Self	–	–
TM40	Aerial Ace	Flying	Physical	60	–	20	Normal	○	○
TM42	Facade	Normal	Physical	70	100	20	Normal	–	○
TM44	Rest	Psychic	Status	–	–	10	Self	–	–
TM45	Attract	Normal	Status	–	100	15	Normal	–	–
TM48	Round	Normal	Special	60	100	15	Normal	–	–
TM53	Energy Ball	Grass	Special	80	100	10	Normal	–	–
TM84	Poison Jab	Poison	Physical	80	100	20	Normal	–	○
TM86	Grass Knot	Grass	Special	–	100	20	Normal	–	–
TM87	Swagger	Normal	Status	–	90	15	Normal	–	–
TM90	Substitute	Normal	Status	–	–	10	Self	–	–

● MAIN WAYS TO OBTAIN

POKÉMON BLACK VERSION	1	Desert Resort Entrance
	2	Desert Resort Back

POKÉMON WHITE VERSION	1	Desert Resort Entrance
	2	Desert Resort Back

POKÉMON BLACK VERSION
It uses an up-tempo song and dance to drive away the bird Pokémon that prey on its flower seeds.

POKÉMON WHITE VERSION
Arid regions are their habitat. They move rhythmically, making a sound similar to maracas.

ABILITIES
● Water Absorb
● Chlorophyll

EGG GROUP Grass

STATS
HP ●●●
ATTACK ●●●●
DEFENSE ●●●
SP. ATTACK ●●●●●
SP. DEFENSE ●●●
SPEED ●●●

Dwebble

● TYPE Bug Rock

● HEIGHT: 1'00"
● WEIGHT: 32.0 lbs.
● GENDER: Both ♂♀ exist
● ITEMS:
  • Hard Stone
  • Rare Bone

● MALE/FEMALE HAVE SAME FORM

● FOOTPRINT

● LEVEL-UP AND LEARNED MOVES

Lv.	Name	Type	Kind	Pow.	Acc.	PP	Range	Long	DA
1	Fury Cutter	Bug	Physical	20	95	20	Normal	–	○
5	Rock Blast	Rock	Physical	25	90	10	Normal	–	–
7	Withdraw	Water	Status	–	–	40	Self	–	–
11	Sand-Attack	Ground	Status	–	100	15	Normal	–	–
13	Faint Attack	Dark	Physical	60	–	20	Normal	–	○
17	Smack Down	Rock	Physical	50	100	15	Normal	–	–
19	Rock Polish	Rock	Status	–	–	20	Self	–	–
23	Bug Bite	Bug	Physical	60	100	20	Normal	–	○
24	Stealth Rock	Rock	Status	–	–	20	Other Side	–	–
29	Rock Slide	Rock	Physical	75	90	10	Many Others	–	–
31	Slash	Normal	Physical	70	100	20	Normal	–	○
35	X-Scissor	Bug	Physical	80	100	15	Normal	–	○
37	Shell Smash	Normal	Status	–	–	15	Self	–	–
41	Flail	Normal	Physical	–	100	15	Normal	–	–
43	Rock Wrecker	Rock	Physical	150	90	5	Normal	–	–

● MOVES TAUGHT BY PEOPLE

Name	Type	Kind	Pow.	Acc.	PP	Range	Long	DA

● EGG MOVES

Name	Type	Kind	Pow.	Acc.	PP	Range	Long	DA
Endure	Normal	Status	–	–	10	Self	–	–
Iron Defense	Steel	Status	–	–	15	Self	–	–
Night Slash	Dark	Physical	70	100	15	Normal	–	○
Sand Tomb	Ground	Physical	35	85	15	Normal	–	–
Counter	Fighting	Physical	–	100	20	Varies	–	○
Curse	Ghost	Status	–	–	10	Varies	–	–
Spikes	Ground	Status	–	–	20	Other Side	–	–
Block	Normal	Status	–	–	5	Normal	–	–

EVOLUTION

	Lv. 34	
Dwebble		Crustle

● TM & HM MOVES

No.	Name	Type	Kind	Pow.	Acc.	PP	Range	Long	DA
TM01	Hone Claws	Dark	Status	–	–	15	Self	–	–
TM06	Toxic	Poison	Status	–	90	10	Normal	–	–
TM10	Hidden Power	Normal	Special	–	100	15	Normal	–	–
TM17	Protect	Normal	Status	–	–	10	Self	–	–
TM21	Frustration	Normal	Physical	–	100	20	Normal	–	○
TM22	SolarBeam	Grass	Special	120	100	10	Normal	–	–
TM23	Smack Down	Rock	Physical	50	100	15	Normal	–	–
TM26	Earthquake	Ground	Physical	100	100	10	Adjacent	–	–
TM27	Return	Normal	Physical	–	100	20	Normal	–	○
TM28	Dig	Ground	Physical	80	100	10	Normal	–	○
TM32	Double Team	Normal	Status	–	–	15	Self	–	–
TM37	Sandstorm	Rock	Status	–	–	10	Both Sides	–	–
TM39	Rock Tomb	Rock	Physical	50	80	10	Normal	–	–
TM40	Aerial Ace	Flying	Physical	60	–	20	Normal	○	○
TM42	Facade	Normal	Physical	70	100	20	Normal	–	○
TM44	Rest	Psychic	Status	–	–	10	Self	–	–
TM45	Attract	Normal	Status	–	100	15	Normal	–	–
TM48	Round	Normal	Special	60	100	15	Normal	–	–
TM65	Shadow Claw	Ghost	Physical	70	100	15	Normal	–	○
TM69	Rock Polish	Rock	Status	–	–	20	Self	–	–
TM71	Stone Edge	Rock	Physical	100	80	5	Normal	–	–
TM75	Swords Dance	Normal	Status	–	–	30	Self	–	–
TM76	Struggle Bug	Bug	Special	30	100	20	Many Others	–	–
TM78	Bulldoze	Ground	Physical	60	100	20	Adjacent	–	–
TM80	Rock Slide	Rock	Physical	75	90	10	Many Others	–	–
TM81	X-Scissor	Bug	Physical	80	100	15	Normal	–	○
TM84	Poison Jab	Poison	Physical	80	100	20	Normal	–	○
TM87	Swagger	Normal	Status	–	90	15	Normal	–	–
TM90	Substitute	Normal	Status	–	–	10	Self	–	–
TM94	Rock Smash	Fighting	Physical	40	100	15	Normal	–	○
HM01	Cut	Normal	Physical	50	95	30	Normal	–	○
HM04	Strength	Normal	Physical	80	100	15	Normal	–	○

● MAIN WAYS TO OBTAIN

POKÉMON BLACK VERSION	1	Desert Resort Entrance
	2	Route 18

POKÉMON WHITE VERSION	1	Desert Resort Entrance
	2	Route 18

POKÉMON BLACK VERSION
This Pokémon can easily melt holes in hard rocks with a liquid secreted from its mouth.

POKÉMON WHITE VERSION
It makes a hole in a suitable rock. If that rock breaks, the Pokémon remains agitated until it locates a replacement.

ABILITIES
● Sturdy
● Shell Armor

EGG GROUPS Bug Mineral

STATS
HP ●●
ATTACK ●●●
DEFENSE ●●●●
SP. ATTACK ●
SP. DEFENSE ●
SPEED ●●●

Crustle

● TYPE Bug Rock

● LEVEL-UP AND LEARNED MOVES

Lv.	Name	Type	Kind	Pow.	Acc.	PP	Range	Long	DA
1	Shell Smash	Normal	Status	—	—	15	Self	—	—
1	Rock Blast	Rock	Physical	25	90	10	Normal	—	—
1	Withdraw	Water	Status	—	—	40	Self	—	—
1	Sand-Attack	Ground	Status	—	100	15	Normal	—	—
5	Rock Blast	Rock	Physical	25	90	10	Normal	—	—
7	Withdraw	Water	Status	—	—	40	Self	—	—
11	Sand-Attack	Ground	Status	—	100	15	Normal	—	—
13	Faint Attack	Dark	Physical	60	—	20	Normal	—	○
17	Smack Down	Rock	Physical	50	100	15	Normal	—	—
19	Rock Polish	Rock	Status	—	—	20	Self	—	—
23	Bug Bite	Bug	Physical	60	100	20	Normal	—	—
24	Stealth Rock	Rock	Status	—	—	20	Other Side	—	—
29	Rock Slide	Rock	Physical	75	90	10	Many Others	—	—
31	Slash	Normal	Physical	70	100	20	Normal	—	○
38	X-Scissor	Bug	Physical	80	100	15	Normal	—	○
43	Shell Smash	Normal	Status	—	—	15	Self	—	—
50	Flail	Normal	Physical	—	100	15	Normal	—	—
55	Rock Wrecker	Rock	Physical	150	90	5	Normal	—	—

● MOVES TAUGHT BY PEOPLE

Name	Type	Kind	Pow.	Acc.	PP	Range	Long	DA

● TM & HM MOVES

No.	Name	Type	Kind	Pow.	Acc.	PP	Range	Long	DA
TM01	Hone Claws	Dark	Status	—	—	15	Self	—	—
TM06	Toxic	Poison	Status	—	90	10	Normal	—	—
TM10	Hidden Power	Normal	Special	—	100	15	Normal	—	—
TM15	Hyper Beam	Normal	Special	150	90	5	Normal	—	—
TM17	Protect	Normal	Status	—	—	10	Self	—	—
TM21	Frustration	Normal	Physical	—	100	20	Normal	—	○
TM22	SolarBeam	Grass	Special	120	100	10	Normal	—	—
TM23	Smack Down	Rock	Physical	50	100	15	Normal	—	—
TM26	Earthquake	Ground	Physical	100	100	10	Adjacent	—	—
TM27	Return	Normal	Physical	—	100	20	Normal	—	○
TM28	Dig	Ground	Physical	80	100	10	Normal	—	—
TM32	Double Team	Normal	Status	—	—	15	Self	—	—
TM37	Sandstorm	Rock	Status	—	—	10	Both Sides	—	—
TM39	Rock Tomb	Rock	Physical	50	80	10	Normal	—	—
TM40	Aerial Ace	Flying	Physical	60	—	20	Normal	○	○
TM42	Facade	Normal	Physical	70	100	20	Normal	—	○
TM44	Rest	Psychic	Status	—	—	10	Self	—	—
TM45	Attract	Normal	Status	—	100	15	Normal	—	—
TM48	Round	Normal	Special	60	100	15	Normal	—	—
TM65	Shadow Claw	Ghost	Physical	70	100	15	Normal	—	○
TM68	Giga Impact	Normal	Physical	150	90	5	Normal	—	—
TM69	Rock Polish	Rock	Status	—	—	20	Self	—	—
TM71	Stone Edge	Rock	Physical	100	80	5	Normal	—	—
TM75	Swords Dance	Normal	Status	—	—	30	Self	—	—
TM76	Struggle Bug	Bug	Special	30	100	20	Many Others	—	—
TM78	Bulldoze	Ground	Physical	60	100	20	Adjacent	—	—
TM80	Rock Slide	Rock	Physical	75	90	10	Many Others	—	—
TM81	X-Scissor	Bug	Physical	80	100	15	Normal	—	○
TM84	Poison Jab	Poison	Physical	80	100	20	Normal	—	—
TM87	Swagger	Normal	Status	—	90	15	Normal	—	—
TM90	Substitute	Normal	Status	—	—	10	Self	—	—
TM94	Rock Smash	Fighting	Physical	40	100	15	Normal	—	—
HM01	Cut	Normal	Physical	50	95	30	Normal	—	—
HM04	Strength	Normal	Physical	80	100	15	Normal	—	—

● FOOTPRINT

● HEIGHT: 4'07"
● WEIGHT: 440.9 lbs.
● GENDER: Both ♂♀ exist
● ITEMS:
  • Hard Stone
  • Rare Bone

● MALE/FEMALE HAVE SAME FORM

EVOLUTION

Lv. 34

Dwebble → Crustle

POKÉMON BLACK VERSION
Competing for territory, Crustle fight viciously. The one whose boulder is broken is the loser of the battle.

POKÉMON WHITE VERSION
It possesses legs of enormous strength, enabling it to carry heavy slabs for many days, even when crossing arid land.

● MAIN WAYS TO OBTAIN

| POKÉMON BLACK VERSION | 1 | Route 18 (Dark Grass) |
| | 2 | Level up Dwebble to Lv. 34 |

| POKÉMON WHITE VERSION | 1 | Route 18 (Dark Grass) |
| | 2 | Level up Dwebble to Lv. 34 |

ABILITIES
● Sturdy
● Shell Armor

EGG GROUPS
Bug
Mineral

STATS
HP ●●●
ATTACK ●●●●
DEFENSE ●●●●●
SP. ATTACK ●●●
SP. DEFENSE ●●●
SPEED ●●

Scraggy

● TYPE Dark Fighting

● LEVEL-UP AND LEARNED MOVES

Lv.	Name	Type	Kind	Pow.	Acc.	PP	Range	Long	DA
1	Leer	Normal	Status	—	100	30	Many Others	—	—
1	Low Kick	Fighting	Physical	—	100	20	Normal	—	○
5	Sand-Attack	Ground	Status	—	100	15	Normal	—	—
9	Faint Attack	Dark	Physical	60	—	20	Normal	—	○
12	Headbutt	Normal	Physical	70	100	15	Normal	—	—
16	Swagger	Normal	Status	—	90	15	Normal	—	—
20	Brick Break	Fighting	Physical	75	100	15	Normal	—	○
23	Payback	Dark	Physical	50	100	10	Normal	—	○
27	Chip Away	Normal	Physical	70	100	20	Normal	—	○
31	Hi Jump Kick	Fighting	Physical	130	90	10	Normal	—	○
34	Scary Face	Normal	Status	—	100	10	Normal	—	—
38	Crunch	Dark	Physical	80	100	15	Normal	—	○
42	Facade	Normal	Physical	70	100	20	Normal	—	○
45	Rock Climb	Normal	Physical	90	85	20	Normal	—	○
49	Focus Punch	Fighting	Physical	150	100	20	Normal	—	○
53	Head Smash	Rock	Physical	150	80	5	Normal	—	—

● MOVES TAUGHT BY PEOPLE

Name	Type	Kind	Pow.	Acc.	PP	Range	Long	DA

● EGG MOVES

Name	Type	Kind	Pow.	Acc.	PP	Range	Long	DA
Drain Punch	Fighting	Physical	75	100	10	Normal	—	○
Counter	Fighting	Physical	—	100	20	Varies	—	—
Dragon Dance	Dragon	Status	—	—	20	Self	—	—
Detect	Fighting	Status	—	—	5	Self	—	—
Fake Out	Normal	Physical	40	100	10	Normal	—	—
Fire Punch	Fire	Physical	75	100	15	Normal	—	○
Ice Punch	Ice	Physical	75	100	15	Normal	—	○
ThunderPunch	Electric	Physical	75	100	15	Normal	—	○
Amnesia	Psychic	Status	—	—	20	Self	—	—
Faint Attack	Dark	Physical	60	—	20	Normal	—	○
Zen Headbutt	Psychic	Physical	80	90	15	Normal	—	○

● TM & HM MOVES

No.	Name	Type	Kind	Pow.	Acc.	PP	Range	Long	DA
TM02	Dragon Claw	Dragon	Physical	80	100	15	Normal	—	○
TM05	Roar	Normal	Status	—	100	20	Normal	—	—
TM06	Toxic	Poison	Status	—	90	10	Normal	—	—
TM08	Bulk Up	Fighting	Status	—	—	20	Self	—	—
TM10	Hidden Power	Normal	Special	—	100	15	Normal	—	—
TM11	Sunny Day	Fire	Status	—	—	5	Both Sides	—	—
TM12	Taunt	Dark	Status	—	100	20	Normal	—	—
TM17	Protect	Normal	Status	—	—	10	Self	—	—
TM18	Rain Dance	Water	Status	—	—	5	Both Sides	—	—
TM21	Frustration	Normal	Physical	—	100	20	Normal	—	○
TM23	Smack Down	Rock	Physical	50	100	15	Normal	—	—
TM27	Return	Normal	Physical	—	100	20	Normal	—	○
TM28	Dig	Ground	Physical	80	100	10	Normal	—	—
TM31	Brick Break	Fighting	Physical	75	100	15	Normal	—	○
TM32	Double Team	Normal	Status	—	—	15	Self	—	—
TM36	Sludge Bomb	Poison	Special	90	100	10	Normal	—	—
TM39	Rock Tomb	Rock	Physical	50	80	10	Normal	—	—
TM41	Torment	Dark	Status	—	100	15	Normal	—	—
TM42	Facade	Normal	Physical	70	100	20	Normal	—	○
TM44	Rest	Psychic	Status	—	—	10	Self	—	—
TM45	Attract	Normal	Status	—	100	15	Normal	—	—
TM47	Low Sweep	Fighting	Physical	60	100	20	Normal	—	○
TM48	Round	Normal	Special	60	100	15	Normal	—	—
TM52	Focus Blast	Fighting	Special	120	70	5	Normal	—	—
TM56	Fling	Dark	Physical	—	100	10	Normal	—	—
TM59	Incinerate	Fire	Special	30	100	15	Many Others	—	—
TM66	Payback	Dark	Physical	50	100	10	Normal	—	○
TM67	Retaliate	Normal	Physical	70	100	5	Normal	—	—
TM71	Stone Edge	Rock	Physical	100	80	5	Normal	—	—
TM80	Rock Slide	Rock	Physical	75	90	10	Many Others	—	—
TM82	Dragon Tail	Dragon	Physical	60	90	10	Normal	—	—
TM83	Work Up	Normal	Status	—	—	30	Self	—	—
TM84	Poison Jab	Poison	Physical	80	100	20	Normal	—	—
TM86	Grass Knot	Grass	Special	—	100	20	Normal	—	—
TM87	Swagger	Normal	Status	—	90	15	Normal	—	—
TM90	Substitute	Normal	Status	—	—	10	Self	—	—
TM94	Rock Smash	Fighting	Physical	40	100	15	Normal	—	—
HM04	Strength	Normal	Physical	80	100	15	Normal	—	—

● FOOTPRINT

● HEIGHT: 2'00"
● WEIGHT: 26.0 lbs.
● GENDER: Both ♂♀ exist
● ITEMS:
  • Shed Shell

● MALE/FEMALE HAVE SAME FORM

EVOLUTION

Lv. 39

Scraggy → Scrafty

POKÉMON BLACK VERSION
Its skin has a rubbery elasticity, so it can reduce damage by defensively pulling its skin up to its neck.

POKÉMON WHITE VERSION
It immediately headbutts anyone that makes eye contact with it. Its skull is massively thick.

● MAIN WAYS TO OBTAIN

| POKÉMON BLACK VERSION | 1 | Route 4 |
| | 2 | Desert Resort Entrance |

| POKÉMON WHITE VERSION | 1 | Route 4 |
| | 2 | Desert Resort Entrance |

ABILITIES
● Shed Skin
● Moxie

EGG GROUPS
Field
Dragon

STATS
HP ●●
ATTACK ●●●
DEFENSE ●●●
SP. ATTACK ●
SP. DEFENSE ●●●
SPEED ●●

Scrafty

● LEVEL-UP AND LEARNED MOVES

Lv.	Name	Type	Kind	Pow.	Acc.	PP	Range	Long	DA
1	Leer	Normal	Status	–	100	30	Many Others	–	–
1	Low Kick	Fighting	Physical	–	100	20	Normal	–	○
1	Sand-Attack	Ground	Status	–	100	15	Normal	–	–
4	Faint Attack	Dark	Physical	60	–	20	Normal	–	–
5	Sand-Attack	Ground	Status	–	100	15	Normal	–	–
9	Faint Attack	Dark	Physical	60	–	20	Normal	–	–
12	Headbutt	Normal	Physical	70	100	15	Normal	–	○
16	Swagger	Normal	Status	–	90	15	Normal	–	–
20	Brick Break	Fighting	Physical	75	100	15	Normal	–	–
23	Payback	Dark	Physical	50	100	10	Normal	–	○
27	Chip Away	Normal	Physical	70	100	20	Normal	–	○
31	Hi Jump Kick	Fighting	Physical	130	90	10	Normal	–	○
34	Scary Face	Normal	Status	–	90	10	Normal	–	–
38	Crunch	Dark	Physical	80	100	15	Normal	–	○
45	Facade	Normal	Physical	70	100	20	Normal	–	–
51	Rock Climb	Normal	Physical	90	85	20	Normal	–	○
58	Focus Punch	Fighting	Physical	150	100	20	Normal	–	–
65	Head Smash	Rock	Physical	150	80	5	Normal	–	–

● MOVES TAUGHT BY PEOPLE

Name	Type	Kind	Pow.	Acc.	PP	Range	Long	DA

● TM & HM MOVES

No.	Name	Type	Kind	Pow.	Acc.	PP	Range	Long	DA
TM02	Dragon Claw	Dragon	Physical	80	100	15	Normal	–	○
TM05	Roar	Normal	Status	–	–	20	Normal	–	–
TM06	Toxic	Poison	Status	–	90	10	Normal	–	–
TM08	Bulk Up	Fighting	Status	–	–	20	Self	–	–
TM10	Hidden Power	Normal	Special	–	100	15	Normal	–	–
TM11	Sunny Day	Fire	Status	–	–	5	Both Sides	–	–
TM12	Taunt	Dark	Status	–	100	20	Normal	–	–
TM15	Hyper Beam	Normal	Special	150	90	5	Normal	–	–
TM17	Protect	Normal	Status	–	–	10	Self	–	–
TM18	Rain Dance	Water	Status	–	–	5	Both Sides	–	–
TM21	Frustration	Normal	Physical	–	100	20	Normal	–	○
TM23	Smack Down	Rock	Physical	50	100	15	Normal	–	–
TM27	Return	Normal	Physical	–	100	20	Normal	–	○
TM28	Dig	Ground	Physical	80	100	10	Normal	–	○
TM31	Brick Break	Fighting	Physical	75	100	15	Normal	–	–
TM32	Double Team	Normal	Status	–	–	15	Self	–	–
TM36	Sludge Bomb	Poison	Special	90	100	10	Normal	–	–
TM39	Rock Tomb	Rock	Physical	50	80	10	Normal	–	–
TM41	Torment	Dark	Status	–	100	15	Normal	–	–
TM42	Facade	Normal	Physical	70	100	20	Normal	–	–
TM44	Rest	Psychic	Status	–	–	10	Self	–	–
TM45	Attract	Normal	Status	–	100	15	Normal	–	–
TM46	Thief	Dark	Physical	40	100	10	Normal	–	○
TM47	Low Sweep	Fighting	Physical	60	100	20	Normal	–	–
TM48	Round	Normal	Special	60	100	15	Normal	–	–
TM52	Focus Blast	Fighting	Special	120	70	5	Normal	–	–
TM56	Fling	Dark	Physical	–	100	10	Normal	–	–
TM59	Incinerate	Fire	Special	30	100	15	Many Others	–	–
TM66	Payback	Dark	Physical	50	100	10	Normal	–	○
TM67	Retaliate	Normal	Physical	70	100	5	Normal	–	–
TM68	Giga Impact	Normal	Physical	150	90	5	Normal	–	–
TM71	Stone Edge	Rock	Physical	100	80	5	Normal	–	–
TM80	Rock Slide	Rock	Physical	75	90	10	Many Others	–	–
TM82	Dragon Tail	Dragon	Physical	60	90	10	Normal	–	○
TM83	Work Up	Normal	Status	–	–	30	Self	–	–
TM84	Poison Jab	Poison	Physical	80	100	20	Normal	–	–
TM86	Grass Knot	Grass	Special	–	100	20	Normal	–	–
TM87	Swagger	Normal	Status	–	90	15	Normal	–	–
TM90	Substitute	Normal	Status	–	–	10	Self	–	–
TM94	Rock Smash	Fighting	Physical	40	100	15	Normal	–	○
HM04	Strength	Normal	Physical	80	100	15	Normal	–	–

● TYPE **Dark** **Fighting**

● FOOTPRINT

● MALE/FEMALE HAVE SAME FORM

- HEIGHT: 3'07"
- WEIGHT: 66.1 lbs.
- GENDER: Both ♂♀ exist
- ITEMS:
  • None

POKÉMON BLACK VERSION
Groups of them beat up anything that enters their territory. Each can spit acidic liquid from its mouth.

POKÉMON WHITE VERSION
It can smash concrete blocks with its kicking attacks. The one with the biggest crest is the group leader.

EVOLUTION

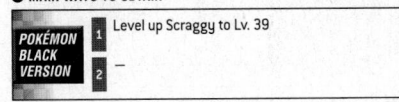

Scraggy → Lv. 39 → Scrafty

ABILITIES
● Shed Skin
● Moxie

EGG GROUPS
Field
Dragon

STATS
- HP ●●
- ATTACK ●●●●
- DEFENSE ●●●●●
- SP. ATTACK ●●●
- SP. DEFENSE ●●●●●
- SPEED ●●●

● MAIN WAYS TO OBTAIN

POKÉMON BLACK VERSION
1 Level up Scraggy to Lv. 39
2 –

POKÉMON WHITE VERSION
1 Level up Scraggy to Lv. 39
2 –

Unova Pokédex ⬡ 067 | Avianoid Pokémon

Sigilyph

● LEVEL-UP AND LEARNED MOVES

Lv.	Name	Type	Kind	Pow.	Acc.	PP	Range	Long	DA
1	Gust	Flying	Special	40	100	35	Normal	○	–
1	Miracle Eye	Psychic	Status	–	–	40	Normal	–	–
4	Hypnosis	Psychic	Status	–	60	20	Normal	–	–
8	Psywave	Psychic	Special	–	80	15	Normal	–	–
11	Tailwind	Flying	Status	–	–	30	Your Side	–	–
14	Whirlwind	Normal	Status	–	100	20	Normal	–	–
18	Psybeam	Psychic	Special	65	100	20	Normal	–	–
21	Air Cutter	Flying	Special	55	95	25	Many Others	–	–
24	Light Screen	Psychic	Status	–	–	30	Your Side	–	–
28	Reflect	Psychic	Status	–	–	20	Your Side	–	–
31	Synchronoise	Psychic	Special	70	100	15	Adjacent	–	–
34	Mirror Move	Flying	Status	–	–	20	Normal	–	–
38	Gravity	Psychic	Status	–	–	5	Both Sides	–	–
41	Air Slash	Flying	Special	75	95	20	Normal	○	–
44	Psychic	Psychic	Special	90	100	10	Normal	–	–
48	Cosmic Power	Psychic	Status	–	–	20	Self	–	–
51	Sky Attack	Flying	Physical	140	90	5	Normal	–	–

● MOVES TAUGHT BY PEOPLE

Name	Type	Kind	Pow.	Acc.	PP	Range	Long	DA

● EGG MOVES

Name	Type	Kind	Pow.	Acc.	PP	Range	Long	DA
Stored Power	Psychic	Special	20	100	10	Normal	–	–
Psycho Shift	Psychic	Status	–	90	10	Normal	–	–
AncientPower	Rock	Special	60	100	5	Normal	–	○
Steel Wing	Steel	Physical	70	90	25	Normal	–	–
Roost	Flying	Status	–	–	10	Self	–	–
Skill Swap	Psychic	Status	–	–	10	Normal	–	–

● TM & HM MOVES

No.	Name	Type	Kind	Pow.	Acc.	PP	Range	Long	DA
TM03	Psyshock	Psychic	Special	80	100	10	Normal	–	–
TM04	Calm Mind	Psychic	Status	–	–	20	Self	–	–
TM06	Toxic	Poison	Status	–	90	10	Normal	–	–
TM10	Hidden Power	Normal	Special	–	100	15	Normal	–	–
TM13	Ice Beam	Ice	Special	95	100	10	Normal	–	–
TM15	Hyper Beam	Normal	Special	150	90	5	Normal	–	–
TM16	Light Screen	Psychic	Status	–	–	30	Your Side	–	–
TM17	Protect	Normal	Status	–	–	10	Self	–	–
TM18	Rain Dance	Water	Status	–	–	5	Both Sides	–	–
TM19	Telekinesis	Psychic	Status	–	–	15	Normal	–	–
TM20	Safeguard	Normal	Status	–	–	25	Your Side	–	–
TM21	Frustration	Normal	Physical	–	100	20	Normal	–	○
TM22	SolarBeam	Grass	Special	120	100	10	Normal	–	–
TM23	Smack Down	Rock	Physical	50	100	15	Normal	–	–
TM27	Return	Normal	Physical	–	100	20	Normal	–	○
TM29	Psychic	Psychic	Special	90	100	10	Normal	–	–
TM30	Shadow Ball	Ghost	Special	80	100	15	Normal	–	–
TM32	Double Team	Normal	Status	–	–	15	Self	–	–
TM33	Reflect	Psychic	Status	–	–	20	Your Side	–	–
TM40	Aerial Ace	Flying	Physical	60	–	20	Normal	○	○
TM42	Facade	Normal	Physical	70	100	20	Normal	–	–
TM44	Rest	Psychic	Status	–	–	10	Self	–	–
TM45	Attract	Normal	Status	–	100	15	Normal	–	–
TM46	Thief	Dark	Physical	40	100	10	Normal	–	○
TM48	Round	Normal	Special	60	100	15	Normal	–	–
TM53	Energy Ball	Grass	Special	80	100	10	Normal	–	–
TM57	Charge Beam	Electric	Special	50	90	10	Normal	–	–
TM70	Flash	Normal	Status	–	100	20	Normal	–	–
TM73	Thunder Wave	Electric	Status	–	100	20	Normal	–	–
TM77	Psych Up	Normal	Status	–	–	10	Self	–	–
TM85	Dream Eater	Psychic	Special	100	100	15	Normal	–	–
TM87	Swagger	Normal	Status	–	90	15	Normal	–	–
TM88	Pluck	Flying	Physical	60	100	20	Normal	○	–
TM90	Substitute	Normal	Status	–	–	10	Self	–	–
TM91	Flash Cannon	Steel	Special	80	100	10	Normal	–	–
TM92	Trick Room	Psychic	Status	–	–	5	Both Sides	–	–
HM02	Fly	Flying	Physical	90	95	15	Normal	○	–

● TYPE **Psychic** **Flying**

● FOOTPRINT

● MALE/FEMALE HAVE SAME FORM

- HEIGHT: 4'07"
- WEIGHT: 30.9 lbs.
- GENDER: Both ♂♀ exist
- ITEMS:
  • None

POKÉMON BLACK VERSION
They never vary the route they fly, because their memories of guarding an ancient city remain steadfast.

POKÉMON WHITE VERSION
The guardians of an ancient city, they use their psychic power to attack enemies that invade their territory.

EVOLUTION

Does not evolve

ABILITIES
● Wonder Skin
● Magic Guard

EGG GROUP
Flying

STATS
- HP ●●●
- ATTACK ●●
- DEFENSE ●●●
- SP. ATTACK ●●●●●
- SP. DEFENSE ●●●
- SPEED ●●●●

● MAIN WAYS TO OBTAIN

POKÉMON BLACK VERSION
1 Desert Resort Back
2 –

POKÉMON WHITE VERSION
1 Desert Resort Back
2 –

Yamask

● TYPE Ghost

● HEIGHT: 1'08"
● WEIGHT: 3.3 lbs.
● GENDER: Both ♂♀ exist
● ITEMS:
• Spell Tag

● MALE/FEMALE HAVE SAME FORM

POKÉMON BLACK VERSION
Each of them carries a mask that used to be its face when it was human. Sometimes they look at it and cry.

POKÉMON WHITE VERSION
These Pokémon arose from the spirits of people interred in graves in past ages. Each retains memories of its former life.

● LEVEL-UP AND LEARNED MOVES

Lv.	Name	Type	Kind	Pow.	Acc.	PP	Range	Long	DA
1	Astonish	Ghost	Physical	30	100	15	Normal	—	○
1	Protect	Normal	Status	—	—	10	Self	—	—
5	Disable	Normal	Status	—	100	20	Normal	—	—
9	Haze	Ice	Status	—	—	30	Both Sides	—	—
13	Night Shade	Ghost	Special	—	100	15	Normal	—	—
17	Hex	Ghost	Special	50	100	10	Normal	—	—
21	Will-O-Wisp	Fire	Status	—	75	15	Normal	—	—
25	Ominous Wind	Ghost	Special	60	100	5	Normal	—	—
29	Curse	Ghost	Status	—	—	10	Varies	—	—
33	Power Split	Psychic	Status	—	—	10	Normal	—	—
33	Guard Split	Psychic	Status	—	—	10	Normal	—	—
37	Shadow Ball	Ghost	Special	80	100	15	Normal	—	—
41	Grudge	Ghost	Status	—	—	5	Self	—	—
45	Mean Look	Normal	Status	—	—	5	Normal	—	—
49	Destiny Bond	Ghost	Status	—	—	5	Self	—	—

● MOVES TAUGHT BY PEOPLE

Name	Type	Kind	Pow.	Acc.	PP	Range	Long	DA

● EGG MOVES

Name	Type	Kind	Pow.	Acc.	PP	Range	Long	DA
Memento	Dark	Status	—	100	10	Normal	—	—
Fake Tears	Dark	Status	—	100	20	Normal	—	—
Nasty Plot	Dark	Status	—	—	20	Self	—	—
Endure	Normal	Status	—	—	10	Self	—	—
Heal Block	Psychic	Status	—	100	15	Many Others	—	—
Imprison	Psychic	Status	—	—	10	Self	—	—
Nightmare	Ghost	Status	—	100	15	Normal	—	—
Disable	Normal	Status	—	100	20	Normal	—	—

● TM & HM MOVES

No.	Name	Type	Kind	Pow.	Acc.	PP	Range	Long	DA
TM04	Calm Mind	Psychic	Status	—	—	20	Self	—	—
TM06	Toxic	Poison	Status	—	90	10	Normal	—	—
TM10	Hidden Power	Normal	Special	—	100	15	Normal	—	—
TM17	Protect	Normal	Status	—	—	10	Self	—	—
TM18	Rain Dance	Water	Status	—	—	5	Both Sides	—	—
TM19	Telekinesis	Psychic	Status	—	—	15	Normal	—	—
TM20	Safeguard	Normal	Status	—	—	25	Your Side	—	—
TM21	Frustration	Normal	Physical	—	100	20	Normal	—	○
TM27	Return	Normal	Physical	—	100	20	Normal	—	○
TM29	Psychic	Psychic	Special	90	100	10	Normal	—	—
TM30	Shadow Ball	Ghost	Special	80	100	15	Normal	—	—
TM32	Double Team	Normal	Status	—	—	15	Self	—	—
TM42	Facade	Normal	Physical	70	100	20	Normal	—	○
TM44	Rest	Psychic	Status	—	—	10	Self	—	—
TM45	Attract	Normal	Status	—	100	15	Normal	—	—
TM46	Thief	Dark	Physical	40	100	10	Normal	—	○
TM48	Round	Normal	Special	60	100	15	Normal	—	—
TM53	Energy Ball	Grass	Special	80	100	10	Normal	—	—
TM61	Will-O-Wisp	Fire	Status	—	75	15	Normal	—	—
TM63	Embargo	Dark	Status	—	100	15	Normal	—	—
TM66	Payback	Dark	Physical	50	100	10	Normal	—	○
TM70	Flash	Normal	Status	—	100	20	Normal	—	—
TM77	Psych Up	Normal	Status	—	—	10	Normal	—	—
TM85	Dream Eater	Psychic	Special	100	100	15	Normal	—	—
TM87	Swagger	Normal	Status	—	90	15	Normal	—	—
TM90	Substitute	Normal	Status	—	—	10	Self	—	—
TM92	Trick Room	Psychic	Status	—	—	5	Both Sides	—	—

● EVOLUTION

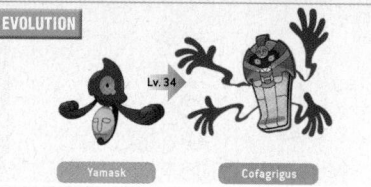

Yamask → (Lv. 34) → Cofagrigus

● ABILITY ● Mummy

● EGG GROUPS: Mineral / Amorphous

● STATS
HP ●
ATTACK ●●
DEFENSE ●●●
SP. ATTACK ●●
SP. DEFENSE ●●
SPEED ●

● MAIN WAYS TO OBTAIN

POKÉMON BLACK VERSION
1 Relic Castle 1F
2 Relic Castle Tower 1F

POKÉMON WHITE VERSION
1 Relic Castle 1F
2 Relic Castle Tower 1F

Cofagrigus

● TYPE Ghost

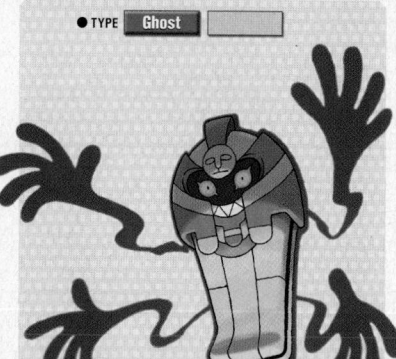

● HEIGHT: 5'07"
● WEIGHT: 168.7 lbs.
● GENDER: Both ♂♀ exist
● ITEMS:
• Spell Tag

● MALE/FEMALE HAVE SAME FORM

POKÉMON BLACK VERSION
It has been said that they swallow those who get too close and turn them into mummies. They like to eat gold nuggets.

POKÉMON WHITE VERSION
They pretend to be elaborate coffins to teach lessons to grave robbers. Their bodies are covered in pure gold.

● LEVEL-UP AND LEARNED MOVES

Lv.	Name	Type	Kind	Pow.	Acc.	PP	Range	Long	DA
1	Astonish	Ghost	Physical	30	100	15	Normal	—	○
1	Protect	Normal	Status	—	—	10	Self	—	—
1	Disable	Normal	Status	—	100	20	Normal	—	—
1	Haze	Ice	Status	—	—	30	Both Sides	—	—
5	Disable	Normal	Status	—	100	20	Normal	—	—
9	Haze	Ice	Status	—	—	30	Both Sides	—	—
13	Night Shade	Ghost	Special	—	100	15	Normal	—	—
17	Hex	Ghost	Special	50	100	10	Normal	—	—
21	Will-O-Wisp	Fire	Status	—	75	15	Normal	—	—
25	Ominous Wind	Ghost	Special	60	100	5	Normal	—	—
29	Curse	Ghost	Status	—	—	10	Varies	—	—
33	Power Split	Psychic	Status	—	—	10	Normal	—	—
33	Guard Split	Psychic	Status	—	—	10	Normal	—	—
34	Scary Face	Normal	Status	—	100	10	Normal	—	—
39	Shadow Ball	Ghost	Special	80	100	15	Normal	—	—
45	Grudge	Ghost	Status	—	—	5	Self	—	—
51	Mean Look	Normal	Status	—	—	5	Normal	—	—
57	Destiny Bond	Ghost	Status	—	—	5	Self	—	—

● MOVES TAUGHT BY PEOPLE

Name	Type	Kind	Pow.	Acc.	PP	Range	Long	DA

● TM & HM MOVES

No.	Name	Type	Kind	Pow.	Acc.	PP	Range	Long	DA
TM04	Calm Mind	Psychic	Status	—	—	20	Self	—	—
TM06	Toxic	Poison	Status	—	90	10	Normal	—	—
TM10	Hidden Power	Normal	Special	—	100	15	Normal	—	—
TM15	Hyper Beam	Normal	Special	150	90	5	Normal	—	—
TM17	Protect	Normal	Status	—	—	10	Self	—	—
TM18	Rain Dance	Water	Status	—	—	5	Both Sides	—	—
TM19	Telekinesis	Psychic	Status	—	—	15	Normal	—	—
TM20	Safeguard	Normal	Status	—	—	25	Your Side	—	—
TM21	Frustration	Normal	Physical	—	100	20	Normal	—	○
TM27	Return	Normal	Physical	—	100	20	Normal	—	○
TM29	Psychic	Psychic	Special	90	100	10	Normal	—	—
TM30	Shadow Ball	Ghost	Special	80	100	15	Normal	—	—
TM32	Double Team	Normal	Status	—	—	15	Self	—	—
TM42	Facade	Normal	Physical	70	100	20	Normal	—	○
TM44	Rest	Psychic	Status	—	—	10	Self	—	—
TM45	Attract	Normal	Status	—	100	15	Normal	—	—
TM46	Thief	Dark	Physical	40	100	10	Your Side	—	○
TM48	Round	Normal	Special	60	100	15	Normal	—	—
TM53	Energy Ball	Grass	Special	80	100	10	Normal	—	—
TM61	Will-O-Wisp	Fire	Status	—	75	15	Normal	—	—
TM63	Embargo	Dark	Status	—	100	15	Normal	—	—
TM66	Payback	Dark	Physical	50	100	10	Normal	—	○
TM68	Giga Impact	Normal	Physical	150	90	5	Normal	—	—
TM70	Flash	Normal	Status	—	100	20	Normal	—	—
TM77	Psych Up	Normal	Status	—	—	10	Normal	—	—
TM85	Dream Eater	Psychic	Special	100	100	15	Normal	—	—
TM86	Grass Knot	Grass	Special	—	100	20	Normal	—	—
TM87	Swagger	Normal	Status	—	90	15	Normal	—	—
TM90	Substitute	Normal	Status	—	—	10	Self	—	—
TM92	Trick Room	Psychic	Status	—	—	5	Both Sides	—	—

● EVOLUTION

Yamask → (Lv. 34) → Cofagrigus

● ABILITY ● Mummy

● EGG GROUPS: Mineral / Amorphous

● STATS
HP ●●
ATTACK ●●
DEFENSE ●●●●●
SP. ATTACK ●●●●
SP. DEFENSE ●●●●
SPEED ●

● MAIN WAYS TO OBTAIN

POKÉMON BLACK VERSION
1 Relic Castle B2F
2 Level up Yamask to Lv. 34

POKÉMON WHITE VERSION
1 Relic Castle B2F
2 Level up Yamask to Lv. 34

Tirtouga

● TYPE Water Rock

● LEVEL-UP AND LEARNED MOVES

Lv.	Name	Type	Kind	Pow.	Acc.	PP	Range	Long	DA
1	Bide	Normal	Physical	—	—	10	Self	—	—
1	Withdraw	Water	Status	—	—	40	Self	—	—
1	Water Gun	Water	Special	40	100	25	Normal	—	—
5	Rollout	Rock	Physical	30	90	20	Normal	—	○
8	Bite	Dark	Physical	60	100	25	Normal	—	○
11	Protect	Normal	Status	—	—	10	Self	—	—
15	Aqua Jet	Water	Physical	40	100	20	Normal	—	○
18	AncientPower	Rock	Special	60	100	5	Normal	—	○
21	Crunch	Dark	Physical	80	100	15	Normal	—	○
25	Wide Guard	Rock	Status	—	—	10	Your Side	—	—
28	Brine	Water	Special	65	100	10	Normal	—	—
31	Smack Down	Rock	Physical	50	100	15	Normal	—	—
35	Curse	Ghost	Status	—	—	10	Varies	—	—
38	Shell Smash	Normal	Status	—	—	15	Self	—	—
41	Aqua Tail	Water	Physical	90	90	10	Normal	—	—
45	Rock Slide	Rock	Physical	75	90	10	Many Others	—	—
48	Rain Dance	Water	Status	—	—	5	Both Sides	—	—
51	Hydro Pump	Water	Special	120	80	5	Normal	—	—

● MOVES TAUGHT BY PEOPLE

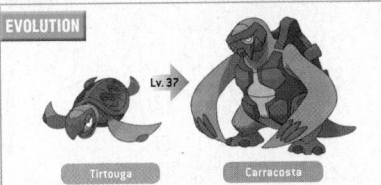

Name	Type	Kind	Pow.	Acc.	PP	Range	Long	DA

● EGG MOVES

Name	Type	Kind	Pow.	Acc.	PP	Range	Long	DA
Water Pulse	Water	Special	60	100	20	Normal	○	○
Knock Off	Dark	Physical	20	100	20	Normal	—	○
Rock Throw	Rock	Physical	50	90	15	Normal	—	—
Slam	Normal	Physical	80	75	20	Normal	—	—
Iron Defense	Steel	Status	—	—	15	Self	—	—
Flail	Normal	Physical	—	100	15	Normal	—	—
Whirlpool	Water	Special	35	85	15	Normal	—	—
Body Slam	Normal	Physical	85	100	15	Normal	—	—
Bide	Normal	Physical	—	—	10	Self	—	—

● TM & HM MOVES

No.	Name	Type	Kind	Pow.	Acc.	PP	Range	Long	DA
TM06	Toxic	Poison	Status	—	90	10	Normal	—	—
TM10	Hidden Power	Normal	Special	—	100	15	Normal	—	—
TM13	Ice Beam	Ice	Special	95	100	10	Normal	—	—
TM14	Blizzard	Ice	Special	120	70	5	Many Others	—	—
TM17	Protect	Normal	Status	—	—	10	Self	—	—
TM18	Rain Dance	Water	Status	—	—	5	Both Sides	—	—
TM21	Frustration	Normal	Physical	—	100	20	Normal	—	○
TM23	Smack Down	Rock	Physical	50	100	15	Normal	—	—
TM26	Earthquake	Ground	Physical	100	100	10	Adjacent	—	—
TM27	Return	Normal	Physical	—	100	20	Normal	—	○
TM28	Dig	Ground	Physical	80	100	10	Normal	—	○
TM32	Double Team	Normal	Status	—	—	15	Self	—	—
TM37	Sandstorm	Rock	Status	—	—	10	Both Sides	—	—
TM39	Rock Tomb	Rock	Physical	50	80	10	Normal	—	—
TM42	Facade	Normal	Physical	70	100	20	Normal	—	○
TM44	Rest	Psychic	Status	—	—	10	Self	—	—
TM45	Attract	Normal	Status	—	100	15	Normal	—	—
TM48	Round	Normal	Special	60	100	15	Normal	—	—
TM55	Scald	Water	Special	80	100	15	Normal	—	—
TM69	Rock Polish	Rock	Status	—	—	20	Self	—	—
TM71	Stone Edge	Rock	Physical	100	80	5	Normal	—	—
TM78	Bulldoze	Ground	Physical	60	100	20	Adjacent	—	—
TM80	Rock Slide	Rock	Physical	75	90	10	Many Others	—	—
TM87	Swagger	Normal	Status	—	90	15	Normal	—	—
TM90	Substitute	Normal	Status	—	—	10	Self	—	—
TM94	Rock Smash	Fighting	Physical	40	100	15	Normal	—	○
HM03	Surf	Water	Special	95	100	15	Adjacent	—	—
HM04	Strength	Normal	Physical	80	100	15	Normal	—	○
HM05	Waterfall	Water	Physical	80	100	15	Normal	—	○
HM06	Dive	Water	Physical	80	100	10	Normal	—	○

● HEIGHT: 2'04"
● WEIGHT: 36.4 lbs.
● GENDER: Both ♂♀ exist
● ITEMS:
 • None

● FOOTPRINT

● MALE/FEMALE HAVE SAME FORM

POKÉMON BLACK VERSION
Restored from a fossil, this Pokémon can dive to depths beyond half a mile.

POKÉMON WHITE VERSION
About 100 million years ago, these Pokémon swam in oceans. It is thought they also went on land to attack prey.

EVOLUTION

Lv. 37

Tirtouga → Carracosta

ABILITIES
● Solid Rock
● Sturdy

EGG GROUPS
Water 1
Water 3

STATS
HP ●●
ATTACK ●●●
DEFENSE ●●●●●
SP. ATTACK ●●
SP. DEFENSE ●●
SPEED ●

● MAIN WAYS TO OBTAIN

POKÉMON BLACK VERSION
1 Get the Cover Fossil in the Relic Castle and have it restored in the Nacrene Museum
2 —

POKÉMON WHITE VERSION
1 Get the Cover Fossil in the Relic Castle and have it restored in the Nacrene Museum
2 —

Carracosta

● TYPE Water Rock

● LEVEL-UP AND LEARNED MOVES

Lv.	Name	Type	Kind	Pow.	Acc.	PP	Range	Long	DA
1	Bide	Normal	Physical	—	—	10	Self	—	○
1	Withdraw	Water	Status	—	—	40	Self	—	—
1	Water Gun	Water	Special	40	100	25	Normal	—	—
1	Rollout	Rock	Physical	30	90	20	Normal	—	○
5	Rollout	Rock	Physical	30	90	20	Normal	—	○
8	Bite	Dark	Physical	60	100	25	Normal	—	○
11	Protect	Normal	Status	—	—	10	Self	—	—
15	Aqua Jet	Water	Physical	40	100	20	Normal	—	○
18	AncientPower	Rock	Special	60	100	5	Normal	—	○
21	Crunch	Dark	Physical	80	100	15	Normal	—	○
25	Wide Guard	Rock	Status	—	—	10	Your Side	—	—
28	Brine	Water	Special	65	100	10	Normal	—	—
31	Smack Down	Rock	Physical	50	100	15	Normal	—	—
35	Curse	Ghost	Status	—	—	10	Varies	—	—
40	Shell Smash	Normal	Status	—	—	15	Self	—	—
45	Aqua Tail	Water	Physical	90	90	10	Normal	—	—
51	Rock Slide	Rock	Physical	75	90	10	Many Others	—	—
56	Rain Dance	Water	Status	—	—	5	Both Sides	—	—
61	Hydro Pump	Water	Special	120	80	5	Normal	—	—

● MOVES TAUGHT BY PEOPLE

Name	Type	Kind	Pow.	Acc.	PP	Range	Long	DA

● TM & HM MOVES

No.	Name	Type	Kind	Pow.	Acc.	PP	Range	Long	DA
TM06	Toxic	Poison	Status	—	90	10	Normal	—	—
TM10	Hidden Power	Normal	Special	—	100	15	Normal	—	—
TM13	Ice Beam	Ice	Special	95	100	10	Normal	—	—
TM14	Blizzard	Ice	Special	120	70	5	Many Others	—	—
TM15	Hyper Beam	Normal	Special	150	90	5	Normal	—	—
TM17	Protect	Normal	Status	—	—	10	Self	—	—
TM18	Rain Dance	Water	Status	—	—	5	Both Sides	—	—
TM21	Frustration	Normal	Physical	—	100	20	Normal	—	○
TM23	Smack Down	Rock	Physical	50	100	15	Normal	—	—
TM26	Earthquake	Ground	Physical	100	100	10	Adjacent	—	—
TM27	Return	Normal	Physical	—	100	20	Normal	—	○
TM28	Dig	Ground	Physical	80	100	10	Normal	—	○
TM32	Double Team	Normal	Status	—	—	15	Self	—	—
TM37	Sandstorm	Rock	Status	—	—	10	Both Sides	—	—
TM39	Rock Tomb	Rock	Physical	50	80	10	Normal	—	—
TM42	Facade	Normal	Physical	70	100	20	Normal	—	○
TM44	Rest	Psychic	Status	—	—	10	Self	—	—
TM45	Attract	Normal	Status	—	100	15	Normal	—	—
TM48	Round	Normal	Special	60	100	15	Normal	—	—
TM52	Focus Blast	Fighting	Special	120	70	5	Normal	—	—
TM55	Scald	Water	Special	80	100	15	Normal	—	—
TM68	Giga Impact	Normal	Physical	150	90	5	Normal	—	—
TM69	Rock Polish	Rock	Status	—	—	20	Self	—	—
TM71	Stone Edge	Rock	Physical	100	80	5	Normal	—	—
TM78	Bulldoze	Ground	Physical	60	100	20	Adjacent	—	—
TM80	Rock Slide	Rock	Physical	75	90	10	Many Others	—	—
TM87	Swagger	Normal	Status	—	90	15	Normal	—	—
TM90	Substitute	Normal	Status	—	—	10	Self	—	—
TM94	Rock Smash	Fighting	Physical	40	100	15	Normal	—	○
HM03	Surf	Water	Special	95	100	15	Adjacent	—	—
HM04	Strength	Normal	Physical	80	100	15	Normal	—	○
HM05	Waterfall	Water	Physical	80	100	15	Normal	—	○
HM06	Dive	Water	Physical	80	100	10	Normal	—	○

● FOOTPRINT

● MALE/FEMALE HAVE SAME FORM

● HEIGHT: 3'11"
● WEIGHT: 178.6 lbs.
● GENDER: Both ♂♀ exist
● ITEMS:
 • None

POKÉMON BLACK VERSION
They can live both in the ocean and on land. A slap from one of them is enough to open a hole in the bottom of a tanker.

POKÉMON WHITE VERSION
Incredible jaw strength enables them to chew up steel beams and rocks along with their prey.

EVOLUTION

Lv. 37

Tirtouga → Carracosta

ABILITIES
● Solid Rock
● Sturdy

EGG GROUPS
Water 1
Water 3

STATS
HP ●●●
ATTACK ●●●
DEFENSE ●●●●●
SP. ATTACK ●●●
SP. DEFENSE ●●●
SPEED ●

● MAIN WAYS TO OBTAIN

POKÉMON BLACK VERSION
1 Level up Tirtouga to Lv. 37
2 —

POKÉMON WHITE VERSION
1 Level up Tirtouga to Lv. 37
2 —

Archen

● TYPE: Rock / Flying

● LEVEL-UP AND LEARNED MOVES

Lv.	Name	Type	Kind	Pow.	Acc.	PP	Range	Long	DA
1	Quick Attack	Normal	Physical	40	100	30	Normal	—	—
1	Leer	Normal	Status	—	100	30	Many Others	—	—
1	Wing Attack	Flying	Physical	60	100	35	Normal	○	—
4	Rock Throw	Rock	Physical	50	90	15	Normal	—	—
8	Double Team	Normal	Status	—	—	15	Self	—	—
11	Scary Face	Normal	Status	—	100	10	Normal	—	—
15	Pluck	Flying	Physical	60	100	20	Normal	○	○
18	AncientPower	Rock	Special	60	100	5	Normal	—	—
21	Agility	Psychic	Status	—	—	30	Self	—	—
25	Quick Guard	Fighting	Status	—	—	15	Your Side	—	—
28	Acrobatics	Flying	Physical	55	100	15	Normal	○	—
31	DragonBreath	Dragon	Special	60	100	20	Normal	—	—
35	Crunch	Dark	Physical	80	100	15	Normal	—	○
38	Endeavor	Normal	Physical	—	100	5	Normal	—	○
41	U-turn	Bug	Physical	70	100	20	Normal	—	—
45	Rock Slide	Rock	Physical	75	90	10	Many Others	—	—
48	Dragon Claw	Dragon	Physical	80	100	10	Normal	—	○
51	Thrash	Normal	Physical	120	100	10	1 Random	—	—

● MOVES TAUGHT BY PEOPLE

Name	Type	Kind	Pow.	Acc.	PP	Range	Long	DA

● EGG MOVES

Name	Type	Kind	Pow.	Acc.	PP	Range	Long	DA
Steel Wing	Steel	Physical	70	90	25	Normal	—	○
Defog	Flying	Status	—	—	15	Normal	—	○
Dragon Pulse	Dragon	Special	90	100	10	Normal	○	○
Head Smash	Rock	Physical	150	80	5	Normal	—	○
Knock Off	Dark	Physical	20	100	20	Normal	—	○
Earth Power	Ground	Special	90	100	10	Normal	—	○
Bite	Dark	Physical	60	100	25	Normal	—	○

● TM & HM MOVES

No.	Name	Type	Kind	Pow.	Acc.	PP	Range	Long	DA
TM01	Hone Claws	Dark	Status	—	—	15	Self	—	—
TM02	Dragon Claw	Dragon	Physical	80	100	15	Normal	—	○
TM05	Roar	Normal	Status	—	100	20	Normal	—	—
TM06	Toxic	Poison	Status	—	90	10	Normal	—	—
TM10	Hidden Power	Normal	Special	—	100	15	Normal	—	—
TM12	Taunt	Dark	Status	—	100	20	Normal	—	—
TM17	Protect	Normal	Status	—	—	10	Self	—	—
TM21	Frustration	Normal	Physical	—	100	20	Normal	—	○
TM23	Smack Down	Rock	Physical	50	100	15	Normal	—	—
TM26	Earthquake	Ground	Physical	100	100	10	Adjacent	—	—
TM27	Return	Normal	Physical	—	100	20	Normal	—	○
TM28	Dig	Ground	Physical	80	100	10	Normal	—	—
TM32	Double Team	Normal	Status	—	—	15	Self	—	—
TM37	Sandstorm	Rock	Status	—	—	10	Both Sides	—	—
TM39	Rock Tomb	Rock	Physical	50	80	10	Normal	—	—
TM40	Aerial Ace	Flying	Physical	60	—	20	Normal	○	—
TM41	Torment	Dark	Status	—	100	15	Normal	—	—
TM42	Facade	Normal	Physical	70	100	20	Normal	—	—
TM44	Rest	Psychic	Status	—	—	10	Self	—	—
TM45	Attract	Normal	Status	—	100	15	Normal	—	—
TM48	Round	Normal	Special	60	100	15	Normal	—	—
TM62	Acrobatics	Flying	Physical	55	100	15	Normal	○	—
TM65	Shadow Claw	Ghost	Physical	70	100	15	Normal	—	○
TM69	Rock Polish	Rock	Status	—	—	20	Self	—	—
TM71	Stone Edge	Rock	Physical	100	80	5	Normal	—	—
TM78	Bulldoze	Ground	Physical	60	100	20	Adjacent	—	—
TM80	Rock Slide	Rock	Physical	75	90	10	Many Others	—	—
TM87	Swagger	Normal	Status	—	90	15	Normal	—	—
TM88	Pluck	Flying	Physical	60	100	20	Normal	○	○
TM89	U-turn	Bug	Physical	70	100	20	Normal	—	—
TM90	Substitute	Normal	Status	—	—	10	Self	—	—
TM94	Rock Smash	Fighting	Physical	40	100	15	Normal	—	○
HM01	Cut	Normal	Physical	50	95	30	Normal	—	—

● FOOTPRINT

● MALE/FEMALE HAVE SAME FORM

● HEIGHT: 1'08"
● WEIGHT: 20.9 lbs.
● GENDER: Both ♂♀ exist
● ITEMS:
• None

POKÉMON BLACK VERSION
Said to be an ancestor of bird Pokémon, they were unable to fly and moved about by hopping from one branch to another.

POKÉMON WHITE VERSION
Revived from a fossil, this Pokémon is thought to be the ancestor of all bird Pokémon.

● EVOLUTION

Archen → Lv. 37 → Archeops

ABILITY ● Defeatist

EGG GROUPS: Flying / Water 3

STATS
HP ●●
ATTACK ●●●●●
DEFENSE ●●
SP. ATTACK ●●●
SP. DEFENSE ●●
SPEED ●●●

● MAIN WAYS TO OBTAIN

POKÉMON BLACK VERSION
1 Get the Plume Fossil in the Relic Castle and have it restored in the Nacrene Museum
2 —

POKÉMON WHITE VERSION
1 Get the Plume Fossil in the Relic Castle and have it restored in the Nacrene Museum
2 —

Archeops

● TYPE: Rock / Flying

● LEVEL-UP AND LEARNED MOVES

Lv.	Name	Type	Kind	Pow.	Acc.	PP	Range	Long	DA
1	Quick Attack	Normal	Physical	40	100	30	Normal	—	—
1	Leer	Normal	Status	—	100	30	Many Others	—	—
1	Wing Attack	Flying	Physical	60	100	35	Normal	○	—
1	Rock Throw	Rock	Physical	50	90	15	Normal	—	—
5	Rock Throw	Rock	Physical	50	90	15	Normal	—	—
8	Double Team	Normal	Status	—	—	15	Self	—	—
11	Scary Face	Normal	Status	—	100	10	Normal	—	—
15	Pluck	Flying	Physical	60	100	20	Normal	○	○
18	AncientPower	Rock	Special	60	100	5	Normal	—	—
21	Agility	Psychic	Status	—	—	30	Self	—	—
25	Quick Guard	Fighting	Status	—	—	15	Your Side	—	—
28	Acrobatics	Flying	Physical	55	100	15	Normal	○	—
31	DragonBreath	Dragon	Special	60	100	20	Normal	—	—
35	Crunch	Dark	Physical	80	100	15	Normal	—	○
40	Endeavor	Normal	Physical	—	100	5	Normal	—	○
45	U-turn	Bug	Physical	70	100	20	Normal	—	—
51	Rock Slide	Rock	Physical	75	90	10	Many Others	—	—
56	Dragon Claw	Dragon	Physical	80	100	10	Normal	—	○
61	Thrash	Normal	Physical	120	100	10	1 Random	—	—

● MOVES TAUGHT BY PEOPLE

Name	Type	Kind	Pow.	Acc.	PP	Range	Long	DA

● TM & HM MOVES

No.	Name	Type	Kind	Pow.	Acc.	PP	Range	Long	DA
TM01	Hone Claws	Dark	Status	—	—	15	Self	—	—
TM02	Dragon Claw	Dragon	Physical	80	100	15	Normal	—	○
TM05	Roar	Normal	Status	—	100	20	Normal	—	—
TM06	Toxic	Poison	Status	—	90	10	Normal	—	—
TM10	Hidden Power	Normal	Special	—	100	15	Normal	—	—
TM12	Taunt	Dark	Status	—	100	20	Normal	—	—
TM15	Hyper Beam	Normal	Special	150	90	5	Normal	—	—
TM17	Protect	Normal	Status	—	—	10	Self	—	—
TM21	Frustration	Normal	Physical	—	100	20	Normal	—	○
TM23	Smack Down	Rock	Physical	50	100	15	Normal	—	—
TM26	Earthquake	Ground	Physical	100	100	10	Adjacent	—	—
TM27	Return	Normal	Physical	—	100	20	Normal	—	○
TM28	Dig	Ground	Physical	80	100	10	Normal	—	—
TM32	Double Team	Normal	Status	—	—	15	Self	—	—
TM37	Sandstorm	Rock	Status	—	—	10	Both Sides	—	—
TM39	Rock Tomb	Rock	Physical	50	80	10	Normal	—	—
TM40	Aerial Ace	Flying	Physical	60	—	20	Normal	○	—
TM41	Torment	Dark	Status	—	100	15	Normal	—	—
TM42	Facade	Normal	Physical	70	100	20	Normal	—	—
TM44	Rest	Psychic	Status	—	—	10	Self	—	—
TM45	Attract	Normal	Status	—	100	15	Normal	—	—
TM48	Round	Normal	Special	60	100	15	Normal	—	—
TM52	Focus Blast	Fighting	Special	120	70	5	Normal	—	—
TM62	Acrobatics	Flying	Physical	55	100	15	Normal	○	—
TM65	Shadow Claw	Ghost	Physical	70	100	15	Normal	—	○
TM68	Giga Impact	Normal	Physical	150	90	5	Normal	—	—
TM69	Rock Polish	Rock	Status	—	—	20	Self	—	—
TM71	Stone Edge	Rock	Physical	100	80	5	Normal	—	—
TM78	Bulldoze	Ground	Physical	60	100	20	Adjacent	—	—
TM80	Rock Slide	Rock	Physical	75	90	10	Many Others	—	—
TM82	Dragon Tail	Dragon	Physical	60	90	10	Normal	—	—
TM87	Swagger	Normal	Status	—	90	15	Normal	—	—
TM88	Pluck	Flying	Physical	60	100	20	Normal	○	○
TM89	U-turn	Bug	Physical	70	100	20	Normal	—	—
TM90	Substitute	Normal	Status	—	—	10	Self	—	—
TM94	Rock Smash	Fighting	Physical	40	100	15	Normal	—	○
HM01	Cut	Normal	Physical	50	95	30	Normal	—	—
HM02	Fly	Flying	Physical	90	95	15	Normal	—	—

● FOOTPRINT

● MALE/FEMALE HAVE SAME FORM

● HEIGHT: 4'07"
● WEIGHT: 70.5 lbs.
● GENDER: Both ♂♀ exist
● ITEMS:
• None

POKÉMON BLACK VERSION
They are intelligent and will cooperate to catch prey. From the ground, they use a running start to take flight.

POKÉMON WHITE VERSION
It runs better than it flies. It catches prey by running at speeds comparable to those of an automobile.

● EVOLUTION

Archen → Lv. 37 → Archeops

ABILITY ● Defeatist

EGG GROUPS: Flying / Water 3

STATS
HP ●●●
ATTACK ●●●●●●
DEFENSE ●●●
SP. ATTACK ●●●●●
SP. DEFENSE ●●
SPEED ●●●●●

● MAIN WAYS TO OBTAIN

POKÉMON BLACK VERSION
1 Level up Archen to Lv. 37
2 —

POKÉMON WHITE VERSION
1 Level up Archen to Lv. 37
2 —

Trubbish

● TYPE Poison

● HEIGHT: 2'00"
● WEIGHT: 68.3 lbs.
● GENDER: Both ♂♀ exist
● ITEMS:
• Black Sludge
• Nugget

● FOOTPRINT

● MALE/FEMALE HAVE SAME FORM

● LEVEL-UP AND LEARNED MOVES

Lv.	Name	Type	Kind	Pow.	Acc.	PP	Range	Long	DA
1	Pound	Normal	Physical	40	100	35	Normal	—	○
1	Poison Gas	Poison	Status	—	80	40	Many Others	—	—
3	Recycle	Normal	Status	—	—	10	Self	—	—
7	Toxic Spikes	Poison	Status	—	—	20	Other Side	—	—
12	Acid Spray	Poison	Special	40	100	20	Normal	—	—
14	DoubleSlap	Normal	Physical	15	85	10	Normal	—	○
18	Sludge	Poison	Special	65	100	20	Normal	—	—
23	Stockpile	Normal	Status	—	—	20	Self	—	—
23	Swallow	Normal	Status	—	—	10	Self	—	—
25	Take Down	Normal	Physical	90	85	20	Normal	—	○
29	Sludge Bomb	Poison	Special	90	100	10	Normal	—	—
34	Clear Smog	Poison	Special	50	—	15	Normal	—	—
36	Toxic	Poison	Status	—	90	10	Normal	—	—
40	Amnesia	Psychic	Status	—	—	20	Self	—	—
45	Gunk Shot	Poison	Physical	120	70	5	Normal	—	—
47	Explosion	Normal	Physical	250	100	5	Adjacent	—	—

● MOVES TAUGHT BY PEOPLE

Name	Type	Kind	Pow.	Acc.	PP	Range	Long	DA

● EGG MOVES

Name	Type	Kind	Pow.	Acc.	PP	Range	Long	DA
Spikes	Ground	Status	—	—	20	Other Side	—	—
Rollout	Rock	Physical	30	90	20	Normal	—	○
Haze	Ice	Status	—	—	30	Both Sides	—	—
Curse	Ghost	Status	—	—	10	Varies	—	—
Rock Blast	Rock	Physical	25	90	10	Normal	—	—
Sand-Attack	Ground	Status	—	100	15	Normal	—	—
Mud Sport	Ground	Status	—	—	15	Both Sides	—	—
Selfdestruct	Normal	Physical	200	100	5	Adjacent	—	—

● TM & HM MOVES

No.	Name	Type	Kind	Pow.	Acc.	PP	Range	Long	DA
TM06	Toxic	Poison	Status	—	90	10	Normal	—	—
TM09	Venoshock	Poison	Special	65	100	10	Normal	—	—
TM10	Hidden Power	Normal	Special	—	100	15	Normal	—	—
TM11	Sunny Day	Fire	Status	—	—	5	Both Sides	—	—
TM17	Protect	Normal	Status	—	—	10	Self	—	—
TM18	Rain Dance	Water	Status	—	—	5	Both Sides	—	—
TM21	Frustration	Normal	Physical	—	100	20	Normal	—	○
TM27	Return	Normal	Physical	—	100	20	Normal	—	○
TM32	Double Team	Normal	Status	—	—	15	Self	—	—
TM34	Sludge Wave	Poison	Special	95	100	10	Adjacent	—	—
TM36	Sludge Bomb	Poison	Special	90	100	10	Normal	—	—
TM42	Facade	Normal	Physical	70	100	20	Normal	—	○
TM44	Rest	Psychic	Status	—	—	10	Self	—	—
TM45	Attract	Normal	Status	—	100	15	Normal	—	—
TM46	Thief	Dark	Physical	40	100	10	Normal	—	○
TM48	Round	Normal	Special	60	100	15	Normal	—	—
TM64	Explosion	Normal	Physical	250	100	5	Adjacent	—	—
TM66	Payback	Dark	Physical	50	100	10	Normal	—	○
TM87	Swagger	Normal	Status	—	90	15	Normal	—	—
TM90	Substitute	Normal	Status	—	—	10	Self	—	—

EVOLUTION

Trubbish → Lv. 36 → Garbodor

ABILITIES
● Stench
● Sticky Hold

EGG GROUP
Mineral

STATS
HP ●●
ATTACK ●●●
DEFENSE ●●●
SP. ATTACK ●●
SP. DEFENSE ●●
SPEED ●●●

● MAIN WAYS TO OBTAIN

POKÉMON BLACK VERSION	1	Route 16
	2	Route 5

POKÉMON WHITE VERSION	1	Route 16
	2	Route 5

POKÉMON BLACK VERSION: Inhaling the gas they belch will make you sleep for a week. They prefer unsanitary places.

POKÉMON WHITE VERSION: The combination of garbage bags and industrial waste caused the chemical reaction that created this Pokémon.

Garbodor

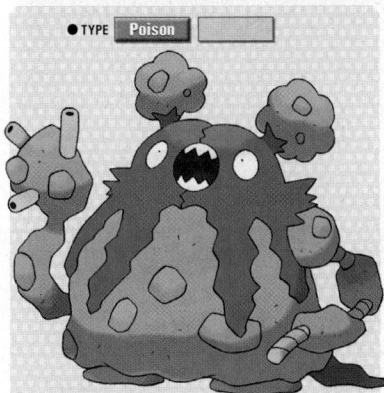

● TYPE Poison

● HEIGHT: 6'03"
● WEIGHT: 236.6 lbs.
● GENDER: Both ♂♀ exist
● ITEMS:
• Black Sludge
• Nugget
• Big Nugget

● FOOTPRINT

● MALE/FEMALE HAVE SAME FORM

● LEVEL-UP AND LEARNED MOVES

Lv.	Name	Type	Kind	Pow.	Acc.	PP	Range	Long	DA
1	Pound	Normal	Physical	40	100	35	Normal	—	○
1	Poison Gas	Poison	Status	—	80	40	Many Others	—	—
1	Recycle	Normal	Status	—	—	10	Self	—	—
1	Toxic Spikes	Poison	Status	—	—	20	Other Side	—	—
3	Recycle	Normal	Status	—	—	10	Self	—	—
7	Toxic Spikes	Poison	Status	—	—	20	Other Side	—	—
12	Acid Spray	Poison	Special	40	100	20	Normal	—	—
14	DoubleSlap	Normal	Physical	15	85	10	Normal	—	○
18	Sludge	Poison	Special	65	100	20	Normal	—	—
23	Stockpile	Normal	Status	—	—	20	Self	—	—
23	Swallow	Normal	Status	—	—	10	Self	—	—
25	Body Slam	Normal	Physical	85	100	15	Normal	—	○
29	Sludge Bomb	Poison	Special	90	100	10	Normal	—	—
34	Clear Smog	Poison	Special	50	—	15	Normal	—	—
39	Toxic	Poison	Status	—	90	10	Normal	—	—
46	Amnesia	Psychic	Status	—	—	20	Self	—	—
54	Gunk Shot	Poison	Physical	120	70	5	Normal	—	—
59	Explosion	Normal	Physical	250	100	5	Adjacent	—	—

● MOVES TAUGHT BY PEOPLE

Name	Type	Kind	Pow.	Acc.	PP	Range	Long	DA

● TM & HM MOVES

No.	Name	Type	Kind	Pow.	Acc.	PP	Range	Long	DA
TM06	Toxic	Poison	Status	—	90	10	Normal	—	—
TM09	Venoshock	Poison	Special	65	100	10	Normal	—	—
TM10	Hidden Power	Normal	Special	—	100	15	Normal	—	—
TM11	Sunny Day	Fire	Status	—	—	5	Both Sides	—	—
TM15	Hyper Beam	Normal	Special	150	90	5	Normal	—	—
TM17	Protect	Normal	Status	—	—	10	Self	—	—
TM18	Rain Dance	Water	Status	—	—	5	Both Sides	—	—
TM21	Frustration	Normal	Physical	—	100	20	Normal	—	○
TM22	SolarBeam	Grass	Special	120	100	15	Normal	—	—
TM23	Smack Down	Rock	Physical	50	100	15	Normal	—	—
TM24	Thunderbolt	Electric	Special	95	100	15	Normal	—	—
TM27	Return	Normal	Physical	—	100	20	Normal	—	○
TM29	Psychic	Psychic	Special	90	100	10	Normal	—	—
TM32	Double Team	Normal	Status	—	—	15	Self	—	—
TM34	Sludge Wave	Poison	Special	95	100	10	Adjacent	—	—
TM36	Sludge Bomb	Poison	Special	90	100	10	Normal	—	—
TM42	Facade	Normal	Physical	70	100	20	Normal	—	○
TM44	Rest	Psychic	Status	—	—	10	Self	—	—
TM45	Attract	Normal	Status	—	100	15	Normal	—	—
TM46	Thief	Dark	Physical	40	100	10	Normal	—	○
TM48	Round	Normal	Special	60	100	15	Normal	—	—
TM52	Focus Blast	Fighting	Special	120	70	5	Normal	—	—
TM56	Fling	Dark	Physical	—	100	10	Normal	—	○
TM64	Explosion	Normal	Physical	250	100	5	Adjacent	—	—
TM66	Payback	Dark	Physical	50	100	10	Normal	—	○
TM68	Giga Impact	Normal	Physical	150	90	5	Normal	—	○
TM69	Rock Polish	Rock	Status	—	—	20	Self	—	—
TM87	Swagger	Normal	Status	—	90	15	Normal	—	—
TM90	Substitute	Normal	Status	—	—	10	Self	—	—

EVOLUTION

Trubbish → Lv. 36 → Garbodor

ABILITIES
● Stench
● Weak Armor

EGG GROUP
Mineral

STATS
HP ●●●
ATTACK ●●●●
DEFENSE ●●●●
SP. ATTACK ●●●
SP. DEFENSE ●●●
SPEED ●●●

● MAIN WAYS TO OBTAIN

POKÉMON BLACK VERSION	1	Route 9
	2	Level up Trubbish to Lv. 36

POKÉMON WHITE VERSION	1	Route 9
	2	Level up Trubbish to Lv. 36

POKÉMON BLACK VERSION: It clenches opponents with its left arm and finishes them off with foul-smelling poison gas belched from its mouth.

POKÉMON WHITE VERSION: They absorb garbage and make it part of their bodies. They shoot a poisonous liquid from their right-hand fingertips.

Zorua

● TYPE Dark

● LEVEL-UP AND LEARNED MOVES

Lv.	Name	Type	Kind	Pow.	Acc.	PP	Range	Long	DA
1	Scratch	Normal	Physical	40	100	35	Normal	—	—
1	Leer	Normal	Status	—	100	30	Many Others	—	—
5	Pursuit	Dark	Physical	40	100	20	Normal	—	○
9	Fake Tears	Dark	Status	—	100	20	Normal	—	○
13	Fury Swipes	Normal	Physical	18	80	15	Normal	—	○
17	Faint Attack	Dark	Physical	60	—	20	Normal	—	○
21	Scary Face	Normal	Status	—	100	10	Normal	—	○
25	Taunt	Dark	Status	—	100	20	Normal	—	○
29	Foul Play	Dark	Physical	95	100	15	Normal	—	○
33	Torment	Dark	Status	—	100	15	Normal	—	○
37	Agility	Psychic	Status	—	—	30	Self	—	—
41	Embargo	Dark	Status	—	100	15	Normal	—	○
45	Punishment	Dark	Physical	—	100	5	Normal	—	○
49	Nasty Plot	Dark	Status	—	—	20	Self	—	—
53	Imprison	Psychic	Status	—	—	10	Self	—	—
57	Night Daze	Dark	Special	85	95	10	Normal	—	○

● MOVES TAUGHT BY PEOPLE

Name	Type	Kind	Pow.	Acc.	PP	Range	Long	DA

● EGG MOVES

Name	Type	Kind	Pow.	Acc.	PP	Range	Long	DA
Detect	Fighting	Status	—	—	5	Self	—	—
Captivate	Normal	Status	—	100	20	Many Others	—	—
Dark Pulse	Dark	Special	80	100	15	Normal	○	—
Snatch	Dark	Status	—	—	10	Self	—	—
Memento	Dark	Status	—	100	10	Normal	—	—
Sucker Punch	Dark	Physical	80	100	5	Normal	—	○
Extrasensory	Psychic	Special	80	100	30	Normal	—	○
Counter	Fighting	Physical	—	100	20	Varies	—	○

● TM & HM MOVES

No.	Name	Type	Kind	Pow.	Acc.	PP	Range	Long	DA
TM01	Hone Claws	Dark	Status	—	—	15	Self	—	—
TM04	Calm Mind	Psychic	Status	—	—	20	Self	—	—
TM05	Roar	Normal	Status	—	100	20	Normal	—	—
TM06	Toxic	Poison	Status	—	90	10	Normal	—	—
TM10	Hidden Power	Normal	Special	—	100	15	Normal	—	—
TM11	Sunny Day	Fire	Status	—	—	5	Both Sides	—	—
TM12	Taunt	Dark	Status	—	100	20	Normal	—	—
TM17	Protect	Normal	Status	—	—	10	Self	—	—
TM18	Rain Dance	Water	Status	—	—	5	Both Sides	—	—
TM21	Frustration	Normal	Physical	—	100	20	Normal	—	○
TM27	Return	Normal	Physical	—	100	20	Normal	—	○
TM28	Dig	Ground	Physical	80	100	10	Normal	—	○
TM30	Shadow Ball	Ghost	Special	80	100	15	Normal	—	○
TM32	Double Team	Normal	Status	—	—	15	Self	—	—
TM40	Aerial Ace	Flying	Physical	60	—	20	Normal	○	○
TM41	Torment	Dark	Status	—	100	15	Normal	—	—
TM42	Facade	Normal	Physical	70	100	20	Normal	—	○
TM44	Rest	Psychic	Status	—	—	10	Self	—	—
TM45	Attract	Normal	Status	—	100	15	Normal	—	—
TM46	Thief	Dark	Physical	40	100	10	Normal	—	○
TM48	Round	Normal	Special	60	100	15	Normal	—	○
TM56	Fling	Dark	Physical	—	100	10	Normal	—	○
TM59	Incinerate	Fire	Special	30	100	15	Many Others	—	—
TM63	Embargo	Dark	Status	—	100	15	Normal	—	—
TM66	Payback	Dark	Physical	50	100	10	Normal	—	○
TM67	Retaliate	Normal	Physical	70	100	5	Normal	—	○
TM75	Swords Dance	Normal	Status	—	—	30	Self	—	—
TM77	Psych Up	Normal	Status	—	—	10	Self	—	—
TM86	Grass Knot	Grass	Special	—	100	20	Normal	—	○
TM87	Swagger	Normal	Status	—	90	15	Normal	—	—
TM89	U-turn	Bug	Physical	70	100	20	Normal	—	○
TM90	Substitute	Normal	Status	—	←	10	Self	—	—
HM01	Cut	Normal	Physical	50	95	30	Normal	—	—

● FOOTPRINT

● MALE/FEMALE HAVE SAME FORM

● HEIGHT: 2'04"
● WEIGHT: 27.6 lbs.
● GENDER: Both ♂♀ exist
● ITEMS:
  • None

POKÉMON BLACK VERSION
It changes into the forms of others to surprise them. Apparently, it often transforms into a silent child.

POKÉMON WHITE VERSION
To protect themselves from danger, they hide their true identities by transforming into people and Pokémon.

EVOLUTION

Zorua — Lv. 30 → Zoroark

ABILITY ● Illusion

EGG GROUP Field

STATS
HP ●
ATTACK ●●●
DEFENSE ●●
SP. ATTACK ●●●●
SP. DEFENSE ●●
SPEED ●●●

● MAIN WAYS TO OBTAIN

POKÉMON BLACK VERSION
1 Cannot be obtained through regular gameplay ●
2 —

POKÉMON WHITE VERSION
1 Cannot be obtained through regular gameplay ●
2 —

● If you received Celebi during the latest distribution to *Pokémon Diamond, Pearl, Platinum, HeartGold,* and *SoulSilver Versions,* transfer it to *Pokémon Black Version* or *Pokémon White Version,* put it in your party, and go to GAME FREAK in Castelia City to let Zorua join your party.

Zoroark

● TYPE Dark

● LEVEL-UP AND LEARNED MOVES

Lv.	Name	Type	Kind	Pow.	Acc.	PP	Range	Long	DA
1	U-turn	Bug	Physical	70	100	20	Normal	—	○
1	Scratch	Normal	Physical	40	100	35	Normal	—	—
1	Leer	Normal	Status	—	100	30	Many Others	—	—
1	Pursuit	Dark	Physical	40	100	20	Normal	—	○
1	Hone Claws	Dark	Status	—	—	15	Self	—	—
5	Pursuit	Dark	Physical	40	100	20	Normal	—	○
9	Hone Claws	Dark	Status	—	—	15	Self	—	—
13	Fury Swipes	Normal	Physical	18	80	15	Normal	—	○
17	Faint Attack	Dark	Physical	60	—	20	Normal	—	○
21	Scary Face	Normal	Status	—	100	10	Normal	—	○
25	Taunt	Dark	Status	—	100	20	Normal	—	○
29	Foul Play	Dark	Physical	95	100	15	Normal	—	○
30	Night Slash	Dark	Physical	70	100	15	Normal	—	○
34	Torment	Dark	Status	—	100	15	Normal	—	○
39	Agility	Psychic	Status	—	—	30	Self	—	—
44	Embargo	Dark	Status	—	100	15	Normal	—	○
49	Punishment	Dark	Physical	—	100	5	Normal	—	○
54	Nasty Plot	Dark	Status	—	—	20	Self	—	—
59	Imprison	Psychic	Status	—	—	10	Self	—	—
64	Night Daze	Dark	Special	85	95	10	Normal	—	○

● MOVES TAUGHT BY PEOPLE

Name	Type	Kind	Pow.	Acc.	PP	Range	Long	DA

● TM & HM MOVES

No.	Name	Type	Kind	Pow.	Acc.	PP	Range	Long	DA
TM01	Hone Claws	Dark	Status	—	—	15	Self	—	—
TM04	Calm Mind	Psychic	Status	—	—	20	Self	—	—
TM05	Roar	Normal	Status	—	100	20	Normal	—	—
TM06	Toxic	Poison	Status	—	90	10	Normal	—	—
TM10	Hidden Power	Normal	Special	—	100	15	Normal	—	—
TM11	Sunny Day	Fire	Status	—	—	5	Both Sides	—	—
TM12	Taunt	Dark	Status	—	100	20	Normal	—	—
TM15	Hyper Beam	Normal	Special	150	90	5	Normal	—	—
TM17	Protect	Normal	Status	—	—	10	Self	—	—
TM18	Rain Dance	Water	Status	—	—	5	Both Sides	—	—
TM21	Frustration	Normal	Physical	—	100	20	Normal	—	○
TM27	Return	Normal	Physical	—	100	20	Normal	—	○
TM28	Dig	Ground	Physical	80	100	10	Normal	—	○
TM30	Shadow Ball	Ghost	Special	80	100	15	Normal	—	○
TM32	Double Team	Normal	Status	—	—	15	Self	—	—
TM35	Flamethrower	Fire	Special	95	100	15	Normal	—	○
TM40	Aerial Ace	Flying	Physical	60	—	20	Normal	○	○
TM41	Torment	Dark	Status	—	100	15	Normal	—	—
TM42	Facade	Normal	Physical	70	100	20	Normal	—	○
TM44	Rest	Psychic	Status	—	—	10	Self	—	—
TM45	Attract	Normal	Status	—	100	15	Normal	—	—
TM46	Thief	Dark	Physical	40	100	10	Normal	—	○
TM47	Low Sweep	Fighting	Physical	60	100	20	Normal	—	○
TM48	Round	Normal	Special	60	100	15	Normal	—	○
TM52	Focus Blast	Fighting	Special	120	70	5	Normal	—	○
TM56	Fling	Dark	Physical	—	100	10	Normal	—	○
TM59	Incinerate	Fire	Special	30	100	15	Many Others	—	—
TM63	Embargo	Dark	Status	—	100	15	Normal	—	—
TM65	Shadow Claw	Ghost	Physical	70	100	15	Normal	—	○
TM66	Payback	Dark	Physical	50	100	10	Normal	—	○
TM67	Retaliate	Normal	Physical	70	100	5	Normal	—	○
TM68	Giga Impact	Normal	Physical	150	90	5	Normal	—	○
TM75	Swords Dance	Normal	Status	—	—	30	Self	—	—
TM77	Psych Up	Normal	Status	—	—	10	Self	—	—
TM86	Grass Knot	Grass	Special	—	100	20	Normal	—	○
TM87	Swagger	Normal	Status	—	90	15	Normal	—	—
TM89	U-turn	Bug	Physical	70	100	20	Normal	—	○
TM90	Substitute	Normal	Status	—	—	10	Self	—	—
TM94	Rock Smash	Fighting	Physical	40	100	15	Normal	—	—
HM01	Cut	Normal	Physical	50	95	30	Normal	—	—

● TYPE Dark

● MALE/FEMALE HAVE SAME FORM

● FOOTPRINT

● HEIGHT: 5'03"
● WEIGHT: 178.8 lbs.
● GENDER: Both ♂♀ exist
● ITEMS:
  • None

POKÉMON BLACK VERSION
Bonds between these Pokémon are very strong. It protects the safety of its pack by tricking its opponents.

POKÉMON WHITE VERSION
Each has the ability to fool a large group of people simultaneously. They protect their lair with illusory scenery.

EVOLUTION

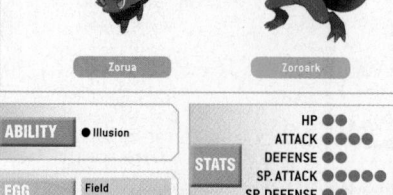

Zorua — Lv. 30 → Zoroark

ABILITY ● Illusion

EGG GROUP Field

STATS
HP ●●
ATTACK ●●●●
DEFENSE ●●
SP. ATTACK ●●●●●
SP. DEFENSE ●●
SPEED ●●●●●

● MAIN WAYS TO OBTAIN

POKÉMON BLACK VERSION
1 Cannot be obtained through regular gameplay ●
2 Level up Zorua to Lv. 30

POKÉMON WHITE VERSION
1 Cannot be obtained through regular gameplay ●
2 Level up Zorua to Lv. 30

● If you received the Shiny Entei, Raikou, or Suicune during the latest distribution to *Pokémon Diamond, Pearl, Platinum, HeartGold,* and *SoulSilver Versions,* transfer it to *Pokémon Black Version* or *Pokémon White Version,* put it in your party, and go to Lostlorn Forest to catch Zoroark.

Minccino

● TYPE **Normal**

● LEVEL-UP AND LEARNED MOVES

Lv.	Name	Type	Kind	Pow.	Acc.	PP	Range	Long	DA
1	Pound	Normal	Physical	40	100	35	Normal	—	○
3	Growl	Normal	Status	—	100	40	Many Others	—	—
7	Helping Hand	Normal	Status	—	—	20	1 Ally	—	—
9	Tickle	Normal	Status	—	100	20	Normal	—	—
13	DoubleSlap	Normal	Physical	15	85	10	Normal	—	—
15	Encore	Normal	Status	—	100	5	Normal	—	—
19	Swift	Normal	Special	60	—	20	Many Others	—	—
21	Sing	Normal	Status	—	55	15	Normal	—	—
25	Tail Slap	Normal	Physical	25	85	10	Normal	—	—
27	Charm	Normal	Status	—	100	20	Normal	—	—
31	Wake-Up Slap	Fighting	Physical	60	100	10	Normal	—	—
33	Echoed Voice	Normal	Special	40	100	15	Normal	—	—
37	Slam	Normal	Physical	80	75	20	Normal	—	—
39	Captivate	Normal	Status	—	100	20	Many Others	—	—
43	Hyper Voice	Normal	Special	90	100	10	Many Others	—	—
45	Last Resort	Normal	Physical	140	100	5	Normal	—	—
49	After You	Normal	Status	—	—	15	Normal	—	—

● MOVES TAUGHT BY PEOPLE

Name	Type	Kind	Pow.	Acc.	PP	Range	Long	DA

● EGG MOVES

Name	Type	Kind	Pow.	Acc.	PP	Range	Long	DA
Iron Tail	Steel	Physical	100	75	15	Normal	—	○
Tail Whip	Normal	Status	—	100	30	Many Others	—	—
Aqua Tail	Water	Physical	90	90	10	Normal	—	—
Mud-Slap	Ground	Special	20	100	10	Normal	—	—
Knock Off	Dark	Physical	20	100	20	Normal	—	—
Fake Tears	Dark	Status	—	100	20	Normal	—	—
Sleep Talk	Normal	Status	—	—	10	Self	—	—
Endure	Normal	Status	—	—	10	Self	—	—
Flail	Normal	Physical	—	100	15	Normal	—	—

● TM & HM MOVES

No.	Name	Type	Kind	Pow.	Acc.	PP	Range	Long	DA
TM04	Calm Mind	Psychic	Status	—	—	20	Self	—	—
TM06	Toxic	Poison	Status	—	90	10	Normal	—	—
TM10	Hidden Power	Normal	Special	—	100	15	Normal	—	—
TM11	Sunny Day	Fire	Status	—	—	5	Both Sides	—	—
TM17	Protect	Normal	Status	—	—	10	Self	—	—
TM18	Rain Dance	Water	Status	—	—	5	Both Sides	—	—
TM20	Safeguard	Normal	Status	—	—	25	Your Side	—	—
TM21	Frustration	Normal	Physical	—	100	20	Normal	—	○
TM24	Thunderbolt	Electric	Special	95	100	15	Normal	—	—
TM27	Return	Normal	Physical	—	100	20	Normal	—	○
TM28	Dig	Ground	Physical	80	100	10	Normal	—	○
TM32	Double Team	Normal	Status	—	—	15	Self	—	—
TM42	Facade	Normal	Physical	70	100	20	Normal	—	○
TM44	Rest	Psychic	Status	—	—	10	Self	—	—
TM45	Attract	Normal	Status	—	100	15	Normal	—	—
TM46	Thief	Dark	Physical	40	100	10	Normal	—	—
TM48	Round	Normal	Special	60	100	15	Normal	—	—
TM49	Echoed Voice	Normal	Special	40	100	15	Normal	—	—
TM56	Fling	Dark	Physical	—	100	10	Normal	—	—
TM67	Retaliate	Normal	Physical	70	100	5	Normal	—	○
TM73	Thunder Wave	Electric	Status	—	100	20	Normal	—	—
TM83	Work Up	Normal	Status	—	—	30	Self	—	—
TM86	Grass Knot	Grass	Special	—	100	20	Normal	—	○
TM87	Swagger	Normal	Status	—	90	15	Normal	—	—
TM89	U-turn	Bug	Physical	70	100	20	Normal	—	○
TM90	Substitute	Normal	Status	—	—	10	Self	—	—

● FOOTPRINT

● MALE/FEMALE HAVE SAME FORM

● HEIGHT: 1'04"
● WEIGHT: 12.8 lbs.
● GENDER: Both ♂♀ exist
● ITEMS:
• Chesto Berry

POKÉMON BLACK VERSION
They greet one another by rubbing each other with their tails, which are always kept well groomed and clean.

POKÉMON WHITE VERSION
These Pokémon prefer a tidy habitat. They are always sweeping and dusting, using their tails as brooms.

EVOLUTION

Use Shiny Stone

Minccino → Cinccino

ABILITIES
● Cute Charm
● Technician

EGG GROUP Field

STATS
HP ●●
ATTACK ●●
DEFENSE ●●
SP. ATTACK ●●
SP. DEFENSE ●●
SPEED ●●●

● MAIN WAYS TO OBTAIN

| POKÉMON BLACK VERSION | 1 | Route 16 |
| | 2 | Route 5 |

| POKÉMON WHITE VERSION | 1 | Route 16 |
| | 2 | Route 5 |

Cinccino

● TYPE **Normal**

● LEVEL-UP AND LEARNED MOVES

Lv.	Name	Type	Kind	Pow.	Acc.	PP	Range	Long	DA
1	Bullet Seed	Grass	Physical	25	100	30	Normal	—	—
1	Rock Blast	Rock	Physical	25	90	10	Normal	—	—
1	Helping Hand	Normal	Status	—	—	20	1 Ally	—	—
1	Tickle	Normal	Status	—	100	20	Normal	—	—
1	Sing	Normal	Status	—	55	15	Normal	—	—
1	Tail Slap	Normal	Physical	25	85	10	Normal	—	○

● MOVES TAUGHT BY PEOPLE

Name	Type	Kind	Pow.	Acc.	PP	Range	Long	DA

● TM & HM MOVES

No.	Name	Type	Kind	Pow.	Acc.	PP	Range	Long	DA
TM04	Calm Mind	Psychic	Status	—	—	20	Self	—	—
TM06	Toxic	Poison	Status	—	90	10	Normal	—	—
TM10	Hidden Power	Normal	Special	—	100	15	Normal	—	—
TM11	Sunny Day	Fire	Status	—	—	5	Both Sides	—	—
TM15	Hyper Beam	Normal	Special	150	90	5	Normal	—	—
TM16	Light Screen	Psychic	Status	—	—	30	Your Side	—	—
TM17	Protect	Normal	Status	—	—	10	Self	—	—
TM18	Rain Dance	Water	Status	—	—	5	Both Sides	—	—
TM20	Safeguard	Normal	Status	—	—	25	Your Side	—	—
TM21	Frustration	Normal	Physical	—	100	20	Normal	—	○
TM24	Thunderbolt	Electric	Special	95	100	15	Normal	—	—
TM25	Thunder	Electric	Special	120	70	10	Normal	—	—
TM27	Return	Normal	Physical	—	100	20	Normal	—	○
TM28	Dig	Ground	Physical	80	100	10	Normal	—	○
TM32	Double Team	Normal	Status	—	—	15	Self	—	—
TM42	Facade	Normal	Physical	70	100	20	Normal	—	○
TM44	Rest	Psychic	Status	—	—	10	Self	—	—
TM45	Attract	Normal	Status	—	100	15	Normal	—	—
TM48	Round	Normal	Special	60	100	15	Normal	—	—
TM49	Echoed Voice	Normal	Special	40	100	15	Normal	—	—
TM52	Focus Blast	Fighting	Special	120	70	5	Normal	—	—
TM56	Fling	Dark	Physical	—	100	10	Normal	—	—
TM67	Retaliate	Normal	Physical	70	100	5	Normal	—	○
TM68	Giga Impact	Normal	Physical	150	90	5	Normal	—	○
TM73	Thunder Wave	Electric	Status	—	100	20	Normal	—	—
TM83	Work Up	Normal	Status	—	—	30	Self	—	—
TM86	Grass Knot	Grass	Special	—	100	20	Normal	—	○
TM87	Swagger	Normal	Status	—	90	15	Normal	—	—
TM89	U-turn	Bug	Physical	70	100	20	Normal	—	○
TM90	Substitute	Normal	Status	—	—	10	Self	—	—

● FOOTPRINT

● MALE/FEMALE HAVE SAME FORM

● HEIGHT: 1'08"
● WEIGHT: 16.5 lbs.
● GENDER: Both ♂♀ exist
● ITEMS:
• Chesto Berry

POKÉMON BLACK VERSION
Their white fur is coated in a special oil that makes it easy for them to deflect attacks.

POKÉMON WHITE VERSION
Their white fur feels amazing to touch. Their fur repels dust and prevents static electricity from building up.

EVOLUTION

Use Shiny Stone

Minccino → Cinccino

ABILITIES
● Cute Charm
● Technician

EGG GROUP Field

STATS
HP ●●●
ATTACK ●●●●
DEFENSE ●●
SP. ATTACK ●●●
SP. DEFENSE ●●
SPEED ●●●●●

● MAIN WAYS TO OBTAIN

| POKÉMON BLACK VERSION | 1 | Route 16 (Rustling Grass) |
| | 2 | Use Shiny Stone on Minccino |

| POKÉMON WHITE VERSION | 1 | Route 16 (Rustling Grass) |
| | 2 | Use Shiny Stone on Minccino |

Gothita

● TYPE Psychic

● HEIGHT: 1'04"
● WEIGHT: 12.8 lbs.
● GENDER: Both ♂♀ exist
● ITEMS:
  • None

● MALE/FEMALE HAVE SAME FORM

● FOOTPRINT

● LEVEL-UP AND LEARNED MOVES

Lv.	Name	Type	Kind	Pow.	Acc.	PP	Range	Long	DA
1	Pound	Normal	Physical	40	100	35	Normal	—	○
3	Confusion	Psychic	Special	50	100	25	Normal	—	—
7	Tickle	Normal	Status	—	100	20	Normal	—	—
10	Fake Tears	Dark	Status	—	100	20	Normal	—	—
14	DoubleSlap	Normal	Physical	15	85	10	Normal	—	○
16	Psybeam	Psychic	Special	65	100	20	Normal	—	—
19	Embargo	Dark	Status	—	100	15	Normal	—	—
24	Faint Attack	Dark	Physical	60	—	20	Normal	—	○
25	Psyshock	Psychic	Special	80	100	10	Normal	—	—
28	Flatter	Dark	Status	—	100	15	Normal	—	—
31	Future Sight	Psychic	Special	100	100	10	Normal	—	—
33	Heal Block	Psychic	Status	—	100	15	Many Others	—	—
37	Psychic	Psychic	Special	90	100	10	Normal	—	—
40	Telekinesis	Psychic	Status	—	—	15	Normal	—	—
46	Charm	Normal	Status	—	100	20	Normal	—	—
48	Magic Room	Psychic	Status	—	—	10	Both Sides	—	—

● MOVES TAUGHT BY PEOPLE

Name	Type	Kind	Pow.	Acc.	PP	Range	Long	DA

● EGG MOVES

Name	Type	Kind	Pow.	Acc.	PP	Range	Long	DA
Mirror Coat	Psychic	Special	—	100	20	Varies	—	—
Uproar	Normal	Special	90	100	10	1 Random	—	—
Miracle Eye	Psychic	Status	—	—	40	Normal	—	—
Captivate	Normal	Status	—	100	20	Many Others	—	—
Mean Look	Normal	Status	—	—	5	Normal	—	—
Dark Pulse	Dark	Special	80	100	15	Normal	○	—

● TM & HM MOVES

No.	Name	Type	Kind	Pow.	Acc.	PP	Range	Long	DA
TM03	Psyshock	Psychic	Special	80	100	10	Normal	—	—
TM04	Calm Mind	Psychic	Status	—	—	20	Self	—	—
TM06	Toxic	Poison	Status	—	90	10	Normal	—	—
TM10	Hidden Power	Normal	Special	—	100	15	Normal	—	—
TM12	Taunt	Dark	Status	—	100	20	Normal	—	—
TM16	Light Screen	Psychic	Status	—	—	30	Your Side	—	—
TM17	Protect	Normal	Status	—	—	10	Self	—	—
TM18	Rain Dance	Water	Status	—	—	5	Both Sides	—	—
TM19	Telekinesis	Psychic	Status	—	—	15	Normal	—	—
TM20	Safeguard	Normal	Status	—	—	25	Your Side	—	—
TM21	Frustration	Normal	Physical	—	100	20	Normal	—	○
TM24	Thunderbolt	Electric	Special	95	100	15	Normal	—	—
TM27	Return	Normal	Physical	—	100	20	Normal	—	○
TM29	Psychic	Psychic	Special	90	100	10	Normal	—	—
TM30	Shadow Ball	Ghost	Special	80	100	15	Normal	—	—
TM32	Double Team	Normal	Status	—	—	15	Self	—	—
TM33	Reflect	Psychic	Status	—	—	20	Your Side	—	—
TM39	Rock Tomb	Rock	Physical	50	80	10	Normal	—	—
TM41	Torment	Dark	Status	—	100	15	Normal	—	—
TM42	Facade	Normal	Physical	70	100	20	Normal	—	○
TM44	Rest	Psychic	Status	—	—	10	Self	—	—
TM45	Attract	Normal	Status	—	100	15	Normal	—	—
TM46	Thief	Dark	Physical	40	100	10	Normal	—	—
TM48	Round	Normal	Special	60	100	15	Normal	—	—
TM53	Energy Ball	Grass	Special	80	100	10	Normal	—	—
TM56	Fling	Dark	Physical	—	100	10	Normal	—	—
TM57	Charge Beam	Electric	Special	50	90	10	Normal	—	—
TM63	Embargo	Dark	Status	—	100	15	Normal	—	—
TM66	Payback	Dark	Physical	50	100	10	Normal	—	—
TM70	Flash	Normal	Status	—	100	20	Normal	—	—
TM73	Thunder Wave	Electric	Status	—	100	20	Normal	—	—
TM77	Psych Up	Normal	Status	—	—	10	Normal	—	—
TM80	Rock Slide	Rock	Physical	75	90	10	Many Others	—	—
TM85	Dream Eater	Psychic	Special	100	100	15	Normal	—	—
TM86	Grass Knot	Grass	Special	—	100	20	Normal	—	○
TM87	Swagger	Normal	Status	—	90	15	Normal	—	—
TM90	Substitute	Normal	Status	—	—	10	Self	—	—
TM92	Trick Room	Psychic	Status	—	—	5	Both Sides	—	—

● EVOLUTION

Gothita → Lv. 32 → Gothorita → Lv. 41 → Gothitelle

ABILITY ● Frisk

EGG GROUP Human-Like

STATS
HP ●●
ATTACK ●●
DEFENSE ●●
SP. ATTACK ●●
SP. DEFENSE ●●
SPEED ●●

POKÉMON BLACK VERSION
Their ribbonlike feelers increase their psychic power. They are always staring at something.

POKÉMON WHITE VERSION
They intently observe both Trainers and Pokémon. Apparently, they are looking at something that only Gothita can see.

● MAIN WAYS TO OBTAIN

POKÉMON BLACK VERSION
1 Route 16
2 Route 5

POKÉMON WHITE VERSION
1 —
2 —

Gothorita

● TYPE Psychic

● HEIGHT: 2'04"
● WEIGHT: 39.7 lbs.
● GENDER: Both ♂♀ exist
● ITEMS:
  • None

● MALE/FEMALE HAVE SAME FORM

● FOOTPRINT

● LEVEL-UP AND LEARNED MOVES

Lv.	Name	Type	Kind	Pow.	Acc.	PP	Range	Long	DA
1	Pound	Normal	Physical	40	100	35	Normal	—	○
1	Confusion	Psychic	Special	50	100	25	Normal	—	—
1	Tickle	Normal	Status	—	100	20	Normal	—	—
1	Fake Tears	Dark	Status	—	100	20	Normal	—	—
3	Confusion	Psychic	Special	50	100	25	Normal	—	—
7	Tickle	Normal	Status	—	100	20	Normal	—	—
10	Fake Tears	Dark	Status	—	100	20	Normal	—	—
14	DoubleSlap	Normal	Physical	15	85	10	Normal	—	○
16	Psybeam	Psychic	Special	65	100	20	Normal	—	—
19	Embargo	Dark	Status	—	100	15	Normal	—	—
24	Faint Attack	Dark	Physical	60	—	20	Normal	—	○
25	Psyshock	Psychic	Special	80	100	10	Normal	—	—
28	Flatter	Dark	Status	—	100	15	Normal	—	—
31	Future Sight	Psychic	Special	100	100	10	Normal	—	—
34	Heal Block	Psychic	Status	—	100	15	Many Others	—	—
39	Psychic	Psychic	Special	90	100	10	Normal	—	—
43	Telekinesis	Psychic	Status	—	—	15	Normal	—	—
50	Charm	Normal	Status	—	100	20	Normal	—	—
53	Magic Room	Psychic	Status	—	—	10	Both Sides	—	—

● MOVES TAUGHT BY PEOPLE

Name	Type	Kind	Pow.	Acc.	PP	Range	Long	DA

● TM & HM MOVES

No.	Name	Type	Kind	Pow.	Acc.	PP	Range	Long	DA
TM03	Psyshock	Psychic	Special	80	100	10	Normal	—	—
TM04	Calm Mind	Psychic	Status	—	—	20	Self	—	—
TM06	Toxic	Poison	Status	—	90	10	Normal	—	—
TM10	Hidden Power	Normal	Special	—	100	15	Normal	—	—
TM12	Taunt	Dark	Status	—	100	20	Normal	—	—
TM16	Light Screen	Psychic	Status	—	—	30	Your Side	—	—
TM17	Protect	Normal	Status	—	—	10	Self	—	—
TM18	Rain Dance	Water	Status	—	—	5	Both Sides	—	—
TM19	Telekinesis	Psychic	Status	—	—	15	Normal	—	—
TM20	Safeguard	Normal	Status	—	—	25	Your Side	—	—
TM21	Frustration	Normal	Physical	—	100	20	Normal	—	○
TM24	Thunderbolt	Electric	Special	95	100	15	Normal	—	—
TM27	Return	Normal	Physical	—	100	20	Normal	—	○
TM29	Psychic	Psychic	Special	90	100	10	Normal	—	—
TM30	Shadow Ball	Ghost	Special	80	100	15	Normal	—	—
TM32	Double Team	Normal	Status	—	—	15	Self	—	—
TM33	Reflect	Psychic	Status	—	—	20	Your Side	—	—
TM39	Rock Tomb	Rock	Physical	50	80	10	Normal	—	—
TM41	Torment	Dark	Status	—	100	15	Normal	—	—
TM42	Facade	Normal	Physical	70	100	20	Normal	—	○
TM44	Rest	Psychic	Status	—	—	10	Self	—	—
TM45	Attract	Normal	Status	—	100	15	Normal	—	—
TM46	Thief	Dark	Physical	40	100	10	Normal	—	—
TM48	Round	Normal	Special	60	100	15	Normal	—	—
TM53	Energy Ball	Grass	Special	80	100	10	Normal	—	—
TM56	Fling	Dark	Physical	—	100	10	Normal	—	—
TM57	Charge Beam	Electric	Special	50	90	10	Normal	—	—
TM63	Embargo	Dark	Status	—	100	15	Normal	—	—
TM66	Payback	Dark	Physical	50	100	10	Normal	—	—
TM70	Flash	Normal	Status	—	100	20	Normal	—	—
TM73	Thunder Wave	Electric	Status	—	100	20	Normal	—	—
TM77	Psych Up	Normal	Status	—	—	10	Normal	—	—
TM80	Rock Slide	Rock	Physical	75	90	10	Many Others	—	—
TM85	Dream Eater	Psychic	Special	100	100	15	Normal	—	—
TM86	Grass Knot	Grass	Special	—	100	20	Normal	—	○
TM87	Swagger	Normal	Status	—	90	15	Normal	—	—
TM90	Substitute	Normal	Status	—	—	10	Self	—	—
TM92	Trick Room	Psychic	Status	—	—	5	Both Sides	—	—

● EVOLUTION

Gothita → Lv. 32 → Gothorita → Lv. 41 → Gothitelle

ABILITY ● Frisk

EGG GROUP Human-Like

STATS
HP ●●
ATTACK ●●●
DEFENSE ●●●
SP. ATTACK ●●●
SP. DEFENSE ●●●
SPEED ●●●

POKÉMON BLACK VERSION
They use hypnosis to control people and Pokémon. Tales of Gothorita leading people astray are told in every corner.

POKÉMON WHITE VERSION
Starlight is the source of their power. At night, they mark star positions by using psychic power to float stones.

● MAIN WAYS TO OBTAIN

POKÉMON BLACK VERSION
1 Route 9
2 Level up Gothita to Lv. 32

POKÉMON WHITE VERSION
1 —
2 —

Gothitelle

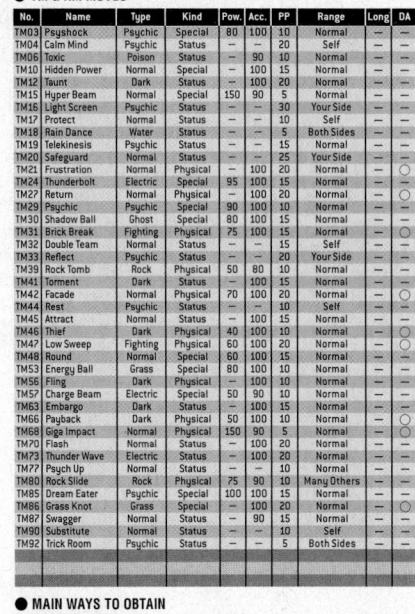

● TYPE Psychic

● HEIGHT: 4'11"
● WEIGHT: 97.0 lbs.
● GENDER: Both ♂♀ exist
● ITEMS:
• None

● FOOTPRINT

● MALE/FEMALE HAVE SAME FORM

POKÉMON BLACK VERSION
Starry skies thousands of light-years away are visible in the space distorted by their intense psychic power.

POKÉMON WHITE VERSION
They can predict the future from the placement and movement of the stars. They can see Trainers' life spans.

● LEVEL-UP AND LEARNED MOVES

Lv.	Name	Type	Kind	Pow.	Acc.	PP	Range	Long	DA
1	Pound	Normal	Physical	40	100	35	Normal	—	○
1	Confusion	Psychic	Special	50	100	25	Normal	—	—
1	Tickle	Normal	Status	—	100	20	Normal	—	—
1	Fake Tears	Dark	Status	—	100	20	Normal	—	—
3	Confusion	Psychic	Special	50	100	25	Normal	—	—
7	Tickle	Normal	Status	—	100	20	Normal	—	—
10	Fake Tears	Dark	Status	—	100	20	Normal	—	—
14	DoubleSlap	Normal	Physical	15	85	10	Normal	—	○
16	Psybeam	Psychic	Special	65	100	10	Normal	—	—
19	Embargo	Dark	Status	—	100	15	Normal	—	—
24	Faint Attack	Dark	Physical	60	—	20	Normal	—	○
25	Psyshock	Psychic	Special	80	100	10	Normal	—	—
28	Flatter	Dark	Status	—	100	15	Normal	—	—
31	Future Sight	Psychic	Special	100	100	10	Normal	—	—
34	Heal Block	Psychic	Status	—	100	15	Many Others	—	—
39	Psychic	Psychic	Special	90	100	10	Normal	—	—
45	Telekinesis	Psychic	Status	—	—	15	Normal	—	—
54	Charm	Normal	Status	—	100	20	Normal	—	—
59	Magic Room	Psychic	Status	—	—	10	Both Sides	—	—

● MOVES TAUGHT BY PEOPLE

Name	Type	Kind	Pow.	Acc.	PP	Range	Long	DA

● TM & HM MOVES

No.	Name	Type	Kind	Pow.	Acc.	PP	Range	Long	DA
TM03	Psyshock	Psychic	Special	80	100	10	Normal	—	—
TM04	Calm Mind	Psychic	Status	—	—	20	Self	—	—
TM06	Toxic	Poison	Status	—	90	10	Normal	—	—
TM10	Hidden Power	Normal	Special	—	100	15	Normal	—	—
TM12	Taunt	Dark	Status	—	100	20	Normal	—	—
TM15	Hyper Beam	Normal	Special	150	90	5	Normal	—	—
TM16	Light Screen	Psychic	Status	—	—	30	Your Side	—	—
TM17	Protect	Normal	Status	—	—	10	Self	—	—
TM18	Rain Dance	Water	Status	—	—	5	Both Sides	—	—
TM19	Telekinesis	Psychic	Status	—	—	15	Normal	—	—
TM20	Safeguard	Normal	Status	—	—	25	Your Side	—	—
TM21	Frustration	Normal	Physical	—	100	20	Normal	—	○
TM24	Thunderbolt	Electric	Special	95	100	15	Normal	—	—
TM27	Return	Normal	Physical	—	100	20	Normal	—	○
TM29	Psychic	Psychic	Special	90	100	10	Normal	—	—
TM30	Shadow Ball	Ghost	Special	80	100	15	Normal	—	—
TM31	Brick Break	Fighting	Physical	75	100	15	Normal	—	○
TM32	Double Team	Normal	Status	—	—	15	Self	—	—
TM33	Reflect	Psychic	Status	—	—	20	Your Side	—	—
TM39	Rock Tomb	Rock	Physical	50	80	10	Normal	—	○
TM41	Torment	Dark	Status	—	100	15	Normal	—	—
TM42	Facade	Normal	Physical	70	100	20	Normal	—	○
TM44	Rest	Psychic	Status	—	—	10	Self	—	—
TM45	Attract	Normal	Status	—	100	15	Normal	—	—
TM46	Thief	Dark	Physical	40	100	10	Normal	—	○
TM47	Low Sweep	Fighting	Physical	60	100	20	Normal	—	○
TM48	Round	Normal	Special	60	100	15	Normal	—	—
TM53	Energy Ball	Grass	Special	80	100	10	Normal	—	—
TM56	Fling	Dark	Physical	—	100	10	Normal	—	○
TM57	Charge Beam	Electric	Special	50	90	10	Normal	—	—
TM63	Embargo	Dark	Status	—	100	15	Normal	—	—
TM66	Payback	Dark	Physical	50	100	10	Normal	—	○
TM68	Giga Impact	Normal	Physical	150	90	5	Normal	—	○
TM70	Flash	Normal	Status	—	100	20	Normal	—	—
TM73	Thunder Wave	Electric	Status	—	100	20	Normal	—	—
TM77	Psych Up	Normal	Status	—	—	10	Normal	—	—
TM80	Rock Slide	Rock	Physical	75	90	10	Many Others	—	○
TM85	Dream Eater	Psychic	Special	100	100	15	Normal	—	—
TM86	Grass Knot	Grass	Special	—	100	20	Normal	—	○
TM87	Swagger	Normal	Status	—	90	15	Normal	—	—
TM90	Substitute	Normal	Status	—	—	10	Self	—	—
TM92	Trick Room	Psychic	Status	—	—	5	Both Sides	—	—

● EVOLUTION

Gothita — Lv. 32 → Gothorita — Lv. 41 → Gothitelle

● ABILITY ● Frisk

● EGG GROUP Human-Like

● STATS
HP ●●●
ATTACK ●●
DEFENSE ●●●●
SP. ATTACK ●●●●
SP. DEFENSE ●●●●
SPEED ●●●

● MAIN WAYS TO OBTAIN

POKÉMON BLACK VERSION
1 Route 9 (Rustling Grass)
2 Level up Gothorita to Lv. 41

POKÉMON WHITE VERSION
1 —
2 —

Solosis

● TYPE Psychic

● HEIGHT: 1'00"
● WEIGHT: 2.2 lbs.
● GENDER: Both ♂♀ exist
● ITEMS:
• None

● FOOTPRINT

● MALE/FEMALE HAVE SAME FORM

POKÉMON BLACK VERSION
They drive away attackers by unleashing psychic power. They can use telepathy to talk with others.

POKÉMON WHITE VERSION
Because their bodies are enveloped in a special liquid, they can survive in any environment.

● LEVEL-UP AND LEARNED MOVES

Lv.	Name	Type	Kind	Pow.	Acc.	PP	Range	Long	DA
1	Psywave	Psychic	Special	—	80	15	Normal	—	—
3	Reflect	Psychic	Status	—	—	20	Your Side	—	—
7	Rollout	Rock	Physical	30	90	20	Normal	—	○
10	Snatch	Dark	Status	—	—	10	Self	—	—
14	Hidden Power	Normal	Special	—	100	15	Normal	—	—
16	Light Screen	Psychic	Status	—	—	30	Your Side	—	—
19	Charm	Normal	Status	—	100	20	Normal	—	—
24	Recover	Normal	Status	—	—	10	Self	—	—
25	Psyshock	Psychic	Special	80	100	10	Normal	—	—
28	Endeavor	Normal	Physical	—	100	5	Normal	—	○
31	Future Sight	Psychic	Special	100	100	10	Normal	—	—
33	Pain Split	Normal	Status	—	—	20	Normal	—	—
37	Psychic	Psychic	Special	90	100	10	Normal	—	—
40	Skill Swap	Psychic	Status	—	—	10	Normal	—	—
46	Heal Block	Psychic	Status	—	100	15	Many Others	—	—
48	Wonder Room	Psychic	Status	—	—	10	Both Sides	—	—

● MOVES TAUGHT BY PEOPLE

Name	Type	Kind	Pow.	Acc.	PP	Range	Long	DA

● EGG MOVES

Name	Type	Kind	Pow.	Acc.	PP	Range	Long	DA
Night Shade	Ghost	Special	—	100	15	Normal	—	—
Astonish	Ghost	Physical	30	100	15	Normal	—	○
Confuse Ray	Ghost	Status	—	100	10	Normal	—	—
Acid Armor	Poison	Status	—	—	40	Self	—	—
Trick	Psychic	Status	—	100	10	Normal	—	—
Imprison	Psychic	Status	—	—	10	Self	—	—
Secret Power	Normal	Physical	70	100	20	Normal	—	○
Astonish	Ghost	Physical	30	100	15	Normal	—	○

● TM & HM MOVES

No.	Name	Type	Kind	Pow.	Acc.	PP	Range	Long	DA
TM03	Psyshock	Psychic	Special	80	100	10	Normal	—	—
TM04	Calm Mind	Psychic	Status	—	—	20	Self	—	—
TM06	Toxic	Poison	Status	—	90	10	Normal	—	—
TM10	Hidden Power	Normal	Special	—	100	15	Normal	—	—
TM16	Light Screen	Psychic	Status	—	—	30	Your Side	—	—
TM17	Protect	Normal	Status	—	—	10	Self	—	—
TM18	Rain Dance	Water	Status	—	—	5	Both Sides	—	—
TM19	Telekinesis	Psychic	Status	—	—	15	Normal	—	—
TM20	Safeguard	Normal	Status	—	—	25	Your Side	—	—
TM21	Frustration	Normal	Physical	—	100	20	Normal	—	○
TM25	Thunder	Electric	Special	120	70	10	Normal	—	—
TM27	Return	Normal	Physical	—	100	20	Normal	—	○
TM29	Psychic	Psychic	Special	90	100	10	Normal	—	—
TM30	Shadow Ball	Ghost	Special	80	100	15	Normal	—	—
TM32	Double Team	Normal	Status	—	—	15	Self	—	—
TM33	Reflect	Psychic	Status	—	—	20	Your Side	—	—
TM39	Rock Tomb	Rock	Physical	50	80	10	Normal	—	○
TM42	Facade	Normal	Physical	70	100	20	Normal	—	○
TM44	Rest	Psychic	Status	—	—	10	Self	—	—
TM45	Attract	Normal	Status	—	100	15	Normal	—	—
TM48	Round	Normal	Special	60	100	15	Normal	—	—
TM53	Energy Ball	Grass	Special	80	100	10	Normal	—	—
TM63	Embargo	Dark	Status	—	100	15	Normal	—	—
TM64	Explosion	Normal	Physical	250	100	5	Adjacent	—	○
TM70	Flash	Normal	Status	—	100	20	Normal	—	—
TM73	Thunder Wave	Electric	Status	—	100	20	Normal	—	—
TM74	Gyro Ball	Steel	Physical	—	100	5	Normal	—	○
TM77	Psych Up	Normal	Status	—	—	10	Normal	—	—
TM80	Rock Slide	Rock	Physical	75	90	10	Many Others	—	○
TM85	Dream Eater	Psychic	Special	100	100	15	Normal	—	—
TM87	Swagger	Normal	Status	—	90	15	Normal	—	—
TM90	Substitute	Normal	Status	—	—	10	Self	—	—
TM91	Flash Cannon	Steel	Special	80	100	10	Normal	—	—
TM92	Trick Room	Psychic	Status	—	—	5	Both Sides	—	—

● EVOLUTION

Solosis — Lv. 32 → Duosion — Lv. 41 → Reuniclus

● ABILITIES ● Overcoat ● Magic Guard

● EGG GROUP Amorphous

● STATS
HP ●●●
ATTACK ●
DEFENSE ●
SP. ATTACK ●●●●●
SP. DEFENSE ●●
SPEED ●

● MAIN WAYS TO OBTAIN

POKÉMON BLACK VERSION
1 —
2 —

POKÉMON WHITE VERSION
1 Route 16
2 Route 5

Duosion

● TYPE Psychic

● FOOTPRINT

● MALE/FEMALE HAVE SAME FORM

● HEIGHT: 2'00"
● WEIGHT: 17.6 lbs.
● GENDER: Both ♂♀ exist
● ITEMS:
  • None

POKÉMON BLACK VERSION
Since they have two divided brains, at times they suddenly try to take two different actions at once.

POKÉMON WHITE VERSION
When their brains, now divided in two, are thinking the same thoughts, these Pokémon exhibit their maximum power.

● LEVEL-UP AND LEARNED MOVES

Lv.	Name	Type	Kind	Pow.	Acc.	PP	Range	Long	DA
1	Psywave	Psychic	Special	—	80	15	Normal	—	—
1	Reflect	Psychic	Status	—	—	20	Your Side	—	—
1	Rollout	Rock	Physical	30	90	20	Normal	—	○
1	Snatch	Dark	Status	—	—	10	Self	—	—
3	Reflect	Psychic	Status	—	—	20	Your Side	—	—
7	Rollout	Rock	Physical	30	90	20	Normal	—	○
10	Snatch	Dark	Status	—	—	10	Self	—	—
14	Hidden Power	Normal	Special	—	100	15	Normal	—	—
16	Light Screen	Psychic	Status	—	—	30	Your Side	—	—
19	Charm	Normal	Status	—	100	20	Normal	—	—
24	Recover	Normal	Status	—	—	10	Self	—	—
25	Psyshock	Psychic	Special	80	100	10	Normal	—	—
28	Endeavor	Normal	Physical	—	100	5	Normal	—	○
31	Future Sight	Psychic	Special	100	100	10	Normal	—	—
34	Pain Split	Normal	Status	—	—	20	Normal	—	—
39	Psychic	Psychic	Special	90	100	10	Normal	—	—
43	Skill Swap	Psychic	Status	—	—	10	Normal	—	—
50	Heal Block	Psychic	Status	—	100	15	Many Others	—	—
53	Wonder Room	Psychic	Status	—	—	10	Both Sides	—	—

● MOVES TAUGHT BY PEOPLE

Name	Type	Kind	Pow.	Acc.	PP	Range	Long	DA

● TM & HM MOVES

No.	Name	Type	Kind	Pow.	Acc.	PP	Range	Long	DA
TM03	Psyshock	Psychic	Special	80	100	10	Normal	—	—
TM04	Calm Mind	Psychic	Status	—	—	20	Self	—	—
TM06	Toxic	Poison	Status	—	90	10	Normal	—	—
TM10	Hidden Power	Normal	Special	—	100	15	Normal	—	—
TM16	Light Screen	Psychic	Status	—	—	30	Your Side	—	—
TM17	Protect	Normal	Status	—	—	10	Self	—	—
TM18	Rain Dance	Water	Status	—	—	5	Both Sides	—	—
TM19	Telekinesis	Psychic	Status	—	—	15	Normal	—	—
TM20	Safeguard	Normal	Status	—	—	25	Your Side	—	—
TM25	Frustration	Normal	Physical	—	100	20	Normal	—	○
TM27	Return	Normal	Physical	—	100	20	Normal	—	○
TM29	Psychic	Psychic	Special	90	100	10	Normal	—	—
TM30	Shadow Ball	Ghost	Special	80	100	15	Normal	—	—
TM32	Double Team	Normal	Status	—	—	15	Self	—	—
TM33	Reflect	Psychic	Status	—	—	20	Your Side	—	—
TM39	Rock Tomb	Rock	Physical	50	80	10	Normal	—	—
TM42	Facade	Normal	Physical	70	100	20	Normal	—	—
TM44	Rest	Psychic	Status	—	—	10	Self	—	—
TM48	Round	Normal	Special	60	100	15	Normal	—	—
TM53	Energy Ball	Grass	Special	80	100	10	Normal	—	—
TM63	Embargo	Dark	Status	—	100	15	Normal	—	—
TM64	Explosion	Normal	Physical	250	100	5	Adjacent	—	○
TM70	Flash	Normal	Status	—	100	20	Normal	—	—
TM73	Thunder Wave	Electric	Status	—	100	20	Normal	—	—
TM74	Gyro Ball	Steel	Physical	—	100	5	Normal	—	○
TM77	Psych Up	Normal	Status	—	—	10	Self	—	—
TM80	Rock Slide	Rock	Physical	75	90	10	Many Others	—	—
TM85	Dream Eater	Psychic	Special	100	100	15	Normal	—	—
TM87	Swagger	Normal	Status	—	90	15	Normal	—	—
TM90	Substitute	Normal	Status	—	—	10	Self	—	—
TM91	Flash Cannon	Steel	Special	80	100	10	Normal	—	—
TM92	Trick Room	Psychic	Status	—	—	5	Both Sides	—	—

● MAIN WAYS TO OBTAIN

POKÉMON BLACK VERSION
1 —
2 —

POKÉMON WHITE VERSION
1 Route 9
2 Level up Solosis to Lv. 32

EVOLUTION

Solosis → Lv. 32 → Duosion → Lv. 41 → Reuniclus

ABILITIES
● Overcoat
● Magic Guard

EGG GROUP
Amorphous

STATS
HP ●●
ATTACK ●●
DEFENSE ●●
SP. ATTACK ●●●●●
SP. DEFENSE ●●●
SPEED ●

Reuniclus

● TYPE Psychic

● FOOTPRINT

● MALE/FEMALE HAVE SAME FORM

● HEIGHT: 3'03"
● WEIGHT: 44.3 lbs.
● GENDER: Both ♂♀ exist
● ITEMS:
  • None

POKÉMON BLACK VERSION
When Reuniclus shake hands, a network forms between their brains, increasing their psychic power.

POKÉMON WHITE VERSION
These remarkably intelligent Pokémon fight by controlling arms that can grip with rock-crushing power.

● LEVEL-UP AND LEARNED MOVES

Lv.	Name	Type	Kind	Pow.	Acc.	PP	Range	Long	DA
1	Psywave	Psychic	Special	—	80	15	Normal	—	—
1	Reflect	Psychic	Status	—	—	20	Your Side	—	—
1	Rollout	Rock	Physical	30	90	20	Normal	—	○
1	Snatch	Dark	Status	—	—	10	Self	—	—
3	Reflect	Psychic	Status	—	—	20	Your Side	—	—
7	Rollout	Rock	Physical	30	90	20	Normal	—	○
10	Snatch	Dark	Status	—	—	10	Self	—	—
14	Hidden Power	Normal	Special	—	100	15	Normal	—	—
16	Light Screen	Psychic	Status	—	—	30	Your Side	—	—
19	Charm	Normal	Status	—	100	20	Normal	—	—
24	Recover	Normal	Status	—	—	10	Self	—	—
25	Psyshock	Psychic	Special	80	100	10	Normal	—	—
28	Endeavor	Normal	Physical	—	100	5	Normal	—	○
31	Future Sight	Psychic	Special	100	100	10	Normal	—	—
34	Pain Split	Normal	Status	—	—	20	Normal	—	—
39	Psychic	Psychic	Special	90	100	10	Normal	—	—
41	Dizzy Punch	Normal	Physical	70	100	10	Normal	—	○
45	Skill Swap	Psychic	Status	—	—	10	Normal	—	—
54	Heal Block	Psychic	Status	—	100	15	Many Others	—	—
59	Wonder Room	Psychic	Status	—	—	10	Both Sides	—	—

● MOVES TAUGHT BY PEOPLE

Name	Type	Kind	Pow.	Acc.	PP	Range	Long	DA

● TM & HM MOVES

No.	Name	Type	Kind	Pow.	Acc.	PP	Range	Long	DA
TM03	Psyshock	Psychic	Special	80	100	10	Normal	—	—
TM04	Calm Mind	Psychic	Status	—	—	20	Self	—	—
TM06	Toxic	Poison	Status	—	90	10	Normal	—	—
TM10	Hidden Power	Normal	Special	—	100	15	Normal	—	—
TM15	Hyper Beam	Normal	Special	150	90	5	Normal	—	—
TM16	Light Screen	Psychic	Status	—	—	30	Your Side	—	—
TM17	Protect	Normal	Status	—	—	10	Self	—	—
TM18	Rain Dance	Water	Status	—	—	5	Both Sides	—	—
TM19	Telekinesis	Psychic	Status	—	—	15	Normal	—	—
TM20	Safeguard	Normal	Status	—	—	25	Your Side	—	—
TM21	Frustration	Normal	Physical	—	100	20	Normal	—	○
TM25	Thunder	Electric	Special	120	70	10	Normal	—	—
TM27	Return	Normal	Physical	—	100	20	Normal	—	○
TM29	Psychic	Psychic	Special	90	100	10	Normal	—	—
TM30	Shadow Ball	Ghost	Special	80	100	15	Normal	—	—
TM32	Double Team	Normal	Status	—	—	15	Self	—	—
TM33	Reflect	Psychic	Status	—	—	20	Your Side	—	—
TM39	Rock Tomb	Rock	Physical	50	80	10	Normal	—	—
TM42	Facade	Normal	Physical	70	100	20	Normal	—	—
TM44	Rest	Psychic	Status	—	—	10	Self	—	—
TM45	Attract	Normal	Status	—	100	15	Normal	—	—
TM48	Round	Normal	Special	60	100	15	Normal	—	—
TM52	Focus Blast	Fighting	Special	120	70	5	Normal	—	—
TM53	Energy Ball	Grass	Special	80	100	10	Normal	—	—
TM56	Fling	Dark	Physical	—	100	10	Normal	—	—
TM63	Embargo	Dark	Status	—	100	15	Normal	—	—
TM64	Explosion	Normal	Physical	250	100	5	Adjacent	—	○
TM68	Giga Impact	Normal	Physical	150	90	5	Normal	—	○
TM70	Flash	Normal	Status	—	100	20	Normal	—	—
TM73	Thunder Wave	Electric	Status	—	100	20	Normal	—	—
TM74	Gyro Ball	Steel	Physical	—	100	5	Normal	—	○
TM77	Psych Up	Normal	Status	—	—	10	Self	—	—
TM80	Rock Slide	Rock	Physical	75	90	10	Many Others	—	—
TM85	Dream Eater	Psychic	Special	100	100	15	Normal	—	—
TM86	Grass Knot	Grass	Special	—	100	20	Normal	—	○
TM87	Swagger	Normal	Status	—	90	15	Normal	—	—
TM90	Substitute	Normal	Status	—	—	10	Self	—	—
TM91	Flash Cannon	Steel	Special	80	100	10	Normal	—	—
TM92	Trick Room	Psychic	Status	—	—	5	Both Sides	—	—
TM94	Rock Smash	Fighting	Physical	40	100	15	Normal	—	○
HM04	Strength	Normal	Physical	80	100	15	Normal	—	○

● MAIN WAYS TO OBTAIN

POKÉMON BLACK VERSION
1 —
2 —

POKÉMON WHITE VERSION
1 Route 9 (Rustling Grass)
2 Level up Duosion to Lv. 41

EVOLUTION

Solosis → Lv. 32 → Duosion → Lv. 41 → Reuniclus

ABILITIES
● Overcoat
● Magic Guard

EGG GROUP
Amorphous

STATS
HP ●●●●
ATTACK ●●●
DEFENSE ●●●
SP. ATTACK ●●●●●
SP. DEFENSE ●●●
SPEED ●●

🔹 Ducklett

● TYPE **Water** **Flying**

● MALE/FEMALE HAVE SAME FORM

- ● HEIGHT: 1'08"
- ● WEIGHT: 12.1 lbs.
- ● GENDER: Both ♂♀ exist
- ● ITEMS:
  - None

● FOOTPRINT

POKÉMON BLACK VERSION
These bird Pokémon are excellent divers. They swim around in the water eating their favorite food—peat moss.

POKÉMON WHITE VERSION
When attacked, it uses its feathers to splash water, escaping under cover of the spray.

● **LEVEL-UP AND LEARNED MOVES**

Lv.	Name	Type	Kind	Pow.	Acc.	PP	Range	Long	DA
1	Water Gun	Water	Special	40	100	25	Normal	—	—
3	Water Sport	Water	Status	—	—	15	Both Sides	—	—
6	Defog	Flying	Status	—	—	15	Normal	—	—
9	Wing Attack	Flying	Physical	60	100	35	Normal	○	○
13	Water Pulse	Water	Special	60	100	20	Normal	○	○
15	Aerial Ace	Flying	Physical	60	—	20	Normal	○	○
19	BubbleBeam	Water	Special	65	100	20	Normal	—	—
21	FeatherDance	Flying	Status	—	100	15	Normal	—	—
24	Aqua Ring	Water	Status	—	—	20	Self	—	—
27	Air Slash	Flying	Special	75	95	20	Normal	○	○
30	Roost	Flying	Status	—	—	10	Self	—	—
34	Rain Dance	Water	Status	—	—	5	Both Sides	—	—
37	Tailwind	Flying	Status	—	—	30	Your Side	—	—
41	Brave Bird	Flying	Physical	120	100	15	Normal	○	○
46	Hurricane	Flying	Special	120	70	10	Normal	○	○

● **MOVES TAUGHT BY PEOPLE**

Name	Type	Kind	Pow.	Acc.	PP	Range	Long	DA

● **EGG MOVES**

Name	Type	Kind	Pow.	Acc.	PP	Range	Long	DA
Steel Wing	Steel	Physical	70	90	25	Normal	—	○
Brine	Water	Special	65	100	10	Normal	—	—
Gust	Flying	Special	40	100	35	Normal	○	—
Air Cutter	Flying	Special	55	95	25	Many Others	○	—
Mirror Move	Flying	Status	—	—	20	Normal	—	—
Me First	Normal	Status	—	—	20	Varies	—	—
Lucky Chant	Normal	Status	—	—	30	Your Side	—	—

● **TM & HM MOVES**

No.	Name	Type	Kind	Pow.	Acc.	PP	Range	Long	DA
TM06	Toxic	Poison	Status	—	90	10	Normal	—	—
TM07	Hail	Ice	Status	—	—	10	Both Sides	—	—
TM10	Hidden Power	Normal	Special	—	100	15	Normal	—	—
TM13	Ice Beam	Ice	Special	95	100	10	Normal	—	—
TM17	Protect	Normal	Status	—	—	10	Self	—	—
TM18	Rain Dance	Water	Status	—	—	5	Both Sides	—	—
TM21	Frustration	Normal	Physical	—	100	20	Normal	—	—
TM27	Return	Normal	Physical	—	100	20	Normal	—	—
TM32	Double Team	Normal	Status	—	—	15	Self	—	—
TM40	Aerial Ace	Flying	Physical	60	—	20	Normal	○	○
TM42	Facade	Normal	Physical	70	100	20	Normal	—	—
TM44	Rest	Psychic	Status	—	—	10	Self	—	—
TM45	Attract	Normal	Status	—	100	15	Normal	—	—
TM48	Round	Normal	Special	60	100	15	Normal	—	—
TM55	Scald	Water	Special	80	100	15	Normal	—	—
TM87	Swagger	Normal	Status	—	90	15	Normal	—	—
TM88	Pluck	Flying	Physical	60	100	20	Normal	—	○
TM90	Substitute	Normal	Status	—	—	10	Self	—	—
HM02	Fly	Flying	Physical	90	95	15	Normal	○	○
HM03	Surf	Water	Special	95	100	15	Adjacent	—	—
HM06	Dive	Water	Physical	80	100	10	Normal	—	○

● **EVOLUTION**

Ducklett → Lv. 35 → Swanna

● **ABILITIES**
- ● Keen Eye
- ● Big Pecks

● **EGG GROUPS**
Water 1
Flying

● **STATS**
- HP ●●
- ATTACK ●●
- DEFENSE ●●
- SP. ATTACK ●●
- SP. DEFENSE ●●
- SPEED ●●●

● **MAIN WAYS TO OBTAIN**

POKÉMON BLACK VERSION
1 Driftveil Drawbridge (Pokémon Shadows)
2 —

POKÉMON WHITE VERSION
1 Driftveil Drawbridge (Pokémon Shadows)
2 —

🔹 Swanna

● TYPE **Water** **Flying**

● MALE/FEMALE HAVE SAME FORM

- ● HEIGHT: 4'03"
- ● WEIGHT: 53.4 lbs.
- ● GENDER: Both ♂♀ exist
- ● ITEMS:
  - None

● FOOTPRINT

POKÉMON BLACK VERSION
Swanna start to dance at dusk. The one dancing in the middle is the leader of the flock.

POKÉMON WHITE VERSION
It administers sharp, powerful pecks with its bill. It whips its long neck to deliver forceful repeated strikes.

● **LEVEL-UP AND LEARNED MOVES**

Lv.	Name	Type	Kind	Pow.	Acc.	PP	Range	Long	DA
1	Water Gun	Water	Special	40	100	25	Normal	—	—
1	Water Sport	Water	Status	—	—	15	Both Sides	—	—
1	Defog	Flying	Status	—	—	15	Normal	—	—
1	Wing Attack	Flying	Physical	60	100	35	Normal	○	○
3	Water Sport	Water	Status	—	—	15	Both Sides	—	—
6	Defog	Flying	Status	—	—	15	Normal	—	—
9	Wing Attack	Flying	Physical	60	100	35	Normal	○	○
13	Water Pulse	Water	Special	60	100	20	Normal	○	○
15	Aerial Ace	Flying	Physical	60	—	20	Normal	○	○
19	BubbleBeam	Water	Special	65	100	20	Normal	—	—
21	FeatherDance	Flying	Status	—	100	15	Normal	—	—
24	Aqua Ring	Water	Status	—	—	20	Self	—	—
27	Air Slash	Flying	Special	75	95	20	Normal	○	○
30	Roost	Flying	Status	—	—	10	Self	—	—
34	Rain Dance	Water	Status	—	—	5	Both Sides	—	—
40	Tailwind	Flying	Status	—	—	30	Your Side	—	—
47	Brave Bird	Flying	Physical	120	100	15	Normal	○	○
55	Hurricane	Flying	Special	120	70	10	Normal	○	○

● **MOVES TAUGHT BY PEOPLE**

Name	Type	Kind	Pow.	Acc.	PP	Range	Long	DA

● **TM & HM MOVES**

No.	Name	Type	Kind	Pow.	Acc.	PP	Range	Long	DA
TM06	Toxic	Poison	Status	—	90	10	Normal	—	—
TM07	Hail	Ice	Status	—	—	10	Both Sides	—	—
TM10	Hidden Power	Normal	Special	—	100	15	Normal	—	—
TM13	Ice Beam	Ice	Special	95	100	10	Normal	—	—
TM15	Hyper Beam	Normal	Special	150	90	5	Normal	—	—
TM17	Protect	Normal	Status	—	—	10	Self	—	—
TM18	Rain Dance	Water	Status	—	—	5	Both Sides	—	—
TM21	Frustration	Normal	Physical	—	100	20	Normal	—	○
TM27	Return	Normal	Physical	—	100	20	Normal	—	○
TM32	Double Team	Normal	Status	—	—	15	Self	—	—
TM40	Aerial Ace	Flying	Physical	60	—	20	Normal	○	○
TM42	Facade	Normal	Physical	70	100	20	Normal	—	—
TM44	Rest	Psychic	Status	—	—	10	Self	—	—
TM45	Attract	Normal	Status	—	100	15	Normal	—	—
TM48	Round	Normal	Special	60	100	15	Normal	—	—
TM55	Scald	Water	Special	80	100	15	Normal	—	—
TM68	Giga Impact	Normal	Physical	150	90	5	Normal	—	○
TM87	Swagger	Normal	Status	—	90	15	Normal	—	—
TM88	Pluck	Flying	Physical	60	100	20	Normal	—	○
TM90	Substitute	Normal	Status	—	—	10	Self	—	—
HM02	Fly	Flying	Physical	90	95	15	Normal	○	○
HM03	Surf	Water	Special	95	100	15	Adjacent	—	—
HM06	Dive	Water	Physical	80	100	10	Normal	—	○

● **EVOLUTION**

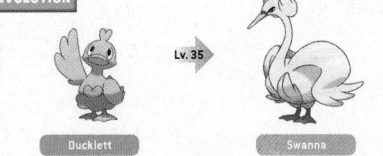 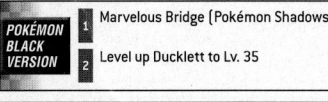

Ducklett → Lv. 35 → Swanna

● **ABILITIES**
- ● Keen Eye
- ● Big Pecks

● **EGG GROUPS**
Water 1
Flying

● **STATS**
- HP ●●●
- ATTACK ●●●●
- DEFENSE ●●●
- SP. ATTACK ●●●●
- SP. DEFENSE ●●●
- SPEED ●●●●

● **MAIN WAYS TO OBTAIN**

POKÉMON BLACK VERSION
1 Marvelous Bridge (Pokémon Shadows)
2 Level up Ducklett to Lv. 35

POKÉMON WHITE VERSION
1 Marvelous Bridge (Pokémon Shadows)
2 Level up Ducklett to Lv. 35

Vanillite

● TYPE Ice

● LEVEL-UP AND LEARNED MOVES

Lv.	Name	Type	Kind	Pow.	Acc.	PP	Range	Long	DA
1	Icicle Spear	Ice	Physical	25	100	30	Normal	—	—
4	Harden	Normal	Status	—	—	30	Self	—	—
7	Astonish	Ghost	Physical	30	100	15	Normal	—	○
10	Uproar	Normal	Special	90	100	10	1 Random	—	—
13	Icy Wind	Ice	Special	55	95	15	Many Others	—	—
16	Mist	Ice	Status	—	—	30	Your Side	—	—
19	Avalanche	Ice	Physical	60	100	10	Normal	—	○
22	Taunt	Dark	Status	—	100	20	Normal	—	—
26	Mirror Shot	Steel	Special	65	85	10	Normal	—	—
31	Acid Armor	Poison	Status	—	—	40	Self	—	—
35	Ice Beam	Ice	Special	95	100	10	Normal	—	—
40	Hail	Ice	Status	—	—	10	Both Sides	—	—
44	Mirror Coat	Psychic	Special	—	100	20	Varies	—	—
49	Blizzard	Ice	Special	120	70	5	Many Others	—	—
53	Sheer Cold	Ice	Special	—	30	5	Normal	—	—

● MOVES TAUGHT BY PEOPLE

Name	Type	Kind	Pow.	Acc.	PP	Range	Long	DA

● EGG MOVES

Name	Type	Kind	Pow.	Acc.	PP	Range	Long	DA
Water Pulse	Water	Special	60	100	20	Normal	○	—
Natural Gift	Normal	Physical	—	100	15	Normal	—	—
Imprison	Psychic	Status	—	—	10	Self	—	—
Autotomize	Steel	Status	—	—	15	Self	—	—
Iron Defense	Steel	Status	—	—	15	Self	—	—
Magnet Rise	Electric	Status	—	—	10	Self	—	—
Ice Shard	Ice	Physical	40	100	30	Normal	—	—
Powder Snow	Ice	Special	40	100	25	Many Others	—	—

● TM & HM MOVES

No.	Name	Type	Kind	Pow.	Acc.	PP	Range	Long	DA
TM06	Toxic	Poison	Status	—	90	10	Normal	—	—
TM07	Hail	Ice	Status	—	—	10	Both Sides	—	—
TM10	Hidden Power	Normal	Special	—	100	15	Normal	—	—
TM12	Taunt	Dark	Status	—	100	20	Normal	—	—
TM13	Ice Beam	Ice	Special	95	100	10	Normal	—	—
TM14	Blizzard	Ice	Special	120	70	5	Many Others	—	—
TM16	Light Screen	Psychic	Status	—	—	30	Your Side	—	—
TM17	Protect	Normal	Status	—	—	10	Self	—	—
TM18	Rain Dance	Water	Status	—	—	5	Both Sides	—	—
TM21	Frustration	Normal	Physical	—	100	20	Normal	—	○
TM27	Return	Normal	Physical	—	100	20	Normal	—	○
TM32	Double Team	Normal	Status	—	—	15	Self	—	—
TM42	Facade	Normal	Physical	70	100	20	Normal	—	○
TM44	Rest	Psychic	Status	—	—	10	Self	—	—
TM45	Attract	Normal	Status	—	100	15	Normal	—	—
TM48	Round	Normal	Special	60	100	15	Normal	—	—
TM64	Explosion	Normal	Physical	250	100	5	Adjacent	—	—
TM79	Frost Breath	Ice	Special	40	90	10	Normal	—	—
TM87	Swagger	Normal	Status	—	90	15	Normal	—	—
TM90	Substitute	Normal	Status	—	—	10	Self	—	—
TM91	Flash Cannon	Steel	Special	80	100	10	Normal	—	—

● FOOTPRINT

● MALE/FEMALE HAVE SAME FORM

● HEIGHT: 1'04"
● WEIGHT: 12.6 lbs.
● GENDER: Both ♂♀ exist
● ITEMS:
　• None

POKÉMON BLACK VERSION
The temperature of their breath is -58° F. They create snow crystals and make snow fall in the areas around them.

POKÉMON WHITE VERSION
This Pokémon formed from icicles bathed in energy from the morning sun. It sleeps buried in snow.

EVOLUTION

Vanillite — Lv. 35 → Vanillish — Lv. 47 → Vanilluxe

ABILITY
● Ice Body

EGG GROUP
Mineral

STATS
HP ●
ATTACK ●●
DEFENSE ●●
SP. ATTACK ●●●
SP. DEFENSE ●●●
SPEED ●●

● MAIN WAYS TO OBTAIN

POKÉMON BLACK VERSION
1 Cold Storage Area
2 Route 6 (winter only)

POKÉMON WHITE VERSION
1 Cold Storage Area
2 Route 6 (winter only)

Vanillish

● TYPE Ice

● LEVEL-UP AND LEARNED MOVES

Lv.	Name	Type	Kind	Pow.	Acc.	PP	Range	Long	DA
1	Icicle Spear	Ice	Physical	25	100	30	Normal	—	—
1	Harden	Normal	Status	—	—	30	Self	—	—
1	Astonish	Ghost	Physical	30	100	15	Normal	—	○
1	Uproar	Normal	Special	90	100	10	1 Random	—	—
4	Harden	Normal	Status	—	—	30	Self	—	—
7	Astonish	Ghost	Physical	30	100	15	Normal	—	○
10	Uproar	Normal	Special	90	100	10	1 Random	—	—
13	Icy Wind	Ice	Special	55	95	15	Many Others	—	—
16	Mist	Ice	Status	—	—	30	Your Side	—	—
19	Avalanche	Ice	Physical	60	100	10	Normal	—	○
22	Taunt	Dark	Status	—	100	20	Normal	—	—
26	Mirror Shot	Steel	Special	65	85	10	Normal	—	—
31	Acid Armor	Poison	Status	—	—	40	Self	—	—
36	Ice Beam	Ice	Special	95	100	10	Normal	—	—
42	Hail	Ice	Status	—	—	10	Both Sides	—	—
47	Mirror Coat	Psychic	Special	—	100	20	Varies	—	—
53	Blizzard	Ice	Special	120	70	5	Many Others	—	—
58	Sheer Cold	Ice	Special	—	30	5	Normal	—	—

● MOVES TAUGHT BY PEOPLE

Name	Type	Kind	Pow.	Acc.	PP	Range	Long	DA

● TM & HM MOVES

No.	Name	Type	Kind	Pow.	Acc.	PP	Range	Long	DA
TM06	Toxic	Poison	Status	—	90	10	Normal	—	—
TM07	Hail	Ice	Status	—	—	10	Both Sides	—	—
TM10	Hidden Power	Normal	Special	—	100	15	Normal	—	—
TM12	Taunt	Dark	Status	—	100	20	Normal	—	—
TM13	Ice Beam	Ice	Special	95	100	10	Normal	—	—
TM14	Blizzard	Ice	Special	120	70	5	Many Others	—	—
TM16	Light Screen	Psychic	Status	—	—	30	Your Side	—	—
TM17	Protect	Normal	Status	—	—	10	Self	—	—
TM18	Rain Dance	Water	Status	—	—	5	Both Sides	—	—
TM21	Frustration	Normal	Physical	—	100	20	Normal	—	○
TM27	Return	Normal	Physical	—	100	20	Normal	—	○
TM32	Double Team	Normal	Status	—	—	15	Self	—	—
TM42	Facade	Normal	Physical	70	100	20	Normal	—	○
TM44	Rest	Psychic	Status	—	—	10	Self	—	—
TM45	Attract	Normal	Status	—	100	15	Normal	—	—
TM48	Round	Normal	Special	60	100	15	Normal	—	—
TM64	Explosion	Normal	Physical	250	100	5	Adjacent	—	—
TM79	Frost Breath	Ice	Special	40	90	10	Normal	—	—
TM87	Swagger	Normal	Status	—	90	15	Normal	—	—
TM90	Substitute	Normal	Status	—	—	10	Self	—	—
TM91	Flash Cannon	Steel	Special	80	100	10	Normal	—	—

● FOOTPRINT

● MALE/FEMALE HAVE SAME FORM

● HEIGHT: 3'07"
● WEIGHT: 90.4 lbs.
● GENDER: Both ♂♀ exist
● ITEMS:
　• None

POKÉMON BLACK VERSION
Snowy mountains are this Pokémon's habitat. During an ancient ice age, they moved to southern areas.

POKÉMON WHITE VERSION
It conceals itself from enemy eyes by creating many small ice particles and hiding among them.

EVOLUTION

Vanillite — Lv. 35 → Vanillish — Lv. 47 → Vanilluxe

ABILITY
● Ice Body

EGG GROUP
Mineral

STATS
HP ●●
ATTACK ●●●
DEFENSE ●●●
SP. ATTACK ●●●
SP. DEFENSE ●●●
SPEED ●●●

● MAIN WAYS TO OBTAIN

POKÉMON BLACK VERSION
1 Dragonspiral Tower Entrance (Dark Grass/winter only)
2 Level up Vanillite to Lv. 35

POKÉMON WHITE VERSION
1 Dragonspiral Tower Entrance (Dark Grass/winter only)
2 Level up Vanillite to Lv. 35

Vanilluxe

● TYPE Ice

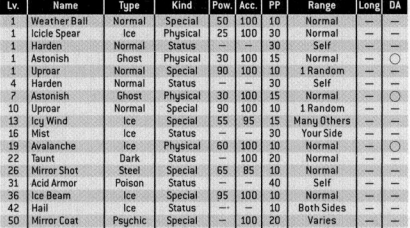

● FOOTPRINT

● MALE/FEMALE HAVE SAME FORM

● HEIGHT: 4'03"
● WEIGHT: 126.8 lbs.
● GENDER: Both ♂♀ exist
● ITEMS:
 • None

● LEVEL-UP AND LEARNED MOVES

Lv.	Name	Type	Kind	Pow.	Acc.	PP	Range	Long	DA
1	Weather Ball	Normal	Special	50	100	10	Normal	—	—
1	Icicle Spear	Ice	Physical	25	100	30	Normal	—	—
1	Harden	Normal	Status	—	—	30	Self	—	—
1	Astonish	Ghost	Physical	30	100	15	Normal	—	○
1	Uproar	Normal	Special	90	100	10	1 Random	—	—
4	Harden	Normal	Status	—	—	30	Self	—	—
7	Astonish	Ghost	Physical	30	100	15	Normal	—	○
10	Uproar	Normal	Special	90	100	10	1 Random	—	—
13	Icy Wind	Ice	Special	55	95	15	Many Others	—	—
16	Mist	Ice	Status	—	—	30	Your Side	—	—
19	Avalanche	Ice	Physical	60	100	10	Normal	—	○
22	Taunt	Dark	Status	—	100	20	Normal	—	—
26	Mirror Shot	Steel	Special	65	85	10	Normal	—	—
31	Acid Armor	Poison	Status	—	—	40	Self	—	—
36	Ice Beam	Ice	Special	95	100	10	Normal	—	—
42	Hail	Ice	Status	—	—	10	Both Sides	—	—
50	Mirror Coat	Psychic	Special	—	100	20	Varies	—	—
59	Blizzard	Ice	Special	120	70	5	Many Others	—	—
67	Sheer Cold	Ice	Special	—	30	5	Normal	—	—

● MOVES TAUGHT BY PEOPLE

Name	Type	Kind	Pow.	Acc.	PP	Range	Long	DA

● TM & HM MOVES

No.	Name	Type	Kind	Pow.	Acc.	PP	Range	Long	DA
TM06	Toxic	Poison	Status	—	90	10	Normal	—	—
TM07	Hail	Ice	Status	—	—	10	Both Sides	—	—
TM10	Hidden Power	Normal	Special	—	100	15	Normal	—	—
TM12	Taunt	Dark	Status	—	100	20	Normal	—	—
TM13	Ice Beam	Ice	Special	95	100	10	Normal	—	—
TM14	Blizzard	Ice	Special	120	70	5	Many Others	—	—
TM15	Hyper Beam	Normal	Special	150	90	5	Normal	—	—
TM16	Light Screen	Psychic	Status	—	—	30	Your Side	—	—
TM17	Protect	Normal	Status	—	—	10	Self	—	—
TM18	Rain Dance	Water	Status	—	—	5	Both Sides	—	—
TM21	Frustration	Normal	Physical	—	100	20	Normal	—	○
TM27	Return	Normal	Physical	—	100	20	Normal	—	○
TM32	Double Team	Normal	Status	—	—	15	Self	—	—
TM42	Facade	Normal	Physical	70	100	20	Normal	—	○
TM44	Rest	Psychic	Status	—	—	10	Self	—	—
TM45	Attract	Normal	Status	—	100	15	Normal	—	—
TM48	Round	Normal	Special	60	100	15	Normal	—	—
TM64	Explosion	Normal	Physical	250	100	5	Adjacent	—	○
TM68	Giga Impact	Normal	Physical	150	90	5	Normal	—	○
TM79	Frost Breath	Ice	Special	40	90	10	Normal	—	—
TM87	Swagger	Normal	Status	—	90	15	Normal	—	—
TM90	Substitute	Normal	Status	—	—	10	Self	—	—
TM91	Flash Cannon	Steel	Special	80	100	10	Normal	—	—

● MAIN WAYS TO OBTAIN

POKÉMON BLACK VERSION	1	Level up Vanillish to Lv. 47
	2	—

POKÉMON WHITE VERSION	1	Level up Vanillish to Lv. 47
	2	—

EVOLUTION

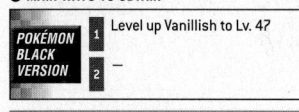

Vanillite — Lv. 35 — Vanillish — Lv. 47 — Vanilluxe

ABILITY
● Ice Body

EGG GROUP
Mineral

STATS
HP ●●●
ATTACK ●●●●
DEFENSE ●●●●
SP. ATTACK ●●●●●
SP. DEFENSE ●●●●
SPEED ●●●●

POKÉMON BLACK VERSION: Swallowing large amounts of water, they make snow clouds inside their bodies and attack their foes with violent blizzards.

POKÉMON WHITE VERSION: If both heads get angry simultaneously, this Pokémon expels a blizzard, burying everything in snow.

Deerling

● TYPE Normal Grass

● MALE/FEMALE HAVE SAME FORM

● SPRING FORM
● SUMMER FORM
● AUTUMN FORM
● WINTER FORM
● FOOTPRINT

● HEIGHT: 2'00"
● WEIGHT: 43.0 lbs.
● GENDER: Both ♂♀ exist
● ITEMS:
 • None

● LEVEL-UP AND LEARNED MOVES

Lv.	Name	Type	Kind	Pow.	Acc.	PP	Range	Long	DA
1	Tackle	Normal	Physical	50	100	35	Normal	—	○
1	Camouflage	Normal	Status	—	—	20	Self	—	—
4	Growl	Normal	Status	—	100	40	Many Others	—	—
7	Sand-Attack	Ground	Status	—	100	15	Normal	—	—
10	Double Kick	Fighting	Physical	30	100	30	Normal	—	—
13	Leech Seed	Grass	Status	—	90	10	Normal	—	—
16	Faint Attack	Dark	Physical	60	—	20	Normal	—	—
20	Take Down	Normal	Physical	90	85	20	Normal	—	○
24	Jump Kick	Fighting	Physical	100	95	10	Normal	—	—
28	Aromatherapy	Grass	Status	—	—	5	Your Party	—	—
32	Energy Ball	Grass	Special	80	100	10	Normal	—	—
36	Charm	Normal	Status	—	100	20	Normal	—	—
41	Nature Power	Normal	Status	—	—	20	Varies	—	—
46	Double-Edge	Normal	Physical	120	100	15	Normal	—	○
51	SolarBeam	Grass	Special	120	100	10	Normal	—	—

● MOVES TAUGHT BY PEOPLE

Name	Type	Kind	Pow.	Acc.	PP	Range	Long	DA

● EGG MOVES

Name	Type	Kind	Pow.	Acc.	PP	Range	Long	DA
Fake Tears	Dark	Status	—	100	20	Normal	—	—
Natural Gift	Normal	Physical	—	100	15	Normal	—	—
Synthesis	Grass	Status	—	—	5	Self	—	—
Worry Seed	Grass	Status	—	100	10	Normal	—	—
Odor Sleuth	Normal	Status	—	—	40	Normal	—	—
Agility	Psychic	Status	—	—	30	Self	—	—
Sleep Talk	Normal	Status	—	—	10	Self	—	—
Baton Pass	Normal	Status	—	—	40	Self	—	—
GrassWhistle	Grass	Status	—	55	15	Normal	—	—

● TM & HM MOVES

No.	Name	Type	Kind	Pow.	Acc.	PP	Range	Long	DA
TM06	Toxic	Poison	Status	—	90	10	Normal	—	—
TM10	Hidden Power	Normal	Special	—	100	15	Normal	—	—
TM11	Sunny Day	Fire	Status	—	—	5	Both Sides	—	—
TM16	Light Screen	Psychic	Status	—	—	30	Your Side	—	—
TM17	Protect	Normal	Status	—	—	10	Self	—	—
TM18	Rain Dance	Water	Status	—	—	5	Both Sides	—	—
TM20	Safeguard	Normal	Status	—	—	25	Your Side	—	—
TM21	Frustration	Normal	Physical	—	100	20	Normal	—	○
TM22	SolarBeam	Grass	Special	120	100	10	Normal	—	—
TM27	Return	Normal	Physical	—	100	20	Normal	—	○
TM30	Shadow Ball	Ghost	Special	80	100	15	Normal	—	—
TM32	Double Team	Normal	Status	—	—	15	Self	—	—
TM42	Facade	Normal	Physical	70	100	20	Normal	—	○
TM44	Rest	Psychic	Status	—	—	10	Self	—	—
TM45	Attract	Normal	Status	—	100	15	Normal	—	—
TM48	Round	Normal	Special	60	100	15	Normal	—	—
TM49	Echoed Voice	Normal	Special	40	100	15	Normal	—	—
TM53	Energy Ball	Grass	Special	80	100	10	Normal	—	—
TM67	Retaliate	Normal	Physical	70	100	5	Normal	—	—
TM70	Flash	Normal	Status	—	100	20	Normal	—	—
TM73	Thunder Wave	Electric	Status	—	100	20	Normal	—	—
TM83	Work Up	Normal	Status	—	—	30	Self	—	—
TM86	Grass Knot	Grass	Special	—	100	20	Normal	—	○
TM87	Swagger	Normal	Status	—	90	15	Normal	—	—
TM90	Substitute	Normal	Status	—	—	10	Self	—	—
TM93	Wild Charge	Electric	Physical	90	100	15	Normal	—	○

● MAIN WAYS TO OBTAIN

POKÉMON BLACK VERSION	1	Route 6
	2	Route 7

POKÉMON WHITE VERSION	1	Route 6
	2	Route 7

EVOLUTION

Deerling — Lv. 34 — Sawsbuck

ABILITIES
● Chlorophyll
● Sap Sipper

EGG GROUP
Field

STATS
HP ●●
ATTACK ●●●
DEFENSE ●●●
SP. ATTACK ●●
SP. DEFENSE ●●
SPEED ●●●

POKÉMON BLACK VERSION: The color and scent of their fur changes to match the mountain grass. When they sense hostility, they hide in the grass.

POKÉMON WHITE VERSION: The turning of the seasons changes the color and scent of this Pokémon's fur. People use it to mark the seasons.

Sawsbuck

● TYPE Normal Grass

● MALE/FEMALE HAVE SAME FORM

● SPRING FORM

● SUMMER FORM

● MALE/FEMALE HAVE SAME FORM

● MALE/FEMALE HAVE SAME FORM

● AUTUMN FORM

● WINTER FORM

- HEIGHT: 6'03"
- WEIGHT: 203.9 lbs.
- GENDER: Both ♂ ♀ exist
- ITEMS:
  • None

● FOOTPRINT

POKÉMON BLACK VERSION
They migrate according to the seasons. People can tell the season by looking at Sawsbuck's horns.

POKÉMON WHITE VERSION
The plants growing on its horns change according to the season. The leaders of the herd possess magnificent horns.

● LEVEL-UP AND LEARNED MOVES

Lv.	Name	Type	Kind	Pow.	Acc.	PP	Range	Long	DA
1	Megahorn	Bug	Physical	120	85	10	Normal	—	○
1	Tackle	Normal	Physical	50	100	35	Normal	—	—
1	Camouflage	Normal	Status	—	—	20	Self	—	—
1	Growl	Normal	Status	—	100	40	Many Others	—	—
4	Growl	Normal	Status	—	100	40	Many Others	—	—
4	Sand-Attack	Ground	Status	—	100	15	Normal	—	—
7	Sand-Attack	Ground	Status	—	100	15	Normal	—	—
10	Double Kick	Fighting	Physical	30	100	30	Normal	—	○
13	Leech Seed	Grass	Status	—	90	10	Normal	—	—
16	Faint Attack	Dark	Physical	60	—	20	Normal	—	—
20	Take Down	Normal	Physical	90	85	20	Normal	—	○
24	Jump Kick	Fighting	Physical	100	95	10	Normal	—	○
28	Aromatherapy	Grass	Status	—	—	5	Your Party	—	—
32	Energy Ball	Grass	Special	80	100	10	Normal	—	○
36	Charm	Normal	Status	—	100	20	Normal	—	—
37	Horn Leech	Grass	Physical	75	100	10	Normal	—	○
44	Nature Power	Normal	Status	—	—	20	Varies	—	—
52	Double-Edge	Normal	Physical	120	100	15	Normal	—	○
60	SolarBeam	Grass	Special	120	100	10	Normal	—	—

● MOVES TAUGHT BY PEOPLE

Name	Type	Kind	Pow.	Acc.	PP	Range	Long	DA

● TM & HM MOVES

No.	Name	Type	Kind	Pow.	Acc.	PP	Range	Long	DA
TM06	Toxic	Poison	Status	—	90	10	Normal	—	—
TM10	Hidden Power	Normal	Special	—	100	15	Normal	—	—
TM11	Sunny Day	Fire	Status	—	—	5	Both Sides	—	—
TM15	Hyper Beam	Normal	Special	150	90	5	Normal	—	—
TM16	Light Screen	Psychic	Status	—	—	30	Your Side	—	—
TM17	Protect	Normal	Status	—	—	10	Self	—	—
TM18	Rain Dance	Water	Status	—	—	5	Both Sides	—	—
TM20	Safeguard	Normal	Status	—	—	25	Your Side	—	—
TM21	Frustration	Normal	Physical	—	100	20	Normal	—	○
TM22	SolarBeam	Grass	Special	120	100	10	Normal	—	—
TM27	Return	Normal	Physical	—	100	20	Normal	—	○
TM30	Shadow Ball	Ghost	Special	80	100	15	Normal	—	—
TM32	Double Team	Normal	Status	—	—	15	Self	—	—
TM42	Facade	Normal	Physical	70	100	20	Normal	—	○
TM44	Rest	Psychic	Status	—	—	10	Self	—	—
TM45	Attract	Normal	Status	—	100	15	Normal	—	—
TM48	Round	Normal	Special	60	100	15	Normal	—	—
TM49	Echoed Voice	Normal	Special	40	100	15	Normal	—	—
TM53	Energy Ball	Grass	Special	80	100	10	Normal	—	○
TM67	Retaliate	Normal	Physical	70	100	5	Normal	—	○
TM68	Giga Impact	Normal	Physical	150	90	5	Normal	—	○
TM70	Flash	Normal	Status	—	100	20	Normal	—	—
TM73	Thunder Wave	Electric	Status	—	100	20	Normal	—	—
TM75	Swords Dance	Normal	Status	—	—	30	Self	—	—
TM83	Work Up	Normal	Status	—	—	30	Self	—	—
TM86	Grass Knot	Grass	Special	—	100	20	Normal	—	○
TM87	Swagger	Normal	Status	—	90	15	Normal	—	—
TM90	Substitute	Normal	Status	—	—	10	Self	—	—
TM93	Wild Charge	Electric	Physical	90	100	15	Normal	—	○
TM94	Rock Smash	Fighting	Physical	40	100	15	Normal	—	○
HM01	Cut	Normal	Physical	50	95	30	Normal	—	—

EVOLUTION

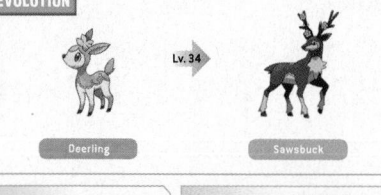

Deerling — Lv. 34 → Sawsbuck

ABILITIES
● Chlorophyll
● Sap Sipper

EGG GROUP Field

STATS
HP ●●●
ATTACK ●●●●
DEFENSE ●●●
SP. ATTACK ●●●
SP. DEFENSE ●●●
SPEED ●●●●

● MAIN WAYS TO OBTAIN

POKÉMON BLACK VERSION
1 Dragonspiral Tower 1F Outside (Dark Grass)
2 Level up Deerling to Lv. 34

POKÉMON WHITE VERSION
1 Dragonspiral Tower 1F Outside (Dark Grass)
2 Level up Deerling to Lv. 34

Emolga

● TYPE Electric Flying

- HEIGHT: 1'04"
- WEIGHT: 11.0 lbs.
- GENDER: Both ♂ ♀ exist
- ITEMS:
  • Cheri Berry

● FOOTPRINT

● MALE/FEMALE HAVE SAME FORM

POKÉMON BLACK VERSION
The energy made in its cheeks' electric pouches is stored inside its membrane and released while it is gliding.

POKÉMON WHITE VERSION
They live on treetops and glide using the inside of a cape-like membrane while discharging electricity.

● LEVEL-UP AND LEARNED MOVES

Lv.	Name	Type	Kind	Pow.	Acc.	PP	Range	Long	DA
1	ThunderShock	Electric	Special	40	100	30	Normal	—	—
4	Quick Attack	Normal	Physical	40	100	30	Normal	—	○
7	Tail Whip	Normal	Status	—	100	30	Many Others	—	—
10	Charge	Electric	Status	—	—	20	Self	—	—
13	Spark	Electric	Physical	65	100	20	Normal	—	○
16	Pursuit	Dark	Physical	40	100	20	Normal	—	○
19	Double Team	Normal	Status	—	—	15	Self	—	—
22	Shock Wave	Electric	Special	60	—	20	Normal	—	—
26	Electro Ball	Electric	Special	—	100	10	Normal	—	—
30	Acrobatics	Flying	Physical	55	100	15	Normal	○	○
34	Light Screen	Psychic	Status	—	—	30	Your Side	—	—
38	Encore	Normal	Status	—	100	5	Normal	—	—
42	Volt Switch	Electric	Special	70	100	20	Normal	—	—
46	Agility	Psychic	Status	—	—	30	Self	—	—
50	Discharge	Electric	Special	80	100	15	Adjacent	—	—

● MOVES TAUGHT BY PEOPLE

Name	Type	Kind	Pow.	Acc.	PP	Range	Long	DA

● EGG MOVES

Name	Type	Kind	Pow.	Acc.	PP	Range	Long	DA
Roost	Flying	Status	—	—	10	Self	—	—
Iron Tail	Steel	Physical	100	75	15	Normal	—	○
Astonish	Ghost	Physical	30	100	15	Normal	—	○
Air Slash	Flying	Special	75	95	20	Normal	○	—
Shock Wave	Electric	Special	60	—	20	Normal	—	—
Charm	Normal	Status	—	100	20	Normal	—	—
Covet	Normal	Physical	60	100	40	Normal	—	○
Tickle	Normal	Status	—	100	20	Normal	—	—
Baton Pass	Normal	Status	—	—	40	Self	—	—

● TM & HM MOVES

No.	Name	Type	Kind	Pow.	Acc.	PP	Range	Long	DA
TM06	Toxic	Poison	Status	—	90	10	Normal	—	—
TM10	Hidden Power	Normal	Special	—	100	15	Normal	—	—
TM12	Taunt	Dark	Status	—	100	20	Normal	—	—
TM16	Light Screen	Psychic	Status	—	—	30	Your Side	—	—
TM17	Protect	Normal	Status	—	—	10	Self	—	—
TM18	Rain Dance	Water	Status	—	—	5	Both Sides	—	—
TM21	Frustration	Normal	Physical	—	100	20	Normal	—	○
TM24	Thunderbolt	Electric	Special	95	100	15	Normal	—	—
TM25	Thunder	Electric	Special	120	70	10	Normal	—	—
TM27	Return	Normal	Physical	—	100	20	Normal	—	○
TM32	Double Team	Normal	Status	—	—	15	Self	—	—
TM40	Aerial Ace	Flying	Physical	60	—	20	Normal	○	○
TM42	Facade	Normal	Physical	70	100	20	Normal	—	○
TM44	Rest	Psychic	Status	—	—	10	Self	—	—
TM45	Attract	Normal	Status	—	100	15	Normal	—	—
TM48	Round	Normal	Special	60	100	15	Normal	—	—
TM56	Fling	Dark	Physical	—	100	10	Normal	—	○
TM57	Charge Beam	Electric	Special	50	90	10	Normal	—	—
TM62	Acrobatics	Flying	Physical	55	100	15	Normal	○	○
TM70	Flash	Normal	Status	—	100	20	Normal	—	—
TM72	Volt Switch	Electric	Special	70	100	20	Normal	—	—
TM73	Thunder Wave	Electric	Status	—	100	20	Normal	—	—
TM87	Swagger	Normal	Status	—	90	15	Normal	—	—
TM89	U-turn	Bug	Physical	70	100	20	Normal	—	○
TM90	Substitute	Normal	Status	—	—	10	Self	—	—
TM93	Wild Charge	Electric	Physical	90	100	15	Normal	—	○
HM01	Cut	Normal	Physical	50	95	30	Normal	—	—

EVOLUTION

Does not evolve

ABILITY
● Static

EGG GROUP Field

STATS
HP ●●
ATTACK ●●●
DEFENSE ●●●
SP. ATTACK ●●●
SP. DEFENSE ●●
SPEED ●●●●●

● MAIN WAYS TO OBTAIN

POKÉMON BLACK VERSION
1 Route 6 (Rustling Grass)
2 Route 16 (Rustling Grass)

POKÉMON WHITE VERSION
1 Route 6 (Rustling Grass)
2 Route 16 (Rustling Grass)

Karrablast

● TYPE **Bug**

● FOOTPRINT

● MALE/FEMALE HAVE SAME FORM

● HEIGHT: 1'08"
● WEIGHT: 13.0 lbs.
● GENDER: Both ♂♀ exist
● ITEMS:
  • None

POKÉMON BLACK VERSION — These mysterious Pokémon evolve when they receive electrical stimulation while they are in the same place as Shelmet.

POKÉMON WHITE VERSION — When they feel threatened, they spit an acidic liquid to drive attackers away. This Pokémon targets Shelmet.

● LEVEL-UP AND LEARNED MOVES

Lv.	Name	Type	Kind	Pow.	Acc.	PP	Range	Long	DA
1	Peck	Flying	Physical	35	100	35	Normal	○	—
4	Leer	Normal	Status	—	100	30	Many Others	—	—
8	Endure	Normal	Status	—	—	10	Self	—	—
13	Fury Cutter	Bug	Physical	20	95	20	Normal	—	○
16	Fury Attack	Normal	Physical	15	85	20	Normal	—	○
20	Headbutt	Normal	Physical	70	100	15	Normal	—	○
25	False Swipe	Normal	Physical	40	100	40	Normal	—	○
28	Bug Buzz	Bug	Special	90	100	10	Normal	—	○
32	Slash	Normal	Physical	70	100	20	Normal	—	○
37	Take Down	Normal	Physical	90	85	20	Normal	—	○
40	Scary Face	Normal	Status	—	100	10	Normal	—	—
44	X-Scissor	Bug	Physical	80	100	15	Normal	—	○
49	Flail	Normal	Physical	—	100	15	Normal	—	○
52	Swords Dance	Normal	Status	—	—	30	Self	—	—
56	Double-Edge	Normal	Physical	120	100	15	Normal	—	○

● MOVES TAUGHT BY PEOPLE

Name	Type	Kind	Pow.	Acc.	PP	Range	Long	DA

● EGG MOVES

Name	Type	Kind	Pow.	Acc.	PP	Range	Long	DA
Megahorn	Bug	Physical	120	85	10	Normal	—	○
Pursuit	Dark	Physical	40	100	20	Normal	—	○
Counter	Fighting	Physical	—	100	20	Varies	—	○
Horn Attack	Normal	Physical	65	100	25	Normal	—	○
Faint Attack	Dark	Physical	60	—	20	Normal	—	○
Bug Bite	Bug	Physical	60	100	20	Normal	—	○
Screech	Normal	Status	—	85	40	Normal	—	—
Knock Off	Dark	Physical	20	100	20	Normal	—	○

● TM & HM MOVES

No.	Name	Type	Kind	Pow.	Acc.	PP	Range	Long	DA
TM06	Toxic	Poison	Status	—	90	10	Normal	—	—
TM10	Hidden Power	Normal	Special	—	100	15	Normal	—	—
TM17	Protect	Normal	Status	—	—	10	Self	—	—
TM18	Rain Dance	Water	Status	—	—	5	Both Sides	—	—
TM27	Return	Normal	Physical	—	100	20	Normal	—	○
TM32	Double Team	Normal	Status	—	—	15	Self	—	—
TM40	Aerial Ace	Flying	Physical	60	—	20	Normal	○	○
TM42	Facade	Normal	Physical	70	100	20	Normal	—	○
TM44	Rest	Psychic	Status	—	—	10	Self	—	—
TM45	Attract	Normal	Status	—	100	15	Normal	—	—
TM48	Round	Normal	Special	60	100	15	Normal	—	—
TM53	Energy Ball	Grass	Special	80	100	10	Normal	—	○
TM54	False Swipe	Normal	Physical	40	100	40	Normal	—	○
TM75	Swords Dance	Normal	Status	—	—	30	Self	—	—
TM76	Struggle Bug	Bug	Special	30	100	20	Many Others	—	—
TM81	X-Scissor	Bug	Physical	80	100	15	Normal	—	○
TM84	Poison Jab	Poison	Physical	80	100	20	Normal	—	○
TM87	Swagger	Normal	Status	—	90	15	Normal	—	—
TM90	Substitute	Normal	Status	—	—	10	Self	—	—
HM01	Cut	Normal	Physical	50	95	30	Normal	—	○

● EVOLUTION

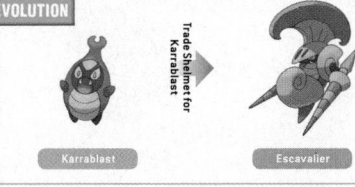

Karrablast → Trade Shelmet for Karrablast → Escavalier

● ABILITIES
  ● Swarm
  ● Shed Skin

● EGG GROUP
  Bug

● STATS
  HP ●●
  ATTACK ●●●
  DEFENSE ●●
  SP. ATTACK ●●
  SP. DEFENSE ●●
  SPEED ●●●

● MAIN WAYS TO OBTAIN

POKÉMON BLACK VERSION
  1 Route 6
  2 Route 11

POKÉMON WHITE VERSION
  1 Route 6
  2 Route 11

Escavalier

● TYPE **Bug** **Steel**

● FOOTPRINT

● MALE/FEMALE HAVE SAME FORM

● HEIGHT: 3'03"
● WEIGHT: 72.8 lbs.
● GENDER: Both ♂♀ exist
● ITEMS:
  • None

POKÉMON BLACK VERSION — They fly around at high speed, striking with their pointed spears. Even when in trouble, they face opponents bravely.

POKÉMON WHITE VERSION — These Pokémon evolve by wearing the shell covering of a Shelmet. The steel armor protects their whole body.

● LEVEL-UP AND LEARNED MOVES

Lv.	Name	Type	Kind	Pow.	Acc.	PP	Range	Long	DA
1	Peck	Flying	Physical	35	100	35	Normal	○	—
1	Leer	Normal	Status	—	100	30	Many Others	—	—
1	Quick Guard	Fighting	Status	—	—	15	Your Side	—	—
1	Twineedle	Bug	Physical	25	100	20	Normal	—	—
4	Leer	Normal	Status	—	100	30	Many Others	—	—
8	Quick Guard	Fighting	Status	—	—	15	Your Side	—	—
13	Twineedle	Bug	Physical	25	100	20	Normal	—	—
16	Fury Attack	Normal	Physical	15	85	20	Normal	—	○
20	Headbutt	Normal	Physical	70	100	15	Normal	—	○
25	False Swipe	Normal	Physical	40	100	40	Normal	—	○
28	Bug Buzz	Bug	Special	90	100	10	Normal	—	○
32	Slash	Normal	Physical	70	100	20	Normal	—	○
37	Iron Head	Steel	Physical	80	100	15	Normal	—	○
40	Iron Defense	Steel	Status	—	—	15	Self	—	—
44	X-Scissor	Bug	Physical	80	100	15	Normal	—	○
49	Reversal	Fighting	Physical	—	100	15	Normal	—	○
52	Swords Dance	Normal	Status	—	—	30	Self	—	—
56	Giga Impact	Normal	Physical	150	90	5	Normal	—	○

● MOVES TAUGHT BY PEOPLE

Name	Type	Kind	Pow.	Acc.	PP	Range	Long	DA

● TM & HM MOVES

No.	Name	Type	Kind	Pow.	Acc.	PP	Range	Long	DA
TM06	Toxic	Poison	Status	—	90	10	Normal	—	—
TM10	Hidden Power	Normal	Special	—	100	15	Normal	—	—
TM15	Hyper Beam	Normal	Special	150	90	5	Normal	—	—
TM17	Protect	Normal	Status	—	—	10	Self	—	—
TM18	Rain Dance	Water	Status	—	—	5	Both Sides	—	—
TM21	Frustration	Normal	Physical	—	100	20	Normal	—	○
TM27	Return	Normal	Physical	—	100	20	Normal	—	○
TM32	Double Team	Normal	Status	—	—	15	Self	—	—
TM40	Aerial Ace	Flying	Physical	60	—	20	Normal	○	○
TM42	Facade	Normal	Physical	70	100	20	Normal	—	○
TM44	Rest	Psychic	Status	—	—	10	Self	—	—
TM45	Attract	Normal	Status	—	100	15	Normal	—	—
TM48	Round	Normal	Special	60	100	15	Normal	—	—
TM52	Focus Blast	Fighting	Special	120	70	5	Normal	—	○
TM53	Energy Ball	Grass	Special	80	100	10	Normal	—	○
TM54	False Swipe	Normal	Physical	40	100	40	Normal	—	○
TM68	Giga Impact	Normal	Physical	150	90	5	Normal	—	○
TM75	Swords Dance	Normal	Status	—	—	30	Self	—	—
TM76	Struggle Bug	Bug	Special	30	100	20	Many Others	—	—
TM81	X-Scissor	Bug	Physical	80	100	15	Normal	—	○
TM84	Poison Jab	Poison	Physical	80	100	20	Normal	—	○
TM87	Swagger	Normal	Status	—	90	15	Normal	—	—
TM90	Substitute	Normal	Status	—	—	10	Self	—	—
TM94	Rock Smash	Fighting	Physical	40	100	15	Normal	—	○
HM01	Cut	Normal	Physical	50	95	30	Normal	—	○

● EVOLUTION

Karrablast → Trade Shelmet for Karrablast → Escavalier

● ABILITIES
  ● Swarm
  ● Shell Armor

● EGG GROUP
  Bug

● STATS
  HP ●●●
  ATTACK ●●●●●●
  DEFENSE ●●●●●
  SP. ATTACK ●●●
  SP. DEFENSE ●●●●
  SPEED ●

● MAIN WAYS TO OBTAIN

POKÉMON BLACK VERSION
  1 Link trade Shelmet for Karrablast
  2 —

POKÉMON WHITE VERSION
  1 Link trade Shelmet for Karrablast
  2 —

Foongus

● TYPE Grass Poison

● LEVEL-UP AND LEARNED MOVES

Lv.	Name	Type	Kind	Pow.	Acc.	PP	Range	Long	DA
1	Absorb	Grass	Special	20	100	25	Normal	—	—
6	Growth	Normal	Status	—	—	40	Self	—	—
8	Astonish	Ghost	Physical	30	100	15	Normal	—	○
12	Bide	Normal	Physical	—	—	10	Self	—	—
15	Mega Drain	Grass	Special	40	100	15	Normal	—	—
18	Ingrain	Grass	Status	—	—	20	Self	—	—
20	Faint Attack	Dark	Physical	60	—	20	Normal	—	○
24	Sweet Scent	Normal	Status	—	100	20	Many Others	—	—
28	Giga Drain	Grass	Special	75	100	10	Normal	—	—
32	Toxic	Poison	Status	—	90	10	Normal	—	—
35	Synthesis	Grass	Status	—	—	5	Self	—	—
39	Clear Smog	Poison	Special	50	—	15	Normal	—	—
43	SolarBeam	Grass	Special	120	100	10	Normal	—	—
45	Rage Powder	Bug	Status	—	—	20	Self	—	—
50	Spore	Grass	Status	—	100	15	Normal	—	—

● MOVES TAUGHT BY PEOPLE

Name	Type	Kind	Pow.	Acc.	PP	Range	Long	DA

● EGG MOVES

Name	Type	Kind	Pow.	Acc.	PP	Range	Long	DA
Gastro Acid	Poison	Status	—	100	10	Normal	—	—
Growth	Normal	Status	—	—	40	Self	—	—
PoisonPowder	Poison	Status	—	75	35	Normal	—	—
Stun Spore	Grass	Status	—	75	30	Normal	—	—
Rollout	Rock	Physical	30	90	20	Normal	—	○
Defense Curl	Normal	Status	—	—	40	Self	—	—
Endure	Normal	Status	—	—	10	Self	—	○
Body Slam	Normal	Physical	85	100	15	Normal	—	○

● TM & HM MOVES

No.	Name	Type	Kind	Pow.	Acc.	PP	Range	Long	DA
TM06	Toxic	Poison	Status	—	90	10	Normal	—	—
TM09	Venoshock	Poison	Special	65	100	10	Normal	—	—
TM10	Hidden Power	Normal	Special	—	100	15	Normal	—	—
TM11	Sunny Day	Fire	Status	—	—	5	Both Sides	—	—
TM17	Protect	Normal	Status	—	—	10	Self	—	—
TM18	Rain Dance	Water	Status	—	—	5	Both Sides	—	—
TM21	Frustration	Normal	Physical	—	100	20	Normal	—	○
TM22	SolarBeam	Grass	Special	120	100	10	Normal	—	—
TM27	Return	Normal	Physical	—	100	20	Normal	—	○
TM32	Double Team	Normal	Status	—	—	15	Self	—	—
TM36	Sludge Bomb	Poison	Special	90	100	10	Normal	—	—
TM42	Facade	Normal	Physical	70	100	20	Normal	—	—
TM44	Rest	Psychic	Status	—	—	10	Self	—	—
TM45	Attract	Normal	Status	—	100	15	Normal	—	—
TM48	Round	Normal	Special	60	100	15	Normal	—	—
TM53	Energy Ball	Grass	Special	80	100	10	Normal	—	—
TM66	Payback	Dark	Physical	50	100	10	Normal	—	○
TM70	Flash	Normal	Status	—	100	20	Normal	—	—
TM86	Grass Knot	Grass	Special	—	100	20	Normal	—	○
TM87	Swagger	Normal	Status	—	90	15	Normal	—	—
TM90	Substitute	Normal	Status	—	—	10	Self	—	—

● FOOTPRINT

● HEIGHT: 0'08"
● WEIGHT: 2.2 lbs.
● GENDER: Both ♂ ♀ exist
● ITEMS:
 • TinyMushroom
 • Big Mushroom
 • BalmMushroom

● MALE/FEMALE HAVE SAME FORM

EVOLUTION

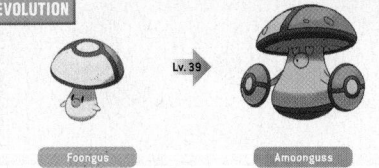

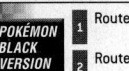 Lv. 39

Foongus → Amoonguss

ABILITY ● Effect Spore

EGG GROUP Grass

STATS
HP ●●●
ATTACK ●●
DEFENSE ●●
SP. ATTACK ●●●
SP. DEFENSE ●●
SPEED ●

POKÉMON BLACK VERSION — It lures people in with its Poké Ball pattern, then releases poison spores. Why it resembles a Poké Ball is unknown.

POKÉMON WHITE VERSION — For some reason, this Pokémon resembles a Poké Ball. They release poison spores to repel those who try to catch them.

● MAIN WAYS TO OBTAIN

POKÉMON BLACK VERSION
1 Route 6
2 Route 7

POKÉMON WHITE VERSION
1 Route 6
2 Route 7

Amoonguss

● TYPE Grass Poison

● LEVEL-UP AND LEARNED MOVES

Lv.	Name	Type	Kind	Pow.	Acc.	PP	Range	Long	DA
1	Absorb	Grass	Special	20	100	25	Normal	—	—
1	Growth	Normal	Status	—	—	40	Self	—	—
1	Astonish	Ghost	Physical	30	100	15	Normal	—	○
1	Bide	Normal	Physical	—	—	10	Self	—	—
6	Growth	Normal	Status	—	—	40	Self	—	—
8	Astonish	Ghost	Physical	30	100	15	Normal	—	○
12	Bide	Normal	Physical	—	—	10	Self	—	—
15	Mega Drain	Grass	Special	40	100	15	Normal	—	—
18	Ingrain	Grass	Status	—	—	20	Self	—	—
20	Faint Attack	Dark	Physical	60	—	20	Normal	—	○
24	Sweet Scent	Normal	Status	—	100	20	Many Others	—	—
28	Giga Drain	Grass	Special	75	100	10	Normal	—	—
32	Toxic	Poison	Status	—	90	10	Normal	—	—
35	Synthesis	Grass	Status	—	—	5	Self	—	—
43	Clear Smog	Poison	Special	50	—	15	Normal	—	—
49	SolarBeam	Grass	Special	120	100	10	Normal	—	—
54	Rage Powder	Bug	Status	—	—	20	Self	—	—
62	Spore	Grass	Status	—	100	15	Normal	—	—

● MOVES TAUGHT BY PEOPLE

Name	Type	Kind	Pow.	Acc.	PP	Range	Long	DA

● TM & HM MOVES

No.	Name	Type	Kind	Pow.	Acc.	PP	Range	Long	DA
TM06	Toxic	Poison	Status	—	90	10	Normal	—	—
TM09	Venoshock	Poison	Special	65	100	10	Normal	—	—
TM10	Hidden Power	Normal	Special	—	100	15	Normal	—	—
TM11	Sunny Day	Fire	Status	—	—	5	Both Sides	—	—
TM15	Hyper Beam	Normal	Special	150	90	5	Normal	—	—
TM17	Protect	Normal	Status	—	—	10	Self	—	—
TM18	Rain Dance	Water	Status	—	—	5	Both Sides	—	—
TM21	Frustration	Normal	Physical	—	100	20	Normal	—	○
TM22	SolarBeam	Grass	Special	120	100	10	Normal	—	—
TM27	Return	Normal	Physical	—	100	20	Normal	—	○
TM32	Double Team	Normal	Status	—	—	15	Self	—	—
TM36	Sludge Bomb	Poison	Special	90	100	10	Normal	—	—
TM42	Facade	Normal	Physical	70	100	20	Normal	—	—
TM44	Rest	Psychic	Status	—	—	10	Self	—	—
TM45	Attract	Normal	Status	—	100	15	Normal	—	—
TM48	Round	Normal	Special	60	100	15	Normal	—	—
TM53	Energy Ball	Grass	Special	80	100	10	Normal	—	—
TM66	Payback	Dark	Physical	50	100	10	Normal	—	○
TM68	Giga Impact	Normal	Physical	150	90	5	Normal	—	○
TM70	Flash	Normal	Status	—	100	20	Normal	—	—
TM86	Grass Knot	Grass	Special	—	100	20	Normal	—	○
TM87	Swagger	Normal	Status	—	90	15	Normal	—	—
TM90	Substitute	Normal	Status	—	—	10	Self	—	—

● FOOTPRINT

● HEIGHT: 2'00"
● WEIGHT: 23.1 lbs.
● GENDER: Both ♂ ♀ exist
● ITEMS:
 • TinyMushroom
 • Big Mushroom
 • BalmMushroom

● MALE/FEMALE HAVE SAME FORM

EVOLUTION

Lv. 39

Foongus → Amoonguss

ABILITY ● Effect Spore

EGG GROUP Grass

STATS
HP ●●●●
ATTACK ●●
DEFENSE ●●●
SP. ATTACK ●●●●
SP. DEFENSE ●●●
SPEED ●

POKÉMON BLACK VERSION — It lures prey close by dancing and waving its arm caps, which resemble Poké Balls, in a swaying motion.

POKÉMON WHITE VERSION — They show off their Poké Ball caps to lure prey, but very few Pokémon are fooled by this.

● MAIN WAYS TO OBTAIN

POKÉMON BLACK VERSION
1 Route 10 (Dark Grass)
2 Level up Foongus to Lv. 39

POKÉMON WHITE VERSION
1 Route 10 (Dark Grass)
2 Level up Foongus to Lv. 39

Frillish

● TYPE Water Ghost

● HEIGHT: 3'11"
● WEIGHT: 72.8 lbs.
● GENDER: Both ♂♀ exist
● ITEMS:
• None

● FOOTPRINT

● MALE FORM   ● FEMALE FORM

● LEVEL-UP AND LEARNED MOVES

Lv.	Name	Type	Kind	Pow.	Acc.	PP	Range	Long	DA
1	Bubble	Water	Special	20	100	30	Many Others	—	—
1	Water Sport	Water	Status	—	—	15	Both Sides	—	—
5	Absorb	Grass	Special	20	100	25	Normal	—	—
9	Night Shade	Ghost	Special	—	100	15	Normal	—	—
13	BubbleBeam	Water	Special	65	100	20	Normal	—	—
17	Recover	Normal	Status	—	—	10	Self	—	—
22	Water Pulse	Water	Special	60	100	20	Normal	○	—
27	Ominous Wind	Ghost	Special	60	100	5	Normal	—	—
32	Brine	Water	Special	65	100	10	Normal	—	—
37	Rain Dance	Water	Status	—	—	5	Both Sides	—	—
43	Hex	Ghost	Special	50	100	10	Normal	—	—
49	Hydro Pump	Water	Special	120	80	5	Normal	—	—
55	Wring Out	Normal	Special	—	100	5	Normal	—	○
61	Water Spout	Water	Special	150	100	5	Many Others	—	—

● MOVES TAUGHT BY PEOPLE

Name	Type	Kind	Pow.	Acc.	PP	Range	Long	DA

● EGG MOVES

Name	Type	Kind	Pow.	Acc.	PP	Range	Long	DA
Acid Armor	Poison	Status	—	—	40	Self	—	—
Confuse Ray	Ghost	Status	—	100	10	Normal	—	—
Pain Split	Normal	Status	—	—	20	Normal	—	—
Mist	Ice	Status	—	—	30	Your Side	—	—
Recover	Normal	Status	—	—	10	Self	—	—
Constrict	Normal	Physical	10	100	35	Normal	—	○

● TM & HM MOVES

No.	Name	Type	Kind	Pow.	Acc.	PP	Range	Long	DA
TM06	Toxic	Poison	Status	—	90	10	Normal	—	—
TM07	Hail	Ice	Status	—	—	10	Both Sides	—	—
TM10	Hidden Power	Normal	Special	—	100	15	Normal	—	—
TM12	Taunt	Dark	Status	—	100	20	Normal	—	—
TM13	Ice Beam	Ice	Special	95	100	10	Normal	—	—
TM14	Blizzard	Ice	Special	120	70	5	Many Others	—	—
TM17	Protect	Normal	Status	—	—	10	Self	—	—
TM18	Rain Dance	Water	Status	—	—	5	Both Sides	—	—
TM20	Safeguard	Normal	Status	—	—	25	Your Side	—	—
TM21	Frustration	Normal	Physical	—	100	20	Normal	—	○
TM27	Return	Normal	Physical	—	100	20	Normal	—	○
TM29	Psychic	Psychic	Special	90	100	10	Normal	—	—
TM30	Shadow Ball	Ghost	Special	80	100	15	Normal	—	—
TM32	Double Team	Normal	Status	—	—	15	Self	—	—
TM34	Sludge Wave	Poison	Special	95	100	10	Adjacent	—	—
TM36	Sludge Bomb	Poison	Special	90	100	10	Normal	—	—
TM42	Facade	Normal	Physical	70	100	20	Normal	—	○
TM44	Rest	Psychic	Status	—	—	10	Self	—	—
TM45	Attract	Normal	Status	—	100	15	Normal	—	—
TM48	Round	Normal	Special	60	100	15	Normal	—	—
TM53	Energy Ball	Grass	Special	80	100	10	Normal	—	—
TM55	Scald	Water	Special	80	100	15	Normal	—	—
TM61	Will-O-Wisp	Fire	Status	—	75	15	Normal	—	—
TM70	Flash	Normal	Status	—	100	20	Normal	—	—
TM77	Psych Up	Normal	Status	—	—	10	Self	—	—
TM85	Dream Eater	Psychic	Special	100	100	15	Normal	—	—
TM87	Swagger	Normal	Status	—	90	15	Normal	—	—
TM90	Substitute	Normal	Status	—	—	10	Self	—	—
TM92	Trick Room	Psychic	Status	—	—	5	Both Sides	—	—
HM03	Surf	Water	Special	95	100	15	Adjacent	—	—
HM05	Waterfall	Water	Physical	80	100	15	Normal	—	○
HM06	Dive	Water	Physical	80	100	10	Normal	—	○

● MAIN WAYS TO OBTAIN

POKÉMON BLACK VERSION
1 Route 17 (Water Surface)
2 Route 4 (Water Surface)

POKÉMON WHITE VERSION
1 Route 17 (Water Surface)
2 Route 4 (Water Surface)

EVOLUTION

Frillish → Lv. 40 → Jellicent

POKÉMON BLACK VERSION
With its thin, veil-like arms wrapped around the body of its opponent, it sinks to the ocean floor.

POKÉMON WHITE VERSION
They paralyze prey with poison, then drag them down to their lairs, five miles below the surface.

ABILITIES
● Water Absorb
● Cursed Body

EGG GROUP
Amorphous

STATS
HP ●●
ATTACK ●●
DEFENSE ●●
SP.ATTACK ●●
SP.DEFENSE ●●●
SPEED ●●

Jellicent

● TYPE Water Ghost

● HEIGHT: 7'03"
● WEIGHT: 297.6 lbs.
● GENDER: Both ♂♀ exist
● ITEMS:
• None

● FOOTPRINT

● MALE FORM   ● FEMALE FORM

● LEVEL-UP AND LEARNED MOVES

Lv.	Name	Type	Kind	Pow.	Acc.	PP	Range	Long	DA
1	Bubble	Water	Special	20	100	30	Many Others	—	—
1	Water Sport	Water	Status	—	—	15	Both Sides	—	—
1	Absorb	Grass	Special	20	100	25	Normal	—	—
1	Night Shade	Ghost	Special	—	100	15	Normal	—	—
5	Absorb	Grass	Special	20	100	25	Normal	—	—
9	Night Shade	Ghost	Special	—	100	15	Normal	—	—
13	BubbleBeam	Water	Special	65	100	20	Normal	—	—
17	Recover	Normal	Status	—	—	10	Self	—	—
22	Water Pulse	Water	Special	60	100	20	Normal	○	—
27	Ominous Wind	Ghost	Special	60	100	5	Normal	—	—
32	Brine	Water	Special	65	100	10	Normal	—	—
37	Rain Dance	Water	Status	—	—	5	Both Sides	—	—
45	Hex	Ghost	Special	50	100	10	Normal	—	—
53	Hydro Pump	Water	Special	120	80	5	Normal	—	—
61	Wring Out	Normal	Special	—	100	5	Normal	—	○
69	Water Spout	Water	Special	150	100	5	Many Others	—	—

● MOVES TAUGHT BY PEOPLE

Name	Type	Kind	Pow.	Acc.	PP	Range	Long	DA

● TM & HM MOVES

No.	Name	Type	Kind	Pow.	Acc.	PP	Range	Long	DA
TM06	Toxic	Poison	Status	—	90	10	Normal	—	—
TM07	Hail	Ice	Status	—	—	10	Both Sides	—	—
TM10	Hidden Power	Normal	Special	—	100	15	Normal	—	—
TM12	Taunt	Dark	Status	—	100	20	Normal	—	—
TM13	Ice Beam	Ice	Special	95	100	10	Normal	—	—
TM14	Blizzard	Ice	Special	120	70	5	Many Others	—	—
TM15	Hyper Beam	Normal	Special	150	90	5	Normal	—	—
TM17	Protect	Normal	Status	—	—	10	Self	—	—
TM18	Rain Dance	Water	Status	—	—	5	Both Sides	—	—
TM20	Safeguard	Normal	Status	—	—	25	Your Side	—	—
TM21	Frustration	Normal	Physical	—	100	20	Normal	—	○
TM27	Return	Normal	Physical	—	100	20	Normal	—	○
TM29	Psychic	Psychic	Special	90	100	10	Normal	—	—
TM30	Shadow Ball	Ghost	Special	80	100	15	Normal	—	—
TM32	Double Team	Normal	Status	—	—	15	Self	—	—
TM34	Sludge Wave	Poison	Special	95	100	10	Adjacent	—	—
TM36	Sludge Bomb	Poison	Special	90	100	10	Normal	—	—
TM42	Facade	Normal	Physical	70	100	20	Normal	—	○
TM44	Rest	Psychic	Status	—	—	10	Self	—	—
TM45	Attract	Normal	Status	—	100	15	Normal	—	—
TM48	Round	Normal	Special	60	100	15	Normal	—	—
TM53	Energy Ball	Grass	Special	80	100	10	Normal	—	—
TM55	Scald	Water	Special	80	100	15	Normal	—	—
TM61	Will-O-Wisp	Fire	Status	—	75	15	Normal	—	—
TM68	Giga Impact	Normal	Physical	150	90	5	Normal	—	○
TM70	Flash	Normal	Status	—	100	20	Normal	—	—
TM77	Psych Up	Normal	Status	—	—	10	Self	—	—
TM85	Dream Eater	Psychic	Special	100	100	15	Normal	—	—
TM87	Swagger	Normal	Status	—	90	15	Normal	—	—
TM90	Substitute	Normal	Status	—	—	10	Self	—	—
TM92	Trick Room	Psychic	Status	—	—	5	Both Sides	—	—
HM03	Surf	Water	Special	95	100	15	Adjacent	—	—
HM05	Waterfall	Water	Physical	80	100	15	Normal	—	○
HM06	Dive	Water	Physical	80	100	10	Normal	—	○

● MAIN WAYS TO OBTAIN

POKÉMON BLACK VERSION
1 Route 17 (Ripples in Water)
2 Level up Frillish to Lv. 40

POKÉMON WHITE VERSION
1 Route 17 (Ripples in Water)
2 Level up Frillish to Lv. 40

EVOLUTION

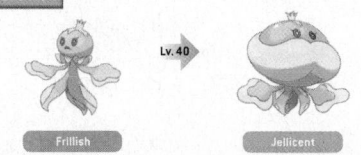

Frillish → Lv. 40 → Jellicent

POKÉMON BLACK VERSION
The fate of the ships and crew that wander into Jellicent's habitat: all sunken, all lost, all vanished.

POKÉMON WHITE VERSION
They propel themselves by expelling absorbed seawater from their bodies. Their favorite food is life energy.

ABILITIES
● Water Absorb
● Cursed Body

EGG GROUP
Amorphous

STATS
HP ●●●●
ATTACK ●●●
DEFENSE ●●●
SP.ATTACK ●●●
SP.DEFENSE ●●●●
SPEED ●●●

Alomomola

● **TYPE** [Water]

● **LEVEL-UP AND LEARNED MOVES**

Lv.	Name	Type	Kind	Pow.	Acc.	PP	Range	Long	DA
1	Pound	Normal	Physical	40	100	35	Normal	—	○
1	Water Sport	Water	Status	—	—	15	Both Sides	—	—
5	Aqua Ring	Water	Status	—	—	20	Self	—	—
9	Aqua Jet	Water	Physical	40	100	20	Normal	—	○
13	DoubleSlap	Normal	Physical	15	85	10	Normal	—	○
17	Heal Pulse	Psychic	Status	—	—	10	Normal	○	—
21	Protect	Normal	Status	—	—	10	Self	—	—
25	Water Pulse	Water	Special	60	100	20	Normal	○	—
29	Wake-Up Slap	Fighting	Physical	60	100	10	Normal	—	○
33	Soak	Water	Status	—	100	20	Normal	—	—
37	Wish	Normal	Status	—	—	10	Self	—	—
41	Brine	Water	Special	65	100	10	Normal	—	—
45	Safeguard	Normal	Status	—	—	25	Your Side	—	—
49	Helping Hand	Normal	Status	—	—	20	1 Ally	—	—
53	Wide Guard	Rock	Status	—	—	10	Your Side	—	—
57	Healing Wish	Psychic	Status	—	—	10	Self	—	—
61	Hydro Pump	Water	Special	120	80	5	Normal	—	—

● **MOVES TAUGHT BY PEOPLE**

Name	Type	Kind	Pow.	Acc.	PP	Range	Long	DA

● **EGG MOVES**

Name	Type	Kind	Pow.	Acc.	PP	Range	Long	DA
Pain Split	Normal	Status	—	—	20	Normal	—	—
Refresh	Normal	Status	—	—	20	Self	—	—
Tickle	Normal	Status	—	100	20	Normal	—	—
Mirror Coat	Psychic	Special	—	100	20	Varies	—	—
Mist	Ice	Status	—	—	30	Your Side	—	—
Endure	Normal	Status	—	—	10	Self	—	—

● **TM & HM MOVES**

No.	Name	Type	Kind	Pow.	Acc.	PP	Range	Long	DA
TM04	Calm Mind	Psychic	Status	—	—	20	Self	—	—
TM06	Toxic	Poison	Status	—	90	10	Normal	—	—
TM07	Hail	Ice	Status	—	—	10	Both Sides	—	—
TM10	Hidden Power	Normal	Special	—	100	15	Normal	—	—
TM13	Ice Beam	Ice	Special	95	100	10	Normal	—	—
TM14	Blizzard	Ice	Special	120	70	5	Many Others	—	—
TM16	Light Screen	Psychic	Status	—	—	30	Your Side	—	—
TM17	Protect	Normal	Status	—	—	10	Self	—	—
TM18	Rain Dance	Water	Status	—	—	5	Both Sides	—	—
TM20	Safeguard	Normal	Status	—	—	25	Your Side	—	—
TM21	Frustration	Normal	Physical	—	100	20	Normal	—	○
TM27	Return	Normal	Physical	—	100	20	Normal	—	○
TM29	Psychic	Psychic	Special	90	100	10	Normal	—	—
TM30	Shadow Ball	Ghost	Special	80	100	15	Normal	—	—
TM32	Double Team	Normal	Status	—	—	15	Self	—	—
TM42	Facade	Normal	Physical	70	100	20	Normal	—	○
TM44	Rest	Psychic	Status	—	—	10	Self	—	—
TM45	Attract	Normal	Status	—	100	15	Normal	—	—
TM48	Round	Normal	Special	60	100	15	Normal	—	—
TM55	Scald	Water	Special	80	100	15	Normal	—	—
TM77	Psych Up	Normal	Status	—	—	10	Normal	—	—
TM87	Swagger	Normal	Status	—	90	15	Normal	—	—
TM90	Substitute	Normal	Status	—	—	10	Self	—	—
HM03	Surf	Water	Special	95	100	15	Adjacent	—	—
HM05	Waterfall	Water	Physical	80	100	15	Normal	—	○
HM06	Dive	Water	Physical	80	100	10	Normal	—	○

● **FOOTPRINT**

● **MALE/FEMALE HAVE SAME FORM**

● HEIGHT: 3'11"
● WEIGHT: 69.7 lbs.
● GENDER: Both ♂♀ exist
● ITEMS:
• None

EVOLUTION

Does not evolve

● **MAIN WAYS TO OBTAIN**

POKÉMON BLACK VERSION	1	Route 17 (Ripples in Water)
	2	Route 4 (Ripples in Water)

POKÉMON WHITE VERSION	1	Route 17 (Ripples in Water)
	2	Route 4 (Ripples in Water)

POKÉMON BLACK VERSION
The special membrane enveloping Alomomola has the ability to heal wounds.

POKÉMON WHITE VERSION
Floating in the open sea is how they live. When they find a wounded Pokémon, they embrace it and bring it to shore.

ABILITIES
● Healer
● Hydration

EGG GROUPS
Water 1
Water 2

STATS
HP ●●●●●●●
ATTACK ●●●
DEFENSE ●●●
SP. ATTACK ●●●
SP. DEFENSE ●●
SPEED ●●●

Joltik

● **TYPE** [Bug] [Electric]

● **LEVEL-UP AND LEARNED MOVES**

Lv.	Name	Type	Kind	Pow.	Acc.	PP	Range	Long	DA
1	String Shot	Bug	Status	—	95	40	Many Others	—	—
1	Leech Life	Bug	Physical	20	100	15	Normal	—	○
1	Spider Web	Bug	Status	—	—	10	Normal	—	—
4	Thunder Wave	Electric	Status	—	100	20	Normal	—	—
7	Screech	Normal	Status	—	85	40	Normal	—	—
12	Fury Cutter	Bug	Physical	20	95	20	Normal	—	○
15	Electroweb	Electric	Special	55	95	15	Many Others	—	—
18	Bug Bite	Bug	Physical	60	100	20	Normal	—	○
23	Gastro Acid	Poison	Status	—	100	10	Normal	—	—
26	Slash	Normal	Physical	70	100	20	Normal	—	○
29	Electro Ball	Electric	Special	—	100	10	Normal	—	—
34	Signal Beam	Bug	Special	75	100	15	Normal	—	—
37	Agility	Psychic	Status	—	—	30	Self	—	—
40	Sucker Punch	Dark	Physical	80	100	5	Normal	—	○
45	Discharge	Electric	Special	80	100	15	Adjacent	—	—
48	Bug Buzz	Bug	Special	90	100	10	Normal	—	—

● **MOVES TAUGHT BY PEOPLE**

Name	Type	Kind	Pow.	Acc.	PP	Range	Long	DA

● **EGG MOVES**

Name	Type	Kind	Pow.	Acc.	PP	Range	Long	DA
Pin Missile	Bug	Physical	14	85	20	Normal	—	—
Poison Sting	Poison	Physical	15	100	35	Normal	—	—
Cross Poison	Poison	Physical	70	100	20	Normal	—	○
Rock Climb	Normal	Physical	90	85	20	Normal	—	○
Pursuit	Dark	Physical	40	100	20	Normal	—	○
Disable	Normal	Status	—	100	20	Normal	—	—
Faint Attack	Dark	Physical	60	—	20	Normal	—	○

● **TM & HM MOVES**

No.	Name	Type	Kind	Pow.	Acc.	PP	Range	Long	DA
TM06	Toxic	Poison	Status	—	90	10	Normal	—	—
TM10	Hidden Power	Normal	Special	—	100	15	Normal	—	—
TM16	Light Screen	Psychic	Status	—	—	30	Your Side	—	—
TM17	Protect	Normal	Status	—	—	10	Self	—	—
TM18	Rain Dance	Water	Status	—	—	5	Both Sides	—	—
TM21	Frustration	Normal	Physical	—	100	20	Normal	—	○
TM24	Thunderbolt	Electric	Special	95	100	15	Normal	—	—
TM27	Return	Normal	Physical	—	100	20	Normal	—	○
TM32	Double Team	Normal	Status	—	—	15	Self	—	—
TM42	Facade	Normal	Physical	70	100	20	Normal	—	○
TM44	Rest	Psychic	Status	—	—	10	Self	—	—
TM45	Attract	Normal	Status	—	100	15	Normal	—	—
TM46	Thief	Dark	Physical	40	100	10	Normal	—	○
TM48	Round	Normal	Special	60	100	15	Normal	—	—
TM53	Energy Ball	Grass	Special	80	100	10	Normal	—	—
TM57	Charge Beam	Electric	Special	50	90	10	Normal	—	—
TM70	Flash	Normal	Status	—	100	20	Normal	—	—
TM72	Volt Switch	Electric	Special	70	100	20	Normal	—	—
TM73	Thunder Wave	Electric	Status	—	100	20	Normal	—	—
TM76	Struggle Bug	Bug	Special	30	100	20	Many Others	—	—
TM81	X-Scissor	Bug	Physical	80	100	15	Normal	—	○
TM84	Poison Jab	Poison	Physical	80	100	20	Normal	—	○
TM87	Swagger	Normal	Status	—	90	15	Normal	—	—
TM90	Substitute	Normal	Status	—	—	10	Self	—	—
TM93	Wild Charge	Electric	Physical	90	100	15	Normal	—	○
HM01	Cut	Normal	Physical	50	95	30	Normal	—	○

● **FOOTPRINT**

● **MALE/FEMALE HAVE SAME FORM**

● HEIGHT: 0'04"
● WEIGHT: 1.3 lbs.
● GENDER: Both ♂♀ exist
● ITEMS:
• None

EVOLUTION

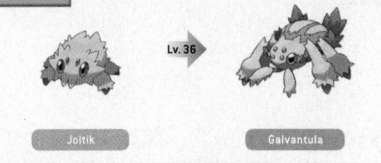

Joltik — Lv. 36 → Galvantula

● **MAIN WAYS TO OBTAIN**

POKÉMON BLACK VERSION	1	Chargestone Cave 1F
	2	—

POKÉMON WHITE VERSION	1	Chargestone Cave 1F
	2	—

POKÉMON BLACK VERSION
Joltik that live in cities have learned a technique for sucking electricity from the outlets in houses.

POKÉMON WHITE VERSION
They attach themselves to large-bodied Pokémon and absorb static electricity, which they store in an electric pouch.

ABILITIES
● Compoundeyes
● Unnerve

EGG GROUP
Bug

STATS
HP ●●
ATTACK ●●
DEFENSE ●●
SP. ATTACK ●●●
SP. DEFENSE ●●
SPEED ●●●

UNOVA POKÉDEX

ALOMOMOLA | 100

JOLTIK | 101

Galvantula

● TYPE Bug Electric

● LEVEL-UP AND LEARNED MOVES

Lv.	Name	Type	Kind	Pow.	Acc.	PP	Range	Long	DA
1	String Shot	Bug	Status	—	95	40	Many Others	—	—
1	Leech Life	Bug	Physical	20	100	15	Normal	—	○
1	Spider Web	Bug	Status	—	—	10	Normal	—	—
1	Thunder Wave	Electric	Status	—	100	20	Normal	—	—
4	Thunder Wave	Electric	Status	—	100	20	Normal	—	—
7	Screech	Normal	Status	—	85	40	Normal	—	—
12	Fury Cutter	Bug	Physical	20	95	20	Normal	—	○
15	Electroweb	Electric	Special	55	95	15	Many Others	—	—
18	Bug Bite	Bug	Physical	60	100	20	Normal	—	○
23	Gastro Acid	Poison	Status	—	100	10	Normal	—	—
26	Slash	Normal	Physical	70	100	20	Normal	—	○
29	Electro Ball	Electric	Special	—	100	10	Normal	—	—
34	Signal Beam	Bug	Special	75	100	15	Normal	—	—
40	Agility	Psychic	Status	—	—	30	Self	—	—
46	Sucker Punch	Dark	Physical	80	100	5	Normal	—	—
54	Discharge	Electric	Special	80	100	15	Adjacent	—	—
60	Bug Buzz	Bug	Special	90	100	10	Normal	—	—

● MOVES TAUGHT BY PEOPLE

Name	Type	Kind	Pow.	Acc.	PP	Range	Long	DA

● TM & HM MOVES

No.	Name	Type	Kind	Pow.	Acc.	PP	Range	Long	DA
TM06	Toxic	Poison	Status	—	90	10	Normal	—	—
TM10	Hidden Power	Normal	Special	—	100	15	Normal	—	—
TM15	Hyper Beam	Normal	Special	150	90	5	Normal	—	—
TM16	Light Screen	Psychic	Status	—	—	30	Your Side	—	—
TM17	Protect	Normal	Status	—	—	10	Self	—	—
TM18	Rain Dance	Water	Status	—	—	5	Both Sides	—	—
TM21	Frustration	Normal	Physical	—	100	20	Normal	—	○
TM24	Thunderbolt	Electric	Special	95	100	15	Normal	—	—
TM25	Thunder	Electric	Special	120	70	10	Normal	—	—
TM27	Return	Normal	Physical	—	100	20	Normal	—	○
TM32	Double Team	Normal	Status	—	—	15	Self	—	—
TM42	Facade	Normal	Physical	70	100	20	Normal	—	—
TM44	Rest	Psychic	Status	—	—	10	Self	—	—
TM45	Attract	Normal	Status	—	100	15	Normal	—	—
TM46	Thief	Dark	Physical	40	100	10	Normal	—	—
TM48	Round	Normal	Special	60	100	15	Normal	—	—
TM53	Energy Ball	Grass	Special	80	100	10	Normal	—	—
TM57	Charge Beam	Electric	Special	50	90	10	Normal	—	—
TM68	Giga Impact	Normal	Physical	150	90	5	Normal	—	—
TM70	Flash	Normal	Status	—	100	20	Normal	—	—
TM72	Volt Switch	Electric	Special	70	100	20	Normal	—	—
TM73	Thunder Wave	Electric	Status	—	100	20	Normal	—	—
TM76	Struggle Bug	Bug	Special	30	100	20	Many Others	—	—
TM81	X-Scissor	Bug	Physical	80	100	15	Normal	—	○
TM84	Poison Jab	Poison	Physical	80	100	20	Normal	—	—
TM87	Swagger	Normal	Status	—	90	15	Normal	—	—
TM90	Substitute	Normal	Status	—	—	10	Self	—	—
TM93	Wild Charge	Electric	Physical	90	100	15	Normal	—	○
HM01	Cut	Normal	Physical	50	95	30	Normal	—	—

● FOOTPRINT

● MALE/FEMALE HAVE SAME FORM

● HEIGHT: 2'07"
● WEIGHT: 31.5 lbs.
● GENDER: Both ♂♀ exist
● ITEMS:
• None

POKÉMON BLACK VERSION
When attacked, they create an electric barrier by spitting out many electrically charged threads.

POKÉMON WHITE VERSION
They employ an electrically charged web to trap their prey. While it is immobilized by shock, they leisurely consume it.

EVOLUTION

Joltik — Lv. 36 → Galvantula

ABILITIES ● Compoundeyes ● Unnerve

EGG GROUP Bug

STATS
HP ●●●
ATTACK ●●●
DEFENSE ●●
SP.ATTACK ●●●
SP.DEFENSE ●●
SPEED ●●●●●

● MAIN WAYS TO OBTAIN

POKÉMON BLACK VERSION
1 Level up Joltik to Lv. 36
2 —

POKÉMON WHITE VERSION
1 Level up Joltik to Lv. 36
2 —

Ferroseed

● TYPE Grass Steel

● LEVEL-UP AND LEARNED MOVES

Lv.	Name	Type	Kind	Pow.	Acc.	PP	Range	Long	DA
1	Tackle	Normal	Physical	50	100	35	Normal	—	○
1	Harden	Normal	Status	—	—	30	Self	—	—
6	Rollout	Rock	Physical	30	90	20	Normal	—	○
9	Curse	Ghost	Status	—	—	10	Varies	—	—
14	Metal Claw	Steel	Physical	50	95	35	Normal	—	○
18	Pin Missile	Bug	Physical	14	85	20	Normal	—	—
21	Gyro Ball	Steel	Physical	—	100	5	Normal	—	○
26	Iron Defense	Steel	Status	—	—	15	Self	—	—
30	Mirror Shot	Steel	Special	65	85	10	Normal	—	—
35	Ingrain	Grass	Status	—	—	20	Self	—	—
38	Selfdestruct	Normal	Physical	200	100	5	Adjacent	—	—
43	Iron Head	Steel	Physical	80	100	15	Normal	—	○
47	Payback	Dark	Physical	50	100	10	Normal	—	○
52	Flash Cannon	Steel	Special	80	100	10	Normal	—	—
55	Explosion	Normal	Physical	250	100	5	Adjacent	—	—

● MOVES TAUGHT BY PEOPLE

Name	Type	Kind	Pow.	Acc.	PP	Range	Long	DA

● EGG MOVES

Name	Type	Kind	Pow.	Acc.	PP	Range	Long	DA
Bullet Seed	Grass	Physical	25	100	30	Normal	—	—
Leech Seed	Grass	Status	—	90	10	Normal	—	—
Spikes	Ground	Status	—	—	20	Other Side	—	—
Worry Seed	Grass	Status	—	100	10	Normal	—	—
Seed Bomb	Grass	Physical	80	100	15	Normal	—	—
Gravity	Psychic	Status	—	—	5	Both Sides	—	—
Rock Climb	Normal	Physical	90	85	20	Normal	—	○
Stealth Rock	Rock	Status	—	—	20	Other Side	—	—

● TM & HM MOVES

No.	Name	Type	Kind	Pow.	Acc.	PP	Range	Long	DA
TM01	Hone Claws	Dark	Status	—	—	15	Self	—	—
TM06	Toxic	Poison	Status	—	90	10	Normal	—	—
TM10	Hidden Power	Normal	Special	—	100	15	Normal	—	—
TM11	Sunny Day	Fire	Status	—	—	5	Both Sides	—	—
TM17	Protect	Normal	Status	—	—	10	Self	—	—
TM21	Frustration	Normal	Physical	—	100	20	Normal	—	○
TM22	SolarBeam	Grass	Special	120	100	10	Normal	—	—
TM24	Thunderbolt	Electric	Special	95	100	15	Normal	—	—
TM27	Return	Normal	Physical	—	100	20	Normal	—	○
TM32	Double Team	Normal	Status	—	—	15	Self	—	—
TM42	Facade	Normal	Physical	70	100	20	Normal	—	—
TM44	Rest	Psychic	Status	—	—	10	Self	—	—
TM48	Round	Normal	Special	60	100	15	Normal	—	—
TM53	Energy Ball	Grass	Special	80	100	10	Normal	—	—
TM64	Explosion	Normal	Physical	250	100	5	Adjacent	—	—
TM66	Payback	Dark	Physical	50	100	10	Normal	—	○
TM69	Rock Polish	Rock	Status	—	—	20	Self	—	—
TM70	Flash	Normal	Status	—	100	20	Normal	—	—
TM73	Thunder Wave	Electric	Status	—	100	20	Normal	—	—
TM74	Gyro Ball	Steel	Physical	—	100	5	Normal	—	○
TM84	Poison Jab	Poison	Physical	80	100	20	Normal	—	—
TM87	Swagger	Normal	Status	—	90	15	Normal	—	—
TM90	Substitute	Normal	Status	—	—	10	Self	—	—
TM91	Flash Cannon	Steel	Special	80	100	10	Normal	—	—
TM94	Rock Smash	Fighting	Physical	40	100	15	Normal	—	—

● FOOTPRINT

● MALE/FEMALE HAVE SAME FORM

● HEIGHT: 2'00"
● WEIGHT: 41.4 lbs.
● GENDER: Both ♂♀ exist
● ITEMS:
• Sticky Barb

POKÉMON BLACK VERSION
When threatened, it attacks by shooting a barrage of spikes, which gives it a chance to escape by rolling away.

POKÉMON WHITE VERSION
They stick their spikes into cave walls and absorb the minerals they find in the rock.

EVOLUTION

Ferroseed — Lv. 40 → Ferrothorn

ABILITY ● Iron Barbs

EGG GROUPS Grass Mineral

STATS
HP ●●
ATTACK ●●
DEFENSE ●●●●
SP.ATTACK ●
SP.DEFENSE ●●●
SPEED ●

● MAIN WAYS TO OBTAIN

POKÉMON BLACK VERSION
1 Chargestone Cave 1F
2 —

POKÉMON WHITE VERSION
1 Chargestone Cave 1F
2 —

Ferrothorn

● TYPE Grass Steel

● LEVEL-UP AND LEARNED MOVES

Lv.	Name	Type	Kind	Pow.	Acc.	PP	Range	Long	DA
1	Rock Climb	Normal	Physical	90	85	20	Normal	—	○
1	Tackle	Normal	Physical	50	100	35	Normal	—	—
1	Harden	Normal	Status	—	—	30	Self	—	—
1	Rollout	Rock	Physical	30	90	20	Normal	—	○
1	Curse	Ghost	Status	—	—	10	Varies	—	—
6	Rollout	Rock	Physical	30	90	20	Normal	—	○
9	Curse	Ghost	Status	—	—	10	Varies	—	—
14	Metal Claw	Steel	Physical	50	95	35	Normal	—	—
18	Pin Missile	Bug	Physical	14	85	20	Normal	—	—
21	Gyro Ball	Steel	Physical	—	100	5	Normal	—	○
26	Iron Defense	Steel	Status	—	—	15	Self	—	—
30	Mirror Shot	Steel	Special	65	85	10	Normal	—	—
35	Ingrain	Grass	Status	—	—	20	Self	—	—
38	Selfdestruct	Normal	Physical	200	100	5	Adjacent	—	—
40	Power Whip	Grass	Physical	120	85	10	Normal	—	○
46	Iron Head	Steel	Physical	80	100	15	Normal	—	○
53	Payback	Dark	Physical	50	100	10	Normal	—	—
61	Flash Cannon	Steel	Special	80	100	10	Normal	—	—
67	Explosion	Normal	Physical	250	100	5	Adjacent	—	—

● MOVES TAUGHT BY PEOPLE

Name	Type	Kind	Pow.	Acc.	PP	Range	Long	DA

● TM & HM MOVES

No.	Name	Type	Kind	Pow.	Acc.	PP	Range	Long	DA
TM01	Hone Claws	Dark	Status	—	—	15	Self	—	—
TM06	Toxic	Poison	Status	—	90	10	Normal	—	—
TM10	Hidden Power	Normal	Special	—	100	15	Normal	—	—
TM11	Sunny Day	Fire	Status	—	—	5	Both Sides	—	—
TM15	Hyper Beam	Normal	Special	150	90	5	Normal	—	—
TM17	Protect	Normal	Status	—	—	10	Self	—	—
TM21	Frustration	Normal	Physical	—	100	20	Normal	—	○
TM22	SolarBeam	Grass	Special	120	100	10	Normal	—	—
TM24	Thunderbolt	Electric	Special	95	100	15	Normal	—	—
TM25	Thunder	Electric	Special	120	70	10	Normal	—	—
TM27	Return	Normal	Physical	—	100	20	Normal	—	○
TM32	Double Team	Normal	Status	—	—	15	Self	—	—
TM37	Sandstorm	Rock	Status	—	—	10	Both Sides	—	—
TM40	Aerial Ace	Flying	Physical	60	—	20	Normal	○	—
TM42	Facade	Normal	Physical	70	100	20	Normal	—	○
TM44	Rest	Psychic	Status	—	—	10	Self	—	—
TM48	Round	Normal	Special	60	100	15	Normal	—	—
TM53	Energy Ball	Grass	Special	80	100	10	Normal	—	—
TM64	Explosion	Normal	Physical	250	100	5	Adjacent	—	—
TM65	Shadow Claw	Ghost	Physical	70	100	15	Normal	—	○
TM66	Payback	Dark	Physical	50	100	10	Normal	—	—
TM68	Giga Impact	Normal	Physical	150	90	5	Normal	—	○
TM69	Rock Polish	Rock	Status	—	—	20	Self	—	—
TM70	Flash	Normal	Status	—	100	20	Normal	—	—
TM73	Thunder Wave	Electric	Status	—	100	20	Normal	—	—
TM74	Gyro Ball	Steel	Physical	—	100	5	Normal	—	○
TM75	Swords Dance	Normal	Status	—	—	30	Self	—	—
TM78	Bulldoze	Ground	Physical	60	100	20	Adjacent	—	—
TM84	Poison Jab	Poison	Physical	80	100	20	Normal	—	—
TM86	Grass Knot	Grass	Special	—	100	20	Normal	—	○
TM87	Swagger	Normal	Status	—	90	15	Normal	—	—
TM90	Substitute	Normal	Status	—	—	10	Self	—	—
TM91	Flash Cannon	Steel	Special	80	100	10	Normal	—	—
TM94	Rock Smash	Fighting	Physical	40	100	15	Normal	—	—
HM01	Cut	Normal	Physical	50	95	30	Normal	—	○
HM04	Strength	Normal	Physical	80	100	15	Normal	—	○

● FOOTPRINT

● MALE/FEMALE HAVE SAME FORM

● HEIGHT: 3'03"
● WEIGHT: 242.5 lbs.
● GENDER: Both ♂ ♀ exist
● ITEMS:
 • None

POKÉMON BLACK VERSION
It fights by swinging around its three spiky feelers. A hit from these steel spikes can reduce a boulder to rubble.

POKÉMON WHITE VERSION
They attach themselves to cave ceilings, firing steel spikes at targets passing beneath them.

EVOLUTION

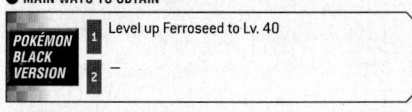

Ferroseed Lv. 40 Ferrothorn

ABILITY ● Iron Barbs

EGG GROUPS Grass Mineral

STATS
HP ●●●
ATTACK ●●●●
DEFENSE ●●●●●
SP. ATTACK ●●●
SP. DEFENSE ●●●●●
SPEED ●

● MAIN WAYS TO OBTAIN

| POKÉMON BLACK VERSION | 1 | Level up Ferroseed to Lv. 40 |
| | 2 | — |

| POKÉMON WHITE VERSION | 1 | Level up Ferroseed to Lv. 40 |
| | 2 | — |

Klink

● TYPE Steel

● LEVEL-UP AND LEARNED MOVES

Lv.	Name	Type	Kind	Pow.	Acc.	PP	Range	Long	DA
1	ViceGrip	Normal	Physical	55	100	30	Normal	—	○
6	Charge	Electric	Status	—	—	20	Self	—	—
11	ThunderShock	Electric	Special	40	100	30	Normal	—	—
16	Gear Grind	Steel	Physical	50	85	15	Normal	—	○
21	Bind	Normal	Physical	15	85	20	Normal	—	—
26	Charge Beam	Electric	Special	50	90	10	Normal	—	—
31	Autotomize	Steel	Status	—	—	15	Self	—	—
36	Mirror Shot	Steel	Special	65	85	10	Normal	—	—
39	Screech	Normal	Status	—	85	40	Normal	—	—
42	Discharge	Electric	Special	80	100	15	Adjacent	—	—
45	Metal Sound	Steel	Status	—	85	40	Normal	—	—
48	Shift Gear	Steel	Status	—	—	10	Self	—	—
51	Lock-On	Normal	Status	—	—	5	Normal	—	—
54	Zap Cannon	Electric	Special	120	50	5	Normal	—	—
57	Hyper Beam	Normal	Special	150	90	5	Normal	—	—

● MOVES TAUGHT BY PEOPLE

Name	Type	Kind	Pow.	Acc.	PP	Range	Long	DA

● EGG MOVES

Name	Type	Kind	Pow.	Acc.	PP	Range	Long	DA

● TM & HM MOVES

No.	Name	Type	Kind	Pow.	Acc.	PP	Range	Long	DA
TM06	Toxic	Poison	Status	—	90	10	Normal	—	—
TM10	Hidden Power	Normal	Special	—	100	15	Normal	—	—
TM15	Hyper Beam	Normal	Special	150	90	5	Normal	—	—
TM17	Protect	Normal	Status	—	—	10	Self	—	—
TM21	Frustration	Normal	Physical	—	100	20	Normal	—	○
TM24	Thunderbolt	Electric	Special	95	100	15	Normal	—	—
TM27	Return	Normal	Physical	—	100	20	Normal	—	○
TM32	Double Team	Normal	Status	—	—	15	Self	—	—
TM37	Sandstorm	Rock	Status	—	—	10	Both Sides	—	—
TM42	Facade	Normal	Physical	70	100	20	Normal	—	○
TM44	Rest	Psychic	Status	—	—	10	Self	—	—
TM48	Round	Normal	Special	60	100	15	Normal	—	—
TM57	Charge Beam	Electric	Special	50	90	10	Normal	—	—
TM69	Rock Polish	Rock	Status	—	—	20	Self	—	—
TM72	Volt Switch	Electric	Special	70	100	20	Normal	—	—
TM73	Thunder Wave	Electric	Status	—	100	20	Normal	—	—
TM87	Swagger	Normal	Status	—	90	15	Normal	—	—
TM90	Substitute	Normal	Status	—	—	10	Self	—	—
TM91	Flash Cannon	Steel	Special	80	100	10	Normal	—	—
TM94	Rock Smash	Fighting	Physical	40	100	15	Normal	—	○

● FOOTPRINT

● GENDER UNKNOWN

● HEIGHT: 1'00"
● WEIGHT: 46.3 lbs.
● GENDER: UNKNOWN
● ITEMS:
 • None

POKÉMON BLACK VERSION
The two minigears that mesh together are predetermined. Each will rebound from other minigears without meshing.

POKÉMON WHITE VERSION
Interlocking two bodies and spinning around generates the energy they need to live.

EVOLUTION

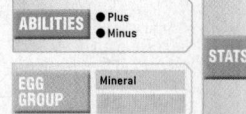

Klink Lv. 38 Klang Lv. 49 Klinklang

ABILITIES ● Plus ● Minus

EGG GROUP Mineral

STATS
HP ●
ATTACK ●●
DEFENSE ●●●
SP. ATTACK ●●
SP. DEFENSE ●●
SPEED ●

● MAIN WAYS TO OBTAIN

| POKÉMON BLACK VERSION | 1 | Chargestone Cave 1F |
| | 2 | P2 Laboratory |

| POKÉMON WHITE VERSION | 1 | Chargestone Cave 1F |
| | 2 | P2 Laboratory |

Klang

● TYPE **Steel**

● FOOTPRINT

● GENDER UNKNOWN

- HEIGHT: 2'00"
- WEIGHT: 112.4 lbs.
- GENDER: UNKNOWN
- ITEMS:
  • None

POKÉMON BLACK VERSION
By changing the direction in which it rotates, it communicates its feelings to others. When angry, it rotates faster.

POKÉMON WHITE VERSION
Spinning minigears are rotated at high speed and repeatedly fired away. It is dangerous if the gears don't return.

● LEVEL-UP AND LEARNED MOVES

Lv.	Name	Type	Kind	Pow.	Acc.	PP	Range	Long	DA
1	ViceGrip	Normal	Physical	55	100	30	Normal	—	○
1	Charge	Electric	Status	—	—	20	Self	—	—
1	ThunderShock	Electric	Special	40	100	30	Normal	—	—
1	Gear Grind	Steel	Physical	50	85	15	Normal	—	○
6	Charge	Electric	Status	—	—	20	Self	—	—
11	ThunderShock	Electric	Special	40	100	30	Normal	—	—
16	Gear Grind	Steel	Physical	50	85	15	Normal	—	○
21	Bind	Normal	Physical	15	85	20	Normal	—	—
26	Charge Beam	Electric	Special	50	90	10	Normal	—	—
31	Autotomize	Steel	Status	—	—	15	Self	—	—
36	Mirror Shot	Steel	Special	65	85	10	Normal	—	—
40	Screech	Normal	Status	—	85	40	Normal	—	—
44	Discharge	Electric	Special	80	100	15	Adjacent	—	—
48	Metal Sound	Steel	Status	—	85	40	Normal	—	—
52	Shift Gear	Steel	Status	—	—	10	Self	—	—
56	Lock-On	Normal	Status	—	—	5	Normal	—	—
60	Zap Cannon	Electric	Special	120	50	5	Normal	—	—
64	Hyper Beam	Normal	Special	150	90	5	Normal	—	—

● MOVES TAUGHT BY PEOPLE

Name	Type	Kind	Pow.	Acc.	PP	Range	Long	DA

● TM & HM MOVES

No.	Name	Type	Kind	Pow.	Acc.	PP	Range	Long	DA
TM06	Toxic	Poison	Status	—	90	10	Normal	—	—
TM10	Hidden Power	Normal	Special	—	100	15	Normal	—	—
TM15	Hyper Beam	Normal	Special	150	90	5	Normal	—	—
TM17	Protect	Normal	Status	—	—	10	Self	—	—
TM21	Frustration	Normal	Physical	—	100	20	Normal	—	○
TM24	Thunderbolt	Electric	Special	95	100	15	Normal	—	—
TM27	Return	Normal	Physical	—	100	20	Normal	—	○
TM32	Double Team	Normal	Status	—	—	15	Self	—	—
TM37	Sandstorm	Rock	Status	—	—	10	Both Sides	—	—
TM42	Facade	Normal	Physical	70	100	20	Normal	—	○
TM44	Rest	Psychic	Status	—	—	10	Self	—	—
TM48	Round	Normal	Special	60	100	15	Normal	—	—
TM57	Charge Beam	Electric	Special	50	90	10	Normal	—	—
TM69	Rock Polish	Rock	Status	—	—	20	Self	—	—
TM72	Volt Switch	Electric	Special	70	100	20	Normal	—	—
TM73	Thunder Wave	Electric	Status	—	100	20	Normal	—	—
TM87	Swagger	Normal	Status	—	90	15	Normal	—	—
TM90	Substitute	Normal	Status	—	—	10	Self	—	—
TM91	Flash Cannon	Steel	Special	80	100	10	Normal	—	—
TM94	Rock Smash	Fighting	Physical	40	100	15	Normal	—	○

EVOLUTION

Klink — Lv. 38 → Klang — Lv. 49 → Klinklang

ABILITIES
- Plus
- Minus

EGG GROUP Mineral

STATS
- HP ●●
- ATTACK ●●●
- DEFENSE ●●●●
- SP. ATTACK ●●●
- SP. DEFENSE ●●●
- SPEED ●●

● MAIN WAYS TO OBTAIN

POKÉMON BLACK VERSION
1 Level up Klink to Lv. 38
2 —

POKÉMON WHITE VERSION
1 Level up Klink to Lv. 38
2 —

Klinklang

● TYPE **Steel**

● FOOTPRINT

● GENDER UNKNOWN

- HEIGHT: 2'00"
- WEIGHT: 178.6 lbs.
- GENDER: UNKNOWN
- ITEMS:
  • None

POKÉMON BLACK VERSION
Its red core functions as an energy tank. It fires the charged energy through its spikes into an area.

POKÉMON WHITE VERSION
The gear with the red core is rotated at high speed for a rapid energy charge.

● LEVEL-UP AND LEARNED MOVES

Lv.	Name	Type	Kind	Pow.	Acc.	PP	Range	Long	DA
1	ViceGrip	Normal	Physical	55	100	30	Normal	—	○
1	Charge	Electric	Status	—	—	20	Self	—	—
1	ThunderShock	Electric	Special	40	100	30	Normal	—	—
1	Gear Grind	Steel	Physical	50	85	15	Normal	—	○
6	Charge	Electric	Status	—	—	20	Self	—	—
11	ThunderShock	Electric	Special	40	100	30	Normal	—	—
16	Gear Grind	Steel	Physical	50	85	15	Normal	—	○
21	Bind	Normal	Physical	15	85	20	Normal	—	—
25	Charge Beam	Electric	Special	50	90	10	Normal	—	—
31	Autotomize	Steel	Status	—	—	15	Self	—	—
36	Mirror Shot	Steel	Special	65	85	10	Normal	—	—
40	Screech	Normal	Status	—	85	40	Normal	—	—
44	Discharge	Electric	Special	80	100	15	Adjacent	—	—
48	Metal Sound	Steel	Status	—	85	40	Normal	—	—
54	Shift Gear	Steel	Status	—	—	10	Self	—	—
60	Lock-On	Normal	Status	—	—	5	Normal	—	—
66	Zap Cannon	Electric	Special	120	50	5	Normal	—	—
72	Hyper Beam	Normal	Special	150	90	5	Normal	—	—

● MOVES TAUGHT BY PEOPLE

Name	Type	Kind	Pow.	Acc.	PP	Range	Long	DA

● TM & HM MOVES

No.	Name	Type	Kind	Pow.	Acc.	PP	Range	Long	DA
TM06	Toxic	Poison	Status	—	90	10	Normal	—	—
TM10	Hidden Power	Normal	Special	—	100	15	Normal	—	—
TM15	Hyper Beam	Normal	Special	150	90	5	Normal	—	—
TM17	Protect	Normal	Status	—	—	10	Self	—	—
TM21	Frustration	Normal	Physical	—	100	20	Normal	—	○
TM24	Thunderbolt	Electric	Special	95	100	15	Normal	—	—
TM25	Thunder	Electric	Special	120	70	10	Normal	—	—
TM27	Return	Normal	Physical	—	100	20	Normal	—	○
TM32	Double Team	Normal	Status	—	—	15	Self	—	—
TM37	Sandstorm	Rock	Status	—	—	10	Both Sides	—	—
TM42	Facade	Normal	Physical	70	100	20	Normal	—	○
TM44	Rest	Psychic	Status	—	—	10	Self	—	—
TM48	Round	Normal	Special	60	100	15	Normal	—	—
TM57	Charge Beam	Electric	Special	50	90	10	Normal	—	—
TM68	Giga Impact	Normal	Physical	150	90	5	Normal	—	○
TM69	Rock Polish	Rock	Status	—	—	20	Self	—	—
TM72	Volt Switch	Electric	Special	70	100	20	Normal	—	—
TM73	Thunder Wave	Electric	Status	—	100	20	Normal	—	—
TM87	Swagger	Normal	Status	—	90	15	Normal	—	—
TM90	Substitute	Normal	Status	—	—	10	Self	—	—
TM91	Flash Cannon	Steel	Special	80	100	10	Normal	—	—
TM92	Trick Room	Psychic	Status	—	—	5	Both Sides	—	○
TM94	Rock Smash	Fighting	Physical	40	100	15	Normal	—	○

EVOLUTION

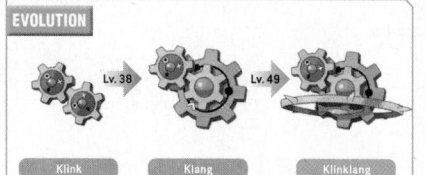

Klink — Lv. 38 → Klang — Lv. 49 → Klinklang

ABILITIES
- Plus
- Minus

EGG GROUP Mineral

STATS
- HP ●●
- ATTACK ●●●
- DEFENSE ●●●●●
- SP. ATTACK ●●●
- SP. DEFENSE ●●●●
- SPEED ●●●●

● MAIN WAYS TO OBTAIN

POKÉMON BLACK VERSION
1 Level up Klang to Lv. 49
2 —

POKÉMON WHITE VERSION
1 Level up Klang to Lv. 49
2 —

Tynamo

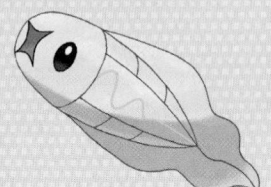

● TYPE Electric

● FOOTPRINT

● MALE/FEMALE HAVE SAME FORM

- HEIGHT: 0'08"
- WEIGHT: 0.7 lbs.
- GENDER: Both ♂♀ exist
- ITEMS:
  • None

POKÉMON BLACK VERSION
While one alone doesn't have much power, a chain of many Tynamo can be as powerful as lightning.

POKÉMON WHITE VERSION
These Pokémon move in schools. They have an electricity-generating organ, so they discharge electricity if in danger.

● LEVEL-UP AND LEARNED MOVES

Lv.	Name	Type	Kind	Pow.	Acc.	PP	Range	Long	DA
1	Tackle	Normal	Physical	50	100	35	Normal	—	○
1	Thunder Wave	Electric	Status	—	100	20	Normal	—	—
1	Spark	Electric	Physical	65	100	20	Normal	—	○
1	Charge Beam	Electric	Special	50	90	10	Normal	—	—

● MOVES TAUGHT BY PEOPLE

Name	Type	Kind	Pow.	Acc.	PP	Range	Long	DA

● EGG MOVES

Name	Type	Kind	Pow.	Acc.	PP	Range	Long	DA

● TM & HM MOVES

No.	Name	Type	Kind	Pow.	Acc.	PP	Range	Long	DA

EVOLUTION

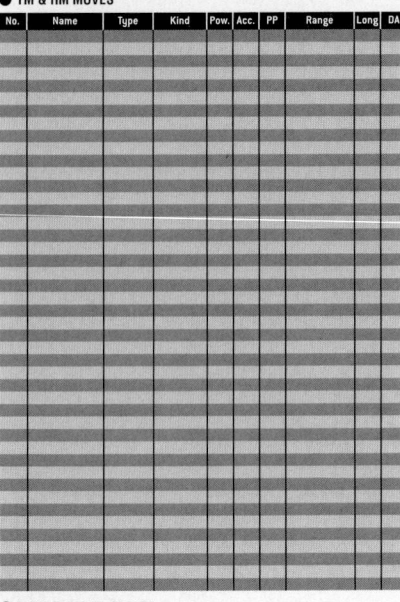

Lv. 39 → Use Thunderstone →

Tynamo → Eelektrik → Eelektross

ABILITY ● Levitate

EGG GROUP Amorphous

STATS
HP ●
ATTACK ●●
DEFENSE ●●
SP. ATTACK ●●
SP. DEFENSE ●●
SPEED ●●●

● MAIN WAYS TO OBTAIN

POKÉMON BLACK VERSION
1 Chargestone Cave B2F
2 Chargestone Cave 1F

POKÉMON WHITE VERSION
1 Chargestone Cave B2F
2 Chargestone Cave 1F

Eelektrik

● TYPE Electric

● FOOTPRINT

● MALE/FEMALE HAVE SAME FORM

- HEIGHT: 3'11"
- WEIGHT: 48.5 lbs.
- GENDER: Both ♂♀ exist
- ITEMS:
  • None

POKÉMON BLACK VERSION
They coil around foes and shock them with electricity-generating organs that seem simply to be circular patterns.

POKÉMON WHITE VERSION
These Pokémon have a big appetite. When they spot their prey, they attack it and paralyze it with electricity.

● LEVEL-UP AND LEARNED MOVES

Lv.	Name	Type	Kind	Pow.	Acc.	PP	Range	Long	DA
1	Headbutt	Normal	Physical	70	100	15	Normal	—	○
1	Thunder Wave	Electric	Status	—	100	20	Normal	—	—
1	Spark	Electric	Physical	65	100	20	Normal	—	○
1	Charge Beam	Electric	Special	50	90	10	Normal	—	—
9	Bind	Normal	Physical	15	85	20	Normal	—	○
19	Acid	Poison	Special	40	100	30	Many Others	—	—
29	Discharge	Electric	Special	80	100	15	Adjacent	—	—
39	Crunch	Dark	Physical	80	100	15	Normal	—	○
44	Thunderbolt	Electric	Special	95	100	15	Normal	—	—
49	Acid Spray	Poison	Special	40	100	20	Normal	—	—
54	Coil	Poison	Status	—	—	20	Self	—	—
59	Wild Charge	Electric	Physical	90	100	15	Normal	—	○
64	Gastro Acid	Poison	Status	—	100	10	Normal	—	—
69	Zap Cannon	Electric	Special	120	50	5	Normal	—	—
74	Thrash	Normal	Physical	120	100	10	1 Random	—	○

● MOVES TAUGHT BY PEOPLE

Name	Type	Kind	Pow.	Acc.	PP	Range	Long	DA

● TM & HM MOVES

No.	Name	Type	Kind	Pow.	Acc.	PP	Range	Long	DA
TM06	Toxic	Poison	Status	—	90	10	Normal	—	—
TM10	Hidden Power	Normal	Special	—	100	15	Normal	—	—
TM16	Light Screen	Psychic	Status	—	—	30	Your Side	—	—
TM17	Protect	Normal	Status	—	—	10	Self	—	—
TM18	Rain Dance	Water	Status	—	—	5	Both Sides	—	—
TM21	Frustration	Normal	Physical	—	100	20	Normal	—	○
TM24	Thunderbolt	Electric	Special	95	100	15	Normal	—	—
TM25	Thunder	Electric	Special	120	70	10	Normal	—	—
TM27	Return	Normal	Physical	—	100	20	Normal	—	○
TM32	Double Team	Normal	Status	—	—	15	Self	—	—
TM42	Facade	Normal	Physical	70	100	20	Normal	—	○
TM44	Rest	Psychic	Status	—	—	10	Self	—	—
TM45	Attract	Normal	Status	—	100	15	Normal	—	—
TM48	Round	Normal	Special	60	100	15	Normal	—	—
TM57	Charge Beam	Electric	Special	50	90	10	Normal	—	—
TM62	Acrobatics	Flying	Physical	55	100	15	Normal	○	○
TM70	Flash	Normal	Status	—	100	20	Normal	—	—
TM72	Volt Switch	Electric	Special	70	100	20	Normal	—	—
TM73	Thunder Wave	Electric	Status	—	100	20	Normal	—	—
TM87	Swagger	Normal	Status	—	90	15	Normal	—	—
TM89	U-turn	Bug	Physical	70	100	20	Normal	—	○
TM90	Substitute	Normal	Status	—	—	10	Self	—	—
TM91	Flash Cannon	Steel	Special	80	100	10	Normal	—	—
TM93	Wild Charge	Electric	Physical	90	100	15	Normal	—	○

EVOLUTION

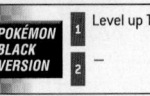

Lv. 39 → Use Thunderstone →

Tynamo → Eelektrik → Eelektross

ABILITY ● Levitate

EGG GROUP Amorphous

STATS
HP ●●
ATTACK ●●●
DEFENSE ●●●●
SP. ATTACK ●●●
SP. DEFENSE ●●●
SPEED ●●

● MAIN WAYS TO OBTAIN

POKÉMON BLACK VERSION
1 Level up Tynamo to Lv. 39
2 —

POKÉMON WHITE VERSION
1 Level up Tynamo to Lv. 39
2 —

Eelektross

● TYPE | Electric |

● LEVEL-UP AND LEARNED MOVES

Lv.	Name	Type	Kind	Pow.	Acc.	PP	Range	Long	DA
1	Crush Claw	Normal	Physical	75	95	10	Normal	—	—
1	Headbutt	Normal	Physical	70	100	15	Normal	—	—
1	Acid	Poison	Special	40	100	30	Many Others	—	—
1	Discharge	Electric	Special	80	100	15	Adjacent	—	—
1	Crunch	Dark	Physical	80	100	15	Normal	—	○

● MOVES TAUGHT BY PEOPLE

Name	Type	Kind	Pow.	Acc.	PP	Range	Long	DA

● TM & HM MOVES

No.	Name	Type	Kind	Pow.	Acc.	PP	Range	Long	DA
TM01	Hone Claws	Dark	Status	—	—	15	Self	—	—
TM02	Dragon Claw	Dragon	Physical	80	100	15	Normal	—	○
TM05	Roar	Normal	Status	—	100	20	Normal	—	—
TM06	Toxic	Poison	Status	—	90	10	Normal	—	—
TM10	Hidden Power	Normal	Special	—	100	15	Normal	—	—
TM15	Hyper Beam	Normal	Special	150	90	5	Normal	—	—
TM16	Light Screen	Psychic	Status	—	—	30	Your Side	—	—
TM17	Protect	Normal	Status	—	—	10	Self	—	—
TM18	Rain Dance	Water	Status	—	—	5	Both Sides	—	—
TM21	Frustration	Normal	Physical	—	100	20	Normal	—	○
TM24	Thunderbolt	Electric	Special	95	100	15	Normal	—	—
TM25	Thunder	Electric	Special	120	70	10	Normal	—	—
TM27	Return	Normal	Physical	—	100	20	Normal	—	○
TM31	Brick Break	Fighting	Physical	75	100	15	Normal	—	○
TM32	Double Team	Normal	Status	—	—	15	Self	—	—
TM35	Flamethrower	Fire	Special	95	100	15	Normal	—	—
TM39	Rock Tomb	Rock	Physical	50	80	10	Normal	—	○
TM42	Facade	Normal	Physical	70	100	20	Normal	—	○
TM44	Rest	Psychic	Status	—	—	10	Self	—	—
TM45	Attract	Normal	Status	—	100	15	Normal	—	—
TM48	Round	Normal	Special	60	100	15	Normal	—	—
TM57	Charge Beam	Electric	Special	50	90	10	Normal	—	—
TM62	Acrobatics	Flying	Physical	55	100	15	Normal	—	○
TM68	Giga Impact	Normal	Physical	150	90	5	Normal	—	○
TM70	Flash	Normal	Status	—	100	20	Normal	—	—
TM72	Volt Switch	Electric	Special	70	100	20	Normal	—	—
TM73	Thunder Wave	Electric	Status	—	100	20	Normal	—	—
TM80	Rock Slide	Rock	Physical	75	90	10	Many Others	—	○
TM82	Dragon Tail	Dragon	Physical	60	90	10	Normal	—	—
TM86	Grass Knot	Grass	Special	—	100	20	Normal	—	—
TM87	Swagger	Normal	Status	—	90	15	Normal	—	—
TM89	U-turn	Bug	Physical	70	100	20	Normal	—	○
TM90	Substitute	Normal	Status	—	—	10	Self	—	—
TM91	Flash Cannon	Steel	Special	80	100	10	Normal	—	—
TM93	Wild Charge	Electric	Physical	90	100	15	Normal	—	○
TM94	Rock Smash	Fighting	Physical	40	100	15	Normal	—	○
HM01	Cut	Normal	Physical	50	95	30	Normal	—	○
HM04	Strength	Normal	Physical	80	100	15	Normal	—	○

● HEIGHT: 6'11"
● WEIGHT: 177.5 lbs.
● GENDER: Both ♂♀ exist
● ITEMS:
 • None

● FOOTPRINT

● MALE/FEMALE HAVE SAME FORM

POKÉMON BLACK VERSION
They crawl out of the ocean using their arms. They will attack prey on shore and immediately drag it into the ocean.

POKÉMON WHITE VERSION
With their sucker mouths, they suck in prey. Then they use their fangs to shock the prey with electricity.

EVOLUTION

Tynamo → Lv. 39 → Eelektrik → Use Thunderstone → Eelektross

ABILITY ● Levitate

EGG GROUP Amorphous

STATS
HP ●●●
ATTACK ●●●●●
DEFENSE ●●●
SP.ATTACK ●●●●●
SP.DEFENSE ●●●●
SPEED ●●

● MAIN WAYS TO OBTAIN

POKÉMON BLACK VERSION
1 Use Thunderstone on Eelektrik
2 —

POKÉMON WHITE VERSION
1 Use Thunderstone on Eelektrik
2 —

Elgyem

● TYPE | Psychic |

● LEVEL-UP AND LEARNED MOVES

Lv.	Name	Type	Kind	Pow.	Acc.	PP	Range	Long	DA
1	Confusion	Psychic	Special	50	100	25	Normal	—	—
4	Growl	Normal	Status	—	100	40	Many Others	—	—
8	Heal Block	Psychic	Status	—	100	15	Many Others	—	—
11	Miracle Eye	Psychic	Status	—	—	40	Normal	—	—
15	Psybeam	Psychic	Special	65	100	20	Normal	—	—
18	Headbutt	Normal	Physical	70	100	15	Normal	—	—
22	Hidden Power	Normal	Special	—	100	15	Normal	—	—
25	Imprison	Psychic	Status	—	—	10	Self	—	—
29	Simple Beam	Normal	Status	—	100	15	Normal	—	—
32	Zen Headbutt	Psychic	Physical	80	90	15	Normal	—	○
36	Psych Up	Normal	Status	—	—	10	Normal	—	—
39	Psychic	Psychic	Special	90	100	10	Normal	—	—
43	Calm Mind	Psychic	Status	—	—	20	Self	—	—
46	Recover	Normal	Status	—	—	10	Self	—	—
50	Guard Split	Psychic	Status	—	—	10	Normal	—	—
50	Power Split	Psychic	Status	—	—	10	Normal	—	—
53	Synchronoise	Psychic	Special	70	100	15	Adjacent	—	—
56	Wonder Room	Psychic	Status	—	—	10	Both Sides	—	—

● MOVES TAUGHT BY PEOPLE

Name	Type	Kind	Pow.	Acc.	PP	Range	Long	DA

● EGG MOVES

Name	Type	Kind	Pow.	Acc.	PP	Range	Long	DA
Teleport	Psychic	Status	—	—	20	Self	—	—
Disable	Normal	Status	—	100	20	Normal	—	—
Astonish	Ghost	Physical	30	100	15	Normal	—	○
Power Swap	Psychic	Status	—	—	10	Normal	—	—
Guard Swap	Psychic	Status	—	—	10	Normal	—	—
Barrier	Psychic	Status	—	—	30	Self	—	—
Nasty Plot	Dark	Status	—	—	20	Self	—	—
Skill Swap	Psychic	Status	—	—	10	Normal	—	—

● TM & HM MOVES

No.	Name	Type	Kind	Pow.	Acc.	PP	Range	Long	DA
TM03	Psyshock	Psychic	Special	80	100	10	Normal	—	—
TM04	Calm Mind	Psychic	Status	—	—	20	Self	—	—
TM06	Toxic	Poison	Status	—	90	10	Normal	—	—
TM10	Hidden Power	Normal	Special	—	100	15	Normal	—	—
TM16	Light Screen	Psychic	Status	—	—	30	Your Side	—	—
TM17	Protect	Normal	Status	—	—	10	Self	—	—
TM18	Rain Dance	Water	Status	—	—	5	Both Sides	—	—
TM19	Telekinesis	Psychic	Status	—	—	15	Normal	—	—
TM20	Safeguard	Normal	Status	—	—	25	Your Side	—	—
TM21	Frustration	Normal	Physical	—	100	20	Normal	—	○
TM24	Thunderbolt	Electric	Special	95	100	15	Normal	—	—
TM27	Return	Normal	Physical	—	100	20	Normal	—	○
TM29	Psychic	Psychic	Special	90	100	10	Normal	—	—
TM30	Shadow Ball	Ghost	Special	80	100	15	Normal	—	—
TM32	Double Team	Normal	Status	—	—	15	Self	—	—
TM33	Reflect	Psychic	Status	—	—	20	Your Side	—	—
TM39	Rock Tomb	Rock	Physical	50	80	10	Normal	—	○
TM42	Facade	Normal	Physical	70	100	20	Normal	—	○
TM44	Rest	Psychic	Status	—	—	10	Self	—	—
TM45	Attract	Normal	Status	—	100	15	Normal	—	—
TM46	Thief	Dark	Physical	40	100	10	Normal	—	—
TM48	Round	Normal	Special	60	100	15	Normal	—	—
TM49	Echoed Voice	Normal	Special	40	100	15	Normal	—	—
TM51	Ally Switch	Psychic	Status	—	—	15	Self	—	—
TM53	Energy Ball	Grass	Special	80	100	10	Normal	—	—
TM57	Charge Beam	Electric	Special	50	90	10	Normal	—	—
TM63	Embargo	Dark	Status	—	100	15	Normal	—	—
TM70	Flash	Normal	Status	—	100	20	Normal	—	—
TM73	Thunder Wave	Electric	Status	—	100	20	Normal	—	—
TM77	Psych Up	Normal	Status	—	—	10	Normal	—	—
TM80	Rock Slide	Rock	Physical	75	90	10	Many Others	—	○
TM85	Dream Eater	Psychic	Special	100	100	15	Normal	—	—
TM87	Swagger	Normal	Status	—	90	15	Normal	—	—
TM90	Substitute	Normal	Status	—	—	10	Self	—	—
TM92	Trick Room	Psychic	Status	—	—	5	Both Sides	—	—

● HEIGHT: 1'08"
● WEIGHT: 19.8 lbs.
● GENDER: Both ♂♀ exist
● ITEMS:
 • None

● FOOTPRINT

● MALE/FEMALE HAVE SAME FORM

POKÉMON BLACK VERSION
It uses its strong psychic power to squeeze its opponent's brain, causing unendurable headaches.

POKÉMON WHITE VERSION
This Pokémon had never been seen until it appeared from far in the desert 50 years ago.

EVOLUTION

Elgyem → Lv. 42 → Beheeyem

ABILITIES ● Telepathy ● Synchronize

EGG GROUP Human-Like

STATS
HP ●●
ATTACK ●●
DEFENSE ●●
SP.ATTACK ●●●
SP.DEFENSE ●●●
SPEED ●

● MAIN WAYS TO OBTAIN

POKÉMON BLACK VERSION
1 Celestial Tower 3F
2 Celestial Tower 4F

POKÉMON WHITE VERSION
1 Celestial Tower 3F
2 Celestial Tower 4F

Beheeyem

● TYPE Psychic

● MALE/FEMALE HAVE SAME FORM

● HEIGHT: 3'03"
● WEIGHT: 76.1 lbs.
● GENDER: Both ♂♀ exist
● ITEMS:
• None

● FOOTPRINT

POKÉMON BLACK VERSION
It can manipulate an opponent's memory. Apparently, it communicates by flashing its three different-colored fingers.

POKÉMON WHITE VERSION
It uses psychic power to control an opponent's brain and tamper with its memories.

● LEVEL-UP AND LEARNED MOVES

Lv.	Name	Type	Kind	Pow.	Acc.	PP	Range	Long	DA
1	Confusion	Psychic	Special	50	100	25	Normal	—	—
1	Growl	Normal	Status	—	100	40	Many Others	—	—
1	Heal Block	Psychic	Status	—	100	15	Many Others	—	—
1	Miracle Eye	Psychic	Status	—	—	40	Normal	—	—
4	Growl	Normal	Status	—	100	40	Many Others	—	—
8	Heal Block	Psychic	Status	—	100	15	Many Others	—	—
11	Miracle Eye	Psychic	Status	—	—	40	Normal	—	—
15	Psybeam	Psychic	Special	65	100	20	Normal	—	—
18	Headbutt	Normal	Physical	70	100	15	Normal	—	○
22	Hidden Power	Normal	Special	—	100	15	Normal	—	—
25	Imprison	Psychic	Status	—	—	10	Self	—	—
29	Simple Beam	Normal	Status	—	100	15	Normal	—	—
32	Zen Headbutt	Psychic	Physical	80	90	15	Normal	—	○
36	Psych Up	Normal	Status	—	—	10	Normal	—	—
39	Psychic	Psychic	Special	90	100	10	Normal	—	—
45	Calm Mind	Psychic	Status	—	—	20	Self	—	—
50	Recover	Normal	Status	—	—	10	Self	—	—
56	Guard Split	Psychic	Status	—	—	10	Normal	—	—
58	Power Split	Psychic	Status	—	—	10	Normal	—	—
63	Synchronoise	Psychic	Special	70	100	15	Adjacent	—	—
68	Wonder Room	Psychic	Status	—	—	10	Both Sides	—	—

● MOVES TAUGHT BY PEOPLE

Name	Type	Kind	Pow.	Acc.	PP	Range	Long	DA

● TM & HM MOVES

No.	Name	Type	Kind	Pow.	Acc.	PP	Range	Long	DA
TM03	Psyshock	Psychic	Special	80	100	10	Normal	—	—
TM04	Calm Mind	Psychic	Status	—	—	20	Self	—	—
TM06	Toxic	Poison	Status	—	90	10	Normal	—	—
TM10	Hidden Power	Normal	Special	—	100	15	Normal	—	—
TM15	Hyper Beam	Normal	Special	150	90	5	Normal	—	—
TM16	Light Screen	Psychic	Status	—	—	30	Your Side	—	—
TM17	Protect	Normal	Status	—	—	10	Self	—	—
TM18	Rain Dance	Water	Status	—	—	5	Both Sides	—	—
TM19	Telekinesis	Psychic	Status	—	—	15	Normal	—	—
TM20	Safeguard	Normal	Status	—	—	25	Your Side	—	—
TM21	Frustration	Normal	Physical	—	100	20	Normal	—	○
TM24	Thunderbolt	Electric	Special	95	100	15	Normal	—	—
TM27	Return	Normal	Physical	—	100	20	Normal	—	○
TM29	Psychic	Psychic	Special	90	100	10	Normal	—	—
TM30	Shadow Ball	Ghost	Special	80	100	15	Normal	—	—
TM32	Double Team	Normal	Status	—	—	15	Self	—	—
TM33	Reflect	Psychic	Status	—	—	20	Your Side	—	—
TM39	Rock Tomb	Rock	Physical	50	80	10	Normal	—	—
TM42	Facade	Normal	Physical	70	100	20	Normal	—	—
TM44	Rest	Psychic	Status	—	—	10	Self	—	—
TM45	Attract	Normal	Status	—	100	15	Normal	—	○
TM48	Round	Normal	Special	60	100	15	Normal	—	—
TM49	Echoed Voice	Normal	Special	40	100	15	Normal	—	—
TM51	Ally Switch	Psychic	Status	—	—	15	Self	—	—
TM53	Energy Ball	Grass	Special	80	100	10	Normal	—	—
TM57	Charge Beam	Electric	Special	50	90	10	Normal	—	—
TM63	Embargo	Dark	Status	—	100	15	Normal	—	—
TM68	Giga Impact	Normal	Physical	150	90	5	Normal	—	—
TM70	Flash	Normal	Status	—	100	20	Normal	—	—
TM77	Psych Up	Normal	Status	—	—	10	Normal	—	—
TM80	Rock Slide	Rock	Physical	75	90	10	Many Others	—	—
TM85	Dream Eater	Psychic	Special	100	100	15	Normal	—	—
TM87	Swagger	Normal	Status	—	90	15	Normal	—	—
TM90	Substitute	Normal	Status	—	—	10	Self	—	—
TM92	Trick Room	Psychic	Status	—	—	5	Both Sides	—	—

EVOLUTION

Elgyem → Lv.42 → Beheeyem

ABILITIES
● Telepathy
● Synchronize

EGG GROUP
Human-Like

STATS
HP ●●●
ATTACK ●●●
DEFENSE ●●●
SP.ATTACK ●●●●
SP.DEFENSE ●●●●●
SPEED ●●

● MAIN WAYS TO OBTAIN

POKÉMON BLACK VERSION
1 Route 14
2 Level up Elgyem to Lv. 42

POKÉMON WHITE VERSION
1 Route 14
2 Level up Elgyem to Lv. 42

Litwick

● TYPE Ghost Fire

● MALE/FEMALE HAVE SAME FORM

● FOOTPRINT

● HEIGHT: 1'00"
● WEIGHT: 6.8 lbs.
● GENDER: Both ♂♀ exist
● ITEMS:
• None

POKÉMON BLACK VERSION
Litwick shines a light that absorbs the life energy of people and Pokémon, which becomes the fuel that it burns.

POKÉMON WHITE VERSION
While shining a light and pretending to be a guide, it leeches off the life force of any who follow it.

● LEVEL-UP AND LEARNED MOVES

Lv.	Name	Type	Kind	Pow.	Acc.	PP	Range	Long	DA
1	Ember	Fire	Special	40	100	25	Normal	—	○
1	Astonish	Ghost	Physical	30	100	15	Normal	—	—
3	Minimize	Normal	Status	—	—	20	Self	—	—
5	Smog	Poison	Special	20	70	20	Normal	—	—
7	Fire Spin	Fire	Special	35	85	15	Normal	—	—
10	Confuse Ray	Ghost	Status	—	100	10	Normal	—	—
13	Night Shade	Ghost	Special	—	100	15	Normal	—	—
16	Will-O-Wisp	Fire	Status	—	75	15	Normal	—	—
20	Flame Burst	Fire	Special	70	100	15	Normal	—	—
24	Imprison	Psychic	Status	—	—	10	Self	—	—
28	Hex	Ghost	Special	50	100	10	Normal	—	—
33	Memento	Dark	Status	—	100	10	Normal	—	—
38	Inferno	Fire	Special	100	50	5	Normal	—	—
43	Curse	Ghost	Status	—	—	10	Varies	—	—
49	Shadow Ball	Ghost	Special	80	100	15	Normal	—	—
55	Pain Split	Normal	Status	—	—	20	Normal	—	—
61	Overheat	Fire	Special	140	90	5	Normal	—	—

● MOVES TAUGHT BY PEOPLE

Name	Type	Kind	Pow.	Acc.	PP	Range	Long	DA

● EGG MOVES

Name	Type	Kind	Pow.	Acc.	PP	Range	Long	DA
Acid Armor	Poison	Status	—	—	40	Self	—	—
Heat Wave	Fire	Special	100	90	10	Many Others	—	—
Haze	Ice	Status	—	—	30	Both Sides	—	—
Endure	Normal	Status	—	—	10	Self	—	—
Captivate	Normal	Status	—	100	20	Many Others	—	—
Acid	Poison	Special	40	100	30	Many Others	—	—
Clear Smog	Poison	Special	50	—	15	Normal	—	—

● TM & HM MOVES

No.	Name	Type	Kind	Pow.	Acc.	PP	Range	Long	DA
TM04	Calm Mind	Psychic	Status	—	—	20	Self	—	—
TM06	Toxic	Poison	Status	—	90	10	Normal	—	—
TM10	Hidden Power	Normal	Special	—	100	15	Normal	—	—
TM11	Sunny Day	Fire	Status	—	—	5	Both Sides	—	—
TM12	Taunt	Dark	Status	—	100	20	Normal	—	—
TM17	Protect	Normal	Status	—	—	10	Self	—	—
TM19	Telekinesis	Psychic	Status	—	—	15	Normal	—	—
TM20	Safeguard	Normal	Status	—	—	25	Your Side	—	—
TM21	Frustration	Normal	Physical	—	100	20	Normal	—	○
TM22	SolarBeam	Grass	Special	120	100	10	Normal	—	—
TM27	Return	Normal	Physical	—	100	20	Normal	—	○
TM29	Psychic	Psychic	Special	90	100	10	Normal	—	—
TM30	Shadow Ball	Ghost	Special	80	100	15	Normal	—	—
TM32	Double Team	Normal	Status	—	—	15	Self	—	—
TM35	Flamethrower	Fire	Special	95	100	15	Normal	—	—
TM38	Fire Blast	Fire	Special	120	85	5	Normal	—	—
TM42	Facade	Normal	Physical	70	100	20	Normal	—	—
TM43	Flame Charge	Fire	Physical	50	100	20	Normal	—	○
TM44	Rest	Psychic	Status	—	—	10	Self	—	—
TM45	Attract	Normal	Status	—	100	15	Normal	—	○
TM46	Thief	Dark	Physical	40	100	10	Normal	—	—
TM48	Round	Normal	Special	60	100	15	Normal	—	—
TM50	Overheat	Fire	Special	140	90	5	Normal	—	—
TM53	Energy Ball	Grass	Special	80	100	10	Normal	—	—
TM59	Incinerate	Fire	Special	30	100	15	Many Others	—	—
TM61	Will-O-Wisp	Fire	Status	—	75	15	Normal	—	—
TM63	Embargo	Dark	Status	—	100	15	Normal	—	—
TM70	Flash	Normal	Status	—	100	20	Normal	—	—
TM77	Psych Up	Normal	Status	—	—	10	Normal	—	—
TM85	Dream Eater	Psychic	Special	100	100	15	Normal	—	—
TM87	Swagger	Normal	Status	—	90	15	Normal	—	—
TM90	Substitute	Normal	Status	—	—	10	Self	—	—
TM92	Trick Room	Psychic	Status	—	—	5	Both Sides	—	—

EVOLUTION

Litwick → Lv.41 → Lampent → Use Dusk Stone → Chandelure

ABILITIES
● Flash Fire
● Flame Body

EGG GROUP
Amorphous

STATS
HP ●●
ATTACK ●●
DEFENSE ●●
SP.ATTACK ●●●
SP.DEFENSE ●●
SPEED ●●

● MAIN WAYS TO OBTAIN

POKÉMON BLACK VERSION
1 Celestial Tower 2F
2 Celestial Tower 3F

POKÉMON WHITE VERSION
1 Celestial Tower 2F
2 Celestial Tower 3F

UNOVA POKÉDEX
112 BEHEEYEM
113 LITWICK

Lampent

● TYPE **Ghost** **Fire**

● FOOTPRINT

● MALE/FEMALE HAVE SAME FORM

● HEIGHT: 2'00"
● WEIGHT: 28.7 lbs.
● GENDER: Both ♂♀ exist
● ITEMS:
• None

POKÉMON BLACK VERSION
This ominous Pokémon is feared. Through cities it wanders, searching for the spirits of the fallen.

POKÉMON WHITE VERSION
It arrives near the moment of death and steals spirit from the body.

● LEVEL-UP AND LEARNED MOVES

Lv.	Name	Type	Kind	Pow.	Acc.	PP	Range	Long	DA
1	Ember	Fire	Special	40	100	25	Normal	—	—
1	Astonish	Ghost	Physical	30	100	15	Normal	—	○
1	Minimize	Normal	Status	—	—	20	Self	—	—
5	Smog	Poison	Special	20	70	20	Normal	—	—
3	Minimize	Normal	Status	—	—	20	Self	—	—
5	Smog	Poison	Special	20	70	20	Normal	—	—
7	Fire Spin	Fire	Special	35	85	15	Normal	—	—
10	Confuse Ray	Ghost	Status	—	100	10	Normal	—	—
13	Night Shade	Ghost	Special	—	100	15	Normal	—	—
16	Will-O-Wisp	Fire	Status	—	75	15	Normal	—	—
20	Flame Burst	Fire	Special	70	100	15	Normal	—	—
24	Imprison	Psychic	Status	—	—	10	Self	—	—
28	Hex	Ghost	Special	50	100	10	Normal	—	—
33	Memento	Dark	Status	—	100	10	Normal	—	—
38	Inferno	Fire	Special	100	50	5	Normal	—	—
45	Curse	Ghost	Status	—	—	10	Varies	—	—
53	Shadow Ball	Ghost	Special	80	100	15	Normal	—	—
61	Pain Split	Normal	Status	—	—	20	Normal	—	—
69	Overheat	Fire	Special	140	90	5	Normal	—	—

● MOVES TAUGHT BY PEOPLE

Name	Type	Kind	Pow.	Acc.	PP	Range	Long	DA

● TM & HM MOVES

No.	Name	Type	Kind	Pow.	Acc.	PP	Range	Long	DA
TM04	Calm Mind	Psychic	Status	—	—	20	Self	—	—
TM06	Toxic	Poison	Status	—	90	10	Normal	—	—
TM10	Hidden Power	Normal	Special	—	100	15	Normal	—	—
TM11	Sunny Day	Fire	Status	—	—	5	Both Sides	—	—
TM12	Taunt	Dark	Status	—	100	20	Normal	—	—
TM17	Protect	Normal	Status	—	—	10	Self	—	—
TM19	Telekinesis	Psychic	Status	—	—	15	Normal	—	—
TM20	Safeguard	Normal	Status	—	—	25	Your Side	—	—
TM21	Frustration	Normal	Physical	—	100	20	Normal	—	○
TM22	SolarBeam	Grass	Special	120	100	10	Normal	—	—
TM27	Return	Normal	Physical	—	100	20	Normal	—	○
TM29	Psychic	Psychic	Special	90	100	10	Normal	—	—
TM30	Shadow Ball	Ghost	Special	80	100	15	Normal	—	—
TM32	Double Team	Normal	Status	—	—	15	Self	—	—
TM35	Flamethrower	Fire	Special	95	100	15	Normal	—	—
TM38	Fire Blast	Fire	Special	120	85	5	Normal	—	—
TM42	Facade	Normal	Physical	70	100	20	Normal	—	○
TM43	Flame Charge	Fire	Physical	50	100	20	Normal	—	○
TM44	Rest	Psychic	Status	—	—	10	Self	—	—
TM45	Attract	Normal	Status	—	100	15	Normal	—	—
TM46	Thief	Dark	Physical	40	100	10	Normal	—	○
TM48	Round	Normal	Special	60	100	15	Normal	—	—
TM50	Overheat	Fire	Special	140	90	5	Normal	—	—
TM53	Energy Ball	Grass	Special	80	100	10	Normal	—	—
TM59	Incinerate	Fire	Special	30	100	15	Many Others	—	—
TM61	Will-O-Wisp	Fire	Status	—	75	15	Normal	—	—
TM63	Embargo	Dark	Status	—	100	15	Normal	—	—
TM66	Payback	Dark	Physical	50	100	10	Normal	—	○
TM70	Flash	Normal	Status	—	100	20	Normal	—	—
TM77	Psych Up	Normal	Status	—	—	10	Normal	—	—
TM85	Dream Eater	Psychic	Special	100	100	15	Normal	—	—
TM87	Swagger	Normal	Status	—	90	15	Normal	—	—
TM90	Substitute	Normal	Status	—	—	10	Self	—	—
TM92	Trick Room	Psychic	Status	—	—	5	Both Sides	—	—

● EVOLUTION

Litwick → Lv. 41 → Lampent → Use Dusk Stone → Chandelure

● ABILITIES
• Flash Fire
• Flame Body

● EGG GROUP
Amorphous

● STATS
HP ●●
ATTACK ●●
DEFENSE ●●
SP. ATTACK ●●●●
SP. DEFENSE ●●●
SPEED ●●●

● MAIN WAYS TO OBTAIN

POKÉMON BLACK VERSION
1 | Level up Litwick to Lv. 41
2 | —

POKÉMON WHITE VERSION
1 | Level up Litwick to Lv. 41
2 | —

Chandelure

● TYPE **Ghost** **Fire**

● FOOTPRINT

● MALE/FEMALE HAVE SAME FORM

● HEIGHT: 3'03"
● WEIGHT: 75.6 lbs.
● GENDER: Both ♂♀ exist
● ITEMS:
• None

POKÉMON BLACK VERSION
It absorbs a spirit, which it then burns. By waving the flames on its arms, it puts its foes into a hypnotic trance.

POKÉMON WHITE VERSION
Being consumed in Chandelure's flame burns up the spirit, leaving the body behind.

● LEVEL-UP AND LEARNED MOVES

Lv.	Name	Type	Kind	Pow.	Acc.	PP	Range	Long	DA
1	Smog	Poison	Special	20	70	20	Normal	—	—
1	Confuse Ray	Ghost	Status	—	100	10	Normal	—	—
1	Flame Burst	Fire	Special	70	100	15	Normal	—	—
1	Hex	Ghost	Special	50	100	10	Normal	—	—

● MOVES TAUGHT BY PEOPLE

Name	Type	Kind	Pow.	Acc.	PP	Range	Long	DA

● TM & HM MOVES

No.	Name	Type	Kind	Pow.	Acc.	PP	Range	Long	DA
TM04	Calm Mind	Psychic	Status	—	—	20	Self	—	—
TM06	Toxic	Poison	Status	—	90	10	Normal	—	—
TM10	Hidden Power	Normal	Special	—	100	15	Normal	—	—
TM11	Sunny Day	Fire	Status	—	—	5	Both Sides	—	—
TM12	Taunt	Dark	Status	—	100	20	Normal	—	—
TM15	Hyper Beam	Normal	Special	150	90	5	Normal	—	—
TM17	Protect	Normal	Status	—	—	10	Self	—	—
TM19	Telekinesis	Psychic	Status	—	—	15	Normal	—	—
TM20	Safeguard	Normal	Status	—	—	25	Your Side	—	—
TM21	Frustration	Normal	Physical	—	100	20	Normal	—	○
TM22	SolarBeam	Grass	Special	120	100	10	Normal	—	—
TM27	Return	Normal	Physical	—	100	20	Normal	—	○
TM29	Psychic	Psychic	Special	90	100	10	Normal	—	—
TM30	Shadow Ball	Ghost	Special	80	100	15	Normal	—	—
TM32	Double Team	Normal	Status	—	—	15	Self	—	—
TM35	Flamethrower	Fire	Special	95	100	15	Normal	—	—
TM38	Fire Blast	Fire	Special	120	85	5	Normal	—	—
TM42	Facade	Normal	Physical	70	100	20	Normal	—	○
TM43	Flame Charge	Fire	Physical	50	100	20	Normal	—	○
TM44	Rest	Psychic	Status	—	—	10	Self	—	—
TM45	Attract	Normal	Status	—	100	15	Normal	—	—
TM46	Thief	Dark	Physical	40	100	10	Normal	—	○
TM48	Round	Normal	Special	60	100	15	Normal	—	—
TM50	Overheat	Fire	Special	140	90	5	Normal	—	—
TM53	Energy Ball	Grass	Special	80	100	10	Normal	—	—
TM59	Incinerate	Fire	Special	30	100	15	Many Others	—	—
TM61	Will-O-Wisp	Fire	Status	—	75	15	Normal	—	—
TM63	Embargo	Dark	Status	—	100	15	Normal	—	—
TM66	Payback	Dark	Physical	50	100	10	Normal	—	○
TM68	Giga Impact	Normal	Physical	150	90	5	Normal	—	○
TM70	Flash	Normal	Status	—	100	20	Normal	—	—
TM77	Psych Up	Normal	Status	—	—	10	Normal	—	—
TM85	Dream Eater	Psychic	Special	100	100	15	Normal	—	—
TM87	Swagger	Normal	Status	—	90	15	Normal	—	—
TM90	Substitute	Normal	Status	—	—	10	Self	—	—
TM92	Trick Room	Psychic	Status	—	—	5	Both Sides	—	—

● EVOLUTION

Litwick → Lv. 41 → Lampent → Use Dusk Stone → Chandelure

● ABILITIES
• Flash Fire
• Flame Body

● EGG GROUP
Amorphous

● STATS
HP ●●
ATTACK ●●
DEFENSE ●●●●
SP. ATTACK ●●●●●
SP. DEFENSE ●●●●
SPEED ●●●

● MAIN WAYS TO OBTAIN

POKÉMON BLACK VERSION
1 | Use Dusk Stone on Lampent
2 | —

POKÉMON WHITE VERSION
1 | Use Dusk Stone on Lampent
2 | —

Axew

● TYPE Dragon

LEVEL-UP AND LEARNED MOVES

Lv.	Name	Type	Kind	Pow.	Acc.	PP	Range	Long	DA
1	Scratch	Normal	Physical	40	100	35	Normal	—	—
4	Leer	Normal	Status	—	100	30	Many Others	—	—
7	Assurance	Dark	Physical	50	100	10	Normal	—	○
10	Dragon Rage	Dragon	Special	—	100	10	Normal	—	—
13	Dual Chop	Dragon	Physical	40	90	15	Normal	—	—
16	Scary Face	Normal	Status	—	100	10	Normal	—	—
20	Slash	Normal	Physical	70	100	20	Normal	—	—
24	False Swipe	Normal	Physical	40	100	40	Normal	—	○
28	Dragon Claw	Dragon	Physical	80	100	15	Normal	—	—
32	Dragon Dance	Dragon	Status	—	—	20	Self	—	—
36	Taunt	Dark	Status	—	100	20	Normal	—	—
41	Dragon Pulse	Dragon	Special	90	100	10	Normal	○	—
46	Swords Dance	Normal	Status	—	—	30	Self	—	—
51	Guillotine	Normal	Physical	—	30	5	Normal	—	—
56	Outrage	Dragon	Physical	120	100	10	1 Random	—	—
61	Giga Impact	Normal	Physical	150	90	5	Normal	—	—

MOVES TAUGHT BY PEOPLE

Name	Type	Kind	Pow.	Acc.	PP	Range	Long	DA
Draco Meteor	Dragon	Special	140	90	5	Normal	—	—

EGG MOVES

Name	Type	Kind	Pow.	Acc.	PP	Range	Long	DA
Counter	Fighting	Physical	—	100	20	Varies	—	○
Focus Energy	Normal	Status	—	—	30	Self	—	—
Reversal	Fighting	Physical	—	100	15	Normal	—	—
Endure	Normal	Status	—	—	10	Self	—	—
Razor Wind	Normal	Special	80	100	10	Many Others	—	—
Night Slash	Dark	Physical	70	100	15	Normal	—	○
Endeavor	Normal	Physical	—	100	5	Normal	—	○
Iron Tail	Steel	Physical	100	75	15	Normal	—	○
Dragon Pulse	Dragon	Special	90	100	10	Normal	○	—
Harden	Normal	Status	—	—	30	Self	—	—

TM & HM MOVES

No.	Name	Type	Kind	Pow.	Acc.	PP	Range	Long	DA
TM01	Hone Claws	Dark	Status	—	—	15	Self	—	—
TM02	Dragon Claw	Dragon	Physical	80	100	15	Normal	—	—
TM05	Roar	Normal	Status	—	100	20	Normal	—	—
TM06	Toxic	Poison	Status	—	90	10	Normal	—	—
TM10	Hidden Power	Normal	Special	—	100	15	Normal	—	—
TM11	Sunny Day	Fire	Status	—	—	5	Both Sides	—	—
TM12	Taunt	Dark	Status	—	100	20	Normal	—	—
TM17	Protect	Normal	Status	—	—	10	Self	—	—
TM18	Rain Dance	Water	Status	—	—	5	Both Sides	—	—
TM21	Frustration	Normal	Physical	—	100	20	Normal	—	○
TM27	Return	Normal	Physical	—	100	20	Normal	—	○
TM28	Dig	Ground	Physical	80	100	10	Normal	—	○
TM32	Double Team	Normal	Status	—	—	15	Self	—	—
TM39	Rock Tomb	Rock	Physical	50	80	10	Normal	—	—
TM40	Aerial Ace	Flying	Physical	60	—	20	Normal	○	○
TM42	Facade	Normal	Physical	70	100	20	Normal	—	—
TM44	Rest	Psychic	Status	—	—	10	Self	—	—
TM45	Attract	Normal	Status	—	100	15	Normal	—	—
TM48	Round	Normal	Special	60	100	15	Normal	—	—
TM54	False Swipe	Normal	Physical	40	100	40	Normal	—	○
TM56	Fling	Dark	Physical	—	100	10	Normal	—	○
TM59	Incinerate	Fire	Special	30	100	15	Many Others	—	—
TM66	Payback	Dark	Physical	50	100	10	Normal	—	○
TM68	Giga Impact	Normal	Physical	150	90	5	Normal	—	—
TM75	Swords Dance	Normal	Status	—	—	30	Self	—	—
TM81	X-Scissor	Bug	Physical	80	100	15	Normal	—	—
TM84	Poison Jab	Poison	Physical	80	100	20	Normal	—	—
TM87	Swagger	Normal	Status	—	90	15	Normal	—	—
TM90	Substitute	Normal	Status	—	—	10	Self	—	—
TM94	Rock Smash	Fighting	Physical	40	100	15	Normal	—	○
HM01	Cut	Normal	Physical	50	95	30	Normal	—	○
HM04	Strength	Normal	Physical	80	100	15	Normal	—	○

MAIN WAYS TO OBTAIN

POKÉMON BLACK VERSION
1 Mistralton Cave 1F
2 Mistralton Cave 2F

POKÉMON WHITE VERSION
1 Mistralton Cave 1F
2 Mistralton Cave 2F

● HEIGHT: 2'00"
● WEIGHT: 39.7 lbs.
● GENDER: Both ♂♀ exist
● ITEMS:
• None

● FOOTPRINT

● MALE/FEMALE HAVE SAME FORM

EVOLUTION

Axew → (Lv. 38) Fraxure → (Lv. 48) Haxorus

POKÉMON BLACK VERSION — They use their tusks to crush the berries they eat. Repeated regrowth makes their tusks strong and sharp.

POKÉMON WHITE VERSION — They mark their territory by leaving gashes in trees with their tusks. If a tusk breaks, a new one grows in quickly.

ABILITIES
● Rivalry
● Mold Breaker

EGG GROUPS
Monster
Dragon

STATS
HP ●●
ATTACK ●●●
DEFENSE ●●●
SP. ATTACK ●
SP. DEFENSE ●
SPEED ●●●

Fraxure

● TYPE Dragon

LEVEL-UP AND LEARNED MOVES

Lv.	Name	Type	Kind	Pow.	Acc.	PP	Range	Long	DA
1	Scratch	Normal	Physical	40	100	35	Normal	—	○
1	Leer	Normal	Status	—	100	30	Many Others	—	—
1	Assurance	Dark	Physical	50	100	10	Normal	—	○
1	Dragon Rage	Dragon	Special	—	100	10	Normal	—	—
4	Leer	Normal	Status	—	100	30	Many Others	—	—
7	Assurance	Dark	Physical	50	100	10	Normal	—	○
10	Dragon Rage	Dragon	Special	—	100	10	Normal	—	—
13	Dual Chop	Dragon	Physical	40	90	15	Normal	—	—
16	Scary Face	Normal	Status	—	100	10	Normal	—	—
20	Slash	Normal	Physical	70	100	20	Normal	—	—
24	False Swipe	Normal	Physical	40	100	40	Normal	—	○
28	Dragon Claw	Dragon	Physical	80	100	15	Many Others	—	—
32	Dragon Dance	Dragon	Status	—	—	20	Self	—	—
36	Taunt	Dark	Status	—	100	20	Normal	—	—
42	Dragon Pulse	Dragon	Special	90	100	10	Normal	○	—
48	Swords Dance	Normal	Status	—	—	30	Self	—	—
54	Guillotine	Normal	Physical	—	30	5	Normal	—	—
60	Outrage	Dragon	Physical	120	100	10	1 Random	—	—
66	Giga Impact	Normal	Physical	150	90	5	Normal	—	—

MOVES TAUGHT BY PEOPLE

Name	Type	Kind	Pow.	Acc.	PP	Range	Long	DA
Draco Meteor	Dragon	Special	140	90	5	Normal	—	—

TM & HM MOVES

No.	Name	Type	Kind	Pow.	Acc.	PP	Range	Long	DA
TM01	Hone Claws	Dark	Status	—	—	15	Self	—	—
TM02	Dragon Claw	Dragon	Physical	80	100	15	Normal	—	—
TM05	Roar	Normal	Status	—	100	20	Normal	—	—
TM06	Toxic	Poison	Status	—	90	10	Normal	—	—
TM10	Hidden Power	Normal	Special	—	100	15	Normal	—	—
TM11	Sunny Day	Fire	Status	—	—	5	Both Sides	—	—
TM12	Taunt	Dark	Status	—	100	20	Normal	—	—
TM17	Protect	Normal	Status	—	—	10	Self	—	—
TM18	Rain Dance	Water	Status	—	—	5	Both Sides	—	—
TM21	Frustration	Normal	Physical	—	100	20	Normal	—	○
TM27	Return	Normal	Physical	—	100	20	Normal	—	○
TM28	Dig	Ground	Physical	80	100	10	Normal	—	○
TM32	Double Team	Normal	Status	—	—	15	Self	—	—
TM39	Rock Tomb	Rock	Physical	50	80	10	Normal	—	—
TM40	Aerial Ace	Flying	Physical	60	—	20	Normal	○	○
TM42	Facade	Normal	Physical	70	100	20	Normal	—	—
TM44	Rest	Psychic	Status	—	—	10	Self	—	—
TM45	Attract	Normal	Status	—	100	15	Normal	—	—
TM48	Round	Normal	Special	60	100	15	Normal	—	—
TM54	False Swipe	Normal	Physical	40	100	40	Normal	—	○
TM56	Fling	Dark	Physical	—	100	10	Normal	—	○
TM59	Incinerate	Fire	Special	30	100	15	Many Others	—	—
TM65	Shadow Claw	Ghost	Physical	70	100	15	Normal	—	○
TM66	Payback	Dark	Physical	50	100	10	Normal	—	○
TM68	Giga Impact	Normal	Physical	150	90	5	Normal	—	—
TM75	Swords Dance	Normal	Status	—	—	30	Self	—	—
TM81	X-Scissor	Bug	Physical	80	100	15	Normal	—	—
TM82	Dragon Tail	Dragon	Physical	60	90	10	Normal	—	—
TM84	Poison Jab	Poison	Physical	80	100	20	Normal	—	—
TM87	Swagger	Normal	Status	—	90	15	Normal	—	—
TM90	Substitute	Normal	Status	—	—	10	Self	—	—
TM94	Rock Smash	Fighting	Physical	40	100	15	Normal	—	○
HM01	Cut	Normal	Physical	50	95	30	Normal	—	○
HM04	Strength	Normal	Physical	80	100	15	Normal	—	○

MAIN WAYS TO OBTAIN

POKÉMON BLACK VERSION
1 Victory Road Outside
2 Level up Axew to Lv. 38

POKÉMON WHITE VERSION
1 Victory Road Outside
2 Level up Axew to Lv. 38

● HEIGHT: 3'03"
● WEIGHT: 79.4 lbs.
● GENDER: Both ♂♀ exist
● ITEMS:
• None

● FOOTPRINT

● MALE/FEMALE HAVE SAME FORM

EVOLUTION

Axew → (Lv. 38) Fraxure → (Lv. 48) Haxorus

POKÉMON BLACK VERSION — Since a broken tusk will not grow back, they diligently sharpen their tusks on river rocks after they've been fighting.

POKÉMON WHITE VERSION — Their tusks can shatter rocks. Territory battles between Fraxure can be intensely violent.

ABILITIES
● Rivalry
● Mold Breaker

EGG GROUPS
Monster
Dragon

STATS
HP ●●
ATTACK ●●●●●
DEFENSE ●●●
SP. ATTACK ●●
SP. DEFENSE ●●
SPEED ●●●

Haxorus

● TYPE **Dragon**

● FOOTPRINT

● HEIGHT: 5'11"
● WEIGHT: 232.6 lbs.
● GENDER: Both ♂ ♀ exist
● ITEMS:
  • None

● MALE/FEMALE HAVE SAME FORM

POKÉMON BLACK VERSION
They are kind but can be relentless when defending territory. They challenge foes with tusks that can cut steel.

POKÉMON WHITE VERSION
Their sturdy tusks will stay sharp even if used to cut steel beams. These Pokémon are covered in hard armor.

● LEVEL-UP AND LEARNED MOVES

Lv.	Name	Type	Kind	Pow.	Acc.	PP	Range	Long	DA
1	Scratch	Normal	Physical	40	100	35	Normal	–	–
1	Leer	Normal	Status	–	100	30	Many Others	–	–
1	Assurance	Dark	Physical	50	100	10	Normal	–	○
1	Dragon Rage	Dragon	Special	–	100	10	Normal	–	–
4	Leer	Normal	Status	–	100	30	Many Others	–	–
7	Assurance	Dark	Physical	50	100	10	Normal	–	○
10	Dragon Rage	Dragon	Special	–	100	10	Normal	–	–
13	Dual Chop	Dragon	Physical	40	90	15	Normal	–	○
16	Scary Face	Normal	Status	–	100	10	Normal	–	–
20	Slash	Normal	Physical	70	100	20	Normal	–	○
24	False Swipe	Normal	Physical	40	100	40	Normal	–	○
28	Dragon Claw	Dragon	Physical	80	100	15	Normal	–	○
32	Dragon Dance	Dragon	Status	–	–	20	Self	–	–
36	Taunt	Dark	Status	–	100	20	Normal	–	–
42	Dragon Pulse	Dragon	Special	90	100	10	Normal	○	–
50	Swords Dance	Normal	Status	–	–	30	Self	–	–
58	Guillotine	Normal	Physical	–	30	5	Normal	–	–
66	Outrage	Dragon	Physical	120	100	10	1 Random	–	○
74	Giga Impact	Normal	Physical	150	90	5	Normal	–	○

● MOVES TAUGHT BY PEOPLE

Name	Type	Kind	Pow.	Acc.	PP	Range	Long	DA
Draco Meteor	Dragon	Special	140	90	5	Normal	–	–

● TM & HM MOVES

No.	Name	Type	Kind	Pow.	Acc.	PP	Range	Long	DA
TM01	Hone Claws	Dark	Status	–	–	15	Self	–	–
TM02	Dragon Claw	Dragon	Physical	80	100	15	Normal	–	○
TM05	Roar	Normal	Status	–	100	20	Normal	–	–
TM06	Toxic	Poison	Status	–	90	10	Normal	–	–
TM10	Hidden Power	Normal	Special	–	100	15	Normal	–	–
TM11	Sunny Day	Fire	Status	–	–	5	Both Sides	–	–
TM12	Taunt	Dark	Status	–	100	20	Normal	–	–
TM15	Hyper Beam	Normal	Special	150	90	5	Normal	–	○
TM17	Protect	Normal	Status	–	–	10	Self	–	–
TM18	Rain Dance	Water	Status	–	–	5	Both Sides	–	–
TM21	Frustration	Normal	Physical	–	100	20	Normal	–	○
TM26	Earthquake	Ground	Physical	100	100	10	Adjacent	–	○
TM27	Return	Normal	Physical	–	100	20	Normal	–	○
TM28	Dig	Ground	Physical	80	100	10	Normal	–	○
TM31	Brick Break	Fighting	Physical	75	100	15	Normal	–	○
TM32	Double Team	Normal	Status	–	–	15	Self	–	–
TM39	Rock Tomb	Rock	Physical	50	80	10	Normal	–	○
TM40	Aerial Ace	Flying	Physical	60	–	20	Normal	–	○
TM42	Facade	Normal	Physical	70	100	20	Normal	–	○
TM44	Rest	Psychic	Status	–	–	10	Self	–	–
TM45	Attract	Normal	Status	–	100	15	Normal	–	–
TM48	Round	Normal	Special	60	100	15	Normal	–	–
TM52	Focus Blast	Fighting	Special	120	70	5	Normal	–	–
TM54	False Swipe	Normal	Physical	40	100	40	Normal	–	○
TM56	Fling	Dark	Physical	–	100	10	Normal	–	○
TM59	Incinerate	Fire	Special	30	100	15	Many Others	–	–
TM65	Shadow Claw	Ghost	Physical	70	100	15	Normal	–	○
TM66	Payback	Dark	Physical	50	100	10	Normal	–	○
TM68	Giga Impact	Normal	Physical	150	90	5	Normal	–	○
TM75	Swords Dance	Normal	Status	–	–	30	Self	–	–
TM78	Bulldoze	Ground	Physical	60	100	20	Adjacent	–	○
TM80	Rock Slide	Rock	Physical	75	90	10	Many Others	–	○
TM81	X-Scissor	Bug	Physical	80	100	15	Normal	–	○
TM82	Dragon Tail	Dragon	Physical	60	90	10	Normal	–	○
TM84	Poison Jab	Poison	Physical	80	100	20	Normal	–	○
TM86	Grass Knot	Grass	Special	–	100	20	Normal	–	○
TM87	Swagger	Normal	Status	–	90	15	Normal	–	–
TM90	Substitute	Normal	Status	–	–	10	Self	–	–
TM94	Rock Smash	Fighting	Physical	40	100	15	Normal	–	○
HM01	Cut	Normal	Physical	50	95	30	Normal	–	○
HM03	Surf	Water	Special	95	100	15	Adjacent	–	–
HM04	Strength	Normal	Physical	80	100	15	Normal	–	○

EVOLUTION

Axew — Lv. 38 → Fraxure — Lv. 48 → Haxorus

● MAIN WAYS TO OBTAIN

POKÉMON BLACK VERSION
1 Level up Fraxure to Lv. 48
2 —

POKÉMON WHITE VERSION
1 Level up Fraxure to Lv. 48
2 —

ABILITIES
● Rivalry
● Mold Breaker

EGG GROUPS
Monster
Dragon

STATS
HP ●●●
ATTACK ●●●●●●
DEFENSE ●●●●
SP. ATTACK ●●●
SP. DEFENSE ●●●
SPEED ●●●●

Cubchoo

● TYPE **Ice**

● FOOTPRINT

● HEIGHT: 1'08"
● WEIGHT: 18.7 lbs.
● GENDER: Both ♂ ♀ exist
● ITEMS:
  • Aspear Berry

● MALE/FEMALE HAVE SAME FORM

POKÉMON BLACK VERSION
When it is not feeling well, its mucus gets watery and the power of its Ice-type moves decreases.

POKÉMON WHITE VERSION
Its nose is always running. It sniffs the snot back up because the mucus provides the raw material for its moves.

● LEVEL-UP AND LEARNED MOVES

Lv.	Name	Type	Kind	Pow.	Acc.	PP	Range	Long	DA
1	Powder Snow	Ice	Special	40	100	25	Many Others	–	–
5	Growl	Normal	Status	–	100	40	Many Others	–	–
9	Bide	Normal	Physical	–	–	10	Self	–	–
13	Icy Wind	Ice	Special	55	95	15	Many Others	–	–
17	Fury Swipes	Normal	Physical	18	80	15	Normal	–	○
21	Brine	Water	Special	65	100	10	Normal	–	–
25	Endure	Normal	Status	–	–	10	Self	–	–
29	Charm	Normal	Status	–	100	20	Normal	–	–
33	Slash	Normal	Physical	70	100	20	Normal	–	○
36	Flail	Normal	Physical	–	100	15	Normal	–	○
41	Rest	Psychic	Status	–	–	10	Self	–	–
45	Blizzard	Ice	Special	120	70	5	Many Others	–	–
49	Hail	Ice	Status	–	–	10	Both Sides	–	–
53	Thrash	Normal	Physical	120	100	10	1 Random	–	○
57	Sheer Cold	Ice	Special	–	30	5	Normal	–	–

● MOVES TAUGHT BY PEOPLE

Name	Type	Kind	Pow.	Acc.	PP	Range	Long	DA

● EGG MOVES

Name	Type	Kind	Pow.	Acc.	PP	Range	Long	DA
Yawn	Normal	Status	–	–	10	Normal	–	–
Avalanche	Ice	Physical	60	100	10	Normal	–	○
Encore	Normal	Status	–	100	5	Normal	–	–
Ice Punch	Ice	Physical	75	100	15	Normal	–	○
Night Slash	Dark	Physical	70	100	15	Normal	–	○
Assurance	Dark	Physical	50	100	10	Normal	–	○
Sleep Talk	Normal	Status	–	–	10	Self	–	–
Focus Punch	Fighting	Physical	150	100	20	Normal	–	○

● TM & HM MOVES

No.	Name	Type	Kind	Pow.	Acc.	PP	Range	Long	DA
TM01	Hone Claws	Dark	Status	–	–	15	Self	–	–
TM06	Toxic	Poison	Status	–	90	10	Normal	–	–
TM07	Hail	Ice	Status	–	–	10	Both Sides	–	–
TM10	Hidden Power	Normal	Special	–	100	15	Normal	–	–
TM13	Ice Beam	Ice	Special	95	100	10	Normal	–	–
TM14	Blizzard	Ice	Special	120	70	5	Many Others	–	–
TM17	Protect	Normal	Status	–	–	10	Self	–	–
TM18	Rain Dance	Water	Status	–	–	5	Both Sides	–	–
TM21	Frustration	Normal	Physical	–	100	20	Normal	–	○
TM27	Return	Normal	Physical	–	100	20	Normal	–	○
TM28	Dig	Ground	Physical	80	100	10	Normal	–	○
TM32	Double Team	Normal	Status	–	–	15	Self	–	–
TM39	Rock Tomb	Rock	Physical	50	80	10	Normal	–	○
TM40	Aerial Ace	Flying	Physical	60	–	20	Normal	–	○
TM42	Facade	Normal	Physical	70	100	20	Normal	–	○
TM44	Rest	Psychic	Status	–	–	10	Self	–	–
TM45	Attract	Normal	Status	–	100	15	Normal	–	–
TM48	Round	Normal	Special	60	100	15	Normal	–	–
TM49	Echoed Voice	Normal	Special	40	100	15	Normal	–	–
TM56	Fling	Dark	Physical	–	100	10	Normal	–	○
TM65	Shadow Claw	Ghost	Physical	70	100	15	Normal	–	○
TM79	Frost Breath	Ice	Special	40	90	10	Normal	–	–
TM86	Grass Knot	Grass	Special	–	100	20	Normal	–	○
TM87	Swagger	Normal	Status	–	90	15	Normal	–	–
TM90	Substitute	Normal	Status	–	–	10	Self	–	–
TM94	Rock Smash	Fighting	Physical	40	100	15	Normal	–	○
HM01	Cut	Normal	Physical	50	95	30	Normal	–	○
HM03	Surf	Water	Special	95	100	15	Adjacent	–	–
HM04	Strength	Normal	Physical	80	100	15	Normal	–	○

EVOLUTION

Cubchoo — Lv. 37 → Beartic

● MAIN WAYS TO OBTAIN

POKÉMON BLACK VERSION
1 Twist Mountain Upper level
2 Route 7 (winter only)

POKÉMON WHITE VERSION
1 Twist Mountain Upper level
2 Route 7 (winter only)

ABILITY
● Snow Cloak

EGG GROUP
Field

STATS
HP ●●
ATTACK ●●●
DEFENSE ●●●
SP. ATTACK ●●●
SP. DEFENSE ●
SPEED ●●

Beartic

● TYPE: Ice

● FOOTPRINT

● MALE/FEMALE HAVE SAME FORM

● HEIGHT: 8'06"
● WEIGHT: 573.2 lbs.
● GENDER: Both ♂♀ exist
● ITEMS:
  • Aspear Berry

POKÉMON BLACK VERSION
It can make its breath freeze at will. Very able in the water, it swims around in northern seas and catches prey.

POKÉMON WHITE VERSION
It freezes its breath to create fangs and claws of ice to fight with. Cold northern areas are its habitat.

● LEVEL-UP AND LEARNED MOVES

Lv.	Name	Type	Kind	Pow.	Acc.	PP	Range	Long	DA
1	Superpower	Fighting	Physical	120	100	5	Normal	–	–
1	Powder Snow	Ice	Special	40	100	25	Many Others	–	–
1	Growl	Normal	Status	–	100	40	Many Others	–	–
1	Bide	Normal	Physical	–	–	10	Self	–	○
1	Icy Wind	Ice	Special	55	95	15	Many Others	–	–
5	Growl	Normal	Status	–	100	40	Many Others	–	–
9	Bide	Normal	Physical	–	–	10	Self	–	○
13	Icy Wind	Ice	Special	55	95	15	Many Others	–	–
17	Fury Swipes	Normal	Physical	18	80	15	Normal	–	○
21	Brine	Water	Special	65	100	10	Normal	–	–
25	Endure	Normal	Status	–	–	10	Self	–	○
29	Swagger	Normal	Status	–	90	15	Normal	–	–
33	Slash	Normal	Physical	70	100	20	Normal	–	–
36	Flail	Normal	Physical	–	100	15	Normal	–	○
37	Icicle Crash	Ice	Physical	85	90	10	Normal	–	–
41	Rest	Psychic	Status	–	–	10	Self	–	–
45	Blizzard	Ice	Special	120	70	5	Many Others	–	–
53	Hail	Ice	Status	–	–	10	Both Sides	–	–
59	Thrash	Normal	Physical	120	100	10	1 Random	–	○
66	Sheer Cold	Ice	Special	–	30	5	Normal	–	–

● MOVES TAUGHT BY PEOPLE

Name	Type	Kind	Pow.	Acc.	PP	Range	Long	DA

● TM & HM MOVES

No.	Name	Type	Kind	Pow.	Acc.	PP	Range	Long	DA
TM01	Hone Claws	Dark	Status	–	–	15	Self	–	–
TM05	Roar	Normal	Status	–	100	20	Normal	–	–
TM06	Toxic	Poison	Status	–	90	10	Normal	–	–
TM07	Hail	Ice	Status	–	–	10	Both Sides	–	–
TM08	Bulk Up	Fighting	Status	–	–	20	Self	–	–
TM10	Hidden Power	Normal	Special	–	100	15	Normal	–	–
TM12	Taunt	Dark	Status	–	100	20	Normal	–	–
TM13	Ice Beam	Ice	Special	95	100	10	Normal	–	–
TM14	Blizzard	Ice	Special	120	70	5	Many Others	–	–
TM15	Hyper Beam	Normal	Special	150	90	5	Normal	–	–
TM17	Protect	Normal	Status	–	–	10	Self	–	–
TM18	Rain Dance	Water	Status	–	–	5	Both Sides	–	–
TM21	Frustration	Normal	Physical	–	100	20	Normal	–	○
TM27	Return	Normal	Physical	–	100	20	Normal	–	○
TM28	Dig	Ground	Physical	80	100	10	Normal	–	○
TM31	Brick Break	Fighting	Physical	75	100	15	Normal	–	–
TM32	Double Team	Normal	Status	–	–	15	Self	–	–
TM39	Rock Tomb	Rock	Physical	50	80	10	Normal	–	–
TM40	Aerial Ace	Flying	Physical	60	–	20	Normal	○	–
TM42	Facade	Normal	Physical	70	100	20	Normal	–	○
TM44	Rest	Psychic	Status	–	–	10	Self	–	–
TM45	Attract	Normal	Status	–	100	15	Normal	–	–
TM48	Round	Normal	Special	60	100	15	Normal	–	–
TM49	Echoed Voice	Normal	Special	40	100	15	Normal	–	–
TM52	Focus Blast	Fighting	Special	120	70	5	Normal	–	–
TM56	Fling	Dark	Physical	–	100	10	Normal	–	–
TM65	Shadow Claw	Ghost	Physical	70	100	15	Normal	–	–
TM68	Giga Impact	Normal	Physical	150	90	5	Normal	–	–
TM71	Stone Edge	Rock	Physical	100	80	5	Normal	–	–
TM75	Swords Dance	Normal	Status	–	–	30	Self	–	–
TM78	Bulldoze	Ground	Physical	60	100	20	Adjacent	–	–
TM79	Frost Breath	Ice	Special	40	90	10	Normal	–	–
TM80	Rock Slide	Rock	Physical	75	90	10	Many Others	–	–
TM86	Grass Knot	Grass	Special	–	100	20	Normal	–	○
TM87	Swagger	Normal	Status	–	90	15	Normal	–	–
TM90	Substitute	Normal	Status	–	–	10	Self	–	–
TM94	Rock Smash	Fighting	Physical	40	100	15	Normal	–	–
HM01	Cut	Normal	Physical	50	95	30	Normal	–	–
HM03	Surf	Water	Special	95	100	15	Adjacent	–	–
HM04	Strength	Normal	Physical	80	100	15	Normal	–	–
HM06	Dive	Water	Physical	80	100	10	Normal	–	–

EVOLUTION

Lv. 37

Cubchoo   Beartic

ABILITY ● Snow Cloak

EGG GROUP Field

STATS
- HP ●●●●
- ATTACK ●●●●
- DEFENSE ●●●
- SP. ATTACK ●●●
- SP. DEFENSE ●●●
- SPEED ●●

● MAIN WAYS TO OBTAIN

POKÉMON BLACK VERSION
1 Dragonspiral Tower 1F Outside (Dark Grass/winter only)
2 Level up Cubchoo to Lv. 37

POKÉMON WHITE VERSION
1 Dragonspiral Tower 1F Outside (Dark Grass/winter only)
2 Level up Cubchoo to Lv. 37

Cryogonal

● TYPE: Ice

● FOOTPRINT

● GENDER UNKNOWN

● HEIGHT: 3'07"
● WEIGHT: 326.3 lbs.
● GENDER: Unknown
● ITEMS:
  • NeverMeltIce

POKÉMON BLACK VERSION
When its body temperature goes up, it turns into steam and vanishes. When its temperature lowers, it returns to ice.

POKÉMON WHITE VERSION
They are born in snow clouds. They use chains made of ice crystals to capture prey.

● LEVEL-UP AND LEARNED MOVES

Lv.	Name	Type	Kind	Pow.	Acc.	PP	Range	Long	DA
1	Bind	Normal	Physical	15	85	20	Normal	–	○
5	Ice Shard	Ice	Physical	40	100	30	Normal	–	–
9	Sharpen	Normal	Status	–	–	30	Self	–	–
13	Rapid Spin	Normal	Physical	20	100	40	Normal	–	–
17	Icy Wind	Ice	Special	55	95	15	Many Others	–	–
21	Mist	Ice	Status	–	–	30	Your Side	–	–
21	Haze	Ice	Status	–	–	30	Both Sides	–	–
25	Aurora Beam	Ice	Special	65	100	20	Normal	–	–
29	Acid Armor	Poison	Status	–	–	40	Self	–	–
33	Ice Beam	Ice	Special	95	100	10	Normal	–	–
37	Light Screen	Psychic	Status	–	–	30	Your Side	–	–
37	Reflect	Psychic	Status	–	–	20	Your Side	–	–
41	Slash	Normal	Physical	70	100	20	Normal	–	–
45	Confuse Ray	Ghost	Status	–	100	10	Normal	–	–
49	Recover	Normal	Status	–	–	10	Self	–	–
53	SolarBeam	Grass	Special	120	100	10	Normal	–	–
57	Night Slash	Dark	Physical	70	100	15	Normal	–	○
61	Sheer Cold	Ice	Special	–	30	5	Normal	–	–

● MOVES TAUGHT BY PEOPLE

Name	Type	Kind	Pow.	Acc.	PP	Range	Long	DA

● TM & HM MOVES

No.	Name	Type	Kind	Pow.	Acc.	PP	Range	Long	DA
TM06	Toxic	Poison	Status	–	90	10	Normal	–	–
TM07	Hail	Ice	Status	–	–	10	Both Sides	–	–
TM10	Hidden Power	Normal	Special	–	100	15	Normal	–	–
TM13	Ice Beam	Ice	Special	95	100	10	Normal	–	–
TM14	Blizzard	Ice	Special	120	70	5	Many Others	–	–
TM15	Hyper Beam	Normal	Special	150	90	5	Normal	–	–
TM16	Light Screen	Psychic	Status	–	–	30	Your Side	–	–
TM17	Protect	Normal	Status	–	–	10	Self	–	–
TM18	Rain Dance	Water	Status	–	–	5	Both Sides	–	–
TM21	Frustration	Normal	Physical	–	100	20	Normal	–	○
TM22	SolarBeam	Grass	Special	120	100	10	Normal	–	–
TM27	Return	Normal	Physical	–	100	20	Normal	–	○
TM32	Double Team	Normal	Status	–	–	15	Self	–	–
TM33	Reflect	Psychic	Status	–	–	20	Your Side	–	–
TM42	Facade	Normal	Physical	70	100	20	Normal	–	○
TM44	Rest	Psychic	Status	–	–	10	Self	–	–
TM45	Attract	Normal	Status	–	100	15	Normal	–	–
TM48	Round	Normal	Special	60	100	15	Normal	–	–
TM62	Acrobatics	Flying	Physical	55	100	15	Normal	○	○
TM64	Explosion	Normal	Physical	250	100	5	Adjacent	–	–
TM79	Frost Breath	Ice	Special	40	90	10	Normal	–	○
TM84	Poison Jab	Poison	Physical	80	100	20	Normal	–	–
TM87	Swagger	Normal	Status	–	90	15	Normal	–	–
TM90	Substitute	Normal	Status	–	–	10	Self	–	–
TM91	Flash Cannon	Steel	Special	80	100	10	Normal	–	–

EVOLUTION

Does not evolve

ABILITY ● Levitate

EGG GROUP Mineral

STATS
- HP ●●●
- ATTACK ●●
- DEFENSE ●
- SP. ATTACK ●●●●
- SP. DEFENSE ●●●●●●
- SPEED ●●●●●

● MAIN WAYS TO OBTAIN

POKÉMON BLACK VERSION
1 Twist Mountain Upper level
2 Twist Mountain Middle level

POKÉMON WHITE VERSION
1 Twist Mountain Upper level
2 Twist Mountain Middle level

Shelmet

● TYPE Bug

● LEVEL-UP AND LEARNED MOVES

Lv.	Name	Type	Kind	Pow.	Acc.	PP	Range	Long	DA
1	Leech Life	Bug	Physical	20	100	15	Normal	–	○
4	Acid	Poison	Special	40	100	30	Many Others	–	–
8	Bide	Normal	Physical	–	–	10	Self	–	○
13	Curse	Ghost	Status	–	–	10	Varies	–	–
16	Struggle Bug	Bug	Special	30	100	20	Many Others	–	–
20	Mega Drain	Grass	Special	40	100	15	Normal	–	–
25	Yawn	Normal	Status	–	–	10	Normal	–	–
28	Protect	Normal	Status	–	–	10	Self	–	–
32	Acid Armor	Poison	Status	–	–	40	Self	–	–
37	Giga Drain	Grass	Special	75	100	10	Normal	–	–
40	Body Slam	Normal	Physical	85	100	15	Normal	–	○
44	Bug Buzz	Bug	Special	90	100	10	Normal	–	–
49	Recover	Normal	Status	–	–	10	Self	–	–
52	Guard Swap	Psychic	Status	–	–	10	Normal	–	–
56	Final Gambit	Fighting	Special	–	100	5	Normal	–	–

● MOVES TAUGHT BY PEOPLE

Name	Type	Kind	Pow.	Acc.	PP	Range	Long	DA

● EGG MOVES

Name	Type	Kind	Pow.	Acc.	PP	Range	Long	DA
Endure	Normal	Status	–	–	10	Self	–	–
Baton Pass	Normal	Status	–	–	40	Self	–	–
Double-Edge	Normal	Physical	120	100	15	Normal	–	○
Encore	Normal	Status	–	100	5	Normal	–	–
Guard Split	Psychic	Status	–	–	10	Normal	–	–
Mind Reader	Normal	Status	–	–	5	Normal	–	–
Mud-Slap	Ground	Special	20	100	10	Normal	–	–
Spikes	Ground	Status	–	–	20	Other Side	–	–
Feint	Normal	Physical	30	100	10	Normal	–	–
Pursuit	Dark	Physical	40	100	20	Normal	–	○

● TM & HM MOVES

No.	Name	Type	Kind	Pow.	Acc.	PP	Range	Long	DA
TM06	Toxic	Poison	Status	–	90	10	Normal	–	–
TM09	Venoshock	Poison	Special	65	100	10	Normal	–	–
TM10	Hidden Power	Normal	Special	–	100	15	Normal	–	–
TM17	Protect	Normal	Status	–	–	10	Self	–	–
TM18	Rain Dance	Water	Status	–	–	5	Both Sides	–	–
TM21	Frustration	Normal	Physical	–	100	20	Normal	–	○
TM27	Return	Normal	Physical	–	100	20	Normal	–	○
TM32	Double Team	Normal	Status	–	–	15	Self	–	–
TM36	Sludge Bomb	Poison	Special	90	100	10	Normal	–	–
TM42	Facade	Normal	Physical	70	100	20	Normal	–	○
TM44	Rest	Psychic	Status	–	–	10	Self	–	–
TM45	Attract	Normal	Status	–	100	15	Normal	–	–
TM48	Round	Normal	Special	60	100	15	Normal	–	–
TM53	Energy Ball	Grass	Special	80	100	10	Normal	–	–
TM76	Struggle Bug	Bug	Special	30	100	20	Many Others	–	–
TM87	Swagger	Normal	Status	–	90	15	Normal	–	–
TM90	Substitute	Normal	Status	–	–	10	Self	–	–

● MAIN WAYS TO OBTAIN

POKÉMON BLACK VERSION
1. Icirrus City (spring/summer/autumn only)
2. Route 8 (spring/summer/autumn only)

POKÉMON WHITE VERSION
1. Icirrus City (spring/summer/autumn only)
2. Route 8 (spring/summer/autumn only)

● FOOTPRINT

● MALE/FEMALE HAVE SAME FORM

● HEIGHT: 1'04"
● WEIGHT: 17.0 lbs.
● GENDER: Both ♂♀ exist
● ITEMS:
  • None

POKÉMON BLACK VERSION
When attacked, it defends itself by closing the lid of its shell. It can spit a sticky, poisonous liquid.

POKÉMON WHITE VERSION
It evolves when bathed in an electric-like energy along with Karrablast. The reason is still unknown.

EVOLUTION
Trade Karrablast for Shelmet
Shelmet → Accelgor

ABILITIES ● Hydration ● Shell Armor

EGG GROUP Bug

STATS
HP ●●
ATTACK ●●
DEFENSE ●●●
SP. ATTACK ●●
SP. DEFENSE ●●
SPEED ●

Accelgor

● TYPE Bug

● LEVEL-UP AND LEARNED MOVES

Lv.	Name	Type	Kind	Pow.	Acc.	PP	Range	Long	DA
1	Leech Life	Bug	Physical	20	100	15	Normal	–	○
1	Acid Spray	Poison	Special	40	100	20	Normal	–	–
1	Double Team	Normal	Status	–	–	15	Self	–	–
1	Quick Attack	Normal	Physical	40	100	30	Normal	–	○
4	Acid Spray	Poison	Special	40	100	20	Normal	–	–
8	Double Team	Normal	Status	–	–	15	Self	–	–
13	Quick Attack	Normal	Physical	40	100	30	Normal	–	○
16	Struggle Bug	Bug	Special	30	100	20	Many Others	–	–
20	Mega Drain	Grass	Special	40	100	15	Normal	–	–
25	Swift	Normal	Special	60	–	20	Many Others	–	–
28	Me First	Normal	Status	–	–	20	Varies	–	–
32	Agility	Psychic	Status	–	–	30	Self	–	–
37	Giga Drain	Grass	Special	75	100	10	Normal	–	–
40	U-turn	Bug	Physical	70	100	20	Normal	–	○
44	Bug Buzz	Bug	Special	90	100	10	Normal	–	–
49	Recover	Normal	Status	–	–	10	Self	–	–
52	Power Swap	Psychic	Status	–	–	10	Normal	–	–
56	Final Gambit	Fighting	Special	–	100	5	Normal	–	○

● MOVES TAUGHT BY PEOPLE

Name	Type	Kind	Pow.	Acc.	PP	Range	Long	DA

● TM & HM MOVES

No.	Name	Type	Kind	Pow.	Acc.	PP	Range	Long	DA
TM06	Toxic	Poison	Status	–	90	10	Normal	–	–
TM09	Venoshock	Poison	Special	65	100	10	Normal	–	–
TM10	Hidden Power	Normal	Special	–	100	15	Normal	–	–
TM15	Hyper Beam	Normal	Special	150	90	5	Normal	–	–
TM17	Protect	Normal	Status	–	–	10	Self	–	–
TM18	Rain Dance	Water	Status	–	–	5	Both Sides	–	–
TM21	Frustration	Normal	Physical	–	100	20	Normal	–	○
TM27	Return	Normal	Physical	–	100	20	Normal	–	○
TM32	Double Team	Normal	Status	–	–	15	Self	–	–
TM36	Sludge Bomb	Poison	Special	90	100	10	Normal	–	–
TM37	Sandstorm	Rock	Status	–	–	10	Both Sides	–	–
TM42	Facade	Normal	Physical	70	100	20	Normal	–	○
TM44	Rest	Psychic	Status	–	–	10	Self	–	–
TM45	Attract	Normal	Status	–	100	15	Normal	–	–
TM48	Round	Normal	Special	60	100	15	Normal	–	–
TM52	Focus Blast	Fighting	Special	120	70	5	Normal	–	–
TM53	Energy Ball	Grass	Special	80	100	10	Normal	–	–
TM68	Giga Impact	Normal	Physical	150	90	5	Normal	–	○
TM76	Struggle Bug	Bug	Special	30	100	20	Many Others	–	–
TM87	Swagger	Normal	Status	–	90	15	Normal	–	–
TM89	U-turn	Bug	Physical	70	100	20	Normal	–	○
TM90	Substitute	Normal	Status	–	–	10	Self	–	–

● MAIN WAYS TO OBTAIN

POKÉMON BLACK VERSION
1. Link trade Karrablast for Shelmet
2. —

POKÉMON WHITE VERSION
1. Link trade Karrablast for Shelmet
2. —

● FOOTPRINT

● MALE/FEMALE HAVE SAME FORM

● HEIGHT: 2'07"
● WEIGHT: 55.8 lbs.
● GENDER: Both ♂♀ exist
● ITEMS:
  • None

POKÉMON BLACK VERSION
When its body dries out, it weakens. So, to prevent dehydration, it wraps itself in many layers of thin membrane.

POKÉMON WHITE VERSION
Having removed its heavy shell, it becomes very light and can fight with ninja-like movements.

EVOLUTION
Trade Karrablast for Shelmet
Shelmet → Accelgor

ABILITIES ● Hydration ● Sticky Hold

EGG GROUP Bug

STATS
HP ●●●
ATTACK ●●●
DEFENSE ●●
SP. ATTACK ●●●●
SP. DEFENSE ●●
SPEED ●●●●●●

Stunfisk

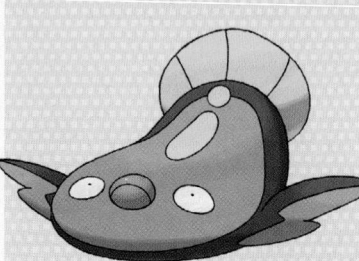

● TYPE Ground Electric

● LEVEL-UP AND LEARNED MOVES

Lv.	Name	Type	Kind	Pow.	Acc.	PP	Range	Long	DA
1	Mud-Slap	Ground	Special	20	100	10	Normal	—	—
1	Mud Sport	Ground	Status	—	—	15	Both Sides	—	—
5	Bide	Normal	Physical	—	—	10	Self	—	○
9	ThunderShock	Electric	Special	40	100	30	Normal	—	—
13	Mud Shot	Ground	Special	55	95	15	Normal	—	—
17	Camouflage	Normal	Status	—	—	20	Self	—	○
21	Mud Bomb	Ground	Special	65	85	10	Normal	—	—
25	Discharge	Electric	Special	80	100	15	Adjacent	—	—
30	Endure	Normal	Status	—	—	10	Self	—	○
35	Bounce	Flying	Physical	85	85	5	Normal	○	○
40	Muddy Water	Water	Special	95	85	10	Many Others	—	—
45	Thunderbolt	Electric	Special	95	100	15	Normal	—	—
50	Revenge	Fighting	Physical	60	100	10	Normal	—	—
55	Flail	Normal	Physical	—	100	15	Normal	—	—
61	Fissure	Ground	Physical	—	30	5	Normal	—	—

● TM & HM MOVES

No.	Name	Type	Kind	Pow.	Acc.	PP	Range	Long	DA
TM06	Toxic	Poison	Status	—	90	10	Normal	—	—
TM10	Hidden Power	Normal	Special	—	100	15	Normal	—	—
TM17	Protect	Normal	Status	—	—	10	Self	—	—
TM18	Rain Dance	Water	Status	—	—	5	Both Sides	—	—
TM21	Frustration	Normal	Physical	—	100	20	Normal	—	—
TM24	Thunderbolt	Electric	Special	95	100	15	Normal	—	—
TM25	Thunder	Electric	Special	120	70	10	Normal	—	—
TM26	Earthquake	Ground	Physical	100	100	10	Adjacent	—	—
TM27	Return	Normal	Physical	—	100	20	Normal	—	○
TM28	Dig	Ground	Physical	80	100	10	Normal	—	—
TM32	Double Team	Normal	Status	—	—	15	Self	—	—
TM34	Sludge Wave	Poison	Special	95	100	10	Adjacent	—	—
TM36	Sludge Bomb	Poison	Special	90	100	10	Normal	—	—
TM37	Sandstorm	Rock	Status	—	—	10	Both Sides	—	—
TM39	Rock Tomb	Rock	Physical	50	80	10	Normal	—	—
TM42	Facade	Normal	Physical	70	100	20	Normal	—	—
TM44	Rest	Psychic	Status	—	—	10	Self	—	—
TM45	Attract	Normal	Status	—	100	15	Normal	—	—
TM48	Round	Normal	Special	60	100	15	Normal	—	—
TM55	Scald	Water	Special	80	100	15	Normal	—	—
TM66	Payback	Dark	Physical	50	100	10	Normal	—	○
TM70	Flash	Normal	Status	—	100	20	Normal	—	—
TM71	Stone Edge	Rock	Physical	100	80	5	Normal	—	—
TM73	Thunder Wave	Electric	Status	—	100	20	Normal	—	—
TM78	Bulldoze	Ground	Physical	60	100	20	Adjacent	—	—
TM80	Rock Slide	Rock	Physical	75	90	10	Many Others	—	—
TM87	Swagger	Normal	Status	—	90	15	Normal	—	—
TM90	Substitute	Normal	Status	—	—	10	Self	—	—
HM03	Surf	Water	Special	95	100	15	Adjacent	—	—

● MOVES TAUGHT BY PEOPLE

Name	Type	Kind	Pow.	Acc.	PP	Range	Long	DA

● EGG MOVES

Name	Type	Kind	Pow.	Acc.	PP	Range	Long	DA
Shock Wave	Electric	Special	60	—	20	Normal	—	—
Earth Power	Ground	Special	90	100	10	Normal	—	—
Yawn	Normal	Status	—	—	10	Normal	—	—
Sleep Talk	Normal	Status	—	—	10	Self	—	—
Astonish	Ghost	Physical	30	100	15	Normal	—	○
Curse	Ghost	Status	—	—	10	Varies	—	—
Spite	Ghost	Status	—	—	10	Normal	—	—
Spark	Electric	Physical	65	100	20	Normal	—	○
Pain Split	Normal	Status	—	—	20	Normal	—	—

● FOOTPRINT

● MALE/FEMALE HAVE SAME FORM

● HEIGHT: 2'04"
● WEIGHT: 24.3 lbs.
● GENDER: Both ♂♀ exist
● ITEMS:
• Soft Sand

EVOLUTION

Does not evolve

● MAIN WAYS TO OBTAIN

POKÉMON BLACK VERSION
1 Icirrus City (Water Surface)
2 Route 8 (Water Surface)

POKÉMON WHITE VERSION
1 Icirrus City (Water Surface)
2 Route 8 (Water Surface)

POKÉMON BLACK VERSION: Its skin is very hard, so it is unhurt even if stepped on by sumo wrestlers. It smiles when transmitting electricity.

POKÉMON WHITE VERSION: It conceals itself in the mud of the seashore. Then it waits. When prey touch it, it delivers a jolt of electricity.

ABILITIES: ● Static ● Limber

EGG GROUPS: Water 1 / Amorphous

STATS:
HP ●●●●
ATTACK ●●●
DEFENSE ●●●
SP. ATTACK ●●●●
SP. DEFENSE ●●●●
SPEED ●

Mienfoo

● TYPE Fighting

● LEVEL-UP AND LEARNED MOVES

Lv.	Name	Type	Kind	Pow.	Acc.	PP	Range	Long	DA
1	Pound	Normal	Physical	40	100	35	Normal	—	○
5	Meditate	Psychic	Status	—	—	40	Self	—	—
9	Detect	Fighting	Status	—	—	5	Self	—	○
13	Fake Out	Normal	Physical	40	100	10	Normal	—	○
17	DoubleSlap	Normal	Physical	15	85	10	Normal	—	—
21	Swift	Normal	Special	60	—	20	Many Others	—	—
25	Calm Mind	Psychic	Status	—	—	20	Self	—	—
29	Force Palm	Fighting	Physical	60	100	10	Normal	—	—
33	Drain Punch	Fighting	Physical	75	100	10	Normal	—	○
37	Jump Kick	Fighting	Physical	100	95	10	Normal	—	—
41	U-turn	Bug	Physical	70	100	20	Normal	—	○
45	Quick Guard	Fighting	Status	—	—	15	Your Side	—	○
49	Bounce	Flying	Physical	85	85	5	Normal	○	○
53	Hi Jump Kick	Fighting	Physical	130	90	10	Normal	—	○
57	Reversal	Fighting	Physical	—	100	15	Normal	—	—
61	Aura Sphere	Fighting	Special	90	—	20	Normal	—	○

● TM & HM MOVES

No.	Name	Type	Kind	Pow.	Acc.	PP	Range	Long	DA
TM04	Calm Mind	Psychic	Status	—	—	20	Self	—	—
TM06	Toxic	Poison	Status	—	90	10	Normal	—	—
TM08	Bulk Up	Fighting	Status	—	—	20	Self	—	—
TM10	Hidden Power	Normal	Special	—	100	15	Normal	—	—
TM11	Sunny Day	Fire	Status	—	—	5	Both Sides	—	—
TM12	Taunt	Dark	Status	—	100	20	Normal	—	—
TM17	Protect	Normal	Status	—	—	10	Self	—	—
TM18	Rain Dance	Water	Status	—	—	5	Both Sides	—	—
TM21	Frustration	Normal	Physical	—	100	20	Normal	—	○
TM27	Return	Normal	Physical	—	100	20	Normal	—	○
TM28	Dig	Ground	Physical	80	100	10	Normal	—	—
TM31	Brick Break	Fighting	Physical	75	100	15	Normal	—	○
TM32	Double Team	Normal	Status	—	—	15	Self	—	—
TM33	Reflect	Psychic	Status	—	—	20	Your Side	—	—
TM39	Rock Tomb	Rock	Physical	50	80	10	Normal	—	—
TM40	Aerial Ace	Flying	Physical	60	—	20	Normal	○	○
TM42	Facade	Normal	Physical	70	100	20	Normal	—	○
TM44	Rest	Psychic	Status	—	—	10	Self	—	—
TM45	Attract	Normal	Status	—	100	15	Normal	—	—
TM47	Low Sweep	Fighting	Physical	60	100	20	Normal	—	○
TM48	Round	Normal	Special	60	100	15	Normal	—	—
TM52	Focus Blast	Fighting	Special	120	70	5	Normal	—	—
TM56	Fling	Dark	Physical	—	100	10	Normal	—	○
TM62	Acrobatics	Flying	Physical	55	100	15	Normal	○	○
TM66	Payback	Dark	Physical	50	100	10	Normal	—	○
TM67	Retaliate	Normal	Physical	70	100	5	Normal	—	—
TM71	Stone Edge	Rock	Physical	100	80	5	Normal	—	—
TM75	Swords Dance	Normal	Status	—	—	30	Self	—	—
TM77	Psych Up	Normal	Status	—	—	10	Self	—	—
TM80	Rock Slide	Rock	Physical	75	90	10	Many Others	—	—
TM83	Work Up	Normal	Status	—	—	30	Self	—	—
TM84	Poison Jab	Poison	Physical	80	100	20	Normal	—	○
TM86	Grass Knot	Grass	Special	—	100	20	Normal	—	—
TM87	Swagger	Normal	Status	—	90	15	Normal	—	—
TM89	U-turn	Bug	Physical	70	100	20	Normal	—	○
TM90	Substitute	Normal	Status	—	—	10	Self	—	—
TM94	Rock Smash	Fighting	Physical	40	100	15	Normal	—	○
HM04	Strength	Normal	Physical	80	100	15	Normal	—	○

● MOVES TAUGHT BY PEOPLE

Name	Type	Kind	Pow.	Acc.	PP	Range	Long	DA

● EGG MOVES

Name	Type	Kind	Pow.	Acc.	PP	Range	Long	DA
Endure	Normal	Status	—	—	10	Self	—	—
Vital Throw	Fighting	Physical	70	—	10	Normal	—	○
Baton Pass	Normal	Status	—	—	40	Self	—	—
SmellingSalt	Normal	Physical	60	100	10	Normal	—	○
Low Kick	Fighting	Physical	—	100	20	Normal	—	○
Feint	Normal	Physical	30	100	10	Normal	—	—
Me First	Normal	Status	—	—	20	Varies	—	—
Knock Off	Dark	Physical	20	100	20	Normal	—	○

● FOOTPRINT

● MALE/FEMALE HAVE SAME FORM

● HEIGHT: 2'11"
● WEIGHT: 44.1 lbs.
● GENDER: Both ♂♀ exist
● ITEMS:
• None

EVOLUTION

Mienfoo — Lv. 50 → Mienshao

● MAIN WAYS TO OBTAIN

POKÉMON BLACK VERSION
1 Dragonspiral Tower Entrance
2 Victory Road Outside

POKÉMON WHITE VERSION
1 Dragonspiral Tower Entrance
2 Victory Road Outside

POKÉMON BLACK VERSION: In fights, they dominate with onslaughts of flowing, continuous attacks. With their sharp claws, they cut enemies.

POKÉMON WHITE VERSION: They have mastered elegant combos. As they concentrate, their battle moves become swifter and more precise.

ABILITIES: ● Inner Focus ● Regenerator

EGG GROUPS: Field / Human-Like

STATS:
HP ●●
ATTACK ●●●●
DEFENSE ●●
SP. ATTACK ●●●
SP. DEFENSE ●●
SPEED ●●●

Mienshao

● TYPE **Fighting**

● LEVEL-UP AND LEARNED MOVES

Lv.	Name	Type	Kind	Pow.	Acc.	PP	Range	Long	DA
1	Pound	Normal	Physical	40	100	35	Normal	–	–
1	Meditate	Psychic	Status	–	–	40	Self	–	–
1	Detect	Fighting	Status	–	–	5	Self	–	–
1	Fake Out	Normal	Physical	40	100	10	Normal	–	○
5	Meditate	Psychic	Status	–	–	40	Self	–	–
9	Detect	Fighting	Status	–	–	5	Self	–	○
13	Fake Out	Normal	Physical	40	100	10	Normal	–	○
17	DoubleSlap	Normal	Physical	15	85	10	Normal	–	–
21	Swift	Normal	Special	60	–	20	Many Others	–	–
25	Calm Mind	Psychic	Status	–	–	20	Self	–	–
29	Force Palm	Fighting	Physical	60	100	10	Normal	–	○
33	Drain Punch	Fighting	Physical	75	100	10	Normal	–	○
37	Jump Kick	Fighting	Physical	100	95	10	Normal	–	○
41	U-turn	Bug	Physical	70	100	20	Normal	–	○
45	Wide Guard	Rock	Status	–	–	10	Your Side	–	–
45	Bounce	Flying	Physical	85	85	5	Normal	○	○
56	Hi Jump Kick	Fighting	Physical	130	90	10	Normal	–	○
63	Reversal	Fighting	Physical	–	100	15	Normal	–	○
70	Aura Sphere	Fighting	Special	90	–	20	Normal	○	–

● MOVES TAUGHT BY PEOPLE

Name	Type	Kind	Pow.	Acc.	PP	Range	Long	DA

● TM & HM MOVES

No.	Name	Type	Kind	Pow.	Acc.	PP	Range	Long	DA
TM04	Calm Mind	Psychic	Status	–	–	20	Self	–	–
TM06	Toxic	Poison	Status	–	90	10	Normal	–	–
TM08	Bulk Up	Fighting	Status	–	–	20	Self	–	–
TM10	Hidden Power	Normal	Special	–	100	15	Normal	–	–
TM11	Sunny Day	Fire	Status	–	–	5	Both Sides	–	–
TM12	Taunt	Dark	Status	–	100	20	Normal	–	–
TM15	Hyper Beam	Normal	Special	150	90	5	Normal	–	–
TM17	Protect	Normal	Status	–	–	10	Self	–	–
TM18	Rain Dance	Water	Status	–	–	5	Both Sides	–	–
TM21	Frustration	Normal	Physical	–	100	20	Normal	–	○
TM27	Return	Normal	Physical	–	100	20	Normal	–	○
TM28	Dig	Ground	Physical	80	100	10	Normal	–	○
TM31	Brick Break	Fighting	Physical	75	100	15	Normal	–	○
TM32	Double Team	Normal	Status	–	–	15	Self	–	–
TM33	Reflect	Psychic	Status	–	–	20	Your Side	–	–
TM39	Rock Tomb	Rock	Physical	50	80	10	Normal	–	○
TM40	Aerial Ace	Flying	Physical	60	–	20	Normal	○	○
TM42	Facade	Normal	Physical	70	100	20	Normal	–	○
TM44	Rest	Psychic	Status	–	–	10	Self	–	–
TM45	Attract	Normal	Status	–	100	15	Normal	–	–
TM47	Low Sweep	Fighting	Physical	60	100	20	Normal	–	○
TM48	Round	Normal	Special	60	100	15	Normal	–	–
TM52	Focus Blast	Fighting	Special	120	70	5	Normal	–	–
TM56	Fling	Dark	Physical	–	100	10	Normal	–	–
TM62	Acrobatics	Flying	Physical	55	100	15	Normal	○	○
TM66	Payback	Dark	Physical	50	100	10	Normal	–	○
TM67	Retaliate	Normal	Physical	70	100	5	Normal	–	○
TM68	Giga Impact	Normal	Physical	150	90	5	Normal	–	○
TM71	Stone Edge	Rock	Physical	100	80	5	Normal	–	○
TM75	Swords Dance	Normal	Status	–	–	30	Self	–	–
TM77	Psych Up	Normal	Status	–	–	10	Normal	–	–
TM80	Rock Slide	Rock	Physical	75	90	10	Many Others	–	○
TM83	Work Up	Normal	Status	–	–	30	Self	–	–
TM84	Poison Jab	Poison	Physical	80	100	20	Normal	–	○
TM86	Grass Knot	Grass	Special	–	100	20	Normal	–	○
TM87	Swagger	Normal	Status	–	90	15	Normal	–	–
TM89	U-turn	Bug	Physical	70	100	20	Normal	–	○
TM90	Substitute	Normal	Status	–	–	10	Self	–	–
TM94	Rock Smash	Fighting	Physical	40	100	15	Normal	–	○
HM04	Strength	Normal	Physical	80	100	15	Normal	–	○

● FOOTPRINT

● MALE/FEMALE HAVE SAME FORM

● HEIGHT: 4'07"
● WEIGHT: 78.3 lbs.
● GENDER: Both ♂♀ exist
● ITEMS:
• None

EVOLUTION

Mienfoo → Lv. 50 → Mienshao

ABILITIES
● Inner Focus
● Regenerator

EGG GROUPS
Field
Human-Like

STATS
HP ●●
ATTACK ●●●●●
DEFENSE ●●
SP. ATTACK ●●●●●
SP. DEFENSE ●●
SPEED ●●●●●

POKÉMON BLACK VERSION
It wields the fur on its arms like a whip. Its arm attacks come with such rapidity that they cannot even be seen.

POKÉMON WHITE VERSION
They use the long fur on their arms as a whip to strike their opponents.

● MAIN WAYS TO OBTAIN

POKÉMON BLACK VERSION
1 Route 14 (Dark Grass)
2 Level up Mienfoo to Lv. 50

POKÉMON WHITE VERSION
1 Route 14 (Dark Grass)
2 Level up Mienfoo to Lv. 50

Druddigon

● TYPE **Dragon**

● LEVEL-UP AND LEARNED MOVES

Lv.	Name	Type	Kind	Pow.	Acc.	PP	Range	Long	DA
1	Leer	Normal	Status	–	100	30	Many Others	–	–
1	Scratch	Normal	Physical	40	100	35	Normal	–	○
5	Hone Claws	Dark	Status	–	–	15	Self	–	–
9	Bite	Dark	Physical	60	100	25	Normal	–	○
13	Scary Face	Normal	Status	–	100	10	Normal	–	–
18	Dragon Rage	Dragon	Special	–	100	10	Normal	–	–
21	Slash	Normal	Physical	70	100	20	Normal	–	○
25	Crunch	Dark	Physical	80	100	15	Normal	–	○
27	Dragon Claw	Dragon	Physical	80	100	15	Normal	–	○
31	Chip Away	Normal	Physical	70	100	20	Normal	–	○
35	Revenge	Fighting	Physical	60	100	10	Normal	–	○
40	Night Slash	Dark	Physical	70	100	15	Normal	–	○
45	Dragon Tail	Dragon	Physical	60	90	10	Normal	–	○
49	Rock Climb	Normal	Physical	90	85	20	Normal	–	○
55	Superpower	Fighting	Physical	120	100	5	Normal	–	○
62	Outrage	Dragon	Physical	120	100	10	1 Random	–	○

● MOVES TAUGHT BY PEOPLE

Name	Type	Kind	Pow.	Acc.	PP	Range	Long	DA
Draco Meteor	Dragon	Special	140	90	5	Normal	–	–

● EGG MOVES

Name	Type	Kind	Pow.	Acc.	PP	Range	Long	DA
Fire Fang	Fire	Physical	65	95	15	Normal	–	○
Thunder Fang	Electric	Physical	65	95	15	Normal	–	○
Crush Claw	Normal	Physical	75	95	10	Normal	–	○
Faint Attack	Dark	Physical	60	–	20	Normal	–	–
Pursuit	Dark	Physical	40	100	20	Normal	–	○
Iron Tail	Steel	Physical	100	75	15	Normal	–	○
Poison Tail	Poison	Physical	50	100	25	Normal	–	○
Snatch	Dark	Status	–	–	10	Self	–	–
Metal Claw	Steel	Physical	50	95	35	Normal	–	○
Glare	Normal	Status	–	90	30	Normal	–	–
Sucker Punch	Dark	Physical	80	100	5	Normal	–	○

● TM & HM MOVES

No.	Name	Type	Kind	Pow.	Acc.	PP	Range	Long	DA
TM01	Hone Claws	Dark	Status	–	–	15	Self	–	–
TM02	Dragon Claw	Dragon	Physical	80	100	15	Normal	–	○
TM05	Roar	Normal	Status	–	100	20	Normal	–	–
TM06	Toxic	Poison	Status	–	90	10	Normal	–	–
TM10	Hidden Power	Normal	Special	–	100	15	Normal	–	–
TM11	Sunny Day	Fire	Status	–	–	5	Both Sides	–	–
TM12	Taunt	Dark	Status	–	100	20	Normal	–	–
TM15	Hyper Beam	Normal	Special	150	90	5	Normal	–	–
TM17	Protect	Normal	Status	–	–	10	Self	–	–
TM18	Rain Dance	Water	Status	–	–	5	Both Sides	–	–
TM21	Frustration	Normal	Physical	–	100	20	Normal	–	○
TM23	Smack Down	Rock	Physical	50	100	15	Normal	–	○
TM26	Earthquake	Ground	Physical	100	100	10	Adjacent	–	○
TM27	Return	Normal	Physical	–	100	20	Normal	–	○
TM28	Dig	Ground	Physical	80	100	10	Normal	–	○
TM32	Double Team	Normal	Status	–	–	15	Self	–	–
TM35	Flamethrower	Fire	Special	95	100	15	Normal	–	–
TM36	Sludge Bomb	Poison	Special	90	100	10	Normal	–	–
TM39	Rock Tomb	Rock	Physical	50	80	10	Normal	–	○
TM40	Aerial Ace	Flying	Physical	60	–	20	Normal	○	○
TM41	Torment	Dark	Status	–	100	15	Normal	–	–
TM42	Facade	Normal	Physical	70	100	20	Normal	–	○
TM44	Rest	Psychic	Status	–	–	10	Self	–	–
TM45	Attract	Normal	Status	–	100	15	Normal	–	–
TM48	Round	Normal	Special	60	100	15	Normal	–	–
TM52	Focus Blast	Fighting	Special	120	70	5	Normal	–	–
TM56	Fling	Dark	Physical	–	100	10	Normal	–	–
TM57	Charge Beam	Electric	Special	50	90	10	Normal	–	–
TM59	Incinerate	Fire	Special	30	100	15	Many Others	–	–
TM65	Shadow Claw	Ghost	Physical	70	100	15	Normal	–	○
TM66	Payback	Dark	Physical	50	100	10	Normal	–	○
TM67	Retaliate	Normal	Physical	70	100	5	Normal	–	○
TM68	Giga Impact	Normal	Physical	150	90	5	Normal	–	○
TM78	Bulldoze	Ground	Physical	60	100	20	Adjacent	–	○
TM80	Rock Slide	Rock	Physical	75	90	10	Many Others	–	○
TM82	Dragon Tail	Dragon	Physical	60	90	10	Normal	–	○
TM87	Swagger	Normal	Status	–	90	15	Normal	–	–
TM90	Substitute	Normal	Status	–	–	10	Self	–	–
TM91	Flash Cannon	Steel	Special	80	100	10	Normal	–	–
TM94	Rock Smash	Fighting	Physical	40	100	15	Normal	–	○
HM01	Cut	Normal	Physical	50	95	30	Normal	–	–
HM03	Surf	Water	Special	95	100	15	Adjacent	–	○
HM04	Strength	Normal	Physical	80	100	15	Normal	–	○

● FOOTPRINT

● MALE/FEMALE HAVE SAME FORM

● HEIGHT: 5'03"
● WEIGHT: 306.4 lbs.
● GENDER: Both ♂♀ exist
● ITEMS:
• Dragon Fang

EVOLUTION

Does not evolve

POKÉMON BLACK VERSION
It warms its body by absorbing sunlight with its wings. When its body temperature falls, it can no longer move.

POKÉMON WHITE VERSION
It races through narrow caves, using its sharp claws to catch prey. The skin on its face is harder than a rock.

ABILITIES
● Rough Skin
● Sheer Force

EGG GROUPS
Dragon
Monster

STATS
HP ●●●
ATTACK ●●●●●
DEFENSE ●●●●●
SP. ATTACK ●●●
SP. DEFENSE ●●●●
SPEED ●●

● MAIN WAYS TO OBTAIN

POKÉMON BLACK VERSION
1 Dragonspiral Tower Entrance (spring/summer/autumn only)
2 Dragonspiral Tower 1F

POKÉMON WHITE VERSION
1 Dragonspiral Tower Entrance (spring/summer/autumn only)
2 Dragonspiral Tower 1F

Golett

● TYPE Ground Ghost

● FOOTPRINT

● GENDER UNKNOWN

● HEIGHT: 3'03"
● WEIGHT: 202.8 lbs.
● GENDER: Unknown
● ITEMS:
 • Light Clay

POKÉMON BLACK VERSION
The energy that burns inside it enables it to move, but no one has yet been able to identify this energy.

POKÉMON WHITE VERSION
These Pokémon are thought to have been created by the science of an ancient and mysterious civilization.

● LEVEL-UP AND LEARNED MOVES

Lv.	Name	Type	Kind	Pow.	Acc.	PP	Range	Long	DA
1	Pound	Normal	Physical	40	100	35	Normal	—	—
1	Astonish	Ghost	Physical	30	100	15	Normal	—	○
1	Defense Curl	Normal	Status	—	—	40	Self	—	—
5	Mud-Slap	Ground	Special	20	100	10	Normal	—	—
9	Rollout	Rock	Physical	30	90	20	Normal	—	○
13	Shadow Punch	Ghost	Physical	60	—	20	Normal	—	—
17	Iron Defense	Steel	Status	—	—	15	Self	—	—
21	Mega Punch	Normal	Physical	80	85	20	Normal	—	—
25	Magnitude	Ground	Physical	—	100	30	Adjacent	—	—
30	DynamicPunch	Fighting	Physical	100	50	5	Normal	—	○
35	Night Shade	Ghost	Special	—	100	15	Normal	—	—
40	Curse	Ghost	Status	—	—	10	Varies	—	—
45	Earthquake	Ground	Physical	100	100	10	Adjacent	—	—
50	Hammer Arm	Fighting	Physical	100	90	10	Normal	—	○
55	Focus Punch	Fighting	Physical	150	100	20	Normal	—	—

● MOVES TAUGHT BY PEOPLE

Name	Type	Kind	Pow.	Acc.	PP	Range	Long	DA

● TM & HM MOVES

No.	Name	Type	Kind	Pow.	Acc.	PP	Range	Long	DA
TM06	Toxic	Poison	Status	—	90	10	Normal	—	—
TM10	Hidden Power	Normal	Special	—	100	15	Normal	—	—
TM13	Ice Beam	Ice	Special	95	100	10	Normal	—	—
TM17	Protect	Normal	Status	—	—	10	Self	—	—
TM18	Rain Dance	Water	Status	—	—	5	Both Sides	—	—
TM19	Telekinesis	Psychic	Status	—	—	15	Normal	—	—
TM20	Safeguard	Normal	Status	—	—	25	Your Side	—	—
TM21	Frustration	Normal	Physical	—	100	20	Normal	—	○
TM26	Earthquake	Ground	Physical	100	100	10	Adjacent	—	—
TM27	Return	Normal	Physical	—	100	20	Normal	—	○
TM29	Psychic	Psychic	Special	90	100	10	Normal	—	—
TM30	Shadow Ball	Ghost	Special	80	100	15	Normal	—	—
TM31	Brick Break	Fighting	Physical	75	100	15	Normal	—	—
TM32	Double Team	Normal	Status	—	—	15	Self	—	—
TM39	Rock Tomb	Rock	Physical	50	80	10	Normal	—	—
TM42	Facade	Normal	Physical	70	100	20	Normal	—	—
TM44	Rest	Psychic	Status	—	—	10	Self	—	—
TM46	Thief	Dark	Physical	40	100	10	Normal	—	○
TM47	Low Sweep	Fighting	Physical	60	100	20	Normal	—	○
TM48	Round	Normal	Special	60	100	15	Normal	—	—
TM52	Focus Blast	Fighting	Special	120	70	5	Normal	—	—
TM56	Fling	Dark	Physical	—	100	10	Normal	—	○
TM69	Rock Polish	Rock	Status	—	—	20	Self	—	—
TM70	Flash	Normal	Status	—	100	20	Normal	—	—
TM74	Gyro Ball	Steel	Physical	—	100	5	Normal	—	—
TM78	Bulldoze	Ground	Physical	60	100	20	Adjacent	—	—
TM80	Rock Slide	Rock	Physical	75	90	10	Many Others	—	—
TM86	Grass Knot	Grass	Special	—	100	20	Normal	—	○
TM87	Swagger	Normal	Status	—	90	15	Normal	—	—
TM90	Substitute	Normal	Status	—	—	10	Self	—	—
TM94	Rock Smash	Fighting	Physical	40	100	15	Normal	—	—
HM04	Strength	Normal	Physical	80	100	15	Normal	—	—

EVOLUTION

Golett → Lv. 43 → Golurk

ABILITIES ● Iron Fist ● Klutz

EGG GROUP Mineral

STATS
HP ●●
ATTACK ●●●
DEFENSE ●●
SP. ATTACK ●●
SP. DEFENSE ●●
SPEED ●●

● MAIN WAYS TO OBTAIN

| **POKÉMON BLACK VERSION** | 1 | Dragonspiral Tower 1F |
| | 2 | Dragonspiral Tower 2F |

| **POKÉMON WHITE VERSION** | 1 | Dragonspiral Tower 1F |
| | 2 | Dragonspiral Tower 2F |

Golurk

● TYPE Ground Ghost

● FOOTPRINT

● GENDER UNKNOWN

● HEIGHT: 9'02"
● WEIGHT: 727.5 lbs.
● GENDER: Unknown
● ITEMS:
 • None

POKÉMON BLACK VERSION
It flies across the sky at Mach speeds. Removing the seal on its chest makes its internal energy go out of control.

POKÉMON WHITE VERSION
It is said that Golurk were ordered to protect people and Pokémon by the ancient people who made them.

● LEVEL-UP AND LEARNED MOVES

Lv.	Name	Type	Kind	Pow.	Acc.	PP	Range	Long	DA
1	Pound	Normal	Physical	40	100	35	Normal	—	—
1	Astonish	Ghost	Physical	30	100	15	Normal	—	○
1	Defense Curl	Normal	Status	—	—	40	Self	—	—
1	Mud-Slap	Ground	Special	20	100	10	Normal	—	—
5	Mud-Slap	Ground	Special	20	100	10	Normal	—	—
9	Rollout	Rock	Physical	30	90	20	Normal	—	○
13	Shadow Punch	Ghost	Physical	60	—	20	Normal	—	—
17	Iron Defense	Steel	Status	—	—	15	Self	—	—
21	Mega Punch	Normal	Physical	80	85	20	Normal	—	—
25	Magnitude	Ground	Physical	—	100	30	Adjacent	—	—
30	DynamicPunch	Fighting	Physical	100	50	5	Normal	—	○
35	Night Shade	Ghost	Special	—	100	15	Normal	—	—
40	Curse	Ghost	Status	—	—	10	Varies	—	—
43	Heavy Slam	Steel	Physical	—	100	10	Normal	—	○
50	Earthquake	Ground	Physical	100	100	10	Adjacent	—	—
60	Hammer Arm	Fighting	Physical	100	90	10	Normal	—	○
70	Focus Punch	Fighting	Physical	150	100	20	Normal	—	—

● MOVES TAUGHT BY PEOPLE

Name	Type	Kind	Pow.	Acc.	PP	Range	Long	DA

● TM & HM MOVES

No.	Name	Type	Kind	Pow.	Acc.	PP	Range	Long	DA
TM06	Toxic	Poison	Status	—	90	10	Normal	—	—
TM10	Hidden Power	Normal	Special	—	100	15	Normal	—	—
TM13	Ice Beam	Ice	Special	95	100	10	Normal	—	—
TM15	Hyper Beam	Normal	Special	150	90	5	Normal	—	—
TM17	Protect	Normal	Status	—	—	10	Self	—	—
TM18	Rain Dance	Water	Status	—	—	5	Both Sides	—	—
TM19	Telekinesis	Psychic	Status	—	—	15	Normal	—	—
TM20	Safeguard	Normal	Status	—	—	25	Your Side	—	—
TM21	Frustration	Normal	Physical	—	100	20	Normal	—	○
TM22	SolarBeam	Grass	Special	120	100	10	Normal	—	—
TM24	Thunderbolt	Electric	Special	95	100	15	Normal	—	—
TM26	Earthquake	Ground	Physical	100	100	10	Adjacent	—	—
TM27	Return	Normal	Physical	—	100	20	Normal	—	○
TM29	Psychic	Psychic	Special	90	100	10	Normal	—	—
TM30	Shadow Ball	Ghost	Special	80	100	15	Normal	—	—
TM31	Brick Break	Fighting	Physical	75	100	15	Normal	—	—
TM32	Double Team	Normal	Status	—	—	15	Self	—	—
TM39	Rock Tomb	Rock	Physical	50	80	10	Normal	—	—
TM42	Facade	Normal	Physical	70	100	20	Normal	—	—
TM44	Rest	Psychic	Status	—	—	10	Self	—	—
TM46	Thief	Dark	Physical	40	100	10	Normal	—	○
TM47	Low Sweep	Fighting	Physical	60	100	20	Normal	—	○
TM48	Round	Normal	Special	60	100	15	Normal	—	—
TM52	Focus Blast	Fighting	Special	120	70	5	Normal	—	—
TM56	Fling	Dark	Physical	—	100	10	Normal	—	○
TM57	Charge Beam	Electric	Special	50	90	10	Normal	—	—
TM68	Giga Impact	Normal	Physical	150	90	5	Normal	—	—
TM69	Rock Polish	Rock	Status	—	—	20	Self	—	—
TM70	Flash	Normal	Status	—	100	20	Normal	—	—
TM71	Stone Edge	Rock	Physical	100	80	5	Normal	—	—
TM74	Gyro Ball	Steel	Physical	—	100	5	Normal	—	—
TM78	Bulldoze	Ground	Physical	60	100	20	Adjacent	—	—
TM80	Rock Slide	Rock	Physical	75	90	10	Many Others	—	—
TM86	Grass Knot	Grass	Special	—	100	20	Normal	—	○
TM87	Swagger	Normal	Status	—	90	15	Normal	—	—
TM90	Substitute	Normal	Status	—	—	10	Self	—	—
TM91	Flash Cannon	Steel	Special	80	100	10	Normal	—	—
TM94	Rock Smash	Fighting	Physical	40	100	15	Normal	—	—
HM02	Fly	Flying	Physical	90	95	15	Normal	—	○
HM04	Strength	Normal	Physical	80	100	15	Normal	—	○

EVOLUTION

Golett → Lv. 43 → Golurk

ABILITIES ● Iron Fist ● Klutz

EGG GROUP Mineral

STATS
HP ●●●
ATTACK ●●●●●
DEFENSE ●●●●
SP. ATTACK ●●●
SP. DEFENSE ●●●
SPEED ●●●

● MAIN WAYS TO OBTAIN

| **POKÉMON BLACK VERSION** | 1 | Level up Golett to Lv. 43 |
| | 2 | — |

| **POKÉMON WHITE VERSION** | 1 | Level up Golett to Lv. 43 |
| | 2 | — |

Pawniard

● TYPE Dark Steel

● LEVEL-UP AND LEARNED MOVES

Lv.	Name	Type	Kind	Pow.	Acc.	PP	Range	Long	DA
1	Scratch	Normal	Physical	40	100	35	Normal	—	—
6	Leer	Normal	Status	—	100	30	Many Others	—	—
9	Fury Cutter	Bug	Physical	20	95	20	Normal	—	○
14	Torment	Dark	Status	—	100	15	Normal	—	—
17	Faint Attack	Dark	Physical	60	—	20	Normal	—	○
22	Scary Face	Normal	Status	—	100	10	Normal	—	—
25	Metal Claw	Steel	Physical	50	95	35	Normal	—	○
30	Slash	Normal	Physical	70	100	20	Normal	—	○
33	Assurance	Dark	Physical	50	100	10	Normal	—	○
38	Metal Sound	Steel	Status	—	85	40	Normal	—	—
41	Embargo	Dark	Status	—	100	15	Normal	—	—
46	Iron Defense	Steel	Status	—	—	15	Self	—	—
49	Night Slash	Dark	Physical	70	100	15	Normal	—	○
53	Iron Head	Steel	Physical	80	100	15	Normal	—	○
57	Swords Dance	Normal	Status	—	—	30	Self	—	—
62	Guillotine	Normal	Physical	—	30	5	Normal	—	○

● MOVES TAUGHT BY PEOPLE

Name	Type	Kind	Pow.	Acc.	PP	Range	Long	DA

● EGG MOVES

Name	Type	Kind	Pow.	Acc.	PP	Range	Long	DA
Revenge	Fighting	Physical	60	100	10	Normal	—	○
Sucker Punch	Dark	Physical	80	100	5	Normal	—	○
Pursuit	Dark	Physical	40	100	20	Normal	—	○
Headbutt	Normal	Physical	70	100	15	Normal	—	○
Stealth Rock	Rock	Status	—	—	20	Other Side	—	—
Psycho Cut	Psychic	Physical	70	100	20	Normal	—	○
Mean Look	Normal	Status	—	—	5	Normal	—	—

● TM & HM MOVES

No.	Name	Type	Kind	Pow.	Acc.	PP	Range	Long	DA
TM01	Hone Claws	Dark	Status	—	—	15	Self	—	—
TM06	Toxic	Poison	Status	—	90	10	Normal	—	—
TM10	Hidden Power	Normal	Special	—	100	15	Normal	—	—
TM12	Taunt	Dark	Status	—	100	20	Normal	—	—
TM17	Protect	Normal	Status	—	—	10	Self	—	—
TM18	Rain Dance	Water	Status	—	—	5	Both Sides	—	—
TM21	Frustration	Normal	Physical	—	100	20	Normal	—	○
TM27	Return	Normal	Physical	—	100	20	Normal	—	○
TM28	Dig	Ground	Physical	80	100	10	Normal	—	○
TM31	Brick Break	Fighting	Physical	75	100	15	Normal	—	○
TM32	Double Team	Normal	Status	—	—	15	Self	—	—
TM37	Sandstorm	Rock	Status	—	—	10	Both Sides	—	—
TM39	Rock Tomb	Rock	Physical	50	80	10	Normal	—	○
TM40	Aerial Ace	Flying	Physical	60	—	20	Normal	○	○
TM41	Torment	Dark	Status	—	100	15	Normal	—	—
TM42	Facade	Normal	Physical	70	100	20	Normal	—	○
TM44	Rest	Psychic	Status	—	—	10	Self	—	—
TM45	Attract	Normal	Status	—	100	15	Normal	—	—
TM46	Thief	Dark	Physical	40	100	10	Normal	—	○
TM47	Low Sweep	Fighting	Physical	60	100	20	Normal	—	○
TM48	Round	Normal	Special	60	100	15	Normal	—	—
TM54	False Swipe	Normal	Physical	40	100	40	Normal	—	○
TM56	Fling	Dark	Physical	—	100	10	Normal	—	○
TM63	Embargo	Dark	Status	—	100	15	Normal	—	—
TM65	Shadow Claw	Ghost	Physical	70	100	15	Normal	—	○
TM66	Payback	Dark	Physical	50	100	10	Normal	—	○
TM67	Retaliate	Normal	Physical	70	100	5	Normal	—	○
TM69	Rock Polish	Rock	Status	—	—	20	Self	—	—
TM73	Thunder Wave	Electric	Status	—	100	20	Normal	—	—
TM75	Swords Dance	Normal	Status	—	—	30	Self	—	—
TM81	X-Scissor	Bug	Physical	80	100	15	Normal	—	○
TM84	Poison Jab	Poison	Physical	80	100	20	Normal	—	○
TM86	Grass Knot	Grass	Special	—	100	20	Normal	—	○
TM87	Swagger	Normal	Status	—	90	15	Normal	—	—
TM90	Substitute	Normal	Status	—	—	10	Self	—	—
TM94	Rock Smash	Fighting	Physical	40	100	15	Normal	—	○
HM01	Cut	Normal	Physical	50	95	30	Normal	—	—

● FOOTPRINT

● MALE/FEMALE HAVE SAME FORM

● HEIGHT: 1'08"
● WEIGHT: 22.5 lbs.
● GENDER: Both ♂♀ exist
● ITEMS:
 • None

POKÉMON BLACK VERSION Blades comprise this Pokémon's entire body. If battling dulls the blades, it sharpens them on stones by the river.

POKÉMON WHITE VERSION They fight at Bisharp's command. They cling to their prey and inflict damage by sinking their blades into it.

● EVOLUTION

Pawniard → Lv. 52 → Bisharp

ABILITIES ● Defiant ● Inner Focus

EGG GROUP Human-Like

STATS
HP ●●
ATTACK ●●●●
DEFENSE ●●●
SP.ATTACK ●●
SP.DEFENSE ●●
SPEED ●●●

● MAIN WAYS TO OBTAIN

POKÉMON BLACK VERSION
1 Route 9
2 —

POKÉMON WHITE VERSION
1 Route 9
2 —

Bisharp

● TYPE Dark Steel

● LEVEL-UP AND LEARNED MOVES

Lv.	Name	Type	Kind	Pow.	Acc.	PP	Range	Long	DA
1	Metal Burst	Steel	Physical	—	100	10	Varies	—	—
1	Scratch	Normal	Physical	40	100	35	Normal	—	○
1	Leer	Normal	Status	—	100	30	Many Others	—	—
1	Fury Cutter	Bug	Physical	20	95	20	Normal	—	○
1	Torment	Dark	Status	—	100	15	Normal	—	—
6	Leer	Normal	Status	—	100	30	Many Others	—	—
9	Fury Cutter	Bug	Physical	20	95	20	Normal	—	○
14	Torment	Dark	Status	—	100	15	Normal	—	—
17	Faint Attack	Dark	Physical	60	—	20	Normal	—	○
22	Scary Face	Normal	Status	—	100	10	Normal	—	—
25	Metal Claw	Steel	Physical	50	95	35	Normal	—	○
30	Slash	Normal	Physical	70	100	20	Normal	—	○
33	Assurance	Dark	Physical	50	100	10	Normal	—	○
38	Metal Sound	Steel	Status	—	85	40	Normal	—	—
41	Embargo	Dark	Status	—	100	15	Normal	—	—
46	Iron Defense	Steel	Status	—	—	15	Self	—	—
49	Night Slash	Dark	Physical	70	100	15	Normal	—	○
57	Iron Head	Steel	Physical	80	100	15	Normal	—	○
63	Swords Dance	Normal	Status	—	—	30	Self	—	—
71	Guillotine	Normal	Physical	—	30	5	Normal	—	○

● MOVES TAUGHT BY PEOPLE

Name	Type	Kind	Pow.	Acc.	PP	Range	Long	DA

● TM & HM MOVES

No.	Name	Type	Kind	Pow.	Acc.	PP	Range	Long	DA
TM01	Hone Claws	Dark	Status	—	—	15	Self	—	—
TM06	Toxic	Poison	Status	—	90	10	Normal	—	—
TM10	Hidden Power	Normal	Special	—	100	15	Normal	—	—
TM12	Taunt	Dark	Status	—	100	20	Normal	—	—
TM15	Hyper Beam	Normal	Special	150	90	5	Normal	—	—
TM17	Protect	Normal	Status	—	—	10	Self	—	—
TM18	Rain Dance	Water	Status	—	—	5	Both Sides	—	—
TM21	Frustration	Normal	Physical	—	100	20	Normal	—	○
TM27	Return	Normal	Physical	—	100	20	Normal	—	○
TM28	Dig	Ground	Physical	80	100	10	Normal	—	○
TM31	Brick Break	Fighting	Physical	75	100	15	Normal	—	○
TM32	Double Team	Normal	Status	—	—	15	Self	—	—
TM37	Sandstorm	Rock	Status	—	—	10	Both Sides	—	—
TM39	Rock Tomb	Rock	Physical	50	80	10	Normal	—	○
TM40	Aerial Ace	Flying	Physical	60	—	20	Normal	○	○
TM41	Torment	Dark	Status	—	100	15	Normal	—	—
TM42	Facade	Normal	Physical	70	100	20	Normal	—	○
TM44	Rest	Psychic	Status	—	—	10	Self	—	—
TM45	Attract	Normal	Status	—	100	15	Normal	—	—
TM46	Thief	Dark	Physical	40	100	10	Normal	—	○
TM47	Low Sweep	Fighting	Physical	60	100	20	Normal	—	○
TM48	Round	Normal	Special	60	100	15	Normal	—	—
TM52	Focus Blast	Fighting	Special	120	70	5	Normal	—	—
TM54	False Swipe	Normal	Physical	40	100	40	Normal	—	○
TM56	Fling	Dark	Physical	—	100	10	Normal	—	○
TM63	Embargo	Dark	Status	—	100	15	Normal	—	—
TM65	Shadow Claw	Ghost	Physical	70	100	15	Normal	—	○
TM66	Payback	Dark	Physical	50	100	10	Normal	—	○
TM67	Retaliate	Normal	Physical	70	100	5	Normal	—	○
TM68	Giga Impact	Normal	Physical	150	90	5	Normal	—	○
TM69	Rock Polish	Rock	Status	—	—	20	Self	—	—
TM71	Stone Edge	Rock	Physical	100	80	5	Normal	—	○
TM73	Thunder Wave	Electric	Status	—	100	20	Normal	—	—
TM75	Swords Dance	Normal	Status	—	—	30	Self	—	—
TM81	X-Scissor	Bug	Physical	80	100	15	Normal	—	○
TM84	Poison Jab	Poison	Physical	80	100	20	Normal	—	○
TM86	Grass Knot	Grass	Special	—	100	20	Normal	—	○
TM87	Swagger	Normal	Status	—	90	15	Normal	—	—
TM90	Substitute	Normal	Status	—	—	10	Self	—	—
TM94	Rock Smash	Fighting	Physical	40	100	15	Normal	—	○
HM01	Cut	Normal	Physical	50	95	30	Normal	—	—

● FOOTPRINT

● MALE/FEMALE HAVE SAME FORM

● HEIGHT: 5'03"
● WEIGHT: 154.3 lbs.
● GENDER: Both ♂♀ exist
● ITEMS:
 • None

POKÉMON BLACK VERSION It leads a group of Pawniard. It battles to become the boss, but will be driven from the group if it loses.

POKÉMON WHITE VERSION Bisharp pursues prey in the company of a large group of Pawniard. Then Bisharp finishes off the prey.

● EVOLUTION

Pawniard → Lv. 52 → Bisharp

ABILITIES ● Defiant ● Inner Focus

EGG GROUP Human-Like

STATS
HP ●●
ATTACK ●●●●●
DEFENSE ●●●●●
SP.ATTACK ●●●
SP.DEFENSE ●●●
SPEED ●●●

● MAIN WAYS TO OBTAIN

POKÉMON BLACK VERSION
1 Route 11 (Dark Grass)
2 Level up Pawniard to Lv. 52

POKÉMON WHITE VERSION
1 Route 11 (Dark Grass)
2 Level up Pawniard to Lv. 52

Bouffalant

● TYPE Normal

● LEVEL-UP AND LEARNED MOVES

Lv.	Name	Type	Kind	Pow.	Acc.	PP	Range	Long	DA
1	Pursuit	Dark	Physical	40	100	20	Normal	—	○
1	Leer	Normal	Status	—	100	30	Many Others	—	—
6	Rage	Normal	Physical	20	100	20	Normal	—	—
11	Fury Attack	Normal	Physical	15	85	20	Normal	—	—
16	Horn Attack	Normal	Physical	65	100	25	Normal	—	—
21	Scary Face	Normal	Status	—	100	10	Normal	—	—
26	Revenge	Fighting	Physical	60	100	10	Normal	—	—
31	Head Charge	Normal	Physical	120	100	15	Normal	—	○
36	Focus Energy	Normal	Status	—	—	30	Self	—	—
41	Megahorn	Bug	Physical	120	85	10	Normal	—	○
46	Reversal	Fighting	Physical	—	100	15	Normal	—	○
51	Thrash	Normal	Physical	120	100	10	1 Random	—	○
56	Swords Dance	Normal	Status	—	—	30	Self	—	—
61	Giga Impact	Normal	Physical	150	90	5	Normal	—	○

● MOVES TAUGHT BY PEOPLE

Name	Type	Kind	Pow.	Acc.	PP	Range	Long	DA

● EGG MOVES

Name	Type	Kind	Pow.	Acc.	PP	Range	Long	DA
Stomp	Normal	Physical	65	100	20	Normal	—	○
Rock Climb	Normal	Physical	90	85	20	Normal	—	○
Headbutt	Normal	Physical	70	100	15	Normal	—	○
Skull Bash	Normal	Physical	100	100	15	Normal	—	○
Mud Shot	Ground	Special	55	95	15	Normal	—	—
Mud-Slap	Ground	Special	20	100	10	Normal	—	—
Iron Head	Steel	Physical	80	100	15	Normal	—	○
Amnesia	Psychic	Status	—	—	20	Self	—	—

● TM & HM MOVES

No.	Name	Type	Kind	Pow.	Acc.	PP	Range	Long	DA
TM06	Toxic	Poison	Status	—	90	10	Normal	—	—
TM10	Hidden Power	Normal	Special	—	100	15	Normal	—	—
TM11	Sunny Day	Fire	Status	—	—	5	Both Sides	—	—
TM12	Taunt	Dark	Status	—	100	20	Normal	—	—
TM17	Protect	Normal	Status	—	—	10	Self	—	—
TM18	Rain Dance	Water	Status	—	—	5	Both Sides	—	—
TM21	Frustration	Normal	Physical	—	100	20	Normal	—	○
TM26	Earthquake	Ground	Physical	100	100	10	Adjacent	—	—
TM27	Return	Normal	Physical	—	100	20	Normal	—	○
TM32	Double Team	Normal	Status	—	—	15	Self	—	—
TM39	Rock Tomb	Rock	Physical	50	80	10	Normal	—	—
TM40	Aerial Ace	Flying	Physical	60	—	20	Normal	○	○
TM42	Facade	Normal	Physical	70	100	20	Normal	—	○
TM44	Rest	Psychic	Status	—	—	10	Self	—	—
TM45	Attract	Normal	Status	—	100	15	Normal	—	—
TM48	Round	Normal	Special	60	100	15	Normal	—	—
TM66	Payback	Dark	Physical	50	100	10	Normal	—	—
TM67	Retaliate	Normal	Physical	70	100	5	Normal	—	—
TM68	Giga Impact	Normal	Physical	150	90	5	Normal	—	○
TM71	Stone Edge	Rock	Physical	100	80	5	Normal	—	—
TM75	Swords Dance	Normal	Status	—	—	30	Self	—	—
TM78	Bulldoze	Ground	Physical	60	100	20	Adjacent	—	—
TM80	Rock Slide	Rock	Physical	75	90	10	Many Others	—	—
TM83	Work Up	Normal	Status	—	—	30	Self	—	—
TM84	Poison Jab	Poison	Physical	80	100	20	Normal	—	—
TM87	Swagger	Normal	Status	—	90	15	Normal	—	—
TM90	Substitute	Normal	Status	—	—	10	Self	—	—
TM93	Wild Charge	Electric	Physical	90	100	15	Normal	—	○
TM94	Rock Smash	Fighting	Physical	40	100	15	Normal	—	○
HM01	Cut	Normal	Physical	50	95	30	Normal	—	—
HM03	Surf	Water	Special	95	100	15	Adjacent	—	—
HM04	Strength	Normal	Physical	80	100	15	Normal	—	—

● FOOTPRINT

● MALE/FEMALE HAVE SAME FORM

● HEIGHT: 5'03"
● WEIGHT: 208.6 lbs.
● GENDER: Both ♂♀ exist
● ITEMS:
• None

POKÉMON BLACK VERSION
Their fluffy fur absorbs damage, even if they strike foes with a fierce headbutt.

POKÉMON WHITE VERSION
They charge wildly and headbutt everything. Their headbutts have enough destructive force to derail a train.

EVOLUTION

Does not evolve

ABILITIES
● Reckless
● Sap Sipper

EGG GROUP Field

STATS
HP ●●●●
ATTACK ●●●●●
DEFENSE ●●●●
SP. ATTACK ●●
SP. DEFENSE ●●●●
SPEED ●●●

● MAIN WAYS TO OBTAIN

POKÉMON BLACK VERSION
1 Route 10
2 Badge Check Gates

POKÉMON WHITE VERSION
1 Route 10
2 Badge Check Gates

Rufflet

● TYPE Normal Flying

● LEVEL-UP AND LEARNED MOVES

Lv.	Name	Type	Kind	Pow.	Acc.	PP	Range	Long	DA
1	Peck	Flying	Physical	35	100	35	Normal	○	—
1	Leer	Normal	Status	—	100	30	Many Others	—	—
5	Fury Attack	Normal	Physical	15	85	20	Normal	—	—
10	Wing Attack	Flying	Physical	60	100	35	Normal	○	—
14	Hone Claws	Dark	Status	—	—	15	Self	—	—
19	Scary Face	Normal	Status	—	100	10	Normal	—	—
23	Aerial Ace	Flying	Physical	60	—	20	Normal	○	○
28	Slash	Normal	Physical	70	100	20	Normal	—	—
32	Defog	Flying	Status	—	—	15	Normal	—	—
37	Tailwind	Flying	Status	—	—	30	Your Side	—	—
41	Air Slash	Flying	Special	75	95	20	Normal	—	○
46	Crush Claw	Normal	Physical	75	95	10	Normal	—	—
50	Sky Drop	Flying	Physical	60	100	10	Normal	○	○
55	Whirlwind	Normal	Status	—	100	20	Normal	—	—
59	Brave Bird	Flying	Physical	120	100	15	Normal	—	○
64	Thrash	Normal	Physical	120	100	10	1 Random	—	○

● MOVES TAUGHT BY PEOPLE

Name	Type	Kind	Pow.	Acc.	PP	Range	Long	DA

● TM & HM MOVES

No.	Name	Type	Kind	Pow.	Acc.	PP	Range	Long	DA
TM01	Hone Claws	Dark	Status	—	—	15	Self	—	—
TM06	Toxic	Poison	Status	—	90	10	Normal	—	—
TM08	Bulk Up	Fighting	Status	—	—	20	Self	—	—
TM10	Hidden Power	Normal	Special	—	100	15	Normal	—	—
TM11	Sunny Day	Fire	Status	—	—	5	Both Sides	—	—
TM17	Protect	Normal	Status	—	—	10	Self	—	—
TM18	Rain Dance	Water	Status	—	—	5	Both Sides	—	—
TM21	Frustration	Normal	Physical	—	100	20	Normal	—	○
TM27	Return	Normal	Physical	—	100	20	Normal	—	○
TM32	Double Team	Normal	Status	—	—	15	Self	—	—
TM39	Rock Tomb	Rock	Physical	50	80	10	Normal	—	—
TM40	Aerial Ace	Flying	Physical	60	—	20	Normal	○	○
TM42	Facade	Normal	Physical	70	100	20	Normal	—	○
TM44	Rest	Psychic	Status	—	—	10	Self	—	—
TM45	Attract	Normal	Status	—	100	15	Normal	—	—
TM48	Round	Normal	Special	60	100	15	Normal	—	—
TM58	Sky Drop	Flying	Physical	60	100	10	Normal	○	○
TM65	Shadow Claw	Ghost	Physical	70	100	15	Normal	—	—
TM67	Retaliate	Normal	Physical	70	100	5	Normal	—	—
TM80	Rock Slide	Rock	Physical	75	90	10	Many Others	—	—
TM83	Work Up	Normal	Status	—	—	30	Self	—	—
TM87	Swagger	Normal	Status	—	90	15	Normal	—	—
TM88	Pluck	Flying	Physical	60	100	20	Normal	—	—
TM89	U-turn	Bug	Physical	70	100	20	Normal	—	○
TM90	Substitute	Normal	Status	—	—	10	Self	—	—
TM94	Rock Smash	Fighting	Physical	40	100	15	Normal	—	○
HM01	Cut	Normal	Physical	50	95	30	Normal	—	—
HM02	Fly	Flying	Physical	90	95	15	Normal	○	○
HM04	Strength	Normal	Physical	80	100	15	Normal	—	—

● FOOTPRINT

● MALE FORM

● HEIGHT: 1'08"
● WEIGHT: 23.1 lbs.
● GENDER: Only ♂ exist
● ITEMS:
• None

POKÉMON BLACK VERSION
They crush berries with their talons. They bravely stand up to any opponent, no matter how strong it is.

POKÉMON WHITE VERSION
They will challenge anything, even strong opponents, without fear. Their frequent fights help them become stronger.

EVOLUTION

Rufflet → Lv. 54 → Braviary

ABILITIES
● Keen Eye
● Sheer Force

EGG GROUP Flying

STATS
HP ●●●
ATTACK ●●●●
DEFENSE ●●
SP. ATTACK ●●
SP. DEFENSE ●●●
SPEED ●●●

● MAIN WAYS TO OBTAIN

POKÉMON BLACK VERSION
1 —
2 —

POKÉMON WHITE VERSION
1 Route 10
2 Victory Road Outside

Braviary

● TYPE Normal Flying

● LEVEL-UP AND LEARNED MOVES

Lv.	Name	Type	Kind	Pow.	Acc.	PP	Range	Long	DA
1	Peck	Flying	Physical	35	100	35	Normal	○	○
1	Leer	Normal	Status	—	100	30	Many Others	—	—
1	Fury Attack	Normal	Physical	15	85	20	Normal	—	○
1	Wing Attack	Flying	Physical	60	100	35	Normal	○	○
1	Fury Attack	Normal	Physical	15	85	20	Normal	—	○
10	Wing Attack	Flying	Physical	60	100	35	Normal	○	○
14	Hone Claws	Dark	Status	—	—	15	Self	—	—
19	Scary Face	Normal	Status	—	100	10	Normal	—	—
23	Aerial Ace	Flying	Physical	60	—	20	Normal	○	○
28	Slash	Normal	Physical	70	100	20	Normal	—	○
32	Defog	Flying	Status	—	—	15	Normal	—	—
37	Tailwind	Flying	Status	—	—	30	Your Side	—	—
41	Air Slash	Flying	Special	75	95	20	Normal	○	—
46	Crush Claw	Normal	Physical	75	95	10	Normal	—	○
50	Sky Drop	Flying	Physical	60	100	10	Normal	○	○
51	Superpower	Fighting	Physical	120	100	5	Normal	—	○
57	Whirlwind	Normal	Status	—	100	20	Normal	—	—
63	Brave Bird	Flying	Physical	120	100	15	Normal	○	○
70	Thrash	Normal	Physical	120	100	10	1 Random	—	○

● MOVES TAUGHT BY PEOPLE

Name	Type	Kind	Pow.	Acc.	PP	Range	Long	DA

● TM & HM MOVES

No.	Name	Type	Kind	Pow.	Acc.	PP	Range	Long	DA
TM01	Hone Claws	Dark	Status	—	—	15	Self	—	—
TM06	Toxic	Poison	Status	—	90	10	Normal	—	—
TM08	Bulk Up	Fighting	Status	—	—	20	Self	—	—
TM10	Hidden Power	Normal	Special	—	100	15	Normal	—	—
TM11	Sunny Day	Fire	Status	—	—	5	Both Sides	—	—
TM15	Hyper Beam	Normal	Special	150	90	5	Normal	—	—
TM17	Protect	Normal	Status	—	—	10	Self	—	—
TM18	Rain Dance	Water	Status	—	—	5	Both Sides	—	—
TM21	Frustration	Normal	Physical	—	100	20	Normal	—	○
TM27	Return	Normal	Physical	—	100	20	Normal	—	○
TM32	Double Team	Normal	Status	—	—	15	Self	—	—
TM39	Rock Tomb	Rock	Physical	50	80	10	Normal	—	—
TM40	Aerial Ace	Flying	Physical	60	—	20	Normal	○	○
TM42	Facade	Normal	Physical	70	100	20	Normal	—	○
TM44	Rest	Psychic	Status	—	—	10	Self	—	—
TM45	Attract	Normal	Status	—	100	15	Normal	—	—
TM48	Round	Normal	Special	60	100	15	Normal	—	—
TM58	Sky Drop	Flying	Physical	60	100	10	Normal	○	○
TM65	Shadow Claw	Ghost	Physical	70	100	15	Normal	—	○
TM67	Retaliate	Normal	Physical	70	100	5	Normal	—	○
TM68	Giga Impact	Normal	Physical	150	90	5	Normal	—	○
TM80	Rock Slide	Rock	Physical	75	90	10	Many Others	—	—
TM83	Work Up	Normal	Status	—	—	30	Self	—	—
TM87	Swagger	Normal	Status	—	90	15	Normal	—	—
TM88	Pluck	Flying	Physical	60	100	20	Normal	—	○
TM89	U-turn	Bug	Physical	70	100	20	Normal	—	○
TM90	Substitute	Normal	Status	—	—	10	Self	—	—
TM94	Rock Smash	Fighting	Physical	40	100	15	Normal	—	○
HM01	Cut	Normal	Physical	50	95	30	Normal	—	○
HM02	Fly	Flying	Physical	90	95	15	Normal	○	○
HM04	Strength	Normal	Physical	80	100	15	Normal	—	○

● FOOTPRINT

● MALE FORM

● HEIGHT: 4'11"
● WEIGHT: 90.4 lbs.
● GENDER: Only ♂ exist
● ITEMS:
 • None

POKÉMON BLACK VERSION
They fight for their friends without any thought about danger to themselves. One can carry a car while flying.

POKÉMON WHITE VERSION
The more scars they have, the more respect these brave soldiers of the sky get from their peers.

EVOLUTION

Rufflet — Lv. 54 → Braviary

ABILITIES ● Keen Eye ● Sheer Force

EGG GROUP Flying

STATS
HP ●●●●
ATTACK ●●●●●
DEFENSE ●●●●
SP. ATTACK ●●
SP. DEFENSE ●●●
SPEED ●●●●

● MAIN WAYS TO OBTAIN

POKÉMON BLACK VERSION
1 —
2 —

POKÉMON WHITE VERSION
1 Route 11 (Dark Grass)
2 Level up Rufflet to Lv. 54

Vullaby

● TYPE Dark Flying

● LEVEL-UP AND LEARNED MOVES

Lv.	Name	Type	Kind	Pow.	Acc.	PP	Range	Long	DA
1	Gust	Flying	Special	40	100	35	Normal	○	—
1	Leer	Normal	Status	—	100	30	Many Others	—	—
5	Fury Attack	Normal	Physical	15	85	20	Normal	—	○
10	Pluck	Flying	Physical	60	100	20	Normal	—	○
14	Nasty Plot	Dark	Status	—	—	20	Self	—	—
19	Flatter	Dark	Status	—	100	15	Normal	—	—
23	Faint Attack	Dark	Physical	60	—	20	Normal	—	○
28	Punishment	Dark	Physical	—	100	5	Normal	—	○
32	Defog	Flying	Status	—	—	15	Normal	—	—
37	Tailwind	Flying	Status	—	—	30	Your Side	—	—
41	Air Slash	Flying	Special	75	95	20	Normal	○	—
46	Dark Pulse	Dark	Special	80	100	15	Normal	○	—
50	Embargo	Dark	Status	—	100	15	Normal	—	—
55	Whirlwind	Normal	Status	—	100	20	Normal	—	—
59	Brave Bird	Flying	Physical	120	100	15	Normal	○	○
64	Mirror Move	Flying	Status	—	—	20	Normal	—	—

● MOVES TAUGHT BY PEOPLE

Name	Type	Kind	Pow.	Acc.	PP	Range	Long	DA

● EGG MOVES

Name	Type	Kind	Pow.	Acc.	PP	Range	Long	DA
Steel Wing	Steel	Physical	70	90	25	Normal	—	○
Mean Look	Normal	Status	—	—	5	Normal	—	—
Roost	Flying	Status	—	—	10	Self	—	—
Scary Face	Normal	Status	—	100	10	Normal	—	—
Knock Off	Dark	Physical	20	100	20	Normal	—	○
Fake Tears	Dark	Status	—	100	20	Normal	—	—

● TM & HM MOVES

No.	Name	Type	Kind	Pow.	Acc.	PP	Range	Long	DA
TM06	Toxic	Poison	Status	—	90	10	Normal	—	—
TM10	Hidden Power	Normal	Special	—	100	15	Normal	—	—
TM11	Sunny Day	Fire	Status	—	—	5	Both Sides	—	—
TM12	Taunt	Dark	Status	—	100	20	Normal	—	—
TM17	Protect	Normal	Status	—	—	10	Self	—	—
TM18	Rain Dance	Water	Status	—	—	5	Both Sides	—	—
TM21	Frustration	Normal	Physical	—	100	20	Normal	—	○
TM27	Return	Normal	Physical	—	100	20	Normal	—	○
TM30	Shadow Ball	Ghost	Special	80	100	15	Normal	—	—
TM32	Double Team	Normal	Status	—	—	15	Self	—	—
TM39	Rock Tomb	Rock	Physical	50	80	10	Normal	—	—
TM40	Aerial Ace	Flying	Physical	60	—	20	Normal	○	○
TM41	Torment	Dark	Status	—	100	15	Normal	—	—
TM42	Facade	Normal	Physical	70	100	20	Normal	—	○
TM44	Rest	Psychic	Status	—	—	10	Self	—	—
TM45	Attract	Normal	Status	—	100	15	Normal	—	—
TM48	Round	Normal	Special	60	100	15	Normal	—	—
TM59	Incinerate	Fire	Special	30	100	15	Many Others	—	—
TM63	Embargo	Dark	Status	—	100	15	Normal	—	—
TM66	Payback	Dark	Physical	50	100	10	Normal	—	○
TM67	Retaliate	Normal	Physical	70	100	5	Normal	—	○
TM77	Psych Up	Normal	Status	—	—	10	Normal	—	—
TM87	Swagger	Normal	Status	—	90	15	Normal	—	—
TM88	Pluck	Flying	Physical	60	100	20	Normal	—	○
TM89	U-turn	Bug	Physical	70	100	20	Normal	—	○
TM90	Substitute	Normal	Status	—	—	10	Self	—	—
TM94	Rock Smash	Fighting	Physical	40	100	15	Normal	—	○
HM01	Cut	Normal	Physical	50	95	30	Normal	—	○
HM02	Fly	Flying	Physical	90	95	15	Normal	○	○

● FOOTPRINT

● FEMALE FORM

● HEIGHT: 1'08"
● WEIGHT: 19.8 lbs.
● GENDER: Only ♀ exist
● ITEMS:
 • None

POKÉMON BLACK VERSION
Its wings are too tiny to allow it to fly. As the time approaches for it to evolve, it discards the bones it was wearing.

POKÉMON WHITE VERSION
They tend to guard their posteriors with suitable bones they have found. They pursue weak Pokémon.

EVOLUTION

Vullaby — Lv. 54 → Mandibuzz

ABILITIES ● Big Pecks ● Overcoat

EGG GROUP Flying

STATS
HP ●●●
ATTACK ●●●
DEFENSE ●●●
SP. ATTACK ●●
SP. DEFENSE ●●●
SPEED ●●●

● MAIN WAYS TO OBTAIN

POKÉMON BLACK VERSION
1 Route 10
2 Victory Road Outside

POKÉMON WHITE VERSION
1 —
2 —

Mandibuzz

● TYPE: Dark Flying

● FOOTPRINT

● FEMALE FORM

- HEIGHT: 3'11"
- WEIGHT: 87.1 lbs.
- GENDER: Only ♀ exist
- ITEMS:
  • None

● LEVEL-UP AND LEARNED MOVES

Lv.	Name	Type	Kind	Pow.	Acc.	PP	Range	Long	DA
1	Gust	Flying	Special	40	100	35	Normal	○	—
1	Leer	Normal	Status	—	100	30	Many Others	—	—
1	Fury Attack	Normal	Physical	15	85	20	Normal	—	○
5	Pluck	Flying	Physical	60	100	20	Normal	—	○
5	Fury Attack	Normal	Physical	15	85	20	Normal	—	○
10	Pluck	Flying	Physical	60	100	20	Normal	○	—
14	Nasty Plot	Dark	Status	—	—	20	Self	—	—
19	Flatter	Dark	Status	—	100	15	Normal	—	○
23	Faint Attack	Dark	Physical	60	—	20	Normal	—	○
28	Punishment	Dark	Physical	—	100	5	Normal	—	○
32	Defog	Flying	Status	—	—	15	Normal	—	—
37	Tailwind	Flying	Status	—	—	30	Your Side	—	—
41	Air Slash	Flying	Special	75	95	20	Normal	○	—
46	Dark Pulse	Dark	Special	80	100	15	Normal	○	—
50	Embargo	Dark	Status	—	100	15	Normal	—	—
51	Bone Rush	Ground	Physical	25	90	10	Normal	—	—
57	Whirlwind	Normal	Status	—	100	20	Normal	—	—
63	Brave Bird	Flying	Physical	120	100	15	Normal	○	—
70	Mirror Move	Flying	Status	—	—	20	Normal	—	—

● MOVES TAUGHT BY PEOPLE

Name	Type	Kind	Pow.	Acc.	PP	Range	Long	DA

● TM & HM MOVES

No.	Name	Type	Kind	Pow.	Acc.	PP	Range	Long	DA
TM06	Toxic	Poison	Status	—	90	10	Normal	—	—
TM10	Hidden Power	Normal	Special	—	100	15	Normal	—	—
TM11	Sunny Day	Fire	Status	—	—	5	Both Sides	—	—
TM12	Taunt	Dark	Status	—	100	20	Normal	—	—
TM15	Hyper Beam	Normal	Special	150	90	5	Normal	—	—
TM17	Protect	Normal	Status	—	—	10	Self	—	—
TM18	Rain Dance	Water	Status	—	—	5	Both Sides	—	—
TM21	Frustration	Normal	Physical	—	100	20	Normal	—	○
TM27	Return	Normal	Physical	—	100	20	Normal	—	○
TM30	Shadow Ball	Ghost	Special	80	100	15	Normal	—	—
TM32	Double Team	Normal	Status	—	—	15	Self	—	—
TM39	Rock Tomb	Rock	Physical	50	80	10	Normal	—	—
TM40	Aerial Ace	Flying	Physical	60	—	20	Normal	○	—
TM41	Torment	Dark	Status	—	100	15	Normal	—	—
TM42	Facade	Normal	Physical	70	100	20	Normal	—	—
TM44	Rest	Psychic	Status	—	—	10	Self	—	—
TM45	Attract	Normal	Status	—	100	15	Normal	—	—
TM46	Thief	Dark	Physical	40	100	10	Normal	—	○
TM48	Round	Normal	Special	60	100	15	Normal	—	—
TM59	Incinerate	Fire	Special	30	100	15	Many Others	—	—
TM63	Embargo	Dark	Status	—	100	15	Normal	—	—
TM66	Payback	Dark	Physical	50	100	10	Normal	—	○
TM67	Retaliate	Normal	Physical	70	100	5	Normal	—	—
TM68	Giga Impact	Normal	Physical	150	90	5	Normal	—	—
TM77	Psych Up	Normal	Status	—	—	10	Normal	—	—
TM87	Swagger	Normal	Status	—	90	15	Normal	—	—
TM88	Pluck	Flying	Physical	60	100	20	Normal	○	—
TM89	U-turn	Bug	Physical	70	100	20	Normal	—	—
TM90	Substitute	Normal	Status	—	—	10	Self	—	—
TM94	Rock Smash	Fighting	Physical	40	100	15	Normal	—	○
HM01	Cut	Normal	Physical	50	95	30	Normal	—	○
HM02	Fly	Flying	Physical	90	95	15	Normal	○	○

EVOLUTION

Vullaby — Lv. 54 → Mandibuzz

POKÉMON BLACK VERSION
It makes a nest out of bones it finds. It grabs weakened prey in its talons and hauls it to its nest of bones.

POKÉMON WHITE VERSION
Watching from the sky, they swoop to strike weakened Pokémon on the ground. They decorate themselves with bones.

ABILITIES: • Big Pecks • Overcoat

EGG GROUP: Flying

STATS:
HP ●●●●
ATTACK ●●●
DEFENSE ●●●●
SP. ATTACK ●●
SP. DEFENSE ●●
SPEED ●●●●

● MAIN WAYS TO OBTAIN

POKÉMON BLACK VERSION
1 Route 11 (Dark Grass)
2 Level up Vullaby to Lv. 54

POKÉMON WHITE VERSION
1 —
2 —

Heatmor

● TYPE: Fire

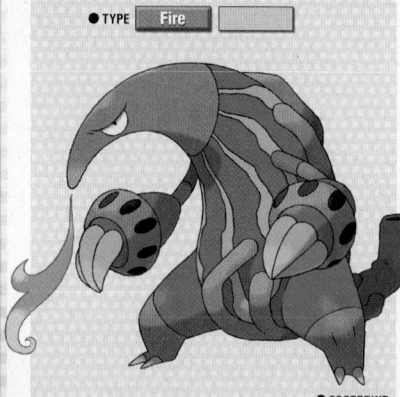

● FOOTPRINT

● MALE/FEMALE HAVE SAME FORM

- HEIGHT: 4'07"
- WEIGHT: 127.9 lbs.
- GENDER: Both ♂ ♀ exist
- ITEMS:
  • None

● LEVEL-UP AND LEARNED MOVES

Lv.	Name	Type	Kind	Pow.	Acc.	PP	Range	Long	DA
1	Incinerate	Fire	Special	30	100	15	Many Others	—	—
1	Lick	Ghost	Physical	20	100	30	Normal	—	○
6	Odor Sleuth	Normal	Status	—	—	40	Normal	—	—
11	Bind	Normal	Physical	15	85	20	Normal	—	○
16	Fire Spin	Fire	Special	35	85	15	Normal	—	—
21	Fury Swipes	Normal	Physical	18	80	15	Normal	—	○
26	Snatch	Dark	Status	—	—	10	Self	—	—
31	Flame Burst	Fire	Special	70	100	15	Normal	—	—
36	Bug Bite	Bug	Physical	60	100	20	Normal	—	○
41	Slash	Normal	Physical	70	100	20	Normal	—	○
46	Amnesia	Psychic	Status	—	—	20	Self	—	—
51	Flamethrower	Fire	Special	95	100	15	Normal	—	—
56	Stockpile	Normal	Status	—	—	20	Self	—	—
56	Spit Up	Normal	Status	—	100	10	Normal	—	—
56	Swallow	Normal	Status	—	—	10	Self	—	—
61	Inferno	Fire	Special	100	50	5	Normal	—	—

● MOVES TAUGHT BY PEOPLE

Name	Type	Kind	Pow.	Acc.	PP	Range	Long	DA

● EGG MOVES

Name	Type	Kind	Pow.	Acc.	PP	Range	Long	DA
Pursuit	Dark	Physical	40	100	20	Normal	—	○
Wrap	Normal	Physical	15	90	20	Normal	—	○
Night Slash	Dark	Physical	70	100	15	Normal	—	○
Curse	Ghost	Status	—	—	10	Varies	—	—
Body Slam	Normal	Physical	85	100	15	Normal	—	○
Heat Wave	Fire	Special	100	90	10	Many Others	—	—
Faint Attack	Dark	Physical	60	—	20	Normal	—	○
Sucker Punch	Dark	Physical	80	100	5	Normal	—	○
Tickle	Normal	Status	—	100	20	Normal	—	—
Sleep Talk	Normal	Status	—	—	10	Self	—	—

● TM & HM MOVES

No.	Name	Type	Kind	Pow.	Acc.	PP	Range	Long	DA
TM01	Hone Claws	Dark	Status	—	—	15	Self	—	—
TM06	Toxic	Poison	Status	—	90	10	Normal	—	—
TM10	Hidden Power	Normal	Special	—	100	15	Normal	—	—
TM11	Sunny Day	Fire	Status	—	—	5	Both Sides	—	—
TM12	Taunt	Dark	Status	—	100	20	Normal	—	—
TM17	Protect	Normal	Status	—	—	10	Self	—	—
TM18	Rain Dance	Water	Status	—	—	5	Both Sides	—	—
TM21	Frustration	Normal	Physical	—	100	20	Normal	—	○
TM22	SolarBeam	Grass	Special	120	100	10	Normal	—	—
TM27	Return	Normal	Physical	—	100	20	Normal	—	○
TM28	Dig	Ground	Physical	80	100	10	Normal	—	○
TM32	Double Team	Normal	Status	—	—	15	Self	—	—
TM35	Flamethrower	Fire	Special	95	100	15	Normal	—	—
TM38	Fire Blast	Fire	Special	120	85	5	Normal	—	—
TM39	Rock Tomb	Rock	Physical	50	80	10	Normal	—	—
TM40	Aerial Ace	Flying	Physical	60	—	20	Normal	○	—
TM42	Facade	Normal	Physical	70	100	20	Normal	—	—
TM44	Rest	Psychic	Status	—	—	10	Self	—	—
TM45	Attract	Normal	Status	—	100	15	Normal	—	—
TM46	Thief	Dark	Physical	40	100	10	Normal	—	○
TM48	Round	Normal	Special	60	100	15	Normal	—	—
TM52	Focus Blast	Fighting	Special	120	70	5	Normal	—	—
TM56	Fling	Dark	Physical	—	100	10	Normal	—	○
TM59	Incinerate	Fire	Special	30	100	15	Many Others	—	—
TM61	Will-O-Wisp	Fire	Status	—	75	15	Normal	—	—
TM65	Shadow Claw	Ghost	Physical	70	100	15	Normal	—	○
TM68	Giga Impact	Normal	Physical	150	90	5	Normal	—	—
TM87	Swagger	Normal	Status	—	90	15	Normal	—	—
TM90	Substitute	Normal	Status	—	—	10	Self	—	—
TM94	Rock Smash	Fighting	Physical	40	100	15	Normal	—	○
HM01	Cut	Normal	Physical	50	95	30	Normal	—	○

EVOLUTION

Does not evolve

POKÉMON BLACK VERSION
It breathes through a hole in its tail while it burns with an internal fire. Durant is its prey.

POKÉMON WHITE VERSION
Using their very hot, flame-covered tongues, they burn through Durant's steel bodies and consume their insides.

ABILITIES: • Gluttony • Flash Fire

EGG GROUP: Field

STATS:
HP ●●●
ATTACK ●●●●
DEFENSE ●●●
SP. ATTACK ●●●●●
SP. DEFENSE ●●
SPEED ●●●

● MAIN WAYS TO OBTAIN

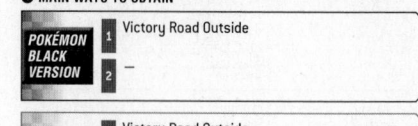

POKÉMON BLACK VERSION
1 Victory Road Outside
2

POKÉMON WHITE VERSION
1 Victory Road Outside
2

Durant

● TYPE Bug   Steel

● LEVEL-UP AND LEARNED MOVES

Lv.	Name	Type	Kind	Pow.	Acc.	PP	Range	Long	DA
1	ViceGrip	Normal	Physical	55	100	30	Normal	—	○
1	Sand-Attack	Ground	Status	—	100	15	Normal	—	—
6	Fury Cutter	Bug	Physical	20	95	20	Normal	—	○
11	Bite	Dark	Physical	60	100	25	Normal	—	○
16	Agility	Psychic	Status	—	—	30	Self	—	—
21	Metal Claw	Steel	Physical	50	95	35	Normal	—	○
26	Bug Bite	Bug	Physical	60	100	20	Normal	—	○
31	Crunch	Dark	Physical	80	100	15	Normal	—	○
36	Iron Head	Steel	Physical	80	100	15	Normal	—	○
41	Dig	Ground	Physical	80	100	10	Normal	—	○
46	Entrainment	Normal	Status	—	100	15	Normal	—	—
51	X-Scissor	Bug	Physical	80	100	15	Normal	—	○
56	Iron Defense	Steel	Status	—	—	15	Self	—	—
61	Guillotine	Normal	Physical	—	30	5	Normal	—	—
66	Metal Sound	Steel	Status	—	85	40	Normal	—	—

● MOVES TAUGHT BY PEOPLE

Name	Type	Kind	Pow.	Acc.	PP	Range	Long	DA

● EGG MOVES

Name	Type	Kind	Pow.	Acc.	PP	Range	Long	DA
Screech	Normal	Status	—	85	40	Normal	—	—
Endure	Normal	Status	—	—	10	Self	—	—
Rock Climb	Normal	Physical	90	85	20	Normal	—	○
Baton Pass	Normal	Status	—	—	40	Self	—	—
Thunder Fang	Electric	Physical	65	95	15	Normal	—	○
Faint Attack	Dark	Physical	60	—	20	Normal	—	○

● TM & HM MOVES

No.	Name	Type	Kind	Pow.	Acc.	PP	Range	Long	DA
TM01	Hone Claws	Dark	Status	—	—	15	Self	—	—
TM06	Toxic	Poison	Status	—	90	10	Normal	—	—
TM10	Hidden Power	Normal	Special	—	100	15	Normal	—	—
TM17	Protect	Normal	Status	—	—	10	Self	—	—
TM21	Frustration	Normal	Physical	—	100	20	Normal	—	○
TM27	Return	Normal	Physical	—	100	20	Normal	—	○
TM28	Dig	Ground	Physical	80	100	10	Normal	—	○
TM32	Double Team	Normal	Status	—	—	15	Self	—	—
TM37	Sandstorm	Rock	Status	—	—	10	Both Sides	—	—
TM39	Rock Tomb	Rock	Physical	50	80	10	Normal	—	○
TM40	Aerial Ace	Flying	Physical	60	—	20	Normal	○	○
TM42	Facade	Normal	Physical	70	100	20	Normal	—	○
TM44	Rest	Psychic	Status	—	—	10	Self	—	—
TM45	Attract	Normal	Status	—	100	15	Normal	—	—
TM48	Round	Normal	Special	60	100	15	Normal	—	—
TM53	Energy Ball	Grass	Special	80	100	10	Normal	—	—
TM65	Shadow Claw	Ghost	Physical	70	100	15	Normal	—	○
TM67	Retaliate	Normal	Physical	70	100	5	Normal	—	○
TM68	Giga Impact	Normal	Physical	150	90	5	Normal	—	○
TM69	Rock Polish	Rock	Status	—	—	20	Self	—	—
TM71	Stone Edge	Rock	Physical	100	80	5	Normal	—	○
TM73	Thunder Wave	Electric	Status	—	100	20	Normal	—	—
TM76	Struggle Bug	Bug	Special	30	100	20	Many Others	—	—
TM80	Rock Slide	Rock	Physical	75	90	10	Many Others	—	—
TM81	X-Scissor	Bug	Physical	80	100	15	Normal	—	○
TM87	Swagger	Normal	Status	—	90	15	Normal	—	—
TM90	Substitute	Normal	Status	—	—	10	Self	—	—
TM91	Flash Cannon	Steel	Special	80	100	10	Normal	—	—
TM94	Rock Smash	Fighting	Physical	40	100	15	Normal	—	○
HM01	Cut	Normal	Physical	50	95	30	Normal	—	○
HM04	Strength	Normal	Physical	80	100	15	Normal	—	○

● FOOTPRINT

● MALE/FEMALE HAVE SAME FORM

● HEIGHT: 1'00"
● WEIGHT: 72.8 lbs.
● GENDER: Both ♂♀ exist
● ITEMS:
 • None

POKÉMON BLACK VERSION
They attack in groups, covering themselves in steel armor to protect themselves from Heatmor.

POKÉMON WHITE VERSION
Durant dig nests in mountains. They build their complicated, interconnected tunnels into mazes.

● EVOLUTION

Does not evolve

ABILITIES ● Swarm ● Hustle

EGG GROUP Bug

STATS
HP ●●
ATTACK ●●●●●
DEFENSE ●●●●●
SP. ATTACK ●●●
SP. DEFENSE ●●
SPEED ●●●●●

● MAIN WAYS TO OBTAIN

POKÉMON BLACK VERSION
1 Victory Road 1F
2 Victory Road 2F

POKÉMON WHITE VERSION
1 Victory Road 1F
2 Victory Road 2F

Deino

● TYPE Dark   Dragon

● LEVEL-UP AND LEARNED MOVES

Lv.	Name	Type	Kind	Pow.	Acc.	PP	Range	Long	DA
1	Tackle	Normal	Physical	50	100	35	Normal	—	—
1	Dragon Rage	Dragon	Special	—	100	10	Normal	—	—
4	Focus Energy	Normal	Status	—	—	30	Self	—	—
9	Bite	Dark	Physical	60	100	25	Normal	—	○
12	Headbutt	Normal	Physical	70	100	15	Normal	—	○
17	DragonBreath	Dragon	Special	60	100	20	Normal	—	—
20	Roar	Normal	Status	—	100	20	Normal	—	—
25	Crunch	Dark	Physical	80	100	15	Normal	—	○
28	Slam	Normal	Physical	80	75	20	Normal	—	○
32	Dragon Pulse	Dragon	Special	90	100	10	Normal	○	—
38	Work Up	Normal	Status	—	—	30	Self	—	—
42	Dragon Rush	Dragon	Physical	100	75	10	Normal	—	○
48	Body Slam	Normal	Physical	85	100	15	Normal	—	○
52	Scary Face	Normal	Status	—	100	10	Normal	—	—
58	Hyper Voice	Normal	Special	90	100	10	Many Others	—	—
62	Outrage	Dragon	Physical	120	100	10	1 Random	—	○

● MOVES TAUGHT BY PEOPLE

Name	Type	Kind	Pow.	Acc.	PP	Range	Long	DA
Draco Meteor	Dragon	Special	140	90	5	Normal	—	—

● EGG MOVES

Name	Type	Kind	Pow.	Acc.	PP	Range	Long	DA
Fire Fang	Fire	Physical	65	95	15	Normal	—	○
Thunder Fang	Electric	Physical	65	95	15	Normal	—	○
Ice Fang	Ice	Physical	65	95	15	Normal	—	○
Double Hit	Normal	Physical	35	90	10	Normal	—	—
Astonish	Ghost	Physical	30	100	15	Normal	—	○
Earth Power	Ground	Special	90	100	10	Normal	—	—
Screech	Normal	Status	—	85	40	Normal	—	—
Head Smash	Rock	Physical	150	80	5	Normal	—	—
Assurance	Dark	Physical	50	100	10	Normal	—	—
Dark Pulse	Dark	Special	80	100	15	Normal	○	—

● TM & HM MOVES

No.	Name	Type	Kind	Pow.	Acc.	PP	Range	Long	DA
TM05	Roar	Normal	Status	—	100	20	Normal	—	—
TM06	Toxic	Poison	Status	—	90	10	Normal	—	—
TM10	Hidden Power	Normal	Special	—	100	15	Normal	—	—
TM11	Sunny Day	Fire	Status	—	—	5	Both Sides	—	—
TM12	Taunt	Dark	Status	—	100	20	Normal	—	—
TM17	Protect	Normal	Status	—	—	10	Self	—	—
TM18	Rain Dance	Water	Status	—	—	5	Both Sides	—	—
TM21	Frustration	Normal	Physical	—	100	20	Normal	—	○
TM27	Return	Normal	Physical	—	100	20	Normal	—	○
TM32	Double Team	Normal	Status	—	—	15	Self	—	—
TM41	Torment	Dark	Status	—	100	15	Normal	—	—
TM42	Facade	Normal	Physical	70	100	20	Normal	—	○
TM44	Rest	Psychic	Status	—	—	10	Self	—	—
TM45	Attract	Normal	Status	—	100	15	Normal	—	—
TM46	Thief	Dark	Physical	40	100	10	Normal	—	○
TM48	Round	Normal	Special	60	100	15	Normal	—	—
TM59	Incinerate	Fire	Special	30	100	15	Many Others	—	—
TM73	Thunder Wave	Electric	Status	—	100	20	Normal	—	—
TM77	Psych Up	Normal	Status	—	—	10	Self	—	—
TM82	Dragon Tail	Dragon	Physical	60	90	10	Normal	—	○
TM83	Work Up	Normal	Status	—	—	30	Self	—	—
TM87	Swagger	Normal	Status	—	90	15	Normal	—	—
TM90	Substitute	Normal	Status	—	—	10	Self	—	—
TM94	Rock Smash	Fighting	Physical	40	100	15	Normal	—	○
HM04	Strength	Normal	Physical	80	100	15	Normal	—	○

● FOOTPRINT

● MALE/FEMALE HAVE SAME FORM

● HEIGHT: 2'07"
● WEIGHT: 38.1 lbs.
● GENDER: Both ♂♀ exist
● ITEMS:
 • None

POKÉMON BLACK VERSION
It tends to bite everything, and it is not a picky eater. Approaching it carelessly is dangerous.

POKÉMON WHITE VERSION
They cannot see, so they tackle and bite to learn about their surroundings. Their bodies are covered in wounds.

● EVOLUTION

Deino → Lv. 50 → Zweilous → Lv. 64 → Hydreigon

ABILITY ● Hustle

EGG GROUP Dragon

STATS
HP ●●
ATTACK ●●●
DEFENSE ●●●
SP. ATTACK ●●●
SP. DEFENSE ●●●
SPEED ●●●

● MAIN WAYS TO OBTAIN

POKÉMON BLACK VERSION
1 Victory Road 1F
2 —

POKÉMON WHITE VERSION
1 Victory Road 1F
2 —

Zweilous

● TYPE **Dark** **Dragon**

● FOOTPRINT

● MALE/FEMALE HAVE SAME FORM

● HEIGHT: 4'07"
● WEIGHT: 110.2 lbs.
● GENDER: Both ♂♀ exist
● ITEMS:
• None

POKÉMON BLACK VERSION
After it has eaten up all the food in its territory, it moves to another area. Its two heads do not get along.

POKÉMON WHITE VERSION
Since their two heads do not get along and compete with each other for food, they always eat too much.

● LEVEL-UP AND LEARNED MOVES

Lv.	Name	Type	Kind	Pow.	Acc.	PP	Range	Long	DA
1	Double Hit	Normal	Physical	35	90	10	Normal	–	○
1	Dragon Rage	Dragon	Special	–	100	10	Normal	–	–
1	Focus Energy	Normal	Status	–	–	30	Self	–	–
1	Bite	Dark	Physical	60	100	25	Normal	–	○
4	Focus Energy	Normal	Status	–	–	30	Self	–	–
9	Bite	Dark	Physical	60	100	25	Normal	–	○
12	Headbutt	Normal	Physical	70	100	15	Normal	–	○
17	DragonBreath	Dragon	Special	60	100	20	Normal	–	–
20	Roar	Normal	Status	–	100	20	Normal	–	–
25	Crunch	Dark	Physical	80	100	15	Normal	–	○
28	Slam	Normal	Physical	80	75	20	Normal	–	○
32	Dragon Pulse	Dragon	Special	90	100	10	Normal	○	–
38	Work Up	Normal	Status	–	–	30	Self	–	–
42	Dragon Rush	Dragon	Physical	100	75	10	Normal	–	○
48	Body Slam	Normal	Physical	85	100	15	Normal	–	○
55	Scary Face	Normal	Status	–	100	10	Normal	–	–
64	Hyper Voice	Normal	Special	90	100	10	Many Others	–	–
71	Outrage	Dragon	Physical	120	100	10	1 Random	–	○

● MOVES TAUGHT BY PEOPLE

Name	Type	Kind	Pow.	Acc.	PP	Range	Long	DA
Draco Meteor	Dragon	Special	140	90	5	Normal	–	–

● TM & HM MOVES

No.	Name	Type	Kind	Pow.	Acc.	PP	Range	Long	DA
TM05	Roar	Normal	Status	–	100	20	Normal	–	–
TM06	Toxic	Poison	Status	–	90	10	Normal	–	–
TM10	Hidden Power	Normal	Special	–	100	15	Normal	–	–
TM11	Sunny Day	Fire	Status	–	–	5	Both Sides	–	–
TM12	Taunt	Dark	Status	–	100	20	Normal	–	–
TM17	Protect	Normal	Status	–	–	10	Self	–	–
TM18	Rain Dance	Water	Status	–	–	5	Both Sides	–	–
TM21	Frustration	Normal	Physical	–	100	20	Normal	–	○
TM27	Return	Normal	Physical	–	100	20	Normal	–	○
TM32	Double Team	Normal	Status	–	–	15	Self	–	–
TM41	Torment	Dark	Status	–	100	15	Normal	–	–
TM42	Facade	Normal	Physical	70	100	20	Normal	–	○
TM44	Rest	Psychic	Status	–	–	10	Self	–	–
TM45	Attract	Normal	Status	–	100	15	Normal	–	–
TM46	Thief	Dark	Physical	40	100	10	Normal	–	○
TM48	Round	Normal	Special	60	100	15	Normal	–	–
TM59	Incinerate	Fire	Special	30	100	15	Many Others	–	–
TM73	Thunder Wave	Electric	Status	–	100	20	Normal	–	–
TM77	Psych Up	Normal	Status	–	–	10	Normal	–	–
TM82	Dragon Tail	Dragon	Physical	60	90	10	Normal	–	○
TM83	Work Up	Normal	Status	–	–	30	Self	–	–
TM87	Swagger	Normal	Status	–	90	15	Normal	–	–
TM90	Substitute	Normal	Status	–	–	10	Self	–	–
TM94	Rock Smash	Fighting	Physical	40	100	15	Normal	–	○
HM04	Strength	Normal	Physical	80	100	15	Normal	–	○

● EVOLUTION

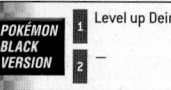

Deino → Lv. 50 → Zweilous → Lv. 64 → Hydreigon

● ABILITY ● Hustle

● EGG GROUP Dragon

● STATS
HP ●●●
ATTACK ●●●●
DEFENSE ●●●
SP. ATTACK ●●●
SP. DEFENSE ●●●
SPEED ●●●

● MAIN WAYS TO OBTAIN

POKÉMON BLACK VERSION
1 Level up Deino to Lv. 50
2 –

POKÉMON WHITE VERSION
1 Level up Deino to Lv. 50
2 –

Hydreigon

● TYPE **Dark** **Dragon**

● FOOTPRINT

● MALE/FEMALE HAVE SAME FORM

● HEIGHT: 5'11"
● WEIGHT: 352.7 lbs.
● GENDER: Both ♂♀ exist
● ITEMS:
• None

POKÉMON BLACK VERSION
This brutal Pokémon travels the skies on its six wings. Anything that moves seems like a foe to it, triggering its attack.

POKÉMON WHITE VERSION
The heads on their arms do not have brains. They use all three heads to consume and destroy everything.

● LEVEL-UP AND LEARNED MOVES

Lv.	Name	Type	Kind	Pow.	Acc.	PP	Range	Long	DA
1	Tri Attack	Normal	Special	80	100	10	Normal	–	–
1	Dragon Rage	Dragon	Special	–	100	10	Normal	–	–
1	Focus Energy	Normal	Status	–	–	30	Self	–	–
1	Bite	Dark	Physical	60	100	25	Normal	–	○
4	Focus Energy	Normal	Status	–	–	30	Self	–	–
9	Bite	Dark	Physical	60	100	25	Normal	–	○
12	Headbutt	Normal	Physical	70	100	15	Normal	–	○
17	DragonBreath	Dragon	Special	60	100	20	Normal	–	–
20	Roar	Normal	Status	–	100	20	Normal	–	–
25	Crunch	Dark	Physical	80	100	15	Normal	–	○
28	Slam	Normal	Physical	80	75	20	Normal	–	○
32	Dragon Pulse	Dragon	Special	90	100	10	Normal	○	–
38	Work Up	Normal	Status	–	–	30	Self	–	–
42	Dragon Rush	Dragon	Physical	100	75	10	Normal	–	○
48	Body Slam	Normal	Physical	85	100	15	Normal	–	○
55	Scary Face	Normal	Status	–	100	10	Normal	–	–
68	Hyper Voice	Normal	Special	90	100	10	Many Others	–	–
79	Outrage	Dragon	Physical	120	100	10	1 Random	–	○

● MOVES TAUGHT BY PEOPLE

Name	Type	Kind	Pow.	Acc.	PP	Range	Long	DA
Draco Meteor	Dragon	Special	140	90	5	Normal	–	–

● TM & HM MOVES

No.	Name	Type	Kind	Pow.	Acc.	PP	Range	Long	DA
TM05	Roar	Normal	Status	–	100	20	Normal	–	–
TM06	Toxic	Poison	Status	–	90	10	Normal	–	–
TM10	Hidden Power	Normal	Special	–	100	15	Normal	–	–
TM11	Sunny Day	Fire	Status	–	–	5	Both Sides	–	–
TM12	Taunt	Dark	Status	–	100	20	Normal	–	–
TM15	Hyper Beam	Normal	Special	150	90	5	Normal	–	–
TM17	Protect	Normal	Status	–	–	10	Self	–	–
TM18	Rain Dance	Water	Status	–	–	5	Both Sides	–	–
TM21	Frustration	Normal	Physical	–	100	20	Normal	–	○
TM26	Earthquake	Ground	Physical	100	100	10	Adjacent	–	–
TM27	Return	Normal	Physical	–	100	20	Normal	–	○
TM32	Double Team	Normal	Status	–	–	15	Self	–	–
TM33	Reflect	Psychic	Status	–	–	20	Your Side	–	–
TM35	Flamethrower	Fire	Special	95	100	15	Normal	–	–
TM38	Fire Blast	Fire	Special	120	85	5	Normal	–	–
TM39	Rock Tomb	Rock	Physical	50	80	10	Normal	–	○
TM41	Torment	Dark	Status	–	100	15	Normal	–	–
TM42	Facade	Normal	Physical	70	100	20	Normal	–	○
TM44	Rest	Psychic	Status	–	–	10	Self	–	–
TM45	Attract	Normal	Status	–	100	15	Normal	–	–
TM46	Thief	Dark	Physical	40	100	10	Normal	–	○
TM48	Round	Normal	Special	60	100	15	Normal	–	–
TM49	Echoed Voice	Normal	Special	40	100	15	Normal	–	–
TM52	Focus Blast	Fighting	Special	120	70	5	Normal	–	–
TM57	Charge Beam	Electric	Special	50	90	10	Normal	–	–
TM59	Incinerate	Fire	Special	30	100	15	Many Others	–	–
TM62	Acrobatics	Flying	Physical	55	100	15	Normal	○	○
TM66	Payback	Dark	Physical	50	100	10	Normal	–	○
TM68	Giga Impact	Normal	Physical	150	90	5	Normal	–	○
TM71	Stone Edge	Rock	Physical	100	80	5	Normal	–	–
TM73	Thunder Wave	Electric	Status	–	100	20	Normal	–	–
TM77	Psych Up	Normal	Status	–	–	10	Normal	–	–
TM78	Bulldoze	Ground	Physical	60	100	20	Adjacent	–	–
TM80	Rock Slide	Rock	Physical	75	90	10	Many Others	–	–
TM82	Dragon Tail	Dragon	Physical	60	90	10	Normal	–	○
TM83	Work Up	Normal	Status	–	–	30	Self	–	–
TM87	Swagger	Normal	Status	–	90	15	Normal	–	–
TM89	U-turn	Bug	Physical	70	100	20	Normal	–	–
TM90	Substitute	Normal	Status	–	–	10	Self	–	–
TM91	Flash Cannon	Steel	Special	80	100	10	Normal	–	–
TM94	Rock Smash	Fighting	Physical	40	100	15	Normal	–	○
HM02	Fly	Flying	Physical	90	95	15	Normal	○	○
HM03	Surf	Water	Special	95	100	15	Adjacent	–	–
HM04	Strength	Normal	Physical	80	100	15	Normal	–	○

● EVOLUTION

Deino → Lv. 50 → Zweilous → Lv. 64 → Hydreigon

● ABILITY ● Levitate

● EGG GROUP Dragon

● STATS
HP ●●●●
ATTACK ●●●●
DEFENSE ●●●●
SP. ATTACK ●●●●●
SP. DEFENSE ●●●●
SPEED ●●●●

● MAIN WAYS TO OBTAIN

POKÉMON BLACK VERSION
1 Level up Zweilous to Lv. 64
2 –

POKÉMON WHITE VERSION
1 Level up Zweilous to Lv. 64
2 –

Larvesta

● LEVEL-UP AND LEARNED MOVES

Lv.	Name	Type	Kind	Pow.	Acc.	PP	Range	Long	DA
1	Ember	Fire	Special	40	100	25	Normal	–	–
1	String Shot	Bug	Status	–	95	40	Many Others	–	–
10	Leech Life	Bug	Physical	20	100	15	Normal	–	○
20	Take Down	Normal	Physical	90	85	20	Normal	–	○
30	Flame Charge	Fire	Physical	50	100	20	Normal	–	○
40	Bug Bite	Bug	Physical	60	100	20	Normal	–	○
50	Double-Edge	Normal	Physical	120	100	15	Normal	–	○
60	Flame Wheel	Fire	Physical	60	100	25	Normal	–	○
70	Bug Buzz	Bug	Special	90	100	10	Normal	–	–
80	Amnesia	Psychic	Status	–	–	20	Self	–	–
90	Thrash	Normal	Physical	120	100	10	1 Random	–	○
100	Flare Blitz	Fire	Physical	120	100	15	Normal	–	○

● MOVES TAUGHT BY PEOPLE

Name	Type	Kind	Pow.	Acc.	PP	Range	Long	DA

● EGG MOVES

Name	Type	Kind	Pow.	Acc.	PP	Range	Long	DA
String Shot	Bug	Status	–	95	40	Many Others	–	–
Harden	Normal	Status	–	–	30	Self	–	–
Foresight	Normal	Status	–	–	40	Normal	–	–
Endure	Normal	Status	–	–	10	Self	–	–
Zen Headbutt	Psychic	Physical	80	90	15	Normal	–	○
Morning Sun	Normal	Status	–	–	5	Self	–	–
Magnet Rise	Electric	Status	–	–	10	Self	–	–

● TM & HM MOVES

No.	Name	Type	Kind	Pow.	Acc.	PP	Range	Long	DA
TM04	Calm Mind	Psychic	Status	–	–	20	Self	–	–
TM06	Toxic	Poison	Status	–	90	10	Normal	–	–
TM10	Hidden Power	Normal	Special	–	100	15	Normal	–	–
TM11	Sunny Day	Fire	Status	–	–	5	Both Sides	–	–
TM17	Protect	Normal	Status	–	–	10	Self	–	–
TM20	Safeguard	Normal	Status	–	–	25	Your Side	–	–
TM21	Frustration	Normal	Physical	–	100	20	Normal	–	○
TM22	SolarBeam	Grass	Special	120	100	10	Normal	–	–
TM27	Return	Normal	Physical	–	100	20	Normal	–	○
TM29	Psychic	Psychic	Special	90	100	10	Normal	–	–
TM32	Double Team	Normal	Status	–	–	15	Self	–	–
TM35	Flamethrower	Fire	Special	95	100	15	Normal	–	–
TM38	Fire Blast	Fire	Special	120	85	5	Normal	–	–
TM42	Facade	Normal	Physical	70	100	20	Normal	–	○
TM43	Flame Charge	Fire	Physical	50	100	20	Normal	–	○
TM44	Rest	Psychic	Status	–	–	10	Self	–	–
TM48	Round	Normal	Special	60	100	15	Normal	–	–
TM50	Overheat	Fire	Special	140	90	5	Normal	–	–
TM59	Incinerate	Fire	Special	30	100	15	Many Others	–	–
TM61	Will-O-Wisp	Fire	Status	–	75	15	Normal	–	–
TM62	Acrobatics	Flying	Physical	55	100	15	Normal	○	○
TM76	Struggle Bug	Bug	Special	30	100	20	Many Others	–	–
TM87	Swagger	Normal	Status	–	90	15	Normal	–	–
TM89	U-turn	Bug	Physical	70	100	20	Normal	–	○
TM90	Substitute	Normal	Status	–	–	10	Self	–	–
TM93	Wild Charge	Electric	Physical	90	100	15	Normal	–	○

● FOOTPRINT

● MALE/FEMALE HAVE SAME FORM

● HEIGHT: 3'07"
● WEIGHT: 63.5 lbs.
● GENDER: Both ♂♀ exist
● ITEMS:
　• None

POKÉMON BLACK VERSION
This Pokémon was believed to have been born from the sun. When it evolves, its entire body is engulfed in flames.

POKÉMON WHITE VERSION
The base of volcanoes is where they make their homes. They shoot fire from their five horns to repel attacking enemies.

EVOLUTION

Larvesta — Lv. 59 → Volcarona

ABILITY
● Flame Body

EGG GROUP
Bug

STATS
HP ●●
ATTACK ●●●●
DEFENSE ●●
SP. ATTACK ●●●
SP. DEFENSE ●●●
SPEED ●●●

● MAIN WAYS TO OBTAIN

POKÉMON BLACK VERSION
1　Hatch the Egg received on Route 18
2　–

POKÉMON WHITE VERSION
1　Hatch the Egg received on Route 18
2　–

Volcarona

● TYPE Bug Fire

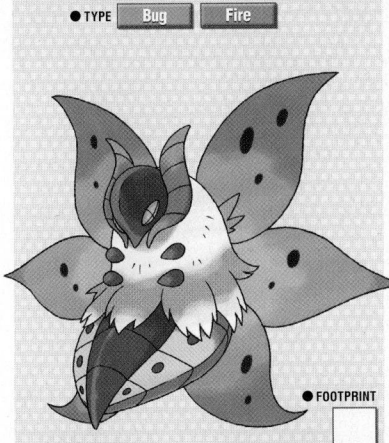

● LEVEL-UP AND LEARNED MOVES

Lv.	Name	Type	Kind	Pow.	Acc.	PP	Range	Long	DA
1	Ember	Fire	Special	40	100	25	Normal	–	–
1	String Shot	Bug	Status	–	95	40	Many Others	–	–
1	Leech Life	Bug	Physical	20	100	15	Normal	–	–
1	Gust	Flying	Special	40	100	35	Normal	○	–
10	Leech Life	Bug	Physical	20	100	15	Normal	–	–
20	Gust	Flying	Special	40	100	35	Normal	○	–
30	Fire Spin	Fire	Special	35	85	15	Normal	–	–
40	Whirlwind	Normal	Status	–	100	20	Normal	–	–
50	Silver Wind	Bug	Special	60	100	5	Normal	–	–
59	Quiver Dance	Bug	Status	–	–	20	Self	–	–
60	Heat Wave	Fire	Special	100	90	10	Many Others	–	–
70	Bug Buzz	Bug	Special	90	100	10	Normal	–	–
80	Rage Powder	Bug	Status	–	–	20	Self	–	–
90	Hurricane	Flying	Special	120	70	10	Normal	○	–
100	Fiery Dance	Fire	Special	80	100	10	Normal	–	–

● MOVES TAUGHT BY PEOPLE

Name	Type	Kind	Pow.	Acc.	PP	Range	Long	DA

● TM & HM MOVES

No.	Name	Type	Kind	Pow.	Acc.	PP	Range	Long	DA
TM04	Calm Mind	Psychic	Status	–	–	20	Self	–	–
TM06	Toxic	Poison	Status	–	90	10	Normal	–	–
TM10	Hidden Power	Normal	Special	–	100	15	Normal	–	–
TM11	Sunny Day	Fire	Status	–	–	5	Both Sides	–	–
TM15	Hyper Beam	Normal	Special	150	90	5	Normal	–	–
TM16	Light Screen	Psychic	Status	–	–	30	Your Side	–	–
TM17	Protect	Normal	Status	–	–	10	Self	–	–
TM20	Safeguard	Normal	Status	–	–	25	Your Side	–	–
TM21	Frustration	Normal	Physical	–	100	20	Normal	–	○
TM22	SolarBeam	Grass	Special	120	100	10	Normal	–	–
TM27	Return	Normal	Physical	–	100	20	Normal	–	○
TM29	Psychic	Psychic	Special	90	100	10	Normal	–	–
TM32	Double Team	Normal	Status	–	–	15	Self	–	–
TM35	Flamethrower	Fire	Special	95	100	15	Normal	–	–
TM38	Fire Blast	Fire	Special	120	85	5	Normal	–	–
TM40	Aerial Ace	Flying	Physical	60	–	20	Normal	○	○
TM42	Facade	Normal	Physical	70	100	20	Normal	–	○
TM43	Flame Charge	Fire	Physical	50	100	20	Normal	–	○
TM44	Rest	Psychic	Status	–	–	10	Self	–	–
TM48	Round	Normal	Special	60	100	15	Normal	–	–
TM50	Overheat	Fire	Special	140	90	5	Normal	–	–
TM59	Incinerate	Fire	Special	30	100	15	Many Others	–	–
TM61	Will-O-Wisp	Fire	Status	–	75	15	Normal	–	–
TM62	Acrobatics	Flying	Physical	55	100	15	Normal	○	○
TM68	Giga Impact	Normal	Physical	150	90	5	Normal	–	–
TM76	Struggle Bug	Bug	Special	30	100	20	Many Others	–	–
TM84	Poison Jab	Poison	Physical	80	100	20	Normal	–	○
TM87	Swagger	Normal	Status	–	90	15	Normal	–	–
TM89	U-turn	Bug	Physical	70	100	20	Normal	–	○
TM90	Substitute	Normal	Status	–	–	10	Self	–	–
TM93	Wild Charge	Electric	Physical	90	100	15	Normal	–	○
HM02	Fly	Flying	Physical	90	95	15	Normal	○	○

● FOOTPRINT

● MALE/FEMALE HAVE SAME FORM

● HEIGHT: 5'03"
● WEIGHT: 101.4 lbs.
● GENDER: Both ♂♀ exist
● ITEMS:
　• SilverPowder

POKÉMON BLACK VERSION
When volcanic ash darkened the atmosphere, it is said that Volcarona's fire provided a replacement for the sun.

POKÉMON WHITE VERSION
A sea of fire engulfs the surroundings of their battles, since they use their six wings to scatter their ember scales.

EVOLUTION

Larvesta — Lv. 59 → Volcarona

ABILITY
● Flame Body

EGG GROUP
Bug

STATS
HP ●●●
ATTACK ●●●
DEFENSE ●●●
SP. ATTACK ●●●●●
SP. DEFENSE ●●●●
SPEED ●●●●

● MAIN WAYS TO OBTAIN

POKÉMON BLACK VERSION
1　Relic Castle (Lowest Floor—Deepest Part)
2　Level up Larvesta to Lv. 59

POKÉMON WHITE VERSION
1　Relic Castle (Lowest Floor—Deepest Part)
2　Level up Larvesta to Lv. 59

Cobalion

● TYPE Steel Fighting

● FOOTPRINT

● GENDER UNKNOWN

● HEIGHT: 6'11"
● WEIGHT: 551.2 lbs.
● GENDER: Unknown
● ITEMS:
  • None

POKÉMON BLACK VERSION
This legendary Pokémon battled against humans to protect Pokémon. Its personality is calm and composed.

POKÉMON WHITE VERSION
It has a body and heart of steel. Its glare is sufficient to make even an unruly Pokémon obey it.

● LEVEL-UP AND LEARNED MOVES

Lv.	Name	Type	Kind	Pow.	Acc.	PP	Range	Long	DA
1	Quick Attack	Normal	Physical	40	100	30	Normal	–	–
1	Leer	Normal	Status	–	100	30	Many Others	–	○
7	Double Kick	Fighting	Physical	30	100	30	Normal	–	○
13	Metal Claw	Steel	Physical	50	95	35	Normal	–	○
19	Take Down	Normal	Physical	90	85	20	Normal	–	–
25	Helping Hand	Normal	Status	–	–	20	1 Ally	–	–
31	Retaliate	Normal	Physical	70	100	5	Normal	–	–
37	Iron Head	Steel	Physical	80	100	15	Normal	–	○
42	Sacred Sword	Fighting	Physical	90	100	20	Normal	–	–
49	Swords Dance	Normal	Status	–	–	30	Self	–	–
55	Quick Guard	Fighting	Status	–	–	15	Your Side	–	–
61	Work Up	Normal	Status	–	–	30	Self	–	–
67	Metal Burst	Steel	Physical	–	100	10	Varies	–	–
73	Close Combat	Fighting	Physical	120	100	5	Normal	–	○

● MOVES TAUGHT BY PEOPLE

Name	Type	Kind	Pow.	Acc.	PP	Range	Long	DA

● TM & HM MOVES

No.	Name	Type	Kind	Pow.	Acc.	PP	Range	Long	DA
TM01	Hone Claws	Dark	Status	–	–	15	Self	–	–
TM04	Calm Mind	Psychic	Status	–	–	20	Self	–	–
TM05	Roar	Normal	Status	–	100	20	Normal	–	–
TM06	Toxic	Poison	Status	–	90	10	Normal	–	–
TM12	Hidden Power	Normal	Special	–	100	15	Normal	–	–
TM15	Hyper Beam	Normal	Special	150	90	5	Normal	–	–
TM17	Protect	Normal	Status	–	–	10	Self	–	–
TM20	Safeguard	Normal	Status	–	–	25	Your Side	–	–
TM21	Frustration	Normal	Physical	–	100	20	Normal	–	○
TM27	Return	Normal	Physical	–	100	20	Normal	–	○
TM32	Double Team	Normal	Status	–	–	15	Self	–	–
TM33	Reflect	Psychic	Status	–	–	20	Your Side	–	–
TM37	Sandstorm	Rock	Status	–	–	10	Both Sides	–	–
TM40	Aerial Ace	Flying	Physical	60	–	20	Normal	○	○
TM42	Facade	Normal	Physical	70	100	20	Normal	–	○
TM44	Rest	Psychic	Status	–	–	10	Self	–	–
TM48	Round	Normal	Special	60	100	15	Normal	–	–
TM52	Focus Blast	Fighting	Special	120	70	5	Normal	–	○
TM54	False Swipe	Normal	Physical	40	100	40	Normal	–	○
TM67	Retaliate	Normal	Physical	70	100	5	Normal	–	–
TM68	Giga Impact	Normal	Physical	150	90	5	Normal	–	○
TM69	Rock Polish	Rock	Status	–	–	20	Self	–	–
TM71	Stone Edge	Rock	Physical	100	80	5	Normal	–	–
TM72	Volt Switch	Electric	Special	70	100	20	Normal	–	–
TM73	Thunder Wave	Electric	Status	–	100	20	Normal	–	–
TM75	Swords Dance	Normal	Status	–	–	30	Self	–	–
TM77	Psych Up	Normal	Status	–	–	10	Normal	–	–
TM81	X-Scissor	Bug	Physical	80	100	15	Normal	–	○
TM83	Work Up	Normal	Status	–	–	30	Self	–	–
TM84	Poison Jab	Poison	Physical	80	100	20	Normal	–	○
TM87	Swagger	Normal	Status	–	90	15	Normal	–	–
TM90	Substitute	Normal	Status	–	–	10	Self	–	–
TM91	Flash Cannon	Steel	Special	80	100	10	Normal	–	–
TM94	Rock Smash	Fighting	Physical	40	100	15	Normal	–	○
HM01	Cut	Normal	Physical	50	95	30	Normal	–	○
HM04	Strength	Normal	Physical	80	100	15	Normal	–	○

● EVOLUTION

Does not evolve

● ABILITY   ● Justified

● EGG GROUPS   No egg has ever been discovered

STATS
HP ●●●
ATTACK ●●●●
DEFENSE ●●●●●
SP.ATTACK ●●●●
SP.DEFENSE ●●●
SPEED ●●●●●

● MAIN WAYS TO OBTAIN

POKÉMON BLACK VERSION
1 Mistralton Cave (Guidance Chamber)
2 –

POKÉMON WHITE VERSION
1 Mistralton Cave (Guidance Chamber)
2 –

Terrakion

● TYPE Rock Fighting

● FOOTPRINT

● GENDER UNKNOWN

● HEIGHT: 6'03"
● WEIGHT: 573.2 lbs.
● GENDER: Unknown
● ITEMS:
  • None

POKÉMON BLACK VERSION
This Pokémon came to the defense of Pokémon that had lost their homes in a war among humans.

POKÉMON WHITE VERSION
Its charge is strong enough to break through a giant castle wall in one blow. This Pokémon is spoken of in legends.

● LEVEL-UP AND LEARNED MOVES

Lv.	Name	Type	Kind	Pow.	Acc.	PP	Range	Long	DA
1	Quick Attack	Normal	Physical	40	100	30	Normal	–	–
1	Leer	Normal	Status	–	100	30	Many Others	–	○
7	Double Kick	Fighting	Physical	30	100	30	Normal	–	○
13	Smack Down	Rock	Physical	50	100	15	Normal	–	–
19	Take Down	Normal	Physical	90	85	20	Normal	–	–
25	Helping Hand	Normal	Status	–	–	20	1 Ally	–	–
31	Retaliate	Normal	Physical	70	100	5	Normal	–	–
37	Rock Slide	Rock	Physical	75	90	10	Many Others	–	–
42	Sacred Sword	Fighting	Physical	90	100	20	Normal	–	–
49	Swords Dance	Normal	Status	–	–	30	Self	–	–
55	Quick Guard	Fighting	Status	–	–	15	Your Side	–	–
61	Work Up	Normal	Status	–	–	30	Self	–	–
67	Stone Edge	Rock	Physical	100	80	5	Normal	–	–
73	Close Combat	Fighting	Physical	120	100	5	Normal	–	○

● MOVES TAUGHT BY PEOPLE

Name	Type	Kind	Pow.	Acc.	PP	Range	Long	DA

● TM & HM MOVES

No.	Name	Type	Kind	Pow.	Acc.	PP	Range	Long	DA
TM04	Calm Mind	Psychic	Status	–	–	20	Self	–	–
TM05	Roar	Normal	Status	–	100	20	Normal	–	–
TM06	Toxic	Poison	Status	–	90	10	Normal	–	–
TM10	Hidden Power	Normal	Special	–	100	15	Normal	–	–
TM12	Taunt	Dark	Status	–	100	20	Normal	–	–
TM15	Hyper Beam	Normal	Special	150	90	5	Normal	–	–
TM17	Protect	Normal	Status	–	–	10	Self	–	–
TM20	Safeguard	Normal	Status	–	–	25	Your Side	–	–
TM21	Frustration	Normal	Physical	–	100	20	Normal	–	○
TM23	Smack Down	Rock	Physical	50	100	15	Normal	–	–
TM26	Earthquake	Ground	Physical	100	100	10	Adjacent	–	–
TM27	Return	Normal	Physical	–	100	20	Normal	–	○
TM32	Double Team	Normal	Status	–	–	15	Self	–	–
TM33	Reflect	Psychic	Status	–	–	20	Your Side	–	–
TM37	Sandstorm	Rock	Status	–	–	10	Both Sides	–	–
TM39	Rock Tomb	Rock	Physical	50	80	10	Normal	–	–
TM40	Aerial Ace	Flying	Physical	60	–	20	Normal	○	○
TM42	Facade	Normal	Physical	70	100	20	Normal	–	○
TM44	Rest	Psychic	Status	–	–	10	Self	–	–
TM48	Round	Normal	Special	60	100	15	Normal	–	–
TM52	Focus Blast	Fighting	Special	120	70	5	Normal	–	○
TM54	False Swipe	Normal	Physical	40	100	40	Normal	–	○
TM67	Retaliate	Normal	Physical	70	100	5	Normal	–	–
TM68	Giga Impact	Normal	Physical	150	90	5	Normal	–	○
TM69	Rock Polish	Rock	Status	–	–	20	Self	–	–
TM71	Stone Edge	Rock	Physical	100	80	5	Normal	–	–
TM75	Swords Dance	Normal	Status	–	–	30	Self	–	–
TM77	Psych Up	Normal	Status	–	–	10	Normal	–	–
TM78	Bulldoze	Ground	Physical	60	100	20	Adjacent	–	–
TM80	Rock Slide	Rock	Physical	75	90	10	Many Others	–	–
TM81	X-Scissor	Bug	Physical	80	100	15	Normal	–	○
TM83	Work Up	Normal	Status	–	–	30	Self	–	–
TM84	Poison Jab	Poison	Physical	80	100	20	Normal	–	○
TM87	Swagger	Normal	Status	–	90	15	Normal	–	–
TM90	Substitute	Normal	Status	–	–	10	Self	–	–
TM94	Rock Smash	Fighting	Physical	40	100	15	Normal	–	○
HM01	Cut	Normal	Physical	50	95	30	Normal	–	○
HM04	Strength	Normal	Physical	80	100	15	Normal	–	○

● EVOLUTION

Does not evolve

● ABILITY   ● Justified

● EGG GROUPS   No egg has ever been discovered

STATS
HP ●●●
ATTACK ●●●●●
DEFENSE ●●●●●
SP.ATTACK ●●●
SP.DEFENSE ●●●
SPEED ●●●●●

● MAIN WAYS TO OBTAIN

POKÉMON BLACK VERSION
1 Victory Road (Trial Chamber)
2 –

POKÉMON WHITE VERSION
1 Victory Road (Trial Chamber)
2 –

Virizion

● TYPE Grass Fighting

LEVEL-UP AND LEARNED MOVES

Lv.	Name	Type	Kind	Pow.	Acc.	PP	Range	Long	DA
1	Quick Attack	Normal	Physical	40	100	30	Normal	—	○
1	Leer	Normal	Status	—	100	10	Many Others	—	—
7	Double Kick	Fighting	Physical	30	100	30	Normal	—	○
13	Magical Leaf	Grass	Special	60	—	20	Normal	—	—
19	Take Down	Normal	Physical	90	85	20	Normal	—	○
25	Helping Hand	Normal	Status	—	—	20	1 Ally	—	—
31	Retaliate	Normal	Physical	70	100	5	Normal	—	○
37	Giga Drain	Grass	Special	75	100	10	Normal	—	—
42	Sacred Sword	Fighting	Physical	90	100	20	Normal	—	○
49	Swords Dance	Normal	Status	—	—	30	Self	—	—
55	Quick Guard	Fighting	Status	—	—	15	Your Side	—	—
61	Work Up	Normal	Status	—	—	30	Self	—	—
67	Leaf Blade	Grass	Physical	90	100	15	Normal	—	○
73	Close Combat	Fighting	Physical	120	100	5	Normal	—	○

MOVES TAUGHT BY PEOPLE

Name	Type	Kind	Pow.	Acc.	PP	Range	Long	DA

TM & HM MOVES

No.	Name	Type	Kind	Pow.	Acc.	PP	Range	Long	DA
TM04	Calm Mind	Psychic	Status	—	—	20	Self	—	—
TM05	Roar	Normal	Status	—	100	20	Normal	—	—
TM06	Toxic	Poison	Status	—	90	10	Normal	—	—
TM10	Hidden Power	Normal	Special	—	100	15	Normal	—	—
TM11	Sunny Day	Fire	Status	—	—	5	Both Sides	—	—
TM12	Taunt	Dark	Status	—	100	20	Normal	—	—
TM15	Hyper Beam	Normal	Special	150	90	5	Normal	—	—
TM16	Light Screen	Psychic	Status	—	—	30	Your Side	—	—
TM17	Protect	Normal	Status	—	—	10	Self	—	—
TM20	Safeguard	Normal	Status	—	—	25	Your Side	—	—
TM21	Frustration	Normal	Physical	—	100	20	Normal	—	○
TM22	SolarBeam	Grass	Special	120	100	10	Normal	—	—
TM27	Return	Normal	Physical	—	100	20	Normal	—	○
TM32	Double Team	Normal	Status	—	—	15	Self	—	—
TM33	Reflect	Psychic	Status	—	—	20	Your Side	—	—
TM40	Aerial Ace	Flying	Physical	60	—	20	Normal	○	○
TM42	Facade	Normal	Physical	70	100	20	Normal	—	○
TM44	Rest	Psychic	Status	—	—	10	Self	—	—
TM48	Round	Normal	Special	60	100	15	Normal	—	—
TM52	Focus Blast	Fighting	Special	120	70	5	Normal	—	—
TM53	Energy Ball	Grass	Special	80	100	10	Normal	—	—
TM54	False Swipe	Normal	Physical	40	100	40	Normal	—	○
TM67	Retaliate	Normal	Physical	70	100	5	Normal	—	○
TM68	Giga Impact	Normal	Physical	150	90	5	Normal	—	○
TM70	Flash	Normal	Status	—	100	20	Normal	—	—
TM71	Stone Edge	Rock	Physical	100	80	5	Normal	—	—
TM75	Swords Dance	Normal	Status	—	—	30	Self	—	—
TM77	Psych Up	Normal	Status	—	—	10	Normal	—	—
TM81	X-Scissor	Bug	Physical	80	100	15	Normal	—	○
TM83	Work Up	Normal	Status	—	—	30	Self	—	—
TM86	Grass Knot	Grass	Special	—	100	20	Normal	—	—
TM87	Swagger	Normal	Status	—	90	15	Normal	—	—
TM90	Substitute	Normal	Status	—	—	10	Self	—	—
TM94	Rock Smash	Fighting	Physical	40	100	15	Normal	—	○
HM01	Cut	Normal	Physical	50	95	30	Normal	—	○
HM04	Strength	Normal	Physical	80	100	15	Normal	—	○

● FOOTPRINT

● GENDER UNKNOWN

● HEIGHT: 6'07"
● WEIGHT: 440.9 lbs.
● GENDER: Unknown
● ITEMS:
• None

EVOLUTION

Does not evolve

POKÉMON BLACK VERSION
This Pokémon fought humans in order to protect its friends. Legends about it continue to be passed down.

POKÉMON WHITE VERSION
Its head sprouts horns as sharp as blades. Using whirlwind-like movements, it confounds and swiftly cuts opponents.

ABILITY: ● Justified

EGG GROUPS: No egg has ever been discovered

STATS
HP ●●●
ATTACK ●●●●
DEFENSE ●●●●
SP. ATTACK ●●●●
SP. DEFENSE ●●●●●
SPEED ●●●●●

MAIN WAYS TO OBTAIN

POKÉMON BLACK VERSION
1 Pinwheel Forest (Rumination Field)
2 —

POKÉMON WHITE VERSION
1 Pinwheel Forest (Rumination Field)
2 —

Tornadus

● TYPE Flying

LEVEL-UP AND LEARNED MOVES

Lv.	Name	Type	Kind	Pow.	Acc.	PP	Range	Long	DA
1	Uproar	Normal	Special	90	100	10	1 Random	—	—
1	Astonish	Ghost	Physical	30	100	15	Normal	—	○
1	Gust	Flying	Special	40	100	35	Normal	○	—
?	Swagger	Normal	Status	—	90	15	Normal	—	—
13	Bite	Dark	Physical	60	100	25	Normal	—	○
19	Revenge	Fighting	Physical	60	100	10	Normal	—	○
25	Air Cutter	Flying	Special	55	95	25	Many Others	—	—
31	Extrasensory	Psychic	Special	80	100	30	Normal	—	—
37	Agility	Psychic	Status	—	—	30	Self	—	—
43	Air Slash	Flying	Special	75	95	20	Normal	○	—
49	Crunch	Dark	Physical	80	100	15	Normal	—	○
55	Tailwind	Flying	Status	—	—	30	Your Side	—	—
61	Rain Dance	Water	Status	—	—	5	Both Sides	—	—
67	Hurricane	Flying	Special	120	70	10	Normal	○	—
73	Dark Pulse	Dark	Special	80	100	15	Normal	—	○
79	Hammer Arm	Fighting	Physical	100	90	10	Normal	—	○
85	Thrash	Normal	Physical	120	100	10	1 Random	—	○

MOVES TAUGHT BY PEOPLE

Name	Type	Kind	Pow.	Acc.	PP	Range	Long	DA

TM & HM MOVES

No.	Name	Type	Kind	Pow.	Acc.	PP	Range	Long	DA
TM06	Toxic	Poison	Status	—	90	10	Normal	—	—
TM08	Bulk Up	Fighting	Status	—	—	20	Self	—	—
TM10	Hidden Power	Normal	Special	—	100	15	Normal	—	—
TM12	Taunt	Dark	Status	—	100	20	Normal	—	—
TM15	Hyper Beam	Normal	Special	150	90	5	Normal	—	—
TM17	Protect	Normal	Status	—	—	10	Self	—	—
TM18	Rain Dance	Water	Status	—	—	5	Both Sides	—	—
TM21	Frustration	Normal	Physical	—	100	20	Normal	—	○
TM23	Smack Down	Rock	Physical	50	100	15	Normal	—	○
TM27	Return	Normal	Physical	—	100	20	Normal	—	○
TM29	Psychic	Psychic	Special	90	100	10	Normal	—	—
TM31	Brick Break	Fighting	Physical	75	100	15	Normal	—	○
TM32	Double Team	Normal	Status	—	—	15	Self	—	—
TM34	Sludge Wave	Poison	Special	95	100	10	Adjacent	—	—
TM36	Sludge Bomb	Poison	Special	90	100	10	Normal	—	—
TM40	Aerial Ace	Flying	Physical	60	—	20	Normal	○	○
TM41	Torment	Dark	Status	—	100	15	Normal	—	—
TM42	Facade	Normal	Physical	70	100	20	Normal	—	○
TM44	Rest	Psychic	Status	—	—	10	Self	—	—
TM45	Attract	Normal	Status	—	100	15	Normal	—	—
TM46	Thief	Dark	Physical	40	100	10	Normal	—	○
TM48	Round	Normal	Special	60	100	15	Normal	—	—
TM52	Focus Blast	Fighting	Special	120	70	5	Normal	—	—
TM56	Fling	Dark	Physical	—	100	10	Normal	—	○
TM58	Sky Drop	Flying	Physical	60	100	10	Normal	—	○
TM59	Incinerate	Fire	Special	30	100	15	Many Others	—	—
TM62	Acrobatics	Flying	Physical	55	100	15	Normal	—	○
TM63	Embargo	Dark	Status	—	100	15	Normal	—	—
TM66	Payback	Dark	Physical	50	100	10	Normal	—	○
TM68	Giga Impact	Normal	Physical	150	90	5	Normal	—	○
TM86	Grass Knot	Grass	Special	—	100	20	Normal	—	—
TM87	Swagger	Normal	Status	—	90	15	Normal	—	—
TM89	U-turn	Bug	Physical	70	100	20	Normal	—	○
TM90	Substitute	Normal	Status	—	—	10	Self	—	—
TM94	Rock Smash	Fighting	Physical	40	100	15	Normal	—	○
HM02	Fly	Flying	Physical	90	95	15	Normal	○	○
HM04	Strength	Normal	Physical	80	100	15	Normal	—	○

● FOOTPRINT

● MALE FORM

● HEIGHT: 4'11"
● WEIGHT: 138.9 lbs.
● GENDER: Only ♂ exist
● ITEMS:
• None

EVOLUTION

Does not evolve

POKÉMON BLACK VERSION
The lower half of its body is wrapped in a cloud of energy. It zooms through the sky at 200 mph.

POKÉMON WHITE VERSION
Tornadus expels massive energy from its tail, causing severe storms. Its power is great enough to blow houses away.

ABILITY: ● Prankster

EGG GROUPS: No egg has ever been discovered

STATS
HP ●●●
ATTACK ●●●●●
DEFENSE ●●●●
SP. ATTACK ●●●●
SP. DEFENSE ●●●
SPEED ●●●●●

MAIN WAYS TO OBTAIN

POKÉMON BLACK VERSION
1 After the encounter on Route 7, it starts moving through the Unova region
2 —

POKÉMON WHITE VERSION
1
2 —

Thundurus

● TYPE Electric Flying

● FOOTPRINT

● MALE FORM

● HEIGHT: 4'11"
● WEIGHT: 134.5 lbs.
● GENDER: Only ♂ exist
● ITEMS:
  • None

POKÉMON BLACK VERSION
Countless charred remains mar the landscape of places through which Thundurus has passed.

POKÉMON WHITE VERSION
The spikes on its tail discharge immense bolts of lightning. It flies around the Unova region firing off lightning bolts.

● LEVEL-UP AND LEARNED MOVES

Lv.	Name	Type	Kind	Pow.	Acc.	PP	Range	Long	DA
1	Uproar	Normal	Special	90	100	10	1 Random	–	–
1	Astonish	Ghost	Physical	30	100	15	Normal	–	○
1	ThunderShock	Electric	Special	40	100	30	Normal	–	–
7	Swagger	Normal	Status	–	90	15	Normal	–	–
13	Bite	Dark	Physical	60	100	25	Normal	–	○
19	Revenge	Fighting	Physical	60	100	10	Normal	–	○
25	Shock Wave	Electric	Special	60	–	20	Normal	–	–
31	Heal Block	Psychic	Status	–	100	15	Many Others	–	–
37	Agility	Psychic	Status	–	–	30	Self	–	–
43	Discharge	Electric	Special	80	100	15	Adjacent	–	–
49	Crunch	Dark	Physical	80	100	15	Normal	–	○
55	Charge	Electric	Status	–	–	20	Self	–	–
61	Nasty Plot	Dark	Status	–	–	20	Self	–	–
67	Thunder	Electric	Special	120	70	10	Normal	–	–
73	Dark Pulse	Dark	Special	80	100	15	Normal	○	–
79	Hammer Arm	Fighting	Physical	100	90	10	Normal	–	○
85	Thrash	Normal	Physical	120	100	10	1 Random	–	–

● MOVES TAUGHT BY PEOPLE

Name	Type	Kind	Pow.	Acc.	PP	Range	Long	DA

● TM & HM MOVES

No.	Name	Type	Kind	Pow.	Acc.	PP	Range	Long	DA
TM06	Toxic	Poison	Status	–	90	10	Normal	–	–
TM08	Bulk Up	Fighting	Status	–	–	20	Self	–	–
TM10	Hidden Power	Normal	Special	–	100	15	Normal	–	–
TM12	Taunt	Dark	Status	–	100	20	Normal	–	–
TM15	Hyper Beam	Normal	Special	150	90	5	Normal	–	–
TM17	Protect	Normal	Status	–	–	10	Self	–	–
TM18	Rain Dance	Water	Status	–	–	5	Both Sides	–	–
TM21	Frustration	Normal	Physical	–	100	20	Normal	–	○
TM23	Smack Down	Rock	Physical	50	100	15	Normal	–	–
TM24	Thunderbolt	Electric	Special	95	100	15	Normal	–	–
TM25	Thunder	Electric	Special	120	70	10	Normal	–	–
TM27	Return	Normal	Physical	–	100	20	Normal	–	○
TM29	Psychic	Psychic	Special	90	100	10	Normal	–	–
TM31	Brick Break	Fighting	Physical	75	100	15	Normal	–	–
TM32	Double Team	Normal	Status	–	–	15	Self	–	–
TM34	Sludge Wave	Poison	Special	95	100	10	Adjacent	–	–
TM36	Sludge Bomb	Poison	Special	90	100	10	Normal	–	–
TM42	Facade	Normal	Physical	70	100	20	Normal	–	○
TM44	Rest	Psychic	Status	–	–	10	Self	–	–
TM45	Attract	Normal	Status	–	100	15	Normal	–	–
TM46	Thief	Dark	Physical	40	100	10	Normal	–	○
TM48	Round	Normal	Special	60	100	15	Normal	–	–
TM52	Focus Blast	Fighting	Special	120	70	5	Normal	–	–
TM56	Fling	Dark	Physical	–	100	10	Normal	–	–
TM57	Charge Beam	Electric	Special	50	90	10	Normal	–	–
TM58	Sky Drop	Flying	Physical	60	100	10	Normal	○	–
TM59	Incinerate	Fire	Special	30	100	15	Many Others	–	–
TM63	Embargo	Dark	Status	–	100	15	Normal	–	–
TM66	Payback	Dark	Physical	50	100	10	Normal	–	○
TM68	Giga Impact	Normal	Physical	150	90	5	Both Sides	–	–
TM72	Volt Switch	Electric	Special	70	100	20	Normal	–	–
TM73	Thunder Wave	Electric	Status	–	100	20	Normal	–	–
TM86	Grass Knot	Grass	Special	–	100	20	Normal	–	○
TM87	Swagger	Normal	Status	–	90	15	Normal	–	–
TM89	U-turn	Bug	Physical	70	100	20	Normal	–	–
TM90	Substitute	Normal	Status	–	–	10	Self	–	–
TM91	Flash Cannon	Steel	Special	80	100	10	Normal	–	–
TM93	Wild Charge	Electric	Physical	90	100	15	Normal	–	–
TM94	Rock Smash	Fighting	Physical	40	100	15	Normal	–	–
HM02	Fly	Flying	Physical	90	95	15	Normal	○	–
HM04	Strength	Normal	Physical	80	100	15	Normal	–	–

EVOLUTION

Does not evolve

ABILITY ● Prankster

EGG GROUPS No egg has ever been discovered

STATS
HP ●●●
ATTACK ●●●●●
DEFENSE ●●●●
SP. ATTACK ●●●●●
SP. DEFENSE ●●●
SPEED ●●●●●

● MAIN WAYS TO OBTAIN

POKÉMON BLACK VERSION
1 —
2

POKÉMON WHITE VERSION
1 After the encounter on Route 7, it starts moving through the Unova region
2

Reshiram

● TYPE Dragon Fire

● FOOTPRINT

● GENDER UNKNOWN

● HEIGHT: 10'06"
● WEIGHT: 727.5 lbs.
● GENDER: Unknown
● ITEMS:
  • None

POKÉMON BLACK VERSION
This Pokémon appears in legends. It sends flames into the air from its tail, burning up everything around it.

POKÉMON WHITE VERSION
When Reshiram's tail flares, the heat energy moves the atmosphere and changes the world's weather.

● LEVEL-UP AND LEARNED MOVES

Lv.	Name	Type	Kind	Pow.	Acc.	PP	Range	Long	DA
1	Fire Fang	Fire	Physical	65	95	15	Normal	–	○
1	Dragon Rage	Dragon	Special	–	100	10	Normal	–	–
8	Imprison	Psychic	Status	–	–	10	Self	–	–
15	AncientPower	Rock	Special	60	100	5	Normal	–	–
22	Flamethrower	Fire	Special	95	100	15	Normal	–	–
29	DragonBreath	Dragon	Special	60	100	20	Normal	–	–
36	Slash	Normal	Physical	70	100	20	Normal	–	○
43	Extrasensory	Psychic	Special	80	100	30	Normal	–	–
50	Fusion Flare	Fire	Special	100	100	5	Normal	–	–
54	Dragon Pulse	Dragon	Special	90	100	10	Normal	○	–
64	Imprison	Psychic	Status	–	–	10	Self	–	–
71	Crunch	Dark	Physical	80	100	15	Normal	–	○
78	Fire Blast	Fire	Special	120	85	5	Normal	–	–
85	Outrage	Dragon	Physical	120	100	10	1 Random	–	–
92	Hyper Voice	Normal	Special	90	100	10	Many Others	–	–
100	Blue Flare	Fire	Special	130	85	5	Normal	–	–

● MOVES TAUGHT BY PEOPLE

Name	Type	Kind	Pow.	Acc.	PP	Range	Long	DA
Draco Meteor	Dragon	Special	140	90	5	Normal	–	–

● TM & HM MOVES

No.	Name	Type	Kind	Pow.	Acc.	PP	Range	Long	DA
TM01	Hone Claws	Dark	Status	–	–	15	Self	–	–
TM02	Dragon Claw	Dragon	Physical	80	100	15	Normal	–	○
TM06	Toxic	Poison	Status	–	90	10	Normal	–	–
TM10	Hidden Power	Normal	Special	–	100	15	Normal	–	–
TM11	Sunny Day	Fire	Status	–	–	5	Both Sides	–	–
TM15	Hyper Beam	Normal	Special	150	90	5	Normal	–	–
TM16	Light Screen	Psychic	Status	–	–	30	Your Side	–	–
TM17	Protect	Normal	Status	–	–	10	Self	–	–
TM20	Safeguard	Normal	Status	–	–	25	Your Side	–	–
TM21	Frustration	Normal	Physical	–	100	20	Normal	–	○
TM22	SolarBeam	Grass	Special	120	100	10	Normal	–	–
TM27	Return	Normal	Physical	–	100	20	Normal	–	○
TM29	Psychic	Psychic	Special	90	100	10	Normal	–	–
TM30	Shadow Ball	Ghost	Special	80	100	15	Normal	–	–
TM32	Double Team	Normal	Status	–	–	15	Self	–	–
TM33	Reflect	Psychic	Status	–	–	20	Your Side	–	–
TM35	Flamethrower	Fire	Special	95	100	15	Normal	–	–
TM38	Fire Blast	Fire	Special	120	85	5	Normal	–	–
TM39	Rock Tomb	Rock	Physical	50	80	10	Normal	–	–
TM42	Facade	Normal	Physical	70	100	20	Normal	–	○
TM43	Flame Charge	Fire	Physical	50	100	20	Normal	–	–
TM44	Rest	Psychic	Status	–	–	10	Self	–	–
TM48	Round	Normal	Special	60	100	15	Normal	–	–
TM49	Echoed Voice	Normal	Special	40	100	15	Normal	–	–
TM50	Overheat	Fire	Special	140	90	5	Normal	–	–
TM52	Focus Blast	Fighting	Special	120	70	5	Normal	–	–
TM56	Fling	Dark	Physical	–	100	10	Many Others	–	–
TM59	Incinerate	Fire	Special	30	100	15	Many Others	–	–
TM61	Will-O-Wisp	Fire	Status	–	75	15	Normal	–	–
TM65	Shadow Claw	Ghost	Physical	70	100	15	Normal	–	○
TM66	Payback	Dark	Physical	50	100	10	Normal	–	○
TM68	Giga Impact	Normal	Physical	150	90	5	Normal	–	–
TM71	Stone Edge	Rock	Physical	100	80	5	Normal	–	–
TM80	Rock Slide	Rock	Physical	75	90	10	Many Others	–	–
TM82	Dragon Tail	Dragon	Physical	60	90	10	Normal	–	○
TM87	Swagger	Normal	Status	–	90	15	Normal	–	–
TM90	Substitute	Normal	Status	–	–	10	Self	–	–
TM94	Rock Smash	Fighting	Physical	40	100	15	Normal	–	–
HM01	Cut	Normal	Physical	50	95	30	Normal	–	–
HM02	Fly	Flying	Physical	90	95	15	Normal	○	–
HM04	Strength	Normal	Physical	80	100	15	Normal	–	–

EVOLUTION

Does not evolve

ABILITY ● Turboblaze

EGG GROUPS No egg has ever been discovered

STATS
HP ●●●●
ATTACK ●●●●●
DEFENSE ●●●●
SP. ATTACK ●●●●●●
SP. DEFENSE ●●●●●
SPEED ●●●●

● MAIN WAYS TO OBTAIN

POKÉMON BLACK VERSION
1 N's Castle
2

POKÉMON WHITE VERSION
1 —
2

Zekrom

● TYPE | Dragon | Electric

● FOOTPRINT

● GENDER UNKNOWN

● HEIGHT: 9'06"
● WEIGHT: 760.6 lbs.
● GENDER: Unknown
● ITEMS:
• None

POKÉMON BLACK VERSION
Concealing itself in lightning clouds, it flies throughout the Unova region. It creates electricity in its tail.

POKÉMON WHITE VERSION
This Pokémon appears in legends. In its tail, it has a giant generator that creates electricity.

● LEVEL-UP AND LEARNED MOVES

Lv.	Name	Type	Kind	Pow.	Acc.	PP	Range	Long	DA
1	Thunder Fang	Electric	Physical	65	95	15	Normal	—	○
1	Dragon Rage	Dragon	Special	—	100	10	Normal	—	—
8	Imprison	Psychic	Status	—	—	10	Self	—	—
15	AncientPower	Rock	Special	60	100	5	Normal	—	○
22	Thunderbolt	Electric	Special	95	100	15	Normal	—	—
29	DragonBreath	Dragon	Special	60	100	20	Normal	—	○
36	Slash	Normal	Physical	70	100	20	Normal	—	—
43	Zen Headbutt	Psychic	Physical	80	90	15	Normal	—	○
50	Fusion Bolt	Electric	Physical	100	100	5	Normal	—	○
54	Dragon Claw	Dragon	Physical	80	100	15	Normal	—	○
64	Imprison	Psychic	Status	—	—	10	Self	—	—
71	Crunch	Dark	Physical	80	100	15	Normal	—	○
78	Thunder	Electric	Special	120	70	10	Normal	—	—
85	Outrage	Dragon	Physical	120	100	5	1 Random	—	—
92	Hyper Voice	Normal	Special	90	100	10	Many Others	—	—
100	Bolt Strike	Electric	Physical	130	85	5	Normal	—	○

● MOVES TAUGHT BY PEOPLE

Name	Type	Kind	Pow.	Acc.	PP	Range	Long	DA
Draco Meteor	Dragon	Special	140	90	5	Normal	—	—

● TM & HM MOVES

No.	Name	Type	Kind	Pow.	Acc.	PP	Range	Long	DA
TM01	Hone Claws	Dark	Status	—	—	15	Self	—	—
TM02	Dragon Claw	Dragon	Physical	80	100	15	Normal	—	○
TM06	Toxic	Poison	Status	—	90	10	Normal	—	—
TM10	Hidden Power	Normal	Special	—	100	15	Normal	—	—
TM15	Hyper Beam	Normal	Special	150	90	5	Normal	—	—
TM16	Light Screen	Psychic	Status	—	—	30	Your Side	—	—
TM17	Protect	Normal	Status	—	—	10	Self	—	—
TM18	Rain Dance	Water	Status	—	—	5	Both Sides	—	—
TM20	Safeguard	Normal	Status	—	—	25	Your Side	—	—
TM21	Frustration	Normal	Physical	—	100	20	Normal	—	○
TM24	Thunderbolt	Electric	Special	95	100	15	Normal	—	—
TM25	Thunder	Electric	Special	120	70	10	Normal	—	—
TM27	Return	Normal	Physical	—	100	20	Normal	—	○
TM29	Psychic	Psychic	Special	90	100	10	Normal	—	—
TM30	Shadow Ball	Ghost	Special	80	100	15	Normal	—	○
TM32	Double Team	Normal	Status	—	—	15	Self	—	—
TM33	Reflect	Psychic	Status	—	—	20	Your Side	—	—
TM39	Rock Tomb	Rock	Physical	50	80	10	Normal	—	—
TM42	Facade	Normal	Physical	70	100	20	Normal	—	○
TM44	Rest	Psychic	Status	—	—	10	Self	—	—
TM48	Round	Normal	Special	60	100	15	Normal	—	—
TM49	Echoed Voice	Normal	Special	40	100	15	Normal	—	—
TM52	Focus Blast	Fighting	Special	120	70	5	Normal	—	—
TM56	Fling	Dark	Physical	—	100	10	Normal	—	—
TM57	Charge Beam	Electric	Special	50	90	10	Normal	—	○
TM65	Shadow Claw	Ghost	Physical	70	100	15	Normal	—	○
TM66	Payback	Dark	Physical	50	100	10	Normal	—	○
TM68	Giga Impact	Normal	Physical	150	90	5	Normal	—	—
TM70	Flash	Normal	Status	—	100	20	Normal	—	—
TM71	Stone Edge	Rock	Physical	100	80	5	Normal	—	—
TM72	Volt Switch	Electric	Special	70	100	20	Normal	—	—
TM73	Thunder Wave	Electric	Status	—	100	20	Normal	—	—
TM80	Rock Slide	Rock	Physical	75	90	10	Many Others	—	—
TM82	Dragon Tail	Dragon	Physical	60	90	10	Normal	—	○
TM87	Swagger	Normal	Status	—	90	15	Normal	—	—
TM90	Substitute	Normal	Status	—	—	10	Self	—	—
TM91	Flash Cannon	Steel	Special	80	100	10	Normal	—	○
TM93	Wild Charge	Electric	Physical	90	100	15	Normal	—	○
TM94	Rock Smash	Fighting	Physical	40	100	15	Normal	—	○
HM01	Cut	Normal	Physical	50	95	30	Normal	—	○
HM02	Fly	Flying	Physical	90	95	15	Normal	○	○
HM04	Strength	Normal	Physical	80	100	15	Normal	—	○

EVOLUTION

Does not evolve

ABILITY ● Teravolt

EGG GROUPS | No egg has ever been discovered

STATS
HP ●●●●
ATTACK ●●●●●
DEFENSE ●●●●●
SP. ATTACK ●●●●●
SP. DEFENSE ●●●●
SPEED ●●●●

● MAIN WAYS TO OBTAIN

POKÉMON BLACK VERSION
1 —
2 —

POKÉMON WHITE VERSION
1 N's Castle
2 —

Landorus

● TYPE | Ground | Flying

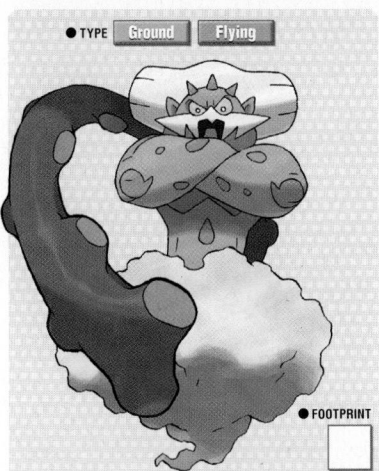

● FOOTPRINT

● MALE FORM

● HEIGHT: 4'11"
● WEIGHT: 149.9 lbs.
● GENDER: Only ♂ exist
● ITEMS:
• None

POKÉMON BLACK VERSION
Lands visited by Landorus grant such bountiful crops that it has been hailed as "The Guardian of the Fields."

POKÉMON WHITE VERSION
The energy that comes pouring from its tail increases the nutrition in the soil, making crops grow to great size.

● LEVEL-UP AND LEARNED MOVES

Lv.	Name	Type	Kind	Pow.	Acc.	PP	Range	Long	DA
1	Block	Normal	Status	—	—	5	Normal	—	—
1	Mud Shot	Ground	Special	55	95	15	Normal	—	—
1	Rock Tomb	Rock	Physical	50	80	10	Normal	—	—
7	Imprison	Psychic	Status	—	—	10	Self	—	—
13	Punishment	Dark	Physical	—	100	5	Normal	—	○
19	Bulldoze	Ground	Physical	60	100	20	Adjacent	—	—
25	Rock Throw	Rock	Physical	50	90	15	Normal	—	—
31	Extrasensory	Psychic	Special	80	100	30	Normal	—	○
37	Swords Dance	Normal	Status	—	—	30	Self	—	—
43	Earth Power	Ground	Special	90	100	10	Normal	—	○
49	Rock Slide	Rock	Physical	75	90	10	Many Others	—	—
55	Earthquake	Ground	Physical	100	100	10	Adjacent	—	—
61	Sandstorm	Rock	Status	—	—	10	Both Sides	—	—
67	Fissure	Ground	Physical	—	30	5	Normal	—	—
73	Stone Edge	Rock	Physical	100	80	5	Normal	—	—
79	Hammer Arm	Fighting	Physical	100	90	10	Normal	—	—
85	Outrage	Dragon	Physical	120	100	10	1 Random	—	—

● MOVES TAUGHT BY PEOPLE

Name	Type	Kind	Pow.	Acc.	PP	Range	Long	DA

● TM & HM MOVES

No.	Name	Type	Kind	Pow.	Acc.	PP	Range	Long	DA
TM04	Calm Mind	Psychic	Status	—	—	20	Self	—	—
TM06	Toxic	Poison	Status	—	90	10	Normal	—	—
TM08	Bulk Up	Fighting	Status	—	—	20	Self	—	—
TM10	Hidden Power	Normal	Special	—	100	15	Normal	—	—
TM15	Hyper Beam	Normal	Special	150	90	5	Normal	—	—
TM17	Protect	Normal	Status	—	—	10	Self	—	—
TM21	Frustration	Normal	Physical	—	100	20	Normal	—	○
TM23	Smack Down	Rock	Physical	50	100	15	Normal	—	—
TM26	Earthquake	Ground	Physical	100	100	10	Adjacent	—	—
TM27	Return	Normal	Physical	—	100	20	Normal	—	○
TM28	Dig	Ground	Physical	80	100	10	Normal	—	—
TM29	Psychic	Psychic	Special	90	100	10	Normal	—	—
TM31	Brick Break	Fighting	Physical	75	100	15	Normal	—	—
TM32	Double Team	Normal	Status	—	—	15	Self	—	—
TM34	Sludge Wave	Poison	Special	95	100	10	Adjacent	—	—
TM36	Sludge Bomb	Poison	Special	90	100	10	Normal	—	—
TM37	Sandstorm	Rock	Status	—	—	10	Both Sides	—	—
TM39	Rock Tomb	Rock	Physical	50	80	10	Normal	—	—
TM42	Facade	Normal	Physical	70	100	20	Normal	—	○
TM44	Rest	Psychic	Status	—	—	10	Self	—	—
TM45	Attract	Normal	Status	—	100	15	Normal	—	—
TM48	Round	Normal	Special	60	100	15	Normal	—	—
TM52	Focus Blast	Fighting	Special	120	70	5	Normal	—	—
TM56	Fling	Dark	Physical	—	100	10	Normal	—	—
TM64	Explosion	Normal	Physical	250	100	5	Adjacent	—	—
TM66	Payback	Dark	Physical	50	100	10	Normal	—	○
TM68	Giga Impact	Normal	Physical	150	90	5	Normal	—	—
TM69	Rock Polish	Rock	Status	—	—	20	Self	—	—
TM71	Stone Edge	Rock	Physical	100	80	5	Normal	—	—
TM75	Swords Dance	Normal	Status	—	—	30	Self	—	—
TM78	Bulldoze	Ground	Physical	60	100	20	Adjacent	—	—
TM80	Rock Slide	Rock	Physical	75	90	10	Many Others	—	—
TM86	Grass Knot	Grass	Special	—	100	20	Normal	—	○
TM87	Swagger	Normal	Status	—	90	15	Normal	—	—
TM89	U-turn	Bug	Physical	70	100	20	Normal	—	○
TM90	Substitute	Normal	Status	—	—	10	Self	—	—
TM94	Rock Smash	Fighting	Physical	40	100	15	Normal	—	○
HM02	Fly	Flying	Physical	90	95	15	Normal	○	○
HM04	Strength	Normal	Physical	80	100	15	Normal	—	○

EVOLUTION

Does not evolve

ABILITY ● Sand Force

EGG GROUPS | No egg has ever been discovered

STATS
HP ●●●
ATTACK ●●●●●
DEFENSE ●●●●
SP. ATTACK ●●●●●
SP. DEFENSE ●●●
SPEED ●●●●

● MAIN WAYS TO OBTAIN

POKÉMON BLACK VERSION
1 Add Tornadus and Thundurus to your party and go to the Abundant Shrine
2 —

POKÉMON WHITE VERSION
1 Add Tornadus and Thundurus to your party and go to the Abundant Shrine
2 —

Kyurem

● TYPE | Dragon | Ice

● FOOTPRINT

● GENDER UNKNOWN

● HEIGHT: 9'10"
● WEIGHT: 716.5 lbs.
● GENDER: Unknown
● ITEMS:
  • None

POKÉMON BLACK VERSION
It generates a powerful, freezing energy inside itself, but its body became frozen when the energy leaked out.

POKÉMON WHITE VERSION
It can produce ultracold air. Its body is frozen.

● LEVEL-UP AND LEARNED MOVES

Lv.	Name	Type	Kind	Pow.	Acc.	PP	Range	Long	DA
1	Icy Wind	Ice	Special	55	95	15	Many Others	—	—
1	Dragon Rage	Dragon	Special	—	100	10	Normal	—	—
8	Imprison	Psychic	Status	—	—	10	Self	—	—
15	AncientPower	Rock	Special	60	100	5	Normal	—	—
22	Ice Beam	Ice	Special	95	100	10	Normal	—	—
29	DragonBreath	Dragon	Special	60	100	20	Normal	—	—
36	Slash	Normal	Physical	70	100	20	Normal	—	○
43	Scary Face	Normal	Status	—	100	10	Normal	—	—
50	Glaciate	Ice	Special	65	95	10	Many Others	—	—
57	Dragon Pulse	Dragon	Special	90	100	10	Normal	○	—
64	Imprison	Psychic	Status	—	—	10	Self	—	—
71	Endeavor	Normal	Physical	—	100	5	Normal	—	○
78	Blizzard	Ice	Special	120	70	5	Many Others	—	—
85	Outrage	Dragon	Physical	120	100	10	1 Random	—	○
92	Hyper Voice	Normal	Special	90	100	10	Many Others	—	—

● MOVES TAUGHT BY PEOPLE

Name	Type	Kind	Pow.	Acc.	PP	Range	Long	DA
Draco Meteor	Dragon	Special	140	90	5	Normal	—	—

● TM & HM MOVES

No.	Name	Type	Kind	Pow.	Acc.	PP	Range	Long	DA
TM01	Hone Claws	Dark	Status	—	—	15	Self	—	—
TM02	Dragon Claw	Dragon	Physical	80	100	15	Normal	—	○
TM06	Toxic	Poison	Status	—	90	10	Normal	—	—
TM07	Hail	Ice	Status	—	—	10	Both Sides	—	—
TM10	Hidden Power	Normal	Special	—	100	15	Normal	—	—
TM11	Sunny Day	Fire	Status	—	—	5	Both Sides	—	—
TM13	Ice Beam	Ice	Special	95	100	10	Normal	—	—
TM14	Blizzard	Ice	Special	120	70	5	Normal	—	—
TM15	Hyper Beam	Normal	Special	150	90	5	Normal	—	—
TM16	Light Screen	Psychic	Status	—	—	30	Your Side	—	—
TM17	Protect	Normal	Status	—	—	10	Self	—	—
TM18	Rain Dance	Water	Status	—	—	5	Both Sides	—	—
TM20	Safeguard	Normal	Status	—	—	25	Your Side	—	—
TM21	Frustration	Normal	Physical	—	100	20	Normal	—	○
TM27	Return	Normal	Physical	—	100	20	Normal	—	○
TM29	Psychic	Psychic	Special	90	100	10	Normal	—	—
TM30	Shadow Ball	Ghost	Special	80	100	15	Normal	—	—
TM32	Double Team	Normal	Status	—	—	15	Self	—	—
TM33	Reflect	Psychic	Status	—	—	20	Your Side	—	—
TM39	Rock Tomb	Rock	Physical	50	80	10	Normal	—	—
TM42	Facade	Normal	Physical	70	100	20	Normal	—	○
TM44	Rest	Psychic	Status	—	—	10	Self	—	—
TM48	Round	Normal	Special	60	100	15	Normal	—	—
TM49	Echoed Voice	Normal	Special	40	100	15	Normal	—	—
TM52	Focus Blast	Fighting	Special	120	70	5	Normal	—	—
TM56	Fling	Dark	Physical	—	100	10	Normal	—	—
TM65	Shadow Claw	Ghost	Physical	70	100	15	Normal	—	○
TM66	Payback	Dark	Physical	50	100	10	Normal	—	○
TM68	Giga Impact	Normal	Physical	150	90	5	Normal	—	○
TM71	Stone Edge	Rock	Physical	100	80	5	Normal	—	—
TM80	Rock Slide	Rock	Physical	75	90	10	Many Others	—	○
TM82	Dragon Tail	Dragon	Physical	60	90	10	Normal	—	○
TM87	Swagger	Normal	Status	—	90	15	Normal	—	—
TM90	Substitute	Normal	Status	—	—	10	Self	—	—
TM91	Flash Cannon	Steel	Special	80	100	10	Normal	—	—
TM94	Rock Smash	Fighting	Physical	40	100	15	Normal	—	○
HM01	Cut	Normal	Physical	50	95	30	Normal	—	○
HM02	Fly	Flying	Physical	90	95	15	Normal	○	○
HM04	Strength	Normal	Physical	80	100	15	Normal	—	○

EVOLUTION

Does not evolve

ABILITY ● Pressure

EGG GROUPS No egg has ever been discovered

STATS
HP ●●●●●
ATTACK ●●●●●●
DEFENSE ●●●●●
SP. ATTACK ●●●●●●●
SP. DEFENSE ●●●●●
SPEED ●●●●●

● MAIN WAYS TO OBTAIN

POKÉMON BLACK VERSION
1 Giant Chasm (Cave's Deepest Part)
2 —

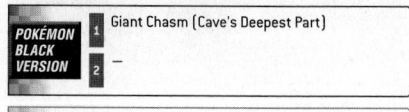

POKÉMON WHITE VERSION
1 Giant Chasm (Cave's Deepest Part)
2 —

UNOVA POKÉDEX ◎ 152 | KYUREM

 Victini

● TYPE Psychic Fire

● FOOTPRINT

● GENDER UNKNOWN

● HEIGHT: 1'04"
● WEIGHT: 8.8 lbs.
● GENDER: Unknown
● ITEMS:
  • None

POKÉMON BLACK VERSION
This Pokémon brings victory. It is said that Trainers with Victini always win, regardless of the type of encounter.

POKÉMON WHITE VERSION
It creates an unlimited supply of energy inside its body, which it shares with those who touch it.

● LEVEL-UP AND LEARNED MOVES

Lv.	Name	Type	Kind	Pow.	Acc.	PP	Range	Long	DA
1	Searing Shot	Fire	Special	100	100	5	Adjacent	—	—
1	Focus Energy	Normal	Status	—	—	30	Self	—	—
1	Confusion	Psychic	Special	50	100	25	Normal	—	—
1	Incinerate	Fire	Special	30	100	15	Many Others	—	—
1	Quick Attack	Normal	Physical	40	100	30	Normal	—	○
9	Endure	Normal	Status	—	—	10	Self	—	—
17	Headbutt	Normal	Physical	70	100	15	Normal	—	○
25	Flame Charge	Fire	Physical	50	100	20	Normal	—	○
33	Reversal	Fighting	Physical	—	100	15	Normal	—	○
41	Flame Burst	Fire	Special	70	100	15	Normal	—	—
49	Zen Headbutt	Psychic	Physical	80	90	15	Normal	—	○
57	Inferno	Fire	Special	100	50	5	Normal	—	—
65	Double-Edge	Normal	Physical	120	100	15	Normal	—	○
73	Flare Blitz	Fire	Physical	120	100	15	Normal	—	○
81	Final Gambit	Fighting	Special	—	100	5	Normal	—	—
89	Stored Power	Psychic	Special	20	100	10	Normal	—	—
97	Overheat	Fire	Special	140	90	5	Normal	—	—

● MOVES TAUGHT BY PEOPLE

Name	Type	Kind	Pow.	Acc.	PP	Range	Long	DA

● TM & HM MOVES

No.	Name	Type	Kind	Pow.	Acc.	PP	Range	Long	DA
TM03	Psyshock	Psychic	Special	80	100	10	Normal	—	—
TM06	Toxic	Poison	Status	—	90	10	Normal	—	—
TM10	Hidden Power	Normal	Special	—	100	15	Normal	—	—
TM11	Sunny Day	Fire	Status	—	—	5	Both Sides	—	—
TM15	Hyper Beam	Normal	Special	150	90	5	Normal	—	—
TM16	Light Screen	Psychic	Status	—	—	30	Your Side	—	—
TM17	Protect	Normal	Status	—	—	10	Self	—	—
TM19	Telekinesis	Psychic	Status	—	—	15	Normal	—	—
TM20	Safeguard	Normal	Status	—	—	25	Your Side	—	—
TM21	Frustration	Normal	Physical	—	100	20	Normal	—	○
TM22	SolarBeam	Grass	Special	120	100	10	Normal	—	—
TM24	Thunderbolt	Electric	Special	95	100	15	Normal	—	—
TM25	Thunder	Electric	Special	120	70	10	Normal	—	—
TM27	Return	Normal	Physical	—	100	20	Normal	—	○
TM29	Psychic	Psychic	Special	90	100	10	Normal	—	—
TM30	Shadow Ball	Ghost	Special	80	100	15	Normal	—	—
TM31	Brick Break	Fighting	Physical	75	100	15	Normal	—	○
TM32	Double Team	Normal	Status	—	—	15	Self	—	—
TM35	Flamethrower	Fire	Special	95	100	15	Normal	—	—
TM38	Fire Blast	Fire	Special	120	85	5	Normal	—	—
TM42	Facade	Normal	Physical	70	100	20	Normal	—	○
TM43	Flame Charge	Fire	Physical	50	100	20	Normal	—	○
TM44	Rest	Psychic	Status	—	—	10	Self	—	—
TM48	Round	Normal	Special	60	100	15	Normal	—	—
TM50	Overheat	Fire	Special	140	90	5	Normal	—	—
TM52	Focus Blast	Fighting	Special	120	70	5	Normal	—	—
TM53	Energy Ball	Grass	Special	80	100	10	Normal	—	—
TM56	Fling	Dark	Physical	—	100	10	Normal	—	—
TM57	Charge Beam	Electric	Special	50	90	10	Normal	—	—
TM59	Incinerate	Fire	Special	30	100	15	Many Others	—	—
TM61	Will-O-Wisp	Fire	Status	—	75	15	Normal	—	—
TM63	Embargo	Dark	Status	—	100	15	Normal	—	—
TM68	Giga Impact	Normal	Physical	150	90	5	Normal	—	○
TM70	Flash	Normal	Status	—	100	20	Normal	—	—
TM73	Thunder Wave	Electric	Status	—	100	20	Normal	—	—
TM77	Psych Up	Normal	Status	—	—	10	Normal	—	—
TM83	Work Up	Normal	Status	—	—	30	Self	—	—
TM86	Grass Knot	Grass	Special	—	100	20	Normal	—	○
TM87	Swagger	Normal	Status	—	90	15	Normal	—	—
TM89	U-turn	Bug	Physical	70	100	20	Normal	—	○
TM90	Substitute	Normal	Status	—	—	10	Self	—	—
TM92	Trick Room	Psychic	Status	—	—	5	Both Sides	—	—
TM93	Wild Charge	Electric	Physical	90	100	15	Normal	—	○
TM94	Rock Smash	Fighting	Physical	40	100	15	Normal	—	○

EVOLUTION

Does not evolve

ABILITY ● Victory Star

EGG GROUPS No egg has ever been discovered

STATS
HP ●●●●○
ATTACK ●●●●○
DEFENSE ●●●●○
SP. ATTACK ●●●●○
SP. DEFENSE ●●●●○
SPEED ●●●●○

● MAIN WAYS TO OBTAIN

POKÉMON BLACK VERSION
| 1 | Cannot be obtained through regular gameplay ● |
| 2 | — |

POKÉMON WHITE VERSION
| 1 | Cannot be obtained through regular gameplay ● |
| 2 | — |

● Victini can be obtained during special distribution periods. Check www.pokemonblackwhite.com to find out if any Pokémon are currently being distributed.

Shiny Pokémon and the Mysterious Pokérus

The world of Pokémon will always have its secrets and mysteries. Among those many mysteries are Pokémon color variations and the microscopic yet beneficial virus, Pokérus, that affects Pokémon development. Keep reading to learn more about these unusual features of Pokémon biology.

Shiny Pokémon — Rarely seen Pokémon with unusual coloration

Shiny Pokémon are so rare that not everyone believes they even exist. These Pokémon have the same stats as any other Pokémon, but their coloration is distinctly different. You'll know you're facing a Shiny Pokémon if you hear a special chime and see stars when the Pokémon appears. Meeting one is pure luck, so if you catch one, treasure it!

Look for the star
A Shiny Pokémon has a star on its "SUMMARY" page.

Congratulations! Your Shelmet evolved into Accelgor!

• Normal Accelgor

Evolution doesn't affect its status
Don't be afraid to evolve a Shiny Pokémon. It stays Shiny even after it evolves.

The Mysterious Pokérus — A strange virus that makes your Pokémon stronger

Pokérus is a beneficial virus that can infect other Pokémon. You can't see it, but the Pokémon Center receptionist will tell you if your Pokémon have it when you bring them in for healing. With Pokérus, a Pokémon's stats increase at a faster rate, making it easier to train. After a few days, Pokérus is no longer contagious and goes away, but its effects remain. If you keep that Pokémon in your party, the Pokérus can be spread to teammates, as well. If you store Pokérus in a PC Box, it won't be spread to other Pokémon, but it won't disappear, either.

Oh... It looks like your Pokémon may be infected with the Pokérus.

Pokérus accelerates stat growth
This is your chance to train your Pokémon and make them strong.

Pokérus leaves after one to four days
When the Pokérus is gone, a smiley face indicates that your Pokémon had it. If you see this mark, you can't spread the Pokérus to teammates anymore.

Unova Pokédex Completion Guide

Complete the Unova Pokédex

Your next adventure—
Completing the Unova Pokédex

After your adventure in the Unova region ends, your next goal is to complete the Unova Pokédex. This is an epic adventure to register the 150 kinds of Pokémon unique to the Unova region in the Pokédex. Completing it gives you a great sense of accomplishment.

Complete the Unova region Pokédex by catching 150 kinds of Pokémon

The requirement for completing the Unova Pokédex in *Pokémon Black* and *Pokémon White* is to register all of the Pokémon. This means catching all Pokémon with Pokédex numbers from 001 to 150 or trading for them with friends and family.

The goal:
Caught number is 150

Pokémon not needed to complete the Unova Pokédex

More than 150 kinds of Pokémon live in the Unova region, but you only need Unova Pokédex numbers 001 to 150 to complete the Pokédex. Landorus, Kyurem, and Victini are not included.

Victini

Landorus

Kyurem

Have Professor Juniper rate your Pokédex's degree of completion

Professor Juniper supports you as you complete the Unova Pokédex. The professor will tell you how complete your Pokédex is. If you register every Pokémon, not including Victini, Landorus, and Kyurem, your Unova Pokédex will be complete.

That is an excellent Pokédex!
Just a little more and it will be full!

Requirements for having Professor Juniper rate your Pokédex's degree of completion

1 The number of seen Pokémon in the Unova Pokédex must be over 150.

2 When you've met the requirement above, she will evaluate the number of caught Pokémon.

The Game Director gives you a certificate for completing your Pokédex

Once you've completed the Unova Pokédex, talk to the Game Director on the 22nd Floor of the GAME FREAK building in Castelia City. He will give you a certificate to recognize your hard work. After that, the award certificate will be placed in your bedroom in Nuvema Town.

Castelia City's GAME FREAK

I will send this award certificate to your house!

Your room in Nuvema Town

It's an award for completing the Unova Pokédex!

● Requirements for getting a certificate from the Game Director

Catch one of every Pokémon in the Unova Pokédex from 001 to 150.

Both *Pokémon Black* and *Pokémon White* Versions are needed to complete the Unova Pokédex

You need to Link Trade between *Pokémon Black* and *Pokémon White* to complete the Unova Pokédex. You have to work together with friends and family and

trade Pokémon for Pokémon you can only get one of, such as the three starter Pokémon or Pokémon that only appear in one version of the game.

If you can't get Zorua and Zoroark, work together with a friend

If you put the distributed Celebi in your party, you can meet Zorua, and if you put the distributed Shiny Raikou, Entei, or Suicune in your party, you can meet Zoroark. You need these two Pokémon to complete the Unova Pokédex. If you don't have the distributed Pokémon, cooperate with your friends and Link Trade to register these Pokémon (p. 114).

1

Techniques for Catching Wild Pokémon

Master these techniques to increase your capture rate

The simplest way to fill out your Pokédex is by catching wild Pokémon with Poké Balls. Master the following techniques to always get the Pokémon you're after.

A wild Sewaddle appeared!

Techniques for Catching **1** ### Push the Pokémon's HP into the red

You could just fling your Poké Ball at a wild Pokémon, but there's a good chance the Pokémon will pop right back out. You won't catch it if it's still full of energy, so use attacks to lower its HP. Once it's weakened, you have a much better chance of sealing the deal.

Lower its HP until the bar is red

When the Pokémon has just a few HP left, your odds of a successful catch are higher.

Techniques for Catching **2** ### Inflict status conditions on wild Pokémon

Use Pokémon moves to inflict status conditions—a target with the Poison or Paralysis condition is easier to catch. That's not all it takes, of course. If you inflict a status condition and lower the Pokémon's HP, you'll maximize your chances of making the catch.

● **Status conditions that aid in capture**

Sleep — Helps a Lot

The target cannot attack (●). Wears off on its own after several turns.

● Some moves that cause Sleep

Sing, Hypnosis

Frozen — Helps a Lot

The target cannot attack. When it tries to use a move, it will sometimes wear off on its own.

● Some moves that cause Frozen status

Powder Snow, Ice Punch

The wild Alomomola is fast asleep.

Paralysis

Lowers Speed, and each turn there's a 25% chance that the target can't attack. Status does not wear off on its own.

● Some moves that cause Paralysis

Thunder Wave, Lick

Poison

Target's HP decreases each turn. Does not wear off on its own.

● Some moves that cause Poison status

PoisonPowder, Poison Gas

Burned

Lowers Attack, and HP decreases each turn. Does not wear off on its own.

● Some moves that cause Burned status

Will-O-Wisp, Scald

● The moves Sleep Talk and Snore are exceptions.

Use the Right Poké Ball at the Right Time

A total of 14 varieties of Poké Balls appear in *Pokémon Black* and *Pokémon White Versions*. Each of these Poké Balls performs differently depending on the particular situation it's used in or type of Pokémon it's used on. Master these differences and get the most out of your Poké Balls.

● Poké Balls you can obtain in the Unova region

Poké Ball

The most basic Poké Ball for catching Pokémon.

● Requirements to purchase

Available from the start

Great Ball

It has a better catch rate than the Poké Ball.

● Requirements to purchase

Get 1 Gym Badge

Ultra Ball

A Poké Ball with a better catch rate than the Great Ball.

● Requirements to purchase

Get 5 Gym Badges

Master Ball

It is the ultimate ball that will surely catch any Pokémon.

● How to get one

Opelucid City (receive from Professor Juniper)

Premier Ball

It has the same performance as a Poké Ball. Received as a bonus.

● How you get them

Buy 10 Poké Balls at once

Heal Ball

A Poké Ball that heals the caught Pokémon's HP and status.

● Poké Marts where they're sold

Striaton City, Nacrene City, etc.

Net Ball

A Poké Ball with a high success rate against Bug- and Water-type Pokémon.

● Poké Marts where they're sold

Nacrene City, Castelia City, etc.

Nest Ball

A Poké Ball that is most effective on weak Pokémon.

● Poké Marts where they're sold

Castelia City, Driftveil City, etc.

Quick Ball

A Poké Ball with a good capture rate when thrown right at the start of battle.

● Poké Marts where they're sold

Opelucid City, Pokémon League, etc.

Timer Ball

A Poké Ball that does better after more turns have elapsed in battle.

● Poké Marts where they're sold

Opelucid City, Pokémon League, etc.

Repeat Ball

A Poké Ball that excels at catching Pokémon you've caught before.

● Poké Mart where they're sold

Pokémon League

Dive Ball

A Poké Ball that does better on Pokémon that live in the water.

● Poké Mart where they're sold

Undella Town

Dusk Ball

A Poké Ball that does better at night and in caves.

● Poké Marts where they're sold

Driftveil City, Opelucid City, etc.

Luxury Ball

A Poké Ball that endears you to caught Pokémon.

● Poké Marts where they're sold

Pokémon League, Undella Town

 **Try the Quick Ball**

Throw the Quick Ball immediately after the battle starts to get the most out of it. No matter how difficult it might be to catch this Pokémon, try throwing a Quick Ball first.

**Unova Pokédex
Completion Tips**

2 Use Pokémon Moves and Abilities

Lure out the Pokémon you're after and keep it from fleeing

Certain Pokémon moves and Abilities come in handy for finding and catching wild Pokémon. Use these moves to increase your chances of catching the Pokémon you're after.

Examples of useful moves for catching Pokémon

Sweet Scent

Use this wherever wild Pokémon appear, such as tall grass or a cave, and wild Pokémon will certainly appear.

● Pokémon who can use this move

Maractus, Foongus, and others

False Swipe

Always leaves at least 1 HP remaining, even if the damage should knock the Pokémon out. Useful for lowering HP as far as it will go without fainting.

● Pokémon who can use this move

Escavalier, Bisharp, and others

Mean Look

The wild Pokémon can't escape. Use this on Pokémon that flee immediately.

● Pokémon who can use this move

Watchog, Cofagrigus, and others

Examples of useful Abilities for catching Pokémon

Illuminate

If the lead Pokémon has this Ability, the wild Pokémon encounter rate rises.

A wild Tynamo appeared!

● Pokémon with this Ability

Watchog

Sticky Hold

An Ability that excels at attracting Pokémon to your fishing pole.

Landed a Pokémon!

● Pokémon with this Ability

Trubbish, Accelgor

Cute Charm

An Ability that's good at attracting Pokémon of the opposite gender.

Pidove   ♂Lv.18

Minccino's Cute Charm

Minccino   ♀Lv.24
4/63

The wild Pidove fell in love!

● Pokémon with this Ability

Minccino, Cinccino

Three great Pokémon for catching wild Pokémon

Some Pokémon have moves that are practically custom-made for catching wild Pokémon. Use these Pokémon from *Pokémon Black* and *Pokémon White* to increase your chances of catching a wild Pokémon.

Case 1 — Watchog's Moves

Patrat, which evolves into Watchog, learns Hypnosis at Lv. 18. It evolves into Watchog at Lv. 20. It learns Super Fang at Lv. 22 and Mean Look at Lv. 36. When trying to catch a Pokémon that flees immediately, such as Tornadus or Thundurus, use Mean Look to keep it from running. Then use Super Fang to keep halving its HP.

● How to Obtain

Catch Patrat on Route 1.
Raise it to Lv. 20.

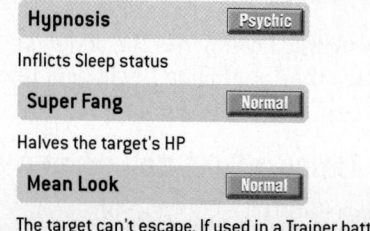

Hypnosis	Psychic

Inflicts Sleep status

Super Fang	Normal

Halves the target's HP

Mean Look	Normal

The target can't escape. If used in a Trainer battle, it prevents opposing Pokémon from switching out.

Baton Pass	Normal

Switches out with an ally Pokémon and passes along any stat changes.

Case 2 — Leavanny's Moves

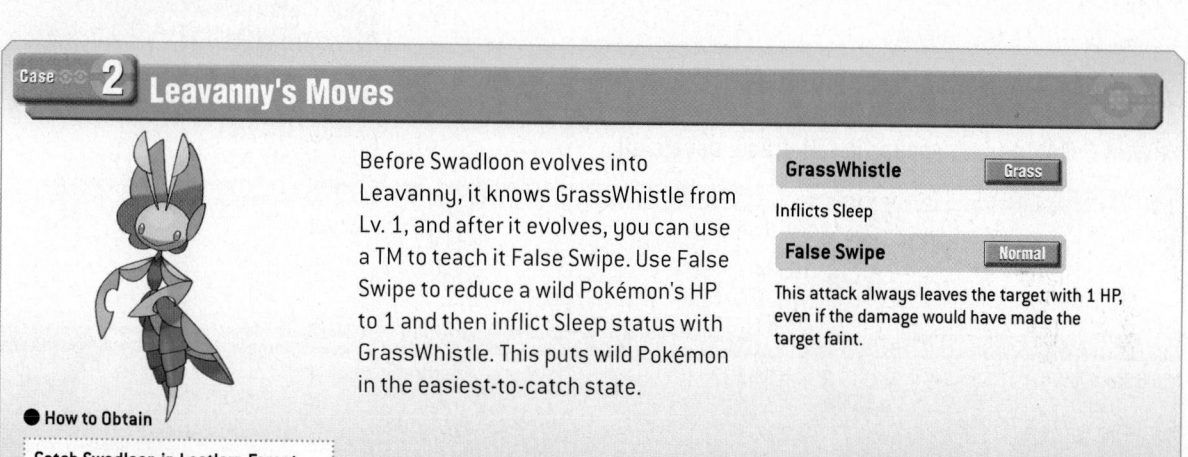

Before Swadloon evolves into Leavanny, it knows GrassWhistle from Lv. 1, and after it evolves, you can use a TM to teach it False Swipe. Use False Swipe to reduce a wild Pokémon's HP to 1 and then inflict Sleep status with GrassWhistle. This puts wild Pokémon in the easiest-to-catch state.

● How to Obtain

Catch Swadloon in Lostlorn Forest and level it up with high friendship.

GrassWhistle	Grass

Inflicts Sleep

False Swipe	Normal

This attack always leaves the target with 1 HP, even if the damage would have made the target faint.

Case 3 — Bisharp's Moves

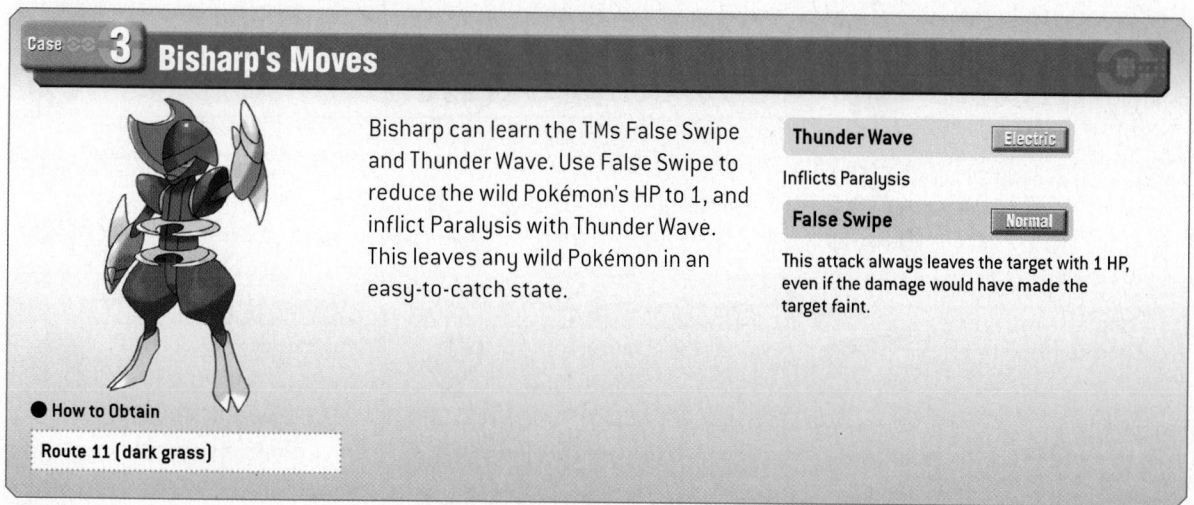

Bisharp can learn the TMs False Swipe and Thunder Wave. Use False Swipe to reduce the wild Pokémon's HP to 1, and inflict Paralysis with Thunder Wave. This leaves any wild Pokémon in an easy-to-catch state.

● How to Obtain

Route 11 (dark grass)

Thunder Wave	Electric

Inflicts Paralysis

False Swipe	Normal

This attack always leaves the target with 1 HP, even if the damage would have made the target faint.

UNOVA POKÉDEX COMPLETION GUIDE

USE POKÉMON MOVES AND ABILITIES

Unova Pokédex Completion Tips

3 Catch Pokémon That Appear in the Wild

Search all over the Unova region for wild Pokémon

Catching wild Pokémon is the simplest way to increase the Caught number in your Unova Pokédex and fill its pages. Some Pokémon that appear in the wild are listed here.

Throw a Poké Ball when you meet a Pokémon

Knowing where and when a Pokémon appears is important when you want to catch a Pokémon you haven't caught yet. Use these tables to track down even the wiliest of wild Pokémon. Once you've caught the Pokémon you were after, check the box by its name.

A wild Beheeyem appeared!

● **Wild Pokémon that appear in tall grass, caves, etc.**

● See p. 103 for Pokémon that appear in rustling grass.

☐ Unova Pokédex No. 010 **Patrat**	☐ Unova Pokédex No. 011 **Watchog**	☐ Unova Pokédex No. 012 **Lillipup**
Route 1 	Route 7 	Route 1 

☐ Unova Pokédex No. 013 **Herdier**	☐ Unova Pokédex No. 015 **Purrloin**	☐ Unova Pokédex No. 016 **Liepard**
Cold Storage Area 	Route 2 	Route 5 

☐ Unova Pokédex No. 023 **Munna**	☐ Unova Pokédex No. 025 **Pidove**	☐ Unova Pokédex No. 026 **Tranquill**
Dreamyard	Route 3 	Lostlorn Forest 

☐ Unova Pokédex No. 028 **Blitzle**	☐ Unova Pokédex No. 029 **Zebstrika**	☐ Unova Pokédex No. 030 **Roggenrola**
Route 3 	Route 7 	Wellspring Cave 1F 

☐ Unova Pokédex No. 031 **Boldore**	☐ Unova Pokédex No. 033 **Woobat**	☐ Unova Pokédex No. 038 **Timburr**
Twist Mountain Upper Level 	Wellspring Cave 1F 	Pinwheel Forest Entrance 

☐ Unova Pokédex No. 039 **Gurdurr**	☐ Unova Pokédex No. 041 **Tympole**	☐ Unova Pokédex No. 042 **Palpitoad**
Twist Mountain Upper Level 	Pinwheel Forest Entrance	Icirrus City (not in winter) 

☐ Unova Pokédex No. 044 **Throh**	☐ Unova Pokédex No. 045 **Sawk**	☐ Unova Pokédex No. 046 **Sewaddle**
Pinwheel Forest Entrance (*Pokémon White Version*) 	Pinwheel Forest Entrance (*Pokémon Black Version*) 	Pinwheel Forest

Unova Pokédex No. 047 **Swadloon**	Unova Pokédex No. 049 **Venipede**	Unova Pokédex No. 050 **Whirlipede**
Lostlorn Forest 	Pinwheel Forest 	Pinwheel Forest (dark grass) 
Unova Pokédex No. 052 **Cottonee**	Unova Pokédex No. 054 **Petilil**	Unova Pokédex No. 057 **Sandile**
Pinwheel Forest (*Pokémon Black Version*) 	Pinwheel Forest (*Pokémon White Version*) 	Route 4 
Unova Pokédex No. 058 **Krokorok**	Unova Pokédex No. 060 **Darumaka**	Unova Pokédex No. 062 **Maractus**
Relic Castle B2F 	Route 4 	Desert Resort Entrance 
Unova Pokédex No. 063 **Dwebble**	Unova Pokédex No. 064 **Crustle**	Unova Pokédex No. 065 **Scraggy**
Desert Resort Entrance 	Route 18 (dark grass) 	Route 4 
Unova Pokédex No. 067 **Sigilyph**	Unova Pokédex No. 068 **Yamask**	Unova Pokédex No. 069 **Cofagrigus**
Desert Resort Back 	Relic Castle 1F 	Relic Castle B2F 
Unova Pokédex No. 074 **Trubbish**	Unova Pokédex No. 075 **Garbodor**	Unova Pokédex No. 078 **Minccino**
Route 16 	Route 9 	Route 16 
Unova Pokédex No. 080 **Gothita**	Unova Pokédex No. 081 **Gothorita**	Unova Pokédex No. 083 **Solosis**
Route 16 (*Pokémon Black Version*) 	Route 9 (*Pokémon Black Version*) 	Route 16 (*Pokémon White Version*)
Unova Pokédex No. 084 **Duosion**	Unova Pokédex No. 088 **Vanillite**	Unova Pokédex No. 089 **Vanillish**
Route 9 (*Pokémon White Version*)	Cold Storage Area 	Dragonspiral Tower entrance (dark grass/winter only) 
Unova Pokédex No. 091 **Deerling**	Unova Pokédex No. 092 **Sawsbuck**	Unova Pokédex No. 094 **Karrablast**
Route 6 	Dragonspiral Tower 1F outside (dark grass) 	Route 6 
Unova Pokédex No. 096 **Foongus**	Unova Pokédex No. 097 **Amoonguss**	Unova Pokédex No. 101 **Joltik**
Route 6	Route 10 (dark grass) 	Chargestone Cave 1F 
Unova Pokédex No. 103 **Ferroseed**	Unova Pokédex No. 105 **Klink**	Unova Pokédex No. 108 **Tynamo**
Chargestone Cave 1F 	Chargestone Cave 1F 	Chargestone Cave B2F 
Unova Pokédex No. 111 **Elgyem**	Unova Pokédex No. 112 **Beheeyem**	Unova Pokédex No. 113 **Litwick**
Celestial Tower 3F 	Route 14 	Celestial Tower 2F 
Unova Pokédex No. 116 **Axew**	Unova Pokédex No. 117 **Fraxure**	Unova Pokédex No. 119 **Cubchoo**
Mistralton Cave 1F 	Victory Road (outside) 	Twist Mountain Upper Level

UNOVA POKÉDEX COMPLETION GUIDE · CATCH POKÉMON THAT APPEAR IN THE WILD

Unova Pokédex No. 120 **Beartic**	Unova Pokédex No. 121 **Cryogonal**	Unova Pokédex No. 122 **Shelmet**
Dragonspiral Tower 1F outside (dark grass/winter only) 	Twist Mountain Upper Level 	Icirrus City (not in winter) 

Unova Pokédex No. 124 **Stunfisk**	Unova Pokédex No. 125 **Mienfoo**	Unova Pokédex No. 126 **Mienshao**
Icirrus City (not in winter) 	Dragonspiral Tower entrance 	Route 14 (dark grass) 

Unova Pokédex No. 127 **Druddigon**	Unova Pokédex No. 128 **Golett**	Unova Pokédex No. 130 **Pawniard**
Dragonspiral Tower entrance (not in winter) 	Dragonspiral Tower 1F 	Route 9 

Unova Pokédex No. 131 **Bisharp**	Unova Pokédex No. 132 **Bouffalant**	Unova Pokédex No. 133 **Rufflet**
Route 11 (dark grass) 	Route 10 	Route 10 (*Pokémon White Version*) 

Unova Pokédex No. 134 **Braviary**	Unova Pokédex No. 135 **Vullaby**	Unova Pokédex No. 136 **Mandibuzz**
Route 11 (dark grass) (*Pokémon White Version*) 	Route 10 (*Pokémon Black Version*) 	Route 11 (dark grass) (*Pokémon Black Version*) 

Unova Pokédex No. 137 **Heatmor**	Unova Pokédex No. 138 **Durant**	Unova Pokédex No. 139 **Deino**
Victory Road (outside) 	Victory Road 1F 	Victory Road 1F 

Attract wild Electric-type Pokémon

Some Pokémon Abilities make it easier to encounter wild Pokémon of a certain type. Two Pokémon in the Unova region—Emolga and Stunfisk—have the Ability Static. If they are at the head of your party, this Ability makes it easier to encounter Electric-type Pokémon. Have them help you catch wild Electric-type Pokémon like Blitzle and Joltik.

● Pokémon with Static

Emolga
Electric | Flying
ABILITY
● Static

Stunfisk
Ground | Electric
ABILITIES
● Static
● Limber

Watch out for Abilities that keep wild Pokémon away

Two Pokémon in the Unova region have the Ability Stench: Trubbish and its evolution Garbodor. If a Pokémon with this Ability is at the head of your party, Stench makes it harder to encounter any wild Pokémon. Make sure you don't have one of these two at the head of your party when you're trying to catch Pokémon!

● Pokémon with Stench

Trubbish
Poison
ABILITIES
● Stench
● Sticky Hold

Garbodor
Poison
ABILITIES
● Stench
● Weak Armor

Catch Pokémon While Surfing

Use the HM Surf to find wild Pokémon

Plenty of Pokémon live in the water, and you'll encounter them while using Surf to move over the water's surface. You won't see any of these Pokémon on land. When you've caught all the Pokémon that appear on land, it's time to catch the Pokémon that live in water.

Catch Pokémon on the water

Three kinds of Pokémon appear on the water surface (not including Pokémon that appear in rippling water). Basculin is one of them, and Basculin (Red-Striped Form) is easier to catch in *Pokémon Black*, and Basculin (Blue-Striped Form) is easier to catch in *Pokémon White*. Both can be caught in either version, but your chances of encountering the other form is lower. You need to catch just one of them to register it in your Pokédex.

A wild Stunfisk appeared!

● Pokémon that appear on the water surface

Unova Pokédex No. 056 Basculin (Red-Striped Form)	Unova Pokédex No. 056 Basculin (Blue-Striped Form)	Unova Pokédex No. 098 Frillish
Route 1 (*Pokémon Black Version*)	Route 1 (*Pokémon White Version*)	Route 17

Unova Pokédex No. 124 Stunfisk
Icirrus City

Use the best kind of Poké Ball for the job

Of course, throwing high-performance Ultra Balls is an effective way to catch Pokémon on the water. But two types of Poké Balls make it even easier to catch Pokémon living in the water, so give the Net Ball and the Dive Ball a try! You can even save money by using the right Poké Ball for the right Pokémon.

● High-performance Poké Balls

Net Ball

Jellicent

Trainer used the Net Ball.

A Poké Ball with a high success rate against Bug- and Water-type Pokémon.

Dive Ball

Basculin

Trainer used the Dive Ball.

This Poké Ball does better on Pokémon that live in the water.

Catch Specially Appearing Wild Pokémon

Don't miss your chance to catch an uncommon Pokémon

Some Pokémon in the Unova region appear in four special places: rustling grass, dust clouds, flying Pokémon's shadows, and rippling water.

Pokémon special appearances

Watch out for the four types of special appearances: rustling grass, dust clouds, flying Pokémon's shadows, and rippling water. The wild Pokémon that appear are all hard-to-find Pokémon that can only be caught in these places. If you see one of these special opportunities, make it your first priority to check it out, even if you're in the middle of your adventure.

A wild Panpour appeared!

● Special Pokémon appearances

Rustling Grass

This occurs in the light-green tall grass, not in the dark grass. Step on the rustling grass and a Pokémon will appear.

Dust Cloud

Occurs inside caves. Step on the dust cloud and a Pokémon will appear, or you will get an item.

Flying Pokémon Shadows

You may see these shadows on the Driftveil Drawbridge and Marvelous Bridge. Step on a shadow and a Pokémon will appear, or you will get an item.

Ripples in Water

Occurs on the water's surface. Surf over it, or cast into that spot, and a Pokémon will appear.

A tip for catching the Pokémon that appear in special places

If you encounter a wild Pokémon while heading for the special appearance, the special appearance disappears. To prevent this, use Repel and immediately head for the grass, shadow, cloud, or ripples.

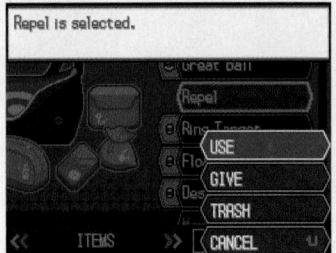

Repel is selected.

● How to meet the Pokémon

1 Go straight to the special location.

2 Avoid encounters with other Pokémon.

3 Don't go into buildings.

4 Don't leave the area.

● Specially Appearing Pokémon

Unova Pokédex No. 014 Stoutland
Cold Storage Area
(rustling grass)

Unova Pokédex No. 017 Pansage
Pinwheel Forest (rustling grass)

Unova Pokédex No. 019 Pansear
Pinwheel Forest
(rustling grass)

Unova Pokédex No. 021 Panpour
Pinwheel Forest
(rustling grass)

Unova Pokédex No. 024 Musharna
Dreamyard (rustling grass)

Unova Pokédex No. 027 Unfezant
Lostlorn Forest (rustling grass)

Unova Pokédex No. 035 Drilbur
Wellspring Cave 1F
(dust cloud)

Unova Pokédex No. 036 Excadrill
Victory Road 1F (dust cloud)

Unova Pokédex No. 037 Audino
Route 1 (rustling grass) ●

Unova Pokédex No. 043 Seismitoad
Icirrus City (rippling water)

Unova Pokédex No. 044 Throh
Pinwheel Forest Entrance
(rustling grass)
(*Pokémon Black Version*)

Unova Pokédex No. 045 Sawk
Pinwheel Forest Entrance
(rustling grass)
(*Pokémon White Version*)

Unova Pokédex No. 048 Leavanny
Lostlorn Forest (rustling grass)

Unova Pokédex No. 053 Whimsicott
Pinwheel Forest (rustling grass)
(*Pokémon Black Version*)

Unova Pokédex No. 055 Lilligant
Pinwheel Forest (rustling grass)
(*Pokémon White Version*)

Unova Pokédex No. 056 Basculin (Red-Striped Form)
Route 1 (rippling water)
(*Pokémon White Version*)

Unova Pokédex No. 056 Basculin (Blue-Striped Form)
Route 1 (rippling water)
(*Pokémon Black Version*)

Unova Pokédex No. 079 Cinccino
Route 16 (rustling grass)

Unova Pokédex No. 082 Gothitelle
Route 9 (rustling grass)
(*Pokémon Black Version*)

Unova Pokédex No. 085 Reuniclus
Route 9 (rustling grass)
(*Pokémon White Version*)

Unova Pokédex No. 086 Ducklett
Driftveil Drawbridge
(Pokémon shadows)

Unova Pokédex No. 087 Swanna
Marvelous Bridge
(Pokémon shadows)

Unova Pokédex No. 093 Emolga
Route 6 (rustling grass)

Unova Pokédex No. 099 Jellicent
Route 17
(rippling water)

Unova Pokédex No. 100 Alomomola
Route 17 (rippling water)

● Audino appears in rustling grass all over the Unova region.

 Items found in dust clouds and Pokémon shadows

You can sometimes find items in two out of the four special appearances—dust clouds and flying Pokémon shadows. Gems and Wings are precious items that can only be found by this method.

● Items found in caves

Items	Rarity
Bug Gem	△
Dark Gem	△
Dragon Gem	△
Electric Gem	△
Everstone	△
Fighting Gem	△
Fire Gem	△
Flying Gem	△
Ghost Gem	△
Grass Gem	△
Ground Gem	△
Ice Gem	△
Normal Gem	△
Poison Gem	△

Items	Rarity
Psychic Gem	△
Rock Gem	△
Steel Gem	△
Water Gem	△
Dawn Stone	▲
Dusk Stone	▲
Fire Stone	▲
Leaf Stone	▲
Moon Stone	▲
Oval Stone	▲
Shiny Stone	▲
Sun Stone	▲
Thunderstone	▲
Water Stone	▲

● Items found on bridges

Items	Rarity
Clever Wing	○
Genius Wing	○
Health Wing	○
Muscle Wing	○
Resist Wing	○
Swift Wing	○
Pretty Wing	△

● Key
○ Appears often
△ Appears rarely
▲ Appears very rarely

Unova Pokédex Completion Tips

6

Obtain Pokémon through Evolution

Battling is the key to evolving certain species of Pokémon

Many Pokémon don't appear in the wild. If you want them, you'll have to level up Pokémon until they evolve. Make sure to use the Pokémon you want to level up in battle frequently.

Some Pokémon evolve when they reach a certain level

Leveling up Pokémon by having them battle is difficult. Use items like the Lucky Egg, which gives you 1.5 times the normal amount of Experience Points, or Exp. Share, which gives half of the battle's Experience Points to a Pokémon, even if it doesn't enter the battle. Also, you can raise Pokémon by leaving ones that haven't evolved yet at the Pokémon Day Care on Route 3.

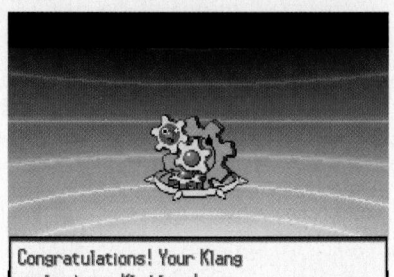

Congratulations! Your Klang evolved into Klinklang!

● Pokémon that evolve by leveling up

Unova Pokédex No. 002 Servine Level up Snivy to Lv. 17 	**Unova Pokédex No. 003 Serperior** Level up Servine to Lv. 36 	**Unova Pokédex No. 005 Pignite** Level up Tepig to Lv. 17 
Unova Pokédex No. 006 Emboar Level up Pignite to Lv. 36 	**Unova Pokédex No. 008 Dewott** Level up Oshawott to Lv. 17 	**Unova Pokédex No. 009 Samurott** Level up Dewott to Lv. 36 
Unova Pokédex No. 011 Watchog Level up Patrat to Lv. 20 	**Unova Pokédex No. 013 Herdier** Level up Lillipup to Lv. 16 	**Unova Pokédex No. 014 Stoutland** Level up Herdier to Lv. 32 
Unova Pokédex No. 016 Liepard Level up Purrloin to Lv. 20 	**Unova Pokédex No. 026 Tranquill** Level up Pidove to Lv. 21 	**Unova Pokédex No. 027 Unfezant** Level up Tranquill to Lv. 32 
Unova Pokédex No. 029 Zebstrika Level up Blitzle to Lv. 27 	**Unova Pokédex No. 031 Boldore** Level up Roggenrola to Lv. 25 	**Unova Pokédex No. 036 Excadrill** Level up Drilbur to Lv. 31 
Unova Pokédex No. 039 Gurdurr Level up Timburr to Lv. 25 	**Unova Pokédex No. 042 Palpitoad** Level up Tympole to Lv. 25 	**Unova Pokédex No. 043 Seismitoad** Level up Palpitoad to Lv. 36 
Unova Pokédex No. 047 Swadloon Level up Sewaddle to Lv. 20 	**Unova Pokédex No. 050 Whirlipede** Level up Venipede to Lv. 22 	**Unova Pokédex No. 051 Scolipede** Level up Whirlipede to Lv. 30 

UNOVA POKÉDEX COMPLETION GUIDE　OBTAIN POKÉMON THROUGH EVOLUTION

Unova Pokédex No. 058 **Krokorok**	Unova Pokédex No. 059 **Krookodile**	Unova Pokédex No. 061 **Darmanitan**
Level up Sandile to Lv. 29 	Level up Krokorok to Lv. 40 	Level up Darumaka to Lv. 35 
Unova Pokédex No. 064 **Crustle**	Unova Pokédex No. 066 **Scrafty**	Unova Pokédex No. 069 **Cofagrigus**
Level up Dwebble to Lv. 34 	Level up Scraggy to Lv. 39 	Level up Yamask to Lv. 34 
Unova Pokédex No. 071 **Carracosta**	Unova Pokédex No. 073 **Archeops**	Unova Pokédex No. 075 **Garbodor**
Level up Tirtouga to Lv. 37 	Level up Archen to Lv. 37 	Level up Trubbish to Lv. 36 
Unova Pokédex No. 081 **Gothorita**	Unova Pokédex No. 082 **Gothitelle**	Unova Pokédex No. 084 **Duosion**
Level up Gothita to Lv. 32 	Level up Gothorita to Lv. 41 	Level up Solosis to Lv. 32
Unova Pokédex No. 085 **Reuniclus**	Unova Pokédex No. 087 **Swanna**	Unova Pokédex No. 089 **Vanillish**
Level up Duosion to Lv. 41 	Level up Ducklett to Lv. 35 	Level up Vanillite to Lv. 35 
Unova Pokédex No. 090 **Vanilluxe**	Unova Pokédex No. 092 **Sawsbuck**	Unova Pokédex No. 097 **Amoonguss**
Level up Vanillish to Lv. 47 	Level up Deerling to Lv. 34 	Level up Foongus to Lv. 39 
Unova Pokédex No. 099 **Jellicent**	Unova Pokédex No. 102 **Galvantula**	Unova Pokédex No. 104 **Ferrothorn**
Level up Frillish to Lv. 40 	Level up Joltik to Lv. 36 	Level up Ferroseed to Lv. 40 
Unova Pokédex No. 106 **Klang**	Unova Pokédex No. 107 **Klinklang**	Unova Pokédex No. 109 **Eelektrik**
Level up Klink to Lv. 38 	Level up Klang to Lv. 49 	Level up Tynamo to Lv. 39 
Unova Pokédex No. 112 **Beheeyem**	Unova Pokédex No. 114 **Lampent**	Unova Pokédex No. 117 **Fraxure**
Level up Elgyem to Lv. 42 	Level up Litwick to Lv. 41 	Level up Axew to Lv. 38 
Unova Pokédex No. 118 **Haxorus**	Unova Pokédex No. 120 **Beartic**	Unova Pokédex No. 126 **Mienshao**
Level up Fraxure to Lv. 48 	Level up Cubchoo to Lv. 37 	Level up Mienfoo to Lv. 50 
Unova Pokédex No. 129 **Golurk**	Unova Pokédex No. 131 **Bisharp**	Unova Pokédex No. 134 **Braviary**
Level up Golett to Lv. 43 	Level up Pawniard to Lv. 52 	Level up Rufflet to Lv. 54 
Unova Pokédex No. 136 **Mandibuzz**	Unova Pokédex No. 140 **Zweilous**	Unova Pokédex No. 141 **Hydreigon**
Level up Vullaby to Lv. 54 	Level up Deino to Lv. 50 	Level up Zweilous to Lv. 64 
Unova Pokédex No. 143 **Volcarona**		
Level up Larvesta to Lv. 59 		

Evolve Pokémon by Using Stones

Some Pokémon evolve using the power of special stones

Some Pokémon evolve from the power hidden in special stones. Collect the stones you need to evolve Pokémon, then use those stones when the time is right for those Pokémon to evolve.

 Stones trigger an instant Evolution

Eight types of stones appear in *Pokémon Black* and *Pokémon White*. You should receive several of each stone by playing through the game up before entering the Hall of Fame. When you get a stone, use it on a Pokémon you want to evolve. But be careful—after evolving, some of these Pokémon can no longer learn moves by leveling up.

● Pokémon that evolve using stones

Unova Pokédex No. 018 **Simisage**  Use a Leaf Stone on Pansage	Unova Pokédex No. 020 **Simisear**  Use a Fire Stone on Pansear	Unova Pokédex No. 022 **Simipour**  Use a Water Stone on Panpour
Unova Pokédex No. 024 **Musharna**  Use a Moon Stone on Munna	Unova Pokédex No. 053 **Whimsicott**  Use a Sun Stone on Cottonee	Unova Pokédex No. 055 **Lilligant**  Use a Sun Stone on Petilil
Unova Pokédex No. 079 **Cinccino**  Use a Shiny Stone on Minccino	Unova Pokédex No. 110 **Eelektross**  Use a Thunderstone on Eelektrik	Unova Pokédex No. 115 **Chandelure**  Use a Dusk Stone on Lampent

● Main ways to get stones

 Leaf Stone
Answer "Pansage" to the man in Castelia City

 Fire Stone
Answer "Pansear" to the man in Castelia City

 Water Stone
Answer "Panpour" to the man in Castelia City

 Thunderstone
Get one in Chargestone Cave B1F

 Moon Stone
Get from Lenora in Pinwheel Forest

 Sun Stone
Get from the boy in the house in Nimbasa City

 Shiny Stone
Get from the girl in the house on Route 6

 Dusk Stone
Get from the man on Route 10

Unova Pokédex Completion Tips

8

Evolve Pokémon through Friendship

Some Pokémon evolve through the power of friendship

Pokémon and their Trainers have a bond of trust, which is called friendship. Some Pokémon evolve when they are leveled up with high enough friendship.

 Make your Pokémon happy

If you make your Pokémon happy, it grows to like you. In *Pokémon Black* and *Pokémon White*, you can use ten main methods to make your Pokémon happy, each of which makes your bond with your Pokémon stronger. For starters, have a Pokémon hold the Soothe Bell from the old lady in the house in Nimbasa City. If you use one of the other nine methods while it is holding the bell, your friendship value goes up more easily.

● **Pokémon obtained through friendship evolution**

☐ Unova Pokédex No. 034 **Swoobat**

Level up Woobat with high friendship

☐ Unova Pokédex No. 048 **Leavanny**

Level up Swadloon with high friendship

● **Main methods for raising a Pokémon's friendship**

 Have your Pokémon hold a Soothe Bell

When a Pokémon is holding the Soothe Bell, its friendship will rise more easily.

Put the Pokémon on your team and walk around

When you go on an adventure with a Pokémon in your party, its friendship will grow.

Level up

Leveling up Pokémon by using them in battle raises their friendship.

Battle with strong Trainers like Gym Leaders

Using Pokémon in big battles, such as the ones with Gym Leaders, raises their friendship.

Participate in the Pokémon Musical

Participating in the Pokémon Musical in Nimbasa City raises the participant's friendship.

Use TMs

Use TMs on a Pokémon to teach it new moves and increase its friendship.

Use stat-raising items

You can raise a Pokémon's friendship by giving it an item that raises its basic stats, such as Protein.

Use battle items

Using items such as X Attack in battle raises the friendship of the Pokémon you use it on.

Use Berries on your Pokémon

Use Berries on your Pokémon, such as the Pomeg Berry or Kelpsy Berry, and its friendship will go up.

Use Sweet Hearts on your Pokémon

Using the Sweet Hearts you get from Infrared Connection Feeling Checks on your Pokémon is also effective (p. 138).

UNOVA POKÉDEX COMPLETION GUIDE

◎ EVOLVE POKÉMON THROUGH FRIENDSHIP

107

Obtain Pokémon by Restoring Fossils

Early Pokémon

You receive a Pokémon Fossil during your adventure. You can revive Fossils like this one into living, breathing Pokémon.

The Fossil you get is one of a pair

You can obtain either the Cover Fossil or the Plume Fossil in the Relic Castle. You can only get one in both *Pokémon Black* and *Pokémon White*. Before obtaining it, check with your friends and family in advance and ask them which Fossil you should get. After you get the Fossil, you can trade to help each other complete the Unova Pokédex.

How reviving Fossils works

Restoring a Pokémon Fossil to its original form by reviving it is easy. Once you've obtained the Fossil in the Relic Castle, all you need to do is go to the Nacrene Museum in Nacrene City. Give the Fossil to the receptionist and she will restore it to a Pokémon.

● Reviving Pokémon from Fossils

1 In the Relic Castle, get the Fossil from the Backpacker

On the first floor of the Relic Castle, a Backpacker asks you if you will take this heavy Fossil off her.

2 Go to the Nacrene Museum

After you get the Fossil from the Backpacker, talk to the receptionist in the Nacrene Museum.

3 Have the Pokémon restored at the museum

She will revive it immediately. If there is space in your party, you can receive the revived Pokémon.

● Pokémon restored from Fossils

Unova Pokédex No. 070 **Tirtouga**	Unova Pokédex No. 072 **Archen**
Get the Cover Fossil in the Relic Castle and have it restored at the Nacrene Museum. 	Get the Plume Fossil in the Relic Castle and have it restored at the Nacrene Museum. 

Get Certain Pokémon during Story Events

Acquire special Pokémon at key points in your journey

Some Pokémon are only encountered during the course of the game, such as the starter Pokémon that Professor Juniper gives you at the beginning of your adventure or the Pokémon the girl at the Dreamyard gives you. They are very hard to obtain otherwise, so make sure to get them when you have a chance.

Many of these Pokémon can't be obtained in other ways

The Pokémon you get during the course of the story are all hard to find, but there are some exceptions. Pansage, Pansear, and Panpour appear in the rustling grass. You can also obtain Volcarona by evolving the Larvesta that hatches from the Egg you pick up on Route 18. Cooperate with your friends and family to trade the starter Pokémon and Reshiram and Zekrom.

Say, do you want this Panpour of mine?

● Pokémon you acquire during the course of the story

Unova Pokédex No. 001 Snivy
Get from Professor Juniper at the start of the adventure

Unova Pokédex No. 004 Tepig
Get from Professor Juniper at the start of the adventure

Unova Pokédex No. 007 Oshawott
Get from Professor Juniper at the start of the adventure

Unova Pokédex No. 017 Pansage
Get from the girl in the Dreamyard (when your starter is Tepig)

Unova Pokédex No. 019 Pansear
Get from the girl in the Dreamyard (when your starter is Oshawott)

Unova Pokédex No. 021 Panpour
Get from the girl in the Dreamyard (when your starter is Snivy)

Unova Pokédex No. 061 Darmanitan
At the Back of the Desert Resort, use the RageCandyBar on the Pokémon statue

Unova Pokédex No. 142 Larvesta
Hatch the Egg from Route 18

Unova Pokédex No. 143 Volcarona
Catch it in the deepest room on the lowest floor of Relic Castle

Unova Pokédex No. 149 Reshiram
Catch it in N's Castle (*Pokémon Black Version*)

Unova Pokédex No. 150 Zekrom
Catch it in N's Castle (*Pokémon White Version*)

Unova Pokédex No. 151 Landorus
Put both Tornadus and Thundurus in your party, go to the Abundant Shrine, and catch it ●

Unova Pokédex No. 152 Kyurem
Catch it in the deepest cave in Giant Chasm

● You must catch Tornadus or Thundurus in your game and then trade for the other one to make Landorus appear.

 ### Take Tornadus and Thundurus to get Landorus

Landorus is in the Abundant Shrine to the west of Route 14. Both Tornadus and Thundurus must be in your party for it to appear.

11 Link Trade for Pokémon

Link up with friends to trade for Pokémon you need

Link Trading for Pokémon is an important way to fill up the pages of your Pokédex. If you work with your friends and family and Link Trade to get Pokémon you haven't obtained or can't obtain, you can register them in your Unova Pokédex. Give it a try!

Choose from a selection with Negotiation Trade

In Link Trades using wireless communications or Nintendo Wi-Fi Connection, you can now use Negotiation Trade. Each person starts by putting up three candidates for trade. Then, after discussion, each person selects and trades one Pokémon.

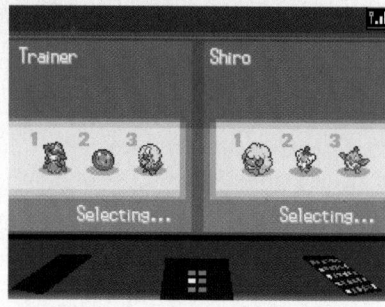

Communication methods for Link Trading Pokémon

Link Trade Pokémon with friends and family in *Pokémon Black* and *Pokémon White Versions* by using one of three methods: infrared trading, wireless trading, or online trading. Learn how they work so you can choose the optimal method.

● Three types of communication methods for Link Trading Pokémon

Infrared	Wireless	Nintendo Wi-Fi Connection
The C-Gear on the Touch Screen	**Pokémon Center's Union Room**	**Pokémon Center's Wi-Fi Club**
Use the C-Gear on the Touch Screen to Link Trade over an Infrared Connection. It's the easiest way to trade—all you have to do is touch IR on the C-Gear and select "Trade" (p. 137).	Wireless trading is useful when you want to Link Trade with someone nearby. You can talk to your friends who have gathered in the Union Room on the Pokémon Center's second floor and Link Trade with them (p. 149).	If Link Trading with friends who are far away, use Nintendo Wi-Fi Connection. Go to the Wi-Fi Club on the second floor of the Pokémon Center. Your friend's Friend Code must be registered already (p. 155).

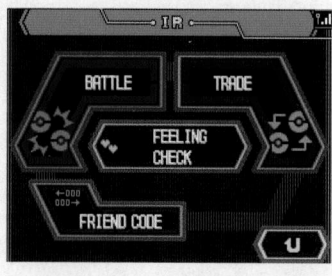
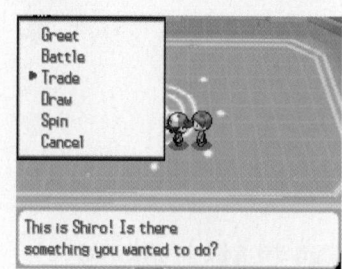
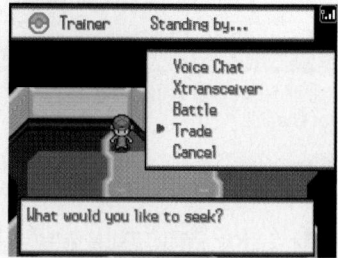

● Pokémon that only appear in *Pokémon Black Version*

Unova Pokédex No. 052 Cottonee
Pinwheel Forest

Unova Pokédex No. 053 Whimsicott
Pinwheel Forest (rustling grass)

Unova Pokédex No. 080 Gothita
Route 16

Unova Pokédex No. 081 Gothorita
Route 9

Unova Pokédex No. 082 Gothitelle
Route 9 (rustling grass)

Unova Pokédex No. 135 Vullaby
Route 10

Unova Pokédex No. 136 Mandibuzz
Route 11 (dark grass)

Unova Pokédex No. 147 Tornadus
After you encounter it on Route 7, you can catch it as it roams around the Unova region

Unova Pokédex No. 149 Reshiram
N's Castle

● Pokémon that only appear in *Pokémon White Version*

Unova Pokédex No. 054 Petilil
Pinwheel Forest

Unova Pokédex No. 055 Lilligant
Pinwheel Forest (rustling grass)

Unova Pokédex No. 083 Solosis
Route 16

Unova Pokédex No. 084 Duosion
Route 9

Unova Pokédex No. 085 Reuniclus
Route 9 (rustling grass)

Unova Pokédex No. 133 Rufflet
Route 10

Unova Pokédex No. 134 Braviary
Route 11 (dark grass)

Unova Pokédex No. 148 Thundurus
After you encounter it on Route 7, you can catch it as it roams around the Unova region

Unova Pokédex No. 150 Zekrom
N's Castle

● The starter Pokémon you get at the beginning of your adventure

Unova Pokédex No. 001 Snivy
Get from Professor Juniper at the start of the adventure

Unova Pokédex No. 004 Tepig
Get from Professor Juniper at the start of the adventure

Unova Pokédex No. 007 Oshawott
Get from Professor Juniper at the start of the adventure

● Pokémon that can be restored from a Fossil you chose

Unova Pokédex No. 070 Tirtouga
Get the Cover Fossil in the Relic Castle and have it restored at the Nacrene Museum

Unova Pokédex No. 072 Archen
Get the Plume Fossil in the Relic Castle and have it restored at the Nacrene Museum

● Pokémon that evolve when traded

Unova Pokédex No. 032 Gigalith
Link Trade Boldore

Unova Pokédex No. 040 Conkeldurr
Link Trade Gurdurr

Unova Pokédex No. 095 Escavalier
Link Trade Karrablast and Shelmet

Unova Pokédex No. 123 Accelgor
Link Trade Shelmet and Karrablast

● Pokémon that you can only get by trading with people in towns

Unova Pokédex No. 052 Cottonee
Get it by trading a Petilil in the house in Nacrene City (*Pokémon White Version*)

Unova Pokédex No. 054 Petilil
Get it by trading a Cottonee in the house in Nacrene City (*Pokémon Black Version*)

12 Catch Cobalion, Terrakion, and Virizion!

Obtain Legendary Pokémon in the Unova region

Cobalion, Terrakion, and Virizion are three Legendary Pokémon that live in the Unova region. You can capture all of them before or after the end of the main story. Compared with other Pokémon, they pop out of Poké Balls more easily and are more difficult to catch.

Encounter Cobalion and you can catch the other two

Cobalion, Terrakion, and Virizion can't be caught in just any order. First, you must encounter Cobalion to remove the seals blocking the way to Terrakion and Virizion. Then you can catch the others. Terrakion and Virizion can be caught in either order.

● Where to find Cobalion, Terrakion, and Virizion

Unova Pokédex No. 144 🔘 *Cobalion*

It lives in Mistralton Cave's Guidance Chamber

Head west from Driftveil City. Use Surf on Route 6 and enter Mistralton Cave. Climb to Mistralton Cave's third floor. It's hiding deep in the third floor.

Kawbraa!

Cobalion Lv. 42

| Steel | Fighting |

ABILITY ● Justified

Unova Pokédex No. 145 🔘 *Terrakion*

It lives in Victory Road's Trial Chamber

Use Fly to go to the Pokémon League and go to the south to enter Victory Road. You'll arrive on the seventh floor, so you need to take the stairs down to the sixth. It's hiding deep in the sixth floor.

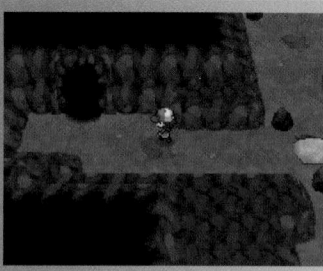

Guroooooohhh!

Terrakion Lv. 42

| Rock | Fighting |

ABILITY ● Justified

Unova Pokédex No. 146 🔘 *Virizion*

It lives in Pinwheel Forest's Rumination Field

Continue west from Nacrene City to Pinwheel Forest. Head north on the paved road and pass through the gap in the fence to the east side. Go east through the tall grass and then north, and it will be hiding there.

Aaapraaa!

Virizion Lv. 42

| Grass | Fighting |

ABILITY ● Justified

13

Catch Tornadus or Thundurus

Get the Pokémon that roam the Unova region

Tornadus appears in *Pokémon Black Version*, and Thundurus appears in *Pokémon White Version*, but they have some common features. Both of them fly all around the Unova region and don't stay in one spot. They have a tendency to flee at the start of a battle. They might be the biggest challenge in your quest to complete the Unova Pokédex.

Learn the behavior of the roaming Pokémon and try to capture them

In order to make Tornadus or Thundurus appear, you need to go to the gate to Route 10 after beating the Opelucid City Gym. Immediately head for Route 7 after you hear about the storm happening there. You will encounter one of them during the storm.

Tornadus appears in a raging windstorm

Whew, what a storm!

Thundurus appears in a violent thunderstorm

Whew, what a storm!

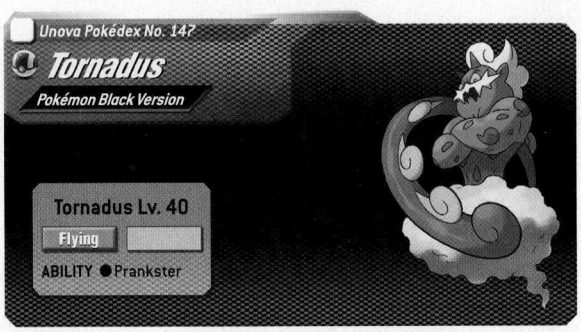

Unova Pokédex No. 147

Tornadus
Pokémon Black Version

Tornadus Lv. 40

Flying

ABILITY ● Prankster

Unova Pokédex No. 148

Thundurus
Pokémon White Version

Thundurus Lv. 40

Electric　Flying

ABILITY ● Prankster

● What you should know about Tornadus and Thundurus

1 They appear in the Unova region's south in the morning, its north in the evening, and in the area around Route 7 at night.

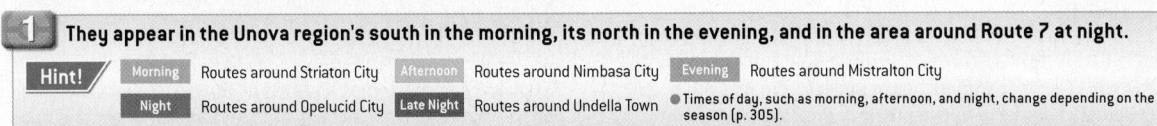

Hint!	Morning	Routes around Striaton City	Afternoon	Routes around Nimbasa City	Evening	Routes around Mistralton City
	Night	Routes around Opelucid City	Late Night	Routes around Undella Town		● Times of day, such as morning, afternoon, and night, change depending on the season (p. 305).

2 Their current position can be checked on the electric bulletin board in the gates. (Sometimes they also disappear.)

3 Both of them appear in the tall grass and on the water surface. You won't find them in caves or other places.

4 Both of them try to run when you encounter them.

5 If you use Fly or the Bicycle to approach them, they will move somewhere else.

Unova Pokédex
Completion Tips

14

Find Zorua
and Zoroark

Get these elusive Pokémon to complete the Unova Pokédex

With the distributed Celebi in your party, you can meet Zorua, and with the distributed Shiny Raikou, Entei, or Suicune in your party, you can meet Zoroark. Both of them are Unova region Pokémon, and they are necessary to complete the Unova Pokédex. If you can't get them, trade for them with family and friends.

◉ Work together with friends and family

In the story of *Pokémon Black* and *Pokémon White Versions*, Zorua and Zoroark don't appear in the wild. This section will show you how to register these two Pokémon as Seen and Caught in the Pokédex, even though you can't get them in the main story.

● **Register the Pokémon as Seen in your Pokédex**

Zorua	It can be seen in GAME FREAK

Talk to the girl on the first floor of the GAME FREAK building in Castelia City, and she will show you a picture of Zorua. This will register Zorua as Seen in the Pokédex.

Zoroark	It can be seen in a battle with N

When you battle N in N's Castle, he uses Zoroark as one of his Pokémon. This will register Zoroark as Seen in the Pokédex.

● **Register the Pokémon as Obtained in your Pokédex**

Link Trade to add Pokémon to the Pokédex

You can Link Trade with friends or family who have Zorua or Zoroark in order to register them in the Pokédex. If you Link Trade for them, you can register them as Caught in the Pokédex.

Zoroark
Dark
ABILITY ● Illusion

Get Pokémon Eggs to add Pokémon to the Pokédex

If you ask someone who has Zorua or Zoroark, they might give you a Zorua Egg. When the Egg hatches, you can register Zorua in the Pokédex. If you level Zorua up to Level 30, it will evolve into Zoroark.

Zorua hatched from the Egg!

Zorua
Dark
ABILITY ● Illusion

Complete the National Pokédex

Realize a Pokémon Trainer's greatest dream

When you complete the Unova Pokédex, your next challenge is to complete the National Pokédex. You'll need help from *Pokémon Diamond, Pearl, Platinum, HeartGold,* or *SoulSilver Version* to complete the National Pokédex, but only Pokémon you can find in *Pokémon Black* and *Pokémon White Versions* will be introduced here.

Complete the National Pokédex by catching 634 kinds of Pokémon

In order to complete the National Pokédex in *Pokémon Black* and *Pokémon White*, you must register 634 kinds of Pokémon. Pokémon given out in special distribution events, such as Mew and Celebi, are not necessary, so anyone can complete the National Pokédex.

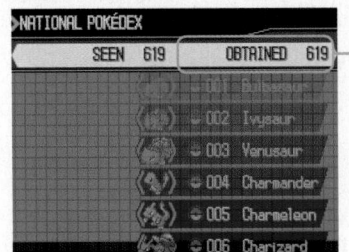

When you're all done, this number will be 634

● Pokémon not needed to complete the National Pokédex

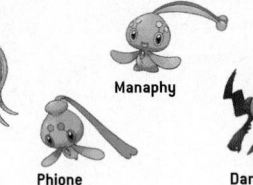

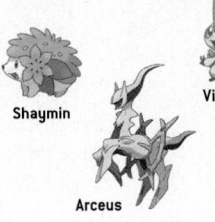

Celebi
Mew
Jirachi
Deoxys
Manaphy
Phione
Shaymin
Darkrai
Arceus
Victini
Landorus
Kyurem

The PC Boxes now number 24

At first, there are only eight Boxes in the PC. But as you catch more Pokémon, the number of Boxes will also increase. The maximum number of Boxes is 24, so make good use of them.

There are 24 Boxes, so you can store a total of 720 Pokémon. With this many Boxes, even collectors don't have to worry about space!

Get the completion certificate from the Game Director

GAME FREAK's Game Director will give you a certificate when you complete the National Pokédex, just like when you completed the Unova Pokédex.

all the Pokémon and completed your Pokédex!

The certificate is different from the one you received when you completed the Unova Pokédex. It's something you need to see with your own eyes. After that, the award certificate will be placed on your dresser in your bedroom in Nuvema Town.

1

Catch Pokémon from Other Regions

Meet other regions' Pokémon after finishing the story

When you defeat Ghetsis in battle, you will see the ending credits. After that, you will start a new journey from your room in Nuvema Town.

Pokémon from other regions will appear in the newly accessible areas.

Catch Pokémon to fill up your National Pokédex

After you complete the main story and continue, Looker, from the International Police, will give you the Super Rod. You will now be able to fish. Now you have another way to encounter Pokémon in addition to the ones you've been using so far, such as walking in tall grass and caves. This means you will be able to catch more types of Pokémon. You'll be surprised to see some of these Pokémon in the wild.

A wild Dragonite appeared!

● **Pokémon from other regions that appear in tall grass, caves, etc.**

National Pokédex No. 011 **Metapod**	National Pokédex No. 012 **Butterfree**	National Pokédex No. 014 **Kakuna**
Route 12 (*Pokémon White Version*) 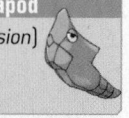	Route 12 (rustling grass) (*Pokémon White Version*) 	Route 12 (*Pokémon Black Version*) 
National Pokédex No. 015 **Beedrill**	National Pokédex No. 020 **Raticate**	National Pokédex No. 022 **Fearow**
Route 12 (rustling grass) (*Pokémon Black Version*) 	Dreamyard Basement (dark grass) 	Route 15 
National Pokédex No. 028 **Sandslash**	National Pokédex No. 035 **Clefairy**	National Pokédex No. 036 **Clefable**
Relic Castle Passageways 	Giant Chasm Crater Forest 	Giant Chasm Crater Forest (rustling grass) 
National Pokédex No. 037 **Vulpix**	National Pokédex No. 038 **Ninetales**	National Pokédex No. 039 **Jigglypuff**
Abundant Shrine 	Abundant Shrine (rustling grass) 	Route 14 
National Pokédex No. 040 **Wigglytuff**	National Pokédex No. 042 **Golbat**	National Pokédex No. 049 **Venomoth**
Route 14 (rustling grass) 	Route 13 	Dreamyard Outside (dark grass) 
National Pokédex No. 055 **Golduck**	National Pokédex No. 075 **Graveler**	National Pokédex No. 078 **Rapidash**
Route 11 	Challenger's Cave 1F 	Route 12 
National Pokédex No. 095 **Onix**	National Pokédex No. 105 **Marowak**	National Pokédex No. 108 **Lickitung**
Relic Castle Passageways 	Route 15 	Challenger's Cave 1F 

National Pokédex No. 114 **Tangela**
Route 13

National Pokédex No. 115 **Kangaskhan**
Route 15

National Pokédex No. 124 **Jynx**
Giant Chasm Caves

National Pokédex No. 127 **Pinsir**
Route 12

National Pokédex No. 132 **Ditto**
Giant Chasm Crater Forest

National Pokédex No. 164 **Noctowl**
Abundant Shrine

National Pokédex No. 166 **Ledian**
Dreamyard Basement (dark grass)

National Pokédex No. 168 **Ariados**
Dreamyard Basement (dark grass)

National Pokédex No. 169 **Crobat**
Route 13 (rustling grass)

National Pokédex No. 191 **Sunkern**
Route 12

National Pokédex No. 192 **Sunflora**
Route 12 (rustling grass)

National Pokédex No. 198 **Murkrow**
Abundant Shrine (*Pokémon Black Version*)

National Pokédex No. 200 **Misdreavus**
Abundant Shrine (*Pokémon White Version*)

National Pokédex No. 206 **Dunsparce**
Route 12

National Pokédex No. 207 **Gligar**
Route 15

National Pokédex No. 213 **Shuckle**
Route 14

National Pokédex No. 214 **Heracross**
Route 12

National Pokédex No. 215 **Sneasel**
Giant Chasm Caves

National Pokédex No. 221 **Piloswine**
Giant Chasm Caves

National Pokédex No. 225 **Delibird**
Giant Chasm Caves

National Pokédex No. 234 **Stantler**
Abundant Shrine

National Pokédex No. 247 **Pupitar**
Route 15

National Pokédex No. 248 **Tyranitar**
Route 15 (rustling grass)

National Pokédex No. 277 **Swellow**
Route 13

National Pokédex No. 302 **Sableye**
Challenger's Cave 1F

National Pokédex No. 303 **Mawile**
Challenger's Cave 1F

National Pokédex No. 334 **Altaria**
Route 14

National Pokédex No. 335 **Zangoose**
Village Bridge

National Pokédex No. 336 **Seviper**
Village Bridge

National Pokédex No. 337 **Lunatone**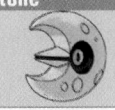
Route 13

National Pokédex No. 338 **Solrock**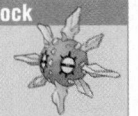
Route 13

National Pokédex No. 344 **Claydol**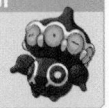
Relic Castle Deepest Room

National Pokédex No. 357 **Tropius**
Route 14

National Pokédex No. 358 **Chimecho**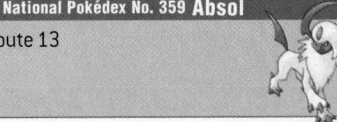
Abundant Shrine

National Pokédex No. 359 **Absol**
Route 13

National Pokédex No. 375 **Metang**
Giant Chasm Crater Forest

National Pokédex No. 376 **Metagross**
Giant Chasm Crater Forest (rustling grass)

National Pokédex No. 400 **Bibarel**
Village Bridge

National Pokédex No. 402 **Kricketune**
Dreamyard Basement (dark grass)

☐ National Pokédex No. 415 **Combee**
Route 12

☐ National Pokédex No. 416 **Vespiquen**
Route 12 (rustling grass)

☐ National Pokédex No. 421 **Cherrim**
Route 12

☐ National Pokédex No. 426 **Drifblim**
Route 13

☐ National Pokédex No. 429 **Mismagius**
Abundant Shrine (rustling grass) (*Pokémon White Version*)

☐ National Pokédex No. 430 **Honchkrow**
Abundant Shrine (rustling grass) (*Pokémon Black Version*)

☐ National Pokédex No. 437 **Bronzong**
Abundant Shrine

☐ National Pokédex No. 447 **Riolu**
Challenger's Cave B1F

☐ National Pokédex No. 465 **Tangrowth**
Route 13 (rustling grass)

☐ National Pokédex No. 472 **Gliscor**
Route 15 (rustling grass)

☐ National Pokédex No. 473 **Mamoswine**
Giant Chasm Crater Forest (rustling grass)

● Pokémon you get by trading with townspeople

● Pokémon you can get with prize money

☐ National Pokédex No. 446 **Munchlax**
Trade a Cinccino for it in Undella Town (summer only)

☐ National Pokédex No. 479 **Rotom**
Trade a Ditto for it in the trailer on Route 15

☐ National Pokédex No. 129 **Magikarp**
Get it for 500 in prize money from the person on Marvelous Bridge

● Pokémon from other regions that appear while surfing

☐ National Pokédex No. 079 **Slowpoke**
Abundant Shrine
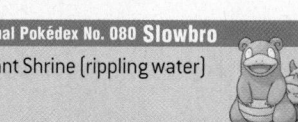

☐ National Pokédex No. 080 **Slowbro**
Abundant Shrine (rippling water)

☐ National Pokédex No. 086 **Seel**
Giant Chasm Caves

☐ National Pokédex No. 087 **Dewgong**
Giant Chasm Caves (rippling water)

☐ National Pokédex No. 120 **Staryu**
Route 13

☐ National Pokédex No. 121 **Starmie**
Route 13 (rippling water)

☐ National Pokédex No. 131 **Lapras**
Village Bridge (rippling water)

☐ National Pokédex No. 199 **Slowking**
Abundant Shrine (rippling water)

☐ National Pokédex No. 222 **Corsola**
Undella Town (rippling water)

☐ National Pokédex No. 226 **Mantine**
Undella Town (rippling water)

☐ National Pokédex No. 278 **Wingull**
Undella Town

☐ National Pokédex No. 279 **Pelipper**
Undella Town

☐ National Pokédex No. 320 **Wailmer**
Undella Town (rippling water)
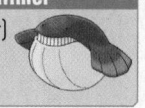

☐ National Pokédex No. 321 **Wailord**
Undella Bay (rippling water)

☐ National Pokédex No. 363 **Spheal**
Undella Bay (winter only)

☐ National Pokédex No. 364 **Sealeo**
Undella Bay (rippling water) (winter only)

☐ National Pokédex No. 365 **Walrein**
Undella Bay (rippling water) (winter only)

☐ National Pokédex No. 418 **Buizel**
Route 14

☐ National Pokédex No. 419 **Floatzel**
Route 14 (rippling water)

☐ National Pokédex No. 458 **Mantyke**
Undella Town

● Pokémon from other regions you can catch by fishing

National Pokédex No. 060 Poliwag
Wellspring Cave 1F

National Pokédex No. 061 Poliwhirl
Wellspring Cave 1F

National Pokédex No. 062 Poliwrath
Wellspring Cave 1F (rippling water)

National Pokédex No. 090 Shellder
Undella Town

National Pokédex No. 091 Cloyster
Undella Town (rippling water)

National Pokédex No. 098 Krabby
Route 4

National Pokédex No. 099 Kingler
Route 4 (rippling water)

National Pokédex No. 116 Horsea
Route 17

National Pokédex No. 117 Seadra
Route 17 (rippling water)

National Pokédex No. 118 Goldeen
Striaton City

National Pokédex No. 119 Seaking
Striaton City (rippling water)

National Pokédex No. 147 Dratini
Dragonspiral Tower 1F Outside

National Pokédex No. 148 Dragonair
Dragonspiral Tower 1F Outside

National Pokédex No. 149 Dragonite
Dragonspiral Tower 1F Outside (rippling water)

National Pokédex No. 170 Chinchou
Driftveil City

National Pokédex No. 171 Lanturn
Driftveil City (rippling water)

National Pokédex No. 186 Politoed
Route 6 (rippling water)

National Pokédex No. 211 Qwilfish
Route 17 (rippling water)

National Pokédex No. 223 Remoraid
Undella Town

National Pokédex No. 224 Octillery
Undella Town (rippling water)

National Pokédex No. 230 Kingdra
Route 17 (rippling water)

National Pokédex No. 318 Carvanha
Village Bridge

National Pokédex No. 319 Sharpedo
Village Bridge (rippling water)

National Pokédex No. 339 Barboach
Icirrus City

National Pokédex No. 340 Whiscash
Icirrus City (rippling water)

National Pokédex No. 349 Feebas
Route 1

National Pokédex No. 350 Milotic
Route 1 (rippling water)

National Pokédex No. 366 Clamperl
Route 4

National Pokédex No. 367 Huntail
Route 4 (rippling water)
(*Pokémon Black Version*)

National Pokédex No. 368 Gorebyss
Route 4 (rippling water)
(*Pokémon White Version*)

National Pokédex No. 369 Relicanth
Route 4 (rippling water)

National Pokédex No. 370 Luvdisc
Route 4
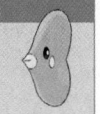

National Pokédex No. 456 Finneon
Route 17

National Pokédex No. 457 Lumineon
Route 17 (rippling water)

● Pokémon from other regions that are restored from Fossils

National Pokédex No. 138 Omanyte
Get the Helix Fossil in the Lower Level of Twist Mountain and have it restored at the Nacrene Museum.

National Pokédex No. 140 Kabuto
Get the Dome Fossil in the Lower Level of Twist Mountain and have it restored at the Nacrene Museum.

National Pokédex No. 142 Aerodactyl
Get the Old Amber in the Lower Level of Twist Mountain and have it restored at the Nacrene Museum.

National Pokédex No. 345 Lileep
Get the Root Fossil in the Lower Level of Twist Mountain and have it restored at the Nacrene Museum.

National Pokédex No. 347 Anorith
Get the Claw Fossil in the Lower Level of Twist Mountain and have it restored at the Nacrene Museum.

National Pokédex No. 408 Cranidos
Get the Skull Fossil in the Lower Level of Twist Mountain and have it restored at the Nacrene Museum.

National Pokédex No. 410 Shieldon
Get the Armor Fossil in the Lower Level of Twist Mountain and have it restored at the Nacrene Museum.

Catch Pokémon during a mass outbreak

A mass outbreak is a peculiar phenomenon in which large numbers of a not-usually-seen Pokémon appear. After you complete the main story, they will occur in a different location daily. The locations of mass outbreaks are displayed on the electric bulletin board placed in each gate.

● Pokémon from other regions that appear in mass outbreaks

National Pokédex No. 046 Paras
Route 11
(*Pokémon White Version*)

National Pokédex No. 056 Mankey
Route 15

National Pokédex No. 083 Farfetch'd
Route 1

National Pokédex No. 084 Doduo
Route 12

National Pokédex No. 102 Exeggcute
Route 18

National Pokédex No. 161 Sentret
Route 7

National Pokédex No. 193 Yanma
Route 14

National Pokédex No. 204 Pineco
Route 16

National Pokédex No. 228 Houndour
Route 9
(*Pokémon Black Version*)

National Pokédex No. 235 Smeargle
Route 5

National Pokédex No. 236 Tyrogue
Route 10

National Pokédex No. 261 Poochyena
Route 9
(*Pokémon White Version*)

National Pokédex No. 285 Shroomish
Route 11
(*Pokémon Black Version*)

National Pokédex No. 311 Plusle
Route 6
(*Pokémon Black Version*)

National Pokédex No. 312 Minun
Route 6
(*Pokémon White Version*)

National Pokédex No. 313 Volbeat
Route 3
(*Pokémon Black Version*)

National Pokédex No. 314 Illumise
Route 3
(*Pokémon White Version*)

National Pokédex No. 353 Shuppet
Route 13

National Pokédex No. 360 Wynaut
Route 2

National Pokédex No. 449 Hippopotas
Route 4

National Pokédex No. 453 Croagunk
Route 8

◎ Catch Pokémon that appear in White Forest (*Pokémon White Version*)

In White Forest, which appears in *Pokémon White Version*, you can catch Pokémon from other regions. The kinds of Pokémon that appear differ according to who is living in your White Forest. Talk to the residents of the forest to learn which kinds of Pokémon you will meet (p. 146).

● Pokémon from other regions that appear in White Forest

National Pokédex No. 016 Pidgey
When Leo is in White Forest

National Pokédex No. 029 Nidoran ♀
When Jacques is in White Forest

National Pokédex No. 032 Nidoran ♂
When Ken is in White Forest

National Pokédex No. 043 Oddish
When Lynette is in White Forest

National Pokédex No. 063 Abra
When Collin is in White Forest

National Pokédex No. 066 Machop
When Ryder is in White Forest

National Pokédex No. 069 Bellsprout
When Piper is in White Forest

National Pokédex No. 081 Magnemite
When Marie is in White Forest

National Pokédex No. 092 Gastly
When Dave is in White Forest

National Pokédex No. 111 Rhyhorn
When Shane is in White Forest

National Pokédex No. 137 Porygon
When Herman is in White Forest

National Pokédex No. 175 Togepi
When Miki is in White Forest

National Pokédex No. 179 Mareep
When Pierce is in White Forest

National Pokédex No. 187 Hoppip
When Britney is in White Forest

National Pokédex No. 194 Wooper
When Lena, Frederic, Herman, or Grace is in White Forest (water surface)

National Pokédex No. 239 Elekid
When Robbie is in White Forest

National Pokédex No. 240 Magby
When Vincent is in White Forest

National Pokédex No. 265 Wurmple
When Silvia is in White Forest

National Pokédex No. 270 Lotad
When Ralph, Ryder, or Karenna is in White Forest (water surface)

National Pokédex No. 273 Seedot
When Miho is in White Forest

National Pokédex No. 280 Ralts
When Lena is in White Forest

National Pokédex No. 283 Surskit
When Leo, Silvia, or Dave is in White Forest (water surface)

National Pokédex No. 287 Slakoth
When Karenna is in White Forest

National Pokédex No. 293 Whismur
When Rosa is in White Forest

National Pokédex No. 298 Azurill
When Molly is in White Forest

National Pokédex No. 304 Aron
When Gene is in White Forest

National Pokédex No. 328 Trapinch
When Eliza is in White Forest

National Pokédex No. 341 Corphish
When Vincent, Carlos, Ken, or Emi is in White Forest (water surface)

National Pokédex No. 371 Bagon
When Grace is in White Forest

National Pokédex No. 396 Starly
When Carlos is in White Forest

National Pokédex No. 403 Shinx
When Doug is in White Forest

National Pokédex No. 406 Budew
When Frederic is in White Forest

National Pokédex No. 440 Happiny
When Emi is in White Forest

Obtain Pokémon by Hatching Eggs

Eggs are found at the Pokémon Day Care

The Pokémon Day Care on Route 3 is a facility that raises Pokémon. After you rescue the Day-Care Man from Team Plasma in Nimbasa City, you can leave up to two Pokémon at the Day Care. Sometimes, when you leave two Pokémon there, an Egg will be found.

Get Pokémon Eggs from the Pokémon Day Care

If you leave two compatible Pokémon at the Day Care, a Pokémon Egg may be found. Finding and hatching Eggs can help you fill out your National Pokédex—in fact, some kinds of Pokémon can only be found if you hatch them from an Egg! However, some species of Pokémon never produce Eggs.

● Steps leading to Egg discovery

Deposit Pokémon	Take the Egg	Hatch the Egg
① 	② 	③ 
You can leave up to two Pokémon at the Pokémon Day Care. Try leaving two Pokémon of opposite genders.	If the male and female Pokémon left at the Day Care get along well, an Egg will be discovered. Take the Egg with you.	Put the Egg in your party and carry it around on your adventure. Eventually, a Pokémon will hatch from the Egg.

 Use Flame Body to make Eggs hatch more quickly

If you add a Pokémon Egg to your party and walk around, a Pokémon will eventually hatch from the Egg. It does take some time for the Pokémon to hatch. If you want the Egg to hatch faster, put a Pokémon with the Ability Flame Body, such as Litwick, Larvesta, or Volcarona, in your party. Being near these Pokémon warms up the Egg and makes it hatch faster than normal.

Larvesta

Litwick

Volcarona

Ability	Flame Body

Main rules for finding Eggs | **1**
Learn how to pair up Pokémon and find Eggs

To find Eggs, you can leave two Pokémon of the same species but opposite genders at the Pokémon Day Care. This is the simplest method, but you can also pair off Pokémon by Egg Group. You can still find an Egg from two different species of Pokémon if they have opposite genders and the same Egg Group.

● Druddigon ♂ and Haxorus ♀

Druddigon ♂
Dragon Group

Haxorus ♀
Dragon Group

● Rules for finding Eggs

1 If you leave two Pokémon of opposite genders from the same Egg Group, an Egg will be found.

2 The Pokémon that hatches from the Egg is either the same species as the female or an earlier evolutionary form.

3 The hatched Pokémon is almost always in its initial evolutionary stage.

Axew

For example, if you leave a male Druddigon and a female Haxorus, both of which are from the Dragon Egg Group, an Axew Egg will be found.

Main rules for finding Eggs | **2**
With Ditto, you can find almost any kind of Egg

Some Pokémon's genders are unknown. Also, some Pokémon species are only male or only female. Under normal circumstances, you can't find Eggs for these Pokémon. But leave one together with a Ditto and you'll find an Egg after all. Ditto can be a big help when you want more Eggs!

● Places where wild Ditto appear

Giant Chasm Crater Forest

● Pokémon of unknown gender that can produce Eggs

Magnemite	Magneton	Voltorb
Electrode	Staryu	Starmie
Porygon	Porygon2	Shedinja
Lunatone	Solrock	Baltoy
Claydol	Beldum	Metang
Metagross	Bronzor	Bronzong
Magnezone	Porygon-Z	Rotom
Klink	Klang	Klinklang
Cryogonal	Golett	Golurk

● Ditto and Klang

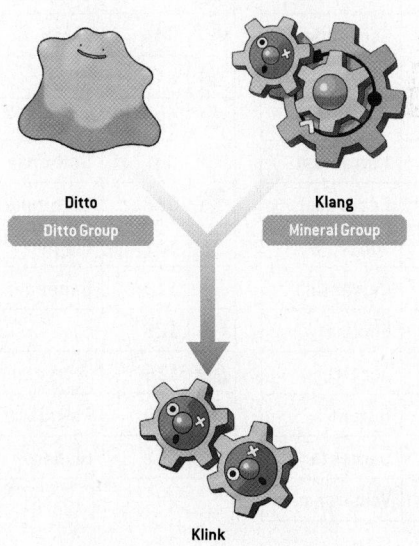

Ditto
Ditto Group

Klang
Mineral Group

Klink

A Klink Egg will be found when you leave Klang, whose gender is unknown, with Ditto.

Pokémon Egg Groups—Unova Pokémon

Grass Group

	001	Snivy
	002	Servine
	003	Serperior
	052	Cottonee
	053	Whimsicott
	054	Petilil
	055	Lilligant
	062	Maractus
	096	Foongus
	097	Amoonguss
	103	Ferroseed
	104	Ferrothorn

Bug Group

	046	Sewaddle
	047	Swadloon
	048	Leavanny
	049	Venipede
	050	Whirlipede
	051	Scolipede
	063	Dwebble
	064	Crustle
	094	Karrablast
	095	Escavalier
	101	Joltik
	102	Galvantula
	122	Shelmet
	123	Accelgor
	138	Durant
	142	Larvesta
	143	Volcarona

Flying Group

	025	Pidove
	026	Tranquill
	027	Unfezant
	033	Woobat
	034	Swoobat
	067	Sigilyph
	072	Archen
	073	Archeops
	086	Ducklett
	087	Swanna
	133	Rufflet
	134	Braviary
	135	Vullaby
	136	Mandibuzz

Human-Like Group

	038	Timburr
	039	Gurdurr
	040	Conkeldurr
	044	Throh
	045	Sawk
	080	Gothita
	081	Gothorita
	082	Gothitelle
	111	Elgyem
	112	Beheeyem
	125	Mienfoo
	126	Mienshao
	130	Pawniard
	131	Bisharp

Monster Group

	116	Axew
	117	Fraxure
	118	Haxorus
	127	Druddigon

Fairy Group

	037	Audino
	052	Cottonee
	053	Whimsicott

Dragon Group

	065	Scraggy
	066	Scrafty
	116	Axew
	117	Fraxure
	118	Haxorus
	127	Druddigon
	139	Deino
	140	Zweilous
	141	Hydreigon

Mineral Group

	030	Roggenrola
	031	Boldore
	032	Gigalith
	063	Dwebble
	064	Crustle
	068	Yamask
	069	Cofagrigus
	074	Trubbish
	075	Garbodor

Continues Above ↗

Mineral Group

	088	Vanillite
	089	Vanillish
	090	Vanilluxe
	103	Ferroseed
	104	Ferrothorn
	105	Klink
	106	Klang
	107	Klinklang
	121	Cryogonal
	128	Golett
	129	Golurk

Field Group

	001	Snivy
	002	Servine
	003	Serperior
	004	Tepig
	005	Pignite
	006	Emboar
	007	Oshawott
	008	Dewott
	009	Samurott
	010	Patrat
	011	Watchog
	012	Lillipup
	013	Herdier
	014	Stoutland
	015	Purrloin
	016	Liepard
	017	Pansage
	018	Simisage

Continues Above ↗

Hatch Eggs faster with Pass Powers

Pass Powers are powers you get for completing Entralink missions (p. 145). You can use Pass Powers on yourself or other people, and you need a friend's help for Hatching Power S and Hatching Power MAX, which can be used when you complete an Entralink mission. The stronger the Pass Power is, the less time it takes for the Pokémon to hatch.

● Pass Powers that make it easier to hatch Eggs

Items	Pass Orb	Time of Effect	Effect
Hatching Power ↑	3	3 min.	Eggs hatch slightly faster
Hatching Power ↑↑	4	3 min.	Eggs hatch much faster
Hatching Power ↑↑↑	5	3 min.	Eggs hatch very fast
Hatching Power S	—	30 min.	Eggs hatch very fast for a long period of time
Hatching Power MAX	—	1 hr.	Eggs hatch very fast for a long period of time

Field Group		
	019	Pansear
	020	Simisear
	021	Panpour
	022	Simipour
	023	Munna
	024	Musharna
	028	Blitzle
	029	Zebstrika
	033	Woobat
	034	Swoobat
	035	Drilbur
	036	Excadrill
	057	Sandile
	058	Krokorok
	059	Krookodile
	060	Darumaka
	061	Darmanitan
	065	Scraggy
	066	Scrafty
	076	Zorua
	077	Zoroark
	078	Minccino
	079	Cinccino
	091	Deerling
	092	Sawsbuck
	093	Emolga
	119	Cubchoo
	120	Beartic
	125	Mienfoo
	126	Mienshao
	132	Bouffalant
	137	Heatmor

Amorphous Group		
	068	Yamask
	069	Cofagrigus
	083	Solosis
	084	Duosion
	085	Reuniclus
	098	Frillish
	099	Jellicent
	108	Tynamo
	109	Eelektrik

Continues Above

Amorphous Group		
	110	Eelektross
	113	Litwick
	114	Lampent
	115	Chandelure
	124	Stunfisk

Water Group ①		
	041	Tympole
	042	Palpitoad
	043	Seismitoad
	070	Tirtouga
	071	Carracosta
	086	Ducklett
	087	Swanna
	100	Alomomola
	124	Stunfisk

Water Group ②		
	056	Basculin
	100	Alomomola

Water Group ③		
	070	Tirtouga
	071	Carracosta
	072	Archen
	073	Archeops

No Eggs Discovered		
	144	Cobalion
	145	Terrakion
	146	Virizion
	147	Tornadus
	148	Thundurus
	149	Reshiram
	150	Zekrom
	151	Landorus
	152	Kyurem
	000	Victini

Pokémon that belong to two Egg Groups are highlighted in ● (orange).

Pokémon with Hidden Abilities

Pokémon with Hidden Abilities appear in *Pokémon Black* and *Pokémon White Versions*. Pokémon you befriend in the Pokémon Global Link often have Hidden Abilities. To find an Egg that can hatch a Pokémon with a Hidden Ability, you must leave a female Pokémon with that Hidden Ability at the Day Care. The Pokémon that hatches isn't guaranteed to have the Hidden Ability, but this is the only method for carrying it over.

● Hatch Pokémon with Hidden Abilities by pairing Pokémon this way

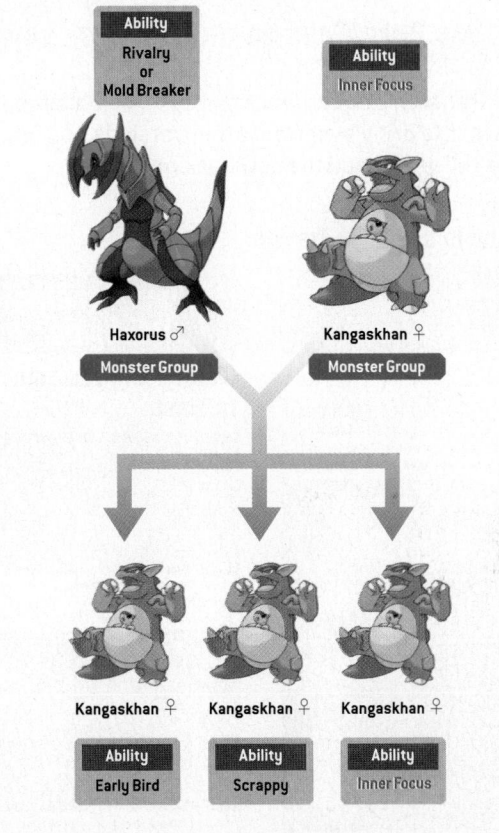

Ability
Rivalry or Mold Breaker

Ability
Inner Focus

Haxorus ♂
Monster Group

Kangaskhan ♀
Monster Group

Kangaskhan ♀ — Ability: Early Bird

Kangaskhan ♀ — Ability: Scrappy

Kangaskhan ♀ — Ability: Inner Focus

See p. 239 for more on hatching Pokémon with Hidden Abilities.

3

Transfer Pokémon with Poké Transfer

Transfer Pokémon from other regions using wireless communications

Poké Transfer is a device that transfers Pokémon from *Pokémon Diamond*, *Pearl*, *Platinum*, *HeartGold*, and *SoulSilver Versions*. You can use it in the Poké Transfer Lab on Route 15. This facility will be invaluable for completing your National Pokédex.

Use Poké Balls on the Pokémon popping out of the tall grass

Poké Transfer is set up like a game. When Pokémon you want to bring over from other versions pop out of the tall grass, pull the bow back and send Poké Balls flying! Hit the purple smoke with the Poké Ball and the Pokémon will fall asleep, making it easier to capture.

● How to use Poké Transfer

Game Receiving Pokémon	Game Sending Pokémon	Game Sending Pokémon	Game Receiving Pokémon
Wireless communications begin	**Choose the Pokémon to send**	**Catch the Pokémon**	**Six Pokémon are put in the Box**

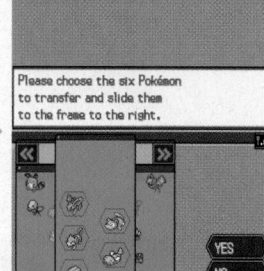
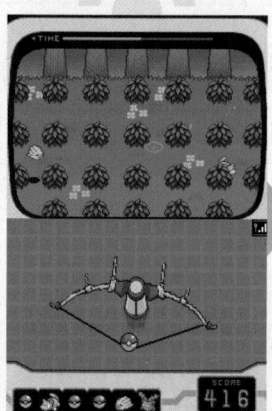

If you choose to use Poké Transfer, communication begins.

Start the Poké Transfer program and select six Pokémon.

Use the stylus to pull the bow and aim the Poké Ball at the Pokémon.

The Pokémon you caught will be sent to the PC Box.

● Poké Transfer rules

1 You need two Nintendo DS systems (Nintendo DS, Nintendo DS Lite, Nintendo DSi, Nintendo DSi XL).

2 You can send Pokémon anytime you want.

3 You don't need to have open space in your party. (The transferred Pokémon are moved to your PC Box.)

4 Items held by Pokémon can't be taken with them.

5 Pokémon that know HMs can't be transferred.

6 Once transferred, a Pokémon can't be returned to the game it came from.

Communication Features Guide

Try the Communication Features

Communication features expand your gameplay

Pokémon Black and *Pokémon White Versions* have four communication functions: IR (Infrared), Wireless, Online (Nintendo Wi-Fi Connection), and PGL (Pokémon Global Link). Each one provides different gameplay features for fresh and thrilling experiences.

Receive the C-Gear from Fennel

The key to these communication features is the C-Gear (p. 130). Once obtained, the C-Gear is displayed on the Touch Screen for quick access. Defeat Team Plasma in the Dreamyard and visit Fennel in Striaton City to receive your C-Gear.

As a token of my appreciation, I will give you this C-Gear to use!

● The C-Gear is displayed on the Touch Screen of your DS system

| C-Gear (for Boys) | C-Gear (for Girls) |

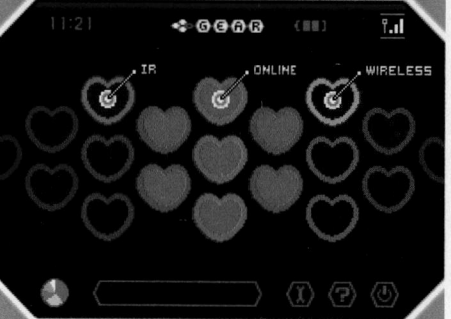

Fennel
the Scientist

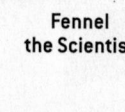

C-Gear screen

● The C-Gear layout may vary but the functions are the same. The frames for boys and girls look different.

Different communication methods provide different game features

Here's a partial list of the features you can use with IR, Wireless, Online, and the Pokémon Global Link. It's not a complete list, but should be enough to see just how much you can do with *Pokémon Black* and *Pokémon White*.

● The four ways to communicate and their main features

IR (Infrared)

You can use these features by linking up with your nearby friends and family members. Compared to the previous generations, it's much easier to trade Pokémon!

Battle

Pokémon trade

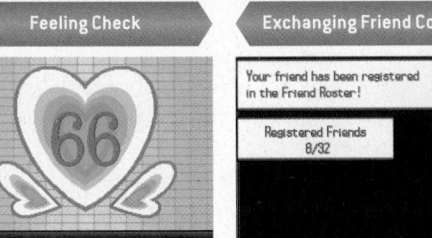

Feeling Check

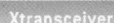

Exchanging Friend Codes

Wireless

You can use these features with people within about 30 feet. You can link up with your good friends and family members or with new people.

Xtransceiver

Entralink

Pass Power

Union Room

Online (Nintendo Wi-Fi Connection)

Set up your DS system for Nintendo WFC and you can use these features. Exchange Friend Codes with your friends and you can have fun with them no matter where they are!

Xtransceiver

Battle with people far away

Trade with people far away

Global Terminal

Pokémon Global Link

Set up access through your PC, with Internet access and Nintendo WFC and you can use these features. Visit the Pokémon Dream World to grow Berries and play new minigames!

Pokémon Dream World

Global Battle Union

E-Z Mail

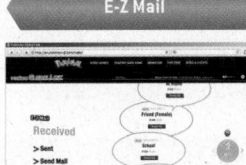

Customize

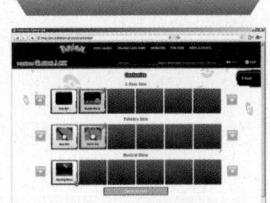

C-Gear

1 How to Use the C-Gear

Just tap the icons in the Touch Screen and off you go!

The C-Gear is your portal device for access to IR, Wireless, Online, and the Pokémon Global Link. It's easy to use—just tap a button for the gameplay you want. The C-Gear is the foundation of Pokémon communication, so learn and enjoy!

The C-Gear Basics

When the C-Gear appears for the first time on the Touch Screen, you may be a little surprised by its unique look. No need to be alarmed, though—the C-Gear is certainly new and innovative, but it's easy to use! Try it out once and you'll know what to do.

● C-Gear

● This image is from a Nintendo DSi system.

Time

ONLINE

IR

Battery icon

Reception icon

WIRELESS

Help icon
Tap to learn detailed information about C-Gear

Pass Power icon
Tap to turn off the C-Gear and disable communications

Survey Radar icon
Tap to display the Survey Radar (p. 132)

Tag Log icon
Tap to display the Tag Log (p. 131)

Customization icon
Tap to change the appearance of the C-Gear

● Reception status

IR	Status
Red (slow blink)	Normal

Wireless	Status
Green (slow blink)	Someone is accessing the Entralink
Green (slow blink)	You've become the target in the Entralink
Green (fast blink)	You can join a mission that someone else started in the Entralink
Yellow (slow blink)	Normal
Yellow (fast blink)	Someone is calling you on the Xtransceiver
Red (slow blink)	Wireless Pokémon distribution available
Blue (slow blink)	Someone is in the Union Room
Pink (slow blink)	Other wireless communications (Tag Mode, Survey Radar) have been detected

Online	Status
Green (slow blink)	Nintendo Wi-Fi Connection available at home, etc.
Blue (slow blink)	Normal or connected to Nintendo Zone or a wireless public network
Red (slow blink)	Free access point available

● The background in the "ONLINE" frame will turn red if the Nintendo Wi-Fi Connection settings are not complete when a wireless Internet connection is detected.

Collect Data
2 Using Tag Mode

Exchange information with other players

Tag Mode enables you to exchange information with other *Pokémon Black* and *Pokémon White* players and check their status. Data is automatically exchanged as long as the DS system is on, even if it's closed.

Tage Mode **1** **Check information as you pass by**

Tap the Tag Log icon, then tap a player's name for more details.

● **Tag Log**

Play time
Their location
Greetings

The rank of statistician
Pass Power
Send message
Thank others

Number of current nearby people

Check the status of other people

Updates on other players are displayed continuously. You can check on information such as who's just caught what kind of Pokémon, and much more.

● **Information about nearby people**

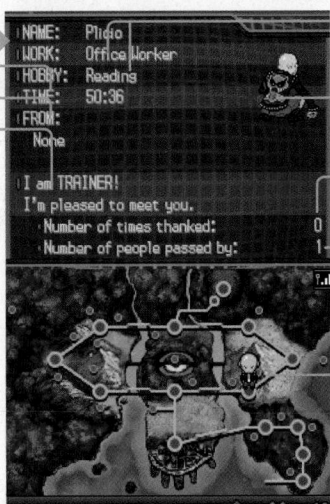

Their occupation and hobby
Picture

Number of times thanked
Number of people passed by

Where they were in-game when you passed them

● **What you can do by tapping the Tag Log icon**

▽ Use Pass Power

You can use the Pass Power you selected in the Entralink (p. 145). You can use it for yourself and people around you.

💬 Send message

Create messages up to eight letters long to send to people you pass by.

😊 Thank others

You can thank people who give you Pass Powers and messages.

2 Join Passerby Analytics

Passerby Analytics HQ is located in Castelia City. Once you join Passerby Analytics, you can accept various requests from the leader and complete them. The leader will reward you with items as you complete his requests. Your rank will go up and you can choose more surveys.

Passerby Analytics HQ
...People pass by as they walk along.

● Passerby Analytics HQ

Pie chart
Check your statistician rank, number of people passed by, number of times thanked, etc.

Answer questionnaires

Enter thank-you messages for Tag Mode

Accept survey requests

Enter your greetings for Tag Mode

● How to complete a Passerby Survey

1 Answer questionnaires and you'll have more surveys for your Survey Radar

Talk to the leader to become a statistician first. Then you can talk to the blonde-haired woman to answer various questionnaires. Answer questionnaires, and more surveys become available for you to conduct. Talk to the woman and answer all the questionnaires if you want the leader to give you lots of surveys.

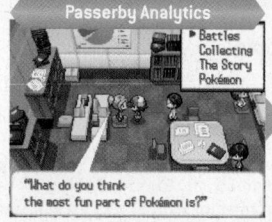

Passerby Analytics

"What do you think the most fun part of Pokémon is?"

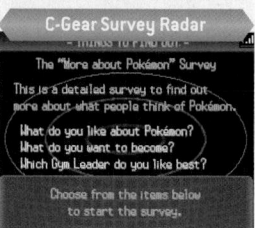

C-Gear Survey Radar

The "More about Pokémon" Survey

This is a detailed survey to find out more about what people think of Pokémon.

What do you like about Pokémon?
What do you want to become?
Which Gym Leader do you like best?

Choose from the items below to start the survey.

2 Accept the survey requests and let your Survey Radar do the job

After answering questionnaires, talk to the leader and accept a request. There are two types of surveys: timed surveys and head-count surveys. Accept the request, select the survey, and complete it.

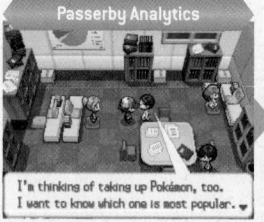

Passerby Analytics

I'm thinking of taking up Pokémon, too. I want to know which one is most popular. ▼

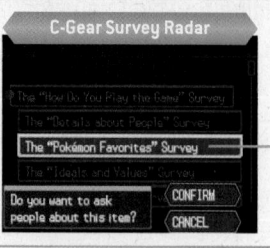

C-Gear Survey Radar

The "How Do You Play the Game" Survey
The "Details about People" Survey
The "Pokémon Favorites" Survey
The "Ideals and Values" Survey

Do you want to ask people about this item?   CONFIRM   CANCEL

Re-select the survey details

3 Rewards for completed surveys

Talk to the leader when you've completed a survey, and he'll reward you with items such as Quick Ball and Nugget. Your rank as a statistician will go up depending on how many surveys you have completed. Complete all the surveys and you'll receive a Rare Candy.

Passerby Analytics

Trainer obtained a Great Ball!

● Statistician Rank

Rank	How to reach this rank	
C	Default, just joined	
B	Complete 4 surveys	
A	Complete 10 surveys	
S	Complete 16 surveys	
S+	Complete 21 surveys	

COMMUNICATION FEATURES GUIDE

COLLECT DATA USING TAG MODE

● Surveys requested by Passerby Analytics HQ

Request No.	Survey	Passerby	Available When	Reward	Request Type	To Complete the Survey
1	How Do You Play the Game	Which version is more popular?	Always available	Great Ball	Timed survey	The survey must be conducted for 2 hours or more for Tag Mode data
					Head-count survey	Collect Tag Mode data from 5 passersby or more
2	How Do You Play the Game	The first Pokémon you picked?	Always available	Net Ball	Timed survey	Collect Tag Mode data for 2 hours or more
					Head-count survey	Collect Tag Mode data from 5 passersby or more
3	How Do You Play the Game	How long have you been playing?	Always available	Timer Ball	Timed survey	Collect Tag Mode data for 4 hours or more
					Head-count survey	Collect Tag Mode data from 10 passersby or more
4	Details About People	More men or more women?	Always available	Dusk Ball	Timed survey	Collect Tag Mode data for 4 hours or more
					Head-count survey	Collect Tag Mode data from 10 passersby or more
5	Details About People	The most common job?	Statistician rank B or higher	Heal Ball	Timed survey	Collect Tag Mode data for 4 hours or more
					Head-count survey	Collect Tag Mode data from 10 passersby or more
6	Details About People	The most common hobby?	Statistician rank B or higher	Quick Ball	Timed survey	Collect Tag Mode data for 4 hours or more
					Head-count survey	Collect Tag Mode data from 10 passersby or more
7	Pokémon Favorites	More popular, battles or trades?	When your statistician rank becomes B	Hyper Potion	Timed survey	Collect Tag Mode data for 8 hours or more
					Head-count survey	Collect Tag Mode data from 20 passersby or more
8	Pokémon Favorites	Favorite kind of Pokémon?	When your statistician rank becomes B	Revive	Timed survey	Collect Tag Mode data for 8 hours or more
					Head-count survey	Collect Tag Mode data from 20 passersby or more
9	Pokémon Favorites	Favorite Pokémon type?	When your statistician rank becomes B	Pearl	Timed survey	Collect Tag Mode data for 8 hours or more
					Head-count survey	Collect Tag Mode data from 20 passersby or more
10	Ideals and Values	Where do people prefer to live?	When your statistician rank becomes B	Stardust	Timed survey	Collect Tag Mode data for 8 hours or more
					Head-count survey	Collect Tag Mode data from 20 passersby or more
11	Ideals and Values	About what's most important	When your statistician rank becomes A	Heart Scale	Timed survey	Collect Tag Mode data for 12 hours or more
					Head-count survey	Collect Tag Mode data from 30 passersby or more
12	Likable People	Favorite kinds of people?	When your statistician rank becomes A	Big Mushroom	Timed survey	Collect Tag Mode data for 12 hours or more
					Head-count survey	Collect Tag Mode data from 30 passersby or more
13	Preferences	About seasons	When your statistician rank becomes A	Big Pearl	Timed survey	Collect Tag Mode data for 12 hours or more
					Head-count survey	Collect Tag Mode data from 30 passersby or more
14	Preferences Entertainment	About art	When your statistician rank becomes A	Star Piece	Timed survey	Collect Tag Mode data for 12 hours or more
					Head-count survey	Collect Tag Mode data from 30 passersby or more
15	Entertainment	Favorite music?	When your statistician rank becomes A	PP Up	Timed survey	Collect Tag Mode data for 16 hours or more
					Head-count survey	Collect Tag Mode data from 40 passersby or more
16	Entertainment	About TV and movies	When your statistician rank becomes A	HP Up	Timed survey	Collect Tag Mode data for 16 hours or more
					Head-count survey	Collect Tag Mode data from 40 passersby or more
17	School Life	Favorite time in school?	When your statistician rank becomes S	Carbos	Timed survey	Collect Tag Mode data for 16 hours or more
					Head-count survey	Collect Tag Mode data from 40 passersby or more
18	School Life	About study	When your statistician rank becomes S	Iron	Timed survey	Collect Tag Mode data for 16 hours or more
					Head-count survey	Collect Tag Mode data from 40 passersby or more
19	Sports and Pastimes	Most popular sport?	When your statistician rank becomes S	Protein	Timed survey	Collect Tag Mode data for 20 hours or more
					Head-count survey	Collect Tag Mode data from 50 passersby or more
20	Sports and Pastimes	About a holiday	When your statistician rank becomes S	Zinc	Timed survey	Collect Tag Mode data for 20 hours or more
					Head-count survey	Collect Tag Mode data from 50 passersby or more
21	More About Pokémon	What do you want to become the most?	When your statistician rank becomes S	Calcium	Timed survey	Collect Tag Mode data for 20 hours or more
					Head-count survey	Collect Tag Mode data from 50 passersby or more
22	More About Pokémon	Most popular Gym Leader?	When your statistician rank becomes S+	Rare Bone	Timed survey	Collect Tag Mode data for 24 hours or more
					Head-count survey	Collect Tag Mode data from 100 passersby or more
23	More About Pokémon	Most fun part of Pokémon?	When your statistician rank becomes S+	Nugget	Timed survey	Collect Tag Mode data for 24 hours or more
					Head-count survey	Collect Tag Mode data from 100 passersby or more

● What you can find out with the surveys using the C-Gear Survey Radar

Survey Name	Questions
How Do You Play the Game	Which version do you play?
	What's your starter Pokémon?
	How long have you been playing?
Details About People	Are you male or female?
	What's your hobby?
	What kind of job do you have?
Pokémon Favorites	Which do you prefer, battle or trade?
	What kind of Pokémon do you like best?
	What Pokémon type do you like best?
Ideals and Values	Would you live in the city or country?
	Which do you wish you had more of?
	What's most important to you?
Likable People	What kind of person do you prefer?
	Which do you value more in a person?
	What kind of people do you like best?

Survey Name	Survey Details
Preferences	What season do you like best?
	What kind of food do you like best?
	What's your favorite color?
Entertainment	What kind of music do you like?
	What kind of TV programs do you like?
	What kind of movies do you like?
School Life	What's your favorite time at school?
	What subject do you like best?
	What subject do you like least?
Sports and Pastimes	Where would you go for a vacation?
	What do you do in your spare time?
	What's your favorite sport?
More About Pokémon	What do you like about Pokémon?
	What do you want to become?
	Which Gym Leader do you like best?

IR
1

Battle over Infrared

Face a friend and you're ready to battle

With IR, you can start a battle quickly with either your party or with the Pokémon from your Battle Box. The levels of all the Pokémon will be equalized, so you don't need to check or swap Pokémon around. Get together with your friends and you're ready to battle!

Serious battles at your fingertips

You can start IR battles by tapping the C-Gear on the Nintendo DS system's Touch Screen. The battle rules are already set up, so there is no need to discuss rules with your friends.

● How to battle through IR

Tap the C-Gear on the Touch Screen to start a battle

Tap "IR" on your C-Gear and then tap "BATTLE." You then choose "BATTLES FOR TWO" or "BATTLES FOR FOUR." If you choose "BATTLES FOR TWO," you'll need to choose the battle format as well. There is no limit to how many Pokémon are allowed for the battles, so the battle begins as soon as you select the battle format. Give it all you've got!

Tap "IR"

Tap "BATTLE"

Decide how many people will participate

Select the Battle mode

Select the Pokémon

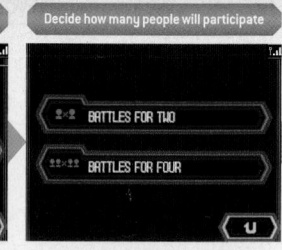

Have fun battling with friends

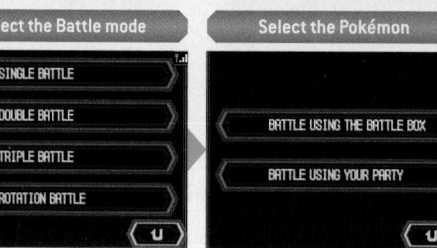

IR battles follow unique battle rules

IR battles have their own unique rules. All your Pokémon are temporarily set to Lv. 50 for the duration of the battle. The Trainers will be equipped with the Wonder Launcher. These rules cannot be changed.

● IR battle rules

1 No limit to the level of the participating Pokémon

2 All the Pokémon are set to Lv. 50 for the duration of the battle

3 Trainers can use the Wonder Launcher

With two-player battles, you and a friend can choose from four battle formats. Each format requires its own strategy, so select the right one for your Pokémon. Here are the details of these four battle formats. Battles over IR have no limit to how many Pokémon can participate. You choose either to battle with your party or with the Pokémon in your Battle Box.

● Battle for two players

Single Battle

In Single Battle format, each player sends out one Pokémon at a time. This is the standard battle format. For Link battles, the "SET" rule is used, so the remaining Pokémon stay in battle when an opponent's Pokémon faints.

The whole party participates

One Pokémon at a time

Double Battle

In Double Battle format, each Trainer sends out two Pokémon at a time. The interplay between your two Pokémon expands the different strategies you can use, giving your battles greater depth.

The whole party participates

Two Pokémon at a time

Triple Battle

In Triple Battle format, each Trainer sends out three Pokémon at a time. Consider each Pokémon's stats and moves as you decide where to position each Pokémon.

The whole party participates

Three Pokémon battle at the same time

Rotation Battle

In Rotation Battles, each Trainer sends out three Pokémon, but only the one in the lead position is battling at any time. The lead position changes as Pokémon rotate. It's an exciting style of battle because no one knows what will happen next!

The whole party participates

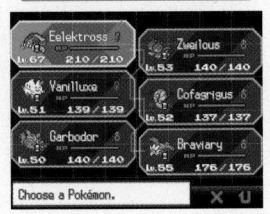

Only the Pokémon in the lead position battles

 If you and your friend didn't choose the same format, the battle format is decided automatically

If you and your friend didn't choose the same format, you don't re-select the formats. Instead, each Battle format has a priority and the higher of the two will be automatically selected.

● The battle format priorities

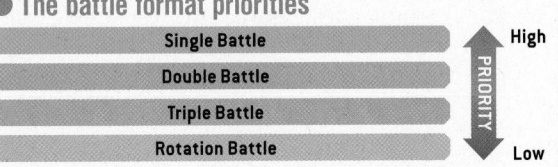

Single Battle	High
Double Battle	
Triple Battle	PRIORITY
Rotation Battle	Low

If you select "BATTLES FOR FOUR" from the IR battle formats, Multi Battle is automatically selected. Two people form a tag team and battle against another team.

You can change your partner or your party to enjoy hundreds of different combinations.

● Battle for four players

Multi Battle

In Multi Battle format, two people form a tag team and battle against another team. You and your tag partner each send out one Pokémon at a time. Work together with your partner's Pokémon just like in regular Double Battles.

One Pokémon sent out at a time

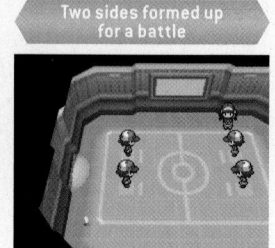
Two sides formed up for a battle

● Multi Battle through IR

Form a tag team, choose a leader, and let the leaders link up

Tap "IR" on the C-Gear, then tap "BATTLES FOR FOUR." Link up with your tag partner with IR. Either you or your partner becomes the tag leader. Once leaders link up with each other, you are ready for a Multi Battle!

Tap "IR"

Tap "BATTLE"

Tap "BATTLES FOR FOUR"

Link up with a partner
Make an Infrared Connection with your partner.
QUIT

Leaders link up with each other
Make an Infrared Connection with your opponents' leader.
QUIT
● Only those who are shown this message need to link up with each other.

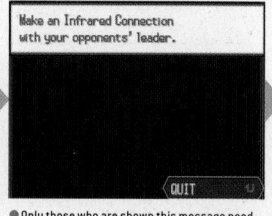
How to enjoy Multi Battles

Have Pokémon ready in the Battle Box

Register some Pokémon in your Battle Box so you can choose between your party and the Pokémon in the Battle Box when you battle others. Keep Pokémon that are strong in battles in this Battle Box.

Register them by using a PC

Register up to 6 Pokémon

Link Trade Pokémon with Infrared

Get ready for a Pokémon trade

With IR, you can trade Pokémon with your friends easily. You do not need to negotiate with them like in the Union Room or at Wi-Fi Club. And you don't need to go to a specific place in the game. All you have to do is turn to face a friend!

Choose between your party or the PC Box for Pokémon trade

You can not only choose one of your party Pokémon but also any Pokémon in your PC Box. You don't need to have it in your party for a trade, so it's super easy.

● How to trade Pokémon using IR

Offer one Pokémon and trade it with a friend

Tap "IR" on your C-Gear and then tap "TRADE." You then choose one Pokémon from either your party or PC Box. Check the Pokémon on the top screen as you and your friend show each other your Pokémon. Select "OFFER" if everything looks good—and your trade is done!

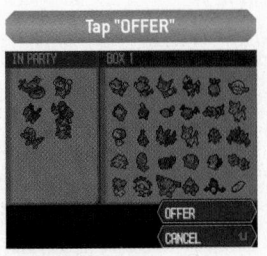

● You cannot trade a party Pokémon that knows a hidden move. You can trade a Pokémon with hidden moves if it is in your PC Box.

Search for Pokémon using the search icon

Tap the search icon in the lower-left corner of the Touch Screen when you are about to select a Pokémon you want to trade. You can search for a Pokémon from your party and PC Boxes by the first letter of Pokémon names. This is especially useful when you have a lot of Pokémon to choose from.

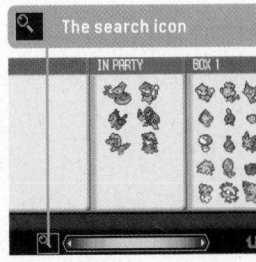

IR
3 Check Compatibility with Feeling Check

See how compatible you are with friends

The Feeling Check is a quick-and-easy way to test your friendship, and it's only available through IR. Get together with your friends for Feeling Checks and see how compatible you are. Compatible friends will receive more Sweet Hearts.

Check your compatibility for Sweet Hearts

Regardless of the check results, you'll receive at least one Sweet Heart at the end of a Feeling Check. Check with many people and collect lots of Sweet Hearts.

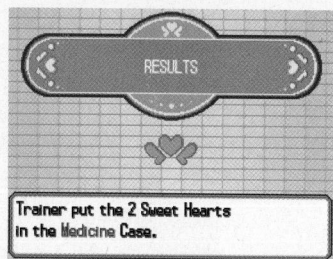

Trainer put the 2 Sweet Hearts in the Medicine Case.

Sweet Heart
It restores the HP of one Pokémon by 20 points.

If you give the girl in Cargo Service in Mistralton City ten Sweet Hearts, she will give you one Heart Scale. Collect lots of them and trade them.

● How to do a Feeling Check through IR

Tap the screen and press your thumbs against it

Tap "IR" on your C-Gear and then tap "FEELING CHECK." Then face each other and follow the on-screen instructions. Your and your friend's score is shown after you each tap the Touch Screen rhythmically and press your thumbs against it. The score decides your rank. The highest score you can achieve is 100.

Tap "IR"

Tap "FEELING CHECK"

Follow the instructions
Tap the Touch Screen ten times in any rhythm you like.

See your results
Your feelings are at Rank B! Everybody's quite envious of you two.

● Feeling Ranks and the number of Sweet Hearts you receive

Message	Score	Sweet Hearts you receive
You are touching the screen incorrectly. Please play according to the guide.	0 to 9	1
Your feelings are at Rank I! Close enough to say a friendly hello.	10 to 19	1
Your feelings are at Rank H! You have an interest in each other.	20 to 29	1
Your feelings are at Rank G! Close enough to go for a walk together.	30 to 39	1
Your feelings are at Rank F! You probably have nicknames for each other.	40 to 49	1
Your feelings are at Rank E! You are as close as best friends.	50 to 59	1

Message	Score	Sweet Hearts you receive
Your feelings are at Rank D! Close enough to make good-night calls.	60 to 69	1
Your feelings are at Rank C! Close enough for traveling together.	70 to 79	1
Your feelings are at Rank B! Everybody's quite envious of you two.	80 to 89	2
Your feelings are at Rank A! You are emotionally united.	90 to 99	2
Your feelings are at Rank S! Undoubtedly a fated pair!	100	3

Exchange Friend Codes with Lots of Friends

IR **4**

You can exchange Friend Codes the moment you've made a new friend

You need your Friend Code when you enter the Wi-Fi Club in the Pokémon Center 2F or to use the Xtransceiver with your friends. With IR, you can exchange Friend Codes in a matter of seconds. Exchange Friend Codes as you make friends and broaden your network of friends.

Use IR for a quick exchange of Friend Codes

Your Friend Code is a 12-digit number. To exchange it, you just face each other and tap a couple buttons on your Touch Screen. It's easy! Once you do, get ready for action with the Wi-Fi Club, the Xtransceiver, and the Pokémon Global Link.

● **How to exchange Friend Codes with IR**

Face each other and tap on the screen twice

Tap "IR" on your C-Gear and then tap "FRIEND CODE." That's all you have to do. Once the exchange is finished, you can check to see how many people are registered.

Tap "IR"	Tap "FRIEND CODE"	Check how many people have registered

How to register Friend Codes manually

You'll need to enter Friend Codes manually if your friends are far away. If the exchange through IR doesn't work for some reason, you'll also need to enter the code manually.

● **How to exchange Friend Codes manually**

You can check Friend Codes in your Pal Pad	Friend Codes can be entered manually
Use the Pal Pad when you want to know your own Friend Code. Select your Friend Code to check it.	Enter your friend's name and his or her 12-digit Friend Code. You both need to register each other's Friend Codes. Let your friend know your Friend Code.
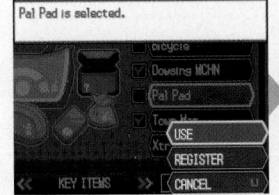 	 

Wireless

1 Talk to Your Friends with the Xtransceiver

Use the high-tech features of Nintendo DSi or Nintendo DSi XL to talk to your friends

Up to four people can talk to each other face-to-face with the Xtransceiver if you use your

Nintendo DSi or Nintendo DSi XL. It's easy to master this amazing function!

Up to 4 people can talk to each other face-to-face

To talk to other people face-to-face with the Xtransceiver, you need to exchange Friend Codes (p. 139). Exchange Friend Codes and you're ready to go.

How to register Friend Codes
- Use IR to exchange Friend Codes
- Register Friend Codes manually

● How to use the Xtransceiver

When you want to call a friend   Tap a friend's name

Tap "WIRELESS" on the C-Gear and select "XTRANSCEIVER" when you want to talk to your friends with the Xtransceiver. Select a name and you are set to talk.

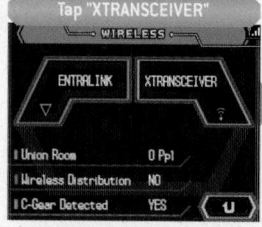
Tap "XTRANSCEIVER"

Select a friend

Tap the name to make the check icon appear.

When someone calls you   "WIRELESS" blinks on the C-Gear

"WIRELESS" on the C-Gear blinks yellow when someone calls you on the Xtransceiver. You'll hear it ring, too. Tap "XTRANSCEIVER" to join a conversation.

The C-Gear blinks yellow

Select a friend

The caller's name is shown.

When you want to join a conversation

You can join a Xtransceiver conversation already in progress with two or three of your friends. Tap a friend's name on the screen to join the conversation.

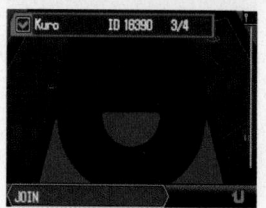

If you're using a Nintendo DS or Nintendo DS Lite

You can even use the Xtransceiver with a Nintendo DS or Nintendo DS Lite, which have no camera functions. It'll be sound only with no visuals, though.

1 Learn how to use the Xtransceiver

All you have to do to chat through the Xtransceiver is to exchange Friend Codes and connect with each other. Press the right buttons on Nintendo DSi and Nintendo DSi XL or tap the icons on the Nintendo DSi and Nintendo DSi XL Touch Screen and off you go.

Xtransceiver buttons for Nintendo DSi and Nintendo DSi XL

A or R   Hold down while you are talking into the microphone

L   Magnify the screen
*For the leader only

● **START**   Pause
● **SELECT**

X   Change to GRAFFITI MODE

B   End Xtransceiver

● "Leader" is the caller.

Use the Control Pad to change the way you look

● UP: Normal
● DOWN: Black and white
● LEFT: Reverse negative and positive
● RIGHT: Sepia

● The Xtransceiver

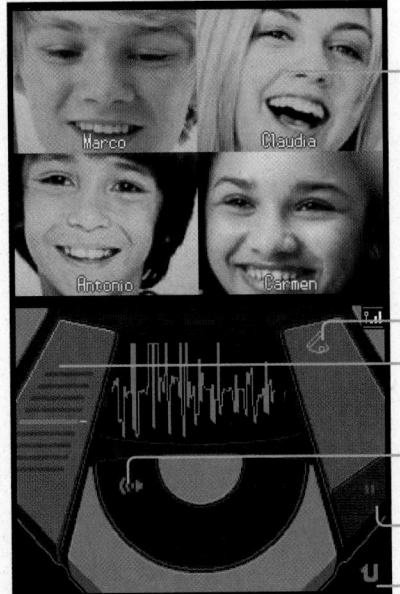

Name and face

GRAFFITI MODE

Voice tuner
You can change the pitch of your voice high and low.

Talk switch
Hold the switch down while you're talking.

Pause

Cancel

2 Mark up your friends' faces with Graffiti Mode

Tap the button for "GRAFFITI MODE," where you can use different graffiti markers on your and your friends' faces.

Tap the Pause button to freeze the picture for easy graffiti.

● Graffiti Mode

 Change marker size

Tap the marker icon, and a window will open to change the marker size. Select a ● to change the marker size.

 Select colors with the dropper

Tap the dropper icon, then tap anywhere on the screen to copy the color from that spot. You can then use that color for graffiti.

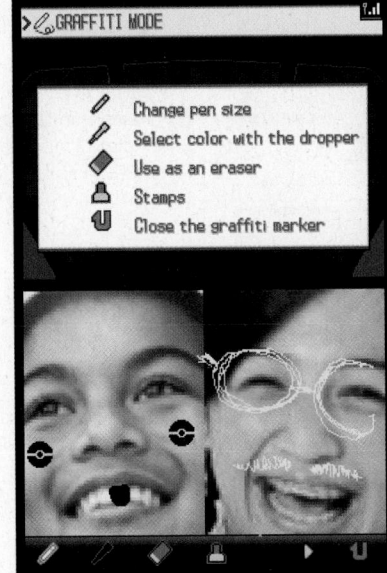

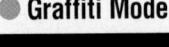 **Use as an eraser**

Tap the eraser icon to switch the marker to an eraser.

Stamps

Tap the Stamp icon, and you'll see five stamps. Choose one, and then tap anywhere on the screen to use that stamp.

2 Explore Other Players' Worlds with the Entralink

You can visit other players' worlds when they are using wireless communications

The Entralink is a place of mysterious power in the middle of the Unova region. You can use it to connect to and visit other players' worlds of *Pokémon Black Version* and *Pokémon White Version*.

You and other players can visit each others' worlds

Go to the Entralink and wait a while on the bridge to connect to other players' worlds to visit there. To connect to those worlds, the player you are visiting needs to be in the city or on the route you can visit on the Entralink.

● Entralink

To the Entree Forest (p. 165)

To the other player's world

To the other player's world

Entree

Go back to your own world

● What you can do in the Entralink

Visit other players' worlds

The Entralink enables you to visit other players' worlds. You can talk to the other players.

You are in Kuro's world. You look different!

Receive Pass Powers from the Entree

Pass Powers can help you in battle, in leveling up your Pokémon, and more (p. 145). Complete a mission and you'll receive a Pass Orb.

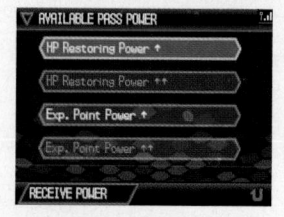

▽ AVAILABLE PASS POWER

HP Restoring Power +
HP Restoring Power ++
Exp. Point Power +
Exp. Point Power ++

RECEIVE POWER

Catch Pokémon in the Entree Forest

The Pokémon you added to your party in Pokémon Global Link will appear in the Entree Forest for you to catch. (p. 165).

The Tangela your Pokémon saw in the dream appeared!

Cities and routes you can visit through the Entralink

Black City	Opelucid City	Route 13
Driftveil City	Route 5	Route 14
Driftveil Drawbridge	Route 6	Route 15
Icirrus City	Route 7	Route 16
Lacunosa Town	Route 8	Tubeline Bridge
Marvelous Bridge	Route 9	Undella Town
Mistralton City	Route 11	White Forest
Nimbasa City	Route 12	

1 You can go to other players' worlds

The fun thing about the Entralink is that you can visit other players' worlds. You can visit not only your friends' and family members' worlds but also the worlds of people with whom you have not exchanged Friend Codes.

● How to visit other players' worlds

Cross the bridge, then tap the city where the other player is

Tap "WIRELESS" and then tap "ENTRALINK" to go to the Entralink. Cross the bridge, and you are there. Tap the Touch Screen and you can move to where the other player is.

Tap "ENTRALINK"

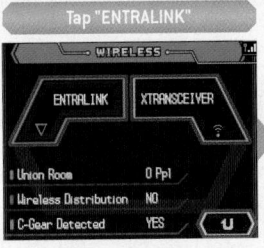

Cross the bridge to the other player's world

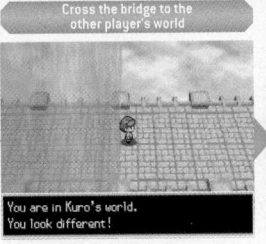

Tap the city where the other player is

● What you can do in the other player's world

1 Check his or her Entree and receive a mission

Check the Entree in the other player's Entralink to receive various missions (p. 144).

2 Check his or her Entree and receive Pass Powers

Check the Entree in the other player's Entralink to receive Pass Powers (p. 145).

3 Go to the cities and routes in the other player's world through the Entralink

Visit Black City and White Forest, both of which are only found in one of the versions (p. 146).

4 Find Pass Orbs in the other player's world

You need Pass Orbs to activate your Pass Powers. You may find Pass Orbs at several places, such as in front of a Pokémon Center.

Your Entree grows

As you complete missions, your Entree will grow. Complete a mission received in *Pokémon Black Version* to raise the "Black Lv." and in *Pokémon White Version* to raise the "White Lv." As the levels go up, the Entree grows.

● Growing taller!

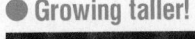

2 ▶ Receiving missions in the other player's world

In the Entralink, you can check the other player's Entree for various missions, including challenging him or her to a battle and selling an item. There are six types of mission. You can try the same mission as many times as you like, so enjoy them often with friends!

● **How to receive missions in the other player's world**

Cross the bridge and check the other player's Entree

Check the other player's Entree for missions as you cannot receive missions from your own Entree. Once you've received a mission, tap the Touch Screen on your Nintendo DS system to go to the city or route where the other player is. Complete the mission and you'll receive Pass Orbs.

● **Mission details** ● The text in parentheses in the missions below could have a different word each time.

SUPPORT MISSION	Talk to (Other Trainer's Name) and give (_____ Power)! Accomplished if you talk to the Trainer, and failed if time runs out or another Trainer completes the mission first.
SUPPORT MISSION	Let (Other Trainer's Name) talk to you and give (_____ Power)! Accomplished if the other Trainer talks to you, and failed if time runs out or another Trainer completes the mission first.
RESCUE MISSION	Talk to (Other Trainer's Name) in a battle and give HP Restoring Power. Accomplished if you talk to the Trainer, and failed if time runs out or another Trainer completes the mission first.
ITEM MISSION	Stash one (Item Name) (In a Certain Location)! Accomplished if you reach the place to stash the item, and failed if time runs out.
ITEM MISSION	Sell one (Item Name) to (Other Trainer's Name) at a reasonable price! Note: This is not available when three people are connected. Accomplished if you sell the item, and failed if time runs out or if the Trainer did not buy the item.
BATTLE MISSION	Challenge (Other Trainer's Name) to a battle! Note: This is not available when three people are connected. Accomplished if you battle, regardless of the battle results, and failed if time runs out or the Trainer turns you down.

Complete all the missions and you'll get a special reward!

Where you receive a mission, the screen indicates completed missions with either black or white dots, depending on the versions of the players who completed the missions. When the sixth mission is completed, the Black and White levels go up by the corresponding number of dots. If five missions have white or black dots already, you'll receive a special reward when you complete the last mission.

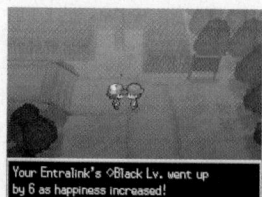

3 Receive a Pass Power from the Entree

A Pass Power can help you find Pokémon, battle them, and more. The Pass Orbs you receive when you complete missions enable you to use Pass Powers. You'll be able to use more powerful Pass Powers as your Entree's level goes up.

● How to receive Pass Powers from the Entree

Check the Entree and select "RECEIVE POWER"

You can receive Pass Powers from your or other players' Entrees. Use it through the Tag Log (p. 131). The effect is shared by all the members on the Tag Log, including you.

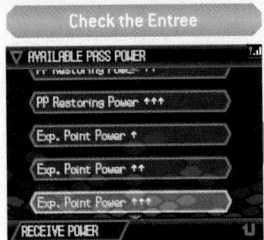
Check the Entree

Select a player on the Tag Log

Share it through C-Gear

● Pass Powers you can receive from the Entree

Pass Power	Pass Orb	Effective period of time	Effect	Minimum level to receive this Power	
				Black Lv.	White Lv.
Bargain Power ↑	3	3 minutes	Poké Mart gives a 10% discount	13	0
Bargain Power ↑ ↑	4	3 minutes	Poké Mart gives a 25% discount	22	0
Bargain Power ↑ ↑ ↑	5	3 minutes	Poké Mart gives a 50% discount	30	0
Befriending Power ↑	2	3 minutes	Helps Pokémon grow friendly a little faster	0	7
Befriending Power ↑ ↑	3	3 minutes	Helps Pokémon grow friendly faster	0	19
Befriending Power ↑ ↑ ↑	4	3 minutes	Helps Pokémon grow friendly much faster	0	25
Capture Power ↑	4	3 minutes	Increases the chance to catch Pokémon a little	5	5
Capture Power ↑ ↑	5	3 minutes	Increases the chance to catch Pokémon	11	11
Capture Power ↑ ↑ ↑	6	3 minutes	Increases the chance to catch Pokémon a lot	30	30
Encounter Power ↑	2	3 minutes	Increases the chance of encountering wild Pokémon a little	9	3
Encounter Power ↑ ↑	3	3 minutes	Increases the chance of encountering wild Pokémon	12	8
Encounter Power ↑ ↑ ↑	4	3 minutes	Increases the chance of encountering wild Pokémon a lot	19	14
Encounter Power ↓	2	3 minutes	Decreases the chance of encountering wild Pokémon a little	0	5
Encounter Power ↓ ↓	3	3 minutes	Decreases the chance of encountering wild Pokémon	0	10
Encounter Power ↓ ↓ ↓	4	3 minutes	Decreases the chance of encountering wild Pokémon a lot	0	26
Exp. Point Power ↑	2	3 minutes	Increases the Exp. Points from a battle a little	0	0
Exp. Point Power ↑ ↑	3	3 minutes	Increases the Exp. Points from a battle	2	0
Exp. Point Power ↑ ↑ ↑	4	3 minutes	Increases the Exp. Points from a battle a lot	16	0
Exp. Point Power ↓	2	3 minutes	Decreases the Exp. Points from a battle a little	3	9
Exp. Point Power ↓ ↓	3	3 minutes	Decreases the Exp. Points from a battle	8	12
Exp. Point Power ↓ ↓ ↓	4	3 minutes	Decreases the Exp. Points from a battle a lot	14	19
Hatching Power ↑	3	3 minutes	Helps Eggs hatch a little faster	0	13
Hatching Power ↑ ↑	4	3 minutes	Helps Eggs hatch faster	0	22
Hatching Power ↑ ↑ ↑	5	3 minutes	Helps Eggs hatch much faster	0	30
HP Restoring Power ↑	2	0 minutes	Restores the HP of the lead Pokémon by 20	0	0
HP Restoring Power ↑ ↑	3	0 minutes	Restores the HP of the lead Pokémon by 50	0	2
HP Restoring Power ↑ ↑ ↑	4	0 minutes	Restores the HP of the lead Pokémon by 200	0	16
PP Restoring Power ↑	2	0 minutes	Restores the PP of all the moves of the lead Pokémon by 5	7	0
PP Restoring Power ↑ ↑	3	0 minutes	Restores the PP of all the moves of the lead Pokémon by 10	19	0
PP Restoring Power ↑ ↑ ↑	4	0 minutes	Fully restores the PP of all the moves of the lead Pokémon	25	0
Prize Money Power ↑	2	3 minutes	The prize money from a battle becomes 150% the usual amount	5	0
Prize Money Power ↑ ↑	3	3 minutes	The prize money from a battle becomes 200% the usual amount	10	0
Prize Money Power ↑ ↑ ↑	4	3 minutes	The prize money from a battle becomes 300% the usual amount	26	0

 Some Pass Powers are only available through Support Missions

Some of the Pass Powers become available only through Support Missions. Such powers include Hatching Power S and Hatching Power MAX. The "S" powers last 30 minutes, while "MAX" powers last as long as an hour. Take advantage of them!

3 Expand Black City or White Forest

These people like to move from one place to another

Black City is found in *Pokémon Black Version* and White Forest is found in *Pokémon White Version*.

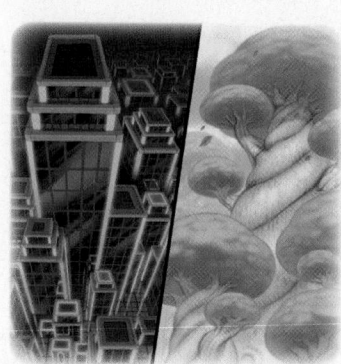

Develop Black City (or White Forest) by having people move in!

Use the Entralink, and people will come to Black City or White Forest.

● **How to let people move in through the Entralink**

Go to someone else's Black City or White Forest

In order to let people move into your Black City or White Forest, you'll need to go to the Entralink. When you talk to the people in another player's Black City or White Forest, some of them may show interest in moving to your world. Answer "YES" to let them move in.

Tap "ENTRALINK"

Cross the bridge to the other player's world

Tap the Touch Screen to move to Black City (or White Forest)

Tap where the adventurer is to warp to that place.

Talk to the people

I want to go to White Forest where I can be more in my natural state.

Listen to their wishes

I can be more in my natural state. Would you take me?

Black City and White Forest grow larger

● **How they look before and after development**

When you let people move in, your city or forest grows larger. However, you can only let up to 10 people live there, and two people with the same name cannot live in the same place.

Black City (not developed)

Black City (developed)

White Forest (not developed)

White Forest (developed)

4 Greet Other Players in the Union Room

The first step to Union Room communications

At the Union Room in Pokémon Center 2F, players can gather to participate in various games.

Surprise your friends with your Trainer Card

The first step in Union Room interactions is greetings. When you greet someone there, you can show your Trainer Card.

● **How to greet others**

Greet each other and show off your Trainer Cards

To show your Trainer Card to a friend, talk to the friend in the Union Room and select "Greet." You can then offer to show your Trainer Card.

Talk to a friend
Talking to Shiro...

Select "Greet"
▶ Greet / Battle / Trade / Draw / Spin / Cancel
This is Shiro! Is there something you wanted to do?

Show your Trainer Cards
Sure thing! Let me show you my Trainer Card.

● **You can check both sides of your Trainer Card**

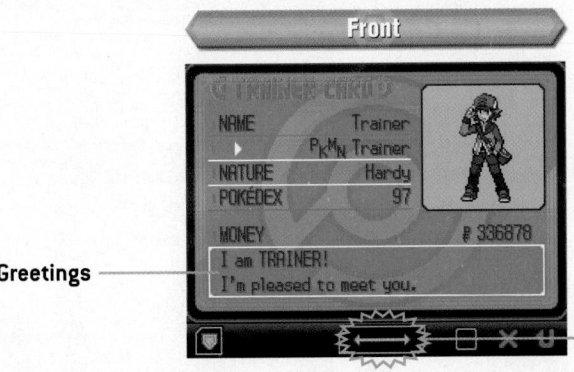

Front

NAME   Trainer
        PᴋᴍN Trainer
NATURE Hardy
POKÉDEX 97
MONEY   ₽ 336878
I am TRAINER!
I'm pleased to meet you.

Greetings ——

Back

ID No.   32561
TIME   50:59
ADVENTURE STARTED
                3/6/2011

Trainer

—— Signature

● Tap it and you can check the back of your Trainer Card.

You can animate your signature on the back of your Trainer Card

The back of your Trainer Card has a blank box. You can use the stylus to sign your name there. You can animate your signed name on the Trainer Card. Write two words side by side and press the arrow button for animation.

Wireless

5 Enjoy Battles in the Union Room

Up to four people can battle together with their favorite Pokémon

One of the good things about the Pokémon Wireless Club Union Room is that you can battle anyone who is in the same Union Room. You'll see your battle friends there. You may even come across people you least expect!

Up to five different formats are available, depending on the number of participants

In the Union Room, you can choose from five battle formats: Single Battle, Double Battle, Triple Battle, Rotation Battle, and Multi Battle. You can also set detailed rules, such as limiting the battling Pokémon's levels.

● How to battle

Select the number of participants and the battle format

To enjoy Pokémon battles, you need to talk to a friend in the Union Room and select "Battle." Then select the number of participants, the battle format, and any additional rules.

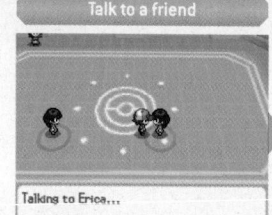

Talk to a friend

Talking to Erica...

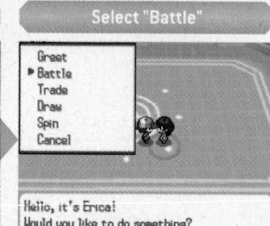

Select "Battle"

Greet
▶Battle
Trade
Draw
Spin
Cancel

Hello, it's Erica!
Would you like to do something?

Select the number of participants

▶Battles for two
Battles for four
Cancel

Hello, it's Erica!
Would you like to do something?

● Available battle formats depend on the number of participants

Single Battle — Battles for two

The basic battle format, where two Pokémon battle one-on-one.

Double Battle — Battles for two

Two Pokémon on each side are sent out for a battle. Combinations between the two become key.

Triple Battle — Battles for two

Three Pokémon on each side are sent out for a battle. This format requires you to think about the range of your team's moves.

Rotation Battle — Battles for two

Send out three Pokémon and let one of them fight every turn.

Multi Battle — Battles for four

This is a format where two friends form a tag team for two-on-two battles. One Pokémon is sent out at a time.

Help your Pokémon in battle with the Wonder Launcher

The Wonder Launcher is an item that enables Trainers to use items, such as Potions and X Attacks, on their Pokémon (p. 182).

Trainer launched the Dire Hit toward Samurott!

COMMUNICATION FEATURES GUIDE

ENJOY BATTLES IN THE UNION ROOM

6 Link Trade Pokémon in the Union Room

Pokémon in PC Boxes can be traded, too!

Trading in the Pokémon Wireless Club Union Room is called Negotiation Trade. You get to select up to three Pokémon and negotiate a one-to-one trade with another player.

You can check each other's Pokémon before the trade begins

Negotiation Trade is a new way to trade Pokémon, just introduced in *Pokémon Black* and *Pokémon White*. You and the other Trainer both offer up to three Pokémon for a fair trade. Depending on the offer by the other Trainer, you may experience unusual Pokémon Trades.

● **How to trade Pokémon**

Offer up to three Pokémon for a Negotiation Trade

To start a Negotiation Trade, you need to talk to a friend in the Union Room and select "Trade." You then select up to three Pokémon to offer. You can select from the PC Boxes as well as from your party for easy trading. Once you and the other Trainer are both happy with the offer, choose one each for a trade.

Use icons to show how you feel about the other Trainer's offer

Once you've offered up to three Pokémon, you can use four icons to communicate with the other Trainer. You can use the smiley or frowning face icon, for example.

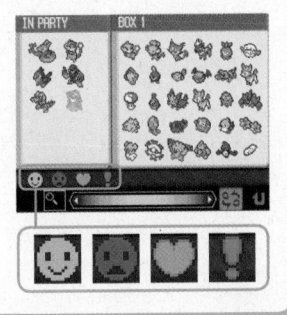

7 Have Fun Drawing in the Union Room

Up to five people can have fun drawing together

At the Pokémon Wireless Club Union Room, up to five people can enjoy drawing at once. Try drawing your favorite Pokémon and Trainers.

Have fun sending messages to each other while you draw with your friends

The cool thing about drawing with up to five people is that you can have fun discussing what to draw. It's also interesting to watch how the drawing progresses, because everyone can draw freely. Whether it's going to be a masterpiece, or an utter failure... That'll keep you excited while drawing.

● Draw together

Anyone can join in anytime for a drawing party of up to five people

To start drawing, you need to talk to a friend in the Union Room and select "Draw." If you want to join a drawing party that's already started, talk to the person who started it.

Talk to a friend	Select "Draw"	You can join a drawing party that's already happening anytime
Talking to Kuro...	Great / Battle / Trade / ▸ Draw / Spin / Cancel — This is Kuro! Is there something you wanted to do?	1 Trainer / 2 Kuro / 3 Shiro

● How to draw

Members

1 Trainer
2 Kuro
3 Shiro
4 Erica
5 Allie

Change line thickness
Choose from three thicknesses from fine to thick.

Pen tip
Each tip is numbered to show which one belongs to which player.

Palette
Tap to change the pen color. There are eight colors available.

Cancel

8 Spin Trade Eggs in the Union Room

Egg trading could make your day

In a Spin Trade, up to five players each bring a Pokémon Egg to trade. The table turns as the game begins, so nobody knows where each Egg ends up.

You'll never know which Egg you'll receive!

Spin Trades can be full of fun and surprises. You could even give away a rare Pokémon Egg to really surprise your friends! If you're eager to give Spin Trades a whirl, see pages 122 through 125 to learn how to find Pokémon Eggs.

● How to do a Spin Trade

Up to five people can participate in a Spin Trade

To start a Spin Trade, you need to talk to a friend in the Union Room and select "Spin." If you want to join a Spin Trade, just talk to the person who initiated it. Spin Trade is available for two to five people. Tap the Touch Screen as the table with the Eggs starts to rotate. This bounces the Eggs on the table, and you may end up with an Egg in the bonus area.

Talk to a friend	Select "Spin"	Look for trade buddies
	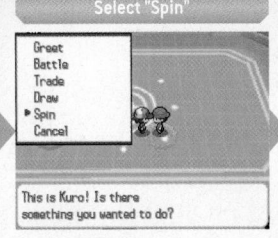	

The Eggs start to spin	The Eggs are shuffling...	You'll receive a friend's Egg!
	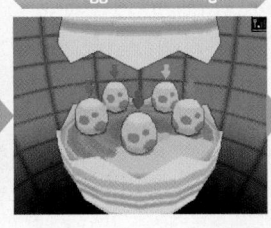	

Land in the bonus area to get a Berry

The table has a bonus area. When the spinning ends, the player who receives an Egg that landed on the bonus area will also receive a Berry as a bonus.

● Bonus area

For two people

Half the table is the bonus area

For three people

Two-thirds of the table is the bonus area

For four people

Half the table is the bonus area

For five people

Three-fifths of the table is the bonus area

● Bonus area Berries

Number of traders	Bonus Berries
Two or three	Figy Berry, Wiki Berry, Mago Berry, Aguav Berry, or Iapapa Berry
Four	Cheri Berry, Chesto Berry, Pecha Berry, Rawst Berry, or Aspear Berry
Five	Pomeg Berry, Kelpsy Berry, Qualot Berry, Hondew Berry, Grepa Berry, or Tamato Berry

ONLINE

1 Accessing Nintendo Wi-Fi Connection

Connect to Nintendo Wi-Fi Connection to trade and battle

You can connect your *Pokémon Black Version* or *Pokémon White Version* to Nintendo Wi-Fi Connection to battle and trade Pokémon with your friends in faraway places and even players you've never met. Get Nintendo Wi-Fi Connection set up for more gameplay.

 Connecting to Nintendo Wi-Fi Connection **1** **Get ready to play online**

To access Nintendo Wi-Fi Connection, you'll need a PC that is connected to the Internet and a wireless router. The wireless router will connect you to Nintendo Wi-Fi Connection so you can play online!

● **The devices you need for Nintendo Wi-Fi Connection**

Computer

Wireless Router

 Connecting to Nintendo Wi-Fi Connection **2** **Set up your Nintendo DS system for Nintendo Wi-Fi Connection**

Once Nintendo Wi-Fi Connection is available, set up your Nintendo DS for connection. Go to System Settings with a Nintendo DSi or Nintendo DSi XL for setup. Select "NINTENDO WFC SETTINGS" from the main menu with a Nintendo DS or Nintendo DS Lite.

● **How to set up Nintendo Wi-Fi Connection** ● This image is from a Nintendo DSi system.

Follow the instructions on screen for easy set up

Select "Connection Settings" and choose Connection 1, 2, or 3 to set up an Access Point.

Select "Connection Settings"

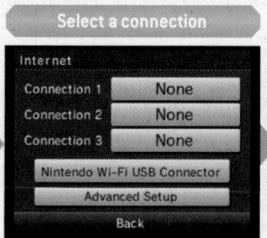

Select a connection

Set up the connection

 Nintendo Wi-Fi Connection gameplay features are found at any Pokémon Center

Drop by any Pokémon Center during your adventure to visit the Wi-Fi Club or the Global Terminal. Go to the reception area on any Pokémon Center 2F. Note that you'll need to have already exchanged Friend Codes to have fun in the Wi-Fi Club.

● **Pokémon Center**

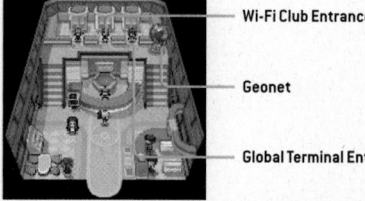

Wi-Fi Club Entrance

Geonet

Global Terminal Entrance

ONLINE

2 Use the Xtransceiver in the Wi-Fi Club

You and distant friends can talk to each other face-to-face

At the Wi-Fi Club, you can talk to your friends over the Xtransceiver. And if you and your friends are playing with the Nintendo DSi or Nintendo DSi XL, you can talk to each other face-to-face, no matter how far apart you are.

Have one-on-one conversations at the Wi-Fi Club

You can enjoy one-on-one communication with a friend with the Xtransceiver over Nintendo Wi-Fi Connection. However, you cannot have a four-way conversation. You can look for someone to chat with or wait for someone to approach you to chat so you can start talking on the Xtransceiver.

● Icons

People who are talking to someone else with the Xtransceiver

People who are looking for someone to talk with using the Xtransceiver

● How to use the Xtransceiver at the Wi-Fi Club

Talk to a friend in the lobby and use the Xtransceiver

Talk to a friend and use the Xtransceiver. You'll hear your friend's voice over the speaker through Nintendo Wi-Fi Connection. With Nintendo DSi and Nintendo DSi XL, you can use graffiti mode, too.

Talk to a friend	Select "Xtransceiver"	You can talk to a friend
		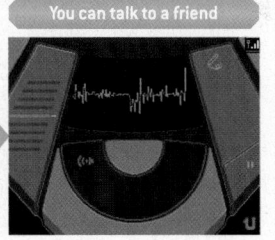

See p. 140 for how to use the Xtransceiver ▶

Have fun talking over voice chat

You can use Voice Chat with a friend in the Wi-Fi Club. You can select "Voice Chat" from the menu. Voice Chat works even when you're in the middle of Wi-Fi Club activities like battling or trading. You can press the X Button to turn it off.

● How to use Voice Chat

Talk to a friend	Select "Voice Chat"	Have fun talking!
		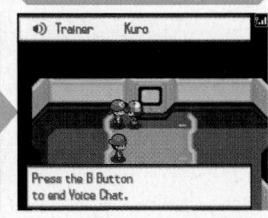

● Icons 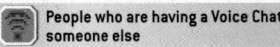 People who are having a Voice Chat with someone else   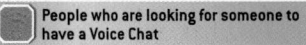 People who are looking for someone to have a Voice Chat

ONLINE

3 Enjoy Battles in the Wi-Fi Club

You can battle with your friends in the Wi-Fi Club

In the Wi-Fi Club, two people can battle each other. You can choose from various battle formats and

rules. Every battle will be different, even with the same friend!

Send out your favorite Pokémon for serious battles

In the Wi-Fi Club, battles are held between two players, so Multi Battles are not available. You can look for someone to chat with or wait for someone to approach you to chat so you can start a battle.

● **Icons**

■	People who are battling with someone else
■	People who are looking for someone to battle

● How to battle in the Wi-Fi Club

Talk to a friend for Pokémon battles

Talk to a friend and select "Battle." Choose a battle format and select either "No restrictions" or "Flat rule." Then decide whether you want to use the Wonder Launcher or not. Once everything is agreed upon, select your Pokémon for the battle. Take a look at the table below for battle formats and rules.

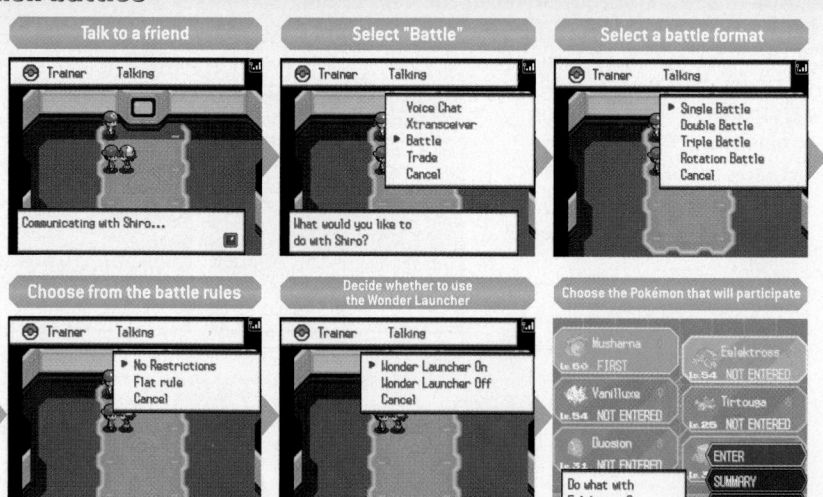

● Battle rules available in the Wi-Fi Club

Battle Format		Single Battle, Double Battle, Triple Battle, Rotation Battle
Battle Rule	No restrictions	Pokémon of any level can battle. There are no restrictions on what Pokémon or items you can use.
	Flat rule	Any Pokémon above Level 50 will be set to Level 50 for the battle. Special Pokémon cannot be used, and your team cannot have duplicate Pokémon or duplicate held items.
Wonder Launcher		ON or OFF

● Special Pokémon: Mewtwo, Mew, Lugia, Ho-Oh, Celebi, Kyogre, Groudon, Rayquaza, Jirachi, Deoxys, Dialga, Palkia, Giratina, Phione, Manaphy, Darkrai, Shaymin, Arceus, Victini, Reshiram, Zekrom, Kyurem, and Eggs.

◉ See p. 135 for the format details ▶

Link Trade Pokémon in the Wi-Fi Club

4

You can use Negotiation Trade with your distant friends

You can trade Pokémon with your friends in the Wi-Fi Club. The Wi-Fi Club uses Negotiation

Trade, where three Pokémon are selected and negotiated for a one-to-one trade.

You can choose one of the three offered Pokémon to trade

In the Wi-Fi Club, you'll choose one of the three offered Pokémon to trade. You can look for someone to chat with or wait for someone to approach you to chat so you can trade.

● **Icons**

People who are trading with someone else

People who are looking for someone to trade with

● How to trade Pokémon in the Wi-Fi Club

Decide which one of the Pokémon on the top screen you want

Talk to a friend and select "Trade." Select three Pokémon from your party or PC Boxes and use the stylus to show them on the top screen. Use icons to show how you feel as the other person offers three Pokémon. Once you and the other person express your feelings, tap 🎮. Tap the Pokémon you want and the trade begins.

Talk to a friend

Select "Trade"

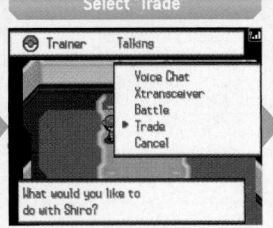

Select up to three Pokémon

Share how you feel

Tap 🎮

Select the one you want

See p. 149 for the icon details

 Trading Pokémon is an important part of the game

Trading Pokémon has many benefits. Trade Pokémon whenever you have the chance, and it'll help you with your adventure and battles.

● **Perks of trading**

1 You can get closer to completing the Pokédex

2 Traded Pokémon gain more Experience Points

3 Eggs are more likely to be found when a traded Pokémon and your own Pokémon are left at the Pokémon Day Care

5

Battle Trainers Worldwide with Random Matchups

You and a distant Trainer can battle head-to-head

Random Matchup at the Global Terminal enables battles with strangers. You will be randomly matched up with another player as you connect to Nintendo Wi-Fi Connection. You'll have no idea what Pokémon team you'll be facing or what strategy your opponent will use. Take up this serious challenge!

Battle with Trainers worldwide

Random Matchup is played through Global Terminal and there is no need to exchange Friend Codes. Talk to the receptionist at the Global Terminal to connect to Nintendo Wi-Fi Connection and you are ready to battle.

How to use Random Matchup

You'll be randomly matched with another player as you connect to Nintendo Wi-Fi Connection

Talk to the reception at the Global Terminal and select "Random Matchup." Choose from Single Battle, Double Battle, Rotation Battle, or Launcher Battle, then select either Free Mode or Rating Mode. Finally, select the Pokémon to participate, and you are ready to battle.

Select "Random Matchup"

Select a battle format
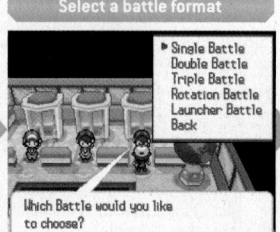

Select a mode
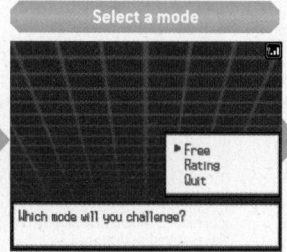

Choose the Pokémon that will participate
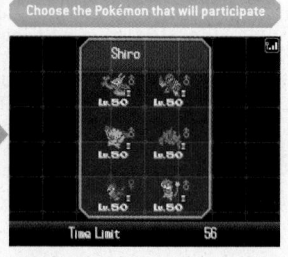

How to play Random Matchup

1 Choose the mode that suits you

Random Matchup has two modes for you to choose from. Free Mode will pair you randomly with another Trainer who has selected Free Mode. Rating Mode is recommended to those who prefer serious and tough battles.

Two modes available at Random Matchup

Free Mode

Anyone can participate in battles as long as they have access to Nintendo Wi-Fi Connection. Players are matched up randomly.
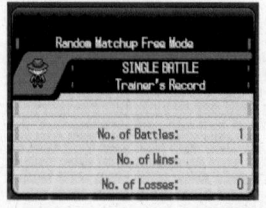

Rating Mode

Players are matched according to their current Ratings. Your Rating is a number that goes up or down depending on battle results.
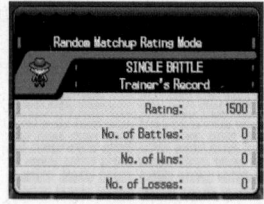

The Ratings and Rankings can be checked through the GBU when you play with Trainers all over the world through Rating Mode. See p. 177 for more on the GBU

2 Learn the unique rules of Random Matchup

Random Matchup has a few unique rules. Unlike in other Link Battles, certain steps of a Random Matchup battle have time limits. Certain items are banned, and Pokémon nicknames are not shown. Check the table below for a full list of special rules.

Battle Time and Command Time are tracked

Battle Time, how long the battle has left, and Command Time, how long you have to choose a move, are displayed during a battle. Check to make sure they don't run out.

● Random Matchup battle formats and rules

Single Battle	Party size	Pokémon level	Level adjustment	Same Pokémon	Same items	Banned Pokémon
	3	Lv. 50	Yes	not allowed	not allowed	Special Pokémon
	Banned item	**Battle Time**	**Command Time**	**Pokémon nickname**	**Reveal Pokémon**	**Pokémon Reveal time**
	Soul Dew	60 minutes	2 minutes	not displayed	Yes	90 sec.

Double Battle	Party size	Pokémon level	Level adjustment	Same Pokémon	Same items	Banned Pokémon
	4	Lv. 50	Yes	not allowed	not allowed	Special Pokémon
	Banned item	**Battle Time**	**Command Time**	**Pokémon nickname**	**Reveal Pokémon**	**Pokémon Reveal time**
	Soul Dew	60 minutes	3 minutes	not displayed	Yes	90 sec.

Triple Battle	Party size	Pokémon level	Level adjustment	Same Pokémon	Same items	Banned Pokémon
	6	Lv. 50	Yes	not allowed	not allowed	Special Pokémon
	Banned item	**Battle Time**	**Command Time**	**Pokémon nickname**	**Reveal Pokémon**	**Pokémon Reveal time**
	Soul Dew	60 minutes	3 minutes	not displayed	Yes	90 sec.

Rotation Battle	Party size	Pokémon level	Level adjustment	Same Pokémon	Same items	Banned Pokémon
	4	Lv. 50	Yes	not allowed	not allowed	Special Pokémon
	Banned item	**Battle Time**	**Command Time**	**Pokémon nickname**	**Reveal Pokémon**	**Pokémon Reveal time**
	Soul Dew	60 minutes	3 minutes	not displayed	Yes	90 sec.

Launcher Battle (Triple Battle with the Wonder Launcher)	Party size	Pokémon level	Level adjustment	Same Pokémon	Same items	Banned Pokémon
	6	Lv. 50	Yes	not allowed	not allowed	Special Pokémon
	Banned item	**Battle Time**	**Command Time**	**Pokémon nickname**	**Reveal Pokémon**	**Pokémon Reveal time**
	Soul Dew	60 minutes	3 minutes	not displayed	Yes	90 sec.

● "Level adjustment" means any Pokémon at Lv. 50 or higher will be automatically set to Lv. 50 for the battle.

● Special Pokémon: Mewtwo, Mew, Lugia, Ho-Oh, Celebi, Kyogre, Groudon, Rayquaza, Jirachi, Deoxys, Chatot, Dialga, Palkia, Giratina, Phione, Manaphy, Darkrai, Shaymin, Arceus, Victini, Reshiram, Zekrom, and Kyurem

◉ See p. 135 for the format details ▶

 ## Find your Game Sync ID

You'll need to register your Game Sync ID before you can use Random Matchup Rating Mode. Tap "ONLINE" on the C-Gear to connect to Nintendo Wi-Fi Connection and have your Game Sync ID issued. Once your Game Sync ID is issued, register it at the Pokémon Global Link.

◉ See p. 163 for how to register your Game Sync ID ▶

Warning!

Your Rating data will be lost if you switch Nintendo DS systems

Once you've launched Nintendo Wi-Fi Connection playing the game, certain data such as the Rating Mode data and Friend Codes will be lost if you play the game with a Nintendo DS system other than the one you usually use.

● There is a way to move your data to another Nintendo DS system. Check your Nintendo Wi-Fi Connection Instruction Booklet for details.

ONLINE

6 Trade Pokémon Worldwide Using GTS

You don't need to exchange Friend Codes to trade Pokémon

At the Global Terminal, you can select "Global Trade" for Pokémon trades with people you don't know. There are two ways to trade: GTS, where you set the conditions of the trade, and GTS Negotiations, where you set the rough conditions to search for people to trade with.

How to use Global Trade   **1** **Two ways to trade Pokémon**

There are two ways to trade Pokémon with GTS. One is to offer a Pokémon and wait for the trade to happen automatically. The other is to search to see if the Pokémon you want is already offered by other people. But you can only choose a Pokémon from your current Pokédex.

 Two different ways to trade Pokémon with GTS

---

1 **DEPOSIT POKÉMON**

Select "Global Trade" at the Global Terminal reception and then select "GTS." Connect to Nintendo Wi-Fi Connection and select "DEPOSIT POKÉMON." Then choose a Pokémon from your party or PC Boxes. After that, decide what kind of Pokémon you want, its gender, and its level. The trade will be completed automatically.

Select "GTS"	Select "DEPOSIT POKÉMON"	Select Pokémon to deposit	Decide what Pokémon you want

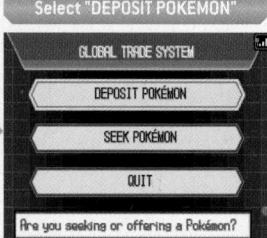 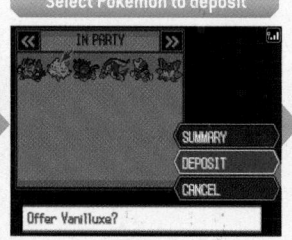 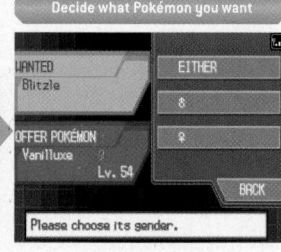

---

2 **SEEK POKÉMON**

Select "Global Trade" at the Global Terminal reception and then select "GTS." Connect to Nintendo Wi-Fi Connection and select "SEEK POKÉMON." Then decide what kind of Pokémon you want, its gender, etc. The people that match your search will be displayed, along with their trade requirements. Choose the person that best suits your preferences and trade.

Select "GTS"	Select "SEEK POKÉMON"	Decide what kind of Pokémon you want	Select one person from the candidates

 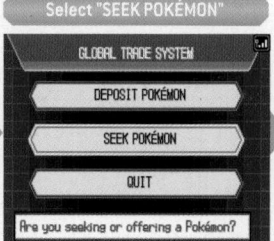 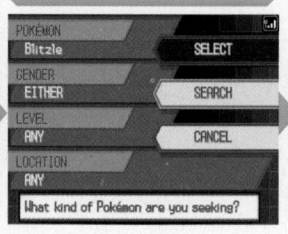 

2 **Trade Pokémon through GTS Negotiations**

In GTS Negotiations, you choose keywords such as "COOL" and "CUTE." Once the right person is found, you'll do a Negotiation Trade with three Pokémon each. There are two ways to search for people: "TRADE WITH ANYONE," where you are paired up automatically, and "TRADE RENDEZVOUS" where you can choose from people you've traded with before.

◉ See p. 149 for more on Negotiation Trade ▶

● **Two different ways to trade Pokémon with GTS Negotiations**

1 **TRADE WITH ANYONE**

Select "Global Trade" at the Global Terminal reception and then select "GTS Negotiations." Connect to Nintendo Wi-Fi Connection and select "TRADE WITH ANYONE." Then decide what kind of Pokémon you want and what kind you want to offer, as well as the level range you are looking for. Finally, select "SEARCH" to find the right person to trade with.

Select "GTS Negotiations"	Select "TRADE WITH ANYONE"	Decide on the trade conditions	Select "SEARCH"
		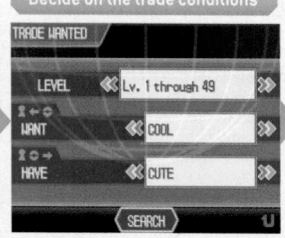	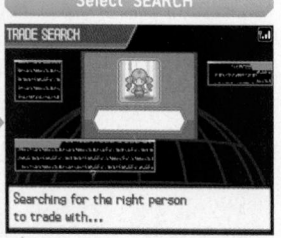

2 **TRADE RENDEZVOUS**

Select "Global Trade" at the Global Terminal reception and then select "GTS Negotiations." Connect to Nintendo Wi-Fi Connection and select "TRADE RENDEZVOUS." Then choose a person from the list on the Touch Screen.

Select "GTS Negotiations"	Select "TRADE RENDEZVOUS"	Select a person to trade with
		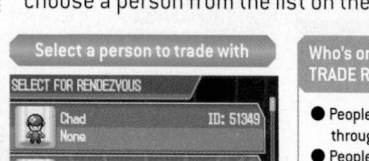

Who's on your TRADE RENDEZVOUS list?

● People you've traded with through IR
● People you've traded with at the Wi-Fi Club
● People you've traded with in the Union Room
● People you've traded with through GTS or GTS Negotiations

🐵 Register yourself on Geonet and tell where others are

Geonet is a high-tech globe that lets you register where you live. Once you've registered your location, you'll see a symbol marking your location. Geonet also shows the locations of Trainers you've traded with using Global Trade. Place the green cursor over those symbols and tap "VIEW" or press the X Button. Then the name of the place will be shown on the Top Screen.

● **How to register yourself on Geonet**

Select your location	A dot is displayed
	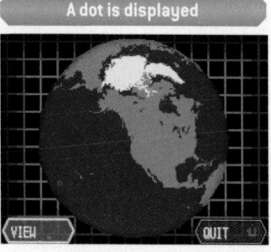

7 ▷ Check Out Other Players' Musical Photos

Enjoy Musical Photos from around the world

Musical Photos are the photos you get after participating in the Pokémon Musical. Go to the Global Terminal and select "Musical Photos" to check or post photos.

See how other people Dress Up their Pokémon

Once you get the Vs. Recorder and the Prop Case in Nimbasa City, you can access Musical Photos at the Global Terminal to see how other Trainers Dress Up their Pokémon.

● How to view and post Musical Photos

VIEW PHOTOS

Select "Musical Photos" at the Global Terminal reception and the Vs. Recorder will be launched. Tap "VIEW PHOTOS" and search for the kind of Pokémon you want to view.

Select "Musical Photos"

Select "VIEW PHOTOS"

Search by Pokémon name

Check out the photos!

SEND PHOTOS

Select "Musical Photos" at the Global Terminal reception and the Vs. Recorder will be launched. Tap "SEND PHOTOS" and send your Musical Photo.

Select "Musical Photos"

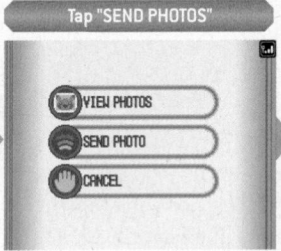
Tap "SEND PHOTOS"

Tap "SEND"

 You can take Musical Photos in Nimbasa City

If you want other people to see your Musical Photos, go to the Musical Theater in Nimbasa City. Dress Up your Pokémon with Props and you can get great photos (p. 260).

Watch Other Players' Battle Videos

Enjoy Battle Videos from around the world

Once you've obtained the Vs. Recorder in Nimbasa City, you can record battles as you battle against a friend or battles in the Battle Subway. Go to the Global Terminal and select "Battle Videos" to check the videos posted by other Trainers around the world or to post your own.

● See how top Trainers play!

You can study how other Trainers are battling with Battle Videos at the Global Terminal. Watch lots of them to examine different battle styles. You should be able to learn strategies you can use to improve your battle skills.

● How to view and post Battle Videos

VIEW BATTLE VIDEOS

Select "Battle Videos" at the Global Terminal reception and the Vs. Recorder will be launched. Tap "VIEW BATTLE VIDEOS" and choose from "SEARCH BY RANKING," "SEARCH," or "SEARCH BY NO." You can save up to three of your favorite videos.

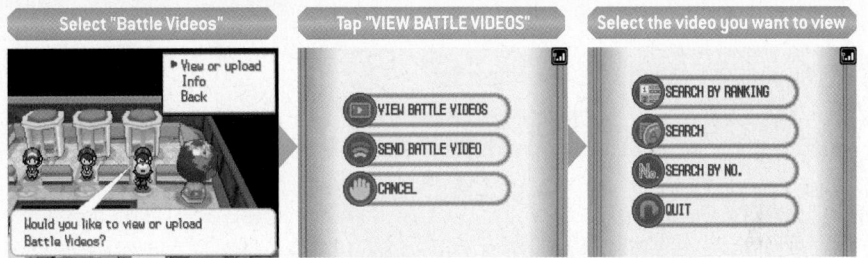

● How to select a Battle Video

Search method		Explanation
SEARCH BY RANKING	NEWEST 30	You can choose from the 30 latest Battle Videos.
	LINK BATTLES	You can choose from the 30 popular Battle Videos from Link Battle.
	BATTLE SUBWAY	You can choose from the 30 popular Battle Videos from the Battle Subway.
SEARCH	SEARCH BY FACILITY	Narrow down the Battle Videos by type and place, such as Random Matchup and the Battle Subway.
	SEARCH BY POKÉMON	Use the first letter of Pokémon to narrow down the Battle Videos.
	SEARCH YOUR LOCATION	Limit the Battle Video search to your location.
SEARCH BY NO.		If you're looking for a specific video, enter the number here.

SEND BATTLE VIDEO

Select "Battle Videos" at the Global Terminal reception and the Vs. Recorder will be launched. Tap "SEND BATTLE VIDEO" to send your saved video.

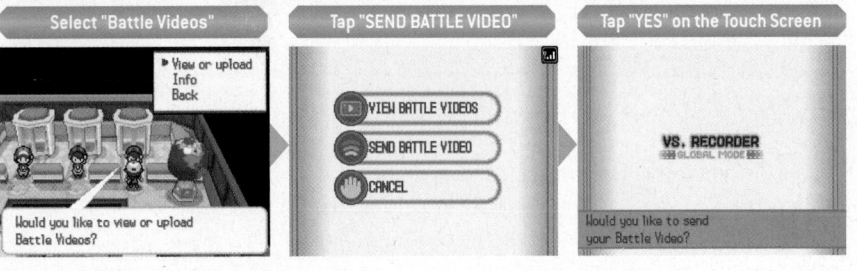

9 Use the Vs. Recorder to Record Battles

Save your battles in Link Battles and at the Battle Subway

When you are about to enter the Battle Subway in Nimbasa City for the first time, a woman of mystery gives you the Vs. Recorder. It's a high-tech device that lets you record battles with your friends and from your rides on the Battle Subway.

You can save one of your own Battle Videos and three more

You can save one of your own Battle Videos with the Vs. Recorder. If you go to the Global Terminal and select Battle Videos, you can save up to three Battle Videos of other players. You can also view your own Battle Subway and Random Matchup results.

Select "Vs. Recorder" from the Key Items Case in your Bag and tap "USE." You can watch videos whenever you like.

● What you can do with the Vs. Recorder

Save one of your Battle Videos

You can choose to save a Battle Video after a Link Battle with a friend or in the Battle Subway.

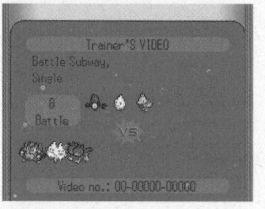

Save three other Battle Videos

If you go to the Global Terminal and select Battle Videos, you can also save up to three Battle Videos of other people.

Check your Battle Subway records and BP

You can check the Battle Subway records of each train as well as the BP you've earned.

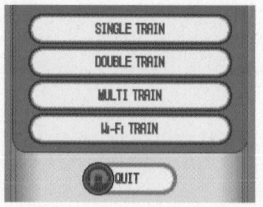

How to check your Random Matchup records

You can check the Global Terminal Random Matchup results for each mode. You can also check your current Rating.

 You can change the color of the Vs. Recorder screen

Tap the bottom-left or bottom-right corner of the Touch Screen after you've launched the Vs. Recorder. You can change the color of the screen from the usual green to pink, gray, yellow, red, brown, or orange. Tap a few times and the color changes every time you tap. Customize it to your preferences.

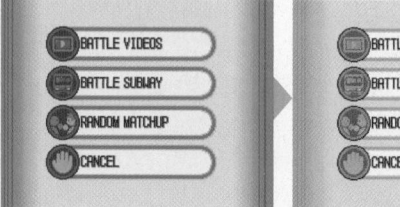

Access the Pokémon Global Link

PGL

1

Pokémon Trainers can visit every day!

The Pokémon Global Link (PGL) is a website that can be connected to your game. This is a brand-new feature packed with lots of fun things. You can visit every day to get cool stuff for your copy of *Pokémon Black* or *Pokémon White*!

Connecting to the PGL 1 Prepare to play online

To access Nintendo Wi-Fi Connection, you'll need a PC that is connected to the Internet and a wireless router. The wireless router will connect you to Nintendo Wi-Fi Connection so you can play online!

● **The devices you need for the Pokémon Global Link**

Computer

Wireless Router

The required specifications (If you need help, please read over the below with your parent or guardian)

■ **System requirements**

Windows®: Microsoft® Windows XP SP3/Windows Vista™/Windows 7
Macintosh®: Mac™ OS X v10.5 Leopard or later
Screen resolution: 1024 x 768 screen resolution or higher
Plug-ins: Adobe® Flash® Player version 10.1.53.64 or higher

*In order to update Flash Player, you'll need the administrator privileges on your computer. If necessary, please talk to your parent or guardian before you try to update it.

*Please be aware that the PGL may not be displayed correctly even when the recommended system requirements below are met depending on your browser or other settings.

Windows®: Intel® Core™ Duo or Intel Core Solo processor or higher
Macintosh®: Intel® processor or higher
Memory: 512 MB RAM or more

■ **Browser requirements**

The Pokémon Global Link is optimized for the browsers below. Please note that other browsers may not properly display it.
Windows®: Internet Explorer® 7 or higher
Macintosh®: Safari® 5 or higher

● Trademarks and registered trademarks are the property of their respective owners.

Connecting to the PGL 2 Sign up for the Pokémon Trainer Club

To access the Pokémon Global Link, you'll need to sign up for the Pokémon Trainer Club. (There is no membership fee.)

Pokémon Trainer Club

www.pokemon.com

Pokémon Global Link

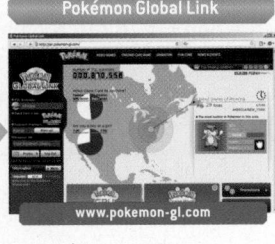

www.pokemon-gl.com

What you need to register at the PGL

● Pokémon Trainer Club Username
● Pokémon Trainer Club Password

 ### Have your Game Sync ID issued

Tap "ONLINE" on the C-Gear and select "GAME SYNC" to have your Game Sync ID issued. Tuck in a Pokémon, then access the PGL to register so you can log in.

1 Tap "GAME SYNC"

2 Your Game Sync ID is issued

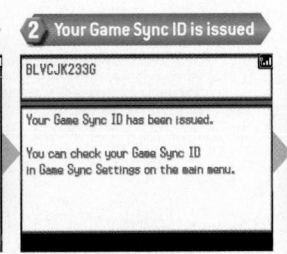

BLYCJK233G

Your Game Sync ID has been issued.

You can check your Game Sync ID in Game Sync Settings on the main menu.

3 Tuck in a Pokémon

Patrat fell asleep. It's sleeping soundly!

● Be sure to write down your Game Sync ID.
● You can select "GAME SYNC SETTINGS" from the main menu to check your Game Sync ID.

2 Befriend Pokémon in the Pokémon Dream World

Tuck in a Pokémon using Game Sync, then go to the Pokémon Dream World

The Pokémon Dream World is a magical place that you can visit by tucking in a Pokémon. The best part is you can take a Pokémon that you befriended in the Pokémon Dream World to *Pokémon Black Version* or *Pokémon White Version*.

Once you've befriended a Pokémon in the dream world, you can take it with you

A lot of the Pokémon that you can befriend in the Pokémon Dream World don't inhabit the Unova region. Take them to *Pokémon Black Version* or *Pokémon White Version*, and you will get closer to the completion of the National Pokédex (p. 116).

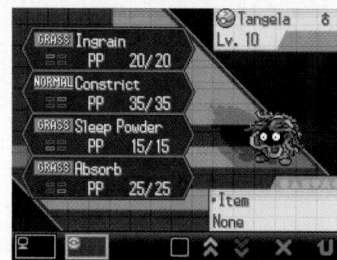

Befriended Pokémon have special Abilities called Hidden Abilities

Pokémon you meet in the dream world often have Hidden Abilities different from the usual Abilities.

 How to add a Pokémon to your party **1** **Meet Pokémon in the Island of Dreams**

In the Pokémon Dream World, there is a place called the Island of Dreams. The island is rich in verdant nature. If you go to the Island of Dreams, you can befriend Pokémon. On the Island of Dreams, make your way across the island to the Tree of Dreams. If you meet a Pokémon, you get to play a minigame to befriend the Pokémon. If you achieve the goal of the minigame, you can become friends with the Pokémon.

● **How to take befriended Pokémon out of the dream world**

Meet and become friends with Pokémon by playing minigames

Tap "ONLINE" on your C-Gear, then tap "GAME SYNC." Choose a Pokémon to tuck in and take to the Pokémon Dream World. Then, when you visit the Island of Dreams, you can enjoy minigames, and make a wish at the Tree of Dreams by offering a Berry. When you wake up your Pokémon, the Pokémon you made the wish for will then show up in the Entree Forest.

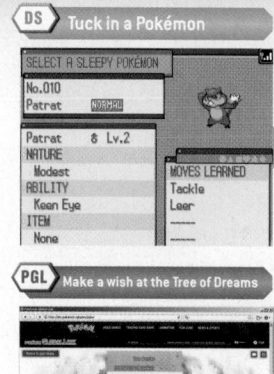
DS Tuck in a Pokémon

PGL The tucked-in Pokémon shows up

PGL Play minigames

PGL Make a wish at the Tree of Dreams

PGL Leave the Pokémon Dream World

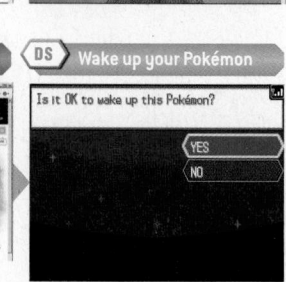
DS Wake up your Pokémon

If you take a Pokémon that you befriended in the Pokémon Dream World to *Pokémon Black Version* or *Pokémon White Version*, it will show up in the Entree Forest. When you catch it, it will be registered in your Pokédex. Add it to your party, and take it along on your adventure.

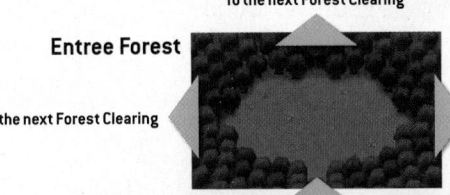
Tap "ENTRALINK"

Go to the Entree Forest

● **Entralink and Entree Forest**

To the next Forest Clearing

Entree Forest

To the next Forest Clearing

To the next Forest Clearing

The Entree Forest is huge, but the place where a Pokémon shows up is the first Forest Clearing. When the number of Pokémon increases, they will show up in other Forest Clearings.

The boy who gives you item(s)
If you have chosen item(s) that you got in the Pokémon Dream World from the Treasure Chest and clicked "Send," a boy will show up. Speak to the boy, and he will give you the item(s) you sent.

Return to your own world

● **How to catch a Pokémon in the Entree Forest**

Catch a Pokémon without fail in the Entralink

Tap "WIRELESS" on your C-Gear, then tap "ENTRALINK." When you arrive in the world of the Entralink, go to the Entree Forest located on its north side. If the Pokémon you befriended in the Pokémon Dream World is in the Entree Forest, a Dream Ball has been added to your Bag. As its name suggests, it's a Poké Ball that can be used only in the Entree Forest.

Go to the Entree Forest

Find the Pokémon

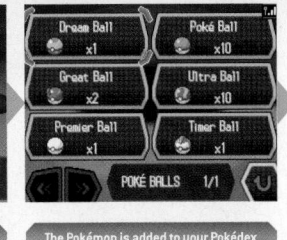
Choose a Poké Ball

Throw the Poké Ball

Catch the Pokémon

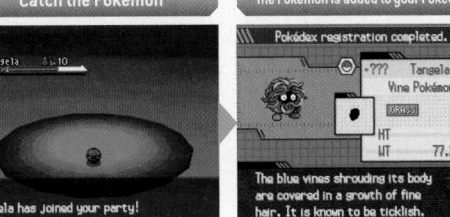
The Pokémon is added to your Pokédex

Areas in the Island of Dreams, and the Pokémon found there, increase over time

At first, the only place you can go on the Island of Dreams is the Pleasant Forest. However, depending on points called "Dream Points" that you can get in dreams, and the progress of your registered *Pokémon Black Version* or *Pokémon White Version*, you can explore new areas and find more kinds of items and Pokémon.

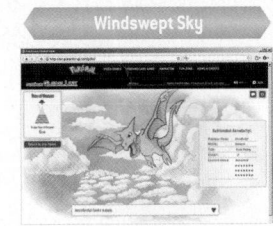
Windswept Sky

Sparkling Sea

Bring Back Pokémon from Other Regions in the Pokémon Dream World

Pokémon you can befriend in the Pokémon Dream World are ones that live in regions other than the Unova region. Most of them have Abilities that are different from the ones they would usually have. This page introduces some of these Pokémon. The Abilities written in red are these Hidden Abilities.

● **Some Pokémon you can bring from the Pokémon Dream World**

National Pokédex 077 **Ponyta**
● TYPE Fire
ABILITIES
Run Away
Flash Fire
Flame Body

National Pokédex 083 **Farfetch'd**
● TYPE Normal Flying
ABILITIES
Keen Eye
Inner Focus
Defiant

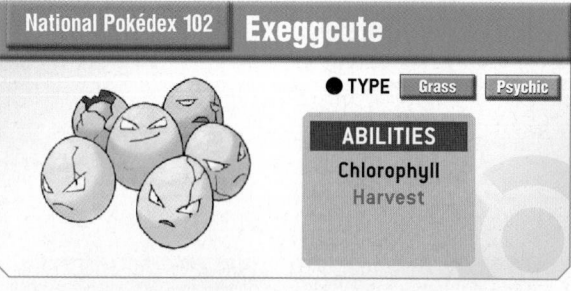

National Pokédex 102 **Exeggcute**
● TYPE Grass Psychic
ABILITIES
Chlorophyll
Harvest

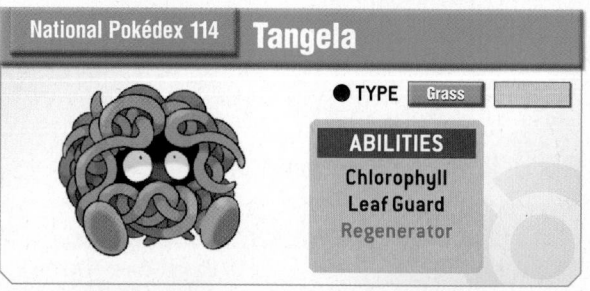

National Pokédex 114 **Tangela**
● TYPE Grass
ABILITIES
Chlorophyll
Leaf Guard
Regenerator

National Pokédex 115 **Kangaskhan**
● TYPE Normal
ABILITIES
Early Bird
Scrappy
Inner Focus

National Pokédex 174 **Igglybuff**
● TYPE Normal
ABILITIES
Cute Charm
Friend Guard

National Pokédex 187 **Hoppip**
● TYPE Grass
ABILITIES
Chlorophyll
Leaf Guard
Infiltrator

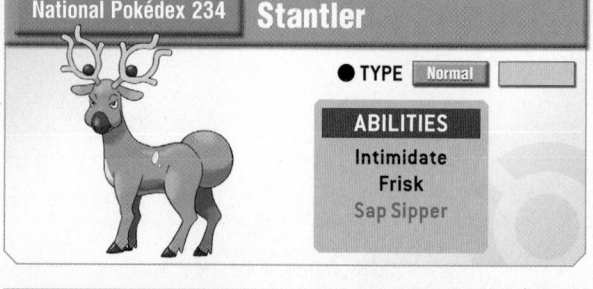

National Pokédex 234 **Stantler**
● TYPE Normal
ABILITIES
Intimidate
Frisk
Sap Sipper

National Pokédex 261 **Poochyena**
● TYPE Dark
ABILITIES
Run Away
Quick Feet
Rattled

National Pokédex 399 **Bidoof**
● TYPE Normal
ABILITIES
Simple
Unaware
Moody

3 Minigames in the Pokémon Dream World

Become friends with Pokémon by playing minigames on the Island of Dreams

If you play a minigame with a Pokémon that you met in the Pokémon Dream World and get a good result, the Pokémon will become your friend. All minigames are fun to play, so enjoy the games and make friends with lots of Pokémon. If you get a high score in a minigame, the Pokémon you befriended may know an uncommon move.

The first four kinds of minigames

The first four minigames in the Pokémon Dream World are Sky Race, Wailord's Water Spout, Pokémon Seek, and Ice Cream Scoop. Keep checking back because more minigames are expected to be added in the future. You may need a Berry, depending on the minigame.

If you meet a Pokémon, make sure to play the minigames

When a Pokémon jumps out, it's a chance to become friends. Play the minigame and do your best.

Complete the goal or the Pokémon won't be your friend

Each minigame has a goal or an objective. If you haven't practiced enough yet to achieve the goal or the objective, you can't become friends with the Pokémon.

● How to play the minigames

Sky Race

In this game, you use hand flags to guide a Pokémon's flight path to the goal. There are obstacles such as clouds and Delay Energy symbols in the race, and if the Pokémon hits them, its speed drops. Increase the Pokémon's speed by hitting three Boost Energy symbols that match the Pokémon's type, and guide the flying Pokémon to the goal.

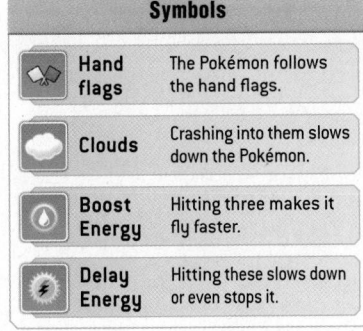

Symbols		
	Hand flags	The Pokémon follows the hand flags.
	Clouds	Crashing into them slows down the Pokémon.
	Boost Energy	Hitting three makes it fly faster.
	Delay Energy	Hitting these slows down or even stops it.

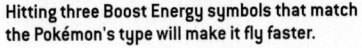

Try to speed up

Hitting three Boost Energy symbols that match the Pokémon's type will make it fly faster.

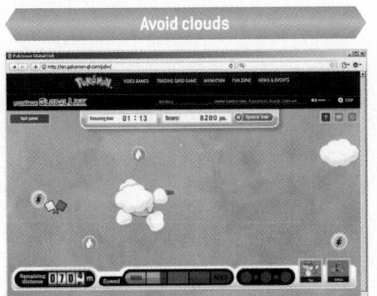

Avoid clouds

Crashing into clouds will slow down the Pokémon even if it has gained speed.

Wailord's Water Spout

Open more of the balls than the target amount. If a Pokémon hits a ball that matches its colors, the ball will open. Wailord will follow the mouse cursor. Left-click the mouse, and the Pokémon on the spout will be launched into the air to try to hit a ball. If a Pokémon falls into the sea, the multiplier will go down.

Combination of Pokémon and balls

Aim at the balls that match the Pokémon's colors and pattern. Study the combination before starting the game.

Pikachu and the yellow ball

Piplup and the blue ball

Meowth and the brown ball

Buizel and the orange ball

Open more of the balls than the target amount

A ball counter and the target amount are shown in the upper right corner of the screen.

Light up five lamps

When a Pokémon hits a ball, a lamp lights up, and when five lamps are lit, the multiplier goes up.

Pokémon Seek

Find one of a variety of missing Pokémon. They get lost in all kinds of places, such as the land, the sky, and the sea. For a clue, click "Listen carefully" and you will know whether the Pokémon is far away or close. Also, try to find the item that the missing Pokémon has lost to score more points.

Find the missing Pokémon

The missing Pokémon is different each time you play.

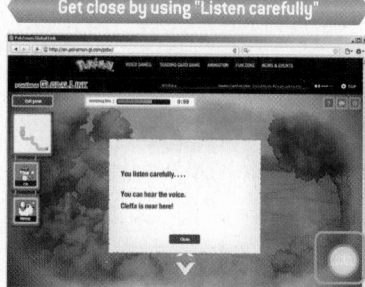
Get close by using "Listen carefully"

You may hear the Pokémon's voice when you click "Listen carefully."

Different Pokémon also show up

If you find a Pokémon that's not the one you're looking for, continue to seek!

Ice Cream Scoop

Pile three kinds of ice cream in the bowl, and aim at the target height. If you click and hold the scoop on one of the ice cream trays, the scoop will get bigger. If you make bite-size scoops, you will score more points. Move the ice cream to the bowl with the mouse, and pile the scoops up high. Pile the ice cream until the time is up.

Characteristics of ice cream (Example)

You need a Berry to play this minigame. The types of ice cream change depending on the Berry.

Blue Ice cream	Easy to scoop ★★★★★
	Stickiness ★★★★★
Yellow Ice cream	Easy to scoop ★★★★★
	Stickiness ★★★★★
Pink Ice cream	Easy to scoop ★★★★★
	Stickiness ★★★★★

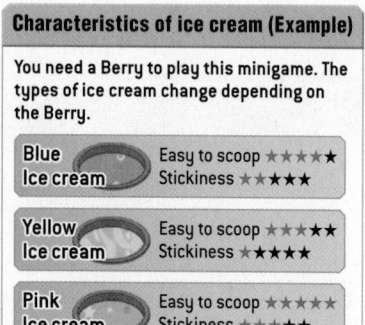

The target line is 20 in.

The first target line is 20 in. Try to pile your scoops higher than 20 in.

Make bite-size scoops

Bite-size scoops increase your score, but it's up to you to figure out the easiest size to pile up the scoops. Hint: It depends on the type of ice cream.

4 Grow Berries in Your Garden

Grow and get more Berries essential for Pokémon battles

Your home has a garden, and you can grow Berries there. In your garden, you can grow Berries that you find on the Island of Dreams in the Pokémon Dream World. Be sure to plant a lot of Berries.

❮❮ Plant Berries in your garden and harvest lots of them

Click on soft soil to plant a Berry in your garden, and a list of Berries will be displayed. Pick a Berry from the list and plant it. Berries will grow as time goes by.

What does "Current garden bed" mean?

A garden bed is a row with patches of soft soil. If you gain enough Dream Points, the number of garden beds increases.

● How to grow and harvest Berries

Grow Berries by watering them

If you water your plants, you will harvest more Berries. If the soil is dry, click on a Berry to water it.

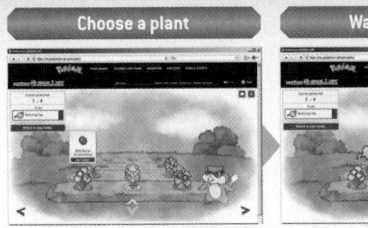
Choose a plant

Water the plant

If the plants sparkle, it's time to harvest

If the plants sparkle when you visit your garden, it means the Berries are ready. Click on the Berries to harvest them.

See the plants sparkle!

Click on the plants

Use the Treasure Chest to take Berries with you

You can use the Treasure Chest at home to take Berries back to your *Pokémon Black* or *Pokémon White* game. Speak to the boy at the entrance of the Entree Forest, and you can get Berries you brought back.

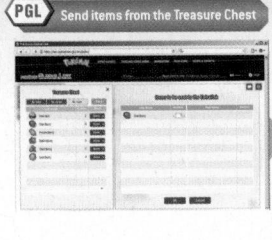
PGL Send items from the Treasure Chest

DS Wake up your Pokémon

The Pokémon is being woken up... Don't turn off the power.

DS Receive items in the Entralink

Trainer received the item(s)!

● When you leave the Pokémon Dream World, click the button in the upper right corner of the screen and wake up your Pokémon.

PGL

5 Decorate Your Home

Collect Décor items to decorate your home

Go to the Pokémon Dream World, and you'll have your own home, which you can redecorate by collecting Décor items. Collect Berries and trade them for Décor items.

Choose a Décor item from your Dream Catalogue and swap for it with Berries

You can decorate your home with class! To swap for Décor items, you need various kinds of Berries (p. 171). Get Berries on the Island of Dreams in the Pokémon Dream World and grow them in your garden (p. 169).

You can place your Décor items wherever you like

Click "Redecorate," then touch a Décor item to change its position.

● How to get a Décor item from your Dream Catalogue

Your Dream Catalogue shows when you have enough Berries

Your Dream Catalogue contains the Décor items for which you can swap Berries. You'll find your Dream Catalogue in your house. If you have enough Berries to get a Décor item, the icon "Swap" will appear next to the Décor item. If you click the icon, the Décor item will be placed in your home.

Click your Dream Catalogue	See what Décor items are available	Swap Berries for a Décor item	The Décor item will be placed
	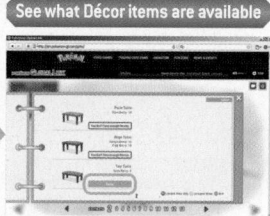		

Answer Loblolly's question in Nacrene City, and more Décor items appear in your Dream Catalogue

Speak to Loblolly in Nacrene City, and you can increase the number of Décor items in your Dream Catalogue. Access the Pokémon Dream World after choosing a Décor item you like, and the Décor item will be displayed in your Dream Catalogue.

DS ▸ Choose a Décor item	DS ▸ Use Game Sync	PGL ▸ The item appears in your Dream Catalogue
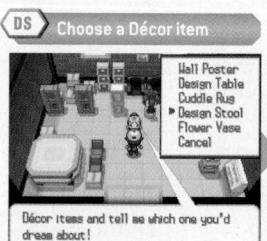		

● If you speak to Loblolly and choose a Décor item while you have a Pokémon tucked in with Game Sync, the Décor item won't be added to your Dream Catalogue. Wake up your Pokémon before you speak to Loblolly, then tuck in a Pokémon via Game Sync. The Décor item you chose will be added to your Dream Catalogue.

Dream Catalogue

Your Dream Catalogue lists Décor items with which you can decorate your home. You can get a Décor item by swapping Berries for it, and place it in your home. Collect a lot of Décor items, and decorate your home as you like, or surprise your friends who visit your home. New Décor items will be added to the Pokémon Dream World. Check the Dream Catalogue to see what Décor items have been added.

● **Some Décor items you can get from your Dream Catalogue and Berries needed to get them**

Type	Décor item	Required Berries	Number you need
Tables	Plain Table	Oran Berry	10
		—	—
	Huge Table	Iapapa Berry	15
		Figy Berry	15
		—	—
	Tiny Table	Oran Berry	8
Chairs	Plain Chair	Oran Berry	5
		—	—
	Huge Chair	Aguav Berry	10
		Figy Berry	10
Rugs	Bolt Rug	Wiki Berry	35
		Persim Berry	35
		Figy Berry	35
Pillows	Soft Pillow	Figy Berry	15
		—	—
Plants	Spiky Plant	Aspear Berry	100
		Sitrus Berry	100
	Leafy Plant	Persim Berry	65
		Lum Berry	65
Beds	Plain Bed	Sitrus Berry	20
		Cheri Berry	40
		Pecha Berry	40
Shelves	Plain Shelf	Oran Berry	10
		Cheri Berry	15
		—	—

Type	Décor item	Required Berries	Number you need
Sofa	Plain Sofa	Cheri Berry	45
		Pecha Berry	45
		—	—
Houses and Islands	Log Cabin	Aspear Berry	150
		Persim Berry	150
		Sitrus Berry	150
	Modern House	Rawst Berry	220
		Chesto Berry	220
		Oran Berry	220
	Cozy Cottage	Initial Décor item	—
Misc.	Arch Window	Aguav Berry	40
		Iapapa Berry	40
	Light Window	Wiki Berry	50
		Mago Berry	50
	Round Window	Oran Berry	10
		Pecha Berry	15
	Treasure Chest	Initial Décor item	
	Friend Board	Initial Décor item	
Watering Systems	Watering Can	Initial Décor item	
Share Shelf	Share Shelf	Initial Décor item	

PGL

6 Swap Items on Share Shelves

Collect Berries and items by swapping them with others

In the Pokémon Dream World, you can swap Berries and items such as Pass Orbs with other players. Use your Share Shelf at your home to swap items.

Here's where you can learn how!

On the Island of Dreams, you can find and swap items, such as Berries, Pass Orbs, and Poké Balls. Swap for Berries to plant so you can get your favorite Décor items to decorate your home.

● How to swap items on Share Shelves

Give Items to other users

To swap items with other users, place items you want to trade on your Share Shelf. The Share Shelf can hold up to nine items.

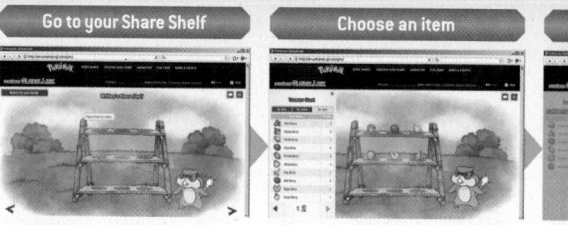

Go to your Share Shelf → Choose an item → Place the item

Swap Berries and items with other users

If you want to get items from other users, go to Share Shelves at other users' homes. If you find an item you want, swap your item for it.

Go to another user's home

Go to the user's Share Shelf

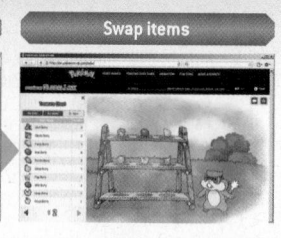
Swap items

Visit other users' homes

In the Pokémon Dream World, you can visit other users' homes, water their gardens, and swap for items on their Share Shelves.

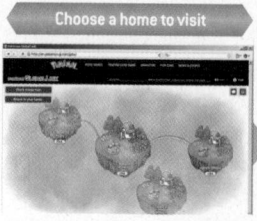
Choose a home to visit

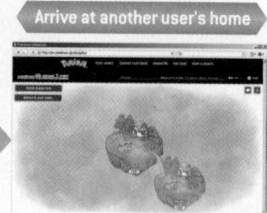
Arrive at another user's home

Visit the home

7 Bring Back Berries and Items

You can bring back Berries and items from the Pokémon Dream World

In the Pokémon Dream World, not only can you become friends with Pokémon, but you can also get Berries and items. You can bring those Berries and items back to *Pokémon Black Version* or *Pokémon White Version*. Here's where you can learn how!

⟪ Learn how to bring back Berries and items

Berries and items you got in the Pokémon Dream World will be stored in the Treasure Chest in your house. When you want to bring them back to *Pokémon Black Version* or *Pokémon White Version*, just use the Treasure Chest.

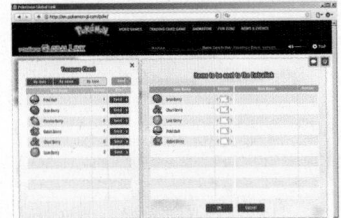

● **How to take Berries and items to *Pokémon Black Version* or *Pokémon White Version***

Use the Treasure Chest to take Berries with you

Choose Berries and items that you want to bring back to *Pokémon Black Version* or *Pokémon White Version* from the Treasure Chest, and click "Send." Choose how many of each item you want to send, click "OK," click "Yes," then click "Close." Leave the Pokémon Dream World, and wake up your Pokémon. Now head over to the Entralink and speak to the boy there. You can receive Berries and items from him.

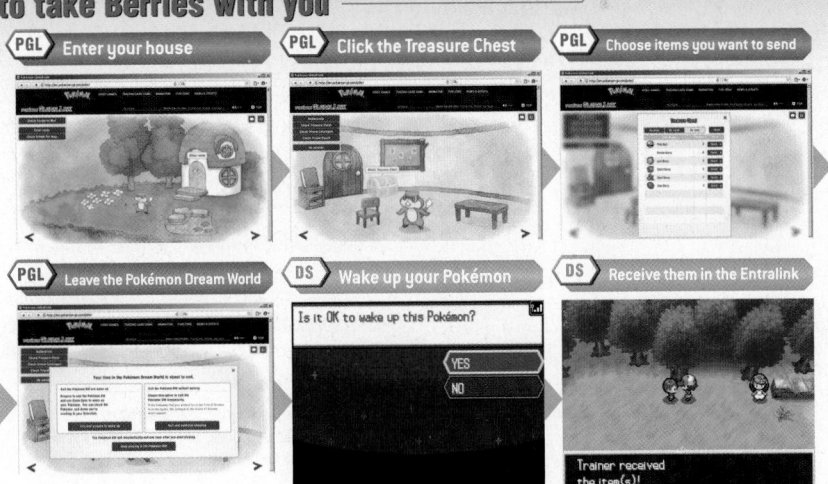

PGL Enter your house | PGL Click the Treasure Chest | PGL Choose items you want to send

PGL Leave the Pokémon Dream World | DS Wake up your Pokémon | DS Receive them in the Entralink

Is it OK to wake up this Pokémon?
YES
NO

Trainer received the item(s)!

Make sure to leave the Pokémon Dream World before waking up your Pokémon

If you want to bring back Pokémon you befriended and made a wish for, as well as items and Berries, make sure to click the button in the upper right corner of the screen to leave the Pokémon Dream World. Then, wake up your Pokémon.

Set Up Your Profile

You can check how much you've played the Pokémon Global Link

You can check your PGL Profile page to see how much time you've spent playing *Pokémon Black Version* or *Pokémon White Version*. If you click a name in your Game Pal Roster, you can also see that person's Profile.

◎ Check Profile

The Profile page shows the records of *Pokémon Black Version* or *Pokémon White Version*, the Pokémon Dream World, and the Global Battle Union. It is fun to watch your records improve and see how much you've played the game, so give it a look.

● **Profile**

● Information may not be updated immediately even if you use Game Sync.

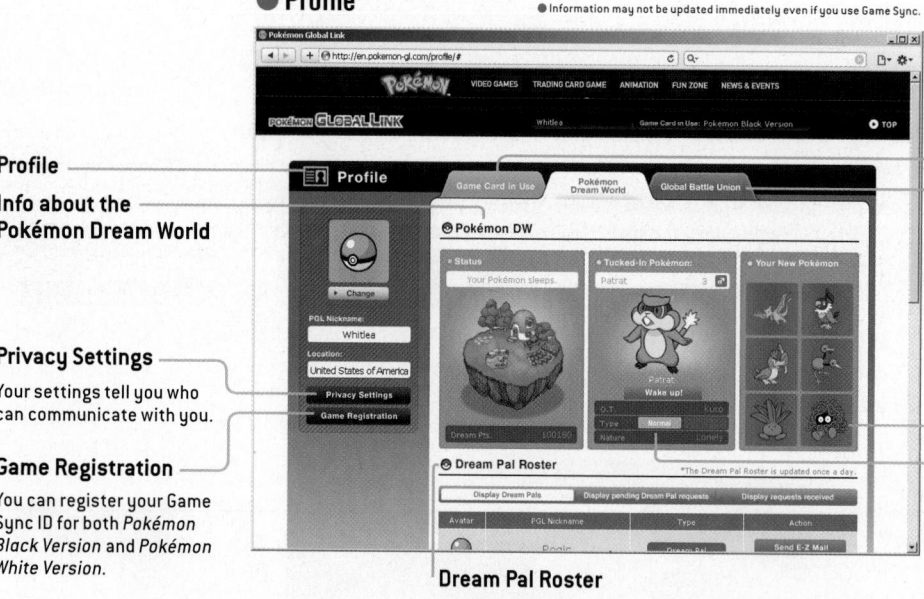

Profile

Info about the Pokémon Dream World

Privacy Settings
Your settings tell you who can communicate with you.

Game Registration
You can register your Game Sync ID for both *Pokémon Black Version* and *Pokémon White Version*.

Dream Pal Roster
See your Dream Pal requests sent or received, along with a list of your Dream Pals and the Delete button to remove Dream Pals.

Game Card in Use
Check info such as your Game Sync ID and your Game Pal Roster.

Info about the Global Battle Union
Check your battle records and register your favorite Battle Video.

Your New Pokémon

Tucked-In Pokémon
Shows you which Pokémon has been tucked in and is in the Pokémon Dream World.

● This screen shows info about the Pokémon Dream World.

● **What you can access in the Profile page**

Privacy settings
You set your privacy settings when you sign up for a Pokémon Trainer Club account. You can change these settings anytime at Pokemon.com.

Set your avatar
You can choose an avatar such as a Poké Ball, item, or Berry.

Game Pal Roster
Game Pals such as those who exchanged Friend Codes are displayed.

Switch Game Cards
You can switch Game Cards on the Game Sync ID registration screen at the Profile page.

9 Communicate with Your Game Pals with E-Z Mail

Enjoy talking with your Pals about Pokémon

E-Z Mail is a tool for Game Pals of *Pokémon Black Version* or *Pokémon White Version* and Dream Pals of the Pokémon Dream World to exchange mail with one another. Have fun exchanging mail with your Pals!

Send a lot of mail easily

Using E-Z Mail, you can exchange mail with your Pals, and you never have to worry about receiving mail from total strangers.

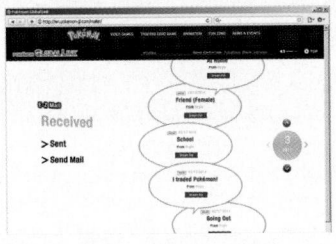

You can send mail to your Pals

Game Pals	Users who exchanged Friend Codes or traded Pokémon with you in *Pokémon Black Version* or *Pokémon White Version*
Dream Pals	Users who have become friends in the Pokémon Dream World

● You may or may not be able to send mail depending on each other's Profile's setting. You can change your Profile settings at Pokemon.com.

● **How to send mail to your Pals**

You can create mail easily by using fixed phrases

Click "Send Mail" to send mail to a Game Pal or Dream Pal. Then, choose a Pal you want to send mail to. Next, choose a method of writing mail. Because fixed phrases are provided for mail, anyone can create mail, even someone who's not good at typing.

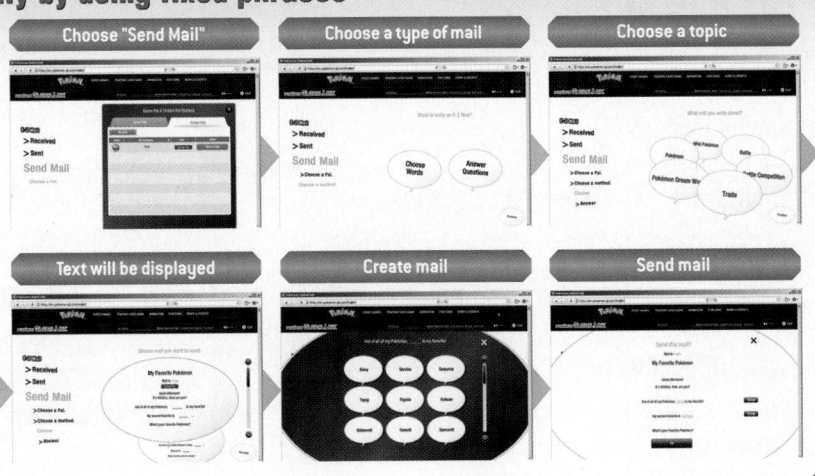

Choose "Send Mail" · Choose a type of mail · Choose a topic
Text will be displayed · Create mail · Send mail

● **Phrases and topics you can choose**

Write mail by choosing words

Choose a topic such as Battle, Trade, or Pokémon Dream World, and fill words in the blanks. Your mail will be done in just a few seconds.

Write mail by answering questions

Choose a topic such as "Friend" or "Going Out." Then a question will be displayed. Answer the question, and presto, your mail is done.

10 Customize the Game

Make the game all your own

Click the "Customize" button, and you can download data to customize your *Pokémon* *Black Version* or *Pokémon White Version* from the Pokémon Global Link.

Make your *Pokémon Black Version* and *Pokémon White Version* even cooler

You can customize your C-Gear skin and Pokédex skin, and add new Musical shows. Check the site often because new customizations will be added over time.

C-Gear Skin

You can change the design of your C-Gear cover. Below is a special skin available on the PGL for a limited time called "Meadow Munna."

Pokédex Skin

You can change the design of your Pokédex's cover. This is a skin called "Starter Pals."

Musical Show

You can add a show for the Pokémon Musical (p. 260), and enjoy a musical with a new song.

● How to customize

Stylize Your C-Gear with Munna!

Use this password at the Pokémon Global Link to access a special digital Munna skin for your C-Gear!

Password: PGLDR34M

Enter your password at www.pokemon-gl.com. Access to the Pokémon Global Link website requires a free Pokémon Trainer Club account and a broadband Internet connection. To download the Munna C-Gear skin, you'll need a copy of either the *Pokémon Black Version* or *Pokémon White Version* game and a system in the Nintendo DS family of systems.

(Offer expires October 2012.)

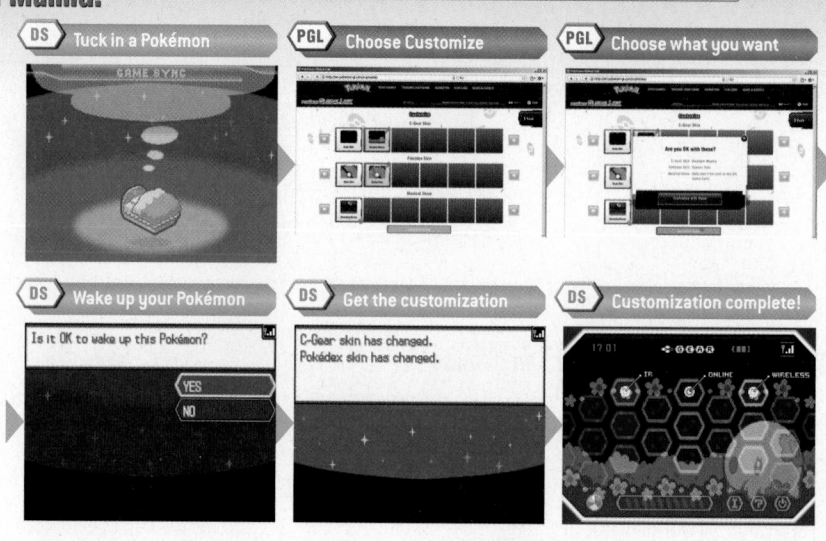

DS Tuck in a Pokémon

PGL Choose Customize

PGL Choose what you want

DS Wake up your Pokémon

DS Get the customization

DS Customization complete!

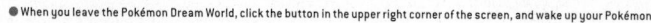

● When you leave the Pokémon Dream World, click the button in the upper right corner of the screen, and wake up your Pokémon.

11 Check Your Ranking at the Global Battle Union

Check your Ranking in battles

At the Global Battle Union, you can check your current Ranking among all the players in the GBU.

You can also check the battle records of strong Trainers such as the Top 3 Trainers.

Go for the top Ranking if you love battles

The results of Random Matchups using Rating Mode at the Global Terminal are displayed in the Global Battle Union. Rankings are calculated regularly.

● **Global Battle Union (GBU)**

Recent Battles
Shows the results of recent battles.

Battle Records
Shows your Ranking by battle format and area.

Details
Click "Details," and your battle records will be displayed.

Overall Ranking: Top 3
You can see the Overall Ranking Top 3.

● **What you can check at the Global Battle Union**

Your battle records	Ranking	Wi-Fi Competition info
You can see the results by battle format and area. The results are displayed by Ratings, which determine what skill level of Trainer you will battle against, and Rankings, which show how you compare to other Trainers.	You can check high-rank Trainers by battle format. If you click their names, their battle records will be displayed.	If info about a current or upcoming Wi-Fi Competition is available, the details will be displayed here.
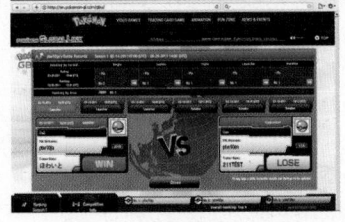		

For details on Random Matchups at the Global Terminal, see p. 156

Use Battle-Combo Moves That the Three Starter Pokémon Can Learn

Battle-combo moves are moves that have special effects if they're used consecutively in one turn, giving you an edge with their powerful effects.

They can be used in Double Battles, Triple Battles, and Multi Battles.

Have strong bonds with the three starter Pokémon and teach them battle-combo moves

Some of the Pokémon in the Unova Pokédex that can learn battle-combo moves are the starter Pokémon, Snivy, Tepig, and Oshawott and their evolutions. If you

have strong bonds with these Pokémon, a man in the Move Tutor's House in Driftveil City will teach them battle-combo moves.

● Battle-combo moves for the Unova starter Pokémon

● **Battle-combo move that Snivy, Servine, and Serperior can learn**

Grass Pledge `Grass`

When combined with Fire Pledge or Water Pledge, the power and effect change.

● **Battle-combo move that Tepig, Pignite, and Emboar can learn**

Fire Pledge `Fire`

When combined with Water Pledge or Grass Pledge, the power and effect change.

● **Battle-combo move that Oshawott, Dewott, and Samurott can learn**

Water Pledge `Water`

When combined with Grass Pledge or Fire Pledge, the power and effect change.

Combine battle-combo moves to exert their powerful effects

Combine battle-combo moves, and the power grows to an overwhelming 150, with additional battle effects, along with visual effects.

| Grass Pledge | + | Water Pledge | Fire Pledge | + | Grass Pledge | Water Pledge | + | Fire Pledge |

● Battle-combo moves and their effects

Combination of moves	Type	Effect
Grass Pledge + Water Pledge	Grass	The power will become 150. The surrounding area will become a wetland. The Speed of opposing Pokémon in the wetland decreases for three turns.
Fire Pledge + Grass Pledge	Fire	The power will become 150. The surrounding area will become a sea of fire. Pokémon, except Fire-type Pokémon, suffer damage as they would with the Burned status condition for this and the next three turns.
Water Pledge + Fire Pledge	Water	The power will become 150. A rainbow forms in the sky. There's an improved chance that additional effects of your team's moves will occur.

Pokémon
Battle Primer

New Pokémon Battles in the Unova Region

New moves and Abilities give battles a twist

Lots of new elements have been added to Pokémon battles in *Pokémon Black Version* and *Pokémon White Version*. New moves, Abilities, items you've never seen before, plus new Pokémon—it all adds up to make battling hotter than ever!

1 Check out new ways to battle and convenient new functions NEW!

Try out the new three-on-three Triple Battles and Rotation Battles. Take your time and get comfortable with the new battle formats, because you'll need to develop new strategies. In the past, Trainers couldn't use items during Link Battles, but now Trainers can support their Pokémon with the help of a Wonder Launcher. Also new in this game is the Battle Box. You can save time getting ready for battles by registering the Pokémon you like to use in battle in your Battle Box.

● **New battle elements in *Pokémon Black Version* and *Pokémon White Version***

Triple Battle

You and the opposing Trainer send out three Pokémon each. This is a powerful and exciting battle format, where six Pokémon battle at once!

Rotation Battle

Pokémon rotate positions, and the Pokémon using a move steps forward. Having to predict what the opposing Trainer is going to do next makes the battle an interesting challenge.

Wonder Launcher

What's so great about the Wonder Launcher? It gives Trainers the power to use items in Link Battles! Think of all the items with powerful effects you could use to enhance your team.

Battle Box

Once you've raised and equipped your team of heavy hitters, register them in your Battle Box and you'll be all set for your next battle.

2 Powerful new moves, Abilities, and items

This game offers attack moves with new effects and easy-to-use status moves. In addition, some familiar moves have surprising new effects! With all these new moves, Abilities, and items, your battle strategies could change completely. Whenever you obtain or learn something new, be sure to experiment and figure out how you can use it to turn the opposing Trainer's strategies upside down and inside out!

● Examples of new moves

Dwebble   Roggenrola

Smack Down   `Rock`

Knock a Flying-type Pokémon (or one with the Levitate Ability) right out of the sky, making it vulnerable to Ground-type moves!

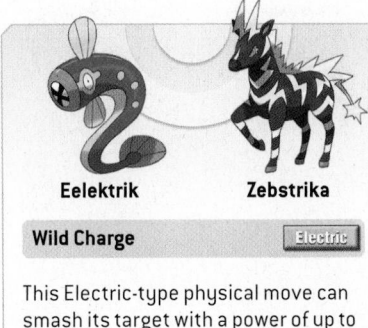

Eelektrik   Zebstrika

Wild Charge   `Electric`

This Electric-type physical move can smash its target with a power of up to 90, but the user suffers some of the damage as well.

Patrat   Herdier

Work Up   `Normal`

This move increases both the Pokémon's Attack and Sp. Atk by one level.

● Examples of new Abilities

Solosis   Vullaby

`Ability` **Overcoat**

Protects the Pokémon from damage from the Sandstorm and Hail weather conditions.

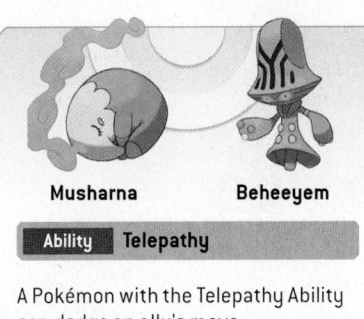

Musharna   Beheeyem

`Ability` **Telepathy**

A Pokémon with the Telepathy Ability can dodge an ally's move.

Timburr   Rufflet

`Ability` **Sheer Force**

Although none of an attack's additional effects happen, the move's power increases by 1.3 times.

● Examples of new items

 Rocky Helmet

If the holder of this item takes damage, the attacker is also damaged on contact.

 **Normal Gem**

When held by a Pokémon, this single-use item boosts the power of a Normal-type move by 1.5 times.

 **Red Card**

When the holder is struck by an attack move, the attacker is removed from battle. It is single-use.

Reshiram and Zekrom's battle-combo moves gain more power

If Reshiram's Fusion Flare and Zekrom's Fusion Bolt are used in succession during the same turn, the power of the move that goes second will be doubled.

Fusion Flare   `Fire`   Fusion Bolt   `Electric`

Fusion Bolt `Electric`	Fusion Flare `Fire`
▼	▼
Fusion Flare `Fire`	Fusion Bolt `Electric`

3 # Use the Wonder Launcher during a battle

The Wonder Launcher is a device that enables Trainers to use items on Pokémon during battles. Select "Wonder Launcher On" to use it during a Link Battle. Using energy that charges every turn, it can boost a Pokémon's stats and the accuracy of a move, restore a Pokémon's HP, or cure status conditions. The more energy you use, the more effective the items you can use. If you use 14 energy points, you can even revive a fainted Pokémon and fully restore its HP!

If you restore a Pokémon's HP, you'll have a chance to fight back

Wonder Launchers can create a huge change in battle conditions. It's great to fully restore one Pokémon's HP, making you feel as though you have an additional Pokémon in this battle.

● How to use the Wonder Launcher

1 Charge energy each turn

Your launcher gains one energy point at the beginning of a turn. If you want to use a powerful item, you need to wait until enough energy is charged.

2 Use the Wonder Launcher

When you have enough energy to use the item you want, choose "LAUNCHER" to use it. The item will be launched at the target.

● How charging energy works

1 One energy point will be charged at the beginning of your turn.

2 In a Triple Battle, if you have fewer than three Pokémon on your team, more energy will be charged.

3 When you use an item, the energy decreases by the amount you use. Even if it fails and no effect results, that energy is spent.

● Places you can use the Wonder Launcher

 **IR** ### Battle

If you battle using IR on your C-Gear, the Wonder Launcher is always available. Experiment with the Wonder Launcher in the different battle formats (p. 134).

WIRELESS ### Union Room in a Pokémon Center

You can use the Wonder Launcher by selecting "Wonder Launcher On" when choosing the rules for battle. Try using the Wonder Launcher in various battle formats (p. 148).

ONLINE ### Pokémon Wi-Fi Club in a Pokémon Center

Select "Wonder Launcher On" when choosing the rules for battle. By battling with your friends many times, you'll find the best ways to use the Wonder Launcher (p. 154).

ONLINE ### Random Matchup at the Global Terminal

If you choose "Launcher Battle," you can use the Wonder Launcher in Triple Battles. Pay attention to how those you battle use Wonder Launchers (p. 157).

● Wonder Launcher items and energy requirements

Energy	Item	Effect
1	Item Urge	Makes an ally Pokémon use its held item
2	Potion	Restores the HP of one Pokémon by 20 points
3	Ability Urge	Activates an Ability that normally has an effect when a Pokémon joins a battle
	X Attack	Raises the Attack stat of a target Pokémon by one level
	X Defend	Raises the Defense stat of a target Pokémon by one level
	X Special	Raises the Sp. Atk stat of a target Pokémon by one level
	X Sp. Def	Raises the Sp. Def stat of a target Pokémon by one level
	X Speed	Raises the Speed of a target Pokémon by one level
	X Accuracy	Raises the accuracy of a target Pokémon by one level
	Dire Hit	Raises the critical-hit ratio of a target Pokémon significantly, but can be used only once
	Guard Spec.	Prevents stat reduction among the Trainer's party Pokémon for five turns
4	Super Potion	Restores the HP of one Pokémon by 50 points
	Ice Heal	Defrosts a Pokémon that has been Frozen
	Antidote	Lifts the effect of Poison from a Pokémon
	Awakening	Awakens a Pokémon from Sleep
	Parlyz Heal	Eliminates Paralysis from a Pokémon
	Burn Heal	Heals a Pokémon that is Burned
5	Item Drop	Makes an ally Pokémon drop a held item
	X Attack 2	Raises the Attack stat of a target Pokémon by two levels
	X Defend 2	Raises the Defense stat of a target Pokémon by two levels
	X Special 2	Raises the Sp. Atk stat of a target Pokémon by two levels
	X Sp. Def 2	Raises the Sp. Def stat of a target Pokémon by two levels
	X Speed 2	Raises the Speed of a target Pokémon by two levels
	X Accuracy 2	Raises the accuracy of a target Pokémon by two levels
	Dire Hit 2	Raises the critical-hit ratio of a target Pokémon (with the effect increasing every time it's used)
6	Full Heal	Cures all status conditions
7	X Attack 3	Raises the Attack stat of a target Pokémon by three levels
	X Defend 3	Raises the Defense stat of a target Pokémon by three levels
	X Special 3	Raises the Sp. Atk stat of a target Pokémon by three levels
	X Sp. Def 3	Raises the Sp. Def stat of a target Pokémon by three levels
	X Speed 3	Raises the Speed of a target Pokémon by three levels
	X Accuracy 3	Raises the accuracy of a target Pokémon by three levels
	Dire Hit 3	Greatly raises the critical-hit ratio of a target Pokémon (with the effect increasing every time it's used)
8	Hyper Potion	Restores the HP of one Pokémon by 200 points
9	Reset Urge	Restores any stat changes of an ally Pokémon
10	Max Potion	Completely restores the HP of a single Pokémon
11	Revive	Revives a fainted Pokémon and restores half its HP
12	Ether	Restores the PP of a Pokémon's move by 10 points
	X Attack 6	Raises the Attack stat of a target Pokémon by six levels
	X Defend 6	Raises the Defense stat of a target Pokémon by six levels
	X Special 6	Raises the Sp. Atk stat of a target Pokémon by six levels
	X Sp. Def 6	Raises the Sp. Def stat of a target Pokémon by six levels
	X Speed 6	Raises the Speed of a target Pokémon by six levels
	X Accuracy 6	Raises the accuracy of a target Pokémon by six levels
13	Full Restore	Fully restores the HP and heals any status conditions of a single Pokémon
14	Max Revive	Revives a fainted Pokémon and fully restores its HP

● Item Urge has no effect on Pokémon with the Klutz Ability. If you use Item Urge on a Pokémon holding a Berry that has no effect in battle, or use it when a Pokémon with the Unnerve Ability is in the battle, you will fail in using the item but the energy is spent.

 ## Some Wonder Launcher items have exclusive effects

Some items for the Wonder Launcher have effects not offered by standard items. Check out Reset Urge, for example. Also, some items are similar to standard items but much more effective, like X Speed 6. Let your situation be your guide in choosing which items to use.

Pokémon Battle Basics

1

Master All the Battle Formats to Win

Review the battle formats so you can win in every one

When battle formats change, battle strategies must also change. That means Pokémon selection, team formation, and the best ways of raising Pokémon also change. Learn to battle well with your Pokémon in any format!

Single Battles **1** ## Single Battles are one-on-one battles

Single Battles are the simplest battle format. In the battlefield, only two Pokémon are involved, yours and the opposing Trainer's. You don't need to wonder what to do next, as in Double Battles or Triple Battles. If you become proficient at Single Battles, you'll be well on your way to Pokémon battle mastery.

● Single Battle basic effect ranges

When attacking

A Pokémon attacks the opposing Trainer's one Pokémon. Remember, there's a chance the Pokémon could be switched with a waiting party Pokémon.

When a Pokémon uses a status move on itself

● The move Reflect, for example

Effect of a status move

With no allies in the battlefield, a status move affects only the user, not your entire party.

● Other things to know about Single Battles

One Pokémon uses a combo

Making a combo (a combination of two moves) with only one Pokémon takes two turns.

Bouffalant ♂Lv.50

Musharna ♀Lv.50
107/195

Musharna used Dream Eater!

Attacks affect only one Pokémon

Even if a move could affect more than one opposing Pokémon at a time, in Single Battles it can inflict damage only on the single one you face.

Watchog ♀Lv.50

Seismitoad ♂Lv.50
169/169

Seismitoad used Hyper Voice!

Double Battles are two-on-two battles

In Double Battles, you and the opposing Trainer send out two Pokémon each, making a total of four Pokémon on the battlefield. The Pokémon at the head of your party stands on the left, and the second Pokémon stands on the right. You have twice as many Pokémon present compared to Single Battles, but the number is not the only difference. With certain attacks, one of your Pokémon may be able to hit both of the opposing Trainer's Pokémon, and one of his or her Pokémon may be able to attack both your Pokémon. You'll need to think ahead carefully and choose your next move from multiple options. But if you've learned the basics in Single Battles, you'll know what to do!

● Double Battle basic effect ranges

When the Pokémon on the left attacks

A Pokémon in a Double Battle can attack either of the opposing Trainer's Pokémon.

When the Pokémon on the right attacks

A Pokémon in a Double Battle can attack either of the opposing Trainer's Pokémon.

When the range is adjacent

● The move Earthquake, for example

Depending on a move's range, it might affect not only the opposing Trainer's two Pokémon, but also your Pokémon in the battlefield.

When a Pokémon uses a status move on its ally

● The move Helping Hand, for example

Effect of a status move

When you have an ally on the battlefield, a status move can affect the user or the ally.

● Other things to know about Double Battles

Combine two Pokémon's moves and Abilities to create dynamic combo moves

In Double Battles, you can make your turn really count by combining the moves, Abilities, and items of both your Pokémon. If you pull together the right combination, you can find ways to take advantage of strong moves that usually affect your ally as well as your enemies.

Excadrill used Earthquake!

It doesn't affect Eelektross...

Triple Battles ① **Position matters in three-on-three Triple Battles**

In Triple Battles, you and the opposing Trainer send out three Pokémon each, making six Pokémon in the battlefield. The Pokémon at the head of your party is placed on the left, the second Pokémon in the middle, and the third Pokémon on the right. Position matters. The Pokémon in the middle can target any of the opposing Trainer's three Pokémon. The

Pokémon on the left and right have a limited range. Each can target only the Pokémon right in front of itself and the Pokémon in the middle, not the Pokémon on the far side of its position. As in Double Battles, a Pokémon can use a status move on an ally. Keep positioning in mind as you work out your Triple Battle strategies.

● **Triple Battle basic effect ranges**

When the Pokémon on the left attacks

The Pokémon on the left in Triple Battles can reach the Pokémon directly across from it and the Pokémon in the middle.

When the Pokémon on the right attacks

The Pokémon on the right in Triple Battles can reach the Pokémon directly across from it and the Pokémon in the middle.

When the Pokémon in the middle attacks

Only the Pokémon in the middle can use a move on any of the opposing Trainer's three Pokémon.

When a move has a long effect range

Moves with a long-range effect are an exception and can reach the Pokémon on the opposite far side. The move Gust, for example, can reach all three targets.

● **Other things to know about Triple Battles**

When choosing a move, pay attention to the range

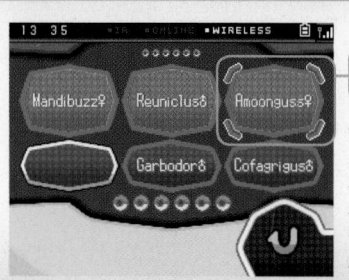

"Long" moves can reach the opposite far side

When a move has a long-range effect, the display includes the opposing Trainer's Pokémon on the far side.

Use Shift effectively

"SHIFT" switches the Pokémon with the middle Pokémon

The Pokémon on the left or right side can switch with the Pokémon in the middle. That's how Shift works!

Train Pokémon for Triple Battles

Strategies for Triple Battles differ from those for Single Battles and Double Battles. Moves that were unremarkable in Single Battles can be strikingly effective in Triple Battles. Abilities that were somewhat useful in Double Battles can grow much more significant.

To be a star in Triple Battles, you'll need to train Pokémon that have the potential to shine in this format. It's up to you to develop strategies for Triple Battles, find the Pokémon to fill the roles in your strategies, and train each Pokémon with care.

● Examples of Pokémon that perform well in Triple Battles

Wide Guard protects allies from attack

Carracosta

Wide Guard	Rock

This move protects from multiple-targeting physical and special moves for one turn. If used for more than one turn in a row, its chance of failing rises.

Telepathy protects the Pokémon from being damaged by ally moves

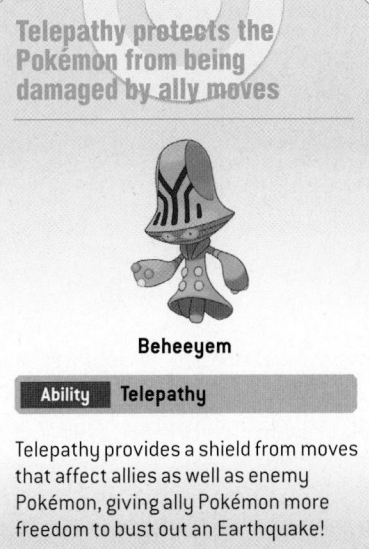

Beheeyem

Ability	Telepathy

Telepathy provides a shield from moves that affect allies as well as enemy Pokémon, giving ally Pokémon more freedom to bust out an Earthquake!

Healer heals allies' status conditions

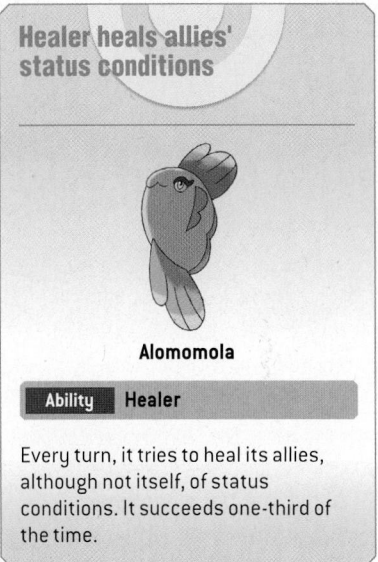

Alomomola

Ability	Healer

Every turn, it tries to heal its allies, although not itself, of status conditions. It succeeds one-third of the time.

Develop a Triple Battle formation

In Triple Battles, a Pokémon's position is a critical factor you need to know to sort out attacks. The Pokémon in the middle can target any of the opposing Trainer's three Pokémon, and it is vulnerable to attack by all three opposing Pokémon. That central position means that the Pokémon in the middle has a different role to play than those on the right and left. Invest some time in practice battles to learn the best way to position your Pokémon and make the most of their special powers.

● Good positioning in Triple Battles

The Pokémon in the middle must withstand attacks and can attack all enemies

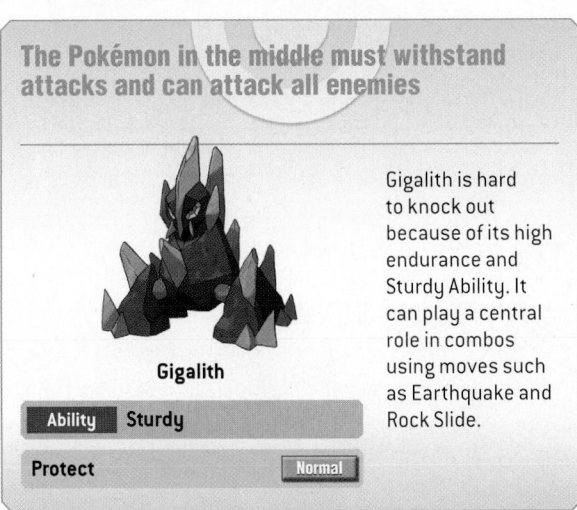

Gigalith

Ability	Sturdy
Protect	Normal

Gigalith is hard to knock out because of its high endurance and Sturdy Ability. It can play a central role in combos using moves such as Earthquake and Rock Slide.

Place Pokémon with long-range moves on the right and left

Whimsicott

Gust	Flying
Hurricane	Flying

Pokémon that know long-range moves can really help out when placed on the left or right side. The opposing Trainer may think the Pokémon farthest away is unreachable, but you'll soon dispel that illusion!

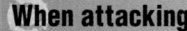

1 Rotation Battles are three-on-three battles that focus on move choices

In Rotation Battles, you and the opposing Trainer send out three Pokémon each, for a total of six Pokémon in the battlefield. The Pokémon at the head of your party is placed in front, and the remaining two in back. You can choose to use a move from any of your Pokémon, front or back. If you choose a move from one of the Pokémon in back, that Pokémon will rotate to the front. Only the Pokémon in front can be attacked.

● Rotation Battle basic effect ranges

When attacking

Your front Pokémon can reach only one Pokémon, the one at the front of the opposing Pokémon's formation.

When being attacked

Your front Pokémon can be attacked by only one Pokémon, the one at the front of the opposing Pokémon's formation.

● About the back positions

When you choose a move from a Pokémon in back

To use a move, a Pokémon rotates to the front.

If you choose a move of a Pokémon in back, that Pokémon rotates to the front and uses the move.

Rotating a Pokémon to the back won't remove its status conditions

When it returns to the back, it remains Confused.

For example, a Pokémon affected by the Confused condition will stay Confused even if it's rotated to the back. If it's withdrawn from the battlefield, however, its status condition will go away.

● You have two ways of changing out the front Pokémon

When to rotate and when to switch

Rotation

If you want to use one of the moves of a Pokémon in back, choose Rotation. Then you can use the move that same turn.

Switch

It takes one turn to Switch a Pokémon with a waiting Pokémon. But, depending on the situation, it's sometimes more effective than Rotation.

POKÉMON BATTLE PRIMER

MASTER ALL THE BATTLE FORMATS TO WIN

2 ## Use moves effective against all opposing Pokémon

In Rotation Battles, not only your Pokémon but also the opposing Trainer's Pokémon can rotate freely. You don't know which of his or her Pokémon will be affected by the move your Pokémon uses. Your best bet is to pick moves that are effective against all three Pokémon, so you benefit no matter which of the opposing Trainer's Pokémon winds up in front.

● **Example of choosing a move depending on the opposing Trainer's Pokémon types**

When there are common supereffective moves

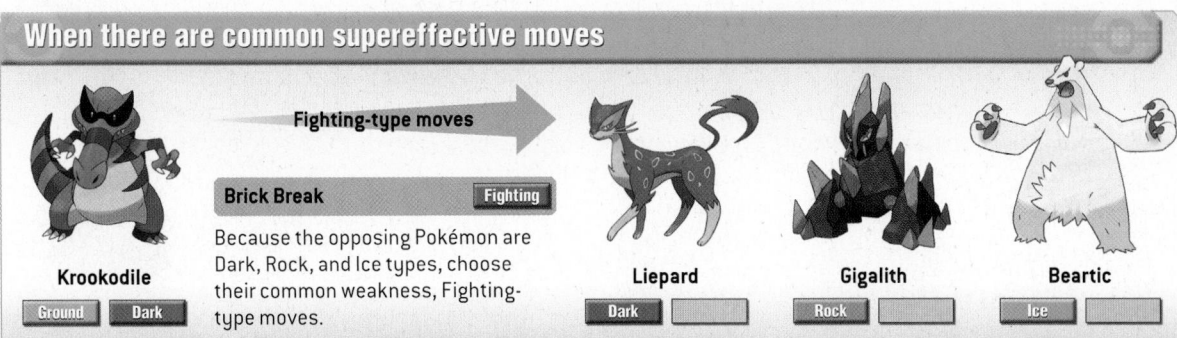

Fighting-type moves

| Brick Break | Fighting |

Because the opposing Pokémon are Dark, Rock, and Ice types, choose their common weakness, Fighting-type moves.

Krookodile
Ground Dark

Liepard
Dark

Gigalith
Rock

Beartic
Ice

When there are no common supereffective moves

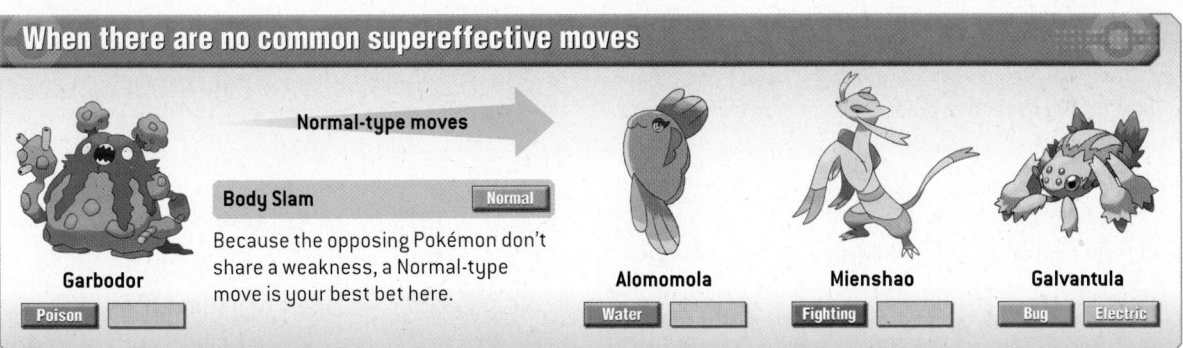

Normal-type moves

| Body Slam | Normal |

Because the opposing Pokémon don't share a weakness, a Normal-type move is your best bet here.

Garbodor
Poison

Alomomola
Water

Mienshao
Fighting

Galvantula
Bug Electric

3 ## Compose your team with a creative eye

Some Abilities block all damage from moves of a certain type. For example, Sap Sipper provides complete damage protection from Grass-type moves. If you place a Pokémon that might have a protective Ability in back, you'll make the opposing Trainer think twice. Will he or she dare to use a move that might be completely wasted?

● **Abilities that provide protection from damage by certain types**

Grass-type moves don't hurt a bit

When a Grass-type move lands on a Pokémon with the Sap Sipper Ability, the Pokémon does not take damage and its Attack stat goes up a level!

Bouffalant

Sawsbuck (Spring Form)

Ability   Sap Sipper

Fire-type moves provide welcome warmth

Fire-type moves against a Pokémon with the Flash Fire Ability won't damage it, but will increase the power of its Fire-type moves by 1.5 times.

Chandelure

Heatmor

Ability   Flash Fire

Water-type moves are a shower of health

When a Water-type move lands on a Pokémon with the Water Absorb Ability, it takes no damage. In fact, its HP is restored!

Maractus

Jellicent

Ability   Water Absorb

Electric-type moves put a spark in your step

The Motor Drive Ability protects a Pokémon from Electric-type moves, meaning it doesn't take damage. Even better, its Speed goes up!

Blitzle

Zebstrika

Ability   Motor Drive

Connect with Link Battle and Battle Anyone

Choose the right approach for any situation

Pokémon Black Version and *Pokémon White Version* are loaded with ways to battle your friends and others. Choose the right way to battle for any connection and every occasion.

Different kinds of Link Battles **1** **Try Random Matchup and battle people you've never met**

When you participate in Pokémon Battle Competitions, you'll face people you don't know. To get used to battling people you've never met before, try Random Matchup and you'll battle against someone completely unexpected. You'll be able to study other Trainers' Pokémon and strategies.

Online **Random Matchup at the Global Terminal**

Test your skills with Random Matchup. You can choose either the Free mode or Rating mode, though you must register your Game Sync ID to play the Rating mode. Choose the Free mode if you haven't registered your Game Sync ID.

▶ Single Battle
Double Battle
Triple Battle
Rotation Battle
Launcher Battle
Back

Which Battle would you like to choose?

Check your own strength

You can have fun with Random Matchups at the Global Terminal on Pokémon Center 2F.

● **Battle formats available from Random Matchup**

- Single Battle
- Rotation Battle
- Double Battle
- Launcher Battle
- Triple Battle

Keep winning in the Rating mode and you'll face tougher challengers

In the Rating mode, your Rating number goes up or down. If you win a battle, your Rating goes up. If you lose, it'll go down. You will be facing Trainers with Ratings similar to yours, so you can expect a good challenge every time. The more you win, the tougher it gets! Check your battle results and also your current Ranking as compared to all the other Trainers in the Rating mode at the Global Battle Union (GBU).

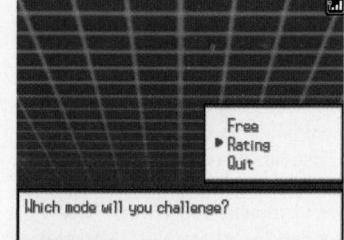

Free
▶ Rating
Quit

Which mode will you challenge?

See p. 156 for Random Matchup details. See p. 177 for GBU details. ▶

2 Battle against your friends every day

Battle against the same player many times and you will be able to hone your skills together. There are three ways to battle your friends. You can still use the Union Room for battle, and you can now use IR for quick and easy face-to-face battles. If your friends are far away, you can still battle them through Nintendo Wi-Fi Connection with Friend Codes.

IR Battle using the C-Gear

Using the C-Gear, battle your friends face-to-face (p. 134). The C-Gear on the Touch Screen can be used at many places in the Unova region. You can accept challenges even in the middle of adventuring around the region. You'll always be able to use the Wonder Launcher with this type of battle.

Battle your friends when you see them

Always keep some Pokémon in your Battle Box so you are ready to accept challenges.

● **Battle formats available with the C-Gear**

Single Battle	Rotation Battle
Double Battle	Multi Battle
Triple Battle	

Wireless Union Room battles

Go to the Union Room at Pokémon Center 2F and touch the battle button on the Touch Screen. Other Trainers who also want to battle will jump up and you'll know who wants to battle (p. 148).

Find people who want to battle and challenge them

In the Union Room, you can battle people you don't know. Don't hesitate to challenge them.

● **Battle formats available in the Union Room**

Single Battle	Rotation Battle
Double Battle	Multi Battle
Triple Battle	

Online Battles at the Wi-Fi Club

You can battle distant friends at the Wi-Fi Club located at Pokémon Center 2F. When you enter the Wi-Fi Club, talk to a Trainer who's seeking for battles or use the monitor at the far end of the room to seek participants (p. 154).

Battle with distant friends

To enjoy the Wi-Fi Club, you'll need access to Nintendo Wi-Fi Connection (p. 139) and to have exchanged Friend Codes with your friends.

● **Battle formats available at the Wi-Fi Club**

Single Battle	Triple Battle
Double Battle	Rotation Battle

Master Type Matchups

Master how Pokémon and move types work and you'll enjoy Pokémon battles even more

Let's review the relationship between Pokémon types and move types. When you know the other Pokémon's type, you should be able to use the right move to defeat it even if it seemed too tough to beat before.

Type Technique 1 Know both Pokémon types and move types

There are two things to consider when thinking of types: Pokémon types and move types. When a Pokémon uses moves of its own type, those moves inflict more damage.

Depending on the type of move used and the type of the Pokémon receiving it, damage can increase or decrease.

● **Pokémon types and move types**

Check Pokémon and move types in the Pokédex

The Pokémon's type

There are 17 Pokémon types in total. Some Pokémon have two types.

The move's type

Every move has its own type. Pokémon can learn moves that are of different types from its own.

● **Both move type and the defending Pokémon type determine effectiveness**

1 Attacker's move type and the defending Pokémon type determine the matchup

Electric-type moves deal normal damage to Ice-type Pokémon. Fire-type moves match up well against Ice-type Pokémon.

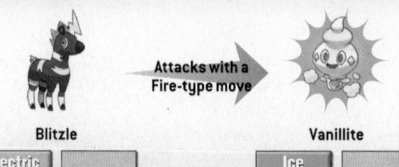

Blitzle
Electric

Attacks with a Fire-type move

Vanillite
Ice

Fire-type moves have a good matchup against Ice-type Pokémon, so its damage is doubled.

2 Depending on the matchup, moves can inflict normal damage

Grass-type moves have a bad matchup against Fire-type Pokémon. Try moves of different types than Grass to avoid the bad matchup.

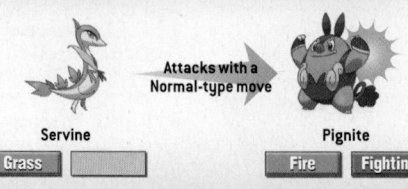

Servine
Grass

Attacks with a Normal-type move

Pignite
Fire   Fighting

Normal-type moves deal just the usual damage to Fire-type Pokémon.

POKÉMON BATTLE PRIMER — MASTER TYPE MATCHUPS

Use types to increase move damage

One of the most basic battle techniques is to increase the damage your Pokémon deal. You can increase damage by using moves that have a good type matchup against the opposing Pokémon. Reduce the other Pokémon's HP to zero faster so your Pokémon will take fewer hits!

● Basic methods to increase damage

1 A move does double damage when used on a Pokémon who's weak against that move's type

A move does double damage when used on a Pokémon who's weak against that move's type. Make it a habit to check the types of the moves and their targets.

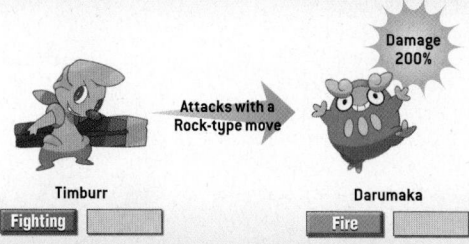

Rock-type moves offer a good matchup against Fire-type Pokémon, so damage is doubled.

2 When a Pokémon uses moves of its own type, those moves do 50% more damage

When a Pokémon uses moves of its own type, those moves do 50% more damage. Even when the matchup is not favorable, you can expect more damage if a Pokémon uses moves of its own type.

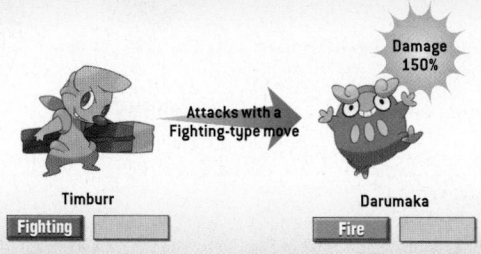

Both the Pokémon type and the move type are Fighting so the move inflicts 50% more damage.

● When the defending Pokémon is of two types

1 A move that is super effective against both types does 4 times the usual damage

When a defending Pokémon has two types, you can sometimes do much more damage than usual. When your Pokémon's move is super effective against both its types, the damage is 4 times normal.

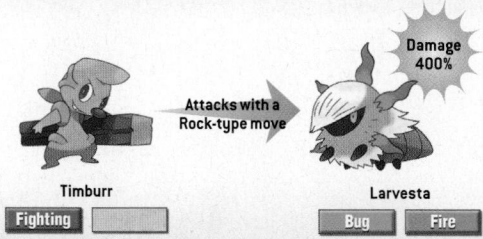

Rock-type moves are super effective on both Bug type and Fire type, so the damage will be 4 times normal.

2 A move that is not very effective against both types does 1/4 the usual damage

When a defending Pokémon has two types, you can sometimes do much less damage than normal. A move that is not very effective against either type deals just 1/4 the usual damage.

Grass-type moves are not very effective on both Bug type and Fire type, so the damage drops to 1/4 normal.

See the Pokémon Weakness Chart on p. 340 for more details on type matchups ▶

POKÉMON BATTLE PRIMER

◎ MASTER TYPE MATCHUPS

Type Technique ❸ **Check type matchup and build a well-balanced team**

Teamwork is the key to Pokémon battles. One way to form a strong team is to figure out the right mix of Pokémon types to tackle any challenge. As the example below shows, a team of various types can handle a wide range of Pokémon types.

● **An example of how to form a good team around your main Pokémon**

If your main Pokémon is Zebstrika:

As an Electric-type Pokémon, Zebstrika is weak against Ground-type moves. That's why you want Seismitoad to add its Water-type moves to the team—they are especially good against Ground-type Pokémon. Seismitoad is weak against Grass-type moves. That's why you want to have Darmanitan with its Fire-type moves. Darmanitan is weak against Water-type moves. For those Water-type Pokémon, you have Zebstrika with its Electric-type moves.

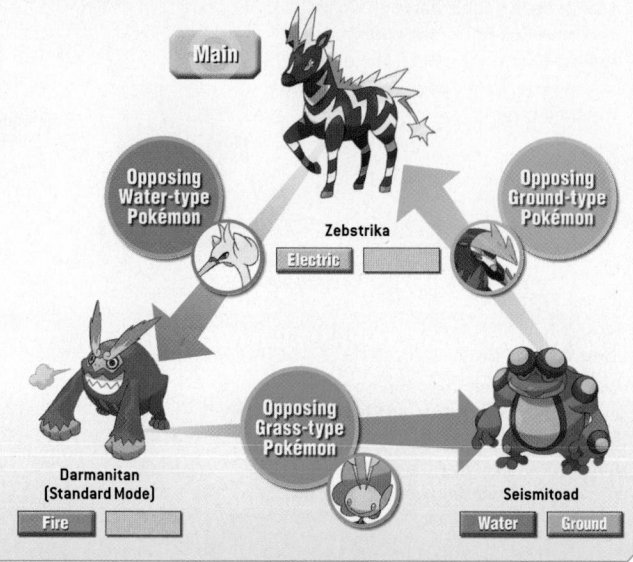

If your main Pokémon is Bisharp:

As a Steel-type Pokémon, Bisharp is weak against Fire-type moves. That's why you want Gigalith on your team with its Rock-type moves, which are good against Fire-type Pokémon. However, Gigalith is weak against Grass-type moves. So you want Garbodor with its Poison-type moves against Grass-type Pokémon. Garbodor is weak against Psychic-type moves. For those Psychic-type Pokémon, you have Bisharp with its Dark-type moves.

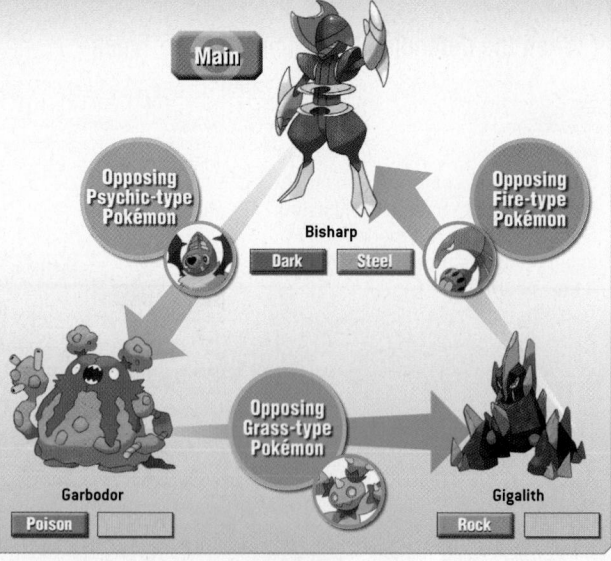

Some Pokémon types are not affected by moves of certain types. For example, Ghost-type Pokémon are not affected at all by Normal- or Fighting-type moves, and Flying-type Pokémon are not affected by Ground-type moves. Also, some Pokémon types prevent certain status conditions. For instance, Fire-type Pokémon cannot be Burned, and Ice-type Pokémon cannot be Frozen. Knowing these things, you can nullify some moves and stay a step ahead in battle.

● Pokémon immunities to move types and status conditions

Type	Description
Normal	Immune to all Ghost-type moves
Fire	Does not become Burned
Grass	Immune to Leech Seed
Ice	Does not become Frozen and takes no damage from the Hail weather condition
Poison	Immune to the Poison and Badly Poisoned conditions Nullifies the effect of Toxic Spikes as it gets sent out (●)
Ground	Immune to all Electric-type moves Immune to Thunder Wave (●) Takes no damage from the Sandstorm weather condition
Flying	Immune to all Ground-type moves Not affected by Spikes or Toxic Spikes
Rock	Takes no damage from the Sandstorm weather condition
Ghost	Immune to Normal- and Fighting-type moves
Dark	Immune to all Psychic-type moves
Steel	Immune to all Poison-type moves and takes no damage from the Sandstorm weather condition Immune to the Poison and Badly Poisoned conditions

● Poison-type Pokémon with the Levitate Ability, and Pokémon that are both Poison type and Flying type, will not nullify the effect of Toxic Spikes.

● Normally, status moves are not affected by types. The exception to this rule is Thunder Wave. It has no effect on Ground-type Pokémon.

 ## Ways to use moves on Pokémon that are otherwise immune to them

In some cases, the defending Pokémon may be immune to all of your Pokémon's moves. You should be prepared to deal with such cases. To cause damage to those Pokémon who are otherwise immune to these moves, use the move Odor Sleuth or the item Ring Target. Surprise the other Trainers who don't expect your counterattack.

Cause damage with certain moves

Stoutland

Odor Sleuth	Normal

The move Odor Sleuth lets Normal- and Fighting-type moves cause damage to Ghost-type Pokémon.

Cause damage with certain items

Pidove

 Ring Target

Use the move Bestow to give the Ring Target to other Pokémon. Moves will cause damage to Pokémon that are usually immune to them.

Pokémon Battle Basics

4

Know Stats for Battling and Raising Pokémon

Understand your Pokémon's stats to help it shine in battles

Each Pokémon has stats such as Attack and Defense. There are six stats, and the higher the number, the better. Understanding stats helps you raise and battle with Pokémon.

Stats Technique 1 Overall strength depends on six stats

Your Pokémon's stats determine crucial battle elements, such as the damage when hit or the order of Pokémon moves within a turn in battle. When a Pokémon levels up, its stats also go up.

● The six Pokémon stats

HP

The Pokémon's health. If attacks reduce its HP to 0, the Pokémon faints.

SPEED

The higher this number, the better your chance to use moves before others.

Stats affecting physical moves:

ATTACK

The higher this stat, the more damage the Pokémon does with physical moves.

DEFENSE

The higher this stat, the less damage the Pokémon takes from physical moves.

Stats affecting special moves:

SP. ATTACK

The higher this number, the more damage the Pokémon does with special moves.

SP. DEFENSE

The higher this stat, the less damage the Pokémon takes from special moves.

● Stats affecting physical and special moves

Stats that affect physical moves:

The Attack stat of the attacking Pokémon and the Defense stat of the defending Pokémon affect the result.

 **ATTACK** → **Physical** → **DEFENSE**

Stats that affect special moves:

The Sp. Attack stat of the attacking Pokémon and the Sp. Defense stat of the defending Pokémon affect the result.

 SP. ATTACK → **Special** →  **SP. DEFENSE**

Stats Technique ② The must-have Pokémon of the Unova region

Let high-stats Pokémon join your battle party. These are the top three Pokémon in the Unova region for each of the six stats. Consider how to raise them, battle with them, and battle against them.

● High-stat Pokémon

Pokémon with high HP

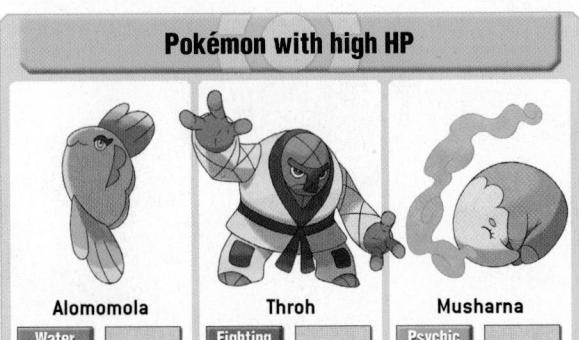

Alomomola — Water
STATS
HP ●●●●●●
ATTACK ●●●
DEFENSE ●●●
SP. ATTACK ●●
SP. DEFENSE ●●
SPEED ●●●

Throh — Fighting
STATS
HP ●●●●●
ATTACK ●●●●●
DEFENSE ●●●
SP. ATTACK ●
SP. DEFENSE ●●●
SPEED ●●

Musharna — Psychic
STATS
HP ●●●●●
ATTACK ●●
DEFENSE ●●●
SP. ATTACK ●●●●●
SP. DEFENSE ●●●●
SPEED ●

Pokémon with high Speed

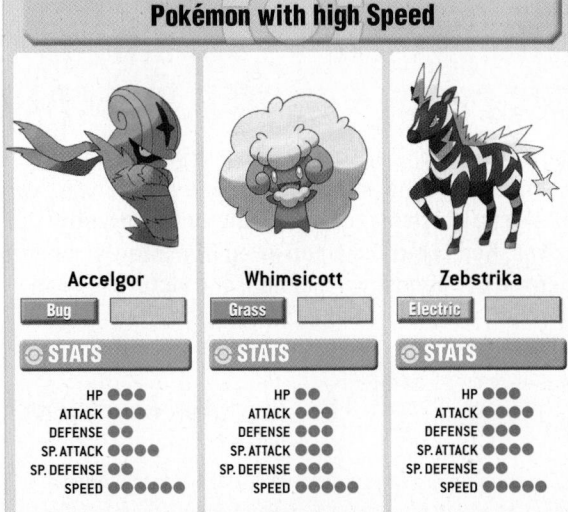

Accelgor — Bug
STATS
HP ●●●
ATTACK ●●●
DEFENSE ●●
SP. ATTACK ●●●●
SP. DEFENSE ●●
SPEED ●●●●●●

Whimsicott — Grass
STATS
HP ●●
ATTACK ●●
DEFENSE ●●●●
SP. ATTACK ●●●
SP. DEFENSE ●●●
SPEED ●●●●●

Zebstrika — Electric
STATS
HP ●●●
ATTACK ●●●●
DEFENSE ●●●
SP. ATTACK ●●●
SP. DEFENSE ●●
SPEED ●●●●●

Pokémon with high Attack

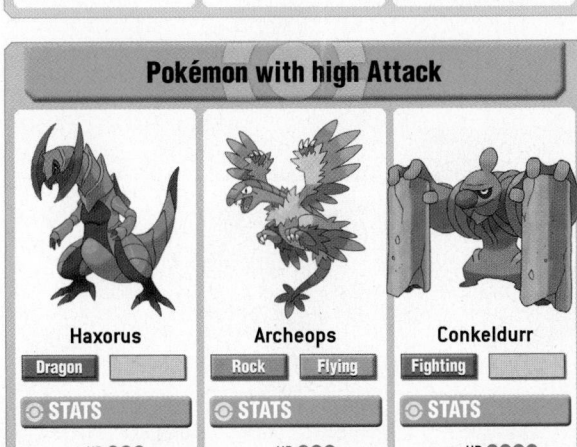

Haxorus — Dragon
STATS
HP ●●●
ATTACK ●●●●●●
DEFENSE ●●●●
SP. ATTACK ●●●
SP. DEFENSE ●●●
SPEED ●●●●

Archeops — Rock / Flying
STATS
HP ●●●
ATTACK ●●●●●●
DEFENSE ●●●
SP. ATTACK ●●●●●
SP. DEFENSE ●●
SPEED ●●●●●

Conkeldurr — Fighting
STATS
HP ●●●●
ATTACK ●●●●●●
DEFENSE ●●●●
SP. ATTACK ●●
SP. DEFENSE ●●●
SPEED ●●

Pokémon with high Sp. Attack

Chandelure — Ghost / Fire
STATS
HP ●●
ATTACK ●●
DEFENSE ●●●●
SP. ATTACK ●●●●●●
SP. DEFENSE ●●●●
SPEED ●●●●

Volcarona — Bug / Fire
STATS
HP ●●●
ATTACK ●●
DEFENSE ●●●
SP. ATTACK ●●●●●●
SP. DEFENSE ●●●●
SPEED ●●●●

Reuniclus — Psychic
STATS
HP ●●●●
ATTACK ●●●
DEFENSE ●●●
SP. ATTACK ●●●●●
SP. DEFENSE ●●●
SPEED ●

Pokémon with high Defense

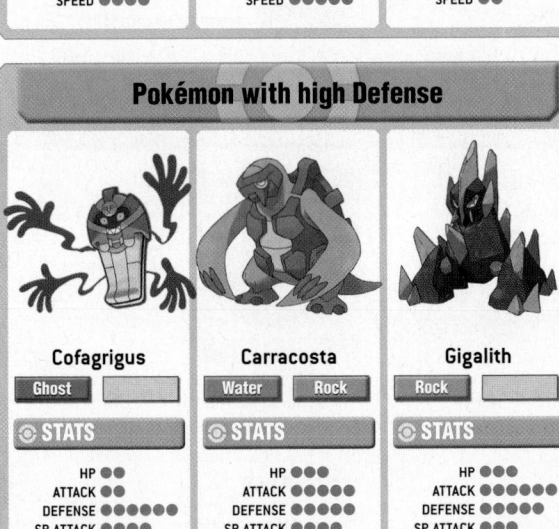

Cofagrigus — Ghost
STATS
HP ●●
ATTACK ●●
DEFENSE ●●●●●●
SP. ATTACK ●●●●
SP. DEFENSE ●●●●
SPEED ●

Carracosta — Water / Rock
STATS
HP ●●●
ATTACK ●●●●●
DEFENSE ●●●●●●
SP. ATTACK ●●●
SP. DEFENSE ●●●
SPEED ●

Gigalith — Rock
STATS
HP ●●●
ATTACK ●●●●●●
DEFENSE ●●●●●●
SP. ATTACK ●●●
SP. DEFENSE ●●●
SPEED ●

Pokémon with high Sp. Defense

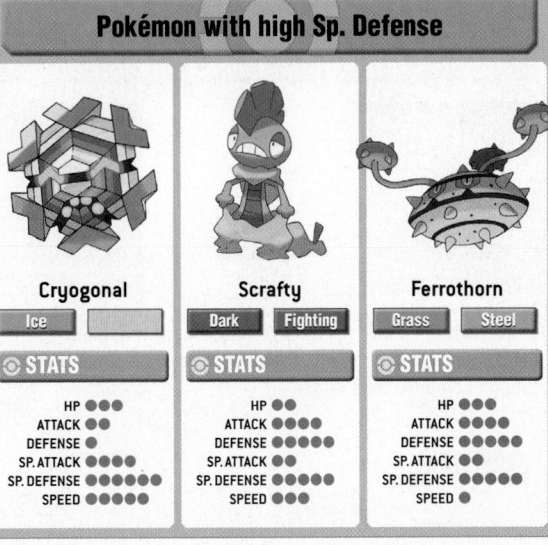

Cryogonal — Ice
STATS
HP ●●●
ATTACK ●●
DEFENSE ●
SP. ATTACK ●●●
SP. DEFENSE ●●●●●●
SPEED ●●●●●

Scrafty — Dark / Fighting
STATS
HP ●●
ATTACK ●●●●
DEFENSE ●●●●●
SP. ATTACK ●●
SP. DEFENSE ●●●●●
SPEED ●●●

Ferrothorn — Grass / Steel
STATS
HP ●●●
ATTACK ●●●●
DEFENSE ●●●●●
SP. ATTACK ●●●
SP. DEFENSE ●●●●
SPEED ●

Pokémon Battle Basics

5

Inflict Status Conditions to Get an Edge

Inflicting status conditions brings you one step closer to victory

Status conditions are unfavorable in general and include Poison, which reduces the affected Pokémon's HP a little every turn, and Paralysis, which makes it difficult for the affected Pokémon to use moves. Keep your Pokémon away from status conditions and inflict them on the opposing Pokémon, and victory is near.

Status Condition Technique **1** **Basic status conditions**

When they have status conditions, Pokémon will not be able to perform to their full potential, failing to use moves or losing HP every turn. It is a lot easier to face such Pokémon than healthy ones. Use moves and Abilities that inflict status conditions to your advantage.

● Status conditions at a glance

Sleep

The affected Pokémon closes its eyes.

You can still choose a move to use, but most times, your Pokémon is unable to use it for a few turns.

| Pros | The affected Pokémon is unable to use moves. |

Poison

The affected Pokémon turns purple.

The affected Pokémon loses a little HP at the end of each turn. Does not wear off on its own, though some Abilities end it.

| Pros | Reduces the target's HP gradually. |

Paralysis

The affected Pokémon turns yellow.

The affected Pokémon's Speed goes down. There's a 25% chance that the Pokémon can't attack. Does not wear off on its own.

| Pros | Lowers the target's Speed. |

Burned

The affected Pokémon turns red.

Lowers Attack, and HP decreases each turn. Does not wear off on its own, though some Abilities end it.

| Pros | Lowers Attack. |

Frozen

The affected Pokémon turns blue.

Unable to use most moves. It may recover on its own as it tries to use a move.

| Pros | The affected Pokémon is unable to use moves. |

Confused

The affected Pokémon's color doesn't change.

For several turns, the affected Pokémon may attack itself. The affected Pokémon recovers when it switches out.

| Pros | The affected Pokémon may attack itself. |

Inflict status conditions on opposing Pokémon to get closer to victory

Use moves and Abilities to inflict status conditions. Some moves that inflict status conditions are purely support moves, and others are attack moves that have additional effects to inflict status conditions. Some useful

Abilities are the ones that cause status conditions as the attacking Pokémon makes physical contact with the defending Pokémon. These are some of the strategies you can consider.

● Moves and Abilities that cause status conditions

Sample move that inflicts Sleep status

Hypnosis `Psychic`

Munna, Musharna, and some other Pokémon learn Hypnosis, a move which inflicts Sleep if it hits. The move's accuracy is not especially high, though, at just 60.

Musharna

Sample Ability that inflicts Poison status

`Ability` **Poison Point**

Whirlipede, Scolipede, and some other Pokémon have the Ability Poison Point, which has a 30% chance of inflicting Poison on attacking Pokémon on contact.

Scolipede

Your Pokémon will be hard to defeat if you can prevent status conditions

Just as you try to inflict status conditions, the opposing Trainer is thinking how to inflict status conditions on your Pokémon. Some moves and Abilities can fix those status

conditions, so stay cool and be ready to use them. Once the opposing Trainer has found out you have ways to fix status conditions, he or she will consider a new strategy.

● Moves and Abilities can prevent or help Pokémon recover from status conditions

Sample move that prevents status conditions

Safeguard `Normal`

Safeguard is a move that prevents your side from being affected by status conditions for five turns. The effect remains even if the user switches out.

Alomomola

Sample Ability that helps allies recover

`Ability` **Healer**

Healer is an Ability that gives an ally a one-third chance of recovering from status conditions.

Audino

● Some moves and Abilities benefit from status conditions

Sample move that benefits from status conditions

Facade `Normal`

Facade's power is doubled if the user is poisoned, paralyzed, or burned. It's a helpful move when your Pokémon is affected by status conditions.

Throh

Sample Ability that benefits from status conditions

`Ability` **Guts**

Guts is an Ability that increases the Pokémon's Attack by 50% when it's affected by status conditions. It'll make the opposing Trainer think twice about using moves that inflict status conditions. .

Conkeldurr

Pokémon Battle Basics

6 Become a Pokémon Move Master

Knowing the features and effects of moves is the key to victory

While landing big damage with powerful attack moves is crucial, moves that inflict status or special conditions are also an essential way to tip the battle in your favor. Understand each move's effects, and you'll know what to do when the situation calls for just the right move.

Move Technique 1 Teach your Pokémon moves

Pokémon learn moves in a variety of ways. Leveling up is the most common, but you can teach your Pokémon some moves only by other, more unusual methods. Use those moves to hit the opposing Pokémon with surprises they weren't expecting.

● Ways to teach moves to Pokémon

◎ Learn by leveling up

Sometimes Pokémon learn moves by leveling up. More powerful moves are usually learned at higher levels. Level up to learn powerful moves.

◎ Use TMs and HMs

TMs can teach Pokémon moves they can't learn by leveling up. The TMs you can use will depend on the Pokémon, as not every Pokémon can use every TM.

◎ Learn moves faster by stopping evolution

You can press the B Button to cancel evolution when a Pokémon is evolving. When you do this, the Pokémon can learn moves it would normally learn after evolving at a lower level.

◎ Have moves taught to your Pokémon

The starter Pokémon and Dragon-type Pokémon can learn special moves in places like Driftveil City and Opelucid City. You must, however, have a very strong bond with your Pokémon (p. 178, 258).

◎ Remember a move

Give the "reminder girl" in Mistralton City a Heart Scale, and she will help your Pokémon recall a move it's forgotten.

◎ Egg moves

Pokémon hatched from Eggs can inherit moves from the Pokémon who were at the Pokémon Day Care when the Egg was discovered (p. 237).

Master moves by understanding their elements

Moves have many elements other than their types. Each move has fixed elements such as power, range, and accuracy. Accuracy becomes important when battling opposing Pokémon with high evasion. Also, in Double and Triple Battles, range really matters. Figure out the features of moves, and teach your Pokémon moves that fit your battle style.

● Elements of a move

Element 1 Power

Attack moves have a numeric value called power. This element is critical for determining how much damage is done to the target. The larger this number is, the more damage your Pokémon does.

1	Each attack move has a power value
2	The more power the move has, the more damage it will do
3	Other elements besides power determine damage

Element 2 Range

Moves have different ranges, such as moves that affect only one Pokémon, moves that affect two Pokémon at once, or moves that affect yourself. In Double Battles and Triple Battles, moves that affect two or more Pokémon at the same time are very useful.

1	Range is the area the move's effects reach
2	Each move has a fixed range
3	Some moves even hit your allies

Element 3 Accuracy

Accuracy indicates how easily a move will land. The larger the value, the more often the move hits. For example, a move with an accuracy of 50 lands only 50 out of 100 times.

1	Use items to raise accuracy
2	You can lower the accuracy of opposing Pokémon with moves
3	Some moves always land regardless of accuracy

Element 4 PP (Power Points)

The number of times a move can be used is called PP. Every time you use a move, its PP decreases by one. When no PP are left, your Pokémon can't use that move. Generally, moves with fewer PP tend to be more powerful.

1	Use Ether to restore PP
2	Increase the maximum PP with PP Up
3	When PP for every move is exhausted, use Struggle

Element 5 Physical Moves and Special Moves

Attack moves are divided into two types: physical and special moves. Physical moves are related to a Pokémon's Attack stat, and special moves are related to the Sp. Attack stat.

1	Physical moves are related to the Attack and Defense stats
2	Special moves are related to the Sp. Attack and Sp. Defense stats
3	Some items and Abilities are related to types of attacks

Element 6 Direct Attacks

Direct attacks make physical contact with the target Pokémon. When a direct attack move hits, it can be influenced by the target Pokémon's Ability, item, and more.

1	Most direct attacks are physical moves
2	A few of them are special moves
3	Direct attacks can trigger items and Abilities

Move Technique 3 Use moves to inflict status conditions

Some moves inflict status conditions on the target. Status condition moves might not do much damage at first, but they can seal off the opposing Pokémon's moves, lower stats, or slowly erode its HP to give you an advantage. Inflicting status conditions can give you the opening you need.

● Advantage of status condition-inflicting moves

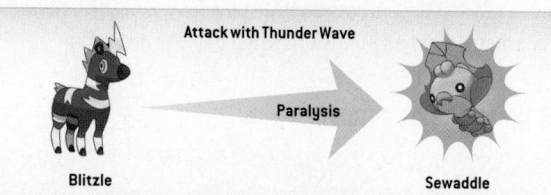

Attack with Thunder Wave

Paralysis

Blitzle

Sewaddle

Inflicting the Paralysis condition lowers the target's Speed and reduces the chance that you'll be hit by an attack.

● Examples of status condition-inflicting moves

Move	Type	Power	Accuracy	Effect	Examples of Pokémon that can learn it
Confuse Ray	Ghost	—	100	Inflicts the Confused condition on the target	Watchog, Litwick, and others
Glare	Normal	—	90	Inflicts Paralysis	Snivy, Druddigon
GrassWhistle	Grass	—	55	Inflicts the Sleep status on the target	Swadloon, Deerling, and others
Hypnosis	Psychic	—	60	Inflicts the Sleep status on the target	Patrat, Munna, and others
Spore	Grass	—	100	Inflicts the Sleep status on the target	Foongus, Amoonguss
Stun Spore	Grass	—	75	Inflicts Paralysis	Cottonee, Petilil, and others
Supersonic	Normal	—	55	Inflicts the Confused condition on the target	Woobat, Tympole, and others
Teeter Dance	Normal	—	100	Inflicts the Confused condition on the target	Lilligant
Thunder Wave	Electric	—	100	Inflicts Paralysis	Blitzle, Joltik, and others
Will-O-Wisp	Fire	—	75	Burns the target	Yamask, Litwick, and others

Move Technique 4 Alter your Pokémon's stats with support moves

Moves can be used to raise and lower stats of your battling Pokémon. For example, if you raise Attack or Sp. Attack, you can do more damage to your target. Also, if you raise Speed enough, you can move before your opponent. Put yourself in an advantageous position by changing stats.

● Advantages of raising stats

Use the move Work Up

Attack and Sp. Attack both rise

Herdier

When you raise Attack and Sp. Attack, you can do massive damage with both physical and special attacks.

● Examples of moves that raise your stats

Move	Type	Power	Accuracy	Effect	Examples of Pokémon that can learn it
Coil	Poison	—	—	Raises Attack, Defense, and accuracy by 1	Serperior, Eelektrik, and others
Cotton Guard	Grass	—	—	Raises the user's Defense by 3	Cottonee, Maractus
Hone Claws	Dark	—	—	Raises Attack and accuracy by 1	Druddigon, Braviary, and others
Quiver Dance	Bug	—	—	Raises the user's Sp. Attack, Sp. Defense, and Speed by 1	Lilligant, Volcarona
Work Up	Normal	—	—	Raises Attack and Sp. Attack by 1	Herdier, Zweilous, and others

● Examples of moves that lower target's stats

Move	Type	Power	Accuracy	Effect	Examples of Pokémon that can learn it
Cotton Spore	Grass	—	100	Lowers target's Speed by 2	Cottonee, Maractus, and others
Fake Tears	Dark	—	100	Lowers target's Sp. Defense by 2	Gothita, Gothorita, and others
FeatherDance	Flying	—	100	Lowers target's Attack by 2	Unfezant, Ducklett, and others
Scary Face	Normal	—	100	Lowers target's Speed by 2	Basculin, Krokorok, and others
Tickle	Normal	—	100	Lowers target's Attack and Defense by 1	Minccino, Gothita, and others

● Pokémon that learn a move as an Egg move or by TM are listed when there aren't any Pokémon that learn the move through leveling up.

● Pokémon who are not in the Unova Pokédex may be needed for a move to be learned as an Egg move.

Frustrate the opposing Trainer with moves that have additional effects

The additional effects some attack moves have let them do more than just damage the target. Get an advantage in battle with the additional effects! There are many effects such as lowering your target's stats, raising your own stats, or inflicting status conditions on the target. For example, the move Electroweb has an additional effect that lowers the target's Speed.

● **Advantage of moves with additional effects**

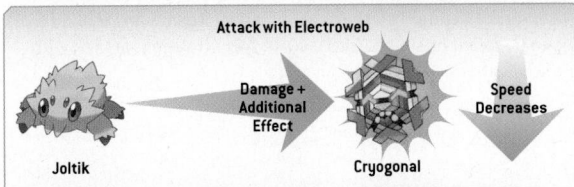

The target's Speed is lowered at the same time as the attack. This makes it easier to use moves before the opposing Pokémon.

● **Examples of moves with a stat-related additional effect**

Move	Type	Power	Accuracy	Effect	Examples of Pokémon that can learn it
Acid Spray	Poison	40	100	100% chance of lowering target's Sp. Defense by 2	Trubbish, Accelgor, and others
Bulldoze	Ground	60	100	100% chance of lowering target's Speed by 1	Palpitoad, Landorus, and others
Electroweb	Electric	55	95	100% chance of lowering target's Speed by 1	Joltik, Galvantula
Flame Charge	Fire	50	100	100% chance of raising the user's Speed by 1	Tepig, Blitzle, and others
Low Sweep	Fighting	60	100	100% chance of lowering target's Speed by 1	Timburr, Sawk, and others
Razor Shell	Water	75	95	50% chance of lowering target's Defense by 1	Oshawott, Dewott, and others
Struggle Bug	Bug	30	100	100% chance of lowering target's Sp. Attack by 1	Sewaddle, Shelmet, and others

● **Examples of moves that deliver status conditions**

Move	Type	Power	Accuracy	Effect	Examples of Pokémon that can learn it
Heart Stamp	Psychic	60	100	30% chance of making target flinch (unable to use moves that turn)	Woobat, Swoobat
Icicle Crash	Ice	85	90	30% chance of making target flinch (unable to use moves that turn)	Beartic
Inferno	Fire	100	50	100% chance of inflicting Burn	Litwick, Heatmor, and others
Scald	Water	80	100	30% chance of inflicting Burn	Emboar, Panpour, and others
Sludge Wave	Poison	95	100	10% chance of inflicting Poison	Trubbish, Frillish, and others

Strike before opposing Pokémon

Speed determines which Pokémon attacks first in battle. But that doesn't mean a Pokémon with low Speed is always stuck playing catch-up. Moves like Quick Attack or Aqua Jet can hit first regardless of Speed. You can get the drop on an opposing Pokémon with very high Speed.

● **Advantages to attacking first**

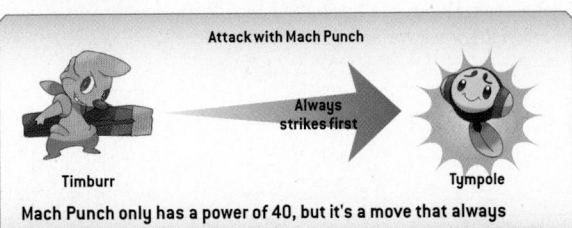

Mach Punch only has a power of 40, but it's a move that always strikes first.

● **Examples of moves that always attack first**

Move	Type	Power	Accuracy	Effect	Examples of Pokémon that can learn it
Aqua Jet	Water	40	100	Always strikes first	Dewott, Alomomola, and others
ExtremeSpeed	Normal	80	100	Always strikes first (faster than other moves that strike first)	—
Fake Out	Normal	40	100	Strikes first and makes the target flinch (only works on first turn)	Liepard, Mienfoo, and others
Ice Shard	Ice	40	100	Always strikes first	Vanillite, Cryogonal
Mach Punch	Fighting	40	100	Always strikes first	Timburr
Quick Attack	Normal	40	100	Always strikes first	Pidove, Blitzle, and others
Sucker Punch	Dark	80	100	Strikes first if target's chosen move is an attack move	Maractus, Galvantula, and others

● When the opposing Pokémon uses a similar move at the same time, the user's Speed decides which attack goes first. The move Fake Out is always the fastest.

● Pokémon that learn ExtremeSpeed appear after you complete the main story.

Move Technique 7 — ## Strike accurately with sure-hit moves

A move's accuracy determines its chances of hitting a target, but opposing Pokémon can raise their evasion with moves or even lower your Pokémon's accuracy, which makes it hard to land a move even if it has high accuracy. In this situation, attack with sure-hit moves.

● Advantage of sure-hit moves

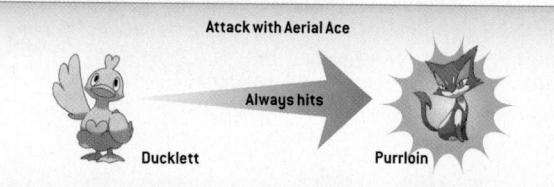

The Flying-type move Aerial Ace even hits targets with raised evasion.

● Examples of sure-hit moves

Move	Type	Power	Accuracy	Effect	Examples of Pokémon that can learn it
Aerial Ace	Flying	60	—	Sure hit	Ducklett, Rufflet, and others
Aura Sphere	Fighting	90	—	Sure hit	Mienfoo, Mienshao
Faint Attack	Dark	60	—	Sure hit	Scraggy, Foongus, and others
Magical Leaf	Grass	60	—	Sure hit	Petilil, Virizion, and others
Shadow Punch	Ghost	60	—	Sure hit	Golett, Golurk
Shock Wave	Electric	60	—	Sure hit	Blitzle, Emolga, and others
Swift	Normal	60	—	Sure hit	Minccino, Accelgor, and others
Trump Card	Normal	—	—	Sure hit and the move's power increases as its PP decreases	Oshawott
Vital Throw	Fighting	70	—	Always strikes later than normal, but has perfect accuracy	Throh, Mienfoo

● Moves that make the next move a sure-hit move

Move	Type	Power	Accuracy	Effect	Examples of Pokémon that can learn it
Lock-On	Normal	—	—	The user's next move is a sure hit during the next turn	Klang, Klinklang, and others
Mind Reader	Normal	—	—	The user's next move is a sure hit during the next turn	Sewaddle, Shelmet
Telekinesis	Psychic	—	—	For three turns, most moves will hit the target	Munna, Gothitelle, and others

Move Technique 8 — ## Accuracy changes the tides of battle

A move's accuracy determines its chances of hitting a target. The higher the target's evasion, the easier it is for the target to dodge the move. You can create an ideal situation by lowering the opposing Pokémon's accuracy and raising your Pokémon's evasion to attack without getting hit.

● Advantages of lowering accuracy

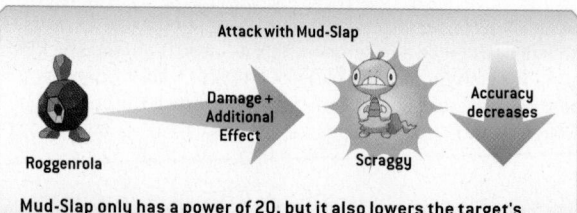

Mud-Slap only has a power of 20, but it also lowers the target's accuracy.

● Examples of accuracy-related moves

Move	Type	Power	Accuracy	Effect	Examples of Pokémon that can learn it
Coil	Poison	—	—	Raises Attack, Defense, and accuracy by 1	Serperior, Eelektrik, and others
Hone Claws	Dark	—	—	Raises Attack and accuracy by 1	Drilbur, Druddigon, and others
Leaf Tornado	Grass	65	90	50% chance of lowering target's accuracy by 1	Snivy, Servine, and others
Mud-Slap	Ground	20	100	100% chance of lowering target's accuracy by 1	Roggenrola, Stunfisk, and others
Sand-Attack	Ground	—	100	Lowers target's accuracy by 1	Purrloin, Sandile, and others

● Examples of evasion-related moves

Move	Type	Power	Accuracy	Effect	Examples of Pokémon that can learn it
Foresight	Normal	—	—	Attacks land easily regardless of the target's evasion	Patrat, Timburr, and others
Minimize	Normal	—	—	Raises the user's evasion by 2	Litwick, Lampent
Miracle Eye	Psychic	—	—	Attacks land easily regardless of the target's evasion	Sigilyph, Elgyem, and others
Odor Sleuth	Normal	—	—	Attacks land easily regardless of the target's evasion	Tepig, Lillipup, and others
Sweet Scent	Normal	—	100	Lowers target's evasion by 1	Maractus, Foongus, and others

Move Technique 9 — Recovery moves get you out of trouble

Pokémon lose HP every time they are hit by an attack. Once a Pokémon's HP drops to 0, it faints and can no longer battle. So it's a good idea to have a Pokémon who knows HP-restoring moves or even moves that cure status conditions. As long as you have some healing power on your team, you'll be ready for long battles.

Advantage of status recovery moves

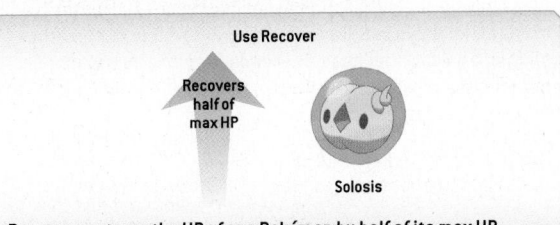

Recover restores the HP of one Pokémon by half of its max HP.

Examples of HP recovery moves

Move	Type	Power	Accuracy	Effect	Examples of Pokémon that can learn it
Drain Punch	Fighting	75	100	Restores HP by up to half of the damage dealt to the target	Seismitoad, Mienfoo, and others
Heal Pulse	Psychic	—	—	Restores the target's HP by up to half of its max HP	Audino, Alomomola
Horn Leech	Grass	75	100	Restores HP by up to half of the damage dealt to the target	Sawsbuck
Leech Seed	Grass	—	90	Each turn, recovers HP by the amount drained from the target (this move's effects continue even if the user is switched out)	Pansage, Deerling, and others
Pain Split	Normal	—	—	The user and target's HP is added, then equally shared	Duosion, Lampent, and others
Recover	Normal	—	—	Restores HP by up to half of the user's max HP	Solosis, Cryogonal, and others
Rest	Psychic	—	—	Fully restores HP, but puts the user to sleep for two turns	Karrablast, Cubchoo, and others

Examples of status recovery moves

Move	Type	Power	Accuracy	Effect	Examples of Pokémon that can learn it
Aromatherapy	Grass	—	—	Heals status conditions of all your party Pokémon	Petilil, Deerling, and others
Heal Bell	Normal	—	—	Heals status conditions of all your party Pokémon	Audino
Healing Wish	Psychic	—	—	User faints, but fully heals the next Pokémon's HP and status conditions	Audino, Petilil, Alomomola
Psycho Shift	Psychic	—	90	Shifts the user's Poisoned, Badly Poisoned, Sleep, Paralyze, or Burned condition to the target and heals the user	Sigilyph
Refresh	Normal	—	—	Heals Poisoned, Paralyzed, and Burned conditions	Audino, Tympole, and others

Move Technique 10 — Prevent damage with protective moves

Some moves keep opposing Pokémon's moves from affecting your Pokémon that turn. Well-timed use of Detect can stop a move—no matter how high its power. Moves such as Quick Guard can protect all of your allies in Double Battles and Triple Battles.

Advantages of protective moves

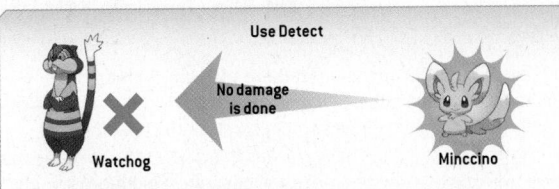

Detect prevents damage from the opposing Pokémon's moves during that turn.

Examples of protective moves

Move	Type	Power	Accuracy	Effect	Examples of Pokémon that can learn it
Detect	Fighting	—	—	Protects the user from moves that target it	Patrat, Tranquill, and others
Protect	Normal	—	—	Protects the user from moves that target it	Swadloon, Venipede, and others
Quick Guard	Fighting	—	—	Protects the user and all allies from first-strike moves	Sawk, Archen, and others
Wide Guard	Rock	—	—	Protects the user and allies from moves that target multiple Pokémon	Throh, Tirtouga, and others

● Using protective moves consecutively makes them more likely to fail.

Examples of moves that remove protecting effects

Move	Type	Power	Accuracy	Effect	Examples of Pokémon that can learn it
Feint	Normal	30	100	Hits even targets protected by Protect, Detect, Quick Guard, and Wide Guard and removes their effects	Shelmet, Mienfoo

Move Technique 11 | Manipulate the weather to power up moves

Some moves can be used to change the weather, and other moves have effects that change depending on the weather. For example, the move Blizzard always hits when the weather condition is Hail. When the weather condition is Sunny, the amount of HP healed by Synthesis increases. Try building a team that uses the weather as an ally.

● **Advantages of weather moves**

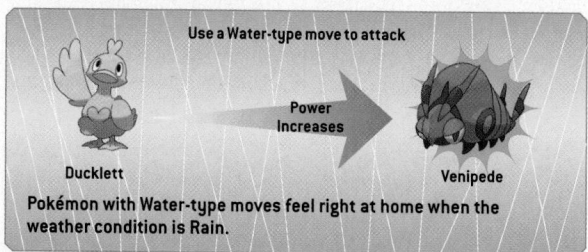

Use a Water-type move to attack

Power Increases

Ducklett → Venipede

Pokémon with Water-type moves feel right at home when the weather condition is Rain.

● **Examples of weather-changing moves**

Move	Type	Power	Accuracy	Effect	Examples of Pokémon that can learn it
Hail	Ice	—	—	The Hail weather condition is in effect for five turns. All Pokémon other than Ice-type Pokémon take damage each turn.	Vanillish, Frillish, Beartic, Cryogonal, and others
Rain Dance	Water	—	—	The Rain weather condition is in effect for five turns. The power of Water-type moves is boosted.	Palpitoad, Carracosta, Ducklett, Frillish, and others
Sandstorm	Rock	—	—	The Sandstorm weather condition is in effect for five turns. All Pokémon other than Rock-, Steel-, and Ground-type Pokémon take damage each turn. Rock-type Pokémon's Sp. Defense goes up.	Boldore, Excadrill, Krookodile, Landorus, and others
Sunny Day	Fire	—	—	The Sunny weather condition is in effect for five turns. The power of Fire-type moves is boosted.	Cottonee, Petilil, Maractus, Larvesta, and others

● **Examples of moves affected by weather**

Move	Type	Power	Accuracy	Effect	Examples of Pokémon that can learn it
Blizzard	Ice	120	70	Always hits when the weather condition is Hail.	Vanilluxe, Cubchoo, and others
Growth	Normal	—	—	Raises Attack and Sp. Attack by 1. Raises by 2 when the weather condition is Sunny.	Snivy, Cottonee, Petilil, Foongus, and others
Hurricane	Flying	120	70	Always hits when the weather condition is Rain. Accuracy lowers by 50% when the weather condition is Sunny.	Whimsicott, Swanna, Volcarona, Tornadus, and others
SolarBeam	Grass	120	100	Usually requires one turn to charge, but goes off right away when the weather condition is Sunny.	Sawsbuck, Cryogonal, and others
Synthesis	Grass	—	—	Recovers HP. Effect changes depending on the weather.	Petilil, Maractus, and others
Thunder	Electric	120	70	Always hits when the weather condition is Rain. Accuracy lowers by 50% when the weather condition is Sunny.	Zebstrika, Klinklang, Thundurus, Zekrom, and others

Move Technique 12 | Limit the opposing Pokémon's actions

You can disrupt the opposing Trainer's plans by limiting the moves he or she can use. Using moves that prevent the opposing Trainer from choosing moves freely can turn the tide of battle your way. For example, Encore forces the target to keep using the same move. If you use this while the opposing Pokémon is using a support move, it won't be able to attack.

● **Advantage to moves that limit the target's moves**

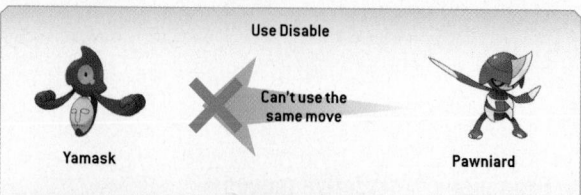

Use Disable

Can't use the same move

Yamask   Pawniard

Disable prevents the target from using the move it used before it was hit by Disable for four turns.

● **Examples of moves that limit your opponent's moves**

Move	Type	Power	Accuracy	Effect	Examples of Pokémon that can learn it
Disable	Normal	—	100	Target can't use the move it just used for four turns	Yamask, Cofagrigus, and others
Embargo	Dark	—	100	Target can't use items for five turns and its Trainer can't use items on that Pokémon	Krookodile, Gothita, Pawniard, Vullaby, and others
Encore	Normal	—	100	Target must use the move it used last for three turns	Samurott, Minccino, and others
Heal Block	Psychic	—	100	Targets cannot restore HP for five turns	Reuniclus, Elgyem, and others
Torment	Dark	—	100	Target cannot use the same move twice in a row	Purrloin, Pansage, and others

Move Technique 13 Use switching moves to take control of the battle

Switching is an important tactic in battles. Normally, you can only switch Pokémon at the start of your turn, but some moves let you switch in your party Pokémon in the middle of your turn. Also, some moves force the opposing Trainer to switch Pokémon. Use moves like these when you are facing an unfavorable matchup.

● Advantages of switching moves

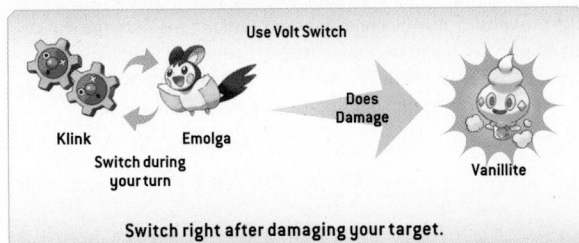

Use Volt Switch

Klink   Emolga   Does Damage   Vanillite

Switch during your turn

Switch right after damaging your target.

● Examples of moves that let you switch Pokémon

Move	Type	Power	Accuracy	Effect	Examples of Pokémon that can learn it
Ally Switch	Psychic	—	—	User switches places with an ally but fails if user is in the center position in a Triple Battle	Elgyem, Beheeyem
Baton Pass	Normal	—	—	User switches with a party Pokémon and passes stat changes to it	Watchog, Scolipede, and others
U-turn	Bug	70	100	User switches with a party Pokémon after attacking	Accelgor, Mienfoo, and others
Volt Switch	Electric	70	100	User switches with a party Pokémon after attacking	Zebstrika, Emolga, and others

● Examples of moves that make the opposing Trainer switch Pokémon

Move	Type	Power	Accuracy	Effect	Examples of Pokémon that can learn it
Circle Throw	Fighting	60	90	Forces the opposing Trainer to switch Pokémon	Throh
Dragon Tail	Dragon	60	90	Forces the opposing Trainer to switch Pokémon	Serperior, Druddigon, and others
Roar	Normal	—	100	Forces the opposing Trainer to switch Pokémon	Emboar, Herdier, and others
Whirlwind	Normal	—	100	Forces the opposing Trainer to switch Pokémon	Sigilyph, Volcarona, and others

● Examples of moves that prevent Pokémon switching

Move	Type	Power	Accuracy	Effect	Examples of Pokémon that can learn it
Block	Normal	—	—	Prevents the target from being switched in Trainer battles	Dwebble, Landorus
Mean Look	Normal	—	—	Prevents the target from being switched in Trainer battles	Watchog, Cofagrigus, and others
Spider Web	Bug	—	—	Prevents the target from being switched in Trainer battles	Joltik, Galvantula

● Moves that switch, or force switching of, Pokémon won't cause them to switch if there are no Pokémon that can be switched into battle.

Move Technique 14 Affect items with moves

Having a Pokémon hold an item gives it an advantage in battle. No doubt, your foe's strategy will make use of held items. Disrupting your foe's tactics with moves that make your opponent's held items unusable—or steal them instantly—makes it easier to fight.

● Advantage of moves that affect items

Attack with Thief

Do damage and steal items

Woobat   Lillipup

Steal your target's held item with Thief.

● Examples of moves related to items

Move	Type	Power	Accuracy	Effect	Examples of Pokémon that can learn it
Acrobatics	Flying	55	100	If the user isn't holding an item, attack does double damage	Archen, Emolga, and others
Fling	Dark	—	100	User attacks by throwing a held item at the target, and power and effect varies depending on the item	Pansage, Pansear, Panpour, Druddigon, and others
Incinerate	Fire	30	100	Burns the Berry being held by the target, making it unusable	Pansear, Darumaka, and others
Magic Room	Psychic	—	—	Held items have no effect for five turns and cannot be thrown with the move Fling	Gothita, Gothorita, Gothitelle
Recycle	Normal	—	—	A previously used held item can be used again	Pansage, Panpour, and others
Thief	Dark	40	100	When the target is holding an item and the user is not, the user can steal that item	Purrloin, Woobat, Krokorok, Darumaka, and others

Move Technique 15 Change Abilities with moves

Each Pokémon has a special Ability. One of the basics of Pokémon battles is using these Pokémon Abilities, which have effects like preventing status conditions or reducing the damage done by moves. They can turn the battle in your favor (p. 210). Use moves that change Abilities to alter the Abilities of the opposing Pokémon, and you can disrupt the opposing Trainer's plans.

● Advantage of changing Abilities

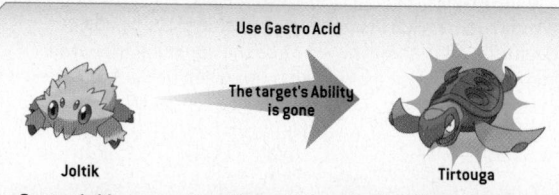

Use Gastro Acid

The target's Ability is gone

Joltik   Tirtouga

Gastro Acid removes the effects of the target's Ability as long as it is in battle.

● Examples of Ability-changing moves

Move	Type	Power	Accuracy	Effect	Examples of Pokémon that can learn it
Entrainment	Normal	—	100	Makes the target's Ability the same as the user's	Leavanny, Durant, and others
Gastro Acid	Poison	—	100	Disables the target's Ability	Joltik, Eelektrik, and others
Role Play	Psychic	—	—	Copies the target's Ability	Pansage, Pansear, etc.
Simple Beam	Normal	—	100	Changes the target's Ability to Simple	Audino, Elgyem, and others
Skill Swap	Psychic	—	—	Swaps Abilities with the target	Sigilyph, Solosis, and others
Worry Seed	Grass	—	100	Changes the target's Ability to Insomnia	Ferroseed, Deerling, and others

● Targets with certain Abilities are immune to these kinds of moves.

Move Technique 16 Come from behind with a one-hit knockout

Even if your opponent's Pokémon has a lot of HP left, certain moves can make it faint in just one blow. Their accuracy is a low 30, but if these moves hit, they can get you out of a dangerous situation. Also, some moves—such as Explosion—will make the user faint in exchange for doing big damage. When your Pokémon's HP is dwindling, these moves may turn the battle around.

● Advantages to one-hit KO moves

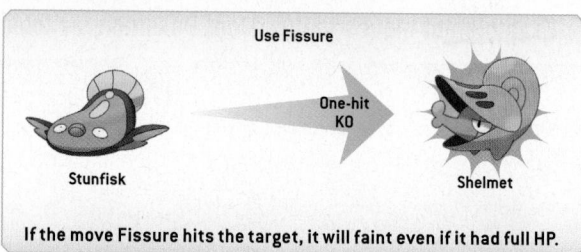

Use Fissure

One-hit KO

Stunfisk   Shelmet

If the move Fissure hits the target, it will faint even if it had full HP.

● One-hit KO moves

Move	Type	Power	Accuracy	Effect	Examples of Pokémon that can learn it
Fissure	Ground	—	30	Target faints with one hit	Excadrill, Stunfisk, and others
Guillotine	Normal	—	30	Target faints with one hit	Haxorus, Bisharp, and others
Horn Drill	Normal	—	30	Target faints with one hit	Excadrill
Sheer Cold	Ice	—	30	Target faints with one hit	Beartic, Cryogonal, and others

● If the target's level is higher than the user's, these moves will not hit.

● Move that make the user faint

Move	Type	Power	Accuracy	Effect	Examples of Pokémon that can learn it
Explosion	Normal	250	100	The user faints after using	Boldore, Garbodor, and others
Final Gambit	Fighting	—	100	Does damage to the target equal to the user's remaining HP, but if the move hits, the user faints	Basculin, Shelmet, Accelgor
Healing Wish	Psychic	—	—	The user faints, but the next Pokémon's HP and status are fully healed	Audino, Petilil, Alomomola
Memento	Dark	—	100	The user faints and lowers the target's Attack and Sp. Attack by 2	Yamask, Litwick, Lampent, and others
Selfdestruct	Normal	200	100	The user faints after using	Trubbish, Ferroseed, and others

In Triple Battles, both you and the opposing Trainer put three Pokémon into battle. Normally, the Pokémon on the far left can't hit the Pokémon on the far right, and the Pokémon on the far right can't hit the Pokémon on the far left. If you use a long-range move, you can hit the Pokémon on the other side. These attacks are very useful when you want to focus your attacks on one of the opposing Pokémon and make it faint as quickly as possible. Make sure to have your Pokémon learn them before attempting Triple Battles.

● **Advantages of long-range attacks**

Attack with Acrobatics

Pansear Trubbish Dwebble

The Pokémon on the opposite side can be attacked.

Archen Ferroseed Karrablast

Acrobatics is a long-range move, so attacks will reach the Pokémon on the opposite side.

● **Examples of long-range attacks**

Move	Type	Power	Accuracy	Effect	Examples of Pokémon that can learn it
Acrobatics	Flying	55	100	If the user isn't holding an item, this move's power doubles	Pansage, Pansear, and others
Aura Sphere	Fighting	90	—	Sure hit	Mienfoo, Mienshao
Dark Pulse	Dark	80	100	20% chance of making target flinch (unable to use a move on that turn)	Vullaby, Tornadus, and others
Heal Pulse	Psychic	—	—	Restores the target's HP by up to half of its max HP	Audino, Alomomola
Hurricane	Flying	120	70	30% chance of inflicting the Confused condition	Whimsicott, Swanna, and others
Water Pulse	Water	60	100	20% chance of inflicting the Confused condition	Dewott, Jellicent, and others

Moves that change based on circumstances

Some moves are influenced by other elements. For example, Grass Knot's power increases against a heavier target, and Return's power grows with greater friendship between the user and its Trainer. Use moves where the power changes according to the user or target to back the opposing Trainer into a corner.

1 Moves that change depending on the target's weight

Grass Knot [Grass]

The more the target weighs, the more Grass Knot's power increases. Low Kick is a similar move.

Pansage

2 Moves that change depending on the user's friendship

Return [Normal]

The higher the user's friendship, the more power Return has. Raise friendship as high as it will go before battle.

Woobat

3 Moves that change depending on the battlefield

Nature Power [Normal]

The land where the battle takes place influences this move. During Link Battles, the land is "normal" so the move will be Earthquake.

Sawsbuck
(Spring Form)

4 Moves that require Speed for best damage

Electro Ball [Electric]

Electro Ball's power increases depending on how much faster the user is than the target.

Emolga

POKÉMON BATTLE PRIMER

BECOME A POKÉMON MOVE MASTER

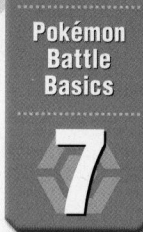

Pokémon Battle Basics

7

Take Advantage of Pokémon Abilities

Know the opposing Pokémon's Abilities and get the edge in battle

Pokémon Abilities have a variety of effects, such as increasing the amount of damage done to Pokémon by an attack or inflicting status conditions on the attacker when receiving an attack. If you can master Abilities, you will always have the edge over others in battle.

Ability Technique **1** **A Pokémon's Ability is determined by its species**

Every Pokémon has an Ability, which is determined by that Pokémon's species. Even if the species has two possible Abilities, each individual Pokémon will have only one of those Abilities. Also, what moves are useful can vary depending on the Pokémon's Ability. Look for ways to take advantage of the effects of the Pokémon's Ability when battling.

 Abilities change based on Pokémon species

Garbodor's Abilities

ABILITY Stench

When the Pokémon with this Ability damages a target with a move, there's a 10% chance it will flinch—preventing it from using any move this turn.

ABILITY Weak Armor

When the Pokémon is hit by a physical attack, Defense drops by 1, but Speed goes up by 1.

Lilligant's Abilities

ABILITY Chlorophyll

The Pokémon's Speed doubles when the weather condition is Sunny.

ABILITY Own Tempo

This Ability prevents the Pokémon from being affected by the Confused status condition.

 Categories of Abilities sorted by when they activate

1 Abilities that activate when the Pokémon enters a battle

2 Abilities that activate when the Pokémon uses a move

3 Abilities that activate when the Pokémon is hit by a move

4 Abilities that work continuously while the Pokémon is in battle

Abilities that activate when entering battle

Some Abilities activate as soon as the Pokémon enters a battle. For example, when a Pokémon with the Intimidate Ability comes into battle, the opposing Pokémon's Attack goes down one level. These Abilities activate when the battle starts or when the Pokémon with this kind of Ability is switched into battle. This is an important point when choosing a Pokémon to put at the head of your party or making tactics that include switching.

● **Advantages of Abilities that activate upon entering battle**

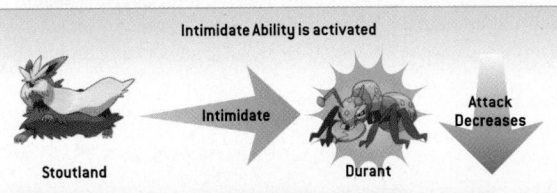

Put a Pokémon with the Intimidate Ability in battle to lower the opposing Pokémon's Attack by one level.

● **Examples of Abilities that activate when a Pokémon enters a battle**

Ability	Effect	Pokémon with this Ability
Forewarn	Determines one of the opposing Pokémon's moves when the Pokémon enters battle. Damaging moves with high power are prioritized	Munna, Musharna
Frisk	Checks an opposing Pokémon's held item when the Pokémon enters battle	Gothorita, Gothitelle, and others
Illusion	Appears in battle disguised as the last Pokémon in the party	Zorua, Zoroark
Intimidate	Lowers an opposing Pokémon's Attack by 1 when the Pokémon enters battle	Stoutland, Krookodile, and others

Take advantage of Abilities that power up particular move types

Some Abilities raise the power of moves if certain conditions are met. For example, Torrent increases the power of Water-type moves when HP is low. Knowing about Abilities like this can help you when you're in trouble.

● **Abilities that raise moves' power**

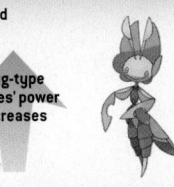

Use Bug-type moves aggressively when your Pokémon has little HP remaining. Power is higher than normal.

● **Examples of Abilities that power up particular move types**

Ability	Effect	Pokémon with this Ability
Adaptability	Powers up moves of the same type as the Pokémon	Basculin
Blaze	Raises the power of Fire-type moves by 50% when the Pokémon's HP drops to 1/3 or less	Pignite, Emboar, and others
Overgrow	Raises the power of Grass-type moves by 50% when the Pokémon's HP drops to 1/3 or less	Servine, Serperior, and others
Sand Force	When the weather condition is Sandstorm, the power of Ground-, Rock-, and Steel-type moves increases by 30%. Sandstorm does not damage Pokémon with this Ability	Excadrill, Landorus, and others
Swarm	Raises the power of Bug-type moves by 50% when the Pokémon's HP drops to 1/3 or less	Leavanny, Scolipede, and others
Torrent	Raises the power of Water-type moves by 50% when the Pokémon's HP drops to 1/3 or less	Dewott, Samurott, and others

Make the opposing Trainer hesitate with Pokémon that have two Abilities

Even if the species has two or more Abilities, each individual Pokémon will have only one of those Abilities. Usually, however, the opposing Trainer won't know which one it is. For example, Scolipede could have the Poison Point Ability, so even if your Scolipede actually has the Swarm Ability, the opposing Trainer will think twice before using direct attacks.

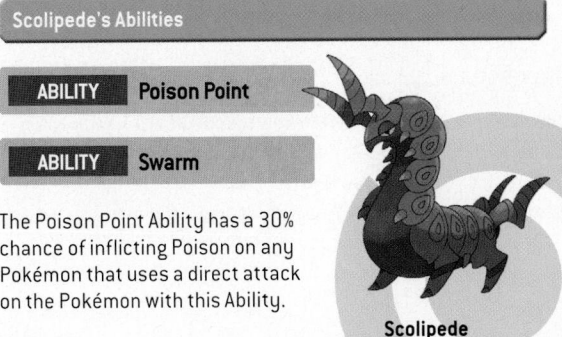

Scolipede's Abilities

ABILITY Poison Point

ABILITY Swarm

The Poison Point Ability has a 30% chance of inflicting Poison on any Pokémon that uses a direct attack on the Pokémon with this Ability.

Scolipede

Ability Technique **4** ## Use Abilities that activate when attacking

Some Abilities activate when the Pokémon with that Ability uses a move. For example, when a Pokémon with the Super Luck Ability damages an opposing Pokémon, its critical-hit ratio increases. In the same way, the Compoundeyes Ability raises the accuracy of moves. Combine Abilities with moves that take advantage of them for a devastating attack.

● **Advantages of offensive Abilities**

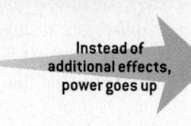

Sheer Force Ability is activated

Instead of additional effects, power goes up

Braviary

Swoobat

When a Pokémon uses a move with an additional effect, the effect goes away, but in exchange its power goes up by 30%.

● **Examples of Abilities that activate on using a move**

Ability	Effect	Pokémon with this Ability
Compoundeyes	Raises accuracy by 30%	Joltik, Galvantula
Guts	Attack stat rises by 50% when the Pokémon is affected by a status condition	Conkeldurr, Throh, and others
Hustle	Raises Attack by 50%, but lowers the accuracy of physical moves by 20%	Darumaka, Durant, and others
Infiltrator	Moves can hit even if the target used Reflect, Light Screen, Safeguard, or Mist	Cottonee, Whimsicott
Iron Fist	Increases the power of punching moves	Golett, Golurk
Mold Breaker	Use moves on targets regardless of their Abilities	Fraxure, Haxorus, and others
Poison Touch	30% chance of inflicting the Poison condition when the Pokémon uses a direct attack	Seismitoad
Prankster	Gives priority to status moves	Whimsicott, Tornadus, and others
Reckless	Raises the power of moves with recoil damage	Basculin, Bouffalant
Rivalry	If the target is the same gender, the power of the Pokémon's move goes up. Against the opposite gender, the move's power goes down, and if the target's gender is unknown, the move's power doesn't change	Fraxure, Haxorus, and others
Sheer Force	When moves with an additional effect is used, power increases by 30%, but the additional effect is lost	Druddigon, Braviary, and others
Stench	10% chance the target will flinch when the Pokémon damages the target with a move (preventing it from using any move this turn)	Trubbish, Garbodor
Super Luck	Heightens the critical-hit ratio of the Pokémon's moves	Tranquill, Unfezant, and others
Technician	If the move's power is 60 or below, its power will increase by 50%	Minccino, Cinccino

Ability Technique **5** ## Use damage-preventing Abilities to get an edge

Some Abilities prevent damage from particular move types. For example, Pokémon with the Sap Sipper Ability don't take damage from Grass-type attacks. When switching Pokémon or using combos in Double Battles and Triple Battles, knowing these Abilities is essential.

● **Advantages of damage-preventing Abilities**

Levitate Ability is activated

The Ground-type move Earthquake

Eelektross

Golurk

Pokémon with the Levitate Ability are not damaged by Ground-type attacks.

● **Examples of damage-preventing Abilities**

Ability	Effect	Pokémon with this Ability
Flash Fire	When the Pokémon is hit by a Fire-type move, it doesn't take damage and the power of its Fire-type moves increases by 50%	Chandelure, Heatmor, and others
Levitate	Gives full immunity to all Ground-type moves	Eelektross, Hydreigon, and others
Lightningrod	Draws all Electric-type moves to the Pokémon. When the Pokémon is hit by an Electric-type move, it doesn't take damage and its Sp. Attack goes up by 1	Blitzle, Zebstrika
Motor Drive	When the Pokémon is hit by a Electric-type move, it doesn't take damage and its Speed goes up by 1	Blitzle, Zebstrika
Sap Sipper	When the Pokémon is hit by a Grass-type move, it doesn't take damage and its Attack goes up by 1	Sawsbuck, Bouffalant, and others
Telepathy	Prevents damage from allies	Musharna, Beheeyem, and others
Water Absorb	When the Pokémon is hit by a Water-type move, it doesn't take damage and its HP is restored	Maractus, Jellicent, and others

Confound your opponent with Abilities that activate upon taking hits

Some Pokémon's Abilities activate when a move hits them. For example, Iron Barbs and Rough Skin lower an opponent's HP when the Pokémon with these Abilities are hit by a direct attack. The Solid Rock Ability reduces damage done by moves of the type the Pokémon with this Ability is weak against. These Abilities make it harder for the foe to use the moves he or she wants to use and give you a clear advantage.

● Advantages of hit-activated Abilities

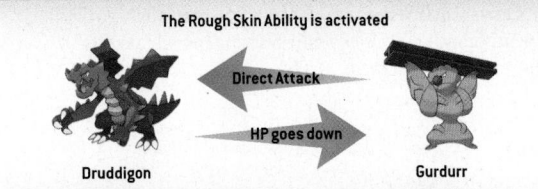

The Rough Skin Ability is activated

Direct Attack

HP goes down

Druddigon   Gurdurr

The Rough Skin Ability reduces the HP of opponents that hit the Pokémon with a direct attack.

● Examples of Abilities that activate when hit

Ability	Effect	Pokémon with this Ability
Cursed Body	30% chance of disabling the move used to hit the Pokémon	Frillish, Jellicent
Cute Charm	30% chance of making the attacker infatuated when hit by a direct attack	Minccino, Cinccino
Effect Spore	30% chance of inflicting the Poison, Paralysis, or Sleep condition on the attacker when hit by a direct attack	Foongus, Amoonguss
Flame Body	30% chance of inflicting the Burn condition on the attacker when hit by a direct attack	Chandelure, Volcarona, and others
Iron Barbs	Slightly reduces the HP of an opponent that hits the Pokémon with a direct attack	Ferroseed, Ferrothorn
Justified	When the Pokémon is hit by a Dark-type move, Attack goes up by 1	Cobalion, Terrakion, and others
Mummy	Changes the attacker's Ability to Mummy when hit by a direct attack	Yamask, Cofagrigus
Poison Point	30% chance of inflicting the Poison condition on the attacker when hit by a direct attack	Whirlipede, Scolipede, and others
Pressure	When the Pokémon is hit by an opponent's move, depletes 1 additional PP from that move	Kyurem
Rough Skin	Slightly reduces the HP of an opponent that hits the Pokémon with a direct attack	Druddigon
Shell Armor	Opponent's moves will not land a critical hit	Crustle, Escavalier, and others
Solid Rock	Minimizes the damage from supereffective moves	Tirtouga, Carracosta
Static	30% chance of inflicting the Paralysis condition on the attacker when hit by a direct attack	Emolga, Stunfisk
Sturdy	Protects the Pokémon against one-hit KO moves, such as Horn Drill and Sheer Cold. Leaves the Pokémon with 1 HP if hit by a move that would knock it out when its HP is full	Gigalith, Sawk, Crustle, Carracosta, and others
Weak Armor	When the Pokémon is hit by a physical attack, Defense goes down by 1, but Speed goes up by 1	Garbodor

Battle with reliable Abilities that prevent status conditions

Abilities can prevent certain status conditions or heal them after they are inflicted. For example, the Limber Ability prevents the Paralysis condition, and the Shed Skin Ability can sometimes heal status conditions. These Abilities can save your bacon when you are facing a foe trying to inflict status conditions.

● Advantages of Abilities that prevent status conditions

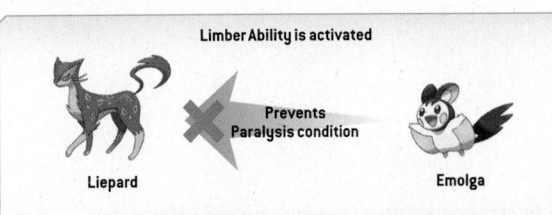

Limber Ability is activated

Prevents Paralysis condition

Liepard   Emolga

Pokémon with the Limber Ability are immune to Paralysis.

● Examples of status condition-related Abilities

Ability	Effect	Pokémon with this Ability
Guts	Attack stat rises by 50% when affected by a status condition	Conkeldurr, Throh, and others
Healer	33% chance every turn that each ally Pokémon's status condition will be healed	Audino, Alomomola
Limber	Protects against the Paralysis condition	Liepard, Stunfisk, and others
Own Tempo	Protects against the Confused condition	Petilil, Lilligant
Shed Skin	33% chance every turn that a status condition will be healed	Scrafty, Karrablast, and others
Synchronize	When the Pokémon receives the Poison, Paralysis, or Burned condition, this inflicts the same condition on the attacker	Musharna, Beheeyem, and others
Vital Spirit	Protects against the Sleep condition	Lillipup

Ability Technique 8 Pokémon with stat-changing Abilities thrive

Abilities can raise a Pokémon's stats, lower an opposing Pokémon's stats, and even protect a Pokémon from having its stats lowered. One great advantage of these Abilities is that they work automatically. Unlike stat-altering moves, you don't have to spend a turn to use them.

● Advantage of Abilities that raise stats

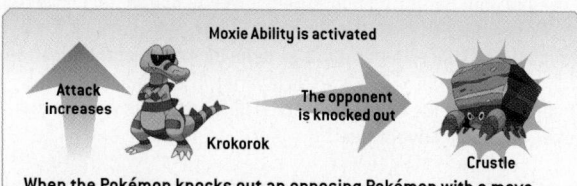

Moxie Ability is activated

Attack increases

Krokorok

The opponent is knocked out

Crustle

When the Pokémon knocks out an opposing Pokémon with a move, its Attack goes up by 1. This gives the Pokémon an advantage over the next Pokémon it faces in battle.

● Examples of stat-related Abilities

Ability	Effect	Pokémon with this Ability
Big Pecks	Prevents Defense from being lowered	Unfezant, Vullaby, etc.
Defeatist	Attack and Sp. Attack are halved when HP is half or less of maximum	Archen, Archeops
Defiant	When an opponent's move or Ability lowers the Pokémon's stats, its Attack goes up by 2	Pawniard, Bisharp
Hustle	Raises Attack by 50%, but lowers the accuracy of the Pokémon's physical moves by 20%	Durant, Zweilous, and others
Justified	When the Pokémon is hit by a Dark-type move, its Attack goes up by 1	Cobalion, Terrakion, and others
Minus	Raises Sp. Attack by 50% if an ally Pokémon has the Minus or Plus Ability	Klang, Klinklang, and others
Moxie	When the Pokémon knocks out an opposing Pokémon with a move, its Attack goes up by 1	Krookodile, Scrafty, and others
Plus	Raises Sp. Attack by 50% if an ally Pokémon has the Plus or Minus Ability	Klang, Klinklang, and others
Rivalry	If the target is the same gender, the power of the Pokémon's move goes up. If the target is of the opposite gender, the move's power goes down, and if the target's gender is unknown, the move's power doesn't change.	Fraxure, Haxorus, and others
Unaware	Ignores the stat changes of the opposing Pokémon	Woobat, Swoobat
Unburden	Doubles Speed if the Pokémon loses or consumes a held item. Its Speed returns to normal if the Pokémon holds another item. No effect if the Pokémon starts out with no held item.	Purrloin, Liepard
Weak Armor	When the Pokémon is hit by a physical attack, its Defense drops by 1, but its Speed goes up by 1	Garbodor

Ability Technique 9 Be a rainmaker with weather-related Abilities

Weather affects Abilities as well as moves. For example, Seismitoad's Swift Swim Ability doubles its Speed in the Rain weather condition. You can combine Abilities and weather conditions to create a situation that strongly favors your team.

● Advantages of weather-related Abilities

Sand Rush Ability is activated

Speed increases

Excadrill

Excadrill's Sand Rush Ability doubles its Speed when the weather condition is Sandstorm.

● Examples of weather-related Abilities

Ability	Effect	Pokémon with this Ability
Chlorophyll	Doubles Speed in the Sunny weather condition	Leavanny, Lilligant, and others
Hydration	Cures status conditions at the end of the turn in the Rain weather condition	Alomomola, Accelgor, and others
Ice Body	Gradually restores HP in the Hail weather condition Hail does not damage the Pokémon	Vanillish, Vanilluxe, and others
Overcoat	Prevents damage from the Sandstorm and Hail weather conditions	Reuniclus, Mandibuzz, and others
Sand Force	Raises the power of Ground-, Rock-, and Steel-type moves by 30% in the Sandstorm weather condition. Sandstorm does not damage the Pokémon.	Drilbur, Excadrill, Landorus
Sand Rush	Doubles Speed in the Sandstorm weather condition Sandstorm does not damage the Pokémon	Herdier, Stoutland, Drilbur, Excadrill
Snow Cloak	Raises evasion in the Hail weather condition Hail does not damage the Pokémon	Cubchoo, Beartic
Swift Swim	Doubles Speed in the Rain weather condition	Palpitoad, Seismitoad, and others

Pokémon Battle Basics

8 Use Items to Develop New Strategies

Held items make your Pokémon even stronger

A Pokémon can hold only one item. Many items are useful in battle. The effects vary by each type of item, so look for items that fit your battle style.

Item Technique **Pokémon can hold many different types of items**

You'll find many different items in the game, all with different uses and characteristics. For example, some item effects work as long as the item is held, while other effects go away after being used once. Also, some items enhance Pokémon's strengths, while others compensate for their weaknesses. Many species of Pokémon can excel in battle if they are given an item to hold.

● **Examples of items for battles**

Items that work as long as they are held	Items that are consumed after one use
Eviolite	Air Balloon
Rocky Helmet	Red Card
Choice Specs	Absorb Bulb
Leftovers	White Herb
Life Orb	Fire Gem

● **Tips for held items**

1 Each Pokémon can only hold one item at a time

2 Held items are useful in battle

3 Some items can harm the holder

4 Some moves and Abilities mean the Pokémon can fight more effectively if it doesn't hold an item

5 Items used up in battles with friends or on the Battle Subway will return after the battle

---

 Pokémon can't use some items on their own

Some items will have no effect when held by a Pokémon. They are meant to be used by Trainers on Pokémon. Some examples are the many kinds of Potions, which restore HP, or Ether, which restores PP. They won't do anything when held by Pokémon.

Use items to boost the power of attacks. For example, when a Pokémon holds the Muscle Band, it raises the power of its moves. These items can speed up battles by reducing the number of turns needed to defeat an opposing Pokémon. Learn the effects of items to do massive damage to opposing Pokémon.

● Advantages of damage-increasing items

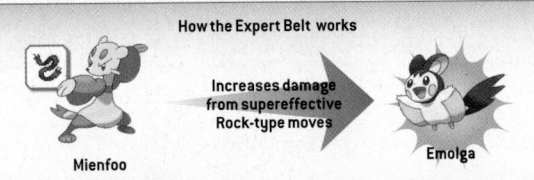

How the Expert Belt works

Increases damage from supereffective Rock-type moves

Mienfoo

Emolga

When a Pokémon holding an Expert Belt uses a supereffective move, the move's power increases.

● Examples of items for attacking

Item	Effect
Big Root	Increases the HP restored by the holder's HP-draining moves, such as Giga Drain or Horn Leech
Binding Band	Doubles the damage done every turn by moves like Bind or Wrap
Black Belt	Raises the power of Fighting-type moves
BlackGlasses	Raises the power of Dark-type moves
Draco Plate	Raises the power of Dragon-type moves
Expert Belt	Raises the power of supereffective moves
King's Rock	Sometimes makes the target flinch (unable to use a move that turn)
Magnet	Raises the power of Electric-type moves
Metal Coat	Raises the power of Steel-type moves
Metronome	Raises the power of a move used in consecutive turns
Miracle Seed	Raises the power of Grass-type moves
Muscle Band	Raises the power of physical moves
Mystic Water	Raises the power of Water-type moves
Power Herb	The holder can immediately use moves that require a one-turn charge. Goes away after use.
Razor Claw	Raises the critical-hit ratio of the holder's attacks
Razor Fang	Sometimes makes the target flinch (unable to use a move that turn)
Rock Incense	Raises the power of Rock-type moves
Scope Lens	Raises the critical-hit ratio of the holder's attacks
Sharp Beak	Raises the power of Flying-type moves
Silk Scarf	Raises the power of Normal-type moves
Soft Sand	Raises the power of Ground-type moves
Spell Tag	Raises the power of Ghost-type moves
TwistedSpoon	Raises the power of Psychic-type moves
Wave Incense	Raises the power of Water-type moves
Wide Lens	Raises the accuracy of the holder's moves
Wise Glasses	Raises the power of special moves
Zoom Lens	Raises the holder's accuracy when it moves after the opposing Pokémon

● Gems that increase the power of attacks when held

Item	Effect
Bug Gem	When held, raises the power of a Bug-type move by 50%. Goes away after use.
Dark Gem	When held, raises the power of a Dark-type move by 50%. Goes away after use.
Dragon Gem	When held, raises the power of a Dragon-type move by 50%. Goes away after use.
Electric Gem	When held, raises the power of an Electric-type move by 50%. Goes away after use.
Fighting Gem	When held, raises the power of a Fighting-type move by 50%. Goes away after use.
Fire Gem	When held, raises the power of a Fire-type move by 50%. Goes away after use.
Flying Gem	When held, raises the power of a Flying-type move by 50%. Goes away after use.
Ghost Gem	When held, raises the power of a Ghost-type move by 50%. Goes away after use.
Grass Gem	When held, raises the power of a Grass-type move by 50%. Goes away after use.
Ground Gem	When held, raises the power of a Ground-type move by 50%. Goes away after use.
Ice Gem	When held, raises the power of an Ice-type move by 50%. Goes away after use.
Normal Gem	When held, raises the power of a Normal-type move by 50%. Goes away after use.
Poison Gem	When held, raises the power of a Poison-type move by 50%. Goes away after use.
Psychic Gem	When held, raises the power of a Psychic-type move by 50%. Goes away after use.
Rock Gem	When held, raises the power of a Rock-type move by 50%. Goes away after use.
Steel Gem	When held, raises the power of a Steel-type move by 50%. Goes away after use.
Water Gem	When held, raises the power of a Water-type move by 50%. Goes away after use.

Held items can help with defense

Items can also prevent your Pokémon from being knocked out or can reduce the damage done by types of moves the holder is weak against. Winning without being affected by a move is impossible. Have your Pokémon hold items that help when they are hit by moves to keep your team out of trouble.

● Advantages of damage-reducing items

How the Coba Berry works

Larvesta — Reduces damage from supereffective Flying-type moves → Tranquill

A Pokémon holding a Coba Berry takes less damage from a super-effective Flying-type move.

● Examples of items for defending

Item	Effect
Absorb Bulb	When the holder is hit by a Water-type move, its Sp. Attack goes up by 1. Goes away after use.
Air Balloon	The holder floats in the air. The balloon pops when the holder is hit by an attack.
BrightPowder	Raises evasion
Cell Battery	When the holder is hit by an Electric-type move, its Attack goes up by 1. Goes away after use.
Eviolite	Raises Defense and Sp. Defense by 50% when held by a Pokémon that can still evolve
Focus Band	The holder is sometimes left with 1 HP when it receives damage that would KO it
Focus Sash	Leaves the holder with 1 HP when hit by a move that would KO it when its HP is full
Lax Incense	Raises evasion
Rocky Helmet	Does damage to Pokémon that hit the holder with a direct attack

● Examples of Berries that reduce damage from attacks

Item	Effect
Charti Berry	Halves damage taken from a supereffective Rock-type move. Goes away after use.
Coba Berry	Halves damage taken from a supereffective Flying-type move. Goes away after use.
Colbur Berry	Halves damage taken from a supereffective Dark-type move. Goes away after use.
Occa Berry	Halves damage taken from a supereffective Fire-type move. Goes away after use.
Passho Berry	Halves damage taken from a supereffective Water-type move. Goes away after use.
Rindo Berry	Halves damage taken from a supereffective Grass-type move. Goes away after use.
Shuca Berry	Halves damage taken from a supereffective Ground-type move. Goes away after use.
Wacan Berry	Halves damage taken from a supereffective Electric-type move. Goes away after use.
Yache Berry	Halves damage taken from a supereffective Ice-type move. Goes away after use.

Item Technique **4** Berries can turn a crisis into an opportunity

Some Berries work when the Pokémon holding it has just a little HP left, or they restore PP when it is gone. The Sitrus Berry, for example, restores HP by up to 1/4 of the holder's max HP. Items that work in a bad situation can give your team a chance for a come-from-behind victory!

● Advantages of Berries that work in a pinch

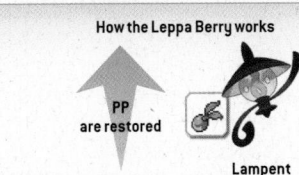

How the Leppa Berry works

PP are restored

Lampent

Lampent restores 10 PP thanks to the Leppa Berry, which gives it a chance to strike back.

● Examples of Berries that activate when HP or PP is low

Item	Effect
Lansat Berry	Raises the holder's critical-hit rate when its HP is low
Leppa Berry	Restores PP by 10 when PP of a holder's move is 0. Goes away after use.
Oran Berry	Restores HP by 10 when the holder's HP falls to half or lower. Goes away after use.
Sitrus Berry	Restores HP by 1/4 of the holder's max HP when its HP falls to half or lower. Goes away after use.
Starf Berry	Raises a stat 2 levels when the holder's HP is low

Item Technique 5 — Heal HP and status conditions with items

Some items can heal HP and status conditions. For example, Leftovers restores a little HP every turn. If you use these items, you can get out of a bad situation or stand tough with Pokémon that are hard to knock out.

Advantages of status condition-healing items

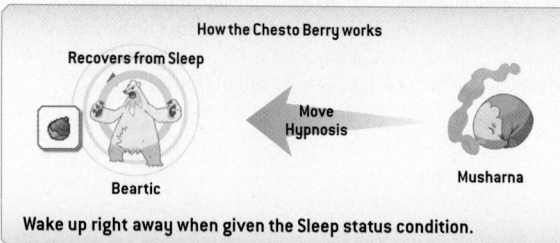

How the Chesto Berry works

Recovers from Sleep

Move Hypnosis

Beartic

Musharna

Wake up right away when given the Sleep status condition.

Examples of moves related to HP and status conditions

Item	Effect
Leftovers	Restores a little HP every turn
Mental Herb	The holder cures itself when moves like Taunt, Encore, Disable, Heal Block, or Attract make it unable to use moves freely. Goes away after use.
White Herb	Restores lowered stats. Goes away after use.

Examples of Berries that heal status conditions

Item	Effect
Aspear Berry	The holder is cured when given the Frozen status condition. Goes away after use.
Cheri Berry	The holder is cured when given the Paralysis status condition. Goes away after use.
Chesto Berry	The holder is cured when given the Sleep status condition. Goes away after use.
Lum Berry	The holder is cured of all status conditions. Goes away after use.
Pecha Berry	The holder is cured when given the Poison status condition. Goes away after use.
Persim Berry	The holder is cured when given the Confused status condition. Goes away after use.
Rawst Berry	The holder is cured when given the Burned status condition. Goes away after use.

Item Technique 6 — Items with negative effects

Some items don't help your Pokémon when held. For example, Life Orb raises the holder's attacking power, but lowers its HP. You can put the opposing Trainer at a disadvantage by using Bestow to stick an opposing Pokémon with one of these items.

Advantages of items with harmful effects

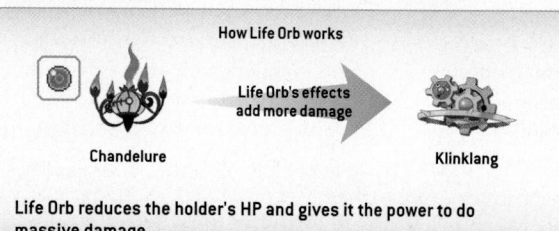

How Life Orb works

Life Orb's effects add more damage

Chandelure

Klinklang

Life Orb reduces the holder's HP and gives it the power to do massive damage.

Examples of harmful held items

Item	Effect
Choice Band	The holder can use only one move, but Attack increases by 50%
Choice Scarf	The holder can use only one move, but Speed increases by 50%
Choice Specs	The holder can use only one move, but Sp. Attack increases by 50%
Flame Orb	Inflicts Burn on the holder during battle
Full Incense	The holder strikes last
Iron Ball	Lowers Speed. If the holder has the Levitate Ability or is a Flying-type Pokémon, Ground-type moves will now hit it.
Lagging Tail	The holder strikes last
Life Orb	Lowers the holder's HP each time it attacks, but raises the power of moves
Ring Target	Moves that would otherwise have no effect will hit the holder
Sticky Barb	Damages the holder every turn. It can stick to an opposing Pokémon that touches the holder with a direct attack.
Toxic Orb	Inflicts Badly Poisoned status on the holder during battle

Berries that can cause Confusion

Item	Effect
Aguav Berry	Restores HP but can inflict the Confused status condition if the Pokémon dislikes Bitter flavors. Goes away after use.
Figy Berry	Restores HP but can inflict the Confused status condition if the Pokémon dislikes Spicy flavors. Goes away after use.
Iapapa Berry	Restores HP but can inflict the Confused status condition if the Pokémon dislikes Sour flavors. Goes away after use.
Mago Berry	Restores HP but can inflict the Confused status condition if the Pokémon dislikes Sweet flavors. Goes away after use.
Wiki Berry	Restores HP but can inflict the Confused status condition if the Pokémon dislikes Dry flavors. Goes away after use.

Item Technique 7 Use items to extend the duration of moves

A few select items extend the duration of a move's effects. Some moves have effects that last several turns, such as Rain Dance, which changes the weather condition to Rain, or Reflect, which halves damage done by physical attacks. Using certain held items makes these effects last longer than usual. Extend these favorable situations even a little longer to put victory in your grasp.

● Advantages of items that affect move duration

How Icy Rock works

Hail lasts longer

Vanilluxe

When a Pokémon holding Icy Rock uses Hail, the weather condition Hail continues longer.

Examples of items that affect move duration

Item	Effect
Damp Rock	Extends the duration of the move Rain Dance
Grip Claw	Extends the duration of moves like Bind and Wrap
Heat Rock	Extends the duration of the move Sunny Day
Icy Rock	Extends the duration of the move Hail
Light Clay	Extends the duration of moves like Reflect and Light Screen
Smooth Rock	Extends the duration of the move Sandstorm

Item Technique 8 Escape from danger with switching-related items

Pokémon can also take advantage of held items related to switching. The Shed Shell lets the holder switch out even when a move that prevents switching, like Mean Look, was used on it. Items can help you swap in a different party member—or force an opposing Pokémon to switch out—and create a favorable situation.

● Advantages of switching-enabling items

Eject Button is activated

Receive attack

Cryogonal   Fraxure
Swaps out that turn

Druddigon

A Pokémon holding the Eject Button can be swapped out with a Pokémon waiting in your party.

● Switching-related items

Item	Effect
Eject Button	If the holder is hit by an attack, its action is canceled and it switches with a party Pokémon. Goes away after use.
Red Card	If the holder is hit by an attack, the opposing Trainer must switch Pokémon. Goes away after use.
Shed Shell	The holder can always be switched out

Other kinds of held items

Many items have unique effects. Float Stone halves a Pokémon's weight. Sticky Barb can stick to an opposing Pokémon that uses a direct attack on the holder. Many other strange items like these exist. Figuring out how they all work may be difficult, but it's worth it to give them all a try.

Ex. 1 Items that change a Pokémon's weight

 Float Stone

Halves the weight of the Pokémon holding it. This can change the effects of weight-influenced moves such as Grass Knot and Low Kick.

Ex. 2 Items related to direct attacks

Sticky Barb

Sticky Barb sometimes sticks to opposing Pokémon who strike the holder with a direct attack. If it sticks, the opposing Pokémon will receive a little damage every turn.

Adapt Your Strategy to Win Battles

Defeat opponents quickly and prevent damage to your Pokémon

Battles are tough. Nobody wants to lose, least of all your foe. So when it's all on the line, what strategy works best to conserve your team's HP while taking out your foes? Study the tips below and experiment to find your own best techniques.

Battle Strategy 1 — Take these actions in Pokémon Battles

While teaching moves and raising Pokémon are important, those things alone aren't enough to win battles. Your actions in battle are very important. Even a single bad decision can cost you the battle. Making the right decision

at the right time many times in a battle will raise your win-loss ratio. Strong Trainers choose actions that will keep them from losing, no matter what the situation.

● Basic actions for winning Pokémon battles

Action 1 — Do as much damage as possible

Knocking out all of your foe's Pokémon is the condition for winning a battle. When you understand which moves do the most damage to your opponent, battles become much more fun.

Action 2 — Reduce damage taken as much as possible

While you want to damage your opponents, your foe will choose moves that deliver big damage to your Pokémon as well. That's why you need to think up ways to reduce damage.

Action 3 — Anticipate your foe's actions

When you try thinking from your foe's perspective, sometimes you can guess what they'll try next. Imagine the types of moves your foe could use, or if they are likely to switch Pokémon. Then you will know what you need to do.

Action 4 — Disrupt your foe's tactics

Defeating even one of the Pokémon at the center of your foe's strategy gives you a huge advantage. You can disrupt combos by preventing an opponent from using a single move. Bring victory your way by disrupting your opponent's tactics.

Battle Strategy 2 — Switch Pokémon to gain a type advantage

Sometimes, the Pokémon you have in battle won't know any moves that take advantage of the opponent's weaknesses. At times like these, you can often defeat an opponent more quickly by switching in another Pokémon from your party. Also, you're better off switching in a different Pokémon if the opponent is likely to use a move that is super effective against your Pokémon.

Usually, switching a party Pokémon into battle takes a turn, but sometimes it's better to switch another Pokémon in rather than keep fighting with the Pokémon currently in battle.

● Switch in Pokémon to get a type advantage

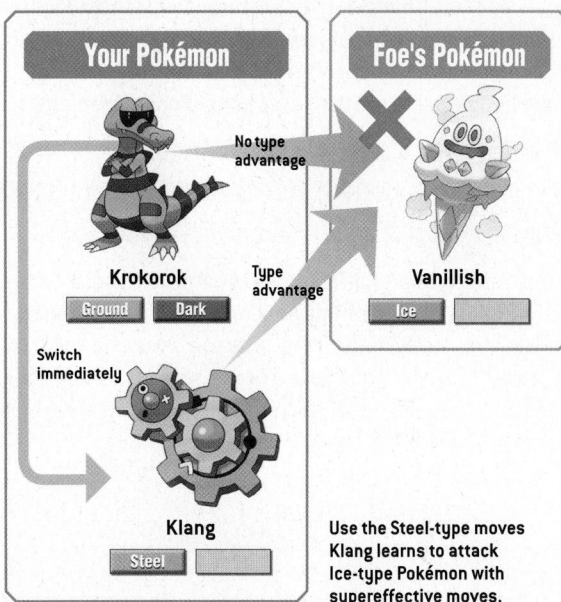

Your Pokémon

Krokorok — Ground · Dark

No type advantage

Type advantage

Switch immediately

Klang — Steel

Foe's Pokémon

Vanillish — Ice

Use the Steel-type moves Klang learns to attack Ice-type Pokémon with supereffective moves.

Battle Strategy 3 — Switch in Pokémon immune to your opponent's attacks

So now you know to switch out your Pokémon if your opponent has a type advantage in order to reduce the amount of damage your Pokémon take. But you should also try to predict what moves your opponent will use, and send out a Pokémon who's strong against—or even completely immune to—those moves. If you successfully switch in a Pokémon whose type isn't affected by the opponent's moves, you'll be in great shape.

A Pokémon often takes damage when it is switching in. But if your Pokémon is immune to the foe's move types, you can switch in without taking any damage at all.

● Switch in Pokémon that are immune to your opponent's attacks

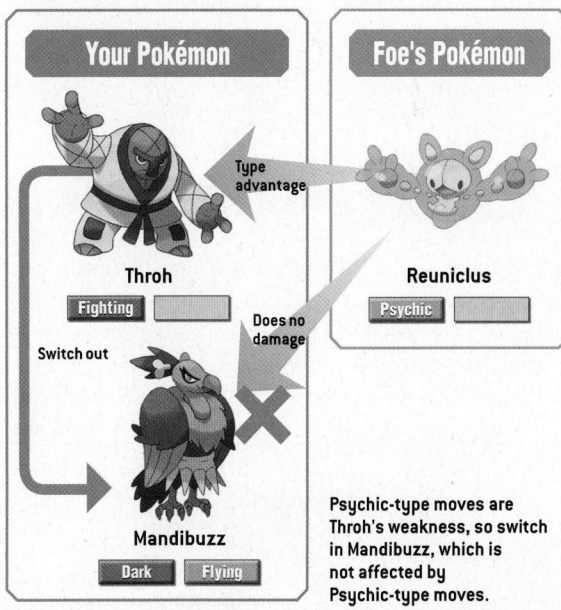

Your Pokémon

Throh — Fighting

Type advantage

Switch out

Does no damage

Mandibuzz — Dark · Flying

Foe's Pokémon

Reuniclus — Psychic

Psychic-type moves are Throh's weakness, so switch in Mandibuzz, which is not affected by Psychic-type moves.

 ### Learn your opponent's moves before you switch out

If the opponent has moves that are strong against your Pokémon, they're bound to get used. You can stick around and use Protect or Detect to negate your opponent's attacks. Once you've seen these moves, you'll know which Pokémon to switch in.

Battle Strategy **4** **Predict your foe's next move**

The turn when a foe switches Pokémon can be used any way you want. That's why it's important to pay attention to when an opponent may switch out. Put yourself in your opponent's shoes and try to predict the next move. For example, if the foe thinks his or her Pokémon might get hit by a move it's weak against, he or she is probably thinking about switching that Pokémon out. You really want to anticipate your foe's move in these situations! Anticipating each other's moves is one of the fun aspects of Pokémon battling.

● **When a foe will likely switch Pokémon**

1 **When your Pokémon might use supereffective moves**

You put a Grass-type Pokémon in battle, and your foe chose a Water- and Ground-type Pokémon. Water- and Ground-type Pokémon are weak against Grass-type attacks. Your foe will probably expect you to use a Grass-type attack. If your foe doesn't have any other tricks in store, it's very likely he or she will switch Pokémon.

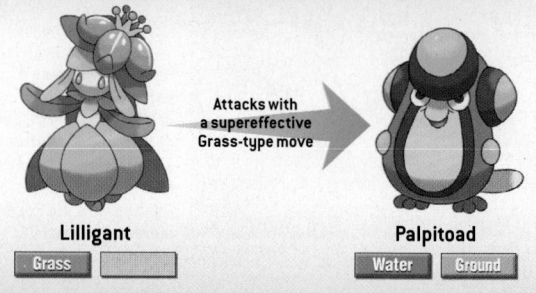

Lilligant
Grass

Attacks with a supereffective Grass-type move

Palpitoad
Water | Ground

2 **When a Pokémon is taking damage each turn from Leech Seed or similar moves**

Leech Seed damages the target every turn and restores your Pokémon's HP. However, if the Pokémon affected by Leech Seed is swapped out, the move's effects go away. In a situation like this, your foe will probably be thinking about switching Pokémon.

Whimsicott
Grass

Attacks with Leech Seed

Gurdurr
Fighting

Battle Strategy **5** **What to do when you think the opposing Trainer is switching Pokémon**

Don't let your guard down—even when you can strike your opponent's weakness. If your foe switches Pokémon to a type that your Pokémon's move has no effect on, you may find yourself in big trouble. When you think a switch is coming up, try to predict what Pokémon will be used next. You also have to consider, however, that the foe might not switch Pokémon.

Excadrill used Slash!

If you think your foe will switch in a Pokémon that's strong against your move, you can use a completely different move, such as a Normal-type move that can damage most opponents.

● **Anticipate switching and attack**

Your Pokémon

Excadrill
Ground | Steel

Foe's Pokémon

Zebstrika
Electric

Switch out

Normal-type Attack

Braviary
Normal | Flying

POKÉMON BATTLE PRIMER

ADAPT YOUR STRATEGY TO WIN BATTLES

Battle Strategy 6 — Snatch victory out of the jaws of defeat

Don't give up if your Pokémon's HP gets low. The moment when it looks like your Pokémon will be knocked out is the time to step up actions to defeat your opponent. If you teach your Pokémon moves that get stronger when it's in trouble, you will always have a chance to come back from behind.

● Examples of moves that work better when the user's HP is low

Come from behind with big damage

Flail — Normal

The lower the user's HP, the more damage Flail does. Its power is maximized when the user has 1 HP and is just about to be defeated.

Restore HP at the last second

Pain Split — Normal

Pain Split adds the user's HP and the target's, then splits the total between them. When the target still has lots of HP, your Pokémon can recover quickly.

Battle Strategy 7 — Change the weather to turn the tides of battle

Weather influences some Pokémon moves and Abilities. If you choose moves that change the weather, you can create a favorable situation for yourself while putting your opponent at a disadvantage, and send victory your way. Create teams that take advantage of the weather!

● Main features of special weather conditions

Sunny

1. Raises the power of Fire-type moves
2. Lowers the power of Water-type moves
3. Doubles the effect of the move Growth
4. SolarBeam can be used on the first turn
5. Increases the amount of HP recovered with Synthesis
6. Increases Speed of Pokémon with the Chlorophyll Ability
7. Makes Pokémon with Leaf Guard Ability immune to status conditions
8. Prevents the Frozen condition

Rain

1. Raises the power of Water-type moves
2. Lowers the power of Fire-type moves
3. The move Thunder always hits
4. The move Hurricane always hits
5. Increases Speed of Pokémon with the Swift Swim Ability
6. Heals status conditions of Pokémon with the Hydration Ability

Sandstorm

1. Damages all Pokémon except for Ground, Rock, and Steel types
2. Raises Rock-type Pokémon's Sp. Def
3. Pokémon with the Magic Guard Ability are not damaged
4. Pokémon with the Overcoat Ability are not damaged
5. Increases Speed of Pokémon with the Sand Rush Ability
6. Raises the power of some moves if Pokémon has the Sand Force Ability

Hail

1. Damages all Pokémon except for Ice types
2. Pokémon with the Magic Guard Ability are not damaged
3. Pokémon with the Overcoat Ability are not damaged
4. Raises evasion of Pokémon with the Snow Cloak Ability
5. Restores HP of Pokémon with the Ice Body Ability
6. The move Blizzard always hits

Master the Art of the Combo

Take what you know about moves, Abilities, and items, and put it all together in a winning strategy

A combo is a combination of Pokémon moves, Abilities, or held items. When you use them together in just the right way, it makes a big difference in battle.

Combo Technique **1** **Combine different elements to create clever combos**

Combos are a tactic for winning the battle that exhibit even more powerful effects than normal moves by combining many different elements, such as moves and Abilities. So many different combos exist, surely some of them are still unknown. Try creating combos by putting together moves, Abilities, and items that seem like they might work. Then, give them a try in battle.

● The elements of combos

1 Move

2 Ability

3 Item

4 Type

● The elements of combos

Move **+ Combo** **Move**

One move can make another move more powerful or compensate for another move's weakness.

Move **+ Combo** **Items**

Giving the Pokémon an item to hold makes moves powerful or compensates for the weakness of those moves.

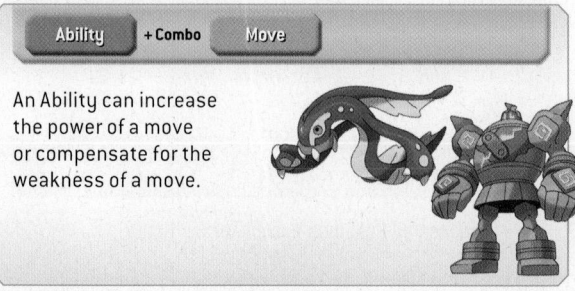

Ability **+ Combo** **Move**

An Ability can increase the power of a move or compensate for the weakness of a move.

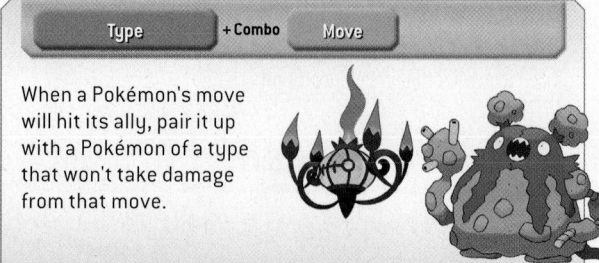

Type **+ Combo** **Move**

When a Pokémon's move will hit its ally, pair it up with a Pokémon of a type that won't take damage from that move.

● Main advantages of combos

1 Pull off bigger effects by combining different elements such as moves, Abilities, and items

2 Sometimes Pokémon can avoid damage from attacks that should have hit them

3 Sometimes the negative effects of moves, Abilities, or items can be neutralized

Telekinesis + Inferno

The move Telekinesis makes every move a sure hit for three turns. Usually, the accuracy of the move Inferno is 50, but it will always hit while Telekinesis is in effect. Inferno has a power of 100, so that's a lot of guaranteed damage!

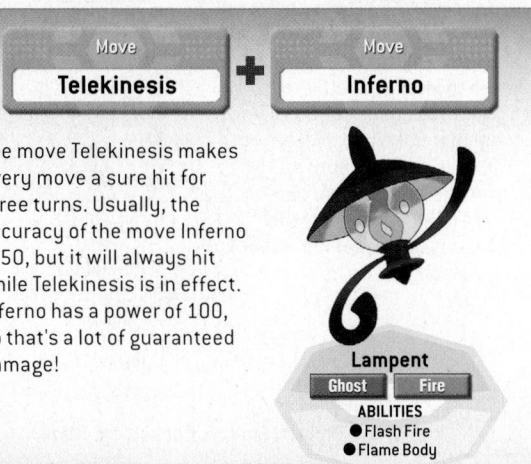

Lampent
Ghost | Fire
ABILITIES
● Flash Fire
● Flame Body

Pokémon that can use this combo: Litwick, Lampent, and others

Mold Breaker + Earthquake

With Mold Breaker, a Pokémon can hit a target that is normally protected by its Ability. So Earthquake, a Ground-type move, would hit Pokémon with the Levitate Ability. Use this combo to shake up any Trainers who thought their Pokémon were safe.

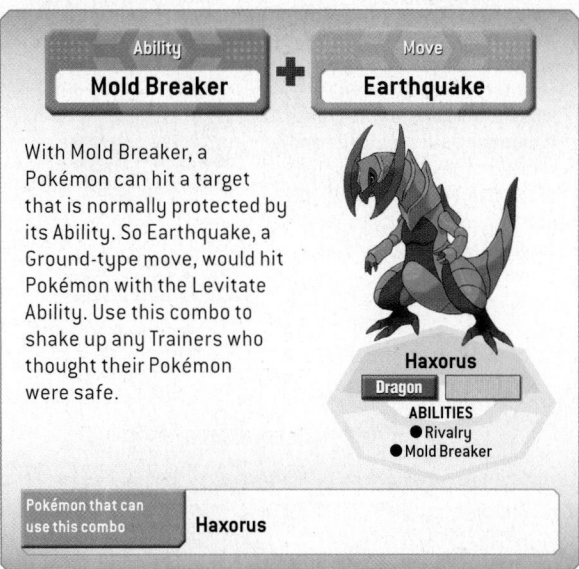

Haxorus
Dragon
ABILITIES
● Rivalry
● Mold Breaker

Pokémon that can use this combo: Haxorus

Toxic + Venoshock

Venoshock does double damage to a target that has the Poisoned or Badly Poisoned status condition. Pile it on your foe by doing massive damage to a target that is already Badly Poisoned by the effects of Toxic.

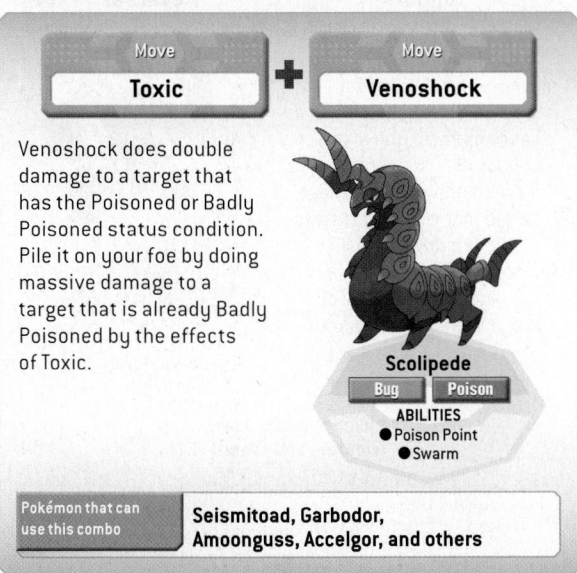

Scolipede
Bug | Poison
ABILITIES
● Poison Point
● Swarm

Pokémon that can use this combo: Seismitoad, Garbodor, Amoonguss, Accelgor, and others

Rest + Chesto Berry

Rest completely restores HP, but the user is afflicted with the Sleep status condition. Have the user hold a Chesto Berry so it wakes up right away. Since it wakes up immediately, it can move during the next turn.

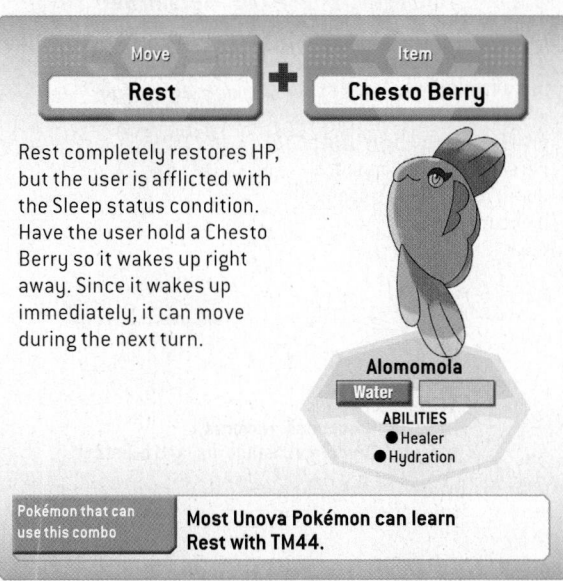

Alomomola
Water
ABILITIES
● Healer
● Hydration

Pokémon that can use this combo: Most Unova Pokémon can learn Rest with TM44.

Mean Look + Curse

When Ghost-type Pokémon use Curse, it reduces the target's HP by a quarter of its max HP every turn. When the Pokémon is swapped out, however, the effect goes away. Combine this move with Mean Look, which keeps the target from being switched out.

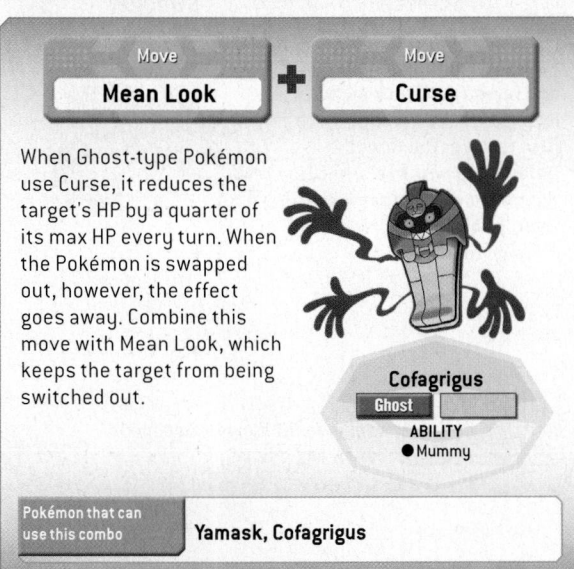

Cofagrigus
Ghost
ABILITY
● Mummy

Pokémon that can use this combo: Yamask, Cofagrigus

Will-O-Wisp + Hex

Hex does double its normal damage to any target afflicted by a status condition. Inflict the Burned condition on a target with the move Will-O-Wisp, and then use Hex on the next turn for big damage.

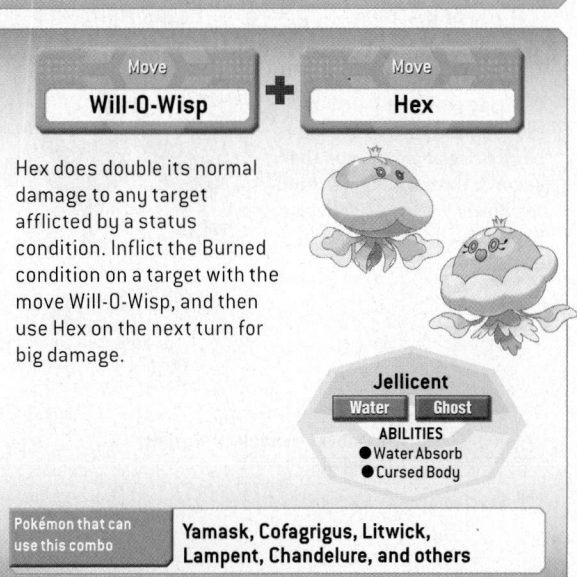

Jellicent
Water | Ghost
ABILITIES
● Water Absorb
● Cursed Body

Pokémon that can use this combo: Yamask, Cofagrigus, Litwick, Lampent, Chandelure, and others

Move: Hypnosis + Move: Dream Eater

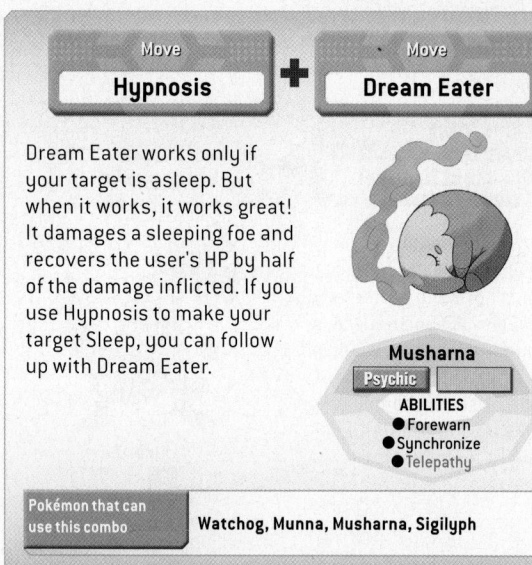

Dream Eater works only if your target is asleep. But when it works, it works great! It damages a sleeping foe and recovers the user's HP by half of the damage inflicted. If you use Hypnosis to make your target Sleep, you can follow up with Dream Eater.

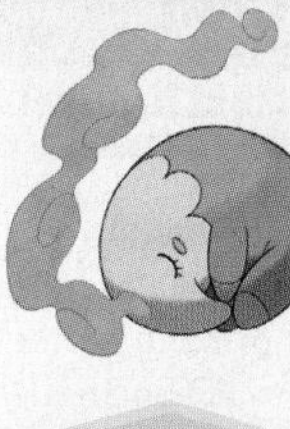

Musharna
Psychic
ABILITIES
- Forewarn
- Synchronize
- Telepathy

Pokémon that can use this combo: Watchog, Munna, Musharna, Sigilyph

Ability: Guts + Item: Flame Orb

The Guts Ability raises Attack when the holder is afflicted by a status condition. So hand that Pokémon a Flame Orb, which inflicts Burned status on its holder. To turn up the heat, add the Facade move—the power of the move increases when its user is Burned.

Conkeldurr
Fighting
ABILITIES
- Guts
- Sheer Force

Pokémon that can use this combo: Timburr, Gurdurr, Conkeldurr, Throh

Move: Outrage + Item: Persim Berry

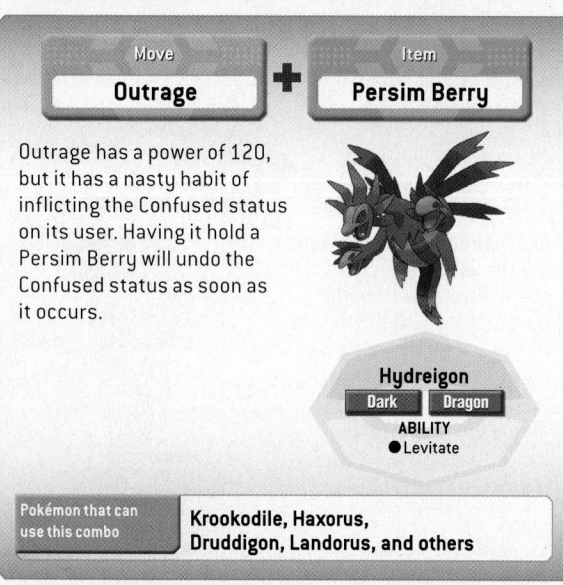

Outrage has a power of 120, but it has a nasty habit of inflicting the Confused status on its user. Having it hold a Persim Berry will undo the Confused status as soon as it occurs.

Hydreigon
Dark | Dragon
ABILITY
- Levitate

Pokémon that can use this combo: Krookodile, Haxorus, Druddigon, Landorus, and others

Move: Endure + Move: Reversal

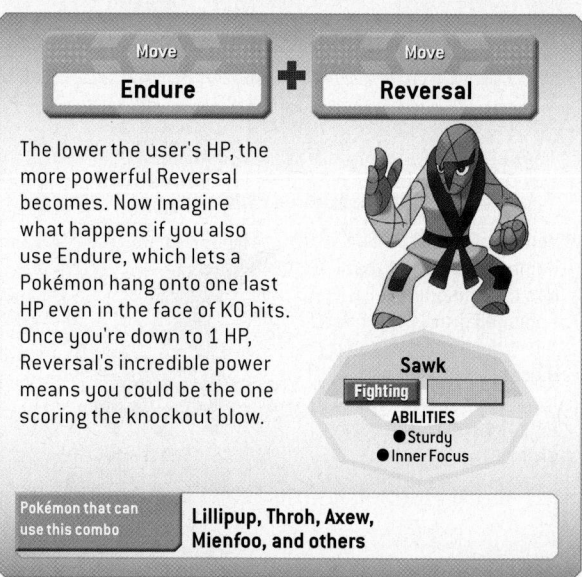

The lower the user's HP, the more powerful Reversal becomes. Now imagine what happens if you also use Endure, which lets a Pokémon hang onto one last HP even in the face of KO hits. Once you're down to 1 HP, Reversal's incredible power means you could be the one scoring the knockout blow.

Sawk
Fighting
ABILITIES
- Sturdy
- Inner Focus

Pokémon that can use this combo: Lillipup, Throh, Axew, Mienfoo, and others

Move: Sky Attack + Item: Power Herb

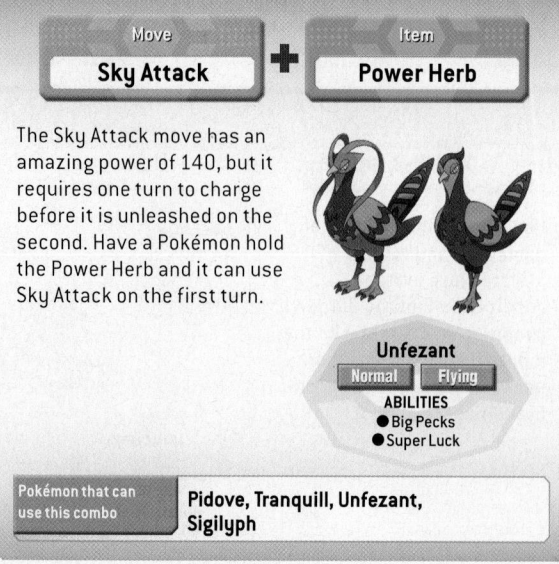

The Sky Attack move has an amazing power of 140, but it requires one turn to charge before it is unleashed on the second. Have a Pokémon hold the Power Herb and it can use Sky Attack on the first turn.

Unfezant
Normal | Flying
ABILITIES
- Big Pecks
- Super Luck

Pokémon that can use this combo: Pidove, Tranquill, Unfezant, Sigilyph

Move: Screech + Move: Swagger

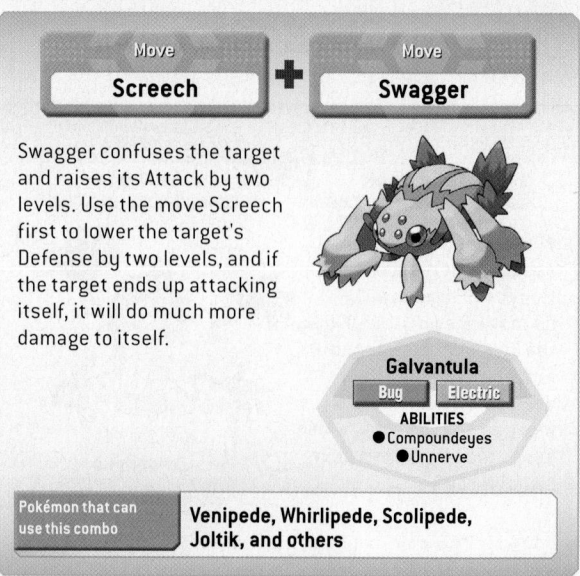

Swagger confuses the target and raises its Attack by two levels. Use the move Screech first to lower the target's Defense by two levels, and if the target ends up attacking itself, it will do much more damage to itself.

Galvantula
Bug | Electric
ABILITIES
- Compoundeyes
- Unnerve

Pokémon that can use this combo: Venipede, Whirlipede, Scolipede, Joltik, and others

Steel + Sludge Wave

Sludge Wave is a powerful move, but it also hits ally Pokémon. It's a Poison-type move, however, so any Steel-type Pokémon on your team won't get a scratch.

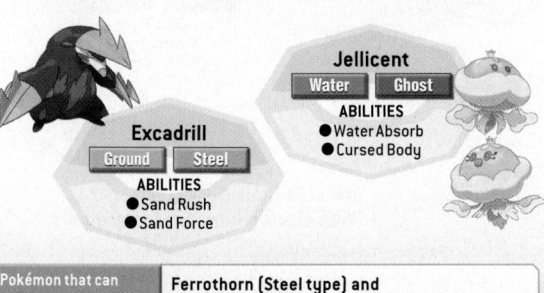

Jellicent
Water | Ghost
ABILITIES
● Water Absorb
● Cursed Body

Excadrill
Ground | Steel
ABILITIES
● Sand Rush
● Sand Force

Pokémon that can use this combo | Ferrothorn (Steel type) and Seismitoad (Sludge Wave), and others

Flying + Earthquake

Earthquake is a powerful move that will also hurt ally Pokémon, so partner up with a Flying-type Pokémon, which won't be hit by Ground-type moves. Then the damage ends up where it belongs: solely on your opponents.

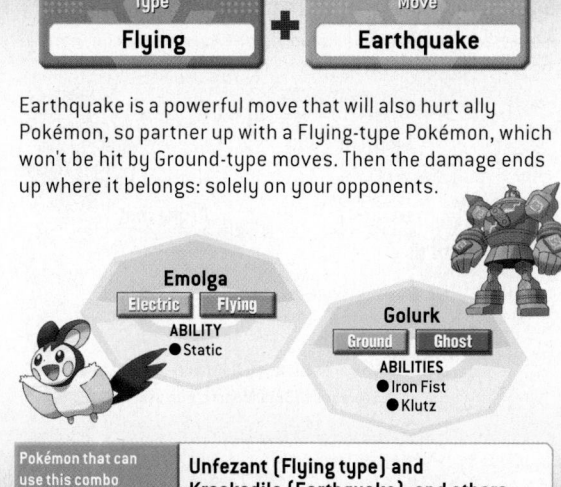

Emolga
Electric | Flying
ABILITY
● Static

Golurk
Ground | Ghost
ABILITIES
● Iron Fist
● Klutz

Pokémon that can use this combo | Unfezant (Flying type) and Krookodile (Earthquake), and others

Motor Drive + Discharge

Discharge hits ally Pokémon, but if an ally Pokémon has the Motor Drive Ability, this Electric-type attack will boost its Speed rather than doing damage.

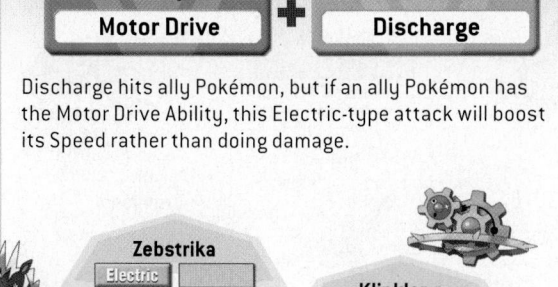

Zebstrika
Electric
ABILITIES
● Lightningrod
● Motor Drive

Klinklang
Steel
ABILITIES
● Plus
● Minus

Pokémon that can use this combo | Blitzle (Motor Drive Ability) and Eelektrik (Discharge), and others

Water Absorb + Surf

Surf soaks both foes and allies, but if an ally has the Water Absorb Ability, being hit by a Water-type attack restores its HP instead of doing damage.

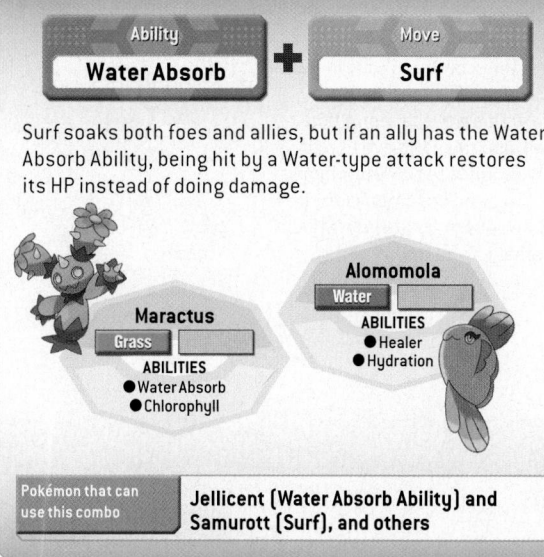

Maractus
Grass
ABILITIES
● Water Absorb
● Chlorophyll

Alomomola
Water
ABILITIES
● Healer
● Hydration

Pokémon that can use this combo | Jellicent (Water Absorb Ability) and Samurott (Surf), and others

Telepathy + Explosion

If a Pokémon has the Telepathy Ability, it won't take collateral damage from allies. Having a partner with this Ability lets you use Explosion, which does incredible damage to every Pokémon in battle, without worry.

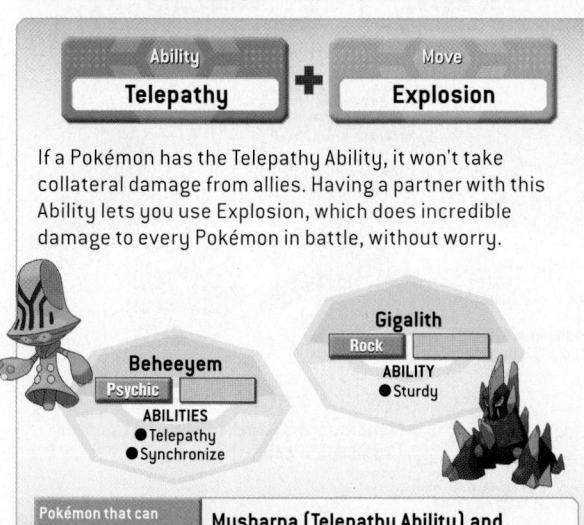

Beheeyem
Psychic
ABILITIES
● Telepathy
● Synchronize

Gigalith
Rock
ABILITY
● Sturdy

Pokémon that can use this combo | Musharna (Telepathy Ability) and Garbodor (Explosion), and others

Belly Drum + Heal Pulse

A Pokémon can use Belly Drum to maximize its Attack at the expense of half of its HP. Use Heal Pulse to restore that Pokémon's HP and reduce the chances of it being targeted and knocked out while its HP is low.

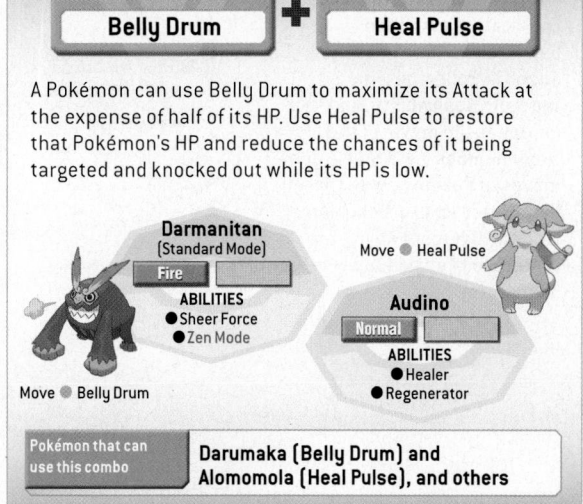

Move ● Heal Pulse

Darmanitan
(Standard Mode)
Fire
ABILITIES
● Sheer Force
● Zen Mode

Audino
Normal
ABILITIES
● Healer
● Regenerator

Move ● Belly Drum

Pokémon that can use this combo | Darumaka (Belly Drum) and Alomomola (Heal Pulse), and others

Move		Move
Sunny Day	+	**SolarBeam**

The move Sunny Day makes the weather condition Sunny. SolarBeam, which usually needs one turn to charge, can now be used right away.

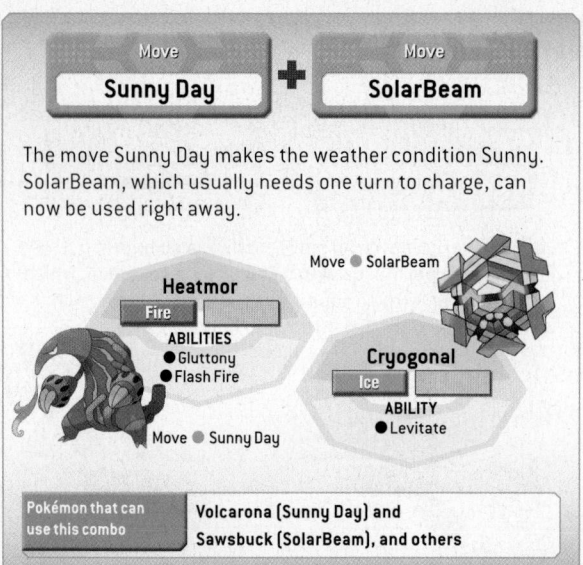

Heatmor
Fire
ABILITIES
● Gluttony
● Flash Fire
Move ● Sunny Day

Cryogonal
Ice
ABILITY
● Levitate

Move ● SolarBeam

Pokémon that can use this combo	Volcarona (Sunny Day) and Sawsbuck (SolarBeam), and others

Move		Move
Rain Dance	+	**Hurricane**

The move Hurricane hits every time when the weather condition is Rain. This combo raises evasion and makes it easy to do big damage to a target that is usually hard to hit.

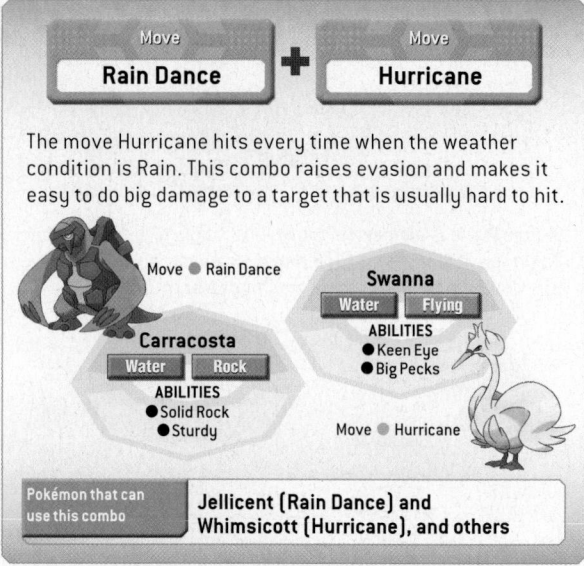

Move ● Rain Dance

Carracosta
Water Rock
ABILITIES
● Solid Rock
● Sturdy

Swanna
Water Flying
ABILITIES
● Keen Eye
● Big Pecks
Move ● Hurricane

Pokémon that can use this combo	Jellicent (Rain Dance) and Whimsicott (Hurricane), and others

Move		Ability		Ability		Move
Hail	+	**Snow Cloak**	+	**Magic Guard**	+	**Blizzard**

The move Hail makes the weather condition Hail. In Hail, the move Blizzard always hits. This weather condition will also raise the evasion of Pokémon with the Snow Cloak Ability, and Pokémon with the Magic Guard Ability won't take damage from Hail.

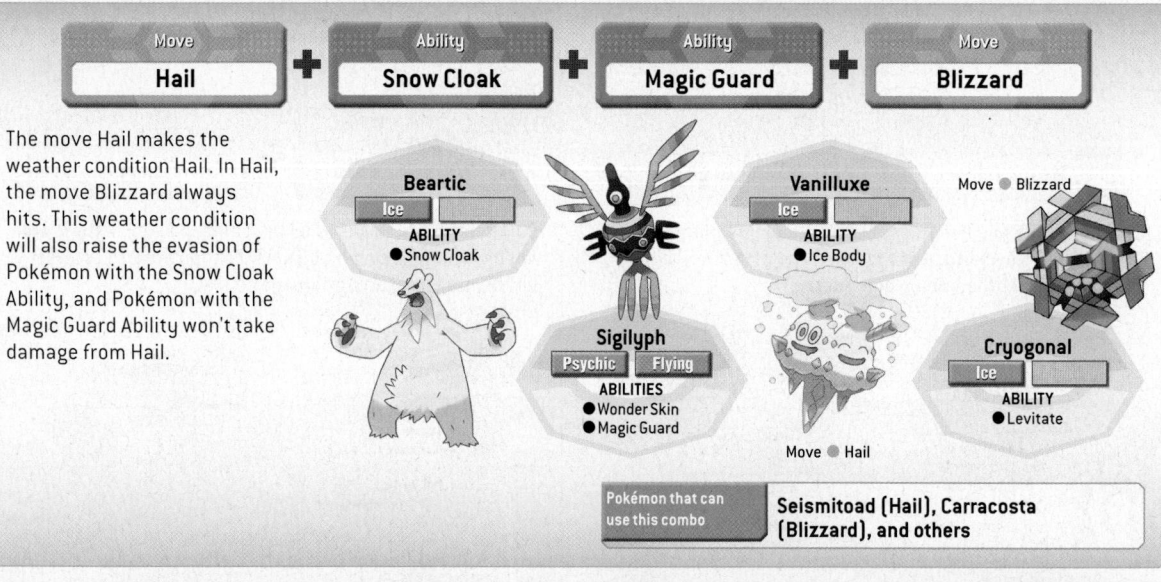

Beartic
Ice
ABILITY
● Snow Cloak

Sigilyph
Psychic Flying
ABILITIES
● Wonder Skin
● Magic Guard

Vanilluxe
Ice
ABILITY
● Ice Body

Cryogonal
Ice
ABILITY
● Levitate

Move ● Blizzard
Move ● Hail

Pokémon that can use this combo	Seismitoad (Hail), Carracosta (Blizzard), and others

Move		Ability		Ability		Ability
Sandstorm	+	**Overcoat**	+	**Sand Rush**	+	**Sand Force**

The move Sandstorm makes the weather condition Sandstorm. This raises the Speed of Pokémon with the Sand Rush Ability, and improves the power of the Ground-, Rock-, and Steel-type moves of Pokémon with the Sand Force Ability. Pokémon with the Overcoat Ability are protected from damage by Sandstorm.

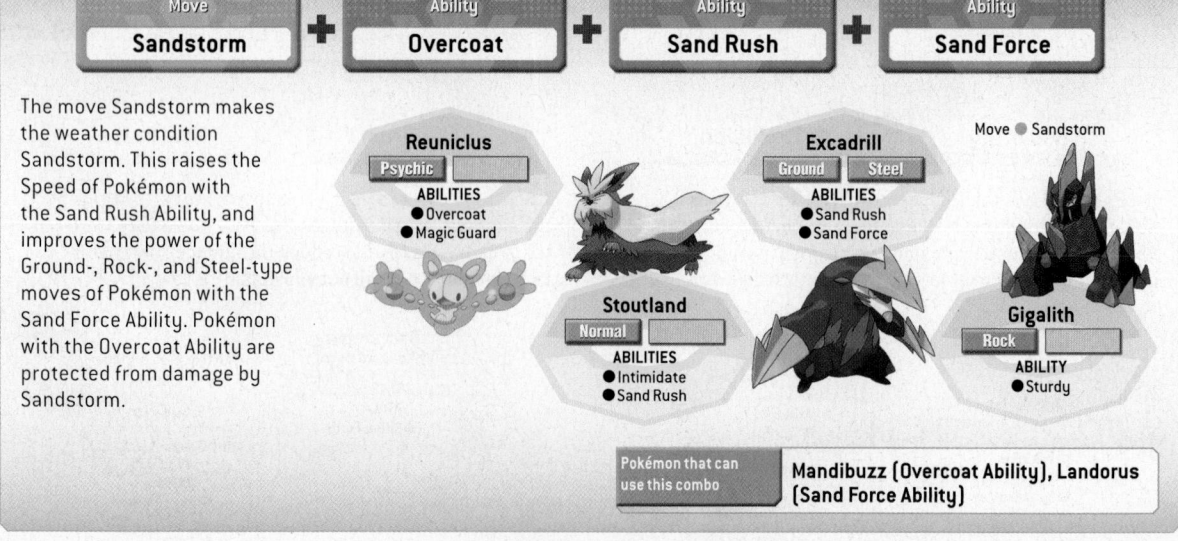

Reuniclus
Psychic
ABILITIES
● Overcoat
● Magic Guard

Stoutland
Normal
ABILITIES
● Intimidate
● Sand Rush

Excadrill
Ground Steel
ABILITIES
● Sand Rush
● Sand Force

Gigalith
Rock
ABILITY
● Sturdy

Move ● Sandstorm

Pokémon that can use this combo	Mandibuzz (Overcoat Ability), Landorus (Sand Force Ability)

Protect yourself from your foe's combos

A foe who is used to battling will probably have several combos at the ready. You should have some ways to protect yourself when your foe starts to use a combo. Many methods are effective when disrupting combos.

For example, you could make the foe's Pokémon unable to use moves, prevent them from using items, or force them to switch Pokémon. Choose the optimal means depending on your opponent.

● **Ways to counter combos**

Overcome item-based combos

If a foe is using an item-based combo, keep your foe's Pokémon from using items. The foe can't use items if you use a move like Thief, which steals the item, or one like Embargo, which makes the opponent unable to use items. Either way, you disrupt the combo.

Thief	Dark
Embargo	Dark
Magic Room	Psychic

Gothitelle

Prevent two-Pokémon combos

Forcing your foe to switch a Pokémon is one trick for disrupting combos that require a combination of two Pokémon's moves or Abilities. The moves Roar and Dragon Tail can force a switch, and the two-Pokémon combo won't work anymore.

Dragon Tail	Dragon
Roar	Normal

Druddigon

Prevent foes from using moves freely

Another effective method of dealing with this is creating a situation in which the foe can't use moves freely. Torment keeps an opponent from using the same move twice, and Taunt prevents a target from using status moves. This will disrupt your foe's tactics.

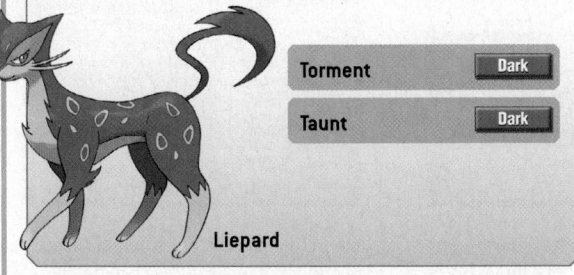

Torment	Dark
Taunt	Dark

Liepard

Dodge moves you sense are coming

When the foe has set up a combo, and you suspect an attack is coming during the next turn, use a move that protects your Pokémon from damage. A carefully timed Detect or Protect can prevent damage and give you a chance to counterattack.

Mienshao

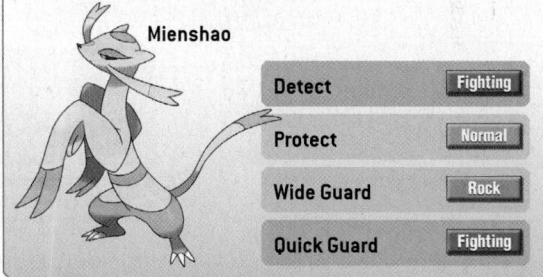

Detect	Fighting
Protect	Normal
Wide Guard	Rock
Quick Guard	Fighting

Use Imprison as a countermeasure

Imprison prevents the target from using any moves that the user knows. If you can keep a move that is part of your foe's combo from being used, it will give you an advantage.

Imprison	Psychic

Swoobat

Disrupt combos that use Abilities

Use the move Simple Beam, which changes the target's Ability to Simple, or Entrainment, which makes the target's Ability the same as the user's. By doing this, you can block the opposing Trainer from setting up a combo that uses an Ability.

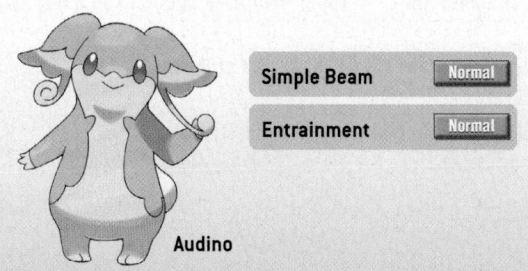

Simple Beam	Normal
Entrainment	Normal

Audino

When a Battle Is Lost, Consider This

Always believe you can win and never give up

You will do your best, but the opposing Trainer will be coming at you with everything he or she's got as well—so there's no such thing as an easy victory, no matter what kind of battle it is. Try and try again until victory is in your grasp. When you just can't win, you might want to rethink your strategy.

Point to Reconsider 1 **Try changing your Pokémon's moves**

Try changing the combination of the four moves you can teach a Pokémon. Teaching a Pokémon an unusual move can let you get the drop on opposing Trainers. When you test moves, sometimes you think of new ways to battle.

In addition to TMs, consider some moves that can be remembered or taught by tutors. When you want to forget an HM, visit the Move Deleter in Mistralton City.

● Examples of ways to teach new moves

Use TMs to teach new moves	Trade Heart Scales to remember moves	Use items like PP Up to increase PP
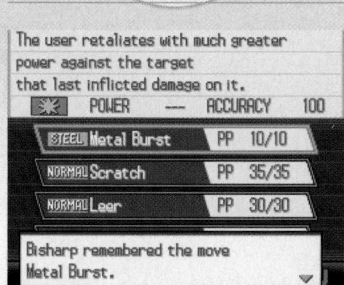		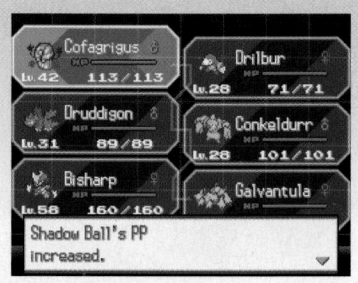
TMs are useful items that let you teach a move as often as you like. Teach moves to many Pokémon and test the move's effects in actual battles.	Mistralton City's reminder girl will help your Pokémon remember a move for one Heart Scale.	When the max PP for a move is low, you might use all of the PP in battle. Use PP Up to increase maximum number of PP.

● Examples of useful attack moves

1 Moves that are super effective against opposing Pokémon you have trouble with

2 Moves that are super effective against the same type as your Pokémon

3 Moves that always hit or that strike first

4 Moves that inflict status conditions

Change your Pokémon's held item

Your Pokémon's held items can easily sway a contest. Depending on the item's effect, it can strengthen your Pokémon's strong points, or compensate for its weaknesses. Change items to bring out your Pokémon's untapped potential.

● **Examples of rethinking items**

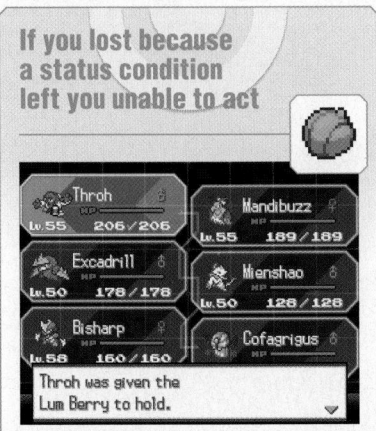

If you lost because a status condition left you unable to act

When afflicted by a status condition, you can't always take the action you want to take. Have your Pokémon hold the Lum Berry to heal status conditions.

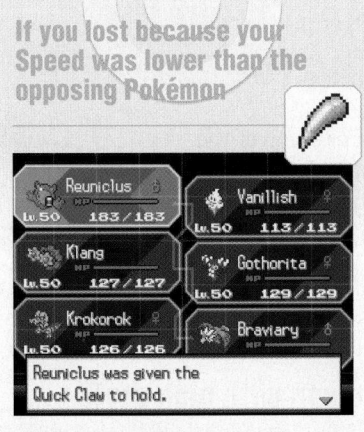

If you lost because your Speed was lower than the opposing Pokémon

If you are losing because you can't strike first, try having your Pokémon hold the Quick Claw, which sometimes let you strike first.

If you lost because you took a lot of damage from a big move

If you lose because the opposing Pokémon's moves are just too strong, try the Focus Sash, which leaves the holder with 1 HP.

Point to Reconsider 3 **Change the lead Pokémon**

Sometimes the Pokémon at the front of your party can make it easier to battle. It's ideal if it can hit the opposing Pokémon with an effective move or use a move that inflicts a status condition. If the opposing Trainer feels pressured to swap Pokémon on the first turn, you have an immediate advantage. Lead with your best!

● **Examples of the difference the lead Pokémon makes**

Let a Pokémon that knows multiple move types lead your party

Teach it multiple move types and you can use supereffective moves against many Pokémon types.

Stoutland

Thunder Fang	Electric
Ice Fang	Ice
Fire Fang	Fire

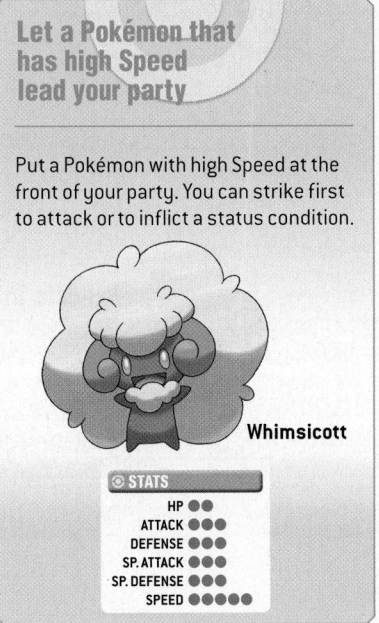

Let a Pokémon that has high Speed lead your party

Put a Pokémon with high Speed at the front of your party. You can strike first to attack or to inflict a status condition.

Whimsicott

Let a Pokémon that knows a switching move lead your party

It's often useful to use moves that let you attack while switching, or those that force the opposing Trainer to switch Pokémon.

Emolga

Volt Switch	Electric
U-turn	Bug

Find the Right Pokémon to Train

You have many Pokémon to choose from, but not all of them have the qualities you're looking for

Each Pokémon is unique. Even among Pokémon of the same species, no two have the same stats and Nature. Look for one Pokémon that is best for your strategy.

Selection Tip 1 **Look for Pokémon with high stats**

Stats differ significantly depending on the species of Pokémon involved. If you want to use strong moves one after another, you should catch Pokémon with high Attack and Sp. Atk stats. If you want to get the first attack and use a support move, the Speed stat is important. Pokémon that perform well must differ depending on your strategy. Choose Pokémon that fit your strategy, and form your own team.

● **Stats differ depending on the species of Pokémon**

Conkeldurr have a high Attack stat

STATS
HP	●●●●
ATTACK	●●●●●●
DEFENSE	●●●●
SP. ATTACK	●●
SP. DEFENSE	●●●
SPEED	●●

Conkeldurr

A Pokémon with a high Attack stat inflicts great damage on its target with physical moves such as Hammer Arm and Stone Edge.

Chandelure have a high Sp. Atk stat

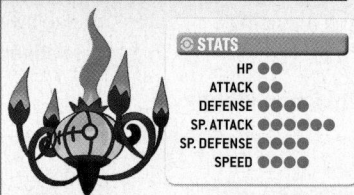

STATS
HP	●●
ATTACK	●●
DEFENSE	●●●
SP. ATTACK	●●●●●●
SP. DEFENSE	●●●
SPEED	●●●●

Chandelure

A Pokémon with a high Sp. Atk stat inflicts great damage on its target with special moves such as Shadow Ball and Overheat.

Accelgor have a high Speed stat

STATS
HP	●●●
ATTACK	●●●
DEFENSE	●●
SP. ATTACK	●●●●
SP. DEFENSE	●●
SPEED	●●●●●●

Accelgor

A Pokémon with a high Speed stat has a better chance to get the first attack. It can take the lead using moves with special effects such as U-turn and Power Swap.

● **Elements relevant to stats**

◎ Species of Pokémon	◎ Nature
◎ Inherent strength	◎ Base stats
◎ Characteristic	◎ Level

● **Elements irrelevant to stats**

◎ Gender
◎ Ability
◎ Friendship

◎ For each Pokémon's stats, see the Unova Pokédex on p. 12. ▷

Selection Tip **2** ## Catch multiples of the same Pokémon and compare them

Even within the same species, stats differ from one Pokémon to another because each Pokémon has inherent strengths for each stat. Catch many Pokémon and compare them. If two Pokémon are at the same level, the Pokémon with higher stats has higher inherent strength. If a Pokémon has higher inherent strength, its stats grow faster when it levels up.

● Inherent strength is different even among Pokémon of the same species

Comparison of stats among Tympole

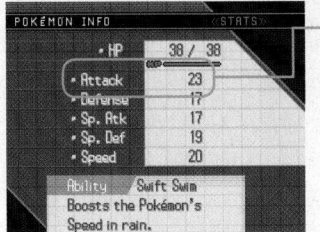

High Attack

When this Tympole uses a physical move such as Return or Facade, it inflicts major damage on opposing Pokémon.

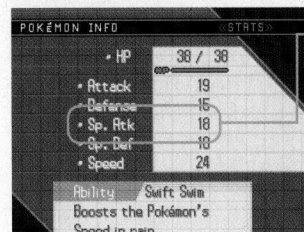

High Sp. Atk

This Tympole can inflict more damage with special moves such as Hydro Pump and Hyper Voice.

Selection Tip **3** ## Check the strengths of your Pokémon

After you finish the main story, a person called the Judge will show up in the Battle Subway in Nimbasa City. The Judge will tell you the inherent strength of individual Pokémon. He will tell you the overall inherent strength and the especially high stat among them.

If you'd like, I could judge the intriguing potential of your Pokémon.

The Judge shows up after the main story

You'll find the Judge in the area near the bottom of the stairs in the Gear Station.

● What the Judge in the Battle Subway in Nimbasa City tells you

1 **Overall evaluation of stats**

I see, I see...
This Pokémon's potential is
(This Pokémon has)
●●●.
That's my determination, and it's final.

Words that fill ●●●

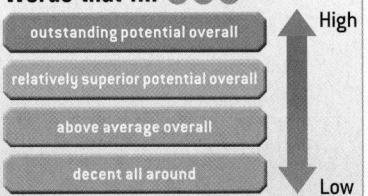

outstanding potential overall	⬆ High
relatively superior potential overall	
above average overall	
decent all around	⬇ Low

2 **The most outstanding stat(s)**

Incidentally, I would say the best potential lies in its ●●●.
And its ●●●
is also good.

- If two or more stats are equally high, he will tell you about those, too.

Words that fill ●●●

HP	Sp. Atk stat
Attack stat	Sp. Def stat
Defense stat	Speed stat

3 **Last, whether 2 is high or low**

●●● in that regard.
That's how
I judged it.

Words that fill ●●●

It can't be better	⬆ High
It's fantastic	
It's very good	
It's rather decent	⬇ Low

Check Pokémon's Characteristics and Natures

The SUMMARY screen in the Pokédex shows the Pokémon's Characteristic and Nature. The Pokémon's Characteristic tells you which stat is inherently high. The Pokémon's Nature tells you which stat grows faster when it levels up.

● **Use characteristics to guess inherent strength of Pokémon**

Comparison of Sandile's Characteristics

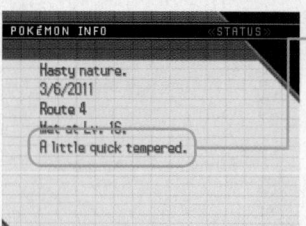

Characteristic with a superior Attack stat

"Quick tempered" indicates the Pokémon's inherent strength lies in its Attack.

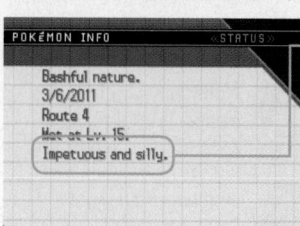

Characteristic with a superior Speed stat

"Impetuous and silly" indicates the Pokémon's inherent strength lies in its Speed.

● **Natures affect Pokémon's stat growth**

"Brave" boosts the growth of the Attack stat

• Nature Brave

High Attack stat

Low Speed stat

Karrablast

A Brave Pokémon's Attack stat grows faster.

"Mild" boosts the growth of the Sp. Atk stat

• Nature Mild

High Sp. Atk stat

Low Defense stat

Deino

A Mild Pokémon's Sp. Atk stat grows faster.

"Timid" boosts the growth of the Speed stat

• Nature Timid

High Speed stat

Low Attack stat

Venipede

A Timid Pokémon's Speed stat grows faster.

◎ See p. 291 for more on Characteristics and Natures ▷

Use Abilities to help you find Pokémon

Certain attributes of Pokémon help you find wild Pokémon. If a Pokémon with a certain Ability is at the head of your party, Pokémon you are looking for are more likely to show up. For example, if you get help from a Pokémon with the Static Ability, you can find more wild Electric-type Pokémon, such as Emolga.

● **Main attributes to help you meet certain Pokémon**

Electric-type Pokémon

Ability Static

The lead Pokémon with this Ability increases the chance to encounter Electric-type Pokémon.

Stunfisk

Pokémon of the opposite gender

Ability Cute Charm

The lead Pokémon with this Ability increases the chance to encounter Pokémon of the opposite gender.

Cinccino

Pokémon with the same Nature

Ability Synchronize

The lead Pokémon with this Ability increases the chance to encounter Pokémon with the same Nature.

Elgyem

2 Raise Pokémon from Eggs

Pokémon can learn unusual moves depending the combination of Pokémon you leave at the Day Care

You can get Pokémon Eggs from the Pokémon Day Care. Pokémon hatched from Eggs may already know moves that wild Pokémon usually wouldn't learn, and they can inherit high stats. So if you raise them, they can perform very well in battles.

Tip to raise Pokémon from Eggs **1** ## Leave Pokémon at the Pokémon Day Care and find Eggs

Leave one ♂ (male) and one ♀ (female) Pokémon at the Pokémon Day Care. If the two belong to the same Egg group, an Egg will be found after a while. If the two are the same species, or if you got either of the Pokémon by trade, you are likely to find an Egg sooner.

Trainer's ID

The "ID" line tells you if you caught the Pokémon

If you don't remember whether you caught the Pokémon yourself or got it in a trade, check the SUMMARY screen.

● **What the Day-Care Man says:**

1 The two seem to get along very well!

2 The two seem to get along.

3 The two don't really seem to like each other much.

4 The two prefer to play with other Pokémon more than with each other.

• If he says **4**, no Egg will be found with these two Pokémon.

Meet the Day-Care Man

After receiving a Bicycle from the Day-Care Man in Nimbasa City, you can leave two Pokémon at the Pokémon Day Care.

If you'd like us to raise your Pokémon, have a word with my wife.

● **Better chance to find an Egg:**

1 Leave Pokémon of the same species

If you leave male and female Pokémon of the same species at the Day Care, the chance to find an Egg will be higher.

♂ Pokémon
Unfezant

♀ Pokémon
Unfezant

2 Leave a Pokémon you got by trade

If you leave one Pokémon that you got by trading, there's a better chance to find an Egg.

Whimsicott

Lilligant

For more information on Eggs, see p. 122 to p. 125.

Tip to raise Pokémon from Eggs **2** **Have a Pokémon inherit traits**

A Pokémon hatched from an Egg may have traits that wild Pokémon wouldn't have because it can inherit moves, Nature, and inherent strength of the Pokémon left at the Day Care. Find an Egg that inherited your favorite Pokémon's traits, and get a strong Pokémon.

Benefits of raising Pokémon from Eggs

1 Hatched Pokémon may already know Egg moves.

2 Hatched Pokémon may inherit high stats.

3 Hatched Pokémon may inherit a Nature.

4 Hatched Pokémon starts with high friendship.

Traits that a hatched Pokémon can inherit

Traits that a Vullaby hatched from an Egg may inherit

♂ Pokémon — Braviary

♀ Pokémon — Mandibuzz

Egg → Vullaby

• Inherited traits
Moves
Stats
Nature

Tip to raise Pokémon from Eggs **3** **Have a Pokémon inherit moves**

Pass on a move that the two Pokémon you left at the Pokémon Day Care have learned to a Pokémon to be hatched. Usually, newly hatched Pokémon only know the moves that they know at Lv. 1. However, depending on the two Pokémon you left at the Day Care, the combination of the moves of the hatched Pokémon may differ. For example, hatched Pokémon sometimes already know a move that they usually learn by leveling up. This is because both of the two Pokémon you left at the Day Care have learned the move. Also, Pokémon may hatch with a move that is usually learned from a TM. This is because the male Pokémon you left at the Day Care has learned the move.

Moves that the hatched Pokémon can know

1 Moves that the Pokémon knows at Lv. 1.

2 If both Pokémon at the Pokémon Day Care have the same level-up move, the hatched Pokémon may have that level-up move.

3 A move that the male Pokémon knows and that the hatched Pokémon could learn from a TM.

Rules to inherit moves

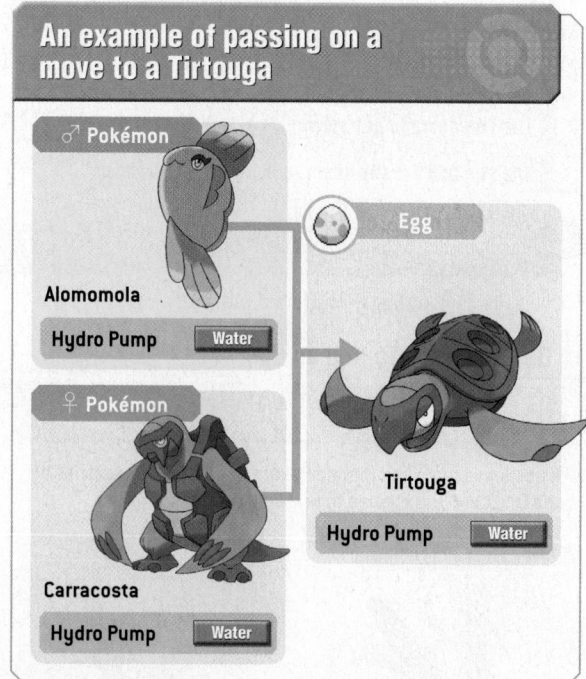

An example of passing on a move to a Tirtouga

♂ Pokémon — Alomomola
Hydro Pump | Water

♀ Pokémon — Carracosta
Hydro Pump | Water

Egg → Tirtouga
Hydro Pump | Water

For Egg Groups of Pokémon, see p. 124. ▶

Tip to raise Pokémon from Eggs **4** **Pokémon can hatch knowing special moves**

Pokémon may hatch from Eggs already knowing moves that they usually wouldn't learn. These moves are called Egg moves. For example, Ducklett doesn't learn Mirror Move by leveling up. However, if a male Pokémon left at the Day Care knows Mirror Move, a Pokémon hatched from that Egg may inherit the move. Because there are many unexpected Egg moves, you can surprise the opposing Trainer in battle.

● **A Rule of Egg moves**

1 A move that the male Pokémon knows and that the hatched Pokémon can learn as an Egg move

● **A Rule of Egg moves**

An Egg move for Ducklett

♂ Pokémon — Sigilyph — Mirror Move — Flying

♀ Pokémon — Swanna

Egg → Ducklett — Mirror Move — Flying

 Tip to raise Pokémon from Eggs **5** **Have a Pokémon inherit a high stat**

There are ways to pass inherent strength on to a Pokémon that hatches from an Egg. For example, when you leave a Pokémon that has high inherent strength in Attack at the Day Care, let it hold a Power Bracer. It passes the holder's inherent strength in Attack on to the Egg. When you raise Pokémon for battles, find many Eggs using this method, hatch them, and find a Pokémon with overall high stats among the hatched Pokémon.

● **Rules to inherit a stat**

Passing on a high stat

♂ Pokémon — Rufflet — High Attack stat

♀ Pokémon — Archeops

Egg → Archen — High Attack stat

● **Items that pass on inherent strengths**

 Power Weight
Passes the holder's inherent strength in HP on to the Pokémon that hatches from the Egg

 Power Lens
Passes the holder's inherent strength in Sp. Atk on to the Pokémon that hatches from the Egg

 Power Bracer
Passes the holder's inherent strength in Attack on to the Pokémon that hatches from the Egg

 Power Band
Passes the holder's inherent strength in Sp. Def on to the Pokémon that hatches from the Egg

 Power Belt
Passes the holder's inherent strength in Defense on to the Pokémon that hatches from the Egg

 Power Anklet
Passes the holder's inherent strength in Speed on to the Pokémon that hatches from the Egg

A hatched Pokémon can inherit a Nature

To raise a Pokémon to have high stats, both its inherent strength and its Nature are important. The stat increases quickly when the Pokémon levels up is determined by its Nature. For example, if you want to pass on the Jolly Nature of the Pokémon you left at the Day Care to a hatched Pokémon, let the Pokémon hold an Everstone. The hatched Pokémon will have that Nature 50% of the time.

● An item for inheriting a Nature

Everstone

The Nature of the Pokémon holding it is passed on to the Egg 50% of the time.

● Either the male or the female Pokémon can hold the Everstone for this effect.

● Rules to inherit a nature

Passing on a Nature

♂ Pokémon

Scrafty

Nature Jolly

♀ Pokémon

Haxorus

Egg

Axew

Nature Jolly

You can't control the hatched Pokémon's Ability

If a Pokémon species has two possible Abilities, a Pokémon hatched from an Egg may have either. For example, Patrat's Ability can be either Run Away or Keen Eye. A Patrat with the Run Away Ability will evolve into a Watchog with the Illuminate Ability, and a Patrat with the Keen Eye Ability will keep that Ability when it evolves into a Watchog. No matter which Ability the Pokémon you leave at the Day Care has, the hatched Patrat may have either of its species' Abilities.

● Relationship between Abilities and evolution

Examples of Patrat and Watchog

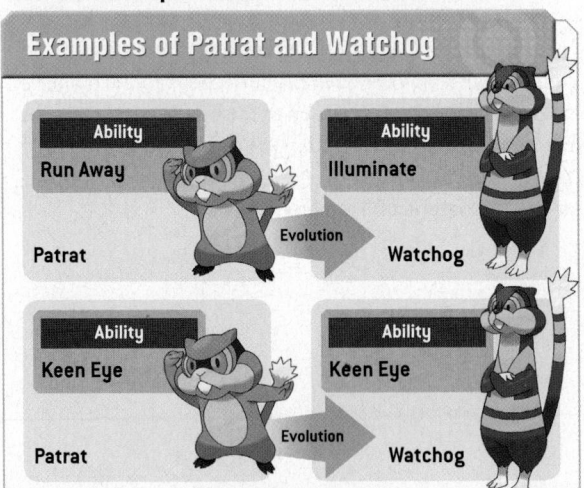

Ability		Ability
Run Away	Evolution	Illuminate
Patrat		Watchog

Ability		Ability
Keen Eye	Evolution	Keen Eye
Patrat		Watchog

● Abilities of Pokémon left at the Day Care don't influence the Abilities of Pokémon hatched from Eggs

1 A Watchog with the Illuminate Ability

♀ Pokémon
Ability
Illuminate

Watchog

Egg
Ability
Run Away
Patrat

Egg
Ability
Keen Eye
Patrat

2 A Watchog with the Keen Eye Ability

♀ Pokémon
Ability
Keen Eye

Watchog

Egg
Ability
Run Away
Patrat

Egg
Ability
Keen Eye
Patrat

Hidden Abilities can be inherited

Two of the Pokémon you'll find in the game have Hidden Abilities: the Musharna that shows up in the Dreamyard every Friday after you finish the main story, and the Darmanitan that awakens from a statue with a RageCandyBar in the Desert Resort. If you leave a Musharna with the Hidden Ability Telepathy at the Pokémon Day Care, you may find an Egg of a Munna with the same Hidden Ability. If you leave a Darmanitan with the Hidden Ability Zen Mode, you may find an Egg of a Darumaka with the Hidden Ability Inner Focus.

Musharna	Darmanitan
Field Group	Field Group

● How to pass on Darmanitan's Ability

1 How to hatch a Darumaka with the normal Ability

♀ Pokémon · Egg
Darmanitan
Darumaka
Ability: Sheer Force → Ability: Hustle

If the female Darmanitan left at the Day Care has the Sheer Force Ability, the Darumaka will have its normal Ability, Hustle.

2 How to hatch a Darumaka with the Hidden Ability

♀ Pokémon · Egg
Darmanitan
Ability: Inner Focus → Darumaka
Ability: Zen Mode
Egg
Ability: Hustle → Darumaka

If the female Darmanitan has the Hidden Ability Zen Mode, the Darumaka may have the Hidden Ability Inner Focus—or its normal Ability, Hustle.

● How to pass on Musharna's Ability

1 How to hatch a Munna with the normal Ability (1)

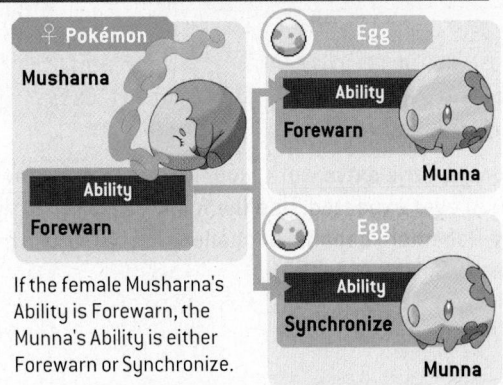

♀ Pokémon
Musharna
Ability: Forewarn
Egg
Ability: Forewarn → Munna
Egg
Ability: Synchronize → Munna

If the female Musharna's Ability is Forewarn, the Munna's Ability is either Forewarn or Synchronize.

2 How to hatch a Munna with the normal Ability (2)

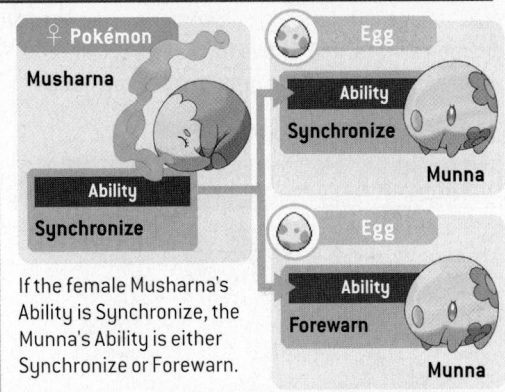

♀ Pokémon
Musharna
Ability: Synchronize
Egg
Ability: Synchronize → Munna
Egg
Ability: Forewarn → Munna

If the female Musharna's Ability is Synchronize, the Munna's Ability is either Synchronize or Forewarn.

3 How to hatch a Munna with the Hidden Ability

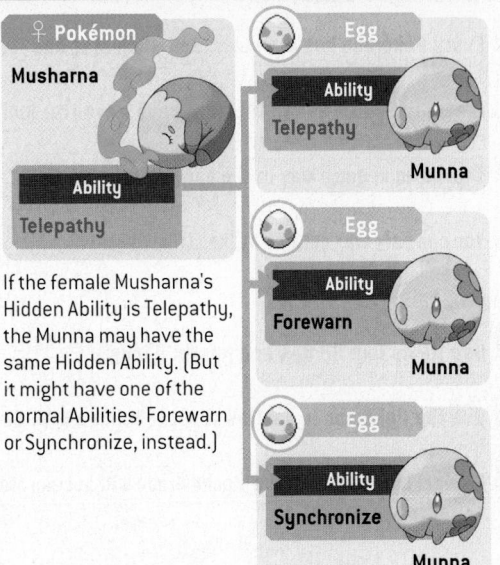

♀ Pokémon
Musharna
Ability: Telepathy
Egg
Ability: Telepathy → Munna
Egg
Ability: Forewarn → Munna
Egg
Ability: Synchronize → Munna

If the female Musharna's Hidden Ability is Telepathy, the Munna may have the same Hidden Ability. (But it might have one of the normal Abilities, Forewarn or Synchronize, instead.)

● If the male Pokémon has a Hidden Ability, or if you leave a Pokémon with a Ditto, the Hidden Ability won't be passed on.

Pokémon Battle Training

3

Master the Art of Strengthening Pokémon

Battling a lot of wild Pokémon is very important to raise strong Pokémon

With only a little extra work, your Pokémon can grow up tougher than you ever expected. Use the following training tips to raise strong Pokémon, capable of challenging both your friends and the Battle Subway (p. 250).

Training Tip **1** **Max out base stats to maximize Pokémon stats**

Stats make a huge difference in a Pokémon battle. To raise your Pokémon's stats, you'll have to raise its six base stats, which determine its stat growth. You may notice the benefits of base stats as a Pokémon's stats increase with each level-up.

● Effect of raising base stats

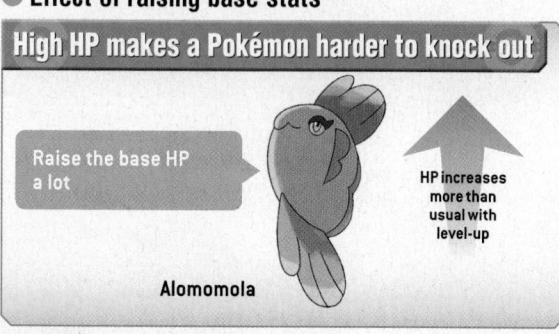

High HP makes a Pokémon harder to knock out

Raise the base HP a lot

HP increases more than usual with level-up

Alomomola

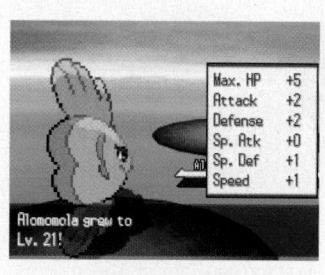

Alomomola grew to Lv. 21!

Max. HP	+5
Attack	+2
Defense	+2
Sp. Atk	+0
Sp. Def	+1
Speed	+1

Higher base stats mean faster growth

Raise the base HP by battling lots of wild Pokémon, and you may notice HP increases faster than usual.

● Rules for base stats

1 Every Pokémon has six stats, and each stat has its own base stat number.

2 A stat with high base stats will have a greater increase when the Pokémon levels up.

3 There's no in-game way to see base stats.

4 You can only max out two of the six base stats.

● How to raise base stats

1 Use items like HP Ups and Health Wings.

2 Use the Pokémon in battles or let it hold an Exp. Share.

3 Pokérus and items like the Macho Brace will accelerate how fast base stats are accumulated.

2 **Use items on Pokémon to raise base stats faster**

Items can raise base stats. There's an item for every stat category, such as HP Up to raise the base HP or Protein to raise the base Attack stat. They are effective even when you use them on Pokémon that have not battled yet.

● **Effect of raising base stats**

Higher base stats mean higher stat gain

Leveling up a Pokémon after giving Calcium and Carbos

Sp. Atk and Speed stats go up

Vanilluxe

● **An example of increased base stats**

Combine nutritious drinks and other methods to raise base stats

You can use up to ten nutritious drinks on one Pokémon for each stat category. However, you can raise base stats even higher with battles and Wings.

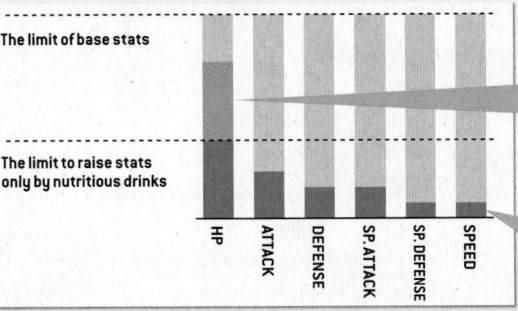

The limit of base stats

The limit to raise stats only by nutritious drinks

HP · ATTACK · DEFENSE · SP.ATTACK · SP.DEFENSE · SPEED

To raise stats over the limit for nutritious drinks, use Wings or have your Pokémon defeat other Pokémon

The base stat has risen from battles against other Pokémon

● **Nutritious drinks that raise base stats**

 HP Up
It raises the base HP.

 Calcium
It raises the base Sp. Atk stat.

 **Protein**
It raises the base Attack stat.

 Zinc
It raises the base Sp. Def stat.

 **Iron**
It raises the base Defense stat.

 Carbos
It raises the base Speed stat.

● **Wings that raise base stats**

 Health Wing
It slightly increases the base HP.
It can be used up to the limit for the base stat.

 Genius Wing
It slightly increases the base Sp. Atk stat.
It can be used up to the limit for the base stat.

 Muscle Wing
It slightly increases the base Attack stat.
It can be used up to the limit for the base stat.

 Clever Wing
It slightly increases the base Sp. Def stat.
It can be used up to the limit for the base stat.

 Resist Wing
It slightly increases the base Defense stat.
It can be used up to the limit for the base stat.

 Swift Wing
It slightly increases the base Speed stat.
It can be used up to the limit for the base stat.

● **Characteristics of items to raise base stats**

1 You can raise base stats up to a certain limit by using nutritious drinks.

2 You can raise base stats up to the maximum by using Wings.

POKÉMON BATTLE PRIMER ◇ MASTER THE ART OF STRENGTHENING POKÉMON

Training Tip ③ Pick your battles based on the stats you want to maximize

A Pokémon raises its base stats when it defeats other Pokémon in battle. Which base stat gets raised depends on which Pokémon your Pokémon defeat. Examples of Pokémon that raise each base stat are shown below. Defeat lots of Pokémon that raise the base stat you want to raise.

● Examples of Pokémon that raise specific base stats

Pokémon that raise HP

Munna
- Best location
Dreamyard

Ducklett
- Location
Driftveil Drawbridge
(Pokémon shadows)

Pokémon that raise Attack

Patrat
- Best location
Route 1

Lillipup
- Best location
Route 1

Pokémon that raise Defense

Roggenrola
- Best location
Wellspring Cave

Sewaddle
- Best location
Pinwheel Forest

Pokémon that raise Sp. Atk

Litwick
- Location
Celestial Tower
2F to 5F

Elgyem
- Location
Celestial Tower
3F to 5F

Pokémon that raise Sp. Def

Frillish
- Best location
Driftveil City
(water surface)

Jellicent
- Best location
Driftveil City
(rippling water)

Pokémon that raise Speed

Purrloin
- Best location
Dreamyard

Blitzle
- Location
Route 3

● Although the appearances of Frillish and Jellicent differ depending on the gender, your Pokémon's base Sp. Def will go up whichever it defeats.

● Items that increase base stat growth depending on the Pokémon the holder defeats in battles

Macho Brace

Increases the amount base stats are raised, depending on which Pokémon the holder defeats

Training Tip ④ Give items to raise the base stat you want to raise

Some held items will boost the amount base stats are raised in battles. Take the Power Bracer, for example. It reduces the Speed stat, but it promotes Attack gain. The holder also can get normal base stats according to the Pokémon it defeats.

● Items to raise a certain base stat when held in battles

Power Weight
Promotes HP gain

Power Lens
Promotes Sp. Atk gain

Power Bracer
Promotes Attack gain

Power Band
Promotes Sp. Def gain

Power Belt
Promotes Defense gain

Power Anklet
Promotes Speed gain

Training Tip 5 Take advantage of the mysterious power of Pokérus

The mysterious Pokérus virus infrequently infects Pokémon in your party when they keep battling wild Pokémon. Pokémon with Pokérus raise their base stats gained in battles by an increased amount. If you're lucky enough to have Pokérus in your party, use it to raise your Pokémon!

While infected, Pokémon are said to grow exceptionally well.

Keep Pokérus in your PC
Keep a Pokémon infected with Pokérus in your PC. The Pokérus will stick around indefinitely.

● Pokérus rules

1. Infrequently infects your Pokémon when they battle wild Pokémon

2. Increases the amount base stats go up in battle

3. Battling can cause it to spread to adjacent party Pokémon

4. Disappears after one to four days, but increase in the amount base stats go up won't change for infected Pokémon

5. Doesn't disappear while the Pokémon is stored in a PC Box

Training Tip 6 Once you've maxed out base stats, go level up

You can only get the base stats so high. There is a limit for each base stat, and there is also a limit for the total six base stats. Once you've maxed out base stats, it's time to earn Experience Points and level up your Pokémon!

put in a great effort!

● This is an image from *Pokémon Black Version*.

Ask a girl in Opelucid City
A girl in a house in Opelucid City tells you if your Pokémon's base stats are maxed out.

● Items related to Experience Points

Lucky Egg
Earns extra Experience Points (Earns 1.5 times the amount of Experience Points it normally would)

Exp. Share
Get some of the Experience Points even if the holder is not in battle

● Good ways to earn Experience Points

1. Challenge the Elite Four and the Champion in the Pokémon League again, and battle against high-level wild Pokémon.

2. After finishing the main story, revisit Big Stadium and Small Court in Nimbasa City to challenge Trainers who have gotten stronger.

3. Leave Pokémon at the Pokémon Day Care.

4. Trade Pokémon with your friends and raise each other's Pokémon.

 Use Rare Candy wisely

A Rare Candy is an item to raise the level of a single Pokémon by one. Use it right after a Pokémon levels up by battling to avoid wasting Experience Points!

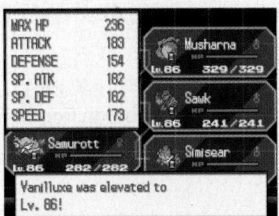

MAX HP	236
ATTACK	183
DEFENSE	154
SP. ATK	182
SP. DEF	182
SPEED	173

Musharna Lv.86 329/329
Sawk Lv.86 241/241
Samurott Lv.86 282/282
Simisear

Vanilluxe was elevated to Lv. 86!

Training Tip **7** **Use Berries to adjust the levels of base stats**

You can't max out all six base stats. You can only max out two stats at most. So when you train, focus on just two or three stats, building up your Pokémon's strengths. When your Pokémon earn base stats that you don't care about, give them Berries to cut down on those unnecessary base stats. You can reduce base stats that once went up and raise different base stats.

● **Effect of items to lower base stats**

You can raise Pokémon suitable for your strategy by lowering base stats

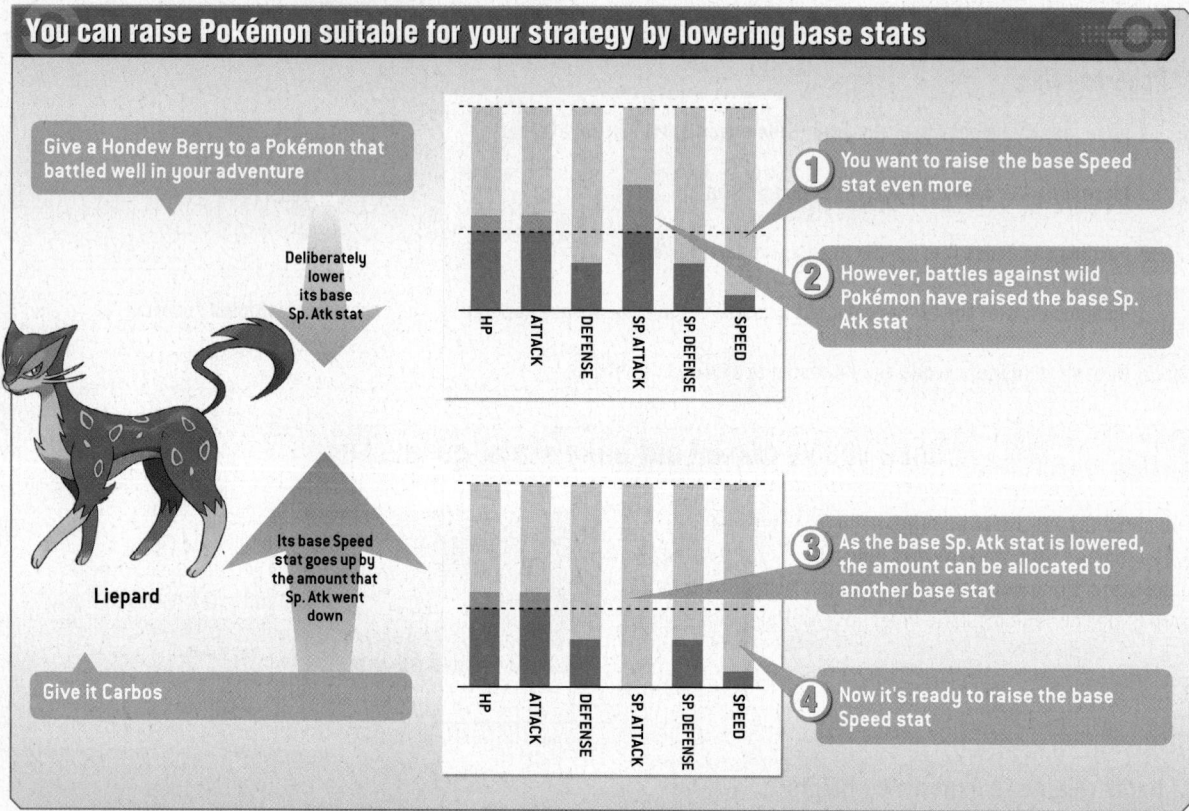

Give a Hondew Berry to a Pokémon that battled well in your adventure

Deliberately lower its base Sp. Atk stat

Liepard

Give it Carbos

Its base Speed stat goes up by the amount that Sp. Atk went down

HP ATTACK DEFENSE SP.ATTACK SP. DEFENSE SPEED

① You want to raise the base Speed stat even more

② However, battles against wild Pokémon have raised the base Sp. Atk stat

③ As the base Sp. Atk stat is lowered, the amount can be allocated to another base stat

④ Now it's ready to raise the base Speed stat

● **Berries that lower base stats**

Pomeg Berry
It lowers the base HP.
It makes the Pokémon more friendly.

Hondew Berry
It lowers the base Sp. Atk stat.
It makes the Pokémon more friendly.

Kelpsy Berry
It lowers the base Attack stat.
It makes the Pokémon more friendly.

Grepa Berry
It lowers the base Sp. Def stat.
It makes the Pokémon more friendly.

Qualot Berry
It lowers the base Defense stat.
It makes the Pokémon more friendly.

Tamato Berry
It lowers the base Speed stat.
It makes the Pokémon more friendly.

 Get Berries that lower base stats by Spin Trade

You can get Berries that lower base stats as a bonus in a five-player Spin Trade in the Union Room. These Berries are hard to find, so cooperate with your friends and family to get them (p. 151).

Landed on a Bonus Area!
Received a free Kelpsy Berry!

| Training Tip | 8 | Build up each Pokémon's strengths even more |

The stats you should raise are different depending on how you battle. It would be ideal to raise all base stats to maximum, but that's not possible. You need to decide on which base stats to focus on. If you raise an originally high stat even more, you can enhance traits different from other Pokémon, and make the best use of your Pokémon's strengths.

● Examples of building up Pokémon's strengths in base stats

An example of an Excadrill whose Attack and Speed stats were raised

As Excadrill have a high Attack stat, you can have a strategy to attack the opposing Pokémon with physical moves. Also, to get the first attack, the base Speed stat was raised.

| Drill Run | Ground |

Excadrill

| Ground | Steel |

ABILITIES
- Sand Rush
- Sand Force

⊙ STATS

HP ●●●●
ATTACK ●●●●●●
DEFENSE ●●
SP. ATTACK ●●●
SP. DEFENSE ●●
SPEED ●●●●

● Base stats

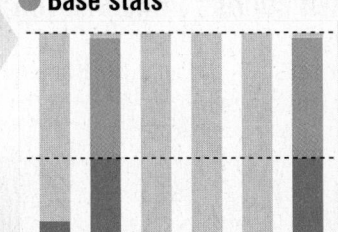

HP | ATTACK | DEFENSE | SP.ATTACK | SP.DEFENSE | SPEED

An example of an Eelektross whose HP and Sp. Atk stats were raised

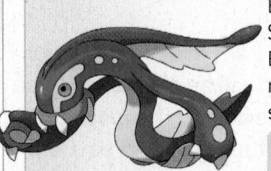

Eelektross have high Attack and Sp. Atk stats. However, in this Eelektross's case, mainly special moves were taught and its Attack stat was deliberately kept low.

| Discharge | Electric |

Eelektross

| Electric | |

ABILITY
- Levitate

⊙ STATS

HP ●●●
ATTACK ●●●●●
DEFENSE ●●●
SP. ATTACK ●●●●●
SP. DEFENSE ●●●
SPEED ●●

● Base stats

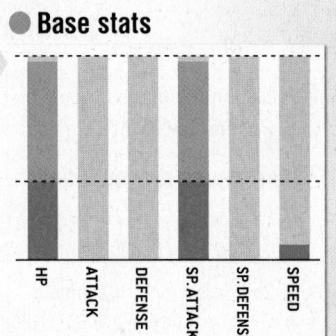

HP | ATTACK | DEFENSE | SP.ATTACK | SP.DEFENSE | SPEED

Pokémon can still do well with low stats

You don't have to raise every single stat of your Pokémon. For example, if a Pokémon battles with only special moves and doesn't learn any physical moves, it cannot make use of its Attack stat no matter how high it is. Raise your Pokémon so they can make full use of their strengths.

Ex. 1 — Moves to make use of high stats

If your Pokémon battles only with physical moves, you don't have to raise its Sp. Atk, which influences special moves. Instead, raise its Attack stat.

Ex. 2 — Moves that inflict fixed damage

Stats of a Pokémon do not affect a move that inflicts fixed damage on its target, such as Dragon Rage.

Ex. 3 — Moves that share stats with the opposing Pokémon

The higher the opposing Pokémon's stats than the user, the more effective the moves like Guard Split and Power Split get.

Ex. 4 — Moves that get stronger when the Pokémon is slow

The slower the user is compared to its target, the more damage it can inflict with the move Gyro Ball.

Plan Ahead to Raise Pokémon that Fit Your Strategy

Plan carefully and raise your Pokémon thoroughly, and they will do even better

Depending on the strategy you want to develop, which Pokémon you use and how you raise them will be different. Raise your Pokémon while imagining how to battle. The more thoroughly you raise your Pokémon, the better they will do in battles.

Raising Plan 1 Determine your goal first, then choose Pokémon to raise

Select Pokémon species based on moves you want to use, or pick Pokémon with Abilities suitable for your strategy.

It's easier to create a plan if you visualize your ideal battle strategy.

● **What moves do you want?**

If you want to use Head Charge

Head Charge is a move that only Bouffalant can learn. Because it is a physical move, raise a Bouffalant to have a high Attack stat.

Head Charge	Normal

Bouffalant

If you want to use Ally Switch

You want to use Ally Switch in Triple Battles. But few Pokémon can learn the move. You could choose a Beheeyem.

Ally Switch	Psychic

Beheeyem

If you want to use Horn Leech

Only Sawsbuck can learn Horn Leech. The user can attack and restore HP at the same time, so it makes the Pokémon difficult to be knocked out.

Horn Leech	Grass

Sawsbuck (Spring Form)

If you want to use Soak

To wreck the opposing Trainer's strategy, raise an Alomomola that can learn Soak. The move can change its target to the Water type.

Soak	Water

Alomomola

● **What Abilities are most helpful?**

When you choose an Ability of Leavanny

If your team is strongest in Sunny weather, pick a Leavanny with the Chlorophyll Ability. It'll get a Speed boost in harsh sunlight.

Leavanny

Ability	Swarm	Ability	Chlorophyll

When you choose an Ability of Golurk

The Iron Fist Ability is suitable when you use punching moves such as Focus Punch and Hammer Arm.

Golurk

Ability	Iron Fist	Ability	Klutz

Raising Plan 2 ## Find out the strengths in attack

A Pokémon with a high Attack stat gives greater damage when it attacks using physical moves, and a Pokémon with a high Sp. Atk stat gives greater damage when it uses special moves. Look at the Pokémon's stats to figure out which moves will be most effective.

● **Types of moves also change how you raise your Pokémon's stats**

Raise the Attack stat for Pokémon that mainly use physical moves

Gigalith have a high Attack stat. Because they learn a lot of physical moves, train them by focusing on raising the base Attack stat.

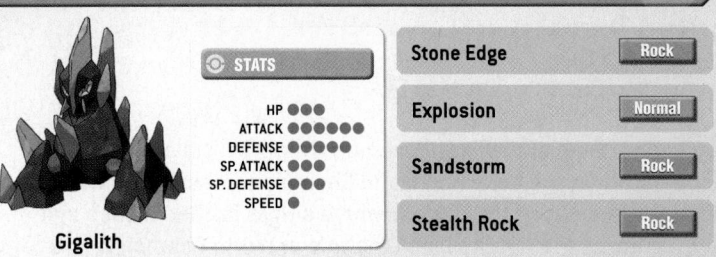

STATS

HP ●●●
ATTACK ●●●●●●
DEFENSE ●●●●●
SP. ATTACK ●●●
SP. DEFENSE ●●●
SPEED ●

Gigalith

Stone Edge	Rock
Explosion	Normal
Sandstorm	Rock
Stealth Rock	Rock

Raise the Sp. Atk stat for Pokémon that mainly use special moves

Lilligant have a high Sp. Atk stat. Because they learn a lot of special moves, train them by focusing on raising the base Sp. Atk stat.

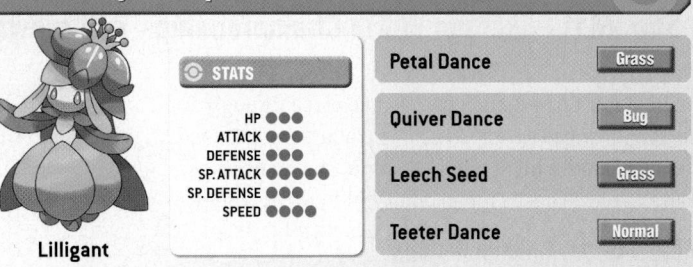

STATS

HP ●●●
ATTACK ●●●
DEFENSE ●●●
SP. ATTACK ●●●●●
SP. DEFENSE ●●●
SPEED ●●●●

Lilligant

Petal Dance	Grass
Quiver Dance	Bug
Leech Seed	Grass
Teeter Dance	Normal

Raising Plan 3 ## Change learned moves depending on your strategy

Deciding on a combination of leaned moves can be a real challenge. However, if you have a grasp of the basics, it will help you decide moves.

● **Important points for combination of moves**

1 **Strategies and learned moves differ depending on the Pokémon's stats and Abilities.**

2 **Single Battles, Double Battles, and Triple Battles all require different strategies and learned moves.**

3 **Teaching both attack moves and support moves provides a good balance.**

4 **If your Pokémon have multiple types of attack moves, they can face various types of opposing Pokémon.**

● **An example of learned moves**

A Scolipede for Single Battles

The strategy is to poison the opposing Pokémon, then guard itself with Protect while the opposing Pokémon's HP drops. In a battle against Steel-type Pokémon, which are immune to Poison-type moves, use the Ground-type move Earthquake.

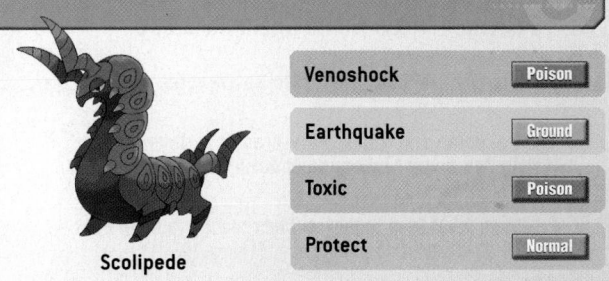

Scolipede

Venoshock	Poison
Earthquake	Ground
Toxic	Poison
Protect	Normal

Put Your Team to the Ultimate Test at the Pokémon World Championships

Face challengers from around the world, with battle strategies that you may have never seen before

Each year, some of the best Pokémon Trainers from around the globe gather at the Pokémon World Championships to test their mettle. At the end of the tournament, a single Trainer in each age division earns the right to claim the title of World Champion. You could be that Trainer!

The 2011 Pokémon World Championships will crown the world's best players.

The Regional Championships will take place throughout the US starting in spring 2011. Top players from these events will move on to the US National Championships, where they will battle for an opportunity to represent their country in the 2011 World Championships this summer. Brush up on your Double Battle skills with the new Pokémon from the Unova region and earn your place on the world stage.

● Flow of the Championships

Regional Championships

Top players at the Regional Championships will receive invitations to participate in the National Championships in Indianapolis, Indiana.

National Championships

The best of the best will compete at the National Championships to earn the right to represent their country in the World Championships.

World Championships

This year, the World Championships will be held in San Diego, California, to determine the World Champion in each of three age divisions.

The 2010 National Championships

Be prepared for anything opposing Trainers may throw at you!

The 2010 World Championships

When it comes to Pokémon, fans all speak the same language, no matter what country they're from.

● Main rules for the 2011 Pokémon Video Game Championships

1. Each battle will use the Double Battle rules.
2. The Pokémon and items registered in a player's Battle Box cannot be changed during the tournament.
3. Pokémon level 51 or higher will be reduced to level 50 for the duration of each battle.
4. Pokémon cannot hold duplicate items.

● Eligible Pokémon for the 2011 Video Game Championships

1. Pokémon from the Unova Pokédex, numbers 001–148 and number 151.
2. Pokémon obtained during normal game play, or that were received at an official event or promotion.
3. Two or more Pokémon with the same Pokédex number cannot be registered in a player's Battle Box.

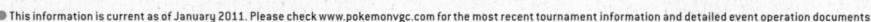

● This information is current as of January 2011. Please check www.pokemonvgc.com for the most recent tournament information and detailed event operation documents.

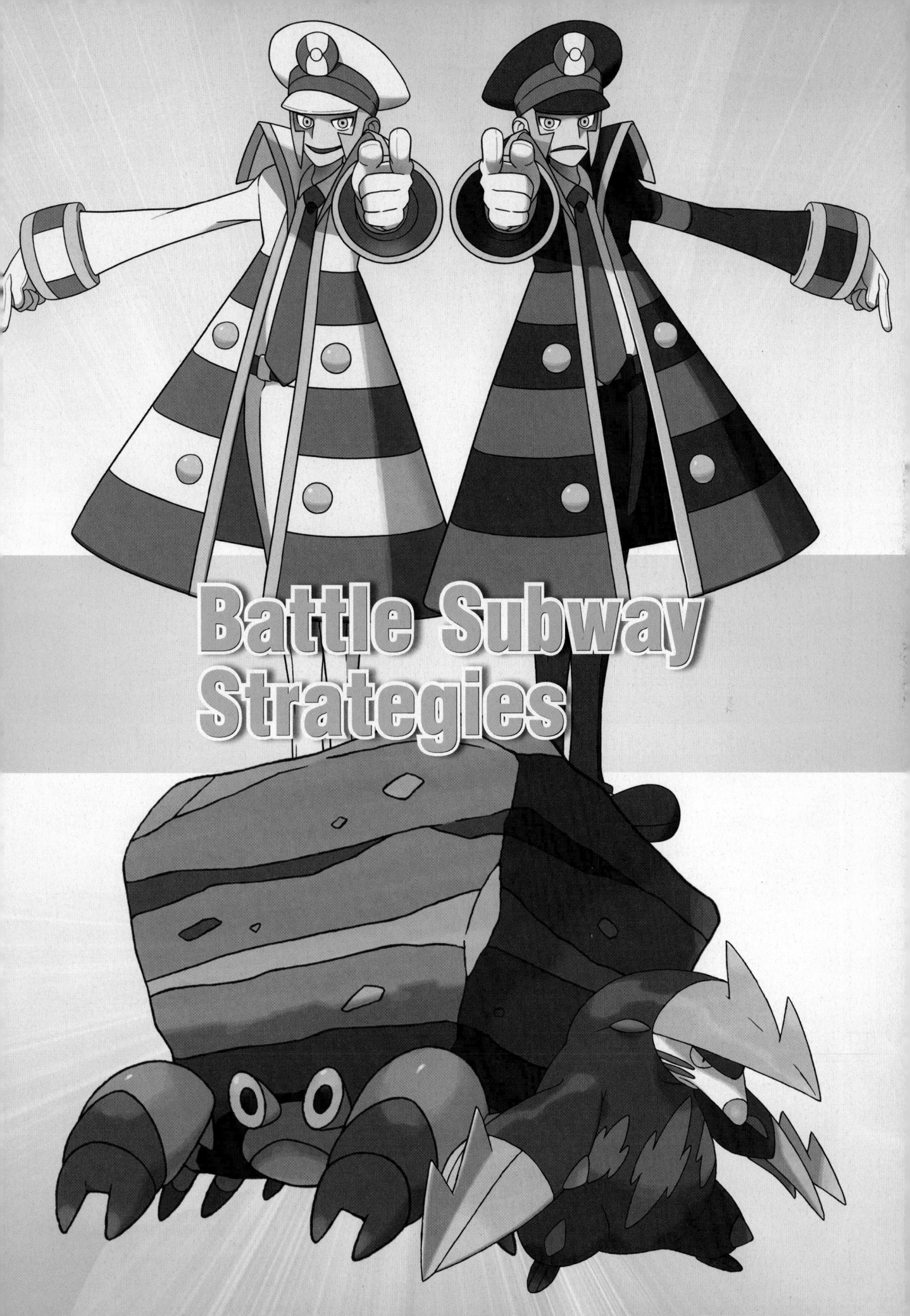

Battle Subway Strategies

Win on the Battle Subway

Join forces with your star Pokémon and take on the subway challenge

On the Battle Subway you can duke it out in any battle format from Single, Double, and Multi Battles, and even battles over Nintendo Wi-Fi Connection. Gather up your strongest Pokémon, and see the ones you raised with great care keep winning and winning!

Learn Battle Subway Basics

Battle Subway Basics **1** **The Battle Subway is in Nimbasa City**

You can take the Battle Subway challenge from the Gear Station in Nimbasa City. The Gear Station is a circular building surrounded by train platforms. You can try different battle formats by boarding different trains.

■ Gear Station

Platform for Trains to Anville Town

Platform for Super Multi Trains

Platform for Multi Trains

Platform for Wi-Fi Trains

Platform for Super Double Trains

Platform for Double Trains

Platform for Super Single Trains

Platform for Single Trains

■ Exchange Service Corner

Each platform has an Exchange

n the Gear Station, seven different trains offer you ifferent Pokémon battles. Each train has its own rules, nd a few special rules apply to the whole Battle Subway.

Learn all the rules of battle so you can challenge yourself and win on all the trains.

Seven different battle formats

❶ Single Train
❷ Super Single Train

The Single Trains are for Single Battles. You can take three Pokémon from your party or your Battle Box.

❸ Double Train
❹ Super Double Train

The Double Trains are for Double Battles. You can take four Pokémon from your party or your Battle Box.

❺ Multi Train
❻ Super Multi Train

Multi Trains are for Multi Battles. You can take two Pokémon from your party or your Battle Box.

❼ Wi-Fi Train

The Wi-Fi Train lets you challenge Trainers from all over the world through Nintendo Wi-Fi Connection. The Pokémon and strategies they use change every time you ride the Wi-Fi Train. Develop your own strategies to show your team is unbeatable by anyone.

Common rules for all trains

1 Levels	• Pokémon of any level can participate. All Pokémon are set to Lv. 50 during a challenge. (After battles in the Battle Subway, their levels return to their original levels.)
2 Battle rules	• Each challenge consists of seven consecutive battles. You cannot get off the train in the middle of a challenge. • If you win against seven Trainers in a row, the train stops at a station.
3 Eligible Pokémon	• All participating Pokémon must be of different species, and they cannot hold duplicate items.
4 Ineligible Pokémon	Mewtwo, Mew, Lugia, Ho-Oh, Celebi, Kyogre, Groudon, Rayquaza, Jirachi, Deoxys, Dialga, Palkia, Giratina, Phione, Manaphy, Darkrai, Shaymin, Arceus, Victini, Reshiram, Zekrom, Kyurem, and Eggs

 ery strong Trainers ride he Super Single Train, Super ouble Train, and Super Multi Train. If you have 49 straight wins there, you vill receive a trophy as a commemorative gift.

A trophy proving you defeated the Single Master

It's a trophy proving you defeated the Single Master in the Battle Subway!

A trophy proving you defeated the Double Master

It's a trophy proving you defeated the Double Master in the Battle Subway!

A trophy proving you defeated the Multi Master

It's a trophy proving you defeated the Multi Master in the Battle Subway!

Basics 4 Exchange BP for Items

You earn Battle Points (BP) every time you have seven straight wins, and you can trade these BP for useful battle items at an Exchange Service Corner. If you collect a lot of BP, you can get powerful TMs.

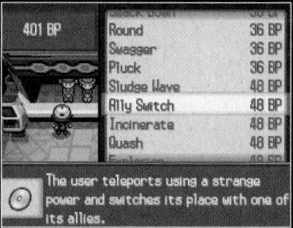

If you win against Ingo in the Single Train, you can get more BP

If you win against Emmet in the Double Train, you can get more BP

● BP you earn from successful battles

Battle	1st round	2nd round	3rd round	4th round	5th round	6th round	7th round	8th round	9th round	10th round
Single Train	3 BP	3 BP	10 BP	—	—	—	—	—	—	—
Super Single Train	5 BP	6 BP	7 BP	8 BP	9 BP	10 BP	30 BP	10 BP	10 BP	10 BP
Double Train	3 BP	3 BP	10 BP	—	—	—	—	—	—	—
Super Double Train	5 BP	6 BP	7 BP	8 BP	9 BP	10 BP	30 BP	10 BP	10 BP	10 BP
Multi Train	3 BP	3 BP	10 BP	—	—	—	—	—	—	—
Super Multi Train	5 BP	6 BP	7 BP	8 BP	9 BP	10 BP	30 BP	10 BP	10 BP	10 BP

Battle	Rank 1	Rank 2	Rank 3	Rank 4	Rank 5	Rank 6	Rank 7	Rank 8	Rank 9	Rank 10
Wi-Fi Train	10 BP	10 BP	10 BP	10 BP	10 BP	10 BP	10 BP	10 BP	10 BP	10 BP
Wi-Fi Train (earlier train)	5 BP	5 BP	5 BP	5 BP	5 BP	5 BP	5 BP	5 BP	5 BP	5 BP

● Items available at the Exchange Service Corner
(Left clerk)   **(Right clerk)**

Prize	BP needed
Pluck	36 BP
Round	36 BP
Smack Down	36 BP
Swagger	36 BP
Ally Switch	48 BP
Explosion	48 BP
Incinerate	48 BP
Psych Up	48 BP
Quash	48 BP
Sludge Wave	48 BP

Prize	BP needed
Calcium	1 BP
Carbos	1 BP
HP Up	1 BP
Iron	1 BP
Protein	1 BP
Zinc	1 BP
Flame Orb	16 BP
Power Anklet	16 BP
Power Band	16 BP
Power Belt	16 BP
Power Bracer	16 BP
Power Lens	16 BP
Power Weight	16 BP

Prize	BP needed
Toxic Orb	16 BP
Absorb Bulb	32 BP
Cell Battery	32 BP
Eject Button	32 BP
Power Herb	32 BP
Red Card	32 BP
White Herb	32 BP
Air Balloon	48 BP
Binding Band	48 BP
BrightPowder	48 BP
Choice Band	48 BP
Choice Scarf	48 BP
Choice Specs	48 BP

Prize	BP needed
Focus Band	48 BP
Focus Sash	48 BP
Iron Ball	48 BP
Life Orb	48 BP
Muscle Band	48 BP
Rare Candy	48 BP
Razor Claw	48 BP
Razor Fang	48 BP
Scope Lens	48 BP
Wide Lens	48 BP
Wise Glasses	48 BP
Zoom Lens	48 BP

Battle Subway Basics 5 Sometimes Trainers at stations give you items

In the Battle Subway, you arrive at a station every time you have seven straight wins. At some stations, you'll find Trainers who give you items. Make sure to speak to them, because they will give you valuable items for raising Pokémon, such as a Rare Candy.

● Station Trainers (for all Single, Double, and Multi Battles)

Train	Number of rounds	Item	Train	Number of rounds	Item
Normal Train	1st round	—	Super Train	9th round	—
Normal Train	2nd round	—	Super Train	10th round	—
Normal Train	3rd round	PP Up	Super Train	11th round	—
Super Train	1st round	—	Super Train	12th round	—
Super Train	2nd round	—	Super Train	13th round	—
Super Train	3rd round	PP Up	Super Train	14th round	—
Super Train	4th round	Rare Candy	Super Train	15th round	Lansat Berry
Super Train	5th round	—	Super Train	21st round	—
Super Train	6th round	—	Super Train	29th round	Starf Berry
Super Train	7th round	—	Super Train	43rd round	—
Super Train	8th round	—	Super Train	143rd round	—

Take On the Single and Super Single Trains

Keep winning against strong Trainers and battle Subway Boss Ingo

The Single Train and the Super Single Train are the most basic trains where you keep battling until you lose. The rules are simple, but the opposing Trainers use various strategies for battles. Challenge them with your strongest Pokémon!

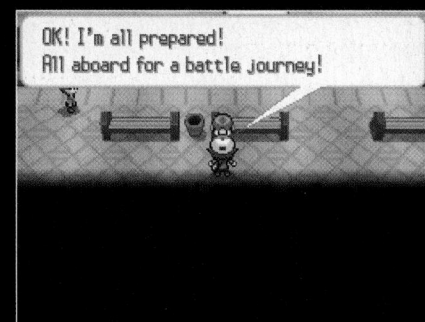

> OK! I'm all prepared! All aboard for a battle journey!

● Rules in the Single Train and the Super Single Train

1 Conditions for challenge	Single Train	You can challenge it anytime.
	Super Single Train	You can challenge it if you have 21 straight wins in the Single Train after finishing the main story.

2 Conditions for battles	You can choose three Pokémon from your party or your Battle Box. The battle format is one-on-one.

On the Single Train — The opposing Trainer's Pokémon get stronger for each seven straight wins

Battles in trains are divided into seven-match challenges—and every time you have seven straight wins, the opposing Trainer's Pokémon get stronger. If a Trainer is too strong for you, you may need to choose other Pokémon to participate in battles. Find the right combination of Pokémon for seven straight wins, and extend your record.

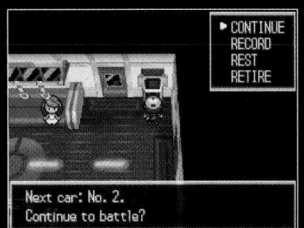

Every time you win, you choose whether to continue battling or not.

If you have seven straight wins, you can pick up BP at a station.

On the Super Single Train — The Pokémon are stronger than in the Single Train

In the Super Single Train, the stats of the opposing Trainers' Pokémon are significantly higher. It's important to attack the opposing Pokémon by targeting their weaknesses.

Metagross
Steel | Psychic

Lilligant
Grass |

Bisharp
Dark | Steel

Swampert
Water | Ground

Battle Subway Boss Ingo!

His Chandelure will use Overheat, and his Excadrill will use Earthquake. These moves are especially strong because they match the type of the user. Fight against Ingo's Pokémon with powerful moves, and defeat him as quickly as you can.

● **Single Train, 21st match**

◎ Garbodor	Lv. 50	Poison	
◎ Crustle	Lv. 50	Bug	Rock
◎ Klinklang	Lv. 50	Steel	
◎			
◎			
◎			

● **Super Single Train, 49th match**

◎ Chandelure	Lv. 50	Ghost	Fire
◎ Excadrill	Lv. 50	Ground	Steel
◎ Haxorus	Lv. 50	Dragon	
◎			
◎			

Take On the Double and Super Double Trains

Keep your winning streak going and challenge Subway Boss Emmet

In the Double Train and the Super Double Train, you battle in two-on-two Double Battles. Strategies specific to Double Battles, such as attacking one of the opposing Trainers' two Pokémon or using moves that attack multiple opponents at once, are important.

Now, please board the Double Train!

● Rules in the Double Train and the Super Double Train

1 Conditions for challenge	Double Train	You can challenge it anytime.
	Super Double Train	You can challenge it if you have 21 straight wins in the Double Train after finishing the main story.

2 Conditions for battles	Choose four Pokémon from your party or your Battle Box. The battle format is two-on-two.

On the Double Train — You need strategies specific to Double Battles

To win more Double Battles, you must create effective combinations with your Pokémon's moves. To keep winning over the long run, you must also tailor some effective combos to the opposing Pokémon. By using moves that attack multiple Pokémon at once, such as Surf and Earthquake, you will dramatically increase your odds of winning.

Get an edge in a battle with moves that attack multiple Pokémon.

Use held items to your advantage. Items that allow your Pokémon to attack first are especially useful.

On the Super Double Train — Strong opposing Pokémon with high stats show up

A lot of Pokémon with high Attack and Sp. Atk stats show up. Bring the Pokémon you've trained hard so that they won't be knocked out by major damage.

Charizard	Mienshao	Braviary	Musharna
Fire Flying	Fighting	Normal Flying	Psychic

Battle Subway Boss Emmet!

On the Double Train, targeting the weaknesses of Emmet's two Bug-type Pokémon is most effective. In the Super Double Train, you could add Flying-type Pokémon—his Excadrill's Earthquake won't affect them.

● Double Train, 21st match

⊚ Crustle	Lv. 50	Bug	Rock
⊚ Durant	Lv. 50	Bug	Steel
⊚ Garbodor	Lv. 50	Poison	
⊚ Klinklang	Lv. 50	Steel	
⊚			
⊚			

● Super Double Train, 49th match

⊚ Chandelure	Lv. 50	Ghost	Fire
⊚ Excadrill	Lv. 50	Ground	Steel
⊚ Haxorus	Lv. 50	Dragon	
⊚ Eelektross	Lv. 50	Electric	
⊚			
⊚			

Take On the Multi and Super Multi Trains

Battle in total sync with your partner and move ahead to battle the Subway Bosses

In the Multi Train and the Super Multi Train, two Trainers must cooperate and battle together. You'll have a partner for every challenge. Your own skills, plus your ability to coordinate with your partner, will determine the outcome of the battle.

All right!
I will show you my power!

◗ Rules for the Multi Train and the Super Multi Train

1	Conditions for challenge	Multi Train	You can challenge it anytime.
		Super Multi Train	You can challenge it if you have 21 straight wins in the Multi Train after finishing the main story.

2	Conditions for battles	Choose two Pokémon from your party or your Battle Box. Two Trainers team up for a two-on-two battle.

On the Multi Train — Working well with your partner determines the outcome of the battle

Just like on the Double Train, how to utilize combos is important, but you cannot choose your partner's Pokémon or moves. If you predict your partner's moves and choose the best matching moves, you will easily extend your winning streak. It's also good to assign the attacking, supporting, and defending roles in advance.

What kinds of Pokémon should I enter?

At the station, you and your partner select a strategy.

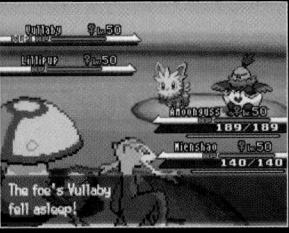

The foe's Vullaby fell asleep!

You can play the supporting role and let your partner do the heavy hitting.

On the Super Multi Train — Face off against fully evolved Pokémon

Many fully evolved Pokémon with high stats will confront you in the Super Multi Train. Switch Pokémon during a battle so the opposing Pokémon cannot target your Pokémon's weaknesses with powerful moves.

Torterra	Blaziken	Registeel	Gallade
Grass · Ground	Fire · Fighting	Steel	Psychic · Fighting

Battle Subway Bosses Ingo and Emmet!

Both Haxorus and Excadrill use Earthquake, so try to beat them early in the battle. If you focus on one of the bosses to knock his team out first, you can battle two-on-one afterward to get an edge in the battle.

● Multi Train, 21st match

◎ Garbodor	Lv. 50	Poison	
◎ Klinklang	Lv. 50	Steel	
◎ Durant	Lv. 50	Bug	Steel
◎ Galvantula	Lv. 50	Bug	Electric
◎			
◎			

● Super Multi Train, 49th match

◎ Excadrill	Lv. 50	Ground	Steel
◎ Haxorus	Lv. 50	Dragon	
◎ Eelektross	Lv. 50	Electric	
◎ Archeops	Lv. 50	Rock	Flying
◎			
◎			

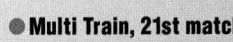

Take On the Wi-Fi Train

Compete with Trainers from all over the world

In the Wi-Fi Train, you will battle against Trainers from all over the world. If you keep winning, your Rank will go up. Aim for high Rank and keep winning.

Your opponents will come from around the world via Nintendo Wi-Fi Connection.

● Rules for the Wi-Fi Train

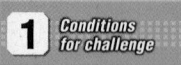
1 Conditions for challenge You can participate whenever you are connected to Nintendo Wi-Fi Connection.

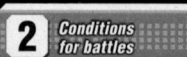
2 Conditions for battles Choose three Pokémon from your party or your Battle Box. The battle format is one-on-one.

On the Wi-Fi Train ① Trainers from all over the world will be your rivals

The battle format is the same as on the Single Trains, but on the Wi-Fi Train, you will face Trainers from all over the world. As new Trainers show up one after another, a strategy that worked well before may not work on new Trainers. You must adapt your strategies depending on the opposing Trainers.

The foe's Patrat fainted!

SUCCESSIVE TRAINERS
Rank 3   Train Number 1
WF04
• LOCATION
Japan
Hokkaido (Hakodate)
• TRAINER'S QUOTE
NO. 1?
Wow, I'm so glad!

The opposing Trainer changes every time. Sometimes, unfamiliar Pokémon will show surprising strength and get in your way.

You can check the Trainer profiles of the opposing Trainers on the Wi-Fi Train at the entrance of the Wi-Fi Train platform.

On the Wi-Fi Train ② Keep winning and your Rank goes up

In the Wi-Fi Train, your Rank improves if you keep winning. When your Rank goes up, you can battle against Trainers with the same Rank as you. On the other hand, if you keep losing, your Rank drops. The higher your Rank is, the stricter the conditions for demotion. To reach the highest Rank, you need strong Pokémon you've trained very hard, and you must have extensive knowledge of battles.

● Conditions to change Ranks

Rank	Promotion	Demotion
Rank 1	A 7-win streak	—
Rank 2	A 7-win streak	5 consecutive failures in a 7-win streak
Rank 3	A 7-win streak	4 consecutive failures in a 7-win streak
Rank 4	A 7-win streak	4 consecutive failures in a 7-win streak
Rank 5	A 7-win streak	3 consecutive failures in a 7-win streak
Rank 6	A 7-win streak	3 consecutive failures in a 7-win streak
Rank 7	A 7-win streak	2 consecutive failures in a 7-win streak
Rank 8	A 7-win streak	2 consecutive failures in a 7-win streak
Rank 9	A 7-win streak	A failure in a 7-win streak
Rank 10	—	A failure in a 7-win streak

Trainer, you have been promoted to Rank 3!

The higher your Rank, the stronger your rivals

Your Rank improves if you win against seven Trainers in a row. You can battle strong Trainers who have prevailed in fierce battles to reach the same Rank as you.

Techniques for Winning on the Battle Subway

Create a balanced team with Pokémon that can have an edge in battles

Two to four Pokémon can participate in the Battle Subway. So you need to plan carefully which Pokémon you use and moves that you teach them. Master these important elements to keep winning.

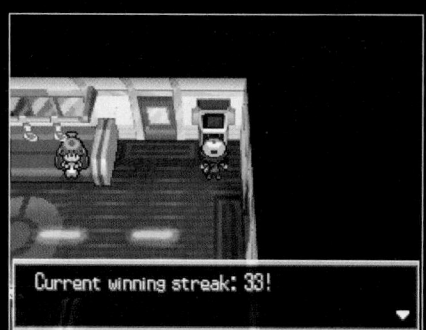

Current winning streak: 33!

BATTLE SUBWAY STRATEGIES   TECHNIQUES FOR WINNING ON THE BATTLE SUBWAY

Battle Subway Techniques 1 — Use Pokémon with high Speed stats

If your Pokémon can act before the opposing Trainer's Pokémon, it can inflict a status condition on it, or make it faint without allowing it to fight back. Choose Pokémon with naturally high Speed stats, and raise them to boost that Speed even higher. Also, it is effective to let a Pokémon hold a Quick Claw.

● Examples of Pokémon with high Speed stats

Serperior	Durant	Accelgor
Grass	Bug / Steel	Bug

Battle Subway Techniques 2 — Prepare various moves and target the opposing Pokémon's weaknesses

Teach moves of various types to one Pokémon. It increases the chances to inflict major damage by targeting the opposing Pokémon's weaknesses, no matter which Pokémon shows up.

● Examples of Pokémon with various-type moves

Druddigon — Dragon

• An example of learned moves

Move	Type
Rock Climb	Normal
Night Slash	Dark
Dragon Tail	Dragon
Superpower	Fighting

Excadrill — Ground / Steel

• An example of learned moves

Move	Type
Slash	Normal
Metal Claw	Steel
Rock Slide	Rock
Earthquake	Ground

Battle Subway Techniques 3 — Get an upper hand in battle with powerful combos

If you use combos that match up powerful moves and effective Abilities, you always have an edge in battle. Inflict major damage on the opposing Pokémon by incorporating a powerful move and get an upper hand in battle.

● An example of a Single Battle combo

Move		Move
Dragon Dance	+	Outrage

Raise its Attack and Speed stats, and use Outrage, which has a power of 120. You can get the first attack and inflict major damage. You could also raise the Attack stat by two levels with Swords Dance.

Haxorus — Dragon

● An example of a Double Battle combo

Move		Type
Earthquake	+	Flying-type

Earthquake's power is strong, but unfortunately it attacks your allied Pokémon, too. However, if you use a Flying-type Pokémon as an ally, Earthquake will damage only the opposing Trainer's Pokémon.

Archeops — Rock / Flying

◎ For more on combos, see p. 224. ▶

Teach Your Pokémon the Ultimate Move

The strongest move of each type is known as an ultimate move. Because these ultimate moves are so powerful, they're not easy to learn—you must have a strong bond with your Pokémon first. If you do have that bond, your Pokémon will soon be using these powerful moves in battles.

Fully evolved forms of the three starter Pokémon

Have a strong bond with your Pokémon and have it learn the ultimate move

The fully evolved forms of the three starter Pokémon—Serperior, Emboar, and Samurott—can learn the ultimate move that matches its type. The Pokémon has to have a very strong bond with you to learn the move. If it does, the old man in the ultimate move tutor's house on Route 13 teaches your Pokémon the move.

Shall I teach them to your Pokémon?

● Pokémon that learn the ultimate moves

• Serperior's ultimate move

Frenzy Plant	Grass

The move's power is 150. The user can't move during the next turn.

• Emboar's ultimate move

Blast Burn	Fire

The move's power is 150. The user can't move during the next turn.

• Samurott's ultimate move

Hydro Cannon	Water

The move's power is 150. The user can't move during the next turn.

Dragon-type Pokémon

A strong bond with your Pokémon helps it learn the strongest move

Dragon-type Pokémon can learn the strongest Dragon-type move, Draco Meteor. The Pokémon has to have a very strong bond with you to learn the move. After you finish the main story, your Pokémon can learn the move in Drayden's house in Opelucid City.

Pokémon Black Version

I can teach you the strongest Dragon-type move!

Pokémon White Version

Drayden: If you wish, I can teach your Pokémon the strongest

● Pokémon that learn the strongest move

Axew	Fraxure	Haxorus	Druddigon	Deino	Zweilous	Hydreigon	Reshiram	Zekrom	Kyurem

• The strongest move for Dragon-type Pokémon

Draco Meteor	Dragon

The move's power is 140. It reduces the user's Sp. Atk by two levels.

Pokémon Musical Strategies

Be a Star in the Pokémon Musical

Become a wonderful stylist and help your Pokémon stand out on stage

The Pokémon Musical in Nimbasa City is a fun event where you put Props on one of your Pokémon and let it dance on stage. Which Prop to choose? How do you make your Pokémon stand out on stage? Test your skills as a stylist.

Learn All About the Pokémon Musical

How to stand out in the Pokémon Musical **1** **Musical Theater is in Nimbasa City**

The bright lights of the Musical Theater shine in the northern part of Nimbasa City—where the Pokémon Musical is held. When you visit it for the first time, you'll receive the Prop Case from the theater owner. After that, your Pokémon can participate in the Pokémon Musical anytime you like.

● Musical Theater

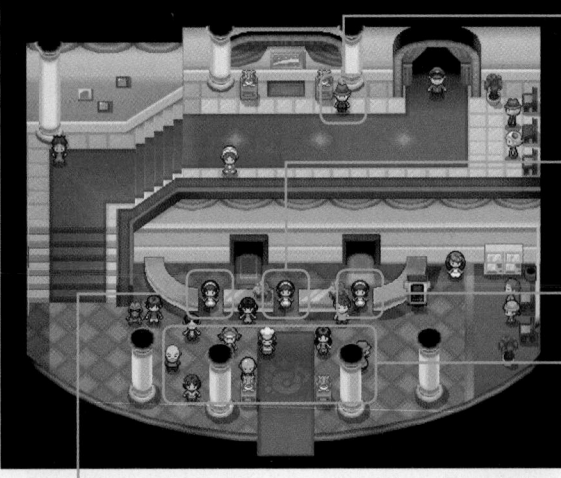

Participating with your friends

Talk to this receptionist when you want to enjoy the Pokémon Musical with your friends through IR or Wireless communications.

Musical Theater Owner

Talk to the owner and he'll give you new Props when you've met certain conditions, such as receiving the highest recognition five times or ten times.

Participating alone

When you want to participate in the Pokémon Musical alone, talk to the receptionist. Other participants will be selected automatically. The more you participate, the better the others become.

The changing room

You can Dress Up your Pokémon without having to participate in the Musical. Come here to see what Props you have and consider which Pokémon should participate.

Fans

After the show, your fans will gather in the reception area. Sometimes you'll receive a Prop when you talk to them. You can have up to ten fans.

Four shows and four styles

Pokémon Musical shows go together with certain prop styles. There are four styles: Cool, Cute, Elegant, and Unique.

Keep in mind which style goes well with which show.

● Shows and their preferred styles

Show **Stardom**

This stage is equipped with a huge monitor and searchlights like the ones for musicians. Up-tempo pop music plays.

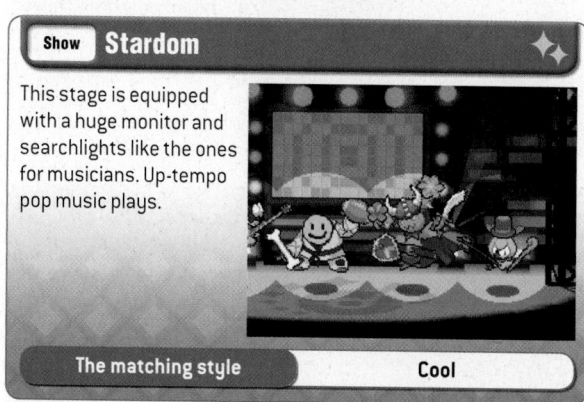

| The matching style | Cool |

Show **Forest Stroll**

Trees and colorful flowers cover the stage. The music is slow and calm. It fits the theme of strolling nicely. It may remind you of a children's song.

| The matching style | Cute |

Show **A Sweet Soirée**

This stage is full of stained-glass windows and expensive furniture. With classical music playing, it has some grown-up style.

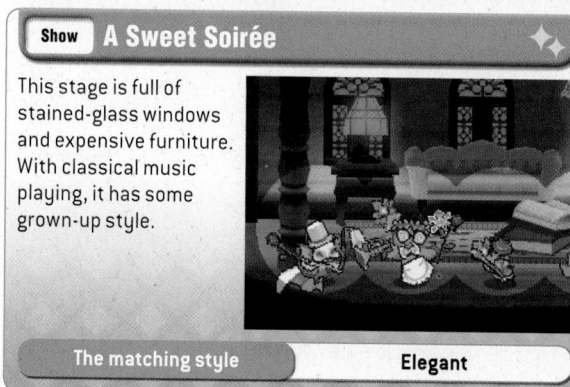

| The matching style | Elegant |

Show **Exciting Nimbasa**

This is a rocky wasteland with the sun setting in the back. Its tango music accentuates the desolateness of the stage.

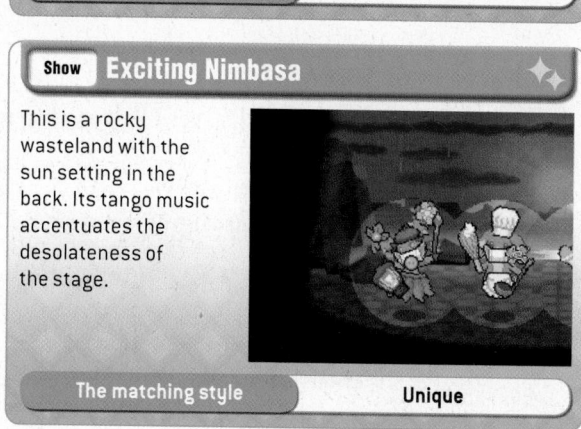

| The matching style | Unique |

The more you try, the more Props you'll receive

The more Props you put on your Pokémon, the more fun it will be to watch. You can obtain Props in three ways, though your fans will give you most of them. Try the Pokémon Musical often and collect all the Props!

● Common ways to pick up new Props

1 After the Pokémon Musical, talk to the fans

Received the Beret!

You may not receive anything if the fans didn't like your Pokémon's performance.

2 Talk to the old man in a house in Opelucid City

Received the Gift Box!

You'll receive four Props. Talk to him every day until you have all four.

3 Talk to the owner when you've tried the Musical often

Received the Crown!

Talk to him after you've received the highest recognition five times and ten times.

How to stand out in the Pokémon Musical **4** | ## Each Prop has its own style

Each Prop you can put on your Pokémon has its own style. You will receive higher recognition when you use the right Props for the show. Check their styles to choose the right ones.

Overall, totally cute!

Check the actual style afterwards

The man to the left of the reception desk will tell you how it went.

● **Props and their styles**

Pirate Hat
● Style
Cool

Tambourine
● Style
Cute

Snow Crystal
● Style
Elegant

Googly Specs
● Style
Unique

See p. 308 for full Prop details. ▶

How to stand out in the Pokémon Musical **5** | ## Dress Up and Appeal are judged

How well you Dress Up your Pokémon with Props and how well it appeals to the audience decide the rating of the overall performance. Check the flow of the Pokémon Musical so you know what to do.

● **The flow of the Pokémon Musical**

Step 1 — **Choose a Pokémon**
Talk to the receptionist and you'll choose which Pokémon will participate in the musical. Choose one from your party.

Step 2 — **Choose the show**
Choose one of the four shows. If you've obtained another show from the Pokémon Global Link, you can choose that one, too (p. 176).

Step 3 — **Dress Up your Pokémon with Props**

Dress Up the Pokémon you selected. Choose from the Props you have to pick the perfect ones for the show. Press "OK!" when you're done with the Props. Check and make sure everything's good—when you press "OK!", the show begins!

OK!

Step 4 — **Appeal to the audience so your Pokémon stands out with its Props**

Check the dancing Pokémon and the other participants once the show begins. You can appeal to the audience if your Pokémon wears a Prop on its arm. Tap the "APPEAL" icon on the Touch Screen to let it rotate or throw its arm Prop to appeal to the audience.

Step 5 — **Receive a Musical Photo and letters from your fans**
When the show is finished, the Musical Photo will be taken. You'll also receive fan letters from the owner.

Dress Up Your Pokémon

Dress Up your Pokémon with the right Props for each show

Dress Up is the most important part of the Pokémon Musical. Which Props your Pokémon wears for which show greatly affects the overall performance. Check your look, and remember how to score high.

OK!

Dress Up Technique 1 **Know how many Props you can put on a Pokémon and where**

There are six body parts for Props: Head, ear, face, arm, body, and waist. For ears and arms, you can put on two Props. Your Pokémon can wear a total of eight Props maximum. As a general rule, the more Props a Pokémon wears, the better its score.

● Prop types and locations

1 Head

There are 23 different Props such as hats. All four styles are available.

2 Ear (two Props)

There are ten different Props such as barrettes and flowers. No "Cool" Props are available.

3 Face

There are nine different Props such as glasses and masks. No "Cute" Props are available.

4 Arm (two Props)

There are 39 different Props such as a wand and a parasol. All four styles are available.

5 Body

There are 14 different Props such as a scarf and ties. No "Unique" Props are available.

6 Waist

There are five different Props such as belts and an apron. No "Cute" Props are available.

Choose the Pokémon that can wear the most Props

Although it depends on the other participants as well, more Props means a better score in general. Some Pokémon can have all eight kinds of Props on them. Choose those Pokémon and put on as many Props as you can.

OK!

Some Pokémon have trouble wearing Props

For example, Pokémon with four feet cannot hold arm Props.

Dress Up Technique **2** | **Learn how to put on Props**

Pokémon Dress Up is done on a special screen where Props are displayed. Learn the screen layout and how to put on Props for a smooth start to the show. Beware that

the Prop images are not shown on this screen. Check p. 308 for effective Dress Up.

● **Dress Up screen**

Prop name

Tap one of the Props and you'll see its name and what body part it goes on.

Scarlet Hat: A Prop that looks nice on the head.

Props you have

A ring of Props you have is shown around your Pokémon. Slide the ring around.

Keep good candidates outside the ring

You can place Props freely outside the ring of Props. It may be a good idea to keep some that you like out of the ring.

Newly obtained Props

When you Dress Up a Pokémon after you obtain a new Prop, "new" is displayed on it.

---

1 | **Slide Props with the stylus to put them on**

Choose one of the ring of Props and slide it onto your Pokémon with the stylus. It'll get put on the right body part. Some Pokémon cannot wear certain types of Props depending on their body shapes. Press "OK" when you are done adding Props.

2 | **Final touch-up**

Final touch-up is done here to check all the Props. Slide the Props left-to-right and adjust their angles.

Before the real show, practice Dress Up in the changing room

Talk to the far-right receptionist at the Musical Theater and you can enter the changing room where you simply enjoy Dress Up. You can use this practice changing room to see which Pokémon should get on stage or what Props you have.

This is a changing room for Dress Up only. Would you like to Dress Up your Pokémon?

▶ Yes
  No
  Info

You can use this room to decide which Pokémon to put on stage

You can also check what Props go on which Pokémon.

How your Props do depends on their style

When putting Props on your Pokémon you should try to choose the right style of Props—and put on as many Props as possible. In addition, the way other participants Dress Up their Pokémon affects your score as well. Keep in mind the rules on how they are evaluated and choose the Props carefully.

● Prop scoring rules

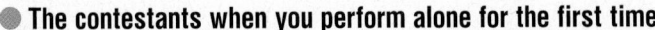

1 Props score high when their style is right for the show

2 Props don't score high when other participants use the same Props

3 When the same Props are used, the Pokémon with more Props will score higher

4 Props score high when no other Pokémon wears the same Prop

● The contestants when you perform alone for the first time

Prop styles: ● Cool ● Cute ● Elegant ● Unique

Show Stardom

Contestant **1** Eugene
- Props
  - Cowboy Hat
  - Crimson Scarf
  - Rose

Contestant **2** Hudson
- Props
  - Fake Bone
  - Football
  - Smiley-Face Mask

Contestant **3** Gilda
- Props
  - Trident
  - Magic Wand
  - Top Hat

Show Forest Stroll

Contestant **1** Linda
- Props
  - Red Flower
  - Green Barrette
  - Gentleman's Hat

Contestant **2** Noa
- Props
  - Pennant
  - Red Barrette
  - Small Barrette

Contestant **3** Amino
- Props
  - Frying Pan
  - Pink Barrette
  - Lace Cap

Show A Sweet Soirée

Contestant **1** Kayla
- Props
  - Paintbrush
  - Green Barrette
  - Red Flower
  - Fedora

Contestant **2** Lima
- Props
  - Red Parasol
  - Scarlet Hat
  - Scarlet Cape

Contestant **3** Leon
- Props
  - Blue Flower
  - Gorgeous Flower
  - Lantern
  - Small Barrette

Show Exciting Nimbasa

Contestant **1** Sedgley
- Props
  - Green Barrette
  - Candy
  - Top Hat
  - Smiley-Face Mask

Contestant **2** Teljin
- Props
  - Racket
  - Blue Flower
  - Square Glasses

Contestant **3** Rose
- Props
  - Microphone
  - Blue Flower
  - Straw Hat
  - Round Button

POKÉMON MUSICAL STRATEGIES ◉ BE A STAR IN THE POKÉMON MUSICAL

Try using the basic Props to Dress Up your Pokémon

You start with 15 Props in your Prop Case. Here are some ideas for how to earn good reviews with those first 15 Props. This is based on the participants data on p. 265. Check it out.

Great work! I saw your Pokémon up there today!

Get good reviews and receive more Props

You can achieve good reviews with just the first 15 Props. If you do well, your fans will give you more Props.

● **Examples of Props that go well with each show**

Prop styles	● Cool ● Cute
	● Elegant ● Unique

Show Stardom

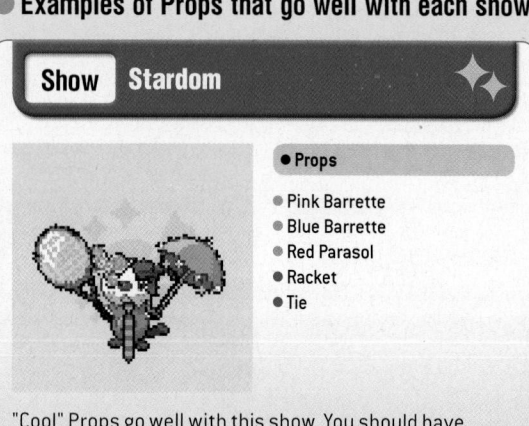

● **Props**
- Pink Barrette
- Blue Barrette
- Red Parasol
- Racket
- Tie

"Cool" Props go well with this show. You should have at least two of them. Only one other participant uses a "Cute" Prop, so have as many of those as you can on your Pokémon for a good review.

Show Forest Stroll

● **Props**
- Blue Barrette
- Small Barrette
- Microphone
- Red Parasol
- Square Glasses
- Top Hat
- Bow Tie

"Cute" Props go well with this show. One of the other participants uses two of them, so your Pokémon should have at least three of them. Put on two more Props of any style for a higher score.

Show A Sweet Soirée

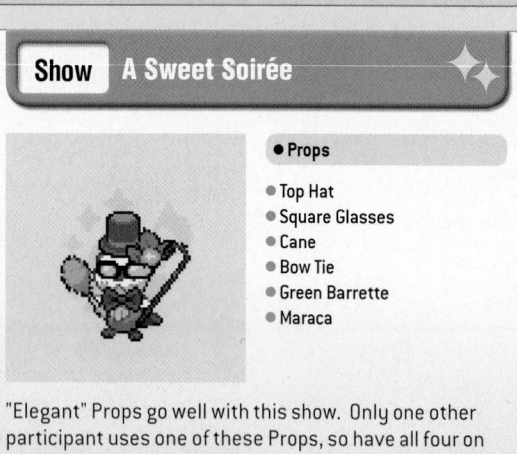

● **Props**
- Top Hat
- Square Glasses
- Cane
- Bow Tie
- Green Barrette
- Maraca

"Elegant" Props go well with this show. Only one other participant uses one of these Props, so have all four on your Pokémon for a good review. Put on two more Props of any style for a higher score, too.

Show Exciting Nimbasa

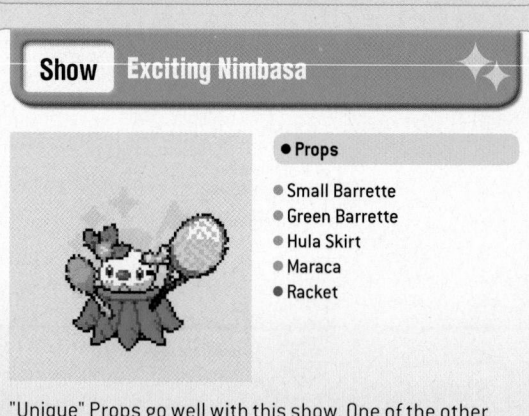

● **Props**
- Small Barrette
- Green Barrette
- Hula Skirt
- Maraca
- Racket

"Unique" Props go well with this show. One of the other participants uses two of them, so your Pokémon should have all three. As for the rest, put on as many Props as possible for even higher reviews.

Eventually, you'll face up to six participants

When you participate alone, you'll initially face the three participants on p. 265. As you keep performing, the number of participants grows and eventually reaches six. Experienced stylists start to appear and it'll be difficult for you to get the best review.

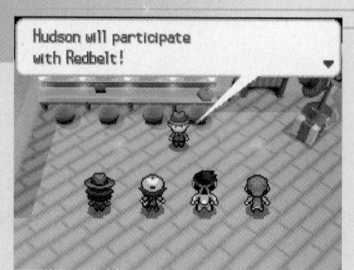

Hudson will participate with Redbelt!

Try it many times and get good reviews

Participate many times to learn what Props other people use.

Give Performances for Good Reviews

Appeal to the audience at the right time

When the Pokémon Dress Up is finished, your Pokémon will go on stage and perform in front of the audience. Your Pokémon can appeal to the audience if it has an arm Prop. Use Props to appeal to the audience and get a good review.

Musical Technique 1 — Appeal to the audience with the arm Props

When they are up on stage, the Pokémon will dance to music and perform the Pokémon Musical. Players are mostly watching the show while their Pokémon dance except that they can appeal to the audience with the arm Props. "APPEAL" will be displayed when your Pokémon is wearing an arm Prop. Tap it and your Pokémon will rotate or throw its arm Prop to appeal to the audience. Learn the rules and use it at the right time.

Pokémon on stage

Pokémon on stage are in spotlights. Sometimes only one Pokémon is in a spotlight.

APPEAL

Tap these icons and your Pokémon will be the only one in the spotlight, getting all the attention from the audience.

● The rules on appealing

 Your Pokémon can appeal to the audience by using the arm Prop.

 A successful appeal is rewarded with the audience's applause.

 When no other Pokémon tries to appeal at the same time as your Pokémon, it'll be successful.

 Musical Technique 2 — Interrupt another Pokémon's appeal

If two appeals happen at the same time, they fail. You can use this rule to interrupt another appeal. When you see another Pokémon starting to appeal, tap "APPEAL." It'll make the Pokémon's appeal fail.

Put on two arm Props

You should have two arm Props on your Pokémon. Use one to appeal to the audience and the second to interrupt another Pokémon's appeal.

After the Pokémon Musical Performance

Check the review with the Musical Photos and fan letters

Exciting Nimbasa

03/06/11

When the Pokémon Musical ends, the Musical Photo is taken. You'll also receive a fan letter from the owner. Check these things to see how well your Pokémon did.

● **After the Pokémon Musical**

 ### The Musical Photo

Forest Stroll

03/06/11

The Musical Photo taken is of the Pokémon that received the best review when it jumped. If you see your Pokémon jumping, the Pokémon Musical was successful. Select "YES" to have the Musical Photo displayed in the Musical Theater. You can only save one photo this way.

 ### A fan letter from the owner

Trainer's Dress Up performance was very unique!

After you take a look at the Musical Photo, you'll come to the backstage area. That's where the owner gives each participant a fan letter. You can tell from the letter what image the Props gave to your Pokémon. Listen carefully to the owner reading the other fan letters and get your Pokémon better prepared for the next show.

 ### Your fans gather in the reception area to give you Props

Your performance... Before I knew what was happening, I was drawn into it.

Your fans are waiting for you in the reception area. Talk to each of them. You can receive new Props from your fans if the review is good enough. The number of Props you receive is not determined by whether your Pokémon did better than others, but by how good the review was. Receiving the best review doesn't mean you receive Props from everyone.

 ### Your Musical Photo on display

There is a Musical Photo saved from last time!

Save the Musical Photo and go take a look at it. Go upstairs to where the owner is. To his left you'll see the Musical Photo displayed. Press the A Button in front of the photo on the wall to see the latest Musical Photo. Keep the photo of your Pokémon jumping from when it received the highest review.

Perform with Your Friends

Compete against your friends in the Pokémon Musical

You can participate in the Pokémon Musical with your friends and family members as well. Compete with each other using the Props you have and see who gets the most attention from the audience. You can receive Props from your fans just like when you participate alone.

● **How it works**

1 Select one of your party Pokémon

Talk to the far-left receptionist and select a Pokémon from your party to participate in the Pokémon Musical.

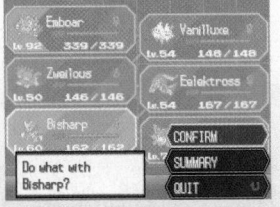

2 Select IR or Wireless communication

You can select either Infrared Connection or wireless communications. Discuss among yourselves to see which communication is better.

3 The leader chooses the show

Choose to become the leader or join as a member. One of you must become the leader, and that leader decides which show to perform.

4 Participate in the Pokémon Musical with your friends

Once everyone's ready, the Pokémon Musical begins. Dress Up your Pokémon and get all the attention from the audience.

 Download a new show

Access the PGL, go to "Customize" and you can download a musical show (p. 176).

 Talk to the owner on your birthday for a special Prop

Talk to the owner on the birthday you set on your Nintendo DS System and you'll receive a Toy Cake. You can also receive a Tiara the first time you play the Musical through Infrared Connection or wireless communications.

On your birthday

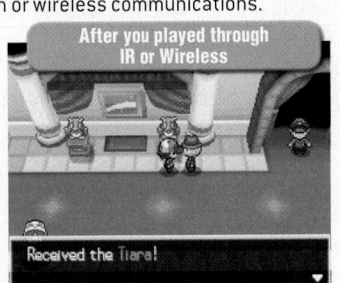
After you played through IR or Wireless

Upgrade Your Trainer Card

Your Trainer Card gets an upgrade each time you rack up a major achievement, such as seeing the ending credits and completing the National Pokédex. With each upgrade, the card changes color. Meet these conditions and show it off to your friends.

The six Trainer Card levels

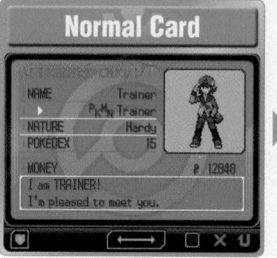

Pokémon Black Version

Pokémon White Version

Level up your Trainer Card

Your Trainer Card levels up whenever you fulfill one of the five conditions below. There's no set order, so you can do these in any order you want. Keep playing Pokémon Black Version and Pokémon White Version to get the Black or White Card—the ultimate Trainer Card!

● How to level up your Trainer Card

1. Defeat Ghetsis in battle and see the ending credits

2. Complete the National Pokédex

3. Obtain the trophies from both the Super Single Train and Super Double Train in the Battle Subway

4. Raise the Black and White levels of your Entree at the Entralink to 30 or above

5. Collect all the Pokémon Musical Props

Watch your Trainer Card change colors as you reach your goals!

Adventure
Data

Pokémon Moves

◆ A

Move	Type	Kind	Pow.	Acc.	PP	Range	Long	DA	Effect
Absorb	GRS	Special	20	100	25	Normal	—	—	Restores HP by up to half of the damage dealt to the target.
Acid	PSN	Special	40	100	30	Many Others	—	—	A 10% chance of lowering the targets' Sp. Defense by 1. Its power is weaker when it hits multiple Pokémon.
Acid Armor	PSN	Status	—	—	40	Self	—	—	Raises the user's Defense by 2.
Acid Spray	PSN	Status	40	100	20	Normal	—	—	Lowers the target's Sp. Defense by 2.
Acrobatics	FLY	Physical	55	100	15	Normal	○	○	If the user isn't holding an item, this attack's power is doubled.
Acupressure	NRM	Status	—	—	30	Self/Ally	—	—	Raises a random stat by 2.
Aerial Ace	FLY	Physical	60	—	20	Normal	○	○	A sure hit.
Aeroblast	FLY	Special	100	95	5	Normal	○	—	Critical hits land more easily.
After You	NRM	Status	—	—	15	Normal	—	—	The user helps the target and makes it use its move right after the user, regardless of its Speed. It fails if the target was going to use its move right after anyway, or if the target has already used its move this turn.
Agility	PSY	Status	—	—	30	Self	—	—	Raises the user's Speed by 2.
Air Cutter	FLY	Special	55	95	25	Many Others	—	—	Critical hits land more easily. Its power is weaker when it hits multiple Pokémon.
Air Slash	FLY	Special	75	95	20	Normal	○	—	A 30% chance of making the target flinch (unable to use moves on that turn).
Ally Switch	PSY	Status	—	—	15	Self	—	—	The user switches places with an ally. It fails if the user is in the middle (works only when the target is on the other end).
Amnesia	PSY	Status	—	—	20	Self	—	—	Raises the user's Sp. Defense by 2.
AncientPower	RCK	Special	60	100	5	Normal	—	—	A 10% chance of raising the user's Attack, Defense, Speed, Sp. Attack, and Sp. Defense stats by 1.
Aqua Jet	WTR	Physical	40	100	20	Normal	—	○	Always strikes first (the user with the higher Speed goes first if similar moves are used).
Aqua Ring	WTR	Status	—	—	20	Self	—	—	Restores a little HP every turn.
Aqua Tail	WTR	Physical	90	90	10	Normal	—	○	A regular attack.
Arm Thrust	FTG	Physical	15	100	20	Normal	—	○	Attacks 2–5 times in a row.
Aromatherapy	GRS	Status	—	—	5	Your Party	—	—	Heals status conditions of all your Pokémon, including those in your party.
Assist	NRM	Status	—	—	20	Self	—	—	Uses a random move from one of the Pokémon in your party.
Assurance	DRK	Physical	50	100	10	Normal	—	○	If the target has already taken some damage in the same turn, this attack's power is doubled.
Astonish	GHO	Physical	30	100	15	Normal	—	○	A 30% chance of making the target flinch (unable to use moves on that turn).
Attack Order	BUG	Physical	90	100	15	Normal	—	—	Critical hits land more easily.
Attract	NRM	Status	—	100	15	Normal	—	—	Leaves the target unable to attack 50% of the time. Only works if the user and the target are of different genders.
Aura Sphere	FTG	Special	90	—	20	Normal	○	—	A sure hit.
Aurora Beam	ICE	Special	65	100	20	Normal	—	—	A 10% chance of lowering the target's Attack by 1.
Autotomize	STL	Status	—	—	15	Self	—	—	Raises the user's Speed by 2 and lowers its weight by 220 lb.
Avalanche	ICE	Physical	60	100	10	Normal	—	○	Its power is doubled if the user has taken damage from the target that turn.

◆ B

Move	Type	Kind	Pow.	Acc.	PP	Range	Long	DA	Effect
Barrage	NRM	Physical	15	85	20	Normal	—	—	Attacks 2–5 times in a row.
Barrier	PSY	Status	—	—	30	Self	—	—	Raises the user's Defense by 2.
Baton Pass	NRM	Status	—	—	40	Self	—	—	Swaps out with an ally Pokémon and passes along any stat changes.
Beat Up	DRK	Physical	—	100	10	Normal	—	—	Attacks once for each Pokémon in your party, including the user. Does not count Pokémon that have fainted or have status conditions.
Belly Drum	NRM	Status	—	—	10	Self	—	—	The user loses half its max HP, but raises its Attack to the maximum.
Bestow	NRM	Status	—	—	15	Normal	—	—	If the target is not holding an item and the user is, the user can give that item to the target. Fails if the user is not holding an item or the target is holding an item.
Bide	NRM	Physical	—	—	10	Self	—	○	Inflicts twice the damage received in the next 2 turns. Cannot choose moves those 2 turns.
Bind	NRM	Physical	15	85	20	Normal	—	○	Inflicts damage over 4–5 turns. The target cannot flee during that time.
Bite	DRK	Physical	60	100	25	Normal	—	○	A 30% chance of making the target flinch (unable to use moves on that turn).
Blast Burn	FIR	Special	150	90	5	Normal	—	—	The user can't move during the next turn. If the target is Frozen, it will be thawed.
Blaze Kick	FIR	Physical	85	90	10	Normal	—	○	A 10% chance of inflicting the Burned condition on the target. If the target is Frozen, it will be thawed. Critical hits land more easily.
Blizzard	ICE	Special	120	70	5	Many Others	—	—	A 10% chance of inflicting the Frozen status condition. Its power is weaker when it hits multiple Pokémon.
Block	NRM	Status	—	—	5	Normal	—	—	The target can't escape. If used in a Trainer battle, it prevents the opposing Trainer from switching out a Pokémon.
Blue Flare	FIR	Special	130	85	5	Normal	—	—	A 20% chance of inflicting the Burned status condition.
Body Slam	NRM	Physical	85	100	15	Normal	—	—	A 30% chance of inflicting Paralysis on the target.
Bolt Strike	ELC	Physical	130	85	5	Normal	—	○	A 20% chance of inflicting Paralysis on the target.
Bone Club	GRD	Physical	65	85	20	Normal	—	○	A 10% chance of making the target flinch (unable to use moves on that turn).
Bone Rush	GRD	Physical	25	90	10	Normal	—	—	Attacks 2–5 times in a row.
Bonemerang	GRD	Physical	50	90	10	Normal	—	—	Attacks twice in a row in a single turn.
Bounce	FLY	Physical	85	85	5	Normal	○	○	The user flies into the air on the first turn and attacks on the second. A 30% chance of inflicting Paralysis on the target.
Brave Bird	FLY	Physical	120	100	15	Normal	○	○	The user takes 1/3 of the damage inflicted.
Brick Break	FTG	Physical	75	100	15	Normal	—	○	This move is not affected by Reflect. It removes the effect of Reflect and Light Screen.
Brine	WTR	Special	65	100	10	Normal	—	—	This move's power doubles if the targets' HP is half or below.
Bubble	WTR	Special	20	100	30	Many Others	—	—	A 10% chance of lowering the targets' Speed by 1. Its power is weaker when it hits multiple Pokémon.
BubbleBeam	WTR	Special	65	100	20	Normal	—	—	A 10% chance of lowering the target's Speed by 1.
Bug Bite	BUG	Physical	60	100	20	Normal	—	○	If the target is holding a Berry with a battle effect, the user eats that Berry and uses its effect.
Bug Buzz	BUG	Special	90	100	10	Normal	—	—	A 10% chance of lowering the target's Sp. Defense by 1.

Move	Type	Kind	Pow.	Acc.	PP	Range	Long	DA	Effect
Bulk Up	FTG	Status	—	—	20	Self	—	—	Raises the user's Attack and Defense by 1.
Bulldoze	GRD	Physical	60	100	20	Adjacent	—	—	Lowers the targets' Speed by 1. Its power is weaker when it hits multiple Pokémon.
Bullet Punch	STL	Physical	40	100	30	Normal	—	○	Always strikes first (the user with the higher Speed goes first if similar moves are used).
Bullet Seed	GRS	Physical	25	100	30	Normal	—	—	Attacks 2–5 times in a row.

◈ C

Move	Type	Kind	Pow.	Acc.	PP	Range	Long	DA	Effect
Calm Mind	PSY	Status	—	—	20	Self	—	—	Raises the user's Sp. Attack and Sp. Defense by 1.
Camouflage	NRM	Status	—	—	20	Self	—	—	Changes the user's type to match the environment. Tall grass/Lawn: Grass type. Path/Sand/Entralink/Swamp: Ground type. Cave: Rock type. Water surface/Puddle/Shoal: Water type. Snow/Ice: Ice type. Indoors: Normal type.
Captivate	NRM	Status	—	100	20	Many Others	—	—	Lowers the targets' Sp. Attack by 2. Only works if the user and the target are of different genders.
Charge	ELC	Status	—	—	20	Self	—	—	Doubles attack power of an Electric-type move used the next turn. Raises the user's Sp. Defense by 1.
Charge Beam	ELC	Special	50	90	10	Normal	—	—	A 70% chance of raising the user's Sp. Attack by 1.
Charm	NRM	Status	—	100	20	Normal	—	—	Lowers the target's Attack by 2.
Chatter	FLY	Special	60	100	20	Normal	○	—	May inflict the Confused status condition on the target. Chance depends on the volume of the sound you recorded (Chatot only).
Chip Away	NRM	Physical	70	100	20	Normal	—	○	The target's stat changes don't affect this move.
Circle Throw	FTG	Physical	60	90	10	Normal	—	○	Attacks and then ends wild Pokémon battles. In a Double Battle with wild Pokémon or if the wild Pokémon's level is higher than the user's, there is no additional effect. In a battle with a Trainer, this move forces another Pokémon to switch in. If there is no Pokémon to switch in, no additional effect takes place.
Clamp	WTR	Physical	35	85	15	Normal	—	○	Inflicts damage over 4–5 turns. The target cannot flee during that time.
Clear Smog	PSN	Special	50	—	15	Normal	—	—	Eliminates every stat change of the target.
Close Combat	FTG	Physical	120	100	5	Normal	—	○	Lowers the user's Defense and Sp. Defense by 1.
Coil	PSN	Status	—	—	20	Self	—	—	Raises Attack, Defense, and accuracy by 1.
Comet Punch	NRM	Physical	18	85	15	Normal	—	○	Attacks 2–5 times in a row.
Confuse Ray	GHO	Status	—	100	10	Normal	—	—	Inflicts the Confused status condition on the target.
Confusion	PSY	Special	50	100	25	Normal	—	—	A 10% chance of inflicting the Confused status condition on the target.
Constrict	NRM	Physical	10	100	35	Normal	—	○	A 10% chance of lowering the target's Speed by 1.
Conversion	NRM	Status	—	—	30	Self	—	—	Changes the user's type to that of one of its moves.
Conversion 2	NRM	Status	—	—	30	Normal	—	—	Changes the user's type to one that is strong against the last move the target used.
Copycat	NRM	Status	—	—	20	Self	—	—	Uses the last move used.
Cosmic Power	PSY	Status	—	—	20	Self	—	—	Raises the user's Defense and Sp. Defense by 1.
Cotton Guard	GRS	Status	—	—	10	Self	—	—	Raises the user's Defense by 3.
Cotton Spore	GRS	Status	—	100	40	Normal	—	—	Lowers the target's Speed by 2.
Counter	FTG	Physical	—	100	20	Varies	—	○	If the user is attacked physically, this move inflicts twice the damage done to the user. Always strikes last.
Covet	NRM	Physical	60	100	40	Normal	—	○	When the target is holding an item and the user is not, the user can steal that item. A regular attack if the target is not holding an item.
Crabhammer	WTR	Physical	90	90	10	Normal	—	○	Critical hits land more easily.
Cross Chop	FTG	Physical	100	80	5	Normal	—	○	Critical hits land more easily.
Cross Poison	PSN	Physical	70	100	20	Normal	—	○	Critical hits land more easily. A 10% chance of inflicting Poison on the target.
Crunch	DRK	Physical	80	100	15	Normal	—	○	A 20% chance of lowering the target's Defense by 1.
Crush Claw	NRM	Physical	75	95	10	Normal	—	○	A 50% chance of lowering the target's Defense by 1.
Crush Grip	NRM	Physical	—	100	5	Normal	—	○	The more HP the target has left, the higher the power of this attack (maximum power: 120).
Curse	GHO	Status	—	—	10	Varies	—	—	Lowers the user's Speed by 1 and raises its Attack and Defense by 1. If used by a Ghost-type Pokémon, the user loses half its max HP, but lowers the target's HP by 1/4 of maximum every turn.
Cut	NRM	Physical	50	95	30	Normal	—	○	A regular attack.

◈ D

Move	Type	Kind	Pow.	Acc.	PP	Range	Long	DA	Effect
Dark Pulse	DRK	Special	80	100	15	Normal	○	—	A 20% chance of making the target flinch (unable to use moves on that turn).
Dark Void	DRK	Status	—	80	10	Many Others	—	—	Inflicts the Sleep status condition on the targets.
Defend Order	BUG	Status	—	—	10	Self	—	—	Raises the user's Defense and Sp. Defense by 1.
Defense Curl	NRM	Status	—	—	40	Self	—	—	Raises the user's Defense by 1.
Defog	FLY	Status	—	—	15	Normal	—	—	Lowers the target's evasion by 1. Nullifies the effects of Light Screen, Reflect, Safeguard, Mist, Spikes, Toxic Spikes, and Stealth Rock on the target's side.
Destiny Bond	GHO	Status	—	—	5	Self	—	—	If the user faints due to damage from a Pokémon, that Pokémon faints as well.
Detect	FTG	Status	—	—	5	Self	—	—	The user evades all attacks that turn. If used in succession, its chance of failing rises.
Dig	GRD	Physical	80	100	10	Normal	—	○	The user burrows underground on the first turn and attacks on the second.
Disable	NRM	Status	—	100	20	Normal	—	—	The target can't use the move it just used for 4 turns.
Discharge	ELC	Special	80	100	15	Adjacent	—	—	This move has a 30% chance of inflicting Paralysis on the targets. Its power is weaker when it hits multiple Pokémon.
Dive	WTR	Physical	80	100	10	Normal	—	○	Dives deep on the first turn and attacks on the second.
Dizzy Punch	NRM	Physical	70	100	10	Normal	—	○	A 20% chance of inflicting Confused status condition.
Doom Desire	STL	Special	140	100	5	Normal	—	—	Attacks the target after 2 turns. This move is affected by the target's type.
Double Hit	NRM	Physical	35	90	10	Normal	—	○	Attacks twice in a row in a single turn.
Double Kick	FTG	Physical	30	100	30	Normal	—	○	Attacks twice in a row in a single turn.

D

Move	Type	Kind	Pow.	Acc.	PP	Range	Long	DA	Effect
Double Team	NRM	Status	—	—	15	Self	—	—	Raises the user's evasion by 1.
Double-Edge	NRM	Physical	120	100	15	Normal	—	○	The user takes 1/3 of the damage inflicted.
DoubleSlap	NRM	Physical	15	85	10	Normal	—	○	Attacks 2–5 times in a row.
Draco Meteor	DRG	Special	140	90	5	Normal	—	—	Lowers the user's Sp. Attack by 2.
Dragon Claw	DRG	Physical	80	100	15	Normal	—	○	A regular attack.
Dragon Dance	DRG	Status	—	—	20	Self	—	—	Raises the user's Attack and Speed by 1.
Dragon Pulse	DRG	Special	90	100	10	Normal	○	—	A regular attack.
Dragon Rage	DRG	Special	—	100	10	Normal	—	—	Deals a fixed 40 points of damage.
Dragon Rush	DRG	Physical	100	75	10	Normal	—	○	A 20% chance of making the target flinch (unable to use moves on that turn).
Dragon Tail	DRG	Physical	60	90	10	Normal	—	○	Attacks and then ends wild Pokémon battles. In a Double Battle with wild Pokémon or if the wild Pokémon's level is higher than the user's, there is no additional effect. In a battle with a Trainer, this move forces another Pokémon to switch in. If there is no Pokémon to switch in, no additional effect takes place.
DragonBreath	DRG	Special	60	100	20	Normal	—	—	A 30% chance of inflicting the Paralysis status condition on the target.
Drain Punch	FTG	Physical	75	100	10	Normal	—	○	Restores HP by up to half of the damage dealt to the target.
Dream Eater	PSY	Special	100	100	15	Normal	—	—	Only works when the target is asleep. Restores HP by up to half of the damage dealt to the target.
Drill Peck	FLY	Physical	80	100	20	Normal	○	○	A regular attack.
Drill Run	GRD	Physical	80	95	10	Normal	—	○	Critical hits land more easily.
Dual Chop	DRG	Physical	40	90	15	Normal	—	○	Attacks twice in a row in a single turn.
DynamicPunch	FTG	Physical	100	50	5	Normal	—	○	Inflicts Confused status condition.

E

Move	Type	Kind	Pow.	Acc.	PP	Range	Long	DA	Effect
Earth Power	GRD	Special	90	100	10	Normal	—	—	A 10% chance of lowering the target's Sp. Defense by 1.
Earthquake	GRD	Physical	100	100	10	Adjacent	—	—	Does double damage to the targets using Dig. Its power is weaker when it hits multiple Pokémon.
Echoed Voice	NRM	Special	40	100	15	Normal	—	—	If this move is used every turn, no matter which Pokémon uses it, its power increases (max. 200). If no Pokémon uses it in a turn, the power returns to normal.
Egg Bomb	NRM	Physical	100	75	10	Normal	—	—	A regular attack.
Electro Ball	ELC	Special	—	100	10	Normal	—	—	The faster the user is than the target, the greater the attack's power (max. 150).
Electroweb	ELC	Special	55	95	15	Many Others	—	—	Lowers the targets' Speed by 1. Its power is weaker when it hits multiple Pokémon.
Embargo	DRK	Status	—	100	15	Normal	—	—	The target can't use items for 5 turns. The Trainer also can't use items on that Pokémon.
Ember	FIR	Special	40	100	25	Normal	—	—	A 10% chance of inflicting the Burned status condition on the target. If the target is Frozen, it will be thawed.
Encore	NRM	Status	—	100	5	Normal	—	—	The target is forced to keep using the last move it used. This effect lasts 3 turns.
Endeavor	NRM	Physical	—	100	5	Normal	—	○	Inflicts damage equal to the target's HP minus the user's HP.
Endure	NRM	Status	—	—	10	Self	—	—	Leaves the user with 1 HP when hit by a move that would KO it. If used in succession, its chance of failing rises.
Energy Ball	GRS	Special	80	100	10	Normal	—	—	A 10% chance of lowering the target's Sp. Defense by 1.
Entrainment	NRM	Status	—	100	15	Normal	—	—	Makes the target's Ability the same as the user's. It does not change certain Abilities, such as Truant.
Eruption	FIR	Special	150	100	5	Many Others	—	—	If the user's HP is low, this move has lower attack power. If the targets are Frozen, they will be thawed. This move's power is weaker when it hits multiple Pokémon.
Explosion	NRM	Physical	250	100	5	Adjacent	—	—	The user faints after using it. Its power is weaker when it hits multiple Pokémon.
Extrasensory	PSY	Special	80	100	30	Normal	—	—	A 10% chance of making the target flinch (unable to use moves on that turn).
ExtremeSpeed	NRM	Physical	80	100	5	Normal	—	○	Always strikes first. Faster than other moves that strike first, except Fake Out. (If two Pokémon use this move, the one with higher Speed goes first.)

F

Move	Type	Kind	Pow.	Acc.	PP	Range	Long	DA	Effect
Facade	NRM	Physical	70	100	20	Normal	—	○	This move's power is doubled if the user has a Paralysis, Poison, or Burned status condition.
Faint Attack	DRK	Physical	60	—	20	Normal	—	○	A sure hit.
Fake Out	NRM	Physical	40	100	10	Normal	—	○	Always strikes first and makes the target flinch (unable to use moves on that turn). Only works on the turn the user is sent out.
Fake Tears	DRK	Status	—	100	20	Normal	—	—	Lowers the target's Sp. Defense by 2.
False Swipe	NRM	Physical	40	100	40	Normal	—	○	Always leaves 1 HP, even if the damage would have made the target faint.
FeatherDance	FLY	Status	—	100	15	Normal	—	—	Lowers the target's Attack by 2.
Feint	NRM	Physical	30	100	10	Normal	—	—	Can hit targets using Protect, Detect, Quick Guard, or Wide Guard, and eliminates the effects of those moves.
Fiery Dance	FIR	Special	80	100	10	Normal	—	—	A 50% chance of raising the user's Sp. Attack by 1.
Final Gambit	FTG	Special	—	100	5	Normal	—	○	Does damage to the target equal to the user's remaining HP. If the move lands, the user faints.
Fire Blast	FIR	Special	120	85	5	Normal	—	—	This move has a 10% chance of inflicting the Burned status condition on the target. If the target is Frozen, it will be thawed.
Fire Fang	FIR	Physical	65	95	15	Normal	—	○	A 10% chance of inflicting the Burned status condition or making the target flinch (unable to use moves on that turn). If the target is Frozen, it will be thawed.

POKÉMON MOVES ◈ ADVENTURE DATA

Move	Type	Kind	Pow.	Acc.	PP	Range	Long	DA	Effect
Fire Pledge	FIR	Special	50	100	10	Normal	—	—	When combined with Water Pledge or Grass Pledge, the power and effect change. If it is combined with Water Pledge, the power is 150 and it becomes a Water-type move. It will create a rainbow that turn that lasts for the next 3 turns and makes it more likely that your team's moves will have additional effects. If it is combined with Grass Pledge, the power is 150. The surrounding area will become a sea of fire that damages opposing Pokémon, except Fire types, that turn and the next 3 turns.
Fire Punch	FIR	Physical	75	100	15	Normal	—	○	A 10% chance of inflicting the Burned status condition on the target. If the target is Frozen, it will be thawed.
Fire Spin	FIR	Special	35	85	15	Normal	—	—	Inflicts damage and prevents the target from fleeing over 4–5 turns. If the target is Frozen, it will be thawed.
Fissure	GRD	Physical	—	30	5	Normal	—	—	The target faints with one hit if the user's level is equal to or greater than the target's level. The higher the user's level is compared to the target's, the more accurate it is.
Flail	NRM	Physical	—	100	15	Normal	—	○	The lower the user's HP is, the more damage this move does to the target.
Flame Burst	FIR	Special	70	100	15	Normal	—	—	In Double Battles and Triple Battles, it damages the Pokémon next to the target as well.
Flame Charge	FIR	Physical	50	100	20	Normal	—	○	Raises the user's Speed by 1.
Flame Wheel	FIR	Physical	60	100	25	Normal	—	○	A 10% chance of inflicting the Burned status condition on the target. If the target is Frozen, it will be thawed. This move can be used even if the user is Frozen. If the user is Frozen, this also thaws the user.
Flamethrower	FIR	Special	95	100	15	Normal	—	—	A 10% chance of inflicting the Burned status condition on the target. If the target is Frozen, it will be thawed.
Flare Blitz	FIR	Physical	120	100	15	Normal	—	○	The user takes 1/3 of the damage inflicted. A 10% chance of inflicting Burned status condition. If the target is Frozen, it will be thawed. This move can be used even if the user is Frozen. If the user is Frozen, this also thaws the user.
Flash	NRM	Status	—	100	20	Normal	—	—	Lowers the target's accuracy by 1.
Flash Cannon	STL	Special	80	100	10	Normal	—	—	A 10% chance of lowering the target's Sp. Defense by 1.
Flatter	DRK	Status	—	100	15	Normal	—	—	Inflicts the Confused status condition on the target, but raises its Sp. Attack by 1.
Fling	DRK	Physical	—	100	10	Normal	—	—	The user attacks by throwing its held item at the target. Power and effect varies depending on the item.
Fly	FLY	Physical	90	95	15	Normal	○	○	The user flies into the air on the first turn and attacks on the second.
Focus Blast	FTG	Special	120	70	5	Normal	—	—	A 10% chance of lowering the target's Sp. Defense by 1.
Focus Energy	NRM	Status	—	—	30	Self	—	—	Heightens the critical-hit ratio of the user's subsequent moves.
Focus Punch	FTG	Physical	150	100	20	Normal	—	○	Always strikes last. The move misses if the user is hit before this move lands.
Follow Me	NRM	Status	—	—	20	Self	—	—	This move is given priority. Opposing Pokémon aim only at the user.
Force Palm	FTG	Physical	60	100	10	Normal	—	○	A 30% chance of inflicting Paralysis status condition on the target.
Foresight	NRM	Status	—	—	40	Normal	—	—	Attacks land easily regardless of the target's evasion. Makes Ghost-type Pokémon vulnerable to Normal- and Fighting-type moves.
Foul Play	DRK	Physical	95	100	15	Normal	—	○	The user turns the target's power against it. Damage varies depending on the target's Attack and Defense.
Frenzy Plant	GRS	Special	150	90	5	Normal	—	—	The user can't move during the next turn.
Frost Breath	ICE	Special	40	90	10	Normal	—	—	Always results in a critical hit.
Frustration	NRM	Physical	—	100	20	Normal	—	○	The lower the user's friendship, the higher the attack's power.
Fury Attack	NRM	Physical	15	85	20	Normal	—	○	Attacks 2–5 times in a row.
Fury Cutter	BUG	Physical	20	95	20	Normal	—	○	This move doubles in power every time it strikes (up to 5 strikes). Power returns to normal once it misses.
Fury Swipes	NRM	Physical	18	80	15	Normal	—	○	Attacks 2–5 times in a row.
Fusion Bolt	ELC	Physical	100	100	5	Normal	—	—	Its power doubles if used immediately after Fusion Flare.
Fusion Flare	FIR	Special	100	100	5	Normal	—	—	Its power doubles if used immediately after Fusion Bolt.
Future Sight	PSY	Special	100	100	10	Normal	—	—	Attacks the target after 2 turns. This move is affected by the target's type.

◈ **G**

Move	Type	Kind	Pow.	Acc.	PP	Range	Long	DA	Effect
Gastro Acid	PSN	Status	—	100	10	Normal	—	—	Disables the target's Ability.
Gear Grind	STL	Physical	50	85	15	Normal	—	○	Attacks twice in a row in a single turn.
Giga Drain	GRS	Special	75	100	10	Normal	—	—	Restores HP by up to half of the damage dealt to the target.
Giga Impact	NRM	Physical	150	90	5	Normal	—	○	The user can't move during the next turn.
Glaciate	ICE	Special	65	95	10	Many Others	—	—	Lowers the targets' Speed by 1. Its power is weaker when it hits multiple Pokémon.
Glare	NRM	Status	—	90	30	Normal	—	—	Inflicts the Paralysis status condition.
Grass Knot	GRS	Special	—	100	20	Normal	—	○	Has higher attack power against heavier targets.
Grass Pledge	GRS	Special	50	100	10	Normal	—	—	When combined with Water Pledge or Fire Pledge, the power and effect change. If it is combined with Water Pledge, the power is 150. The surrounding area will become a swamp, which lowers the Speed of opposing Pokémon that turn that lasts for the next 3 turns. If it is combined with Fire Pledge, the power is 150 and it becomes a Fire-type move. The surrounding area will become a sea of fire that damages opposing Pokémon, except Fire types, that turn and the next 3 turns.
GrassWhistle	GRS	Status	—	55	15	Normal	—	—	Inflicts Sleep status condition on the target.
Gravity	PSY	Status	—	—	5	Both Sides	—	—	Raises the accuracy of all Pokémon in battle for 5 turns. Ground-type moves will now hit a Pokémon with Levitate Ability or a Flying-type Pokémon. Prevents use of Fly, Splash, Bounce, and Magnet Rise. Pulls any airborne Pokémon to the ground.
Growl	NRM	Status	—	100	40	Many Others	—	—	Lowers the targets' Attack by 1.
Growth	NRM	Status	—	—	40	Self	—	—	Raises the user's Attack and Sp. Attack by 1. Raises them by 2 when the weather condition is Sunny.
Grudge	GHO	Status	—	—	5	Self	—	—	If the user faints because of a move, that move's PP drops to 0.
Guard Split	PSY	Status	—	—	10	Normal	—	—	The user and the target's Defense and Sp. Defense are added up, then divided equally between them.

G

Move	Type	Kind	Pow.	Acc.	PP	Range	Long	DA	Effect
Guard Swap	PSY	Status	—	—	10	Normal	—	—	Swaps Defense and Sp. Defense changes between the user and the target.
Guillotine	NRM	Physical	—	30	5	Normal	—	○	The target faints with one hit if the user's level is equal to or greater than the target's level. The higher the user's level is compared to the target's, the more accurate it is.
Gunk Shot	PSN	Physical	120	70	5	Normal	—	—	A 30% chance of inflicting Poison status condition.
Gust	FLY	Special	40	100	35	Normal	○	—	Does twice the usual damage if the target is using Fly or Bounce when it hits.
Gyro Ball	STL	Physical	—	100	5	Normal	—	○	The slower the user is than the target, the greater the attack's power (max. 150).

H

Move	Type	Kind	Pow.	Acc.	PP	Range	Long	DA	Effect
Hail	ICE	Status	—	—	10	Both Sides	—	—	Changes the weather condition to Hail for 5 turns, damaging all Pokémon except Ice types every turn.
Hammer Arm	FTG	Physical	100	90	10	Normal	—	○	Lowers the user's Speed by 1.
Harden	NRM	Status	—	—	30	Self	—	—	Raises the user's Defense by 1.
Haze	ICE	Status	—	—	30	Both Sides	—	—	Restores the stats of all Pokémon to their original state.
Head Charge	NRM	Physical	120	100	15	Normal	—	○	The user takes 1/4 of the damage inflicted.
Head Smash	RCK	Physical	150	80	5	Normal	—	○	The user takes 1/2 of the damage inflicted.
Headbutt	NRM	Physical	70	100	15	Normal	—	○	A 30% chance of making the target flinch (unable to use moves on that turn).
Heal Bell	NRM	Status	—	—	5	Your Party	—	—	Heals status conditions of all your Pokémon, including those in your party.
Heal Block	PSY	Status	—	100	15	Many Others	—	—	Targets cannot have HP restored by moves, etc. for 5 turns.
Heal Order	BUG	Status	—	—	10	Self	—	—	Restores HP by up to half of the user's max HP.
Heal Pulse	PSY	Status	—	—	10	Normal	○	—	Restores HP by up to half of the target's max HP.
Healing Wish	PSY	Status	—	—	10	Self	—	—	The user faints, but fully heals the next Pokémon's HP and status conditions.
Heart Stamp	PSY	Physical	60	100	25	Normal	—	○	A 30% chance of making the target flinch (unable to use moves on that turn).
Heart Swap	PSY	Status	—	—	10	Normal	—	—	Swaps all stat changes between the user and the target.
Heat Crash	FIR	Physical	—	100	10	Normal	—	○	The heavier the user is than the target, the greater the attack's power (max. 120).
Heat Wave	FIR	Special	100	90	10	Many Others	—	—	A 10% chance of inflicting the Burned status condition on the targets. If the targets are Frozen, they will be thawed. Its power is weaker when it hits multiple Pokémon.
Heavy Slam	STL	Physical	—	100	10	Normal	—	○	The heavier the user is than the target, the greater the attack's power (max. 120).
Helping Hand	NRM	Status	—	—	20	1 Ally	—	—	Strengthens an ally's attack power by 50%.
Hex	GHO	Special	50	100	10	Normal	—	—	Deals double the damage to a target affected by status conditions.
Hi Jump Kick	FTG	Physical	130	90	10	Normal	—	○	If this move misses, the user loses half its max HP.
Hidden Power	NRM	Special	—	100	15	Normal	—	—	Type and attack power change depending on the user.
Hone Claws	DRK	Status	—	—	15	Self	—	—	Raises Attack and accuracy by 1.
Horn Attack	NRM	Physical	65	100	25	Normal	—	○	A regular attack.
Horn Drill	NRM	Physical	—	30	5	Normal	—	○	The target faints with one hit if the user's level is equal to or greater than the target's level. The higher the user's level is compared to the target's, the more accurate it is.
Horn Leech	GRS	Physical	75	100	10	Normal	—	○	Restores HP by up to half of the damage dealt to the target.
Howl	NRM	Status	—	—	40	Self	—	—	Raises the user's Attack by 1.
Hurricane	FLY	Special	120	70	10	Normal	○	—	A 30% chance of inflicting Confused status condition. Is 100% accurate in the Rain weather condition, and 50% accurate in the Sunny weather condition. It hits even Pokémon that are in the sky by using moves such as Fly and Bounce.
Hydro Cannon	WTR	Special	150	90	5	Normal	—	—	The user can't move during the next turn.
Hydro Pump	WTR	Special	120	80	5	Normal	—	—	A regular attack.
Hyper Beam	NRM	Special	150	90	5	Normal	—	—	The user can't move during the next turn.
Hyper Fang	NRM	Physical	80	90	15	Normal	—	○	A 10% chance of making the target flinch (unable to use moves on that turn).
Hyper Voice	NRM	Special	90	100	10	Many Others	—	—	Its power is weaker when it hits multiple Pokémon.
Hypnosis	PSY	Status	—	60	20	Normal	—	—	Inflicts Sleep status condition on the target.

I

Move	Type	Kind	Pow.	Acc.	PP	Range	Long	DA	Effect
Ice Ball	ICE	Physical	30	90	20	Normal	—	○	Attacks consecutively over 5 turns or until it misses. Cannot choose other moves. Inflicts greater damage with every successful hit. Inflicts twice the damage if used after Defense Curl.
Ice Beam	ICE	Special	95	100	10	Normal	—	—	A 10% chance of inflicting Frozen status condition.
Ice Fang	ICE	Physical	65	95	15	Normal	—	○	A 10% chance of inflicting Frozen status condition or making the target flinch (unable to use moves on that turn).
Ice Punch	ICE	Physical	75	100	15	Normal	—	○	A 10% chance of inflicting Frozen status condition.
Ice Shard	ICE	Physical	40	100	30	Normal	—	—	Always strikes first. The user with the higher Speed goes first if similar moves are used.
Icicle Crash	ICE	Physical	85	90	10	Normal	—	—	A 30% chance of making the target flinch (unable to use moves on that turn).
Icicle Spear	ICE	Physical	25	100	30	Normal	—	—	Attacks 2–5 times in a row.
Icy Wind	ICE	Special	55	95	15	Many Others	—	—	Lowers the targets' Speed by 1. Its power is weaker when it hits multiple Pokémon.
Imprison	PSY	Status	—	—	10	Self	—	—	Opposing Pokémon cannot use a move if the user knows that move as well.
Incinerate	FIR	Special	30	100	15	Many Others	—	—	Burns up the Berry being held by each of the targets, which makes the Berries unusable. Its power is weaker when it hits multiple Pokémon.
Inferno	FIR	Special	100	50	5	Normal	—	—	Inflicts the Burned status condition.
Ingrain	GRS	Status	—	—	20	Self	—	—	Restores a little HP each turn. The user cannot be switched out after using this move. Ground-type moves will now hit the user even if it is a Flying-type Pokémon or has the Levitate Ability.
Iron Defense	STL	Status	—	—	15	Self	—	—	Raises the user's Defense by 2.

Move	Type	Kind	Pow.	Acc.	PP	Range	Long	DA	Effect
Iron Head	STL	Physical	80	100	15	Normal	—	○	A 30% chance of making the target flinch (unable to use moves on that turn).
Iron Tail	STL	Physical	100	75	15	Normal	—	○	A 30% chance of lowering the target's Defense by 1.

◈ J

Move	Type	Kind	Pow.	Acc.	PP	Range	Long	DA	Effect
Judgment	NRM	Special	100	100	10	Normal	—	—	This move's type changes according to the Plate Arceus is holding.
Jump Kick	FTG	Physical	100	95	10	Normal	—	○	If this move misses, the user loses half its max HP.

◈ K

Move	Type	Kind	Pow.	Acc.	PP	Range	Long	DA	Effect
Karate Chop	FTG	Physical	50	100	25	Normal	—	○	Critical hits land more easily.
Kinesis	PSY	Status	—	80	15	Normal	—	—	Lowers the target's accuracy by 1.
Knock Off	DRK	Physical	20	100	20	Normal	—	○	The target drops its held item. It gets the item back after the battle.

◈ L

Move	Type	Kind	Pow.	Acc.	PP	Range	Long	DA	Effect
Last Resort	NRM	Physical	140	100	5	Normal	—	○	Fails unless the user has used each of its other moves at least once.
Lava Plume	FIR	Special	80	100	15	Adjacent	—	—	This move has a 30% chance of inflicting the Burned status condition on the targets. If the targets are Frozen, they will be thawed. Its power is weaker when it hits multiple Pokémon.
Leaf Blade	GRS	Physical	90	100	15	Normal	—	○	Critical hits land more easily.
Leaf Storm	GRS	Special	140	90	5	Normal	—	—	Lowers the user's Sp. Attack by 2.
Leaf Tornado	GRS	Special	65	90	10	Normal	—	—	A 50% chance of lowering the target's accuracy by 1.
Leech Life	BUG	Physical	20	100	15	Normal	—	○	Restores HP by up to half of the damage dealt to the target.
Leech Seed	GRS	Status	—	90	10	Normal	—	—	Steals HP from the target every turn. Keeps working after the user switches out.
Leer	NRM	Status	—	100	30	Many Others	—	—	Lowers the targets' Defense by 1.
Lick	GHO	Physical	20	100	30	Normal	—	○	A 30% chance of inflicting Paralysis status condition on the target.
Light Screen	PSY	Status	—	—	30	Your Side	—	—	Halves damage to the Pokémon on your side from special moves. Effect lasts 5 turns even if the user is switched out. Effect is weaker in Double Battles and Triple Battles.
Lock-On	NRM	Status	—	—	5	Normal	—	—	The user's next move is a sure hit during the next turn.
Lovely Kiss	NRM	Status	—	75	10	Normal	—	—	Inflicts Sleep status condition on the target.
Low Kick	FTG	Physical	—	100	20	Normal	—	○	The heavier the target, the higher the attack power becomes.
Low Sweep	FTG	Physical	60	100	20	Normal	—	○	Lowers the target's Speed by 1.
Lucky Chant	NRM	Status	—	—	30	Your Side	—	—	The Pokémon on your side take no critical hits for 5 turns.
Lunar Dance	PSY	Status	—	—	10	Self	—	—	The user faints, but fully heals the next Pokémon's HP, PP, and status conditions.
Luster Purge	PSY	Special	70	100	5	Normal	—	—	A 50% chance of lowering the target's Sp. Defense by 1.

◈ M

Move	Type	Kind	Pow.	Acc.	PP	Range	Long	DA	Effect
Mach Punch	FTG	Physical	40	100	30	Normal	—	○	Always strikes first. The user with the higher Speed goes first if similar moves are used.
Magic Coat	PSY	Status	—	—	15	Self	—	—	Reflects moves with effects like Leech Seed or those that inflict the Sleep, Poison, Paralysis, or Confused status conditions.
Magic Room	PSY	Status	—	—	10	Both Sides	—	—	No held items have any effect for 5 turns. Fling cannot be used to throw items while it is in effect.
Magical Leaf	GRS	Special	60	—	20	Normal	—	—	A sure hit.
Magma Storm	FIR	Special	120	75	5	Normal	—	—	Inflicts damage over 4–5 turns. The target cannot flee during that time. If the target is Frozen, it will be thawed.
Magnet Bomb	STL	Physical	60	—	20	Normal	—	—	A sure hit.
Magnet Rise	ELC	Status	—	—	10	Self	—	—	Nullifies Ground-type moves for 5 turns.
Magnitude	GRD	Physical	—	100	30	Adjacent	—	—	Attack power shifts between 10, 30, 50, 70, 90, 110, and 150. Does double damage if the targets are using Dig. Its power is weaker when it hits multiple Pokémon.
Me First	NRM	Status	—	—	20	Varies	—	—	Copies the target's chosen move and uses it with increased power. Fails if it does not strike first.
Mean Look	NRM	Status	—	—	5	Normal	—	—	The target can't escape. If used in a Trainer battle, it prevents the opposing Trainer from switching out a Pokémon.
Meditate	PSY	Status	—	—	40	Self	—	—	Raises the user's Attack by 1.
Mega Drain	GRS	Special	40	100	15	Normal	—	—	Restores HP by up to half of the damage dealt to the target.
Mega Kick	NRM	Physical	120	75	5	Normal	—	○	A regular attack.
Mega Punch	NRM	Physical	80	85	20	Normal	—	○	A regular attack.
Megahorn	BUG	Physical	120	85	10	Normal	—	○	A regular attack.
Memento	DRK	Status	—	100	10	Normal	—	—	The user faints, but the target's Attack and Sp. Attack are lowered by 2.
Metal Burst	STL	Physical	—	100	10	Varies	—	—	Targets the Pokémon that most recently damaged the user with a move. Inflicts 1.5 times the damage taken.
Metal Claw	STL	Physical	50	95	35	Normal	—	○	A 10% chance of raising the user's Attack by 1.
Metal Sound	STL	Status	—	85	40	Normal	—	—	Lowers the target's Sp. Defense by 2.
Meteor Mash	STL	Physical	100	85	10	Normal	—	○	A 20% chance of raising the user's Attack by 1.
Metronome	NRM	Status	—	—	10	Self	—	—	Uses one move randomly chosen from all possible moves.
Milk Drink	NRM	Status	—	—	10	Self	—	—	Restores HP by up to half of the user's max HP.
Mimic	NRM	Status	—	—	10	Normal	—	—	Copies the target's last-used move (copied move has a PP of 5).

M

Move	Type	Kind	Pow.	Acc.	PP	Range	Long	DA	Effect
Mind Reader	NRM	Status	—	—	5	Normal	—	—	The user's next move is a sure hit during the next turn.
Minimize	NRM	Status	—	—	20	Self	—	—	Raises the user's evasion by 2.
Miracle Eye	PSY	Status	—	—	40	Normal	—	—	Attacks land easily regardless of the target's evasion. Dark-type Pokémon become vulnerable to Psychic-type moves.
Mirror Coat	PSY	Special	—	100	20	Varies	—	—	If the user is attacked with a special move, this move inflicts twice the damage. Always strikes last.
Mirror Move	FLY	Status	—	—	20	Normal	—	—	Uses the last move that the target used.
Mirror Shot	STL	Special	65	85	10	Normal	—	—	A 30% chance of lowering the target's accuracy by 1.
Mist	ICE	Status	—	—	30	Your Side	—	—	For 5 turns, this move protects against stat-lowering moves and additional effects.
Mist Ball	PSY	Special	70	100	5	Normal	—	—	A 50% chance of lowering the target's Sp. Attack by 1.
Moonlight	NRM	Status	—	—	5	Self	—	—	Recovers 1/2 of the user's max HP. In Sunny weather, recovers 2/3 of the user's max HP. In Rain/Sandstorm/Hail weather, recovers 1/4 of the user's max HP.
Morning Sun	NRM	Status	—	—	5	Self	—	—	Recovers 1/2 of the user's max HP. In Sunny weather, recovers 2/3 of the user's max HP. In Rain/Sandstorm/Hail weather, recovers 1/4 of the user's max HP.
Mud Bomb	GRD	Special	65	85	10	Normal	—	—	A 30% chance of lowering the target's accuracy by 1.
Mud Shot	GRD	Special	55	95	15	Normal	—	—	Lowers the target's Speed by 1.
Mud Sport	GRD	Status	—	—	15	Both Sides	—	—	As long as the user is in play, the power of Electric-type moves drops to 1/3 of normal.
Muddy Water	WTR	Special	95	85	10	Many Others	—	—	A 30% chance of lowering the targets' accuracy by 1. Its power is weaker when it hits multiple Pokémon.
Mud-Slap	GRD	Special	20	100	10	Normal	—	—	Lowers the target's accuracy by 1.

N

Move	Type	Kind	Pow.	Acc.	PP	Range	Long	DA	Effect
Nasty Plot	DRK	Status	—	—	20	Self	—	—	Raises the user's Sp. Attack by 2.
Natural Gift	NRM	Physical	—	100	15	Normal	—	—	Type and attack power change according to the Berry held by the user. The Berry is consumed when this move is used. This move fails if the user is not holding a Berry.
Nature Power	NRM	Status	—	—	20	Varies	—	—	Move varies depending on the environment. Tall grass/Lawn: Seed Bomb. Path/Sand/Entralink: Earthquake. Cave: Rock Slide. Swamp: Mud Bomb. Water surface/Puddle/Shoal: Hydro Pump. Snow: Blizzard. Ice: Ice Beam. Indoors: Tri Attack.
Needle Arm	GRS	Physical	60	100	15	Normal	—	◯	A 30% chance of making the target flinch (unable to use moves on that turn).
Night Daze	DRK	Special	85	95	10	Normal	—	—	A 40% chance of lowering the target's accuracy by 1.
Night Shade	GHO	Special	—	100	15	Normal	—	—	Deals fixed damage equal to the user's level.
Night Slash	DRK	Physical	70	100	15	Normal	—	◯	Critical hits land more easily.
Nightmare	GHO	Status	—	100	15	Normal	—	—	Lowers the target's HP by 1/4 of maximum every turn. Fails if the target is not asleep.

O

Move	Type	Kind	Pow.	Acc.	PP	Range	Long	DA	Effect
Octazooka	WTR	Special	65	85	10	Normal	—	—	A 50% chance of lowering the target's accuracy by 1.
Odor Sleuth	NRM	Status	—	—	40	Normal	—	—	Attacks land easily regardless of the target's evasion. Ghost-type Pokémon become vulnerable to Normal- and Fighting-type moves.
Ominous Wind	GHO	Special	60	100	5	Normal	—	—	A 10% chance of raising the user's Attack, Defense, Speed, Sp. Attack, and Sp. Defense stats by 1.
Outrage	DRG	Physical	120	100	10	1 Random	—	◯	Attacks consecutively over 2–3 turns. Cannot choose other moves. Then the user becomes Confused.
Overheat	FIR	Special	140	90	5	Normal	—	—	Lowers the user's Sp. Attack by 2. If the target is Frozen, it will be thawed.

P

Move	Type	Kind	Pow.	Acc.	PP	Range	Long	DA	Effect
Pain Split	NRM	Status	—	—	20	Normal	—	—	The user and the target's HP are added, then divided equally between them.
Pay Day	NRM	Physical	40	100	20	Normal	—	—	Increases the prize money received after battle (the user's level, multiplied by number of attacks, multiplied by 5).
Payback	DRK	Physical	50	100	10	Normal	—	◯	Power doubles if the user strikes after the target.
Peck	FLY	Physical	35	100	35	Normal	◯	◯	A regular attack.
Perish Song	NRM	Status	—	—	5	Adjacent	◯	—	All adjacent Pokémon in battle will faint after 3 turns, unless switched out.
Petal Dance	GRS	Special	120	100	10	1 Random	—	◯	Attacks consecutively over 2–3 turns. Cannot choose other moves. Then the user becomes Confused.
Pin Missile	BUG	Physical	14	85	20	Normal	—	—	Attacks 2–5 times in a row.
Pluck	FLY	Physical	60	100	20	Normal	◯	◯	If the target is holding a Berry with a battle effect, the user eats that Berry and uses its effect.
Poison Fang	PSN	Physical	50	100	15	Normal	—	◯	A 30% chance of inflicting the Badly Poisoned condition. Damage from being Badly Poisoned increases with every turn.
Poison Gas	PSN	Status	—	80	40	Many Others	—	—	Inflicts Poison status condition.
Poison Jab	PSN	Physical	80	100	20	Normal	—	◯	A 30% chance of inflicting Poison.
Poison Sting	PSN	Physical	15	100	35	Normal	—	—	A 30% chance of inflicting Poison.
Poison Tail	PSN	Physical	50	100	25	Normal	—	◯	A 10% chance of inflicting Poison. Critical hits land more easily.
PoisonPowder	PSN	Status	—	75	35	Normal	—	—	Inflicts Poison status condition.
Pound	NRM	Physical	40	100	35	Normal	—	◯	A regular attack.
Powder Snow	ICE	Special	40	100	25	Many Others	—	—	A 10% chance of inflicting Frozen status condition. Its power is weaker when it hits multiple Pokémon.
Power Gem	RCK	Special	70	100	20	Normal	—	—	A regular attack.
Power Split	PSY	Status	—	—	10	Normal	—	—	The user and the target's Attack and Sp. Attack are added, then divided equally between them.
Power Swap	PSY	Status	—	—	10	Normal	—	—	Swaps Attack and Sp. Attack changes between the user and the target.
Power Trick	PSY	Status	—	—	10	Self	—	—	Swaps original Attack and Defense stats (does not swap stat changes).
Power Whip	GRS	Physical	120	85	10	Normal	—	◯	A regular attack.

◈ P

Move	Type	Kind	Pow.	Acc.	PP	Range	Long	DA	Effect
Present	NRM	Physical	—	90	15	Normal	—	—	Attack power varies: 40 (40% chance), 80 (30% chance), 120 (10% chance). A 20% chance of healing the target by 1/4 of max HP.
Protect	NRM	Status	—	—	10	Self	—	—	The user evades all attacks that turn. If used in succession, its chance of failing rises.
Psybeam	PSY	Special	65	100	20	Normal	—	—	A 10% chance of inflicting Confused status condition.
Psych Up	NRM	Status	—	—	10	Normal	—	—	Copies the target's stat changes to the user.
Psychic	PSY	Special	90	100	10	Normal	—	—	A 10% chance of lowering the target's Sp. Defense by 1.
Psycho Boost	PSY	Special	140	90	5	Normal	—	—	Lowers the user's Sp. Attack by 2.
Psycho Cut	PSY	Physical	70	100	20	Normal	—	—	Critical hits land more easily.
Psycho Shift	PSY	Status	—	90	10	Normal	—	—	Shifts the user's Paralysis, Poison, Badly Poisoned, Burned, or Sleep status conditions to the target and heals the user.
Psyshock	PSY	Special	80	100	10	Normal	—	—	Damage depends on the user's Sp. Attack and the target's Defense.
Psystrike	PSY	Special	100	100	10	Normal	—	—	Damage depends on the user's Sp. Attack and the target's Defense.
Psywave	PSY	Special	—	80	15	Normal	—	—	Inflicts damage equal to the user's level multiplied by a random number between 0.5 and 1.5.
Punishment	DRK	Physical	—	100	5	Normal	—	○	The higher the target's stats are, the more powerful it becomes.
Pursuit	DRK	Physical	40	100	20	Normal	—	○	Does twice the usual damage if the target is switching out.

◈ Q

Move	Type	Kind	Pow.	Acc.	PP	Range	Long	DA	Effect
Quash	DRK	Status	—	100	15	Normal	—	—	The user suppresses the target and makes it move last that turn. Fails if the target has already used its move that turn.
Quick Attack	NRM	Physical	40	100	30	Normal	—	○	Always strikes first. The user with the higher Speed goes first if similar moves are used.
Quick Guard	FTG	Status	—	—	15	Your Side	—	—	The user protects itself and its allies from first-strike moves. If used in succession, its chance of failing rises.
Quiver Dance	BUG	Status	—	—	20	Self	—	—	Raises the user's Sp. Attack, Sp. Defense, and Speed by 1.

◈ R

Move	Type	Kind	Pow.	Acc.	PP	Range	Long	DA	Effect
Rage	NRM	Physical	20	100	20	Normal	—	○	Attack power rises as the user takes hits.
Rage Powder	BUG	Status	—	—	20	Self	—	—	This move is given priority. Opposing Pokémon aim only at the user.
Rain Dance	WTR	Status	—	—	5	Both Sides	—	—	Changes the weather condition to Rain for 5 turns, strengthening Water-type moves.
Rapid Spin	NRM	Physical	20	100	40	Normal	—	○	Releases the user from moves such as Bind, Wrap, Leech Seed, and Spikes.
Razor Leaf	GRS	Physical	55	95	25	Many Others	—	—	Critical hits land more easily. Its power is weaker when it hits multiple Pokémon.
Razor Shell	WTR	Physical	75	95	10	Normal	—	○	A 50% chance of lowering the target's Defense by 1.
Razor Wind	NRM	Special	80	100	10	Many Others	—	—	Builds power on the first turn and attacks on the second. Critical hits land more easily. Its power is weaker when it hits multiple Pokémon.
Recover	NRM	Status	—	—	10	Self	—	—	Restores HP by up to half of the user's max HP.
Recycle	NRM	Status	—	—	10	Self	—	—	A held item that has been used can be used again.
Reflect	PSY	Status	—	—	20	Your Side	—	—	Halves damage to the Pokémon on your side from physical moves. Effect lasts 5 turns even if the user is switched out. Effect is weaker in Double Battles and Triple Battles.
Reflect Type	NRM	Status	—	—	15	Normal	—	—	The user becomes the same type as the target.
Refresh	NRM	Status	—	—	20	Self	—	—	Heals Paralysis, Poison, and Burned status conditions.
Rest	PSY	Status	—	—	10	Self	—	—	Fully restores HP, but makes the user Sleep for 2 turns.
Retaliate	NRM	Physical	70	100	5	Normal	—	○	If an ally fainted in the previous turn, this attack's power is doubled.
Return	NRM	Physical	—	100	20	Normal	—	○	The higher the user's friendship, the higher the power becomes.
Revenge	FTG	Physical	60	100	10	Normal	—	○	Its power is doubled if the user has taken damage from the target that turn.
Reversal	FTG	Physical	—	100	15	Normal	—	○	If the user's HP is low, this move does more damage to the target.
Roar	NRM	Status	—	100	20	Normal	—	—	Ends wild Pokémon battles. In a battle with a Trainer, this move forces that Trainer to switch Pokémon. When there is no Pokémon to switch in, this move fails.
Roar of Time	DRG	Special	150	90	5	Normal	—	—	The user can't move during the next turn.
Rock Blast	RCK	Physical	25	90	10	Normal	—	—	Attacks 2–5 times in a row.
Rock Climb	NRM	Physical	90	85	20	Normal	—	○	A 20% chance of inflicting Confused status condition.
Rock Polish	RCK	Status	—	—	20	Self	—	—	Raises the user's Speed by 2.
Rock Slide	RCK	Physical	75	90	10	Many Others	—	—	A 30% chance of making the targets flinch (unable to use moves on that turn). Its power is weaker when it hits multiple Pokémon.
Rock Smash	FTG	Physical	40	100	15	Normal	—	○	A 50% chance of lowering the target's Defense by 1.
Rock Throw	RCK	Physical	50	90	15	Normal	—	—	A regular attack.
Rock Tomb	RCK	Physical	50	80	10	Normal	—	—	Lowers the target's Speed by 1.
Rock Wrecker	RCK	Physical	150	90	5	Normal	—	—	The user can't move during the next turn.
Role Play	PSY	Status	—	—	10	Normal	—	—	Copies the target's Ability (cannot copy Wonder Guard or Multitype).
Rolling Kick	FTG	Physical	60	85	15	Normal	—	○	A 30% chance of making the target flinch (unable to use moves on that turn).
Rollout	RCK	Physical	30	90	20	Normal	—	○	Attacks consecutively over 5 turns or until it misses. Cannot choose other moves. Inflicts greater damage with every successful hit. Inflicts twice the damage if used after Defense Curl.
Roost	FLY	Status	—	—	10	Self	—	—	Restores half of maximum HP, and pulls Flying-type Pokémon to the ground during that turn.
Round	NRM	Special	60	100	15	Normal	—	—	When multiple Pokémon use this move in a turn, the first one to use it is followed immediately by others. Its power is doubled when following another Pokémon using it.

◈ **S**

Move	Type	Kind	Pow.	Acc.	PP	Range	Long	DA	Effect
Sacred Fire	FIR	Physical	100	95	5	Normal	—	—	A 50% chance of inflicting the Burned status condition on the target. If the target is Frozen, it will be thawed. This move can be used even if the user is Frozen. If the user is Frozen, this also thaws the user.
Sacred Sword	FTG	Physical	90	100	20	Normal	—	○	The target's stat changes don't affect this move.
Safeguard	NRM	Status	—	—	25	Your Side	—	—	Protects the Pokémon on your side from status conditions for 5 turns. Effects last even if the user switches out.
Sand Tomb	GRD	Physical	35	85	15	Normal	—	—	Inflicts damage over 4–5 turns. Target cannot flee during that time.
Sand-Attack	GRD	Status	—	100	15	Normal	—	—	Lowers target's accuracy by 1.
Sandstorm	RCK	Status	—	—	10	Both Sides	—	—	Changes the weather condition to Sandstorm for 5 turns. The Sp. Defense of Rock-type Pokémon increases. All Pokémon other than Rock, Steel, and Ground types take damage each turn.
Scald	WTR	Special	80	100	15	Normal	—	—	A 30% chance of inflicting Burned status condition.
Scary Face	NRM	Status	—	100	10	Normal	—	—	Lowers target's Speed by 2.
Scratch	NRM	Physical	40	100	35	Normal	—	○	A regular attack.
Screech	NRM	Status	—	85	40	Normal	—	—	Lowers target's Defense by 2.
Searing Shot	FIR	Special	100	100	5	Adjacent	—	—	A 30% chance of inflicting the Burned status condition on the targets. If the targets are Frozen, they will be thawed. Its power is weaker when it hits multiple Pokémon.
Secret Power	NRM	Physical	70	100	20	Normal			A 30% chance of one of the following additional effects, depending on the environment: Tall grass/Lawn: Sleep status condition. Path/Sand/Entralink: lowers accuracy by 1. Cave: the target flinches. Water surface/Puddle/Shoal: lowers Attack by 1. Swamp: lowers Speed by 1. Snow/Ice: Frozen status condition. Indoors: Paralysis status condition.
Seed Bomb	GRS	Physical	80	100	15	Normal	—	—	A regular attack.
Seed Flare	GRS	Special	120	85	5	Normal	—	—	A 40% chance of lowering the target's Sp. Defense by 2.
Seismic Toss	FTG	Physical	—	100	20	Normal	—	○	Deals fixed damage equal to the user's level.
Selfdestruct	NRM	Physical	200	100	5	Adjacent	—	—	The user faints after using it. Its power is weaker when it hits multiple Pokémon.
Shadow Ball	GHO	Special	80	100	15	Normal	—	—	A 20% chance of lowering the target's Sp. Defense by 1.
Shadow Claw	GHO	Physical	70	100	15	Normal	—	○	Critical hits land more easily.
Shadow Force	GHO	Physical	120	100	5	Normal	—	○	Makes the user invisible on the first turn and attacks on the second. Strikes the target even if it is using Protect or Detect.
Shadow Punch	GHO	Physical	60	—	20	Normal	—	○	A sure hit.
Shadow Sneak	GHO	Physical	40	100	30	Normal	—	○	Always strikes first. The user with the higher Speed goes first if similar moves are used.
Sharpen	NRM	Status	—	—	30	Self	—	—	Raises the user's Attack by 1.
Sheer Cold	ICE	Special	—	30	5	Normal	—	—	The target faints with one hit if the user's level is equal to or greater than the target's level. The higher the user's level is compared to the target's, the more accurate it is.
Shell Smash	NRM	Status	—	—	15	Self	—	—	Lowers the user's Defense and Sp. Defense by 1 and raises the user's Attack, Sp. Attack, and Speed by 2.
Shift Gear	STL	Status	—	—	10	Self	—	—	Raises the user's Speed by 2 and Attack by 1.
Shock Wave	ELC	Special	60	—	20	Normal	—	—	A sure hit.
Signal Beam	BUG	Special	75	100	15	Normal	—	—	A 10% chance of inflicting Confused status condition.
Silver Wind	BUG	Special	60	100	5	Normal	—	—	A 10% chance of raising the user's Attack, Defense, Speed, Sp. Attack, and Sp. Defense stats by 1.
Simple Beam	NRM	Status	—	100	15	Normal	—	—	Changes the target's Ability to Simple. It fails to change certain Abilities such as Truant.
Sing	NRM	Status	—	55	15	Normal	—	—	Inflicts Sleep status condition on the target.
Sketch	NRM	Status	—	—	1	Normal	—	—	Copies the last move used by the target. The user then forgets Sketch and learns the new move.
Skill Swap	PSY	Status	—	—	10	Normal	—	—	Swaps Abilities between the user and target (cannot swap Wonder Guard or Multitype).
Skull Bash	NRM	Physical	100	100	15	Normal	—	○	Builds power on the first turn and attacks on the second. It raises the user's Defense stat by 1 on the first turn.
Sky Attack	FLY	Physical	140	90	5	Normal	○	—	Builds power on the first turn and attacks on the second. A 30% chance of making the target flinch (unable to use moves on that turn). Critical hits land more easily.
Sky Drop	FLY	Physical	60	100	10	Normal	○	○	The user takes the target into the sky, then damages it by dropping it during the next turn. Does not damage Flying-type Pokémon.
Sky Uppercut	FTG	Physical	85	90	15	Normal	—	○	It hits even Pokémon that are in the sky by using moves such as Fly and Bounce.
Slack Off	NRM	Status	—	—	10	Self	—	—	Restores HP by up to half of the user's max HP.
Slam	NRM	Physical	80	75	20	Normal	—	○	A regular attack.
Slash	NRM	Physical	70	100	20	Normal	—	○	Critical hits land more easily.
Sleep Powder	GRS	Status	—	75	15	Normal	—	—	Inflicts Sleep status condition on the target.
Sleep Talk	NRM	Status	—	—	10	Self	—	—	Only works when the user is asleep. Randomly uses one of the user's moves.
Sludge	PSN	Special	65	100	20	Normal	—	—	A 30% chance of inflicting Poison status condition.
Sludge Bomb	PSN	Special	90	100	10	Normal	—	—	A 30% chance of inflicting Poison status condition.
Sludge Wave	PSN	Special	95	100	10	Adjacent	—	—	A 10% chance of inflicting Poison status condition. Its power is weaker when it hits multiple Pokémon.
Smack Down	RCK	Physical	50	100	15	Normal	—	—	Ground-type moves will now hit a Pokémon with Levitate Ability or a Flying-type Pokémon. It hits even Pokémon that are in the sky by using moves such as Fly and Bounce.
SmellingSalt	NRM	Physical	60	100	10	Normal	—	○	This move does twice the usual damage against targets with Paralysis, but heals this status condition.
Smog	PSN	Special	20	70	20	Normal	—	—	A 40% chance of inflicting Poison status condition.
SmokeScreen	NRM	Status	—	100	20	Normal	—	—	Lowers the target's accuracy by 1.
Snatch	DRK	Status	—	—	10	Self	—	—	Steals the effects of recovery or stat-changing moves used by the target on that turn.
Snore	NRM	Special	40	100	15	Normal	—	—	Only works when the user is asleep. A 30% chance of making the target flinch (unable to use moves on that turn).
Soak	WTR	Status	—	100	20	Normal	—	—	Changes the target's type to Water.
Softboiled	NRM	Status	—	—	10	Self	—	—	Restores HP by up to half of the user's max HP.

Move	Type	Kind	Pow.	Acc.	PP	Range	Long	DA	Effect
SolarBeam	GRS	Special	120	100	10	Normal	—	—	Builds power on the first turn and attacks on the second. In Sunny weather, attacks on first turn. In Rain/Sandstorm/Hail weather, power is halved.
SonicBoom	NRM	Special	—	90	20	Normal	—	—	This move deals a fixed 20 points of damage.
Spacial Rend	DRG	Special	100	95	5	Normal	—	—	Critical hits land more easily.
Spark	ELC	Physical	65	100	20	Normal	—	○	A 30% chance of inflicting Paralysis status condition on the target.
Spider Web	BUG	Status	—	—	10	Normal	—	—	The target can't escape. If used in a Trainer battle, it prevents the opposing Trainer from switching out a Pokémon.
Spike Cannon	NRM	Physical	20	100	15	Normal	—	—	Attacks 2–5 times in a row.
Spikes	GRD	Status	—	—	20	Other Side	—	—	Damages Pokémon as they are sent out to the opposing side. Power rises with each use, up to 3 times. Ineffective against Flying-type Pokémon and Pokémon with the Levitate Ability.
Spit Up	NRM	Special	—	100	10	Normal	—	—	Deals damage determined by how many times the user has used Stockpile. Fails if the user has not used Stockpile first. Nullifies Defense and Sp. Defense stat increases caused by Stockpile.
Spite	GHO	Status	—	100	10	Normal	—	—	Takes 4 points from the PP of the target's last move used.
Splash	NRM	Status	—	—	40	Self	—	—	No effect.
Spore	GRS	Status	—	100	15	Normal	—	—	Inflicts Sleep status condition on the target.
Stealth Rock	RCK	Status	—	—	20	Other Side	—	—	Damages Pokémon as they are sent out to the opposing side. Damage is subject to type matchups.
Steamroller	BUG	Physical	65	100	20	Normal	—	○	A 30% chance of making the target flinch (unable to use moves on that turn). Double damage if the target has used Minimize.
Steel Wing	STL	Physical	70	90	25	Normal	—	○	A 10% chance of raising the user's Defense by 1.
Stockpile	NRM	Status	—	—	20	Self	—	—	Raises the user's Defense and Sp. Defense by 1. Can be used up to 3 times.
Stomp	NRM	Physical	65	100	20	Normal	—	○	A 30% chance of making the target flinch (unable to use moves on that turn). Double damage if the target has used Minimize.
Stone Edge	RCK	Physical	100	80	5	Normal	—	—	Critical hits land more easily.
Stored Power	PSY	Special	20	100	10	Normal	—	—	The higher the user's stat stages, the more powerful it becomes.
Storm Throw	FTG	Physical	40	100	10	Normal	—	○	Always results in a critical hit.
Strength	NRM	Physical	80	100	15	Normal	—	○	A regular attack.
String Shot	BUG	Status	—	95	40	Many Others	—	—	Lowers the targets' Speed by 1.
Struggle	NRM	Physical	50	—	1	Normal	—	○	This move becomes available when all other moves are out of PP. The user takes damage equal to 1/4 of its maximum HP. Inflicts damage regardless of type matchup.
Struggle Bug	BUG	Special	30	100	20	Many Others	—	—	Lowers the targets' Sp. Attack by 1. Its power is weaker when it hits multiple Pokémon.
Stun Spore	GRS	Status	—	75	30	Normal	—	—	Inflicts Paralysis status condition.
Submission	FTG	Physical	80	80	25	Normal	—	○	The user takes 1/4 of the damage inflicted.
Substitute	NRM	Status	—	—	10	Self	—	—	Uses 1/4 of maximum HP to create a copy of the user.
Sucker Punch	DRK	Physical	80	100	5	Normal	—	○	This move attacks first and deals damage only if the target's chosen move is an attack move.
Sunny Day	FIR	Status	—	—	5	Both Sides	—	—	Changes the weather condition to Sunny for 5 turns, strengthening Fire-type moves.
Super Fang	NRM	Physical	—	90	10	Normal	—	○	Halves the target's HP.
Superpower	FTG	Physical	120	100	5	Normal	—	○	Lowers the user's Attack and Defense by 1.
Supersonic	NRM	Status	—	55	20	Normal	—	—	Inflicts the Confused status condition on the target.
Surf	WTR	Special	95	100	15	Adjacent	—	—	Double damage if the targets are using Dive when attacked. Its power is weaker when it hits multiple Pokémon.
Swagger	NRM	Status	—	90	15	Normal	—	—	Inflicts the Confused status condition on the target but raises its Attack by 2.
Swallow	NRM	Status	—	—	10	Self	—	—	Restores HP, the amount of which is determined by how many times the user has used Stockpile. Fails if the user has not used Stockpile first. Nullifies Defense and Sp. Defense stat increases caused by Stockpile.
Sweet Kiss	NRM	Status	—	75	10	Normal	—	—	Inflicts the Confused status condition on the target.
Sweet Scent	NRM	Status	—	100	20	Many Others	—	—	Lowers the targets' evasion by 1.
Swift	NRM	Special	60	—	20	Many Others	—	—	A sure hit. Its power is weaker when it hits multiple Pokémon.
Switcheroo	DRK	Status	—	100	10	Normal	—	—	Swaps items between the user and the target.
Swords Dance	NRM	Status	—	—	30	Self	—	—	Raises the user's Attack by 2.
Synchronoise	PSY	Special	70	100	15	Adjacent	—	—	Inflicts damage on any Pokémon of the same type as the user. Its power is weaker when it hits multiple Pokémon.
Synthesis	GRS	Status	—	—	5	Self	—	—	Recovers 1/2 of the user's max HP. In Sunny weather, recovers 2/3 of the user's max HP. In Rain/Sandstorm/Hail weather, recovers 1/4 of the user's max HP.

◈ **T**

Move	Type	Kind	Pow.	Acc.	PP	Range	Long	DA	Effect
Tackle	NRM	Physical	50	100	35	Normal	—	○	A regular attack.
Tail Glow	BUG	Status	—	—	20	Self	—	—	Raises the user's Sp. Attack by 3.
Tail Slap	NRM	Physical	25	85	10	Normal	—	○	Attacks 2–5 times in a row.
Tail Whip	NRM	Status	—	100	30	Many Others	—	—	Lowers the targets' Defense by 1.
Tailwind	FLY	Status	—	—	30	Your Side	—	—	Doubles the Speed of the Pokémon on your side for 4 turns.
Take Down	NRM	Physical	90	85	20	Normal	—	○	The user takes 1/4 of the damage inflicted.
Taunt	DRK	Status	—	100	20	Normal	—	—	Prevents the target from using anything other than attack moves for 3 turns.
Teeter Dance	NRM	Status	—	100	20	Adjacent	—	—	Inflicts the Confused status condition on the targets.
Telekinesis	PSY	Status	—	—	15	Normal	—	—	The target floats for 3 turns. All moves land regardless of their accuracy except Ground-type moves and one-hit KO moves, such as Sheer Cold and Horn Drill.
Teleport	PSY	Status	—	—	20	Self	—	—	Ends wild Pokémon battles.

T

Move	Type	Kind	Pow.	Acc.	PP	Range	Long	DA	Effect
Thief	DRK	Physical	40	100	10	Normal	—	○	When the target is holding an item and the user is not, the user can steal that item.
Thrash	NRM	Physical	120	100	10	1 Random	—	○	Attacks consecutively over 2–3 turns. Cannot choose other moves. Then the user becomes Confused.
Thunder	ELC	Special	120	70	10	Normal	—	—	A 30% chance of inflicting Paralysis status condition on the target. Is 100% accurate in the Rain weather condition and 50% accurate in the Sunny weather condition. It hits even Pokémon that are in the sky by using moves such as Fly and Bounce.
Thunder Fang	ELC	Physical	65	95	15	Normal	—	○	A 10% chance of inflicting Paralysis or making the target flinch (unable to use moves on that turn).
Thunder Wave	ELC	Status	—	100	20	Normal	—	—	Inflicts Paralysis status condition.
Thunderbolt	ELC	Special	95	100	15	Normal	—	—	A 10% chance of inflicting Paralysis on the target.
ThunderPunch	ELC	Physical	75	100	15	Normal	—	○	A 10% chance of inflicting Paralysis on the target.
ThunderShock	ELC	Special	40	100	30	Normal	—	—	A 10% chance of inflicting Paralysis on the target.
Tickle	NRM	Status	—	100	20	Normal	—	—	Lowers the target's Attack and Defense by 1.
Torment	DRK	Status	—	100	15	Normal	—	—	Makes the target unable to use the same move twice in a row.
Toxic	PSN	Status	—	90	10	Normal	—	—	Inflicts the Badly Poisoned condition on the target. Damage from being Badly Poisoned increases with every turn.
Toxic Spikes	PSN	Status	—	—	20	Other Side	—	—	Lays a trap of poison spikes on the opposing side that inflict the Poison condition on Pokémon that switch into battle. Using Toxic Spikes twice will inflict the Badly Poisoned condition. Toxic Spikes' effect ends when a Poison-type Pokémon switches into battle. Ineffective against Flying-type Pokémon and Pokémon with the Levitate Ability.
Transform	NRM	Status	—	—	10	Normal	—	—	The user transforms into the target. The user has the same moves and Ability as the target (all moves have 5 PP).
Tri Attack	NRM	Special	80	100	10	Normal	—	—	A 20% chance of inflicting the Paralysis, Burned, or Frozen status condition on the target.
Trick	PSY	Status	—	100	10	Normal	—	—	Swaps items between the user and the target.
Trick Room	PSY	Status	—	—	5	Both Sides	—	—	For 5 turns, the Pokémon with lower Speed go first. First-strike moves still go first. If used again while Trick Room is still in effect, it cancels the effect.
Triple Kick	FTG	Physical	10	90	10	Normal	—	○	Attacks 3 times in a row in a single turn. Power rises from 10 to 20 to 30 as long as it continues to hit.
Trump Card	NRM	Special	—	—	5	Normal	—	○	A sure hit. The move's power increases as its PP decreases.
Twineedle	BUG	Physical	25	100	20	Normal	—	—	Attacks twice in a row in a single turn. A 20% chance of inflicting Poison status condition.
Twister	DRG	Special	40	100	20	Many Others	—	—	A 20% chance of making the targets flinch (unable to use moves on that turn). This does twice the damage if the targets are using Fly, Bounce, etc. when it hits. Its power is weaker when it hits multiple Pokémon.

U

Move	Type	Kind	Pow.	Acc.	PP	Range	Long	DA	Effect
Uproar	NRM	Special	90	100	10	1 Random	—	—	The user makes an uproar for 3 turns. During that time, no Pokémon can fall asleep.
U-turn	BUG	Physical	70	100	20	Normal	—	○	After attacking, the user switches out with another Pokémon in the party.

V

Move	Type	Kind	Pow.	Acc.	PP	Range	Long	DA	Effect
Vacuum Wave	FTG	Special	40	100	30	Normal	—	—	Always strikes first. The user with the higher Speed goes first if similar moves are used.
Venoshock	PSN	Special	65	100	10	Normal	—	—	Its power is doubled if the target has the Poison or Badly Poisoned status condition.
ViceGrip	NRM	Physical	55	100	30	Normal	—	○	A regular attack.
Vine Whip	GRS	Physical	35	100	15	Normal	—	○	A regular attack.
Vital Throw	FTG	Physical	70	—	10	Normal	—	○	A sure hit. Always strikes last.
Volt Switch	ELC	Special	70	100	20	Normal	—	—	After attacking, the user switches out with another Pokémon in the party.
Volt Tackle	ELC	Physical	120	100	15	Normal	—	○	The user takes 1/3 of the damage inflicted. A 10% chance of inflicting Paralysis on the target.

W

Move	Type	Kind	Pow.	Acc.	PP	Range	Long	DA	Effect
Wake-Up Slap	FTG	Physical	60	100	10	Normal	—	○	This move does twice the damage against an asleep target, but heals the Sleep status condition.
Water Gun	WTR	Special	40	100	25	Normal	—	—	A regular attack.
Water Pledge	WTR	Special	50	100	10	Normal	—	—	When combined with Fire Pledge or Grass Pledge, the power and effect change. If it is combined with Fire Pledge, the power is 150. It will create a rainbow that turn that lasts for the next 3 turns and makes it more likely that your team's moves will have additional effects. If it is combined with Grass Pledge, the power is 150 and it becomes a Grass-type move. The surrounding area will become a swamp, which lowers the Speed of opposing Pokémon that turn and the next 3 turns.
Water Pulse	WTR	Special	60	100	20	Normal	○	—	A 20% chance of inflicting Confused status condition.
Water Sport	WTR	Status	—	—	15	Both Sides	—	—	As long as the user is in play, the power of Fire-type moves drops to 1/3.
Water Spout	WTR	Special	150	100	5	Many Others	—	—	If the user's HP is low, this move has lower attack power. Its power is weaker when it hits multiple Pokémon.
Waterfall	WTR	Physical	80	100	15	Normal	—	○	A 20% chance of making the target flinch (unable to use moves on that turn).
Weather Ball	NRM	Special	50	100	10	Normal	—	—	In special weather conditions, this move's type changes and its attack power doubles. Sunny weather condition: Fire type. Rain weather condition: Water type. Hail weather condition: Ice type. Sandstorm weather condition: Rock type.
Whirlpool	WTR	Special	35	85	15	Normal	—	—	Inflicts damage over 4–5 turns. The target cannot flee during that time. Double damage if the target is using Dive when attacked.
Whirlwind	NRM	Status	—	100	20	Normal	—	—	Ends wild Pokémon battles. In a battle with a Trainer, this move forces the opposing Trainer to switch Pokémon. When there is no Pokémon to switch in, this move fails.
Wide Guard	RCK	Status	—	—	10	Your Side	—	—	Protects from special and physical moves that target multiple Pokémon. If used 2 turns in succession, its chance of failing rises.
Wild Charge	ELC	Physical	90	100	15	Normal	—	○	The user takes 1/4 of the damage inflicted.

Move	Type	Kind	Pow.	Acc.	PP	Range	Long	DA	Effect
Will-O-Wisp	FIR	Status	—	75	15	Normal	—	—	Inflicts the Burned status condition on the target.
Wing Attack	FLY	Physical	60	100	35	Normal	○	○	A regular attack.
Wish	NRM	Status	—	—	10	Self	—	—	Restores 1/2 of maximum HP at the end of the next turn. Works even if the user has switched out.
Withdraw	WTR	Status	—	—	40	Self	—	—	Raises the user's Defense by 1.
Wonder Room	PSY	Status	—	—	10	Both Sides	—	—	Each Pokémon's Defense and Sp. Def stats are swapped for 5 turns.
Wood Hammer	GRS	Physical	120	100	15	Normal	—	○	The user takes 1/3 of the damage inflicted.
Work Up	NRM	Status	—	—	30	Self	—	—	Raises the user's Attack and Sp. Attack by 1.
Worry Seed	GRS	Status	—	100	10	Normal	—	—	Changes the target's Ability to Insomnia. It fails to change certain Abilities such as Truant.
Wrap	NRM	Physical	15	90	20	Normal	—	○	Inflicts damage over 4–5 turns. The target cannot flee during that time.
Wring Out	NRM	Special	—	100	5	Normal	—	○	The more HP the target has left, the greater the move's power becomes (max attack power: 120).

X

Move	Type	Kind	Pow.	Acc.	PP	Range	Long	DA	Effect
X-Scissor	BUG	Physical	80	100	15	Normal	—	○	A regular attack.

Y

Move	Type	Kind	Pow.	Acc.	PP	Range	Long	DA	Effect
Yawn	NRM	Status	—	—	10	Normal	—	—	Inflicts the Sleep status condition on the target on the next turn unless the target switches out.

Z

Move	Type	Kind	Pow.	Acc.	PP	Range	Long	DA	Effect
Zap Cannon	ELC	Special	120	50	5	Normal	—	—	Inflicts the Paralysis status condition on the target.
Zen Headbutt	PSY	Physical	80	90	15	Normal	—	○	A 20% chance of making the target flinch (unable to use moves on that turn).

Field moves

Move	Field effect
Chatter	You can record your voice. It's played in battle.
Cut	Cuts down small trees so your party may pass.
Dig	Pulls you out of spaces like caves, returning you to the last entrance you went through.
Dive	In patches of darker water, you can dive to the bottom to explore the seafloor.
Flash	Illuminates dark caves.
Fly	Whisks you instantly to a town or city you've visited before.
Milk Drink	Distributes part of the user's own HP among teammates.
Softboiled	Distributes part of the user's own HP among teammates.
Strength	Moves large rocks and pushes them into holes to create a new path.
Surf	Lets you move across water.
Sweet Scent	Attracts wild Pokémon and makes them appear.
Teleport	Transports you to the last Pokémon Center you used (cannot be used in caves or similar places).
Waterfall	Lets you climb up and down waterfalls.

Moves learned from people

Move	How to obtain
Blast Burn	Ultimate Move Tutor's House on Route 13 (Talk to the old man)
Draco Meteor	Drayden's House in Opelucid City (Talk to Iris in *Pokémon Black Version* and Drayden in *Pokémon White Version*)
Fire Pledge	Move Tutor's House in Driftveil City (Talk to the man)
Frenzy Plant	Ultimate Move Tutor's House on Route 13 (Talk to the old man)
Grass Pledge	Move Tutor's House in Driftveil City (Talk to the man)
Hydro Cannon	Ultimate Move Tutor's House on Route 13 (Talk to the old man)
Water Pledge	Move Tutor's House in Driftveil City (Talk to the man)

◈TMs

No.	Move	How to Obtain	Price
1	Hone Claws	From Zinzolin, one of the Seven Sages, hiding in the Cold Storage (after finishing the main story)	—
2	Dragon Claw	Victory Road 3F	—
3	Psyshock	Giant Chasm Crater Forest	—
4	Calm Mind	From Ryoku, one of the Seven Sages, hiding in the Relic Castle (after finishing the main story)	—
5	Roar	Route 10	—
6	Toxic	Route 17	—
7	Hail	Mistralton City Poké Mart	50,000
8	Bulk Up	From Giallo, one of the Seven Sages, hiding on Route 14 (after finishing the main story)	—
9	Venoshock	Route 15	—
10	Hidden Power	From Professor Juniper in Nuvema Town (when the number of Pokémon seen on your Pokédex is 115 or above)	—
11	Sunny Day	Mistralton City Poké Mart	50,000
12	Taunt	Victory Road Outside	—
13	Ice Beam	Giant Chasm Crater Forest	—
14	Blizzard	Icirrus City Poké Mart	70,000
15	Hyper Beam	Shopping Mall 2F on Route 9	90,000
16	Light Screen	Nimbasa City Poké Mart	30,000
17	Protect	From Professor Juniper in Nuvema Town (when the number of Pokémon SEEN on your Pokédex is 60 or above)	—
18	Rain Dance	Mistralton City Poké Mart	50,000
19	Telekinesis	Route 18	—
20	Safeguard	Nimbasa City Poké Mart	30,000
21	Frustration	Nimbasa City Poké Mart	10,000
22	SolarBeam	Pinwheel Forest	—
23	Smack Down	Receive for 36 BP at the Battle Subway	—
24	Thunderbolt	At P2 Laboratory	—
25	Thunder	Icirrus City Poké Mart	70,000
26	Earthquake	Relic Castle tower 1F (after finishing the main story)	—
27	Return	Nimbasa City Poké Mart	10,000
28	Dig	From a Worker in the prefab house on Route 4	—
29	Psychic	Route 13	—
30	Shadow Ball	Relic Castle B2F	—
31	Brick Break	From an old woman in the Pokémon Center in Icirrus City	—
32	Double Team	From Rood, one of the Seven Sages, hiding on Route 18 (after finishing the main story)	—
33	Reflect	Nimbasa City Poké Mart	30,000
34	Sludge Wave	Receive for 48 BP at the Battle Subway	—
35	Flamethrower	Abundant Shrine	—
36	Sludge Bomb	Route 8	—
37	Sandstorm	Mistralton City Poké Mart	50,000
38	Fire Blast	Icirrus City Poké Mart	70,000
39	Rock Tomb	Desert Resort	—
40	Aerial Ace	Talk to a boy in a house in Mistralton City and you'll find it in the field to the south of the runway (after obtaining the Mistralton City Gym Badge)	—
41	Torment	Route 4	—
42	Facade	From a Parasol Lady on Route 8	—
43	Flame Charge	From a Battle Girl on Tubeline Bridge	—
44	Rest	From a Hiker in a building in Castelia City	—
45	Attract	From a girl in a building in Castelia City	—
46	Thief	Wellspring Cave 1F	—
47	Low Sweep	Wellspring Cave B1F	—
48	Round	Receive for 36 BP at the Battle Subway	—
49	Echoed Voice	From a woman at the Musical Theater in Nimbasa City	—
50	Overheat	Route 11	—
51	Ally Switch	Receive for 48 BP at the Battle Subway	—
52	Focus Blast	Wellspring Cave B1F	—
53	Energy Ball	Route 12	—
54	False Swipe	Receive from Professor Juniper in Nuvema Town (when the number of Pokémon SEEN on your Pokédex is 25 or above)	—

No.	Move	How to Obtain	Price
55	Scald	Cold Storage	—
56	Fling	An Infielder throws it at you on Route 9	—
57	Charge Beam	From a Battle Girl on Route 7	—
58	Sky Drop	Mistralton City	—
59	Incinerate	Receive for 48 BP at the Battle Subway	—
60	Quash	Receive for 48 BP at the Battle Subway	—
61	Will-O-Wisp	Celestial Tower 2F	—
62	Acrobatics	Defeat Skyla at the Mistralton City Pokémon Gym	—
63	Embargo	Dragonspiral Tower Outside	—
64	Explosion	Receive for 48 BP at the Battle Subway	—
65	Shadow Claw	Celestial Tower 4F	—
66	Payback	Route 16	—
67	Retaliate	Defeat Lenora at the Nacrene City Pokémon Gym	—
68	Giga Impact	Shopping Mall 2F on Route 9	90,000
69	Rock Polish	From Bronius, one of the Seven Sages, hiding in the Chargestone Cave (after finishing the main story)	—
70	Flash	From a man with sunglasses in Castelia City	—
71	Stone Edge	Challenger's Cave B2F	—
72	Volt Switch	Defeat Elesa at the Nimbasa City Pokémon Gym	—
73	Thunder Wave	Nimbasa City Poké Mart	10,000
74	Gyro Ball	Nimbasa City Poké Mart	10,000
75	Swords Dance	From Gorm, one of the Seven Sages, hiding in the Dreamyard (after finishing the main story)	—
76	Struggle Bug	Defeat Burgh at the Castelia City Pokémon Gym	—
77	Psych Up	Receive for 48 BP at the Battle Subway	—
78	Bulldoze	Defeat Clay at the Driftveil City Pokémon Gym and receive it from him in front of the Chargestone Cave	—
79	Frost Breath	Defeat Brycen at the Icirrus City Pokémon Gym	—
80	Rock Slide	Mistralton Cave 2F	—
81	X-Scissor	Route 7	—
82	Dragon Tail	Defeat Drayden (in *Pokémon Black Version*) or Iris (in *Pokémon White Version*) at the Opelucid City Pokémon Gym	—
83	Work Up	Defeat the Gym Leader at the Striaton City Pokémon Gym (Gym Leader is chosen depending on your starter)	—
84	Poison Jab	Route 6	—
85	Dream Eater	Dreamyard basement (after finishing the main story)	—
86	Grass Knot	Pinwheel Forest	—
87	Swagger	Receive for 36 BP at the Battle Subway	—
88	Pluck	Receive for 36 BP at the Battle Subway	—
89	U-turn	Collect Gram 1, Gram 2, and Gram 3 and return them to Wingull on Route 13	—
90	Substitute	Twist Mountain Middle Level (in the winter)	—
91	Flash Cannon	Twist Mountain Lowest Level	—
92	Trick Room	Abundant Shrine	—
93	Wild Charge	Victory Road Outside	—
94	Rock Smash	From a Battle Girl in the Pinwheel Forest	—

◈ HMs

No.	Move	How to Obtain	Price
1	Cut	From Fennel in Striaton City (after defeating the Gym Leader)	—
2	Fly	From Bianca in Driftveil City (after defeating her)	—
3	Surf	From Alder at Twist Mountain	—
4	Strength	From the man in the house in Nimbasa City	—
5	Waterfall	Route 18	—
6	Dive	From a woman in Undella Town	—

Pokémon Abilities

A

Ability	Effect in battle	Effect when the Pokémon is the lead in your party
Adaptability	Increases the power boost received by using a move of same type as the Pokémon.	—
Aftermath	Knocks off 1/4 of the attacking Pokémon's HP when a direct attack causes the Pokémon to faint.	—
Air Lock	Eliminates effects of weather on Pokémon.	—
Analytic	The power of its move is increased by 30% when the Pokémon moves last.	—
Anger Point	Raises the Pokémon's Attack to the maximum when hit by a critical hit.	—
Anticipation	Warns if your foe's Pokémon has supereffective moves or one-hit KO moves.	—
Arena Trap	Prevents the foe's Pokémon from fleeing or switching out. Ineffective against Flying-type Pokémon and Pokémon with the Levitate Ability.	Raises wild Pokémon encounter rate.

B

Ability	Effect in battle	Effect when the Pokémon is the lead in your party
Bad Dreams	Slightly lowers the HP of sleeping Pokémon every turn.	
Battle Armor	Opposing Pokémon's moves will not hit critically.	
Big Pecks	Prevents Defense from being lowered.	
Blaze	Raises the power of Fire-type moves by 50% when the Pokémon's HP drops to 1/3 or less.	

C

Ability	Effect in battle	Effect when the Pokémon is the lead in your party
Chlorophyll	Double Speed in the Sunny weather condition.	—
Clear Body	Protects against stat-lowering moves and Abilities.	—
Cloud Nine	Eliminates effects of weather on Pokémon.	—
Color Change	Changes the Pokémon's type into the type of the move that just hit it.	—
Compoundeyes	Raises accuracy by 30%.	Raises encounter rate with wild Pokémon holding items.
Contrary	Makes stat changes have an opposite effect (increase instead of decrease and vice versa).	—
Cursed Body	A 30% chance of inflicting Disable on the move the opponent used to hit the Pokémon.	—
Cute Charm	A 30% chance of counter-inflicting the Infatuated condition when hit with a direct attack.	Raises encounter rate of wild Pokémon of the opposite gender.

D

Ability	Effect in battle	Effect when the Pokémon is the lead in your party
Damp	Pokémon on neither side can use Selfdestruct and Explosion. Nullifies the Aftermath Ability.	—
Defeatist	The Pokémon's Attack and Sp. Attack gets halved when HP becomes half or less.	—
Defiant	When an opponent's move or Ability lowers the Pokémon's stats, the Pokémon's Attack rises by 2.	—
Download	When the Pokémon enters battle, this Ability raises its Attack by 1 if the foe's Pokémon's Defense is lower than its Sp. Defense, and raises it's Sp. Attack by 1 if the foe's Pokémon's Sp. Defense is lower than its Defense.	—
Drizzle	Makes the weather Rain when the Pokémon enters battle.	—
Drought	Makes the weather Sunny when the Pokémon enters battle.	—
Dry Skin	Restores HP when the Pokémon is hit by a Water-type move. Restores HP in the Rain weather condition. However, the Pokémon receives increased damage from Fire-type moves. Takes damage every turn when in the Sunny weather condition.	—

E

Ability	Effect in battle	Effect when the Pokémon is the lead in your party
Early Bird	The Pokémon wakes quickly from the Sleep condition.	—
Effect Spore	A 30% chance of inflicting the Poison, Paralysis, or Sleep status conditions when hit with a direct attack.	—

F

Ability	Effect in battle	Effect when the Pokémon is the lead in your party
Filter	Minimizes the damage received from supereffective moves.	—
Flame Body	A 30% chance of inflicting the Burn status condition when hit with a direct attack.	Facilitates hatching Eggs in your party.
Flare Boost	Increases the power of special moves by 50% when Burned.	—
Flash Fire	When the Pokémon is hit by a Fire-type move, its Fire-type moves increase Power by 50% rather than taking damage.	—
Flower Gift	Raises Attack and Sp. Defense of the Pokémon in the Sunny weather condition.	—
Forecast	Changes Castform's form and type. Sunny weather condition: changes to Fire type. Rain weather condition: changes to Water type. Hail weather condition: changes to Ice type.	—
Forewarn	Reveals a move an opponent knows when the Pokémon enters battle. Damaging moves with high power are prioritized.	—
Friend Guard	Reduces damage done to allies by 25%.	—
Frisk	Checks an opponent's held item when the Pokémon enters battle.	

G

Ability	Effect in battle	Effect when the Pokémon is the lead in your party
Gluttony	Allows the Pokémon to use its held Berry sooner when it has low HP.	—
Guts	Attack stat rises by 50% when the Pokémon is affected by a status condition.	—

H

Ability	Effect in battle	Effect when the Pokémon is the lead in your party
Harvest	A 50% chance of restoring the Berry the Pokémon used at turn end and 100% chance when the weather condition is Sunny.	—
Healer	A 33% chance every turn that an ally Pokémon's status condition will be healed.	—
Heatproof	Halves damage from Fire-type moves and from the Burned status condition.	—
Heavy Metal	Doubles the Pokémon's weight.	—
Honey Gather	If the Pokémon isn't holding an item, it will sometimes be left holding Honey after a battle (even if it didn't participate). Its chance of finding Honey increases with its level.	—
Huge Power	Doubles the Pokémon's Attack.	—
Hustle	Raises Attack by 50%, but lowers the accuracy of the Pokémon's physical moves by 20%.	Raises encounter rate with high-level wild Pokémon.
Hydration	Cures status conditions at the end of the turn in the Rain weather condition.	—
Hyper Cutter	Prevents Attack from being lowered.	—

I

Ability	Effect in battle	Effect when the Pokémon is the lead in your party
Ice Body	Gradually restores HP in the Hail weather condition instead of taking damage.	—
Illuminate	No effect.	Raises wild Pokémon encounter rate.
Illusion	Appears in battle disguised as the last Pokémon in the party.	—
Immunity	Protects against the Poison condition.	—
Imposter	Transforms itself into the Pokémon it is facing as it enters battle.	—
Infiltrator	Moves can hit even if the target used Reflect, Light Screen, Safeguard, or Mist.	—
Inner Focus	The Pokémon doesn't flinch by additional effect of a move.	—
Insomnia	Protects against the Sleep status condition.	—
Intimidate	Lowers opponents' Attack by 1 when the Pokémon enters battle.	Lowers encounter rate with low-level wild Pokémon.
Iron Barbs	Slightly reduces the HP of an opponent that hits the Pokémon with a direct attack.	—
Iron Fist	Increases the power of Ice Punch, Fire Punch, ThunderPunch, Mach Punch, Mega Punch, Comet Punch, Bullet Punch, Sky Uppercut, Drain Punch, Focus Punch, Dizzy Punch, DynamicPunch, Hammer Arm, Meteor Mash, and Shadow Punch.	—

J

Ability	Effect in battle	Effect when the Pokémon is the lead in your party
Justified	When the Pokémon is hit by a Dark-type move, Attack goes up by 1.	—

K

Ability	Effect in battle	Effect when the Pokémon is the lead in your party
Keen Eye	Prevents accuracy from being lowered.	Lowers encounter rate with low-level wild Pokémon.
Klutz	The Pokémon's held items have no effect.	—

L

Ability	Effect in battle	Effect when the Pokémon is the lead in your party
Leaf Guard	Protects the Pokémon from status conditions when in the Sunny weather condition.	—
Levitate	Gives full immunity to all Ground-type moves.	—
Light Metal	Halves the Pokémon's weight.	—
Lightningrod	Draws all Electric-type moves to the Pokémon. When the Pokémon is hit by an Electric-type move, Sp. Attack goes up by 1 rather than taking damage.	—
Limber	Protects against the Paralysis status condition.	—
Liquid Ooze	When an opposing Pokémon uses an HP-draining move, it damages the user instead.	—

M

Ability	Effect in battle	Effect when the Pokémon is the lead in your party
Magic Bounce	Reflects status moves.	—
Magic Guard	The Pokémon will not take damage from anything other than a direct attack. Nullifies the Liquid Ooze, Aftermath, Rough Skin, and Iron Barbs Abilities, the Sandstorm and Hail weather conditions, as well as status conditions such as Poison, Badly Poisoned, Burned, Nightmare, Curse, Leech Seed, Bind, Sand Tomb, Fire Spin, Clamp, and Magma Storm. The effects of Stealth Rock, Spikes, Wrap, Flame Burst, and Fire Pledge are negated as are the item effects from Black Sludge, Sticky Barb, Life Orb, and Rocky Helmet. The Pokémon also receives no recoil or move-failure damage from attacks.	—
Magma Armor	Prevents the Frozen status condition.	Facilitates hatching Eggs in your party.
Magnet Pull	Prevents Steel-type Pokémon from fleeing or switching out.	Raises encounter rate with wild Steel-type Pokémon.

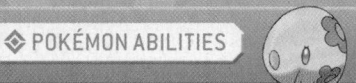

M

Ability	Effect in battle	Effect when the Pokémon is the lead in your party
Marvel Scale	Defense stat increases by 50% when the Pokémon is affected by a status condition.	—
Minus	Raises Sp. Attack by 50% when another ally has the Ability Plus or Minus.	—
Mold Breaker	Use moves on targets regardless of their Abilities. Does not nullify Abilities that have effects after an attack. For example, the Pokémon can score a critical hit against the target with Battle Armor, but it will still take damage from Rough Skin.	—
Moody	Raises one stat by 2 and lowers another by 1 at turn end.	—
Motor Drive	When the Pokémon is hit by a Electric-type move, Speed goes up by 1 rather than taking damage.	—
Moxie	When the Pokémon knocks out an opponent with a move, Attack goes up 1.	—
Multiscale	Halves damage when HP is full.	—
Multitype	Type changes according to the Plate Arceus is holding.	—
Mummy	Changes the Ability of the opponent that hits the Pokémon with a direct attack to Mummy.	—

N

Ability	Effect in battle	Effect when the Pokémon is the lead in your party
Natural Cure	Cures the Pokémon's status conditions when it switches out.	—
No Guard	Moves used by or against the Pokémon always strike their targets.	Raises wild Pokémon encounter rate.
Normalize	All of the Pokémon's moves become Normal-type moves.	—

O

Ability	Effect in battle	Effect when the Pokémon is the lead in your party
Oblivious	Protects against the Infatuated condition.	—
Overcoat	Protects the Pokémon from weather damage, such as Sandstorm and Hail.	—
Overgrow	Raises the power of Grass-type moves by 50% when the Pokémon's HP drops to 1/3 or less.	—
Own Tempo	Protects against the Confused status condition.	—

P

Ability	Effect in battle	Effect when the Pokémon is the lead in your party
Pickpocket	Steals an item when hit with a direct attack. It fails if the user is already holding an item.	—
Pickup	Picks up the item the foe's Pokémon used that turn at turn end. Fails if the user is already holding an item.	If the Pokémon has no held item, it sometimes picks one up after battle (even if it didn't participate). It picks up different items depending on its level.
Plus	Raises Sp. Attack by 50% when another ally has the Ability Plus or Minus.	—
Poison Heal	Restores HP every turn if the Pokémon is inflicted with the Poison status condition.	—
Poison Point	A 30% chance of counter-inflicting the Poison status condition when hit with a direct attack.	—
Poison Touch	A 30% chance of inflicting the Poison status condition when the Pokémon uses a direct attack.	—
Prankster	Gives priority to status moves.	—
Pressure	When the Pokémon is hit by an opponent's move, it depletes 1 additional PP from that move.	Raises encounter rate with high-level wild Pokémon.
Pure Power	Doubles the Pokémon's Attack.	—

Q

Ability	Effect in battle	Effect when the Pokémon is the lead in your party
Quick Feet	Increases Speed by 50% when the Pokémon is affected with status conditions.	Lowers wild Pokémon encounter rate.

R

Ability	Effect in battle	Effect when the Pokémon is the lead in your party
Rain Dish	Gradually restores HP in the Rain weather condition.	—
Rattled	When the Pokémon is hit by a Ghost-, Dark-, or Bug-type move, Speed goes up by 1.	—
Reckless	Raises the power of moves with recoil damage.	—
Regenerator	Restores 1/3 its HP when withdrawn from battle.	—
Rivalry	If the target is the same gender, the power of the Pokémon's move goes up. If the target is of the opposite gender, the move's power goes down. No effect when the gender is unknown.	—
Rock Head	No recoil damage from moves like Take Down and Double-Edge.	—
Rough Skin	Slightly reduces the HP of an opponent that hits the Pokémon with a direct attack.	—
Run Away	The Pokémon can always escape from a battle with a wild Pokémon.	—

S

Ability	Effect in battle	Effect when the Pokémon is the lead in your party
Sand Force	Raises the power of Ground-, Rock-, and Steel-type moves by 30% in the Sandstorm weather condition. Sandstorm does not damage the Pokémon.	—
Sand Rush	Doubles Speed in the Sandstorm weather condition. Sandstorm does not damage the Pokémon.	—

Ability	Effect in battle	Effect when the Pokémon is the lead in your party
Sand Stream	Makes the weather Sandstorm when the Pokémon enters battle.	—
Sand Veil	Raises evasion in the Sandstorm weather condition. Sandstorm does not damage the Pokémon.	Lowers encounter rate with wild Pokémon in the Sandstorm weather condition.
Sap Sipper	When the Pokémon is hit by a Grass-type move, Attack goes up by 1 rather than taking damage.	—
Scrappy	Lets the Pokémon hit Ghost-type Pokémon with Normal- and Fighting-type moves.	—
Serene Grace	Doubles chances of moves inflicting additional effects.	—
Shadow Tag	Prevents the opposing Pokémon from fleeing or switching out. If both your and the opposing Pokémon have this Ability, the effect is canceled.	—
Shed Skin	A 33% chance every turn of curing the Pokémon's status conditions.	—
Sheer Force	When moves with an additional effect are used, power increases by 30%, but the additional effect is lost.	—
Shell Armor	Opponent's moves will not hit critically.	—
Shield Dust	Protects the Pokémon from additional effects of moves.	—
Simple	The effects of stat changes become more powerful.	—
Skill Link	Moves that strike successively strike the maximum number of times (2–5 times means it always strikes 5 times).	—
Slow Start	Halves Attack and Speed for 5 turns after the Pokémon enters battle.	—
Sniper	Moves that deliver a critical hit deal a great amount of damage.	—
Snow Cloak	Raises evasion in the Hail weather condition. Hail does not damage the Pokémon.	Lowers encounter rate with wild Pokémon in the Hail weather condition.
Snow Warning	Makes the weather Hail when the Pokémon enters battle.	—
Solar Power	Raises Sp. Attack by 50%, but takes damage every turn in the Sunny weather condition.	—
Solid Rock	Minimizes the damage received from supereffective moves.	—
Soundproof	Protects the Pokémon from sound-based moves: Snore, Heal Bell, Screech, Sing, Chatter, Metal Sound, GrassWhistle, Uproar, Supersonic, Growl, Hyper Voice, Roar, Perish Song, Bug Buzz, Round, and Echoed Voice.	—
Speed Boost	Raises Speed by 1 every turn.	—
Stall	The Pokémon's moves are used last in the turn.	—
Static	A 30% chance of counter-inflicting the Paralysis status condition when hit with a direct attack.	Raises encounter rate with wild Electric-type Pokémon.
Steadfast	Raises Speed by 1 every time the Pokémon flinches.	—
Stench	A 10% chance of making the target flinch as the Pokémon uses a move to deal damage.	Lowers wild Pokémon encounter rate.
Sticky Hold	The Pokémon's held item cannot be stolen.	Makes Pokémon bite more often when fishing.
Storm Drain	Draws all Water-type moves to the Pokémon. When the Pokémon is hit by a Water-type move, Sp. Attack goes up by 1 rather than taking damage.	—
Sturdy	Protects the Pokémon against one-hit KO moves like Horn Drill and Sheer Cold. Leaves the Pokémon with 1 HP if hit by a move that would knock it out when its HP is full.	—
Suction Cups	Nullifies moves like Whirlwind and Roar, which would force Pokémon to switch out.	Makes Pokémon bite more often when fishing.
Super Luck	Heightens the critical-hit ratio of the Pokémon's moves.	—
Swarm	Raises the power of Bug-type moves by 50% when the Pokémon's HP drops to 1/3 or less.	—
Swift Swim	Doubles Speed in the Rain weather condition.	—
Synchronize	When the Pokémon receives the Poison, Paralysis, or Burned status condition, this inflicts the same condition.	Raises encounter rate with wild Pokémon with the same Nature.

◈ T

Ability	Effect in battle	Effect when the Pokémon is the lead in your party
Tangled Feet	Raises evasion when the Pokémon is in the Confused status condition.	—
Technician	If the move's power is 60 or less, its power will increase by 50%. Also takes effect if a move's power is altered by itself or by another move.	—
Telepathy	Prevents damage from allies.	—
Teravolt	Use moves on targets regardless of their Abilities. Does not nullify Abilities that have effects after an attack. For example, the Pokémon can score a critical hit against the target with Battle Armor, but will still take damage from Rough Skin.	—
Thick Fat	Halves damage from Fire- and Ice-type moves.	—
Tinted Lens	Nullifies the type disadvantage of the Pokémon's not-very-effective moves: 1/2 damage turns into regular damage, 1/4 damage turns into 1/2 damage.	—
Torrent	Raises the power of Water-type moves by 50% when the Pokémon's HP drops to 1/3 or less.	—
Toxic Boost	Increases the power of physical moves by 50% when it has the Poison status condition.	—
Trace	Makes the Pokémon's Ability the same as the opponent's, except for certain Abilities like Forecast and Trace.	—
Truant	The Pokémon can use a move only once every other turn.	—
Turboblaze	Use moves on targets regardless of their Abilities. Does not nullify Abilities that have effects after an attack. For example, the Pokémon can score a critical hit against the target with Battle Armor, but it will still take damage from a target with Rough Skin.	

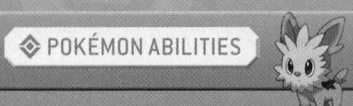

U

Ability	Effect in battle	Effect when the Pokémon is the lead in your party
Unaware	Ignores the stat changes of the opposing Pokémon, except Speed.	—
Unburden	Doubles Speed if the Pokémon loses or consumes a held item. Its Speed returns to normal if the Pokémon holds another item. No effect if the Pokémon starts out with no held item.	—
Unnerve	Prevent the opponent from eating Berries.	—

V

Ability	Effect in battle	Effect when the Pokémon is the lead in your party
Victory Star	The accuracy of its allies and itself is 10% higher.	—
Vital Spirit	Protects against the Sleep status condition.	Raises encounter rate with high-level wild Pokémon.
Volt Absorb	When the Pokémon is hit by an Electric-type move, HP is restored rather than taking damage.	—

W

Ability	Effect in battle	Effect when the Pokémon is the lead in your party
Water Absorb	When the Pokémon is hit by a Water-type move, HP is restored rather than taking damage.	—
Water Veil	Prevents the Burn status condition.	—
Weak Armor	When the Pokémon is hit by a physical attack, Defense goes down 1, but Speed goes up 1.	—
White Smoke	Protects against stat-lowering moves and Abilities.	Lowers wild Pokémon encounter rate.
Wonder Guard	Protects the Pokémon against all moves except supereffective ones.	—
Wonder Skin	Makes status moves more likely to miss.	—

Z

Ability	Effect in battle	Effect when the Pokémon is the lead in your party
Zen Mode	When over half its HP is lost, it changes form.	—

◇ Items obtained with the Pickup Ability

Item	Level of Pokémon with Pickup Ability									
	Low									High
Potion	◎									
Antidote	○	◎								
Super Potion	○	○	◎							
Great Ball	○	○	○	◎						
Repel	○	○	○	○	◎					
Escape Rope	○	○	○	○	○	◎				
Full Heal	○	○	○	○	○	○	◎			
Hyper Potion	○	○	○	○	○	○	○	◎		
Ultra Ball	△	△	○	○	○	○	○	○	◎	
Revive		△	△	○	○	○	○	○	○	◎
Rare Candy			△	△	○	○	○	○	○	○
Sun Stone				△	△	○	○	○	○	○
Moon Stone					△	△	○	○	○	○
Heart Scale						△	△	○	○	○
Full Restore			▲	▲				△	△	○	○
Max Revive								△	△	○
PP Up									△	△
Max Elixir										△
Nugget	▲	▲								
King's Rock		▲	▲							
Ether				▲	▲					
Iron Ball					▲	▲				
Prism Scale						▲	▲	▲	▲	▲
Elixir						▲	▲			
Leftovers									▲	▲

◎ Often found　○ Sometimes found　△ Rarely found　▲ Almost never found

Pokémon's Natures

Each individual Pokémon has a Nature, which affects how its stats grow when it levels up.

Pokémon's stats	ATTACK	DEFENSE	SPEED	SP. ATTACK	SP. DEFENSE
Adamant	○			▲	
Bashful					
Bold	▲	○			
Brave	○		▲		
Calm	▲				○
Careful				▲	○
Docile					
Gentle		▲			○
Hardy					
Hasty		▲	○		
Impish		○		▲	
Jolly			○	▲	
Lax		○			▲
Lonely	○	▲			
Mild		▲		○	
Modest	▲			○	
Naive			○		▲
Naughty	○				▲
Quiet			▲	○	
Quirky					
Rash				○	▲
Relaxed		○	▲		
Sassy			▲		○
Serious					
Timid	▲		○		

○ Gains more upon leveling up
▲ Gains less upon leveling up

Pokémon's Characteristics

On top of having a Nature, each individual Pokémon has a Characteristic. This also affects how the Pokémon's stats grow when it levels up.

Stat that grows easily	Characteristic	Stat that grows easily	Characteristic	Stat that grows easily	Characteristic
HP	Loves to eat.	ATTACK	Proud of its power.	DEFENSE	Sturdy body.
	Often dozes off.		Likes to thrash about.		Capable of taking hits.
	Often scatters things.		A little quick tempered.		Highly persistent.
	Scatters things often.		Likes to fight.		Good endurance.
	Likes to relax.		Quick tempered.		Good perseverance.

Stat that grows easily	Characteristic	Stat that grows easily	Characteristic	Stat that grows easily	Characteristic
SPEED	Likes to run.	SP. ATTACK	Highly curious.	SP. DEFENSE	Strong willed.
	Alert to sounds.		Mischievous.		Somewhat vain.
	Impetuous and silly.		Thoroughly cunning.		Strongly defiant.
	Somewhat of a clown.		Often lost in thought.		Hates to lose.
	Quick to flee.		Very finicky.		Somewhat stubborn.

Items

A

Item	Explanation	Main Ways to Obtain	Price
Absorb Bulb	Raises the holder's Sp. Attack by 1 when it is hit by a Water-type move. Goes away after use.	Exchange for 32 BP in the Battle Subway	—
Adamant Orb	When held by Dialga, raises the power of Dragon- and Steel-type moves.	From the Shadow Triad on the Marvelous Bridge	—
Air Balloon	The holder floats. The balloon pops when the holder is hit by an attack.	Exchange for 48 BP in the Battle Subway	—
Amulet Coin	If the holder takes part in a battle, the received prize money is doubled.	From Mickey after gathering the three Dancers in Castelia City	—
Antidote	Cures Poison.	Poké Mart (after obtaining one Gym Badge) or Route 9 Shopping Mall 1F	100
Armor Fossil	A Pokémon Fossil. When restored, it becomes Shieldon.	Receive from the Worker in the lower level of Twist Mountain (after finishing the main story)	—
Awakening	Cures Sleep.	Poké Mart (after obtaining one Gym Badge) or Route 9 Shopping Mall 1F	250

B

Item	Explanation	Main Ways to Obtain	Price
BalmMushroom	A fragrant mushroom. Can be sold to the Maid on Route 5 for 25,000.	Wild Foongus and Amoonguss very rarely hold this item	—
Berry Juice	Restores the HP of one Pokémon by 20 points.	Battle all three Trainers on the Royal Unova (Tuesdays)/Black City (*Pokémon Black Version*)	1,500
Big Mushroom	A big mushroom. Can be sold to the Poké Mart for 2,500. Can be sold to the Maid on Route 5 for 5,000.	Lostlorn Forest/Held by wild Foongus and Amoonguss/Black City (*Pokémon Black Version*)	20,000
Big Nugget	A big nugget of pure gold. Can be sold to the old gentleman in Icirrus City for 30,000.	Undella Town/Very rarely held by wild Garbodor	—
Big Pearl	A big pearl. Can be sold to the Poké Mart for 3,750. Can be sold to the old gentleman in Icirrus City for 7,500.	Driftveil City/Receive from a Fisherman in Striaton City/Receive from the sunglasses-wearing man on Route 13/Black City (*Pokémon Black Version*)	38,000
Big Root	Increases the amount of HP recovered when the holder uses an HP-draining move.	Pinwheel Forest	—
Binding Band	Doubles the damage done every turn by moves like Bind or Wrap when held.	Exchange for 48 BP in the Battle Subway	—
Black Belt	When held by a Pokémon, it boosts the power of Fighting-type moves.	Challenger's Cave B2F/Sometimes held by wild Throh and Sawk	—
Black Flute	A glass flute. Can be sold to the billionaire in Undella Town for 8,000.	From the sunglasses-wearing man on Route 13	—
Black Sludge	If the holder is a Poison-type Pokémon, it restores HP during battle. If the holder is any other type, it reduces HP during battle instead.	Sometimes held by wild Trubbish and often held by wild Garbodor	—
BlackGlasses	When held by a Pokémon, it boosts the power of Dark-type moves.	Desert Resort	—
Blue Flute	A glass flute. Can be sold to the billionaire in Undella Town for 7,000.	From the sunglasses-wearing man on Route 13	—
Blue Shard	Part of an ancient implement. Can be sold to the old gentleman in Icirrus City for 200.	Black City (*Pokémon Black Version*)	3,000
BrightPowder	When held by a Pokémon, this item raises evasion.	Chargestone Cave B2F/Exchange for 48 BP in the Battle Subway	—
Bug Gem	When held by a Pokémon, it boosts the power of a Bug-type move by 50%. Goes away after use.	Found in dust clouds inside caves	—
Burn Heal	Cures Burn.	Poké Mart (after obtaining one Gym Badge)/Route 9 Shopping Mall 1F	250

C

Item	Explanation	Main Ways to Obtain	Price
Calcium	Raises the base Sp. Attack stat of a Pokémon.	Victory Road/Exchange for 1 BP in the Battle Subway/Route 9 Shopping Mall 3F/Village Bridge	9,800
Carbos	Raises the base Speed stat of a Pokémon.	Exchange for 1 BP in the Battle Subway/Moor of Icirrus/Route 9 Shopping Mall 3F/Giant Chasm	9,800
Casteliacone	Castelia City's famous ice cream. Cures all status conditions.	Castelia City's Casteliacone stand (Tuesdays: spring, summer, and autumn only)	100
Cell Battery	When the holder is hit by an Electric-type move, Attack goes up by 1. Goes away after use.	Exchange for 32 BP in the Battle Subway	—
Charcoal	When held by a Pokémon, it boosts the power of Fire-type moves.	From the woman in the house in Nacrene City (when you answer Tepig)/Route 16	—

● Please note that some items found in this section are obtained in places that are not reachable until after the main story.

◆ It has not yet been revealed how to obtain this item in *Pokémon Black Version* and *Pokémon White Version*.

Item	Explanation	Main Ways to Obtain	Price
Choice Band	The holder can only use one move, but Attack increases by 50%.	Exchange for 48 BP in the Battle Subway	—
Choice Scarf	The holder can only use one move, but Speed increases by 50%.	From the sunglasses-wearing man in Castelia City's Pokémon Center (when you have 30 or more Pokémon with different OTs)/Exchange for 48 BP in the Battle Subway	—
Choice Specs	The holder can only use one move, but Sp. Attack increases by 50%.	Exchange for 48 BP in the Battle Subway	—
Claw Fossil	A Pokémon Fossil. When restored, it becomes Anorith.	From the Worker in the lower level of Twist Mountain (after finishing the main story)	—
Cleanse Tag	Helps keep wild Pokémon away if the holder is the first one in the party.	From the chairman of Icirrus City's Pokémon Fan Club (when you show him a Pokémon you've raised 50 to 98 levels)	—
Clever Wing	Raises the base Sp. Defense stat of a Pokémon by a little. Can be used until the stat reaches its maximum value.	Step on the shadows of flying Pokémon (Driftveil Drawbridge/Marvelous Bridge)	—
Comet Shard	A shard that fell to the ground when a comet approached. Can be sold to the old gentleman in Icirrus City for 60,000.	Giant Chasm	—
Cover Fossil	A Pokémon Fossil. When restored, it becomes Tirtouga.	From the Backpacker in Relic Castle 1F	—

◈ D

Item	Explanation	Main Ways to Obtain	Price
Damp Rock	Extends the duration of the move Rain Dance when held.	From the woman on Route 8 (talk to her during the morning)	—
Dark Gem	When held by a Pokémon, it boosts the power of a Dark-type move by 50%. Goes away after use.	Found in dust clouds inside caves	—
Dawn Stone	Evolves certain Pokémon.	Route 10/Found in dust clouds inside caves/Black City (*Pokémon Black Version*)	10,000
DeepSeaScale	When held by Clamperl, it doubles Sp. Defense. Link trade Clamperl while it holds the DeepSeaScale to evolve it into Gorebyss.	Route 13/Sometimes held by wild Basculin (Blue-Striped Form)/Receive from the sunglasses-wearing man on Route 13	—
DeepSeaTooth	When held by Clamperl, it doubles Sp. Attack. Link trade Clamperl while it holds the DeepSeaScale to evolve it into Huntail.	Route 17/Sometimes held by wild Basculin (Red-Striped Form)/Receive from the sunglasses-wearing man on Route 13	—
Destiny Knot	When held, it shares the Infatuation condition when it is afflicted by it.	Receive from the woman in the house in Opelucid City.	—
Dire Hit	Significantly raises the critical-hit ratio of the Pokémon on which it is used (can be used only once).	Nacrene City's store/Route 9 Shopping Mall 3F	650
Dome Fossil	A Pokémon Fossil. When restored, it becomes a Kabuto.	From the Worker in the lower level of Twist Mountain (after finishing the main story)	—
Draco Plate	When held by a Pokémon, it boosts the power of Dragon-type moves. When held by Arceus, it shifts Arceus's type to Dragon type.	From the man in the house on Route 13	—
Dragon Fang	When held by a Pokémon, it boosts the power of Dragon-type moves.	Dragonspiral Tower 4F/Sometimes held by wild Druddigon	—
Dragon Gem	When held by a Pokémon, it boosts the power of a Dragon-type move by 50%. Goes away after use.	Found in dust clouds inside caves	—
Dragon Scale	Link trade Seadra while it holds the Dragon Scale to evolve it into Kingdra.	Route 18/From the sunglasses-wearing man on Route 13	—
Dread Plate	When held by a Pokémon, it boosts the power of Dark-type moves. When held by Arceus, it shifts Arceus's type to Dark type.	??? (◆)	—
Dubious Disc	Link trade Porygon2 while it holds the Dubious Disc to evolve it into Porygon-Z.	P2 Laboratory/From the sunglasses-wearing man on Route 13	—
Dusk Stone	Evolves certain Pokémon.	Mistralton Cave—Guidance Chamber/Route 10/Found in dust clouds in caves/Black City (*Pokémon Black Version*)	10,000

◈ E

Item	Explanation	Main Ways to Obtain	Price
Earth Plate	When held by a Pokémon, it boosts the power of Ground-type moves. When held by Arceus, it shifts Arceus's type to Ground type.	??? (◆)	—
Eject Button	If the holder is hit by an attack, its action is canceled, and it switches places with a party Pokémon. Goes away after use.	Exchange for 32 BP in the Battle Subway	—
Electirizer	Link trade Electabuzz while it holds the Electirizer to evolve it into Electivire.	Route 13/From the sunglasses-wearing man on Route 13	—
Electric Gem	When held by a Pokémon, it boosts the power of an Electric-type move by 50%. Goes away after use.	Found in dust clouds inside caves	—
Elixir	It restores the PP of all of a Pokémon's moves by 10 points.	Wellspring Cave 1F/Route 6	—

E

Item	Explanation	Main Ways to Obtain	Price
Energy Root	Restores the HP of one Pokémon by 200 points. Very bitter.	Driftveil City Market	800
EnergyPowder	Restores the HP of one Pokémon by 50 points. Very bitter.	Driftveil Market	500
Escape Rope	Use it to escape instantly from a cave or a dungeon.	Poké Mart (after obtaining one Gym Badge)/Route 9 Shopping Mall 1F	550
Ether	Restores the PP of a Pokémon's move by 10 points.	Pinwheel Forest/Route 4/Cold Storage/Twist Mountain	—
Everstone	Prevents Pokémon evolution when held.	Often held by wild Roggenrola and Boldore/ From the sunglasses-wearing man in Castelia City's Pokémon Center (when you have 10 or more Pokémon with different OTs)	—
Eviolite	Raises Defense and Sp. Defense by 50% when held by a Pokémon that can still evolve.	From the researcher in the building in Castelia City (when the number of SEEN Pokémon in the Pokédex is 20 or more)	—
Exp. Share	The holder earns Experience Points without even going into battle.	Defeat the Janitor in Castelia City's Battle Company/From the chairman of Icirrus City's Pokémon Fan Club (show him a Pokémon you raised 25 to 49 levels)	—
Expert Belt	Raises the power of supereffective moves.	From the man in Driftveil City's market (when you have a Pokémon of Lv. 30 or above in your party)/Very rarely held by wild Throh and Sawk	—

F

Item	Explanation	Main Ways to Obtain	Price
Fighting Gem	When held by a Pokémon, it boosts the power of a Fighting-type move by 50%. Goes away after use.	Found in dust clouds inside caves	—
Fire Gem	When held by a Pokémon, it boosts the power of a Fire-type move by 50%. Goes away after use.	Found in dust clouds inside caves	—
Fire Stone	Evolves certain Pokémon.	When your answer to the man in Castelia City's question is Pansear/Desert Resort/Found in dust clouds in caves/Black City (Pokémon Black Version)	10,000
Fist Plate	When held by a Pokémon, it boosts the power of Fighting-type moves. When held by Arceus, it shifts Arceus's type to Fighting type.	??? (◆)	—
Flame Orb	Inflicts Burned status condition on the holder during battle.	Exchange for 16 BP in the Battle Subway	—
Flame Plate	When held by a Pokémon, it boosts the power of Fire-type moves. When held by Arceus, it shifts Arceus's type to Fire type.	??? (◆)	—
Float Stone	Halves the holder's weight.	From the Linebacker in the house in Opelucid City	—
Fluffy Tail	Allows the holder to always run away from a wild Pokémon encounter.	Black City (Pokémon Black Version)	15,000
Flying Gem	When held by a Pokémon, it boosts the power of a Flying-type move by 50%. Goes away after use.	Found in dust clouds inside caves	—
Focus Band	The holder is sometimes left with 1 HP when it receives damage that would KO it.	Exchange for 48 BP in the Battle Subway	—
Focus Sash	Leaves the holder with 1 HP when hit by a move that would KO it when its HP is full. Goes away after use.	Exchange for 48 BP in the Battle Subway	—
Fresh Water	Restores the HP of one Pokémon by 50 points.	Vending machines/Receive from Clyde at Pokémon Gyms	200
Full Heal	Cures all status conditions.	Poké Mart (after obtaining five Gym Badges)/Route 9 Shopping Mall 1F	600
Full Incense	When held by a Pokémon, it makes them move later.	Driftveil City Market (after finishing the main story)	9,600
Full Restore	Fully restores the HP and heals any status conditions of a single Pokémon.	Poké Mart (after obtaining eight Gym Badges)	3,000

G

Item	Explanation	Main Ways to Obtain	Price
Genius Wing	Raises the base Sp. Attack stat of a Pokémon by a little. Can be used until the stat reaches its maximum value.	Step on the shadows of flying Pokémon (Driftveil Drawbridge/Marvelous Bridge)	—
Ghost Gem	When held by a Pokémon, it boosts the power of a Ghost-type move by 50%. Goes away after use.	Found in dust clouds inside caves	—
Grass Gem	When held by a Pokémon, it boosts the power of a Grass-type move by 50%. Goes away after use.	Found in dust clouds inside caves	—
Green Shard	Part of an ancient implement. Can be sold to the old gentleman in Icirrus City for 200.	Black City (Pokémon Black Version)	3,000
Grip Claw	Extends the duration of moves like Bind and Wrap.	Wild Sneasel, who appear after the main story is completed, will often be holding this item	—

◆ It has not yet been revealed how to obtain this item in Pokémon Black Version and Pokémon White Version.

Item	Explanation	Main Ways to Obtain	Price
Griseous Orb	When held by Giratina, it changes it into its Origin Forme, and boosts the power of Dragon- and Ghost-type moves.	Receive from the Shadow Triad on the Marvelous Bridge	—
Ground Gem	When held by a Pokémon, it boosts the power of a Ground-type move by 50%. Goes away after use.	Found in dust clouds inside caves	—
Guard Spec.	Prevents stat reduction among the Trainer's party Pokémon for five turns.	Nacrene City's store/Route 9 Shopping Mall 3F	700

H

Item	Explanation	Main Ways to Obtain	Price
Hard Stone	When held by a Pokémon, it boosts the power of Rock-type moves.	Mistralton Cave 2F/Sometimes held by wild Roggenrola and Boldore/Sometimes held by wild Dwebble and Crustle	—
Heal Powder	Cures all status conditions. Very bitter.	Driftveil City Market	450
Health Wing	Raises the base HP stat of a Pokémon by a little. Can be used until the stat reaches its maximum value.	Step on the shadows of flying Pokémon (Driftveil Drawbridge/Marvelous Bridge)	—
Heart Scale	Give one to the reminder girl in Mistralton City, and she will have your Pokémon remember a move it has forgotten.	Cold Storage/Desert Resort/Route 18/By showing the woman in Driftveil City the Pokémon she wants to see/Black City (Pokémon Black Version)	10,000
Heat Rock	Extends the duration of the move Sunny Day when held.	Receive from the woman on Route 8 (talk to her during the afternoon)	—
Helix Fossil	A Pokémon Fossil. When restored, it becomes an Omanyte.	Receive from the Worker in the lower level of Twist Mountain (after finishing the main story)	—
Honey	Use in tall grass or in a cave to make wild Pokémon appear.	Wild Combee, who appear after the main story is completed, will always be holding this item	—
HP Up	Raises the base HP stat of a Pokémon.	Route 3/ Route 9/ Exchange for 1 BP in the Battle Subway/Route 9 Shopping Mall 3F	9,800
Hyper Potion	Restores the HP of one Pokémon by 200 points.	Poké Mart (after obtaining three Gym Badges)/Route 9 Shopping Mall 1F	1200

I

Item	Explanation	Main Ways to Obtain	Price
Ice Gem	When held by a Pokémon, it boosts the power of an Ice-type move by 50%. Goes away after use.	Found in dust clouds inside caves	—
Ice Heal	Cures the Frozen status condition.	Poké Mart (after obtaining one Gym Badge)/Route 9 Shopping Mall 1F	250
Icicle Plate	When held by a Pokémon, it boosts the power of Ice-type moves. When held by Arceus, it shifts Arceus's type to Ice type.	??? (◆)	—
Icy Rock	Extends the duration of the move Hail when held.	Receive from the woman on Route 8 (talk to her during the night)	—
Insect Plate	When held by a Pokémon, it boosts the power of Bug-type moves. When held by Arceus, it shifts Arceus's type to Bug type.	??? (◆)	—
Iron	Raises the base Defense stat of a Pokémon.	Chargestone Cave 1F/Mistralton Cave 2F/Exchange for 1 BP in the Battle Subway/Route 9 Shopping Mall 3F	9,800
Iron Ball	Lowers the holder's Speed. If the holder has the Levitate Ability or is a Flying-type Pokémon, Ground-type moves now hit it.	Exchange for 48 BP in the Battle Subway	—
Iron Plate	When held by a Pokémon, it boosts the power of Steel-type moves. When held by Arceus, it shifts Arceus's type to Steel type.	??? (◆)	—

K

Item	Explanation	Main Ways to Obtain	Price
King's Rock	Sometimes the target of the holder's attack move flinches.	From the chairman of Icirrus City's Pokémon Fan Club (when you show him a Pokémon you raised 99 levels)/From the sunglasses-wearing man on Route 13	—

L

Item	Explanation	Main Ways to Obtain	Price
Lagging Tail	When held by a Pokémon, it makes them move later.	Wild Slowpoke and Lickitung, which appear after you finish the main story, sometimes hold this item	—
Lava Cookie	Lavaridge Town's famous specialty. It cures all status conditions.	Battle four Trainers on the Royal Unova (Monday, Wednesday, and Friday)	—
Lax Incense	When held by a Pokémon, this item raises evasion.	Driftveil City Market (after finishing the main story)	9,600
Leaf Stone	Evolves certain Pokémon.	When your answer to the man in Castelia City's question is Pansage/Route 6/Found in dust clouds in caves/Black City (Pokémon Black Version)	10,000

◈ ITEMS

L

Item	Explanation	Main Ways to Obtain	Price
Leftovers	Restores a little of the holder's HP every turn.	Held by the Munchlax you can trade for in Undella Town (summer only)/Village Bridge (Dowsing MCHN)	—
Lemonade	Restores the HP of one Pokémon by 80 points.	Vending machines/Receive from the man in Castelia City's Café Sonata	350
Life Orb	Lowers the holder's HP each time it attacks, but raises the power of moves.	Exchange for 48 BP in the Battle Subway	—
Light Clay	Extends the duration of moves like Reflect and Light Screen.	Sometimes held by wild Golett	—
Luck Incense	Doubles prize money from a battle if the holding Pokémon joins in.	Driftveil City Market (after finishing the main story)	9,600
Lucky Egg	Slightly increases the number of Experience Points received from battle.	From Professor Juniper on Chargestone Cave 1F/From the sunglasses-wearing man on Route 13	—
Lucky Punch	When held by Chansey, it raises the critical hit ratio of its moves.	From the sunglasses-wearing man on Route 13	—
Lustrous Orb	When held by Palkia, it raises the power of Dragon- and Water-type moves.	From the Shadow Triad on the Marvelous Bridge	—

M

Item	Explanation	Main Ways to Obtain	Price
Macho Brace	Halves Speed, but makes it easier to raise base stats.	From the Infielder in the Nimbasa City gate	—
Magmarizer	Link trade Magmar while it holds the Magmarizer, to evolve it into Magmortar.	From the sunglasses-wearing man on Route 13	—
Magnet	When held by a Pokémon, it boosts the power of Electric-type moves.	Chargestone Cave 1F	—
Max Elixir	Restores the PP of all of a Pokémon's moves completely.	Route 18/Dragonspiral Tower/Moor of Icirrus/Held by the Rotom you can trade for on Route 15/Giant Chasm	—
Max Ether	Restores the PP of a Pokémon's move completely.	Route 7/ Route 1/ Route 3/Route 13	—
Max Potion	Completely restores the HP of a single Pokémon.	Poké Mart (after obtaining seven Gym Badges)/Route 9 Shopping Mall 1F	2,500
Max Repel	Prevents weak wild Pokémon from appearing for 250 steps after its use.	Poké Mart (after obtaining five Gym Badges)/Route 9 Shopping Mall 1F	700
Max Revive	Revives a fainted Pokémon and fully restores its HP.	Relic Castle B3F/Moor of Icirrus/From Bianca on Route 10/Victory Road/N's Castle/Giant Chasm	—
Meadow Plate	When held by a Pokémon, boosts the power of Grass-type moves. When held by Arceus, it shifts Arceus's type to Grass type.	??? (◆)	—
Mental Herb	The holder cures itself when moves like Taunt, Encore, Disable, Heal Block, or Attract make it unable to use moves freely. Goes away when used.	Sometimes held by wild Sewaddle, Swadloon, and Leavanny	—
Metal Coat	When held by a Pokémon, boosts the power of Steel-type moves.	Twist Mountain (winter)/From the sunglasses-wearing man on Route 13	—
Metal Powder	When held by Ditto, Defense doubles.	From the sunglasses-wearing man on Route 13	—
Metronome	Raises the power of a move used consecutively when held.	Wild Kricketune, who appear after the main story is completed, will sometimes be holding this item	—
Mind Plate	When held by a Pokémon, boosts the power of Psychic-type moves. When held by Arceus, it shifts Arceus's type to Psychic type.	??? (◆)	—
Miracle Seed	When held by a Pokémon, boosts the power of Grass-type moves.	From the woman in the house in Nacrene City (when you answer Snivy)/Pinwheel Forest/Sometimes held by wild Maractus	—
Moomoo Milk	Restores the HP of one Pokémon by 100 points.	Driftveil City Market	500
Moon Stone	Evolves certain Pokémon.	From Lenora in Pinwheel Forest/Twist Mountain/Found in dust clouds in caves/Black City (*Pokémon Black Version*)	10,000
Muscle Band	When held by a Pokémon, boosts the power of physical moves.	Exchange for 48 BP in the Battle Subway	—
Muscle Wing	Raises the base Attack stat of a Pokémon by a little. Can be used until the stat reaches its maximum value.	Step on the shadows of flying Pokémon (Driftveil Drawbridge/Marvelous Bridge)	—
Mystic Water	When held by a Pokémon, boosts the power of Water-type moves.	From the woman in the house in Nacrene City (when you answer Oshawott)/Wellspring Cave B1F	—

◆ It has not yet been revealed how to obtain this item in *Pokémon Black Version* and *Pokémon White Version*.

N

Item	Explanation	Main Ways to Obtain	Price
NeverMeltIce	When held by a Pokémon, boosts the power of Ice-type moves.	Cold Storage/Sometimes held by wild Cryogonal	—
Normal Gem	When held by a Pokémon, boosts the power of a Normal-type move by 50%. Goes away after use.	Found in dust clouds inside caves	—
Nugget	A nugget of pure gold. Can be sold to the Poké Mart for 5,000. Can be sold to the old gentleman in Icirrus City for 10,000.	From the men in Chargestone Cave B1F/Twist Mountain/Victory Road/Black City (*Pokémon Black Version*)	50,000

O

Item	Explanation	Main Ways to Obtain	Price
Odd Incense	When held by a Pokémon, boosts the power of Psychic-type moves.	Driftveil City Market (after finishing the main story)	9,600
Old Amber	A piece of amber that contains genetic material. When restored, it becomes Aerodactyl.	From the worker in the lower level of Twist Mountain (after finishing the main story)	—
Old Gateau	Old Chateau's hidden specialty. It cures all status conditions.	From Cedric Juniper in Dragonspiral Tower/Battle all five Trainers on the *Royal Unova* (Thursday)	—
Oval Stone	Evolves certain Pokémon.	Challenger's Cave B2F/Found in dust clouds in caves/Black City (*Pokémon Black Version*)	10,000

P

Item	Explanation	Main Ways to Obtain	Price
Parlyz Heal	Cures Paralysis.	Poké Mart (after obtaining one Gym Badge)/Route 9 Shopping Mall 1F	200
Pass Orb	A mysterious orb that generates Pass Powers.	Successfully complete missions in the Entralink	—
Pearl	A pretty pearl. Can be sold to the Poké Mart for 700. Can be sold to the old gentleman in Icirrus City for 1,400.	Route 1/Black City (*Pokémon Black Version*)	6,000
Pearl String	Very large pearls that sparkle in a pretty silver color. Can be sold to the old gentleman in Icirrus City for 25,000.	Route 13 (Dowsing MCHN)	—
Plume Fossil	A Pokémon Fossil. When restored, it becomes Archen.	From the Backpacker in Relic Castle 1F	—
Poison Barb	When held by a Pokémon, it boosts the power of Poison-type moves.	Route 8/Sometimes held by wild Venipede and Whirlipede	—
Poison Gem	When held by a Pokémon, it boosts the power of a Poison-type move by 50%. Goes away after use.	Found in dust clouds inside caves	—
Poké Doll	The holder can always run away from a wild Pokémon encounter.	Black City (*Pokémon Black Version*)	18,000
Poké Toy	The holder can always run away from a wild Pokémon encounter.	Route 9 Shopping Mall 1F	1,000
Potion	Restores the HP of one Pokémon by 20 points.	Poké Mart (from the start)/Route 9 Shopping Mall 1F	300
Power Anklet	Lowers Speed, but makes the Speed base stat easier to raise.	Exchange for 16 BP in the Battle Subway	—
Power Band	Lowers Speed, but makes the Sp. Defense base stat easier to raise.	Exchange for 16 BP in the Battle Subway	—
Power Belt	Lowers Speed, but makes the Defense base stat easier to raise.	Exchange for 16 BP in the Battle Subway	—
Power Bracer	Lowers Speed, but makes the Attack base stat easier to raise.	Exchange for 16 BP in the Battle Subway	—
Power Herb	The holder can immediately use moves that require a one-turn charge. Goes away after use.	Exchange for 32 BP in the Battle Subway	—
Power Lens	Lowers Speed, but makes the Sp. Attack base stat easier to raise.	Exchange for 16 BP in the Battle Subway	—
Power Weight	Lowers Speed, but makes the HP base stat easier to raise.	Exchange for 16 BP in the Battle Subway	—
PP Max	Increases the max number of PP as high as it will go.	From the sunglasses-wearing man in Castelia City's Pokémon Center (when you have 40 or more Pokémon with different OTs)	—
PP Up	Increases the max number of PP by 1 level.	Route 7/Twist Mountain/Relic Castle B3F/Obtainable in Route 9 Shopping Mall/Challenger's Cave B1F	—
Pretty Wing	A pretty wing. Can be sold to the Poké Mart for 100.	Step on the shadows of flying Pokémon (Driftveil Drawbridge/Marvelous Bridge)	—
Prism Scale	Link trade Feebas while it holds the Prism Scale to evolve it into Milotic.	Route 13/Receive from the man in Undella Town's Pokémon Center	—

P

	Item	Explanation	Main Ways to Obtain	Price
	Protector	Link trade Rhydon while it holds the Protector to evolve it into Rhyperior.	Route 11/Receive from the sunglasses-wearing man on Route 13	—
	Protein	Raises the base Attack stat of a Pokémon.	Cold Storage/Exchange for 1 BP in the Battle Subway/Route 9 Shopping Mall 3F/Challenger's Cave B2F	9,800
	Psychic Gem	When held by a Pokémon, boosts the power of a Psychic-type move by 50%. Goes away after use.	Found in dust clouds inside caves	—
	Pure Incense	Helps keep wild Pokémon away if the holder is the first one in the party.	Driftveil City Market (after finishing the main story)	9,600

Q

	Item	Explanation	Main Ways to Obtain	Price
	Quick Claw	Allows the holder to strike first sometimes.	From the Hiker on the Skyarrow Bridge	—
	Quick Powder	When held by Ditto, it raises Speed.	Wild Ditto, who appear after the main story is completed, will often be holding this item	—

R

	Item	Explanation	Main Ways to Obtain	Price
	RageCandyBar	Mahogany Town's famous snack. It cures all status conditions. Use it on the Pokémon statues in Desert Resort to wake up Darmanitan.	From Professor Juniper in the Desert Resort (after the ending)/From the woman in the house in Icirrus City (winter only)	—
	Rare Bone	A rare bone. Can be sold to the sunglasses-wearing man on Route 18 for 10,000 in prize money.	Very rarely held by wild Crustle/Black City (Pokémon Black Version)	30,000
	Rare Candy	Raises a Pokémon's level by 1.	Chargestone Cave B2F/Anville Town/Route 16/Lostlorn Forest/Route 2/Icirrus City (winter only)/Victory Road	—
	Razor Claw	Boosts the holder's critical-hit ratio.	Exchange for 48 BP in the Battle Subway/Route 13/From the sunglasses-wearing man on Route 13	—
	Razor Fang	When the holder hits a target with an attack, the target will sometimes flinch.	Exchange for 48 BP in the Battle Subway/Abundant Shrine/From the sunglasses-wearing man on Route 13	—
	Reaper Cloth	Link trade Dusclops while it holds the Reaper Cloth to evolve it into Dusknoir.	Route 14/From the sunglasses-wearing man on Route 13	—
	Red Card	If the holder is hit by an attack, the opposing Trainer is forced to switch out the attacking Pokémon. Goes away after use.	Exchange for 32 BP in the Battle Subway	—
	Red Flute	A glass flute. Can be sold to the billionaire in Undella Town for 7,500.	From the sunglasses-wearing man on Route 13	—
	Red Shard	Part of an ancient implement. Can be sold to the old gentleman in Icirrus City for 200.	Black City (Pokémon Black Version)	3,000
	Relic Band	A bracelet made by a civilization about 3,000 years ago. The billionaire in Undella Town will buy it for a great deal of prize money.	??? (◆)	—
	Relic Copper	A copper coin made by a civilization about 3,000 years ago. The billionaire in Undella Town will buy it for a great deal of prize money.	??? (◆)	—
	Relic Crown	A crown made by a civilization about 3,000 years ago. The billionaire in Undella Town will buy it for a great deal of prize money.	??? (◆)	—
	Relic Gold	A gold coin made by a civilization about 3,000 years ago. The billionaire in Undella Town will buy it for a great deal of prize money.	??? (◆)	—
	Relic Silver	A silver coin made by a civilization about 3,000 years ago. The billionaire in Undella Town will buy it for a great deal of prize money.	??? (◆)	—
	Relic Statue	A stone figure made by a civilization about 3,000 years ago. The billionaire in Undella Town will buy it for a great deal of prize money.	??? (◆)	—
	Relic Vase	A vase made by a civilization about 3,000 years ago. The billionaire in Undella Town will buy it for a great deal of prize money.	??? (◆)	—
	Repel	Prevents weak wild Pokémon from appearing for 100 steps after its use.	Poké Mart (after obtaining one Gym Badge)/Route 9 Shopping Mall 1F	350
	Resist Wing	Raises the base Defense stat of a Pokémon by a little. Can be used until the stat reaches its maximum value.	Step on the shadows of flying Pokémon (Driftveil Drawbridge/Marvelous Bridge)	—
	Revival Herb	Revives a fainted Pokémon. Very bitter.	Driftveil City Market	2,800
	Revive	Revives a fainted Pokémon and restores half of its HP.	Poké Mart (after obtaining three Gym Badges)/Route 9 Shopping Mall 1F	1,500
	Ring Target	Moves that would otherwise have no effect will hit the holder.	From the woman in the house in Opelucid City	—

◆ It has not yet been revealed how to obtain this item in Pokémon Black Version and Pokémon White Version.

Item	Explanation	Main Ways to Obtain	Price
Rock Gem	When held by a Pokémon, boosts the power of a Rock-type move by 50%. Goes away after use.	Found in dust clouds inside caves	—
Rock Incense	When held by a Pokémon, boosts the power of Rock-type moves.	Driftveil City Market (after finishing the main story)	9,600
Rocky Helmet	Does damage to the Pokémon that hit the holder with a direct attack.	From the Worker in the Cold Storage area	—
Root Fossil	A Pokémon Fossil. When restored, it becomes Lileep.	From the Worker in the lower level of Twist Mountain (after finishing the main story)	—
Rose Incense	When held by a Pokémon, boosts the power of Grass-type moves.	Driftveil City Market (after finishing the main story)	9,600

◈ S

Item	Explanation	Main Ways to Obtain	Price
Scope Lens	Boosts the holder's critical-hit ratio.	From the man on 47F of Castelia City's Battle Company/Exchange for 48 BP in the Battle Subway	—
Sea Incense	When held by a Pokémon, boosts the power of Water-type moves.	Driftveil City Market (after finishing the main story)	9,600
Sharp Beak	When held by a Pokémon, boosts the power of Flying-type moves.	From the woman in Mistralton City's Cargo Service	—
Shed Shell	The holder can always be switched out.	Sometimes held by wild Scraggy	—
Shell Bell	Restores the holder's HP by up to 1/8th of the damage dealt to the target.	From the old man in the house in Driftveil City (when the number of SEEN Pokémon in the Pokédex is 50 or more)	—
Shiny Stone	Evolves certain Pokémon.	From the girl in the house on Route 6/Dragonspiral Tower 4F/Found in dust clouds in caves/Black City (*Pokémon Black Version*)	10,000
Shoal Salt	Salt found in the Shoal Cave. Can be sold to the Maid on Route 5 for 7,000.	From the sunglasses-wearing man on Route 13	—
Shoal Shell	A seashell found in the Shoal Cave. Can be sold to the old gentleman in Icirrus City for 7,000.	From the sunglasses-wearing man on Route 13	—
Silk Scarf	When held by a Pokémon, boosts the power of Normal-type moves.	Route 6	—
SilverPowder	When held by a Pokémon, boosts the power of Bug-type moves.	Pinwheel Forest/Always held by wild Volcarona	—
Skull Fossil	A Pokémon Fossil. When restored, it becomes Cranidos.	From the Worker in the lower level of Twist Mountain (after finishing the main story)	—
Sky Plate	When held by a Pokémon, boosts the power of Flying-type moves. When held by Arceus, it shifts Arceus's type to Flying type.	??? (◆)	—
Smoke Ball	Allows the holder to always run away from wild Pokémon.	Team Plasma's base in Castelia City (after Bianca's Pokémon has been returned)	—
Smooth Rock	Extends the duration of the move Sandstorm when held.	From the woman on Route 8 (talk to her during the evening)	—
Soda Pop	Restores the HP of one Pokémon by 60 points.	Vending machine/Receive from the waitress in Nacrene City's Café Warehouse on Wednesdays/Answer all of survey questions in Castelia City's Passerby Analytics HQ	300
Soft Sand	When held by a Pokémon, it boosts the power of Ground-type moves.	From the sunglasses-wearing man in the Desert Resort/Sometimes held by wild Stunfisk	—
Soothe Bell	The holder's friendship improves more quickly.	From the old lady in the house in Nimbasa City (when the lead Pokémon in your party has high friendship)	—
Spell Tag	When held by a Pokémon, boosts the power of Ghost-type moves.	Celestial Tower 3F/Sometimes held by wild Yamask and Cofagrigus	—
Splash Plate	When held by a Pokémon, boosts the power of Water-type moves. When held by Arceus, it shifts Arceus's type to Water type.	From the man in the house on Route 13	—
Spooky Plate	When held by a Pokémon, boosts the power of Ghost-type moves. When held by Arceus, it shifts Arceus's type to Ghost type.	??? (◆)	—
Star Piece	A shard of a pretty gem that sparkles in a red color. Can be sold to the Poké Mart for 4,900. Can be sold to the old gentleman in Icirrus City for 9,800.	Smash the challenge rock in Pinwheel Forest (when you have a Fighting-type in your party)/Dragonspiral Tower 5F/Black City (*Pokémon Black Version*)	48,000
Stardust	Lovely, red-colored sand. Can be sold to the Poké Mart for 1,000. Can be sold to the old gentleman in Icirrus City for 2,000.	Dragonspiral Tower/Black City (*Pokémon Black Version*)	10,000
Steel Gem	When held by a Pokémon, it boosts the power of a Steel-type move by 50%. Goes away after use.	Found in dust clouds inside caves	—
Stick	When held by Farfetch'd, it raises the critical hit ratio of its moves.	From the sunglasses-wearing man on Route 13	—

S

Item	Explanation	Main Ways to Obtain	Price
Sticky Barb	Damages the holder every turn. It can stick to an opponent that touches the holder with a direct attack.	Sometimes held by wild Ferroseed	—
Stone Plate	When held by a Pokémon, boosts the power of Rock-type moves. When held by Arceus, it shifts Arceus's type to Rock type.	??? (◆)	—
Sun Stone	Evolves certain Pokémon.	From the boy in a house in Nimbasa City/Relic Castle B4F/Found in dust clouds in caves/Black City (*Pokémon Black Version*)	10,000
Super Potion	Restores the HP of one Pokémon by 50 points.	Poké Mart (after obtaining one Gym Badge)/Route 9 Shopping Mall 1F	700
Super Repel	Prevents weak wild Pokémon from appearing for 200 steps after its use.	Poké Mart (after obtaining three Gym Badges)/Route 9 Shopping Mall 1F	500
Sweet Heart	Restores the HP of one Pokémon by 20 points.	Use the Feeling Check feature with Infrared Connection	—
Swift Wing	Raises the base Speed stat of a Pokémon a little. Can be used until the stat reaches its maximum value.	Step on the shadows of flying Pokémon (Driftveil Drawbridge/Marvelous Bridge)	—

T

Item	Explanation	Main Ways to Obtain	Price
Thick Club	When held by Cubone or Marowak, Attack is doubled.	From the sunglasses-wearing man on Route 13	—
Thunderstone	Evolves certain Pokémon.	Chargestone Cave B1F/Receive from a man on 3F of Route 9 Shopping Mall/Black City (*Pokémon Black Version*)	10,000
TinyMushroom	A tiny mushroom. Can be sold to the Poké Mart for 250. Can be sold to the Maid on Route 5 for 500.	Often held by wild Foongus and Amoonguss/Black City (*Pokémon Black Version*)	3,000
Toxic Orb	Inflicts the Badly Poisoned status condition on the holder during battle.	Exchange for 16 BP in the Battle Subway	—
Toxic Plate	When held by a Pokémon, boosts the power of Poison-type moves. When held by Arceus, it shifts Arceus's type to Poison type.	??? (◆)	—
TwistedSpoon	When held by a Pokémon, boosts the power of Psychic-type moves.	Dreamyard Basement (after finishing the main story)	—

U

Item	Explanation	Main Ways to Obtain	Price
Up-Grade	Link trade Porygon while it holds the Up-Grade to evolve it into Porygon2.	Route 15/From the sunglasses-wearing man on Route 13	—

W

Item	Explanation	Main Ways to Obtain	Price
Water Gem	When held by a Pokémon, boosts the power of a Water-type move by 50%. Goes away after use.	Found in dust clouds inside caves	—
Water Stone	Evolves certain Pokémon.	When your answer to the man in Castelia City's question is Panpour/Driftveil City/Found in dust clouds in caves/ Black City (*Pokémon Black Version*)	10,000
Wave Incense	When held by a Pokémon, boosts the power of Water-type moves.	Driftveil City Market (after finishing the main story)	9,600
White Flute	A glass flute. Can be sold to the billionaire in Undella Town for 8,000.	From the sunglasses-wearing man on Route 13	—
White Herb	Restores lowered stats. Goes away after use.	Exchange for 32 BP in the Battle Subway	—
Wide Lens	Raises the holder's accuracy.	From the sunglasses-wearing man in Castelia City's Pokémon Center (when you have five or more Pokémon with different OTs)/Exchange for 48 BP in the Battle Subway	—
Wise Glasses	When held by a Pokémon, it boosts the power of special moves.	Exchange for 48 BP in the Battle Subway	—

X

Item	Explanation	Main Ways to Obtain	Price
X Accuracy	Raises the accuracy of a Pokémon on which it was used.	Nacrene City's store/Route 9 Shopping Mall 3F	950
X Attack	Raises the Attack stat of a Pokémon on which it was used by one level.	Nacrene City's store/Route 9 Shopping Mall 3F	500
X Defend	Raises the Defense stat of a Pokémon on which it was used by one level.	Nacrene City's store/Route 9 Shopping Mall 3F	550
X Sp. Def	Raises the Sp. Def stat of a Pokémon on which it was used by one level.	Nacrene City's store/Route 9 Shopping Mall 3F	350

◆ It has not yet been revealed how to obtain this item in *Pokémon Black Version* and *Pokémon White Version*.

Item	Explanation	Main Ways to Obtain	Price
X Special	Raises the Sp. Attack of a Pokémon on which it was used by one level.	Nacrene City's store/Route 9 Shopping Mall 3F	350
X Speed	Raises the Speed of a Pokémon on which it was used by one level.	Nacrene City's store/Route 9 Shopping Mall 3F	350

Y

Item	Explanation	Main Ways to Obtain	Price
Yellow Flute	A glass flute. Can be sold to the billionaire in Undella Town for 7,500.	From the sunglasses-wearing man on Route 13	—
Yellow Shard	Part of an ancient implement. Can be sold to the old gentleman in Icirrus City for 200.	Black City (*Pokémon Black Version*)	3,000

Z

Item	Explanation	Main Ways to Obtain	Price
Zap Plate	When held by a Pokémon, it boosts the power of Electric-type moves. When held by Arceus, it shifts Arceus's type to Electric type.	??? [◆]	—
Zinc	Raises the base Sp. Defense stat of a Pokémon.	Exchange for 1 BP in the Battle Subway/Route 5/Route 9 Shopping Mall 3F	9,800
Zoom Lens	Raises the holder's accuracy when it moves after the opposing Pokémon.	From the sunglasses-wearing man in Castelia City's Pokémon Center (when you have 20 or more Pokémon with different OTs)/Exchange for 48 BP in the Battle Subway	—

Mail

Item	Explanation	Main Way to Obtain	Price
BridgeMail D	Stationary featuring a print of a red drawbridge.	Driftveil City's Poké Mart	50
BridgeMail M	Stationary featuring a print of an arched bridge.	Poké Marts in Black City (*Pokémon Black Version*) or White Forest (*Pokémon White Version*)	50
BridgeMail S	Stationary featuring a print of a sky-piercing bridge.	Castelia City's Poké Mart	50
BridgeMail T	Stationary featuring a print of a steel suspension bridge.	Opelucid City's Poké Mart	50
BridgeMail V	Stationary featuring a print of a brick bridge.	Lacunosa Town's Poké Mart	50
Favored Mail	Stationary designed for writing about your favorite things.	All Poké Marts other than the ones at Nimbasa City, Mistralton City, Icirrus City, and the Pokémon League/Route 9 Shopping Mall 2F	50
Greet Mail	Stationary designed for introductory greetings.	All Poké Marts other than the ones at Nimbasa City, Mistralton City, Icirrus City, and the Pokémon League/Route 9 Shopping Mall 2F	50
Inquiry Mail	Stationary designed for writing questions.	All Poké Marts other than the ones at Nimbasa City, Mistralton City, Icirrus City, and the Pokémon League/Route 9 Shopping Mall 2F	50
Like Mail	Stationary designed for writing recommendations.	All Poké Marts other than the ones at Nimbasa City, Mistralton City, Icirrus City, and the Pokémon League/Route 9 Shopping Mall 2F	50
Reply Mail	Stationary designed for writing a reply.	All Poké Marts other than the ones at Nimbasa City, Mistralton City, Icirrus City, and the Pokémon League/Route 9 Shopping Mall 2F	50
RSVP Mail	Stationary designed for invitations.	All Poké Marts other than the ones at Nimbasa City, Mistralton City, Icirrus City, and the Pokémon League/Route 9 Shopping Mall 2F	50
Thanks Mail	Stationary designed for a thank-you note.	All Poké Marts other than the ones at Nimbasa City, Mistralton City, Icirrus City, and the Pokémon League/Route 9 Shopping Mall 2F	50

◇ Key Items

Item	Explanation	Main Way to Obtain	Price
Bicycle	A folding Bicycle that lets you travel faster than running.	Receive from the Day-Care Man in Nimbasa City	—
Dark Stone	Zekrom's body was destroyed and changed into this stone. It's waiting for a hero to appear.	Receive from Lenora in Nacrene City after investigating the Relic Castle (*Pokémon White Version*)	—
Dowsing MCHN	A cutting-edge device that alerts you to hidden items.	Receive from Bianca in Nacrene City	—
Dragon Skull	A skull of a Pokémon that flew freely through the skies.	Take back from Team Plasma in Pinwheel Forest	—
Gracidea	Shaymin can change Formes when holding this item (except at night).	Receive from the woman in Lacunosa Town's Pokémon Center (when Shaymin is in your party and you don't have the Gracidea)	—
Gram 1	An important letter Wingull delivers.	Receive from the older man on Route 13 (after hearing Wingull's story)	—
Gram 2	An important letter Wingull delivers.	Route 13 (after hearing Wingull's story)	—
Gram 3	An important letter Wingull delivers.	Receive from the Parasol Lady on Route 13 (after hearing Wingull's story)	—
Light Stone	Reshiram's body was destroyed and changed into this stone. It's waiting for a hero to appear.	Receive from Lenora in Nacrene City after investigating the Relic Castle (*Pokémon Black Version*)	—
Pal Pad	A useful pad that records friends and good times.	Receive from Amanita in Striaton City	—
Prop Case	A lovely case for the props for your Pokémon to wear in the Musical.	Receive from the owner at the Musical Theater in Nimbasa City	—
Super Rod	The best fishing rod. Use it to catch Pokémon from the waterside.	Receive from Looker in Nuvema Town (after finishing the main story)	—
Town Map	A very convenient map that can be viewed anytime.	Receive from your mom in Nuvema Town	—
Vs. Recorder	Records your battles with friends and in battle facilities.	Get from a woman in Nimbasa City	—
Xtransceiver	A cutting-edge transceiver with a camera that lets you chat with up to three other people.	Receive from your mom in Nuvema Town	—

◇ Poké Balls

Item	Explanation	Main Way to Obtain	Price
Poké Ball	An item for capturing wild Pokémon.	Poké Mart (from the start)/Route 9 Shopping Mall 2F	200
Dive Ball	A Poké Ball that makes it easier to catch Pokémon that live in the water.	Undella Town's Poké Mart	1,000
Dream Ball	A Poké Ball that magically appears in your bag in the Entree Forest.	Only appears in your bag when you are catching Pokémon in the Entree Forest.	—
Dusk Ball	A Poké Ball that does better at night and in caves.	Poké Marts in Driftveil City, Opelucid City, and the Pokémon League/Route 9 Shopping Mall 2F	1,000
Great Ball	A Poké Ball that provides a higher Pokémon catch rate than a standard Poké Ball.	Poké Mart (after obtaining one Gym Badge)/Route 9 Shopping Mall 2F	600
Heal Ball	A gentle Poké Ball that heals the caught Pokémon's HP and status.	Poké Marts in Striaton City, Nacrene City, Castelia City, and the Pokémon League/Route 9 Shopping Mall 2F	300
Luxury Ball	A Poké Ball that endears you to caught Pokémon.	Pokémon League/Undella Town Poké Mart	1,000
Master Ball	It is the ultimate Poké Ball that will surely catch any wild Pokémon.	Receive from Professor Juniper in Opelucid City/Receive from the sunglasses-wearing man in Castelia City's Pokémon Center (when you have 50 or more Pokémon with different OTs)	—
Nest Ball	A Poké Ball where the weaker the wild Pokémon is the more the catch rate increases.	Poké Marts in Castelia City, Driftveil City, and the Pokémon League/Route 9 Shopping Mall 2F	1,000
Net Ball	A Poké Ball with a high success rate against Bug- and Water-type Pokémon.	Poké Marts in Nacrene City, Castelia City, Driftveil City, and the Pokémon League/Route 9 Shopping Mall 2F	1,000
Premier Ball	A rare Poké Ball made in commemoration of an event.	Buy 10 or more Poké Balls at once	—
Quick Ball	A Poké Ball with a good capture rate when thrown right at the start of battle.	Opelucid City, Pokémon League Poké Mart/Route 9 Shopping Mall 2F	1,000
Repeat Ball	A Poké Ball that excels at catching Pokémon you've caught before.	Pokémon League's Poké Mart	1,000
Timer Ball	A Poké Ball that does better after more turns have elapsed in battle.	Opelucid City, Pokémon League Poké Mart/Route 9 Shopping Mall 2F	1,000
Ultra Ball	A Poké Ball that provides a higher Pokémon catch rate than a Great Ball.	Poké Mart (after obtaining five Gym Badges)/Route 9 Shopping Mall 2F	1,200

⬡ Berries

Item	Explanation	Main Way to Obtain	Price
Cheri Berry	Holder can heal itself of the Paralysis status condition.	Route 6 (after defeating Pokémon Ranger Shanti or Richard)/Show the Harlequin in Castelia City's Studio Castelia the Pokémon he wants to see	—
Chesto Berry	Holder can heal itself of the Sleep status condition.	Pinwheel Forest (after defeating Pokémon Ranger Forrest or Audra)/Show the Harlequin in Castelia City's Studio Castelia the Pokémon he wants to see	—
Pecha Berry	Holder can heal itself of the Poison status condition.	Pinwheel Forest (after defeating Pokémon Ranger Irene or Miguel)/Route 8 (after defeating Pokémon Ranger Lewis or Annie)	—
Rawst Berry	Holder can heal itself of the Burned status condition.	Desert Resort (after defeating Pokémon Ranger Mylene or Jaden)/Show the Harlequin in Castelia City's Studio Castelia the Pokémon he wants to see	—
Aspear Berry	Holder can heal itself of the Frozen status condition.	Route 7 (after defeating Pokémon Ranger Mary or Pedro)/Show the Harlequin in Castelia City's Studio Castelia the Pokémon he wants to see	—
Leppa Berry	Holder restores 10 PP to a move when that move's PP reaches 0.	Route 11 (after defeating Pokémon Ranger Crofton or Thalia)/Show the mayor of White Forest the Pokémon he wants to see (*Pokémon White Version*)	—
Oran Berry	Holder restores 10 of its own HP when its HP falls to half or less.	Route 3 (after defeating Pokémon Breeder Adelaide)/Receive from Cheren in Striaton City (after defeating him in a Pokémon Battle)	—
Persim Berry	Holder can heal itself of the Confused status condition.	Route 1 (after defeating Pokémon Ranger Brenda or Claude)	—
Lum Berry	Holder can heal itself of any status condition.	Route 3 (after defeating Pokémon Breeder Galen)/Successfully complete the job at the Village Bridge/Show the mayor of White Forest the Pokémon he wants to see (*Pokémon White Version*)	—
Sitrus Berry	Holder restores its own max HP by 1/4 its max HP when its HP falls to half or less.	Moor of Icirrus (after defeating Pokémon Ranger Chloris or Harry)/Route 12 (after defeating Pokémon Breeder Eustace or Ethel)	—
Figy Berry	Holder restores its own HP when its HP falls to half or less, but if the holder dislikes Spicy flavors, it gains the Confused status condition.	Prize for Spin Trades in the Union Room	—
Wiki Berry	Holder restores some of its own HP when its HP falls to half or less, but if the holder dislikes Dry flavors, it gains the Confused status condition.	Prize for Spin Trades in the Union Room	—
Mago Berry	Holder restores some of its own HP when its HP falls to half or less, but if the holder dislikes Sweet flavors, it gains the Confused status condition.	Prize for Spin Trades in the Union Room	—
Aguav Berry	Holder restores some of its own HP when its HP falls to half or less, but if the holder dislikes Bitter flavors, it gains the Confused status condition.	Prize for Spin Trades in the Union Room	—
Iapapa Berry	Holder restores some of its own HP when its HP falls to half or less, but if the holder dislikes Sour flavors, it gains the Confused status condition.	Prize for Spin Trades in the Union Room	—
Razz Berry	Can be sold to the Maid on Route 5 for 500 in prize money.	Not obtainable in these versions	—
Bluk Berry	Can be sold to the Maid on Route 5 for 500 in prize money.	Show the mayor of White Forest the Pokémon he wants to see (*Pokémon White Version*)	—
Nanab Berry	Can be sold to the Maid on Route 5 for 500 in prize money.	Not obtainable in these versions	—
Wepear Berry	Can be sold to the Maid on Route 5 for 500 in prize money.	Not obtainable in these versions	—
Pinap Berry	Can be sold to the Maid on Route 5 for 500 in prize money.	Not obtainable in these versions	—
Pomeg Berry	Slightly raises the Pokémon's friendship, but lowers its base HP stat.	Prize for Spin Trades in the Union Room	—
Kelpsy Berry	Slightly raises the Pokémon's friendship, but lowers its base Attack stat.	Prize for Spin Trades in the Union Room	—
Qualot Berry	Slightly raises the Pokémon's friendship, but lowers its base Defense stat.	Prize for Spin Trades in the Union Room	—
Hondew Berry	Slightly raises the Pokémon's friendship, but lowers its base Sp. Attack stat.	Prize for Spin Trades in the Union Room	—

◈ Berries

Item	Explanation	Main Way to Obtain	Price
Grepa Berry	Slightly raises the Pokémon's friendship, but lowers its base Sp. Defense stat.	Prize for Spin Trades in the Union Room	—
Tamato Berry	Slightly raises the Pokémon's friendship, but lowers its base Speed stat.	Prize for Spin Trades in the Union Room	—
Cornn Berry	Can be sold to the Maid on Route 5 for 500 in prize money.	Not obtainable in these versions	—
Magost Berry	Can be sold to the Maid on Route 5 for 500 in prize money.	Not obtainable in these versions	—
Rabuta Berry	Can be sold to the Maid on Route 5 for 500 in prize money.	Not obtainable in these versions	—
Nomel Berry	Can be sold to the Maid on Route 5 for 500 in prize money.	Not obtainable in these versions	—
Spelon Berry	Can be sold to the Maid on Route 5 for 500 in prize money.	Not obtainable in these versions	—
Pamtre Berry	Can be sold to the Maid on Route 5 for 500 in prize money.	Not obtainable in these versions	—
Watmel Berry	Can be sold to the Maid on Route 5 for 500 in prize money.	Not obtainable in these versions	—
Durin Berry	Can be sold to the Maid on Route 5 for 500 in prize money.	Not obtainable in these versions	—
Belue Berry	Can be sold to the Maid on Route 5 for 500 in prize money.	Not obtainable in these versions	—
Occa Berry	Halves damage the holder takes from supereffective Fire-type moves.	Sometimes held by wild Pansage	—
Passho Berry	Halves damage the holder takes from supereffective Water-type moves.	Sometimes held by wild Pansear	—
Wacan Berry	Halves damage the holder takes from supereffective Electric-type moves.	Wild Buizel and Floatzel, who appear after the main story is completed, will sometimes be holding this item.	—
Rindo Berry	Halves damage the holder takes from supereffective Grass-type moves.	Sometimes held by wild Panpour	—
Yache Berry	Halves damage the holder takes from supereffective Ice-type moves.	From Iris in Castelia City	—
Chople Berry	Halves damage the holder takes from supereffective Fighting-type moves.	Not obtainable in these versions	—
Kebia Berry	Halves damage the holder takes from supereffective Poison-type moves.	Shroomish, who appear during a Pokémon outbreak in *Pokémon Black Version*, will sometimes be holding this item.	—
Shuca Berry	Halves damage the holder takes from supereffective Ground-type moves.	Wild Rapidash, who appear after the main story is completed, will sometimes be holding this item.	—
Coba Berry	Halves damage the holder takes from supereffective Flying-type moves.	Wild Sunkern, who appear after the main story is completed, will sometimes be holding this item.	—
Payapa Berry	Halves damage the holder takes from supereffective Psychic-type moves.	Mankey, who appear during a Pokémon outbreak, will sometimes be holding this item.	—
Tanga Berry	Halves damage the holder takes from supereffective Bug-type moves.	Not obtainable in these versions	—
Charti Berry	Halves damage the holder takes from supereffective Rock-type moves.	Wild Swellow, who appear after the main story is completed, will sometimes be holding this item.	—
Kasib Berry	Halves damage the holder takes from supereffective Ghost-type moves.	Not obtainable in these versions	—

Item	Explanation	Main Way to Obtain	Price
Haban Berry	Halves damage the holder takes from supereffective Dragon-type moves.	Not obtainable in these versions	—
Colbur Berry	Halves damage the holder takes from supereffective Dark-type moves.	Wild Chimecho, who appear after the main story is completed, will sometimes be holding this item.	—
Babiri Berry	Halves damage the holder takes from supereffective Steel-type moves.	Not obtainable in these versions	—
Chilan Berry	Halves damage the holder takes from Normal-type moves.	Wild Raticate, who appear after the main story is completed, will sometimes be holding this item.	—
Liechi Berry	Holder raises its Attack stat by 1 when its HP becomes low.	Not obtainable in these versions	—
Ganlon Berry	Holder raises its Defense stat by 1 when its HP becomes low.	Not obtainable in these versions	—
Salac Berry	Holder raises its Speed stat by 1 when its HP becomes low.	Not obtainable in these versions	—
Petaya Berry	Holder raises its Sp. Attack stat by 1 when its HP becomes low.	Not obtainable in these versions	—
Apicot Berry	Holder's Sp. Defense goes up 1 when its HP falls to half or less.	Not obtainable in these versions	—
Lansat Berry	Raises the critical-hit ratio of the holder's attacks when its HP falls to half or less.	From a Trainer on the platform you visit after you win enough battles in a row on the Battle Subway.	—
Starf Berry	Raises one of the holder's stats by 2 when its HP falls to half or less.	From a Trainer on the platform you visit after you win enough battles in a row on the Battle Subway.	—
Enigma Berry	When the holder is damaged by a supereffective attack, some HP is restored.	Not obtainable in these versions	—
Micle Berry	Raises the accuracy of the holder's moves by 20% the turn when its HP becomes low.	Not obtainable in these versions	—
Custap Berry	The holder's move is more likely to strike first during the next turn when its HP becomes low.	Not obtainable in these versions	—
Jaboca Berry	When the holder takes damage from a physical attack the opponent who landed the attack is also damaged.	Not obtainable in these versions	—
Rowap Berry	When the holder takes damage from a special attack the opponent who landed the attack is also damaged.	Not obtainable in these versions	—

● Changes in time due to the seasons

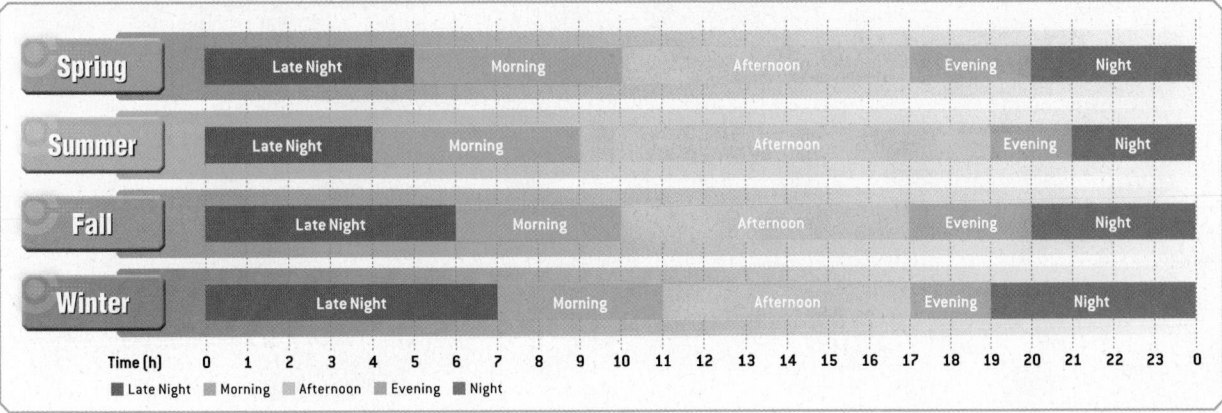

Items held by wild Pokémon: Unova Pokémon

Some wild Pokémon are holding items. When you catch a Pokémon with an item, you also get that item. Some items can only be obtained this way, such as the Shed Shell held by Scraggy, or the Black Sludge held by Trubbish and Garbodor. The many ways to get the items held by Pokémon from other regions that you can meet after finishing the main story are listed on pages 292–301.

Unova Region	Pokémon	Always holding	Often holding	Sometimes holding	Rarely holding
017	Pansage	—	Oran Berry	Occa Berry	—
019	Pansear	—	Oran Berry	Passho Berry	—
021	Panpour	—	Oran Berry	Rindo Berry	—
028	Blitzle	—	Cheri Berry	—	—
029	Zebstrika	—	Cheri Berry	—	—
030	Roggenrola	—	Everstone	Hard Stone	—
031	Boldore	—	Everstone	Hard Stone	—
037	Audino	—	Oran Berry	Sitrus Berry	—
041	Tympole	—	Persim Berry	—	—
042	Palpitoad	—	Persim Berry	—	—
043	Seismitoad	—	Persim Berry	—	—
044	Throh	—	—	Black Belt	Expert Belt
045	Sawk	—	—	Black Belt	Expert Belt
046	Sewaddle	—	—	Mental Herb	—
047	Swadloon	—	—	Mental Herb	—
048	Leavanny	—	—	Mental Herb	—
049	Venipede	—	Pecha Berry	Poison Barb	—
050	Whirlipede	—	Pecha Berry	Poison Barb	—
056	Basculin (Red-Striped Form)	—	—	DeepSeaTooth	—
056	Basculin (Blue-Striped Form)	—	—	DeepSeaScale	—
060	Darumaka	—	Rawst Berry	—	—
061	Darmanitan	—	Rawst Berry	—	—
062	Maractus	—	—	Miracle Seed	—
063	Dwebble	—	—	Hard Stone	—
064	Crustle	—	—	Hard Stone	Rare Bone
065	Scraggy	—	—	Shed Shell	—
068	Yamask	—	—	Spell Tag	—
069	Cofagrigus	—	—	Spell Tag	—
074	Trubbish	—	—	Black Sludge	Nugget
075	Garbodor	—	Black Sludge	Nugget	Big Nugget
078	Minccino	—	Chesto Berry	—	—
079	Cinccino	—	Chesto Berry	—	—
093	Emolga	Cheri Berry	—	—	—
096	Foongus	—	TinyMushroom	Big Mushroom	BalmMushroom
097	Amoonguss	—	TinyMushroom	Big Mushroom	BalmMushroom
103	Ferroseed	—	—	Sticky Barb	—
119	Cubchoo	—	Aspear Berry	—	—
120	Beartic	—	Aspear Berry	—	—
121	Cryogonal	—	—	NeverMeltIce	—
124	Stunfisk	—	—	Soft Sand	—
127	Druddigon	—	—	Dragon Fang	—
128	Golett	—	—	Light Clay	—
143	Volcarona	SilverPowder	—	—	—

● Pokémon holding items listed in the "Rarely holding" column appear only in the dark grass.

306

Items that certain people will buy from you

There are people in the Unova region who will buy certain items, and they will pay handsomely for them. If you sell items to these people, they will pay twice what the Poké Mart will buy the item for. Some items, such as BalmMushroom and Pearl String, are only purchased by these people.

■ Items the Maid in the trailer on Route 5 buys

Item	Price	Item	Price	Item	Price
Cheri Berry	20	Shuca Berry	20	Cornn Berry	500
Chesto Berry	20	Coba Berry	20	Magost Berry	500
Pecha Berry	20	Payapa Berry	20	Rabuta Berry	500
Rawst Berry	20	Tanga Berry	20	Nomel Berry	500
Aspear Berry	20	Charti Berry	20	Spelon Berry	500
Leppa Berry	20	Kasib Berry	20	Pamtre Berry	500
Oran Berry	20	Haban Berry	20	Watmel Berry	500
Persim Berry	20	Colbur Berry	20	Durin Berry	500
Lum Berry	20	Babiri Berry	20	Belue Berry	500
Sitrus Berry	20	Chilan Berry	20	Honey	500
Figy Berry	20	Liechi Berry	20	TinyMushroom	500
Wiki Berry	20	Ganlon Berry	20	Berry Juice	1,500
Mago Berry	20	Salac Berry	20	Casteliacone	2,000
Aguav Berry	20	Petaya Berry	20	Lava Cookie	4,000
Iapapa Berry	20	Apicot Berry	20	Old Gateau	4,000
Pomeg Berry	20	Sweet Heart	100	Big Mushroom	5,000
Kelpsy Berry	20	Lucky Egg	200	RageCandyBar	6,000
Qualot Berry	20	Leftovers	200	Shoal Salt	7,000
Hondew Berry	20	Stick	200	Rare Candy	10,000
Grepa Berry	20	Fresh Water	200	BalmMushroom	25,000
Tamato Berry	20	Soda Pop	300	Lansat Berry	30,000
Occa Berry	20	Lemonade	350	Starf Berry	30,000
Passho Berry	20	Moomoo Milk	500	Enigma Berry	30,000
Wacan Berry	20	Razz Berry	500	Micle Berry	30,000
Rindo Berry	20	Bluk Berry	500	Custap Berry	30,000
Yache Berry	20	Nanab Berry	500	Jaboca Berry	30,000
Chople Berry	20	Wepear Berry	500	Rowap Berry	30,000
Kebia Berry	20	Pinap Berry	500		

■ Items the old gentleman in Icirrus City's Pokémon Center buys

Item	Price	Item	Price	Item	Price
Red Shard	200	Ghost Gem	200	Water Stone	3,000
Blue Shard	200	Dragon Gem	200	Dawn Stone	3,000
Yellow Shard	200	Dark Gem	200	Thunderstone	3,000
Green Shard	200	Steel Gem	200	Shiny Stone	3,000
Fire Gem	200	Normal Gem	200	Dusk Stone	3,000
Water Gem	200	Hard Stone	500	Sun Stone	3,000
Electric Gem	200	Everstone	1,000	Moon Stone	3,000
Grass Gem	200	Icy Rock	1,000	Shoal Shell	7,000
Ice Gem	200	Smooth Rock	1,000	Big Pearl	7,500
Fighting Gem	200	Heat Rock	1,000	Star Piece	9,800
Poison Gem	200	Damp Rock	1,000	Nugget	10,000
Ground Gem	200	Float Stone	1,000	Pearl String	25,000
Flying Gem	200	Pearl	1,400	Big Nugget	30,000
Psychic Gem	200	Oval Stone	1,500	Comet Shard	60,000
Bug Gem	200	Stardust	2,000		
Rock Gem	200	Fire Stone	3,000		

■ Items the sunglasses-wearing man in the prefab house on Route 18 buys

Item	Price
Rare Bone	10,000

■ Items the billionaire in the big villa in Undella Town buys

Item	Price	Item	Price	Item	Price
Blue Flute	7,000	Black Flute	8,000	Relic Vase	???
Red Flute	7,500	Relic Copper	???	Relic Band	???
Yellow Flute	7,500	Relic Silver	???	Relic Statue	???
White Flute	8,000	Relic Gold	???	Relic Crown	???

PprOKÉMON MUSICAL PROPS ◆ ADVENTURE DATA

Props for the Head

Style ● Cool	Style ● Cool	Style ● Cool	Style ● Cool	Style ● Cool	Style ● Cute	Style ● Cute
Chef's Hat	**Cowboy Hat**	**Horned Helm**	**Pirate Hat**	**Wig**	**Big Barrette**	**Decorative Ribbon**

● How to obtain	● How to obtain	● How to obtain	● How to obtain	● How to obtain	● How to obtain	● How to obtain
Receive from a fan after participating in a musical	Receive from a fan after participating in a musical	Receive from a fan after participating in a musical	Receive from a fan after participating in a musical	Receive from a fan after participating in a musical	Receive from a fan after participating in a musical	Receive from a fan after participating in a musical

Style ● Cute	Style ● Cute	Style ● Elegant	Style ● Elegant	Style ● Elegant	Style ● Elegant	Style ● Elegant	Style ● Elegant
Fedora	**Headband**	**Crown**	**Gentleman's Hat**	**Lace Cap**	**Laurel Wreath**	**Tiara**	**Top Hat**
● How to obtain	● How to obtain	● How to obtain	● How to obtain	● How to obtain	● How to obtain	● How to obtain	● How to obtain
Receive from a fan after participating in a musical	Receive from a fan after participating in a musical	Talk to the owner after getting the highest reviews five or more times	Receive from a fan after participating in a musical	Receive from a fan after participating in a musical	Receive from a fan after participating in a musical	Talk to the owner after participating in a musical with friends via IR or wireless	Get right away

Style ● Unique	Style ● Unique	Style ● Unique	Style ● Unique	Style ● Unique	Style ● Unique	Style ● Unique	Style ● Unique
Beret	**Helmet**	**Jester's Cap**	**Professor Hat**	**Scarlet Hat**	**Straw Hat**	**Windup Key**	**Witchy Hat**
● How to obtain	● How to obtain	● How to obtain	● How to obtain	● How to obtain	● How to obtain	● How to obtain	● How to obtain
Receive from a fan after participating in a musical	Receive from a fan after participating in a musical	Receive from a fan after participating in a musical	Receive from a fan after participating in a musical	Receive from the old man who loves musicals in Opelucid City	Receive from a fan after participating in a musical	Receive from a fan after participating in a musical	Receive from a fan after participating in a musical

Props for the Ears

Style ● Cute	Style ● Cute	Style ● Cute	Style ● Cute	Style ● Cute	Style ● Cute	Style ● Cute
Blue Barrette	**Blue Flower**	**Pink Barrette**	**Red Barrette**	**Red Flower**	**Striped Barrette**	**Small Barrette**
● How to obtain	● How to obtain	● How to obtain	● How to obtain	● How to obtain	● How to obtain	● How to obtain
Get right away	Receive from a fan after participating in a musical	Get right away	Receive from a fan after participating in a musical	Receive from a fan after participating in a musical	Receive from a fan after participating in a musical	Get right away

Style ● Elegant	Style ● Elegant	Style ● Unique		Style ● Cool	Style ● Elegant	Style ● Elegant	Style ● Elegant
Gorgeous Flower	**Snow Crystal**	**Green Barrette**	**Props for the Face**	**White Domino Mask**	**Fluffy Beard**	**Gorgeous Specs**	**Monocle**
● How to obtain	● How to obtain	● How to obtain		● How to obtain	● How to obtain	● How to obtain	● How to obtain
Receive from a fan after participating in a musical	Receive from a fan after participating in a musical	Get right away		Receive from a fan after participating in a musical	Receive from the old man who loves musicals in Opelucid City	Receive from a fan after participating in a musical	Receive from a fan after participating in a musical

Style ● Elegant	Style ● Unique	Style ● Unique	Style ● Unique	Style ● Unique		Style ● Cool	Style ● Cool
Square Glasses	**Germ Mask**	**Googly Specs**	**Red Nose**	**Smiley-Face Mask**	**Props for the Arms**	**Electric Guitar**	**Football**
● How to obtain	● How to obtain	● How to obtain	● How to obtain	● How to obtain		● How to obtain	● How to obtain
Get right away	Receive from a fan after participating in a musical	Receive from a fan after participating in a musical	Receive from a fan after participating in a musical	Receive from a fan after participating in a musical		Defeat Musician Preston on Route 5	Receive from a fan after participating in a musical

Style ● Cool	Style ● Cool	Style ● Cool	Style ● Cool	Style ● Cool	Style ● Cool	Style ● Cool	Style ● Cool
Frying Pan	**Lantern**	**Racket**	**Rigid Shield**	**Shuriken**	**Standing Mike**	**Toy Cutlass**	**Toy Fishing Rod**
● How to obtain	● How to obtain	● How to obtain	● How to obtain	● How to obtain	● How to obtain	● How to obtain	● How to obtain
Receive from a fan after participating in a musical	Receive from a fan after participating in a musical	Get right away	Receive from a fan after participating in a musical	Receive from a fan after participating in a musical	Receive from a fan after participating in a musical	Receive from a fan after participating in a musical	Receive from a fan after participating in a musical

Style	Prop	Image	How to obtain
● Cool	Toy Sword		Receive from a fan after participating in a musical
● Cool	Trident		Receive from a fan after participating in a musical
● Cool	Wrench		Receive from a fan after participating in a musical
● Cute	Candy		Receive from a fan after participating in a musical
● Cute	Colorful Parasol		Receive from a fan after participating in a musical
● Cute	Gift Box		Receive from the old man who loves musicals in Opelucid City
● Cute	Microphone		Get right away
● Cute	Purse		Receive from a fan after participating in a musical
● Cute	Red Parasol		Get right away
● Cute	Tambourine		Receive from a fan after participating in a musical
● Cute	Toy Cake		Talk to the owner on the birthday registered in your Nintendo DS system
● Cute	Whisk		Receive from a fan after participating in a musical
● Cute	White Pompom		Receive from a fan after participating in a musical
● Elegant	Bouquet		Receive from a fan after participating in a musical
● Elegant	Cane		Get right away
● Elegant	Lonely Flower		Receive from a fan after participating in a musical
● Elegant	Pocket Watch		Receive from a fan after participating in a musical
● Elegant	Rose		Receive from a fan after participating in a musical
● Elegant	Trumpet		Receive from a fan after participating in a musical
● Unique	Big Bag		Receive from the old man who loves musicals in Opelucid City
● Unique	Fake Bone		Receive from a fan after participating in a musical
● Unique	Ladle		Receive from a fan after participating in a musical
● Unique	Magic Wand		Receive from a fan after participating in a musical
● Unique	Mallet		Receive from a fan after participating in a musical
● Unique	Maraca		Get right away
● Unique	Paintbrush		Receive from a fan after participating in a musical
● Unique	Pennant		Receive from a fan after participating in a musical
● Unique	Round Mushroom		Receive from a fan after participating in a musical
● Unique	Thick Book		Receive from a fan after participating in a musical

Props for the Waist

Style	Prop	Image	How to obtain
● Cool	Umber Belt		Get right away
● Cool	Winner's Belt		Talk to the owner after getting the highest reviews ten times or more

Style	Prop	Image	How to obtain
● Elegant	Frilly Apron		Receive from a fan after participating in a musical
● Unique	Fake Bellybutton		Receive from a fan after participating in a musical
● Unique	Hula Skirt		Get right away

Props for the Body

Style	Prop	Image	How to obtain
● Cool	Black Wings		Receive from a fan after participating in a musical
● Cool	Scarlet Cape		Receive from a fan after participating in a musical
● Cool	Striped Tie		Receive from a fan after participating in a musical
● Cool	Tie		Get right away
● Cute	Bib		Receive from a fan after participating in a musical
● Cute	Crimson Scarf		Receive from a fan after participating in a musical
● Cute	Round Button		Receive from a fan after participating in a musical
● Cute	White Wings		Receive from a fan after participating in a musical
● Elegant	Black Cape		Receive from a fan after participating in a musical
● Elegant	Black Tie		Receive from a fan after participating in a musical
● Elegant	Bow Tie		Get right away
● Elegant	Dressy Tie		Receive from a fan after participating in a musical
● Elegant	Necklace		Receive from a fan after participating in a musical
● Elegant	White Cape		Receive from a fan after participating in a musical

In this section you can look up all the Pokémon that can learn a certain move, searching by move. The numbers in the brackets are the level at which the Pokémon learns the move, [TM] is a Technical Machine, and [HM] is a Hidden Machine. Also, [E] is an Egg Move, and [T] is a move that someone teaches the Pokémon.

◈ A

Move	Pokémon that can learn it					
Absorb	052 Cottonee [1]	054 Petilil [1]	062 Maractus [1]	096 Foongus [1]	097 Amoonguss [1]	098 Frillish [5]
	099 Jellicent [1, 5]					
Acid	043 Seismitoad [36]	109 Eelektrik [19]	110 Eelektross [1]	113 Litwick [E]	122 Shelmet [4]	
Acid Armor	083 Solosis [E]	088 Vanillite [31]	089 Vanillish [31]	090 Vanilluxe [31]	098 Frillish [E]	113 Litwick [E]
	121 Cryogonal [29]	122 Shelmet [32]				
Acid Spray	074 Trubbish [12]	075 Garbodor [12]	109 Eelektrik [49]	123 Accelgor [1, 4]		
Acrobatics	017 Pansage [31, TM]	018 Simisage [TM]	019 Pansear [31, TM]	020 Simisear [TM]	021 Panpour [31, TM]	022 Simipour [TM]
	033 Woobat [TM]	034 Swoobat [TM]	072 Archen [28, TM]	073 Archeops [28, TM]	093 Emolga [30, TM]	109 Eelektrik [TM]
	110 Eelektross [TM]	121 Cryogonal [TM]	125 Mienfoo [TM]	126 Mienshao [TM]	141 Hydreigon [TM]	142 Larvesta [TM]
	143 Volcarona [TM]	147 Tornadus [TM]				
Acupressure	062 Maractus [29]					
Aerial Ace	001 Snivy [TM]	002 Servine [TM]	003 Serperior [TM]	007 Oshawott [TM]	008 Dewott [TM]	009 Samurott [TM]
	012 Lillipup [TM]	013 Herdier [TM]	014 Stoutland [TM]	015 Purrloin [TM]	016 Liepard [TM]	025 Pidove [TM]
	026 Tranquill [TM]	027 Unfezant [TM]	033 Woobat [TM]	034 Swoobat [TM]	035 Drilbur [TM]	036 Excadrill [TM]
	048 Leavanny [TM]	059 Krookodile [TM]	062 Maractus [TM]	063 Dwebble [TM]	064 Crustle [TM]	067 Sigilyph [TM]
	072 Archen [TM]	073 Archeops [TM]	076 Zorua [TM]	077 Zoroark [TM]	086 Ducklett [15, TM]	087 Swanna [15, TM]
	093 Emolga [TM]	094 Karrablast [TM]	095 Escavalier [TM]	104 Ferrothorn [TM]	116 Axew [TM]	117 Fraxure [TM]
	118 Haxorus [TM]	119 Cubchoo [TM]	120 Beartic [TM]	125 Mienfoo [TM]	126 Mienshao [TM]	127 Druddigon [TM]
	130 Pawniard [TM]	131 Bisharp [TM]	132 Bouffalant [TM]	133 Rufflet [23, TM]	134 Braviary [23, TM]	135 Vullaby [TM]
	136 Mandibuzz [TM]	137 Heatmor [TM]	138 Durant [TM]	143 Volcarona [TM]	144 Cobalion [TM]	145 Terrakion [TM]
	146 Virizion [TM]	147 Tornadus [TM]				
Aeroblast	—					
After You	010 Patrat [23]	011 Watchog [25]	037 Audino [40]	054 Petilil [44]	062 Maractus [57]	078 Minccino [49]
Agility	028 Blitzle [36]	029 Zebstrika [42]	046 Sewaddle [E]	049 Venipede [29]	050 Whirlipede [32]	051 Scolipede [33]
	056 Basculin [E]	072 Archen [21]	073 Archeops [21]	076 Zorua [37]	077 Zoroark [39]	091 Deerling [E]
	093 Emolga [46]	101 Joltik [37]	102 Galvantula [40]	123 Accelgor [32]	138 Durant [16]	147 Tornadus [37]
	148 Thundurus [37]					
Air Cutter	025 Pidove [15]	026 Tranquill [15]	027 Unfezant [15]	033 Woobat [21]	034 Swoobat [21]	067 Sigilyph [21]
	086 Ducklett [E]	147 Tornadus [25]				
Air Slash	007 Oshawott [E]	025 Pidove [29]	026 Tranquill [32]	027 Unfezant [33]	033 Woobat [32]	034 Swoobat [32]
	046 Sewaddle [E]	067 Sigilyph [41]	086 Ducklett [27]	087 Swanna [27]	093 Emolga [E]	133 Rufflet [41]
	134 Braviary [41]	135 Vullaby [41]	136 Mandibuzz [41]	147 Tornadus [43]		
Ally Switch	111 Elgyem [TM]	112 Beheeyem [TM]				
Amnesia	019 Pansear [25]	033 Woobat [29]	034 Swoobat [29]	037 Audino [E]	065 Scraggy [E]	074 Trubbish [40]
	075 Garbodor [46]	132 Bouffalant [E]	137 Heatmor [46]	142 Larvesta [80]		
AncientPower	067 Sigilyph [E]	070 Tirtouga [18]	071 Carracosta [18]	072 Archen [18]	073 Archeops [18]	149 Reshiram [15]
	150 Zekrom [15]	152 Kyurem [15]				
Aqua Jet	007 Oshawott [29]	008 Dewott [33]	009 Samurott [33]	056 Basculin [13]	070 Tirtouga [15]	071 Carracosta [15]
	100 Alomomola [9]					
Aqua Ring	021 Panpour [E]	041 Tympole [20]	042 Palpitoad [20]	043 Seismitoad [20]	086 Ducklett [24]	087 Swanna [24]
	100 Alomomola [5]					
Aqua Tail	007 Oshawott [35]	008 Dewott [41]	009 Samurott [45]	021 Panpour [E]	056 Basculin [28]	070 Tirtouga [41]
	071 Carracosta [45]	078 Minccino [E]				
Arm Thrust	005 Pignite [17]	006 Emboar [17]				
Aromatherapy	054 Petilil [28]	091 Deerling [28]	092 Sawsbuck [28]			
Assist	015 Purrloin [6]	016 Liepard [1, 6]				
Assurance	004 Tepig [31]	005 Pignite [36]	006 Emboar [38]	007 Oshawott [E]	010 Patrat [E]	015 Purrloin [28]
	016 Liepard [31]	033 Woobat [12]	034 Swoobat [1, 12]	057 Sandile [16]	058 Krokorok [16]	059 Krookodile [16]
	116 Axew [7]	117 Fraxure [1, 7]	118 Haxorus [1, 7]	119 Cubchoo [E]	130 Pawniard [33]	131 Bisharp [33]
	139 Deino [E]					
Astonish	017 Pansage [E]	019 Pansear [E]	021 Panpour [E]	068 Yamask [1]	069 Cofagrigus [1]	083 Solosis [E]
	088 Vanillite [7]	089 Vanillish [1, 7]	090 Vanilluxe [1, 7]	093 Emolga [E]	096 Foongus [8]	097 Amoonguss [1, 8]
	111 Elgyem [E]	113 Litwick [1]	114 Lampent [1]	124 Stunfisk [E]	128 Golett [1]	129 Golurk [1]
	139 Deino [E]	147 Tornadus [1]	148 Thundurus [1]			
Attack Order	—					
Attract	001 Snivy [TM]	002 Servine [TM]	003 Serperior [TM]	004 Tepig [TM]	005 Pignite [TM]	006 Emboar [TM]
	007 Oshawott [TM]	008 Dewott [TM]	009 Samurott [TM]	010 Patrat [TM]	011 Watchog [TM]	012 Lillipup [TM]
	013 Herdier [TM]	014 Stoutland [TM]	015 Purrloin [TM]	016 Liepard [TM]	017 Pansage [TM]	018 Simisage [TM]
	019 Pansear [TM]	020 Simisear [TM]	021 Panpour [TM]	022 Simipour [TM]	023 Munna [TM]	024 Musharna [TM]
	025 Pidove [TM]	026 Tranquill [TM]	027 Unfezant [TM]	028 Blitzle [TM]	029 Zebstrika [TM]	030 Roggenrola [TM]
	031 Boldore [TM]	032 Gigalith [TM]	033 Woobat [25, TM]	034 Swoobat [25, TM]	035 Drilbur [TM]	036 Excadrill [TM]
	037 Audino [15, TM]	038 Timburr [TM]	039 Gurdurr [TM]	040 Conkeldurr [TM]	041 Tympole [TM]	042 Palpitoad [TM]

Move	Pokémon that can learn it					
Attract (continued)	043 Seismitoad [TM]	044 Throh [TM]	045 Sawk [TM]	046 Sewaddle [TM]	047 Swadloon [TM]	048 Leavanny [TM]
	049 Venipede [TM]	050 Whirlipede [TM]	051 Scolipede [TM]	052 Cottonee [TM]	053 Whimsicott [TM]	054 Petilil [TM]
	055 Lilligant [TM]	056 Basculin [TM]	057 Sandile [TM]	058 Krokorok [TM]	059 Krookodile [TM]	060 Darumaka [TM]
	061 Darmanitan [TM]	062 Maractus [TM]	063 Dwebble [TM]	064 Crustle [TM]	065 Scraggy [TM]	066 Scrafty [TM]
	067 Sigilyph [TM]	068 Yamask [TM]	069 Cofagrigus [TM]	070 Tirtouga [TM]	071 Carracosta [TM]	072 Archen [TM]
	073 Archeops [TM]	074 Trubbish [TM]	075 Garbodor [TM]	076 Zorua [TM]	077 Zoroark [TM]	078 Minccino [TM]
	079 Cinccino [TM]	080 Gothita [TM]	081 Gothorita [TM]	082 Gothitelle [TM]	083 Solosis [TM]	084 Duosion [TM]
	085 Reuniclus [TM]	086 Ducklett [TM]	087 Swanna [TM]	088 Vanillite [TM]	089 Vanillish [TM]	090 Vanilluxe [TM]
	091 Deerling [TM]	092 Sawsbuck [TM]	093 Emolga [TM]	094 Karrablast [TM]	095 Escavalier [TM]	096 Foongus [TM]
	097 Amoonguss [TM]	098 Frillish [TM]	099 Jellicent [TM]	100 Alomomola [TM]	101 Joltik [TM]	102 Galvantula [TM]
	109 Eelektrik [TM]	110 Eelektross [TM]	111 Elgyem [TM]	112 Beheeyem [TM]	113 Litwick [TM]	114 Lampent [TM]
	115 Chandelure [TM]	116 Axew [TM]	117 Fraxure [TM]	118 Haxorus [TM]	119 Cubchoo [TM]	120 Beartic [TM]
	121 Cryogonal [TM]	122 Shelmet [TM]	123 Accelgor [TM]	124 Stunfisk [TM]	125 Mienfoo [TM]	126 Mienshao [TM]
	127 Druddigon [TM]	130 Pawniard [TM]	131 Bisharp [TM]	132 Bouffalant [TM]	133 Rufflet [TM]	134 Braviary [TM]
	135 Vullaby [TM]	136 Mandibuzz [TM]	137 Heatmor [TM]	138 Durant [TM]	139 Deino [TM]	140 Zweilous [TM]
	141 Hydreigon [TM]	147 Tornadus [TM]	148 Thundurus [TM]	151 Landorus [TM]		
Aura Sphere	125 Mienfoo [61]	126 Mienshao [70]				
Aurora Beam	121 Cryogonal [25]					
Autotomize	030 Roggenrola [E]	088 Vanillite [E]	105 Klink [31]	106 Klang [31]	107 Klinklang [31]	
Avalanche	088 Vanillite [19]	089 Vanillish [19]	090 Vanilluxe [19]	119 Cubchoo [E]		

◈◈ **B**

Move	Pokémon that can learn it					
Barrage	—					
Barrier	023 Munna [E]	111 Elgyem [E]				
Baton Pass	010 Patrat [33]	011 Watchog [39]	023 Munna [E]	046 Sewaddle [E]	051 Scolipede [30]	091 Deerling [E]
	093 Emolga [E]	122 Shelmet [E]	125 Mienfoo [E]	138 Durant [E]		
Beat Up	052 Cottonee [E]	057 Sandile [E]				
Belly Drum	060 Darumaka [30]	061 Darmanitan [30]				
Bestow	025 Pidove [E]	037 Audino [E]				
Bide	010 Patrat [8]	011 Watchog [8]	038 Timburr [8]	039 Gurdurr [1, 8]	040 Conkeldurr [1, 8]	044 Throh [5]
	045 Sawk [5]	054 Petilil [E]	070 Tirtouga [1, E]	071 Carracosta [1]	096 Foongus [12]	097 Amoonguss [1, 12]
	119 Cubchoo [9]	120 Beartic [1, 9]	122 Shelmet [8]	124 Stunfisk [5]		
Bind	044 Throh [1]	105 Klink [21]	106 Klang [21]	107 Klinklang [21]	109 Eelektrik [9]	121 Cryogonal [1]
	137 Heatmor [11]					
Bite	010 Patrat [6]	011 Watchog [1, 6]	012 Lillipup [8]	013 Herdier [1, 8]	014 Stoutland [1, 8]	017 Pansage [19]
	019 Pansear [19]	021 Panpour [19]	056 Basculin [10]	057 Sandile [4]	058 Krokorok [1, 4]	059 Krookodile [1, 4]
	070 Tirtouga [8]	071 Carracosta [8]	072 Archen [E]	127 Druddigon [9]	138 Durant [11]	139 Deino [9]
	140 Zweilous [1, 9]	141 Hydreigon [1, 9]	147 Tornadus [13]	148 Thundurus [13]		
Blast Burn	006 Emboar [T]					
Blaze Kick						
Blizzard	007 Oshawott [TM]	008 Dewott [TM]	009 Samurott [TM]	021 Panpour [TM]	022 Simipour [TM]	037 Audino [TM]
	070 Tirtouga [TM]	071 Carracosta [TM]	088 Vanillite [49, TM]	089 Vanillish [53, TM]	090 Vanilluxe [59, TM]	098 Frillish [TM]
	099 Jellicent [TM]	100 Alomomola [TM]	119 Cubchoo [45, TM]	120 Beartic [45, TM]	121 Cryogonal [TM]	152 Kyurem [78, TM]
Block	063 Dwebble [E]	151 Landorus [1]				
Blue Flare	149 Reshiram [100]					
Body Slam	004 Tepig [E]	044 Throh [29]	070 Tirtouga [E]	075 Garbodor [25]	096 Foongus [E]	122 Shelmet [40]
	137 Heatmor [E]	139 Deino [48]	140 Zweilous [48]	141 Hydreigon [48]		
Bolt Strike	150 Zekrom [100]					
Bone Club	—					
Bone Rush	136 Mandibuzz [51]					
Bonemerang	—					
Bounce	062 Maractus [E]	124 Stunfisk [35]	125 Mienfoo [49]	126 Mienshao [49]		
Brave Bird	086 Ducklett [41]	087 Swanna [47]	133 Rufflet [59]	134 Braviary [63]	135 Vullaby [59]	136 Mandibuzz [63]
Brick Break	000 Victini [TM]	005 Pignite [TM]	006 Emboar [TM]	018 Simisage [TM]	020 Simisear [TM]	022 Simipour [TM]
	035 Drilbur [TM]	036 Excadrill [TM]	038 Timburr [TM]	039 Gurdurr [TM]	040 Conkeldurr [TM]	043 Seismitoad [TM]
	044 Throh [TM]	045 Sawk [29, TM]	058 Krokorok [TM]	059 Krookodile [TM]	060 Darumaka [TM]	061 Darmanitan [TM]
	065 Scraggy [20, TM]	066 Scrafty [20, TM]	082 Gothitelle [TM]	110 Eelektross [TM]	118 Haxorus [TM]	120 Beartic [TM]
	125 Mienfoo [TM]	126 Mienshao [TM]	128 Golett [TM]	129 Golurk [TM]	130 Pawniard [TM]	131 Bisharp [TM]
	147 Tornadus [TM]	148 Thundurus [TM]	151 Landorus [TM]			
Brine	007 Oshawott [E]	021 Panpour [34]	056 Basculin [E]	070 Tirtouga [28]	071 Carracosta [28]	086 Ducklett [E]
	098 Frillish [32]	099 Jellicent [32]	100 Alomomola [41]	119 Cubchoo [21]	120 Beartic [21]	
Bubble	041 Tympole [1]	042 Palpitoad [1]	043 Seismitoad [1]	098 Frillish [1]	099 Jellicent [1]	
BubbleBeam	041 Tympole [12]	042 Palpitoad [12]	043 Seismitoad [12]	056 Basculin [E]	086 Ducklett [19]	087 Swanna [19]
	098 Frillish [13]	099 Jellicent [13]				

B

Move	Pokémon that can learn it				
Bug Bite	046 Sewaddle [8]	047 Swadloon [1]	048 Leavanny [1, 8]	049 Venipede [22]	050 Whirlipede [23]	051 Scolipede [23]
	063 Dwebble [23]	064 Crustle [23]	094 Karrablast [E]	101 Joltik [18]	102 Galvantula [18]	137 Heatmor [36]
	138 Durant [26]	142 Larvesta [40]				
Bug Buzz	046 Sewaddle [36]	094 Karrablast [28]	095 Escavalier [28]	101 Joltik [48]	102 Galvantula [60]	122 Shelmet [44]
	123 Accelgor [44]	142 Larvesta [70]	143 Volcarona [70]			
Bulk Up	006 Emboar [TM]	038 Timburr [28, TM]	039 Gurdurr [29, TM]	040 Conkeldurr [29, TM]	044 Throh [33, TM]	045 Sawk [33, TM]
	059 Krookodile [TM]	061 Darmanitan [TM]	065 Scraggy [TM]	066 Scrafty [TM]	120 Beartic [TM]	125 Mienfoo [TM]
	126 Mienshao [TM]	133 Rufflet [TM]	134 Braviary [TM]	147 Tornadus [TM]	148 Thundurus [TM]	151 Landorus [TM]
Bulldoze	005 Pignite [TM]	006 Emboar [TM]	030 Roggenrola [TM]	031 Boldore [TM]	032 Gigalith [TM]	035 Drilbur [TM]
	036 Excadrill [TM]	040 Conkeldurr [TM]	042 Palpitoad [TM]	043 Seismitoad [TM]	044 Throh [TM]	045 Sawk [TM]
	051 Scolipede [TM]	057 Sandile [TM]	058 Krokorok [TM]	059 Krookodile [TM]	061 Darmanitan [TM]	063 Dwebble [TM]
	064 Crustle [TM]	070 Tirtouga [TM]	071 Carracosta [TM]	072 Archen [TM]	073 Archeops [TM]	104 Ferrothorn [TM]
	118 Haxorus [TM]	120 Beartic [TM]	124 Stunfisk [TM]	127 Druddigon [TM]	128 Golett [TM]	129 Golurk [TM]
	132 Bouffalant [TM]	141 Hydreigon [TM]	145 Terrakion [TM]	151 Landorus [19, TM]		
Bullet Punch	—					
Bullet Seed	017 Pansage [E]	062 Maractus [E]	079 Cinccino [1]	103 Ferroseed [E]		

C

Move	Pokémon that can learn it				
Calm Mind	001 Snivy [TM]	002 Servine [TM]	003 Serperior [TM]	023 Munna [35, TM]	024 Musharna [TM]	033 Woobat [29, TM]
	034 Swoobat [29, TM]	037 Audino [TM]	046 Sewaddle [TM]	047 Swadloon [TM]	048 Leavanny [TM]	067 Sigilyph [TM]
	068 Yamask [TM]	069 Cofagrigus [TM]	076 Zorua [TM]	077 Zoroark [TM]	078 Minccino [TM]	079 Cinccino [TM]
	080 Gothita [TM]	081 Gothorita [TM]	082 Gothitelle [TM]	083 Solosis [TM]	084 Duosion [TM]	085 Reuniclus [TM]
	100 Alomomola [TM]	111 Elgyem [43, TM]	112 Beheeyem [45, TM]	113 Litwick [TM]	114 Lampent [TM]	115 Chandelure [TM]
	125 Mienfoo [25, TM]	126 Mienshao [25, TM]	142 Larvesta [TM]	143 Volcarona [TM]	144 Cobalion [TM]	145 Terrakion [TM]
	146 Virizion [TM]	151 Landorus [TM]				
Camouflage	046 Sewaddle [E]	091 Deerling [1]	092 Sawsbuck [1]	124 Stunfisk [17]		
Captivate	001 Snivy [E]	015 Purrloin [33]	076 Zorua [E]	078 Minccino [39]	080 Gothita [E]	113 Litwick [E]
Charge	028 Blitzle [8]	029 Zebstrika [1, 8]	093 Emolga [10]	105 Klink [6]	106 Klang [1, 6]	107 Klinklang [1, 6]
	148 Thundurus [55]					
Charge Beam	000 Victini [TM]	023 Munna [TM]	024 Musharna [TM]	028 Blitzle [TM]	029 Zebstrika [TM]	033 Woobat [TM]
	034 Swoobat [TM]	037 Audino [TM]	067 Sigilyph [TM]	080 Gothita [TM]	081 Gothorita [TM]	082 Gothitelle [TM]
	093 Emolga [TM]	101 Joltik [TM]	102 Galvantula [TM]	105 Klink [26, TM]	106 Klang [26, TM]	107 Klinklang [25, TM]
	108 Tynamo [1]	109 Eelektrik [1, TM]	110 Eelektross [TM]	111 Elgyem [TM]	112 Beheeyem [TM]	127 Druddigon [TM]
	129 Golurk [TM]	141 Hydreigon [TM]	148 Thundurus [TM]	150 Zekrom [TM]		
Charm	012 Lillipup [E]	015 Purrloin [E]	033 Woobat [E]	052 Cottonee [28]	054 Petilil [E]	078 Minccino [27]
	080 Gothita [46]	081 Gothorita [50]	082 Gothitelle [54]	083 Solosis [19]	084 Duosion [19]	085 Reuniclus [19]
	091 Deerling [36]	092 Sawsbuck [36]	093 Emolga [E]	119 Cubchoo [29]		
Chatter	—					
Chip Away	038 Timburr [24]	039 Gurdurr [24]	040 Conkeldurr [24]	056 Basculin [16]	065 Scraggy [27]	066 Scrafty [27]
	127 Druddigon [31]					
Circle Throw	044 Throh [37]					
Clamp	—					
Clear Smog	074 Trubbish [34]	075 Garbodor [34]	096 Foongus [39]	097 Amoonguss [43]	113 Litwick [E]	
Close Combat	045 Sawk [49]	144 Cobalion [73]	145 Terrakion [73]	146 Virizion [73]		
Coil	001 Snivy [31]	002 Servine [36]	003 Serperior [38]	109 Eelektrik [54]		
Comet Punch	038 Timburr [E]					
Confuse Ray	011 Watchog [20]	083 Solosis [E]	098 Frillish [E]	113 Litwick [10]	114 Lampent [10]	115 Chandelure [1]
	121 Cryogonal [45]					
Confusion	000 Victini [1]	033 Woobat [1]	034 Swoobat [1]	080 Gothita [3]	081 Gothorita [1, 3]	082 Gothitelle [1, 3]
	111 Elgyem [1]	112 Beheeyem [1]				
Constrict	098 Frillish [E]					
Conversion	—					
Conversion2	—					
Copycat	007 Oshawott [E]					
Cosmic Power	067 Sigilyph [48]					
Cotton Guard	052 Cottonee [37]	062 Maractus [55]				
Cotton Spore	052 Cottonee [17]	053 Whimsicott [1]	062 Maractus [18]			
Counter	038 Timburr [E]	045 Sawk [21]	057 Sandile [E]	063 Dwebble [E]	065 Scraggy [E]	076 Zorua [E]
	094 Karrablast [E]	116 Axew [E]				
Covet	004 Tepig [E]	015 Purrloin [E]	017 Pansage [E]	019 Pansear [E]	021 Panpour [E]	093 Emolga [E]
Crabhammer	—					
Cross Chop	—					
Cross Poison	101 Joltik [E]					
Crunch	010 Patrat [16]	011 Watchog [16]	012 Lillipup [22]	013 Herdier [24]	014 Stoutland [24]	017 Pansage [43]

Move	Pokémon that can learn it					
Crunch (continued)	019 Pansear [43]	021 Panpour [43]	056 Basculin [24]	057 Sandile [28]	058 Krokorok [28]	059 Krookodile [28]
	065 Scraggy [38]	066 Scrafty [38]	070 Tirtouga [21]	071 Carracosta [21]	072 Archen [35]	073 Archeops [35]
	109 Eelektross [39]	110 Eelektross [1]	127 Druddigon [25]	138 Durant [31]	139 Deino [25]	140 Zweilous [25]
	141 Hydreigon [25]	147 Tornadus [49]	148 Thundurus [49]	149 Reshiram [71]	150 Zekrom [71]	
Crush Claw	035 Drilbur [E]	110 Eelektross [1]	127 Druddigon [E]	133 Rufflet [46]	134 Braviary [46]	
Crush Grip	—					
Curse	004 Tepig [E]	023 Munna [E]	030 Roggenrola [E]	063 Dwebble [E]	068 Yamask [29]	069 Cofagrigus [29]
	070 Tirtouga [35]	071 Carracosta [35]	074 Trubbish [E]	103 Ferroseed [9]	104 Ferrothorn [1, 9]	113 Litwick [43]
	114 Lampent [45]	122 Shelmet [13]	124 Stunfisk [E]	128 Golett [40]	129 Golurk [40]	137 Heatmor [E]
Cut	001 Snivy [HM]	002 Servine [HM]	003 Serperior [HM]	007 Oshawott [HM]	008 Dewott [HM]	009 Samurott [HM]
	010 Patrat [HM]	011 Watchog [HM]	015 Purrloin [HM]	016 Liepard [HM]	017 Pansage [HM]	018 Simisage [HM]
	019 Pansear [HM]	020 Simisear [HM]	021 Panpour [HM]	022 Simipour [HM]	035 Drilbur [HM]	036 Excadrill [HM]
	046 Sewaddle [HM]	047 Swadloon [HM]	048 Leavanny [HM]	051 Scolipede [HM]	054 Petilil [HM]	055 Lilligant [HM]
	056 Basculin [HM]	057 Sandile [HM]	058 Krokorok [HM]	059 Krookodile [HM]	063 Dwebble [HM]	064 Crustle [HM]
	072 Archen [HM]	073 Archeops [HM]	076 Zorua [HM]	077 Zoroark [HM]	092 Sawsbuck [HM]	093 Emolga [HM]
	094 Karrablast [HM]	095 Escavalier [HM]	101 Joltik [HM]	102 Galvantula [HM]	104 Ferrothorn [HM]	110 Eelektross [HM]
	116 Axew [HM]	117 Fraxure [HM]	118 Haxorus [HM]	119 Cubchoo [HM]	120 Beartic [HM]	127 Druddigon [HM]
	130 Pawniard [HM]	131 Bisharp [HM]	132 Bouffalant [HM]	133 Rufflet [HM]	134 Braviary [HM]	135 Vullaby [HM]
	136 Mandibuzz [HM]	137 Heatmor [HM]	138 Durant [HM]	144 Cobalion [HM]	145 Terrakion [HM]	146 Virizion [HM]
	149 Reshiram [HM]	150 Zekrom [HM]	152 Kyurem [HM]			

◈ **D**

Move	Pokémon that can learn it					
Dark Pulse	076 Zorua [E]	080 Gothita [E]	135 Vullaby [46]	136 Mandibuzz [46]	139 Deino [E]	147 Tornadus [73]
	148 Thundurus [73]					
Dark Void	—					
Defend Order	—					
Defense Curl	004 Tepig [13]	005 Pignite [13]	006 Emboar [13]	023 Munna [1]	024 Musharna [1]	049 Venipede [1]
	050 Whirlipede [1]	051 Scolipede [1]	096 Foongus [E]	128 Golett [1]	129 Golurk [1]	
Defog	072 Archen [E]	086 Ducklett [6]	087 Swanna [1, 6]	133 Rufflet [32]	134 Braviary [32]	135 Vullaby [32]
	136 Mandibuzz [32]					
Destiny Bond	068 Yamask [49]	069 Cofagrigus [57]				
Detect	007 Oshawott [E]	010 Patrat [11]	011 Watchog [11]	025 Pidove [22]	026 Tranquill [23]	027 Unfezant [23]
	038 Timburr [E]	065 Scraggy [E]	076 Zorua [E]	125 Mienfoo [9]	126 Mienshao [1, 9]	
Dig	007 Oshawott [TM]	008 Dewott [TM]	009 Samurott [TM]	010 Patrat [TM]	011 Watchog [TM]	012 Lillipup [TM]
	013 Herdier [TM]	014 Stoutland [TM]	017 Pansage [TM]	018 Simisage [TM]	019 Pansear [TM]	020 Simisear [TM]
	021 Panpour [TM]	022 Simipour [TM]	035 Drilbur [19, TM]	036 Excadrill [19, TM]	037 Audino [TM]	038 Timburr [TM]
	039 Gurdurr [TM]	040 Conkeldurr [TM]	043 Seismitoad [TM]	044 Throh [TM]	045 Sawk [TM]	051 Scolipede [TM]
	057 Sandile [31, TM]	058 Krokorok [32, TM]	059 Krookodile [32, TM]	060 Darumaka [TM]	061 Darmanitan [TM]	063 Dwebble [TM]
	064 Crustle [TM]	065 Scraggy [TM]	066 Scrafty [TM]	070 Tirtouga [TM]	071 Carracosta [TM]	072 Archen [TM]
	073 Archeops [TM]	076 Zorua [TM]	077 Zoroark [TM]	078 Minccino [TM]	079 Cinccino [TM]	116 Axew [TM]
	117 Fraxure [TM]	118 Haxorus [TM]	119 Cubchoo [TM]	120 Beartic [TM]	124 Stunfisk [TM]	125 Mienfoo [TM]
	126 Mienshao [TM]	127 Druddigon [TM]	130 Pawniard [TM]	131 Bisharp [TM]	137 Heatmor [TM]	138 Durant [41, TM]
	151 Landorus [TM]					
Disable	068 Yamask [5, E]	069 Cofagrigus [1, 5]	101 Joltik [E]	111 Elgyem [E]		
Discharge	028 Blitzle [32]	029 Zebstrika [36]	093 Emolga [50]	101 Joltik [45]	102 Galvantula [54]	105 Klink [42]
	106 Klang [44]	107 Klinklang [44]	109 Eelektrik [29]	110 Eelektross [1]	124 Stunfisk [25]	148 Thundurus [43]
Dive	007 Oshawott [HM]	008 Dewott [HM]	009 Samurott [HM]	021 Panpour [HM]	022 Simipour [HM]	056 Basculin [HM]
	070 Tirtouga [HM]	071 Carracosta [HM]	086 Ducklett [HM]	087 Swanna [HM]	098 Frillish [HM]	099 Jellicent [HM]
	100 Alomomola [HM]	120 Beartic [HM]				
Dizzy Punch	085 Reuniclus [41]					
Doom Desire	—					
Double Hit	139 Deino [E]	140 Zweilous [1]				
Double Kick	028 Blitzle [E]	045 Sawk [13]	091 Deerling [10]	092 Sawsbuck [10]	144 Cobalion [?]	145 Terrakion [?]
	146 Virizion [?]					
Double Team	000 Victini [TM]	001 Snivy [TM]	002 Servine [TM]	003 Serperior [TM]	004 Tepig [TM]	005 Pignite [TM]
	006 Emboar [TM]	007 Oshawott [TM]	008 Dewott [TM]	009 Samurott [TM]	010 Patrat [TM]	011 Watchog [TM]
	012 Lillipup [TM]	013 Herdier [TM]	014 Stoutland [TM]	015 Purrloin [TM]	016 Liepard [TM]	017 Pansage [TM]
	018 Simisage [TM]	019 Pansear [TM]	020 Simisear [TM]	021 Panpour [TM]	022 Simipour [TM]	023 Munna [TM]
	024 Musharna [TM]	025 Pidove [TM]	026 Tranquill [TM]	027 Unfezant [TM]	028 Blitzle [TM]	029 Zebstrika [TM]
	030 Roggenrola [TM]	031 Boldore [TM]	032 Gigalith [TM]	033 Woobat [TM]	034 Swoobat [TM]	035 Drilbur [TM]
	036 Excadrill [TM]	037 Audino [TM]	038 Timburr [TM]	039 Gurdurr [TM]	040 Conkeldurr [TM]	041 Tympole [TM]
	042 Palpitoad [TM]	043 Seismitoad [TM]	044 Throh [TM]	045 Sawk [TM]	046 Sewaddle [TM]	047 Swadloon [TM]
	048 Leavanny [TM]	049 Venipede [TM]	050 Whirlipede [TM]	051 Scolipede [TM]	052 Cottonee [TM]	053 Whimsicott [TM]
	054 Petilil [TM]	055 Lilligant [TM]	056 Basculin [TM]	057 Sandile [TM]	058 Krokorok [TM]	059 Krookodile [TM]

◇ D

Move	Pokémon that can learn it				
Double Team (continued)	060 Darumaka [TM]	061 Darmanitan [TM]	062 Maractus [TM]	063 Dwebble [TM]	064 Crustle [TM]	065 Scraggy [TM]
	066 Scrafty [TM]	067 Sigilyph [TM]	068 Yamask [TM]	069 Cofagrigus [TM]	070 Tirtouga [TM]	071 Carracosta [TM]
	072 Archen [8, TM]	073 Archeops [8, TM]	074 Trubbish [TM]	075 Garbodor [TM]	076 Zorua [TM]	077 Zoroark [TM]
	078 Minccino [TM]	079 Cinccino [TM]	080 Gothita [TM]	081 Gothorita [TM]	082 Gothitelle [TM]	083 Solosis [TM]
	084 Duosion [TM]	085 Reuniclus [TM]	086 Ducklett [TM]	087 Swanna [TM]	088 Vanillite [TM]	089 Vanillish [TM]
	090 Vanilluxe [TM]	091 Deerling [TM]	092 Sawsbuck [TM]	093 Emolga [19, TM]	094 Karrablast [TM]	095 Escavalier [TM]
	096 Foongus [TM]	097 Amoonguss [TM]	098 Frillish [TM]	099 Jellicent [TM]	100 Alomomola [TM]	101 Joltik [TM]
	102 Galvantula [TM]	103 Ferroseed [TM]	104 Ferrothorn [TM]	105 Klink [TM]	106 Klang [TM]	107 Klinklang [TM]
	109 Eelektrik [TM]	110 Eelektross [TM]	111 Elgyem [TM]	112 Beheeyem [TM]	113 Litwick [TM]	114 Lampent [TM]
	115 Chandelure [TM]	116 Axew [TM]	117 Fraxure [TM]	118 Haxorus [TM]	119 Cubchoo [TM]	120 Beartic [TM]
	121 Cryogonal [TM]	122 Shelmet [TM]	123 Accelgor [1, 8, TM]	124 Stunfisk [TM]	125 Mienfoo [TM]	126 Mienshao [TM]
	127 Druddigon [TM]	128 Golett [TM]	129 Golurk [TM]	130 Pawniard [TM]	131 Bisharp [TM]	132 Bouffalant [TM]
	133 Rufflet [TM]	134 Braviary [TM]	135 Vullaby [TM]	136 Mandibuzz [TM]	137 Heatmor [TM]	138 Durant [TM]
	139 Deino [TM]	140 Zweilous [TM]	141 Hydreigon [TM]	142 Larvesta [TM]	143 Volcarona [TM]	144 Cobalion [TM]
	145 Terrakion [TM]	146 Virizion [TM]	147 Tornadus [TM]	148 Thundurus [TM]	149 Reshiram [TM]	150 Zekrom [TM]
	151 Landorus [TM]	152 Kyurem [TM]				
Double-Edge	000 Victini [65]	028 Blitzle [E]	037 Audino [50]	049 Venipede [43]	050 Whirlipede [50]	051 Scolipede [55]
	056 Basculin [36]	057 Sandile [E]	091 Deerling [46]	092 Sawsbuck [52]	094 Karrablast [56]	122 Shelmet [E]
	142 Larvesta [50]					
DoubleSlap	037 Audino [10]	074 Trubbish [14]	075 Garbodor [14]	078 Minccino [13]	080 Gothita [14]	081 Gothorita [14]
	082 Gothitelle [14]	100 Alomomola [13]	125 Mienfoo [17]	126 Mienshao [17]		
Draco Meteor	116 Axew [T]	117 Fraxure [T]	118 Haxorus [T]	127 Druddigon [T]	139 Deino [T]	140 Zweilous [T]
	141 Hydreigon [T]	149 Reshiram [T]	150 Zekrom [T]	152 Kyurem [T]		
Dragon Claw	059 Krookodile [TM]	065 Scraggy [TM]	066 Scrafty [TM]	072 Archen [48, TM]	073 Archeops [56, TM]	110 Eelektross [TM]
	116 Axew [28, TM]	117 Fraxure [28, TM]	118 Haxorus [28, TM]	127 Druddigon [27, TM]	149 Reshiram [TM]	150 Zekrom [54, TM]
	152 Kyurem [TM]					
Dragon Dance	065 Scraggy [E]	116 Axew [32]	117 Fraxure [32]	118 Haxorus [32]		
Dragon Pulse	072 Archen [E]	116 Axew [41, E]	117 Fraxure [42]	118 Haxorus [42]	139 Deino [32]	140 Zweilous [32]
	141 Hydreigon [32]	149 Reshiram [54]	152 Kyurem [57]			
Dragon Rage	116 Axew [10]	117 Fraxure [1, 10]	118 Haxorus [1, 10]	127 Druddigon [18]	139 Deino [1]	140 Zweilous [1]
	141 Hydreigon [1]	149 Reshiram [1]	150 Zekrom [1]	152 Kyurem [1]		
Dragon Rush	139 Deino [42]	140 Zweilous [42]	141 Hydreigon [42]			
Dragon Tail	003 Serperior [TM]	009 Samurott [TM]	059 Krookodile [TM]	065 Scraggy [TM]	066 Scrafty [TM]	073 Archeops [TM]
	110 Eelektross [TM]	117 Fraxure [TM]	118 Haxorus [TM]	127 Druddigon [45, TM]	139 Deino [TM]	140 Zweilous [TM]
	141 Hydreigon [TM]	149 Reshiram [TM]	150 Zekrom [TM]	152 Kyurem [TM]		
DragonBreath	072 Archen [31]	073 Archeops [31]	139 Deino [17]	140 Zweilous [17]	141 Hydreigon [17]	149 Reshiram [29]
	150 Zekrom [29]	152 Kyurem [29]				
Drain Punch	038 Timburr [E]	043 Seismitoad [44]	065 Scraggy [E]	125 Mienfoo [33]	126 Mienshao [33]	
Dream Eater	011 Watchog [TM]	015 Purrloin [TM]	016 Liepard [TM]	023 Munna [41, TM]	024 Musharna [TM]	033 Woobat [TM]
	034 Swoobat [TM]	037 Audino [TM]	046 Sewaddle [TM]	047 Swadloon [TM]	048 Leavanny [TM]	052 Cottonee [TM]
	053 Whimsicott [TM]	054 Petilil [TM]	055 Lilligant [TM]	067 Sigilyph [TM]	068 Yamask [TM]	069 Cofagrigus [TM]
	080 Gothita [TM]	081 Gothorita [TM]	082 Gothitelle [TM]	083 Solosis [TM]	084 Duosion [TM]	085 Reuniclus [TM]
	098 Frillish [TM]	099 Jellicent [TM]	111 Elgyem [TM]	112 Beheeyem [TM]	113 Litwick [TM]	114 Lampent [TM]
	115 Chandelure [TM]					
Drill Peck	—					
Drill Run	035 Drilbur [43]	036 Excadrill [55]				
Dual Chop	116 Axew [13]	117 Fraxure [13]	118 Haxorus [13]			
DynamicPunch	038 Timburr [34]	039 Gurdurr [37]	040 Conkeldurr [37]	128 Golett [30]	129 Golurk [30]	

◇ E

Move	Pokémon that can learn it				
Earth Power	035 Drilbur [E]	041 Tympole [E]	072 Archen [E]	124 Stunfisk [E]	139 Deino [E]	151 Landorus [43]
Earthquake	006 Emboar [TM]	030 Roggenrola [TM]	031 Boldore [TM]	032 Gigalith [TM]	035 Drilbur [33, TM]	036 Excadrill [36, TM]
	040 Conkeldurr [TM]	043 Seismitoad [TM]	044 Throh [TM]	045 Sawk [TM]	051 Scolipede [TM]	057 Sandile [43, TM]
	058 Krokorok [48, TM]	059 Krookodile [54, TM]	061 Darmanitan [TM]	063 Dwebble [TM]	064 Crustle [TM]	070 Tirtouga [TM]
	071 Carracosta [TM]	072 Archen [TM]	073 Archeops [TM]	118 Haxorus [TM]	124 Stunfisk [TM]	127 Druddigon [TM]
	128 Golett [45, TM]	129 Golurk [50, TM]	132 Bouffalant [TM]	141 Hydreigon [TM]	145 Terrakion [TM]	151 Landorus [55, TM]
Echoed Voice	004 Tepig [TM]	005 Pignite [TM]	006 Emboar [TM]	015 Purrloin [TM]	016 Liepard [TM]	025 Pidove [TM]
	026 Tranquill [TM]	027 Unfezant [TM]	037 Audino [TM]	041 Tympole [38, TM]	042 Palpitoad [42, TM]	043 Seismitoad [49, TM]
	078 Minccino [33, TM]	079 Cinccino [TM]	091 Deerling [TM]	092 Sawsbuck [TM]	111 Elgyem [TM]	112 Beheeyem [TM]
	119 Cubchoo [TM]	120 Beartic [TM]	141 Hydreigon [TM]	149 Reshiram [TM]	150 Zekrom [TM]	152 Kyurem [TM]
Egg Bomb	—					
Electro Ball	093 Emolga [26]	101 Joltik [29]	102 Galvantula [29]			
Electroweb	101 Joltik [15]	102 Galvantula [15]				
Embargo	000 Victini [TM]	015 Purrloin [TM]	016 Liepard [TM]	033 Woobat [TM]	034 Swoobat [TM]	057 Sandile [22, TM]

Move	Pokémon that can learn it					
Embargo (continued)	058 Krokorok [22, TM]	059 Krookodile [22, TM]	068 Yamask [TM]	069 Cofagrigus [TM]	076 Zorua [41, TM]	077 Zoroark [44, TM]
	080 Gothita [19, TM]	081 Gothorita [19, TM]	082 Gothitelle [19, TM]	083 Solosis [TM]	084 Duosion [TM]	085 Reuniclus [TM]
	111 Elgyem [TM]	112 Beheeyem [TM]	113 Litwick [TM]	114 Lampent [TM]	115 Chandelure [TM]	130 Pawniard [41, TM]
	131 Bisharp [41, TM]	135 Vullaby [50, TM]	136 Mandibuzz [50, TM]	147 Tornadus [TM]	148 Thundurus [TM]	
Ember	004 Tepig [7]	005 Pignite [1, 7]	006 Emboar [1, 7]	113 Litwick [1]	114 Lampent [1]	142 Larvesta [1]
	143 Volcarona [1]					
Encore	007 Oshawott [31]	008 Dewott [36]	009 Samurott [38]	015 Purrloin [E]	037 Audino [E]	052 Cottonee [E]
	060 Darumaka [E]	078 Minccino [15]	093 Emolga [38]	119 Cubchoo [E]	122 Shelmet [E]	
Endeavor	004 Tepig [E]	033 Woobat [47]	034 Swoobat [47]	052 Cottonee [44]	072 Archen [38]	073 Archeops [40]
	083 Solosis [28]	084 Duosion [28]	085 Reuniclus [28]	116 Axew [E]	152 Kyurem [71]	
Endure	000 Victini [9]	012 Lillipup [E]	028 Blitzle [E]	038 Timburr [E]	044 Throh [41]	045 Sawk [41]
	046 Sewaddle [29]	054 Petilil [E]	060 Darumaka [E]	063 Dwebble [E]	068 Yamask [E]	078 Minccino [E]
	094 Karrablast [8]	096 Foongus [E]	100 Alomomola [E]	113 Litwick [E]	116 Axew [E]	119 Cubchoo [25]
	120 Beartic [25]	122 Shelmet [E]	124 Stunfisk [30]	125 Mienfoo [E]	138 Durant [E]	142 Larvesta [E]
Energy Ball	000 Victini [TM]	001 Snivy [TM]	002 Servine [TM]	003 Serperior [TM]	017 Pansage [TM]	018 Simisage [TM]
	023 Munna [TM]	024 Musharna [TM]	033 Woobat [TM]	034 Swoobat [TM]	046 Sewaddle [TM]	047 Swadloon [TM]
	048 Leavanny [TM]	052 Cottonee [35, TM]	053 Whimsicott [TM]	054 Petilil [35, TM]	055 Lilligant [TM]	062 Maractus [TM]
	067 Sigilyph [TM]	068 Yamask [TM]	069 Cofagrigus [TM]	080 Gothita [TM]	081 Gothorita [TM]	082 Gothitelle [TM]
	083 Solosis [TM]	084 Duosion [TM]	085 Reuniclus [TM]	091 Deerling [32, TM]	092 Sawsbuck [32, TM]	094 Karrablast [TM]
	095 Escavalier [TM]	096 Foongus [TM]	097 Amoonguss [TM]	098 Frillish [TM]	099 Jellicent [TM]	101 Joltik [TM]
	102 Galvantula [TM]	103 Ferroseed [TM]	104 Ferrothorn [TM]	111 Elgyem [TM]	112 Beheeyem [TM]	113 Litwick [TM]
	114 Lampent [TM]	115 Chandelure [TM]	122 Shelmet [TM]	123 Accelgor [TM]	138 Durant [TM]	146 Virizion [TM]
Entrainment	037 Audino [25]	048 Leavanny [43]	054 Petilil [37]	138 Durant [46]		
Eruption	—					
Explosion	030 Roggenrola [40, TM]	031 Boldore [55, TM]	032 Gigalith [55, TM]	074 Trubbish [47, TM]	075 Garbodor [59, TM]	083 Solosis [TM]
	084 Duosion [TM]	085 Reuniclus [TM]	088 Vanillite [TM]	089 Vanillish [TM]	090 Vanilluxe [TM]	103 Ferroseed [55, TM]
	104 Ferrothorn [67, TM]	121 Cryogonal [TM]	151 Landorus [TM]			
Extrasensory	076 Zorua [E]	147 Tornadus [31]	149 Reshiram [43]	151 Landorus [31]		
ExtremeSpeed	—					

◈ F

Move	Pokémon that can learn it					
Facade	000 Victini [TM]	001 Snivy [TM]	002 Servine [TM]	003 Serperior [TM]	004 Tepig [TM]	005 Pignite [TM]
	006 Emboar [TM]	007 Oshawott [TM]	008 Dewott [TM]	009 Samurott [TM]	010 Patrat [TM]	011 Watchog [TM]
	012 Lillipup [TM]	013 Herdier [TM]	014 Stoutland [TM]	015 Purrloin [TM]	016 Liepard [TM]	017 Pansage [TM]
	018 Simisage [TM]	019 Pansear [TM]	020 Simisear [TM]	021 Panpour [TM]	022 Simipour [TM]	023 Munna [TM]
	024 Musharna [TM]	025 Pidove [43, TM]	026 Tranquill [50, TM]	027 Unfezant [55, TM]	028 Blitzle [TM]	029 Zebstrika [TM]
	030 Roggenrola [TM]	031 Boldore [TM]	032 Gigalith [TM]	033 Woobat [TM]	034 Swoobat [TM]	035 Drilbur [TM]
	036 Excadrill [TM]	037 Audino [TM]	038 Timburr [TM]	039 Gurdurr [TM]	040 Conkeldurr [TM]	041 Tympole [TM]
	042 Palpitoad [TM]	043 Seismitoad [TM]	044 Throh [TM]	045 Sawk [TM]	046 Sewaddle [TM]	047 Swadloon [TM]
	048 Leavanny [TM]	049 Venipede [TM]	050 Whirlipede [TM]	051 Scolipede [TM]	052 Cottonee [TM]	053 Whimsicott [TM]
	054 Petilil [TM]	055 Lilligant [TM]	056 Basculin [TM]	057 Sandile [TM]	058 Krokorok [TM]	059 Krookodile [TM]
	060 Darumaka [19, TM]	061 Darmanitan [19, TM]	062 Maractus [TM]	063 Dwebble [TM]	064 Crustle [TM]	065 Scraggy [42, TM]
	066 Scrafty [45, TM]	067 Sigilyph [TM]	068 Yamask [TM]	069 Cofagrigus [TM]	070 Tirtouga [TM]	071 Carracosta [TM]
	072 Archen [TM]	073 Archeops [TM]	074 Trubbish [TM]	075 Garbodor [TM]	076 Zorua [TM]	077 Zoroark [TM]
	078 Minccino [TM]	079 Cinccino [TM]	080 Gothita [TM]	081 Gothorita [TM]	082 Gothitelle [TM]	083 Solosis [TM]
	084 Duosion [TM]	085 Reuniclus [TM]	086 Ducklett [TM]	087 Swanna [TM]	088 Vanillite [TM]	089 Vanillish [TM]
	090 Vanilluxe [TM]	091 Deerling [TM]	092 Sawsbuck [TM]	093 Emolga [TM]	094 Karrablast [TM]	095 Escavalier [TM]
	096 Foongus [TM]	097 Amoonguss [TM]	098 Frillish [TM]	099 Jellicent [TM]	100 Alomomola [TM]	101 Joltik [TM]
	102 Galvantula [TM]	103 Ferroseed [TM]	104 Ferrothorn [TM]	105 Klink [TM]	106 Klang [TM]	107 Klinklang [TM]
	109 Eelektrik [TM]	110 Eelektross [TM]	111 Elgyem [TM]	112 Beheeyem [TM]	113 Litwick [TM]	114 Lampent [TM]
	115 Chandelure [TM]	116 Axew [TM]	117 Fraxure [TM]	118 Haxorus [TM]	119 Cubchoo [TM]	120 Beartic [TM]
	121 Cryogonal [TM]	122 Shelmet [TM]	123 Accelgor [TM]	124 Stunfisk [TM]	125 Mienfoo [TM]	126 Mienshao [TM]
	127 Druddigon [TM]	128 Golett [TM]	129 Golurk [TM]	130 Pawniard [TM]	131 Bisharp [TM]	132 Bouffalant [TM]
	133 Rufflet [TM]	134 Braviary [TM]	135 Vullaby [TM]	136 Mandibuzz [TM]	137 Heatmor [TM]	138 Durant [TM]
	139 Deino [TM]	140 Zweilous [TM]	141 Hydreigon [TM]	142 Larvesta [TM]	143 Volcarona [TM]	144 Cobalion [TM]
	145 Terrakion [TM]	146 Virizion [TM]	147 Tornadus [TM]	148 Thundurus [TM]	149 Reshiram [TM]	150 Zekrom [TM]
	151 Landorus [TM]	152 Kyurem [TM]				
Faint Attack	015 Purrloin [E]	063 Dwebble [13]	064 Crustle [13]	065 Scraggy [9, E]	066 Scrafty [1, 9]	076 Zorua [17]
	077 Zoroark [17]	080 Gothita [24]	081 Gothorita [24]	082 Gothitelle [24]	091 Deerling [16]	092 Sawsbuck [16]
	094 Karrablast [E]	096 Foongus [20]	097 Amoonguss [20]	101 Joltik [E]	127 Druddigon [E]	130 Pawniard [17]
	131 Bisharp [17]	135 Vullaby [23]	136 Mandibuzz [23]	137 Heatmor [E]	138 Durant [E]	
Fake Out	015 Purrloin [21]	016 Liepard [22]	065 Scraggy [E]	125 Mienfoo [13]	126 Mienshao [1, 13]	
Fake Tears	015 Purrloin [E]	033 Woobat [E]	052 Cottonee [E]	068 Yamask [E]	076 Zorua [9]	078 Minccino [E]
	080 Gothita [10]	081 Gothorita [1, 10]	082 Gothitelle [1, 10]	091 Deerling [E]	135 Vullaby [E]	

◇ F

Move	Pokémon that can learn it					
False Swipe	007 Oshawott [TM]	008 Dewott [TM]	009 Samurott [TM]	048 Leavanny [1, TM]	094 Karrablast [25, TM]	095 Escavalier [25, TM]
	116 Axew [24, TM]	117 Fraxure [24, TM]	118 Haxorus [24, TM]	130 Pawniard [TM]	131 Bisharp [TM]	144 Cobalion [TM]
	145 Terrakion [TM]	146 Virizion [TM]				
FeatherDance	025 Pidove [36]	026 Tranquill [41]	027 Unfezant [44]	086 Ducklett [21]	087 Swanna [21]	
Feint	122 Shelmet [E]	125 Mienfoo [E]				
Fiery Dance	143 Volcarona [100]					
Final Gambit	000 Victini [81]	056 Basculin [51]	122 Shelmet [56]	123 Accelgor [56]		
Fire Blast	000 Victini [TM]	004 Tepig [TM]	005 Pignite [TM]	006 Emboar [TM]	019 Pansear [34, TM]	020 Simisear [TM]
	037 Audino [TM]	060 Darumaka [TM]	061 Darmanitan [TM]	113 Litwick [TM]	114 Lampent [TM]	115 Chandelure [TM]
	137 Heatmor [TM]	141 Hydreigon [TM]	142 Larvesta [TM]	143 Volcarona [TM]	149 Reshiram [78, TM]	
Fire Fang	012 Lillipup [E]	014 Stoutland [1]	057 Sandile [E]	060 Darumaka [11]	061 Darmanitan [11]	127 Druddigon [E]
	139 Deino [E]	149 Reshiram [1]				
Fire Pledge	004 Tepig [T]	005 Pignite [T]	006 Emboar [T]			
Fire Punch	019 Pansear [E]	060 Darumaka [22]	061 Darmanitan [22]	065 Scraggy [E]		
Fire Spin	019 Pansear [E]	113 Litwick [7]	114 Lampent [7]	137 Heatmor [16]	143 Volcarona [30]	
Fissure	035 Drilbur [47]	036 Excadrill [62]	124 Stunfisk [61]	151 Landorus [67]		
Flail	010 Patrat [E]	041 Tympole [34]	042 Palpitoad [37]	043 Seismitoad [39]	046 Sewaddle [43]	056 Basculin [46]
	063 Dwebble [41]	064 Crustle [50]	070 Tirtouga [E]	078 Minccino [E]	094 Karrablast [49]	119 Cubchoo [36]
	120 Beartic [36]	124 Stunfisk [55]				
Flame Burst	000 Victini [41]	019 Pansear [22]	020 Simisear [1]	113 Litwick [20]	114 Lampent [20]	115 Chandelure [1]
	137 Heatmor [31]					
Flame Charge	000 Victini [25, TM]	004 Tepig [15, TM]	005 Pignite [15, TM]	006 Emboar [15, TM]	019 Pansear [TM]	020 Simisear [TM]
	028 Blitzle [18, TM]	029 Zebstrika [18, TM]	060 Darumaka [TM]	061 Darmanitan [TM]	113 Litwick [TM]	114 Lampent [TM]
	115 Chandelure [TM]	142 Larvesta [30, TM]	143 Volcarona [TM]	149 Reshiram [TM]		
Flame Wheel	060 Darumaka [E]	142 Larvesta [60]				
Flamethrower	000 Victini [TM]	004 Tepig [33, TM]	005 Pignite [39, TM]	006 Emboar [43, TM]	011 Watchog [TM]	019 Pansear [TM]
	020 Simisear [TM]	037 Audino [TM]	060 Darumaka [TM]	061 Darmanitan [TM]	077 Zoroark [TM]	110 Eelektross [TM]
	113 Litwick [TM]	114 Lampent [TM]	115 Chandelure [TM]	127 Druddigon [TM]	137 Heatmor [51, TM]	
	141 Hydreigon [TM]	142 Larvesta [TM]	143 Volcarona [TM]	149 Reshiram [22, TM]		
Flare Blitz	000 Victini [73]	004 Tepig [43]	005 Pignite [52]	006 Emboar [62]	060 Darumaka [33]	061 Darmanitan [33]
	142 Larvesta [100]					
Flash	000 Victini [TM]	001 Snivy [TM]	002 Servine [TM]	003 Serperior [TM]	011 Watchog [TM]	017 Pansage [TM]
	018 Simisage [TM]	023 Munna [TM]	024 Musharna [TM]	028 Blitzle [TM]	029 Zebstrika [TM]	033 Woobat [TM]
	034 Swoobat [TM]	037 Audino [TM]	046 Sewaddle [TM]	047 Swadloon [TM]	048 Leavanny [TM]	052 Cottonee [TM]
	053 Whimsicott [TM]	054 Petilil [TM]	055 Lilligant [TM]	067 Sigilyph [TM]	068 Yamask [TM]	069 Cofagrigus [TM]
	080 Gothita [TM]	081 Gothorita [TM]	082 Gothitelle [TM]	083 Solosis [TM]	084 Duosion [TM]	085 Reuniclus [TM]
	091 Deerling [TM]	092 Sawsbuck [TM]	093 Emolga [TM]	096 Foongus [TM]	097 Amoonguss [TM]	098 Frillish [TM]
	099 Jellicent [TM]	101 Joltik [TM]	102 Galvantula [TM]	103 Ferroseed [TM]	104 Ferrothorn [TM]	109 Eelektrik [TM]
	110 Eelektross [TM]	111 Elgyem [TM]	112 Beheeyem [TM]	113 Litwick [TM]	114 Lampent [TM]	115 Chandelure [TM]
	124 Stunfisk [TM]	128 Golett [TM]	129 Golurk [TM]	146 Virizion [TM]	150 Zekrom [TM]	
Flash Cannon	030 Roggenrola [TM]	031 Boldore [TM]	032 Gigalith [TM]	067 Sigilyph [TM]	083 Solosis [TM]	084 Duosion [TM]
	085 Reuniclus [TM]	088 Vanillite [TM]	089 Vanillish [TM]	090 Vanilluxe [TM]	103 Ferroseed [52, TM]	104 Ferrothorn [61, TM]
	105 Klink [TM]	106 Klang [TM]	107 Klinklang [TM]	109 Eelektrik [TM]	110 Eelektross [TM]	121 Cryogonal [TM]
	127 Druddigon [TM]	129 Golurk [TM]	138 Durant [TM]	141 Hydreigon [TM]	144 Cobalion [TM]	148 Thundurus [TM]
	150 Zekrom [TM]	152 Kyurem [TM]				
Flatter	033 Woobat [E]	080 Gothita [28]	081 Gothorita [28]	082 Gothitelle [28]	135 Vullaby [19]	136 Mandibuzz [19]
Fling	000 Victini [TM]	005 Pignite [TM]	006 Emboar [TM]	007 Oshawott [TM]	008 Dewott [TM]	009 Samurott [TM]
	010 Patrat [TM]	011 Watchog [TM]	017 Pansage [28, TM]	018 Simisage [TM]	019 Pansear [28, TM]	020 Simisear [TM]
	021 Panpour [28, TM]	022 Simipour [TM]	035 Drilbur [TM]	036 Excadrill [TM]	037 Audino [TM]	038 Timburr [TM]
	039 Gurdurr [TM]	040 Conkeldurr [TM]	043 Seismitoad [TM]	044 Throh [TM]	045 Sawk [TM]	053 Whimsicott [TM]
	058 Krokorok [TM]	059 Krookodile [TM]	060 Darumaka [TM]	061 Darmanitan [TM]	065 Scraggy [TM]	066 Scrafty [TM]
	075 Garbodor [TM]	076 Zorua [TM]	077 Zoroark [TM]	078 Minccino [TM]	079 Cinccino [TM]	080 Gothita [TM]
	081 Gothorita [TM]	082 Gothitelle [TM]	085 Reuniclus [TM]	093 Emolga [TM]	116 Axew [TM]	117 Fraxure [TM]
	118 Haxorus [TM]	119 Cubchoo [TM]	120 Beartic [TM]	125 Mienfoo [TM]	126 Mienshao [TM]	127 Druddigon [TM]
	128 Golett [TM]	129 Golurk [TM]	130 Pawniard [TM]	131 Bisharp [TM]	137 Heatmor [TM]	147 Tornadus [TM]
	148 Thundurus [TM]	149 Reshiram [TM]	150 Zekrom [TM]	151 Landorus [TM]	152 Kyurem [TM]	
Fly	025 Pidove [HM]	026 Tranquill [HM]	027 Unfezant [HM]	033 Woobat [HM]	034 Swoobat [HM]	067 Sigilyph [HM]
	073 Archeops [HM]	086 Ducklett [HM]	087 Swanna [HM]	129 Golurk [HM]	133 Rufflet [HM]	134 Braviary [HM]
	135 Vullaby [HM]	136 Mandibuzz [HM]	141 Hydreigon [HM]	143 Volcarona [HM]	147 Tornadus [HM]	148 Thundurus [HM]
	149 Reshiram [HM]	150 Zekrom [HM]	151 Landorus [HM]	152 Kyurem [HM]		
Focus Blast	000 Victini [TM]	005 Pignite [TM]	006 Emboar [TM]	011 Watchog [TM]	018 Simisage [TM]	020 Simisear [TM]
	022 Simipour [TM]	036 Excadrill [TM]	038 Timburr [TM]	039 Gurdurr [TM]	040 Conkeldurr [TM]	043 Seismitoad [TM]
	044 Throh [TM]	045 Sawk [TM]	059 Krookodile [TM]	061 Darmanitan [TM]	065 Scraggy [TM]	066 Scrafty [TM]
	071 Carracosta [TM]	073 Archeops [TM]	075 Garbodor [TM]	077 Zoroark [TM]	079 Cinccino [TM]	085 Reuniclus [TM]
	095 Escavalier [TM]	118 Haxorus [TM]	120 Beartic [TM]	123 Accelgor [TM]	125 Mienfoo [TM]	126 Mienshao [TM]
	127 Druddigon [TM]	128 Golett [TM]	129 Golurk [TM]	131 Bisharp [TM]	137 Heatmor [TM]	141 Hydreigon [TM]

Move	Pokémon that can learn it					
Focus Blast (continued)	144 Cobalion [TM]	145 Terrakion [TM]	146 Virizion [TM]	147 Tornadus [TM]	148 Thundurus [TM]	149 Reshiram [TM]
	150 Zekrom [TM]	151 Landorus [TM]	152 Kyurem [TM]			
Focus Energy	000 Victini [1]	007 Oshawott [13]	008 Dewott [13]	009 Samurott [13]	038 Timburr [4]	039 Gurdurr [1, 4]
	040 Conkeldurr [1, 4]	044 Throh [9]	045 Sawk [9]	057 Sandile [E]	060 Darumaka [E]	116 Axew [E]
	132 Bouffalant [36]	139 Deino [4]	140 Zweilous [1, 4]	141 Hydreigon [1, 4]		
Focus Punch	038 Timburr [46]	039 Gurdurr [53]	040 Conkeldurr [53]	060 Darumaka [E]	065 Scraggy [49]	066 Scrafty [58]
	119 Cubchoo [E]	128 Golett [55]	129 Golurk [70]			
Follow Me	—					
Force Palm	038 Timburr [E]	125 Mienfoo [29]	126 Mienshao [29]			
Foresight	010 Patrat [E]	038 Timburr [E]	142 Larvesta [E]			
Foul Play	015 Purrloin [E]	057 Sandile [37]	058 Krokorok [40]	059 Krookodile [42]	076 Zorua [29]	077 Zoroark [29]
Frenzy Plant	003 Serperior [T]					
Frost Breath	088 Vanillite [TM]	089 Vanillish [TM]	090 Vanilluxe [TM]	119 Cubchoo [TM]	120 Beartic [TM]	121 Cryogonal [TM]
Frustration	000 Victini [TM]	001 Snivy [TM]	002 Servine [TM]	003 Serperior [TM]	004 Tepig [TM]	005 Pignite [TM]
	006 Emboar [TM]	007 Oshawott [TM]	008 Dewott [TM]	009 Samurott [TM]	010 Patrat [TM]	011 Watchog [TM]
	012 Lillipup [TM]	013 Herdier [TM]	014 Stoutland [TM]	015 Purrloin [TM]	016 Liepard [TM]	017 Pansage [TM]
	018 Simisage [TM]	019 Pansear [TM]	020 Simisear [TM]	021 Panpour [TM]	022 Simipour [TM]	023 Munna [TM]
	024 Musharna [TM]	025 Pidove [TM]	026 Tranquill [TM]	027 Unfezant [TM]	028 Blitzle [TM]	029 Zebstrika [TM]
	030 Roggenrola [TM]	031 Boldore [TM]	032 Gigalith [TM]	033 Woobat [TM]	034 Swoobat [TM]	035 Drilbur [TM]
	036 Excadrill [TM]	037 Audino [TM]	038 Timburr [TM]	039 Gurdurr [TM]	040 Conkeldurr [TM]	041 Tympole [TM]
	042 Palpitoad [TM]	043 Seismitoad [TM]	044 Throh [TM]	045 Sawk [TM]	046 Sewaddle [TM]	047 Swadloon [TM]
	048 Leavanny [TM]	049 Venipede [TM]	050 Whirlipede [TM]	051 Scolipede [TM]	052 Cottonee [TM]	053 Whimsicott [TM]
	054 Petilil [TM]	055 Lilligant [TM]	056 Basculin [TM]	057 Sandile [TM]	058 Krokorok [TM]	059 Krookodile [TM]
	060 Darumaka [TM]	061 Darmanitan [TM]	062 Maractus [TM]	063 Dwebble [TM]	064 Crustle [TM]	065 Scraggy [TM]
	066 Scrafty [TM]	067 Sigilyph [TM]	068 Yamask [TM]	069 Cofagrigus [TM]	070 Tirtouga [TM]	071 Carracosta [TM]
	072 Archen [TM]	073 Archeops [TM]	074 Trubbish [TM]	075 Garbodor [TM]	076 Zorua [TM]	077 Zoroark [TM]
	078 Minccino [TM]	079 Cinccino [TM]	080 Gothita [TM]	081 Gothorita [TM]	082 Gothitelle [TM]	083 Solosis [TM]
	084 Duosion [TM]	085 Reuniclus [TM]	086 Ducklett [TM]	087 Swanna [TM]	088 Vanillite [TM]	089 Vanillish [TM]
	090 Vanilluxe [TM]	091 Deerling [TM]	092 Sawsbuck [TM]	093 Emolga [TM]	094 Karrablast [TM]	095 Escavalier [TM]
	096 Foongus [TM]	097 Amoonguss [TM]	098 Frillish [TM]	099 Jellicent [TM]	100 Alomomola [TM]	101 Joltik [TM]
	102 Galvantula [TM]	103 Ferroseed [TM]	104 Ferrothorn [TM]	105 Klink [TM]	106 Klang [TM]	107 Klinklang [TM]
	109 Eelektrik [TM]	110 Eelektross [TM]	111 Elgyem [TM]	112 Beheeyem [TM]	113 Litwick [TM]	114 Lampent [TM]
	115 Chandelure [TM]	116 Axew [TM]	117 Fraxure [TM]	118 Haxorus [TM]	119 Cubchoo [TM]	120 Beartic [TM]
	121 Cryogonal [TM]	122 Shelmet [TM]	123 Accelgor [TM]	124 Stunfisk [TM]	125 Mienfoo [TM]	126 Mienshao [TM]
	127 Druddigon [TM]	128 Golett [TM]	129 Golurk [TM]	130 Pawniard [TM]	131 Bisharp [TM]	132 Bouffalant [TM]
	133 Rufflet [TM]	134 Braviary [TM]	135 Vullaby [TM]	136 Mandibuzz [TM]	137 Heatmor [TM]	138 Durant [TM]
	139 Deino [TM]	140 Zweilous [TM]	141 Hydreigon [TM]	142 Larvesta [TM]	143 Volcarona [TM]	144 Cobalion [TM]
	145 Terrakion [TM]	146 Virizion [TM]	147 Tornadus [TM]	148 Thundurus [TM]	149 Reshiram [TM]	150 Zekrom [TM]
	151 Landorus [TM]	152 Kyurem [TM]				
Fury Attack	094 Karrablast [16]	095 Escavalier [16]	132 Bouffalant [11]	133 Rufflet [5]	134 Braviary [1, 5]	135 Vullaby [5]
	136 Mandibuzz [1, 5]					
Fury Cutter	007 Oshawott [19]	008 Dewott [20]	009 Samurott [20]	063 Dwebble [1]	094 Karrablast [13]	101 Joltik [12]
	102 Galvantula [12]	130 Pawniard [9]	131 Bisharp [1, 9]	138 Durant [6]		
Fury Swipes	015 Purrloin [12]	016 Liepard [12]	017 Pansage [13]	018 Simisage [1]	019 Pansear [13]	020 Simisear [1]
	021 Panpour [13]	022 Simipour [1]	035 Drilbur [12]	036 Excadrill [12]	076 Zorua [13]	077 Zoroark [13]
	119 Cubchoo [17]	120 Beartic [17]	137 Heatmor [21]			
Fusion Bolt	150 Zekrom [50]					
Fusion Flare	149 Reshiram [50]					
Future Sight	023 Munna [31]	033 Woobat [36]	034 Swoobat [36]	080 Gothita [31]	081 Gothorita [31]	082 Gothitelle [31]
	083 Solosis [31]	084 Duosion [31]	085 Reuniclus [31]			

G

Move	Pokémon that can learn it					
Gastro Acid	001 Snivy [40]	002 Servine [48]	003 Serperior [56]	096 Foongus [E]	101 Joltik [23]	102 Galvantula [23]
	109 Eelektrik [64]					
Gear Grind	105 Klink [16]	106 Klang [1, 16]	107 Klinklang [1, 16]			
Giga Drain	001 Snivy [34]	002 Servine [40]	003 Serperior [44]	052 Cottonee [26]	054 Petilil [26]	062 Maractus [26]
	096 Foongus [28]	097 Amoonguss [28]	122 Shelmet [37]	123 Accelgor [37]	146 Virizion [37]	
Giga Impact	000 Victini [TM]	003 Serperior [TM]	006 Emboar [TM]	009 Samurott [TM]	011 Watchog [TM]	012 Lillipup [40, TM]
	013 Herdier [47, TM]	014 Stoutland [59, TM]	016 Liepard [TM]	018 Simisage [TM]	020 Simisear [TM]	022 Simipour [TM]
	024 Musharna [TM]	027 Unfezant [TM]	029 Zebstrika [TM]	032 Gigalith [TM]	034 Swoobat [TM]	036 Excadrill [TM]
	040 Conkeldurr [TM]	043 Seismitoad [TM]	044 Throh [TM]	045 Sawk [TM]	048 Leavanny [TM]	051 Scolipede [TM]
	053 Whimsicott [TM]	055 Lilligant [TM]	059 Krookodile [TM]	061 Darmanitan [TM]	064 Crustle [TM]	066 Scrafty [TM]
	069 Cofagrigus [TM]	071 Carracosta [TM]	073 Archeops [TM]	075 Garbodor [TM]	077 Zoroark [TM]	079 Cinccino [TM]
	082 Gothitelle [TM]	085 Reuniclus [TM]	087 Swanna [TM]	090 Vanilluxe [TM]	092 Sawsbuck [TM]	095 Escavalier [56, TM]
	097 Amoonguss [TM]	099 Jellicent [TM]	102 Galvantula [TM]	104 Ferrothorn [TM]	107 Klinklang [TM]	110 Eelektross [TM]

G

Move	Pokémon that can learn it					
Giga Impact	112 Beheeyem [TM]	115 Chandelure [TM]	116 Axew [61, TM]	117 Fraxure [66, TM]	118 Haxorus [74, TM]	120 Beartic [TM]
	123 Accelgor [TM]	126 Mienshao [TM]	127 Druddigon [TM]	129 Golurk [TM]	131 Bisharp [TM]	132 Bouffalant [61, TM]
	134 Braviary [TM]	136 Mandibuzz [TM]	137 Heatmor [TM]	138 Durant [TM]	141 Hydreigon [TM]	143 Volcarona [TM]
	144 Cobalion [TM]	145 Terrakion [TM]	146 Virizion [TM]	147 Tornadus [TM]	148 Thundurus [TM]	149 Reshiram [TM]
	150 Zekrom [TM]	151 Landorus [TM]	152 Kyurem [TM]			
Glaciate	152 Kyurem [50]					
Glare	001 Snivy [E]	127 Druddigon [E]				
Grass Knot	000 Victini [TM]	001 Snivy [TM]	002 Servine [TM]	003 Serperior [TM]	004 Tepig [TM]	005 Pignite [TM]
	006 Emboar [TM]	007 Oshawott [TM]	008 Dewott [TM]	009 Samurott [TM]	010 Patrat [TM]	011 Watchog [TM]
	015 Purrloin [TM]	016 Liepard [TM]	017 Pansage [34, TM]	018 Simisage [TM]	019 Pansear [TM]	020 Simisear [TM]
	021 Panpour [TM]	022 Simipour [TM]	037 Audino [TM]	038 Timburr [TM]	039 Gurdurr [TM]	040 Conkeldurr [TM]
	043 Seismitoad [TM]	044 Throh [TM]	045 Sawk [TM]	046 Sewaddle [TM]	047 Swadloon [TM]	048 Leavanny [TM]
	052 Cottonee [TM]	053 Whimsicott [TM]	054 Petilil [TM]	055 Lilligant [TM]	058 Krokorok [TM]	059 Krookodile [TM]
	060 Darumaka [TM]	061 Darmanitan [TM]	062 Maractus [TM]	065 Scraggy [TM]	066 Scrafty [TM]	069 Cofagrigus [TM]
	076 Zorua [TM]	077 Zoroark [TM]	078 Minccino [TM]	079 Cinccino [TM]	080 Gothita [TM]	081 Gothorita [TM]
	082 Gothitelle [TM]	085 Reuniclus [TM]	091 Deerling [TM]	092 Sawsbuck [TM]	096 Foongus [TM]	097 Amoonguss [TM]
	104 Ferrothorn [TM]	110 Eelektross [TM]	118 Haxorus [TM]	119 Cubchoo [TM]	120 Beartic [TM]	125 Mienfoo [TM]
	126 Mienshao [TM]	128 Golett [TM]	129 Golurk [TM]	130 Pawniard [TM]	131 Bisharp [TM]	146 Virizion [TM]
	147 Tornadus [TM]	148 Thundurus [TM]	151 Landorus [TM]			
Grass Pledge	001 Snivy [T]	002 Servine [T]	003 Serperior [T]			
GrassWhistle	017 Pansage [E]	047 Swadloon [1]	052 Cottonee [E]	054 Petilil [E]	062 Maractus [E]	091 Deerling [E]
Gravity	030 Roggenrola [E]	067 Sigilyph [38]	103 Ferroseed [E]			
Growl	015 Purrloin [3]	016 Liepard [1, 3]	025 Pidove [4]	026 Tranquill [1, 4]	027 Unfezant [1, 4]	037 Audino [1]
	041 Tympole [1]	042 Palpitoad [1]	043 Seismitoad [1]	078 Minccino [3]	091 Deerling [4]	092 Sawsbuck [1, 4]
	111 Elgyem [4]	112 Beheeyem [1, 4]	119 Cubchoo [5]	120 Beartic [1, 5]		
Growth	001 Snivy [13]	002 Servine [13]	003 Serperior [13]	052 Cottonee [4]	053 Whimsicott [1]	054 Petilil [4]
	055 Lilligant [1]	062 Maractus [6]	096 Foongus [6, E]	097 Amoonguss [1, 6]		
Grudge	068 Yamask [41]	069 Cofagrigus [45]				
Guard Split	068 Yamask [33]	069 Cofagrigus [33]	111 Elgyem [50]	112 Beheeyem [56]	122 Shelmet [E]	
Guard Swap	111 Elgyem [E]	122 Shelmet [52]				
Guillotine	116 Axew [51]	117 Fraxure [54]	118 Haxorus [58]	130 Pawniard [62]	131 Bisharp [71]	138 Durant [61]
Gunk Shot	074 Trubbish [45]	075 Garbodor [54]				
Gust	025 Pidove [1]	026 Tranquill [1]	027 Unfezant [1]	033 Woobat [8]	034 Swoobat [1, 8]	053 Whimsicott [10]
	067 Sigilyph [1]	086 Ducklett [E]	135 Vullaby [1]	136 Mandibuzz [1]	143 Volcarona [1, 20]	147 Tornadus [1]
Gyro Ball	004 Tepig [TM]	005 Pignite [TM]	006 Emboar [TM]	023 Munna [TM]	024 Musharna [TM]	033 Woobat [TM]
	034 Swoobat [TM]	049 Venipede [TM]	050 Whirlipede [TM]	051 Scolipede [TM]	060 Darumaka [TM]	061 Darmanitan [TM]
	083 Solosis [TM]	084 Duosion [TM]	085 Reuniclus [TM]	103 Ferroseed [21, TM]	104 Ferrothorn [21, TM]	128 Golett [TM]
	129 Golurk [TM]					

H

Move	Pokémon that can learn it					
Hail	007 Oshawott [TM]	008 Dewott [TM]	009 Samurott [TM]	021 Panpour [TM]	022 Simipour [TM]	041 Tympole [TM]
	042 Palpitoad [TM]	043 Seismitoad [TM]	056 Basculin [TM]	086 Ducklett [TM]	087 Swanna [TM]	088 Vanillite [40, TM]
	089 Vanillish [42, TM]	090 Vanilluxe [42, TM]	098 Frillish [TM]	099 Jellicent [TM]	100 Alomomola [TM]	119 Cubchoo [49, TM]
	120 Beartic [53, TM]	121 Cryogonal [TM]	152 Kyurem [TM]			
Hammer Arm	006 Emboar [1]	038 Timburr [40]	039 Gurdurr [45]	040 Conkeldurr [45]	060 Darumaka [E]	061 Darmanitan [35]
	128 Golett [50]	129 Golurk [60]	147 Tornadus [79]	148 Thundurus [79]	151 Landorus [79]	
Harden	030 Roggenrola [4]	031 Boldore [1, 4]	032 Gigalith [1, 4]	088 Vanillite [4]	089 Vanillish [1, 4]	090 Vanilluxe [1, 4]
	103 Ferroseed [1]	104 Ferrothorn [1]	116 Axew [E]	142 Larvesta [E]		
Haze	068 Yamask [9]	069 Cofagrigus [1, 9]	074 Trubbish [E]	113 Litwick [E]	121 Cryogonal [21]	
Head Charge	132 Bouffalant [31]					
Head Smash	004 Tepig [37]	005 Pignite [44]	006 Emboar [50]	065 Scraggy [53]	066 Scrafty [65]	072 Archen [E]
	139 Deino [E]					
Headbutt	000 Victini [17]	030 Roggenrola [10]	031 Boldore [1, 10]	032 Gigalith [1, 10]	056 Basculin [7]	060 Darumaka [14]
	061 Darmanitan [14]	065 Scraggy [12]	066 Scrafty [12]	094 Karrablast [20]	095 Escavalier [20]	109 Eelektrik [1]
	110 Eelektross [1]	111 Elgyem [18]	112 Beheeyem [18]	130 Pawniard [E]	132 Bouffalant [E]	139 Deino [12]
	140 Zweilous [12]	141 Hydreigon [12]				
Heal Bell	037 Audino [E]					
Heal Block	068 Yamask [E]	080 Gothita [33]	081 Gothorita [34]	082 Gothitelle [34]	083 Solosis [46]	084 Duosion [50]
	085 Reuniclus [54]	111 Elgyem [8]	112 Beheeyem [1, 8]	148 Thundurus [31]		
Heal Order	—					
Heal Pulse	037 Audino [35]	100 Alomomola [17]				
Healing Wish	037 Audino [E]	054 Petilil [E]	100 Alomomola [57]			
Heart Stamp	033 Woobat [15]	034 Swoobat [15]				
Heart Swap	—					

Move	Pokémon that can learn it				
Heat Crash	004 Tepig [27]	005 Pignite [31]	006 Emboar [31]		
Heat Wave	019 Pansear [E]	113 Litwick [E]	137 Heatmor [E]	143 Volcarona [60]	
Heavy Slam	004 Tepig [E]	030 Roggenrola [E]	129 Golurk [43]		
Helping Hand	012 Lillipup [12]	013 Herdier [12]	014 Stoutland [12]	023 Munna [E]	033 Woobat [E]	037 Audino [1]
	048 Leavanny [32]	052 Cottonee [31]	054 Petilil [31]	078 Minccino [7]	079 Cinccino [1]	100 Alomomola [49]
	144 Cobalion [25]	145 Terrakion [25]	146 Virizion [25]			
Hex	068 Yamask [17]	069 Cofagrigus [17]	098 Frillish [43]	099 Jellicent [45]	113 Litwick [28]	114 Lampent [28]
	115 Chandelure [1]					
Hi Jump Kick	065 Scraggy [31]	066 Scrafty [31]	125 Mienfoo [53]	126 Mienshao [56]		
Hidden Power	000 Victini [TM]	001 Snivy [TM]	002 Servine [TM]	003 Serperior [TM]	004 Tepig [TM]	005 Pignite [TM]
	006 Emboar [TM]	007 Oshawott [TM]	008 Dewott [TM]	009 Samurott [TM]	010 Patrat [TM]	011 Watchog [TM]
	012 Lillipup [TM]	013 Herdier [TM]	014 Stoutland [TM]	015 Purrloin [TM]	016 Liepard [TM]	017 Pansage [TM]
	018 Simisage [TM]	019 Pansear [TM]	020 Simisear [TM]	021 Panpour [TM]	022 Simipour [TM]	023 Munna [TM]
	024 Musharna [TM]	025 Pidove [TM]	026 Tranquill [TM]	027 Unfezant [TM]	028 Blitzle [TM]	029 Zebstrika [TM]
	030 Roggenrola [TM]	031 Boldore [TM]	032 Gigalith [TM]	033 Woobat [TM]	034 Swoobat [TM]	035 Drilbur [TM]
	036 Excadrill [TM]	037 Audino [TM]	038 Timburr [TM]	039 Gurdurr [TM]	040 Conkeldurr [TM]	041 Tympole [TM]
	042 Palpitoad [TM]	043 Seismitoad [TM]	044 Throh [TM]	045 Sawk [TM]	046 Sewaddle [TM]	047 Swadloon [TM]
	048 Leavanny [TM]	049 Venipede [TM]	050 Whirlipede [TM]	051 Scolipede [TM]	052 Cottonee [TM]	053 Whimsicott [TM]
	054 Petilil [TM]	055 Lilligant [TM]	056 Basculin [TM]	057 Sandile [TM]	058 Krokorok [TM]	059 Krookodile [TM]
	060 Darumaka [TM]	061 Darmanitan [TM]	062 Maractus [TM]	063 Dwebble [TM]	064 Crustle [TM]	065 Scraggy [TM]
	066 Scrafty [TM]	067 Sigilyph [TM]	068 Yamask [TM]	069 Cofagrigus [TM]	070 Tirtouga [TM]	071 Carracosta [TM]
	072 Archen [TM]	073 Archeops [TM]	074 Trubbish [TM]	075 Garbodor [TM]	076 Zorua [TM]	077 Zoroark [TM]
	078 Minccino [TM]	079 Cinccino [TM]	080 Gothita [TM]	081 Gothorita [TM]	082 Gothitelle [TM]	083 Solosis [14, TM]
	084 Duosion [14, TM]	085 Reuniclus [14, TM]	086 Ducklett [TM]	087 Swanna [TM]	088 Vanillite [TM]	089 Vanillish [TM]
	090 Vanilluxe [TM]	091 Deerling [TM]	092 Sawsbuck [TM]	093 Emolga [TM]	094 Karrablast [TM]	095 Escavalier [TM]
	096 Foongus [TM]	097 Amoonguss [TM]	098 Frillish [TM]	099 Jellicent [TM]	100 Alomomola [TM]	101 Joltik [TM]
	102 Galvantula [TM]	103 Ferroseed [TM]	104 Ferrothorn [TM]	105 Klink [TM]	106 Klang [TM]	107 Klinklang [TM]
	109 Eelektrik [TM]	110 Eelektross [TM]	111 Elgyem [22, TM]	112 Beheeyem [22, TM]	113 Litwick [TM]	114 Lampent [TM]
	115 Chandelure [TM]	116 Axew [TM]	117 Fraxure [TM]	118 Haxorus [TM]	119 Cubchoo [TM]	120 Beartic [TM]
	121 Cryogonal [TM]	122 Shelmet [TM]	123 Accelgor [TM]	124 Stunfisk [TM]	125 Mienfoo [TM]	126 Mienshao [TM]
	127 Druddigon [TM]	128 Golett [TM]	129 Golurk [TM]	130 Pawniard [TM]	131 Bisharp [TM]	132 Bouffalant [TM]
	133 Rufflet [TM]	134 Braviary [TM]	135 Vullaby [TM]	136 Mandibuzz [TM]	137 Heatmor [TM]	138 Durant [TM]
	139 Deino [TM]	140 Zweilous [TM]	141 Hydreigon [TM]	142 Larvesta [TM]	143 Volcarona [TM]	144 Cobalion [TM]
	145 Terrakion [TM]	146 Virizion [TM]	147 Tornadus [TM]	148 Thundurus [TM]	149 Reshiram [TM]	150 Zekrom [TM]
	151 Landorus [TM]	152 Kyurem [TM]				
Hone Claws	015 Purrloin [24, TM]	016 Liepard [26, TM]	017 Pansage [TM]	018 Simisage [TM]	019 Pansear [TM]	020 Simisear [TM]
	021 Panpour [TM]	022 Simipour [TM]	035 Drilbur [22, TM]	036 Excadrill [22, TM]	048 Leavanny [TM]	057 Sandile [TM]
	058 Krokorok [TM]	059 Krookodile [TM]	063 Dwebble [TM]	064 Crustle [TM]	072 Archen [TM]	073 Archeops [TM]
	076 Zorua [TM]	077 Zoroark [1, 9, TM]	103 Ferroseed [TM]	104 Ferrothorn [TM]	110 Eelektross [TM]	116 Axew [TM]
	117 Fraxure [TM]	118 Haxorus [TM]	119 Cubchoo [TM]	120 Beartic [TM]	127 Druddigon [5, TM]	130 Pawniard [TM]
	131 Bisharp [TM]	133 Rufflet [14, TM]	134 Braviary [14, TM]	137 Heatmor [TM]	138 Durant [TM]	144 Cobalion [TM]
	149 Reshiram [TM]	150 Zekrom [TM]	152 Kyurem [TM]			
Horn Attack	094 Karrablast [E]	132 Bouffalant [16]				
Horn Drill	036 Excadrill [31]					
Horn Leech	092 Sawsbuck [37]					
Howl	012 Lillipup [E]					
Hurricane	053 Whimsicott [46]	086 Ducklett [46]	087 Swanna [55]	143 Volcarona [90]	147 Tornadus [67]	
Hydro Cannon	009 Samurott [T]					
Hydro Pump	007 Oshawott [43]	008 Dewott [52]	009 Samurott [62]	021 Panpour [E]	041 Tympole [42]	042 Palpitoad [47]
	043 Seismitoad [53]	070 Tirtouga [51]	071 Carracosta [61]	098 Frillish [49]	099 Jellicent [53]	100 Alomomola [61]
Hyper Beam	000 Victini [TM]	003 Serperior [TM]	006 Emboar [TM]	009 Samurott [TM]	011 Watchog [TM]	014 Stoutland [TM]
	016 Liepard [TM]	018 Simisage [TM]	020 Simisear [TM]	022 Simipour [TM]	024 Musharna [TM]	027 Unfezant [TM]
	029 Zebstrika [TM]	032 Gigalith [TM]	034 Swoobat [TM]	036 Excadrill [TM]	037 Audino [TM]	040 Conkeldurr [TM]
	043 Seismitoad [TM]	048 Leavanny [TM]	051 Scolipede [TM]	053 Whimsicott [TM]	055 Lilligant [TM]	059 Krookodile [TM]
	061 Darmanitan [TM]	064 Crustle [TM]	066 Scrafty [TM]	067 Sigilyph [TM]	069 Cofagrigus [TM]	071 Carracosta [TM]
	073 Archeops [TM]	075 Garbodor [TM]	077 Zoroark [TM]	079 Cinccino [TM]	082 Gothitelle [TM]	085 Reuniclus [TM]
	087 Swanna [TM]	090 Vanilluxe [TM]	092 Sawsbuck [TM]	095 Escavalier [TM]	097 Amoonguss [TM]	099 Jellicent [TM]
	102 Galvantula [TM]	104 Ferrothorn [TM]	105 Klink [57, TM]	106 Klang [64, TM]	107 Klinklang [72, TM]	110 Eelektross [TM]
	112 Beheeyem [TM]	115 Chandelure [TM]	118 Haxorus [TM]	120 Beartic [TM]	121 Cryogonal [TM]	123 Accelgor [TM]
	126 Mienshao [TM]	127 Druddigon [TM]	129 Golurk [TM]	131 Bisharp [TM]	134 Braviary [TM]	136 Mandibuzz [TM]
	141 Hydreigon [TM]	143 Volcarona [TM]	144 Cobalion [TM]	145 Terrakion [TM]	146 Virizion [TM]	147 Tornadus [TM]
	148 Thundurus [TM]	149 Reshiram [TM]	150 Zekrom [TM]	151 Landorus [TM]	152 Kyurem [TM]	
Hyper Fang	010 Patrat [28]	011 Watchog [32]				
Hyper Voice	041 Tympole [45]	042 Palpitoad [51]	043 Seismitoad [59]	078 Minccino [43]	139 Deino [58]	140 Zweilous [64]
	141 Hydreigon [68]	149 Reshiram [92]	150 Zekrom [92]	152 Kyurem [92]		
Hypnosis	010 Patrat [18]	011 Watchog [18]	023 Munna [19]	024 Musharna [1]	025 Pidove [E]	067 Sigilyph [4]

I

Move	Pokémon that can learn it					
Ice Ball	—					
Ice Beam	007 Oshawott [TM]	008 Dewott [TM]	009 Samurott [TM]	021 Panpour [TM]	022 Simipour [TM]	037 Audino [TM]
	056 Basculin [TM]	067 Sigilyph [TM]	070 Tirtouga [TM]	071 Carracosta [TM]	086 Ducklett [TM]	087 Swanna [TM]
	088 Vanillite [35, TM]	089 Vanillish [36, TM]	090 Vanilluxe [36, TM]	098 Frillish [TM]	099 Jellicent [TM]	100 Alomomola [TM]
	119 Cubchoo [TM]	120 Beartic [TM]	121 Cryogonal [33, TM]	128 Golett [TM]	129 Golurk [TM]	152 Kyurem [22, TM]
Ice Fang	012 Lillipup [E]	014 Stoutland [1]	139 Deino [E]			
Ice Punch	065 Scraggy [E]	119 Cubchoo [E]				
Ice Shard	088 Vanillite [E]	121 Cryogonal [5]				
Icicle Crash	120 Beartic [37]					
Icicle Spear	088 Vanillite [1]	089 Vanillish [1]	090 Vanilluxe [1]			
Icy Wind	088 Vanillite [13]	089 Vanillish [13]	090 Vanilluxe [13]	119 Cubchoo [13]	120 Beartic [1, 13]	121 Cryogonal [17]
	152 Kyurem [1]					
Imprison	023 Munna [13]	033 Woobat [19]	034 Swoobat [19]	068 Yamask [E]	076 Zorua [53]	077 Zoroark [59]
	083 Solosis [E]	088 Vanillite [E]	111 Elgyem [25]	112 Beheeyem [25]	113 Litwick [24]	114 Lampent [24]
	149 Reshiram [8, 64]	150 Zekrom [8, 64]	151 Landorus [?]	152 Kyurem [8, 64]		
Incinerate	000 Victini [1, TM]	004 Tepig [TM]	005 Pignite [TM]	006 Emboar [TM]	019 Pansear [10, TM]	020 Simisear [TM]
	037 Audino [TM]	057 Sandile [TM]	058 Krokorok [TM]	059 Krookodile [TM]	060 Darumaka [6, TM]	061 Darmanitan [1, 6, TM]
	065 Scraggy [TM]	066 Scrafty [TM]	076 Zorua [TM]	077 Zoroark [TM]	113 Litwick [TM]	114 Lampent [TM]
	115 Chandelure [TM]	116 Axew [TM]	117 Fraxure [TM]	118 Haxorus [TM]	127 Druddigon [TM]	135 Vullaby [TM]
	136 Mandibuzz [TM]	137 Heatmor [1, TM]	139 Deino [TM]	140 Zweilous [TM]	141 Hydreigon [TM]	142 Larvesta [TM]
	143 Volcarona [TM]	147 Tornadus [TM]	148 Thundurus [TM]	149 Reshiram [TM]		
Inferno	000 Victini [57]	113 Litwick [38]	114 Lampent [38]	137 Heatmor [61]		
Ingrain	054 Petilil [E]	062 Maractus [33]	096 Foongus [18]	097 Amoonguss [18]	103 Ferroseed [35]	104 Ferrothorn [35]
Iron Defense	030 Roggenrola [20]	031 Boldore [20]	032 Gigalith [20]	035 Drilbur [E]	050 Whirlipede [22]	063 Dwebble [E]
	070 Tirtouga [E]	088 Vanillite [E]	095 Escavalier [40]	103 Ferroseed [26]	104 Ferrothorn [26]	128 Golett [17]
	129 Golurk [17]	130 Pawniard [46]	131 Bisharp [46]	138 Durant [56]		
Iron Head	095 Escavalier [37]	103 Ferroseed [43]	104 Ferrothorn [46]	130 Pawniard [54]	131 Bisharp [57]	132 Bouffalant [E]
	138 Durant [36]	144 Cobalion [37]				
Iron Tail	001 Snivy [E]	010 Patrat [E]	078 Minccino [E]	093 Emolga [E]	116 Axew [E]	127 Druddigon [E]

J

Move	Pokémon that can learn it			
Judgment	—			
Jump Kick	091 Deerling [24]	092 Sawsbuck [24]	125 Mienfoo [37]	126 Mienshao [37]

K

Move	Pokémon that can learn it					
Karate Chop	045 Sawk [25]					
Kinesis	—					
Knock Off	033 Woobat [E]	070 Tirtouga [E]	072 Archen [E]	078 Minccino [E]	094 Karrablast [E]	125 Mienfoo [E]
	135 Vullaby [E]					

L

Move	Pokémon that can learn it					
Last Resort	012 Lillipup [36]	013 Herdier [42]	014 Stoutland [51]	037 Audino [55]	078 Minccino [45]	
Lava Plume	—					
Leaf Blade	001 Snivy [28]	002 Servine [32]	003 Serperior [32]	048 Leavanny [36]	146 Virizion [67]	
Leaf Storm	001 Snivy [43]	002 Servine [52]	003 Serperior [62]	017 Pansage [E]	048 Leavanny [50]	054 Petilil [46]
Leaf Tornado	001 Snivy [16]	002 Servine [16]	003 Serperior [16]			
Leech Life	101 Joltik [1]	102 Galvantula [1]	122 Shelmet [1]	123 Accelgor [1]	142 Larvesta [10]	143 Volcarona [1, 10]
Leech Seed	001 Snivy [19]	002 Servine [20]	003 Serperior [20]	017 Pansage [16]	052 Cottonee [8]	053 Whimsicott [1]
	054 Petilil [8]	055 Lilligant [1]	062 Maractus [E]	091 Deerling [13]	092 Sawsbuck [13]	103 Ferroseed [E]
Leer	001 Snivy [4]	002 Servine [1, 4]	003 Serperior [1, 4]	010 Patrat [3]	011 Watchog [1, 3]	012 Lillipup [1]
	013 Herdier [1]	014 Stoutland [1]	017 Pansage [4]	018 Simisage [1]	019 Pansear [4]	020 Simisear [1]
	021 Panpour [4]	022 Simipour [1]	025 Pidove [8]	026 Tranquill [1, 8]	027 Unfezant [1, 8]	038 Timburr [1]
	039 Gurdurr [1]	040 Conkeldurr [1]	044 Throh [1]	045 Sawk [1]	057 Sandile [1]	058 Krokorok [1]
	059 Krookodile [1]	065 Scraggy [1]	066 Scrafty [1]	072 Archen [1]	073 Archeops [1]	076 Zorua [1]
	077 Zoroark [1]	094 Karrablast [4]	095 Escavalier [1, 4]	116 Axew [4]	117 Fraxure [1, 4]	118 Haxorus [1, 4]
	127 Druddigon [1]	130 Pawniard [6]	131 Bisharp [1, 6]	132 Bouffalant [1]	133 Rufflet [1]	134 Braviary [1]
	135 Vullaby [1]	136 Mandibuzz [1]	144 Cobalion [1]	145 Terrakion [1]	146 Virizion [1]	
Lick	012 Lillipup [E]	017 Pansage [?]	018 Simisage [1]	019 Pansear [?]	020 Simisear [1]	021 Panpour [?]
	022 Simipour [1]	137 Heatmor [1]				
Light Screen	000 Victini [TM]	001 Snivy [TM]	002 Servine [TM]	003 Serperior [TM]	011 Watchog [TM]	023 Munna [TM]
	024 Musharna [TM]	028 Blitzle [TM]	029 Zebstrika [TM]	033 Woobat [TM]	034 Swoobat [TM]	037 Audino [TM]
	046 Sewaddle [TM]	047 Swadloon [TM]	048 Leavanny [TM]	053 Whimsicott [TM]	055 Lilligant [TM]	067 Sigilyph [24, TM]

Move	Pokémon that can learn it					
Light Screen (continued)	079 Cinccino [TM]	080 Gothita [TM]	081 Gothorita [TM]	082 Gothitelle [TM]	083 Solosis [16, TM]	084 Duosion [16, TM]
	085 Reuniclus [16, TM]	088 Vanillite [TM]	089 Vanillish [TM]	090 Vanilluxe [TM]	091 Deerling [TM]	092 Sawsbuck [TM]
	093 Emolga [34, TM]	100 Alomomola [TM]	101 Joltik [TM]	102 Galvantula [TM]	109 Eelektrik [TM]	110 Eelektross [TM]
	111 Elgyem [TM]	112 Beheeyem [TM]	121 Cryogonal [37, TM]	142 Larvesta [TM]	143 Volcarona [TM]	146 Virizion [TM]
	149 Reshiram [TM]	150 Zekrom [TM]	152 Kyurem [TM]			
Lock-On	030 Roggenrola [E]	105 Klink [51]	106 Klang [56]	107 Klinklang [60]		
Lovely Kiss	—					
Low Kick	011 Watchog [1]	017 Pansage [E]	019 Pansear [E]	021 Panpour [E]	038 Timburr [12]	039 Gurdurr [12]
	040 Conkeldurr [12]	065 Scraggy [1]	066 Scrafty [1]	125 Mienfoo [E]		
Low Sweep	005 Pignite [TM]	006 Emboar [TM]	017 Pansage [TM]	018 Simisage [TM]	019 Pansear [TM]	020 Simisear [TM]
	021 Panpour [TM]	022 Simipour [TM]	038 Timburr [TM]	039 Gurdurr [TM]	040 Conkeldurr [TM]	044 Throh [TM]
	045 Sawk [17, TM]	058 Krokorok [TM]	059 Krookodile [TM]	065 Scraggy [TM]	066 Scrafty [TM]	077 Zoroark [TM]
	082 Gothitelle [TM]	125 Mienfoo [TM]	126 Mienshao [TM]	128 Golett [TM]	129 Golurk [TM]	130 Pawniard [TM]
	131 Bisharp [TM]					
Lucky Chant	023 Munna [5]	024 Musharna [1]	025 Pidove [E]	037 Audino [E]	086 Ducklett [E]	
Lunar Dance	—					
Luster Purge	—					

◈ **M**

Move	Pokémon that can learn it					
Mach Punch	038 Timburr [E]					
Magic Coat	023 Munna [E]					
Magic Room	080 Gothita [48]	081 Gothorita [53]	082 Gothitelle [59]			
Magical Leaf	001 Snivy [E]	017 Pansage [E]	054 Petilil [19]	146 Virizion [13]		
Magma Storm	—					
Magnet Bomb	—					
Magnet Rise	088 Vanillite [E]	142 Larvesta [E]				
Magnitude	004 Tepig [E]	030 Roggenrola [E]	128 Golett [25]	129 Golurk [25]		
Me First	028 Blitzle [E]	046 Sewaddle [E]	086 Ducklett [E]	123 Accelgor [28]	125 Mienfoo [E]	
Mean Look	001 Snivy [E]	010 Patrat [31]	011 Watchog [36]	057 Sandile [E]	068 Yamask [45]	069 Cofagrigus [51]
	080 Gothita [E]	130 Pawniard [E]	135 Vullaby [E]			
Meditate	125 Mienfoo [5]	126 Mienshao [1, 5]				
Mega Drain	001 Snivy [22]	002 Servine [24]	003 Serperior [24]	052 Cottonee [13]	053 Whimsicott [1]	054 Petilil [13]
	055 Lilligant [1]	062 Maractus [13]	096 Foongus [15]	097 Amoonguss [15]	122 Shelmet [20]	123 Accelgor [20]
Mega Kick	—					
Mega Punch	128 Golett [21]	129 Golurk [21]				
Megahorn	009 Samurott [1]	051 Scolipede [1]	092 Sawsbuck [1]	094 Karrablast [E]	132 Bouffalant [41]	
Memento	052 Cottonee [E]	068 Yamask [E]	076 Zorua [E]	113 Litwick [33]	114 Lampent [33]	
Metal Burst	131 Bisharp [1]	144 Cobalion [67]				
Metal Claw	035 Drilbur [15]	036 Excadrill [15]	103 Ferroseed [14]	104 Ferrothorn [14]	127 Druddigon [E]	130 Pawniard [25]
	131 Bisharp [25]	138 Durant [21]	144 Cobalion [13]			
Metal Sound	035 Drilbur [E]	105 Klink [45]	106 Klang [48]	107 Klinklang [48]	130 Pawniard [38]	131 Bisharp [38]
	138 Durant [66]					
Meteor Mash	—					
Metronome	—					
Milk Drink	—					
Mimic	—					
Mind Reader	046 Sewaddle [E]	122 Shelmet [E]				
Minimize	113 Litwick [3]	114 Lampent [1, 3]				
Miracle Eye	067 Sigilyph [1]	080 Gothita [E]	111 Elgyem [11]	112 Beheeyem [1, 11]		
Mirror Coat	001 Snivy [E]	080 Gothita [E]	088 Vanillite [44]	089 Vanillish [47]	090 Vanilluxe [50]	100 Alomomola [E]
Mirror Move	067 Sigilyph [34]	086 Ducklett [E]	135 Vullaby [64]	136 Mandibuzz [70]		
Mirror Shot	088 Vanillite [26]	089 Vanillish [26]	090 Vanilluxe [26]	103 Ferroseed [30]	104 Ferrothorn [30]	105 Klink [36]
	106 Klang [36]	107 Klinklang [36]				
Mist	041 Tympole [E]	088 Vanillite [16]	089 Vanillish [16]	090 Vanilluxe [16]	098 Frillish [E]	100 Alomomola [E]
	121 Cryogonal [21]					
Mist Ball	—					
Moonlight	023 Munna [17]					
Morning Sun	025 Pidove [E]	142 Larvesta [E]				
Mud Bomb	041 Tympole [E]	124 Stunfisk [21]				
Mud Shot	041 Tympole [16]	042 Palpitoad [16]	043 Seismitoad [16]	056 Basculin [E]	124 Stunfisk [13]	132 Bouffalant [E]
	151 Landorus [1]					
Mud Sport	021 Panpour [E]	035 Drilbur [1]	036 Excadrill [1]	041 Tympole [E]	074 Trubbish [E]	124 Stunfisk [1]
Muddy Water	041 Tympole [27]	042 Palpitoad [28]	043 Seismitoad [28]	056 Basculin [E]	124 Stunfisk [40]	

M

Move	Pokémon that can learn it				
Mud-Slap	012 Lillipup [E]	030 Roggenrola [17]	031 Boldore [17]	032 Gigalith [17]	035 Drilbur [8]	036 Excadrill [1, 8]
	057 Sandile [19]	058 Krokorok [19]	059 Krookodile [19]	078 Minccino [E]	122 Shelmet [E]	124 Stunfisk [1]
	128 Golett [5]	129 Golurk [1, 5]	132 Bouffalant [E]			

N

Move	Pokémon that can learn it				
Nasty Plot	015 Purrloin [42]	016 Liepard [50]	017 Pansage [E]	019 Pansear [E]	021 Panpour [E]	068 Yamask [E]
	076 Zorua [49]	077 Zoroark [54]	111 Elgyem [E]	135 Vullaby [14]	136 Mandibuzz [14]	148 Thundurus [61]
Natural Gift	001 Snivy [E]	017 Pansage [40]	019 Pansear [40]	021 Panpour [40]	052 Cottonee [E]	054 Petilil [E]
	088 Vanillite [E]	091 Deerling [E]				
Nature Power	091 Deerling [41]	092 Sawsbuck [44]				
Needle Arm	062 Maractus [22]					
Night Daze	076 Zorua [57]	077 Zoroark [64]				
Night Shade	068 Yamask [13]	069 Cofagrigus [13]	083 Solosis [E]	098 Frillish [9]	099 Jellicent [1, 9]	113 Litwick [13]
	114 Lampent [13]	128 Golett [35]	129 Golurk [35]			
Night Slash	007 Oshawott [E]	015 Purrloin [37]	016 Liepard [43]	063 Dwebble [E]	077 Zoroark [30]	116 Axew [E]
	119 Cubchoo [E]	121 Cryogonal [57]	127 Druddigon [40]	130 Pawniard [49]	131 Bisharp [49]	137 Heatmor [E]
Nightmare	023 Munna [29]	068 Yamask [E]				

O

Move	Pokémon that can learn it				
Octazooka	—					
Odor Sleuth	004 Tepig [9]	005 Pignite [1, 9]	006 Emboar [1, 9]	012 Lillipup [5]	013 Herdier [1, 5]	014 Stoutland [1, 5]
	033 Woobat [4]	034 Swoobat [1, 4]	091 Deerling [E]	137 Heatmor [6]		
Ominous Wind	068 Yamask [25]	069 Cofagrigus [25]	098 Frillish [27]	099 Jellicent [27]		
Outrage	059 Krookodile [60]	116 Axew [56]	117 Fraxure [60]	118 Haxorus [66]	127 Druddigon [62]	139 Deino [62]
	140 Zweilous [71]	141 Hydreigon [79]	149 Reshiram [85]	150 Zekrom [85]	151 Landorus [85]	152 Kyurem [85]
Overheat	000 Victini [97, TM]	004 Tepig [TM]	005 Pignite [TM]	006 Emboar [TM]	019 Pansear [TM]	020 Simisear [TM]
	029 Zebstrika [TM]	060 Darumaka [42, TM]	061 Darmanitan [54, TM]	113 Litwick [61, TM]	114 Lampent [69, TM]	115 Chandelure [TM]
	142 Larvesta [TM]	143 Volcarona [TM]	149 Reshiram [TM]			

P

Move	Pokémon that can learn it				
Pain Split	083 Solosis [33]	084 Duosion [34]	085 Reuniclus [34]	098 Frillish [E]	100 Alomomola [E]	113 Litwick [55]
	114 Lampent [61]	124 Stunfisk [E]				
Pay Day	015 Purrloin [E]					
Payback	013 Herdier [TM]	014 Stoutland [TM]	015 Purrloin [TM]	016 Liepard [TM]	017 Pansage [TM]	018 Simisage [TM]
	019 Pansear [TM]	020 Simisear [TM]	021 Panpour [TM]	022 Simipour [TM]	038 Timburr [TM]	039 Gurdurr [TM]
	040 Conkeldurr [TM]	043 Seismitoad [TM]	044 Throh [TM]	045 Sawk [TM]	046 Sewaddle [TM]	047 Swadloon [TM]
	048 Leavanny [TM]	049 Venipede [TM]	050 Whirlipede [TM]	051 Scolipede [TM]	057 Sandile [TM]	058 Krokorok [TM]
	059 Krookodile [TM]	061 Darmanitan [TM]	065 Scraggy [23, TM]	066 Scrafty [23, TM]	068 Yamask [TM]	069 Cofagrigus [TM]
	074 Trubbish [TM]	075 Garbodor [TM]	076 Zorua [TM]	077 Zoroark [TM]	080 Gothita [TM]	081 Gothorita [TM]
	082 Gothitelle [TM]	096 Foongus [TM]	097 Amoonguss [TM]	103 Ferroseed [47, TM]	104 Ferrothorn [53, TM]	113 Litwick [TM]
	114 Lampent [TM]	115 Chandelure [TM]	116 Axew [TM]	117 Fraxure [TM]	118 Haxorus [TM]	124 Stunfisk [TM]
	125 Mienfoo [TM]	126 Mienshao [TM]	127 Druddigon [TM]	130 Pawniard [TM]	131 Bisharp [TM]	132 Bouffalant [TM]
	135 Vullaby [TM]	136 Mandibuzz [TM]	141 Hydreigon [TM]	147 Tornadus [TM]	148 Thundurus [TM]	149 Reshiram [TM]
	150 Zekrom [TM]	151 Landorus [TM]	152 Kyurem [TM]			
Peck	062 Maractus [1]	094 Karrablast [1]	095 Escavalier [1]	133 Rufflet [1]	134 Braviary [1]	
Perish Song	—					
Petal Dance	055 Lilligant [46]	062 Maractus [38]				
Pin Missile	049 Venipede [E]	062 Maractus [10]	101 Joltik [E]	103 Ferroseed [18]	104 Ferrothorn [18]	
Pluck	025 Pidove [TM]	026 Tranquill [TM]	027 Unfezant [TM]	033 Woobat [TM]	034 Swoobat [TM]	067 Sigilyph [TM]
	072 Archen [15, TM]	073 Archeops [15, TM]	086 Ducklett [TM]	087 Swanna [TM]	133 Rufflet [TM]	134 Braviary [TM]
	135 Vullaby [10, TM]	136 Mandibuzz [1, 10, TM]				
Poison Fang	—					
Poison Gas	074 Trubbish [1]	075 Garbodor [1]				
Poison Jab	005 Pignite [TM]	006 Emboar [TM]	035 Drilbur [TM]	036 Excadrill [TM]	038 Timburr [TM]	039 Gurdurr [TM]
	040 Conkeldurr [TM]	043 Seismitoad [TM]	044 Throh [TM]	045 Sawk [TM]	048 Leavanny [TM]	049 Venipede [TM]
	050 Whirlipede [TM]	051 Scolipede [TM]	062 Maractus [TM]	063 Dwebble [TM]	064 Crustle [TM]	065 Scraggy [TM]
	066 Scrafty [TM]	094 Karrablast [TM]	095 Escavalier [TM]	101 Joltik [TM]	102 Galvantula [TM]	103 Ferroseed [TM]
	104 Ferrothorn [TM]	116 Axew [TM]	117 Fraxure [TM]	118 Haxorus [TM]	121 Cryogonal [TM]	125 Mienfoo [TM]
	126 Mienshao [TM]	130 Pawniard [TM]	131 Bisharp [TM]	132 Bouffalant [TM]	143 Volcarona [TM]	144 Cobalion [TM]
	145 Terrakion [TM]					
Poison Sting	049 Venipede [5]	050 Whirlipede [1, 5]	051 Scolipede [1, 5]	101 Joltik [E]		
Poison Tail	049 Venipede [19]	050 Whirlipede [19]	051 Scolipede [19]	127 Druddigon [E]		

Move	Pokémon that can learn it					
PoisonPowder	052 Cottonee [22]	096 Foongus [E]				
Pound	037 Audino [1]	038 Timburr [1]	039 Gurdurr [1]	040 Conkeldurr [1]	074 Trubbish [1]	075 Garbodor [1]
	078 Minccino [1]	080 Gothita [1]	081 Gothorita [1]	082 Gothitelle [1]	100 Alomomola [1]	125 Mienfoo [1]
	126 Mienshao [1]	128 Golett [1]	129 Golurk [1]			
Powder Snow	088 Vanillite [E]	119 Cubchoo [1]	120 Beartic [1]			
Power Gem	031 Boldore [25]	032 Gigalith [25]				
Power Split	068 Yamask [33]	069 Cofagrigus [33]	111 Elgyem [50]	112 Beheeyem [58]		
Power Swap	111 Elgyem [E]	123 Accelgor [52]				
Power Trick	—					
Power Whip	104 Ferrothorn [40]					
Present	—					
Protect	000 Victini [TM]	001 Snivy [TM]	002 Servine [TM]	003 Serperior [TM]	004 Tepig [TM]	005 Pignite [TM]
	006 Emboar [TM]	007 Oshawott [TM]	008 Dewott [TM]	009 Samurott [TM]	010 Patrat [TM]	011 Watchog [TM]
	012 Lillipup [TM]	013 Herdier [TM]	014 Stoutland [TM]	015 Purrloin [TM]	016 Liepard [TM]	017 Pansage [TM]
	018 Simisage [TM]	019 Pansear [TM]	020 Simisear [TM]	021 Panpour [TM]	022 Simipour [TM]	023 Munna [TM]
	024 Musharna [TM]	025 Pidove [TM]	026 Tranquill [TM]	027 Unfezant [TM]	028 Blitzle [TM]	029 Zebstrika [TM]
	030 Roggenrola [TM]	031 Boldore [TM]	032 Gigalith [TM]	033 Woobat [TM]	034 Swoobat [TM]	035 Drilbur [TM]
	036 Excadrill [TM]	037 Audino [TM]	038 Timburr [TM]	039 Gurdurr [TM]	040 Conkeldurr [TM]	041 Tympole [TM]
	042 Palpitoad [TM]	043 Seismitoad [TM]	044 Throh [TM]	045 Sawk [TM]	046 Sewaddle [TM]	047 Swadloon [20, TM]
	048 Leavanny [TM]	049 Venipede [15, TM]	050 Whirlipede [15, TM]	051 Scolipede [15, TM]	052 Cottonee [TM]	053 Whimsicott [TM]
	054 Petilil [TM]	055 Lilligant [TM]	056 Basculin [TM]	057 Sandile [TM]	058 Krokorok [TM]	059 Krookodile [TM]
	060 Darumaka [TM]	061 Darmanitan [TM]	062 Maractus [TM]	063 Dwebble [TM]	064 Crustle [TM]	065 Scraggy [TM]
	066 Scrafty [TM]	067 Sigilyph [TM]	068 Yamask [1, TM]	069 Cofagrigus [1, TM]	070 Tirtouga [11, TM]	071 Carracosta [11, TM]
	072 Archen [TM]	073 Archeops [TM]	074 Trubbish [TM]	075 Garbodor [TM]	076 Zorua [TM]	077 Zoroark [TM]
	078 Minccino [TM]	079 Cinccino [TM]	080 Gothita [TM]	081 Gothorita [TM]	082 Gothitelle [TM]	083 Solosis [TM]
	084 Duosion [TM]	085 Reuniclus [TM]	086 Ducklett [TM]	087 Swanna [TM]	088 Vanillite [TM]	089 Vanillish [TM]
	090 Vanilluxe [TM]	091 Deerling [TM]	092 Sawsbuck [TM]	093 Emolga [TM]	094 Karrablast [TM]	095 Escavalier [TM]
	096 Foongus [TM]	097 Amoonguss [TM]	098 Frillish [TM]	099 Jellicent [TM]	100 Alomomola [21, TM]	101 Joltik [TM]
	102 Galvantula [TM]	103 Ferroseed [TM]	104 Ferrothorn [TM]	105 Klink [TM]	106 Klang [TM]	107 Klinklang [TM]
	109 Eelektrik [TM]	110 Eelektross [TM]	111 Elgyem [TM]	112 Beheeyem [TM]	113 Litwick [TM]	114 Lampent [TM]
	115 Chandelure [TM]	116 Axew [TM]	117 Fraxure [TM]	118 Haxorus [TM]	119 Cubchoo [TM]	120 Beartic [TM]
	121 Cryogonal [TM]	122 Shelmet [28, TM]	123 Accelgor [TM]	124 Stunfisk [TM]	125 Mienfoo [TM]	126 Mienshao [TM]
	127 Druddigon [TM]	128 Golett [TM]	129 Golurk [TM]	130 Pawniard [TM]	131 Bisharp [TM]	132 Bouffalant [TM]
	133 Rufflet [TM]	134 Braviary [TM]	135 Vullaby [TM]	136 Mandibuzz [TM]	137 Heatmor [TM]	138 Durant [TM]
	139 Deino [TM]	140 Zweilous [TM]	141 Hydreigon [TM]	142 Larvesta [TM]	143 Volcarona [TM]	144 Cobalion [TM]
	145 Terrakion [TM]	146 Virizion [TM]	147 Tornadus [TM]	148 Thundurus [TM]	149 Reshiram [TM]	150 Zekrom [TM]
	151 Landorus [TM]	152 Kyurem [TM]				
Psybeam	023 Munna [11]	024 Musharna [1]	067 Sigilyph [18]	080 Gothita [16]	081 Gothorita [16]	082 Gothitelle [16]
	111 Elgyem [15]	112 Beheeyem [15]				
Psych Up	000 Victini [TM]	011 Watchog [29, TM]	015 Purrloin [TM]	016 Liepard [TM]	023 Munna [TM]	024 Musharna [TM]
	027 Unfezant [TM]	033 Woobat [TM]	034 Swoobat [TM]	037 Audino [TM]	067 Sigilyph [TM]	068 Yamask [TM]
	069 Cofagrigus [TM]	076 Zorua [TM]	077 Zoroark [TM]	080 Gothita [TM]	081 Gothorita [TM]	082 Gothitelle [TM]
	083 Solosis [TM]	084 Duosion [TM]	085 Reuniclus [TM]	098 Frillish [TM]	099 Jellicent [TM]	100 Alomomola [TM]
	111 Elgyem [36, TM]	112 Beheeyem [36, TM]	113 Litwick [TM]	114 Lampent [TM]	115 Chandelure [TM]	125 Mienfoo [TM]
	126 Mienshao [TM]	135 Vullaby [TM]	136 Mandibuzz [TM]	139 Deino [TM]	140 Zweilous [TM]	141 Hydreigon [TM]
	144 Cobalion [TM]	145 Terrakion [TM]	146 Virizion [TM]			
Psychic	000 Victini [TM]	023 Munna [37, TM]	024 Musharna [TM]	033 Woobat [41, TM]	034 Swoobat [41, TM]	037 Audino [TM]
	053 Whimsicott [TM]	061 Darmanitan [TM]	067 Sigilyph [44, TM]	068 Yamask [TM]	069 Cofagrigus [TM]	075 Garbodor [TM]
	080 Gothita [37, TM]	081 Gothorita [39, TM]	082 Gothitelle [39, TM]	083 Solosis [37, TM]	084 Duosion [39, TM]	085 Reuniclus [39, TM]
	098 Frillish [TM]	099 Jellicent [TM]	100 Alomomola [TM]	111 Elgyem [39, TM]	112 Beheeyem [39, TM]	113 Litwick [TM]
	114 Lampent [TM]	115 Chandelure [TM]	128 Golett [TM]	129 Golurk [TM]	142 Larvesta [TM]	143 Volcarona [TM]
	147 Tornadus [TM]	148 Thundurus [TM]	149 Reshiram [TM]	150 Zekrom [TM]	151 Landorus [TM]	152 Kyurem [TM]
Psycho Boost	—					
Psycho Cut	130 Pawniard [E]					
Psycho Shift	067 Sigilyph [E]					
Psyshock	000 Victini [TM]	023 Munna [TM]	024 Musharna [TM]	033 Woobat [TM]	034 Swoobat [TM]	037 Audino [TM]
	067 Sigilyph [TM]	080 Gothita [25, TM]	081 Gothorita [25, TM]	082 Gothitelle [25, TM]	083 Solosis [25, TM]	084 Duosion [25, TM]
	085 Reuniclus [25, TM]	111 Elgyem [TM]	112 Beheeyem [TM]			
Psystrike	—					
Psywave	023 Munna [1]	067 Sigilyph [8]	083 Solosis [1]	084 Duosion [1]	085 Reuniclus [1]	
Punishment	076 Zorua [45]	077 Zoroark [49]	135 Vullaby [28]	136 Mandibuzz [28]	151 Landorus [13]	
Pursuit	001 Snivy [E]	010 Patrat [E]	012 Lillipup [E]	015 Purrloin [15]	016 Liepard [15]	028 Blitzle [22]
	029 Zebstrika [22]	049 Venipede [12]	050 Whirlipede [12]	051 Scolipede [12]	057 Sandile [E]	076 Zorua [5]
	077 Zoroark [1, 5]	093 Emolga [16]	094 Karrablast [E]	101 Joltik [E]	122 Shelmet [E]	127 Druddigon [E]
	130 Pawniard [E]	132 Bouffalant [1]	137 Heatmor [E]			

Q

Move	Pokémon that can learn it					
Quash	—					
Quick Attack	000 Victini [1]	025 Pidove [11]	026 Tranquill [1, 11]	027 Unfezant [1, 11]	028 Blitzle [1]	029 Zebstrika [1]
	072 Archen [1]	073 Archeops [1]	093 Emolga [4]	123 Accelgor [1, 13]	144 Cobalion [1]	145 Terrakion [1]
	146 Virizion [1]					
Quick Guard	045 Sawk [45]	072 Archen [25]	073 Archeops [25]	095 Escavalier [1, 8]	125 Mienfoo [45]	144 Cobalion [55]
	145 Terrakion [55]	146 Virizion [55]				
Quiver Dance	055 Lilligant [28]	143 Volcarona [59]				

R

Move	Pokémon that can learn it					
Rage	028 Blitzle [E]	056 Basculin [E]	057 Sandile [1]	058 Krokorok [1]	059 Krookodile [1]	060 Darumaka [9]
	061 Darmanitan [1, 9]	132 Bouffalant [6]				
Rage Powder	096 Foongus [45]	097 Amoonguss [54]	143 Volcarona [80]			
Rain Dance	007 Oshawott [TM]	008 Dewott [TM]	009 Samurott [TM]	010 Patrat [TM]	011 Watchog [TM]	012 Lillipup [TM]
	013 Herdier [TM]	014 Stoutland [TM]	015 Purrloin [TM]	016 Liepard [TM]	021 Panpour [TM]	022 Simipour [TM]
	023 Munna [TM]	024 Musharna [TM]	025 Pidove [TM]	026 Tranquill [TM]	027 Unfezant [TM]	028 Blitzle [TM]
	029 Zebstrika [TM]	033 Woobat [TM]	034 Swoobat [TM]	037 Audino [TM]	038 Timburr [TM]	039 Gurdurr [TM]
	040 Conkeldurr [TM]	041 Tympole [31, TM]	042 Palpitoad [33, TM]	043 Seismitoad [33, TM]	044 Throh [TM]	045 Sawk [TM]
	056 Basculin [TM]	065 Scraggy [TM]	066 Scrafty [TM]	067 Sigilyph [TM]	068 Yamask [TM]	069 Cofagrigus [TM]
	070 Tirtouga [48, TM]	071 Carracosta [56, TM]	074 Trubbish [TM]	075 Garbodor [TM]	076 Zorua [TM]	077 Zoroark [TM]
	078 Minccino [TM]	079 Cinccino [TM]	080 Gothita [TM]	081 Gothorita [TM]	082 Gothitelle [TM]	083 Solosis [TM]
	084 Duosion [TM]	085 Reuniclus [TM]	086 Ducklett [34, TM]	087 Swanna [34, TM]	088 Vanillite [TM]	089 Vanillish [TM]
	090 Vanilluxe [TM]	091 Deerling [TM]	092 Sawsbuck [TM]	093 Emolga [TM]	094 Karrablast [TM]	095 Escavalier [TM]
	096 Foongus [TM]	097 Amoonguss [TM]	098 Frillish [37, TM]	099 Jellicent [37, TM]	100 Alomomola [TM]	101 Joltik [TM]
	102 Galvantula [TM]	109 Eelektrik [TM]	110 Eelektross [TM]	111 Elgyem [TM]	112 Beheeyem [TM]	116 Axew [TM]
	117 Fraxure [TM]	118 Haxorus [TM]	119 Cubchoo [TM]	120 Beartic [TM]	121 Cryogonal [TM]	122 Shelmet [TM]
	123 Accelgor [TM]	124 Stunfisk [TM]	125 Mienfoo [TM]	126 Mienshao [TM]	127 Druddigon [TM]	128 Golett [TM]
	129 Golurk [TM]	130 Pawniard [TM]	131 Bisharp [TM]	132 Bouffalant [TM]	133 Rufflet [TM]	134 Braviary [TM]
	135 Vullaby [TM]	136 Mandibuzz [TM]	137 Heatmor [TM]	139 Deino [TM]	140 Zweilous [TM]	141 Hydreigon [TM]
	147 Tornadus [61, TM]	148 Thundurus [TM]	150 Zekrom [TM]	152 Kyurem [TM]		
Rapid Spin	035 Drilbur [5, E]	036 Excadrill [1, 5]	121 Cryogonal [13]			
Razor Leaf	046 Sewaddle [15]	047 Swadloon [1]	048 Leavanny [1, 15]	052 Cottonee [19]		
Razor Shell	007 Oshawott [17]	008 Dewott [17]	009 Samurott [17]			
Razor Wind	025 Pidove [32]	026 Tranquill [36]	027 Unfezant [38]	046 Sewaddle [E]	116 Axew [E]	
Recover	083 Solosis [24]	084 Duosion [24]	085 Reuniclus [24]	098 Frillish [17, E]	099 Jellicent [17]	111 Elgyem [46]
	112 Beheeyem [50]	121 Cryogonal [49]	122 Shelmet [49]	123 Accelgor [49]		
Recycle	017 Pansage [37]	019 Pansear [37]	021 Panpour [37]	074 Trubbish [3]	075 Garbodor [1, 3]	
Reflect	001 Snivy [TM]	002 Servine [TM]	003 Serperior [TM]	023 Munna [TM]	024 Musharna [TM]	033 Woobat [TM]
	034 Swoobat [TM]	037 Audino [TM]	048 Leavanny [TM]	067 Sigilyph [28, TM]	080 Gothita [TM]	081 Gothorita [TM]
	082 Gothitelle [TM]	083 Solosis [3, TM]	084 Duosion [1, 3, TM]	085 Reuniclus [1, 3, TM]	111 Elgyem [TM]	112 Beheeyem [TM]
	121 Cryogonal [37, TM]	125 Mienfoo [TM]	126 Mienshao [TM]	141 Hydreigon [TM]	144 Cobalion [TM]	145 Terrakion [TM]
	146 Virizion [TM]	149 Reshiram [TM]	150 Zekrom [TM]	152 Kyurem [TM]		
Reflect Type	—					
Refresh	037 Audino [5]	041 Tympole [E]	100 Alomomola [E]			
Rest	000 Victini [TM]	001 Snivy [TM]	002 Servine [TM]	003 Serperior [TM]	004 Tepig [TM]	005 Pignite [TM]
	006 Emboar [TM]	007 Oshawott [TM]	008 Dewott [TM]	009 Samurott [TM]	010 Patrat [TM]	011 Watchog [TM]
	012 Lillipup [TM]	013 Herdier [TM]	014 Stoutland [TM]	015 Purrloin [TM]	016 Liepard [TM]	017 Pansage [TM]
	018 Simisage [TM]	019 Pansear [TM]	020 Simisear [TM]	021 Panpour [TM]	022 Simipour [TM]	023 Munna [TM]
	024 Musharna [TM]	025 Pidove [TM]	026 Tranquill [TM]	027 Unfezant [TM]	028 Blitzle [TM]	029 Zebstrika [TM]
	030 Roggenrola [TM]	031 Boldore [TM]	032 Gigalith [TM]	033 Woobat [TM]	034 Swoobat [TM]	035 Drilbur [TM]
	036 Excadrill [TM]	037 Audino [TM]	038 Timburr [TM]	039 Gurdurr [TM]	040 Conkeldurr [TM]	041 Tympole [TM]
	042 Palpitoad [TM]	043 Seismitoad [TM]	044 Throh [TM]	045 Sawk [TM]	046 Sewaddle [TM]	047 Swadloon [TM]
	048 Leavanny [TM]	049 Venipede [TM]	050 Whirlipede [TM]	051 Scolipede [TM]	052 Cottonee [TM]	053 Whimsicott [TM]
	054 Petilil [TM]	055 Lilligant [TM]	056 Basculin [TM]	057 Sandile [TM]	058 Krokorok [TM]	059 Krookodile [TM]
	060 Darumaka [TM]	061 Darmanitan [TM]	062 Maractus [TM]	063 Dwebble [TM]	064 Crustle [TM]	065 Scraggy [TM]
	066 Scrafty [TM]	067 Sigilyph [TM]	068 Yamask [TM]	069 Cofagrigus [TM]	070 Tirtouga [TM]	071 Carracosta [TM]
	072 Archen [TM]	073 Archeops [TM]	074 Trubbish [TM]	075 Garbodor [TM]	076 Zorua [TM]	077 Zoroark [TM]
	078 Minccino [TM]	079 Cinccino [TM]	080 Gothita [TM]	081 Gothorita [TM]	082 Gothitelle [TM]	083 Solosis [TM]
	084 Duosion [TM]	085 Reuniclus [TM]	086 Ducklett [TM]	087 Swanna [TM]	088 Vanillite [TM]	089 Vanillish [TM]
	090 Vanilluxe [TM]	091 Deerling [TM]	092 Sawsbuck [TM]	093 Emolga [TM]	094 Karrablast [TM]	095 Escavalier [TM]
	096 Foongus [TM]	097 Amoonguss [TM]	098 Frillish [TM]	099 Jellicent [TM]	100 Alomomola [TM]	101 Joltik [TM]
	102 Galvantula [TM]	103 Ferroseed [TM]	104 Ferrothorn [TM]	105 Klink [TM]	106 Klang [TM]	107 Klinklang [TM]
	109 Eelektrik [TM]	110 Eelektross [TM]	111 Elgyem [TM]	112 Beheeyem [TM]	113 Litwick [TM]	114 Lampent [TM]
	115 Chandelure [TM]	116 Axew [TM]	117 Fraxure [TM]	118 Haxorus [TM]	119 Cubchoo [41, TM]	120 Beartic [41, TM]
	121 Cryogonal [TM]	122 Shelmet [TM]	123 Accelgor [TM]	124 Stunfisk [TM]	125 Mienfoo [TM]	126 Mienshao [TM]
	127 Druddigon [TM]	128 Golett [TM]	129 Golurk [TM]	130 Pawniard [TM]	131 Bisharp [TM]	132 Bouffalant [TM]

Move	Pokémon that can learn it					
Rest (continued)	133 Rufflet [TM]	134 Braviary [TM]	135 Vullaby [TM]	136 Mandibuzz [TM]	137 Heatmor [TM]	138 Durant [TM]
	139 Deino [TM]	140 Zweilous [TM]	141 Hydreigon [TM]	142 Larvesta [TM]	143 Volcarona [TM]	144 Cobalion [TM]
	145 Terrakion [TM]	146 Virizion [TM]	147 Tornadus [TM]	148 Thundurus [TM]	149 Reshiram [TM]	150 Zekrom [TM]
	151 Landorus [TM]	152 Kyurem [TM]				
Retaliate	007 Oshawott [37, TM]	008 Dewott [44, TM]	009 Samurott [50, TM]	010 Patrat [TM]	011 Watchog [TM]	012 Lillipup [29, TM]
	013 Herdier [33, TM]	014 Stoutland [36, TM]	037 Audino [TM]	038 Timburr [TM]	039 Gurdurr [TM]	040 Conkeldurr [TM]
	044 Throh [TM]	045 Sawk [37, TM]	048 Leavanny [TM]	057 Sandile [TM]	058 Krokorok [TM]	059 Krookodile [TM]
	065 Scraggy [TM]	066 Scrafty [TM]	076 Zorua [TM]	077 Zoroark [TM]	078 Minccino [TM]	079 Cinccino [TM]
	091 Deerling [TM]	092 Sawsbuck [TM]	125 Mienfoo [TM]	126 Mienshao [TM]	127 Druddigon [TM]	130 Pawniard [TM]
	131 Bisharp [TM]	132 Bouffalant [TM]	133 Rufflet [TM]	134 Braviary [TM]	135 Vullaby [TM]	136 Mandibuzz [TM]
	138 Durant [TM]	144 Cobalion [31, TM]	145 Terrakion [31, TM]	146 Virizion [31, TM]		
Return	000 Victini [TM]	001 Snivy [TM]	002 Servine [TM]	003 Serperior [TM]	004 Tepig [TM]	005 Pignite [TM]
	006 Emboar [TM]	007 Oshawott [TM]	008 Dewott [TM]	009 Samurott [TM]	010 Patrat [TM]	011 Watchog [TM]
	012 Lillipup [TM]	013 Herdier [TM]	014 Stoutland [TM]	015 Purrloin [TM]	016 Liepard [TM]	017 Pansage [TM]
	018 Simisage [TM]	019 Pansear [TM]	020 Simisear [TM]	021 Panpour [TM]	022 Simipour [TM]	023 Munna [TM]
	024 Musharna [TM]	025 Pidove [TM]	026 Tranquill [TM]	027 Unfezant [TM]	028 Blitzle [TM]	029 Zebstrika [TM]
	030 Roggenrola [TM]	031 Boldore [TM]	032 Gigalith [TM]	033 Woobat [TM]	034 Swoobat [TM]	035 Drilbur [TM]
	036 Excadrill [TM]	037 Audino [TM]	038 Timburr [TM]	039 Gurdurr [TM]	040 Conkeldurr [TM]	041 Tympole [TM]
	042 Palpitoad [TM]	043 Seismitoad [TM]	044 Throh [TM]	045 Sawk [TM]	046 Sewaddle [TM]	047 Swadloon [TM]
	048 Leavanny [TM]	049 Venipede [TM]	050 Whirlipede [TM]	051 Scolipede [TM]	052 Cottonee [TM]	053 Whimsicott [TM]
	054 Petilil [TM]	055 Lilligant [TM]	056 Basculin [TM]	057 Sandile [TM]	058 Krokorok [TM]	059 Krookodile [TM]
	060 Darumaka [TM]	061 Darmanitan [TM]	062 Maractus [TM]	063 Dwebble [TM]	064 Crustle [TM]	065 Scraggy [TM]
	066 Scrafty [TM]	067 Sigilyph [TM]	068 Yamask [TM]	069 Cofagrigus [TM]	070 Tirtouga [TM]	071 Carracosta [TM]
	072 Archen [TM]	073 Archeops [TM]	074 Trubbish [TM]	075 Garbodor [TM]	076 Zorua [TM]	077 Zoroark [TM]
	078 Minccino [TM]	079 Cinccino [TM]	080 Gothita [TM]	081 Gothorita [TM]	082 Gothitelle [TM]	083 Solosis [TM]
	084 Duosion [TM]	085 Reuniclus [TM]	086 Ducklett [TM]	087 Swanna [TM]	088 Vanillite [TM]	089 Vanillish [TM]
	090 Vanilluxe [TM]	091 Deerling [TM]	092 Sawsbuck [TM]	093 Emolga [TM]	094 Karrablast [TM]	095 Escavalier [TM]
	096 Foongus [TM]	097 Amoonguss [TM]	098 Frillish [TM]	099 Jellicent [TM]	100 Alomomola [TM]	101 Joltik [TM]
	102 Galvantula [TM]	103 Ferroseed [TM]	104 Ferrothorn [TM]	105 Klink [TM]	106 Klang [TM]	107 Klinklang [TM]
	109 Eelektrik [TM]	110 Eelektross [TM]	111 Elgyem [TM]	112 Beheeyem [TM]	113 Litwick [TM]	114 Lampent [TM]
	115 Chandelure [TM]	116 Axew [TM]	117 Fraxure [TM]	118 Haxorus [TM]	119 Cubchoo [TM]	120 Beartic [TM]
	121 Cryogonal [TM]	122 Shelmet [TM]	123 Accelgor [TM]	124 Stunfisk [TM]	125 Mienfoo [TM]	126 Mienshao [TM]
	127 Druddigon [TM]	128 Golett [TM]	129 Golurk [TM]	130 Pawniard [TM]	131 Bisharp [TM]	132 Bouffalant [TM]
	133 Rufflet [TM]	134 Braviary [TM]	135 Vullaby [TM]	136 Mandibuzz [TM]	137 Heatmor [TM]	138 Durant [TM]
	139 Deino [TM]	140 Zweilous [TM]	141 Hydreigon [TM]	142 Larvesta [TM]	143 Volcarona [TM]	144 Cobalion [TM]
	145 Terrakion [TM]	146 Virizion [TM]	147 Tornadus [TM]	148 Thundurus [TM]	149 Reshiram [TM]	150 Zekrom [TM]
	151 Landorus [TM]	152 Kyurem [TM]				
Revenge	007 Oshawott [25]	008 Dewott [28]	009 Samurott [28]	010 Patrat [E]	044 Throh [21]	056 Basculin [E]
	124 Stunfisk [50]	127 Druddigon [35]	130 Pawniard [E]	132 Bouffalant [26]	147 Tornadus [19]	148 Thundurus [19]
Reversal	000 Victini [33]	012 Lillipup [33]	013 Herdier [38]	014 Stoutland [42]	038 Timburr [E]	044 Throh [53]
	045 Sawk [53]	095 Escavalier [49]	116 Axew [E]	125 Mienfoo [63]	126 Mienshao [63]	132 Bouffalant [46]
Roar	004 Tepig [39, TM]	005 Pignite [47, TM]	006 Emboar [55, TM]	012 Lillipup [26, TM]	013 Herdier [29, TM]	014 Stoutland [29, TM]
	057 Sandile [TM]	058 Krokorok [TM]	059 Krookodile [TM]	060 Darumaka [TM]	061 Darmanitan [TM]	065 Scraggy [TM]
	066 Scrafty [TM]	072 Archen [TM]	073 Archeops [TM]	076 Zorua [TM]	077 Zoroark [TM]	110 Eelektross [TM]
	116 Axew [TM]	117 Fraxure [TM]	118 Haxorus [TM]	120 Beartic [TM]	127 Druddigon [TM]	139 Deino [20, TM]
	140 Zweilous [20, TM]	141 Hydreigon [20, TM]	144 Cobalion [TM]	145 Terrakion [TM]	146 Virizion [TM]	
Roar of Time	—					
Rock Blast	030 Roggenrola [14]	031 Boldore [14]	032 Gigalith [14]	063 Dwebble [5]	064 Crustle [1, 5]	074 Trubbish [E]
	079 Cinccino [1]					
Rock Climb	035 Drilbur [E]	049 Venipede [40, E]	050 Whirlipede [46]	051 Scolipede [50]	057 Sandile [E]	065 Scraggy [45]
	066 Scrafty [51]	101 Joltik [E]	103 Ferroseed [E]	104 Ferrothorn [1]	127 Druddigon [49]	132 Bouffalant [E]
	138 Durant [E]					
Rock Polish	030 Roggenrola [TM]	031 Boldore [TM]	032 Gigalith [TM]	063 Dwebble [19, TM]	064 Crustle [19, TM]	070 Tirtouga [TM]
	071 Carracosta [TM]	072 Archen [TM]	073 Archeops [TM]	075 Garbodor [TM]	103 Ferroseed [TM]	104 Ferrothorn [TM]
	105 Klink [TM]	106 Klang [TM]	107 Klinklang [TM]	128 Golett [TM]	129 Golurk [TM]	130 Pawniard [TM]
	131 Bisharp [TM]	138 Durant [TM]	144 Cobalion [TM]	145 Terrakion [TM]	151 Landorus [TM]	
Rock Slide	005 Pignite [TM]	006 Emboar [TM]	018 Simisage [TM]	020 Simisear [TM]	022 Simipour [TM]	023 Munna [TM]
	024 Musharna [TM]	030 Roggenrola [27, TM]	031 Boldore [30, TM]	032 Gigalith [30, TM]	035 Drilbur [29, TM]	036 Excadrill [29, TM]
	038 Timburr [31, TM]	039 Gurdurr [33, TM]	040 Conkeldurr [33, TM]	043 Seismitoad [TM]	044 Throh [TM]	045 Sawk [TM]
	051 Scolipede [TM]	057 Sandile [TM]	058 Krokorok [TM]	059 Krookodile [TM]	060 Darumaka [TM]	061 Darmanitan [TM]
	063 Dwebble [29, TM]	064 Crustle [29, TM]	065 Scraggy [TM]	066 Scrafty [TM]	070 Tirtouga [45, TM]	071 Carracosta [51, TM]
	072 Archen [45, TM]	073 Archeops [51, TM]	080 Gothita [TM]	081 Gothorita [TM]	082 Gothitelle [TM]	083 Solosis [TM]
	084 Duosion [TM]	085 Reuniclus [TM]	110 Eelektross [TM]	111 Elgyem [TM]	112 Beheeyem [TM]	118 Haxorus [TM]
	120 Beartic [TM]	124 Stunfisk [TM]	125 Mienfoo [TM]	126 Mienshao [TM]	127 Druddigon [TM]	128 Golett [TM]
	129 Golurk [TM]	132 Bouffalant [TM]	133 Rufflet [TM]	134 Braviary [TM]	138 Durant [TM]	141 Hydreigon [TM]
	145 Terrakion [37, TM]	149 Reshiram [TM]	150 Zekrom [TM]	151 Landorus [49, TM]	152 Kyurem [TM]	

R

Move	Pokémon that can learn it					
Rock Smash	000 Victini [TM]	003 Serperior [TM]	004 Tepig [TM]	005 Pignite [TM]	006 Emboar [TM]	007 Oshawott [TM]
	008 Dewott [TM]	009 Samurott [TM]	011 Watchog [TM]	012 Lillipup [TM]	013 Herdier [TM]	014 Stoutland [TM]
	016 Liepard [TM]	017 Pansage [TM]	018 Simisage [TM]	019 Pansear [TM]	020 Simisear [TM]	021 Panpour [TM]
	022 Simipour [TM]	029 Zebstrika [TM]	030 Roggenrola [TM]	031 Boldore [TM]	032 Gigalith [TM]	035 Drilbur [TM]
	036 Excadrill [TM]	038 Timburr [TM]	039 Gurdurr [TM]	040 Conkeldurr [TM]	042 Palpitoad [TM]	043 Seismitoad [TM]
	044 Throh [TM]	045 Sawk [1, TM]	049 Venipede [TM]	050 Whirlipede [TM]	051 Scolipede [TM]	058 Krokorok [TM]
	059 Krookodile [TM]	060 Darumaka [TM]	061 Darmanitan [TM]	063 Dwebble [TM]	064 Crustle [TM]	065 Scraggy [TM]
	066 Scrafty [TM]	070 Tirtouga [TM]	071 Carracosta [TM]	072 Archen [TM]	073 Archeops [TM]	077 Zoroark [TM]
	085 Reuniclus [TM]	092 Sawsbuck [TM]	095 Escavalier [TM]	103 Ferroseed [TM]	104 Ferrothorn [TM]	105 Klink [TM]
	106 Klang [TM]	107 Klinklang [TM]	110 Eelektross [TM]	116 Axew [TM]	117 Fraxure [TM]	118 Haxorus [TM]
	119 Cubchoo [TM]	120 Beartic [TM]	125 Mienfoo [TM]	126 Mienshao [TM]	127 Druddigon [TM]	128 Golett [TM]
	129 Golurk [TM]	130 Pawniard [TM]	131 Bisharp [TM]	132 Bouffalant [TM]	133 Rufflet [TM]	134 Braviary [TM]
	135 Vullaby [TM]	136 Mandibuzz [TM]	137 Heatmor [TM]	138 Durant [TM]	139 Deino [TM]	140 Zweilous [TM]
	141 Hydreigon [TM]	144 Cobalion [TM]	145 Terrakion [TM]	146 Virizion [TM]	147 Tornadus [TM]	148 Thundurus [TM]
	149 Reshiram [TM]	150 Zekrom [TM]	151 Landorus [TM]	152 Kyurem [TM]		
Rock Throw	038 Timburr [16]	039 Gurdurr [16]	040 Conkeldurr [16]	070 Tirtouga [E]	072 Archen [5]	073 Archeops [1, 5]
	151 Landorus [25]					
Rock Tomb	004 Tepig [TM]	005 Pignite [TM]	006 Emboar [TM]	012 Lillipup [TM]	013 Herdier [TM]	014 Stoutland [TM]
	017 Pansage [TM]	018 Simisage [TM]	019 Pansear [TM]	020 Simisear [TM]	021 Panpour [TM]	022 Simipour [TM]
	023 Munna [TM]	024 Musharna [TM]	030 Roggenrola [E, TM]	031 Boldore [TM]	032 Gigalith [TM]	035 Drilbur [TM]
	036 Excadrill [TM]	038 Timburr [TM]	039 Gurdurr [TM]	040 Conkeldurr [TM]	043 Seismitoad [TM]	044 Throh [TM]
	045 Sawk [TM]	051 Scolipede [TM]	057 Sandile [TM]	058 Krokorok [TM]	059 Krookodile [TM]	060 Darumaka [TM]
	061 Darmanitan [TM]	063 Dwebble [TM]	064 Crustle [TM]	065 Scraggy [TM]	066 Scrafty [TM]	070 Tirtouga [TM]
	071 Carracosta [TM]	072 Archen [TM]	073 Archeops [TM]	080 Gothita [TM]	081 Gothorita [TM]	082 Gothitelle [TM]
	083 Solosis [TM]	084 Duosion [TM]	085 Reuniclus [TM]	110 Eelektross [TM]	111 Elgyem [TM]	112 Beheeyem [TM]
	116 Axew [TM]	117 Fraxure [TM]	118 Haxorus [TM]	119 Cubchoo [TM]	120 Beartic [TM]	124 Stunfisk [TM]
	125 Mienfoo [TM]	126 Mienshao [TM]	127 Druddigon [TM]	128 Golett [TM]	129 Golurk [TM]	130 Pawniard [TM]
	131 Bisharp [TM]	132 Bouffalant [TM]	133 Rufflet [TM]	134 Braviary [TM]	135 Vullaby [TM]	136 Mandibuzz [TM]
	137 Heatmor [TM]	138 Durant [TM]	141 Hydreigon [TM]	145 Terrakion [TM]	149 Reshiram [TM]	150 Zekrom [TM]
	151 Landorus [1, TM]	152 Kyurem [TM]				
Rock Wrecker	063 Dwebble [43]	064 Crustle [55]				
Role Play	017 Pansage [E]	019 Pansear [E]	021 Panpour [E]			
Rolling Kick	—					
Rollout	004 Tepig [21]	005 Pignite [23]	006 Emboar [23]	049 Venipede [1]	050 Whirlipede [1]	051 Scolipede [1]
	060 Darumaka [3]	061 Darmanitan [1, 3]	070 Tirtouga [5]	071 Carracosta [1, 5]	074 Trubbish [E]	083 Solosis [7]
	084 Duosion [1, 7]	085 Reuniclus [1, 7]	096 Foongus [E]	103 Ferroseed [6]	104 Ferrothorn [1, 6]	128 Golett [9]
	129 Golurk [9]					
Roost	025 Pidove [18]	026 Tranquill [18]	027 Unfezant [18]	033 Woobat [E]	067 Sigilyph [E]	086 Ducklett [30]
	087 Swanna [30]	093 Emolga [E]	135 Vullaby [E]			
Round	000 Victini [TM]	001 Snivy [TM]	002 Servine [TM]	003 Serperior [TM]	004 Tepig [TM]	005 Pignite [TM]
	006 Emboar [TM]	007 Oshawott [TM]	008 Dewott [TM]	009 Samurott [TM]	010 Patrat [TM]	011 Watchog [TM]
	012 Lillipup [TM]	013 Herdier [TM]	014 Stoutland [TM]	015 Purrloin [TM]	016 Liepard [TM]	017 Pansage [TM]
	018 Simisage [TM]	019 Pansear [TM]	020 Simisear [TM]	021 Panpour [TM]	022 Simipour [TM]	023 Munna [TM]
	024 Musharna [TM]	025 Pidove [TM]	026 Tranquill [TM]	027 Unfezant [TM]	028 Blitzle [TM]	029 Zebstrika [TM]
	030 Roggenrola [TM]	031 Boldore [TM]	032 Gigalith [TM]	033 Woobat [TM]	034 Swoobat [TM]	035 Drilbur [TM]
	036 Excadrill [TM]	037 Audino [TM]	038 Timburr [TM]	039 Gurdurr [TM]	040 Conkeldurr [TM]	041 Tympole [9, TM]
	042 Palpitoad [1, 9, TM]	043 Seismitoad [1, 9, TM]	044 Throh [TM]	045 Sawk [TM]	046 Sewaddle [TM]	047 Swadloon [TM]
	048 Leavanny [TM]	049 Venipede [TM]	050 Whirlipede [TM]	051 Scolipede [TM]	052 Cottonee [TM]	053 Whimsicott [TM]
	054 Petilil [TM]	055 Lilligant [TM]	056 Basculin [TM]	057 Sandile [TM]	058 Krokorok [TM]	059 Krookodile [TM]
	060 Darumaka [TM]	061 Darmanitan [TM]	062 Maractus [TM]	063 Dwebble [TM]	064 Crustle [TM]	065 Scraggy [TM]
	066 Scrafty [TM]	067 Sigilyph [TM]	068 Yamask [TM]	069 Cofagrigus [TM]	070 Tirtouga [TM]	071 Carracosta [TM]
	072 Archen [TM]	073 Archeops [TM]	074 Trubbish [TM]	075 Garbodor [TM]	076 Zorua [TM]	077 Zoroark [TM]
	078 Minccino [TM]	079 Cinccino [TM]	080 Gothita [TM]	081 Gothorita [TM]	082 Gothitelle [TM]	083 Solosis [TM]
	084 Duosion [TM]	085 Reuniclus [TM]	086 Ducklett [TM]	087 Swanna [TM]	088 Vanillite [TM]	089 Vanillish [TM]
	090 Vanilluxe [TM]	091 Deerling [TM]	092 Sawsbuck [TM]	093 Emolga [TM]	094 Karrablast [TM]	095 Escavalier [TM]
	096 Foongus [TM]	097 Amoonguss [TM]	098 Frillish [TM]	099 Jellicent [TM]	100 Alomomola [TM]	101 Joltik [TM]
	102 Galvantula [TM]	103 Ferroseed [TM]	104 Ferrothorn [TM]	105 Klink [TM]	106 Klang [TM]	107 Klinklang [TM]
	109 Eelektrik [TM]	110 Eelektross [TM]	111 Elgyem [TM]	112 Beheeyem [TM]	113 Litwick [TM]	114 Lampent [TM]
	115 Chandelure [TM]	116 Axew [TM]	117 Fraxure [TM]	118 Haxorus [TM]	119 Cubchoo [TM]	120 Beartic [TM]
	121 Cryogonal [TM]	122 Shelmet [TM]	123 Accelgor [TM]	124 Stunfisk [TM]	125 Mienfoo [TM]	126 Mienshao [TM]
	127 Druddigon [TM]	128 Golett [TM]	129 Golurk [TM]	130 Pawniard [TM]	131 Bisharp [TM]	132 Bouffalant [TM]
	133 Rufflet [TM]	134 Braviary [TM]	135 Vullaby [TM]	136 Mandibuzz [TM]	137 Heatmor [TM]	138 Durant [TM]
	139 Deino [TM]	140 Zweilous [TM]	141 Hydreigon [TM]	142 Larvesta [TM]	143 Volcarona [TM]	144 Cobalion [TM]
	145 Terrakion [TM]	146 Virizion [TM]	147 Tornadus [TM]	148 Thundurus [TM]	149 Reshiram [TM]	150 Zekrom [TM]
	151 Landorus [TM]	152 Kyurem [TM]				

◈ S

Move	Pokémon that can learn it					
Sacred Fire	—					
Sacred Sword	144 Cobalion [42]	145 Terrakion [42]	146 Virizion [42]			
Safeguard	000 Victini [TM]	001 Snivy [TM]	002 Servine [TM]	003 Serperior [TM]	023 Munna [TM]	024 Musharna [TM]
	033 Woobat [TM]	034 Swoobat [TM]	037 Audino [TM]	046 Sewaddle [TM]	047 Swadloon [TM]	048 Leavanny [TM]
	052 Cottonee [TM]	053 Whimsicott [TM]	054 Petilil [TM]	055 Lilligant [TM]	062 Maractus [TM]	067 Sigilyph [TM]
	068 Yamask [TM]	069 Cofagrigus [TM]	078 Minccino [TM]	079 Cinccino [TM]	080 Gothita [TM]	081 Gothorita [TM]
	082 Gothitelle [TM]	083 Solosis [TM]	084 Duosion [TM]	085 Reuniclus [TM]	091 Deerling [TM]	092 Sawsbuck [TM]
	098 Frillish [TM]	099 Jellicent [TM]	100 Alomomola [45, TM]	111 Elgyem [TM]	112 Beheeyem [TM]	113 Litwick [TM]
	114 Lampent [TM]	115 Chandelure [TM]	128 Golett [TM]	129 Golurk [TM]	142 Larvesta [TM]	143 Volcarona [TM]
	144 Cobalion [TM]	145 Terrakion [TM]	146 Virizion [TM]	149 Reshiram [TM]	150 Zekrom [TM]	152 Kyurem [TM]
Sand Tomb	057 Sandile [13]	058 Krokorok [13]	059 Krookodile [13]	063 Dwebble [E]		
Sand-Attack	010 Patrat [13]	011 Watchog [13]	012 Lillipup [E]	015 Purrloin [10]	016 Liepard [1, 10]	028 Blitzle [E]
	030 Roggenrola [7]	031 Boldore [1, 7]	032 Gigalith [1, 7]	057 Sandile [7]	058 Krokorok [1, 7]	059 Krookodile [1, 7]
	063 Dwebble [11]	064 Crustle [1, 11]	065 Scraggy [5]	066 Scrafty [1, 5]	074 Trubbish [E]	091 Deerling [7]
	092 Sawsbuck [1, 7]	138 Durant [1]				
Sandstorm	030 Roggenrola [33, TM]	031 Boldore [42, TM]	032 Gigalith [42, TM]	035 Drilbur [40, TM]	036 Excadrill [49, TM]	057 Sandile [40, TM]
	058 Krokorok [44, TM]	059 Krookodile [48, TM]	063 Dwebble [TM]	064 Crustle [TM]	070 Tirtouga [TM]	071 Carracosta [TM]
	072 Archen [TM]	073 Archeops [TM]	104 Ferrothorn [TM]	105 Klink [TM]	106 Klang [TM]	107 Klinklang [TM]
	123 Accelgor [TM]	124 Stunfisk [TM]	130 Pawniard [TM]	131 Bisharp [TM]	138 Durant [TM]	144 Cobalion [TM]
	145 Terrakion [TM]	151 Landorus [61, TM]				
Scald	006 Emboar [TM]	007 Oshawott [TM]	008 Dewott [TM]	009 Samurott [TM]	021 Panpour [22, TM]	022 Simipour [1, TM]
	041 Tympole [TM]	042 Palpitoad [TM]	043 Seismitoad [TM]	056 Basculin [TM]	070 Tirtouga [TM]	071 Carracosta [TM]
	086 Ducklett [TM]	087 Swanna [TM]	098 Frillish [TM]	099 Jellicent [TM]	100 Alomomola [TM]	124 Stunfisk [TM]
Scary Face	038 Timburr [37]	039 Gurdurr [41]	040 Conkeldurr [41]	056 Basculin [41]	057 Sandile [34]	058 Krokorok [36]
	059 Krookodile [36]	065 Scraggy [34]	066 Scrafty [34]	069 Cofagrigus [34]	072 Archen [11]	073 Archeops [11]
	076 Zorua [21]	077 Zoroark [21]	094 Karrablast [40]	116 Axew [16]	117 Fraxure [16]	118 Haxorus [16]
	127 Druddigon [13]	130 Pawniard [22]	131 Bisharp [22]	132 Bouffalant [21]	133 Rufflet [19]	134 Braviary [19]
	135 Vullaby [E]	139 Deino [52]	140 Zweilous [55]	141 Hydreigon [55]	152 Kyurem [43]	
Scratch	015 Purrloin [1]	016 Liepard [1]	017 Pansage [1]	019 Pansear [1]	021 Panpour [1]	035 Drilbur [1]
	036 Excadrill [1]	076 Zorua [1]	077 Zoroark [1]	116 Axew [1]	117 Fraxure [1]	118 Haxorus [1]
	127 Druddigon [1]	130 Pawniard [1]	131 Bisharp [1]			
Screech	007 Oshawott [E]	010 Patrat [E]	028 Blitzle [E]	046 Sewaddle [E]	049 Venipede [8]	050 Whirlipede [1, 8]
	051 Scolipede [1, 8]	094 Karrablast [E]	101 Joltik [7]	102 Galvantula [7]	105 Klink [39]	106 Klang [40]
	107 Klinklang [40]	138 Durant [E]	139 Deino [E]			
Searing Shot	000 Victini [1]					
Secret Power	023 Munna [E]	037 Audino [20]	083 Solosis [E]			
Seed Bomb	017 Pansage [22]	018 Simisage [1]	062 Maractus [E]	103 Ferroseed [E]		
Seed Flare	—					
Seismic Toss	044 Throh [13]					
Selfdestruct	074 Trubbish [E]	103 Ferroseed [38]	104 Ferrothorn [38]			
Shadow Ball	000 Victini [TM]	010 Patrat [TM]	011 Watchog [TM]	012 Lillipup [TM]	013 Herdier [TM]	014 Stoutland [TM]
	015 Purrloin [TM]	016 Liepard [TM]	023 Munna [TM]	024 Musharna [TM]	033 Woobat [TM]	034 Swoobat [TM]
	037 Audino [TM]	053 Whimsicott [TM]	067 Sigilyph [TM]	068 Yamask [37, TM]	069 Cofagrigus [39, TM]	076 Zorua [TM]
	077 Zoroark [TM]	080 Gothita [TM]	081 Gothorita [TM]	082 Gothitelle [TM]	083 Solosis [TM]	084 Duosion [TM]
	085 Reuniclus [TM]	091 Deerling [TM]	092 Sawsbuck [TM]	098 Frillish [TM]	099 Jellicent [TM]	100 Alomomola [TM]
	111 Elgyem [TM]	112 Beheeyem [TM]	113 Litwick [TM]	114 Lampent [53, TM]	115 Chandelure [TM]	128 Golett [TM]
	129 Golurk [TM]	135 Vullaby [TM]	136 Mandibuzz [TM]	149 Reshiram [TM]	150 Zekrom [TM]	152 Kyurem [TM]
Shadow Claw	015 Purrloin [TM]	016 Liepard [TM]	017 Pansage [TM]	018 Simisage [TM]	019 Pansear [TM]	020 Simisear [TM]
	021 Panpour [TM]	022 Simipour [TM]	035 Drilbur [TM]	036 Excadrill [TM]	048 Leavanny [TM]	058 Krokorok [TM]
	059 Krookodile [TM]	063 Dwebble [TM]	064 Crustle [TM]	072 Archen [TM]	073 Archeops [TM]	077 Zoroark [TM]
	104 Ferrothorn [TM]	117 Fraxure [TM]	118 Haxorus [TM]	119 Cubchoo [TM]	120 Beartic [TM]	127 Druddigon [TM]
	130 Pawniard [TM]	131 Bisharp [TM]	133 Rufflet [TM]	134 Braviary [TM]	137 Heatmor [TM]	138 Durant [TM]
	149 Reshiram [TM]	150 Zekrom [TM]	152 Kyurem [TM]			
Shadow Force	—					
Shadow Punch	128 Golett [13]	129 Golurk [13]				
Shadow Sneak	—					
Sharpen	121 Cryogonal [9]					
Sheer Cold	088 Vanillite [53]	089 Vanillish [58]	090 Vanilluxe [67]	119 Cubchoo [57]	120 Beartic [66]	121 Cryogonal [61]
Shell Smash	063 Dwebble [37]	064 Crustle [1, 43]	070 Tirtouga [38]	071 Carracosta [40]		
Shift Gear	105 Klink [48]	106 Klang [52]	107 Klinklang [54]			
Shock Wave	028 Blitzle [11, E]	029 Zebstrika [11]	093 Emolga [22, E]	124 Stunfisk [E]	148 Thundurus [25]	
Signal Beam	101 Joltik [34]	102 Galvantula [34]				
Silver Wind	046 Sewaddle [E]	143 Volcarona [50]				
Simple Beam	037 Audino [45]	111 Elgyem [29]	112 Beheeyem [29]			
Sing	078 Minccino [21]	079 Cinccino [1]				
Sketch	—					

◇ S

Move	Pokémon that can learn it				
Skill Swap	067 Sigilyph [E]	083 Solosis [40]	084 Duosion [43]	085 Reuniclus [45]	111 Elgyem [E]	
Skull Bash	035 Drilbur [E]	132 Bouffalant [E]				
Sky Attack	025 Pidove [50]	026 Tranquill [59]	027 Unfezant [66]	067 Sigilyph [51]		
Sky Drop	133 Rufflet [50, TM]	134 Braviary [50, TM]	147 Tornadus [TM]	148 Thundurus [TM]		
Sky Uppercut	—					
Slack Off	—					
Slam	001 Snivy [25]	002 Servine [28]	003 Serperior [28]	010 Patrat [36]	011 Watchog [43]	070 Tirtouga [E]
	078 Minccino [37]	139 Deino [28]	140 Zweilous [28]	141 Hydreigon [28]		
Slash	009 Samurott [36]	015 Purrloin [30]	016 Liepard [34]	035 Drilbur [26]	036 Excadrill [26]	048 Leavanny [29]
	063 Dwebble [31]	064 Crustle [31]	094 Karrablast [32]	095 Escavalier [32]	101 Joltik [26]	102 Galvantula [26]
	116 Axew [20]	117 Fraxure [20]	118 Haxorus [20]	119 Cubchoo [33]	120 Beartic [33]	121 Cryogonal [41]
	127 Druddigon [21]	130 Pawniard [30]	131 Bisharp [30]	133 Rufflet [28]	134 Braviary [28]	137 Heatmor [41]
	149 Reshiram [36]	150 Zekrom [36]	152 Kyurem [36]			
Sleep Powder	054 Petilil [10]					
Sleep Talk	004 Tepig [E]	019 Pansear [E]	023 Munna [E]	037 Audino [E]	041 Tympole [E]	060 Darumaka [E]
	078 Minccino [E]	091 Deerling [E]	119 Cubchoo [E]	124 Stunfisk [E]	137 Heatmor [E]	
Sludge	074 Trubbish [18]	075 Garbodor [18]				
Sludge Bomb	035 Drilbur [TM]	036 Excadrill [TM]	041 Tympole [TM]	042 Palpitoad [TM]	043 Seismitoad [TM]	049 Venipede [TM]
	050 Whirlipede [TM]	051 Scolipede [TM]	057 Sandile [TM]	058 Krokorok [TM]	059 Krookodile [TM]	065 Scraggy [TM]
	066 Scrafty [TM]	074 Trubbish [29, TM]	075 Garbodor [29, TM]	096 Foongus [TM]	097 Amoonguss [TM]	098 Frillish [TM]
	099 Jellicent [TM]	122 Shelmet [TM]	123 Accelgor [TM]	124 Stunfisk [TM]	127 Druddigon [TM]	147 Tornadus [TM]
	148 Thundurus [TM]	151 Landorus [TM]				
Sludge Wave	041 Tympole [TM]	042 Palpitoad [TM]	043 Seismitoad [TM]	074 Trubbish [TM]	075 Garbodor [TM]	098 Frillish [TM]
	099 Jellicent [TM]	124 Stunfisk [TM]	147 Tornadus [TM]	148 Thundurus [TM]	151 Landorus [TM]	
Smack Down	006 Emboar [TM]	030 Roggenrola [23, TM]	031 Boldore [23, TM]	032 Gigalith [23, TM]	038 Timburr [TM]	039 Gurdurr [TM]
	040 Conkeldurr [TM]	059 Krookodile [TM]	061 Darmanitan [TM]	063 Dwebble [17, TM]	064 Crustle [17, TM]	065 Scraggy [TM]
	066 Scrafty [TM]	067 Sigilyph [TM]	070 Tirtouga [31, TM]	071 Carracosta [31, TM]	072 Archen [TM]	073 Archeops [TM]
	075 Garbodor [TM]	127 Druddigon [TM]	145 Terrakion [13, TM]	147 Tornadus [TM]	148 Thundurus [TM]	151 Landorus [TM]
SmellingSalt	038 Timburr [E]	125 Mienfoo [E]				
Smog	004 Tepig [19]	005 Pignite [20]	006 Emboar [20]	113 Litwick [5]	114 Lampent [1, 5]	115 Chandelure [1]
SmokeScreen	—					
Snatch	015 Purrloin [39]	016 Liepard [47]	076 Zorua [E]	083 Solosis [10]	084 Duosion [1, 10]	085 Reuniclus [1, 10]
	127 Druddigon [E]	137 Heatmor [26]				
Snore	041 Tympole [E]					
Soak	056 Basculin [32]	100 Alomomola [33]				
Softboiled	—					
SolarBeam	000 Victini [TM]	001 Snivy [TM]	002 Servine [TM]	003 Serperior [TM]	004 Tepig [TM]	005 Pignite [TM]
	006 Emboar [TM]	017 Pansage [TM]	018 Simisage [TM]	019 Pansear [TM]	020 Simisear [TM]	032 Gigalith [TM]
	037 Audino [TM]	046 Sewaddle [TM]	047 Swadloon [TM]	048 Leavanny [TM]	049 Venipede [TM]	050 Whirlipede [TM]
	051 Scolipede [TM]	052 Cottonee [46, TM]	053 Whimsicott [TM]	054 Petilil [TM]	055 Lilligant [TM]	060 Darumaka [TM]
	061 Darmanitan [TM]	062 Maractus [50, TM]	063 Dwebble [TM]	064 Crustle [TM]	067 Sigilyph [TM]	075 Garbodor [TM]
	091 Deerling [51, TM]	092 Sawsbuck [60, TM]	096 Foongus [43, TM]	097 Amoonguss [49, TM]	103 Ferroseed [TM]	104 Ferrothorn [TM]
	113 Litwick [TM]	114 Lampent [TM]	115 Chandelure [TM]	121 Cryogonal [53, TM]	129 Golurk [TM]	137 Heatmor [TM]
	142 Larvesta [TM]	143 Volcarona [TM]	146 Virizion [TM]	149 Reshiram [TM]		
SonicBoom	023 Munna [E]					
Spacial Rend	—					
Spark	028 Blitzle [25]	029 Zebstrika [25]	093 Emolga [13]	108 Tynamo [1]	109 Eelektrik [1]	124 Stunfisk [E]
Spider Web	101 Joltik [1]	102 Galvantula [1]				
Spike Cannon	—					
Spikes	049 Venipede [E]	062 Maractus [E]	063 Dwebble [E]	074 Trubbish [E]	103 Ferroseed [E]	122 Shelmet [E]
Spit Up	137 Heatmor [56]					
Spite	124 Stunfisk [E]					
Splash	—					
Spore	096 Foongus [50]	097 Amoonguss [62]				
Stealth Rock	030 Roggenrola [30]	031 Boldore [36]	032 Gigalith [36]	063 Dwebble [24]	064 Crustle [24]	103 Ferroseed [E]
	130 Pawniard [E]					
Steamroller	049 Venipede [33]	050 Whirlipede [37]	051 Scolipede [39]			
Steel Wing	025 Pidove [E]	067 Sigilyph [E]	072 Archen [E]	086 Ducklett [E]	135 Vullaby [E]	
Stockpile	074 Trubbish [23]	075 Garbodor [23]	137 Heatmor [56]			
Stomp	028 Blitzle [29]	029 Zebstrika [31]	132 Bouffalant [E]			
Stone Edge	005 Pignite [TM]	006 Emboar [TM]	030 Roggenrola [36, TM]	031 Boldore [48, TM]	032 Gigalith [48, TM]	038 Timburr [43, TM]
	039 Gurdurr [49, TM]	040 Conkeldurr [49, TM]	044 Throh [TM]	045 Sawk [TM]	057 Sandile [TM]	058 Krokorok [TM]
	059 Krookodile [TM]	061 Darmanitan [TM]	063 Dwebble [TM]	064 Crustle [TM]	065 Scraggy [TM]	066 Scrafty [TM]
	070 Tirtouga [TM]	071 Carracosta [TM]	072 Archen [TM]	073 Archeops [TM]	120 Beartic [TM]	124 Stunfisk [TM]
	125 Mienfoo [TM]	126 Mienshao [TM]	129 Golurk [TM]	131 Bisharp [TM]	132 Bouffalant [TM]	138 Durant [TM]

Move	Pokémon that can learn it					
Stone Edge (continued)	141 Hydreigon [TM]	144 Cobalion [TM]	145 Terrakion [67, TM]	146 Virizion [TM]	149 Reshiram [TM]	150 Zekrom [TM]
	151 Landorus [73, TM]	152 Kyurem [TM]				
Stored Power	000 Victini [89]	023 Munna [47]	033 Woobat [E]	067 Sigilyph [E]		
Storm Throw	044 Throh [25]					
Strength	003 Serperior [HM]	004 Tepig [HM]	005 Pignite [HM]	006 Emboar [HM]	009 Samurott [HM]	011 Watchog [HM]
	013 Herdier [HM]	014 Stoutland [HM]	030 Roggenrola [HM]	031 Boldore [HM]	032 Gigalith [HM]	035 Drilbur [HM]
	036 Excadrill [HM]	038 Timburr [HM]	039 Gurdurr [HM]	040 Conkeldurr [HM]	043 Seismitoad [HM]	044 Throh [HM]
	045 Sawk [HM]	051 Scolipede [HM]	058 Krokorok [HM]	059 Krookodile [HM]	060 Darmanitan [HM]	061 Darmanitan [HM]
	063 Dwebble [HM]	064 Crustle [HM]	065 Scraggy [HM]	066 Scrafty [HM]	070 Tirtouga [HM]	071 Carracosta [HM]
	085 Reuniclus [HM]	104 Ferrothorn [HM]	110 Eelektross [HM]	116 Axew [HM]	117 Fraxure [HM]	118 Haxorus [HM]
	119 Cubchoo [HM]	120 Beartic [HM]	125 Mienfoo [HM]	126 Mienshao [HM]	127 Druddigon [HM]	128 Golett [HM]
	129 Golurk [HM]	132 Bouffalant [HM]	133 Rufflet [HM]	134 Braviary [HM]	138 Durant [HM]	139 Deino [HM]
	140 Zweilous [HM]	141 Hydreigon [HM]	144 Cobalion [HM]	145 Terrakion [HM]	146 Virizion [HM]	147 Tornadus [HM]
	148 Thundurus [HM]	149 Reshiram [HM]	150 Zekrom [HM]	151 Landorus [HM]	152 Kyurem [HM]	
String Shot	046 Sewaddle [1]	047 Swadloon [1]	048 Leavanny [1]	101 Joltik [1]	102 Galvantula [1]	142 Larvesta [1, E]
	143 Volcarona [1]					
Struggle	—					
Struggle Bug	046 Sewaddle [22, TM]	047 Swadloon [TM]	048 Leavanny [22, TM]	049 Venipede [TM]	050 Whirlipede [TM]	051 Scolipede [TM]
	063 Dwebble [TM]	064 Crustle [TM]	094 Karrablast [TM]	095 Escavalier [TM]	101 Joltik [TM]	102 Galvantula [TM]
	122 Shelmet [16, TM]	123 Accelgor [16, TM]	138 Durant [TM]	142 Larvesta [TM]	143 Volcarona [TM]	
Stun Spore	052 Cottonee [10]	054 Petilil [22]	096 Foongus [E]			
Submission	035 Drilbur [E]					
Substitute	000 Victini [TM]	001 Snivy [TM]	002 Servine [TM]	003 Serperior [TM]	004 Tepig [TM]	005 Pignite [TM]
	006 Emboar [TM]	007 Oshawott [TM]	008 Dewott [TM]	009 Samurott [TM]	010 Patrat [TM]	011 Watchog [TM]
	012 Lillipup [TM]	013 Herdier [TM]	014 Stoutland [TM]	015 Purrloin [TM]	016 Liepard [TM]	017 Pansage [TM]
	018 Simisage [TM]	019 Pansear [TM]	020 Simisear [TM]	021 Panpour [TM]	022 Simipour [TM]	023 Munna [TM]
	024 Musharna [TM]	025 Pidove [TM]	026 Tranquill [TM]	027 Unfezant [TM]	028 Blitzle [TM]	029 Zebstrika [TM]
	030 Roggenrola [TM]	031 Boldore [TM]	032 Gigalith [TM]	033 Woobat [TM]	034 Swoobat [TM]	035 Drilbur [TM]
	036 Excadrill [TM]	037 Audino [TM]	038 Timburr [TM]	039 Gurdurr [TM]	040 Conkeldurr [TM]	041 Tympole [TM]
	042 Palpitoad [TM]	043 Seismitoad [TM]	044 Throh [TM]	045 Sawk [TM]	046 Sewaddle [TM]	047 Swadloon [TM]
	048 Leavanny [TM]	049 Venipede [TM]	050 Whirlipede [TM]	051 Scolipede [TM]	052 Cottonee [TM]	053 Whimsicott [TM]
	054 Petilil [TM]	055 Lilligant [TM]	056 Basculin [TM]	057 Sandile [TM]	058 Krokorok [TM]	059 Krookodile [TM]
	060 Darumaka [TM]	061 Darmanitan [TM]	062 Maractus [TM]	063 Dwebble [TM]	064 Crustle [TM]	065 Scraggy [TM]
	066 Scrafty [TM]	067 Sigilyph [TM]	068 Yamask [TM]	069 Cofagrigus [TM]	070 Tirtouga [TM]	071 Carracosta [TM]
	072 Archen [TM]	073 Archeops [TM]	074 Trubbish [TM]	075 Garbodor [TM]	076 Zorua [TM]	077 Zoroark [TM]
	078 Minccino [TM]	079 Cinccino [TM]	080 Gothita [TM]	081 Gothorita [TM]	082 Gothitelle [TM]	083 Solosis [TM]
	084 Duosion [TM]	085 Reuniclus [TM]	086 Ducklett [TM]	087 Swanna [TM]	088 Vanillite [TM]	089 Vanillish [TM]
	090 Vanilluxe [TM]	091 Deerling [TM]	092 Sawsbuck [TM]	093 Emolga [TM]	094 Karrablast [TM]	095 Escavalier [TM]
	096 Foongus [TM]	097 Amoonguss [TM]	098 Frillish [TM]	099 Jellicent [TM]	100 Alomomola [TM]	101 Joltik [TM]
	102 Galvantula [TM]	103 Ferroseed [TM]	104 Ferrothorn [TM]	105 Klink [TM]	106 Klang [TM]	107 Klinklang [TM]
	109 Eelektrik [TM]	110 Eelektross [TM]	111 Elgyem [TM]	112 Beheeyem [TM]	113 Litwick [TM]	114 Lampent [TM]
	115 Chandelure [TM]	116 Axew [TM]	117 Fraxure [TM]	118 Haxorus [TM]	119 Cubchoo [TM]	120 Beartic [TM]
	121 Cryogonal [TM]	122 Shelmet [TM]	123 Accelgor [TM]	124 Stunfisk [TM]	125 Mienfoo [TM]	126 Mienshao [TM]
	127 Druddigon [TM]	128 Golett [TM]	129 Golurk [TM]	130 Pawniard [TM]	131 Bisharp [TM]	132 Bouffalant [TM]
	133 Rufflet [TM]	134 Braviary [TM]	135 Vullaby [TM]	136 Mandibuzz [TM]	137 Heatmor [TM]	138 Durant [TM]
	139 Deino [TM]	140 Zweilous [TM]	141 Hydreigon [TM]	142 Larvesta [TM]	143 Volcarona [TM]	144 Cobalion [TM]
	145 Terrakion [TM]	146 Virizion [TM]	147 Tornadus [TM]	148 Thundurus [TM]	149 Reshiram [TM]	150 Zekrom [TM]
	151 Landorus [TM]	152 Kyurem [TM]				
Sucker Punch	015 Purrloin [46]	016 Liepard [55]	062 Maractus [42]	076 Zorua [E]	101 Joltik [40]	102 Galvantula [46]
	127 Druddigon [E]	130 Pawniard [E]	137 Heatmor [E]			
Sunny Day	000 Victini [TM]	001 Snivy [TM]	002 Servine [TM]	003 Serperior [TM]	004 Tepig [TM]	005 Pignite [TM]
	006 Emboar [TM]	010 Patrat [TM]	011 Watchog [TM]	012 Lillipup [TM]	013 Herdier [TM]	014 Stoutland [TM]
	015 Purrloin [TM]	016 Liepard [TM]	017 Pansage [TM]	018 Simisage [TM]	019 Pansear [TM]	020 Simisear [TM]
	025 Pidove [TM]	026 Tranquill [TM]	027 Unfezant [TM]	037 Audino [TM]	038 Timburr [TM]	039 Gurdurr [TM]
	040 Conkeldurr [TM]	044 Throh [TM]	045 Sawk [TM]	046 Sewaddle [TM]	047 Swadloon [TM]	048 Leavanny [TM]
	049 Venipede [TM]	050 Whirlipede [TM]	051 Scolipede [TM]	052 Cottonee [40, TM]	053 Whimsicott [TM]	054 Petilil [40, TM]
	055 Lilligant [TM]	060 Darumaka [TM]	061 Darmanitan [TM]	062 Maractus [45, TM]	065 Scraggy [TM]	066 Scrafty [TM]
	074 Trubbish [TM]	075 Garbodor [TM]	076 Zorua [TM]	077 Zoroark [TM]	078 Minccino [TM]	079 Cinccino [TM]
	091 Deerling [TM]	092 Sawsbuck [TM]	096 Foongus [TM]	097 Amoonguss [TM]	103 Ferroseed [TM]	104 Ferrothorn [TM]
	113 Litwick [TM]	114 Lampent [TM]	115 Chandelure [TM]	116 Axew [TM]	117 Fraxure [TM]	118 Haxorus [TM]
	125 Mienfoo [TM]	126 Mienshao [TM]	127 Druddigon [TM]	132 Bouffalant [TM]	133 Rufflet [TM]	134 Braviary [TM]
	135 Vullaby [TM]	136 Mandibuzz [TM]	137 Heatmor [TM]	139 Deino [TM]	140 Zweilous [TM]	141 Hydreigon [TM]
	142 Larvesta [TM]	143 Volcarona [TM]	146 Virizion [TM]	149 Reshiram [TM]	152 Kyurem [TM]	
Super Fang	010 Patrat [21]	011 Watchog [22]				
Superpower	004 Tepig [E]	038 Timburr [49]	039 Gurdurr [57]	040 Conkeldurr [57]	044 Throh [49]	060 Darumaka [39]
	061 Darmanitan [47]	120 Beartic [1]	127 Druddigon [55]	134 Braviary [51]		

◁ S

Move	Pokémon that can learn it				
Supersonic	033 Woobat [E]	041 Tympole [5]	042 Palpitoad [1, 5]	043 Seismitoad [1, 5]	
Surf	007 Oshawott [HM]	008 Dewott [HM]	009 Samurott [HM]	013 Herdier [HM]	014 Stoutland [HM]	021 Panpour [HM]
	022 Simipour [HM]	037 Audino [HM]	041 Tympole [HM]	042 Palpitoad [HM]	043 Seismitoad [HM]	056 Basculin [HM]
	070 Tirtouga [HM]	071 Carracosta [HM]	086 Ducklett [HM]	087 Swanna [HM]	098 Frillish [HM]	099 Jellicent [HM]
	100 Alomomola [HM]	118 Haxorus [HM]	119 Cubchoo [HM]	120 Beartic [HM]	124 Stunfisk [HM]	127 Druddigon [HM]
	132 Bouffalant [HM]	141 Hydreigon [HM]				
Swagger	000 Victini [TM]	001 Snivy [TM]	002 Servine [TM]	003 Serperior [TM]	004 Tepig [TM]	005 Pignite [TM]
	006 Emboar [TM]	007 Oshawott [TM]	008 Dewott [TM]	009 Samurott [TM]	010 Patrat [TM]	011 Watchog [TM]
	012 Lillipup [TM]	013 Herdier [TM]	014 Stoutland [TM]	015 Purrloin [TM]	016 Liepard [TM]	017 Pansage [TM]
	018 Simisage [TM]	019 Pansear [TM]	020 Simisear [TM]	021 Panpour [TM]	022 Simipour [TM]	023 Munna [TM]
	024 Musharna [TM]	025 Pidove [39, TM]	026 Tranquill [45, TM]	027 Unfezant [49, TM]	028 Blitzle [TM]	029 Zebstrika [TM]
	030 Roggenrola [TM]	031 Boldore [TM]	032 Gigalith [TM]	033 Woobat [TM]	034 Swoobat [TM]	035 Drilbur [TM]
	036 Excadrill [TM]	037 Audino [TM]	038 Timburr [TM]	039 Gurdurr [TM]	040 Conkeldurr [TM]	041 Tympole [TM]
	042 Palpitoad [TM]	043 Seismitoad [TM]	044 Throh [TM]	045 Sawk [TM]	046 Sewaddle [TM]	047 Swadloon [TM]
	048 Leavanny [TM]	049 Venipede [TM]	050 Whirlipede [TM]	051 Scolipede [TM]	052 Cottonee [TM]	053 Whimsicott [TM]
	054 Petilil [TM]	055 Lilligant [TM]	056 Basculin [TM]	057 Sandile [25, TM]	058 Krokorok [25, TM]	059 Krookodile [25, TM]
	060 Darumaka [TM]	061 Darmanitan [17, TM]	062 Maractus [TM]	063 Dwebble [TM]	064 Crustle [TM]	065 Scraggy [16, TM]
	066 Scrafty [16, TM]	067 Sigilyph [TM]	068 Yamask [TM]	069 Cofagrigus [TM]	070 Tirtouga [TM]	071 Carracosta [TM]
	072 Archen [TM]	073 Archeops [TM]	074 Trubbish [TM]	075 Garbodor [TM]	076 Zorua [TM]	077 Zoroark [TM]
	078 Minccino [TM]	079 Cinccino [TM]	080 Gothita [TM]	081 Gothorita [TM]	082 Gothitelle [TM]	083 Solosis [TM]
	084 Duosion [TM]	085 Reuniclus [TM]	086 Ducklett [TM]	087 Swanna [TM]	088 Vanillite [TM]	089 Vanillish [TM]
	090 Vanilluxe [TM]	091 Deerling [TM]	092 Sawsbuck [TM]	093 Emolga [TM]	094 Karrablast [TM]	095 Escavalier [TM]
	096 Foongus [TM]	097 Amoonguss [TM]	098 Frillish [TM]	099 Jellicent [TM]	100 Alomomola [TM]	101 Joltik [TM]
	102 Galvantula [TM]	103 Ferroseed [TM]	104 Ferrothorn [TM]	105 Klink [TM]	106 Klang [TM]	107 Klinklang [TM]
	109 Eelektrik [TM]	110 Eelektross [TM]	111 Elgyem [TM]	112 Beheeyem [TM]	113 Litwick [TM]	114 Lampent [TM]
	115 Chandelure [TM]	116 Axew [TM]	117 Fraxure [TM]	118 Haxorus [TM]	119 Cubchoo [TM]	120 Beartic [29, TM]
	121 Cryogonal [TM]	122 Shelmet [TM]	123 Accelgor [TM]	124 Stunfisk [TM]	125 Mienfoo [TM]	126 Mienshao [TM]
	127 Druddigon [TM]	128 Golett [TM]	129 Golurk [TM]	130 Pawniard [TM]	131 Bisharp [TM]	132 Bouffalant [TM]
	133 Rufflet [TM]	134 Braviary [TM]	135 Vullaby [TM]	136 Mandibuzz [TM]	137 Heatmor [TM]	138 Durant [TM]
	139 Deino [TM]	140 Zweilous [TM]	141 Hydreigon [TM]	142 Larvesta [TM]	143 Volcarona [TM]	144 Cobalion [TM]
	145 Terrakion [TM]	146 Virizion [TM]	147 Tornadus [?, TM]	148 Thundurus [?, TM]	149 Reshiram [TM]	150 Zekrom [TM]
	151 Landorus [TM]	152 Kyurem [TM]				
Swallow	074 Trubbish [23]	075 Garbodor [23]	137 Heatmor [56]			
Sweet Kiss	037 Audino [E]					
Sweet Scent	001 Snivy [E]	054 Petilil [E]	062 Maractus [3]	096 Foongus [24]	097 Amoonguss [24]	
Swift	023 Munna [E]	056 Basculin [E]	078 Minccino [19]	123 Accelgor [25]	125 Mienfoo [21]	126 Mienshao [21]
Switcheroo	052 Cottonee [E]					
Swords Dance	001 Snivy [TM]	002 Servine [TM]	003 Serperior [TM]	007 Oshawott [41, TM]	008 Dewott [49, TM]	009 Samurott [57, TM]
	010 Patrat [TM]	011 Watchog [TM]	035 Drilbur [36, TM]	036 Excadrill [42, TM]	048 Leavanny [46, TM]	051 Scolipede [TM]
	055 Lilligant [TM]	063 Dwebble [TM]	064 Crustle [TM]	076 Zorua [TM]	077 Zoroark [TM]	092 Sawsbuck [TM]
	094 Karrablast [52, TM]	095 Escavalier [52, TM]	104 Ferrothorn [TM]	116 Axew [46, TM]	117 Fraxure [48, TM]	118 Haxorus [50, TM]
	120 Beartic [TM]	125 Mienfoo [TM]	126 Mienshao [TM]	130 Pawniard [57, TM]	131 Bisharp [63, TM]	132 Bouffalant [56, TM]
	144 Cobalion [49, TM]	145 Terrakion [49, TM]	146 Virizion [49, TM]	151 Landorus [37, TM]		
Synchronoise	023 Munna [25]	033 Woobat [E]	067 Sigilyph [31]	111 Elgyem [53]	112 Beheeyem [63]	
Synthesis	054 Petilil [17]	055 Lilligant [1]	062 Maractus [15]	091 Deerling [E]	096 Foongus [35]	097 Amoonguss [35]

◁ T

Move	Pokémon that can learn it				
Tackle	001 Snivy [1]	002 Servine [1]	003 Serperior [1]	004 Tepig [1]	005 Pignite [1]	006 Emboar [1]
	007 Oshawott [1]	008 Dewott [1]	009 Samurott [1]	010 Patrat [1]	011 Watchog [1]	012 Lillipup [1]
	013 Herdier [1]	014 Stoutland [1]	030 Roggenrola [1]	031 Boldore [1]	032 Gigalith [1]	046 Sewaddle [1]
	047 Swadloon [1]	048 Leavanny [1]	056 Basculin [1]	060 Darumaka [1]	061 Darmanitan [1]	091 Deerling [1]
	092 Sawsbuck [1]	103 Ferroseed [1]	104 Ferrothorn [1]	108 Tynamo [1]	139 Deino [1]	
Tail Glow	—					
Tail Slap	078 Minccino [25]	079 Cinccino [1]				
Tail Whip	004 Tepig [3]	005 Pignite [1, 3]	006 Emboar [1, 3]	007 Oshawott [5]	008 Dewott [1, 5]	009 Samurott [1, 5]
	028 Blitzle [4]	029 Zebstrika [1, 4]	078 Minccino [E]	093 Emolga [?]		
Tailwind	025 Pidove [46]	026 Tranquill [54]	027 Unfezant [60]	053 Whimsicott [28]	067 Sigilyph [11]	086 Ducklett [37]
	087 Swanna [40]	133 Rufflet [37]	134 Braviary [37]	135 Vullaby [37]	136 Mandibuzz [37]	147 Tornadus [55]
Take Down	004 Tepig [25]	005 Pignite [28]	006 Emboar [28]	012 Lillipup [15]	013 Herdier [15]	014 Stoutland [15]
	028 Blitzle [E]	030 Roggenrola [E]	037 Audino [30]	049 Venipede [E]	056 Basculin [20]	060 Darumaka [E]
	074 Trubbish [25]	091 Deerling [20]	092 Sawsbuck [20]	094 Karrablast [37]	142 Larvesta [20]	144 Cobalion [19]
	145 Terrakion [19]	146 Virizion [19]				
Taunt	000 Victini [TM]	001 Snivy [TM]	002 Servine [TM]	003 Serperior [TM]	004 Tepig [TM]	005 Pignite [TM]
	006 Emboar [TM]	007 Oshawott [TM]	008 Dewott [TM]	009 Samurott [TM]	015 Purrloin [TM]	016 Liepard [38, TM]
	017 Pansage [TM]	018 Simisage [TM]	019 Pansear [TM]	020 Simisear [TM]	021 Panpour [25, TM]	022 Simipour [TM]

Move	Pokémon that can learn it					
Taunt (continued)	025 Pidove [25, TM]	026 Tranquill [27, TM]	027 Unfezant [27, TM]	033 Woobat [TM]	034 Swoobat [TM]	038 Timburr [TM]
	039 Gurdurr [TM]	040 Conkeldurr [TM]	044 Throh [TM]	045 Sawk [TM]	052 Cottonee [TM]	053 Whimsicott [TM]
	056 Basculin [TM]	057 Sandile [TM]	058 Krokorok [TM]	059 Krookodile [TM]	060 Darumaka [35, TM]	061 Darmanitan [39, TM]
	065 Scraggy [TM]	066 Scrafty [TM]	072 Archen [TM]	073 Archeops [TM]	076 Zorua [25, TM]	077 Zoroark [25, TM]
	080 Gothita [TM]	081 Gothorita [TM]	082 Gothitelle [TM]	088 Vanillite [22, TM]	089 Vanillish [22, TM]	090 Vanilluxe [22, TM]
	093 Emolga [TM]	098 Frillish [TM]	099 Jellicent [TM]	113 Litwick [TM]	114 Lampent [TM]	115 Chandelure [TM]
	116 Axew [36, TM]	117 Fraxure [36, TM]	118 Haxorus [36, TM]	120 Beartic [TM]	125 Mienfoo [TM]	126 Mienshao [TM]
	127 Druddigon [TM]	130 Pawniard [TM]	131 Bisharp [TM]	132 Bouffalant [TM]	135 Vullaby [TM]	136 Mandibuzz [TM]
	137 Heatmor [TM]	139 Deino [TM]	140 Zweilous [TM]	141 Hydreigon [TM]	144 Cobalion [TM]	145 Terrakion [TM]
	146 Virizion [TM]	147 Tornadus [TM]	148 Thundurus [TM]			
Teeter Dance	055 Lilligant [10]					
Telekinesis	000 Victini [TM]	023 Munna [43, TM]	024 Musharna [TM]	033 Woobat [TM]	034 Swoobat [TM]	037 Audino [TM]
	067 Sigilyph [TM]	068 Yamask [TM]	069 Cofagrigus [TM]	080 Gothita [40, TM]	081 Gothorita [43, TM]	082 Gothitelle [45, TM]
	083 Solosis [TM]	084 Duosion [TM]	085 Reuniclus [TM]	111 Elgyem [TM]	112 Beheeyem [TM]	113 Litwick [TM]
	114 Lampent [TM]	115 Chandelure [TM]	128 Golett [TM]	129 Golurk [TM]		
Teleport	111 Elgyem [E]					
Thief	015 Purrloin [TM]	016 Liepard [TM]	017 Pansage [TM]	018 Simisage [TM]	019 Pansear [TM]	020 Simisear [TM]
	021 Panpour [TM]	022 Simipour [TM]	033 Woobat [TM]	034 Swoobat [TM]	053 Whimsicott [TM]	057 Sandile [TM]
	058 Krokorok [TM]	059 Krookodile [TM]	060 Darumaka [TM]	061 Darmanitan [TM]	066 Scrafty [TM]	067 Sigilyph [TM]
	068 Yamask [TM]	069 Cofagrigus [TM]	074 Trubbish [TM]	075 Garbodor [TM]	076 Zorua [TM]	077 Zoroark [TM]
	078 Minccino [TM]	080 Gothita [TM]	081 Gothorita [TM]	082 Gothitelle [TM]	101 Joltik [TM]	102 Galvantula [TM]
	111 Elgyem [TM]	112 Beheeyem [TM]	113 Litwick [TM]	114 Lampent [TM]	115 Chandelure [TM]	128 Golett [TM]
	129 Golurk [TM]	130 Pawniard [TM]	131 Bisharp [TM]	135 Vullaby [TM]	136 Mandibuzz [TM]	137 Heatmor [TM]
	139 Deino [TM]	140 Zweilous [TM]	141 Hydreigon [TM]	147 Tornadus [TM]	148 Thundurus [TM]	
Thrash	004 Tepig [E]	028 Blitzle [43]	029 Zebstrika [53]	056 Basculin [56]	057 Sandile [46]	058 Krokorok [52]
	060 Darumaka [27]	061 Darmanitan [27]	072 Archen [51]	073 Archeops [61]	109 Eelektrik [74]	119 Cubchoo [53]
	120 Beartic [59]	132 Bouffalant [51]	133 Rufflet [64]	134 Braviary [70]	142 Larvesta [90]	147 Tornadus [85]
	148 Thundurus [85]					
Thunder	000 Victini [TM]	011 Watchog [TM]	014 Stoutland [TM]	028 Blitzle [TM]	029 Zebstrika [TM]	037 Audino [TM]
	079 Cinccino [TM]	083 Solosis [TM]	084 Duosion [TM]	085 Reuniclus [TM]	093 Emolga [TM]	102 Galvantula [TM]
	104 Ferrothorn [TM]	107 Klinklang [TM]	109 Eelektrik [TM]	110 Eelektross [TM]	124 Stunfisk [TM]	148 Thundurus [67, TM]
	150 Zekrom [78, TM]					
Thunder Fang	012 Lillipup [E]	014 Stoutland [1]	057 Sandile [E]	127 Druddigon [E]	138 Durant [E]	139 Deino [E]
	150 Zekrom [1]					
Thunder Wave	000 Victini [TM]	011 Watchog [TM]	012 Lillipup [TM]	013 Herdier [TM]	014 Stoutland [TM]	015 Purrloin [TM]
	016 Liepard [TM]	023 Munna [TM]	024 Musharna [TM]	028 Blitzle [15, TM]	029 Zebstrika [1, 15, TM]	033 Woobat [TM]
	034 Swoobat [TM]	037 Audino [TM]	067 Sigilyph [TM]	078 Minccino [TM]	079 Cinccino [TM]	080 Gothita [TM]
	081 Gothorita [TM]	082 Gothitelle [TM]	083 Solosis [TM]	084 Duosion [TM]	085 Reuniclus [TM]	091 Deerling [TM]
	092 Sawsbuck [TM]	093 Emolga [TM]	101 Joltik [4, TM]	102 Galvantula [1, 4, TM]	103 Ferroseed [TM]	104 Ferrothorn [TM]
	105 Klink [TM]	106 Klang [TM]	107 Klinklang [TM]	108 Tynamo [1]	109 Eelektrik [1, TM]	110 Eelektross [TM]
	111 Elgyem [TM]	112 Beheeyem [TM]	124 Stunfisk [TM]	130 Pawniard [TM]	131 Bisharp [TM]	138 Durant [TM]
	139 Deino [TM]	140 Zweilous [TM]	141 Hydreigon [TM]	144 Cobalion [TM]	148 Thundurus [TM]	150 Zekrom [TM]
Thunderbolt	000 Victini [TM]	010 Patrat [TM]	011 Watchog [TM]	012 Lillipup [TM]	013 Herdier [TM]	014 Stoutland [TM]
	028 Blitzle [TM]	029 Zebstrika [TM]	037 Audino [TM]	075 Garbodor [TM]	078 Minccino [TM]	079 Cinccino [TM]
	080 Gothita [TM]	081 Gothorita [TM]	082 Gothitelle [TM]	093 Emolga [TM]	101 Joltik [TM]	102 Galvantula [TM]
	103 Ferroseed [TM]	104 Ferrothorn [TM]	105 Klink [TM]	106 Klang [TM]	107 Klinklang [TM]	109 Eelektrik [44, TM]
	110 Eelektross [TM]	111 Elgyem [TM]	112 Beheeyem [TM]	124 Stunfisk [45, TM]	129 Golurk [TM]	148 Thundurus [TM]
	150 Zekrom [22, TM]					
ThunderPunch	065 Scraggy [E]					
ThunderShock	093 Emolga [1]	105 Klink [11]	106 Klang [1, 11]	107 Klinklang [1, 11]	124 Stunfisk [9]	148 Thundurus [1]
Tickle	017 Pansage [E]	019 Pansear [E]	021 Panpour [E]	052 Cottonee [E]	078 Minccino [9]	079 Cinccino [1]
	080 Gothita [7]	081 Gothorita [1, 7]	082 Gothitelle [1, 7]	093 Emolga [E]	100 Alomomola [E]	137 Heatmor [E]
Torment	001 Snivy [TM]	002 Servine [TM]	003 Serperior [TM]	015 Purrloin [19, TM]	016 Liepard [19, TM]	017 Pansage [25, TM]
	018 Simisage [TM]	019 Pansear [TM]	020 Simisear [TM]	021 Panpour [TM]	022 Simipour [TM]	023 Munna [TM]
	024 Musharna [TM]	033 Woobat [TM]	034 Swoobat [TM]	057 Sandile [10, TM]	058 Krokorok [10, TM]	059 Krookodile [10, TM]
	061 Darmanitan [TM]	065 Scraggy [TM]	066 Scrafty [TM]	072 Archen [TM]	073 Archeops [TM]	076 Zorua [33, TM]
	077 Zoroark [34, TM]	080 Gothita [TM]	081 Gothorita [TM]	082 Gothitelle [TM]	127 Druddigon [TM]	130 Pawniard [14, TM]
	131 Bisharp [1, 14, TM]	135 Vullaby [TM]	136 Mandibuzz [TM]	139 Deino [TM]	140 Zweilous [TM]	141 Hydreigon [TM]
	147 Tornadus [TM]	148 Thundurus [TM]				
Toxic	000 Victini [TM]	001 Snivy [TM]	002 Servine [TM]	003 Serperior [TM]	004 Tepig [TM]	005 Pignite [TM]
	006 Emboar [TM]	007 Oshawott [TM]	008 Dewott [TM]	009 Samurott [TM]	010 Patrat [TM]	011 Watchog [TM]
	012 Lillipup [TM]	013 Herdier [TM]	014 Stoutland [TM]	015 Purrloin [TM]	016 Liepard [TM]	017 Pansage [TM]
	018 Simisage [TM]	019 Pansear [TM]	020 Simisear [TM]	021 Panpour [TM]	022 Simipour [TM]	023 Munna [TM]
	024 Musharna [TM]	025 Pidove [TM]	026 Tranquill [TM]	027 Unfezant [TM]	028 Blitzle [TM]	029 Zebstrika [TM]
	030 Roggenrola [TM]	031 Boldore [TM]	032 Gigalith [TM]	033 Woobat [TM]	034 Swoobat [TM]	035 Drilbur [TM]
	036 Excadrill [TM]	037 Audino [TM]	038 Timburr [TM]	039 Gurdurr [TM]	040 Conkeldurr [TM]	041 Tympole [TM]

◈ T

Move	Pokémon that can learn it					
Toxic (continued)	042 Palpitoad [TM]	043 Seismitoad [TM]	044 Throh [TM]	045 Sawk [TM]	046 Sewaddle [TM]	047 Swadloon [TM]
	048 Leavanny [TM]	049 Venipede [36, TM]	050 Whirlipede [41, TM]	051 Scolipede [44, TM]	052 Cottonee [TM]	053 Whimsicott [TM]
	054 Petilil [TM]	055 Lilligant [TM]	056 Basculin [TM]	057 Sandile [TM]	058 Krokorok [TM]	059 Krookodile [TM]
	060 Darumaka [TM]	061 Darmanitan [TM]	062 Maractus [TM]	063 Dwebble [TM]	064 Crustle [TM]	065 Scraggy [TM]
	066 Scrafty [TM]	067 Sigilyph [TM]	068 Yamask [TM]	069 Cofagrigus [TM]	070 Tirtouga [TM]	071 Carracosta [TM]
	072 Archen [TM]	073 Archeops [TM]	074 Trubbish [36, TM]	075 Garbodor [39, TM]	076 Zorua [TM]	077 Zoroark [TM]
	078 Minccino [TM]	079 Cinccino [TM]	080 Gothita [TM]	081 Gothorita [TM]	082 Gothitelle [TM]	083 Solosis [TM]
	084 Duosion [TM]	085 Reuniclus [TM]	086 Ducklett [TM]	087 Swanna [TM]	088 Vanillite [TM]	089 Vanillish [TM]
	090 Vanilluxe [TM]	091 Deerling [TM]	092 Sawsbuck [TM]	093 Emolga [TM]	094 Karrablast [TM]	095 Escavalier [TM]
	096 Foongus [32, TM]	097 Amoonguss [32, TM]	098 Frillish [TM]	099 Jellicent [TM]	100 Alomomola [TM]	101 Joltik [TM]
	102 Galvantula [TM]	103 Ferroseed [TM]	104 Ferrothorn [TM]	105 Klink [TM]	106 Klang [TM]	107 Klinklang [TM]
	109 Eelektrik [TM]	110 Eelektross [TM]	111 Elgyem [TM]	112 Beheeyem [TM]	113 Litwick [TM]	114 Lampent [TM]
	115 Chandelure [TM]	116 Axew [TM]	117 Fraxure [TM]	118 Haxorus [TM]	119 Cubchoo [TM]	120 Beartic [TM]
	121 Cryogonal [TM]	122 Shelmet [TM]	123 Accelgor [TM]	124 Stunfisk [TM]	125 Mienfoo [TM]	126 Mienshao [TM]
	127 Druddigon [TM]	128 Golett [TM]	129 Golurk [TM]	130 Pawniard [TM]	131 Bisharp [TM]	132 Bouffalant [TM]
	133 Rufflet [TM]	134 Braviary [TM]	135 Vullaby [TM]	136 Mandibuzz [TM]	137 Heatmor [TM]	138 Durant [TM]
	139 Deino [TM]	140 Zweilous [TM]	141 Hydreigon [TM]	142 Larvesta [TM]	143 Volcarona [TM]	144 Cobalion [TM]
	145 Terrakion [TM]	146 Virizion [TM]	147 Tornadus [TM]	148 Thundurus [TM]	149 Reshiram [TM]	150 Zekrom [TM]
	151 Landorus [TM]	152 Kyurem [TM]				
Toxic Spikes	049 Venipede [E]	074 Trubbish [7]	075 Garbodor [1, 7]			
Transform	—					
Tri Attack	141 Hydreigon [1]					
Trick	083 Solosis [E]					
Trick Room	000 Victini [TM]	023 Munna [TM]	024 Musharna [TM]	033 Woobat [TM]	034 Swoobat [TM]	037 Audino [TM]
	053 Whimsicott [TM]	067 Sigilyph [TM]	068 Yamask [TM]	069 Cofagrigus [TM]	080 Gothita [TM]	081 Gothorita [TM]
	082 Gothitelle [TM]	083 Solosis [TM]	084 Duosion [TM]	085 Reuniclus [TM]	098 Frillish [TM]	099 Jellicent [TM]
	107 Klinklang [TM]	111 Elgyem [TM]	112 Beheeyem [TM]	113 Litwick [TM]	114 Lampent [TM]	115 Chandelure [TM]
Triple Kick	—					
Trump Card	007 Oshawott [E]					
Twineedle	049 Venipede [E]	095 Escavalier [1, 13]				
Twister	001 Snivy [E]					

◈ U

Move	Pokémon that can learn it					
Uproar	025 Pidove [E]	041 Tympole [23]	042 Palpitoad [23]	043 Seismitoad [23]	056 Basculin [4]	057 Sandile [E]
	060 Darumaka [17]	080 Gothita [E]	088 Vanillite [10]	089 Vanillish [1, 10]	090 Vanilluxe [1, 10]	147 Tornadus [1]
	148 Thundurus [1]					
U-Turn	000 Victini [TM]	025 Pidove [TM]	026 Tranquill [TM]	027 Unfezant [TM]	033 Woobat [TM]	034 Swoobat [TM]
	053 Whimsicott [TM]	060 Darumaka [TM]	061 Darmanitan [TM]	072 Archen [41, TM]	073 Archeops [45, TM]	076 Zorua [TM]
	077 Zoroark [1, TM]	078 Minccino [TM]	079 Cinccino [TM]	093 Emolga [TM]	109 Eelektrik [TM]	110 Eelektross [TM]
	123 Accelgor [40, TM]	125 Mienfoo [41, TM]	126 Mienshao [41, TM]	133 Rufflet [TM]	134 Braviary [TM]	135 Vullaby [TM]
	136 Mandibuzz [TM]	141 Hydreigon [TM]	142 Larvesta [TM]	143 Volcarona [TM]	147 Tornadus [TM]	148 Thundurus [TM]
	151 Landorus [TM]					

◈ V

Move	Pokémon that can learn it					
Vacuum Wave	—					
Venoshock	043 Seismitoad [TM]	049 Venipede [26, TM]	050 Whirlipede [28, TM]	051 Scolipede [28, TM]	074 Trubbish [TM]	075 Garbodor [TM]
	096 Foongus [TM]	097 Amoonguss [TM]	122 Shelmet [TM]	123 Accelgor [TM]		
ViceGrip	105 Klink [1]	106 Klang [1]	107 Klinklang [1]	138 Durant [1]		
Vine Whip	001 Snivy [7]	002 Servine [1, 7]	003 Serperior [1, 7]	017 Pansage [10]		
Vital Throw	044 Throh [17]	125 Mienfoo [E]				
Volt Switch	028 Blitzle [TM]	029 Zebstrika [TM]	093 Emolga [42, TM]	101 Joltik [TM]	102 Galvantula [TM]	105 Klink [TM]
	106 Klang [TM]	107 Klinklang [TM]	109 Eelektrik [TM]	110 Eelektross [TM]	144 Cobalion [TM]	148 Thundurus [TM]
	150 Zekrom [TM]					
Volt Tackle	—					

◈ W

Move	Pokémon that can learn it					
Wake-Up Slap	038 Timburr [20]	039 Gurdurr [20]	040 Conkeldurr [20]	078 Minccino [31]	100 Alomomola [29]	
Water Gun	007 Oshawott [7]	008 Dewott [1, 7]	009 Samurott [1, 7]	021 Panpour [10]	056 Basculin [1]	070 Tirtouga [1]
	071 Carracosta [1]	086 Ducklett [1]	087 Swanna [1]			
Water Pledge	007 Oshawott [T]	008 Dewott [T]	009 Samurott [T]			
Water Pulse	007 Oshawott [23]	008 Dewott [25]	009 Samurott [25]	041 Tympole [E]	070 Tirtouga [E]	086 Ducklett [13]
	087 Swanna [13]	088 Vanillite [E]	098 Frillish [22]	099 Jellicent [22]	100 Alomomola [25]	

Move	Pokémon that can learn it					
Water Sport	007 Oshawott [11]	008 Dewott [1, 11]	009 Samurott [1, 11]	021 Panpour [16]	086 Ducklett [3]	087 Swanna [1, 3]
	098 Frillish [1]	099 Jellicent [1]	100 Alomomola [1]			
Water Spout	098 Frillish [61]	099 Jellicent [69]				
Waterfall	007 Oshawott [HM]	008 Dewott [HM]	009 Samurott [HM]	021 Panpour [HM]	022 Simipour [HM]	056 Basculin [HM]
	070 Tirtouga [HM]	071 Carracosta [HM]	098 Frillish [HM]	099 Jellicent [HM]	100 Alomomola [HM]	
Weather Ball	090 Vanilluxe [1]					
Whirlpool	056 Basculin [E]	070 Tirtouga [E]				
Whirlwind	067 Sigilyph [14]	133 Rufflet [55]	134 Braviary [57]	135 Vullaby [55]	136 Mandibuzz [57]	143 Volcarona [40]
Wide Guard	038 Timburr [E]	044 Throh [45]	070 Tirtouga [25]	071 Carracosta [25]	100 Alomomola [53]	126 Mienshao [45]
Wild Charge	000 Victini [TM]	004 Tepig [TM]	005 Pignite [TM]	006 Emboar [TM]	012 Lillipup [TM]	013 Herdier [TM]
	014 Stoutland [TM]	028 Blitzle [39, TM]	029 Zebstrika [47, TM]	037 Audino [TM]	091 Deerling [TM]	092 Sawsbuck [TM]
	093 Emolga [TM]	101 Joltik [TM]	102 Galvantula [TM]	109 Eelektrik [59, TM]	110 Eelektross [TM]	132 Bouffalant [TM]
	142 Larvesta [TM]	143 Volcarona [TM]	148 Thundurus [TM]	150 Zekrom [TM]		
Will-O-Wisp	000 Victini [TM]	004 Tepig [TM]	005 Pignite [TM]	006 Emboar [TM]	019 Pansear [TM]	020 Simisear [TM]
	060 Darumaka [TM]	061 Darmanitan [TM]	068 Yamask [21, TM]	069 Cofagrigus [21, TM]	098 Frillish [TM]	099 Jellicent [TM]
	113 Litwick [16, TM]	114 Lampent [16, TM]	115 Chandelure [TM]	137 Heatmor [TM]	142 Larvesta [TM]	143 Volcarona [TM]
	149 Reshiram [TM]					
Wing Attack	072 Archen [1]	073 Archeops [1]	086 Ducklett [9]	087 Swanna [1, 9]	133 Rufflet [10]	134 Braviary [1, 10]
Wish	025 Pidove [E]	037 Audino [E]	100 Alomomola [37]			
Withdraw	063 Dwebble [7]	064 Crustle [1, 7]	070 Tirtouga [1]	071 Carracosta [1]		
Wonder Room	083 Solosis [48]	084 Duosion [53]	085 Reuniclus [59]	111 Elgyem [56]	112 Beheeyem [68]	
Wood Hammer	062 Maractus [E]					
Work Up	000 Victini [TM]	005 Pignite [TM]	006 Emboar [TM]	010 Patrat [26, TM]	011 Watchog [TM]	012 Lillipup [19, TM]
	013 Herdier [20, TM]	014 Stoutland [20, TM]	017 Pansage [TM]	018 Simisage [TM]	019 Pansear [TM]	020 Simisear [TM]
	021 Panpour [TM]	022 Simipour [TM]	025 Pidove [TM]	026 Tranquill [TM]	027 Unfezant [TM]	037 Audino [TM]
	038 Timburr [TM]	039 Gurdurr [TM]	040 Conkeldurr [TM]	044 Throh [TM]	045 Sawk [TM]	060 Darumaka [25, TM]
	061 Darmanitan [25, TM]	065 Scraggy [TM]	066 Scrafty [TM]	078 Minccino [TM]	079 Cinccino [TM]	091 Deerling [TM]
	092 Sawsbuck [TM]	125 Mienfoo [TM]	126 Mienshao [TM]	132 Bouffalant [TM]	133 Rufflet [TM]	134 Braviary [TM]
	139 Deino [38, TM]	140 Zweilous [38, TM]	141 Hydreigon [38, TM]	144 Cobalion [61, TM]	145 Terrakion [61, TM]	146 Virizion [61, TM]
Worry Seed	052 Cottonee [E]	054 Petilil [E]	062 Maractus [E]	091 Deerling [E]	103 Ferroseed [E]	
Wrap	001 Snivy [10]	002 Servine [1, 10]	003 Serperior [1, 10]	137 Heatmor [E]		
Wring Out	001 Snivy [37]	002 Servine [44]	003 Serperior [50]	098 Frillish [55]	099 Jellicent [61]	

◈ **X**

Move	Pokémon that can learn it					
X-Scissor	007 Oshawott [TM]	008 Dewott [TM]	009 Samurott [TM]	035 Drilbur [TM]	036 Excadrill [TM]	048 Leavanny [39, TM]
	051 Scolipede [TM]	063 Dwebble [35, TM]	064 Crustle [38, TM]	094 Karrablast [44, TM]	095 Escavalier [44, TM]	101 Joltik [TM]
	102 Galvantula [TM]	116 Axew [TM]	117 Fraxure [TM]	118 Haxorus [TM]	130 Pawniard [TM]	131 Bisharp [TM]
	138 Durant [51, TM]	144 Cobalion [TM]	145 Terrakion [TM]	146 Virizion [TM]		

◈ **Y**

Move	Pokémon that can learn it					
Yawn	004 Tepig [E]	012 Lillipup [E]	015 Purrloin [E]	019 Pansear [16]	023 Munna [7]	037 Audino [E]
	060 Darumaka [E]	119 Cubchoo [E]	122 Shelmet [25]	124 Stunfisk [E]		

◈ **Z**

Move	Pokémon that can learn it					
Zap Cannon	105 Klink [54]	106 Klang [60]	107 Klinklang [66]	109 Eelektrik [69]		
Zen Headbutt	000 Victini [49]	023 Munna [23]	065 Scraggy [E]	111 Elgyem [32]	112 Beheeyem [32]	142 Larvesta [E]
	150 Zekrom [43]					

A

Ability	Pokémon that have this Ability				
Adaptability	056 Basculin				
Aftermath	—				
Air Lock	—				
Analytic	—				
Anger Point	—				
Anticipation	—				
Arena Trap	—				

B

Ability	Pokémon that have this Ability				
Bad Dreams	—				
Battle Armor	—				
Big Pecks	025 Pidove	026 Tranquill	027 Unfezant	086 Ducklett	087 Swanna	135 Vullaby
	136 Mandibuzz				
Blaze	004 Tepig	005 Pignite	006 Emboar		

C

Ability	Pokémon that have this Ability				
Chlorophyll	046 Sewaddle	047 Swadloon	048 Leavanny	054 Petilil	055 Lilligant	062 Maractus
	091 Deerling	092 Sawsbuck			
Clear Body	—				
Cloud Nine	—				
Color Change	—				
Compoundeyes	101 Joltik	102 Galvantula			
Contrary	—				
Cursed Body	098 Frillish	099 Jellicent			
Cute Charm	078 Minccino	079 Cinccino			

D

Ability	Pokémon that have this Ability	
Damp	—	
Defeatist	072 Archen	073 Archeops
Defiant	130 Pawniard	131 Bisharp
Download	—	
Drizzle	—	
Drought	—	
Dry Skin	—	

E

Ability	Pokémon that have this Ability	
Early Bird	—	
Effect Spore	096 Foongus	097 Amoonguss

F

Ability	Pokémon that have this Ability				
Filter	—				
Flame Body	113 Litwick	114 Lampent	115 Chandelure	142 Larvesta	143 Volcarona
Flare Boost	—				
Flash Fire	113 Litwick	114 Lampent	115 Chandelure	137 Heatmor	
Flower Gift	—				
Forecast	—				
Forewarn	023 Munna	024 Musharna			
Friend Guard	—				
Frisk	080 Gothita	081 Gothorita	082 Gothitelle		

G

Ability	Pokémon that have this Ability				
Gluttony	017 Pansage	018 Simisage	019 Pansear	020 Simisear	021 Panpour	022 Simipour
	137 Heatmor				
Guts	038 Timburr	039 Gurdurr	040 Conkeldurr	044 Throh	

H

Ability	Pokémon that have this Ability				
Harvest	—				
Healer	037 Audino	100 Alomomola			
Heatproof	—				
Heavy Metal	—				
Honey Gather	—				
Huge Power	—				
Hustle	060 Darumaka	138 Durant	139 Deino	140 Zweilous	
Hydration	041 Tympole	042 Palpitoad	100 Alomomola	122 Shelmet	123 Accelgor
Hyper Cutter	—				

I

Ability	Pokémon that have this Ability				
Ice Body	088 Vanillite	089 Vanillish	090 Vanilluxe		
Illuminate	011 Watchog				
Illusion	076 Zorua	077 Zoroark			
Immunity	—				
Imposter	—				
Infiltrator	052 Cottonee	053 Whimsicott			
Inner Focus	044 Throh	045 Sawk	060 Darumaka	125 Mienfoo	126 Mienshao	130 Pawniard
	131 Bisharp				
Insomnia	—				
Intimidate	013 Herdier	014 Stoutland	057 Sandile	058 Krokorok	059 Krookodile
Iron Barbs	103 Ferroseed	104 Ferrothorn			
Iron Fist	128 Golett	129 Golurk			

J

Ability	Pokémon that have this Ability		
Justified	144 Cobalion	145 Terrakion	146 Virizion

K

Ability	Pokémon that have this Ability				
Keen Eye	010 Patrat	011 Watchog	086 Ducklett	087 Swanna	133 Rufflet	134 Braviary
Klutz	033 Woobat	034 Swoobat	128 Golett	129 Golurk	

L

Ability	Pokémon that have this Ability				
Leaf Guard	047 Swadloon				
Levitate	108 Tynamo	109 Eelektrik	110 Eelektross	121 Cryogonal	141 Hydreigon
Light Metal	—				
Lightningrod	028 Blitzle	029 Zebstrika			
Limber	015 Purrloin	016 Liepard	124 Stunfisk		
Liquid Ooze	—				

M

Ability	Pokémon that have this Ability			
Magic Bounce	—			
Magic Guard	067 Sigilyph	083 Solosis	084 Duosion	085 Reuniclus
Magma Armor	—			
Magnet Pull	—			
Marvel Scale	—			
Minus	105 Klink	106 Klang	107 Klinklang	
Mold Breaker	116 Axew	117 Fraxure	118 Haxorus	
Moody	—			
Motor Drive	028 Blitzle	029 Zebstrika		
Moxie	057 Sandile	058 Krokorok	059 Krookodile	065 Scraggy	066 Scrafty
Multiscale	—			
Multitype	—			
Mummy	068 Yamask	069 Cofagrigus		

N

Ability	Pokémon that have this Ability
Natural Cure	—
No Guard	—
Normalize	—

O

Ability	Pokémon that have this Ability				
Oblivious	—				
Overcoat	083 Solosis	084 Duosion	085 Reuniclus	135 Vullaby	136 Mandibuzz
Overgrow	001 Snivy	002 Servine	003 Serperior		
Own Tempo	054 Petilil	055 Lilligant			

P

Ability	Pokémon that have this Ability			
Pickpocket	—			
Pickup	012 Lillipup			
Plus	105 Klink	106 Klang	107 Klinklang	
Poison Heal	—			
Poison Point	049 Venipede	050 Whirlipede	051 Scolipede	
Poison Touch	043 Seismitoad			
Prankster	052 Cottonee	053 Whimsicott	147 Tornadus	148 Thundurus
Pressure	152 Kyurem			
Pure Power	—			

Q

Ability	Pokémon that have this Ability
Quick Feet	—

R

Ability	Pokémon that have this Ability		
Rain Dish	—		
Rattled	—		
Reckless	056 Basculin	132 Bouffalant	
Regenerator	037 Audino	125 Mienfoo	126 Mienshao
Rivalry	116 Axew	117 Fraxure	118 Haxorus
Rock Head	—		
Rough Skin	127 Druddigon		
Run Away	010 Patrat		

S

Ability	Pokémon that have this Ability				
Sand Force	035 Drilbur	036 Excadrill	151 Landorus		
Sand Rush	013 Herdier	014 Stoutland	035 Drilbur	036 Excadrill	
Sand Stream	—				
Sand Veil	—				
Sap Sipper	091 Deerling	092 Sawsbuck	132 Bouffalant		
Scrappy	—				
Serene Grace	—				
Shadow Tag	—				
Shed Skin	065 Scraggy	066 Scrafty	094 Karrablast		
Sheer Force	038 Timburr	039 Gurdurr	040 Conkeldurr	061 Darmanitan	127 Druddigon	133 Rufflet
	134 Braviary				
Shell Armor	063 Dwebble	064 Crustle	095 Escavalier	122 Shelmet	
Shield Dust	—				
Simple	—				
Skill Link	—				
Slow Start	—				
Sniper	—				
Snow Cloak	119 Cubchoo	120 Beartic			
Snow Warning	—				
Solar Power	—				
Solid Rock	070 Tirtouga	071 Carracosta			
Soundproof	—				
Speed Boost	—				
Stall	—				
Static	093 Emolga	124 Stunfisk			
Steadfast	—				
Stench	074 Trubbish	075 Garbodor			
Sticky Hold	074 Trubbish	123 Accelgor			
Storm Drain	—				
Sturdy	030 Roggenrola	031 Boldore	032 Gigalith	045 Sawk	063 Dwebble	064 Crustle

Ability	Pokémon that have this Ability				
Sturdy	070 Tirtouga	071 Carracosta			
Suction Cups	—				
Super Luck	025 Pidove	026 Tranquill	027 Unfezant		
Swarm	046 Sewaddle	048 Leavanny	049 Venipede	050 Whirlipede	051 Scolipede	094 Karrablast
	095 Escavalier	138 Durant			
Swift Swim	041 Tympole	042 Palpitoad	043 Seismitoad		
Synchronize	023 Munna	024 Musharna	111 Elgyem	112 Beheeyem	

T

Ability	Pokémon that have this Ability			
Tangled Feet	—			
Technician	078 Minccino	079 Cinccino		
Telepathy	023 Munna	024 Musharna	111 Elgyem	112 Beheeyem
Teravolt	150 Zekrom			
Thick Fat	—			
Tinted Lens	—			
Torrent	007 Oshawott	008 Dewott	009 Samurott	
Toxic Boost	—			
Trace	—			
Truant	—			
Turboblaze	149 Reshiram			

U

Ability	Pokémon that have this Ability	
Unaware	033 Woobat	034 Swoobat
Unburden	015 Purrloin	016 Liepard
Unnerve	101 Joltik	102 Galvantula

V

Ability	Pokémon that have this Ability
Victory Star	000 Victini
Vital Spirit	012 Lillipup
Volt Absorb	—

W

Ability	Pokémon that have this Ability		
Water Absorb	062 Maractus	098 Frillish	099 Jellicent
Water Veil	—		
Weak Armor	075 Garbodor		
White Smoke	—		
Wonder Guard	—		
Wonder Skin	067 Sigilyph		

Z

Ability	Pokémon that have this Ability
Zen Mode	061 Darmanitan

How and Where to Meet Special Pokémon

Unova Pokédex No.	Pokémon		Level	Location	Item Needed	Conditions to appear
024	Musharna		50	Dreamyard Basement	—	Appears every Friday after you finish the main story
061	Darmanitan		35	Desert Resort	RageCandyBar	Use the RageCandyBar on a Pokémon statue. There are a total of five.
143	Volcarona		70	Relic Castle Lowest floor, deepest room	—	After finishing the main story
144	Cobalion		42	Mistralton Cave Guidance Chamber	—	The HMs Surf and Strength are needed
145	Terrakion		42	Victory Road Trial Chamber	—	If you've battled with Cobalion, you can enter the Trial Chamber.
146	Virizion		42	Pinwheel Forest Rumination Field	—	If you've battled with Cobalion, you can enter Rumination Field.
147	Tornadus		40	After you meet it on Route 7, it will start roaming the Unova region.	—	Only appears in *Pokémon Black Version*
148	Thundurus		40	After you meet it on Route 7, it will start roaming the Unova region.	—	Only appears in *Pokémon White Version*
149	Reshiram		50	N's Castle	Light Stone	Only appears in *Pokémon Black Version*
			50	Dragonspiral Tower	—	Only appears in *Pokémon Black Version* (Appears here for a rematch)
150	Zekrom		50	N's Castle	Dark Stone	Only appears in *Pokémon White Version*
			50	Dragonspiral Tower	—	Only appears in *Pokémon White Version* (Appears here for a rematch)
151	Landorus		70	Abundant Shrine	—	Put both Tornadus and Thundurus in your party. (You must have caught one of the two yourself)
152	Kyurem		75	Giant Chasm Cave's Deepest Part	—	—

Rematch	How to meet it again if you defeat it in battle	How to meet it again if you run from battle	How to meet it again if you lose the battle
Y	Reappears every Friday	Reappears every Friday	Return for a rematch after being returned to the Pokémon Center
None	Will not return	Will not return	Return for a rematch after being returned to the Pokémon Center
Y	Defeat the Elite Four and the Champion at the Pokémon League (comes back until you catch it)	Defeat the Elite Four and the Champion at the Pokémon League (comes back until you catch it)	Return for a rematch after being returned to the Pokémon Center
Y	Finish the main story, or defeat the Elite Four and the Champion at the Pokémon League (comes back until you catch it)	Finish the main story, or defeat the Elite Four and the Champion at the Pokémon League (comes back until you catch it)	Return for a rematch after being returned to the Pokémon Center
Y	Finish the main story, or defeat the Elite Four and the Champion at the Pokémon League (comes back until you catch it)	Finish the main story, or defeat the Elite Four and the Champion at the Pokémon League (comes back until you catch it)	Return for a rematch after being returned to the Pokémon Center
Y	Finish the main story, or defeat the Elite Four and the Champion at the Pokémon League (comes back until you catch it)	Finish the main story, or defeat the Elite Four and the Champion at the Pokémon League (comes back until you catch it)	Return for a rematch after being returned to the Pokémon Center
Y	Finish the main story, or defeat the Elite Four and the Champion at the Pokémon League (comes back until you catch it)	It moves to another location	Return for a rematch after being returned to the Pokémon Center
Y	Finish the main story, or defeat the Elite Four and the Champion at the Pokémon League (comes back until you catch it)	It moves to another location	Return for a rematch after being returned to the Pokémon Center
Y	You can battle with it again at that spot (if your party and Boxes are completely full, you can't have a rematch, and the story continues)	You can battle with it again at that spot (if your party and Boxes are completely full, you can't have a rematch, and the story continues)	Return for a rematch after being returned to the Pokémon Center
Y	Defeat the Elite Four and the Champion at the Pokémon League (comes back until you catch it)	Defeat the Elite Four and the Champion at the Pokémon League (comes back until you catch it)	Return for a rematch after being returned to the Pokémon Center
Y	You can battle with it again at that spot (if your party and Boxes are completely full, you can't have a rematch, and the story continues)	You can battle with it again at that spot (if your party and Boxes are completely full, you can't have a rematch, and the story continues)	Return for a rematch after being returned to the Pokémon Center
Y	Defeat the Elite Four and the Champion at the Pokémon League (comes back until you catch it)	Defeat the Elite Four and the Champion at the Pokémon League (comes back until you catch it)	Return for a rematch after being returned to the Pokémon Center
Y	Defeat the Elite Four and the Champion at the Pokémon League (comes back until you catch it)	Defeat the Elite Four and the Champion at the Pokémon League (comes back until you catch it)	Return for a rematch after being returned to the Pokémon Center
Y	Defeat the Elite Four and the Champion at the Pokémon League (comes back until you catch it)	Defeat the Elite Four and the Champion at the Pokémon League (comes back until you catch it)	Return for a rematch after being returned to the Pokémon Center

A

Pokémon	Unova	National	Type		Ability		Weak against these move types							Immune to these move types		
Abomasnow		460	GRS	ICE	Snow Warning		★FIR	FTG	PSN	FLY	BUG	RCK	STL			
Abra		63	PSY		Synchronize	Inner Focus	BUG	GHO	DRK							
Absol		359	DRK		Pressure	Super Luck	FTG	BUG						PSY		
Accelgor	123	617	BUG		Hydration	Sticky Hold	FIR	FLY	RCK							
Aerodactyl		142	RCK	FLY	Rock Head	Pressure	WTR	ELC	ICE	RCK	STL			GRD		
Aggron		306	STL	RCK	Sturdy	Rock Head	★FTG	★GRD	WTR					PSN		
Aipom		190	NRM		Run Away	Pickup	FTG							GHO		
Alakazam		65	PSY		Synchronize	Inner Focus	BUG	GHO	DRK							
Alomomola	100	594	WTR		Healer	Hydration	GRS	ELC								
Altaria		334	DRG	FLY	Natural Cure		★ICE	RCK	DRG					GRD		
Ambipom		424	NRM		Technician	Pickup	FTG							GHO		
Amoonguss	97	591	GRS	PSN	Effect Spore		FIR	ICE	FLY	PSY						
Ampharos		181	ELC		Static		GRD									
Anorith		347	RCK	BUG	Battle Armor		WTR	RCK	STL							
Arbok		24	PSN		Intimidate	Shed Skin	GRD	PSY								
Arcanine		59	FIR		Intimidate	Flash Fire	WTR	GRD	RCK					FIR*2		
Arceus		493	NRM		Multitype		FTG							GHO		
Arceus		493	FIR		Multitype		WTR	GRD	RCK							
Arceus		493	WTR		Multitype		GRS	ELC								
Arceus		493	GRS		Multitype		FIR	ICE	PSN	FLY	BUG					
Arceus		493	ELC		Multitype		GRD									
Arceus		493	ICE		Multitype		FIR	FTG	RCK	STL						
Arceus		493	FTG		Multitype		FLY	PSY								
Arceus		493	PSN		Multitype		GRD	PSY								
Arceus		493	GRD		Multitype		GRS	WTR	ICE					ELC		
Arceus		493	FLY		Multitype		ELC	ICE	RCK					GRD		
Arceus		493	PSY		Multitype		BUG	GHO	DRK							
Arceus		493	BUG		Multitype		FIR	FLY	RCK							
Arceus		493	RCK		Multitype		GRS	WTR	FTG	GRD	STL					
Arceus		493	GHO		Multitype		GHO	DRK						NRM	FTG	
Arceus		493	DRG		Multitype		ICE	DRG								
Arceus		493	DRK		Multitype		FTG	BUG						PSY		
Arceus		493	STL		Multitype		FIR	FTG	GRD					PSN		
Archen	72	566	RCK	FLY	Defeatist		WTR	ELC	ICE	RCK	STL			GRD		
Archeops	73	567	RCK	FLY	Defeatist		WTR	ELC	ICE	RCK	STL			GRD		
Ariados		168	BUG	PSN	Swarm	Insomnia	FIR	FLY	PSY	RCK						
Armaldo		348	RCK	BUG	Battle Armor		WTR	RCK	STL							
Aron		304	STL	RCK	Sturdy	Rock Head	★FTG	★GRD	WTR					PSN		
Articuno		144	ICE	FLY	Pressure		★RCK	FIR	ELC	STL				GRD		
Audino	37	531	NRM		Healer	Regenerator	FTG							GHO		
Axew	116	610	DRG		Rivalry	Mold Breaker	ICE	DRG								
Azelf		482	PSY		Levitate		BUG	GHO	DRK					GRD*1		
Azumarill		184	WTR		Thick Fat	Huge Power	GRS	ELC								
Azurill		298	NRM		Thick Fat	Huge Power	FTG							GHO		

B

Pokémon	Unova	National	Type		Ability		Weak against these move types							Immune to these move types		
Bagon		371	DRG		Rock Head		ICE	DRG								
Baltoy		343	GRD	PSY	Levitate		GRS	WTR	ICE	BUG	GHO	DRK		ELC	GRD*1	
Banette		354	GHO		Insomnia	Frisk	GHO	DRK						NRM	FTG	
Barboach		339	WTR	GRD	Oblivious	Anticipation	★GRS							ELC		
Basculin	56	550	WTR		Reckless	Adaptability	GRS	ELC								
Bastiodon		411	RCK	STL	Sturdy		★FTG	★GRD	WTR					PSN		
Bayleef		153	GRS		Overgrow		FIR	ICE	PSN	FLY	BUG					
Beartic	120	614	ICE		Snow Cloak		FIR	FTG	RCK	STL						
Beautifly		267	BUG	FLY	Swarm		★RCK	FIR	ELC	ICE	FLY			GRD		
Beedrill		15	BUG	PSN	Swarm		FIR	FLY	PSY	RCK						
Beheeyem	112	606	PSY		Telepathy	Synchronize	BUG	GHO	DRK							
Beldum		374	STL	PSY	Clear Body		FIR	GRD						PSN		
Bellossom		182	GRS		Chlorophyll		FIR	ICE	PSN	FLY	BUG					
Bellsprout		69	GRS	PSN	Chlorophyll		FIR	ICE	FLY	PSY						
Bibarel		400	NRM	WTR	Simple	Unaware	GRS	ELC	FTG					GHO		
Bidoof		399	NRM		Simple	Unaware	FTG							GHO		
Bisharp	131	625	DRK	STL	Defiant	Inner Focus	★FTG	FIR	GRD					PSN	PSY	
Blastoise		9	WTR		Torrent		GRS	ELC								

★ Deals 4 times damage.　　*1 Ability prevents damage.　　*2 May deal damage depending on the Pokémon's Ability.　　*3 Damage may be prevented depending on the Pokémon's Ability.

Pokémon	Unova	National	Type		Ability		Weak against these move types							Immune to these move types		
Blaziken		257	FIR	FTG	Blaze		WTR	GRD	FLY	PSY						
Blissey		242	NRM		Natural Cure	Serene Grace	FTG							GHO		
Blitzle	28	522	ELC		Lightningrod	Motor Drive	GRD							ELC *1		
Boldore	31	525	RCK		Sturdy		WTR	GRS	FTG	GRD	STL					
Bonsly		438	RCK		Sturdy	Rock Head	GRS	WTR	FTG	GRD	STL					
Bouffalant	132	626	NRM		Reckless	Sap Sipper	FTG							GHO	GRS *2	
Braviary	134	628	NRM	FLY	Keen Eye	Sheer Force	ELC	ICE	RCK					GRD	GHO	
Breloom		286	GRS	FTG	Effect Spore	Poison Heal	★ FLY	FIR	ICE	PSN	PSY					
Bronzong		437	STL	PSY	Levitate	Heatproof	FIR	GRD *3						PSN		
Bronzor		436	STL	PSY	Levitate	Heatproof	FIR	GRD *3						PSN		
Budew		406	GRS	PSN	Natural Cure	Poison Point	FIR	ICE	FLY	PSY						
Buizel		418	WTR		Swift Swim		GRS	ELC								
Bulbasaur		1	GRS	PSN	Overgrow		FIR	ICE	FLY	PSY						
Buneary		427	NRM		Run Away	Klutz	FTG							GHO		
Burmy		412	BUG		Shed Skin		FIR	FLY	RCK							
Butterfree		12	BUG	FLY	Compoundeyes		★ RCK	FIR	ELC	ICE	FLY			GRD		

◈ **C**

Pokémon	Unova	National	Type		Ability		Weak against these move types							Immune to these move types		
Cacnea		331	GRS		Sand Veil		FIR	ICE	PSN	FLY	BUG					
Cacturne		332	GRS	DRK	Sand Veil		★ BUG	FIR	ICE	FTG	PSN	FLY		PSY		
Camerupt		323	FIR	GRD	Magma Armor	Solid Rock	★ WTR	GRD						ELC		
Carnivine		455	GRS		Levitate		FIR	ICE	PSN	FLY	BUG			GRD *1		
Carracosta	71	565	WTR	RCK	Solid Rock	Sturdy	★ GRS	ELC	FTG	GRD						
Carvanha		318	WTR	DRK	Rough Skin		GRS	ELC	FTG	BUG				PSY		
Cascoon		268	BUG		Shed Skin		FIR	FLY	RCK							
Castform		351	NRM		Forecast		FTG							GHO		
Caterpie		10	BUG		Shield Dust		FIR	FLY	RCK							
Celebi		251	PSY	GRS	Natural Cure		★ BUG	FIR	ICE	PSN	FLY	GHO	DRK			
Chandelure	115	609	GHO	FIR	Flash Fire	Flame Body	WTR	GRD	RCK	GHO	DRK			NRM	FTG	FIR *2
Chansey		113	NRM		Natural Cure	Serene Grace	FTG							GHO		
Charizard		6	FIR	FLY	Blaze		★ RCK	WTR	ELC					GRD		
Charmander		4	FIR		Blaze		WTR	GRD	RCK							
Charmeleon		5	FIR		Blaze		WTR	GRD	RCK							
Chatot		441	NRM	FLY	Keen Eye	Tangled Feet	ELC	ICE	RCK					GRD	GHO	
Cherrim		421	GRS		Flower Gift		FIR	ICE	PSN	FLY	BUG					
Cherubi		420	GRS		Chlorophyll		FIR	ICE	PSN	FLY	BUG					
Chikorita		152	GRS		Overgrow		FIR	ICE	PSN	FLY	BUG					
Chimchar		390	FIR		Blaze		WTR	GRD	RCK							
Chimecho		358	PSY		Levitate		BUG	GHO	DRK					GRD *1		
Chinchou		170	WTR	ELC	Volt Absorb	Illuminate	GRS	GRD						ELC *2		
Chingling		433	PSY		Levitate		BUG	GHO	DRK					GRD *1		
Cinccino	79	573	NRM		Cute Charm	Technician	FTG							GHO		
Clamperl		366	WTR		Shell Armor		GRS	ELC								
Claydol		344	GRD	PSY	Levitate		GRS	WTR	ICE	BUG	GHO	DRK		ELC	GRD *1	
Clefable		36	NRM		Cute Charm	Magic Guard	FTG							GHO		
Clefairy		35	NRM		Cute Charm	Magic Guard	FTG							GHO		
Cleffa		173	NRM		Cute Charm	Magic Guard	FTG							GHO		
Cloyster		91	WTR	ICE	Shell Armor	Skill Link	GRS	ELC	FTG	RCK						
Cobalion	144	638	STL	FTG	Justified		FIR	FTG	GRD					PSN		
Cofagrigus	69	563	GHO		Mummy		GHO	DRK						NRM	FTG	
Combee		415	BUG	FLY	Honey Gather		★ RCK	FIR	ELC	ICE	FLY			GRD		
Combusken		256	FIR	FTG	Blaze		WTR	GRD	FLY	PSY						
Conkeldurr	40	534	FTG		Guts	Sheer Force	FLY	PSY								
Corphish		341	WTR		Hyper Cutter	Shell Armor	GRS	ELC								
Corsola		222	WTR	RCK	Hustle	Natural Cure	★ GRS	ELC	FTG	GRD						
Cottonee	52	546	GRS		Prankster	Infiltrator	FIR	ICE	PSN	FLY	BUG					
Cradily		346	RCK	GRS	Suction Cups		ICE	FTG	BUG	STL						
Cranidos		408	RCK		Mold Breaker		GRS	WTR	FTG	GRD	STL					
Crawdaunt		342	WTR	DRK	Hyper Cutter	Shell Armor	GRS	ELC	FTG	BUG				PSY		
Cresselia		488	PSY		Levitate		BUG	GHO	DRK					GRD *1		
Croagunk		453	PSN	FTG	Anticipation	Dry Skin	★ PSY	GRD	FLY					WTR *2		
Crobat		169	PSN	FLY	Inner Focus		ELC	ICE	PSY	RCK				GRD		
Croconaw		159	WTR		Torrent		GRS	ELC								
Crustle	64	558	BUG	RCK	Sturdy	Shell Armor	WTR	RCK	STL							

◇ **C**

Pokémon	Unova	National	Type		Ability			Weak against these move types							Immune to these move types		
Cryogonal	121	615	ICE		Levitate			FIR	FTG	RCK	STL				GRD *1		
Cubchoo	119	613	ICE		Snow Cloak			FIR	FTG	RCK	STL						
Cubone		104	GRD		Rock Head	Lightningrod		GRS	WTR	ICE					ELC		
Cyndaquil		155	FIR		Blaze			WTR	GRD	RCK							

◇ **D**

Pokémon	Unova	National	Type		Ability			Weak against these move types							Immune to these move types		
Darkrai		491	DRK		Bad Dreams			FTG	BUG						PSY		
Darmanitan Standard Mode	61	555	FIR		Sheer Force		Zen Mode	WTR	GRD	RCK							
Darmanitan Zen Mode	61	555	FIR	PSY	Sheer Force		Zen Mode	WTR	GRD	RCK	GHO	DRK					
Darumaka	60	554	FIR		Hustle		Inner Focus	WTR	GRD	RCK							
Deerling	91	585	NRM	GRS	Chlorophyll	Sap Sipper		FIR	ICE	FTG	PSN	FLY	BUG		GHO	GRS *2	
Deino	139	633	DRK	DRG	Hustle			ICE	FTG	BUG	DRG				PSY		
Delcatty		301	NRM		Cute Charm	Normalize		FTG							GHO		
Delibird		225	ICE	FLY	Vital Spirit	Hustle		★ RCK	FIR	ELC	STL				GRD		
Deoxys		386	PSY		Pressure			BUG	GHO	DRK							
Dewgong		87	WTR	ICE	Thick Fat	Hydration		GRS	ELC	FTG	RCK						
Dewott	8	502	WTR		Torrent			GRS	ELC								
Dialga		483	STL	DRG	Pressure			FTG	GRD						PSN		
Diglett		50	GRD		Sand Veil	Arena Trap		GRS	WTR	ICE					ELC		
Ditto		132	NRM		Limber			FTG							GHO		
Dodrio		85	NRM	FLY	Run Away	Early Bird		ELC	ICE	RCK					GRD	GHO	
Doduo		84	NRM	FLY	Run Away	Early Bird		ELC	ICE	RCK					GRD	GHO	
Donphan		232	GRD		Sturdy			GRS	WTR	ICE					ELC		
Dragonair		148	DRG		Shed Skin			ICE	DRG								
Dragonite		149	DRG	FLY	Inner Focus			★ ICE	RCK	DRG					GRD		
Drapion		452	PSN	DRK	Battle Armor	Sniper		GRD							PSY		
Dratini		147	DRG		Shed Skin			ICE	DRG								
Drifblim		426	GHO	FLY	Aftermath	Unburden		ELC	ICE	RCK	GHO	DRK			NRM	FTG	GRD
Drifloon		425	GHO	FLY	Aftermath	Unburden		ELC	ICE	RCK	GHO	DRK			NRM	FTG	GRD
Drilbur	35	529	GRD		Sand Rush	Sand Force		WTR	GRS	ICE					ELC		
Drowzee		96	PSY		Insomnia	Forewarn		BUG	GHO	DRK							
Druddigon	127	621	DRG		Rough Skin	Sheer Force		ICE	DRG								
Ducklett	86	580	WTR	FLY	Keen Eye	Big Pecks		★ ELC	RCK						GRD		
Dugtrio		51	GRD		Sand Veil	Arena Trap		GRS	WTR	ICE					ELC		
Dunsparce		206	NRM		Serene Grace	Run Away		FTG							GHO		
Duosion	84	578	PSY		Overcoat	Magic Guard		BUG	GHO	DRK							
Durant	138	632	BUG	STL	Swarm	Hustle		★ FIR							PSN		
Dusclops		356	GHO		Pressure			GHO	DRK						NRM	FTG	
Dusknoir		477	GHO		Pressure			GHO	DRK						NRM	FTG	
Duskull		355	GHO		Levitate			GHO	DRK						NRM	FTG	GRD *1
Dustox		269	BUG	PSN	Shield Dust			FIR	FLY	PSY	RCK						
Dwebble	63	557	BUG	RCK	Sturdy	Shell Armor		WTR	RCK	STL							

◇ **E**

Pokémon	Unova	National	Type		Ability			Weak against these move types							Immune to these move types		
Eelektrik	109	603	ELC		Levitate										GRD *1		
Eelektross	110	604	ELC		Levitate										GRD *1		
Eevee		133	NRM		Run Away	Adaptability		FTG							GHO		
Ekans		23	PSN		Intimidate	Shed Skin		GRD	PSY								
Electabuzz		125	ELC		Static			GRD									
Electivire		466	ELC		Motor Drive			GRD							ELC *1		
Electrike		309	ELC		Static	Lightningrod		GRD							ELC *2		
Electrode		101	ELC		Soundproof	Static		GRD									
Elekid		239	ELC		Static			GRD									
Elgyem	111	605	PSY		Telepathy	Synchronize		BUG	GHO	DRK							
Emboar	6	500	FIR	FTG	Blaze			WTR	GRD	FLY	PSY						
Emolga	93	587	ELC	FLY	Static			ICE	RCK						GRD		
Empoleon		395	WTR	STL	Torrent			ELC	FTG	GRD					PSN		
Entei		244	FIR		Pressure			WTR	GRD	RCK							
Escavalier	95	589	BUG	STL	Swarm	Shell Armor		★ FIR							PSN		
Espeon		196	PSY		Synchronize			BUG	GHO	DRK							
Excadrill	36	530	GRD	STL	Sand Rush	Sand Force		FIR	WTR	FTG	GRD				ELC	PSN	
Exeggcute		102	GRS	PSY	Chlorophyll			★ BUG	FIR	ICE	PSN	FLY	GHO	DRK			

★ Deals 4 times damage.　　*1 Ability prevents damage.　　*2 May deal damage depending on the Pokémon's Ability.　　*3 Damage may be prevented depending on the Pokémon's Ability.

Pokémon	Unova	National	Type		Ability		Weak against these move types							Immune to these move types		
Exeggutor		103	GRS	PSY	Chlorophyll		★BUG	FIR	ICE	PSN	FLY	GHO	DRK			
Exploud		295	NRM		Soundproof		FTG							GHO		

F

Pokémon	Unova	National	Type		Ability		Weak against these move types						Immune to these move types		
Farfetch'd		83	NRM	FLY	Keen Eye	Inner Focus	ELC	ICE	RCK				GRD	GHO	
Fearow		22	NRM	FLY	Keen Eye		ELC	ICE	RCK				GRD	GHO	
Feebas		349	WTR		Swift Swim		GRS	ELC							
Feraligatr		160	WTR		Torrent		GRS	ELC							
Ferroseed	103	597	GRS	STL	Iron Barbs		★FIR	FTG					PSN		
Ferrothorn	104	598	GRS	STL	Iron Barbs		★FIR	FTG					PSN		
Finneon		456	WTR		Swift Swim	Storm Drain	GRS	ELC					WTR *2		
Flaaffy		180	ELC		Static		GRD								
Flareon		136	FIR		Flash Fire		WTR	GRD	RCK				FIR *1		
Floatzel		419	WTR		Swift Swim		GRS	ELC							
Flygon		330	GRD	DRG	Levitate		★ICE	DRG					ELC	GRD *1	
Foongus	96	590	GRS	PSY	Effect Spore		FIR	ICE	FLY	PSY					
Forretress		205	BUG	STL	Sturdy		★FIR						PSN		
Fraxure	117	611	DRG		Rivalry	Mold Breaker	ICE	DRG							
Frillish	98	592	WTR	GHO	Water Absorb	Cursed Body	GRS	ELC	GHO	DRK			NRM	FTG	WTR *2
Froslass		478	ICE	GHO	Snow Cloak		FIR	RCK	GHO	DRK	STL		NRM	FTG	
Furret		162	NRM		Run Away	Keen Eye	FTG						GHO		

G

Pokémon	Unova	National	Type		Ability		Weak against these move types						Immune to these move types		
Gabite		444	DRG	GRD	Sand Veil		★ICE	DRG					ELC		
Gallade		475	PSY	FTG	Steadfast		FLY	GHO							
Galvantula	102	596	BUG	ELC	Compoundeyes	Unnerve	FIR	RCK							
Garbodor	75	569	PSN		Stench	Weak Armor	GRD	PSY							
Garchomp		445	DRG	GRD	Sand Veil		★ICE	DRG					ELC		
Gardevoir		282	PSY		Synchronize	Trace	BUG	GHO	DRK						
Gastly		92	GHO	PSN	Levitate		PSY	GHO	DRK				NRM	FTG	GRD *1
Gastrodon		423	WTR	GRD	Sticky Hold	Storm Drain	★GRS						ELC	WTR *2	
Gengar		94	GHO	PSN	Levitate		PSY	GHO	DRK				NRM	FTG	GRD *1
Geodude		74	RCK	GRD	Rock Head	Sturdy	★GRS	★WTR	ICE	FTG	GRD	STL	ELC		
Gible		443	DRG	GRD	Sand Veil		★ICE	DRG					ELC		
Gigalith	32	526	RCK		Sturdy		WTR	GRS	FTG	GRD	STL				
Girafarig		203	NRM	PSY	Inner Focus	Early Bird	BUG	DRK					GHO		
Giratina (Altered Forme)		487	GHO	DRG	Pressure		ICE	GHO	DRG	DRK			NRM	FTG	
Giratina (Origin Forme)		487	GHO	DRG	Levitate		ICE	GHO	DRG	DRK			NRM	FTG	GRD *1
Glaceon		471	ICE		Snow Cloak		FIR	FTG	RCK	STL					
Glalie		362	ICE		Inner Focus	Ice Body	FIR	FTG	RCK	STL					
Glameow		431	NRM		Limber	Own Tempo	FTG						GHO		
Gligar		207	GRD	FLY	Hyper Cutter	Sand Veil	★ICE	WTR					ELC	GRD	
Gliscor		472	GRD	FLY	Hyper Cutter	Sand Veil	★ICE	WTR					ELC	GRD	
Gloom		44	GRS	PSN	Chlorophyll		FIR	ICE	FLY	PSY					
Golbat		42	PSN	FLY	Inner Focus		ELC	ICE	PSY	RCK			GRD		
Goldeen		118	WTR		Swift Swim	Water Veil	GRS	ELC							
Golduck		55	WTR		Damp	Cloud Nine	GRS	ELC							
Golem		76	RCK	GRD	Rock Head	Sturdy	★GRS	★WTR	ICE	FTG	GRD	STL	ELC		
Golett	128	622	GRD	GHO	Iron Fist	Klutz	WTR	GRS	ICE	GHO	DRK		NRM	ELC	FTG
Golurk	129	623	GRD	GHO	Iron Fist	Klutz	WTR	GRS	ICE	GHO	DRK		NRM	ELC	FTG
Gorebyss		368	WTR		Swift Swim		GRS	ELC							
Gothita	80	574	PSY		Frisk		BUG	GHO	DRK						
Gothitelle	82	576	PSY		Frisk		BUG	GHO	DRK						
Gothorita	81	575	PSY		Frisk		BUG	GHO	DRK						
Granbull		210	NRM		Intimidate	Quick Feet	FTG						GHO		
Graveler		75	RCK	GRD	Rock Head	Sturdy	★GRS	★WTR	ICE	FTG	GRD	STL	ELC		
Grimer		88	PSN		Stench	Sticky Hold	GRD	PSY							
Grotle		388	GRS		Overgrow		FIR	ICE	PSN	FLY	BUG				
Groudon		383	GRD		Drought		GRS	WTR	ICE				ELC		
Grovyle		253	GRS		Overgrow		FIR	ICE	PSN	FLY	BUG				
Growlithe		58	FIR		Intimidate	Flash Fire	WTR	GRD	RCK				FIR *2		
Grumpig		326	PSY		Thick Fat	Own Tempo	BUG	GHO	DRK						

G

Pokémon	Unova	National	Type		Ability		Weak against these move types						Immune to these move types		
Gulpin		316	PSN		Liquid Ooze	Sticky Hold	GRD	PSY							
Gurdurr	39	533	FTG		Guts	Sheer Force	FLY	PSY							
Gyarados		130	WTR	FLY	Intimidate		★ELC	RCK					GRD		

H

Pokémon	Unova	National	Type		Ability		Weak against these move types						Immune to these move types		
Happiny		440	NRM		Natural Cure	Serene Grace	FTG						GHO		
Hariyama		297	FTG		Thick Fat	Guts	FLY	PSY							
Haunter		93	GHO	PSN	Levitate		PSY	GHO	DRK				NRM	FTG	GRD *1
Haxorus	118	612	DRG		Rivalry	Mold Breaker	ICE	DRG							
Heatmor	137	631	FIR		Gluttony	Flash Fire	WTR	GRD	RCK				FIR *2		
Heatran		485	FIR	STL	Flash Fire		★GRD	WTR	FTG				PSN	FIR *1	
Heracross		214	BUG	FTG	Swarm	Guts	★FLY	FIR	PSY						
Herdier	13	507	NRM		Intimidate	Sand Rush	FTG						GHO		
Hippopotas		449	GRD		Sand Stream		GRS	WTR	ICE				ELC		
Hippowdon		450	GRD		Sand Stream		GRS	WTR	ICE				ELC		
Hitmonchan		107	FTG		Keen Eye	Iron Fist	FLY	PSY							
Hitmonlee		106	FTG		Limber	Reckless	FLY	PSY							
Hitmontop		237	FTG		Intimidate	Technician	FLY	PSY							
Honchkrow		430	DRK	FLY	Insomnia	Super Luck	ELC	ICE	RCK				GRD	PSY	
Ho-Oh		250	FIR	FLY	Pressure		★RCK	WTR	ELC				GRD		
Hoothoot		163	NRM	FLY	Insomnia	Keen Eye	ELC	ICE	RCK				GRD	GHO	
Hoppip		187	GRS	FLY	Chlorophyll	Leaf Guard	★ICE	FIR	PSN	FLY	RCK		GRD		
Horsea		116	WTR		Swift Swim	Sniper	GRS	ELC							
Houndoom		229	DRK	FIR	Early Bird	Flash Fire	WTR	FTG	GRD	RCK			PSY	FIR *2	
Houndour		228	DRK	FIR	Early Bird	Flash Fire	WTR	FTG	GRD	RCK			PSY	FIR *2	
Huntail		367	WTR		Swift Swim		GRS	ELC							
Hydreigon	141	635	DRK	DRG	Levitate		ICE	FTG	BUG	DRG			PSY	GRD *1	
Hypno		97	PSY		Insomnia	Forewarn	BUG	GHO	DRK						

I

Pokémon	Unova	National	Type		Ability		Weak against these move types						Immune to these move types		
Igglybuff		174	NRM		Cute Charm		FTG						GHO		
Illumise		314	BUG		Oblivious	Tinted Lens	FIR	FLY	RCK						
Infernape		392	FIR	FTG	Blaze		WTR	GRD	FLY	PSY					
Ivysaur		2	GRS	PSN	Overgrow		FIR	ICE	FLY	PSY					

J

Pokémon	Unova	National	Type		Ability		Weak against these move types						Immune to these move types		
Jellicent	99	593	WTR	GHO	Water Absorb	Cursed Body	GRS	ELC	GHO	DRK			NRM	FTG	WTR *2
Jigglypuff		39	NRM		Cute Charm		FTG						GHO		
Jirachi		385	STL	PSY	Serene Grace		FIR	GRD					PSN		
Jolteon		135	ELC		Volt Absorb		GRD						ELC *1		
Joltik	101	595	BUG	ELC	Compoundeyes	Unnerve	FIR	RCK							
Jumpluff		189	GRS	FLY	Chlorophyll	Leaf Guard	★ICE	FIR	PSN	FLY	RCK		GRD		
Jynx		124	ICE	PSY	Oblivious	Forewarn	FIR	BUG	RCK	GHO	DRK	STL			

K

Pokémon	Unova	National	Type		Ability		Weak against these move types						Immune to these move types		
Kabuto		140	RCK	WTR	Swift Swim	Battle Armor	★GRS	ELC	FTG	GRD					
Kabutops		141	RCK	WTR	Swift Swim	Battle Armor	★GRS	ELC	FTG	GRD					
Kadabra		64	PSY		Synchronize	Inner Focus	BUG	GHO	DRK						
Kakuna		14	BUG	PSN	Shed Skin		FIR	FLY	PSY	RCK					
Kangaskhan		115	NRM		Early Bird	Scrappy	FTG						GHO		
Karrablast	94	588	BUG		Swarm	Shed Skin	FIR	FLY	RCK						
Kecleon		352	NRM		Color Change		FTG						GHO		
Kingdra		230	WTR	DRG	Swift Swim	Sniper	DRG								
Kingler		99	WTR		Hyper Cutter	Shell Armor	GRS	ELC							
Kirlia		281	PSY		Synchronize	Trace	BUG	GHO	DRK						
Klang	106	600	STL		Plus	Minus	FIR	FTG	GRD				PSN		
Klink	105	599	STL		Plus	Minus	FIR	FTG	GRD				PSN		
Klinklang	107	601	STL		Plus	Minus	FIR	FTG	GRD				PSN		
Koffing		109	PSN		Levitate		PSY						GRD *1		
Krabby		98	WTR		Hyper Cutter	Shell Armor	GRS	ELC							
Kricketot		401	BUG		Shed Skin		FIR	FLY	RCK						

★ Deals 4 times damage. *1 Ability prevents damage. *2 May deal damage depending on the Pokémon's Ability. *3 Damage may be prevented depending on the Pokémon's Ability.

Pokémon	Unova	National	Type		Ability		Weak against these move types							Immune to these move types		
Kricketune		402	BUG		Swarm		FIR	FLY	RCK							
Krokorok	58	552	GRD	DRK	Intimidate	Moxie	WTR	GRS	ICE	FTG	BUG			ELC	PSY	
Krookodile	59	553	GRD	DRK	Intimidate	Moxie	WTR	GRS	ICE	FTG	BUG			ELC	PSY	
Kyogre		382	WTR		Drizzle		GRS	ELC								
Kyurem	152	646	DRG	ICE	Pressure		FTG	RCK	DRG	STL						

L

Pokémon	Unova	National	Type		Ability		Weak against these move types							Immune to these move types		
Lairon		305	STL	RCK	Sturdy	Rock Head	★FTG	★GRD	WTR					PSN		
Lampent	114	608	GHO	FIR	Flash Fire	Flame Body	WTR	GRD	RCK	GHO	DRK			NRM	FTG	FIR*2
Landorus	151	645	GRD	FLY	Sand Force		★ICE	WTR						ELC	GRD	
Lanturn		171	WTR	ELC	Volt Absorb	Illuminate	GRS	GRD						ELC*2		
Lapras		131	WTR	ICE	Water Absorb	Shell Armor	GRS	ELC	FTG	RCK				WTR*2		
Larvesta	142	636	BUG	FIR	Flame Body		★RCK	WTR	FLY							
Larvitar		246	RCK	GRD	Guts		★GRS	★WTR	ICE	FTG	GRD	STL		ELC		
Latias		380	DRG	PSY	Levitate		ICE	BUG	GHO	DRG	DRK			GRD*1		
Latios		381	DRG	PSY	Levitate		ICE	BUG	GHO	DRG	DRK			GRD*1		
Leafeon		470	GRS		Leaf Guard		FIR	ICE	PSN	FLY	BUG					
Leavanny	48	542	BUG	GRS	Swarm	Chlorophyll	★FIR	★FLY	ICE	PSN	BUG	RCK				
Ledian		166	BUG	FLY	Swarm	Early Bird	★RCK	FIR	ELC	ICE	FLY			GRD		
Ledyba		165	BUG	FLY	Swarm	Early Bird	★RCK	FIR	ELC	ICE	FLY			GRD		
Lickilicky		463	NRM		Own Tempo	Oblivious	FTG							GHO		
Lickitung		108	NRM		Own Tempo	Oblivious	FTG							GHO		
Liepard	16	510	DRK		Limber	Unburden	FTG	BUG						PSY		
Lileep		345	RCK	GRS	Suction Cups		ICE	FTG	BUG	STL						
Lilligant	55	549	GRS		Chlorophyll	Own Tempo	FIR	ICE	PSN	FLY	BUG					
Lillipup	12	506	NRM		Vital Spirit	Pickup	FTG							GHO		
Linoone		264	NRM		Pickup	Gluttony	FTG							GHO		
Litwick	113	607	GHO	FIR	Flash Fire	Flame Body	WTR	GRD	RCK	GHO	DRK			NRM	FTG	FIR*2
Lombre		271	WTR	GRS	Swift Swim	Rain Dish	PSN	FLY	BUG							
Lopunny		428	NRM		Cute Charm	Klutz	FTG							GHO		
Lotad		270	WTR	GRS	Swift Swim	Rain Dish	PSN	FLY	BUG							
Loudred		294	NRM		Soundproof		FTG							GHO		
Lucario		448	FTG	STL	Steadfast	Inner Focus	FIR	FTG	GRD					PSN		
Ludicolo		272	WTR	GRS	Swift Swim	Rain Dish	PSN	FLY	BUG							
Lugia		249	PSY	FLY	Pressure		ELC	ICE	RCK	GHO	DRK			GRD		
Lumineon		457	WTR		Swift Swim	Storm Drain	GRS	ELC						WTR*2		
Lunatone		337	RCK	PSY	Levitate		GRS	WTR	BUG	GHO	DRK	STL		GRD*1		
Luvdisc		370	WTR		Swift Swim		GRS	ELC								
Luxio		404	ELC		Rivalry	Intimidate	GRD									
Luxray		405	ELC		Rivalry	Intimidate	GRD									

M

Pokémon	Unova	National	Type		Ability		Weak against these move types							Immune to these move types		
Machamp		68	FTG		Guts	No Guard	FLY	PSY								
Machoke		67	FTG		Guts	No Guard	FLY	PSY								
Machop		66	FTG		Guts	No Guard	FLY	PSY								
Magby		240	FIR		Flame Body		WTR	GRD	RCK							
Magcargo		219	FIR	RCK	Magma Armor	Flame Body	★WTR	★GRD	FTG	RCK						
Magikarp		129	WTR		Swift Swim		GRS	ELC								
Magmar		126	FIR		Flame Body		WTR	GRD	RCK							
Magmortar		467	FIR		Flame Body		WTR	GRD	RCK							
Magnemite		81	ELC	STL	Magnet Pull	Sturdy	★GRD	FIR	FTG					PSN		
Magneton		82	ELC	STL	Magnet Pull	Sturdy	★GRD	FIR	FTG					PSN		
Magnezone		462	ELC	STL	Magnet Pull	Sturdy	★GRD	FIR	FTG					PSN		
Makuhita		296	FTG		Thick Fat	Guts	FLY	PSY								
Mamoswine		473	ICE	GRD	Oblivious	Snow Cloak	GRS	FIR	WTR	FTG	STL			ELC		
Manaphy		490	WTR		Hydration		GRS	ELC								
Mandibuzz	136	630	DRK	FLY	Big Pecks	Overcoat	ELC	ICE	RCK					GRD	PSY	
Manectric		310	ELC		Static	Lightningrod	GRD							ELC*2		
Mankey		56	FTG		Vital Spirit	Anger Point	FLY	PSY								
Mantine		226	WTR	FLY	Swift Swim	Water Absorb	★ELC	RCK						GRD	WTR*2	
Mantyke		458	WTR	FLY	Swift Swim	Water Absorb	★ELC	RCK						GRD	WTR*2	
Maractus	62	556	GRS		Water Absorb	Chlorophyll	FIR	ICE	PSN	FLY	BUG			WTR*2		
Mareep		179	ELC		Static		GRD									

◀ M

Pokémon	Unova	National	Type		Ability			Weak against these move types						Immune to these move types		
Marill		183	WTR		Thick Fat	Huge Power		GRS	ELC							
Marowak		105	GRD		Rock Head	Lightningrod		GRS	WTR	ICE				ELC		
Marshtomp		259	WTR	GRD	Torrent			★ GRS						ELC		
Masquerain		284	BUG	FLY	Intimidate			★ RCK	FIR	ELC	ICE	FLY		GRD		
Mawile		303	STL		Hyper Cutter	Intimidate		FIR	FTG	GRD				PSN		
Medicham		308	FTG	PSY	Pure Power			FLY	GHO							
Meditite		307	FTG	PSY	Pure Power			FLY	GHO							
Meganium		154	GRS		Overgrow			FIR	ICE	PSN	FLY	BUG				
Meowth		52	NRM		Pickup	Technician		FTG						GHO		
Mesprit		481	PSY		Levitate			BUG	GHO	DRK				GRD*1		
Metagross		376	STL	PSY	Clear Body			FIR	GRD					PSN		
Metang		375	STL	PSY	Clear Body			FIR	GRD					PSN		
Metapod		11	BUG		Shed Skin			FIR	FLY	RCK						
Mew		151	PSY		Synchronize			BUG	GHO	DRK						
Mewtwo		150	PSY		Pressure			BUG	GHO	DRK						
Mienfoo	125	619	FTG		Inner Focus	Regenerator		FLY	PSY							
Mienshao	126	620	FTG		Inner Focus	Regenerator		FLY	PSY							
Mightyena		262	DRK		Intimidate	Quick Feet		FTG	BUG					PSY		
Milotic		350	WTR		Marvel Scale			GRS	ELC							
Miltank		241	NRM		Thick Fat	Scrappy		FTG						GHO		
Mime Jr.		439	PSY		Soundproof	Filter		BUG	GHO	DRK						
Minccino	78	572	NRM		Cute Charm	Technician		FTG						GHO		
Minun		312	ELC		Minus			GRD								
Misdreavus		200	GHO		Levitate			GHO	DRK					NRM	FTG	GRD *1
Mismagius		429	GHO		Levitate			GHO	DRK					NRM	FTG	GRD *1
Moltres		146	FIR	FLY	Pressure			★ RCK	WTR	ELC				GRD		
Monferno		391	FIR	FTG	Blaze			WTR	GRD	FLY	PSY					
Mothim		414	BUG	FLY	Swarm			★ RCK	FIR	ELC	ICE	FLY		GRD		
Mr. Mime		122	PSY		Soundproof	Filter		BUG	GHO	DRK						
Mudkip		258	WTR		Torrent			GRS	ELC							
Muk		89	PSN		Stench	Sticky Hold		GRD	PSY							
Munchlax		446	NRM		Pickup	Thick Fat		FTG						GHO		
Munna	23	517	PSY		Forewarn	Synchronize	Telepathy	BUG	GHO	DRK						
Murkrow		198	DRK	FLY	Insomnia	Super Luck		ELC	ICE	RCK				GRD	PSY	
Musharna	24	518	PSY		Forewarn	Synchronize	Telepathy	BUG	GHO	DRK						

◀ N

Pokémon	Unova	National	Type		Ability			Weak against these move types						Immune to these move types		
Natu		177	PSY	FLY	Synchronize	Early Bird		ELC	ICE	RCK	GHO	DRK		GRD		
Nidoking		34	PSN	GRD	Poison Point	Rivalry		WTR	ICE	GRD	PSY			ELC		
Nidoqueen		31	PSN	GRD	Poison Point	Rivalry		WTR	ICE	GRD	PSY			ELC		
Nidoran ♀		29	PSN		Poison Point	Rivalry		GRD	PSY							
Nidoran ♂		32	PSN		Poison Point	Rivalry		GRD	PSY							
Nidorina		30	PSN		Poison Point	Rivalry		GRD	PSY							
Nidorino		33	PSN		Poison Point	Rivalry		GRD	PSY							
Nincada		290	BUG	GRD	Compoundeyes			FIR	WTR	ICE	FLY			ELC		
Ninetales		38	FIR		Flash Fire			WTR	GRD	RCK				FIR *1		
Ninjask		291	BUG	FLY	Speed Boost			★ RCK	FIR	ELC	ICE	FLY		GRD		
Noctowl		164	NRM	FLY	Insomnia	Keen Eye		ELC	ICE	RCK				GRD	GHO	
Nosepass		299	RCK		Sturdy	Magnet Pull		GRS	WTR	FTG	GRD	STL				
Numel		322	FIR	GRD	Oblivious	Simple		★ WTR	GRD					ELC		
Nuzleaf		274	GRS	DRK	Chlorophyll	Early Bird		★ BUG	FIR	ICE	FTG	PSN	FLY	PSY		

◀ O

Pokémon	Unova	National	Type		Ability			Weak against these move types						Immune to these move types		
Octillery		224	WTR		Suction Cups	Sniper		GRS	ELC							
Oddish		43	GRS	PSN	Chlorophyll			FIR	ICE	FLY	PSY					
Omanyte		138	RCK	WTR	Swift Swim	Shell Armor		★ GRS	ELC	FTG	GRD					
Omastar		139	RCK	WTR	Swift Swim	Shell Armor		★ GRS	ELC	FTG	GRD					
Onix		95	RCK	GRD	Rock Head	Sturdy		★ GRS	★ WTR	ICE	FTG	GRD	STL	ELC		
Oshawott	7	501	WTR		Torrent			GRS	ELC							

★ Deals 4 times damage.   *1 Ability prevents damage.   *2 May deal damage depending on the Pokémon's Ability.   *3 Damage may be prevented depending on the Pokémon's Ability.

P

Pokémon	Unova	National	Type		Ability		Weak against these move types					Immune to these move types	
Pachirisu		417	ELC		Run Away	Pickup	GRD						
Palkia		484	WTR	DRG	Pressure		DRG						
Palpitoad	42	536	WTR	GRD	Swift Swim	Hydration	★GRS					ELC	
Panpour	21	515	WTR		Gluttony		GRS	ELC					
Pansage	17	511	GRS		Gluttony		FIR	ICE	PSN	FLY	BUG		
Pansear	19	513	FIR		Gluttony		WTR	GRD	RCK				
Paras		46	BUG	GRS	Effect Spore	Dry Skin	★FIR	★FLY	ICE	PSN	BUG	RCK	WTR*2	
Parasect		47	BUG	GRS	Effect Spore	Dry Skin	★FIR	★FLY	ICE	PSN	BUG	RCK	WTR*2	
Patrat	10	504	NRM		Run Away	Keen Eye	FTG					GHO	
Pawniard	130	624	DRK	STL	Defiant	Inner Focus	★FTG	FIR	GRD			PSN	PSY
Pelipper		279	WTR	FLY	Keen Eye		★ELC	RCK				GRD	
Persian		53	NRM		Limber	Technician	FTG					GHO	
Petilil	54	548	GRS		Chlorophyll	Own Tempo	FIR	ICE	PSN	FLY	BUG		
Phanpy		231	GRD		Pickup		GRS	WTR	ICE			ELC	
Phione		489	WTR		Hydration		GRS	ELC					
Pichu		172	ELC		Static		GRD						
Pidgeot		18	NRM	FLY	Keen Eye	Tangled Feet	ELC	ICE	RCK			GRD	GHO
Pidgeotto		17	NRM	FLY	Keen Eye	Tangled Feet	ELC	ICE	RCK			GRD	GHO
Pidgey		16	NRM	FLY	Keen Eye	Tangled Feet	ELC	ICE	RCK			GRD	GHO
Pidove	25	519	NRM	FLY	Big Pecks	Super Luck	ELC	ICE	RCK			GRD	GHO
Pignite	5	499	FIR	FTG	Blaze		WTR	GRD	FLY	PSY			
Pikachu		25	ELC		Static		GRD						
Piloswine		221	ICE	GRD	Oblivious	Snow Cloak	GRS	FIR	WTR	FTG	STL	ELC	
Pineco		204	BUG		Sturdy		FIR	FLY	RCK				
Pinsir		127	BUG		Hyper Cutter	Mold Breaker	FIR	FLY	RCK				
Piplup		393	WTR		Torrent		GRS	ELC					
Plusle		311	ELC		Plus		GRD						
Politoed		186	WTR		Water Absorb	Damp	GRS	ELC				WTR*2	
Poliwag		60	WTR		Water Absorb	Damp	GRS	ELC				WTR*2	
Poliwhirl		61	WTR		Water Absorb	Damp	GRS	ELC				WTR*2	
Poliwrath		62	WTR	FTG	Water Absorb	Damp	GRS	ELC	FLY	PSY		WTR*2	
Ponyta		77	FIR		Run Away	Flash Fire	WTR	GRD	RCK			FIR*2	
Poochyena		261	DRK		Run Away	Quick Feet	FTG	BUG				PSY	
Porygon		137	NRM		Trace	Download	FTG					GHO	
Porygon2		233	NRM		Trace	Download	FTG					GHO	
Porygon-Z		474	NRM		Adaptability	Download	FTG					GHO	
Primeape		57	FTG		Vital Spirit	Anger Point	FLY	PSY					
Prinplup		394	WTR		Torrent		GRS	ELC					
Probopass		476	RCK	STL	Sturdy	Magnet Pull	★FTG	★GRD	WTR			PSN	
Psyduck		54	WTR		Damp	Cloud Nine	GRS	ELC					
Pupitar		247	RCK	GRD	Shed Skin		★GRS	★WTR	ICE	FTG	GRD	STL	ELC
Purrloin	15	509	DRK		Limber	Unburden	FTG	BUG				PSY	
Purugly		432	NRM		Thick Fat	Own Tempo	FTG					GHO	

Q

Pokémon	Unova	National	Type		Ability		Weak against these move types				Immune to these move types	
Quagsire		195	WTR	GRD	Damp	Water Absorb	★GRS				ELC	WTR*2
Quilava		156	FIR		Blaze		WTR	GRD	RCK			
Qwilfish		211	WTR	PSN	Poison Point	Swift Swim	ELC	GRD	PSY			

R

Pokémon	Unova	National	Type		Ability		Weak against these move types					Immune to these move types	
Raichu		26	ELC		Static		GRD						
Raikou		243	ELC		Pressure		GRD						
Ralts		280	PSY		Synchronize	Trace	BUG	GHO	DRK				
Rampardos		409	RCK		Mold Breaker		GRS	WTR	FTG	GRD	STL		
Rapidash		78	FIR		Run Away	Flash Fire	WTR	GRD	RCK			FIR*2	
Raticate		20	NRM		Run Away	Guts	FTG					GHO	
Rattata		19	NRM		Run Away	Guts	FTG					GHO	
Rayquaza		384	DRG	FLY	Air Lock		★ICE	RCK	DRG			GRD	
Regice		378	ICE		Clear Body		FIR	FTG	RCK	STL			
Regigigas		486	NRM		Slow Start		FTG					GHO	
Regirock		377	RCK		Clear Body		GRS	WTR	FTG	GRD	STL		
Registeel		379	STL		Clear Body		FIR	FTG	GRD			PSN	
Relicanth		369	WTR	RCK	Swift Swim	Rock Head	★GRS	ELC	FTG	GRD			

R

Pokémon	Unova	National	Type		Ability		Weak against these move types						Immune to these move types		
Remoraid		223	WTR		Hustle	Sniper	GRS	ELC							
Reshiram	149	643	DRG	FIR	Turboblaze		GRD	RCK	DRG						
Reuniclus	85	579	PSY		Overcoat	Magic Guard	BUG	GHO	DRK						
Rhydon		112	GRD	RCK	Lightningrod	Rock Head	★GRS	★WTR	ICE	FTG	GRD	STL	ELC		
Rhyhorn		111	GRD	RCK	Lightningrod	Rock Head	★GRS	★WTR	ICE	FTG	GRD	STL	ELC		
Rhyperior		464	GRD	RCK	Lightningrod	Solid Rock	★GRS	★WTR	ICE	FTG	GRD	STL	ELC		
Riolu		447	FTG		Steadfast	Inner Focus	FLY	PSY							
Roggenrola	30	524	RCK		Sturdy		WTR	GRS	FTG	GRD	STL				
Roselia		315	GRS	PSN	Natural Cure	Poison Point	FIR	ICE	FLY	PSY					
Roserade		407	GRS	PSN	Natural Cure	Poison Point	FIR	ICE	FLY	PSY					
Rotom		479	ELC	GHO	Levitate		GHO	DRK					NRM	FTG	GRD*1
Rotom Fan Rotom		479	ELC	FLY	Levitate		ICE	RCK					GRD*1		
Rotom Frost Rotom		479	ELC	ICE	Levitate		FIR	FTG	RCK				GRD*1		
Rotom Heat Rotom		479	ELC	FIR	Levitate		WTR	RCK					GRD*1		
Rotom Mow Rotom		479	ELC	GRS	Levitate		FIR	ICE	PSN	BUG			GRD*1		
Rotom Wash Rotom		479	ELC	WTR	Levitate		GRS						GRD*1		
Rufflet	133	627	NRM	FLY	Keen Eye	Sheer Force	ELC	ICE	RCK				GRD	GHO	

S

Pokémon	Unova	National	Type		Ability		Weak against these move types						Immune to these move types		
Sableye		302	DRK	GHO	Keen Eye	Stall							NRM	FTG	PSY
Salamence		373	DRG	FLY	Intimidate		★ICE	RCK	DRG				GRD		
Samurott	9	503	WTR		Torrent		GRS	ELC							
Sandile	57	551	GRD	DRK	Intimidate	Moxie	WTR	GRS	ICE	FTG	BUG		ELC	PSY	
Sandshrew		27	GRD		Sand Veil		GRS	WTR	ICE				ELC		
Sandslash		28	GRD		Sand Veil		GRS	WTR	ICE				ELC		
Sawk	45	539	FTG		Sturdy	Inner Focus	FLY	PSY							
Sawsbuck	92	586	NRM	GRS	Chlorophyll	Sap Sipper	FIR	ICE	FTG	PSN	FLY	BUG	GHO	GRS*2	
Sceptile		254	GRS		Overgrow		FIR	ICE	PSN	FLY	BUG				
Scizor		212	BUG	STL	Swarm	Technician	★FIR						PSN		
Scolipede	51	545	BUG	PSN	Poison Point	Swarm	FIR	FLY	PSY	RCK					
Scrafty	66	560	DRK	FTG	Shed Skin	Moxie	FTG	FLY					PSY		
Scraggy	65	559	DRK	FTG	Shed Skin	Moxie	FTG	FLY					PSY		
Scyther		123	BUG	FLY	Swarm	Technician	★RCK	FIR	ELC	ICE	FLY		GRD		
Seadra		117	WTR		Poison Point	Sniper	GRS	ELC							
Seaking		119	WTR		Swift Swim	Water Veil	GRS	ELC							
Sealeo		364	ICE	WTR	Thick Fat	Ice Body	GRS	ELC	FTG	RCK					
Seedot		273	GRS		Chlorophyll	Early Bird	FIR	ICE	PSN	FLY	BUG				
Seel		86	WTR		Thick Fat	Hydration	GRS	ELC							
Seismitoad	43	537	WTR	GRD	Swift Swim	Poison Touch	★GRS						ELC		
Sentret		161	NRM		Run Away	Keen Eye	FTG						GHO		
Serperior	3	497	GRS		Overgrow		FIR	ICE	PSN	FLY	BUG				
Servine	2	496	GRS		Overgrow		FIR	ICE	PSN	FLY	BUG				
Seviper		336	PSN		Shed Skin		GRD	PSY							
Sewaddle	46	540	BUG	GRS	Swarm	Chlorophyll	★FIR	★FLY	ICE	PSN	BUG	RCK			
Sharpedo		319	WTR	DRK	Rough Skin		GRS	ELC	FTG	BUG			PSY		
Shaymin (Land Forme)		492	GRS		Natural Cure		FIR	ICE	PSN	FLY	BUG				
Shaymin (Sky Forme)		492	GRS	FLY	Serene Grace		★ICE	FIR	PSN	FLY	RCK		GRD		
Shedinja		292	BUG	GHO	Wonder Guard		FIR	FLY	RCK	GHO	DRK		Type *1 outside of the five to the left		
Shelgon		372	DRG		Rock Head		ICE	DRG							
Shellder		90	WTR		Shell Armor	Skill Link	GRS	ELC							
Shellos		422	WTR		Sticky Hold	Storm Drain	GRS	ELC					WTR*2		
Shelmet	122	616	BUG		Hydration	Shell Armor	FIR	FLY	RCK						
Shieldon		410	RCK	STL	Sturdy		★FTG	★GRD	WTR				PSN		
Shiftry		275	GRS	DRK	Chlorophyll	Early Bird	★BUG	FIR	ICE	FTG	PSN	FLY	PSY		
Shinx		403	ELC		Rivalry	Intimidate	GRD								
Shroomish		285	GRS		Effect Spore	Poison Heal	FIR	ICE	PSN	FLY	BUG				
Shuckle		213	BUG	RCK	Sturdy	Gluttony	WTR	RCK	STL						

★ Deals 4 times damage.   *1 Ability prevents damage.   *2 May deal damage depending on the Pokémon's Ability.   *3 Damage may be prevented depending on the Pokémon's Ability.

Pokémon	Unova	National	Type		Ability		Weak against these move types							Immune to these move types		
Shuppet		353	GHO		Insomnia	Frisk	GHO	DRK						NRM	FTG	
Sigilyph	67	561	PSY	FLY	Wonder Skin	Magic Guard	ELC	ICE	RCK	GHO	DRK			GRD		
Silcoon		266	BUG		Shed Skin		FIR	FLY	RCK							
Simipour	22	516	WTR		Gluttony		GRS	ELC								
Simisage	18	512	GRS		Gluttony		FIR	ICE	PSN	FLY	BUG					
Simisear	20	514	FIR		Gluttony		WTR	GRD	RCK							
Skarmory		227	STL	FLY	Keen Eye	Sturdy	FIR	ELC						PSN	GRD	
Skiploom		188	GRS	FLY	Chlorophyll	Leaf Guard	★ICE	FIR	PSN	FLY	RCK			GRD		
Skitty		300	NRM		Cute Charm	Normalize	FTG							GHO		
Skorupi		451	PSN	BUG	Battle Armor	Sniper	FIR	FLY	PSY	RCK						
Skuntank		435	PSN	DRK	Stench	Aftermath	GRD							PSY		
Slaking		289	NRM		Truant		FTG							GHO		
Slakoth		287	NRM		Truant		FTG							GHO		
Slowbro		80	WTR	PSY	Oblivious	Own Tempo	GRS	ELC	BUG	GHO	DRK					
Slowking		199	WTR	PSY	Oblivious	Own Tempo	GRS	ELC	BUG	GHO	DRK					
Slowpoke		79	WTR	PSY	Oblivious	Own Tempo	GRS	ELC	BUG	GHO	DRK					
Slugma		218	FIR		Magma Armor	Flame Body	WTR	GRD	RCK							
Smeargle		235	NRM		Own Tempo	Technician	FTG							GHO		
Smoochum		238	ICE	PSY	Oblivious	Forewarn	FIR	BUG	RCK	GHO	DRK	STL				
Sneasel		215	DRK	ICE	Inner Focus	Keen Eye	★FTG	FIR	BUG	RCK	STL			PSY		
Snivy	1	495	GRS		Overgrow		FIR	ICE	PSN	FLY	BUG					
Snorlax		143	NRM		Immunity	Thick Fat	FTG							GHO		
Snorunt		361	ICE		Inner Focus	Ice Body	FIR	FTG	RCK	STL						
Snover		459	GRS	ICE	Snow Warning		★FIR	FTG	PSN	FLY	BUG	RCK	STL			
Snubbull		209	NRM		Intimidate	Run Away	FTG							GHO		
Solosis	83	577	PSY		Overcoat	Magic Guard	BUG	GHO	DRK							
Solrock		338	RCK	PSY	Levitate		GRS	WTR	BUG	GHO	DRK	STL		GRD *1		
Spearow		21	NRM	FLY	Keen Eye		ELC	ICE	RCK					GRD	GHO	
Spheal		363	ICE	WTR	Thick Fat	Ice Body	GRS	ELC	FTG	RCK						
Spinarak		167	BUG	PSN	Swarm	Insomnia	FIR	FLY	PSY	RCK						
Spinda		327	NRM		Own Tempo	Tangled Feet	FTG							GHO		
Spiritomb		442	GHO	DRK	Pressure									NRM	FTG	PSY
Spoink		325	PSY		Thick Fat	Own Tempo	BUG	GHO	DRK							
Squirtle		7	WTR		Torrent		GRS	ELC								
Stantler		234	NRM		Intimidate	Frisk	FTG							GHO		
Staraptor		398	NRM	FLY	Intimidate		ELC	ICE	RCK					GRD	GHO	
Staravia		397	NRM	FLY	Intimidate		ELC	ICE	RCK					GRD	GHO	
Starly		396	NRM	FLY	Keen Eye		ELC	ICE	RCK					GRD	GHO	
Starmie		121	WTR	PSY	Illuminate	Natural Cure	GRS	ELC	BUG	GHO	DRK					
Staryu		120	WTR		Illuminate	Natural Cure	GRS	ELC								
Steelix		208	STL	GRD	Rock Head	Sturdy	FIR	WTR	FTG	GRD				ELC	PSN	
Stoutland	14	508	NRM		Intimidate	Sand Rush	FTG							GHO		
Stunfisk	124	618	GRD	ELC	Static	Limber	WTR	GRS	ICE	GRD				ELC		
Stunky		434	PSN	DRK	Stench	Aftermath	GRD							PSY		
Sudowoodo		185	RCK		Sturdy	Rock Head	GRS	WTR	FTG	GRD	STL					
Suicune		245	WTR		Pressure		GRS	ELC								
Sunflora		192	GRS		Chlorophyll	Solar Power	FIR	ICE	PSN	FLY	BUG					
Sunkern		191	GRS		Chlorophyll	Solar Power	FIR	ICE	PSN	FLY	BUG					
Surskit		283	BUG	WTR	Swift Swim		ELC	FLY	RCK							
Swablu		333	NRM	FLY	Natural Cure		ELC	ICE	RCK					GRD	GHO	
Swadloon	47	541	BUG	GRS	Leaf Guard	Chlorophyll	★FIR	★FLY	ICE	PSN	BUG	RCK				
Swalot		317	PSN		Liquid Ooze	Sticky Hold	GRD	PSY								
Swampert		260	WTR	GRD	Torrent		★GRS							ELC		
Swanna	87	581	WTR	FLY	Keen Eye	Big Pecks	★ELC	RCK						GRD		
Swellow		277	NRM	FLY	Guts		ELC	ICE	RCK					GRD	GHO	
Swinub		220	ICE	GRD	Oblivious	Snow Cloak	GRS	FIR	WTR	FTG	STL			ELC		
Swoobat	34	528	PSY	FLY	Unaware	Klutz	ELC	ICE	RCK	GHO	DRK			GRD		

◈ **T**

Pokémon	Unova	National	Type		Ability		Weak against these move types							Immune to these move types		
Taillow		276	NRM	FLY	Guts		ELC	ICE	RCK					GRD	GHO	
Tangela		114	GRS		Chlorophyll	Leaf Guard	FIR	ICE	PSN	FLY	BUG					
Tangrowth		465	GRS		Chlorophyll	Leaf Guard	FIR	ICE	PSN	FLY	BUG					
Tauros		128	NRM		Intimidate	Anger Point	FTG							GHO		
Teddiursa		216	NRM		Pickup	Quick Feet	FTG							GHO		

◈ T

Pokémon	Unova	National	Type		Ability		◯ Weak against these move types						✕ Immune to these move types	
Tentacool		72	WTR	PSN	Clear Body	Liquid Ooze	ELC	GRD	PSY					
Tentacruel		73	WTR	PSN	Clear Body	Liquid Ooze	ELC	GRD	PSY					
Tepig	4	498	FIR		Blaze		WTR	GRD	RCK					
Terrakion	145	639	RCK	FTG	Justified		WTR	GRS	FTG	GRD	PSY	STL		
Throh	44	538	FTG		Guts	Inner Focus	FLY	PSY						
Thundurus	148	642	ELC	FLY	Prankster		ICE	RCK					GRD	
Timburr	38	532	FTG		Guts	Sheer Force	FLY	PSY						
Tirtouga	70	564	WTR	RCK	Solid Rock	Sturdy	★ GRS	ELC	FTG	GRD				
Togekiss		468	NRM	FLY	Hustle	Serene Grace	ELC	ICE	RCK				GRD	GHO
Togepi		175	NRM		Hustle	Serene Grace	FTG						GHO	
Togetic		176	NRM	FLY	Hustle	Serene Grace	ELC	ICE	RCK				GRD	GHO
Torchic		255	FIR		Blaze		WTR	GRD	RCK					
Torkoal		324	FIR		White Smoke		WTR	GRD	RCK					
Tornadus	147	641	FLY		Prankster		ELC	ICE	RCK				GRD	
Torterra		389	GRS	GRD	Overgrow		★ ICE	FIR	FLY	BUG			ELC	
Totodile		158	WTR		Torrent		GRS	ELC						
Toxicroak		454	PSN	FTG	Anticipation	Dry Skin	★ PSY	GRD	FLY				WTR *2	
Tranquill	26	520	NRM	FLY	Big Pecks	Super Luck	ELC	ICE	RCK				GRD	GHO
Trapinch		328	GRD		Hyper Cutter	Arena Trap	GRS	WTR	ICE				ELC	
Treecko		252	GRS		Overgrow		FIR	ICE	PSN	FLY	BUG			
Tropius		357	GRS	FLY	Chlorophyll	Solar Power	★ ICE	FIR	PSN	FLY	RCK		GRD	
Trubbish	74	568	PSN		Stench	Sticky Hold	GRD	PSY						
Turtwig		387	GRS		Overgrow		FIR	ICE	PSN	FLY	BUG			
Tympole	41	535	WTR		Swift Swim	Hydration	GRS	ELC						
Tynamo	108	602	ELC		Levitate								GRD *1	
Typhlosion		157	FIR		Blaze		WTR	GRD	RCK					
Tyranitar		248	RCK	DRK	Sand Stream		★ FTG	GRS	WTR	GRD	BUG	STL	PSY	
Tyrogue		236	FTG		Guts	Steadfast	FLY	PSY						

◈ U

Pokémon	Unova	National	Type		Ability		◯ Weak against these move types					✕ Immune to these move types	
Umbreon		197	DRK		Synchronize		FTG	BUG				PSY	
Unfezant	27	521	NRM	FLY	Big Pecks	Super Luck	ELC	ICE	RCK			GRD	GHO
Unown		201	PSY		Levitate		BUG	GHO	DRK			GRD *1	
Ursaring		217	NRM		Guts	Quick Feet	FTG					GHO	
Uxie		480	PSY		Levitate		BUG	GHO	DRK			GRD *1	

◈ V

Pokémon	Unova	National	Type		Ability		◯ Weak against these move types					✕ Immune to these move types	
Vanillish	89	583	ICE		Ice Body		FIR	FTG	RCK	STL			
Vanillite	88	582	ICE		Ice Body		FIR	FTG	RCK	STL			
Vanilluxe	90	584	ICE		Ice Body		FIR	FTG	RCK	STL			
Vaporeon		134	WTR		Water Absorb		GRS	ELC				WTR *1	
Venipede	49	543	BUG	PSN	Poison Point	Swarm	FIR	FLY	PSY	RCK			
Venomoth		49	BUG	PSN	Shield Dust	Tinted Lens	FIR	FLY	PSY	RCK			
Venonat		48	BUG	PSN	Compoundeyes	Tinted Lens	FIR	FLY	PSY	RCK			
Venusaur		3	GRS	PSN	Overgrow		FIR	ICE	FLY	PSY			
Vespiquen		416	BUG	FLY	Pressure		★ RCK	FIR	ELC	ICE	FLY	GRD	
Vibrava		329	GRD	DRG	Levitate		★ ICE	DRG				ELC	GRD *1
Victini	0	494	PSY	FIR	Victory Star		WTR	GRD	RCK	GHO	DRK		
Victreebel		71	GRS	PSN	Chlorophyll		FIR	ICE	FLY	PSY			
Vigoroth		288	NRM		Vital Spirit		FTG					GHO	
Vileplume		45	GRS	PSN	Chlorophyll		FIR	ICE	FLY	PSY			
Virizion	146	640	GRS	FTG	Justified		★ FLY	FIR	ICE	PSN	PSY		
Volbeat		313	BUG		Illuminate	Swarm	FIR	FLY	RCK				
Volcarona	143	637	BUG	FIR	Flame Body		★ RCK	WTR	FLY				
Voltorb		100	ELC		Soundproof	Static	GRD						
Vullaby	135	629	DRK	FLY	Big Pecks	Overcoat	ELC	ICE	RCK			GRD	PSY
Vulpix		37	FIR		Flash Fire		WTR	GRD	RCK			FIR *1	

◈ W

Pokémon	Unova	National	Type		Ability		◯ Weak against these move types			✕ Immune to these move types	
Wailmer		320	WTR		Water Veil	Oblivious	GRS	ELC			
Wailord		321	WTR		Water Veil	Oblivious	GRS	ELC			

★ Deals 4 times damage.   *1 Ability prevents damage.   *2 May deal damage depending on the Pokémon's Ability.   *3 Damage may be prevented depending on the Pokémon's Ability.

Pokémon	Unova	National	Type		Ability		Weak against these move types						Immune to these move types	
Walrein		365	ICE	WTR	Thick Fat	Ice Body	GRS	ELC	FTG	RCK				
Wartortle		8	WTR		Torrent		GRS	ELC						
Watchog	11	505	NRM		Illuminate	Keen Eye	FTG						GHO	
Weavile		461	DRK	ICE	Pressure		★FTG	FIR	BUG	RCK	STL		PSY	
Weedle		13	BUG	PSN	Shield Dust		FIR	FLY	PSY	RCK				
Weepinbell		70	GRS	PSN	Chlorophyll		FIR	ICE	FLY	PSY				
Weezing		110	PSN		Levitate		PSY						GRD *1	
Whimsicott	53	547	GRS		Prankster	Infiltrator	FIR	ICE	PSN	FLY	BUG			
Whirlipede	50	544	BUG	PSN	Poison Point	Swarm	FIR	FLY	PSY	RCK				
Whiscash		340	WTR	GRD	Oblivious	Anticipation	★GRS						ELC	
Whismur		293	NRM		Soundproof		FTG						GHO	
Wigglytuff		40	NRM		Cute Charm		FTG						GHO	
Wingull		278	WTR	FLY	Keen Eye		★ELC	RCK					GRD	
Wobbuffet		202	PSY		Shadow Tag		BUG	GHO	DRK					
Woobat	33	527	PSY	FLY	Unaware	Klutz	ELC	ICE	RCK	GHO	DRK		GRD	
Wooper		194	WTR	GRD	Damp	Water Absorb	★GRS						ELC	WTR *2
Wormadam Plant Cloak		413	BUG	GRS	Anticipation		★FIR	★FLY	ICE	PSN	BUG	RCK		
Wormadam Sandy Cloak		413	BUG	GRD	Anticipation		FIR	WTR	ICE	FLY			ELC	
Wormadam Trash Cloak		413	BUG	STL	Anticipation		★FIR						PSN	
Wurmple		265	BUG		Shield Dust		FIR	FLY	RCK					
Wynaut		360	PSY		Shadow Tag		BUG	GHO	DRK					

◈ X

Pokémon	Unova	National	Type		Ability		Weak against these move types						Immune to these move types	
Xatu		178	PSY	FLY	Synchronize	Early Bird	ELC	ICE	RCK	GHO	DRK		GRD	

◈ Y

Pokémon	Unova	National	Type		Ability		Weak against these move types						Immune to these move types	
Yamask	68	562	GHO		Mummy		GHO	DRK					NRM	FTG
Yanma		193	BUG	FLY	Speed Boost	Compoundeyes	★RCK	FIR	ELC	ICE	FLY		GRD	
Yanmega		469	BUG	FLY	Speed Boost	Tinted Lens	★RCK	FIR	ELC	ICE	FLY		GRD	

◈ Z

Pokémon	Unova	National	Type		Ability		Weak against these move types						Immune to these move types	
Zangoose		335	NRM		Immunity		FTG						GHO	
Zapdos		145	ELC	FLY	Pressure		ICE	RCK					GRD	
Zebstrika	29	523	ELC		Lightningrod	Motor Drive	GRD						ELC *1	
Zekrom	150	644	DRG	ELC	Teravolt		ICE	GRD	DRG					
Zigzagoon		263	NRM		Pickup	Gluttony	FTG						GHO	
Zoroark	77	571	DRK		Illusion		FTG	BUG					PSY	
Zorua	76	570	DRK		Illusion		FTG	BUG					PSY	
Zubat		41	PSN	FLY	Inner Focus		ELC	ICE	PSY	RCK			GRD	
Zweilous	140	634	DRK	DRG	Hustle		ICE	FTG	BUG	DRG			PSY	

Type Matchup Chart

Types are assigned both to moves and to the Pokémon themselves. These types can greatly affect the amount of damage dealt or received in battle, so learn how they line up against one another and give yourself the edge in battle.

Attacking Pokémon's Move Type (rows) vs **Defending Pokémon's Type** (columns)

Attacking ↓ / Defending →	Normal	Fire	Water	Grass	Electric	Ice	Fighting	Poison	Ground	Flying	Psychic	Bug	Rock	Ghost	Dragon	Dark	Steel
Normal													△	×			△
Fire		△	△	◉		◉						◉	△		△		◉
Water		◉	△	△					◉				◉		△		
Grass		△	◉	△					◉	△		△	◉		△		△
Electric			◉	△	△				×	◉					△		
Ice		△	△	◉		△			◉	◉					◉		△
Fighting	◉					◉		△		△	△	△	◉	×		◉	◉
Poison				◉				△	△				△	△			×
Ground		◉		△	◉			◉		×		△	◉				◉
Flying				◉	△		◉					◉	△				△
Psychic							◉	◉			△					×	△
Bug		△		◉			△	△		△	◉			△		◉	△
Rock		◉				◉	△		△	◉		◉					△
Ghost	×										◉			◉		△	△
Dragon															◉		△
Dark							△				◉			◉		△	△
Steel		△	△		△	◉							◉				△

Legend

Symbol	Meaning	Multiplier
◉	Very effective — "It's super effective!"	×2
[No Icon]	Normal Damage	×1
△	Not too effective — "It's not very effective..."	×0.5
×	No effect — "It doesn't affect..."	×0

- Fire-type Pokémon cannot be afflicted with the Burned condition.
- Grass-type Pokémon are immune to Leech Seed.
- Ice-type Pokémon are immune to the Frozen condition, and take no damage from the Hail weather condition.
- Poison-type Pokémon are immune to the Poison and Badly Poisoned conditions, even when switching in with Toxic Spikes in play. Poison-type Pokémon nullify Toxic Spikes (unless these Pokémon are also Flying type or have the Levitate Ability).
- Ground-type Pokémon are immune to Thunder Wave and take no damage from the Sandstorm weather condition.
- Flying-type Pokémon cannot be damaged by Spikes when switching in, or become afflicted with a Poison or Badly Poisoned condition due to switching in with Toxic Spikes in play.
- Rock-type Pokémon are immune to the Sandstorm weather condition. Their Sp. Def also goes up in the Sandstorm weather condition.
- Steel-type Pokémon are immune to the Sandstorm weather condition. They are also immune to the Poison and Badly Poisoned conditions. Even if switched in with Toxic Spikes in play, they will not be afflicted by the Poison or Badly Poisoned condition.

Jingle Bells 120

Jingle, Jingle, Jingle 123

Jolly Old St. Nicholas 126

Joy to the World 128

The Last Month of the Year (What Month Was Jesus Born In?) 130

Let It Snow! Let It Snow! Let It Snow! 132

Little Saint Nick 138

Lo, How a Rose E'er Blooming 135

A Marshmallow World 142

Mary's Little Boy Child 145

Merry Christmas, Darling 148

Merry Christmas from the Family 152

The Merry Christmas Polka 158

A Merry, Merry Christmas to You 163

The Most Wonderful Day of the Year................166

My Favorite Things 172

The Night Before Christmas Song 176

Noel! Noel! 180

Nuttin' for Christmas 182

O Christmas Tree 171

O Come, All Ye Faithful (Adeste Fideles) 186

O Come, Little Children 188

O Come, O Come Immanuel 190

O Holy Night 192

O Little Town of Bethlehem 196

O Sanctissima 189

Old Toy Trains 198

Parade of the Wooden Soldiers 204

Pretty Paper 201

Rockin' Around the Christmas Tree 208

Rudolph the Red-Nosed Reindeer 211

Santa, Bring My Baby Back (To Me) 214

Shake Me I Rattle (Squeeze Me I Cry) 216

Silent Night 222

Silver and Gold 219

Silver Bells 224

Sleep, Holy Babe 230

Some Children See Him 232

The Star Carol 234

Still, Still, Still 236

Suzy Snowflake 238

That Christmas Feeling 240

Toyland 242

The Twelve Days of Christmas..........................244

Up on the Housetop..248

We Three Kings of Orient Are 250

We Wish You a Merry Christmas.......................252

What Child Is This? 254

When Santa Claus Gets Your Letter..................227

While Shepherds Watched Their Flocks 256

The White World of Winter 257

Who Would Imagine a King...............................260

Wonderful Christmastime 264

The Wonderful World of Christmas 270

A CAROLING WE GO

Music and Lyrics by
JOHNNY MARKS

5

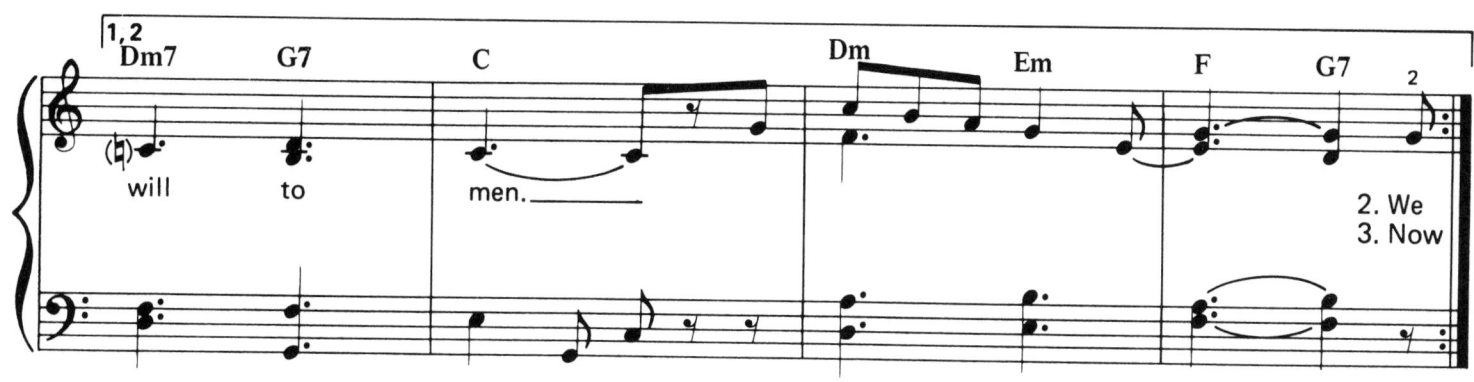

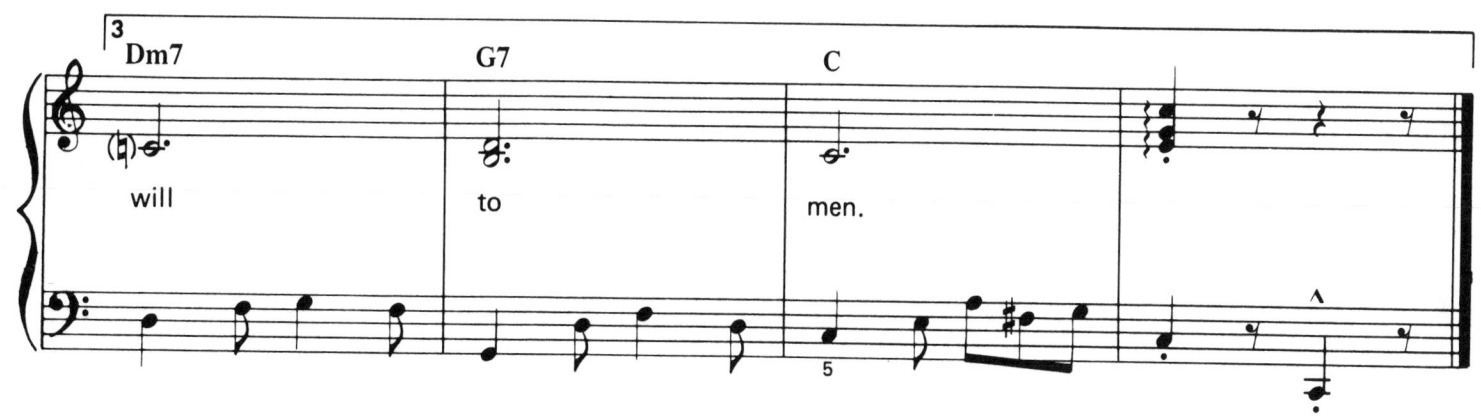

ALMOST DAY

Words and Music by
HUDDIE LEDBETTER

Square Dance Tempo (= 1 beat)

Chick-ens a-crowin' for mid-night, It's al-most day;

Chick-ens a-crowin' for mid-night, It's al-most day.

Can-dy canes and sug-ar plums On Christ-mas day;

Can-dy canes and sug-ar plums On Christ-mas day.

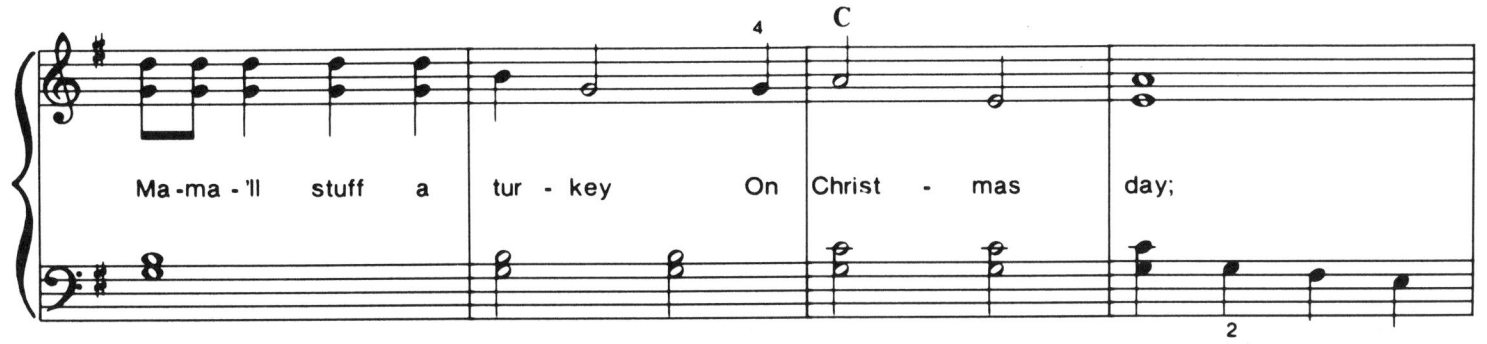

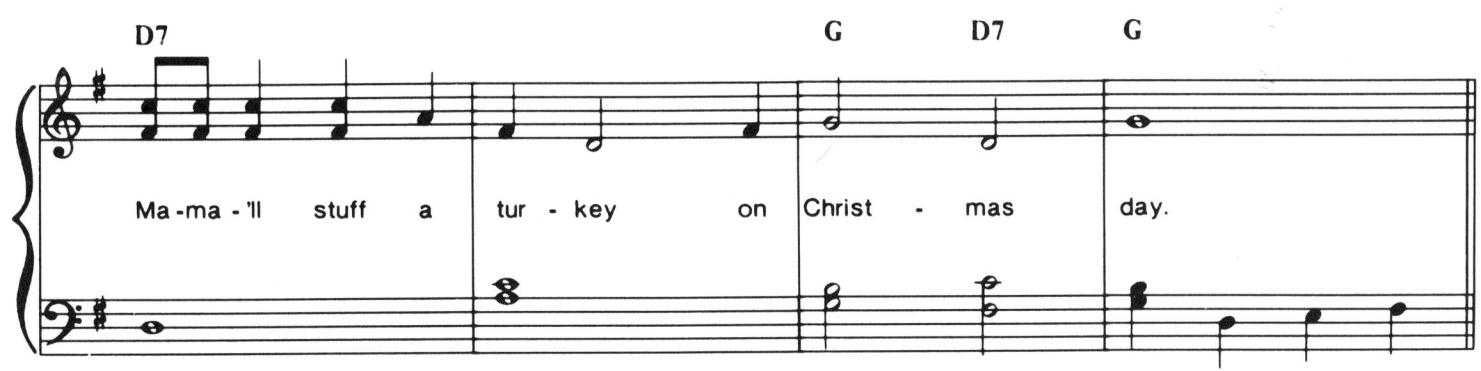

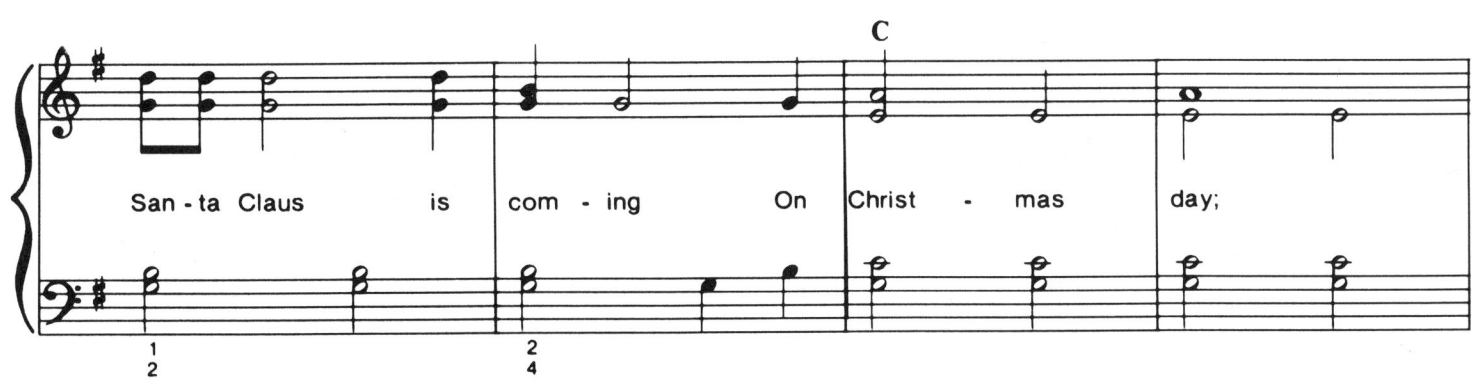

ANGELS FROM THE REALMS OF GLORY

Words by JAMES MONTGOMERY
Music by HENRY T. SMART